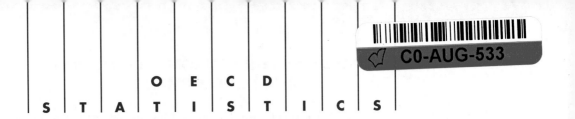

INDUSTRIAL STRUCTURE STATISTICS

Core Data

STATISTIQUES DES STRUCTURES INDUSTRIELLES

Données de base

1998 EDITION V O L U M E I **ÉDITION 1998**

ORGANISATION FOR ECONOMIC CO-OPERATION AND DEVELOPMENT

ORGANISATION DE COOPÉRATION ET DE DÉVELOPPEMENT ÉCONOMIQUES

ORGANISATION FOR ECONOMIC CO-OPERATION AND DEVELOPMENT

Pursuant to Article 1 of the Convention signed in Paris on 14th December 1960, and which came into force on 30th September 1961, the Organisation for Economic Co-operation and Development (OECD) shall promote policies designed:

- to achieve the highest sustainable economic growth and employment and a rising standard of living in Member countries, while maintaining financial stability, and thus to contribute to the development of the world economy;
- to contribute to sound economic expansion in Member as well as non-member countries in the process of economic development; and
- to contribute to the expansion of world trade on a multilateral, non-discriminatory basis in accordance with international obligations.

The original Member countries of the OECD are Austria, Belgium, Canada, Denmark, France, Germany, Greece, Iceland, Ireland, Italy, Luxembourg, the Netherlands, Norway, Portugal, Spain, Sweden, Switzerland, Turkey, the United Kingdom and the United States. The following countries became Members subsequently through accession at the dates indicated hereafter: Japan (28th April 1964), Finland (28th January 1969), Australia (7th June 1971), New Zealand (29th May 1973), Mexico (18th May 1994), the Czech Republic (21st December 1995), Hungary (7th May 1996), Poland (22nd November 1996) and Korea (12th December 1996). The Commission of the European Communities takes part in the work of the OECD (Article 13 of the OECD Convention).

ORGANISATION DE COOPÉRATION ET DE DÉVELOPPEMENT ÉCONOMIQUES

En vertu de l'article 1er de la Convention signée le 14 décembre 1960, à Paris, et entrée en vigueur le 30 septembre 1961, l'Organisation de Coopération et de Développement Économiques (OCDE) a pour objectif de promouvoir des politiques visant :

- à réaliser la plus forte expansion de l'économie et de l'emploi et une progression du niveau de vie dans les pays Membres, tout en maintenant la stabilité financière, et à contribuer ainsi au développement de l'économie mondiale ;
- à contribuer à une saine expansion économique dans les pays Membres, ainsi que les pays non membres, en voie de développement économique ;
- à contribuer à l'expansion du commerce mondial sur une base multilatérale et non discriminatoire conformément aux obligations internationales.

Les pays Membres originaires de l'OCDE sont : l'Allemagne, l'Autriche, la Belgique, le Canada, le Danemark, l'Espagne, les États-Unis, la France, la Grèce, l'Irlande, l'Islande, l'Italie, le Luxembourg, la Norvège, les Pays-Bas, le Portugal, le Royaume-Uni, la Suède, la Suisse et la Turquie. Les pays suivants sont ultérieurement devenus Membres par adhésion aux dates indiquées ci-après : le Japon (28 avril 1964), la Finlande (28 janvier 1969), l'Australie (7 juin 1971), la Nouvelle-Zélande (29 mai 1973), le Mexique (18 mai 1994), la République tchèque (21 décembre 1995), la Hongrie (7 mai 1996), la Pologne (22 novembre 1996) et la Corée (12 décembre 1996). La Commission des Communautés européennes participe aux travaux de l'OCDE (article 13 de la Convention de l'OCDE).

FOREWORD

This issue of Industrial Structure Statistics comes in two volumes. Volume 1 provides detailed annual statistics on production, value added, employment, exports/imports, etc. for manufacturing and non-manufacturing sectors. This data facilitates an assessment of the evolution of the industrial structure of OECD Member countries. The publication was prepared by the Main Economic Indicators Division of the Statistics Directorate in the OECD Secretariat under the auspices of the Statistical Working Party on Industrial Statistics of the Industry Committee. The Secretariat wishes to thank the representatives of all the national authorities who have assisted in the preparation of this publication.

All series published, as well as data for earlier years, are held on the database Information System on Industrial Structures (ISIS), and are available on diskette (Industrial Structure Statistics - Vol. 1: Core Data, 1998). These statistics are published on the responsibility of the Secretary-General of the OECD.

Volume 2 presents annual energy consumption data in manufacturing sectors. It was prepared by the Energy Statistics Division of the International Energy Agency (IEA). The energy data have been collected during the Pilot phase of the project which was launched in 1995 under the auspices of the Statistical Working Party on Industrial Statistics of the Industry Committee.

The data are also available on diskette (Industrial Structure Statistics - Vol. 2: Energy Consumption, 1998).

AVANT-PROPOS

Cette édition des Statistiques des structures industrielles comprend deux volumes. Le volume 1 présente des données structurelles détaillées relatives a la production, la valeur ajoutée, l'emploi, les exportations et les importations, etc. pour les secteurs manufacturier et non-manufacturier. Ces données permettent d'évaluer l'évolution de la structure industrielle des pays Membres de l'OCDE. Cette publication a été préparée par la Division des principaux indicateurs économiques de la Direction Statistique du Secrétariat de l'OCDE sous l'égide du Groupe de travail sur les Statistiques industrielles du Comité de l'industrie. Le Secrétariat tient a remercier les représentants de toutes les administrations nationales qui ont apporté leur concours à la préparation de cette publication.

L'ensemble des statistiques publiées ainsi que celles portant sur des années antérieures sont contenues dans la base de données Système d'Information sur les Structures Industrielles (SISI) et sont disponibles sur disquette (Statistiques des structures industrielles - Vol. 1 : Données de base, 1998).

Ces statistiques sont publiées sous la responsabilité du Secrétaire général de l'OCDE.

Le volume 2 présente des données annuelles de consommation d'énergie dans l'industrie manufacturière. Il a été préparé par la division des statistiques de l'énergie de l'Agence Internationale de l'Energie (AIE). Les données sur l'énergie ont été collectées dans le cadre de la phase pilote du projet lancé en 1995 sous l'égide du Groupe de travail sur les Statistiques industrielles du Comité de l'industrie.

Ces données sont également disponibles sur disquette (Statistiques des structures industrielles - Vol. 2 : Consommation d'énergie, 1998).

Table of contents - Table des matières

INTRODUCTION

OECD industrial statistics

The OECD Secretariat compiles a wide range of industrial statistics, most of them under the auspices of the Statistical Working Party of the Industry Committee. The quarterly *Indicators of Industrial Activity* gives an overall view of the most recent short-term economic development, and presents monthly indices of output, deliveries, orders, prices and employment as well as qualitative information from business tendency surveys. More detailed official annual data derived from industrial surveys, foreign trade sources or national accounts and covering a number of structural variables are given in *Industrial Structure Statistics*. The OECD estimated *Database for Structural Analysis (STAN)*, based on *Industrial Structure Statistics* and developed to ensure international comparability of survey-based national industrial statistics as well as their compatibility with national accounts contains a limited list of variables for most OECD countries. In addition, aggregate data for industrial production and producer prices are presented in the monthly publication, *Main Economic Indicators*.

Trends and structural shifts in industry, presented in numerous detailed statistical tables and graphs, are examined in two other OECD publications, issued alternatively every two years, *Science, Technology and Industry Outlook* and *Industry and Technology: Scoreboard of Indicators*, for use by policy makers and analysts.

Output from the computerised statistical databases is available both as printed publications, and in computer-readable form such as microcomputer diskettes. Further information on these databases is available on the World Wide Web at http://www.oecd.org/std *or* at http://www.oecd/org/dsti/eas/.

Process of Data Collection since 1995

The United Nations Statistical Commission, at its twenty-seventh session, recommended that OECD, in collaboration with the United Nations Industrial Development Organisation (UNIDO), take responsibility for the collection and dissemination of world-wide industrial statistics. As a result, new information is obtained from national statistical offices through a joint OECD/UNIDO questionnaire, with OECD responsible for collecting data from its Member countries. Also, historical datasets have been unified.

Much of the new data for OECD countries appearing in UNIDO publications have been initially collected and processed by OECD. At the same time, the electronic edition (diskette) of Industrial Structure Statistics contains data for earlier years which were collected by the Statistical Division of the United Nations Secretariat (UNSD). However, certain distinctions between the two datasets will remain. To meet its own analytical needs, the OECD collects data for an extended number of variables not treated by UNIDO: investment in machinery and equipment; employment of operatives; hours worked; supplements to wages and salaries; wages and salaries for operatives; labour costs including supplements to wages and salaries for operatives. Furthermore, data collection of foreign trade and national accounts statistics disaggregated by industry, together with constant price series, is specific to OECD.

Methodological Notes

The previous edition of *Industrial Structure Statistics* included data classified according to ISIC, Revision 2, adopted in 1968 by the United Nations Organisation (*Statistical Papers, Series M, No. 4, Rev. 2, Add. 1*, New York, 1971). This edition was accompanied by a free supplement which showed a selection of industrial statistical data, collected by the OECD since 1995, classified according to ISIC Revision 3, adopted in February 1989 by the United Nations Organisation (*Statistical Papers, Series M, No. 4, Rev. 3*, New York, 1990).

In the current paper edition of *Industrial Structure Statistics*, data are classified according to both versions of the *International Standard Industrial Classification*, ISIC Revision 2 and ISIC Revision 3. Some tables with ISIC Revision 2 data have been suppressed, generally where data have not been updated for more than two years. By way of compensation, some new ISIC Revision 3 tables are presented for the first time.

Industrial Structure Statistics are divided in three parts: the first contains statistics according to ISIC Revision 2 and a detailed description of ISIC Revision 2; the second contains statistics according to ISIC Revision 3 and a detailed description of ISIC Revision 3; the third provides available methodological information. In keeping with earlier years, statistics in the two first parts are presented in two sections. The first section contains data derived directly from industrial surveys and foreign trade data. The second section provides data from national accounts disaggregated by industry. For the same variable, including the foreign trade information, the figures may vary depending on the source used. Differences may result, *inter alia*, from the way in which smaller units, taxes and subsidies and transactions by residents and non-residents are treated.

The electronic edition of this publication contains data for Revisions 2 and 3 of the ISIC classification.

Industrial survey figures (Section I of Parts A and B) comprise the results of sample surveys conducted by national statistical organisations. Since the sampling procedures vary, the percentage of the economy covered will vary between countries. Some, but not all, countries "gross up" the data to account for the unsampled portion. Here again there is no uniform procedure, though any information made available to the Secretariat is described in Section I of Part C. For this reason, the data presented in Section I of Parts A and B are more suitable for cross-sectional intra-country analyses than for analyses of levels between countries.

Foreign trade statistics (also shown in Section I of Parts A and B) are normally derived from customs figures and are product-based. Roughly speaking, this means that a particular shipment of goods is classified directly to an industry. Survey results, whether the base unit is the establishment or the enterprise, allocate an entire unit's transactions to one industry according to its principal activity (i.e. they are industry-based). An adjustment to reallocate the unit's secondary activities to a more appropriate industry may or may not have been made, depending on the country.

National account estimates (Section II of Parts A and B) are intended to be economy wide. Individual industries are calculated by breaking down higher level figures. Thus, the dataset is derived using a "top-down" approach, whereas industrial surveys use a "bottom-up" approach.

There are various conceptual differences between definitions of the same variables for industrial survey and national accounts purposes. For industrial survey concepts and definitions, readers may refer to the *International Recommendations for Industrial Statistics* [Statistical Papers Series M, No. 4/Rev. 2 (United Nations publication, Sales No. E.83.XVII.8)]. Principles and concepts of national accounting are set out in *A System of National Accounts* [Studies in Methods Series F, No. 2/Rev. 3 (United Nations publication, Sales No. E.69.XVII.3] and the new *System of National Accounts 1993* (EUROSTAT, International Monetary Fund, OECD, UN and World Bank joint publication, ISBN 92-1-161352-2).

All qualitative information made known to the Secretariat, in particular all amendments to previously published information made to take into account the change in classifications used in countries, is given in Section I of Part C. It includes, when available, deviations from recommended practice.

INTRODUCTION

Statistiques industrielles de l'OCDE

Le Secrétariat de l'OCDE compile une large gamme de statistiques, le plus souvent sous l'égide du Groupe de Travail Statistique du Comité de l'industrie. La publication trimestrielle *Indicateurs des activités industrielles* donne un aperçu général de l'évolution économique à court terme la plus récente et présente des indices mensuels de production, livraisons, commandes, prix et emploi ainsi que des données tirées d'enquêtes de conjoncture. Des données annuelles plus détaillées résultant d'enquêtes industrielles, de sources sur le commerce extérieur ou des comptes nationaux et couvrant un certain nombre de variables structurelles sont présentées dans les *Statistiques des structures industrielles*. La *Base de données* estimées d'*Analyse Structurelle* de l'OCDE (*STAN*) fondée sur les *Statistiques des structures industrielles* et développée dans le but d'assurer la comparabilité internationale des statistiques issues des enquêtes industrielles effectuées dans les pays Membres ainsi que leur compatibilité avec les comptes nationaux comprend un nombre limité de variables pour la plupart des pays de l'OCDE. En outre, des données agrégées de production industrielle et de prix à la production sont présentés dans la publication mensuelle *Principaux indicateurs économiques*.

Les tendances et les mutations structurelles de l'industrie, présentées dans de nombreux tableaux et graphiques détaillés, sont examinées dans deux autres publications de l'OCDE, diffusées alternativement tous les deux ans, *Les perspectives de la science, de la technologie et de l'industrie* et *Industrie et technologie : tableau de bord d'indicateurs,* à l'usage des décideurs politiques et analystes.

Les résultats provenant de ces banques de données sont non seulement disponibles sous forme de publications imprimées, mais aussi sur supports lisibles par ordinateur tels que disquette de micro-ordinateur. De plus amples informations sur ces bases de données sont disponibles sur le site Internet aux adresses suivantes http://www.oecd.org/std ou http://www.oecd/org/dsti/eas/.

Processus pour la collecte des données depuis 1995

La Commission Statistique des Nations Unies, lors de sa vingt-septième réunion, a recommandé que l'OCDE, en collaboration avec l'Organisation des Nations Unies pour le Développement Industriel (ONUDI), prenne la responsabilité de la collecte et de la diffusion des statistiques industrielles au niveau mondial. En conséquence, de nouvelles informations sont demandées aux instituts nationaux statistiques au moyen d'un questionnaire commun à l'OCDE et à l'ONUDI, l'OCDE étant chargée de la collecte des statistiques de ses pays Membres. Les bases de données historiques ont été uniformisées.

La plupart des données nouvelles relatives aux pays Membres de l'OCDE qui paraissent dans les publications de l'ONUDI ont été traitées par l'OCDE. Dans le même temps, l'édition électronique (disquette) des *Statistiques des structures industrielles* contient les données antérieurement recueillies par la division statistique du secrétariat des Nations Unies (UNSD). Cependant, certaines différences subsistent. Afin de satisfaire ses propres besoins analytiques, l'OCDE recueille des variables additionnelles que l'ONUDI ne collecte pas : les investissements en machines et équipement, l'emploi des ouvriers, les heures ouvrées, les suppléments aux salaires et traitements, les salaires des ouvriers, les coûts de la main d'œuvre y compris les compléments salariaux pour les ouvriers. En outre, la collecte des données tirées des statistiques du commerce extérieur et des comptes nationaux désagrégés par industrie, et celle des séries à prix constants restent propres à l'OCDE.

Notes méthodologiques

L'édition précédente des *Statistiques des structures industrielles* contenait des données selon la CITI Révision 2, adoptée en 1968 par l'Organisation des Nations Unies – ONU (*Etudes Statistiques, Série M, n° 4, Rév. 2, Add. 1*, New York, 1975). Elle était accompagnée d'un supplément gratuit présentant une sélection de données industrielles recueillies par l'OCDE depuis 1995, classées selon la CITI Révision 3, adoptée en février 1989 par l'ONU (*Etudes Statistiques, Série M, n° 4, Rév. 3*, New York, 1990).

Dans la présente publication papier *Statistiques des structures industrielles*, les données sont publiées selon les deux versions de la Classification Internationale Type par Industrie, la CITI Révision 2 et la CITI Révision 3. Quelques tableaux de données en CITI Révision 2 ont été supprimés, généralement parce qu'ils n'avaient pas été mis à jour depuis plus de deux ans. En revanche, de nouveaux tableaux présentant des données en CITI Révision 3 sont inclus pour la première fois dans cette édition.

Les *Statistiques des structures industrielles* sont divisées en trois parties. La première partie présente les statistiques en CITI Révision 2 ainsi que la description détaillée de la CITI Révision 2, la deuxième présente les statistiques en CITI Révision 3 ainsi que la description détaillée de la CITI Révision 3, la troisième contient les informations méthodologiques disponibles. Comme dans les éditions précédentes, les statistiques publiées dans chacune des deux premières parties sont regroupées en deux sections. La première section comprend les données provenant directement des enquêtes statistiques industrielles et des données sur le commerce extérieur. La seconde section reprend les données des comptes nationaux désagrégées par industrie. Pour une même variable, y compris pour les données sur le commerce extérieur, les chiffres peuvent varier selon la source utilisée. Des différences peuvent résulter notamment de la manière dont sont traitées les petites unités de base, les taxes et subventions, et les transactions des non-résidents et des résidents.

Depuis la dernière édition de cette publication, l'édition électronique des *Statistiques des Structures Industrielles* contient des données selon les Révisions 2 et 3 de la classification CITI.

Les résultats d'enquêtes industrielles (section 1, parties A et B) proviennent d'enquêtes par échantillon menées par les instituts nationaux de statistiques. Etant donné la variété des méthodes d'échantillonnage, le pourcentage des industries couvertes varie d'un pays à l'autre. Certains pays «gonflent» les données pour prendre en compte la portion non couverte par l'enquête. Là encore, il n'existe pas de procédure uniforme, mais toute information connue du Secrétariat est décrite dans la section I de la partie C. Pour cette raison, les données présentées dans les sections I des parties A et B sont mieux adaptées à des analyses intersectorielles dans chaque pays qu'à des analyses de niveaux entre pays.

Les statistiques du commerce extérieur (également en section 1, parties A et B) sont issues des sources douanières et sont fondées sur une classification par produit. Cela signifie, à peu près, qu'une marchandise est affectée directement à une classe industrielle. Pour les résultats d'enquêtes, quelle que soit l'unité de base -- établissement ou entreprise --, l'ensemble des transactions d'une unité est alloué à une industrie suivant l'activité principale (c'est-à-dire en fonction de l'industrie). Quelques pays procèdent à un ajustement pour allouer les activités secondaires d'une unité à une classe industrielle plus appropriée.

Les estimations à partir des comptes nationaux (section II des parties A et B) ont pour but de couvrir l'ensemble de l'économie. Les données par industrie sont calculées par décomposition des données plus agrégées. Cet ensemble d'informations est donc fondé sur une approche allant «du haut vers le bas» tandis que les enquêtes industrielles utilisent une approche allant «du bas vers le haut».

Il existe un certain nombre de différences de concepts dans les définitions de variables identiques entrant dans les enquêtes industrielles et les comptes nationaux. Pour les concepts et définitions des enquêtes industrielles, le lecteur peut se référer aux *Recommandations internationales concernant les statistiques industrielles* [Etudes statistiques série M, No. 48 (publication des Nations Unies, numéro de vente F.68.XVII.10)]. Les principes et concepts de la comptabilité nationale sont présentés dans *Un Système de Comptabilité Nationale* [Etudes sméthodologiques Série F, No. 2/Rév 3 (publication des Nations Unies, numéro de vente F.69.XVIII.3)] et dans le nouveau *Système de Comptabilité Nationale 1993* (publication commune de l'EUROSTAT, du Fonds Monétaire International, de l'OCDE, des Nations Unies et de la Banque Mondiale, ISBN 92-1-161352-2).

Toutes les informations qualitatives fournies au Secrétariat, en particulier toutes celles qui résultent des changements de classifications utilisées dans les pays et qui modifient les informations précédemment publiées, sont détaillées dans la section I de la partie C. Elles incluent les déviations par rapport aux normes lorsqu'elles ont été transmises par les pays.

CONVENTIONAL SIGNS AND ABBREVIATIONS
SIGNES ET ABREVIATIONS CONVENTIONNELS

Units

Units
Thousands
Millions
Billions

Unités

Unités
Milliers
Millions
Milliards

Other signs

. .   Not available
0   Nil or negligible
.   Decimal point

Autres signes

. .   Non disponible
0   Nul ou négligeable
.   Point décimal

Currency   Monnaie

Australia	A$	Australie
Austria	Sch	Autriche
Belgium	BF	Belgique
Canada	C$	Canada
Czech Republic	CK	République Tchèque
Denmark	DKr	Danemark
Finland	Mk	Finlande
France	FF	France
Germany	DM	Allemagne
Greece	Dr	Grèce
Hungary	Ft	Hongrie
Iceland	IKr	Islande
Ireland	Ir£	Irlande
Italy	L	Italie
Japan	Y	Japon
Korea	Won	Corée
Luxembourg	LF	Luxembourg
Mexico	NM$	Mexique
Netherlands	Gld	Pays-Bas
New Zealand	NZ$	Nouvelle-Zélande
Norway	NKr	Norvège
Poland	PLN	Pologne
Portugal	Esc	Portugal
Spain	Ptas	Espagne
Sweden	SKr	Suède
Switzerland	SF	Suisse
Turkey	TL	Turquie
United Kingdom	£	Royaume-Uni
United States	$	États-Unis

ISIC REVISION 2

CITI REVISION 2

Section I

Industrial survey and foreign trade statistics
Statistiques des enquêtes industrielles et du commerce extérieur

List of countries
Liste des pays

Statistiques des Structures Industrielles
OCDE, © 1998   OECD OCDE

Millions of C$ (Current Prices)

ISIC2	Industry	PRODUCTION									
		1987	1988	1989	1990	1991	1992	1993	1994	1995	1996
31	Food, Beverages & Tobacco	51 260	53 470	54 350	54 810	54 800	56 660	58 450	62 220	..	..
311.2	Food	42 550	44 030	45 190	46 020	45 730	46 870	48 570	51 270	..	..
313	Beverages	6 230	6 820	6 430	5 960	6 180	6 760	6 970	7 080	..	..
314	Tobacco	2 480	2 620	2 730	2 830	2 890	3 030	2 910	3 870	..	..
32	Textiles, Apparel & Leather	16 240	16 790	17 460	16 650	15 230	15 030	15 530	16 960	..	..
321	Textiles	8 350	8 650	8 910	8 380	7 880	7 860	8 210	9 390	..	..
3213	Knitting Mills	1 130	1 120	1 120	990	990	970	1 000	1 130	..	..
322	Wearing Apparel	6 390	6 680	7 120	6 960	6 280	6 110	6 220	6 370	..	..
323	Leather & Products	490	520	530	470	360	350	330	350	..	..
324	Footwear	1 010	940	900	840	710	710	770	850	..	..
33	Wood Products & Furniture	19 130	20 240	20 970	19 750	17 210	19 100	23 560	28 090	..	..
331	Wood Products	14 460	15 220	15 630	14 600	12 870	14 780	18 990	23 000	..	..
332	Furnitures & Fixtures	4 670	5 020	5 340	5 150	4 340	4 320	4 570	5 090	..	..
34	Paper, Paper Products & Printing	35 150	39 470	40 800	38 870	35 190	34 610	35 640	41 190	..	..
341	Paper & Products	23 460	26 340	26 630	24 490	21 490	21 130	22 080	26 950	..	..
3411	Pulp, Paper & Board	18 350	20 680	20 750	18 830	16 010	15 690	16 380	20 650	..	..
342	Printing & Publishing	11 690	13 130	14 170	14 380	13 700	13 480	13 560	14 240	..	..
35	Chemical Products	53 480	54 870	57 670	60 520	55 940	57 410	61 830	58 090	..	..
351	Industrial Chemicals	12 640	14 950	15 370	14 940	13 080	12 880	14 070	16 840	..	..
3511	Basic Industrial Chemicals	7 790	9 580	9 680	9 610	8 380	7 970	7 750	9 120	..	..
3512	Fertilizers & Pesticides	1 890	1 770	1 960	1 720	1 470	1 510	1 820	2 090	..	..
3513	Synthetic Resins	2 960	3 600	3 730	3 610	3 230	3 400	4 500	5 630	..	..
352	Other Chemicals	11 950	12 920	13 570	13 590	13 630	14 210	15 000	15 940	..	..
3521	Paints, Varnishes & Lacquers	1 500	1 890	1 950	1 820	1 720	1 800	1 870	2 060	..	..
3522	Drugs & Medicines	3 680	3 990	4 060	4 490	4 460	5 040	5 490	5 630	..	..
3523	Soap & Cleaning Preparations	2 890	3 050	3 410	3 230	3 070	3 070	3 190	3 370	..	..
3529	Chemical Products, nec	3 880	3 990	4 150	4 050	4 180	4 300	4 450	4 880	..	..
353	Petroleum Refineries	17 520	14 420	15 580	19 630	17 730	17 370	17 380	7 900	..	..
354	Petroleum & Coal Products	880	790	940	840	760	780	780	860	..	..
355	Rubber Products	3 360	3 590	3 780	3 800	3 510	4 710	6 110	6 880	..	..
356	Plastic Products, nec	7 130	8 200	8 430	7 720	7 230	7 460	8 490	9 670	..	..
36	Non-Metallic Mineral Products	8 390	8 850	9 140	8 530	7 190	6 820	6 850	7 380	..	..
361	Pottery, China etc	200	160	140	130	120	130	110	100	..	..
362	Glass & Products	1 570	1 590	1 640	1 610	1 420	1 410	1 330	1 460	..	..
369	Non-Metallic Products, nec	6 620	7 100	7 360	6 790	5 650	5 280	5 410	5 820	..	..
37	Basic Metal Industries	19 740	23 810	23 880	19 690	18 460	18 330	20 180	23 940	..	..
371	Iron & Steel	10 450	12 130	12 480	10 000	9 420	9 440	11 070	12 980	..	..
372	Non-Ferrous Metals	9 290	11 680	11 400	9 690	9 040	8 890	9 110	10 960	..	..
38	Fabricated Metal Products	108 000	124 140	129 820	122 100	117 570	122 440	140 930	166 600	..	..
381	Metal Products	16 410	17 590	18 600	17 050	14 910	14 100	14 330	16 220	..	..
3813	Structural Metal Products	4 970	5 490	6 130	5 620	4 980	4 300	4 250	5 000	..	..
382	Non-Electrical Machinery	16 120	19 060	20 470	19 640	17 990	18 150	19 870	25 280	..	..
3821	Engines & Turbines	..	..	..	..	..	..	..	..	..	..
3822	Agricultural Machinery	880	1 040	1 250	1 280	820	910	1 180	1 760	..	..
3823	Metal & Wood working Machinery	1 030	1 120	1 250	1 200	1 060	1 110	1 370	1 820	..	..
3824	Special Industrial Machinery	3 390	3 870	4 080	3 710	2 870	2 620	2 990	3 710	..	..
3825	Office & Computing Machinery	2 650	3 540	3 650	3 730	3 790	4 070	4 110	6 130	..	..
3829	Machinery & Equipment, nec	8 170	9 490	10 240	9 720	9 450	9 440	10 220	11 860	..	..
383	Electrical Machinery	14 960	16 630	17 940	17 140	18 040	18 830	19 120	21 210	..	..
3831	Electrical Industrial Machinery	2 770	3 050	3 420	3 360	3 150	3 050	3 400	3 850	..	..
3832	Radio, TV & Communication Equipment	7 280	8 190	9 000	8 810	10 570	12 000	11 840	12 940	..	..
3833	Electrical Appliances & Housewares	810	600	740	550	490	400	370	430	..	..
3839	Electrical Apparatus, nec	4 100	4 790	4 780	4 420	3 830	3 380	3 510	3 990	..	..
384	Transport Equipment	58 700	68 900	70 760	66 240	64 610	69 480	85 660	101 790	..	..
3841	Shipbuilding & Repairing	1 360	1 760	2 100	1 980	1 740	1 390	1 460	1 300	..	..
3842	Railroad Equipment	1 460	1 410	1 870	1 590	1 340	1 470	1 360	2 310	..	..
3843	Motor Vehicles	51 600	60 770	60 920	56 120	55 360	60 580	76 860	91 130	..	..
3844	Motorcycles & Bicycles	..	..	..	..	..	..	..	..	..	..
3845	Aircraft	4 010	4 670	5 490	6 220	5 830	5 490	5 190	5 930	..	..
3849	Transport Equipment, nec	270	290	380	330	340	550	790	1 120	..	..
385	Professional Goods	1 810	1 960	2 050	2 030	2 020	1 880	1 950	2 100	..	..
3851	Professional Equipment	1 560	1 670	1 730	1 710	1 700	1 570	1 650	1 770	..	..
3852	Photographic & Optical Goods	220	250	280	280	280	270	260	290	..	..
3853	Watches & Clocks	30	40	40	40	40	40	40	40	..	..
39	Other Manufacturing, nes	3 320	3 690	3 910	3 810	3 620	3 510	3 560	4 150	..	..
3901	Jewellery	400	440	480	500	430	390	420	540	..	..
3	Total Manufacturing	314 710	345 320	358 020	344 740	325 190	333 910	366 510	408 620	..	..
1	Agric., Hunting, Forestry, Fishing	..	..	..				..		..	..
2	Mining & Quarrying	33 170	33 870	37 060	..		..	..		..	..
21	Coal Mining	1 560	1 760	1 660		1 760	1 470	1 650	1 590	..	..
22	Crude Petroleum & Natural Gas	19 130	16 410	18 270	21 480	18 350	19 180	21 440	21 870	..	..
23.29	Other Mining	12 480	15 700	17 130		..		..		..	..
3	Total Manufacturing	314 710	345 320	358 020	344 740	325 190	333 910	366 510	408 620	..	..
4	Electricity, Gas & Water	29 600	31 290	31 190	34 450	36 780	..	41 560	43 170	..	..
5	Construction	..	..	..	..	..	..	..	..	..	..
6.9	Services	..	..	..	..	..	..	..	..	..	..
0000	Grand Total	..	..	..	..	..	..	..	..	..	..

Note: ISIC 3829 includes 3821; 3832 includes 3902; 39 includes 3232 and 3844.

Millions of C$

(Current Prices)

ISIC2	Industry	VALUE ADDED									
		1987	1988	1989	1990	1991	1992	1993	1994	1995	1996
31	Food, Beverages & Tobacco	17 050	17 930	18 350	19 400	20 300	21 610	21 330	22 660	..	..
311.2	Food	12 810	13 250	13 660	14 820	15 480	16 200	15 900	16 820	..	..
313	Beverages	3 260	3 660	3 610	3 440	3 620	4 140	4 210	4 210	..	..
314	Tobacco	980	1 020	1 080	1 140	1 200	1 270	1 220	1 630	..	..
32	Textiles, Apparel & Leather	7 140	7 360	7 700	7 350	6 830	6 770	6 960	7 480	..	..
321	Textiles	3 440	3 610	3 690	3 470	3 340	3 420	3 600	3 990	..	..
3213	Knitting Mills	490	480	500	440	440	440	450	520	..	..
322	Wearing Apparel	3 040	3 120	3 370	3 300	3 010	2 870	2 860	2 950	..	..
323	Leather & Products	180	200	220	190	150	140	140	140	..	..
324	Footwear	480	430	420	390	330	340	360	400	..	..
33	Wood Products & Furniture	8 440	8 280	8 600	7 830	6 730	7 820	10 190	12 200	..	..
331	Wood Products	6 140	5 850	5 980	5 210	4 580	5 620	7 880	9 630	..	..
332	Furnitures & Fixtures	2 300	2 430	2 620	2 620	2 150	2 200	2 310	2 570	..	..
34	Paper, Paper Products & Printing	17 840	20 100	20 220	19 160	16 400	16 210	16 390	19 860	..	..
341	Paper & Products	10 750	12 270	11 730	10 210	7 890	7 590	7 890	10 910	..	..
3411	Pulp, Paper & Board	8 850	10 180	9 550	8 040	5 770	5 530	5 670	8 460	..	..
342	Printing & Publishing	7 090	7 830	8 490	8 950	8 510	8 620	8 500	8 950	..	..
35	Chemical Products	17 190	20 230	20 250	20 910	19 200	20 010	21 320	24 370	..	..
351	Industrial Chemicals	4 500	6 320	6 300	5 610	4 380	4 560	5 010	6 630	..	..
3511	Basic Industrial Chemicals	3 030	4 460	4 490	3 900	2 950	3 030	3 210	4 140	..	..
3512	Fertilizers & Pesticides	510	500	630	580	480	520	600	800	..	..
3513	Synthetic Resins	960	1 360	1 180	1 130	950	1 010	1 200	1 690	..	..
352	Other Chemicals	6 110	6 650	7 050	7 300	7 430	7 600	7 850	8 110	..	..
3521	Paints, Varnishes & Lacquers	700	880	920	830	790	830	830	880	..	..
3522	Drugs & Medicines	2 230	2 500	2 570	2 930	3 000	3 140	3 370	3 250	..	..
3523	Soap & Cleaning Preparations	1 510	1 600	1 790	1 760	1 660	1 650	1 690	1 790	..	..
3529	Chemical Products, nec	1 670	1 670	1 770	1 780	1 980	1 980	1 960	2 190	..	..
353	Petroleum Refineries	1 960	2 190	1 610	2 650	2 380	2 040	2 250	2 620	..	..
354	Petroleum & Coal Products	310	300	330	340	270	330	310	330	..	..
355	Rubber Products	1 420	1 540	1 580	1 630	1 510	2 030	2 140	2 370	..	..
356	Plastic Products, nec	2 890	3 230	3 380	3 380	3 230	3 450	3 760	4 310	..	..
36	Non-Metallic Mineral Products	4 160	4 470	4 460	4 100	3 410	3 270	3 400	3 670	..	..
361	Pottery, China etc	130	100	90	80	70	70	60	50	..	..
362	Glass & Products	870	870	820	750	660	690	700	780	..	..
369	Non-Metallic Products, nec	3 160	3 500	3 550	3 270	2 680	2 510	2 640	2 840	..	..
37	Basic Metal Industries	8 440	10 330	9 550	7 530	6 920	6 890	7 790	9 430	..	..
371	Iron & Steel	4 290	4 930	4 990	3 770	3 490	3 570	4 320	4 920	..	..
372	Non-Ferrous Metals	4 150	5 400	4 560	3 760	3 430	3 320	3 470	4 510	..	..
38	Fabricated Metal Products	36 420	41 350	44 580	42 640	39 230	40 000	44 500	51 880	..	..
381	Metal Products	7 160	7 610	7 930	7 530	6 660	6 260	6 290	7 170	..	..
3813	Structural Metal Products	2 400	2 580	2 790	2 690	2 350	2 020	1 930	2 220	..	..
382	Non-Electrical Machinery	7 270	8 640	9 100	8 840	7 810	7 900	9 130	10 700	..	..
3821	Engines & Turbines	..	..	..	..	..	..	..	..	..	..
3822	Agricultural Machinery	360	450	560	610	350	470	570	770	..	..
3823	Metal & Wood working Machinery	610	670	770	780	670	730	900	1 190	..	..
3824	Special Industrial Machinery	1 330	1 540	1 650	1 590	1 200	1 140	1 350	1 660	..	..
3825	Office & Computing Machinery	1 220	1 580	1 460	1 290	1 090	1 040	1 290	1 350	..	..
3829	Machinery & Equipment, nec	3 750	4 400	4 660	4 570	4 500	4 520	5 020	5 730	..	..
383	Electrical Machinery	7 300	8 120	8 870	8 710	8 060	8 270	8 520	9 630	..	..
3831	Electrical Industrial Machinery	1 300	1 500	1 680	1 640	1 480	1 470	1 660	1 870	..	..
3832	Radio, TV & Communication Equipment	3 890	4 340	4 840	4 800	4 830	5 220	5 170	5 810	..	..
3833	Electrical Appliances & Housewares	350	280	300	280	240	170	160	210	..	..
3839	Electrical Apparatus, nec	1 760	2 000	2 050	1 990	1 510	1 410	1 530	1 740	..	..
384	Transport Equipment	13 770	15 970	17 630	16 480	15 570	16 520	19 430	23 180	..	..
3841	Shipbuilding & Repairing	500	690	880	810	770	740	920	780	..	..
3842	Railroad Equipment	750	710	800	620	660	650	520	930	..	..
3843	Motor Vehicles	10 110	12 130	12 830	11 500	10 860	11 650	14 510	17 430	..	..
3844	Motorcycles & Bicycles	..	..	..	..	..	..	..	..	..	..
3845	Aircraft	2 280	2 320	2 950	3 400	3 120	3 240	3 130	3 530	..	..
3849	Transport Equipment, nec	130	120	170	150	160	240	350	510	..	..
385	Professional Goods	920	1 010	1 050	1 080	1 130	1 050	1 130	1 200	..	..
3851	Professional Equipment	810	880	890	920	970	900	970	1 030	..	..
3852	Photographic & Optical Goods	100	110	140	140	140	130	140	150	..	..
3853	Watches & Clocks	10	20	20	20	20	20	20	20	..	..
39	Other Manufacturing, nes	1 640	1 860	1 980	1 990	1 870	1 870	1 890	2 220	..	..
3901	Jewellery	170	190	220	240	200	190	190	260	..	..
3	Total Manufacturing	118 360	131 920	135 690	130 930	120 890	124 410	133 780	153 790	..	..
1	Agric., Hunting, Forestry, Fishing	..	..	..	..	..	..	..	..	..	..
2	Mining & Quarrying	26 310	25 910	28 710	29 650	25 240	25 510	26 900	31 070	..	..
21	Coal Mining	1 140	1 280	1 200	1 320	1 250	1 000	1 210	1 130	..	..
22	Crude Petroleum & Natural Gas	17 340	14 210	15 880	19 140	16 160	16 950	19 120	22 000	..	..
23 29	Other Mining	7 830	10 420	11 630	9 190	7 830	7 560	6 570	7 940	..	..
3	Total Manufacturing	118 360	131 920	135 690	130 930	120 890	124 410	133 780	153 790	..	..
4	Electricity, Gas & Water	15 340	32 840	15 090	18 390	18 400	..	21 270	22 190	..	..
5	Construction	..	..	..	..	..	..	..	..	..	..
6.9	Services	..	..	..	..	..	..	..	..	..	..
0000	Grand Total	..	..	..	..	..	..	..	..	..	..

Note: ISIC 3829 includes 3821; 3832 includes 3902; 39 includes 3232 and 3844.

Thousands

Table CA.4 **CANADA**

ISIC2	Industry	EMPLOYMENT - EMPLOYEES									
		1987	1988	1989	1990	1991	1992	1993	1994	1995	1996
31	**Food, Beverages & Tobacco**	235.0	238.0	234.0	227.0	219.0	227.0	221.0	220.0	..	..
311.2	Food	197.0	201.0	202.0	198.0	192.0	195.0	189.0	189.0		
313	Beverages	32.0	31.0	27.0	24.0	22.0	27.0	27.0	26.0		
314	Tobacco	6.0	6.0	5.0	5.0	5.0	5.0	5.0	5.0		
32	**Textiles, Apparel & Leather**	199.0	204.0	198.0	182.0	167.0	151.0	148.0	149.0		
321	Textiles	76.0	79.0	76.0	72.0	69.0	62.0	60.0	63.0		
3213	Knitting Mills	14.0	14.0	13.0	12.0	12.0	11.0	10.0	11.0		
322	Wearing Apparel	101.0	105.0	103.0	94.0	84.0	76.0	75.0	73.0		
323	Leather & Products	6.0	6.0	6.0	5.0	5.0	4.0	3.0	3.0		
324	Footwear	16.0	14.0	13.0	11.0	9.0	9.0	10.0	10.0		
33	**Wood Products & Furniture**	177.0	179.0	182.0	170.0	146.0	143.0	150.0	159.0		
331	Wood Products	112.0	113.0	113.0	104.0	91.0	94.0	100.0	107.0		
332	Furnitures & Fixtures	65.0	66.0	69.0	66.0	55.0	49.0	50.0	52.0		
34	**Paper, Paper Products & Printing**	245.0	253.0	260.0	256.0	243.0	233.0	226.0	223.0		
341	Paper & Products	117.0	119.0	119.0	114.0	109.0	104.0	101.0	100.0		
3411	Pulp, Paper & Board	80.0	81.0	81.0	78.0	75.0	70.0	68.0	67.0		
342	Printing & Publishing	128.0	134.0	141.0	142.0	134.0	129.0	125.0	123.0		
35	**Chemical Products**	195.0	208.0	212.0	206.0	197.0	197.0	198.0	195.0		
351	Industrial Chemicals	32.0	33.0	32.0	33.0	32.0	31.0	31.0	28.0		
3511	Basic Industrial Chemicals	19.0	21.0	20.0	22.0	21.0	20.0	17.0	15.0		
3512	Fertilizers & Pesticides	6.0	5.0	5.0	4.0	4.0	4.0	5.0	4.0		
3513	Synthetic Resins	7.0	7.0	7.0	7.0	7.0	7.0	9.0	9.0		
352	Other Chemicals	65.0	68.0	70.0	68.0	66.0	68.0	66.0	64.0		
3521	Paints, Varnishes & Lacquers	7.0	8.0	9.0	8.0	7.0	8.0	7.0	7.0		
3522	Drugs & Medicines	19.0	19.0	19.0	20.0	21.0	21.0	22.0	20.0		
3523	Soap & Cleaning Preparations	18.0	19.0	19.0	18.0	15.0	16.0	15.0	15.0		
3529	Chemical Products, nec	21.0	22.0	23.0	22.0	23.0	23.0	22.0	22.0		
353	Petroleum Refineries	14.0	14.0	15.0	15.0	14.0	12.0	13.0	12.0		
354	Petroleum & Coal Products	3.0	3.0	3.0	3.0	2.0	3.0	3.0	2.0		
355	Rubber Products	24.0	26.0	26.0	25.0	23.0	23.0	23.0	24.0		
356	Plastic Products, nec	57.0	64.0	66.0	62.0	60.0	60.0	62.0	65.0		
36	**Non-Metallic Mineral Products**	57.0	57.0	57.0	54.0	50.0	45.0	43.0	42.0		
361	Pottery, China etc	2.0	2.0	1.0	1.0	1.0	1.0	1.0	1.0		
362	Glass & Products	14.0	13.0	13.0	12.0	11.0	10.0	10.0	9.0		
369	Non-Metallic Products, nec	41.0	42.0	43.0	41.0	38.0	34.0	32.0	32.0		
37	**Basic Metal Industries**	104.0	109.0	107.0	97.0	92.0	87.0	85.0	84.0		
371	Iron & Steel	59.0	62.0	60.0	53.0	51.0	47.0	46.0	46.0		
372	Non-Ferrous Metals	45.0	47.0	47.0	44.0	41.0	40.0	39.0	38.0		
38	**Fabricated Metal Products**	608.0	652.0	672.0	627.0	579.0	553.0	539.0	557.0		
381	Metal Products	133.0	141.0	147.0	135.0	123.0	109.0	106.0	109.0		
3813	Structural Metal Products	44.0	47.0	51.0	48.0	44.0	37.0	35.0	35.0		
382	Non-Electrical Machinery	141.0	156.0	164.0	148.0	138.0	128.0	129.0	140.0		
3821	Engines & Turbines	..	..	..	..	..	..	..	..		
3822	Agricultural Machinery	9.0	10.0	10.0	10.0	8.0	8.0	9.0	10.0		
3823	Metal & Wood working Machinery	13.0	14.0	17.0	15.0	14.0	12.0	14.0	16.0		
3824	Special Industrial Machinery	25.0	27.0	29.0	25.0	22.0	20.0	20.0	21.0		
3825	Office & Computing Machinery	17.0	18.0	18.0	16.0	16.0	17.0	15.0	16.0		
3829	Machinery & Equipment, nec	77.0	87.0	90.0	82.0	78.0	71.0	71.0	77.0		
383	Electrical Machinery	122.0	129.0	128.0	123.0	114.0	110.0	104.0	101.0		
3831	Electrical Industrial Machinery	28.0	29.0	30.0	29.0	26.0	24.0	24.0	23.0		
3832	Radio, TV & Communication Equipment	61.0	67.0	66.0	64.0	60.0	62.0	58.0	57.0		
3833	Electrical Appliances & Housewares	7.0	5.0	5.0	4.0	4.0	3.0	3.0	3.0		
3839	Electrical Apparatus, nec	26.0	28.0	27.0	26.0	24.0	21.0	19.0	18.0		
384	Transport Equipment	194.0	207.0	215.0	204.0	188.0	192.0	187.0	193.0		
3841	Shipbuilding & Repairing	14.0	16.0	18.0	16.0	13.0	14.0	12.0	11.0		
3842	Railroad Equipment	8.0	8.0	8.0	7.0	7.0	7.0	7.0	8.0		
3843	Motor Vehicles	130.0	137.0	142.0	133.0	123.0	127.0	130.0	135.0		
3844	Motorcycles & Bicycles										
3845	Aircraft	40.0	44.0	45.0	46.0	43.0	42.0	36.0	36.0		
3849	Transport Equipment, nec	2.0	2.0	2.0	2.0	2.0	2.0	2.0	3.0		
385	Professional Goods	18.0	19.0	18.0	17.0	16.0	14.0	13.0	14.0		
3851	Professional Equipment	15.0	16.0	15.0	14.0	13.0	12.0	11.0	11.0		
3852	Photographic & Optical Goods	3.0	3.0	3.0	3.0	3.0	2.0	2.0	3.0		
3853	Watches & Clocks	..	..	..	..	..		0.0	0.0		
39	**Other Manufacturing, nes**	43.0	47.0	51.0	49.0	45.0	39.0	38.0	40.0		
3901	Jewellery	5.0	5.0	6.0	6.0	5.0	4.0	5.0	5.0		
3	**Total Manufacturing**	1 865.0	1 947.0	1 969.0	1 869.0	1 738.0	1 674.0	1 647.0	1 670.0	..	..
1	**Agric., Hunting, Forestry, Fishing**	..	..	..	..	..	..	..	..	..	..
2	**Mining & Quarrying**	113.0	118.0	117.0	113.0	108.0	97.0	93.0	93.0	..	..
21	Coal Mining	10.0	11.0	11.0	12.0	11.0	10.0	9.0	9.0		
22	Crude Petroleum & Natural Gas	40.0	41.0	40.0	39.0	39.0	35.0	34.0	35.0		
23.29	Other Mining	63.0	66.0	66.0	62.0	58.0	52.0	50.0	49.0		
3	**Total Manufacturing**	1 865.0	1 947.0	1 969.0	1 869.0	1 738.0	1 674.0	1 647.0	1 670.0	..	..
4	**Electricity, Gas & Water**	101.0	93.0	101.0	102.0	108.0	108.0	..	..	..	..
5	**Construction**	..	..	..	..	..	..		..	..	..
6.9	**Services**	..	..	..	..	..	..			..	..
0000	**Grand Total**	..	..	..	..	..	..			..	..

Note: ISIC 3829 includes 3821; 3832 includes 3902; 39 includes 3232 and 3844.

Millions of C$

(Current Prices)

ISIC2	Industry	WAGES & SALARIES - EMPLOYEES									
		1987	1988	1989	1990	1991	1992	1993	1994	1995	1996
31	Food, Beverages & Tobacco	6 236	6 595	6 771	6 828	6 899	7 322	7 301	7 357	..	..
311.2	Food	4 926	5 265	5 503	5 639	5 652	5 905	5 875	5 925	..	..
313	Beverages	1 067	1 100	1 031	947	995	1 154	1 168	1 161	..	..
314	Tobacco	243	230	237	242	252	263	258	271	..	..
32	Textiles, Apparel & Leather	3 745	3 973	4 068	3 941	3 706	3 537	3 560	3 696	..	..
321	Textiles	1 705	1 831	1 858	1 799	1 765	1 701	1 736	1 844	..	..
3213	Knitting Mills	251	258	256	240	248	229	241	264	..	..
322	Wearing Apparel	1 664	1 778	1 861	1 799	1 653	1 561	1 539	1 554	..	..
323	Leather & Products	100	105	110	109	94	80	75	77	..	..
324	Footwear	276	259	239	234	194	195	210	221	..	..
33	Wood Products & Furniture	4 382	4 687	4 910	4 796	4 281	4 404	4 735	5 194	..	..
331	Wood Products	3 085	3 272	3 376	3 255	2 946	3 136	3 438	3 826	..	..
332	Furnitures & Fixtures	1 297	1 415	1 534	1 541	1 335	1 268	1 297	1 368	..	..
34	Paper, Paper Products & Printing	7 663	8 444	9 090	9 320	9 227	9 085	9 054	9 204	..	..
341	Paper & Products	4 123	4 419	4 631	4 639	4 648	4 566	4 578	4 729	..	..
3411	Pulp, Paper & Board	3 114	3 332	3 491	3 497	3 525	3 402	3 428	3 519	..	..
342	Printing & Publishing	3 540	4 025	4 459	4 681	4 579	4 519	4 476	4 475	..	..
35	Chemical Products	5 966	6 578	6 987	7 219	7 114	7 183	7 443	7 710	..	..
351	Industrial Chemicals	1 299	1 371	1 421	1 549	1 502	1 496	1 495	1 489	..	..
3511	Basic Industrial Chemicals	850	936	950	1 067	1 039	999	880	852	..	..
3512	Fertilizers & Pesticides	203	175	184	164	150	162	199	182	..	..
3513	Synthetic Resins	246	260	287	318	313	335	416	455	..	..
352	Other Chemicals	1 910	2 118	2 281	2 343	2 410	2 463	2 526	2 622	..	..
3521	Paints, Varnishes & Lacquers	194	256	278	281	258	268	263	279	..	..
3522	Drugs & Medicines	593	652	679	734	815	851	903	938	..	..
3523	Soap & Cleaning Preparations	485	537	586	574	512	531	542	553	..	..
3529	Chemical Products, nec	638	673	738	754	825	813	818	852	..	..
353	Petroleum Refineries	680	692	741	766	721	657	721	690	..	..
354	Petroleum & Coal Products	90	93	93	89	78	92	92	91	..	..
355	Rubber Products	715	804	821	839	802	835	843	903	..	..
356	Plastic Products, nec	1 272	1 500	1 630	1 633	1 601	1 640	1 766	1 915	..	..
36	Non-Metallic Mineral Products	1 670	1 775	1 842	1 810	1 658	1 566	1 535	1 523	..	..
361	Pottery, China etc	53	40	39	35	34	36	28	25	..	..
362	Glass & Products	406	413	398	387	366	349	352	337	..	..
369	Non-Metallic Products, nec	1 211	1 322	1 405	1 388	1 258	1 181	1 155	1 161	..	..
37	Basic Metal Industries	3 856	4 228	4 399	4 162	4 161	4 133	4 096	4 085	..	..
371	Iron & Steel	2 207	2 410	2 445	2 261	2 270	2 180	2 197	2 272	..	..
372	Non-Ferrous Metals	1 649	1 818	1 954	1 901	1 891	1 953	1 899	1 813	..	..
38	Fabricated Metal Products	17 497	19 518	21 034	20 779	19 956	19 913	20 247	21 818	..	..
381	Metal Products	3 331	3 723	4 115	4 023	3 767	3 452	3 356	3 584	..	..
3813	Structural Metal Products	1 128	1 259	1 486	1 482	1 404	1 222	1 127	1 169	..	..
382	Non-Electrical Machinery	3 743	4 273	4 698	4 624	4 477	4 309	4 538	5 100	..	..
3821	Engines & Turbines	..	..	..	..	..	..	..	..	..	..
3822	Agricultural Machinery	246	251	272	278	234	242	261	307	..	..
3823	Metal & Wood working Machinery	382	426	501	487	485	459	514	614	..	..
3824	Special Industrial Machinery	666	772	853	821	736	670	694	765	..	..
3825	Office & Computing Machinery	504	531	564	538	565	595	611	638	..	..
3829	Machinery & Equipment, nec	1 945	2 293	2 508	2 500	2 457	2 343	2 458	2 776	..	..
383	Electrical Machinery	3 452	3 780	3 970	4 023	3 909	3 993	3 875	3 927	..	..
3831	Electrical Industrial Machinery	729	795	855	881	844	815	830	829	..	..
3832	Radio, TV & Communication Equipment	1 867	2 086	2 169	2 200	2 191	2 380	2 285	2 321	..	..
3833	Electrical Appliances & Housewares	154	113	132	122	97	91	88	108	..	..
3839	Electrical Apparatus, nec	702	786	814	820	777	707	672	669	..	..
384	Transport Equipment	6 494	7 217	7 719	7 574	7 283	7 670	8 006	8 722	..	..
3841	Shipbuilding & Repairing	387	469	534	526	455	511	476	419	..	..
3842	Railroad Equipment	262	272	295	269	270	263	272	370	..	..
3843	Motor Vehicles	4 466	4 882	5 184	4 923	4 757	5 084	5 594	6 197	..	..
3844	Motorcycles & Bicycles	..	..	..	..	..	..	..	..	..	..
3845	Aircraft	1 321	1 534	1 638	1 791	1 745	1 746	1 590	1 649	..	..
3849	Transport Equipment, nec	58	60	68	65	56	66	74	87	..	..
385	Professional Goods	477	525	532	535	520	489	472	485	..	..
3851	Professional Equipment	406	447	449	451	437	414	398	403	..	..
3852	Photographic & Optical Goods	65	72	76	77	75	67	67	73	..	..
3853	Watches & Clocks	6	6	7	7	8	8	7	9	..	..
39	Other Manufacturing, nes	835	993	1 112	1 136	1 082	1 015	1 008	1 055	..	..
3901	Jewellery	97	110	128	136	132	109	116	125	..	..
3	Total Manufacturing	51 850	56 792	60 210	59 992	58 083	58 157	58 979	61 638	..	..
1	Agric., Hunting, Forestry, Fishing	..	..	..	..	..	..	..	..	..	..
2	Mining & Quarrying	4 767	5 320	5 632	5 696	6 818	5 493	5 185	5 460	..	..
21	Coal Mining	430	476	520	550	489	418	418	460	..	..
22	Crude Petroleum & Natural Gas	1 937	2 127	2 202	2 248	2 562	2 356	2 258	2 440	..	..
23.29	Other Mining	2 400	2 717	2 910	2 898	3 767	2 719	2 509	2 560	..	..
3	Total Manufacturing	51 850	56 792	60 210	59 992	58 083	58 157	58 979	61 638	..	..
4	Electricity, Gas & Water	3 473	3 835	4 389	4 625	5 333	5 292	..	..	..	..
5	Construction	..	..	..	..	..	..	..	..	..	..
6.9	Services	..	..	..	..	..	..	..	..	..	..
0000	Grand Total	..	..	..	..	..	..	..	..	..	..

Note: ISIC 3829 includes 3821; 3832 includes 3902; 39 includes 3232 and 3844.

Table CA.8 **CANADA**

ISIC2	Industry	HOURS WORKED									
		1987	1988	1989	1990	1991	1992	1993	1994	1995	1996
31	**Food, Beverages & Tobacco**	..	305 000	301 000	293 000	284 000	290 000	286 000	285 000	..	..
311.2	Food	..	267 000	267 000	264 000	256 000	260 000	257 000	257 000	..	..
313	Beverages	..	33 000	30 000	25 000	24 000	26 000	25 000	24 000	..	..
314	Tobacco	..	5 000	4 000	4 000	4 000	4 000	4 000	4 000	..	..
32	**Textiles, Apparel & Leather**	..	337 000	317 000	290 000	258 000	230 000	231 000	231 000	..	..
321	Textiles	..	126 000	124 000	114 000	106 000	95 000	95 000	98 000	..	..
3213	Knitting Mills	..	24 000	21 000	20 000	20 000	18 000	18 000	19 000	..	..
322	Wearing Apparel	..	177 000	162 000	149 000	130 000	117 000	117 000	113 000	..	..
323	Leather & Products	..	10 000	10 000	9 000	8 000	5 000	5 000	5 000	..	..
324	Footwear	..	24 000	21 000	18 000	14 000	13 000	14 000	15 000	..	..
33	**Wood Products & Furniture**	..	303 000	303 000	278 000	205 000	226 000	235 000	254 000	..	..
331	Wood Products	..	189 000	186 000	168 000	112 000	150 000	157 000	172 000	..	..
332	Furnitures & Fixtures	..	114 000	117 000	110 000	93 000	76 000	78 000	82 000	..	..
34	**Paper, Paper Products & Printing**	..	319 000	327 000	315 000	305 000	287 000	277 000	273 000	..	..
341	Paper & Products	..	168 000	169 000	160 000	157 000	149 000	146 000	145 000	..	..
3411	Pulp, Paper & Board	..	116 000	116 000	110 000	109 000	100 000	98 000	97 000	..	..
342	Printing & Publishing	..	151 000	158 000	155 000	148 000	138 000	131 000	128 000	..	..
35	**Chemical Products**	..	257 000	264 000	248 000	239 000	245 000	250 000	255 000	..	..
351	Industrial Chemicals	..	37 000	37 000	38 000	36 000	35 000	36 000	36 000	..	..
3511	Basic Industrial Chemicals	..	24 000	25 000	26 000	25 000	23 000	20 000	19 000	..	..
3512	Fertilizers & Pesticides	..	5 000	5 000	4 000	4 000	4 000	5 000	5 000	..	..
3513	Synthetic Resins	..	8 000	7 000	8 000	7 000	8 000	11 000	12 000	..	..
352	Other Chemicals	..	69 000	71 000	66 000	64 000	69 000	68 000	66 000	..	..
3521	Paints, Varnishes & Lacquers	..	9 000	9 000	8 000	7 000	8 000	8 000	8 000	..	..
3522	Drugs & Medicines	..	15 000	16 000	16 000	16 000	19 000	18 000	16 000	..	..
3523	Soap & Cleaning Preparations	..	19 000	19 000	17 000	15 000	15 000	15 000	15 000	..	..
3529	Chemical Products, nec	..	26 000	27 000	25 000	26 000	27 000	27 000	27 000	..	..
353	Petroleum Refineries	..	12 000	12 000	12 000	11 000	11 000	11 000	11 000	..	..
354	Petroleum & Coal Products	..	4 000	4 000	4 000	3 000	4 000	4 000	4 000	..	..
355	Rubber Products	..	36 000	36 000	33 000	31 000	32 000	32 000	34 000	..	..
356	Plastic Products, nec	..	99 000	104 000	95 000	94 000	94 000	99 000	104 000	..	..
36	**Non-Metallic Mineral Products**	..	89 000	89 000	84 000	75 000	66 000	62 000	62 000	..	..
361	Pottery, China etc	..	2 000	2 000	2 000	2 000	2 000	1 000	1 000	..	..
362	Glass & Products	..	20 000	20 000	18 000	17 000	16 000	15 000	15 000	..	..
369	Non-Metallic Products, nec	..	67 000	67 000	64 000	56 000	48 000	46 000	46 000	..	..
37	**Basic Metal Industries**	..	160 000	153 000	140 000	136 000	130 000	128 000	131 000	..	..
371	Iron & Steel	..	96 000	87 000	77 000	77 000	70 000	70 000	75 000	..	..
372	Non-Ferrous Metals	..	64 000	66 000	63 000	59 000	60 000	58 000	56 000	..	..
38	**Fabricated Metal Products**	..	957 000	992 000	896 000	828 000	784 000	780 000	830 000	..	..
381	Metal Products	..	220 000	230 000	202 000	188 000	160 000	157 000	163 000	..	..
3813	Structural Metal Products	..	70 000	78 000	71 000	66 000	54 000	50 000	49 000	..	..
382	Non-Electrical Machinery	..	229 000	243 000	218 000	202 000	180 000	185 000	203 000	..	..
3821	Engines & Turbines	..	..	..	..	..	..	..	..	..	..
3822	Agricultural Machinery	..	15 000	16 000	15 000	12 000	12 000	13 000	15 000	..	..
3823	Metal & Wood working Machinery	..	25 000	30 000	25 000	25 000	21 000	23 000	28 000	..	..
3824	Special Industrial Machinery	..	40 000	42 000	36 000	31 000	28 000	29 000	30 000	..	..
3825	Office & Computing Machinery	..	17 000	16 000	16 000	15 000	17 000	17 000	18 000	..	..
3829	Machinery & Equipment, nec	..	132 000	139 000	126 000	119 000	102 000	103 000	112 000	..	..
383	Electrical Machinery	..	171 000	170 000	161 000	148 000	147 000	139 000	144 000	..	..
3831	Electrical Industrial Machinery	..	40 000	41 000	41 000	36 000	34 000	35 000	35 000	..	..
3832	Radio, TV & Communication Equipment	..	88 000	87 000	81 000	76 000	80 000	73 000	79 000	..	..
3833	Electrical Appliances & Housewares	..	6 000	6 000	5 000	5 000	4 000	4 000	4 000	..	..
3839	Electrical Apparatus, nec	..	37 000	36 000	34 000	31 000	29 000	27 000	26 000	..	..
384	Transport Equipment	..	313 000	325 000	294 000	270 000	279 000	282 000	303 000	..	..
3841	Shipbuilding & Repairing	..	23 000	26 000	23 000	19 000	20 000	18 000	17 000	..	..
3842	Railroad Equipment	..	10 000	11 000	8 000	8 000	8 000	8 000	12 000	..	..
3843	Motor Vehicles	..	223 000	229 000	202 000	187 000	195 000	207 000	225 000	..	..
3844	Motorcycles & Bicycles	..	..	..	..	..	..	..	..	..	..
3845	Aircraft	..	55 000	56 000	59 000	54 000	54 000	46 000	46 000	..	..
3849	Transport Equipment, nec	..	2 000	3 000	2 000	2 000	2 000	3 000	3 000	..	..
385	Professional Goods	..	24 000	24 000	21 000	20 000	18 000	17 000	17 000	..	..
3851	Professional Equipment	..	18 000	18 000	15 000	15 000	14 000	12 000	12 000	..	..
3852	Photographic & Optical Goods	..	6 000	6 000	6 000	5 000	4 000	5 000	5 000	..	..
3853	Watches & Clocks	..	..	..	..	..	..	0	0	..	..
39	**Other Manufacturing, nes**	..	71 000	76 000	78 000	69 000	56 000	54 000	56 000	..	..
3901	Jewellery	..	8 000	9 000	10 000	9 000	7 000	7 000	7 000	..	..
3	**Total Manufacturing**	..	2 798 000	2 823 000	2 616 000	2 400 000	2 317 000	2 306 000	2 374 000	..	..
1	**Agric., Hunting, Forestry, Fishing**	..	..	..	..	..	..	..	..	..	..
2	**Mining & Quarrying**	107 000	113 000	93 000	..	..	..	..	..	..	..
21	Coal Mining	15 000	16 000	..	..	18 000	15 000	15 000	16 000	..	..
22	Crude Petroleum & Natural Gas	..	..	..	..	..	..	..	..	..	..
23.29	Other Mining	92 000	97 000	93 000	..	..	..	..	25 000	..	..
3	**Total Manufacturing**	..	2 798 000	2 823 000	2 616 000	2 400 000	2 317 000	2 306 000	2 374 000	..	..
4	**Electricity, Gas & Water**	..	..	..	..	..	..	..	..	..	..
5	**Construction**	..	..	..	..	..	..	..	..	..	..
6.9	**Services**	..	..	..	..	..	..	..	..	..	..
0000	**Grand Total**	..	..	..	..	..	..	..	..	..	..

Note: Hours worked is hours paid.
ISIC 3829 includes 3821; 3832 includes 3902; 39 includes 3232 and 3844.

Units

ISIC2	Industry	ESTABLISHMENTS									
		1987	1988	1989	1990	1991	1992	1993	1994	1995	1996
31	Food, Beverages & Tobacco	3 465	3 619	3 678	3 675	3 426	3 299	3 219	3 163	..	..
311.2	Food	3 144	3 313	3 385	3 397	3 176	3 068	3 008	2 957	..	..
313	Beverages	296	287	274	260	234	214	194	189	..	..
314	Tobacco	25	19	19	18	16	17	17	17	..	..
32	Textiles, Apparel & Leather	3 867	4 410	4 206	4 331	3 752	3 400	3 115	2 873	..	..
321	Textiles	1 230	1 364	1 305	1 337	1 206	1 117	1 057	983	..	..
3213	Knitting Mills	203	203	201	199	184	169	157	146	..	..
322	Wearing Apparel	2 253	2 677	2 548	2 656	2 274	2 033	1 828	1 674	..	..
323	Leather & Products	210	219	218	204	165	150	135	124	..	..
324	Footwear	174	150	135	134	107	100	95	92	..	..
33	Wood Products & Furniture	5 169	5 505	5 142	5 279	4 684	4 362	4 166	4 044	..	..
331	Wood Products	2 725	2 889	2 697	2 672	2 426	2 288	2 201	2 205	..	..
332	Furnitures & Fixtures	2 444	2 616	2 445	2 607	2 258	2 074	1 965	1 839	..	..
34	Paper, Paper Products & Printing	5 951	6 319	5 935	6 237	5 735	5 561	5 306	5 128	..	..
341	Paper & Products	675	701	728	715	668	667	651	656	..	..
3411	Pulp, Paper & Board	144	145	147	146	155	156	158	162	..	..
342	Printing & Publishing	5 276	5 618	5 207	5 522	5 067	4 894	4 655	4 472	..	..
35	Chemical Products	2 969	3 318	3 347	3 330	3 081	2 999	2 960	2 958	..	..
351	Industrial Chemicals	416	450	477	475	446	435	436	444	..	..
3511	Basic Industrial Chemicals	180	193	205	210	202	198	195	211	..	..
3512	Fertilizers & Pesticides	142	157	175	165	153	152	150	144	..	..
3513	Synthetic Resins	94	100	97	100	91	85	91	89	..	..
352	Other Chemicals	1 021	1 173	1 145	1 154	1 034	1 003	960	961	..	..
3521	Paints, Varnishes & Lacquers	131	151	146	140	129	131	127	130	..	..
3522	Drugs & Medicines	139	148	145	136	122	117	119	112	..	..
3523	Soap & Cleaning Preparations	214	237	237	240	209	205	192	189	..	..
3529	Chemical Products, nec	537	637	617	638	574	550	522	530	..	..
353	Petroleum Refineries	64	68	75	62	61	60	62	61	..	..
354	Petroleum & Coal Products	81	90	106	92	92	102	108	119	..	..
355	Rubber Products	164	182	193	178	172	176	173	175	..	..
356	Plastic Products, nec	1 223	1 355	1 351	1 369	1 276	1 223	1 221	1 198	..	..
36	Non-Metallic Mineral Products	1 547	1 663	1 688	1 691	1 593	1 550	1 519	1 522	..	..
361	Pottery, China etc	56	53	48	48	39	37	34	31	..	..
362	Glass & Products	176	201	196	196	174	163	155	150	..	..
369	Non-Metallic Products, nec	1 315	1 409	1 444	1 447	1 380	1 350	1 330	1 341	..	..
37	Basic Metal Industries	437	517	547	493	454	438	417	413	..	..
371	Iron & Steel	187	211	229	214	195	192	187	185	..	..
372	Non-Ferrous Metals	250	306	318	279	259	246	230	228	..	..
38	Fabricated Metal Products	10 871	12 045	11 963	11 980	11 094	10 568	10 084	9 826	..	..
381	Metal Products	3 584	3 857	3 919	3 913	3 653	3 467	3 287	3 186	..	..
3813	Structural Metal Products	1 205	1 324	1 381	1 371	1 295	1 245	1 185	1 131	..	..
382	Non-Electrical Machinery	4 169	4 749	4 599	4 694	4 345	4 157	4 000	3 910	..	..
3821	Engines & Turbines	..	..	..	..	..	..	..	..	..	..
3822	Agricultural Machinery	246	259	246	238	219	213	196	196	..	..
3823	Metal & Wood working Machinery	603	657	646	615	572	552	526	518	..	..
3824	Special Industrial Machinery	533	595	598	606	555	541	521	505	..	..
3825	Office & Computing Machinery	187	247	232	225	189	190	182	173	..	..
3829	Machinery & Equipment, nec	2 600	2 991	2 877	3 010	2 810	2 661	2 575	2 518	..	..
383	Electrical Machinery	1 256	1 382	1 383	1 378	1 281	1 223	1 176	1 142	..	..
3831	Electrical Industrial Machinery	309	335	347	339	331	327	317	306	..	..
3832	Radio, TV & Communication Equipment	572	633	614	629	566	541	523	516	..	..
3833	Electrical Appliances & Housewares	67	69	67	61	55	52	48	48	..	..
3839	Electrical Apparatus, nec	308	345	355	349	329	303	288	272	..	..
384	Transport Equipment	1 370	1 519	1 537	1 469	1 346	1 273	1 224	1 210	..	..
3841	Shipbuilding & Repairing	382	429	383	373	306	287	250	240	..	..
3842	Railroad Equipment	29	27	28	28	27	23	22	21	..	..
3843	Motor Vehicles	750	846	920	854	800	758	748	747	..	..
3844	Motorcycles & Bicycles	..	..	..	..	..	..	..	..	..	..
3845	Aircraft	185	202	194	199	199	189	182	177	..	..
3849	Transport Equipment, nec	24	15	12	15	14	16	22	25	..	..
385	Professional Goods	492	538	525	526	469	448	397	378	..	..
3851	Professional Equipment	248	291	285	289	261	247	233	224	..	..
3852	Photographic & Optical Goods	223	227	220	220	191	184	147	139	..	..
3853	Watches & Clocks	21	20	20	17	17	17	17	15	..	..
39	Other Manufacturing, nes	2 514	2 866	2 644	2 848	2 520	2 334	2 157	2 047	..	..
3901	Jewellery	380	426	379	408	342	323	304	288	..	..
3	Total Manufacturing	36 790	40 262	39 150	39 864	36 339	34 511	32 943	31 974	..	..
1	Agric., Hunting, Forestry, Fishing	..	..	..	..	..	..	..	..	..	..
2	Mining & Quarrying	1 279	1 340	1 259	1 232	1 172	1 103	1 084	1 241	..	..
21	Coal Mining	31	27	29	29	33	35	33	32	..	..
22	Crude Petroleum & Natural Gas	738	801	725	714	674	634	626	686	..	..
23.29	Other Mining	510	512	505	489	465	434	425	523	..	..
3	Total Manufacturing	36 790	40 262	39 150	39 864	36 339	34 511	32 943	31 974	..	..
4	Electricity, Gas & Water	321	320	320	320	..	321	..	..	..	..
5	Construction	..	..	..	..	..	..	..	..	..	..
6.9	Services	..	..	..	..	..	..	..	..	..	..
0000	Grand Total	..	..	..	..	..	..	..	..	..	..

Note: ISIC 3829 includes 3821; 3832 includes 3902; 39 includes 3232 and 3844.

Millions of Mk

(Current Prices)

ISIC2	Industry	PRODUCTION									
		1987	1988	1989	1990	1991	1992	1993	1994	1995	1996
31	**Food, Beverages & Tobacco**	44 541	47 077	48 595	50 659	50 351	49 041	49 501	48 546	..	..
311.2	Food	40 078	42 169	43 240	44 751	44 113	43 212	44 209	43 329	..	..
313	Beverages	3 611	3 936	4 413	4 788	5 140	4 800	4 303	4 243	..	..
314	Tobacco	852	973	943	1 119	1 096	1 028	989	974	..	..
32	**Textiles, Apparel & Leather**	11 234	9 916	9 164	8 254	6 621	5 988	6 155	7 005	..	..
321	Textiles	4 297	3 983	3 824	3 489	2 944	3 009	3 229	3 644	..	..
3213	Knitting Mills	1 431	1 331	1 282	1 190	996	982	1 009	1 171	..	..
322	Wearing Apparel	4 909	4 173	3 946	3 437	2 605	2 001	1 945	2 300	..	..
323	Leather & Products	667	594	488	462	392	380	378	383	..	..
324	Footwear	1 360	1 166	906	865	680	598	604	679	..	..
33	**Wood Products & Furniture**	16 791	18 191	21 373	21 370	16 606	16 300	18 002	22 187	..	..
331	Wood Products	13 317	14 550	17 395	17 452	13 316	13 327	15 234	19 144	..	..
332	Furnitures & Fixtures	3 474	3 642	3 978	3 918	3 290	2 973	2 768	3 043	..	..
34	**Paper, Paper Products & Printing**	56 479	59 711	65 545	62 705	58 247	59 147	63 763	72 020	..	..
341	Paper & Products	41 922	43 729	48 032	44 506	40 964	43 685	48 746	56 174	..	..
3411	Pulp, Paper & Board	36 450	37 230	42 967	39 382	35 818	37 944	42 331	49 134	..	..
342	Printing & Publishing	14 558	15 982	17 513	18 200	17 283	15 462	15 016	15 847	..	..
35	**Chemical Products**	29 088	29 393	32 930	36 171	33 242	33 438	36 686	39 204	..	..
351	Industrial Chemicals	11 539	12 168	13 826	13 513	11 873	11 999	13 160	14 765	..	..
3511	Basic Industrial Chemicals	4 624	4 978	5 658	5 461	4 870	4 731	5 631	6 611	..	..
3512	Fertilizers & Pesticides	2 256	2 303	2 440	2 500	2 096	2 239	1 824	1 858	..	..
3513	Synthetic Resins	4 660	4 887	5 728	5 552	4 908	5 029	5 705	6 297	..	..
352	Other Chemicals	4 742	5 240	5 812	5 937	6 145	6 150	6 682	6 866	..	..
3521	Paints, Varnishes & Lacquers	1 019	1 205	1 346	1 304	1 163	1 141	1 225	1 379	..	..
3522	Drugs & Medicines	1 546	1 743	1 954	2 103	2 339	2 420	2 232	2 320	..	..
3523	Soap & Cleaning Preparations	1 092	1 154	1 278	1 256	1 187	1 112	1 125	1 089	..	..
3529	Chemical Products, nec	1 085	1 139	1 234	1 275	1 455	1 477	2 100	2 077	..	..
353	Petroleum Refineries	8 821	7 136	8 015	11 099	10 183	10 188	11 083	10 960	..	..
354	Petroleum & Coal Products	928	894	1 014	1 081	1 266	1 224	1 528	1 776	..	..
355	Rubber Products	910	1 155	1 090	1 063	888	999	1 186	1 462	..	..
356	Plastic Products, nec	2 149	2 801	3 174	3 477	2 887	2 878	3 048	3 374	..	..
36	**Non-Metallic Mineral Products**	7 991	8 772	10 118	10 285	8 552	7 052	6 527	7 102	..	..
361	Pottery, China etc	351	398	456	435	390	357	360	440	..	..
362	Glass & Products	1 114	1 267	1 358	1 327	1 300	1 397	1 559	1 607	..	..
369	Non-Metallic Products, nec	6 526	7 106	8 304	8 523	6 862	5 298	4 608	5 056	..	..
37	**Basic Metal Industries**	15 178	19 526	22 489	19 848	18 067	21 525	24 465	27 129	..	..
371	Iron & Steel	10 113	12 343	13 744	12 382	11 447	13 682	15 971	17 610	..	..
372	Non-Ferrous Metals	5 065	7 183	8 745	7 466	6 620	7 842	8 494	9 519	..	..
38	**Fabricated Metal Products**	59 411	64 160	71 640	74 345	61 374	64 594	74 853	89 137	..	..
381	Metal Products	11 086	12 359	14 834	14 662	12 844	11 878	13 278	14 355	..	..
3813	Structural Metal Products	5 125	5 445	7 063	6 843	5 933	5 405	5 915	5 930	..	..
382	Non-Electrical Machinery	21 568	23 429	25 843	27 727	21 761	22 728	25 718	30 028	..	..
3821	Engines & Turbines	193	206	238	247		299	280	307	..	..
3822	Agricultural Machinery	1 313	1 508	1 834	1 867	1 008	888	906	1 355	..	..
3823	Metal & Wood working Machinery	1 413	1 569	1 286	1 568	1 373	1 179	1 423	1 763	..	..
3824	Special Industrial Machinery	8 329	9 438	10 609	11 171	7 700	8 343	9 072	10 742	..	..
3825	Office & Computing Machinery	2 169	2 527	2 336	2 847	2 114	3 830	4 954	5 345	..	..
3829	Machinery & Equipment, nec	8 152	8 161	9 549	10 010	9 302	8 188	9 083	10 516	..	..
383	Electrical Machinery	11 462	12 131	14 141	14 678	11 851	13 883	19 018	26 127	..	..
3831	Electrical Industrial Machinery	3 418	3 955	4 468	4 673	4 233	4 808	5 589	6 575	..	..
3832	Radio, TV & Communication Equipment	5 439	5 110	6 311	6 888	5 091	6 540	10 927	16 633	..	..
3833	Electrical Appliances & Housewares	249	309	269	283	253	210	270	277	..	..
3839	Electrical Apparatus, nec	2 356	2 757	3 093	2 834	2 274	2 326	2 232	2 642	..	..
384	Transport Equipment	13 545	14 046	14 445	14 776	12 337	13 389	13 544	14 963	..	..
3841	Shipbuilding & Repairing	6 243	6 380	6 318	6 626	5 906	7 571	8 281	9 308	..	..
3842	Railroad Equipment	1 214	1 268	1 264	1 349	1 089	883	929	865	..	..
3843	Motor Vehicles	5 292	5 479	5 849	5 529	4 112	3 783	3 019	3 327	..	..
3844	Motorcycles & Bicycles	176	214	230	315	316	238	187	210	..	..
3845	Aircraft	580	625	694	870	870	861	1 075	1 196	..	..
3849	Transport Equipment, nec	40	81	91	86	44	53	53	58	..	..
385	Professional Goods	1 750	2 195	2 378	2 503	2 580	2 716	3 296	3 665	..	..
3851	Professional Equipment	1 685	2 151	2 339	2 456	2 520	2 645	3 203	3 588	..	..
3852	Photographic & Optical Goods	64	44	39	47	60	71	92	76	..	..
3853	Watches & Clocks	..	..	..	..	..	..	..	..	..	..
39	**Other Manufacturing, nes**	1 115	1 254	1 288	1 239	1 269	1 329	1 416	1 500	..	..
3901	Jewellery	268	322	387	406	402	393	345	378	..	..
3	**Total Manufacturing**	241 828	258 001	283 142	284 876	254 329	258 413	281 370	313 832	..	..
1	**Agric., Hunting, Forestry, Fishing**	..	..	..	..	..			..	..	..
2	**Mining & Quarrying**	2 170	2 630	3 261	2 744	2 584	2 584	2 533	2 779	..	..
21	Coal Mining	..	..	..	..	..	..	..	..	..	..
22	Crude Petroleum & Natural Gas	..	..	..	..	..	..	..	..	..	..
23.29	Other Mining	2 170	2 630	3 261	2 744	2 584	2 584	2 533	2 779	..	..
3	**Total Manufacturing**	241 828	258 001	283 142	284 876	254 329	258 413	281 370	313 832	..	..
4	**Electricity, Gas & Water**	29 060	29 303	29 610	32 739	33 872	35 048	37 460	38 952	..	..
5	**Construction**	..	..	..	..	..	..	..	..	..	..
6.9	**Services**	..	..	..	302	399	261	246	263	..	..
0000	**Grand Total**	273 059	289 934	316 013	320 661	291 184	296 306	321 609	355 826	..	..

Note: Unless given separately, ISIC 3852 includes 3853.

Millions of Mk   (Current Prices)

ISIC2	Industry	VALUE ADDED									
		1987	1988	1989	1990	1991	1992	1993	1994	1995	1996
31	**Food, Beverages & Tobacco**	10 834	12 078	12 555	13 070	13 838	13 087	13 435	12 464	..	..
311.2	Food	8 389	9 401	9 567	9 849	10 211	10 166	10 679	10 029	..	..
313	Beverages	1 982	2 131	2 476	2 546	2 955	2 363	2 221	1 911	..	..
314	Tobacco	464	544	512	675	672	559	534	523	..	..
32	**Textiles, Apparel & Leather**	5 016	4 406	4 263	3 649	2 986	2 772	2 850	3 231	..	..
321	Textiles	1 919	1 789	1 790	1 476	1 196	1 306	1 383	1 672	..	..
3213	Knitting Mills	699	642	646	527	442	469	493	603	..	..
322	Wearing Apparel	2 283	1 947	1 868	1 638	1 343	1 027	1 026	1 094	..	..
323	Leather & Products	248	212	186	182	171	155	164	157	..	..
324	Footwear	567	458	419	354	276	283	278	308	..	..
33	**Wood Products & Furniture**	6 060	6 642	7 988	8 004	5 371	5 844	6 883	8 494	..	..
331	Wood Products	4 364	4 895	5 952	6 036	3 847	4 545	5 666	7 216	..	..
332	Furnitures & Fixtures	1 696	1 747	2 036	1 969	1 525	1 299	1 217	1 278	..	..
34	**Paper, Paper Products & Printing**	19 282	23 113	24 830	21 860	18 778	20 373	23 276	27 108	..	..
341	Paper & Products	12 391	15 620	16 864	13 778	11 154	13 515	16 616	19 980	..	..
3411	Pulp, Paper & Board	10 446	13 230	15 073	11 906	9 358	11 333	14 261	17 503	..	..
342	Printing & Publishing	6 891	7 494	7 966	8 082	7 624	6 859	6 661	7 128	..	..
35	**Chemical Products**	10 042	10 142	12 645	13 124	11 272	11 537	12 438	13 684	..	..
351	Industrial Chemicals	4 416	4 814	5 352	5 244	4 052	4 824	5 042	5 504	..	..
3511	Basic Industrial Chemicals	2 092	2 454	2 730	2 498	1 820	1 810	2 266	2 709	..	..
3512	Fertilizers & Pesticides	723	775	916	1 028	770	1 153	690	596	..	..
3513	Synthetic Resins	1 601	1 586	1 705	1 717	1 462	1 861	2 085	2 199	..	..
352	Other Chemicals	2 077	2 325	2 672	2 703	2 685	2 774	3 105	3 167	..	..
3521	Paints, Varnishes & Lacquers	370	398	471	451	414	432	483	538	..	..
3522	Drugs & Medicines	738	884	1 048	1 098	1 213	1 216	1 104	1 160	..	..
3523	Soap & Cleaning Preparations	442	475	505	481	383	423	434	430	..	..
3529	Chemical Products, nec	527	566	648	672	676	703	1 084	1 039	..	..
353	Petroleum Refineries	1 845	850	2 279	2 579	2 351	1 658	1 825	2 256	..	..
354	Petroleum & Coal Products	278	308	402	463	449	399	488	515	..	..
355	Rubber Products	424	620	534	509	387	492	550	660	..	..
356	Plastic Products, nec	1 003	1 225	1 406	1 626	1 348	1 390	1 429	1 583	..	..
36	**Non-Metallic Mineral Products**	3 743	4 328	5 069	4 930	3 974	3 190	3 074	3 366	..	..
361	Pottery, China etc	246	267	311	281	227	203	216	271	..	..
362	Glass & Products	509	596	661	622	619	692	772	765	..	..
369	Non-Metallic Products, nec	2 988	3 464	4 097	4 027	3 128	2 296	2 086	2 330	..	..
37	**Basic Metal Industries**	3 734	4 992	5 954	4 638	4 229	5 497	6 659	7 284	..	..
371	Iron & Steel	3 022	3 796	4 044	3 251	3 016	4 088	4 948	5 323	..	..
372	Non-Ferrous Metals	711	1 195	1 910	1 388	1 213	1 409	1 711	1 961	..	..
38	**Fabricated Metal Products**	27 381	28 867	31 489	33 252	26 503	27 929	31 069	33 065	..	..
381	Metal Products	5 038	5 886	6 919	6 728	5 863	5 289	5 544	5 996	..	..
3813	Structural Metal Products	1 999	2 309	3 008	2 803	2 516	2 111	2 166	2 319	..	..
382	Non-Electrical Machinery	10 443	11 415	11 326	12 828	9 433	9 580	10 339	10 913	..	..
3821	Engines & Turbines	74	96	110	106	112	122	128	142	..	..
3822	Agricultural Machinery	634	499	593	682	238	288	280	420	..	..
3823	Metal & Wood working Machinery	612	719	467	673	556	479	604	677	..	..
3824	Special Industrial Machinery	3 949	4 762	4 849	5 098	3 676	3 765	4 300	4 671	..	..
3825	Office & Computing Machinery	1 304	1 419	764	1 493	605	1 142	1 152	947	..	..
3829	Machinery & Equipment, nec	3 871	3 920	4 543	4 776	5 159	6 420	8 159	9 007	..	..
383	Electrical Machinery	5 648	5 811	6 736	7 007	4 246	3 784	3 875	4 056	..	..
3831	Electrical Industrial Machinery	1 885	2 158	2 493	2 446	2 282	2 717	3 137	2 685	..	..
3832	Radio, TV & Communication Equipment	2 599	2 318	2 913	3 349	1 971	2 696	3 973	5 311	..	..
3833	Electrical Appliances & Housewares	114	157	129	126	124	80	120	127	..	..
3839	Electrical Apparatus, nec	1 049	1 178	1 201	1 085	781	927	930	884	..	..
384	Transport Equipment	5 356	4 619	5 237	5 374	4 704	5 185	5 292	5 413	..	..
3841	Shipbuilding & Repairing	2 578	1 753	2 105	2 313	2 111	2 744	3 077	2 812	..	..
3842	Railroad Equipment	476	578	460	526	386	310	446	312	..	..
3843	Motor Vehicles	1 816	1 785	2 037	1 877	1 467	1 484	999	1 449	..	..
3844	Motorcycles & Bicycles	66	69	96	173	153	105	82	96	..	..
3845	Aircraft	403	394	492	442	565	513	660	712	..	..
3849	Transport Equipment, nec	18	39	46	43	22	29	29	33	..	..
385	Professional Goods	896	1 136	1 271	1 316	1 344	1 455	1 734	1 736	..	..
3851	Professional Equipment	856	1 110	1 246	1 286	1 310	1 412	1 683	1 699	..	..
3852	Photographic & Optical Goods	39	26	25	30	34	43	52	37	..	..
3853	Watches & Clocks	..	..	..	..	..	..	..	..	..	..
39	**Other Manufacturing, nes**	588	686	676	643	648	697	739	790	..	..
3901	Jewellery	142	171	172	194	185	175	162	187	..	..
3	**Total Manufacturing**	86 680	95 253	105 467	103 170	87 598	90 926	100 424	109 487	..	..
1	**Agric., Hunting, Forestry, Fishing**	..	..	..	..	..	..	..	..	..	..
2	**Mining & Quarrying**	1 061	1 437	1 941	1 406	1 376	1 393	1 353	1 531	..	..
21	Coal Mining	..	..	..	..	..	..	..	..	..	..
22	Crude Petroleum & Natural Gas	..	..	..	..	..	..	..	..	..	..
23.29	Other Mining	1 061	1 437	1 941	1 406	1 376	1 393	1 353	1 531	..	..
3	**Total Manufacturing**	86 680	95 253	105 467	103 170	87 598	90 926	100 424	109 487	..	..
4	**Electricity, Gas & Water**	10 674	11 361	11 921	11 554	11 778	12 485	12 792	13 302	..	..
5	**Construction**	..	..	..						..	..
6.9	**Services**	..	..	..	179	-151	146	105	114	..	..
0000	**Grand Total**	98 415	108 052	119 330	116 309	100 601	104 950	114 674	124 433	..	..

Note: Unless given separately, ISIC 3852 includes 3853.

Thousands

Table FN.3 **FINLAND**

ISIC2	Industry	EMPLOYMENT									
		1987	**1988**	**1989**	**1990**	**1991**	**1992**	**1993**	**1994**	**1995**	**1996**
31	**Food, Beverages & Tobacco**	57.0	56.1	53.9	53.6	51.6	47.8	43.9	41.6	..	..
311.2	Food	50.8	50.1	47.9	47.1	45.1	41.8	38.8	36.5	..	..
313	Beverages	4.9	4.8	4.8	5.5	5.4	4.9	4.2	4.2	..	..
314	Tobacco	1.2	1.2	1.2	1.1	1.1	1.0	0.9	0.9	..	..
32	**Textiles, Apparel & Leather**	48.0	41.0	36.0	30.5	24.8	19.7	17.6	16.6	..	..
321	Textiles	14.9	13.4	12.3	11.0	9.3	8.3	7.4	7.1	..	..
3213	Knitting Mills	6.3	5.7	5.2	4.7	3.9	3.6	3.0	2.9	..	..
322	Wearing Apparel	24.8	20.5	18.5	14.8	11.7	8.3	7.3	6.6	..	..
323	Leather & Products	2.2	1.8	1.5	1.5	1.2	1.0	1.0	0.9	..	..
324	Footwear	6.1	5.2	3.7	3.3	2.6	2.1	2.0	2.0	..	..
33	**Wood Products & Furniture**	44.9	43.3	44.7	41.9	38.2	33.4	30.9	31.7	..	..
331	Wood Products	32.1	31.1	32.7	30.8	27.7	24.4	22.9	24.2	..	..
332	Furnitures & Fixtures	12.8	12.2	12.0	11.1	10.6	9.0	8.0	7.5	..	..
34	**Paper, Paper Products & Printing**	80.5	80.2	84.2	82.3	78.1	73.1	69.3	67.5	..	..
341	Paper & Products	41.7	41.2	45.5	44.4	41.8	40.1	39.0	38.7	..	..
3411	Pulp, Paper & Board	32.6	31.3	37.6	37.1	34.6	32.1	31.2	30.9	..	..
342	Printing & Publishing	38.8	39.0	38.7	37.9	36.3	33.0	30.3	28.9	..	..
35	**Chemical Products**	38.6	38.6	38.1	38.1	37.0	34.7	33.1	33.1	..	..
351	Industrial Chemicals	15.2	14.2	13.9	13.7	13.3	12.6	11.9	11.6	..	..
3511	Basic Industrial Chemicals	5.3	5.0	5.1	4.9	5.0	5.4	4.7	4.6	..	..
3512	Fertilizers & Pesticides	2.3	2.3	2.3	2.3	2.1	1.4	1.7	1.4	..	..
3513	Synthetic Resins	7.5	6.8	6.5	6.5	6.2	5.8	5.5	5.6	..	..
352	Other Chemicals	10.0	10.1	10.1	10.3	10.2	9.3	9.3	9.3	..	..
3521	Paints, Varnishes & Lacquers	1.6	1.7	1.8	1.7	1.6	1.5	1.4	1.5	..	..
3522	Drugs & Medicines	3.5	3.5	3.5	3.8	3.8	3.9	3.7	3.7	..	..
3523	Soap & Cleaning Preparations	2.3	2.1	2.3	2.2	2.3	1.8	1.5	1.5	..	..
3529	Chemical Products, nec	2.7	2.8	2.6	2.5	2.5	2.2	2.7	2.6	..	..
353	Petroleum Refineries	2.8	3.6	3.2	3.1	3.1	3.1	3.0	2.7	..	..
354	Petroleum & Coal Products	0.8	0.8	0.8	0.7	0.9	0.8	0.7	0.9	..	..
355	Rubber Products	3.3	3.0	2.8	2.6	2.5	2.3	2.2	2.6	..	..
356	Plastic Products, nec	6.4	7.0	7.2	7.6	7.0	6.5	6.0	6.1	..	..
36	**Non-Metallic Mineral Products**	20.3	19.9	20.3	20.2	18.4	15.3	12.3	11.9	..	..
361	Pottery, China etc	1.4	1.4	1.4	1.3	1.3	1.1	0.9	1.0	..	..
362	Glass & Products	3.4	3.3	3.3	3.2	3.1	3.0	2.7	2.8	..	..
369	Non-Metallic Products, nec	15.5	15.2	15.6	15.7	14.0	11.3	8.6	8.2	..	..
37	**Basic Metal Industries**	17.8	17.4	16.9	17.2	16.2	15.6	15.5	15.8	..	..
371	Iron & Steel	12.9	12.7	12.5	12.8	12.0	11.4	11.2	11.6	..	..
372	Non-Ferrous Metals	4.9	4.7	4.5	4.4	4.2	4.2	4.2	4.2	..	..
38	**Fabricated Metal Products**	158.2	155.3	151.1	146.8	136.1	122.3	117.0	123.2	..	..
381	Metal Products	31.0	31.8	33.5	32.1	30.2	24.8	23.0	23.5	..	..
3813	Structural Metal Products	12.3	12.7	13.8	12.8	12.0	9.5	8.7	8.7	..	..
382	Non-Electrical Machinery	55.0	53.5	51.0	52.5	47.8	43.1	40.6	41.8	..	..
3821	Engines & Turbines	0.6	0.6	0.6	0.6	0.8	0.7	0.6	0.6	..	..
3822	Agricultural Machinery	3.4	3.2	3.4	3.3	2.6	1.8	1.5	1.6	..	..
3823	Metal & Wood working Machinery	3.8	3.8	3.3	3.1	3.1	2.5	2.6	2.7	..	..
3824	Special Industrial Machinery	19.2	20.8	18.3	18.4	16.3	16.0	15.1	15.5	..	..
3825	Office & Computing Machinery	3.3	4.1	3.7	5.0	2.9	3.5	3.4	3.8	..	..
3829	Machinery & Equipment, nec	24.7	21.0	21.6	22.2	22.1	18.5	17.4	17.5	..	..
383	Electrical Machinery	31.4	30.9	29.3	28.6	26.0	24.4	24.3	28.2	..	..
3831	Electrical Industrial Machinery	12.9	12.0	10.2	10.5	9.3	9.2	8.8	9.4	..	..
3832	Radio, TV & Communication Equipment	11.6	11.9	12.1	11.5	11.0	10.5	11.5	14.5	..	..
3833	Electrical Appliances & Housewares	0.9	1.0	0.6	0.6	0.5	0.5	0.6	0.6	..	..
3839	Electrical Apparatus, nec	6.0	6.0	6.4	5.9	5.2	4.2	3.4	3.6	..	..
384	Transport Equipment	35.5	33.2	31.4	27.8	26.4	24.8	23.7	24.0	..	..
3841	Shipbuilding & Repairing	17.6	16.5	14.3	11.6	11.3	10.9	10.7	11.2	..	..
3842	Railroad Equipment	3.6	3.5	3.6	3.1	3.3	3.1	2.9	2.7	..	..
3843	Motor Vehicles	10.8	9.6	9.9	8.9	7.9	6.9	6.5	6.5	..	..
3844	Motorcycles & Bicycles	0.5	0.5	0.5	0.6	0.6	0.5	0.4	0.4	..	..
3845	Aircraft	2.8	2.7	2.9	3.2	3.2	3.2	3.1	3.0	..	..
3849	Transport Equipment, nec	0.2	0.3	0.3	0.3	0.2	0.2	0.2	0.2	..	..
385	Professional Goods	5.3	5.9	5.9	5.8	5.6	5.2	5.4	5.7	..	..
3851	Professional Equipment	5.0	5.7	5.7	5.7	5.5	5.1	5.2	5.5	..	..
3852	Photographic & Optical Goods	0.2	0.2	0.1	0.1	0.2	0.1	0.2	0.2	..	..
3853	Watches & Clocks		..	..			..	..		..	..
39	**Other Manufacturing, nes**	4.4	4.3	4.0	3.7	3.6	3.3	3.3	3.2	..	..
3901	Jewellery	0.9	0.9	0.9	0.9	0.9	0.7	0.7	0.6	..	..
3	**Total Manufacturing**	469.6	455.9	449.1	434.4	403.9	365.4	342.8	344.8	..	..
I	**Agric., Hunting, Forestry, Fishing**	..	..	..	..	..	..	..	..	..	..
2	**Mining & Quarrying**	5.4	4.7	4.3	3.9	3.8	3.6	3.1	2.8	..	..
21	Coal Mining	..	..	..	..	..	..	..	..	..	..
22	Crude Petroleum & Natural Gas	..	..	..	..	..	..	..	..	..	..
23.29	Other Mining	5.4	4.7	4.4	3.9	3.8	3.6	3.1	2.8	..	..
3	**Total Manufacturing**	469.6	455.9	449.1	434.4	403.9	365.4	342.8	344.8	..	..
4	**Electricity, Gas & Water**	28.1	28.0	27.4	26.8	26.2	25.2	22.8	21.3	..	..
5	**Construction**	..	..	..	..	..	..	..	..	..	..
6.9	**Services**					0.8	1.5	0.7	0.7	0.6	..
0000	**Grand Total**	503.1	488.6	480.8	465.9	435.4	394.9	369.4	369.5	..	..

Note: Unless given separately, ISIC 3852 includes 3853.

Table FN.4 **FINLAND**

Thousands

ISIC2	Industry	EMPLOYMENT - EMPLOYEES									
		1987	1988	1989	1990	1991	1992	1993	1994	1995	1996
31	Food, Beverages & Tobacco	56.4	55.5	53.4	53.2	51.1	47.4	43.6	41.3	..	..
311.2	Food	50.2	49.5	47.3	46.6	44.7	41.4	38.5	36.2	..	..
313	Beverages	4.9	4.8	4.8	5.5	5.4	4.9	4.2	4.2	..	..
314	Tobacco	1.2	1.2	1.2	1.1	1.1	1.0	0.9	0.9	..	..
32	Textiles, Apparel & Leather	47.5	40.5	35.6	30.2	24.6	19.5	17.4	16.5	..	..
321	Textiles	14.8	13.3	12.2	10.9	9.2	8.2	7.3	7.1	..	..
3213	Knitting Mills	6.3	5.7	5.1	4.6	3.9	3.5	3.0	2.9	..	..
322	Wearing Apparel	24.6	20.4	18.3	14.7	11.5	8.2	7.2	6.6	..	..
323	Leather & Products	2.1	1.8	1.4	1.4	1.2	1.0	0.9	0.9	..	..
324	Footwear	6.0	5.1	3.6	3.2	2.6	2.1	1.9	2.0	..	..
33	Wood Products & Furniture	44.1	42.6	44.1	41.3	37.7	32.9	30.6	31.4	..	..
331	Wood Products	31.6	30.6	32.3	30.4	27.3	24.1	22.7	24.0	..	..
332	Furnitures & Fixtures	12.5	12.0	11.8	10.9	10.4	8.8	7.9	7.4	..	..
34	Paper, Paper Products & Printing	80.3	80.0	84.0	82.2	77.9	73.0	69.2	67.5	..	..
341	Paper & Products	41.7	41.2	45.5	44.4	41.8	40.1	39.0	38.7	..	..
3411	Pulp, Paper & Board	32.6	31.3	37.6	37.1	34.6	32.1	31.2	30.9	..	..
342	Printing & Publishing	38.6	38.8	38.5	37.8	36.1	32.9	30.2	28.8	..	..
35	Chemical Products	38.5	38.5	38.0	38.0	36.9	34.6	33.1	33.1	..	..
351	Industrial Chemicals	15.2	14.2	13.9	13.7	13.3	12.6	11.9	11.6	..	..
3511	Basic Industrial Chemicals	5.3	5.0	5.1	4.9	4.9	5.4	4.7	4.6	..	..
3512	Fertilizers & Pesticides	2.3	2.3	2.3	2.3	2.1	1.4	1.7	1.4	..	..
3513	Synthetic Resins	7.5	6.8	6.4	6.5	6.2	5.8	5.5	5.6	..	..
352	Other Chemicals	10.0	10.1	10.1	10.3	10.2	9.3	9.3	9.3	..	..
3521	Paints, Varnishes & Lacquers	1.6	1.7	1.8	1.7	1.6	1.5	1.4	1.5	..	..
3522	Drugs & Medicines	3.5	3.5	3.5	3.8	3.8	3.9	3.7	3.7	..	..
3523	Soap & Cleaning Preparations	2.3	2.1	2.3	2.2	2.3	1.8	1.5	1.5	..	..
3529	Chemical Products, nec	2.7	2.7	2.6	2.5	2.4	2.2	2.7	2.6	..	..
353	Petroleum Refineries	2.8	3.6	3.2	3.1	3.1	3.1	3.0	2.7	..	..
354	Petroleum & Coal Products	0.8	0.8	0.8	0.7	0.9	0.8	0.7	0.9	..	..
355	Rubber Products	3.3	3.0	2.8	2.6	2.5	2.3	2.2	2.5	..	..
356	Plastic Products, nec	6.4	6.9	7.2	7.6	7.0	6.5	6.0	6.0	..	..
36	Non-Metallic Mineral Products	20.1	19.7	20.1	20.1	18.2	15.2	12.2	11.9	..	..
361	Pottery, China etc	1.4	1.4	1.4	1.3	1.3	1.1	0.9	1.0	..	..
362	Glass & Products	3.4	3.3	3.3	3.2	3.1	2.9	2.7	2.8	..	..
369	Non-Metallic Products, nec	15.4	15.0	15.5	15.6	13.9	11.2	8.5	8.1	..	..
37	Basic Metal Industries	17.8	17.4	16.9	17.1	16.2	15.6	15.5	15.8	..	..
371	Iron & Steel	12.9	12.7	12.5	12.8	12.0	11.4	11.2	11.6	..	..
372	Non-Ferrous Metals	4.9	4.7	4.4	4.3	4.2	4.2	4.2	4.2	..	..
38	Fabricated Metal Products	157.4	154.5	150.5	146.3	135.5	121.9	116.6	122.9	..	..
381	Metal Products	30.7	31.5	33.2	31.9	29.9	24.6	22.8	23.4	..	..
3813	Structural Metal Products	12.1	12.6	13.7	12.7	11.9	9.4	8.7	8.7	..	..
382	Non-Electrical Machinery	54.7	53.3	50.8	52.4	47.7	42.9	40.5	41.8	..	..
3821	Engines & Turbines	0.6	0.6	0.6	0.6	0.8	0.7	0.6	0.6	..	..
3822	Agricultural Machinery	3.4	3.2	3.4	3.3	2.6	1.8	1.5	1.6	..	..
3823	Metal & Wood working Machinery	3.8	3.7	3.3	3.0	3.1	2.5	2.6	2.7	..	..
3824	Special Industrial Machinery	19.2	20.7	18.2	18.3	16.3	16.0	15.1	15.5	..	..
3825	Office & Computing Machinery	3.2	4.1	3.7	5.0	2.9	3.5	3.4	3.8	..	..
3829	Machinery & Equipment, nec	24.6	21.0	21.6	22.1	22.1	18.4	17.3	17.5	..	..
383	Electrical Machinery	31.4	30.9	29.3	28.5	25.9	24.4	24.3	28.2	..	..
3831	Electrical Industrial Machinery	12.9	12.0	10.2	10.5	9.3	9.2	8.8	9.4	..	..
3832	Radio, TV & Communication Equipment	11.6	11.9	12.1	11.5	11.0	10.5	11.5	14.5	..	..
3833	Electrical Appliances & Housewares	0.9	1.0	0.6	0.6	0.5	0.5	0.6	0.6	..	..
3839	Electrical Apparatus, nec	6.0	6.0	6.4	5.9	5.2	4.2	3.4	3.6	..	..
384	Transport Equipment	35.3	33.0	31.3	27.7	26.4	24.7	23.6	24.0	..	..
3841	Shipbuilding & Repairing	17.5	16.5	14.3	11.6	11.2	10.9	10.6	11.2	..	..
3842	Railroad Equipment	3.6	3.5	3.6	3.1	3.3	3.1	2.9	2.7	..	..
3843	Motor Vehicles	10.7	9.6	9.8	8.9	7.9	6.8	6.5	6.5	..	..
3844	Motorcycles & Bicycles	0.5	0.5	0.5	0.6	0.6	0.5	0.4	0.4	..	..
3845	Aircraft	2.8	2.7	2.9	3.2	3.2	3.2	3.1	3.0	..	..
3849	Transport Equipment, nec	0.2	0.3	0.3	0.3	0.2	0.2	0.2	0.2	..	..
385	Professional Goods	5.2	5.8	5.8	5.8	5.6	5.2	5.4	5.6	..	..
3851	Professional Equipment	5.0	5.7	5.7	5.7	5.5	5.1	5.2	5.5	..	..
3852	Photographic & Optical Goods	0.2	0.2	0.1	0.1	0.2	0.1	0.2	0.2	..	..
3853	Watches & Clocks	..	..	..	..	..	..	..	..	..	..
39	Other Manufacturing, nes	4.3	4.2	3.9	3.6	3.5	3.3	3.3	3.2	..	..
3901	Jewellery	0.9	0.9	0.9	0.9	0.9	0.7	0.7	0.6	..	..
3	Total Manufacturing	466.5	453.2	446.6	432.1	401.7	363.6	341.4	343.6	..	..
1	Agric., Hunting, Forestry, Fishing	..	..	..	..	..	..	..	..	..	..
2	Mining & Quarrying	5.3	4.7	4.3	3.9	3.8	3.5	3.0	2.8	..	..
21	Coal Mining	..	..	..	..	..	..	..	..	..	..
22	Crude Petroleum & Natural Gas	..	..	..	..	..	..	..	..	..	..
23.29	Other Mining	5.3	4.7	4.3	3.9	3.8	3.5	3.0	2.8	..	..
3	Total Manufacturing	466.5	453.2	446.6	432.1	401.7	363.6	341.4	343.6	..	..
4	Electricity, Gas & Water	28.1	28.0	27.4	26.8	26.2	25.2	22.8	21.3	..	..
5	Construction	..	..	..	..	..	..	..	..	..	..
6.9	Services	..	..	..	0.8	1.5	0.7	0.7	0.6	..	..
0000	Grand Total	500.0	485.8	478.8	463.6	433.2	393.0	367.9	368.3	..	..

Note: Unless given separately, ISIC 3852 includes 3853.

Millions of Mk

Table FN.5 FINLAND

(Current Prices)

ISIC2	Industry	INVESTMENT									
		1987	1988	1989	1990	1991	1992	1993	1994	1995	1996
31	Food, Beverages & Tobacco	1 954	1 835	1 670	2 414	1 944	2 742	1 363	1 414	..	..
311.2	Food	1 338	1 601	1 320	1 841	1 437	1 788	1 051	1 131	..	..
313	Beverages	410	174	282	499	459	881	276	259	..	..
314	Tobacco	206	61	68	74	47	73	35	23		
32	Textiles, Apparel & Leather	419	335	353	366	150	118	211	188		
321	Textiles	211	249	224	287	117	80	179	141	..	..
3213	Knitting Mills	36	91	80	93	27	21	23	32		
322	Wearing Apparel	162	57	76	56	17	23	15	20		
323	Leather & Products	16	6	30	26	12	11	9	13	..	..
324	Footwear	30	23	23	-3	4	4	8	15		
33	Wood Products & Furniture	816	863	1 882	1 430	1 142	884	781	1 074		
331	Wood Products	606	702	1 513	1 249	1 001	714	730	989		
332	Furnitures & Fixtures	210	161	369	181	142	171	51	85		
34	Paper, Paper Products & Printing	5 579	6 436	8 344	8 108	6 229	5 201	4 520	4 224		
341	Paper & Products	4 642	5 551	7 165	6 805	5 264	4 316	3 995	3 470	..	..
3411	Pulp, Paper & Board	4 304	5 148	6 727	6 505	4 662	4 114	3 805	3 199	..	..
342	Printing & Publishing	937	884	1 179	1 303	965	885	525	754		
35	Chemical Products	3 032	2 414	2 719	2 367	1 865	1 833	2 039	1 783		
351	Industrial Chemicals	1 912	1 400	1 353	1 273	742	666	1 038	990		
3511	Basic Industrial Chemicals	843	788	417	745	330	393	479	584		
3512	Fertilizers & Pesticides	424	88	77	90	65	41	35	52		
3513	Synthetic Resins	645	524	859	439	347	232	524	354	..	..
352	Other Chemicals	460	295	578	504	330	302	229	319	..	..
3521	Paints, Varnishes & Lacquers	125	138	108	100	41	26	17	29	..	..
3522	Drugs & Medicines	271	74	184	274	175	171	120	174		
3523	Soap & Cleaning Preparations	13	48	50	32	30	36	21	12		
3529	Chemical Products, nec	51	35	236	98	84	69	71	105		
353	Petroleum Refineries	442	396	457	269	411	249	511	103		
354	Petroleum & Coal Products	21	50	23	28	225	465	60	35		
355	Rubber Products	58	66	62	89	34	60	29	106		
356	Plastic Products, nec	139	207	245	204	123	91	171	231		
36	Non-Metallic Mineral Products	701	617	868	1 114	437	412	314	345		
361	Pottery, China etc	25	16	21	28	24	147	16	32	..	..
362	Glass & Products	208	91	91	88	60	57	61	130	..	..
369	Non-Metallic Products, nec	468	510	756	998	353	208	237	183	..	..
37	Basic Metal Industries	1 510	1 301	1 207	1 032	1 034	655	692	746		
371	Iron & Steel	1 143	1 037	935	819	717	486	383	532		
372	Non-Ferrous Metals	367	264	272	214	317	169	309	214		
38	Fabricated Metal Products	3 118	2 813	3 952	4 069	2 554	2 010	2 146	3 648		
381	Metal Products	563	652	1 090	903	640	320	319	386		
3813	Structural Metal Products	185	243	428	364	332	128	90	60		
382	Non-Electrical Machinery	1 122	947	1 350	1 431	916	663	229	724	..	..
3821	Engines & Turbines	15	12	7	12	1	7	9	12		
3822	Agricultural Machinery	61	72	43	76	16	9	10	23		
3823	Metal & Wood working Machinery	42	61	187	251	163	157	46	79		
3824	Special Industrial Machinery	464	445	579	543	328	226	-110	254		
3825	Office & Computing Machinery	72	109	92	49	39	57	91	107		
3829	Machinery & Equipment, nec	469	249	442	499	368	207	183	249		
383	Electrical Machinery	765	676	719	703	383	594	787	1 554		
3831	Electrical Industrial Machinery	164	144	185	253	135	185	214	319		
3832	Radio, TV & Communication Equipment	482	377	383	272	241	306	514	1 123		
3833	Electrical Appliances & Housewares	6	13	21	23	-9	7	6	22		
3839	Electrical Apparatus, nec	112	142	130	154	17	96	54	90		
384	Transport Equipment	620	503	664	884	514	339	679	838		
3841	Shipbuilding & Repairing	339	183	199	221	119	170	485	653		
3842	Railroad Equipment	21	15	18	14	17	8	9	8		
3843	Motor Vehicles	213	246	270	245	258	89	61	57		
3844	Motorcycles & Bicycles	2	5	4	17	8	4	2	3		
3845	Aircraft	44	51	171	382	111	67	118	115		
3849	Transport Equipment, nec	1	4	4	4	1	2	3	3		
385	Professional Goods	50	35	129	149	101	94	132	146		
3851	Professional Equipment	46	33	122	148	99	94	138	137		
3852	Photographic & Optical Goods	4	2	7	1	2	1	-6	9	..	..
3853	Watches & Clocks	..	..	..	..	..	..			..	..
39	Other Manufacturing, nes	53	72	39	63	44	57	39	54	..	..
3901	Jewellery	6	21	-4	18	17	18	6	12	..	..
3	Total Manufacturing	17 181	16 686	21 034	20 962	15 398	13 911	12 103	13 476	..	..
1	Agric., Hunting, Forestry, Fishing	..	..	..	..	..	..	..	..	..	..
2	Mining & Quarrying	187	176	340	244	144	117	96	126	..	..
21	Coal Mining	..	..	..	..	..	..	..	..	..	..
22	Crude Petroleum & Natural Gas	..	..	..	..	..	..	..	..	..	..
23.29	Other Mining	187	176	340	244	144	117	96	126	..	..
3	Total Manufacturing	17 181	16 686	21 034	20 962	15 398	13 911	12 103	13 476	..	..
4	Electricity, Gas & Water	4 167	3 731	5 521	5 613	5 793	5 229	4 077	4 748	..	..
5	Construction	..	..	..	..	..	..	..	..	..	..
6.9	Services	..	..	..	49	-3 164	19	9	50	..	..
0000	Grand Total	21 536	20 592	26 895	26 868	18 172	19 275	16 285	18 400	..	..

Note: Unless given separately, ISIC 3852 includes 3853.

Millions of Mk (Current Prices)

ISIC2	Industry	INVESTMENT IN MACHINERY & EQUIPMENT									
		1987	1988	1989	1990	1991	1992	1993	1994	1995	1996
31	Food, Beverages & Tobacco	1 248	1 413	1 129	1 395	1 301	1 567	1 033	1 064	..	..
311.2	Food	875	1 176	853	1 085	993	986	714	843	..	..
313	Beverages	302	196	213	275	268	512	287	199	..	..
314	Tobacco	71	41	63	35	40	69	32	23	..	..
32	Textiles, Apparel & Leather	326	291	305	249	125	86	190	133	..	..
321	Textiles	192	197	194	190	93	58	166	97	..	..
3213	Knitting Mills	49	67	67	43	22	14	24	30	..	..
322	Wearing Apparel	97	67	66	41	18	15	10	17	..	..
323	Leather & Products	13	11	29	18	10	9	5	7	..	..
324	Footwear	25	15	16	0	3	5	8	11	..	..
33	Wood Products & Furniture	559	731	1 115	1 081	799	626	550	768	..	..
331	Wood Products	422	571	923	946	695	563	514	707	..	..
332	Furnitures & Fixtures	136	160	192	135	104	63	36	61	..	..
34	Paper, Paper Products & Printing	4 584	5 618	6 829	6 423	4 524	3 900	3 598	3 598	..	..
341	Paper & Products	3 833	4 663	5 890	5 442	3 774	3 187	3 123	2 922	..	..
3411	Pulp, Paper & Board	3 522	4 339	5 565	5 183	3 216	3 006	2 945	2 675	..	..
342	Printing & Publishing	751	955	939	980	750	712	476	676	..	..
35	Chemical Products	2 298	2 259	2 004	1 724	1 243	1 398	1 630	1 396	..	..
351	Industrial Chemicals	1 532	1 191	993	1 031	548	503	850	804	..	..
3511	Basic Industrial Chemicals	698	718	323	604	251	318	392	488	..	..
3512	Fertilizers & Pesticides	346	72	65	74	53	35	26	40	..	..
3513	Synthetic Resins	488	402	605	353	244	150	433	276	..	..
352	Other Chemicals	262	243	394	246	205	196	148	205	..	..
3521	Paints, Varnishes & Lacquers	63	87	65	52	33	17	13	27	..	..
3522	Drugs & Medicines	154	71	100	112	108	108	73	104	..	..
3523	Soap & Cleaning Preparations	7	39	34	22	24	24	20	8	..	..
3529	Chemical Products, nec	39	46	195	60	41	47	43	66	..	..
353	Petroleum Refineries	295	457	345	177	126	171	416	73	..	..
354	Petroleum & Coal Products	14	28	32	27	209	395	51	28	..	..
355	Rubber Products	49	122	58	76	31	39	25	99	..	..
356	Plastic Products, nec	147	218	183	167	124	94	141	187	..	..
36	Non-Metallic Mineral Products	522	472	611	824	335	213	230	266	..	..
361	Pottery, China etc	23	10	17	22	21	12	15	20	..	..
362	Glass & Products	170	62	77	70	48	47	55	106	..	..
369	Non-Metallic Products, nec	328	400	517	733	266	155	160	140	..	..
37	Basic Metal Industries	1 372	1 109	1 071	885	876	610	646	605	..	..
371	Iron & Steel	1 025	868	831	690	594	367	361	428	..	..
372	Non-Ferrous Metals	347	241	240	195	282	244	285	177	..	..
38	Fabricated Metal Products	2 262	2 398	2 862	2 973	2 078	1 637	1 913	2 831	..	..
381	Metal Products	382	545	724	664	513	258	256	277	..	..
3813	Structural Metal Products	135	176	271	272	263	107	84	21	..	..
382	Non-Electrical Machinery	815	876	1 092	1 122	703	534	430	567	..	..
3821	Engines & Turbines	12	11	7	7	4	5	3	10	..	..
3822	Agricultural Machinery	47	50	47	65	11	6	9	20	..	..
3823	Metal & Wood working Machinery	32	122	147	225	135	154	38	48	..	..
3824	Special Industrial Machinery	326	325	444	391	236	135	139	189	..	..
3825	Office & Computing Machinery	59	78	88	49	39	49	92	97	..	..
3829	Machinery & Equipment, nec	338	290	360	385	279	185	148	203	..	..
383	Electrical Machinery	659	561	597	583	383	507	691	1 353	..	..
3831	Electrical Industrial Machinery	140	144	157	221	124	136	137	301	..	..
3832	Radio, TV & Communication Equipment	409	295	362	241	203	279	498	950	..	..
3833	Electrical Appliances & Housewares	6	10	20	14	-10	7	6	16	..	..
3839	Electrical Apparatus, nec	104	111	58	107	67	84	50	87	..	..
384	Transport Equipment	368	332	351	495	398	271	458	530	..	..
3841	Shipbuilding & Repairing	175	127	106	195	76	126	291	358	..	..
3842	Railroad Equipment	13	8	12	13	16	9	11	8	..	..
3843	Motor Vehicles	142	160	165	157	206	66	48	50	..	..
3844	Motorcycles & Bicycles	2	5	4	17	8	4	2	3	..	..
3845	Aircraft	36	29	61	109	92	65	104	109	..	..
3849	Transport Equipment, nec	1	3	5	4	1	2	2	3	..	..
385	Professional Goods	38	85	99	109	80	68	79	104	..	..
3851	Professional Equipment	35	83	97	109	79	67	85	97	..	..
3852	Photographic & Optical Goods	4	2	1	1	1	1	-6	7	..	..
3853	Watches & Clocks	..	..	..	..	..	..	..	..	..	..
39	Other Manufacturing, nes	46	58	45	46	44	42	37	47	..	..
3901	Jewellery	9	21	17	13	15	17	6	9	..	..
3	Total Manufacturing	13 216	14 348	15 971	15 599	11 324	10 080	9 827	10 708	..	..
1	Agric., Hunting, Forestry, Fishing	..	..	..	..	..	..	..	..	..	..
2	Mining & Quarrying	127	117	230	150	80	53	35	61	..	..
21	Coal Mining	..	..	..	..	..	..	..	..	..	..
22	Crude Petroleum & Natural Gas	..	..	..	..	..	..	..	..	..	..
23.29	Other Mining	127	117	230	150	80	53	35	61	..	..
3	Total Manufacturing	13 216	14 348	15 971	15 599	11 324	10 080	9 827	10 708	..	..
4	Electricity, Gas & Water	1 856	1 700	2 612	2 435	2 483	2 297	1 641	2 536	..	..
5	Construction	..	..	..	..	..	..	..	..	..	..
6.9	Services	..	..	..	24	-2 385	11	6	27	..	..
0000	Grand Total	15 198	16 164	18 813	18 208	11 502	12 441	11 508	13 332	..	..

Note: Unless given separately, ISIC 3852 includes 3853.

Millions of Mk

(Current Prices)

ISIC2	Industry	WAGES & SALARIES - EMPLOYEES									
		1987	1988	1989	1990	1991	1992	1993	1994	1995	1996
31	Food, Beverages & Tobacco	4 530	4 855	5 086	5 563	5 562	5 446	5 107	5 028	..	..
311.2	Food	3 977	4 275	4 459	4 744	4 738	4 648	4 384	4 301	..	..
313	Beverages	429	444	483	670	678	662	595	602	..	..
314	Tobacco	124	136	144	149	146	137	128	126	..	..
32	Textiles, Apparel & Leather	2 962	2 713	2 550	2 318	1 974	1 634	1 529	1 546	..	..
321	Textiles	992	947	941	898	790	740	717	730	..	..
3213	Knitting Mills	392	376	373	355	318	301	278	279	..	..
322	Wearing Apparel	1 480	1 304	1 258	1 070	885	649	573	570	..	..
323	Leather & Products	134	122	105	109	96	82	82	86	..	..
324	Footwear	356	340	246	241	203	163	157	160	..	..
33	Wood Products & Furniture	3 157	3 299	3 763	3 828	3 440	3 097	3 026	3 372	..	..
331	Wood Products	2 297	2 398	2 810	2 860	2 509	2 304	2 322	2 627	..	..
332	Furnitures & Fixtures	860	901	954	967	931	793	704	744	..	..
34	Paper, Paper Products & Printing	8 010	8 476	9 813	10 465	10 341	9 881	9 657	9 851	..	..
341	Paper & Products	4 337	4 515	5 594	5 938	5 891	5 802	5 818	6 082	..	..
3411	Pulp, Paper & Board	3 489	3 546	4 739	5 087	5 016	4 831	4 815	5 000	..	..
342	Printing & Publishing	3 673	3 961	4 219	4 527	4 450	4 080	3 840	3 769	..	..
35	Chemical Products	3 459	3 790	4 070	4 472	4 548	4 384	4 346	4 506	..	..
351	Industrial Chemicals	1 452	1 498	1 602	1 718	1 729	1 708	1 669	1 696	..	..
3511	Basic Industrial Chemicals	527	534	587	626	640	763	673	695	..	..
3512	Fertilizers & Pesticides	244	263	278	305	301	180	260	225	..	..
3513	Synthetic Resins	681	701	737	787	787	765	736	776	..	..
352	Other Chemicals	865	944	1 035	1 163	1 220	1 124	1 145	1 209	..	..
3521	Paints, Varnishes & Lacquers	144	178	195	213	210	203	193	214	..	..
3522	Drugs & Medicines	295	320	350	421	448	465	439	485	..	..
3523	Soap & Cleaning Preparations	198	203	238	261	287	203	186	190	..	..
3529	Chemical Products, nec	229	243	252	268	276	254	327	320	..	..
353	Petroleum Refineries	329	450	445	464	494	507	503	469	..	..
354	Petroleum & Coal Products	74	77	88	89	119	115	108	122	..	..
355	Rubber Products	252	248	252	256	245	244	256	310	..	..
356	Plastic Products, nec	487	573	649	782	742	686	665	700	..	..
36	Non-Metallic Mineral Products	1 631	1 752	1 973	2 208	2 000	1 644	1 396	1 430	..	..
361	Pottery, China etc	105	118	123	127	133	116	97	119	..	..
362	Glass & Products	283	282	316	350	343	321	341	366	..	..
369	Non-Metallic Products, nec	1 244	1 352	1 534	1 731	1 523	1 207	958	945	..	..
37	Basic Metal Industries	1 703	1 766	1 901	2 114	2 028	2 093	2 120	2 248	..	..
371	Iron & Steel	1 237	1 295	1 406	1 575	1 491	1 516	1 520	1 620	..	..
372	Non-Ferrous Metals	467	471	495	540	537	577	601	628	..	..
38	Fabricated Metal Products	13 822	14 780	15 594	16 711	15 581	14 678	14 323	16 082	..	..
381	Metal Products	2 525	2 808	3 289	3 427	3 224	2 728	2 623	2 844	..	..
3813	Structural Metal Products	1 040	1 162	1 422	1 422	1 332	1 057	1 010	1 077	..	..
382	Non-Electrical Machinery	5 040	5 363	5 555	6 222	5 615	5 296	5 180	5 636	..	..
3821	Engines & Turbines	55	57	63	69	91	81	75	82	..	..
3822	Agricultural Machinery	279	284	330	346	269	174	153	193	..	..
3823	Metal & Wood working Machinery	329	351	335	346	353	305	316	371	..	..
3824	Special Industrial Machinery	1 829	2 125	2 054	2 195	1 920	2 010	1 974	2 160	..	..
3825	Office & Computing Machinery	323	444	443	670	363	449	421	490	..	..
3829	Machinery & Equipment, nec	2 225	2 102	2 331	2 596	2 619	2 276	2 241	2 340	..	..
383	Electrical Machinery	2 601	2 799	2 945	3 103	2 938	2 920	3 040	3 748	..	..
3831	Electrical Industrial Machinery	1 030	1 081	1 009	1 157	1 061	1 078	1 085	1 233	..	..
3832	Radio, TV & Communication Equipment	986	1 094	1 247	1 249	1 259	1 300	1 486	1 972	..	..
3833	Electrical Appliances & Housewares	63	73	52	58	45	44	60	62	..	..
3839	Electrical Apparatus, nec	523	552	638	640	574	498	408	481	..	..
384	Transport Equipment	3 187	3 245	3 176	3 266	3 119	3 038	2 760	3 062	..	..
3841	Shipbuilding & Repairing	1 633	1 665	1 438	1 466	1 393	1 451	1 321	1 541	..	..
3842	Railroad Equipment	317	346	374	351	375	322	299	316	..	..
3843	Motor Vehicles	900	872	959	935	850	762	625	690	..	..
3844	Motorcycles & Bicycles	37	43	46	58	56	44	40	43	..	..
3845	Aircraft	287	299	335	430	430	443	458	454	..	..
3849	Transport Equipment, nec	13	21	23	26	15	16	17	19	..	..
385	Professional Goods	470	566	629	694	685	697	721	791	..	..
3851	Professional Equipment	453	554	618	680	670	681	697	769	..	..
3852	Photographic & Optical Goods	17	12	11	14	16	16	25	22	..	..
3853	Watches & Clocks	..	..	..	..	..	..	..	..	..	..
39	Other Manufacturing, nes	308	329	337	341	343	333	332	334	..	..
3901	Jewellery	73	82	90	99	99	82	78	73	..	..
3	Total Manufacturing	39 583	41 762	45 085	48 020	45 815	43 191	41 836	44 396	..	..
1	Agric., Hunting, Forestry, Fishing	..	..	..	..	..	..	..	..	..	..
2	Mining & Quarrying	474	446	435	431	448	426	384	374	..	..
21	Coal Mining	..	..	..	..	..	..	..	..	..	..
22	Crude Petroleum & Natural Gas	..	..	..	..	..	..	..	..	..	..
23.29	Other Mining	474	446	435	431	448	426	384	374	..	..
3	Total Manufacturing	39 583	41 762	45 085	48 020	45 815	43 191	41 836	44 396	..	..
4	Electricity, Gas & Water	2 719	2 956	3 166	3 358	3 521	3 476	3 120	3 049	..	..
5	Construction	..	..	..	..	..	..	..	..	..	..
6.9	Services	..	..	..	73	227	57	51	46	..	..
0000	Grand Total	42 775	45 164	48 686	51 881	50 011	47 149	45 391	47 865	..	..

Note: Unless given separately, ISIC 3852 includes 3853.

Millions of Mk   (Current Prices)

ISIC2	Industry	SOCIAL COSTS									
		1987	1988	1989	1990	1991	1992	1993	1994	1995	1996
31	Food, Beverages & Tobacco	1 117	1 258	1 345	1 497	1 480	1 425	1 465	1 477	..	..
311.2	Food	970	1 098	1 161	1 260	1 243	1 214	1 264	1 261	..	..
313	Beverages	113	125	143	202	197	175	164	174	..	..
314	Tobacco	33	35	40	35	40	36	36	42	..	..
32	Textiles, Apparel & Leather	673	620	595	565	492	403	413	428	..	..
321	Textiles	237	228	232	228	213	190	204	207	..	..
3213	Knitting Mills	91	88	89	86	84	76	77	78	..	..
322	Wearing Apparel	323	291	283	254	207	152	149	153	..	..
323	Leather & Products	30	28	24	25	23	21	20	22	..	..
324	Footwear	83	73	55	58	50	40	41	45	..	..
33	Wood Products & Furniture	789	826	968	1 025	886	807	883	1 028	..	..
331	Wood Products	592	615	737	781	659	609	688	805	..	..
332	Furnitures & Fixtures	197	211	231	244	228	197	195	223	..	..
34	Paper, Paper Products & Printing	1 914	2 068	2 484	2 751	2 652	2 589	2 685	2 904	..	..
341	Paper & Products	1 091	1 159	1 485	1 632	1 578	1 600	1 655	1 842	..	..
3411	Pulp, Paper & Board	878	910	1 264	1 395	1 343	1 339	1 359	1 506	..	..
342	Printing & Publishing	824	909	999	1 120	1 074	989	1 030	1 062	..	..
35	Chemical Products	863	962	1 148	1 214	1 156	1 090	1 264	1 329	..	..
351	Industrial Chemicals	366	405	460	499	448	433	507	505	..	..
3511	Basic Industrial Chemicals	135	144	172	180	168	191	204	204	..	..
3512	Fertilizers & Pesticides	62	82	88	101	73	47	79	69	..	..
3513	Synthetic Resins	168	180	201	218	207	195	225	232	..	..
352	Other Chemicals	215	241	264	299	288	258	315	342	..	..
3521	Paints, Varnishes & Lacquers	42	44	51	54	53	47	58	65	..	..
3522	Drugs & Medicines	71	80	88	109	106	105	120	135	..	..
3523	Soap & Cleaning Preparations	46	50	56	61	57	46	46	48	..	..
3529	Chemical Products, nec	57	68	70	76	72	60	92	94	..	..
353	Petroleum Refineries	72	99	171	148	148	140	153	149	..	..
354	Petroleum & Coal Products	18	20	25	25	34	35	34	37	..	..
355	Rubber Products	80	62	67	55	61	60	74	93	..	..
356	Plastic Products, nec	112	135	161	189	177	165	181	203	..	..
36	Non-Metallic Mineral Products	424	460	512	570	512	436	404	425	..	..
361	Pottery, China etc	24	27	30	31	30	32	30	39	..	..
362	Glass & Products	73	69	83	89	86	85	97	108	..	..
369	Non-Metallic Products, nec	327	364	400	450	396	319	276	278	..	..
37	Basic Metal Industries	436	465	513	595	543	529	607	695	..	..
371	Iron & Steel	321	345	389	445	417	412	448	495	..	..
372	Non-Ferrous Metals	115	120	124	150	126	118	159	201	..	..
38	Fabricated Metal Products	3 253	3 563	3 840	4 346	3 923	3 627	3 948	4 682	..	..
381	Metal Products	598	676	828	906	819	680	732	834	..	..
3813	Structural Metal Products	252	280	372	383	352	266	287	321	..	..
382	Non-Electrical Machinery	1 201	1 298	1 392	1 698	1 446	1 339	1 438	1 682	..	..
3821	Engines & Turbines	12	12	15	18	24	23	21	23	..	..
3822	Agricultural Machinery	73	68	83	91	70	48	42	53	..	..
3823	Metal & Wood working Machinery	78	88	85	91	84	77	92	110	..	..
3824	Special Industrial Machinery	434	500	511	656	544	523	559	697	..	..
3825	Office & Computing Machinery	74	111	118	171	76	103	109	131	..	..
3829	Machinery & Equipment, nec	531	520	582	671	648	565	614	667	..	..
383	Electrical Machinery	631	675	703	750	703	682	798	1 058	..	..
3831	Electrical Industrial Machinery	251	261	235	274	256	242	269	352	..	..
3832	Radio, TV & Communication Equipment	232	255	293	299	285	301	395	542	..	..
3833	Electrical Appliances & Housewares	14	17	13	15	12	11	17	17	..	..
3839	Electrical Apparatus, nec	135	142	162	162	151	129	117	147	..	..
384	Transport Equipment	719	780	774	826	795	762	783	887	..	..
3841	Shipbuilding & Repairing	334	360	310	344	356	365	386	432	..	..
3842	Railroad Equipment	92	109	119	102	103	89	87	100	..	..
3843	Motor Vehicles	200	207	232	235	200	181	167	197	..	..
3844	Motorcycles & Bicycles	8	10	10	13	13	11	12	13	..	..
3845	Aircraft	82	90	96	124	119	112	126	140	..	..
3849	Transport Equipment, nec	3	5	6	7	4	4	5	6	..	..
385	Professional Goods	104	134	143	166	161	163	198	221	..	..
3851	Professional Equipment	100	131	140	163	157	160	191	214	..	..
3852	Photographic & Optical Goods	4	3	3	3	4	3	6	7	..	..
3853	Watches & Clocks	..	..	..	..	..	..	..	..	..	..
39	Other Manufacturing, nes	67	73	80	84	85	85	94	94	..	..
3901	Jewellery	15	18	21	23	25	21	20	20	..	..
3	Total Manufacturing	9 535	10 294	11 485	12 647	11 728	10 991	11 761	13 060	..	..
1	Agric., Hunting, Forestry, Fishing	..	..	..	..	..	..	..	..	..	..
2	Mining & Quarrying	118	117	112	114	119	113	119	119	..	..
21	Coal Mining	..	..	..	..	..	..	..	..	..	..
22	Crude Petroleum & Natural Gas	..	..	..	..	..	..	..	..	..	..
23.29	Other Mining	118	117	112	114	119	113	119	119	..	..
3	Total Manufacturing	9 535	10 294	11 485	12 647	11 728	10 991	11 761	13 060	..	..
4	Electricity, Gas & Water	656	738	810	903	965	987	965	1 004	..	..
5	Construction	..	..	..	..	..	..	..	..	..	..
6.9	Services	..	..	..	21	84	16	16	15	..	..
0000	Grand Total	10 309	11 149	12 407	13 685	12 896	12 106	12 860	14 198	..	..

Note: Unless given separately, ISIC 3852 includes 3853.

Millions of Mk

(Current Prices)

ISIC2	Industry	WAGES & SALARIES + SOCIAL COSTS - EMPLOYEES									
		1987	1988	1989	1990	1991	1992	1993	1994	1995	1996
31	**Food, Beverages & Tobacco**	5 646	6 113	6 430	7 060	7 042	6 871	6 572	6 505	..	..
311.2	Food	4 948	5 373	5 620	6 005	5 981	5 862	5 648	5 562	..	..
313	Beverages	542	569	626	872	876	836	760	776	..	..
314	Tobacco	157	171	185	183	186	174	164	167	..	..
32	**Textiles, Apparel & Leather**	3 634	3 333	3 145	2 883	2 466	2 037	1 942	1 974	..	..
321	Textiles	1 229	1 175	1 173	1 127	1 003	930	921	937	..	..
3213	Knitting Mills	483	463	463	441	402	377	355	356	..	..
322	Wearing Apparel	1 803	1 595	1 541	1 324	1 092	801	721	723	..	..
323	Leather & Products	164	150	129	134	119	103	102	109	..	..
324	Footwear	439	413	301	299	253	203	198	205	..	..
33	**Wood Products & Furniture**	3 947	4 126	4 732	4 852	4 326	3 903	3 909	4 400	..	..
331	Wood Products	2 889	3 013	3 547	3 641	3 168	2 913	3 009	3 432	..	..
332	Furnitures & Fixtures	1 058	1 112	1 185	1 211	1 158	990	899	968	..	..
34	**Paper, Paper Products & Printing**	9 924	10 544	12 297	13 216	12 992	12 471	12 342	12 754	..	..
341	Paper & Products	5 428	5 674	7 079	7 570	7 469	7 402	7 472	7 924	..	..
3411	Pulp, Paper & Board	4 367	4 456	6 003	6 482	6 358	6 170	6 174	6 506	..	..
342	Printing & Publishing	4 497	4 870	5 218	5 646	5 524	5 069	4 870	4 831	..	..
35	**Chemical Products**	4 323	4 752	5 218	5 686	5 704	5 475	5 610	5 835	..	..
351	Industrial Chemicals	1 817	1 904	2 061	2 216	2 177	2 141	2 177	2 200	..	..
3511	Basic Industrial Chemicals	662	678	758	806	808	954	877	899	..	..
3512	Fertilizers & Pesticides	306	345	365	406	375	227	339	294	..	..
3513	Synthetic Resins	850	881	938	1 005	995	960	960	1 008	..	..
352	Other Chemicals	1 081	1 185	1 299	1 462	1 508	1 382	1 459	1 551	..	..
3521	Paints, Varnishes & Lacquers	186	222	246	267	262	250	250	280	..	..
3522	Drugs & Medicines	365	400	437	530	554	570	559	620	..	..
3523	Soap & Cleaning Preparations	244	253	294	322	344	249	232	238	..	..
3529	Chemical Products, nec	287	310	322	344	348	314	419	414	..	..
353	Petroleum Refineries	401	549	616	612	642	647	656	618	..	..
354	Petroleum & Coal Products	92	98	113	114	153	149	142	159	..	..
355	Rubber Products	332	310	318	311	305	304	330	403	..	..
356	Plastic Products, nec	600	708	810	971	918	851	846	904	..	..
36	**Non-Metallic Mineral Products**	2 055	2 212	2 485	2 778	2 511	2 080	1 799	1 854	..	..
361	Pottery, China etc	128	145	153	158	163	148	127	158	..	..
362	Glass & Products	356	351	399	440	429	406	438	473	..	..
369	Non-Metallic Products, nec	1 571	1 717	1 934	2 181	1 919	1 526	1 234	1 223	..	..
37	**Basic Metal Industries**	2 139	2 232	2 414	2 710	2 570	2 622	2 727	2 943	..	..
371	Iron & Steel	1 558	1 640	1 794	2 020	1 907	1 927	1 968	2 115	..	..
372	Non-Ferrous Metals	582	591	619	690	663	695	760	829	..	..
38	**Fabricated Metal Products**	17 074	18 343	19 433	21 057	19 504	18 305	18 271	20 763	..	..
381	Metal Products	3 122	3 484	4 117	4 333	4 042	3 409	3 354	3 678	..	..
3813	Structural Metal Products	1 292	1 442	1 794	1 804	1 684	1 323	1 297	1 398	..	..
382	Non-Electrical Machinery	6 240	6 661	6 947	7 920	7 061	6 635	6 618	7 318	..	..
3821	Engines & Turbines	66	69	78	87	114	104	96	105	..	..
3822	Agricultural Machinery	352	352	412	437	338	222	196	246	..	..
3823	Metal & Wood working Machinery	407	438	420	438	438	382	408	481	..	..
3824	Special Industrial Machinery	2 263	2 625	2 564	2 851	2 464	2 533	2 534	2 857	..	..
3825	Office & Computing Machinery	397	555	561	840	439	552	530	622	..	..
3829	Machinery & Equipment, nec	2 756	2 621	2 913	3 267	3 267	2 840	2 855	3 007	..	..
383	Electrical Machinery	3 232	3 474	3 648	3 853	3 641	3 603	3 837	4 806	..	..
3831	Electrical Industrial Machinery	1 281	1 341	1 244	1 431	1 316	1 320	1 355	1 585	..	..
3832	Radio, TV & Communication Equipment	1 217	1 349	1 540	1 547	1 544	1 601	1 881	2 514	..	..
3833	Electrical Appliances & Housewares	77	90	65	73	57	55	77	80	..	..
3839	Electrical Apparatus, nec	657	694	799	802	724	627	525	628	..	..
384	Transport Equipment	3 906	4 025	3 950	4 091	3 914	3 799	3 543	3 949	..	..
3841	Shipbuilding & Repairing	1 967	2 025	1 748	1 810	1 749	1 816	1 707	1 973	..	..
3842	Railroad Equipment	409	456	494	453	478	411	386	415	..	..
3843	Motor Vehicles	1 099	1 078	1 191	1 171	1 050	943	792	887	..	..
3844	Motorcycles & Bicycles	45	52	56	71	69	55	52	56	..	..
3845	Aircraft	369	388	432	554	550	555	584	593	..	..
3849	Transport Equipment, nec	16	26	29	32	19	20	21	25	..	..
385	Professional Goods	574	700	771	860	846	860	919	1 012	..	..
3851	Professional Equipment	553	685	758	843	827	840	888	983	..	..
3852	Photographic & Optical Goods	21	16	13	17	19	20	31	29	..	..
3853	Watches & Clocks	..	..	..	..	..	..	..	..	..	..
39	**Other Manufacturing, nes**	375	402	417	425	427	418	426	428	..	..
3901	Jewellery	88	99	111	122	124	103	98	93	..	..
3	**Total Manufacturing**	49 118	52 057	56 570	60 667	57 543	54 182	53 597	57 456	..	..
1	**Agric., Hunting, Forestry, Fishing**	..	..	..	..				..	..	..
2	**Mining & Quarrying**	592	563	547	545	567	538	502	493	..	..
21	Coal Mining	..	..	..	..	..	..	..	..	..	..
22	Crude Petroleum & Natural Gas	..	..	..	..	..	..	..	..	..	..
23.29	Other Mining	592	563	547	545	567	538	502	493	..	..
3	**Total Manufacturing**	49 118	52 057	56 570	60 667	57 543	54 182	53 597	57 456	..	..
4	**Electricity, Gas & Water**	3 374	3 694	3 976	4 260	4 486	4 463	4 085	4 054	..	..
5	**Construction**	..	..	..	..			..	..	..	..
6.9	**Services**	..	..	..	94	312	73	67	60	..	..
0000	**Grand Total**	53 084	56 313	61 093	65 567	62 908	59 256	58 252	62 062	..	..

Note: Unless given separately, ISIC 3852 includes 3853.

Table FN.10 **FINLAND**

Thousands

ISIC2	Industry	|HOURS WORKED| 1987	1988	1989	1990	1991	1992	1993	1994	1995	1996
31	Food, Beverages & Tobacco	97 423	95 604	91 194	88 117	82 869	77 237	71 150	68 465	..	..
311.2	Food	86 870	85 207	81 112	77 534	72 860	67 711	63 028	60 399	..	..
313	Beverages	8 494	8 338	8 171	8 856	8 344	7 943	6 687	6 694	..	..
314	Tobacco	2 059	2 059	1 911	1 727	1 665	1 583	1 435	1 372	..	..
32	Textiles, Apparel & Leather	77 306	66 118	57 855	47 748	37 254	29 754	26 846	26 018	..	..
321	Textiles	24 080	21 540	19 656	16 952	13 721	12 290	11 346	11 307	..	..
3213	Knitting Mills	9 898	8 930	8 149	7 082	5 780	5 146	4 598	4 560	..	..
322	Wearing Apparel	39 979	33 330	29 907	23 237	17 536	12 513	10 975	10 162	..	..
323	Leather & Products	3 442	2 827	2 317	2 287	1 862	1 572	1 443	1 461	..	..
324	Footwear	9 805	8 421	5 975	5 272	4 135	3 379	3 082	3 088	..	..
33	Wood Products & Furniture	74 573	72 736	74 130	67 370	57 159	49 598	47 848	51 158	..	..
331	Wood Products	53 426	52 432	54 312	49 576	40 919	36 098	35 776	39 146	..	..
332	Furnitures & Fixtures	21 147	20 304	19 818	17 794	16 240	13 500	12 072	12 012	..	..
34	Paper, Paper Products & Printing	131 958	131 080	137 102	129 983	120 748	111 348	107 191	106 155	..	..
341	Paper & Products	70 524	69 255	76 402	72 068	66 372	63 274	62 292	62 754	..	..
3411	Pulp, Paper & Board	55 122	52 396	63 018	60 498	54 989	50 935	49 893	50 186	..	..
342	Printing & Publishing	61 434	61 825	60 700	57 915	54 376	48 074	44 899	43 401	..	..
35	Chemical Products	64 824	64 858	63 619	62 857	59 787	55 997	54 467	54 658	..	..
351	Industrial Chemicals	25 186	23 642	23 082	22 332	21 416	20 405	19 490	19 156	..	..
3511	Basic Industrial Chemicals	8 758	8 205	8 430	7 891	7 995	8 767	7 857	7 631	..	..
3512	Fertilizers & Pesticides	3 572	3 876	3 745	3 685	3 402	2 232	2 666	2 322	..	..
3513	Synthetic Resins	12 856	11 561	10 907	10 756	10 019	9 406	8 967	9 203	..	..
352	Other Chemicals	16 960	16 992	17 202	17 006	16 774	15 092	15 369	15 142	..	..
3521	Paints, Varnishes & Lacquers	2 710	2 980	3 124	2 851	2 831	2 573	2 384	2 528	..	..
3522	Drugs & Medicines	5 752	5 672	5 922	6 253	5 957	6 053	6 021	5 935	..	..
3523	Soap & Cleaning Preparations	3 966	3 743	3 838	3 755	3 997	2 848	2 577	2 488	..	..
3529	Chemical Products, nec	4 532	4 597	4 318	4 147	3 989	3 618	4 387	4 191	..	..
353	Petroleum Refineries	5 015	6 360	5 334	5 102	5 035	5 066	4 826	4 430	..	..
354	Petroleum & Coal Products	1 438	1 376	1 396	1 256	1 479	1 397	1 288	1 453	..	..
355	Rubber Products	5 350	4 867	4 499	4 095	3 615	3 647	3 592	4 241	..	..
356	Plastic Products, nec	10 875	11 621	12 106	13 066	11 468	10 390	9 902	10 236	..	..
36	Non-Metallic Mineral Products	34 788	34 044	34 516	33 378	28 657	23 183	18 980	19 024	..	..
361	Pottery, China etc	2 298	2 343	2 204	2 136	1 979	1 717	1 405	1 607	..	..
362	Glass & Products	5 746	5 507	5 545	5 327	4 920	4 481	4 405	4 613	..	..
369	Non-Metallic Products, nec	26 744	26 194	26 767	25 915	21 758	16 985	13 170	12 804	..	..
37	Basic Metal Industries	30 538	29 332	28 631	28 424	26 085	25 502	25 537	26 368	..	..
371	Iron & Steel	22 262	21 621	21 255	21 250	19 313	18 672	18 596	19 468	..	..
372	Non-Ferrous Metals	8 276	7 711	7 376	7 174	6 772	6 830	6 941	6 900	..	..
38	Fabricated Metal Products	270 458	264 710	255 656	243 787	214 938	192 302	183 067	200 079	..	..
381	Metal Products	52 863	54 263	56 676	52 932	47 447	38 848	36 450	38 114	..	..
3813	Structural Metal Products	21 437	21 944	23 681	21 490	18 733	14 708	13 825	13 855	..	..
382	Non-Electrical Machinery	95 351	92 298	87 604	87 965	75 405	67 372	64 570	68 812	..	..
3821	Engines & Turbines	1 039	1 056	1 054	1 057	1 199	1 073	948	1 081	..	..
3822	Agricultural Machinery	5 615	5 398	5 778	5 478	4 002	2 568	2 326	2 708	..	..
3823	Metal & Wood working Machinery	6 602	6 442	5 651	5 128	4 830	4 002	4 131	4 671	..	..
3824	Special Industrial Machinery	33 726	36 215	31 813	30 585	25 280	24 732	23 693	25 257	..	..
3825	Office & Computing Machinery	5 720	7 367	6 477	8 650	4 823	5 747	5 569	6 248	..	..
3829	Machinery & Equipment, nec	42 649	35 820	36 831	37 067	35 271	29 250	27 903	28 847	..	..
383	Electrical Machinery	54 495	52 919	50 284	47 246	41 778	39 209	39 901	47 344	..	..
3831	Electrical Industrial Machinery	22 466	20 819	17 870	17 645	15 096	14 629	14 282	15 900	..	..
3832	Radio, TV & Communication Equipment	20 366	20 614	20 907	19 115	17 966	17 106	19 285	24 485	..	..
3833	Electrical Appliances & Housewares	1 494	1 544	1 014	969	731	718	956	974	..	..
3839	Electrical Apparatus, nec	10 169	9 942	10 493	9 517	7 985	6 756	5 378	5 985	..	..
384	Transport Equipment	59 058	54 969	50 786	45 639	40 909	38 299	33 227	36 366	..	..
3841	Shipbuilding & Repairing	29 107	27 545	22 429	19 555	17 764	17 711	15 816	17 879	..	..
3842	Railroad Equipment	5 660	5 322	5 421	4 708	4 582	3 881	3 610	3 678	..	..
3843	Motor Vehicles	18 476	16 296	16 741	14 457	11 918	10 229	8 164	9 320	..	..
3844	Motorcycles & Bicycles	838	953	987	1 072	991	731	592	640	..	..
3845	Aircraft	4 685	4 400	4 733	5 409	5 412	5 493	4 799	4 586	..	..
3849	Transport Equipment, nec	292	453	475	438	242	254	246	263	..	..
385	Professional Goods	8 691	10 261	10 306	10 005	9 399	8 574	8 919	9 443	..	..
3851	Professional Equipment	8 302	9 976	10 067	9 742	9 132	8 325	8 584	9 147	..	..
3852	Photographic & Optical Goods	389	285	239	263	267	249	335	296	..	..
3853	Watches & Clocks	..	..	..	..	..	..	..	..	..	..
39	Other Manufacturing, nes	7 334	7 291	6 775	6 039	5 727	5 259	5 279	5 105	..	..
3901	Jewellery	1 459	1 490	1 475	1 435	1 420	1 117	1 000	957	..	..
3	Total Manufacturing	789 202	765 773	749 478	707 703	633 224	570 180	540 365	557 030	..	..
1	Agric., Hunting, Forestry, Fishing	..	..	..	..	..	..	..	..	..	..
2	Mining & Quarrying	9 009	7 726	7 097	6 402	6 063	5 558	4 998	4 622	..	..
21	Coal Mining	..	..	..	..	..	..	..	..	..	..
22	Crude Petroleum & Natural Gas	..	..	..	..	..	..	..	..	..	..
23.29	Other Mining	9 009	7 726	7 097	6 402	6 063	5 558	4 998	4 622	..	..
3	Total Manufacturing	789 202	765 773	749 478	707 703	633 224	570 180	540 365	557 030	..	..
4	Electricity, Gas & Water	47 869	47 075	45 879	44 157	42 851	40 508	36 444	34 182	..	..
5	Construction	..	..	..	..	..	..	..	..	..	..
6.9	Services	..	..	..	1 343	2 545	1 163	1 024	863	..	..
0000	Grand Total	846 080	820 574	802 454	759 605	684 683	617 409	582 831	596 697	..	..

Note: Unless given separately, ISIC 3852 includes 3853.

Table FN.11 **FINLAND**

ISIC2	Industry	ESTABLISHMENTS									
		1987	1988	1989	1990	1991	1992	1993	1994	1995	1996
31	**Food, Beverages & Tobacco**	958	931	859	813	825	765	718	690	..	..
311.2	Food	930	901	831	785	799	738	693	665	..	..
313	Beverages	24	26	24	24	22	23	21	21	..	..
314	Tobacco	4	4	4	4	4	4	4	4	..	..
32	**Textiles, Apparel & Leather**	786	707	637	579	545	462	433	383	..	..
321	Textiles	253	239	229	204	206	186	171	158	..	..
3213	Knitting Mills	89	90	85	77	70	58	54	53	..	..
322	Wearing Apparel	379	339	296	265	238	186	172	147	..	..
323	Leather & Products	65	57	54	54	46	39	37	34	..	..
324	Footwear	89	72	58	56	55	51	53	44	..	..
33	**Wood Products & Furniture**	931	905	941	897	919	826	749	719	..	..
331	Wood Products	576	557	585	560	561	507	466	455	..	..
332	Furnitures & Fixtures	355	348	356	337	358	319	283	264	..	..
34	**Paper, Paper Products & Printing**	894	845	834	816	884	835	799	767	..	..
341	Paper & Products	187	151	151	148	162	165	162	159	..	..
3411	Pulp, Paper & Board	112	78	78	74	78	72	72	72	..	..
342	Printing & Publishing	707	694	683	668	722	670	637	608	..	..
35	**Chemical Products**	459	440	441	456	497	479	455	450	..	..
351	Industrial Chemicals	175	152	154	160	165	157	147	151	..	..
3511	Basic Industrial Chemicals	62	56	57	56	59	57	57	57	..	..
3512	Fertilizers & Pesticides	12	11	11	13	12	11	7	9	..	..
3513	Synthetic Resins	101	85	86	91	94	89	83	85	..	..
352	Other Chemicals	97	89	90	92	110	105	107	103	..	..
3521	Paints, Varnishes & Lacquers	15	13	12	12	17	16	15	14	..	..
3522	Drugs & Medicines	16	15	15	16	19	21	19	19	..	..
3523	Soap & Cleaning Preparations	33	27	26	28	28	26	25	22	..	..
3529	Chemical Products, nec	33	34	37	36	46	42	48	48	..	..
353	Petroleum Refineries	2	4	4	4	4	4	3	3	..	..
354	Petroleum & Coal Products	22	21	20	20	20	20	17	20	..	..
355	Rubber Products	18	24	26	26	29	29	28	32	..	..
356	Plastic Products, nec	145	150	147	154	169	164	153	141	..	..
36	**Non-Metallic Mineral Products**	407	405	416	424	463	406	350	325	..	..
361	Pottery, China etc	12	12	12	13	13	10	9	9	..	..
362	Glass & Products	45	43	45	49	49	46	38	37	..	..
369	Non-Metallic Products, nec	350	350	359	362	401	350	303	279	..	..
37	**Basic Metal Industries**	88	75	72	73	78	77	73	73	..	..
371	Iron & Steel	56	50	48	51	55	56	54	54	..	..
372	Non-Ferrous Metals	32	25	24	22	23	21	19	19	..	..
38	**Fabricated Metal Products**	2 015	1 910	1 939	1 957	2 176	2 001	1 931	1 892	..	..
381	Metal Products	702	732	750	740	831	721	698	672	..	..
3813	Structural Metal Products	291	294	314	306	338	289	294	278	..	..
382	Non-Electrical Machinery	730	615	632	648	733	707	657	665	..	..
3821	Engines & Turbines	18	18	17	17	20	17	16	15	..	..
3822	Agricultural Machinery	58	42	44	45	49	47	39	38	..	..
3823	Metal & Wood working Machinery	67	64	58	55	59	54	50	49	..	..
3824	Special Industrial Machinery	230	216	207	220	232	237	223	225	..	..
3825	Office & Computing Machinery	33	29	27	21	24	27	25	25	..	..
3829	Machinery & Equipment, nec	324	246	279	290	349	325	304	313	..	..
383	Electrical Machinery	229	228	221	236	250	257	266	264	..	..
3831	Electrical Industrial Machinery	107	105	98	110	111	118	120	120	..	..
3832	Radio, TV & Communication Equipment	64	66	64	66	79	74	83	85	..	..
3833	Electrical Appliances & Housewares	11	12	11	11	10	12	13	11	..	..
3839	Electrical Apparatus, nec	47	45	48	49	50	53	50	48	..	..
384	Transport Equipment	268	246	243	239	259	214	198	179	..	..
3841	Shipbuilding & Repairing	93	93	89	85	97	76	73	65	..	..
3842	Railroad Equipment	8	8	7	6	14	14	15	14	..	..
3843	Motor Vehicles	149	125	129	129	130	105	93	83	..	..
3844	Motorcycles & Bicycles	4	6	5	6	7	5	5	5	..	..
3845	Aircraft	7	7	7	8	8	9	7	7	..	..
3849	Transport Equipment, nec	7	7	6	5	3	5	5	5	..	..
385	Professional Goods	86	89	93	94	103	102	112	112	..	..
3851	Professional Equipment	75	81	86	88	97	94	103	105	..	..
3852	Photographic & Optical Goods	10	8	7	6	6	8	9	7	..	..
3853	Watches & Clocks	1	..	..	..	..	..	..	..	..	..
39	**Other Manufacturing, nes**	95	98	98	86	93	91	87	80	..	..
3901	Jewellery	30	29	29	26	31	29	28	25	..	..
3	**Total Manufacturing**	6 633	6 316	6 237	6 101	6 480	5 942	5 595	5 379	..	..
1	**Agric., Hunting, Forestry, Fishing**	..	..	..	..	..	..	..	..	..	..
2	**Mining & Quarrying**	145	133	150	138	136	129	121	121	..	..
21	Coal Mining	..	..	..	..	..	..	..	..	..	..
22	Crude Petroleum & Natural Gas	..	..	..	..	..	..	..	..	..	..
23.29	Other Mining	145	133	150	138	136	129	121	121	..	..
3	**Total Manufacturing**	6 633	6 316	6 237	6 101	6 480	5 942	5 595	5 379	..	..
4	**Electricity, Gas & Water**	532	522	520	527	536	525	514	510	..	..
5	**Construction**	..	..	..	..	..	..	..	..	..	..
6.9	**Services**	..	..	..	7	13	13	10	9	..	..
0000	**Grand Total**	7 310	6 971	6 907	6 773	7 165	6 609	6 240	6 019	..	..

Note: Unless given separately, ISIC 3852 includes 3853.

Thousands

ISIC2	Industry	EMPLOYMENT - EMPLOYEES									
		1987	1988	1989	1990	1991	1992	1993	1994	1995	1996
31	Food, Beverages & Tobacco	213.5	218.9	208.4	208.9	202.1	197.8	198.3	200.3	200.6	..
311.2	Food	174.2	181.1	174.7	177.7	176.5	173.7	175.2	177.4	177.9	..
313	Beverages	29.1	28.5	26.2	24.0	18.7	17.6	17.3	17.4	17.4	..
314	Tobacco	10.2	9.3	7.5	7.2	6.9	6.5	5.8	5.5	5.3	..
32	Textiles, Apparel & Leather	769.6	762.3	724.1	649.6	675.9	643.1	613.3	578.9	568.8	..
321	Textiles	415.7	410.3	384.4	349.0	333.1	315.9	307.6	295.7	295.0	..
3213	Knitting Mills	54.0	52.5	45.9	38.7	..	..	..	..	..	..
322	Wearing Apparel	271.4	275.7	262.5	231.5	198.1	187.0	196.7	190.2	192.4	..
323	Leather & Products	46.3	42.4	44.9	40.5	38.6	33.7	31.5	30.1	27.4	..
324	Footwear	36.3	33.9	32.3	28.6	106.2	106.7	77.5	62.9	54.0	..
33	Wood Products & Furniture	69.2	79.4	83.1	82.8	86.6	82.5	88.9	87.3	87.2	..
331	Wood Products	37.8	41.2	40.1	40.6	40.5	37.3	40.5	39.6	39.5	..
332	Furnitures & Fixtures	31.4	38.2	43.0	42.2	46.0	45.1	48.4	47.7	47.7	..
34	Paper, Paper Products & Printing	121.5	129.4	134.5	131.1	132.0	136.2	146.6	152.1	161.7	..
341	Paper & Products	59.0	61.4	63.0	59.8	60.0	59.1	60.0	63.2	64.9	..
3411	Pulp, Paper & Board	22.9	24.1	24.2	22.0	..	..	..	..	..	..
342	Printing & Publishing	62.5	68.0	71.5	71.3	72.0	77.1	86.6	88.9	96.8	..
35	Chemical Products	407.0	417.4	422.2	428.3	282.4	283.6	298.8	304.5	311.7	..
351	Industrial Chemicals	43.5	47.8	50.8	52.3	46.1	46.7	54.6	56.0	56.7	..
3511	Basic Industrial Chemicals	30.0	33.7	36.6	36.3	..	..	..	..	..	..
3512	Fertilizers & Pesticides	7.2	7.2	6.6	6.1	..	..	..	..	..	..
3513	Synthetic Resins	6.3	6.9	7.6	9.9	..	..	..	..	..	..
352	Other Chemicals	73.7	76.7	76.3	76.0	75.0	77.5	75.6	76.4	77.9	..
3521	Paints, Varnishes & Lacquers	7.5	7.9	8.1	9.2	..	..	..	..	..	..
3522	Drugs & Medicines	28.9	32.0	29.8	31.6	..	..	..	..	..	..
3523	Soap & Cleaning Preparations	11.5	12.3	14.1	14.0	..	..	..	..	..	..
3529	Chemical Products, nec	25.8	24.5	24.4	21.2	..	..	..	..	..	..
353	Petroleum Refineries	4.5	5.3	6.0	7.1	7.3	7.7	7.9	8.2	8.6	..
354	Petroleum & Coal Products	13.1	12.4	11.9	11.0	10.3	9.1	8.1	7.1	7.0	..
355	Rubber Products	188.0	185.2	181.6	182.0	31.3	31.4	32.9	33.4	33.5	..
356	Plastic Products, nec	84.2	90.0	95.6	99.9	112.5	111.2	119.8	123.3	128.0	..
36	Non-Metallic Mineral Products	115.6	117.9	121.3	124.6	131.2	130.8	131.7	129.2	132.5	..
361	Pottery, China etc	19.3	18.0	17.4	16.0	15.7	15.0	15.5	15.6	15.9	..
362	Glass & Products	22.9	24.0	24.5	25.5	24.6	25.3	24.8	25.4	26.0	..
369	Non-Metallic Products, nec	73.4	75.9	79.4	83.1	91.0	90.5	91.4	88.2	90.6	..
37	Basic Metal Industries	106.8	117.7	116.9	120.8	119.5	114.9	115.8	116.0	120.0	..
371	Iron & Steel	81.3	85.3	85.9	88.3	88.0	85.0	86.2	86.7	89.4	..
372	Non-Ferrous Metals	25.5	32.4	31.0	32.5	31.5	30.0	29.6	29.3	30.6	..
38	Fabricated Metal Products	1 020.6	1 105.2	1 117.2	1 121.0	1 112.6	1 081.6	1 148.7	1 222.1	1 321.9	..
381	Metal Products	155.5	177.4	173.6	175.3	172.7	164.8	185.4	198.8	211.9	..
3813	Structural Metal Products	34.5	48.1	41.1	45.1	..	..	..	..	..	..
382	Non-Electrical Machinery	169.3	188.1	202.5	209.2	258.8	248.6	272.3	290.6	322.5	..
3821	Engines & Turbines	0.3	0.3	0.3	0.3	..	..	..	..	..	..
3822	Agricultural Machinery	11.2	9.3	10.1	12.5	..	..	..	..	..	..
3823	Metal & Wood working Machinery	38.0	45.7	50.9	52.4	..	..	..	..	..	..
3824	Special Industrial Machinery	32.5	33.8	34.7	43.5	..	..	..	..	..	..
3825	Office & Computing Machinery	17.0	22.9	22.6	18.6	..	..	..	..	..	..
3829	Machinery & Equipment, nec	70.3	76.1	84.0	81.9	..	..	..	..	..	..
383	Electrical Machinery	445.9	474.1	463.4	448.9	404.3	392.1	395.0	408.6	436.4	..
3831	Electrical Industrial Machinery	39.7	41.8	41.8	39.7	..	..	..	..	..	..
3832	Radio, TV & Communication Equipment	202.0	209.8	193.0	187.2	..	..	..	..	..	..
3833	Electrical Appliances & Housewares	36.4	38.7	41.8	35.9	..	..	..	..	..	..
3839	Electrical Apparatus, nec	167.9	183.8	186.8	186.2	..	..	..	..	..	..
384	Transport Equipment	202.4	212.3	226.4	242.9	243.6	245.3	263.1	289.2	314.0	..
3841	Shipbuilding & Repairing	66.9	50.4	56.8	53.3	..	..	..	..	..	..
3842	Railroad Equipment	2.5	3.4	3.8	3.8	..	..	..	..	..	..
3843	Motor Vehicles	123.8	146.7	156.7	174.7	..	..	..	..	..	..
3844	Motorcycles & Bicycles	7.9	8.3	7.1	6.6	..	..	..	..	..	..
3845	Aircraft	..	..	..	0.3	..	..	..	..	..	..
3849	Transport Equipment, nec	1.3	3.5	2.0	4.2	..	..	..	..	..	..
385	Professional Goods	47.4	53.3	51.3	44.7	33.2	30.8	32.9	34.9	37.1	..
3851	Professional Equipment	15.1	18.1	17.7	19.0	..	..	..	..	..	..
3852	Photographic & Optical Goods	14.8	17.4	19.4	16.0	..	..	..	..	..	..
3853	Watches & Clocks	17.6	17.7	14.2	9.7	..	..	..	..	..	..
39	Other Manufacturing, nes	127.2	118.2	106.2	90.8	76.6	64.5	61.0	56.1	62.7	..
3901	Jewellery	8.2	9.2	6.6	6.1	..	..	..	..	..	..
3	Total Manufacturing	2 951.1	3 066.4	3 033.9	2 957.9	2 818.9	2 735.0	2 803.0	2 846.5	2 967.1	..
1	Agric., Hunting, Forestry, Fishing	..	..	..	..	..	..	..	..	..	..
2	Mining & Quarrying	..	..	..	58.6	..	..	..	..	..	..
21	Coal Mining	..	..	..	37.9	..	..	..	..	..	..
22	Crude Petroleum & Natural Gas	..	..	..	..	..	..	..	..	..	..
23.29	Other Mining	..	..	..	20.7	..	..	..	..	..	..
3	Total Manufacturing	2 951.1	3 066.4	3 033.9	2 957.9	2 818.9	2 735.0	2 803.0	2 846.5	2 967.1	..
4	Electricity, Gas & Water	..	..	..	..	..	..	..	..	..	..
5	Construction	..	..	..	..	..	..	..	..	..	..
6.9	Services	..	..	..	..	..	..	..	..	..	..
0000	Grand Total	2 951.1	3 066.4	3 033.9	3 016.5	2 818.9	2 735.0	2 803.0	2 846.5	2 967.1	..

Millions of Won

(Current Prices)

ISIC2	Industry	WAGES & SALARIES - EMPLOYEES									
		1987	1988	1989	1990	1991	1992	1993	1994	1995	1996
31	**Food, Beverages & Tobacco**	794 447	923 929	1 089 432	1 240 296	1 434 878	1 574 194	1 804 543	1 978 543	2 081 205	..
311.2	Food	588 679	701 368	843 686	979 809	1 167 489	1 295 415	1 510 008	1 661 015	1 747 946	..
313	Beverages	135 716	148 253	174 030	185 038	176 982	181 974	196 463	222 696	237 093	..
314	Tobacco	70 052	74 308	71 716	75 449	90 407	96 805	98 072	94 832	96 166	..
32	**Textiles, Apparel & Leather**	2 321 967	2 704 790	3 170 175	3 379 095	4 221 514	4 628 456	4 948 521	5 199 693	5 295 221	..
321	Textiles	1 325 819	1 550 183	1 790 499	1 932 806	2 188 422	2 450 834	2 624 917	2 788 845	2 848 709	..
3213	Knitting Mills	158 600	181 179	198 500	199 354						
322	Wearing Apparel	736 436	865 336	1 016 967	1 059 409	1 090 314	1 188 623	1 444 705	1 584 729	1 703 047	..
323	Leather & Products	151 989	169 718	219 600	244 032	281 231	288 631	292 551	308 795	294 000	..
324	Footwear	107 723	119 553	143 109	142 848	661 547	700 368	586 348	517 324	449 465	..
33	**Wood Products & Furniture**	229 619	314 646	410 306	491 460	661 106	705 529	832 493	896 755	929 664	..
331	Wood Products	123 000	161 445	197 540	244 326	310 888	323 807	378 054	418 383	433 077	..
332	Furnitures & Fixtures	106 619	153 201	212 766	247 134	350 218	381 722	454 439	478 372	496 587	..
34	**Paper, Paper Products & Printing**	547 792	664 567	868 899	978 949	1 129 723	1 357 608	1 641 804	1 871 544	2 191 813	..
341	Paper & Products	242 391	296 108	361 285	410 479	495 178	568 408	625 101	731 438	815 879	..
3411	Pulp, Paper & Board	102 148	134 737	162 697	178 619						
342	Printing & Publishing	305 401	368 459	507 614	568 470	634 545	789 200	1 016 703	1 140 106	1 375 934	..
35	**Chemical Products**	1 570 927	1 891 325	2 387 401	2 818 384	2 525 965	2 875 748	3 410 656	3 877 727	4 300 761	..
351	Industrial Chemicals	245 174	317 026	437 904	509 460	497 803	590 000	760 995	855 582	954 381	..
3511	Basic Industrial Chemicals	169 224	216 732	310 090	363 261						
3512	Fertilizers & Pesticides	43 651	51 779	52 657	50 292	..	..	..	..	..	..
3513	Synthetic Resins	32 299	48 515	75 157	95 907						
352	Other Chemicals	352 361	410 253	502 973	574 944	654 875	766 121	857 565	967 063	1 075 830	..
3521	Paints, Varnishes & Lacquers	41 411	49 118	60 156	68 073						
3522	Drugs & Medicines	142 993	173 877	185 285	237 009	..	..	..	..	..	..
3523	Soap & Cleaning Preparations	49 397	58 957	89 290	98 895	..	..	..	..	..	..
3529	Chemical Products, nec	118 560	128 301	168 242	170 967						
353	Petroleum Refineries	43 625	51 836	79 576	105 250	101 587	117 319	135 869	170 409	201 316	..
354	Petroleum & Coal Products	61 373	68 647	77 505	83 409	96 418	96 583	93 717	91 613	108 414	..
355	Rubber Products	569 619	670 644	799 725	947 206	256 601	288 031	344 389	381 113	424 534	..
356	Plastic Products, nec	298 775	372 919	489 718	598 115	918 681	1 017 694	1 218 121	1 411 947	1 536 286	..
36	**Non-Metallic Mineral Products**	458 069	578 892	742 401	891 797	1 130 245	1 316 996	1 438 149	1 560 541	1 727 839	..
361	Pottery, China etc	56 151	65 993	74 813	81 916	94 143	101 361	119 790	134 143	148 555	..
362	Glass & Products	98 868	129 318	168 329	218 992	245 865	294 979	313 209	346 566	383 445	..
369	Non-Metallic Products, nec	303 050	383 581	499 259	590 889	790 237	920 656	1 005 150	1 079 832	1 195 839	..
37	**Basic Metal Industries**	549 167	739 151	931 844	1 083 849	1 294 699	1 385 232	1 487 621	1 694 347	1 950 527	..
371	Iron & Steel	416 372	576 956	728 336	841 140	1 016 312	1 076 621	1 164 106	1 329 259	1 531 474	..
372	Non-Ferrous Metals	132 795	162 195	203 508	242 709	278 387	308 611	323 515	365 088	419 053	..
38	**Fabricated Metal Products**	4 163 077	5 474 952	6 805 575	8 200 115	9 727 981	10 904 244	12 726 685	15 146 601	18 317 105	..
381	Metal Products	592 768	851 105	986 708	1 171 657	1 409 223	1 516 061	1 910 034	2 290 465	2 712 030	..
3813	Structural Metal Products	155 254	279 539	273 509	348 385						
382	Non-Electrical Machinery	720 674	937 241	1 261 062	1 523 189	2 246 913	2 508 838	2 974 372	3 488 803	4 268 402	..
3821	Engines & Turbines	984	1 144	1 750	1 970	..	..	..	..	..	..
3822	Agricultural Machinery	45 936	40 852	54 014	88 791						
3823	Metal & Wood working Machinery	157 827	220 873	311 549	360 635	..	..	..	..	..	..
3824	Special Industrial Machinery	132 218	164 466	206 972	334 774	..	..	..	..	..	..
3825	Office & Computing Machinery	53 360	92 222	105 848	109 871	..	..	..	..	..	..
3829	Machinery & Equipment, nec	330 349	417 684	580 929	627 148						
383	Electrical Machinery	1 616 676	2 109 497	2 595 205	2 903 124	3 206 054	3 475 051	3 790 441	4 307 743	5 243 560	..
3831	Electrical Industrial Machinery	159 526	204 640	246 828	281 141	..	..	..	..	..	..
3832	Radio, TV & Communication Equipment	712 892	921 274	1 067 308	1 206 030	..	..	..	..	..	..
3833	Electrical Appliances & Housewares	123 065	163 864	230 483	232 023	..	..	..	..	..	..
3839	Electrical Apparatus, nec	621 193	819 719	1 050 586	1 183 930						
384	Transport Equipment	1 074 018	1 352 738	1 690 521	2 333 289	2 623 279	3 148 831	3 747 778	4 710 899	5 683 057	..
3841	Shipbuilding & Repairing	417 602	381 513	463 676	628 092	..	..	..	..	..	..
3842	Railroad Equipment	14 604	19 361	28 470	37 919	..	..	..	..	..	..
3843	Motor Vehicles	608 333	889 999	1 143 571	1 572 581	..	..	..	..	..	..
3844	Motorcycles & Bicycles	26 532	33 607	38 283	46 854	..	..	..	..	..	..
3845	Aircraft	..	..	..	2 046	..	..	..	..	..	..
3849	Transport Equipment, nec	6 947	28 258	16 521	45 797	..	..	..	..	..	..
385	Professional Goods	158 941	224 371	272 079	268 856	242 512	255 463	304 060	348 691	410 056	..
3851	Professional Equipment	51 011	76 030	85 955	112 867	..	..	..	..	..	..
3852	Photographic & Optical Goods	50 412	72 121	111 520	98 928	..	..	..	..	..	..
3853	Watches & Clocks	57 518	76 220	74 604	57 061						
39	**Other Manufacturing, nes**	397 360	436 299	479 525	495 593	504 315	497 331	532 829	542 741	708 464	..
3901	Jewellery	27 191	33 668	30 802	32 933	..	..	..	..	..	..
3	**Total Manufacturing**	11 032 425	13 728 551	16 885 558	19 579 538	22 630 426	25 245 338	28 823 301	32 768 492	37 502 598	..
I	**Agric., Hunting, Forestry, Fishing**	..	..	..	..	..	..	..	..	..	..
2	**Mining & Quarrying**	..	..	..	..	..	..	..	..	..	..
21	Coal Mining	..	..	..	..	..	..	..	..	..	..
22	Crude Petroleum & Natural Gas	..	..	..	..	..	..	..	..	..	..
23.29	Other Mining	..	..	..	..	..	..	..	..	..	..
3	**Total Manufacturing**	11 032 425	13 728 551	16 885 558	19 579 538	22 630 426	25 245 338	28 823 301	32 768 492	37 502 598	..
4	**Electricity, Gas & Water**	..	..	..	..	..	..	..	..	..	..
5	**Construction**	..	..	..	..	..	..	..	..	..	..
6.9	**Services**	..	..	..	..	..	..	..	..	..	..
0000	**Grand Total**	11 032 425	13 728 551	16 885 558	19 579 538	22 630 426	25 245 338	28 823 301	32 768 492	37 502 598	..

Millions of NM$ (Current Prices)

ISIC2	Industry	PRODUCTION									
		1987	1988	1989	1990	1991	1992	1993	1994	1995	1996
31	Food, Beverages & Tobacco	11 083	22 418	28 465	35 959	44 892	52 897	56 457	64 224	86 203	..
311.2	Food	6 486	13 201	16 909	21 262	25 063	29 284	30 552	34 546	48 259	..
313	Beverages	3 627	7 574	9 479	12 196	16 173	18 743	20 091	23 370	29 505	..
314	Tobacco	969	1 643	2 077	2 501	3 655	4 871	5 815	6 309	8 439	..
32	Textiles, Apparel & Leather	2 664	5 277	6 240	7 325	7 498	7 839	7 423	7 405	8 790	..
321	Textiles	1 857	3 596	4 273	4 949	5 054	5 196	4 853	4 897	6 441	..
3213	Knitting Mills	160	350	384	566	721	728	712	817	887	..
322	Wearing Apparel	506	1 040	1 194	1 445	1 381	1 487	1 450	1 478	1 482	..
323	Leather & Products	..	..	..	..	..	..	..	..		..
324	Footwear	301	641	774	931	1 063	1 156	1 120	1 030	866	..
33	Wood Products & Furniture	290	559	718	865	950	1 041	1 085	1 180	1 373	..
331	Wood Products	132	248	313	364	356	352	349	386	628	..
332	Furnitures & Fixtures	158	311	405	501	594	689	736	794	745	..
34	Paper, Paper Products & Printing	2 869	5 885	6 908	7 693	8 366	8 771	9 017	9 890	15 229	..
341	Paper & Products	2 508	5 108	5 959	6 569	7 079	7 378	7 710	8 552	13 323	..
3411	Pulp, Paper & Board	1 786	3 616	4 191	4 629	4 917	4 984	5 706	6 319	9 239	..
342	Printing & Publishing	361	776	949	1 123	1 287	1 393	1 307	1 338	1 905	..
35	Chemical Products	11 846	23 812	28 795	34 997	40 373	43 033	41 634	49 653	78 852	..
351	Industrial Chemicals	5 425	10 773	12 324	14 428	16 260	16 143	14 764	16 917	34 547	..
3511	Basic Industrial Chemicals	2 341	4 695	5 569	6 427	6 972	7 341	6 605	7 228	16 529	..
3512	Fertilizers & Pesticides	784	1 568	1 980	2 522	3 120	2 453	2 758	3 140	5 046	..
3513	Synthetic Resins	2 300	4 510	4 775	5 479	6 168	6 349	5 401	6 550	12 972	..
352	Other Chemicals	3 971	8 071	10 546	13 368	16 242	18 726	19 093	23 396	31 151	..
3521	Paints, Varnishes & Lacquers	424	923	1 143	1 522	1 821	2 178	2 109	2 300	2 855	..
3522	Drugs & Medicines	1 354	2 736	3 608	4 612	5 383	6 359	8 148	9 679	13 737	..
3523	Soap & Cleaning Preparations	1 744	3 436	4 565	5 809	7 185	8 292	6 973	9 371	11 632	..
3529	Chemical Products, nec	450	976	1 230	1 426	1 853	1 897	1 863	2 046	2 927	..
353	Petroleum Refineries	..	..	..	..	..	..	..	..		..
354	Petroleum & Coal Products	529	1 009	1 201	1 597	1 799	1 785	1 825	2 261	3 406	..
355	Rubber Products	996	2 075	2 319	2 837	3 130	3 107	2 789	3 352	4 638	..
356	Plastic Products, nec	925	1 883	2 405	2 767	2 942	3 272	3 163	3 727	5 109	..
36	Non-Metallic Mineral Products	3 176	6 152	7 039	9 158	11 770	13 787	14 591	15 738	18 952	..
361	Pottery, China etc	206	456	507	640	755	939	931	1 024	1 358	..
362	Glass & Products	1 062	2 036	2 547	3 177	3 767	3 947	4 214	4 494	6 285	..
369	Non-Metallic Products, nec	1 909	3 660	3 985	5 340	7 247	8 902	9 446	10 221	11 309	..
37	Basic Metal Industries	7 901	16 926	19 351	22 946	21 950	21 791	21 207	23 440	45 618	..
371	Iron & Steel	5 044	11 435	12 876	15 787	16 358	16 402	16 271	17 451	33 603	..
372	Non-Ferrous Metals	2 856	5 492	6 475	7 159	5 592	5 389	4 936	5 989	12 015	..
38	Fabricated Metal Products	14 822	31 454	40 047	53 441	65 718	77 107	71 780	76 959	125 661	..
381	Metal Products	1 998	4 198	5 002	6 230	7 104	7 900	7 173	7 897	11 635	..
3813	Structural Metal Products	236	477	615	780	911	1 184	1 334	1 157	1 182	..
382	Non-Electrical Machinery	1 442	3 254	3 909	4 818	5 163	5 685	5 696	7 972	12 739	..
3821	Engines & Turbines	..	..	..	..	..	..	..	..		..
3822	Agricultural Machinery	189	527	580	664	584	764	616	896	1 013	..
3823	Metal & Wood working Machinery	320	763	924	1 043	1 059	1 217	874	760	1 593	..
3824	Special Industrial Machinery	..	..	..	..	..	..	..	..		..
3825	Office & Computing Machinery	510	1 112	1 373	1 841	2 114	2 008	2 558	4 041	7 748	..
3829	Machinery & Equipment, nec	422	852	1 032	1 270	1 406	1 696	1 648	2 274	2 385	..
383	Electrical Machinery	3 043	5 907	7 585	9 291	8 953	10 443	9 633	10 550	13 868	..
3831	Electrical Industrial Machinery	1 059	2 246	2 713	3 158	3 486	3 758	3 195	3 358	4 666	..
3832	Radio, TV & Communication Equipment	1 215	2 253	3 076	3 944	2 901	3 942	3 650	4 002	5 161	..
3833	Electrical Appliances & Housewares	383	689	789	932	1 229	1 377	1 262	1 485	2 055	..
3839	Electrical Apparatus, nec	386	719	1 007	1 258	1 337	1 366	1 526	1 705	1 987	..
384	Transport Equipment	8 202	17 807	23 139	32 531	43 771	52 320	48 140	49 569	86 022	..
3841	Shipbuilding & Repairing	44	71	79	92	47	31	37	50	89	..
3842	Railroad Equipment	116	184	146	245	204	36	192	153	84	..
3843	Motor Vehicles	7 979	17 415	22 726	31 978	43 315	52 030	47 708	49 148	85 656	..
3844	Motorcycles & Bicycles	63	137	188	217	206	223	203	218	194	..
3845	Aircraft	..	..	..	..	..	..	..	..		..
3849	Transport Equipment, nec	137	290	411	570	726	758	1 138	971	1 396	..
385	Professional Goods	..	..	..	..	..	..	..			..
3851	Professional Equipment	..	..	..	..	..	..	..	..		..
3852	Photographic & Optical Goods	..	..	..	..	..	..	..	..		..
3853	Watches & Clocks	..	..	..	..	..	..	..	..		..
39	Other Manufacturing, nes	159	328	411	514	628	709	700	804	848	..
3901	Jewellery	..	..	..	..	..	..	..			..
3	Total Manufacturing	54 809	112 810	137 975	172 897	202 144	226 975	223 894	249 293	381 525	..
1	Agric., Hunting, Forestry, Fishing	..	..	..	..	..	..	..	..		..
2	Mining & Quarrying	..	..	..	..	..	..	..	..		..
21	Coal Mining	..	..	..	..	..	..	..	..		..
22	Crude Petroleum & Natural Gas	..	..	..	..	..	..	..	..		..
23.29	Other Mining	..	..	..	..	..	..	..	..		..
3	Total Manufacturing	54 809	112 810	137 975	172 897	202 144	226 975	223 894	249 293	381 525	..
4	Electricity, Gas & Water	..	..	..	..	..	..	..	..		..
5	Construction	..	..	..	..	..	..	..	..		..
6.9	Services	..	..	..	..	..	..	..	..		..
0000	Grand Total	..	..	..	..	..	..	..	..		..

Note: Data for ISIC 323, 353, 3821 and 3845 are not available. ISIC 3823 includes part of 3824 (manufacture, assembly and repair of machinery and equipment including tractors for the construction, extraction -- i.e. mining -- and other industries); 3849 is allocated to 3823 and 3843.

Table ME.2 **MEXICO**

ISIC2	Industry	VALUE ADDED									
		1987	1988	1989	1990	1991	1992	1993	1994	1995	1996
31	**Food, Beverages & Tobacco**	4 395	8 867	11 092	14 251	18 757	22 601	24 291	27 485	..	..
311.2	Food	1 808	3 698	4 703	6 124	7 478	8 719	9 077	10 385	..	..
313	Beverages	1 826	3 908	4 799	6 215	8 420	10 174	10 719	12 228	..	..
314	Tobacco	761	1 261	1 590	1 912	2 859	3 708	4 495	4 873	..	..
32	**Textiles, Apparel & Leather**	1 166	2 311	2 730	3 164	3 578	3 677	3 490	3 423	..	..
321	Textiles	815	1 593	1 876	2 154	2 389	2 357	2 215	2 173	..	..
3213	Knitting Mills	87	197	206	312	408	318	304	335	..	..
322	Wearing Apparel	217	444	520	610	704	816	783	798	..	..
323	Leather & Products	..	..	..	..	..	..			..	..
324	Footwear	134	275	334	400	484	503	492	452	..	..
33	**Wood Products & Furniture**	115	221	282	341	391	411	425	469	..	..
331	Wood Products	55	102	129	150	155	147	141	158	..	..
332	Furnitures & Fixtures	60	119	154	191	236	264	284	311	..	..
34	**Paper, Paper Products & Printing**	956	1 945	2 210	2 463	2 795	2 929	2 850	3 059	..	..
341	Paper & Products	802	1 609	1 807	1 985	2 222	2 300	2 250	2 441	..	..
3411	Pulp, Paper & Board	561	1 108	1 233	1 365	1 519	1 501	1 575	1 702	..	..
342	Printing & Publishing	154	336	403	478	573	628	600	618	..	..
35	**Chemical Products**	5 000	10 100	12 085	14 604	16 952	18 755	18 154	22 236	..	..
351	Industrial Chemicals	2 238	4 468	5 021	5 878	6 646	6 992	6 138	7 246	..	..
3511	Basic Industrial Chemicals	1 107	2 229	2 619	3 032	3 287	3 406	2 878	3 091	..	..
3512	Fertilizers & Pesticides	193	373	474	623	782	842	926	1 055	..	..
3513	Synthetic Resins	937	1 866	1 928	2 223	2 577	2 744	2 334	3 100	..	..
352	Other Chemicals	1 734	3 538	4 595	5 696	6 887	8 188	8 721	10 988	..	..
3521	Paints, Varnishes & Lacquers	178	369	457	608	788	856	824	918	..	..
3522	Drugs & Medicines	722	1 496	1 920	2 422	2 791	3 382	4 434	5 482	..	..
3523	Soap & Cleaning Preparations	615	1 202	1 626	1 978	2 455	3 002	2 518	3 553	..	..
3529	Chemical Products, nec	219	471	592	687	853	948	945	1 035	..	..
353	Petroleum Refineries	..	..	..	..	..	..			..	..
354	Petroleum & Coal Products	163	303	356	485	572	590	543	660	..	..
355	Rubber Products	457	947	1 057	1 305	1 424	1 400	1 230	1 520	..	..
356	Plastic Products, nec	407	843	1 057	1 241	1 423	1 586	1 521	1 822	..	..
36	**Non-Metallic Mineral Products**	1 743	3 371	3 789	4 945	6 553	7 641	8 183	8 873	..	..
361	Pottery, China etc	131	292	321	409	478	592	591	645	..	..
362	Glass & Products	600	1 154	1 424	1 763	2 161	2 330	2 510	2 672	..	..
369	Non-Metallic Products, nec	1 011	1 924	2 044	2 773	3 914	4 719	5 082	5 556	..	..
37	**Basic Metal Industries**	2 455	5 184	5 906	7 047	7 001	7 244	7 251	8 211	..	..
371	Iron & Steel	1 680	3 677	4 100	5 060	5 194	5 179	5 230	5 916	..	..
372	Non-Ferrous Metals	775	1 507	1 807	1 987	1 807	2 065	2 021	2 294	..	..
38	**Fabricated Metal Products**	5 779	11 835	14 720	18 836	23 166	26 410	24 549	26 430	..	..
381	Metal Products	870	1 819	2 134	2 658	3 180	3 401	3 114	3 362	..	..
3813	Structural Metal Products	97	196	252	322	461	490	572	442	..	..
382	Non-Electrical Machinery	635	1 423	1 718	2 097	2 309	2 501	2 250	2 950	..	..
3821	Engines & Turbines	..	..	..	..	..	..			..	..
3822	Agricultural Machinery	53	150	167	191	183	240	177	252	..	..
3823	Metal & Wood working Machinery	180	433	522	585	636	718	492	440	..	..
3824	Special Industrial Machinery	..	..	..	..	..	..			..	..
3825	Office & Computing Machinery	196	431	522	689	739	663	749	1 114	..	..
3829	Machinery & Equipment, nec	206	409	507	632	753	880	832	1 143	..	..
383	Electrical Machinery	1 444	2 833	3 577	4 333	4 729	5 366	4 952	5 518	..	..
3831	Electrical Industrial Machinery	532	1 144	1 304	1 511	1 724	1 907	1 601	1 706	..	..
3832	Radio, TV & Communication Equipment	600	1 125	1 566	1 952	1 959	2 366	2 266	2 543	..	..
3833	Electrical Appliances & Housewares	153	272	296	350	481	524	487	578	..	..
3839	Electrical Apparatus, nec	159	292	412	520	565	570	598	691	..	..
384	Transport Equipment	2 773	5 642	7 127	9 520	12 654	14 853	13 824	14 250	..	..
3841	Shipbuilding & Repairing	24	39	40	45	49	35	40	49	..	..
3842	Railroad Equipment	71	110	89	144	211	12	101	76	..	..
3843	Motor Vehicles	2 656	5 444	6 928	9 254	12 320	14 724	13 612	14 049	..	..
3844	Motorcycles & Bicycles	23	49	69	76	74	81	72	76	..	..
3845	Aircraft	..	..	..	..	..	..			..	..
3849	Transport Equipment, nec	..	..	..	..	..	..			..	..
385	Professional Goods	58	118	164	229	294	289	409	349	..	..
3851	Professional Equipment	..	..	..	..	..	..			..	..
3852	Photographic & Optical Goods	..	..	..	..	..	..			..	..
3853	Watches & Clocks	..	..	..	..	..	..			..	..
39	**Other Manufacturing, nes**	80	168	216	270	328	362	361	408	..	..
3901	Jewellery	..	..	..	..	..	..			..	..
3	**Total Manufacturing**	21 689	44 002	53 031	65 923	79 520	90 030	89 553	100 593	..	..
1	**Agric., Hunting, Forestry, Fishing**	..	..	..	..	..	..			..	..
2	**Mining & Quarrying**	..	..	..	..	..	..			..	..
21	Coal Mining	..	..	..	..	..	..			..	..
22	Crude Petroleum & Natural Gas	..	..	..	..	..	..			..	..
23.29	Other Mining	..	..	..	..	..	..			..	..
3	**Total Manufacturing**	21 689	44 002	53 031	65 923	79 520	90 030	89 553	100 593	..	..
4	**Electricity, Gas & Water**	..	..	..	..	..	..			..	..
5	**Construction**	..	..	..	..	..	..			..	..
6.9	**Services**	..	..	..	..	..	..			..	..
0000	**Grand Total**	..	..	..	..	..	..			..	..

Note: Data for ISIC 323, 353, 3821 and 3845 are not available. ISIC 3823 includes part of 3824 (manufacture, assembly and repair of machinery and equipment including tractors for the construction, extraction -- i.e. mining -- and other industries); 3849 is allocated to 3823 and 3843.

Table ME.3 **MEXICO**

Thousands

ISIC2	Industry	EMPLOYMENT - EMPLOYEES									
		1987	1988	1989	1990	1991	1992	1993	1994	1995	1996
31	**Food, Beverages & Tobacco**	179.5	177.3	182.4	188.1	188.7	193.7	188.7	182.1	171.5	..
311.2	Food	95.6	93.3	96.7	97.5	96.4	97.5	94.8	88.3	85.7	..
313	Beverages	78.2	77.3	80.6	85.3	86.8	90.6	88.1	88.6	80.7	..
314	Tobacco	5.7	6.7	5.2	5.3	5.5	5.7	5.8	5.2	5.0	..
32	**Textiles, Apparel & Leather**	124.7	122.7	120.9	115.7	108.9	103.7	88.1	81.5	80.5	..
321	Textiles	73.9	73.4	72.1	68.1	63.6	60.2	48.9	43.8	43.1	..
3213	Knitting Mills	5.9	5.4	5.5	5.4	5.2	5.2	5.0	4.7	4.3	..
322	Wearing Apparel	31.2	31.3	31.3	31.1	28.9	28.3	25.3	24.2	26.2	..
323	Leather & Products	..	..	..	..	..	..	..	..	..	..
324	Footwear	19.6	18.1	17.4	16.4	16.3	15.2	13.9	13.4	11.2	..
33	**Wood Products & Furniture**	13.4	13.0	12.6	12.2	11.9	11.3	9.9	9.9	8.8	..
331	Wood Products	6.0	5.9	5.3	5.0	4.6	4.2	3.3	3.1	3.7	..
332	Furnitures & Fixtures	7.4	7.1	7.3	7.2	7.3	7.1	6.6	6.8	5.1	..
34	**Paper, Paper Products & Printing**	43.7	43.1	44.7	44.2	43.3	42.0	37.5	33.7	34.2	..
341	Paper & Products	32.3	31.9	33.4	33.1	32.2	31.1	28.1	24.1	25.8	..
3411	Pulp, Paper & Board	21.7	21.3	22.2	21.3	20.7	19.5	17.7	14.7	16.4	..
342	Printing & Publishing	11.4	11.2	11.2	11.1	11.1	10.9	9.4	9.6	8.4	..
35	**Chemical Products**	175.5	177.4	179.5	179.6	175.8	168.0	145.7	141.3	145.7	..
351	Industrial Chemicals	58.2	58.6	57.6	56.8	55.2	49.7	40.5	36.6	40.5	..
3511	Basic Industrial Chemicals	20.0	20.5	20.5	20.2	19.1	18.5	15.2	12.4	14.2	..
3512	Fertilizers & Pesticides	11.8	11.6	12.1	11.8	11.0	8.3	6.2	6.6	6.6	..
3513	Synthetic Resins	26.3	26.4	25.0	24.8	25.1	22.9	19.1	17.5	19.6	..
352	Other Chemicals	62.0	62.4	65.5	67.3	67.6	67.5	62.9	62.6	62.5	..
3521	Paints, Varnishes & Lacquers	6.3	6.5	6.8	7.1	7.1	7.1	7.3	7.1	6.3	..
3522	Drugs & Medicines	25.2	25.5	26.5	27.1	26.9	27.6	27.8	27.3	26.9	..
3523	Soap & Cleaning Preparations	23.7	23.3	25.0	26.0	26.4	25.7	21.9	22.2	23.8	..
3529	Chemical Products, nec	6.8	7.1	7.2	7.1	7.2	7.0	6.0	6.0	5.5	..
353	Petroleum Refineries	..	..	..	..	..	..	..	..	..	..
354	Petroleum & Coal Products	4.9	4.6	4.4	4.4	4.1	3.7	3.8	3.8	3.7	..
355	Rubber Products	17.0	17.2	17.7	17.1	16.6	15.9	13.6	12.7	12.4	..
356	Plastic Products, nec	33.4	34.5	34.2	34.0	32.2	31.2	24.9	25.6	26.6	..
36	**Non-Metallic Mineral Products**	61.9	61.4	62.7	63.0	61.0	58.9	52.6	49.7	45.4	..
361	Pottery, China etc	6.7	7.0	7.4	7.4	7.0	7.2	6.7	6.6	6.9	..
362	Glass & Products	23.0	22.4	23.3	24.4	23.7	22.8	20.4	19.2	18.4	..
369	Non-Metallic Products, nec	32.2	32.0	32.1	31.2	30.2	28.9	25.6	24.0	20.1	..
37	**Basic Metal Industries**	70.8	70.7	69.7	65.3	61.2	53.2	44.1	40.2	40.8	..
371	Iron & Steel	52.9	52.8	51.6	47.2	43.4	37.8	30.8	28.0	29.3	..
372	Non-Ferrous Metals	17.9	17.9	18.1	18.1	17.7	15.5	13.3	12.2	11.6	..
38	**Fabricated Metal Products**	275.5	279.8	290.9	296.7	295.5	282.1	236.6	224.1	215.1	..
381	Metal Products	50.3	50.1	51.6	52.8	51.5	48.6	41.4	40.6	36.4	..
3813	Structural Metal Products	8.6	8.5	8.4	8.4	9.0	7.9	6.8	7.1	6.8	..
382	Non-Electrical Machinery	33.0	34.9	33.6	32.7	31.4	30.4	23.3	23.2	22.7	..
3821	Engines & Turbines	..	..	..	..	..	..	..	..	..	..
3822	Agricultural Machinery	2.8	3.1	2.6	2.7	3.1	2.9	2.1	2.2	2.6	..
3823	Metal & Wood working Machinery	13.1	14.2	13.1	12.6	11.4	10.5	7.0	6.1	6.9	..
3824	Special Industrial Machinery	..	..	..	..	..	..	..	..	..	..
3825	Office & Computing Machinery	4.2	4.6	4.2	4.2	3.9	3.3	3.0	2.7	2.6	..
3829	Machinery & Equipment, nec	12.9	13.0	13.6	13.2	13.0	13.7	11.2	12.2	10.6	..
383	Electrical Machinery	94.5	92.7	96.2	94.1	92.0	90.6	77.4	75.4	76.5	..
3831	Electrical Industrial Machinery	27.2	28.6	30.7	30.8	30.8	30.3	24.8	23.9	27.1	..
3832	Radio, TV & Communication Equipment	46.7	44.1	44.5	41.5	39.8	39.8	36.1	35.6	35.1	..
3833	Electrical Appliances & Housewares	10.7	10.0	10.1	11.1	10.5	10.3	7.9	7.4	7.0	..
3839	Electrical Apparatus, nec	10.0	10.1	10.9	10.7	10.8	10.1	8.7	8.4	7.3	..
384	Transport Equipment	95.4	99.8	107.2	114.4	117.8	110.1	91.8	82.7	77.6	..
3841	Shipbuilding & Repairing	4.8	4.2	3.5	2.5	2.7	1.6	1.0	1.2	0.5	..
3842	Railroad Equipment	5.7	6.0	4.3	3.4	3.5	1.1	1.0	0.9	1.0	..
3843	Motor Vehicles	81.6	86.0	96.2	105.2	108.3	104.4	87.5	78.6	74.9	..
3844	Motorcycles & Bicycles	3.4	3.6	3.2	3.3	3.3	2.9	2.3	2.0	1.2	..
3845	Aircraft	..	..	..	..	..	..	..	..	..	..
3849	Transport Equipment, nec	..	..	..	..	..	..	..	..	..	..
385	Professional Goods	2.3	2.2	2.4	2.6	2.8	2.5	2.7	2.2	1.9	..
3851	Professional Equipment	..	..	..	..	..	..	..	..	..	..
3852	Photographic & Optical Goods	..	..	..	..	..	..	..	..	..	..
3853	Watches & Clocks	..	..	..	..	..	..	..	..	..	..
39	**Other Manufacturing, nes**	5.6	5.5	6.0	6.4	6.4	6.7	6.3	6.7	5.4	..
3901	Jewellery	..	..	..	..	..	..	..	..	..	..
3	**Total Manufacturing**	950.5	950.8	969.4	971.1	952.7	919.8	809.5	769.1	747.5	..
I	**Agric., Hunting, Forestry, Fishing**	..	..	..	..	..	..	..	..	..	..
2	**Mining & Quarrying**	..	..	..	..	..	..	..	..	..	..
21	Coal Mining	..	..	..	..	..	..	..	..	..	..
22	Crude Petroleum & Natural Gas	..	..	..	..	..	..	..	..	..	..
23.29	Other Mining	..	..	..	..	..	..	..	..	..	..
3	**Total Manufacturing**	950.5	950.8	969.4	971.1	952.7	919.8	809.5	769.1	747.5	..
4	**Electricity, Gas & Water**	..	..	..	..	..	..	..	..	..	..
5	**Construction**	..	..	..	..	..	..	..	..	..	..
6.9	**Services**	..	..	..	..	..	..	..	..	..	..
0000	**Grand Total**	..	..	..	..	..	..	..	..	..	..

Note: Data for ISIC 323, 353, 3821 and 3845 are not available. ISIC 3823 includes part of 3824 (manufacture, assembly and repair of machinery and equipment including tractors for the construction, extraction -- i.e. mining -- and other industries); 3849 is allocated to 3823 and 3843.

Millions of NM$ (Current Prices)

ISIC2	Industry	INVESTMENT									
		1987	1988	1989	1990	1991	1992	1993	1994	1995	1996
31	**Food, Beverages & Tobacco**	198	307	500	1 033	1 532	804	474	429	..	..
311.2	Food	105	169	278	625	921	93	47	-96	..	..
313	Beverages	82	120	206	370	584	323	182	254	..	..
314	Tobacco	11	18	16	39	27	122	141	220	..	..
32	**Textiles, Apparel & Leather**	67	227	241	226	276	206	235	-25	..	..
321	Textiles	55	192	206	184	219	122	192	-27	..	..
3213	Knitting Mills	2	11	8	12	11	31	21	4	..	..
322	Wearing Apparel	5	22	22	25	28	29	45	9	..	..
323	Leather & Products	..				..		..	..	..	..
324	Footwear	7	13	12	16	29	56	-1	-7	..	..
33	**Wood Products & Furniture**	4	11	11	14	16	15	6	27	..	..
331	Wood Products	3	5	5	5	7	10	-1	15	..	..
332	Furnitures & Fixtures	1	6	6	10	10	6	7	11	..	..
34	**Paper, Paper Products & Printing**	83	106	189	362	667	14	55	176	..	..
341	Paper & Products	69	88	157	292	598	14	35	123	..	..
3411	Pulp, Paper & Board	59	71	144	257	557	14	23	75	..	..
342	Printing & Publishing	14	18	31	70	69	-1	20	53	..	..
35	**Chemical Products**	363	621	963	1 009	1 453	234	399	1 083	..	..
351	Industrial Chemicals	216	343	574	500	805	46	-31	260	..	..
3511	Basic Industrial Chemicals	61	159	206	178	203	101	27	217	..	..
3512	Fertilizers & Pesticides	93	91	134	87	90	-109	-125	87	..	..
3513	Synthetic Resins	63	93	234	235	512	54	67	-44	..	..
352	Other Chemicals	103	168	253	358	398	165	374	682	..	..
3521	Paints, Varnishes & Lacquers	9	15	21	60	42	33	-6	79	..	..
3522	Drugs & Medicines	36	69	132	163	212	184	220	383	..	..
3523	Soap & Cleaning Preparations	38	41	68	95	93	-49	149	203	..	..
3529	Chemical Products, nec	19	43	32	41	51	-3	11	17	..	..
353	Petroleum Refineries	..				..		..	..	..	..
354	Petroleum & Coal Products	5	10	11	10	44	-32	25	41	..	..
355	Rubber Products	13	38	51	45	99	4	4	49	..	..
356	Plastic Products, nec	26	61	74	96	107	51	27	51	..	..
36	**Non-Metallic Mineral Products**	95	218	320	403	2 471	158	-31	210	..	..
361	Pottery, China etc	8	35	14	60	37	28	20	-8	..	..
362	Glass & Products	40	93	91	147	695	131	-90	137	..	..
369	Non-Metallic Products, nec	47	91	215	196	1 738	-1	38	80	..	..
37	**Basic Metal Industries**	76	140	118	296	357	-73	-60	313	..	..
371	Iron & Steel	60	97	48	203	238	109	-96	175	..	..
372	Non-Ferrous Metals	16	43	69	93	119	-182	37	138	..	..
38	**Fabricated Metal Products**	424	727	793	1 160	2 129	1 321	-344	1 252	..	..
381	Metal Products	44	88	102	172	304	86	-68	180	..	..
3813	Structural Metal Products	3	6	6	13	20	15	-12	31	..	..
382	Non-Electrical Machinery	34	85	80	104	120	98	91	144	..	..
3821	Engines & Turbines	..	..			..	..			..	..
3822	Agricultural Machinery	7	6	11	14	15	73	5	-61	..	..
3823	Metal & Wood working Machinery	13	43	31	27	21	3	-12	64	..	..
3824	Special Industrial Machinery	..	..			..	..			..	..
3825	Office & Computing Machinery	6	13	6	33	28	-10	52	47	..	..
3829	Machinery & Equipment, nec	8	23	32	30	57	32	46	93	..	..
383	Electrical Machinery	71	113	173	214	420	98	-25	101	..	..
3831	Electrical Industrial Machinery	17	37	66	73	102	-2	-3	7	..	..
3832	Radio, TV & Communication Equipment	34	45	64	66	133	42	-8	76	..	..
3833	Electrical Appliances & Housewares	7	11	10	35	61	29	-10	-11	..	..
3839	Electrical Apparatus, nec	13	20	33	40	124	29	-5	30	..	..
384	Transport Equipment	272	433	436	663	1 283	1 020	-330	819	..	..
3841	Shipbuilding & Repairing	1	0	1	2	0	2	11	13	..	..
3842	Railroad Equipment	2	3	3	2	3	-3	2	2	..	..
3843	Motor Vehicles	266	426	430	654	1 277	1 012	-347	786	..	..
3844	Motorcycles & Bicycles	2	4	2	5	3	10	4	19	..	..
3845	Aircraft	..	..	..	..	..	..	..	..	..	..
3849	Transport Equipment, nec	..	..	..	..	..	..	..	..	..	..
385	Professional Goods	4	7	2	7	2	19	-12	8	..	..
3851	Professional Equipment						19	-12	8	..	..
3852	Photographic & Optical Goods	..	..	..	..	..	..	..	..	..	..
3853	Watches & Clocks	..	..	..	..	..	..	..	..	..	..
39	**Other Manufacturing, nes**	4	6	11	11	22	24	32	43	..	..
3901	Jewellery	..	..	..	..	..	..	..	..	..	..
3	**Total Manufacturing**	1 316	2 363	3 145	4 515	8 922	2 703	765	3 508	..	..
1	**Agric., Hunting, Forestry, Fishing**	..	..	..	..	..	..	..	..	..	..
2	**Mining & Quarrying**	..	..	..	..	..	..	..	..	..	..
21	Coal Mining	..	..	..	..	..	..	..	..	..	..
22	Crude Petroleum & Natural Gas	..	..	..	..	..	..	..	..	..	..
23.29	Other Mining	..	..	..	..	..	..	..	..	..	..
3	**Total Manufacturing**	1 316	2 363	3 145	4 515	8 922	2 703	765	3 508	..	..
4	**Electricity, Gas & Water**	..	..	..	..	..	..	..	..	..	..
5	**Construction**	..	..	..	..	..	..	..	..	..	..
6.9	**Services**	..	..	..	..	..	..	..	..	..	..
0000	**Grand Total**	..	..	..	..	..	..	..	..	..	..

Note: Data for ISIC 323, 353, 3821 and 3845 are not available. ISIC 3823 includes part of 3824 (manufacture, assembly and repair of machinery and equipment including tractors for the construction, extraction -- i.e. mining -- and other industries); 3849 is allocated to 3823 and 3843.

Table ME.5 **MEXICO**

Millions of NM$ (Current Prices)

ISIC2	Industry	INVESTMENT IN MACHINERY & EQUIPMENT									
		1987	1988	1989	1990	1991	1992	1993	1994	1995	1996
31	**Food, Beverages & Tobacco**	114	158	257	537	859	1 302	1 253	1 352	..	..
311.2	Food	62	99	157	347	588	668	733	707	..	..
313	Beverages	45	43	96	170	257	621	480	579	..	..
314	Tobacco	7	16	4	19	13	13	40	66	..	..
32	**Textiles, Apparel & Leather**	50	171	199	187	214	303	224	181	..	..
321	Textiles	44	161	183	164	189	263	181	125	..	..
3213	Knitting Mills	2	8	7	9	10	63	18	9	..	..
322	Wearing Apparel	3	5	10	11	12	16	27	39	..	..
323	Leather & Products	..	..	..	..	..	..	..	..	..	..
324	Footwear	4	5	7	13	13	24	16	17	..	..
33	**Wood Products & Furniture**	2	6	6	8	9	7	21	10	..	..
331	Wood Products	1	2	3	3	4	3	10	3	..	..
332	Furnitures & Fixtures	1	4	3	5	5	4	11	7	..	..
34	**Paper, Paper Products & Printing**	56	77	141	285	866	268	376	364	..	..
341	Paper & Products	45	64	120	225	805	173	183	313	..	..
3411	Pulp, Paper & Board	40	53	111	199	775	141	142	227	..	..
342	Printing & Publishing	11	12	21	60	61	94	193	51	..	..
35	**Chemical Products**	217	371	635	692	1 039	1 844	1 361	2 347	..	..
351	Industrial Chemicals	137	223	415	409	677	1 288	842	937	..	..
3511	Basic Industrial Chemicals	42	122	166	131	153	296	436	159	..	..
3512	Fertilizers & Pesticides	46	39	60	65	55	367	79	112	..	..
3513	Synthetic Resins	48	62	190	213	469	625	327	666	..	..
352	Other Chemicals	51	75	127	171	167	326	271	1 068	..	..
3521	Paints, Varnishes & Lacquers	3	4	6	33	25	25	31	50	..	..
3522	Drugs & Medicines	14	33	69	71	87	146	132	924	..	..
3523	Soap & Cleaning Preparations	24	14	35	50	40	121	86	76	..	..
3529	Chemical Products, nec	9	24	17	17	15	33	22	18	..	..
353	Petroleum Refineries	..	..	..	..	..	..	..	..	..	..
354	Petroleum & Coal Products	4	6	6	5	21	60	93	31	..	..
355	Rubber Products	8	25	31	29	84	59	45	137	..	..
356	Plastic Products, nec	17	41	55	78	90	111	110	174	..	..
36	**Non-Metallic Mineral Products**	54	139	201	246	1 972	626	918	1 522	..	..
361	Pottery, China etc	7	26	9	50	23	88	45	27	..	..
362	Glass & Products	25	74	62	102	516	214	249	414	..	..
369	Non-Metallic Products, nec	22	39	130	94	1 434	324	624	1 081	..	..
37	**Basic Metal Industries**	49	99	73	202	211	376	382	341	..	..
371	Iron & Steel	41	69	26	134	122	248	315	239	..	..
372	Non-Ferrous Metals	9	30	47	68	90	128	67	102	..	..
38	**Fabricated Metal Products**	231	435	495	711	1 015	1 255	1 636	2 079	..	..
381	Metal Products	29	56	71	121	225	456	287	161	..	..
3813	Structural Metal Products	2	2	3	7	9	46	32	24	..	..
382	Non-Electrical Machinery	16	60	50	52	60	62	119	65	..	..
3821	Engines & Turbines	..	..	..	..	..	..	..	..	..	..
3822	Agricultural Machinery	4	4	7	6	0	7	5	11	..	..
3823	Metal & Wood working Machinery	5	36	22	17	10	20	16	14	..	..
3824	Special Industrial Machinery	..	..	..	..	..	..	..	..	..	..
3825	Office & Computing Machinery	3	9	3	16	24	20	27	12	..	..
3829	Machinery & Equipment, nec	4	12	18	13	26	16	71	28	..	..
383	Electrical Machinery	58	81	109	158	254	229	341	295	..	..
3831	Electrical Industrial Machinery	12	25	46	46	58	87	117	119	..	..
3832	Radio, TV & Communication Equipment	33	41	38	47	94	57	29	69	..	..
3833	Electrical Appliances & Housewares	6	5	7	30	40	29	147	57	..	..
3839	Electrical Apparatus, nec	6	10	19	34	62	56	48	51	..	..
384	Transport Equipment	126	233	263	376	476	505	881	1 557	..	..
3841	Shipbuilding & Repairing	1	0	1	2	0	0	2	0	..	..
3842	Railroad Equipment	1	2	2	1	2	0	1	5	..	..
3843	Motor Vehicles	122	227	259	370	472	497	874	1 549	..	..
3844	Motorcycles & Bicycles	1	3	2	3	2	7	4	4	..	..
3845	Aircraft	..	..	..	..	..	..	..	..	..	..
3849	Transport Equipment, nec	..	..	..	..	..	3	8	0	..	..
385	Professional Goods	2	5	1	5	1	3	8	0	..	..
3851	Professional Equipment	..	..	..	..	..	..	..	..	..	..
3852	Photographic & Optical Goods	..	..	..	..	..	..	..	..	..	..
3853	Watches & Clocks	..	..	..	..	..	..	..	..	..	..
39	**Other Manufacturing, nes**	2	3	6	7	18	22	17	17	..	..
3901	Jewellery	..	..	..	..	..	..	..	..	..	..
3	**Total Manufacturing**	775	1 458	2 014	2 874	6 204	6 002	6 187	8 213	..	..
1	**Agric., Hunting, Forestry, Fishing**	..	..	..	..	..	..	..	..		
2	**Mining & Quarrying**	..	..	..	..	..	..	..	..		
21	Coal Mining	..	..	..	..	..	..	..	..		
22	Crude Petroleum & Natural Gas	..	..	..	..	..	..	..	..		
23.29	Other Mining	..	..	..	..	..	..	..	..		
3	**Total Manufacturing**	775	1 458	2 014	2 874	6 204	6 002	6 187	8 213		
4	**Electricity, Gas & Water**	..	..	..	..	..	..	..	..		
5	**Construction**	..	..	..	..	..	..	..	..		
6.9	**Services**	..	..	..	..	..	..	..	..		
0000	**Grand Total**	..	..	..	..	..	..	..	..		

Note: Data for ISIC 323, 353, 3821 and 3845 are not available. ISIC 3823 includes part of 3824 (manufacture, assembly and repair of machinery and equipment including tractors for the construction, extraction -- i.e. mining -- and other industries); 3849 is allocated to 3823 and 3843.

Millions of NM$ (Current Prices)

ISIC2	Industry	WAGES & SALARIES - EMPLOYEES									
		1987	1988	1989	1990	1991	1992	1993	1994	1995	1996
31	**Food, Beverages & Tobacco**	595	1 198	1 641	2 186	2 912	3 697	4 278	4 546	4 901	..
311.2	Food	301	619	814	1 099	1 462	1 830	1 984	2 115	2 367	..
313	Beverages	265	528	763	1 004	1 331	1 692	2 077	2 199	2 259	..
314	Tobacco	28	51	63	82	119	174	217	232	275	..
32	**Textiles, Apparel & Leather**	368	748	962	1 132	1 350	1 536	1 486	1 489	1 511	..
321	Textiles	245	504	616	697	820	921	868	852	872	..
3213	Knitting Mills	19	37	46	53	71	86	94	103	102	..
322	Wearing Apparel	78	153	201	256	316	354	366	377	442	..
323	Leather & Products	..	..	..	..	..	..	..	..	..	..
324	Footwear	46	91	146	179	214	261	251	260	197	..
33	**Wood Products & Furniture**	37	72	87	111	143	169	163	170	152	..
331	Wood Products	17	35	38	43	53	56	48	47	57	..
332	Furnitures & Fixtures	19	37	48	68	91	113	115	123	95	..
34	**Paper, Paper Products & Printing**	189	379	505	629	779	938	931	923	1 040	..
341	Paper & Products	145	286	390	479	579	677	679	645	763	..
3411	Pulp, Paper & Board	102	199	268	325	385	437	445	398	482	..
342	Printing & Publishing	45	93	116	151	200	261	252	278	277	..
35	**Chemical Products**	851	1 840	2 435	3 207	4 143	4 937	5 028	5 423	6 795	..
351	Industrial Chemicals	293	634	816	1 049	1 305	1 455	1 366	1 365	1 763	..
3511	Basic Industrial Chemicals	117	263	336	440	532	639	600	564	680	..
3512	Fertilizers & Pesticides	56	117	159	214	249	207	209	253	295	..
3513	Synthetic Resins	120	254	321	394	523	609	557	548	788	..
352	Other Chemicals	327	727	1 009	1 372	1 844	2 350	2 521	2 810	3 637	..
3521	Paints, Varnishes & Lacquers	29	67	97	125	175	231	256	278	294	..
3522	Drugs & Medicines	139	299	414	569	761	949	1 184	1 296	1 608	..
3523	Soap & Cleaning Preparations	122	278	385	526	706	929	828	973	1 441	..
3529	Chemical Products, nec	36	84	113	153	201	242	252	263	294	..
353	Petroleum Refineries	..	..	..	..	..	..	..	..	..	..
354	Petroleum & Coal Products	19	40	49	67	84	101	115	143	156	..
355	Rubber Products	109	221	282	354	446	504	530	553	564	..
356	Plastic Products, nec	103	218	279	364	464	527	495	553	675	..
36	**Non-Metallic Mineral Products**	293	599	789	1 058	1 340	1 656	1 687	1 775	1 943	..
361	Pottery, China etc	22	45	66	86	115	147	163	152	190	..
362	Glass & Products	111	232	300	413	515	657	680	671	782	..
369	Non-Metallic Products, nec	160	322	423	558	710	852	844	952	971	..
37	**Basic Metal Industries**	322	717	863	1 083	1 228	1 397	1 300	1 320	1 590	..
371	Iron & Steel	245	548	653	808	869	1 025	920	927	1 188	..
372	Non-Ferrous Metals	77	169	211	275	359	371	381	393	402	..
38	**Fabricated Metal Products**	1 096	2 249	3 045	4 196	5 307	6 315	6 060	6 415	7 042	..
381	Metal Products	186	379	502	672	873	1 031	1 011	1 088	1 135	..
3813	Structural Metal Products	29	64	80	111	155	182	175	202	211	..
382	Non-Electrical Machinery	152	332	417	524	647	768	698	756	854	..
3821	Engines & Turbines	..	..	..	..	..	..	..	..	..	..
3822	Agricultural Machinery	13	31	36	46	66	94	84	86	118	..
3823	Metal & Wood working Machinery	59	134	168	201	222	243	194	180	231	..
3824	Special Industrial Machinery	..	..	..	..	..	..	..	..	..	..
3825	Office & Computing Machinery	25	57	70	87	105	117	124	129	133	..
3829	Machinery & Equipment, nec	55	109	143	191	254	314	296	361	371	..
383	Electrical Machinery	333	662	884	1 140	1 367	1 544	1 476	1 491	1 965	..
3831	Electrical Industrial Machinery	102	220	305	390	493	597	575	521	708	..
3832	Radio, TV & Communication Equipment	148	285	386	505	548	565	540	599	838	..
3833	Electrical Appliances & Housewares	41	73	80	101	132	170	142	140	157	..
3839	Electrical Apparatus, nec	42	84	113	144	194	212	219	231	263	..
384	Transport Equipment	415	856	1 212	1 821	2 371	2 918	2 832	3 033	3 035	..
3841	Shipbuilding & Repairing	18	30	32	33	42	37	29	35	12	..
3842	Railroad Equipment	25	48	47	43	51	25	33	45	44	..
3843	Motor Vehicles	362	757	1 110	1 716	2 242	2 817	2 735	2 920	2 953	..
3844	Motorcycles & Bicycles	10	20	24	30	37	39	36	34	26	..
3845	Aircraft	..	..	..	..	..	..	..	..	..	..
3849	Transport Equipment, nec	..	..	..	..	..	..	..	..	..	..
385	Professional Goods	11	21	29	38	49	54	43	48	54	..
3851	Professional Equipment	..	..	..	..	..	..	..	..	..	..
3852	Photographic & Optical Goods	..	..	..	..	..	..	..	..	..	..
3853	Watches & Clocks	..	..	..	..	..	..	..	..	..	..
39	**Other Manufacturing, nes**	20	43	55	76	98	131	144	158	163	..
3901	Jewellery	..	..	..	..	..	..	..	..	..	..
3	**Total Manufacturing**	3 771	7 844	10 382	13 678	17 302	20 775	21 077	22 219	25 137	..
1	**Agric., Hunting, Forestry, Fishing**	..	..	..	..	..	..	..	..	..	..
2	**Mining & Quarrying**	..	..	..	..	..	..	..	..	..	..
21	Coal Mining	..	..	..	..	..	..	..	..	..	..
22	Crude Petroleum & Natural Gas	..	..	..	..	..	..	..	..	..	..
23.29	Other Mining	..	..	..	..	..	..	..	..	..	..
3	**Total Manufacturing**	3 771	7 844	10 382	13 678	17 302	20 775	21 077	22 219	25 137	..
4	**Electricity, Gas & Water**	..	..	..	..	..	..	..	..	..	..
5	**Construction**	..	..	..	..	..	..	..	..	..	..
6.9	**Services**	..	..	..	..	..	..	..	..	..	..
0000	**Grand Total**	..	..	..	..	..	..	..	..	..	..

Note: Data for ISIC 323, 353, 3821 and 3845 are not available. ISIC 3823 includes part of 3824 (manufacture, assembly and repair of machinery and equipment including tractors for the construction, extraction -- i.e. mining -- and other industries); 3849 is allocated to 3823 and 3843.

Table ME.7 **MEXICO**

(Current Prices)

ISIC2	Industry	SUPPLEMENTS TO WAGES & SALARIES									
		1987	1988	1989	1990	1991	1992	1993	1994	1995	1996
31	Food, Beverages & Tobacco	207	440	669	824	1 121	1 450	1 628	2 040	2 024	..
311.2	Food	102	226	336	430	564	747	782	972	974	..
313	Beverages	93	190	299	350	498	620	741	947	931	..
314	Tobacco	12	24	34	44	59	83	106	121	119	..
32	Textiles, Apparel & Leather	125	260	347	439	510	613	574	615	582	..
321	Textiles	91	192	248	296	325	375	344	351	327	..
3213	Knitting Mills	6	12	16	18	27	34	37	41	36	..
322	Wearing Apparel	19	39	57	80	106	127	134	152	167	..
323	Leather & Products	..	..	..	..	..	..	..	..	..	..
324	Footwear	15	29	42	63	79	111	97	113	88	..
33	Wood Products & Furniture	10	21	28	33	47	51	54	63	54	..
331	Wood Products	5	11	12	14	21	21	23	24	27	..
332	Furnitures & Fixtures	5	11	16	19	26	30	31	39	27	..
34	Paper, Paper Products & Printing	76	163	227	273	353	436	396	421	427	..
341	Paper & Products	60	129	181	223	280	345	302	311	325	..
3411	Pulp, Paper & Board	43	90	126	157	195	236	207	205	227	..
342	Printing & Publishing	15	34	46	50	73	91	95	110	101	..
35	Chemical Products	375	795	1 040	1 356	1 791	2 213	2 230	2 551	2 839	..
351	Industrial Chemicals	149	312	411	532	689	788	730	765	870	..
3511	Basic Industrial Chemicals	57	116	151	196	235	285	259	292	335	..
3512	Fertilizers & Pesticides	22	48	68	100	139	118	111	117	111	..
3513	Synthetic Resins	71	148	192	236	316	385	360	356	424	..
352	Other Chemicals	110	249	371	471	642	865	974	1 166	1 366	..
3521	Paints, Varnishes & Lacquers	8	20	27	33	58	79	93	109	104	..
3522	Drugs & Medicines	52	121	182	238	314	436	529	622	691	..
3523	Soap & Cleaning Preparations	37	78	116	146	201	262	260	337	459	..
3529	Chemical Products, nec	14	30	46	54	69	88	90	99	111	..
353	Petroleum Refineries	..	..	..	..	..	..	..	..	..	..
354	Petroleum & Coal Products	10	21	27	44	44	57	73	85	83	..
355	Rubber Products	74	141	130	166	243	295	271	319	293	..
356	Plastic Products, nec	32	71	101	143	172	209	183	215	227	..
36	Non-Metallic Mineral Products	117	249	378	476	638	787	812	861	950	..
361	Pottery, China etc	9	18	28	37	54	70	77	98	99	..
362	Glass & Products	48	102	166	209	276	323	320	297	331	..
369	Non-Metallic Products, nec	60	128	184	229	307	394	416	466	520	..
37	Basic Metal Industries	177	396	631	707	826	967	830	875	977	..
371	Iron & Steel	143	315	512	573	640	772	649	687	789	..
372	Non-Ferrous Metals	34	81	118	134	186	194	181	188	188	..
38	Fabricated Metal Products	508	1 037	1 437	1 801	2 405	2 891	2 910	3 034	3 352	..
381	Metal Products	68	144	208	258	328	440	420	477	518	..
3813	Structural Metal Products	10	20	29	35	52	76	67	76	71	..
382	Non-Electrical Machinery	52	112	158	207	253	291	278	315	378	..
3821	Engines & Turbines	..	..	..	..	..	..	..	..	..	..
3822	Agricultural Machinery	6	13	18	22	26	44	40	55	66	..
3823	Metal & Wood working Machinery	21	43	55	80	93	89	69	68	92	..
3824	Special Industrial Machinery	..	..	..	..	..	..	..	..	..	..
3825	Office & Computing Machinery	9	22	31	33	46	47	52	53	56	..
3829	Machinery & Equipment, nec	17	34	54	72	88	112	117	139	165	..
383	Electrical Machinery	124	248	366	474	671	720	635	682	990	..
3831	Electrical Industrial Machinery	35	76	105	139	191	244	200	194	297	..
3832	Radio, TV & Communication Equipment	56	107	170	222	321	291	265	301	493	..
3833	Electrical Appliances & Housewares	18	33	40	45	61	78	67	56	84	..
3839	Electrical Apparatus, nec	15	32	51	68	97	107	103	131	117	..
384	Transport Equipment	260	524	694	849	1 137	1 416	1 549	1 528	1 442	..
3841	Shipbuilding & Repairing	6	10	13	15	12	11	16	11	4	..
3842	Railroad Equipment	22	45	48	34	28	7	11	7	30	..
3843	Motor Vehicles	230	464	624	790	1 086	1 384	1 510	1 491	1 399	..
3844	Motorcycles & Bicycles	3	5	8	10	11	13	11	19	9	..
3845	Aircraft	..	..	..	..	..	..	..	..	..	..
3849	Transport Equipment, nec	4	8	11	15	17	23	28	33	23	..
385	Professional Goods	..	..	..	..	..	..	..	..	..	..
3851	Professional Equipment	..	..	..	..	..	..	..	..	..	..
3852	Photographic & Optical Goods	..	..	..	..	..	..	..	..	..	..
3853	Watches & Clocks	..	..	..	..	..	..	..	..	..	..
39	Other Manufacturing, nes	7	12	18	26	37	46	45	67	58	..
3901	Jewellery	..	..	..	..	..	..	..	..	..	..
3	Total Manufacturing	1 603	3 373	4 775	5 935	7 728	9 454	9 480	10 526	11 261	..
1	Agric., Hunting, Forestry, Fishing	..	..	..	..	..	..	..	..	..	..
2	Mining & Quarrying	..	..	..	..	..	..	..	..	..	..
21	Coal Mining	..	..	..	..	..	..	..	..	..	..
22	Crude Petroleum & Natural Gas	..	..	..	..	..	..	..	..	..	..
23.29	Other Mining	..	..	..	..	..	..	..	..	..	..
3	Total Manufacturing	1 603	3 373	4 775	5 935	7 728	9 454	9 480	10 526	11 261	..
4	Electricity, Gas & Water	..	..	..	..	..	..	..	..	..	..
5	Construction	..	..	..	..	..	..	..	..	..	..
6.9	Services	..	..	..	..	..	..	..	..	..	..
0000	Grand Total	..	..	..	..	..	..	..	..	..	..

Note: Data for ISIC 323, 353, 3821 and 3845 are not available. ISIC 3823 includes part of 3824 (manufacture, assembly and repair of machinery and equipment including tractors for the construction, extraction -- i.e. mining -- and other industries); 3849 is allocated to 3823 and 3843.

Millions of NM$

(Current Prices)

ISIC2	Industry	WAGES & SALARIES + SUPPLEMENTS - EMPLOYEES									
		1987	1988	1989	1990	1991	1992	1993	1994	1995	1996
31	**Food, Beverages & Tobacco**	802	1 638	2 310	3 010	3 890	5 146	5 906	6 586	6 926	..
311.2	Food	403	845	1 150	1 530	1 947	2 577	2 766	3 087	3 341	..
313	Beverages	358	718	1 062	1 354	1 759	2 312	2 818	3 146	3 190	..
314	Tobacco	41	75	98	126	184	257	323	353	394	..
32	**Textiles, Apparel & Leather**	493	1 008	1 309	1 571	1 835	2 149	2 060	2 104	2 092	..
321	Textiles	336	696	863	993	1 140	1 296	1 212	1 202	1 198	..
3213	Knitting Mills	25	49	62	72	92	121	132	144	138	..
322	Wearing Apparel	97	192	257	336	402	481	500	529	610	..
323	Leather & Products	..	..	..	..					..	..
324	Footwear	61	120	188	242	293	372	348	373	284	..
33	**Wood Products & Furniture**	47	93	115	144	181	220	217	233	206	..
331	Wood Products	22	46	51	57	70	77	72	71	83	..
332	Furnitures & Fixtures	24	47	64	87	111	143	146	162	123	..
34	**Paper, Paper Products & Printing**	265	542	732	903	1 120	1 374	1 328	1 344	1 466	..
341	Paper & Products	205	415	570	702	854	1 022	980	956	1 088	..
3411	Pulp, Paper & Board	144	289	395	482	581	672	652	603	709	..
342	Printing & Publishing	60	127	162	201	266	352	347	388	378	..
35	**Chemical Products**	1 226	2 634	3 475	4 563	5 893	7 150	7 257	7 974	9 634	..
351	Industrial Chemicals	442	947	1 227	1 581	2 009	2 242	2 096	2 130	2 633	..
3511	Basic Industrial Chemicals	173	378	488	636	777	924	859	856	1 015	..
3512	Fertilizers & Pesticides	78	166	227	314	375	325	320	370	407	..
3513	Synthetic Resins	191	403	513	631	857	994	917	904	1 211	..
352	Other Chemicals	437	976	1 380	1 843	2 466	3 215	3 494	3 976	5 003	..
3521	Paints, Varnishes & Lacquers	38	87	124	158	228	310	350	387	399	..
3522	Drugs & Medicines	190	420	596	807	1 041	1 384	1 714	1 918	2 299	..
3523	Soap & Cleaning Preparations	159	355	501	672	930	1 191	1 089	1 310	1 900	..
3529	Chemical Products, nec	50	114	158	206	268	330	342	361	405	..
353	Petroleum Refineries	..	..	..						..	..
354	Petroleum & Coal Products	29	61	75	112	124	158	188	228	239	..
355	Rubber Products	182	362	412	520	683	799	801	872	856	..
356	Plastic Products, nec	135	289	381	507	611	736	678	768	902	..
36	**Non-Metallic Mineral Products**	411	847	1 167	1 533	1 961	2 443	2 500	2 636	2 893	..
361	Pottery, China etc	31	63	94	123	170	217	240	250	289	..
362	Glass & Products	160	333	465	622	766	979	999	968	1 113	..
369	Non-Metallic Products, nec	221	451	607	788	1 026	1 246	1 260	1 418	1 491	..
37	**Basic Metal Industries**	499	1 113	1 494	1 789	2 059	2 363	2 130	2 194	2 567	..
371	Iron & Steel	388	863	1 165	1 381	1 542	1 798	1 569	1 614	1 976	..
372	Non-Ferrous Metals	111	250	329	408	517	566	561	581	590	..
38	**Fabricated Metal Products**	1 604	3 286	4 482	5 997	7 687	9 206	8 970	9 450	10 394	..
381	Metal Products	254	523	710	929	1 170	1 471	1 431	1 565	1 653	..
3813	Structural Metal Products	39	84	109	146	213	257	242	278	281	..
382	Non-Electrical Machinery	204	444	576	731	878	1 059	976	1 070	1 232	..
3821	Engines & Turbines	..	..								..
3822	Agricultural Machinery	18	44	54	68	102	137	124	140	184	..
3823	Metal & Wood working Machinery	80	177	223	281	289	332	262	247	323	..
3824	Special Industrial Machinery	..	..	..							..
3825	Office & Computing Machinery	34	79	101	120	152	164	176	182	189	..
3829	Machinery & Equipment, nec	72	143	198	263	335	426	413	500	536	..
383	Electrical Machinery	457	910	1 249	1 614	1 981	2 264	2 111	2 173	2 955	..
3831	Electrical Industrial Machinery	137	296	410	528	687	840	775	715	1 005	..
3832	Radio, TV & Communication Equipment	204	392	556	727	817	856	806	899	1 330	..
3833	Electrical Appliances & Housewares	59	106	120	146	203	248	209	196	240	..
3839	Electrical Apparatus, nec	56	116	164	213	275	320	322	362	380	..
384	Transport Equipment	675	1 380	1 906	2 670	3 592	4 334	4 381	4 561	4 478	..
3841	Shipbuilding & Repairing	24	40	44	48	54	48	45	46	17	..
3842	Railroad Equipment	46	93	95	76	172	32	44	52	74	..
3843	Motor Vehicles	592	1 221	1 735	2 506	3 316	4 201	4 245	4 411	4 352	..
3844	Motorcycles & Bicycles	13	25	32	40	50	52	47	53	35	..
3845	Aircraft	..	..	..							..
3849	Transport Equipment, nec	..	..	..							..
385	Professional Goods	15	29	41	53	67	78	71	81	77	..
3851	Professional Equipment	..	..	..							..
3852	Photographic & Optical Goods	..	..	..							..
3853	Watches & Clocks	..	..	..							..
39	**Other Manufacturing, nes**	27	55	73	102	129	178	189	224	221	..
3901	Jewellery	..	..	..							..
3	**Total Manufacturing**	5 374	11 217	15 157	19 613	24 754	30 230	30 556	32 745	36 398	..
1	**Agric., Hunting, Forestry, Fishing**	..	..	..	..	..	..	..	..	..	..
2	**Mining & Quarrying**	..	..	..	..	..	..	..	..	..	..
21	Coal Mining	..	..	..	..	..	..	..	..	..	..
22	Crude Petroleum & Natural Gas	..	..	..	..	..	..	..	..	..	..
23.29	Other Mining	..	..	..	..	..	..	..	..	..	..
3	**Total Manufacturing**	5 374	11 217	15 157	19 613	24 754	30 230	30 556	32 745	36 398	..
4	**Electricity, Gas & Water**	..	..	..	..	..	..	..	..	..	..
5	**Construction**	..	..	..	..	..	..	..	..	..	..
6.9	**Services**	..	..	..	..	..	..	..	..	..	..
0000	**Grand Total**	..	..	..	..	..	..	..	..	..	..

Note: Data for ISIC 323, 353, 3821 and 3845 are not available. ISIC 3823 includes part of 3824 (manufacture, assembly and repair of machinery and equipment including tractors for the construction, extraction -- i.e. mining -- and other industries); 3849 is allocated to 3823 and 3843.

Thousands

ISIC2	Industry	HOURS WORKED									
		1987	1988	1989	1990	1991	1992	1993	1994	1995	1996
31	**Food, Beverages & Tobacco**	425	419	441	453	463	474	450	437	..	..
311.2	Food	225	221	231	235	237	239	216	213	..	..
313	Beverages	187	185	198	204	214	222	221	213	..	..
314	Tobacco	13	13	12	13	12	13	13	12	..	..
32	**Textiles, Apparel & Leather**	276	274	270	259	243	225	195	179	..	..
321	Textiles	160	163	160	150	141	128	110	97	..	..
3213	Knitting Mills	13	12	13	13	13	13	13	11	..	..
322	Wearing Apparel	71	71	69	70	66	63	56	54	..	..
323	Leather & Products	..	..	..	..	..	..	..	..	..	..
324	Footwear	45	41	41	39	36	34	29	27	..	..
33	**Wood Products & Furniture**	31	30	29	29	29	28	23	22	..	..
331	Wood Products	14	13	12	11	11	10	7	6	..	..
332	Furnitures & Fixtures	17	16	17	17	18	17	16	15	..	..
34	**Paper, Paper Products & Printing**	107	106	111	111	107	106	94	85	..	..
341	Paper & Products	80	80	84	84	80	79	71	62	..	..
3411	Pulp, Paper & Board	55	54	57	55	53	51	46	39	..	..
342	Printing & Publishing	27	27	27	27	26	27	23	22	..	..
35	**Chemical Products**	401	403	411	410	402	380	331	324	..	..
351	Industrial Chemicals	142	140	140	136	132	117	95	87	..	..
3511	Basic Industrial Chemicals	49	48	50	49	45	44	35	30	..	..
3512	Fertilizers & Pesticides	28	28	29	27	25	18	14	15	..	..
3513	Synthetic Resins	65	63	60	60	61	55	45	42	..	..
352	Other Chemicals	134	136	142	147	149	148	139	139	..	..
3521	Paints, Varnishes & Lacquers	14	15	16	17	16	16	17	16	..	..
3522	Drugs & Medicines	53	54	56	58	58	58	59	57	..	..
3523	Soap & Cleaning Preparations	51	51	55	56	59	57	50	52	..	..
3529	Chemical Products, nec	16	16	16	16	16	16	14	14	..	..
353	Petroleum Refineries	..	..	..	..	9	8	9	9	..	..
354	Petroleum & Coal Products	11	10	10	10	9	8	9	9	..	..
355	Rubber Products	36	35	36	36	35	33	28	27	..	..
356	Plastic Products, nec	79	81	83	81	77	74	60	62	..	..
36	**Non-Metallic Mineral Products**	152	153	152	155	153	147	131	122	..	..
361	Pottery, China etc	16	17	17	18	17	17	16	16	..	..
362	Glass & Products	58	58	59	61	63	59	51	49	..	..
369	Non-Metallic Products, nec	78	79	76	76	73	70	63	57	..	..
37	**Basic Metal Industries**	159	166	158	154	149	128	107	96	..	..
371	Iron & Steel	117	120	115	111	106	91	76	67	..	..
372	Non-Ferrous Metals	42	46	43	43	42	37	32	29	..	..
38	**Fabricated Metal Products**	607	622	649	659	662	642	537	506	..	..
381	Metal Products	114	115	119	122	119	113	96	95	..	..
3813	Structural Metal Products	20	20	19	20	21	19	16	17	..	..
382	Non-Electrical Machinery	74	79	74	74	71	68	52	51	..	..
3821	Engines & Turbines	..	..	..	..	..	..	..	..	..	..
3822	Agricultural Machinery	6	7	5	6	6	6	4	5	..	..
3823	Metal & Wood working Machinery	30	33	29	29	26	23	16	13	..	..
3824	Special Industrial Machinery	..	..	..	..	..	..	..	..	..	..
3825	Office & Computing Machinery	9	10	9	9	9	7	7	6	..	..
3829	Machinery & Equipment, nec	29	30	30	30	30	31	26	27	..	..
383	Electrical Machinery	208	205	216	209	201	205	177	172	..	..
3831	Electrical Industrial Machinery	62	65	70	70	69	69	56	53	..	..
3832	Radio, TV & Communication Equipment	101	96	99	91	83	90	82	83	..	..
3833	Electrical Appliances & Housewares	23	21	21	24	25	24	18	17	..	..
3839	Electrical Apparatus, nec	22	24	25	24	25	22	21	20	..	..
384	Transport Equipment	206	218	235	247	264	250	206	182	..	..
3841	Shipbuilding & Repairing	11	10	8	6	6	4	2	3	..	..
3842	Railroad Equipment	13	13	10	8	7	2	2	2	..	..
3843	Motor Vehicles	175	186	210	225	244	237	196	173	..	..
3844	Motorcycles & Bicycles	7	8	7	8	7	7	5	4	..	..
3845	Aircraft	..	..	..	..	..	..	..	..	..	..
3849	Transport Equipment, nec	5	5	5	6	6	6	7	5	..	..
385	Professional Goods	..	..	..	..	..	..	..	..	..	..
3851	Professional Equipment	..	..	..	..	..	..	..	..	..	..
3852	Photographic & Optical Goods	..	..	..	..	..	..	..	..	..	..
3853	Watches & Clocks	..	..	..	..	..	..	..	..	..	..
39	**Other Manufacturing, nes**	12	12	14	14	15	15	15	15	..	..
3901	Jewellery	..	..	..	..	..	..	..	..	..	..
3	**Total Manufacturing**	2 170	2 185	2 234	2 242	2 222	2 145	1 884	1 783	..	..
1	**Agric., Hunting, Forestry, Fishing**	..	..	..	..	..	..	..	..	..	..
2	**Mining & Quarrying**	..	..	..	..	..	..	..	..	..	..
21	Coal Mining	..	..	..	..	..	..	..	..	..	..
22	Crude Petroleum & Natural Gas	..	..	..	..	..	..	..	..	..	..
23.29	Other Mining	..	..	..	..	..	..	..	..	..	..
3	**Total Manufacturing**	2 170	2 185	2 234	2 242	2 222	2 145	1 884	1 783	..	..
4	**Electricity, Gas & Water**	..	..	..	..	..	..	..	..	..	..
5	**Construction**	..	..	..	..	..	..	..	..	..	..
6.9	**Services**	..	..	..	..	..	..	..	..	..	..
0000	**Grand Total**	..	..	..	..	..	..	..	..	..	..

Note: Data for ISIC 323, 353, 3821 and 3845 are not available. ISIC 3823 includes part of 3824 (manufacture, assembly and repair of machinery and equipment including tractors for the construction, extraction -- i.e. mining -- and other industries); 3849 is allocated to 3823 and 3843.

Table ME.10 **MEXICO**

ISIC2	Industry	ESTABLISHMENTS									
		1987	1988	1989	1990	1991	1992	1993	1994	1995	1996
31	**Food, Beverages & Tobacco**	585	578	577	577	553	538	528	520	515	..
311.2	Food	423	418	417	417	400	393	388	384	380	..
313	Beverages	155	153	153	153	146	138	133	129	128	..
314	Tobacco	7	7	7	7	7	7	7	7	7	..
32	**Textiles, Apparel & Leather**	498	489	483	480	473	461	437	428	421	..
321	Textiles	251	247	244	243	241	236	229	224	219	..
3213	Knitting Mills	38	36	34	33	33	32	31	30	30	..
322	Wearing Apparel	187	184	182	180	175	171	156	153	151	..
323	Leather & Products	..	..	..	..	..	..	..	..	..	..
324	Footwear	60	58	57	57	57	54	52	51	51	..
33	**Wood Products & Furniture**	90	87	85	84	82	82	82	78	75	..
331	Wood Products	18	17	16	16	14	14	14	14	14	..
332	Furnitures & Fixtures	72	70	69	68	68	68	68	64	61	..
34	**Paper, Paper Products & Printing**	206	206	205	205	204	199	198	193	189	..
341	Paper & Products	132	132	132	132	132	129	128	123	121	..
3411	Pulp, Paper & Board	67	67	67	67	67	65	65	61	59	..
342	Printing & Publishing	74	74	73	73	72	70	70	70	68	..
35	**Chemical Products**	686	680	679	674	665	642	624	610	600	..
351	Industrial Chemicals	178	177	177	177	174	173	169	165	161	..
3511	Basic Industrial Chemicals	77	77	77	77	77	76	75	73	72	..
3512	Fertilizers & Pesticides	51	50	50	50	49	49	47	46	46	..
3513	Synthetic Resins	50	50	50	50	48	48	47	46	43	..
352	Other Chemicals	242	240	239	239	234	219	211	206	204	..
3521	Paints, Varnishes & Lacquers	40	40	40	40	40	38	37	35	35	..
3522	Drugs & Medicines	72	72	72	72	71	71	71	71	71	..
3523	Soap & Cleaning Preparations	66	66	65	65	63	55	51	48	47	..
3529	Chemical Products, nec	64	62	62	62	60	55	52	52	51	..
353	Petroleum Refineries	..	..	..	..	..	..	..	..	..	..
354	Petroleum & Coal Products	23	23	23	23	23	22	21	21	20	..
355	Rubber Products	50	49	49	48	48	46	46	45	43	..
356	Plastic Products, nec	193	191	191	187	186	182	177	173	172	..
36	**Non-Metallic Mineral Products**	198	196	195	193	188	183	178	170	168	..
361	Pottery, China etc	5	5	5	5	5	5	5	5	5	..
362	Glass & Products	24	23	22	22	22	22	21	21	21	..
369	Non-Metallic Products, nec	169	168	168	166	161	156	152	144	142	..
37	**Basic Metal Industries**	121	119	119	119	117	117	112	108	102	..
371	Iron & Steel	96	94	94	94	92	92	88	85	79	..
372	Non-Ferrous Metals	25	25	25	25	25	25	24	23	23	..
38	**Fabricated Metal Products**	752	743	730	728	704	682	652	625	612	..
381	Metal Products	226	224	220	218	212	203	195	188	183	..
3813	Structural Metal Products	52	50	49	49	47	45	43	41	41	..
382	Non-Electrical Machinery	181	179	175	175	169	162	153	145	142	..
3821	Engines & Turbines	..	..	..	..	..	..	..	..	..	..
3822	Agricultural Machinery	11	10	10	10	10	10	10	10	10	..
3823	Metal & Wood working Machinery	72	71	69	69	69	65	61	55	54	..
3824	Special Industrial Machinery	..	..	..	..	..	..	..	..	..	..
3825	Office & Computing Machinery	23	23	22	22	16	14	13	13	13	..
3829	Machinery & Equipment, nec	75	75	74	74	74	73	69	67	65	..
383	Electrical Machinery	182	177	174	174	165	162	153	147	145	..
3831	Electrical Industrial Machinery	65	65	64	64	62	60	58	57	57	..
3832	Radio, TV & Communication Equipment	76	71	70	70	65	64	60	58	56	..
3833	Electrical Appliances & Housewares	18	18	17	17	16	16	15	13	13	..
3839	Electrical Apparatus, nec	23	23	23	23	22	22	20	19	19	..
384	Transport Equipment	157	157	155	155	152	149	145	140	137	..
3841	Shipbuilding & Repairing	7	7	7	7	6	6	5	5	5	..
3842	Railroad Equipment	12	12	12	12	10	8	6	6	5	..
3843	Motor Vehicles	125	125	123	123	123	122	121	118	116	..
3844	Motorcycles & Bicycles	13	13	13	13	13	13	13	11	11	..
3845	Aircraft	..	..	..	..	..	..	..	..	..	..
3849	Transport Equipment, nec	..	..	..	..	..	..	..	..	..	..
385	Professional Goods	6	6	6	6	6	6	6	5	5	..
3851	Professional Equipment	..	..	..	..	..	..	..	..	..	..
3852	Photographic & Optical Goods	..	..	..	..	..	..	..	..	..	..
3853	Watches & Clocks	..	..	..	..	..	..	..	..	..	..
39	**Other Manufacturing, nes**	36	36	36	36	36	34	34	34	33	..
3901	Jewellery	..	..	..	..	..	..	..	..	..	..
3	**Total Manufacturing**	3 172	3 134	3 109	3 096	3 022	2 938	2 845	2 766	2 715	..
1	**Agric., Hunting, Forestry, Fishing**	..	..	..	..	..	..	..	..	..	..
2	**Mining & Quarrying**	..	..	..	..	..	..	..	..	..	..
21	Coal Mining	..	..	..	..	..	..	..	..	..	..
22	Crude Petroleum & Natural Gas	..	..	..	..	..	..	..	..	..	..
23.29	Other Mining	..	..	..	..	..	..	..	..	..	..
3	**Total Manufacturing**	3 172	3 134	3 109	3 096	3 022	2 938	2 845	2 766	2 715	..
4	**Electricity, Gas & Water**	..	..	..	..	..	..	..	..	..	..
5	**Construction**	..	..	..	..	..	..	..	..	..	..
6.9	**Services**	..	..	..	..	..	..	..	..	..	..
0000	**Grand Total**	..	..	..	..	..	..	..	..	..	..

Note: Data for ISIC 323, 353, 3821 and 3845 are not available. ISIC 3823 includes part of 3824 (manufacture, assembly and repair of machinery and equipment including tractors for the construction, extraction -- i.e. mining -- and other industries); 3849 is allocated to 3823 and 3843.

Thousands

ISIC2	Industry	EMPLOYMENT									
		1986-87	1987-88	1988-89	1989-90	1990-91	1991-92	1992-93	1993-94	1994-95	1995-96
31	Food, Beverages & Tobacco	76.0	67.9	68.9	64.7	62.2	61.0	63.6	65.4	65.2	67.1
311.2	Food	70.9	64.6	65.6	60.8	58.4	58.3	59.8	61.8	61.4	63.3
313	Beverages	4.2	2.5	2.4	3.1	3.1	2.1	3.3	3.1	3.2	3.3
314	Tobacco	1.0	0.9	0.9	0.8	0.7	0.6	0.5	0.5	0.5	0.5
32	Textiles, Apparel & Leather	42.5	37.5	32.0	32.3	29.2	27.0	27.4	29.0	29.4	27.3
321	Textiles	15.2	13.5	11.8	12.5	11.3	10.4	10.5	11.1	11.7	11.1
3213	Knitting Mills	3.8	3.9	3.4	3.4	2.9	2.6	2.2	2.1	2.1	1.8
322	Wearing Apparel	20.2	18.4	15.7	14.9	13.7	12.7	12.8	13.3	13.1	12.0
323	Leather & Products	3.6	2.9	2.5	2.5	2.3	2.4	2.5	2.7	2.8	2.6
324	Footwear	3.6	2.7	2.1	2.4	2.0	1.5	1.5	1.9	1.8	1.6
33	Wood Products & Furniture	25.2	22.7	21.7	23.0	21.5	21.2	22.6	25.4	24.7	28.7
331	Wood Products	16.8	15.3	14.7	15.4	14.4	14.4	15.5	17.5	16.3	20.1
332	Furnitures & Fixtures	8.4	7.4	6.9	7.6	7.1	6.8	7.0	7.8	8.4	8.6
34	Paper, Paper Products & Printing	30.8	31.5	29.1	26.4	27.2	25.7	25.3	26.1	27.5	27.2
341	Paper & Products	12.2	13.4	10.3	8.6	9.6	9.0	8.7	8.7	9.4	9.1
3411	Pulp, Paper & Board	7.4	7.2	5.9	4.4	5.0	4.5	4.0	3.9	4.2	3.0
342	Printing & Publishing	18.5	18.2	18.8	17.8	17.6	16.6	16.6	17.4	18.1	18.1
35	Chemical Products	26.4	25.0	24.0	21.2	20.1	20.2	20.6	21.5	21.3	21.3
351	Industrial Chemicals	5.3	5.4	5.5	4.1	4.6	4.6	4.5	4.9	5.0	4.5
3511	Basic Industrial Chemicals	0.5	0.5	1.1	0.5	1.1	1.3	1.0	1.1	1.1	1.1
3512	Fertilizers & Pesticides	1.5	1.3	1.4	1.3	1.2	1.2	1.2	1.2	1.4	1.1
3513	Synthetic Resins	3.4	3.6	3.0	2.3	2.2	2.1	2.3	2.6	2.5	2.2
352	Other Chemicals	8.9	8.4	7.2	6.5	5.6	5.8	6.4	6.4	6.2	6.7
3521	Paints, Varnishes & Lacquers	2.1	2.0	1.6	1.2	0.7	1.0	1.6	1.6	1.1	1.7
3522	Drugs & Medicines	1.6	1.5	1.4	1.3	1.2	1.2	1.4	1.4	1.9	1.7
3523	Soap & Cleaning Preparations	3.8	3.1	2.9	2.7	2.4	2.6	2.4	2.2	2.3	2.2
3529	Chemical Products, nec	1.5	1.9	1.4	1.4	1.2	1.1	1.0	1.2	1.0	1.1
353	Petroleum Refineries	1.0	1.0	0.8	0.8	0.8	0.8	0.7	0.6	0.6	0.6
354	Petroleum & Coal Products	0.6	0.7	0.8	0.1	0.2	0.2	0.2	0.3	0.3	0.2
355	Rubber Products	4.3	2.8	2.4	2.0	2.0	1.9	2.0	2.0	1.9	1.9
356	Plastic Products, nec	6.3	6.8	7.4	7.6	6.9	7.0	6.8	7.4	7.3	7.4
36	Non-Metallic Mineral Products	10.4	9.8	8.0	6.9	6.4	6.2	6.6	6.8	7.3	8.1
361	Pottery, China etc	1.1	1.1	0.8	0.6	0.6	0.6	0.6	0.7	0.7	0.7
362	Glass & Products	2.6	2.2	1.6	1.6	1.3	1.2	1.4	1.5	1.5	1.5
369	Non-Metallic Products, nec	6.7	6.5	5.6	4.6	4.6	4.4	4.5	4.6	5.1	5.8
37	Basic Metal Industries	6.7	6.6	6.4	7.1	6.8	6.1	6.5	7.1	7.4	7.2
371	Iron & Steel	3.4	3.2	3.4	3.7	3.4	3.0	3.1	3.3	3.4	3.3
372	Non-Ferrous Metals	3.2	3.4	3.0	3.4	3.4	3.1	3.4	3.8	4.0	4.0
38	Fabricated Metal Products	71.5	68.8	63.4	69.0	56.4	52.7	53.5	58.6	64.1	65.7
381	Metal Products	27.4	25.6	24.0	22.2	20.0	19.0	19.2	20.9	22.6	24.0
3813	Structural Metal Products	13.0	13.2	12.8	11.5	9.8	9.4	9.0	9.9	11.3	13.3
382	Non-Electrical Machinery	16.9	17.0	16.1	16.2	15.4	14.9	15.1	17.6	18.6	19.1
3821	Engines & Turbines	1.4	1.4	1.4	1.4	1.3	1.3	1.2	1.3	1.3	1.3
3822	Agricultural Machinery	2.3	2.3	2.1	2.1	1.9	1.8	2.0	2.3	2.2	2.2
3823	Metal & Wood working Machinery	1.8	1.6	1.5	1.4	1.5	1.4	1.5	1.6	1.7	1.7
3824	Special Industrial Machinery	11.0	11.0	10.6	10.8	9.9	9.7	9.8	11.8	12.8	13.2
3825	Office & Computing Machinery	0.5	0.6	0.4	0.6	0.7	0.7	0.6	0.7	0.7	0.8
3829	Machinery & Equipment, nec	..	..	..	..	..	..	..	..	..	..
383	Electrical Machinery	13.5	13.6	11.1	11.5	11.3	10.1	10.4	11.6	12.9	12.7
3831	Electrical Industrial Machinery	2.9	3.0	2.0	2.8	2.8	2.5	2.5	2.6	3.1	3.0
3832	Radio, TV & Communication Equipment	3.6	3.7	2.9	3.0	2.5	2.1	2.0	2.4	2.7	2.7
3833	Electrical Appliances & Housewares	4.1	4.1	3.3	3.6	3.5	3.4	3.7	4.4	4.7	4.7
3839	Electrical Apparatus, nec	2.9	2.9	2.9	2.1	2.5	2.2	2.2	2.3	2.3	2.3
384	Transport Equipment	12.4	11.3	11.0	17.9	8.8	7.7	7.8	8.0	9.4	9.3
3841	Shipbuilding & Repairing	2.9	2.9	2.9	2.6	2.4	2.4	2.3	2.6	3.6	3.7
3842	Railroad Equipment				7.5	..	..	..	..	..	..
3843	Motor Vehicles	8.3	7.7	7.3	6.6	5.6	4.4	4.6	4.4	4.8	4.6
3844	Motorcycles & Bicycles	0.5	0.1	0.1	0.3	0.1	0.0	0.0	0.1	0.0	0.0
3845	Aircraft	0.5	0.4	0.7	0.8	0.6	0.7	0.7	0.8	0.8	0.8
3849	Transport Equipment, nec	0.2	0.2	0.2	0.2	0.2	0.2	0.1	0.1	0.1	0.1
385	Professional Goods	1.3	1.4	1.2	1.3	1.0	1.0	1.2	0.6	0.6	0.7
3851	Professional Equipment	0.7	0.9	0.9	0.9	0.6	0.7	0.9	0.4	0.4	0.5
3852	Photographic & Optical Goods	0.6	0.5	0.3	0.4	0.3	0.3	0.2	0.2	0.2	0.2
3853	Watches & Clocks	..	..	..	..	..	..	..	..	..	..
39	Other Manufacturing, nes	4.4	4.2	3.8	4.5	4.0	4.0	4.0	4.5	4.6	4.4
3901	Jewellery	..	..	..	..	..	..	..	..	..	..
3	Total Manufacturing	293.8	274.0	257.1	254.9	233.8	223.9	230.0	244.3	251.4	257.0
1	Agric., Hunting, Forestry, Fishing	160.9	151.4	157.4	182.0	165.5	158.9	159.4	155.2	166.1	175.3
2	Mining & Quarrying	5.8	4.6	4.5	4.1	4.4	4.2	3.9	4.2	4.3	4.4
21	Coal Mining	2.2	1.3	1.1	1.0	1.0	0.9	0.8	0.8	0.9	0.8
22	Crude Petroleum & Natural Gas	0.9	0.8	..	0.8	0.9	0.9	0.8	0.9	1.0	0.9
23.29	Other Mining	3.2	..	..	2.5	2.6	2.5	2.4	2.6	2.7	2.9
3	Total Manufacturing	293.8	274.0	257.1	254.9	233.8	223.9	230.0	244.3	251.4	257.0
4	Electricity, Gas & Water	14.5	14.8	15.8	13.0	13.2	12.5	11.2	11.2	10.1	9.9
5	Construction	89.6	90.2	82.2	79.7	75.5	70.1	69.4	74.4	85.4	93.4
6.9	Services	820.8	..	..	801.1	808.3	797.2	794.1	843.2	881.9	904.2
0000	Grand Total	1 377.0	1 345.1	1 316.5	1 334.7	1 300.7	1 266.9	1 268.0	1 332.4	1 399.3	1 444.1

Note: Data refer to fiscal year ending 31 March.
Data are expressed as full-time equivalent.
Unless given separately, ISIC 313 includes 314; 322 includes 323 and 324; 3829 includes 3824; 3849 includes 3842 and 3844.
ISIC 3 includes a figure for ancillary units. Prior to 1995-96 ISIC 1 covers forestry, logging and fishing only; 4 covers gas only.

Table NZ.4 **NEW ZEALAND**

ISIC2	Industry	EMPLOYMENT - EMPLOYEES									
		1986-87	1987-88	1988-89	1989-90	1990-91	1991-92	1992-93	1993-94	1994-95	1995-96
31	**Food, Beverages & Tobacco**	74.2	66.1	66.3	62.6	60.1	58.5	61.2	62.8	62.3	64.4
311.2	Food	69.2	62.9	63.1	58.8	56.5	56.1	57.6	59.4	58.8	60.8
313	Beverages	4.1	2.4	2.3	3.0	3.0	1.9	3.1	2.9	3.0	3.1
314	Tobacco	0.9	0.9	0.9	0.8	0.7	0.6	0.5	0.5	0.5	0.5
32	**Textiles, Apparel & Leather**	39.9	34.6	29.2	29.6	26.6	24.2	24.6	26.1	26.4	24.4
321	Textiles	14.4	12.5	10.8	11.6	10.4	9.5	9.6	10.1	10.6	10.0
3213	Knitting Mills	3.6	3.7	3.2	3.2	2.7	2.4	2.0	1.9	2.0	1.6
322	Wearing Apparel	18.7	16.8	14.2	13.5	12.3	11.2	11.3	11.8	11.5	10.4
323	Leather & Products	3.3	2.6	2.2	2.2	2.1	2.2	2.3	2.4	2.6	2.4
324	Footwear	3.5	2.6	1.9	2.3	1.9	1.4	1.4	1.8	1.7	1.5
33	**Wood Products & Furniture**	21.7	19.1	18.0	19.4	17.7	17.3	18.6	21.1	20.2	24.1
331	Wood Products	15.0	13.4	12.8	13.5	12.5	12.3	13.4	15.2	13.9	17.6
332	Furnitures & Fixtures	6.7	5.7	5.2	5.9	5.3	5.0	5.2	5.9	6.3	6.5
34	**Paper, Paper Products & Printing**	29.1	29.8	27.2	24.5	25.3	23.8	23.4	24.1	25.4	25.1
341	Paper & Products	12.1	13.2	10.1	8.5	9.5	8.9	8.6	8.6	9.3	9.0
3411	Pulp, Paper & Board	7.4	7.2	5.9	4.4	5.0	4.5	4.0	3.9	4.1	3.0
342	Printing & Publishing	17.0	16.6	17.1	16.1	15.8	14.9	14.8	15.5	16.0	16.2
35	**Chemical Products**	25.4	24.0	23.1	20.2	19.1	19.1	19.6	20.4	20.1	20.1
351	Industrial Chemicals	5.2	5.3	5.4	3.9	4.4	4.4	4.4	4.7	4.8	4.2
3511	Basic Industrial Chemicals	0.4	0.5	1.1	0.4	1.1	1.2	1.0	1.1	1.1	1.1
3512	Fertilizers & Pesticides	1.5	1.3	1.4	1.3	1.2	1.2	1.1	1.2	1.3	1.1
3513	Synthetic Resins	3.3	3.6	2.9	2.2	2.2	2.0	2.2	2.5	2.4	2.1
352	Other Chemicals	8.6	8.1	7.0	6.3	5.4	5.6	6.2	6.1	5.9	6.4
3521	Paints, Varnishes & Lacquers	2.0	1.9	1.6	1.2	0.7	0.9	1.6	1.6	1.0	1.7
3522	Drugs & Medicines	1.5	1.4	1.3	1.3	1.2	1.2	1.4	1.3	1.8	1.6
3523	Soap & Cleaning Preparations	3.7	3.0	2.8	2.6	2.3	2.5	2.3	2.1	2.2	2.1
3529	Chemical Products, nec	1.4	1.8	1.4	1.3	1.2	1.0	1.0	1.1	0.9	1.0
353	Petroleum Refineries	1.0	1.0	0.8	0.8	0.8	0.8	0.7	0.6	0.6	0.6
354	Petroleum & Coal Products	0.6	0.7	0.8	0.1	0.2	0.2	0.2	0.2	0.2	0.2
355	Rubber Products	4.2	2.7	2.3	1.9	1.9	1.8	1.9	1.9	1.8	1.8
356	Plastic Products, nec	5.9	6.3	6.9	7.2	6.4	6.4	6.3	6.9	6.8	6.9
36	**Non-Metallic Mineral Products**	9.5	8.9	7.1	6.0	5.6	5.4	5.7	5.9	6.3	7.1
361	Pottery, China etc	0.8	0.8	0.5	0.3	0.3	0.3	0.4	0.4	0.4	0.4
362	Glass & Products	2.4	2.0	1.4	1.4	1.1	1.0	1.2	1.2	1.2	1.3
369	Non-Metallic Products, nec	6.3	6.1	5.2	4.3	4.2	4.1	4.2	4.2	4.7	5.4
37	**Basic Metal Industries**	6.5	6.5	6.2	6.9	6.6	5.9	6.3	6.8	7.2	7.0
371	Iron & Steel	3.4	3.2	3.3	3.6	3.3	2.9	3.0	3.2	3.3	3.1
372	Non-Ferrous Metals	3.2	3.3	2.9	3.3	3.3	3.0	3.3	3.7	3.9	3.9
38	**Fabricated Metal Products**	63.4	60.1	54.8	60.4	47.9	44.0	44.8	49.7	54.6	55.7
381	Metal Products	24.3	22.4	20.9	19.1	17.0	16.0	16.1	17.7	19.3	20.6
3813	Structural Metal Products	11.6	11.7	11.3	10.1	8.5	8.0	7.6	8.5	9.8	11.7
382	Non-Electrical Machinery	13.8	13.6	12.6	12.6	11.8	11.2	11.5	13.8	14.6	14.8
3821	Engines & Turbines	1.1	1.1	1.0	1.0	1.0	0.9	0.8	0.8	0.9	0.9
3822	Agricultural Machinery	1.8	1.7	1.6	1.6	1.5	1.3	1.5	1.8	1.7	1.7
3823	Metal & Wood working Machinery	1.4	1.3	1.2	1.1	1.2	1.1	1.1	1.3	1.4	1.4
3824	Special Industrial Machinery	9.2	9.0	8.5	8.5	7.7	7.4	7.6	9.4	10.2	10.3
3825	Office & Computing Machinery	0.3	0.5	0.3	0.5	0.5	0.5	0.4	0.5	0.5	0.5
3829	Machinery & Equipment, nec	..	..	..	..	..	..	..	..	..	..
383	Electrical Machinery	12.7	12.8	10.4	10.8	10.6	9.4	9.7	10.8	12.0	11.9
3831	Electrical Industrial Machinery	2.6	2.7	1.7	2.5	2.4	2.2	2.2	2.3	2.8	2.7
3832	Radio, TV & Communication Equipment	3.3	3.4	2.7	2.7	2.3	1.8	1.8	2.1	2.4	2.5
3833	Electrical Appliances & Housewares	4.1	4.0	3.2	3.6	3.5	3.3	3.6	4.3	4.7	4.6
3839	Electrical Apparatus, nec	2.7	2.7	2.8	2.0	2.4	2.0	2.0	2.1	2.1	2.2
384	Transport Equipment	11.3	10.1	9.9	16.8	7.7	6.5	6.6	6.8	8.1	8.0
3841	Shipbuilding & Repairing	2.3	2.2	2.2	1.9	1.7	1.7	1.7	2.0	2.9	2.9
3842	Railroad Equipment	..	..	..	7.5	..	..	..	..	..	..
3843	Motor Vehicles	8.0	7.3	6.9	6.3	5.3	4.0	4.2	4.0	4.4	4.2
3844	Motorcycles & Bicycles	0.5	0.1	0.0	0.2	0.0	0.0	0.0	0.0	0.0	0.0
3845	Aircraft	0.4	0.4	0.6	0.7	0.5	0.6	0.6	0.7	0.7	0.7
3849	Transport Equipment, nec	0.2	0.2	0.2	0.2	0.2	0.2	0.1	0.1	0.1	0.1
385	Professional Goods	1.2	1.3	1.1	1.2	0.9	0.9	1.1	0.5	0.5	0.5
3851	Professional Equipment	0.7	0.9	0.8	0.8	0.5	0.6	0.8	0.3	0.3	0.4
3852	Photographic & Optical Goods	0.6	0.4	0.3	0.4	0.3	0.3	0.2	0.2	0.2	0.1
3853	Watches & Clocks	..	..	..	..	..	..	..	..	..	..
39	**Other Manufacturing, nes**	3.4	3.1	2.8	3.5	2.9	2.7	2.7	3.2	3.2	3.0
3901	Jewellery	0.9	0.6	0.5	0.6	0.7	0.6	0.6	0.6	0.5	0.5
3	**Total Manufacturing**	273.2	252.1	234.6	233.0	211.9	201.0	206.8	220.0	225.5	230.9
1	**Agric., Hunting, Forestry, Fishing**	41.7	39.7	59.1	60.0	63.1	60.4	63.4	64.7	65.7	74.4
2	**Mining & Quarrying**	5.5	4.2	4.1	3.7	3.9	3.8	3.5	3.8	3.9	3.9
21	Coal Mining	2.2	1.2	1.1	1.0	1.0	0.9	0.8	0.7	0.8	0.8
22	Crude Petroleum & Natural Gas	0.9	0.8	0.8	0.7	0.8	0.8	0.7	0.9	0.9	0.8
23.29	Other Mining	2.8	..	..	2.1	2.2	2.2	2.1	2.2	2.3	2.5
3	**Total Manufacturing**	273.2	252.1	234.6	233.0	211.9	201.0	206.8	220.0	225.5	230.9
4	**Electricity, Gas & Water**	14.5	14.8	15.8	13.0	13.2	12.5	11.2	11.1	10.1	9.8
5	**Construction**	61.5	59.9	52.8	50.0	44.5	38.8	38.4	43.8	49.8	55.0
6.9	**Services**	688.1	702.0	683.7	681.4	685.0	663.6	657.2	687.2	724.2	742.0
0000	**Grand Total**	1 104.9	1 072.8	1 050.1	1 041.0	1 021.7	980.0	980.4	1 043.4	1 079.3	1 116.0

Note: Data refer to fiscal year ending 31 March.
Data are expressed as full-time equivalent.
Unless given separately, ISIC 313 includes 314; 322 includes 323 and 324; 3829 includes 3824; 3849 includes 3842 and 3844.
ISIC 3 includes a figure for ancillary units. Prior to 1995-96 ISIC 1 covers forestry, logging and fishing only; 4 covers gas only.

Units

Table NZ.11 NEW ZEALAND

ISIC2	Industry	ENTERPRISES									
		1986-87	1987-88	1988-89	1989-90	1990-91	1991-92	1992-93	1993-94	1994-95	1995-96
31	**Food, Beverages & Tobacco**	1 603	1 607	1 676	1 671	1 697	1 790	1 816	1 914	2 061	2 020
311.2	Food	1 481	1 493	1 556	1 553	1 565	1 658	1 668	1 743	1 870	1 814
313	Beverages	116	109	115	114	128	128	145	168	189	204
314	Tobacco	6	5	5	4	4	4	3	3	2	2
32	**Textiles, Apparel & Leather**	2 150	2 216	2 148	2 094	2 099	2 148	2 176	2 157	2 294	2 256
321	Textiles	714	755	769	745	734	760	774	767	833	824
3213	Knitting Mills	145	154	146	134	135	137	128	120	120	102
322	Wearing Apparel	1 112	1 146	1 085	1 065	1 087	1 127	1 143	1 132	1 205	1 188
323	Leather & Products	229	223	205	194	191	186	187	187	186	178
324	Footwear	95	92	89	90	87	75	72	71	70	66
33	**Wood Products & Furniture**	2 718	2 825	2 788	2 763	2 868	2 918	3 004	3 118	3 438	3 476
331	Wood Products	1 475	1 511	1 511	1 492	1 551	1 562	1 622	1 697	1 841	1 881
332	Furnitures & Fixtures	1 243	1 314	1 277	1 271	1 317	1 356	1 382	1 421	1 597	1 595
34	**Paper, Paper Products & Printing**	1 216	1 273	1 370	1 346	1 384	1 415	1 451	1 486	1 554	1 477
341	Paper & Products	123	141	150	119	118	119	114	121	110	93
3411	Pulp, Paper & Board	18	20	19	17	15	13	16	19	13	13
342	Printing & Publishing	1 093	1 132	1 220	1 227	1 266	1 296	1 337	1 365	1 444	1 384
35	**Chemical Products**	954	933	909	898	890	934	893	908	977	967
351	Industrial Chemicals	143	143	140	147	139	146	149	174	197	194
3511	Basic Industrial Chemicals	41	39	36	39	35	37	35	38	42	39
3512	Fertilizers & Pesticides	35	36	36	45	40	46	46	52	69	57
3513	Synthetic Resins	67	68	68	63	64	63	68	84	86	98
352	Other Chemicals	286	271	250	240	234	241	243	244	281	281
3521	Paints, Varnishes & Lacquers	52	53	43	40	42	40	39	34	38	38
3522	Drugs & Medicines	50	52	43	41	40	50	54	55	64	67
3523	Soap & Cleaning Preparations	108	94	95	94	90	89	88	83	96	92
3529	Chemical Products, nec	76	72	69	65	62	62	62	72	83	84
353	Petroleum Refineries	11	10	8	10	7	7	3	2	2	2
354	Petroleum & Coal Products	21	22	23	17	21	19	23	23	28	25
355	Rubber Products	92	84	81	85	84	95	91	89	91	77
356	Plastic Products, nec	401	403	407	399	405	426	384	376	378	388
36	**Non-Metallic Mineral Products**	791	744	709	680	662	652	688	656	737	726
361	Pottery, China etc	243	225	202	198	193	203	209	190	204	206
362	Glass & Products	187	166	165	161	156	162	182	173	210	197
369	Non-Metallic Products, nec	361	353	342	321	313	287	297	293	323	323
37	**Basic Metal Industries**	153	170	171	160	157	162	166	203	211	215
371	Iron & Steel	68	77	77	72	73	68	70	106	119	122
372	Non-Ferrous Metals	85	93	94	88	84	94	96	97	92	93
38	**Fabricated Metal Products**	6 527	6 821	6 793	6 651	6 699	6 830	6 779	6 684	7 256	7 566
381	Metal Products	2 488	2 531	2 431	2 324	2 316	2 362	2 389	2 329	2 488	2 568
3813	Structural Metal Products	1 092	1 132	1 103	1 030	1 016	1 026	1 038	1 025	1 087	1 105
382	Non-Electrical Machinery	2 419	2 592	2 700	2 697	2 757	2 837	2 774	2 788	3 039	3 233
3821	Engines & Turbines	247	263	270	263	267	269	273	294	282	280
3822	Agricultural Machinery	397	402	376	364	356	349	371	355	372	350
3823	Metal & Wood working Machinery	265	259	253	243	237	230	238	207	209	211
3824	Special Industrial Machinery	1 423	1 577	1 699	1 715	1 770	1 832	1 745	1 786	2 011	2 207
3825	Office & Computing Machinery	87	91	102	112	127	157	147	146	165	185
3829	Machinery & Equipment, nec								..	..	..
383	Electrical Machinery	631	631	590	592	607	615	585	587	623	617
3831	Electrical Industrial Machinery	244	258	250	253	275	279	252	242	241	236
3832	Radio, TV & Communication Equipment	218	210	189	189	182	187	178	194	226	228
3833	Electrical Appliances & Housewares	48	47	38	38	37	35	31	35	37	35
3839	Electrical Apparatus, nec	121	116	113	112	113	114	124	116	119	118
384	Transport Equipment	901	983	985	950	933	932	947	899	1 007	1 037
3841	Shipbuilding & Repairing	505	571	578	566	558	544	525	484	536	578
3842	Railroad Equipment				1			..	..	..	..
3843	Motor Vehicles	303	317	309	284	276	288	317	300	333	325
3844	Motorcycles & Bicycles	14	13	11	13	10	8	8	10	13	9
3845	Aircraft	57	62	67	67	71	75	82	88	107	106
3849	Transport Equipment, nec	22	20	20	19	18	17	15	17	18	19
385	Professional Goods	88	84	87	88	86	84	84	81	99	111
3851	Professional Equipment	65	64	64	64	60	60	59	61	76	86
3852	Photographic & Optical Goods	23	20	23	24	26	24	25	20	23	25
3853	Watches & Clocks							..	..	..	..
39	**Other Manufacturing, nes**	826	824	809	823	880	954	1 003	938	1 033	1 033
3901	Jewellery	242	231	237	246	254	255	262	261	286	285
3	**Total Manufacturing**	16 938	17 413	17 373	17 086	17 336	17 803	17 976	18 064	19 561	19 736
1	**Agric., Hunting, Forestry, Fishing**	87 183	88 592	89 054	86 972	86 574	87 708	89 148	76 970	77 805	75 492
2	**Mining & Quarrying**	476	528	542	529	524	516	487	473	483	491
21	Coal Mining	40	51	50	45	41	39	37	35	34	27
22	Crude Petroleum & Natural Gas	100	115	122	127	137	146	143	143	153	155
23.29	Other Mining				422	415	399	372	393	373	389
3	**Total Manufacturing**	16 938	17 413	17 373	17 086	17 336	17 803	17 976	18 064	19 561	19 736
4	**Electricity, Gas & Water**	62	62	81	76	78	85	92	104	108	116
5	**Construction**	23 872	25 195	24 875	24 503	25 664	26 099	25 506	24 238	28 321	30 664
6.9	**Services**	89 517	91 354	96 957	101 786	106 986	115 975	117 594	121 287	135 369	139 303
0000	**Grand Total**	218 048	223 144	228 882	230 952	237 162	248 186	250 803	241 136	261 647	265 802

Note: Data refer to fiscal year ending 31 March.
Unless given separately, ISIC 313 includes 314; 322 includes 323 and 324; 3829 includes 3824; 3849 includes 3842 and 3844.
ISIC 3 includes a figure for ancillary units. Prior to 1995-96 ISIC 1 covers forestry, logging and fishing only; 4 covers gas only.

Millions of Esc

Table PO.1 **PORTUGAL**

(Current Prices)

ISIC2	Industry	PRODUCTION									
		1987	**1988**	**1989**	**1990**	**1991**	**1992**	**1993**	**1994**	**1995**	**1996**
31	**Food, Beverages & Tobacco**	685 517	755 883	866 705	1 330 006	1 475 895	1 552 386	1 580 760	1 755 909	1 770 180	..
311.2	Food	593 921	653 174	739 747	1 041 936	1 152 557	1 195 666	1 191 318	1 341 173	1 320 091	..
313	Beverages	60 283	71 703	91 584	188 818	207 833	224 081	240 458	269 621	308 190	..
314	Tobacco	31 313	31 006	35 374	99 252	115 505	132 639	148 984	145 115	141 899	..
32	**Textiles, Apparel & Leather**	696 441	736 519	806 080	1 484 453	1 563 773	1 600 332	1 684 894	1 864 972	1 873 579	..
321	Textiles	445 945	463 600	485 882	726 602	722 081	735 005	744 960	823 743	853 076	..
3213	Knitting Mills	110 462	110 245	122 170	188 490	202 782	212 792	228 991	250 341	254 964	..
322	Wearing Apparel	132 531	145 534	168 890	442 294	497 965	529 005	531 841	561 309	573 320	..
323	Leather & Products	43 215	45 093	49 830	79 862	77 809	70 587	78 005	87 946	77 838	..
324	Footwear	74 750	82 293	101 478	235 695	265 918	265 735	330 088	391 974	369 345	..
33	**Wood Products & Furniture**	141 742	166 914	203 567	426 546	489 790	485 695	496 980	546 159	599 650	..
331	Wood Products	118 423	140 074	173 566	328 449	356 173	336 840	355 243	401 982	444 787	..
332	Furnitures & Fixtures	23 318	26 840	30 000	98 097	133 617	148 855	141 737	144 177	154 863	..
34	**Paper, Paper Products & Printing**	269 868	325 464	378 684	465 642	513 995	532 937	533 992	606 656	766 091	..
341	Paper & Products	192 520	230 019	264 451	269 483	267 592	271 866	254 292	322 925	440 219	..
3411	Pulp, Paper & Board	152 470	184 792	218 231	214 896	195 117	200 761	171 755	224 792	322 895	..
342	Printing & Publishing	77 348	95 445	114 232	196 159	246 403	261 071	279 700	283 731	325 872	..
35	**Chemical Products**	737 682	884 741	935 704	1 057 511	1 152 160	1 207 157	1 265 044	1 416 327	1 602 189	..
351	Industrial Chemicals	240 595	317 995	272 108	218 537	186 069	192 604	184 660	200 726	244 469	..
3511	Basic Industrial Chemicals	118 949	163 566	117 107	68 388	71 838	75 054	71 555	61 557	63 672	..
3512	Fertilizers & Pesticides	40 094	44 353	48 852	49 127	20 613	32 609	29 112	33 036	39 080	..
3513	Synthetic Resins	81 551	110 077	106 149	101 022	93 618	84 941	83 993	106 133	141 717	..
352	Other Chemicals	176 445	200 283	222 868	268 126	297 771	322 301	316 696	319 902	357 746	..
3521	Paints, Varnishes & Lacquers	25 581	31 651	37 708	51 082	57 013	60 626	63 162	65 622	77 836	..
3522	Drugs & Medicines	51 087	57 313	60 764	80 594	99 381	115 208	115 787	128 739	139 726	..
3523	Soap & Cleaning Preparations	46 443	54 851	61 841	70 542	65 290	76 402	78 905	77 583	78 604	..
3529	Chemical Products, nec	53 334	56 468	62 555	65 908	76 087	70 065	58 842	47 958	61 580	..
353	Petroleum Refineries	230 095	263 132	323 393	..	..	..	592 232	694 880	755 907	..
354	Petroleum & Coal Products	0	0	0	..	..	..	5 722	6 045	6 406	..
355	Rubber Products	28 295	31 756	32 229	35 607	30 045	36 815	38 975	49 160	57 891	..
356	Plastic Products, nec	62 251	71 574	85 106	114 887	120 853	126 838	126 759	145 614	179 770	..
36	**Non-Metallic Mineral Products**	184 104	220 822	253 985	396 821	458 336	485 023	515 661	570 821	617 379	..
361	Pottery, China etc	36 645	42 365	45 846	84 135	89 493	99 469	111 783	127 783	135 873	..
362	Glass & Products	32 820	42 246	48 194	60 772	69 330	76 212	74 345	82 998	95 682	..
369	Non-Metallic Products, nec	114 640	136 211	159 945	251 914	299 513	309 342	329 533	360 040	385 824	..
37	**Basic Metal Industries**	97 098	114 185	126 854	179 248	157 309	147 854	157 264	159 125	222 713	..
371	Iron & Steel	79 125	91 607	104 811	126 697	108 753	103 287	114 426	107 632	167 182	..
372	Non-Ferrous Metals	17 973	22 578	22 043	52 551	48 556	44 567	42 838	51 493	55 531	..
38	**Fabricated Metal Products**	534 458	623 612	741 975	1 323 646	1 470 327	1 499 132	1 542 349	1 695 621	2 084 756	..
381	Metal Products	120 358	133 715	154 474	363 812	436 449	448 949	449 548	475 381	542 655	..
3813	Structural Metal Products	14 862	15 667	17 911	53 529	62 354	78 126	101 619	137 332	145 657	..
382	Non-Electrical Machinery	70 101	75 135	85 467	221 625	267 617	246 798	270 823	285 227	311 252	..
3821	Engines & Turbines	48	3 794	5 817	9 885	11 712	14 364	11 511	1 979	2 306	..
3822	Agricultural Machinery	7 649	9 397	10 673	23 307	27 734	25 688	22 021	26 166	27 615	..
3823	Metal & Wood working Machinery	5 674	6 603	8 176	12 037	11 481	12 707	12 252	12 653	13 084	..
3824	Special Industrial Machinery	16 186	19 101	21 381	66 333	65 646	59 056	73 950	94 219	106 335	..
3825	Office & Computing Machinery	6 989	1 106	1 334	6 318	9 395	5 819	8 602	12 917	11 755	..
3829	Machinery & Equipment, nec	33 555	35 134	38 085	103 745	141 649	129 164	142 487	137 293	150 157	..
383	Electrical Machinery	160 104	191 517	229 571	374 743	413 421	430 585	467 892	517 697	584 996	..
3831	Electrical Industrial Machinery	21 635	24 573	32 983	63 582	68 940	74 826	79 494	49 710	46 756	..
3832	Radio, TV & Communication Equipment	74 978	86 949	98 753	170 309	198 646	201 834	217 696	251 594	272 751	..
3833	Electrical Appliances & Housewares	13 580	19 178	21 654	35 661	32 984	29 136	31 723	20 782	29 300	..
3839	Electrical Apparatus, nec	49 911	60 817	76 181	105 191	112 851	124 789	138 979	195 611	236 189	..
384	Transport Equipment	176 008	215 360	263 165	349 006	329 712	347 815	325 277	382 587	608 022	..
3841	Shipbuilding & Repairing	35 369	41 606	46 699	63 379	76 759	63 123	55 745	49 840	78 121	..
3842	Railroad Equipment	..	..	..	..	1 632	1 812	1 758	23 344	26 926	..
3843	Motor Vehicles	129 755	160 617	200 618	269 565	236 423	266 046	252 953	278 949	470 666	..
3844	Motorcycles & Bicycles	8 716	9 883	11 008	13 742	14 042	16 100	13 954	15 804	18 665	..
3845	Aircraft	0	0	0	558	610	554	672	14 323	11 388	..
3849	Transport Equipment, nec	0	0	0	..	246	180	195	327	2 256	..
385	Professional Goods	7 887	7 885	9 300	14 460	23 128	24 985	28 809	34 729	37 831	..
3851	Professional Equipment	4 493	2 137	2 484	6 814	15 160	16 654	20 040	21 546	23 625	..
3852	Photographic & Optical Goods	3 394	3 928	4 741	6 566	6 699	6 720	7 301	11 742	13 049	..
3853	Watches & Clocks	0	1 819	2 075	1 080	1 269	1 611	1 468	1 441	1 157	..
39	**Other Manufacturing, nes**	5 504	6 558	8 206	64 643	77 294	76 373	91 657	99 148	109 985	..
3901	Jewellery	..	..	..	23 023	33 548	30 104	37 006	39 139	47 151	..
3	**Total Manufacturing**	3 352 414	3 834 697	4 321 760	6 728 516	7 358 879	7 586 889	7 868 601	8 714 738	9 646 522	..
1	**Agric., Hunting, Forestry, Fishing**	..	..	..							
2	**Mining & Quarrying**	27 700	38 266	74 577	117 311	128 731	134 819	135 243	139 925	161 976	..
21	Coal Mining	1 712	1 542	1 245	1 937	1 747	1 833	2 012	1 637	339	..
22	Crude Petroleum & Natural Gas	0	0	0	122	0	0	0	0	..	..
23.29	Other Mining	25 988	36 724	73 332	115 252	126 984	132 986	133 231	138 288	161 637	..
3	**Total Manufacturing**	3 352 414	3 834 697	4 321 760	6 728 516	7 358 879	7 586 889	7 868 601	8 714 738	9 646 522	..
4	**Electricity, Gas & Water**	4 884	149 806	193 401	423 176	517 496	582 625	616 526	1 119 406	1 174 801	..
5	**Construction**	456 117	..	..	1 219 458	1 523 650	1 820 838	2 011 729	2 187 648	2 376 336	..
6.9	**Services**	..	..	..	..	..	..	..	..	..	..
0000	**Grand Total**	3 841 115	4 022 769	4 589 737	8 488 461	9 528 756	10 125 171	10 632 099	12 161 717	13 359 635	..

Note: Break in series between 1989 and 1990, see Sources and Definitions.

Table PO.2 **PORTUGAL**

Millions of Esc

(Current Prices)

ISIC2	Industry	1987	1988	1989	1990	1991	1992	1993	1994	1995	1996
31	**Food, Beverages & Tobacco**	167 087	184 204	222 937	319 476	342 637	407 609	421 409	434 931	442 736	..
311.2	Food	115 490	127 996	157 281	186 068	188 619	228 204	220 580	232 160	231 820	..
313	Beverages	30 265	35 365	42 631	49 011	54 284	61 687	65 514	70 157	80 961	..
314	Tobacco	21 332	20 843	23 025	84 397	99 734	117 718	135 315	132 614	129 955	..
32	**Textiles, Apparel & Leather**	245 083	266 814	280 703	458 593	472 825	474 576	532 706	596 972	582 621	..
321	Textiles	166 502	175 126	178 080	235 817	227 941	224 534	241 224	273 711	262 104	..
3213	Knitting Mills	35 484	35 593	39 930	52 278	56 171	57 028	64 612	71 415	66 496	..
322	Wearing Apparel	46 207	53 023	59 192	140 358	160 593	162 003	178 474	197 163	200 168	..
323	Leather & Products	10 095	10 419	11 553	17 965	17 418	16 670	18 417	21 319	17 556	..
324	Footwear	22 278	28 247	31 878	64 453	66 873	71 369	94 591	104 779	102 793	..
33	**Wood Products & Furniture**	45 663	51 928	61 430	109 014	135 189	134 578	136 772	152 219	160 459	..
331	Wood Products	36 751	40 948	49 043	75 852	88 872	84 342	89 934	102 355	107 424	..
332	Furnitures & Fixtures	8 912	10 979	12 386	33 162	46 317	50 236	46 838	49 864	53 035	..
34	**Paper, Paper Products & Printing**	120 520	140 207	161 856	156 740	162 692	168 616	165 661	216 658	285 929	..
341	Paper & Products	82 574	96 043	111 709	82 209	74 098	71 463	59 083	101 819	152 235	..
3411	Pulp, Paper & Board	71 307	83 359	100 392	71 832	58 450	57 515	43 647	77 686	126 297	..
342	Printing & Publishing	37 947	44 165	50 147	74 531	88 594	97 153	106 578	114 839	133 694	..
35	**Chemical Products**	166 770	205 517	181 510	455 188	455 603	490 224	508 241	566 820	661 797	..
351	Industrial Chemicals	53 030	90 470	55 482	61 624	41 808	44 955	45 932	48 878	60 649	..
3511	Basic Industrial Chemicals	21 868	40 402	27 232	17 766	20 442	23 058	22 791	20 345	21 219	..
3512	Fertilizers & Pesticides	11 255	13 262	12 710	16 721	6 221	9 174	9 708	8 652	11 080	..
3513	Synthetic Resins	19 907	36 806	15 539	27 137	15 145	12 723	13 433	19 881	28 350	..
352	Other Chemicals	56 203	63 015	71 397	68 548	88 897	96 784	92 341	95 671	102 890	..
3521	Paints, Varnishes & Lacquers	7 883	10 408	13 022	14 809	17 758	20 690	21 128	22 496	23 106	..
3522	Drugs & Medicines	21 035	23 480	24 947	26 253	37 300	40 279	38 461	41 348	48 967	..
3523	Soap & Cleaning Preparations	15 422	17 862	19 975	15 570	17 426	18 791	17 474	16 903	16 670	..
3529	Chemical Products, nec	11 863	11 265	13 453	11 916	16 413	17 024	15 278	14 924	14 147	..
353	Petroleum Refineries	24 331	15 726	15 657	..	..	..	313 843	361 511	424 678	..
354	Petroleum & Coal Products	0	0	0				1 376	1 536	1 648	..
355	Rubber Products	11 999	14 036	13 467	7 724	7 665	11 523	14 163	16 232	19 124	..
356	Plastic Products, nec	21 208	22 269	25 508	33 714	36 697	39 408	40 586	42 992	52 808	..
36	**Non-Metallic Mineral Products**	91 200	109 521	122 733	169 402	193 067	201 314	217 237	248 653	264 699	..
361	Pottery, China etc	20 275	22 828	24 222	41 530	43 698	48 160	54 099	63 521	67 020	..
362	Glass & Products	16 207	21 176	23 129	24 720	28 835	30 433	29 697	36 879	40 510	..
369	Non-Metallic Products, nec	54 718	65 517	75 382	103 152	120 534	122 721	133 441	148 253	157 169	..
37	**Basic Metal Industries**	33 736	37 313	40 554	50 359	44 874	37 612	42 385	38 463	46 813	..
371	Iron & Steel	28 578	30 835	34 362	38 849	32 746	24 977	29 703	23 321	31 642	..
372	Non-Ferrous Metals	5 157	6 478	6 192	11 510	12 128	12 635	12 682	15 142	15 171	..
38	**Fabricated Metal Products**	185 381	222 030	257 267	399 987	463 746	462 572	480 344	542 719	617 298	..
381	Metal Products	46 916	51 944	57 841	117 680	147 049	153 606	157 442	170 782	188 224	..
3813	Structural Metal Products	7 277	7 758	8 819	15 205	18 935	24 752	31 955	44 661	47 488	..
382	Non-Electrical Machinery	27 306	30 500	35 289	75 322	92 861	81 712	91 492	98 502	102 702	..
3821	Engines & Turbines	21	1 415	2 246	6 204	6 782	6 798	5 504	548	828	..
3822	Agricultural Machinery	2 613	3 774	4 390	7 280	7 888	7 308	6 858	8 157	8 787	..
3823	Metal & Wood working Machinery	2 651	2 952	3 834	4 440	4 466	5 078	4 995	5 617	6 085	..
3824	Special Industrial Machinery	7 057	8 605	9 539	25 051	26 578	20 575	28 325	38 507	44 048	..
3825	Office & Computing Machinery	2 471	478	552	2 188	2 639	2 158	2 591	3 165	3 166	..
3829	Machinery & Equipment, nec	12 492	13 276	14 728	30 159	44 508	39 795	43 219	42 508	39 788	..
383	Electrical Machinery	59 937	70 222	84 551	118 829	132 587	138 294	149 161	161 096	164 103	..
3831	Electrical Industrial Machinery	10 246	10 799	14 327	23 372	26 354	29 312	25 787	18 742	15 763	..
3832	Radio, TV & Communication Equipment	24 931	28 845	32 819	51 151	64 027	58 601	67 883	67 975	63 169	..
3833	Electrical Appliances & Housewares	2 778	4 906	6 014	7 302	5 709	5 629	6 737	4 486	7 015	..
3839	Electrical Apparatus, nec	21 982	25 672	31 389	37 004	36 497	44 752	48 754	69 893	78 156	..
384	Transport Equipment	47 721	65 737	75 620	83 092	81 504	78 106	69 886	97 343	145 546	..
3841	Shipbuilding & Repairing	16 123	25 645	25 306	27 678	32 444	21 922	23 375	19 338	24 652	..
3842	Railroad Equipment				355	726	657	537	12 220	14 794	..
3843	Motor Vehicles	27 968	34 797	43 553	49 897	42 933	49 805	41 226	52 605	95 304	..
3844	Motorcycles & Bicycles	3 137	3 587	3 869	4 705	5 023	5 433	4 352	4 900	4 644	..
3845	Aircraft	0	0	0	360	279	224	326	8 155	5 518	..
3849	Transport Equipment, nec	0	0	0	97	99	65	70	125	634	..
385	Professional Goods	3 501	3 627	3 966	5 064	9 745	10 854	12 363	14 996	16 723	..
3851	Professional Equipment	2 045	817	965	1 629	6 416	7 099	8 544	9 568	10 838	..
3852	Photographic & Optical Goods	1 456	1 852	1 877	2 990	2 861	3 212	3 388	4 935	5 296	..
3853	Watches & Clocks	0	959	1 125	445	468	543	431	493	589	..
39	**Other Manufacturing, nes**	2 415	2 682	3 163	20 129	22 997	21 867	25 421	28 552	31 126	..
3901	Jewellery	..	..	..	6 487	8 334	7 137	8 223	9 211	11 258	..
3	**Total Manufacturing**	1 057 855	1 220 217	1 332 154	2 138 888	2 293 630	2 398 968	2 530 176	2 825 987	3 093 478	..
1	**Agric., Hunting, Forestry, Fishing**	..	..	..	..	..	..	..	..	..	..
2	**Mining & Quarrying**	..	..	..	60 555	59 535	58 919	59 262	72 924	79 982	..
21	Coal Mining	..	..	..	1 228	1 228	1 316	1 371	1 071	122	..
22	Crude Petroleum & Natural Gas	..	..	..	0	0	0	0	0	..	..
23.29	Other Mining	..	..	..	59 327	58 307	57 603	57 891	71 853	79 860	..
3	**Total Manufacturing**	1 057 855	1 220 217	1 332 154	2 138 888	2 293 630	2 398 968	2 530 176	2 825 987	3 093 478	..
4	**Electricity, Gas & Water**	..	..	..	312 181	387 092	433 802	466 147	463 337	469 704	..
5	**Construction**	209 144	..	..	363 206	458 207	532 956	549 464	623 492	653 177	..
6.9	**Services**	..	..	..	..	..	..	..	..	..	..
0000	**Grand Total**	1 266 999	1 220 217	1 332 154	2 874 830	3 198 464	3 424 645	3 605 049	3 985 740	4 296 341	..

Note: Break in series between 1989 and 1990, see Sources and Definitions.

Thousands

ISIC2	Industry	EMPLOYMENT									
		1987	1988	1989	1990	1991	1992	1993	1994	1995	1996
31	**Food, Beverages & Tobacco**	79.4	76.4	76.5	119.6	123.0	116.3	116.9	122.2	113.8	..
311.2	Food	69.1	66.0	65.9	99.8	102.7	97.2	97.9	103.4	95.9	..
313	Beverages	8.4	8.6	8.8	18.0	18.7	17.6	17.4	17.4	16.6	..
314	Tobacco	1.9	1.8	1.8	1.8	1.6	1.5	1.5	1.4	1.3	..
32	**Textiles, Apparel & Leather**	221.9	220.1	222.0	372.9	383.7	362.7	355.1	350.1	333.9	..
321	Textiles	139.8	135.7	132.4	158.3	151.2	140.4	134.0	127.6	122.3	..
3213	Knitting Mills	32.7	31.9	32.1	42.8	40.5	38.4	38.0	36.4	34.8	..
322	Wearing Apparel	51.2	52.9	55.9	145.3	158.1	151.4	146.2	149.0	141.0	..
323	Leather & Products	5.8	5.8	5.6	9.8	10.2	8.9	9.3	8.3	8.1	..
324	Footwear	25.1	25.7	28.1	59.4	64.1	62.1	65.7	65.1	62.5	..
33	**Wood Products & Furniture**	48.5	47.0	45.2	93.0	107.4	103.1	91.5	91.7	91.6	..
331	Wood Products	36.4	34.8	33.3	54.9	58.1	51.7	51.3	51.1	50.6	..
332	Furnitures & Fixtures	12.1	12.2	11.9	38.1	49.3	51.4	40.2	40.5	41.0	..
34	**Paper, Paper Products & Printing**	39.3	40.2	40.6	52.1	52.3	51.0	52.6	49.7	48.9	..
341	Paper & Products	16.8	16.6	16.7	18.5	17.1	16.8	17.1	14.8	14.4	..
3411	Pulp, Paper & Board	10.8	10.6	10.8	12.2	10.7	10.4	10.2	7.8	7.8	..
342	Printing & Publishing	22.6	23.6	23.9	33.6	35.2	34.2	35.5	35.0	34.5	..
35	**Chemical Products**	56.8	54.4	52.1	65.2	58.9	60.2	57.0	54.1	54.3	..
351	Industrial Chemicals	12.7	11.9	11.1	12.4	8.9	9.7	8.9	7.4	7.2	..
3511	Basic Industrial Chemicals	5.6	5.4	5.1	4.2	4.3	4.2	3.9	3.4	3.3	..
3512	Fertilizers & Pesticides	3.6	3.2	2.9	5.2	1.4	2.5	2.1	1.6	1.5	..
3513	Synthetic Resins	3.4	3.3	3.1	3.0	3.2	3.0	2.9	2.5	2.4	..
352	Other Chemicals	21.5	20.7	19.7	23.8	23.0	23.3	22.2	21.1	21.0	..
3521	Paints, Varnishes & Lacquers	3.4	3.4	3.4	4.9	4.7	4.6	4.6	4.4	4.3	..
3522	Drugs & Medicines	8.0	7.9	7.6	9.2	9.2	9.7	9.0	8.8	8.8	..
3523	Soap & Cleaning Preparations	5.1	5.0	4.6	5.1	4.1	4.0	4.2	4.0	3.9	..
3529	Chemical Products, nec	5.0	4.5	4.1	4.6	4.9	5.0	4.4	3.9	4.0	..
353	Petroleum Refineries	2.2	2.3	2.2	..	..	..	3.7	3.6	3.5	..
354	Petroleum & Coal Products	0.0	0.0	0.0	..	..	..	0.3	0.3	0.3	..
355	Rubber Products	6.8	6.3	6.2	6.6	5.6	6.4	5.9	5.8	5.9	..
356	Plastic Products, nec	13.6	13.2	12.9	16.8	16.9	16.3	16.0	15.9	16.4	..
36	**Non-Metallic Mineral Products**	49.8	49.2	48.1	74.0	75.0	69.2	70.1	69.6	69.9	..
361	Pottery, China etc	15.0	15.3	14.6	25.6	24.0	24.8	24.6	25.5	26.6	..
362	Glass & Products	7.8	7.6	7.5	10.6	10.5	9.2	8.9	9.0	9.3	..
369	Non-Metallic Products, nec	27.0	26.3	25.9	37.8	40.5	35.1	36.5	35.1	34.0	..
37	**Basic Metal Industries**	16.8	16.4	14.5	20.3	19.4	17.6	17.7	13.6	14.0	..
371	Iron & Steel	13.6	13.2	11.8	15.1	13.8	12.0	12.0	8.0	9.4	..
372	Non-Ferrous Metals	3.2	3.2	2.7	5.2	5.6	5.6	5.6	5.6	4.7	..
38	**Fabricated Metal Products**	116.3	115.1	116.3	205.0	212.5	205.0	202.1	203.6	209.1	..
381	Metal Products	33.4	32.6	31.7	79.7	87.9	83.6	80.4	77.7	78.7	..
3813	Structural Metal Products	4.5	4.3	4.1	9.3	10.4	12.4	16.4	20.6	20.6	..
382	Non-Electrical Machinery	19.0	18.3	18.0	40.5	41.0	38.2	38.7	38.6	38.5	..
3821	Engines & Turbines	0.0	1.0	1.1	2.0	1.8	1.7	1.0	0.2	0.3	..
3822	Agricultural Machinery	2.3	2.2	2.1	4.0	4.2	4.0	3.6	3.5	3.6	..
3823	Metal & Wood working Machinery	2.2	2.1	2.0	2.5	2.6	2.5	2.3	2.2	2.1	..
3824	Special Industrial Machinery	6.1	5.9	5.8	13.3	12.1	11.7	13.0	14.7	14.7	..
3825	Office & Computing Machinery	1.4	0.4	0.4	1.1	1.0	0.8	1.0	1.2	1.0	..
3829	Machinery & Equipment, nec	7.0	6.7	6.7	17.6	19.2	17.3	17.9	16.8	16.9	..
383	Electrical Machinery	28.2	28.8	29.8	41.1	44.2	44.8	45.2	45.9	46.6	..
3831	Electrical Industrial Machinery	5.6	5.8	5.9	10.4	9.7	9.2	8.3	5.3	5.0	..
3832	Radio, TV & Communication Equipment	12.3	12.3	13.3	14.7	15.8	16.1	15.6	16.3	14.9	..
3833	Electrical Appliances & Housewares	2.2	2.1	2.2	3.5	3.5	3.1	3.4	2.2	2.5	..
3839	Electrical Apparatus, nec	8.0	8.6	8.4	12.5	15.3	16.4	17.9	22.2	24.2	..
384	Transport Equipment	33.2	33.0	34.2	39.5	34.4	33.5	32.7	36.2	39.8	..
3841	Shipbuilding & Repairing	15.7	14.4	13.4	11.5	11.8	11.6	10.9	7.5	9.1	..
3842	Railroad Equipment				0.2	0.2	0.2	0.1	3.1	3.0	..
3843	Motor Vehicles	13.8	15.1	17.4	24.9	19.4	19.0	19.0	20.9	23.6	..
3844	Motorcycles & Bicycles	2.7	2.6	2.5	2.7	2.8	2.6	2.5	2.4	2.4	..
3845	Aircraft	0.0	0.0	0.0	0.2	0.2	0.1	0.2	2.3	1.4	..
3849	Transport Equipment, nec	0.0	0.0	0.0	0.1	0.1	0.0	0.1	0.1	0.4	..
385	Professional Goods	2.5	2.4	2.5	4.2	5.1	4.8	5.0	5.3	5.5	..
3851	Professional Equipment	1.4	0.5	0.6	2.1	3.1	2.9	3.2	3.1	3.3	..
3852	Photographic & Optical Goods	1.1	1.1	1.2	1.8	1.6	1.6	1.5	1.8	1.9	..
3853	Watches & Clocks	0.0	0.7	0.7	0.4	0.4	0.4	0.3	0.4	0.3	..
39	**Other Manufacturing, nes**	2.3	2.4	2.5	15.0	15.7	13.5	14.1	14.4	13.2	..
3901	Jewellery	..	..	..	3.8	4.6	4.0	4.4	4.5	4.4	..
3	**Total Manufacturing**	631.1	621.1	617.7	1 017.1	1 047.9	998.6	977.1	969.1	948.8	..
1	**Agric., Hunting, Forestry, Fishing**	..	..	..	..	..	..	..	..	..	..
2	**Mining & Quarrying**	12.6	13.5	13.1	18.3	19.0	18.2	17.6	15.7	15.1	..
21	Coal Mining	1.0	0.9	0.8	0.9	0.8	0.7	0.6	0.6	0.1	..
22	Crude Petroleum & Natural Gas	0.0	0.0	0.0	0.0	0.0	0.0	0.0	0.0		..
23.29	Other Mining	11.6	12.5	12.2	17.4	18.3	17.5	17.0	15.1	15.0	..
3	**Total Manufacturing**	631.1	621.1	617.7	1 017.1	1 047.9	998.6	977.1	969.1	948.8	..
4	**Electricity, Gas & Water**	27.2	26.6	22.2	25.8	24.6	22.9	21.8	20.1	19.8	..
5	**Construction**	217.0	..	..	210.1	222.4	222.3	232.8	244.8	232.5	..
6.9	**Services**	..	..	..	..	..	..	..	..	..	..
0000	**Grand Total**	887.8	661.2	653.1	1 271.3	1 313.9	1 262.1	1 249.3	1 249.6	1 216.2	..

Note: Break in series between 1989 and 1990, see Sources and Definitions.

Thousands

Table PO.4 **PORTUGAL**

ISIC2	Industry	EMPLOYMENT - EMPLOYEES									
		1987	1988	1989	1990	1991	1992	1993	1994	1995	1996
31	Food, Beverages & Tobacco	75.5	73.1	73.0	60.0	60.3	57.6	54.8	53.7	50.0	..
311.2	Food	65.3	62.7	62.5	46.3	46.9	45.5	42.7	41.4	39.2	..
313	Beverages	8.3	8.5	8.7	11.8	11.8	10.5	10.6	10.8	9.6	..
314	Tobacco	1.9	1.8	1.8	1.8	1.6	1.5	1.5	1.4	1.3	..
32	Textiles, Apparel & Leather	221.2	219.5	221.4	194.9	194.2	181.9	173.8	166.0	156.3	..
321	Textiles	139.4	135.4	132.1	110.7	100.8	91.3	85.6	78.7	73.8	..
3213	Knitting Mills	32.6	31.7	31.9	23.8	21.3	19.2	19.4	16.7	15.8	..
322	Wearing Apparel	51.1	52.8	55.8	54.4	61.3	59.5	55.3	56.9	53.1	..
323	Leather & Products	5.8	5.7	5.6	2.0	1.8	1.9	1.8	1.5	1.6	..
324	Footwear	25.0	25.6	28.0	27.8	30.3	29.3	31.1	28.9	27.8	..
33	Wood Products & Furniture	46.5	45.0	43.4	17.0	16.3	14.6	14.2	14.3	14.3	..
331	Wood Products	34.7	33.2	31.8	12.8	12.9	11.3	10.5	10.6	10.6	..
332	Furnitures & Fixtures	11.8	11.8	11.5	4.1	3.3	3.3	3.7	3.7	3.6	..
34	Paper, Paper Products & Printing	38.9	39.7	40.3	24.9	22.2	22.0	21.1	18.2	18.1	..
341	Paper & Products	16.7	16.5	16.7	12.9	11.2	11.5	11.3	8.6	8.7	..
3411	Pulp, Paper & Board	10.8	10.6	10.8	10.6	9.2	9.2	8.6	6.4	6.6	..
342	Printing & Publishing	22.2	23.2	23.6	12.1	11.0	10.4	9.8	9.6	9.4	..
35	Chemical Products	56.3	53.9	51.6	39.8	32.5	34.6	31.4	28.5	27.7	..
351	Industrial Chemicals	12.7	11.9	11.1	9.5	5.8	6.9	6.3	4.9	4.8	..
3511	Basic Industrial Chemicals	5.6	5.4	5.1		2.7	2.9	2.8	2.2	2.1	..
3512	Fertilizers & Pesticides	3.6	3.2	2.9		1.0	..	..	..	..	..
3513	Synthetic Resins	3.4	3.3	3.1	1.9	2.1					..
352	Other Chemicals	21.2	20.4	19.4	15.4	13.8	13.8	12.9	12.3	11.9	..
3521	Paints, Varnishes & Lacquers	3.4	3.4	3.4	2.8	2.6	2.4	2.3	2.1	1.9	..
3522	Drugs & Medicines	8.0	7.9	7.6	7.2	7.0	7.2	6.9	6.8	6.7	..
3523	Soap & Cleaning Preparations	5.1	4.9	4.6	3.3	2.3	2.1	2.0	1.9	1.8	..
3529	Chemical Products, nec	4.7	4.2	3.9	2.0	1.9	..	1.7	1.6	1.6	..
353	Petroleum Refineries	2.2	2.3	2.2	5.2	4.2	..	3.7	3.6	3.5	..
354	Petroleum & Coal Products	0.0	0.0	0.0	0.0	0.0	..	0.0	0.0		..
355	Rubber Products	6.7	6.2	6.1	3.5	2.4	..	2.9	2.7	2.5	..
356	Plastic Products, nec	13.6	13.2	12.9	6.1	6.1	6.3	5.5	5.0	5.0	..
36	Non-Metallic Mineral Products	49.3	48.8	47.7	32.5	31.4	30.3	29.1	28.8	28.9	..
361	Pottery, China etc	14.9	15.3	14.6	13.1	13.0	13.6	13.4	13.8	14.2	..
362	Glass & Products	7.8	7.6	7.5	7.5	6.9	6.1	5.6	5.4	5.6	..
369	Non-Metallic Products, nec	26.6	25.9	25.6	11.9	11.5	10.6	10.1	9.7	9.2	..
37	Basic Metal Industries	16.7	16.3	14.5	13.7	12.5	10.8	10.5	7.5	8.2	..
371	Iron & Steel	13.6	13.2	11.8	11.5	10.2	8.7	8.3	4.8	6.3	..
372	Non-Ferrous Metals	3.1	3.1	2.7	2.2	2.4	2.2	2.2	2.7	1.9	..
38	Fabricated Metal Products	115.9	114.8	116.0	102.0	99.4	98.5	94.6	94.4	98.2	..
381	Metal Products	33.2	32.4	31.6	21.3	21.7	21.1	20.3	18.1	18.0	..
3813	Structural Metal Products	4.5	4.3	4.1	2.3	3.1	3.9	3.7	4.5	3.8	..
382	Non-Electrical Machinery	19.0	18.2	18.0	16.3	16.4	15.7	14.0	11.2	10.8	..
3821	Engines & Turbines	0.0	1.0	1.1					0.0		..
3822	Agricultural Machinery	2.3	2.2	2.1	1.1	1.2	1.2	0.9	0.8	0.7	..
3823	Metal & Wood working Machinery	2.2	2.1	2.0	1.1	1.2	1.1	0.8			..
3824	Special Industrial Machinery	6.1	5.9	5.8	5.9	5.3	5.2	4.8	3.7	3.6	..
3825	Office & Computing Machinery	1.4	0.4	0.4							..
3829	Machinery & Equipment, nec	7.0	6.7	6.7	5.9	6.7	6.2	6.4	5.5	5.2	..
383	Electrical Machinery	28.1	28.8	29.7	31.1	32.9	34.6	34.7	34.8	36.2	..
3831	Electrical Industrial Machinery	5.6	5.8	5.9	7.9	7.1	12.0	5.6	2.6	2.6	..
3832	Radio, TV & Communication Equipment	12.3	12.3	13.3	12.3	12.7	13.4	13.0	13.2	12.4	..
3833	Electrical Appliances & Housewares	2.2	2.1	2.2	1.9	2.0	1.8	1.8	1.3	1.7	..
3839	Electrical Apparatus, nec	8.0	8.6	8.4	9.0	11.1	7.3	14.3	17.6	19.5	..
384	Transport Equipment	33.1	33.0	34.2	30.9	25.4	24.3	22.5	27.2	30.2	..
3841	Shipbuilding & Repairing	15.6	14.3	13.4	9.3	8.9	8.9	8.1	5.3	6.6	..
3842	Railroad Equipment	..	..	..			0.2	0.1	3.0	3.0	..
3843	Motor Vehicles	13.8	15.1	17.4	19.6	14.3	13.6	12.9	15.4	17.8	..
3844	Motorcycles & Bicycles	2.7	2.6	2.5	1.7	1.9	1.6	1.4			..
3845	Aircraft	0.0	0.0	0.0			0.0	0.0			..
3849	Transport Equipment, nec	0.0	0.0	0.0	0.0	0.0	0.0	0.0	0.0		..
385	Professional Goods	2.5	2.3	2.5	2.4	3.0	3.0	3.0	3.2	3.2	..
3851	Professional Equipment	1.4	0.5	0.6			1.4	1.5	1.3	1.3	..
3852	Photographic & Optical Goods	1.1	1.1	1.2	1.5	1.3	..	..	..	..	..
3853	Watches & Clocks	0.0	0.7	0.7							..
39	Other Manufacturing, nes	2.2	2.4	2.5	3.9	3.5	3.7	3.1	3.1	2.6	..
3901	Jewellery	..	..	..			0.7	0.6	0.6	0.6	..
3	Total Manufacturing	622.6	613.5	610.4	488.8	472.2	454.0	432.5	414.6	404.2	..
1	Agric., Hunting, Forestry, Fishing	..	..	..							..
2	Mining & Quarrying	12.4	13.3	13.0	7.8	7.0	7.0	5.9	4.7	3.9	..
21	Coal Mining	1.0	0.9	0.8	0.8	0.7	0.7	0.6	0.5		..
22	Crude Petroleum & Natural Gas	0.0	0.0	0.0	0.0	0.0	0.0	0.0	0.0		..
23.29	Other Mining	11.4	12.4	12.2	7.0	6.3	6.4	5.3	4.1	3.9	..
3	Total Manufacturing	622.6	613.5	610.4	488.8	472.2	454.0	432.5	414.6	404.2	..
4	Electricity, Gas & Water	27.1	26.6	22.2	25.4	24.2	22.2	21.0	19.3	19.0	..
5	Construction	205.6	..	..	72.2	69.3	67.5	67.5	66.1	60.6	..
6.9	Services	..	..	..							..
0000	Grand Total	867.7	653.4	645.6	594.2	572.6	550.7	526.9	504.7	487.8	..

Note: Break in series between 1989 and 1990, see Sources and Definitions.

Millions of Esc

(Current Prices)

ISIC2	Industry	INVESTMENT									
		1987	1988	1989	1990	1991	1992	1993	1994	1995	1996
31	**Food, Beverages & Tobacco**	25 348	34 779	41 990	80 962	79 679	76 845	68 272	108 545	63 903	..
311.2	Food	17 657	23 890	27 955	52 255	54 109	56 986	42 158	80 350	42 968	..
313	Beverages	5 137	9 844	12 980	27 277	24 465	18 763	24 013	27 452	21 350	
314	Tobacco	2 554	1 045	1 055	1 430	1 105	1 096	2 101	743	-415	..
32	**Textiles, Apparel & Leather**	42 715	50 434	54 527	93 765	98 724	92 115	65 070	110 280	87 207	
321	Textiles	31 715	38 759	43 014	53 234	58 915	49 633	30 994	58 274	49 369	
3213	Knitting Mills	6 489	6 501	6 576	14 311	15 691	11 869	11 603	18 755	11 361	
322	Wearing Apparel	5 178	6 637	7 361	26 592	23 249	24 620	19 963	30 362	21 765	
323	Leather & Products	1 888	1 673	910	2 539	3 587	2 886	2 380	3 767	2 019	
324	Footwear	3 935	3 364	3 242	11 400	12 973	14 976	11 733	17 877	14 054	
33	**Wood Products & Furniture**	9 246	8 522	9 528	32 967	27 525	30 317	25 175	42 420	27 519	
331	Wood Products	7 989	6 777	7 328	25 271	19 259	21 215	14 711	20 975	19 407	
332	Furnitures & Fixtures	1 258	1 745	2 200	7 696	8 266	9 102	10 464	21 445	8 112	
34	**Paper, Paper Products & Printing**	29 440	47 414	46 483	54 473	91 702	39 997	60 937	35 667	36 975	
341	Paper & Products	23 671	40 303	36 491	38 346	71 607	27 656	46 720	8 694	15 093	..
3411	Pulp, Paper & Board	21 014	38 743	32 680	35 078	68 789	23 519	30 253	3 588	8 713	..
342	Printing & Publishing	5 769	7 111	9 992	16 127	20 095	12 341	14 217	26 973	21 882	
35	**Chemical Products**	20 961	19 150	32 729	41 157	36 211	120 298	110 934	49 286	48 042	
351	Industrial Chemicals	6 215	7 415	11 882	10 584	-14 499	26 191	9 953	8 223	10 531	
3511	Basic Industrial Chemicals	3 499	2 948	4 085	9 720	10 131	6 957	4 535	4 473	5 859	..
3512	Fertilizers & Pesticides	408	924	2 546	-4 538	-36 447	6 316	604	1 648	454	..
3513	Synthetic Resins	2 308	3 543	5 250	5 402	11 817	12 918	4 814	2 102	4 218	..
352	Other Chemicals	6 177	6 653	7 639	11 629	12 700	17 486	15 408	16 808	14 647	
3521	Paints, Varnishes & Lacquers	564	829	759	2 787	3 226	3 202	2 863	3 022	3 591	
3522	Drugs & Medicines	2 099	2 364	3 245	4 339	5 958	7 219	6 883	7 404	7 318	
3523	Soap & Cleaning Preparations	1 462	1 396	2 035	2 172	1 703	3 834	3 801	2 909	2 227	
3529	Chemical Products, nec	2 052	2 064	1 600	2 331	1 813	3 231	1 861	3 473	1 511	
353	Petroleum Refineries	1 412	1 908	3 069	..	..	..	62 984	-5 462	8 417	
354	Petroleum & Coal Products	0	0	0	..	..	..	596	191	263	
355	Rubber Products	1 282	2 220	3 148	-4 175	-2 214	7 425	9 931	7 385	3 782	
356	Plastic Products, nec	5 875	955	6 991	9 733	11 662	12 637	12 062	22 141	10 402	..
36	**Non-Metallic Mineral Products**	23 391	21 442	29 144	57 282	81 809	29 239	44 850	46 785	63 224	
361	Pottery, China etc	4 093	6 160	9 767	16 636	8 871	8 793	10 752	12 296	22 798	
362	Glass & Products	12 165	4 076	6 072	11 372	16 524	10 726	7 730	4 547	10 437	
369	Non-Metallic Products, nec	7 132	11 206	13 305	29 274	56 414	9 720	26 368	29 942	29 989	
37	**Basic Metal Industries**	3 403	4 055	8 827	31 335	7 749	21 246	11 841	5 331	7 488	
371	Iron & Steel	2 608	3 186	7 891	27 962	10 199	16 528	7 346	2 008	4 869	
372	Non-Ferrous Metals	795	870	936	3 373	-2 450	4 718	4 495	3 323	2 619	
38	**Fabricated Metal Products**	28 330	32 049	32 980	70 135	98 114	78 679	88 530	160 976	130 009	
381	Metal Products	7 516	8 437	7 806	28 794	29 755	34 356	22 884	36 296	31 869	
3813	Structural Metal Products	1 306	640	644	3 449	2 930	4 591	6 902	14 405	6 293	
382	Non-Electrical Machinery	2 670	3 626	4 158	11 020	14 250	13 017	11 111	16 160	20 511	
3821	Engines & Turbines	0	98	59	41	-1 045	763	-6 750	132	117	
3822	Agricultural Machinery	321	289	636	1 343	2 836	1 944	1 275	1 652	490	
3823	Metal & Wood working Machinery	289	343	823	1 491	1 233	1 179	1 241	870	916	
3824	Special Industrial Machinery	909	1 718	1 439	3 311	3 107	4 046	9 179	8 089	13 874	
3825	Office & Computing Machinery	152	-21	10	190	155	164	130	-848	276	
3829	Machinery & Equipment, nec	999	1 199	1 190	4 644	7 964	4 921	6 036	6 265	4 838	
383	Electrical Machinery	11 698	12 629	13 310	13 372	36 430	19 264	33 550	15 845	23 728	
3831	Electrical Industrial Machinery	950	1 376	2 019	2 162	11 177	583	5 277	1 792	1 682	
3832	Radio, TV & Communication Equipment	6 554	6 681	6 991	4 430	9 908	6 924	16 488	-522	8 786	
3833	Electrical Appliances & Housewares	2 206	1 331	1 166	1 666	1 514	2 463	2 687	1 614	1 425	
3839	Electrical Apparatus, nec	1 988	3 241	3 133	5 114	13 831	9 294	9 098	12 961	11 835	
384	Transport Equipment	5 148	6 901	7 346	15 991	17 085	10 640	20 259	91 069	45 657	
3841	Shipbuilding & Repairing	1 041	1 142	413	3 837	3 018	1 051	-112 364	1 803	-3 521	
3842	Railroad Equipment				77	124	133	198	885	-5 652	
3843	Motor Vehicles	3 497	5 114	6 206	11 313	13 037	8 658	132 030	85 699	52 839	
3844	Motorcycles & Bicycles	385	606	547	749	823	776	417	1 706	1 369	
3845	Aircraft	0	0	0	6	72	17	-25	955	596	
3849	Transport Equipment, nec	0	0	0	9	11	5	3	21	26	
385	Professional Goods	1 297	456	361	958	596	1 402	726	1 606	8 244	
3851	Professional Equipment	796	66	41	556	189	910	348	1 189	6 949	
3852	Photographic & Optical Goods	501	245	161	378	394	219	286	515	1 257	
3853	Watches & Clocks	0	145	159	24	13	273	92	-98	38	
39	**Other Manufacturing, nes**	295	707	559	3 421	3 125	2 914	4 790	7 504	4 628	
3901	Jewellery	..	..	..	629	575	197	1 237	1 732	1 219	
3	**Total Manufacturing**	183 129	218 553	256 769	465 497	524 640	491 650	480 399	566 794	468 995	
1	**Agric., Hunting, Forestry, Fishing**	..	..	..	..	..	..	..	..	..	
2	**Mining & Quarrying**	..	..	..	34 072	32 897	21 276	14 580	20 518	16 512	
21	Coal Mining	..	..	..	83	43	33	3	42	21	
22	Crude Petroleum & Natural Gas	..	..	..	0	0	0	0	0	0	
23.29	Other Mining	..	..	..	33 989	32 854	21 243	14 577	20 476	16 491	
3	**Total Manufacturing**	183 129	218 553	256 769	465 497	524 640	491 650	480 399	566 794	468 995	
4	**Electricity, Gas & Water**	..	..	..	200 216	264 729	342 493	196 053	162 571	168 550	
5	**Construction**	17 861	..	..	60 174	60 009	75 027	64 693	122 210	79 249	
6.9	**Services**	..	..	..	..	..	..	..	..	..	
0000	**Grand Total**	200 990	218 553	256 769	759 959	882 275	930 446	755 725	872 093	733 306	..

Note: Break in series between 1989 and 1990, see Sources and Definitions.

Millions of Esc

(Current Prices)

ISIC2	Industry	INVESTMENT IN MACHINERY & EQUIPMENT									
		1987	1988	1989	1990	1991	1992	1993	1994	1995	1996
31	Food, Beverages & Tobacco	18 493	24 553	27 926	27 511	17 795	20 508	19 548	36 114	15 635	..
311.2	Food	12 207	15 553	17 481	18 505	11 982	14 618	8 163	27 731	11 178	..
313	Beverages	4 187	7 979	10 141	8 382	5 527	5 338	10 540	8 268	4 743	..
314	Tobacco	2 099	1 021	304	624	286	552	845	115	-286	..
32	Textiles, Apparel & Leather	32 247	19 453	42 948	28 783	32 586	28 343	16 008	34 666	25 028	..
321	Textiles	25 059	12 020	35 145	19 624	23 794	17 324	7 990	20 259	16 311	..
3213	Knitting Mills	4 705	4 842	5 046	4 111	6 205	3 166	3 368	6 645	3 057	..
322	Wearing Apparel	3 267	3 975	4 685	6 054	5 297	5 183	4 674	8 287	5 457	..
323	Leather & Products	1 288	1 078	438	194	221	828	52	1 403	205	..
324	Footwear	2 633	2 379	2 680	2 911	3 274	5 008	3 292	4 717	3 055	..
33	Wood Products & Furniture	6 093	4 769	5 256	6 212	4 331	-3 047	4 178	3 643	-608	..
331	Wood Products	5 254	3 798	4 017	5 610	3 741	-3 631	2 859	2 382	-24	..
332	Furnitures & Fixtures	838	971	1 240	602	590	584	1 319	1 261	-584	..
34	Paper, Paper Products & Printing	25 420	19 850	39 535	4 226	46 224	14 080	38 326	584	-2 789	..
341	Paper & Products	21 003	13 982	32 018	-1 261	41 591	12 623	37 348	-3 470	-5 366	..
3411	Pulp, Paper & Board	18 935	13 092	29 238	-2 028	41 308	11 637	30 970	-3 922	-4 940	..
342	Printing & Publishing	4 417	5 868	7 517	5 487	4 633	1 457	978	4 054	2 577	..
35	Chemical Products	15 806	14 399	23 262	11 109	-13 893	51 686	68 724	6 803	16 589	..
351	Industrial Chemicals	5 222	5 283	8 043	885	-26 396	13 658	2 305	1 978	2 883	..
3511	Basic Industrial Chemicals	2 968	1 973	2 136	..	5 292	3 176	654	972	572	..
3512	Fertilizers & Pesticides	317	613	1 181	..	-32 210	..	..	..	..	..
3513	Synthetic Resins	1 937	2 698	4 727	1 761	522	..	..	..	..	..
352	Other Chemicals	4 065	4 328	5 445	4 036	4 114	6 049	5 782	5 626	3 125	..
3521	Paints, Varnishes & Lacquers	346	503	654	1 041	995	421	843	729	715	..
3522	Drugs & Medicines	1 319	1 484	2 400	1 652	2 649	3 377	2 699	3 221	2 395	..
3523	Soap & Cleaning Preparations	1 032	1 033	1 328	734	15	1 571	2 462	1 184	403	..
3529	Chemical Products, nec	1 368	1 308	1 063	609	455	..	-222	492	-388	..
353	Petroleum Refineries	1 150	1 689	2 187	7 465	9 623	..	53 614	-7 444	6 563	..
354	Petroleum & Coal Products	0	0	0	0	0	..	0	0	..	..
355	Rubber Products	965	1 842	2 308	-3 264	-2 787	..	3 226	3 659	1 775	..
356	Plastic Products, nec	4 405	1 257	5 278	1 987	1 553	1 846	3 797	2 984	2 243	..
36	Non-Metallic Mineral Products	16 999	15 591	20 097	16 722	34 846	-566	13 566	9 862	17 995	..
361	Pottery, China etc	3 013	4 561	6 274	6 094	1 545	2 409	2 620	5 256	12 418	..
362	Glass & Products	9 707	3 726	4 938	2 814	7 732	7 213	5 192	-531	2 018	..
369	Non-Metallic Products, nec	4 279	7 304	8 884	7 814	25 569	-10 188	5 754	5 137	3 559	..
37	Basic Metal Industries	2 979	3 250	7 116	7 538	-10 059	7 772	4 096	1 360	1 923	..
371	Iron & Steel	2 376	2 560	6 317	6 415	-6 380	6 723	3 181	818	1 071	..
372	Non-Ferrous Metals	603	690	799	1 123	-3 679	1 049	915	542	852	..
38	Fabricated Metal Products	21 518	26 689	25 902	21 305	28 508	20 791	-28 198	38 815	28 520	..
381	Metal Products	5 757	6 592	6 761	6 252	5 832	6 805	-455	2 150	4 266	..
3813	Structural Metal Products	1 236	542	471	564	323	558	1 686	795	100	..
382	Non-Electrical Machinery	1 529	2 368	2 846	2 191	883	942	-5 166	1 594	4 206	..
3821	Engines & Turbines	0	0	0	..	..	..	..	0	..	..
3822	Agricultural Machinery	101	177	262	146	185	143	304	268	-111	..
3823	Metal & Wood working Machinery	203	273	649	544	266	2	287	..	..	..
3824	Special Industrial Machinery	746	1 111	1 090	805	454	265	1 772	363	2 345	..
3825	Office & Computing Machinery	134	116	63	..	..	..	..	..	..	..
3829	Machinery & Equipment, nec	344	690	781	738	1 645	191	164	866	1 709	..
383	Electrical Machinery	10 000	12 143	10 936	4 108	14 488	8 176	14 667	5 582	12 959	..
3831	Electrical Industrial Machinery	782	1 062	1 392	-298	3 888	2 402	2 185	532	766	..
3832	Radio, TV & Communication Equipment	6 349	6 648	6 005	1 425	3 934	2 318	7 354	1	6 234	..
3833	Electrical Appliances & Housewares	1 049	783	769	498	54	897	768	354	414	..
3839	Electrical Apparatus, nec	1 820	3 650	2 770	2 483	6 612	2 559	4 360	4 695	5 545	..
384	Transport Equipment	3 547	5 192	5 037	8 513	7 184	4 340	-37 080	29 124	6 369	..
3841	Shipbuilding & Repairing	541	657	186	1 490	847	761	-44 779	225	-6 474	..
3842	Railroad Equipment	..	..	..	..	..	90	134	647	-2 216	..
3843	Motor Vehicles	2 535	4 092	4 499	6 718	5 998	3 287	7 521	27 377	14 475	..
3844	Motorcycles & Bicycles	254	408	316	303	278	202	44	..	..	..
3845	Aircraft	0	0	0	..	..	0	0	..	..	..
3849	Transport Equipment, nec	0	0	0	0	0	0	0	0	..	..
385	Professional Goods	685	395	322	241	121	528	-164	365	720	..
3851	Professional Equipment	208	160	178	..	..	269	-307	307	324	..
3852	Photographic & Optical Goods	477	235	144	97	210	..	..	..	..	..
3853	Watches & Clocks	0	0	0	..	..	..	..	..	..	..
39	Other Manufacturing, nes	181	374	398	543	441	453	170	532	148	..
3901	Jewellery	..	..	..	..	..	..	79	-15	155	150	..
3	Total Manufacturing	139 737	128 927	192 442	123 949	140 779	140 020	136 418	132 379	102 441	..
1	Agric., Hunting, Forestry, Fishing	..	..	..	..	..	..	..	..	..	..
2	Mining & Quarrying	..	..	..	11 707	9 816	3 727	2 615	1 712	1 694	..
21	Coal Mining	..	..	..	59	27	16	-1	-18	..	..
22	Crude Petroleum & Natural Gas	..	..	..	0	0	0	0	0	..	..
23.29	Other Mining	..	..	..	11 648	9 789	3 711	2 616	1 730	1 694	..
3	Total Manufacturing	139 737	128 927	192 442	123 949	140 779	140 020	136 418	132 379	102 441	..
4	Electricity, Gas & Water	..	..	..	8 817	14 483	60 245	-90 286	67 399	87 163	..
5	Construction	9 903	..	..	17 755	18 679	20 181	11 210	31 898	18 183	..
6.9	Services	..	..	..	..	..	..	..	..	..	..
0000	Grand Total	149 640	128 927	192 442	162 228	183 757	224 173	59 957	233 388	209 481	..

Note: Break in series between 1989 and 1990, see Sources and Definitions.

Millions of Esc

(Current Prices)

ISIC2	Industry	WAGES & SALARIES - EMPLOYEES									
		1987	1988	1989	1990	1991	1992	1993	1994	1995	1996
31	**Food, Beverages & Tobacco**	57 648	63 961	75 840	66 011	77 959	86 843	89 138	91 005	89 661	..
311.2	Food	47 585	52 523	62 272	48 481	57 558	65 183	65 510	66 789	65 732	..
313	Beverages	7 820	9 124	10 883	14 829	17 521	18 532	19 994	21 415	21 026	..
314	Tobacco	2 243	2 315	2 685	2 701	2 880	3 128	3 634	2 801	2 903	..
32	**Textiles, Apparel & Leather**	134 903	150 688	172 437	142 203	158 257	169 046	173 092	172 305	173 478	..
321	Textiles	89 250	97 612	108 505	85 650	87 015	90 618	90 831	88 176	87 837	..
3213	Knitting Mills	18 417	20 524	23 472	16 326	16 655	17 431	18 700	17 661	17 473	..
322	Wearing Apparel	28 134	32 685	39 185	36 575	46 560	50 508	50 398	52 622	53 550	..
323	Leather & Products	4 197	4 544	5 094	1 962	2 127	2 515	2 548	2 463	2 470	..
324	Footwear	13 322	15 847	19 652	18 016	22 555	25 405	29 315	29 044	29 621	..
33	**Wood Products & Furniture**	26 171	29 508	33 297	14 990	16 594	16 921	17 974	19 748	20 507	..
331	Wood Products	20 255	22 660	25 368	11 571	13 389	13 367	13 300	15 076	15 755	..
332	Furnitures & Fixtures	5 916	6 848	7 929	3 419	3 205	3 554	4 674	4 672	4 752	..
34	**Paper, Paper Products & Printing**	40 149	46 719	55 849	39 106	42 380	47 082	46 037	45 356	49 795	..
341	Paper & Products	19 681	22 526	25 575	21 616	23 256	26 191	23 520	21 735	24 367	..
3411	Pulp, Paper & Board	14 433	16 531	18 953	18 711	20 397	22 222	18 949	17 574	19 835	..
342	Printing & Publishing	20 469	24 193	30 274	17 490	19 124	20 891	22 517	23 621	25 428	..
35	**Chemical Products**	67 170	74 022	80 884	66 377	64 697	77 082	77 803	76 297	80 651	..
351	Industrial Chemicals	18 832	19 819	21 132	16 964	13 588	17 228	16 900	14 586	15 592	..
3511	Basic Industrial Chemicals	8 082	8 694	8 924		6 156	7 379	7 647	6 708	6 995	..
3512	Fertilizers & Pesticides	5 453	5 562	5 870	..	2 499					..
3513	Synthetic Resins	5 297	5 563	6 339	4 146	4 933			..	..	..
352	Other Chemicals	26 345	29 844	32 948	25 777	27 864	32 205	33 629	34 399	36 722	..
3521	Paints, Varnishes & Lacquers	3 806	4 099	4 597	4 435	4 724	5 219	5 166	5 129	4 912	..
3522	Drugs & Medicines	9 800	11 539	13 425	11 798	14 044	16 741	18 295	19 402	21 619	..
3523	Soap & Cleaning Preparations	7 654	8 760	9 310	6 415	5 320	5 894	6 313	6 292	6 445	..
3529	Chemical Products, nec	5 085	5 446	5 616	3 129	3 776		3 855	3 576	3 746	..
353	Petroleum Refineries	4 926	5 534	6 219	13 196	12 659	..	14 853	15 320	15 317	..
354	Petroleum & Coal Products	0	0	0	0	0	..	0	0	..	..
355	Rubber Products	6 165	6 786	7 437	4 309	3 429		4 545	4 480	4 683	..
356	Plastic Products, nec	10 903	12 039	13 147	6 131	7 157	8 482	7 876	7 512	8 337	..
36	**Non-Metallic Mineral Products**	41 136	46 839	53 620	37 183	42 492	48 088	48 482	51 673	54 750	..
361	Pottery, China etc	11 180	13 283	14 442	12 755	14 347	16 478	17 629	19 208	20 850	..
362	Glass & Products	8 619	9 354	10 996	9 527	10 973	12 253	11 774	11 723	12 413	..
369	Non-Metallic Products, nec	21 337	24 201	28 183	14 901	17 172	19 357	19 079	20 742	21 487	..
37	**Basic Metal Industries**	18 589	20 315	20 744	17 605	18 040	17 550	18 114	12 267	16 559	..
371	Iron & Steel	15 983	17 351	17 829	14 953	15 048	14 462	14 891	8 089	13 260	..
372	Non-Ferrous Metals	2 606	2 964	2 915	2 652	2 992	3 088	3 223	4 178	3 299	..
38	**Fabricated Metal Products**	118 320	133 056	156 390	131 596	149 838	164 992	171 380	181 870	202 462	..
381	Metal Products	27 947	31 218	35 124	21 421	26 109	28 505	29 521	29 680	30 855	..
3813	Structural Metal Products	5 350	5 620	6 051	2 659	4 483	5 808	5 958	8 741	8 025	..
382	Non-Electrical Machinery	19 142	20 899	22 566	19 299	23 003	24 235	23 606	19 669	20 749	..
3821	Engines & Turbines	17	1 308	1 341					0		..
3822	Agricultural Machinery	1 796	2 053	2 208	1 239	1 632	1 723	1 396	1 280	1 261	..
3823	Metal & Wood working Machinery	1 845	2 041	2 236	1 097	1 308	1 354	1 175			..
3824	Special Industrial Machinery	5 101	5 709	6 461	6 312	6 653	7 255	7 315	5 761	6 047	..
3825	Office & Computing Machinery	1 887	369	426	..	..					..
3829	Machinery & Equipment, nec	8 496	9 419	9 894	7 101	9 396	9 735	10 628	10 678	11 366	..
383	Electrical Machinery	32 646	36 696	42 793	45 553	54 402	61 327	67 256	67 951	73 873	..
3831	Electrical Industrial Machinery	6 607	7 378	8 972	11 910	11 687	18 079	11 587	7 588	7 319	..
3832	Radio, TV & Communication Equipment	15 060	16 820	19 093	18 150	24 112	27 674	30 667	30 433	32 109	..
3833	Electrical Appliances & Housewares	1 864	2 023	2 600	2 870	3 318	3 374	3 548	1 780	2 575	..
3839	Electrical Apparatus, nec	9 114	10 475	12 124	12 623	15 285	12 200	21 454	28 150	31 870	..
384	Transport Equipment	36 246	42 022	53 183	43 081	42 742	47 052	46 640	59 686	71 759	..
3841	Shipbuilding & Repairing	18 219	20 142	23 893	15 202	17 157	19 173	17 921	12 527	15 930	..
3842	Railroad Equipment						281	213	6 654	7 558	..
3843	Motor Vehicles	14 968	18 405	25 210	25 961	23 169	25 742	26 961	34 476	42 659	..
3844	Motorcycles & Bicycles	1 824	2 128	2 431	1 574	2 051	1 856	1 545			..
3845	Aircraft	0	0	0			0	0	..	..	..
3849	Transport Equipment, nec	0	0	0	0	0	0	0	0	..	..
385	Professional Goods	2 338	2 220	2 724	2 242	3 582	3 873	4 357	4 884	5 226	..
3851	Professional Equipment	1 410	516	545	..		2 090	2 487	2 287	2 360	..
3852	Photographic & Optical Goods	928	943	1 301	1 290	1 394	..	..	..	..	..
3853	Watches & Clocks	0	762	877	..		..	..			..
39	**Other Manufacturing, nes**	1 418	1 665	1 921	3 413	3 527	4 296	4 091	4 280	3 762	..
3901	Jewellery	..	..	..	..		1 175	1 057	1 064	1 154	..
3	**Total Manufacturing**	505 505	566 773	650 981	518 484	573 784	631 900	646 111	654 801	691 625	..
1	**Agric., Hunting, Forestry, Fishing**	..	..	..	..						..
2	**Mining & Quarrying**	9 091	11 088	13 528	10 267	11 503	12 560	11 348	10 681	8 865	..
21	Coal Mining	1 284	1 302	1 336	1 187	1 293	1 328	1 357	2 061	..	..
22	Crude Petroleum & Natural Gas	0	0	0	0	0	0	0	0	..	..
23.29	Other Mining	7 807	9 785	12 192	9 080	10 210	11 232	9 991	8 620	8 865	..
3	**Total Manufacturing**	505 505	566 773	650 981	518 484	573 784	631 900	646 111	654 801	691 625	..
4	**Electricity, Gas & Water**	44 038	48 121	44 697	46 636	52 335	57 667	63 717	59 489	59 435	..
5	Construction	117 999	..	..	80 639	93 135	110 349	121 160	130 641	130 424	..
6.9	Services	..	..	..	..		..		..		..
0000	**Grand Total**	676 633	625 982	709 205	656 026	730 757	812 476	842 336	855 612	890 349	..

Note: Break in series between 1989 and 1990, see Sources and Definitions.
Before 1990, data include social security contributions.

Table PO.8 **PORTUGAL**

Millions of Esc (Current Prices)

ISIC2	Industry	1987	1988	1989	1990	1991	1992	1993	1994	1995	1996
						SUPPLEMENTS TO WAGES & SALARIES					
31	Food, Beverages & Tobacco	11 492	12 314	15 531	25 156	31 497	34 280	35 254	36 876	34 854	..
311.2	Food	9 489	10 057	12 748	17 216	21 378	23 698	23 320	24 078	22 685	..
313	Beverages	1 496	1 712	2 174	5 683	7 890	8 106	9 222	9 227	9 017	..
314	Tobacco	508	546	609	2 257	2 229	2 476	2 712	3 571	3 152	..
32	Textiles, Apparel & Leather	27 136	29 794	33 415	41 614	45 841	48 810	49 987	49 657	48 916	..
321	Textiles	18 014	19 199	21 174	25 361	25 550	26 577	26 652	25 688	24 922	..
3213	Knitting Mills	3 804	4 026	4 603	4 864	4 782	4 814	5 070	5 001	4 768	..
322	Wearing Apparel	5 596	6 488	7 595	10 891	13 717	14 856	14 840	15 603	15 669	..
323	Leather & Products	854	917	1 001	512	553	693	658	620	676	..
324	Footwear	2 672	3 191	3 645	4 850	6 021	6 684	7 837	7 746	7 649	..
33	Wood Products & Furniture	5 848	6 465	7 111	4 904	5 360	5 555	5 989	6 432	6 350	..
331	Wood Products	4 549	4 987	5 470	3 888	4 395	4 275	4 284	4 691	4 912	..
332	Furnitures & Fixtures	1 300	1 478	1 641	1 016	965	1 280	1 705	1 741	1 438	..
34	Paper, Paper Products & Printing	7 473	8 533	10 237	15 743	16 916	19 620	20 476	18 011	19 025	..
341	Paper & Products	3 753	4 152	4 672	9 252	9 856	11 778	12 323	9 135	9 938	..
3411	Pulp, Paper & Board	2 708	3 005	3 407	8 033	8 592	10 440	10 048	7 341	8 177	..
342	Printing & Publishing	3 720	4 380	5 565	6 491	7 060	7 842	8 153	8 876	9 087	..
35	Chemical Products	12 962	14 144	15 124	30 184	29 383	35 905	36 045	35 346	36 000	..
351	Industrial Chemicals	3 630	3 862	3 986	8 116	7 506	9 242	9 992	7 228	6 889	..
3511	Basic Industrial Chemicals	1 649	1 734	1 736	..	2 446	3 568	4 135	2 808	2 773	..
3512	Fertilizers & Pesticides	999	1 052	1 051	..	2 438	..	..	..	..	..
3513	Synthetic Resins	982	1 076	1 199	1 504	2 622	..	..	..	..	..
352	Other Chemicals	5 030	5 515	6 030	10 515	11 811	13 519	14 562	15 020	15 887	..
3521	Paints, Varnishes & Lacquers	765	776	893	1 452	1 704	1 960	2 011	1 917	1 688	..
3522	Drugs & Medicines	1 827	2 069	2 291	4 903	6 120	6 942	7 573	8 724	8 960	..
3523	Soap & Cleaning Preparations	1 441	1 570	1 686	2 837	2 508	2 610	2 915	2 782	2 778	..
3529	Chemical Products, nec	997	1 100	1 160	1 323	1 479	..	2 063	1 597	2 461	..
353	Petroleum Refineries	906	..	..	7 879	6 454	..	7 142	9 108	9 084	..
354	Petroleum & Coal Products	0	..	..	0	0	..	0	0	..	..
355	Rubber Products	1 242	1 364	1 441	1 729	1 458	..	1 731	1 495	1 445	..
356	Plastic Products, nec	2 153	2 385	2 540	1 945	2 154	2 592	2 618	2 495	2 695	..
36	Non-Metallic Mineral Products	8 367	9 427	10 631	14 715	15 499	18 810	17 962	19 058	19 294	..
361	Pottery, China etc	2 288	2 643	2 856	3 868	4 235	4 752	5 124	5 581	5 940	..
362	Glass & Products	1 723	1 892	2 223	3 572	3 955	4 485	4 578	4 162	3 948	..
369	Non-Metallic Products, nec	4 357	4 892	5 553	7 275	7 309	9 573	8 260	9 315	9 406	..
37	Basic Metal Industries	3 662	3 926	4 102	7 116	7 740	8 365	7 566	5 071	6 809	..
371	Iron & Steel	3 130	3 306	3 513	6 151	6 505	7 325	6 442	3 577	5 784	..
372	Non-Ferrous Metals	532	620	589	965	1 235	1 040	1 124	1 494	1 025	..
38	Fabricated Metal Products	23 792	26 016	29 856	50 143	56 516	63 940	63 807	72 194	75 227	..
381	Metal Products	5 809	6 426	7 050	7 898	8 706	9 531	10 144	12 279	11 175	..
3813	Structural Metal Products	1 042	1 106	1 158	994	1 320	1 894	2 030	5 137	3 635	..
382	Non-Electrical Machinery	3 885	4 137	4 346	6 200	6 916	7 670	7 602	6 433	6 599	..
3821	Engines & Turbines	4	5	4	..	..	..	..	0	..	..
3822	Agricultural Machinery	392	438	451	525	658	591	507	487	439	..
3823	Metal & Wood working Machinery	400	428	454	332	443	462	345	..	..	..
3824	Special Industrial Machinery	1 113	1 227	1 335	1 950	1 832	2 070	2 100	1 878	1 868	..
3825	Office & Computing Machinery	354	296	322	..	..	..	..	..	..	..
3829	Machinery & Equipment, nec	1 622	1 744	1 779	2 234	2 806	3 202	3 758	3 419	3 584	..
383	Electrical Machinery	6 709	7 250	8 156	17 813	22 088	26 493	24 659	25 822	24 903	..
3831	Electrical Industrial Machinery	1 348	1 506	1 824	4 711	4 433	7 174	4 695	2 441	2 721	..
3832	Radio, TV & Communication Equipment	3 144	3 357	3 620	7 038	10 215	12 807	10 744	12 677	11 300	..
3833	Electrical Appliances & Housewares	360	416	504	1 211	1 728	1 507	1 376	535	830	..
3839	Electrical Apparatus, nec	1 857	1 971	2 208	4 853	5 712	5 005	7 844	10 169	10 052	..
384	Transport Equipment	6 896	7 747	9 798	17 582	17 710	19 052	19 883	25 765	30 825	..
3841	Shipbuilding & Repairing	3 237	3 370	4 272	6 093	6 464	7 025	6 278	4 844	5 933	..
3842	Railroad Equipment	..	..	..	..	..	105	81	2 367	3 516	..
3843	Motor Vehicles	3 009	3 637	4 681	10 852	10 565	11 363	13 085	16 673	19 766	..
3844	Motorcycles & Bicycles	389	454	507	524	562	558	439	..	..	..
3845	Aircraft	0	0	0	..	..	0	0	0	..	..
3849	Transport Equipment, nec	0	0	0	0	0	0	0	..	..	..
385	Professional Goods	493	455	507	650	1 096	1 194	1 519	1 895	1 725	..
3851	Professional Equipment	297	257	279	..	..	731	1 022	1 167	931	..
3852	Photographic & Optical Goods	196	199	229	318	342	..	..	..	..	..
3853	Watches & Clocks	0	0	0	..	..	..	..	..	..	..
39	Other Manufacturing, nes	296	353	389	1 052	1 018	1 433	1 289	1 296	1 147	..
3901	Jewellery	..	..	..	..	..	369	292	302	288	..
3	Total Manufacturing	101 028	110 973	126 397	190 627	209 770	236 718	238 375	243 941	247 622	..
1	Agric., Hunting, Forestry, Fishing	..	..	..	..	..	..	..	..	..	..
2	Mining & Quarrying	916	1 143	1 324	3 539	3 885	4 477	4 611	3 600	3 158	..
21	Coal Mining	311	307	317	401	410	488	560	424	..	..
22	Crude Petroleum & Natural Gas	0	0	0	0	0	0	0	0	..	..
23.29	Other Mining	605	836	1 007	3 138	3 475	3 989	4 051	3 176	3 158	..
3	Total Manufacturing	101 028	110 973	126 397	190 627	209 770	236 718	238 375	243 941	247 622	..
4	Electricity, Gas & Water	8 360	9 082	7 995	25 403	28 319	32 078	29 919	29 575	28 714	..
5	Construction	24 595	..	..	23 768	27 924	30 658	33 779	37 045	36 702	..
6.9	Services	..	..	..	..	..	..	..	..	..	..
0000	Grand Total	134 899	121 197	135 716	243 337	269 898	303 931	306 684	314 161	316 196	..

Note: Break in series between 1989 and 1990, see Sources and Definitions.

Millions of Esc

(Current Prices)

ISIC2	Industry	WAGES & SALARIES + SUPPLEMENTS - EMPLOYEES									
		1987	1988	1989	1990	1991	1992	1993	1994	1995	1996
31	Food, Beverages & Tobacco	..	..	..	136 434	164 394	182 252	193 953	209 567	..	..
311.2	Food	..	..	..	104 514	125 626	139 804	147 945	161 693	..	..
313	Beverages	..	..	..	26 948	33 659	36 844	39 662	41 503	..	..
314	Tobacco	..	..	..	4 972	5 109	5 604	6 346	6 371	..	..
32	Textiles, Apparel & Leather	..	..	..	308 554	355 787	382 566	401 029	414 274	..	..
321	Textiles	..	..	..	147 871	156 873	167 049	169 913	170 810	..	..
3213	Knitting Mills	..	..	..	34 527	37 240	40 403	42 543	44 198	..	..
322	Wearing Apparel	..	..	..	106 479	132 495	143 044	148 184	156 416	..	..
323	Leather & Products	..	..	..	8 954	10 894	10 927	12 031	11 830	..	..
324	Footwear	..	..	..	45 250	55 525	61 546	70 901	75 218	..	..
33	Wood Products & Furniture	..	..	..	69 953	90 502	94 986	96 345	105 412	..	..
331	Wood Products	..	..	..	45 754	55 634	55 891	59 065	64 256	..	..
332	Furnitures & Fixtures	..	..	..	24 199	34 868	39 095	37 280	41 156	..	..
34	Paper, Paper Products & Printing	..	..	..	84 381	97 350	110 576	118 033	119 636	..	..
341	Paper & Products	..	..	..	36 090	39 555	45 122	43 496	39 993	..	..
3411	Pulp, Paper & Board	..	..	..	28 230	30 509	34 427	30 939	26 726	..	..
342	Printing & Publishing	..	..	..	48 291	57 795	65 454	74 537	79 643	..	..
35	Chemical Products	..	..	..	126 316	131 780	156 469	160 908	161 189	..	..
351	Industrial Chemicals	..	..	..	29 194	26 944	32 482	32 726	27 985	..	..
3511	Basic Industrial Chemicals	..	..	..	9 621	12 320	13 973	14 563	12 531	..	..
3512	Fertilizers & Pesticides	..	..	..	12 481	5 451	8 659	8 592	6 410	..	..
3513	Synthetic Resins	..	..	..	7 092	9 173	9 850	9 571	9 044	..	..
352	Other Chemicals	..	..	..	47 415	54 337	64 065	68 130	68 980	..	..
3521	Paints, Varnishes & Lacquers	..	..	..	8 502	9 690	10 916	12 294	11 958	..	..
3522	Drugs & Medicines	..	..	..	20 136	24 587	29 849	31 668	33 761	..	..
3523	Soap & Cleaning Preparations	..	..	..	11 436	10 787	12 179	13 489	13 636	..	..
3529	Chemical Products, nec	..	..	..	7 341	9 273	11 121	10 679	9 625	..	..
353	Petroleum Refineries	..	..	..	..	..	..	21 995	24 428	..	..
354	Petroleum & Coal Products	..	..	..	..	..	..	830	820	..	..
355	Rubber Products	..	..	..	8 935	8 280	10 590	10 120	10 659	..	..
356	Plastic Products, nec	..	..	..	19 259	22 560	25 806	27 107	28 317	..	..
36	Non-Metallic Mineral Products	..	..	..	90 251	106 745	115 674	123 113	129 249	..	..
361	Pottery, China etc	..	..	..	26 577	28 661	33 089	34 996	38 790	..	..
362	Glass & Products	..	..	..	16 105	18 963	20 385	21 171	21 209	..	..
369	Non-Metallic Products, nec	..	..	..	47 569	59 121	62 200	66 946	69 250	..	..
37	Basic Metal Industries	..	..	..	31 609	33 954	35 575	36 425	26 757	..	..
371	Iron & Steel	..	..	..	25 268	26 172	26 927	27 100	16 605	..	..
372	Non-Ferrous Metals	..	..	..	6 341	7 782	8 648	9 325	10 152	..	..
38	Fabricated Metal Products	..	..	..	279 925	335 297	365 967	392 633	423 902	..	..
381	Metal Products	..	..	..	77 766	100 611	109 088	116 342	123 549	..	..
3813	Structural Metal Products	..	..	..	10 392	14 378	19 010	23 653	35 960	..	..
382	Non-Electrical Machinery	..	..	..	53 127	62 984	66 341	72 632	76 377	..	..
3821	Engines & Turbines	..	..	..	4 072	4 524	4 844	3 431	403	..	..
3822	Agricultural Machinery	..	..	..	4 544	6 065	6 241	5 891	6 077	..	..
3823	Metal & Wood working Machinery	..	..	..	3 076	3 746	4 036	3 887	4 177	..	..
3824	Special Industrial Machinery	..	..	..	17 166	18 094	19 786	22 998	29 316	..	..
3825	Office & Computing Machinery	..	..	..	1 639	1 777	1 559	2 103	2 350	..	..
3829	Machinery & Equipment, nec	..	..	..	22 630	28 778	29 875	34 322	34 054	..	..
383	Electrical Machinery	..	..	..	74 025	92 778	103 189	109 391	112 619	..	..
3831	Electrical Industrial Machinery	..	..	..	19 095	19 779	22 521	20 970	14 712	..	..
3832	Radio, TV & Communication Equipment	..	..	..	28 068	40 086	45 019	46 332	48 990	..	..
3833	Electrical Appliances & Housewares	..	..	..	5 830	7 054	6 610	7 430	3 499	..	..
3839	Electrical Apparatus, nec	..	..	..	21 032	25 859	29 039	34 659	45 418	..	..
384	Transport Equipment	..	..	..	70 161	71 718	79 513	85 360	101 129	..	..
3841	Shipbuilding & Repairing	..	..	..	24 399	27 595	30 039	29 399	22 152	..	..
3842	Railroad Equipment	..	..	..	331	361	387	295	9 098	..	..
3843	Motor Vehicles	..	..	..	42 083	39 884	44 980	51 764	59 850	..	..
3844	Motorcycles & Bicycles	..	..	..	2 976	3 552	3 850	3 487	3 888	..	..
3845	Aircraft	..	..	..	310	256	212	360	6 048	..	..
3849	Transport Equipment, nec	..	..	..	62	70	45	55	93	..	..
385	Professional Goods	..	..	..	4 846	7 206	7 836	8 908	10 228	..	..
3851	Professional Equipment	..	..	..	2 548	4 676	5 099	5 972	6 344	..	..
3852	Photographic & Optical Goods	..	..	..	1 939	2 169	2 300	2 497	3 353	..	..
3853	Watches & Clocks	..	..	..	359	361	437	439	531	..	..
39	Other Manufacturing, nes	..	..	..	13 174	16 305	16 486	18 967	20 321	..	..
3901	Jewellery	..	..	..	3 784	5 278	5 193	5 755	6 221	..	..
3	Total Manufacturing	..	..	..	1 140 597	1 332 114	1 460 551	1 541 406	1 610 307	..	..
1	Agric., Hunting, Forestry, Fishing	..	..	..	..	..	..	..	..	..	..
2	Mining & Quarrying	..	..	..	24 359	29 496	32 403	32 961	31 346	..	..
21	Coal Mining	..	..	..	1 626	1 722	1 844	1 979	2 549	..	..
22	Crude Petroleum & Natural Gas	..	..	..	0	0	0	0	0	..	..
23.29	Other Mining	..	..	..	22 733	27 774	30 559	30 982	28 797	..	..
3	Total Manufacturing	..	..	..	1 140 597	1 332 114	1 460 551	1 541 406	1 610 307	..	..
4	Electricity, Gas & Water	..	..	..	72 614	81 618	90 989	95 295	91 199	..	..
5	Construction	..	..	..	214 330	266 767	314 302	347 331	387 182	..	..
6.9	Services	..	..	..	..	..	..	..	..	..	..
0000	Grand Total	..	..	..	1 451 900	1 709 995	1 898 245	2 016 993	2 120 034	..	..

Table PO.10 PORTUGAL

Thousands

ISIC2	Industry	HOURS WORKED									
		1987	1988	1989	1990	1991	1992	1993	1994	1995	1996
31	Food, Beverages & Tobacco	129 039	124 536	120 686	75 971	75 646	66 425	65 279	63 471	58 701	..
311.2	Food	112 225	107 641	103 667	59 928	60 037	53 116	51 621	50 338	46 742	..
313	Beverages	14 617	14 771	15 003	14 064	14 213	11 906	12 292	11 837	10 761	..
314	Tobacco	2 197	2 124	2 016	1 980	1 396	1 404	1 366	1 297	1 198	..
32	Textiles, Apparel & Leather	392 785	397 523	394 551	314 757	312 001	296 316	274 254	258 002	244 536	..
321	Textiles	248 168	246 411	235 350	181 980	167 586	151 726	137 645	123 819	116 267	..
3213	Knitting Mills	59 644	58 623	58 193	41 684	36 555	29 906	30 391	26 069	24 562	..
322	Wearing Apparel	89 565	93 382	98 541	90 551	97 963	95 442	86 625	87 923	84 195	..
323	Leather & Products	9 622	9 858	9 296	2 769	2 759	2 964	2 754	2 264	2 437	..
324	Footwear	45 430	47 872	51 364	39 457	43 693	46 183	47 229	43 995	41 637	..
33	Wood Products & Furniture	84 639	82 040	77 906	28 145	25 210	21 980	20 585	21 005	19 027	..
331	Wood Products	63 679	60 871	57 530	22 544	20 982	17 803	15 718	15 921	14 141	..
332	Furnitures & Fixtures	20 960	21 169	20 376	5 601	4 228	4 177	4 867	5 084	4 886	..
34	Paper, Paper Products & Printing	60 593	61 521	61 648	26 562	23 702	22 067	21 208	17 493	19 430	..
341	Paper & Products	28 853	28 204	26 961	15 127	13 812	13 970	13 415	10 519	11 695	..
3411	Pulp, Paper & Board	18 954	18 250	17 459	12 292	11 281	10 584	10 155	7 403	8 781	..
342	Printing & Publishing	31 740	33 317	34 687	11 436	9 890	8 096	7 792	6 974	7 736	..
35	Chemical Products	79 399	76 340	72 477	41 818	35 016	36 548	30 785	28 040	28 127	..
351	Industrial Chemicals	19 093	17 916	16 595	11 966	6 824	7 825	6 656	5 548	5 633	..
3511	Basic Industrial Chemicals	7 898	7 362	7 231	..	3 287	3 299	3 104	2 165	2 308	..
3512	Fertilizers & Pesticides	6 264	5 650	4 783	..	416	..	..	..	..	..
3513	Synthetic Resins	4 931	4 904	4 581	2 585	3 120	..	..	..	..	..
352	Other Chemicals	24 197	23 646	22 688	14 630	13 722	11 540	9 552	9 667	9 684	..
3521	Paints, Varnishes & Lacquers	3 795	3 904	3 878	1 967	2 075	1 741	1 521	1 388	1 381	..
3522	Drugs & Medicines	7 684	7 690	7 184	6 290	6 258	5 259	4 550	4 991	5 150	..
3523	Soap & Cleaning Preparations	5 906	5 886	5 619	3 796	2 963	2 139	1 651	1 510	1 501	..
3529	Chemical Products, nec	6 812	6 166	6 007	2 578	2 427	2 401	1 830	1 778	1 652	..
353	Petroleum Refineries	2 738	3 006	2 833	2 607	2 288	..	2 908	2 561	2 419	..
354	Petroleum & Coal Products	0	0	0	0	0	..	0	0	..	..
355	Rubber Products	10 557	9 882	9 415	2 892	2 613	..	3 710	3 211	3 298	..
356	Plastic Products, nec	22 814	21 890	20 946	9 723	9 569	9 364	7 959	7 053	7 092	..
36	Non-Metallic Mineral Products	88 806	88 644	84 956	49 272	47 824	44 522	42 063	41 923	41 292	..
361	Pottery, China etc	28 558	29 900	27 337	20 213	19 680	20 222	19 341	20 424	20 503	..
362	Glass & Products	14 001	13 523	13 036	10 948	10 322	8 478	7 945	7 704	8 098	..
369	Non-Metallic Products, nec	46 247	45 221	44 583	18 111	17 823	15 823	14 777	13 794	12 692	..
37	Basic Metal Industries	26 283	25 580	23 314	18 253	19 065	15 546	14 281	9 867	11 712	..
371	Iron & Steel	20 673	19 901	18 752	14 961	15 206	12 379	10 873	6 080	8 746	..
372	Non-Ferrous Metals	5 610	5 679	4 562	3 292	3 859	3 168	3 408	3 788	2 966	..
38	Fabricated Metal Products	194 476	192 429	189 427	145 303	141 813	136 227	130 955	129 808	129 864	..
381	Metal Products	57 321	56 514	53 990	32 404	33 353	31 103	28 780	25 816	24 445	..
3813	Structural Metal Products	7 012	6 319	6 095	3 172	4 151	5 065	4 991	6 297	5 374	..
382	Non-Electrical Machinery	31 700	30 340	28 186	23 321	23 532	22 204	19 351	15 611	14 339	..
3821	Engines & Turbines	43	1 539	1 215	..	..	..	..	0	..	..
3822	Agricultural Machinery	4 131	3 920	3 509	1 369	1 707	1 683	1 298	1 162	825	..
3823	Metal & Wood working Machinery	3 847	3 616	3 461	1 735	1 872	1 623	1 063	..	..	..
3824	Special Industrial Machinery	10 580	10 217	9 332	8 539	7 767	7 541	7 085	5 440	5 211	..
3825	Office & Computing Machinery	2 212	719	630	..	..	..	..	..	..	..
3829	Machinery & Equipment, nec	10 887	10 329	10 039	8 281	9 053	8 519	8 491	7 468	6 945	..
383	Electrical Machinery	44 315	42 670	43 454	38 577	41 979	44 676	47 927	46 812	47 936	..
3831	Electrical Industrial Machinery	7 192	7 589	8 080	9 459	9 555	8 718	7 253	2 194	2 445	..
3832	Radio, TV & Communication Equipment	20 003	17 851	18 379	14 723	14 121	16 242	15 314	17 286	16 216	..
3833	Electrical Appliances & Housewares	3 546	3 567	3 676	1 940	2 501	2 836	2 527	1 953	2 185	..
3839	Electrical Apparatus, nec	13 574	13 663	13 319	12 454	15 802	16 880	22 833	25 379	27 090	..
384	Transport Equipment	56 389	58 597	59 661	47 334	38 054	33 838	30 760	37 176	39 349	..
3841	Shipbuilding & Repairing	26 632	26 022	24 186	14 515	14 256	12 428	10 928	9 668	8 740	..
3842	Railroad Equipment	..	..	..	..	..	329	196	3 965	4 342	..
3843	Motor Vehicles	23 525	26 558	29 682	29 503	20 202	18 699	17 468	20 020	22 832	..
3844	Motorcycles & Bicycles	4 689	4 613	4 452	2 786	3 166	2 382	2 168	..	..	..
3845	Aircraft	0	0	0	..	..	0	0	..	..	..
3849	Transport Equipment, nec	0	0	0	0	0	0	0	0	..	..
385	Professional Goods	4 751	4 308	4 136	3 668	4 895	4 406	4 137	4 394	3 795	..
3851	Professional Equipment	2 579	901	995	..	..	2 011	1 914	1 857	1 483	..
3852	Photographic & Optical Goods	2 172	2 127	1 930	2 151	2 063	..	..	..	..	..
3853	Watches & Clocks	0	1 280	1 211	..	..	..	..	..	..	..
39	Other Manufacturing, nes	4 124	4 163	4 334	5 789	4 822	5 167	4 446	4 019	3 748	..
3901	Jewellery	..	..	..	..	..	843	675	747	711	..
3	Total Manufacturing	1 060 144	1 052 776	1 029 299	705 870	685 099	644 797	603 853	573 629	556 437	..
1	Agric., Hunting, Forestry, Fishing	..	..	..	..	..	..	..	..	..	..
2	Mining & Quarrying	20 648	22 369	22 868	11 006	10 025	9 909	8 647	6 037	5 060	..
21	Coal Mining	1 815	1 670	1 687	1 255	1 081	1 001	868	740	..	..
22	Crude Petroleum & Natural Gas	0	0	0	0	0	0	0	0	..	..
23.29	Other Mining	18 833	20 699	21 181	9 751	8 943	8 908	7 779	5 297	5 060	..
3	Total Manufacturing	1 060 144	1 052 776	1 029 299	705 870	685 099	644 797	603 853	573 629	556 437	..
4	Electricity, Gas & Water	27 027	27 277	19 569	22 617	18 447	18 041	18 289	16 241	15 370	..
5	Construction	351 444	..	..	109 493	97 258	99 414	101 349	103 938	90 357	..
6.9	Services	..	..	..	..	..	..	..	..	..	..
0000	Grand Total	1 459 263	1 102 422	1 071 736	848 986	810 829	772 161	732 139	699 845	667 224	..

Note: Break in series between 1989 and 1990, see Sources and Definitions.

Table PO.11 **PORTUGAL**

ISIC2	Industry	ENTERPRISES									
		1987	1988	1989	1990	1991	1992	1993	1994	1995	1996
31	Food, Beverages & Tobacco	..	..	..	8 085	7 965	7 487	7 548	8 132	7 686	..
311.2	Food	..	..	..	7 343	7 139	6 830	6 773	7 475	6 956	
313	Beverages	..	..	..	737	822	653	770	652	726	..
314	Tobacco	..	..	..	5	4	4	5	5	4	..
32	Textiles, Apparel & Leather	..	..	..	15 134	15 578	15 309	15 632	15 391	14 702	
321	Textiles	..	..	..	4 300	4 010	4 056	4 241	3 945	4 027	
3213	Knitting Mills	..	..	..	1 706	1 464	1 414	1 662	1 275	1 477	
322	Wearing Apparel	..	..	..	8 273	8 805	8 405	8 471	8 481	7 929	
323	Leather & Products	..	..	..	819	834	746	786	802	807	
324	Footwear	..	..	..	1 742	1 929	2 102	2 134	2 163	1 939	
33	Wood Products & Furniture	..	..	..	14 367	14 237	13 905	14 104	14 192	14 169	
331	Wood Products	..	..	..	7 783	7 426	7 345	7 654	7 477	7 571	
332	Furnitures & Fixtures	..	..	..	6 584	6 811	6 560	6 450	6 715	6 598	
34	Paper, Paper Products & Printing	..	..	..	2 856	2 978	2 968	3 365	3 412	3 401	
341	Paper & Products	..	..	..	423	424	419	442	452	448	
3411	Pulp, Paper & Board	..	..	..	91	97	100	101	84	78	
342	Printing & Publishing	..	..	..	2 433	2 554	2 549	2 923	2 960	2 953	
35	Chemical Products	..	..	..	1 902	1 860	1 863	1 979	2 043	1 967	
351	Industrial Chemicals	..	..	..	174	190	185	208	201	196	
3511	Basic Industrial Chemicals	..	..	..	79	86	87	96	94	94	
3512	Fertilizers & Pesticides	..	..	..	23	30	28	21	19	15	
3513	Synthetic Resins	..	..	..	72	74	70	91	88	87	
352	Other Chemicals	..	..	..	712	693	729	707	701	692	
3521	Paints, Varnishes & Lacquers	..	..	..	120	119	126	140	135	134	
3522	Drugs & Medicines	..	..	..	103	106	111	121	125	121	
3523	Soap & Cleaning Preparations	..	..	..	159	146	151	154	168	159	
3529	Chemical Products, nec	..	..	..	330	322	341	292	273	278	
353	Petroleum Refineries	..	..	..	2	2	2	1	1	1	
354	Petroleum & Coal Products	..	..	..	32	26	23	25	23	18	
355	Rubber Products	..	..	..	267	250	252	243	243	233	
356	Plastic Products, nec	..	..	..	715	699	672	795	874	827	
36	Non-Metallic Mineral Products	..	..	..	4 252	4 203	3 917	4 063	4 104	4 009	
361	Pottery, China etc	..	..	..	957	941	977	954	973	1 026	
362	Glass & Products	..	..	..	484	430	484	504	461	467	
369	Non-Metallic Products, nec	..	..	..	2 811	2 832	2 456	2 605	2 670	2 516	
37	Basic Metal Industries	..	..	..	570	575	604	693	663	607	
371	Iron & Steel	..	..	..	254	267	258	335	295	285	
372	Non-Ferrous Metals	..	..	..	316	308	346	358	368	322	
38	Fabricated Metal Products	..	..	..	16 152	16 083	16 448	16 631	17 018	16 551	
381	Metal Products	..	..	..	11 597	11 485	11 742	11 473	11 521	11 271	
3813	Structural Metal Products	..	..	..	835	845	859	2 649	2 952	3 333	
382	Non-Electrical Machinery	..	..	..	2 407	2 373	2 515	2 795	2 945	2 813	
3821	Engines & Turbines	..	..	..	27	36	36	50	51	50	
3822	Agricultural Machinery	..	..	..	364	361	406	420	419	435	
3823	Metal & Wood working Machinery	..	..	..	91	94	92	117	116	110	
3824	Special Industrial Machinery	..	..	..	538	530	569	890	1 024	950	
3825	Office & Computing Machinery	..	..	..	107	102	88	125	173	171	
3829	Machinery & Equipment, nec	..	..	..	1 280	1 250	1 324	1 193	1 162	1 097	
383	Electrical Machinery	..	..	..	1 173	1 170	1 104	1 227	1 312	1 187	
3831	Electrical Industrial Machinery	..	..	..	401	361	366	396	403	380	
3832	Radio, TV & Communication Equipment	..	..	..	313	327	307	356	392	312	
3833	Electrical Appliances & Housewares	..	..	..	71	81	82	89	80	71	
3839	Electrical Apparatus, nec	..	..	..	388	401	349	386	437	424	
384	Transport Equipment	..	..	..	749	749	772	800	831	862	
3841	Shipbuilding & Repairing	..	..	..	257	262	303	295	267	314	
3842	Railroad Equipment	..	..	..	1	1	1	1	4	4	
3843	Motor Vehicles	..	..	..	419	407	389	418	464	461	
3844	Motorcycles & Bicycles	..	..	..	51	58	56	56	63	54	
3845	Aircraft	..	..	..	10	11	12	15	16	14	
3849	Transport Equipment, nec	..	..	..	11	10	11	15	17	15	
385	Professional Goods	..	..	..	226	306	315	336	409	418	
3851	Professional Equipment	..	..	..	175	251	260	276	345	359	
3852	Photographic & Optical Goods	..	..	..	23	28	28	28	35	34	
3853	Watches & Clocks	..	..	..	28	27	27	32	29	25	
39	Other Manufacturing, nes	..	..	..	2 109	2 053	1 966	1 979	1 988	2 009	
3901	Jewellery	..	..	..	910	899	897	1 026	914	972	
3	Total Manufacturing	..	..	..	65 427	65 532	64 467	65 994	66 943	65 101	..
1	Agric., Hunting, Forestry, Fishing	..	..	..	..	..			..		..
2	Mining & Quarrying	..	..	..	1 388	1 410	1 309	1 622	1 412	1 255	..
21	Coal Mining	..	..	..	8	6	7	12	10	10	..
22	Crude Petroleum & Natural Gas	..	..	..	0	0	0	0	0		
23.29	Other Mining	..	..	..	1 380	1 404	1 302	1 610	1 402	1 245	
3	Total Manufacturing	..	..	..	65 427	65 532	64 467	65 994	66 943	65 101	
4	Electricity, Gas & Water	..	..	..	55	70	72	99	131	125	
5	Construction	..	..	..	21 687	22 841	23 947	28 409	31 406	30 404	
6.9	Services	..	..	..	..	..	..				..
0000	Grand Total	..	..	..	88 557	89 853	89 795	96 124	99 892	96 885	..

Billions of TL (Current Prices)

ISIC2	Industry	PRODUCTION									
		1987	1988	1989	1990	1991	1992	1993	1994	1995	1996
31	Food, Beverages & Tobacco	6 335	11 408	20 547	32 538	60 478	112 069	198 092	393 526	..	..
311.2	Food	4 634	8 163	14 930	23 188	41 860	82 395	144 151	302 081	..	..
313	Beverages	595	1 141	2 190	3 833	7 691	12 552	23 053	42 489	..	..
314	Tobacco	1 106	2 105	3 427	5 516	10 928	17 121	30 888	48 956	..	..
32	Textiles, Apparel & Leather	6 230	10 890	19 264	29 579	47 367	100 935	172 218	441 247	..	..
321	Textiles	4 768	7 990	13 683	20 594	32 427	67 059	114 251	300 162	..	..
3213	Knitting Mills	428	750	1 232	2 078	3 824	11 151	22 183	58 619	..	..
322	Wearing Apparel	1 182	2 566	4 878	7 856	13 219	30 177	51 695	125 698	..	..
323	Leather & Products	170	186	420	567	710	1 812	2 941	9 384	..	..
324	Footwear	110	149	284	562	1 011	1 887	3 332	6 002	..	..
33	Wood Products & Furniture	484	807	1 216	2 064	3 197	7 847	14 832	23 485	..	..
331	Wood Products	384	626	925	1 562	2 440	5 751	10 525	15 881	..	..
332	Furniture & Fixtures	101	182	291	502	756	2 096	4 307	7 604	..	..
34	Paper, Paper Products & Printing	1 245	2 049	3 535	5 755	9 311	18 306	40 216	82 657	..	..
341	Paper & Products	853	1 296	2 348	3 522	5 343	9 591	17 910	43 178	..	..
3411	Pulp, Paper & Board	522	654	1 465	1 924	3 072	6 282	10 780	24 604	..	..
342	Printing & Publishing	392	754	1 187	2 232	3 969	8 715	22 306	39 479	..	..
35	Chemical Products	11 188	20 250	34 537	53 870	80 873	141 110	231 119	510 104	..	..
351	Industrial Chemicals	2 671	5 399	7 244	9 518	14 694	26 064	41 866	96 925	..	..
3511	Basic Industrial Chemicals	441	506	1 046	1 159	1 652	11 390	5 510	8 470	..	..
3512	Fertilizers & Pesticides	948	1 668	2 197	3 582	6 082	8 508	18 929	31 104	..	..
3513	Synthetic Resins	1 282	3 226	4 001	4 777	6 960	6 165	17 428	57 351	..	..
352	Other Chemicals	1 624	2 889	5 888	8 666	14 649	26 374	50 008	111 185	..	..
3521	Paints, Varnishes & Lacquers	394	562	988	1 537	2 426	3 848	7 641	18 826	..	..
3522	Drugs & Medicines	699	1 246	2 597	4 081	7 161	11 783	23 001	47 358	..	..
3523	Soap & Cleaning Preparations	367	712	1 566	1 977	3 397	7 330	12 917	28 123	..	..
3529	Chemical Products, nec	165	369	737	1 070	1 665	3 413	6 449	16 877	..	..
353	Petroleum Refineries	4 397	7 499	13 513	23 676	34 743	59 344	95 285	204 529	..	..
354	Petroleum & Coal Products	1 454	2 410	4 842	7 102	8 350	12 170	13 536	27 571	..	..
355	Rubber Products	559	1 132	1 703	2 371	4 378	8 777	14 827	33 005	..	..
356	Plastic Products, nec	483	922	1 347	2 538	4 058	8 380	15 597	36 889	..	..
36	Non-Metallic Mineral Products	2 237	3 904	6 304	10 669	16 344	31 023	57 527	119 651	..	..
361	Pottery, China etc	354	590	781	1 835	2 953	4 404	8 585	22 340	..	..
362	Glass & Products	476	846	1 474	2 405	3 304	6 448	10 882	22 348	..	..
369	Non-Metallic Products, nec	1 407	2 469	4 050	6 428	10 087	20 171	38 059	74 963	..	..
37	Basic Metal Industries	4 454	8 669	15 229	19 325	29 303	50 503	101 097	239 195	..	..
371	Iron & Steel	3 559	6 962	12 198	15 264	24 593	42 234	86 661	207 373	..	..
372	Non-Ferrous Metals	895	1 707	3 031	4 061	4 711	8 269	14 435	31 822	..	..
38	Fabricated Metal Products	6 964	12 069	18 654	36 136	65 047	126 293	243 832	399 133	..	..
381	Metal Products	1 160	1 933	3 196	5 314	8 874	18 637	32 451	61 398	..	..
3813	Structural Metal Products	211	319	517	1 025	1 672	3 238	7 060	13 221	..	..
382	Non-Electrical Machinery	1 794	3 065	4 328	8 668	15 083	27 583	50 908	95 428	..	..
3821	Engines & Turbines	73	118	155	291	229	499	937	1 524	..	..
3822	Agricultural Machinery	418	716	756	1 602	1 979	3 405	7 103	10 670	..	..
3823	Metal & Wood working Machinery	82	109	162	295	395	979	1 300	2 851	..	..
3824	Special Industrial Machinery	467	262	400	646	1 146	2 133	4 311	8 902	..	..
3825	Office & Computing Machinery	80	12	25	73	100	287	659	1 054	..	..
3829	Machinery & Equipment, nec	675	1 848	2 829	5 761	11 234	20 281	36 596	70 428	..	..
383	Electrical Machinery	1 942	3 090	4 689	9 272	17 743	31 067	54 548	97 196	..	..
3831	Electrical Industrial Machinery	342	554	947	1 630	3 327	5 049	9 744	17 645	..	..
3832	Radio, TV & Communication Equipment	1 058	1 527	2 161	4 687	9 429	16 718	28 926	44 372	..	..
3833	Electrical Appliances & Housewares	42	134	224	679	950	2 417	4 206	7 050	..	..
3839	Electrical Apparatus, nec	500	875	1 357	2 276	4 037	6 884	11 672	28 129	..	..
384	Transport Equipment	2 039	3 861	6 192	12 442	22 562	46 729	101 718	137 079	..	..
3841	Shipbuilding & Repairing	58	89	211	363	643	1 101	1 754	3 442	..	..
3842	Railroad Equipment	73	92	148			1 187	1 808	3 476	..	..
3843	Motor Vehicles	1 874	3 541	5 570	11 471	20 413	42 884	95 039	124 839	..	..
3844	Motorcycles & Bicycles	..	62	..	152	328	808	1 481	2 387	..	..
3845	Aircraft		76	181	..	..	743	1 620	2 896	..	..
3849	Transport Equipment, nec			..			4	18	39	..	..
385	Professional Goods	29	121	249	441	785	2 276	4 207	8 032	..	..
3851	Professional Equipment	13	78	163	270	431	1 083	1 984	3 362	..	..
3852	Photographic & Optical Goods	6	9	..	49	195	179	320	416	..	..
3853	Watches & Clocks	3		..	..	..	8	105	78	..	..
39	Other Manufacturing, nes	81	137	261	411	658	1 296	2 286	4 943	..	..
3901	Jewellery	7	14	22		66	197	347	1 076	..	..
3	Total Manufacturing	39 217	70 184	119 547	190 346	312 579	589 382	1 061 219	2 213 940	..	..
1	Agric., Hunting, Forestry, Fishing	..	..	..	..	..	..	..	..	..	..
2	Mining & Quarrying	1 270	2 138	4 131	6 365	..	..	..	..	..	..
21	Coal Mining	603	861	1 990	2 840	..	..	..	..	..	..
22	Crude Petroleum & Natural Gas	279	358	805	1 854	..	..	..	..	..	..
23.29	Other Mining	388	919	1 336	1 671	..	..	..	..	..	..
3	Total Manufacturing	39 217	70 184	119 547	190 346	312 579	589 382	1 061 219	2 213 940	..	..
4	Electricity, Gas & Water	233	430	872	2 080	..	..	..	..	..	..
5	Construction	2 421	5 132	9 762	14 425	27 305	..	..	..	..	..
6.9	Services	..	..	..	..	..	..	..	..	..	..
0000	Grand Total	..	..	..	..	..	..	..	..	..	..

Note: Break in series between 1991 and 1992, see Sources and Definitions.
Some data are not given for reasons of confidentiality.
ISIC 385 includes a figure for other professional goods (Turkish SIC 3854).

Table TU.2 **TURKEY**

ISIC2	Industry	VALUE ADDED									
		1987	1988	1989	1990	1991	1992	1993	1994	1995	1996
31	**Food, Beverages & Tobacco**	2 347	4 322	7 390	12 017	24 741	43 300	76 584	136 209	..	..
311.2	Food	1 191	2 209	4 245	6 639	13 716	26 741	47 638	91 679	..	..
313	Beverages	387	705	1 324	2 330	4 698	7 441	13 361	23 857	..	..
314	Tobacco	769	1 407	1 822	3 048	6 327	9 119	15 585	20 672	..	..
32	**Textiles, Apparel & Leather**	2 199	3 897	6 597	11 211	18 741	38 583	66 261	159 673	..	..
321	Textiles	1 776	3 029	4 922	8 405	13 809	27 571	46 584	115 248	..	..
3213	Knitting Mills	131	260	416	754	1 363	3 828	8 648	17 876	..	..
322	Wearing Apparel	345	774	1 434	2 471	4 313	9 734	17 395	39 359	..	..
323	Leather & Products	47	44	139	156	222	513	991	2 811	..	..
324	Footwear	30	51	103	180	397	766	1 291	2 255	..	..
33	**Wood Products & Furniture**	168	278	421	700	1 128	2 913	5 547	7 934	..	..
331	Wood Products	132	193	301	489	755	1 998	3 666	4 422	..	..
332	Furnitures & Fixtures	36	85	121	211	373	915	1 882	3 512	..	..
34	**Paper, Paper Products & Printing**	433	806	1 387	2 592	4 126	7 383	16 795	35 888	..	..
341	Paper & Products	267	484	901	1 458	2 322	3 126	6 675	17 753	..	..
3411	Pulp, Paper & Board	168	254	601	816	1 467	1 934	4 355	10 228	..	..
342	Printing & Publishing	166	323	486	1 133	1 804	4 257	10 120	18 135	..	..
35	**Chemical Products**	3 495	7 581	13 046	22 521	36 509	69 174	116 421	246 865	..	..
351	Industrial Chemicals	949	2 326	2 714	3 707	5 516	10 768	16 288	46 108	..	..
3511	Basic Industrial Chemicals	172	199	346	502	812	4 336	2 771	4 635	..	..
3512	Fertilizers & Pesticides	192	541	614	1 077	2 387	3 037	6 419	9 797	..	..
3513	Synthetic Resins	586	1 586	1 755	2 129	2 317	3 395	7 098	31 676	..	..
352	Other Chemicals	612	1 106	2 281	3 779	6 734	12 830	26 399	54 855	..	..
3521	Paints, Varnishes & Lacquers	135	155	241	511	759	1 527	3 257	8 500	..	..
3522	Drugs & Medicines	276	515	1 081	1 931	3 760	6 333	13 298	26 915	..	..
3523	Soap & Cleaning Preparations	136	292	626	880	1 451	3 476	6 947	12 706	..	..
3529	Chemical Products, nec	65	144	333	457	763	1 494	2 896	6 734	..	..
353	Petroleum Refineries	1 374	3 101	6 372	11 805	19 048	35 054	55 211	105 305	..	..
354	Petroleum & Coal Products	212	339	522	1 194	1 519	2 915	4 688	9 704	..	..
355	Rubber Products	203	457	765	1 179	2 209	4 692	7 874	17 341	..	..
356	Plastic Products, nec	145	252	393	856	1 484	2 915	5 960	13 551	..	..
36	**Non-Metallic Mineral Products**	1 181	2 036	3 285	6 161	9 127	17 827	34 754	70 335	..	..
361	Pottery, China etc	254	346	495	1 217	1 962	3 030	5 680	15 363	..	..
362	Glass & Products	274	483	839	1 384	1 780	3 850	6 740	13 396	..	..
369	Non-Metallic Products, nec	652	1 207	1 951	3 560	5 386	10 947	22 334	41 576	..	..
37	**Basic Metal Industries**	1 317	2 778	4 860	5 174	9 237	15 520	33 413	85 386	..	..
371	Iron & Steel	1 023	2 208	3 726	3 660	7 478	12 569	28 696	74 945	..	..
372	Non-Ferrous Metals	294	571	1 134	1 514	1 759	2 951	4 716	10 441	..	..
38	**Fabricated Metal Products**	2 620	4 674	7 407	14 707	26 732	52 568	101 518	176 589	..	..
381	Metal Products	478	824	1 361	2 357	4 031	8 022	14 085	27 036	..	..
3813	Structural Metal Products	75	113	213	462	713	1 320	2 697	4 913	..	..
382	Non-Electrical Machinery	604	1 168	1 842	3 711	5 792	11 704	20 020	43 959	..	..
3821	Engines & Turbines	30	58	77	140	117	244	366	567	..	..
3822	Agricultural Machinery	87	195	197	563	578	1 181	1 902	3 220	..	..
3823	Metal & Wood working Machinery	36	47	80	147	220	491	617	1 449	..	..
3824	Special Industrial Machinery	148	106	133	289	531	927	1 853	4 361	..	..
3825	Office & Computing Machinery	26	5	11	35	42	98	220	225	..	..
3829	Machinery & Equipment, nec	277	759	1 345	2 537	4 304	8 763	15 063	34 137	..	..
383	Electrical Machinery	830	1 234	1 876	3 866	7 648	13 833	25 412	45 686	..	..
3831	Electrical Industrial Machinery	142	255	398	772	1 671	2 491	4 679	8 007	..	..
3832	Radio, TV & Communication Equipment	501	628	921	1 957	4 236	7 730	14 346	23 834	..	..
3833	Electrical Appliances & Housewares	11	43	87	345	297	909	1 529	2 682	..	..
3839	Electrical Apparatus, nec	177	309	470	792	1 443	2 704	4 858	11 163	..	..
384	Transport Equipment	697	1 391	2 204	4 546	8 870	17 826	39 948	56 339	..	..
3841	Shipbuilding & Repairing	37	52	120	194	402	819	1 343	2 515	..	..
3842	Railroad Equipment	18	47	50			895	1 386	2 265	..	..
3843	Motor Vehicles	631	1 240	1 913	4 034	7 632	15 219	35 497	48 434	..	..
3844	Motorcycles & Bicycles	..	23		68	168	379	659	919	..	..
3845	Aircraft	..	29	81			514	1 055	2 190	..	..
3849	Transport Equipment, nec	..					1	8	16	..	..
385	Professional Goods	11	58	123	226	392	1 182	2 053	3 570	..	..
3851	Professional Equipment	4	38	78	141	235	541	914	1 887	..	..
3852	Photographic & Optical Goods	3	4	..	27	95	87	160	261	..	..
3853	Watches & Clocks	1					2	32	15	..	..
39	**Other Manufacturing, nes**	32	52	122	218	314	664	1 020	2 397	..	..
3901	Jewellery	3	6	10	..	32	102	182	509	..	..
3	**Total Manufacturing**	13 790	26 424	44 515	75 301	130 654	247 932	452 313	921 275	..	..
1	**Agric., Hunting, Forestry, Fishing**	..	..	..	..	..				..	..
2	**Mining & Quarrying**	1 030	1 741	3 791	5 418	8 930	..	..	..	..	..
21	Coal Mining	471	646	1 753	1 923	3 695	..	..	..	..	..
22	Crude Petroleum & Natural Gas	246	317	751	1 842	3 062	..	..	..	..	..
23.29	Other Mining	313	778	1 287	1 653	2 173	..	..	..	..	..
3	**Total Manufacturing**	13 790	26 424	44 515	75 301	130 654	247 932	452 313	921 275	..	..
4	**Electricity, Gas & Water**	149	290	543	1 791	3 382	..	..	..	..	..
5	**Construction**	..	..	..	..	..	..	..	..	..	..
6.9	**Services**	..	..	..	..	..	..	..	..	..	..
0000	**Grand Total**	..	..	..	..	..	..	..	..	..	..

Note: Break in series between 1991 and 1992, see Sources and Definitions.
Some data are not given for reasons of confidentiality.
ISIC 385 includes a figure for other professional goods (Turkish SIC 3854).

Thousands

ISIC2	Industry	EMPLOYMENT									
		1987	1988	1989	1990	1991	1992	1993	1994	1995	1996
31	**Food, Beverages & Tobacco**	175.0	175.0	183.0	175.5	171.6	184.8	177.6	168.9	..	..
311.2	Food	128.0	128.0	134.0	129.5	124.5	140.6	134.7	130.9	..	..
313	Beverages	12.0	13.0	14.0	13.9	14.8	13.9	13.7	11.5	..	..
314	Tobacco	35.0	34.0	35.0	32.1	32.3	30.3	29.3	26.5	..	..
32	**Textiles, Apparel & Leather**	242.0	265.0	280.0	283.8	251.3	288.8	292.2	289.1	..	..
321	Textiles	186.0	194.0	198.0	198.1	172.0	188.1	189.6	186.5	..	..
3213	Knitting Mills	16.0	16.0	18.0	18.9	18.8	27.1	33.8	31.4	..	..
322	Wearing Apparel	44.0	62.0	72.0	74.4	69.1	87.2	89.5	89.9	..	..
323	Leather & Products	5.0	4.0	5.0	5.1	4.3	6.0	5.7	6.7	..	..
324	Footwear	6.0	5.0	6.0	6.2	6.0	7.4	7.5	6.0	..	..
33	**Wood Products & Furniture**	19.0	19.0	18.0	18.0	16.2	22.6	22.5	20.9	..	..
331	Wood Products	13.0	14.0	14.0	13.7	12.2	15.4	14.4	13.5	..	..
332	Furnitures & Fixtures	5.0	5.0	5.0	4.4	4.0	7.2	8.2	7.4	..	..
34	**Paper, Paper Products & Printing**	34.0	35.0	34.0	35.2	32.9	35.0	34.5	33.8	..	..
341	Paper & Products	22.0	21.0	21.0	21.6	20.9	20.3	19.6	19.5	..	..
3411	Pulp, Paper & Board	14.0	13.0	13.0	13.3	13.4	14.0	13.4	12.7	..	..
342	Printing & Publishing	12.0	14.0	13.0	13.6	12.0	14.8	14.9	14.2	..	..
35	**Chemical Products**	91.0	92.0	94.0	96.8	89.9	94.8	93.7	90.2	..	..
351	Industrial Chemicals	33.0	31.0	31.0	31.2	28.7	28.1	25.8	24.5	..	..
3511	Basic Industrial Chemicals	9.0	7.0	8.0	7.5	6.2	16.4	5.1	4.3	..	..
3512	Fertilizers & Pesticides	10.0	9.0	9.0	9.5	9.0	5.4	8.1	7.5	..	..
3513	Synthetic Resins	15.0	14.0	14.0	14.1	13.5	6.3	12.6	12.8	..	..
352	Other Chemicals	26.0	26.0	27.0	27.5	26.4	27.0	27.4	25.9	..	..
3521	Paints, Varnishes & Lacquers	5.0	4.0	4.0	4.3	3.8	3.9	3.8	3.9	..	..
3522	Drugs & Medicines	11.0	12.0	13.0	12.5	12.2	12.2	12.6	11.6	..	..
3523	Soap & Cleaning Preparations	5.0	5.0	6.0	5.8	5.6	5.8	5.6	5.0	..	..
3529	Chemical Products, nec	4.0	5.0	4.0	5.0	4.8	5.2	5.3	5.4	..	..
353	Petroleum Refineries	5.0	5.0	5.0	5.0	4.9	4.9	5.1	5.1	..	..
354	Petroleum & Coal Products	4.0	4.0	5.0	5.0	5.2	4.3	4.1	4.8	..	..
355	Rubber Products	12.0	14.0	13.0	12.9	11.0	13.0	13.6	12.8	..	..
356	Plastic Products, nec	11.0	13.0	13.0	15.2	13.7	17.5	17.7	17.1	..	..
36	**Non-Metallic Mineral Products**	74.0	79.0	79.0	74.2	66.2	70.3	66.0	65.0	..	..
361	Pottery, China etc	12.0	13.0	10.0	13.2	10.9	9.9	10.5	11.3	..	..
362	Glass & Products	14.0	15.0	15.0	15.1	13.3	12.1	10.8	10.4	..	..
369	Non-Metallic Products, nec	48.0	51.0	53.0	45.9	42.1	48.4	44.7	43.3	..	..
37	**Basic Metal Industries**	80.0	84.0	83.0	82.4	73.8	71.0	69.3	63.3	..	..
371	Iron & Steel	59.0	63.0	62.0	62.3	58.1	56.1	55.4	51.1	..	..
372	Non-Ferrous Metals	22.0	22.0	22.0	20.1	15.7	14.9	13.9	12.2	..	..
38	**Fabricated Metal Products**	195.0	202.0	191.0	205.8	194.4	212.4	218.0	200.0	..	..
381	Metal Products	40.0	41.0	38.0	40.5	36.5	43.0	44.3	41.0	..	..
3813	Structural Metal Products	7.0	7.0	7.0	7.9	7.4	9.5	10.6	9.9	..	..
382	Non-Electrical Machinery	55.0	54.0	51.0	51.4	45.3	50.2	50.7	48.4	..	..
3821	Engines & Turbines	2.0	2.0	2.0	1.9	1.7	1.6	1.3	0.9	..	..
3822	Agricultural Machinery	10.0	10.0	9.0	9.2	8.7	9.2	8.4	7.9	..	..
3823	Metal & Wood working Machinery	5.0	4.0	4.0	4.0	3.4	4.8	3.4	3.4	..	..
3824	Special Industrial Machinery	14.0	9.0	8.0	7.7	6.7	8.0	8.3	8.2	..	..
3825	Office & Computing Machinery	2.0	0.0	0.0	0.4	0.3	0.5	0.5	0.7	..	..
3829	Machinery & Equipment, nec	22.0	28.0	28.0	28.3	24.6	26.2	28.8	27.2	..	..
383	Electrical Machinery	42.0	43.0	40.0	46.1	43.6	45.9	44.5	39.8	..	..
3831	Electrical Industrial Machinery	12.0	11.0	10.0	12.4	10.4	8.9	10.7	9.8	..	..
3832	Radio, TV & Communication Equipment	15.0	16.0	16.0	18.1	17.9	20.1	18.4	15.3	..	..
3833	Electrical Appliances & Housewares	2.0	2.0	2.0	2.9	3.3	4.9	4.5	3.7	..	..
3839	Electrical Apparatus, nec	13.0	13.0	12.0	12.7	11.9	12.1	11.0	11.0	..	..
384	Transport Equipment	56.0	60.0	58.0	63.3	64.4	68.0	73.0	65.9	..	..
3841	Shipbuilding & Repairing	5.0	5.0	5.0	5.6	5.2	5.2	4.6	4.2	..	..
3842	Railroad Equipment	10.0	10.0	9.0	..		7.5	6.6	6.7	..	..
3843	Motor Vehicles	40.0	42.0	40.0	45.8	47.4	50.9	56.9	50.6	..	..
3844	Motorcycles & Bicycles	..	1.0	..	0.9	1.0	1.7	2.1	1.7	..	..
3845	Aircraft	..	2.0	2.0	..	..	2.7	2.8	2.7	..	..
3849	Transport Equipment, nec	..	..	..	..	..	0.0	0.1	0.1	..	..
385	Professional Goods	2.0	4.0	4.0	4.5	4.7	5.1	5.4	5.0	..	..
3851	Professional Equipment	1.0	3.0	3.0	3.0	2.9	3.2	3.2	2.8	..	..
3852	Photographic & Optical Goods	0.0	0.0	..	0.6	0.7	0.5	0.6	0.5	..	..
3853	Watches & Clocks	0.0	..				0.0	0.2	0.1	..	..
39	**Other Manufacturing, nes**	5.0	5.0	5.0	4.7	4.3	5.2	5.7	5.6	..	..
3901	Jewellery	1.0	1.0	0.0	..	0.6	1.2	1.4	1.6	..	..
3	**Total Manufacturing**	914.0	955.0	968.0	976.4	900.6	984.9	979.5	936.9	..	..
1	**Agric., Hunting, Forestry, Fishing**	..	..	..	..	..	..	..	..	..	..
2	**Mining & Quarrying**	113.0	110.0	114.0	100.0	89.0	..	..	..	..	..
21	Coal Mining	83.0	80.0	81.0	73.0	66.0	..	..	..	..	..
22	Crude Petroleum & Natural Gas	1.0	1.0	1.0	1.0	1.0	..	..	..	..	..
23.29	Other Mining	..	..	..	..	..	..	..	..	..	..
3	**Total Manufacturing**	914.0	955.0	968.0	976.4	900.6	984.9	979.5	936.9	..	..
4	**Electricity, Gas & Water**	27.0	29.0	32.0	37.0	37.0	..	..	..	..	..
5	**Construction**	..	..	..	..	..	..	..	..	..	..
6.9	**Services**	..	..	..	..	..	..	..	..	..	..
0000	**Grand Total**	..	..	..	..	..	..	..	..	..	..

Note: Break in series between 1991 and 1992, see Sources and Definitions.
Some data are not given for reasons of confidentiality.
ISIC 385 includes a figure for other professional goods (Turkish SIC 3854).

Thousands

ISIC2	Industry	EMPLOYMENT - EMPLOYEES								
		1987	1988	1989	1990	1991	1992	1993	1994	1995	1996
31	**Food, Beverages & Tobacco**	..	..	..	175.3	171.4	183.1	176.3	167.8	..	..
311.2	Food	..	..	..	129.2	124.3	138.9	133.4	129.8	..	..
313	Beverages	..	..	..	13.9	14.8	13.9	13.6	11.5	..	..
314	Tobacco	..	..	..	32.1	32.3	30.3	29.3	26.5	..	..
32	**Textiles, Apparel & Leather**	..	..	..	283.5	251.0	287.4	291.1	288.4	..	..
321	Textiles	..	..	..	198.0	171.8	187.5	189.1	186.1	..	..
3213	Knitting Mills	..	..	..	18.9	18.7	27.0	33.7	31.4	..	..
322	Wearing Apparel	..	..	..	74.3	69.0	86.6	89.0	89.6	..	..
323	Leather & Products	..	..	..	5.1	4.3	5.9	5.6	6.7	..	..
324	Footwear	..	..	..	6.1	5.9	7.3	7.5	6.0	..	..
33	**Wood Products & Furniture**	..	..	..	18.0	16.2	22.2	22.2	20.7	..	..
331	Wood Products	..	..	..	13.6	12.2	15.1	14.1	13.4	..	..
332	Furnitures & Fixtures	..	..	..	4.3	4.0	7.0	8.0	7.3	..	..
34	**Paper, Paper Products & Printing**	..	..	..	35.2	32.9	34.9	34.4	33.7	..	..
341	Paper & Products	..	..	..	21.6	20.9	20.2	19.6	19.5	..	..
3411	Pulp, Paper & Board	..	..	..	13.3	13.4	13.9	13.4	12.7	..	..
342	Printing & Publishing	..	..	..	13.6	12.0	14.7	14.8	14.2	..	..
35	**Chemical Products**	..	..	..	96.7	89.9	94.5	93.4	89.9	..	..
351	Industrial Chemicals	..	..	..	31.2	28.7	28.1	25.8	24.5	..	..
3511	Basic Industrial Chemicals	..	..	..	7.5	6.2	16.4	5.1	4.3	..	..
3512	Fertilizers & Pesticides	..	..	..	9.5	9.0	5.4	8.1	7.5	..	..
3513	Synthetic Resins	..	..	..	14.1	13.5	6.3	12.6	12.8	..	..
352	Other Chemicals	..	..	..	27.5	26.4	27.0	27.3	25.9	..	..
3521	Paints, Varnishes & Lacquers	..	..	..	4.3	3.8	3.8	3.8	3.9	..	..
3522	Drugs & Medicines	..	..	..	12.5	12.2	12.2	12.6	11.6	..	..
3523	Soap & Cleaning Preparations	..	..	..	5.8	5.6	5.8	5.5	5.0	..	..
3529	Chemical Products, nec	..	..	..	5.0	4.8	5.2	5.3	5.4	..	..
353	Petroleum Refineries	..	..	..	5.0	4.9	4.9	5.1	5.1	..	..
354	Petroleum & Coal Products	..	..	..	5.0	5.2	4.3	4.1	4.8	..	..
355	Rubber Products	..	..	..	12.9	10.9	12.9	13.5	12.8	..	..
356	Plastic Products, nec	..	..	..	15.1	13.7	17.3	17.6	16.9	..	..
36	**Non-Metallic Mineral Products**	..	..	..	74.0	66.0	69.9	65.5	64.7	..	..
361	Pottery, China etc	..	..	..	13.2	10.9	9.9	10.5	11.3	..	..
362	Glass & Products	..	..	..	15.1	13.2	12.0	10.7	10.4	..	..
369	Non-Metallic Products, nec	..	..	..	45.7	41.9	48.0	44.3	43.0	..	..
37	**Basic Metal Industries**	..	..	..	82.4	73.7	70.9	69.1	63.2	..	..
371	Iron & Steel	..	..	..	62.3	58.1	56.0	55.3	51.1	..	..
372	Non-Ferrous Metals	..	..	..	20.1	15.6	14.8	13.8	12.2	..	..
38	**Fabricated Metal Products**	..	..	..	205.6	194.2	211.1	216.8	199.0	..	..
381	Metal Products	..	..	..	40.4	36.4	42.6	43.8	40.6	..	..
3813	Structural Metal Products	..	..	..	7.9	7.3	9.4	10.5	9.8	..	..
382	Non-Electrical Machinery	..	..	..	51.3	45.2	49.8	50.2	48.0	..	..
3821	Engines & Turbines	..	..	..	1.9	1.7	1.6	1.3	0.9	..	..
3822	Agricultural Machinery	..	..	..	9.2	8.6	9.0	8.3	7.8	..	..
3823	Metal & Wood working Machinery	..	..	..	3.9	3.3	4.8	3.3	3.3	..	..
3824	Special Industrial Machinery	..	..	..	7.7	6.6	7.9	8.2	8.1	..	..
3825	Office & Computing Machinery	..	..	..	0.4	0.3	0.5	0.5	0.7	..	..
3829	Machinery & Equipment, nec	..	..	..	28.3	24.6	26.1	28.7	27.1	..	..
383	Electrical Machinery	..	..	..	46.1	43.5	45.8	44.4	39.7	..	..
3831	Electrical Industrial Machinery	..	..	..	12.4	10.4	8.8	10.6	9.8	..	..
3832	Radio, TV & Communication Equipment	..	..	..	18.1	17.9	20.1	18.4	15.2	..	..
3833	Electrical Appliances & Housewares	..	..	..	2.9	3.3	4.9	4.5	3.7	..	..
3839	Electrical Apparatus, nec	..	..	..	12.7	11.9	12.0	10.9	10.9	..	..
384	Transport Equipment	..	..	..	63.3	64.3	67.9	72.9	65.8	..	..
3841	Shipbuilding & Repairing	..	..	..	5.6	5.2	5.2	4.6	4.2	..	..
3842	Railroad Equipment	..	..	..	8.7	8.3	7.5	6.6	6.7	..	..
3843	Motor Vehicles	..	..	..	45.7	47.4	50.7	56.7	50.4	..	..
3844	Motorcycles & Bicycles	..	..	..	0.9	1.0	1.7	2.0	1.7	..	..
3845	Aircraft	..	..	..	2.3	2.5	2.7	2.8	2.7	..	..
3849	Transport Equipment, nec	..	..	..	0.0	0.0	0.0	0.1	0.1	..	..
385	Professional Goods	..	..	..	4.5	4.7	5.1	5.4	4.9	..	..
3851	Professional Equipment	..	..	..	3.0	2.9	3.2	3.2	2.8	..	..
3852	Photographic & Optical Goods	..	..	..	0.6	0.7	0.5	0.6	0.5	..	..
3853	Watches & Clocks	..	..	..	0.0	0.0	0.0	0.2	0.1	..	..
39	**Other Manufacturing, nes**	..	..	..	4.7	4.3	5.1	5.7	5.6	..	..
3901	Jewellery	..	..	..	0.7	0.6	1.2	1.4	1.6	..	..
3	**Total Manufacturing**	..	..	..	975.2	899.5	979.1	974.5	932.9	..	..
1	**Agric., Hunting, Forestry, Fishing**	..	..	..	..	..	..	..	..	..	..
2	**Mining & Quarrying**	..	..	..	..	..	..	..	..	..	..
21	Coal Mining	..	..	..	..	..	..	..	..	..	..
22	Crude Petroleum & Natural Gas	..	..	..	..	..	..	..	..	..	..
23.29	Other Mining	..	..	..	..	..	..	..	..	..	..
3	**Total Manufacturing**	..	..	..	975.2	899.5	979.1	974.5	932.9	..	..
4	**Electricity, Gas & Water**	..	..	..	..	..	..	..	..	..	..
5	**Construction**	..	..	..	..	..	..	..	..	..	..
6.9	**Services**	..	..	..	..	..	..	..	..	..	..
0000	**Grand Total**	..	..	..	..	..	..	..	..	..	..

Note: Break in series between 1991 and 1992, see Sources and Definitions.
Some data are not given for reasons of confidentiality.
ISIC 385 includes a figure for other professional goods (Turkish SIC 3854).

Billions of TL (Current Prices)

ISIC2	Industry	INVESTMENT									
		1987	1988	1989	1990	1991	1992	1993	1994	1995	1996
31	**Food, Beverages & Tobacco**	175	252	383	794	1 268	2 592	7 035	10 236	..	..
311.2	Food	152	203	335	646	1 052	2 027	4 502	6 826	..	..
313	Beverages	15	19	35	95	155	442	1 766	1 331	..	..
314	Tobacco	8	30	13	52	61	123	767	2 078	..	..
32	**Textiles, Apparel & Leather**	406	1 150	1 262	2 080	2 290	7 001	7 839	20 990	..	..
321	Textiles	369	716	1 126	1 866	1 917	6 221	6 657	16 370	..	..
3213	Knitting Mills	26	49	108	141	188	3 205	995	4 526	..	..
322	Wearing Apparel	29	425	120	173	339	695	1 051	4 165	..	..
323	Leather & Products	6	6	8	30	17	45	71	250	..	..
324	Footwear	2	2	7	11	16	41	60	206	..	..
33	**Wood Products & Furniture**	18	28	45	99	90	371	670	1 436	..	..
331	Wood Products	11	16	33	84	62	329	518	1 253	..	..
332	Furnitures & Fixtures	7	11	12	15	29	42	152	184	..	..
34	**Paper, Paper Products & Printing**	78	113	190	343	877	764	2 835	5 263	..	..
341	Paper & Products	60	72	98	168	407	46	688	1 446	..	..
3411	Pulp, Paper & Board	38	43	50	68	358	230	402	738	..	..
342	Printing & Publishing	18	41	93	175	471	717	2 147	3 817	..	..
35	**Chemical Products**	341	431	831	1 680	2 612	4 514	7 154	16 897	..	..
351	Industrial Chemicals	145	157	301	531	517	1 228	1 926	3 978	..	..
3511	Basic Industrial Chemicals	23	34	51	71	102	545	305	413	..	..
3512	Fertilizers & Pesticides	76	50	131	271	220	289	240	522	..	..
3513	Synthetic Resins	46	73	120	189	194	394	1 381	3 042	..	..
352	Other Chemicals	55	101	172	395	805	865	2 148	3 134	..	..
3521	Paints, Varnishes & Lacquers	5	16	18	37	78	93	251	277	..	..
3522	Drugs & Medicines	28	46	92	253	473	427	1 361	1 177	..	..
3523	Soap & Cleaning Preparations	9	11	36	53	179	100	189	866	..	..
3529	Chemical Products, nec	13	28	27	51	74	246	347	814	..	..
353	Petroleum Refineries	76	30	60	104	321	1 335	580	115	..	..
354	Petroleum & Coal Products	11	9	115	106	320	243	473	1 391	..	..
355	Rubber Products	31	93	111	408	375	425	815	2 339	..	..
356	Plastic Products, nec	23	41	71	137	275	417	1 211	5 940	..	..
36	**Non-Metallic Mineral Products**	248	449	729	1 308	2 212	2 872	4 357	12 160	..	..
361	Pottery, China etc	67	77	69	255	394	477	710	2 429	..	..
362	Glass & Products	39	71	180	596	928	305	1 045	1 639	..	..
369	Non-Metallic Products, nec	142	301	480	456	890	2 090	2 602	8 092	..	..
37	**Basic Metal Industries**	252	936	1 588	3 507	883	2 726	5 340	9 206	..	..
371	Iron & Steel	178	823	1 449	3 304	696	2 451	4 927	8 184	..	..
372	Non-Ferrous Metals	74	112	139	203	187	275	413	1 022	..	..
38	**Fabricated Metal Products**	546	687	884	1 720	3 674	8 721	12 183	28 193	..	..
381	Metal Products	72	145	192	211	348	3 874	2 153	5 191	..	..
3813	Structural Metal Products	8	15	14	25	50	-1	412	2 335	..	..
382	Non-Electrical Machinery	76	114	232	274	602	1 015	2 270	3 284	..	..
3821	Engines & Turbines	6	5	7	25	10	59	12	15	..	..
3822	Agricultural Machinery	14	13	20	35	28	90	307	224	..	..
3823	Metal & Wood working Machinery	10	10	18	14	26	243	37	15	..	..
3824	Special Industrial Machinery	19	8	8	27	-4	89	624	193	..	..
3825	Office & Computing Machinery	1		0	0	1	12	13	10	..	..
3829	Machinery & Equipment, nec	27	78	179	173	540	520	1 277	2 828	..	..
383	Electrical Machinery	91	180	178	587	867	1 225	2 358	4 896	..	..
3831	Electrical Industrial Machinery	28	52	73	334	174	270	673	1 300	..	..
3832	Radio, TV & Communication Equipment	38	65	55	165	525	439	844	1 662	..	..
3833	Electrical Appliances & Housewares	1	9	8	15	45	179	297	152	..	..
3839	Electrical Apparatus, nec	24	53	41	73	124	338	545	1 781	..	..
384	Transport Equipment	306	238	267	607	1 836	2 454	5 235	14 260	..	..
3841	Shipbuilding & Repairing	23	4	12	12	17	19	85	414	..	..
3842	Railroad Equipment	5	5	12	8		28	28	9	..	..
3843	Motor Vehicles	89	194	194	559	1 770	2 310	4 899	13 788	..	..
3844	Motorcycles & Bicycles	..	2	..	5	5	22	127	77	..	..
3845	Aircraft	..	34	46	24	..	75	95	-33	..	..
3849	Transport Equipment, nec	..		..	0			1	6	..	..
385	Professional Goods	2	11	15	41	21	154	166	561	..	..
3851	Professional Equipment	1	6	9	15	15	74	113	412	..	..
3852	Photographic & Optical Goods	0	1	..	20	2	6	15	12	..	..
3853	Watches & Clocks	..		..	0	..		7	2	..	..
39	**Other Manufacturing, nes**	3	5	12	23	21	53	894	428	..	..
3901	Jewellery	..	0	0	1	2	9	29	54	..	..
3	**Total Manufacturing**	2 067	4 049	5 924	11 554	13 927	29 614	48 307	104 809	..	..
1	**Agric., Hunting, Forestry, Fishing**	..	..	..	..	..	..	..	..	..	..
2	**Mining & Quarrying**	266	341	429	489	..	..	..	..	..	..
21	Coal Mining	111	199	224	201	..	..	..	..	..	..
22	Crude Petroleum & Natural Gas	26	66	119	167	..	..	..	..	..	..
23.29	Other Mining	129	76	86	121	..	..	..	..	..	..
3	**Total Manufacturing**	2 067	4 049	5 924	11 554	13 927	29 614	48 307	104 809	..	..
4	**Electricity, Gas & Water**	17	30	407	186	..	..	..	..	..	..
5	**Construction**	..	..	..	..	..	..	..	..	..	..
6.9	**Services**	..	..	..	..	..	..	..	..	..	..
0000	**Grand Total**	..	..	..	..	..	..	..	..	..	..

Note: Break in series between 1991 and 1992, see Sources and Definitions.
Some data are not given for reasons of confidentiality.
ISIC 385 includes a figure for other professional goods (Turkish SIC 3854).

Billions of TL

(Current Prices)

ISIC2	Industry	INVESTMENT IN MACHINERY & EQUIPMENT									
		1987	1988	1989	1990	1991	1992	1993	1994	1995	1996
31	**Food, Beverages & Tobacco**	117	173	271	533	818	1 677	3 341	7 688	..	..
311.2	Food	99	132	238	461	696	1 294	1 869	5 043	..	..
313	Beverages	12	15	24	42	94	326	1 019	965	..	..
314	Tobacco	6	26	9	30	29	57	453	1 680	..	..
32	**Textiles, Apparel & Leather**	359	1 133	1 038	1 805	1 848	5 920	7 013	16 339	..	..
321	Textiles	333	723	960	1 668	1 640	5 499	6 357	13 462	..	..
3213	Knitting Mills	20	40	78	115	158	3 117	1 029	4 000	..	..
322	Wearing Apparel	20	403	68	105	188	364	566	2 592	..	..
323	Leather & Products	5	4	5	23	9	25	45	126	..	..
324	Footwear	1	2	5	9	12	33	45	160	..	..
33	**Wood Products & Furniture**	10	13	27	75	64	314	560	1 144	..	..
331	Wood Products	7	10	21	61	52	289	430	1 034	..	..
332	Furnitures & Fixtures	3	2	7	14	12	25	131	110	..	..
34	**Paper, Paper Products & Printing**	66	89	120	247	719	378	1 909	4 103	..	..
341	Paper & Products	52	61	67	147	381	23	525	1 205	..	..
3411	Pulp, Paper & Board	33	36	29	64	338	202	290	613	..	..
342	Printing & Publishing	14	28	53	100	339	355	1 383	2 898	..	..
35	**Chemical Products**	204	286	566	1 227	1 965	2 864	5 283	11 128	..	..
351	Industrial Chemicals	108	91	214	411	437	1 070	1 767	4 192	..	..
3511	Basic Industrial Chemicals	18	30	37	60	92	518	253	316	..	..
3512	Fertilizers & Pesticides	60	20	89	187	187	178	192	491	..	..
3513	Synthetic Resins	30	42	88	163	159	374	1 322	3 384	..	..
352	Other Chemicals	34	63	102	230	553	607	1 339	1 747	..	..
3521	Paints, Varnishes & Lacquers	3	5	7	15	39	39	124	120	..	..
3522	Drugs & Medicines	16	27	52	139	307	295	805	596	..	..
3523	Soap & Cleaning Preparations	7	8	25	46	156	70	127	458	..	..
3529	Chemical Products, nec	9	23	18	31	51	202	283	574	..	..
353	Petroleum Refineries	9	6	31	74	289	345	284	100	..	..
354	Petroleum & Coal Products	7	10	79	71	137	153	205	905	..	..
355	Rubber Products	28	83	81	333	349	367	681	2 206	..	..
356	Plastic Products, nec	19	33	59	108	199	322	1 008	1 978	..	..
36	**Non-Metallic Mineral Products**	194	357	634	1 095	1 704	2 434	3 509	8 540	..	..
361	Pottery, China etc	54	59	62	230	328	398	567	2 070	..	..
362	Glass & Products	27	61	163	489	694	279	557	1 363	..	..
369	Non-Metallic Products, nec	112	237	410	376	682	1 756	2 385	5 107	..	..
37	**Basic Metal Industries**	190	703	1 403	3 343	613	2 383	3 650	7 727	..	..
371	Iron & Steel	124	615	1 308	3 180	474	2 156	3 295	6 942	..	..
372	Non-Ferrous Metals	66	87	96	163	138	227	355	784	..	..
38	**Fabricated Metal Products**	445	530	619	1 126	3 019	6 743	9 301	22 586	..	..
381	Metal Products	46	115	145	162	259	3 003	1 272	2 922	..	..
3813	Structural Metal Products	6	10	7	16	37	45	91	602	..	..
382	Non-Electrical Machinery	54	86	167	211	403	602	1 866	2 766	..	..
3821	Engines & Turbines	4	5	4	23	7	58	10	6	..	..
3822	Agricultural Machinery	8	8	16	26	23	43	254	136	..	..
3823	Metal & Wood working Machinery	9	6	13	8	17	35	25	-5	..	..
3824	Special Industrial Machinery	12	6	4	18	8	54	542	95	..	..
3825	Office & Computing Machinery	3	0	0	0	0	4	1	2	..	..
3829	Machinery & Equipment, nec	19	61	130	136	348	409	1 034	2 532	..	..
383	Electrical Machinery	74	130	123	264	696	962	1 902	4 224	..	..
3831	Electrical Industrial Machinery	22	40	55	72	133	227	574	1 101	..	..
3832	Radio, TV & Communication Equipment	31	37	26	129	447	326	584	1 393	..	..
3833	Electrical Appliances & Housewares	0	8	5	8	27	142	293	118	..	..
3839	Electrical Apparatus, nec	21	45	36	54	89	267	451	1 613	..	..
384	Transport Equipment	269	189	173	455	1 646	2 036	4 123	12 273	..	..
3841	Shipbuilding & Repairing	17	4	6	8	10	8	43	375	..	..
3842	Railroad Equipment	4	3	9	5	..	23	23	7	..	..
3843	Motor Vehicles	59	160	131	424	1 602	1 957	3 939	11 688	..	..
3844	Motorcycles & Bicycles	..	2	..	4	3	19	55	10	..	..
3845	Aircraft	..	21	24	14	..	28	61	190	..	..
3849	Transport Equipment, nec	..	..	..	0	..	..	1	4	..	..
385	Professional Goods	1	9	11	34	15	140	138	400	..	..
3851	Professional Equipment	1	5	6	10	10	71	94	372	..	..
3852	Photographic & Optical Goods	0	1	..	19	2	5	14	5	..	..
3853	Watches & Clocks	0	..	..	0	0	0	6	1	..	..
39	**Other Manufacturing, nes**	3	3	6	18	17	37	236	383	..	..
3901	Jewellery	0	0	0	0	..	8	25	31	..	..
3	**Total Manufacturing**	1 588	3 287	4 684	9 469	10 767	22 750	34 802	79 637	..	..
1	**Agric., Hunting, Forestry, Fishing**	..	..	..	..	..			..	..	..
2	**Mining & Quarrying**	142	137	99	182	..	..	..	..	..	..
21	Coal Mining	75	98	29	57	..	..	..	..	..	..
22	Crude Petroleum & Natural Gas	8	11	45	89	..	..	..	..	..	..
23.29	Other Mining	59	28	25	36	..	..	..	..	..	..
3	**Total Manufacturing**	1 588	3 287	4 684	9 469	10 767	22 750	34 802	79 637	..	..
4	**Electricity, Gas & Water**	5	18	9	15	..	..	..	..	..	..
5	**Construction**	..	..	..	..	..			..	..	..
6.9	**Services**	..	..	..	..	..			..	..	..
0000	**Grand Total**	..	..	..	..	..			..	..	..

Note: Break in series between 1991 and 1992, see Sources and Definitions.
Some data are not given for reasons of confidentiality.
ISIC 385 includes a figure for other professional goods (Turkish SIC 3854).

Billions of TL   (Current Prices)

ISIC2	Industry	\n WAGES & SALARIES - EMPLOYEES									
		1987	1988	1989	1990	1991	1992	1993	1994	1995	1996
31	**Food, Beverages & Tobacco**	376	570	1 332	2 642	5 515	10 273	16 820	27 591	..	..
311.2	Food	264	415	945	1 898	3 812	7 249	11 736	18 947	..	..
313	Beverages	34	55	123	265	601	968	1 676	2 569	..	..
314	Tobacco	78	100	264	479	1 102	2 056	3 408	6 074	..	..
32	**Textiles, Apparel & Leather**	489	921	1 737	3 041	6 145	9 658	16 905	26 663	..	..
321	Textiles	402	733	1 350	2 319	4 888	7 344	12 844	19 700	..	..
3213	Knitting Mills	28	47	97	163	338	683	1 610	2 305	..	..
322	Wearing Apparel	65	155	323	593	1 040	1 917	3 361	5 752	..	..
323	Leather & Products	8	10	24	45	53	122	205	665	..	..
324	Footwear	13	23	40	84	163	275	495	546	..	..
33	**Wood Products & Furniture**	33	55	111	206	421	846	1 520	2 234	..	..
331	Wood Products	24	41	84	162	336	649	1 097	1 653	..	..
332	Furnitures & Fixtures	9	14	26	44	86	197	423	581	..	..
34	**Paper, Paper Products & Printing**	101	156	371	699	1 282	2 190	3 531	5 837	..	..
341	Paper & Products	59	85	220	440	824	1 320	2 240	3 795	..	..
3411	Pulp, Paper & Board	38	52	154	309	588	1 036	1 731	2 858	..	..
342	Printing & Publishing	43	72	150	260	458	869	1 291	2 042	..	..
35	**Chemical Products**	324	558	1 230	2 496	4 762	8 209	13 607	23 438	..	..
351	Industrial Chemicals	119	187	394	857	1 570	2 664	4 184	7 267	..	..
3511	Basic Industrial Chemicals	27	37	99	166	274	1 517	657	960	..	..
3512	Fertilizers & Pesticides	36	56	95	265	472	548	1 332	2 231	..	..
3513	Synthetic Resins	55	94	200	426	824	599	2 195	4 076	..	..
352	Other Chemicals	105	186	404	756	1 480	2 533	4 374	7 097	..	..
3521	Paints, Varnishes & Lacquers	17	25	46	100	300	297	451	820	..	..
3522	Drugs & Medicines	53	93	203	377	704	1 304	2 300	3 663	..	..
3523	Soap & Cleaning Preparations	20	40	99	165	244	541	940	1 464	..	..
3529	Chemical Products, nec	15	28	56	114	233	391	683	1 150	..	..
353	Petroleum Refineries	22	33	107	186	418	742	1 266	2 324	..	..
354	Petroleum & Coal Products	15	30	62	163	307	462	722	1 290	..	..
355	Rubber Products	38	77	163	325	613	1 167	1 963	3 731	..	..
356	Plastic Products, nec	26	46	100	208	373	641	1 098	1 730	..	..
36	**Non-Metallic Mineral Products**	184	342	703	1 487	2 398	4 261	6 566	10 436	..	..
361	Pottery, China etc	28	51	95	225	355	569	1 060	1 777	..	..
362	Glass & Products	50	87	217	404	710	1 216	1 652	2 650	..	..
369	Non-Metallic Products, nec	106	204	391	858	1 333	2 476	3 854	6 009	..	..
37	**Basic Metal Industries**	267	453	1 055	1 932	4 473	6 950	10 969	17 184	..	..
371	Iron & Steel	205	355	819	1 544	3 756	5 883	9 189	14 704	..	..
372	Non-Ferrous Metals	62	98	236	388	717	1 067	1 780	2 479	..	..
38	**Fabricated Metal Products**	591	982	1 865	3 866	7 660	13 187	23 504	34 644	..	..
381	Metal Products	99	169	310	590	1 111	1 847	3 257	5 257	..	..
3813	Structural Metal Products	18	31	58	112	222	364	705	1 074	..	..
382	Non-Electrical Machinery	167	259	498	913	1 761	2 983	5 023	7 739	..	..
3821	Engines & Turbines	7	11	23	39	76	111	180	212	..	..
3822	Agricultural Machinery	28	47	90	180	308	524	912	1 470	..	..
3823	Metal & Wood working Machinery	13	17	32	66	114	254	318	420	..	..
3824	Special Industrial Machinery	44	35	66	118	225	391	708	1 109	..	..
3825	Office & Computing Machinery	7	2	3	7	12	19	35	56	..	..
3829	Machinery & Equipment, nec	68	148	284	503	1 025	1 683	2 870	4 472	..	..
383	Electrical Machinery	137	232	423	911	1 845	3 203	5 574	7 639	..	..
3831	Electrical Industrial Machinery	36	56	110	238	412	600	1 253	1 879	..	..
3832	Radio, TV & Communication Equipment	59	103	181	408	901	1 719	2 978	3 770	..	..
3833	Electrical Appliances & Housewares	3	9	17	35	65	148	237	323	..	..
3839	Electrical Apparatus, nec	39	64	115	231	466	736	1 107	1 667	..	..
384	Transport Equipment	185	305	598	1 377	2 791	4 892	9 213	13 438	..	..
3841	Shipbuilding & Repairing	19	25	66	124	255	413	668	1 134	..	..
3842	Railroad Equipment	30	42	70			567	1 104	1 889	..	..
3843	Motor Vehicles	134	217	416	1 003	2 012	3 521	6 735	9 171	..	..
3844	Motorcycles & Bicycles	..	6		17	35	95	178	218	..	..
3845	Aircraft		15	38	..	..	296	527	1 022	..	..
3849	Transport Equipment, nec	..	..		..	..	1	2	4	..	..
385	Professional Goods	3	17	36	74	152	261	437	571	..	..
3851	Professional Equipment	2	13	28	56	118	184	297	351	..	..
3852	Photographic & Optical Goods	1	1		6	20	15	23	33	..	..
3853	Watches & Clocks	0	..		..	..	0	7	3	..	..
39	**Other Manufacturing, nes**	9	16	29	54	90	170	293	440	..	..
3901	Jewellery	1	1	2	..	7	39	56	103	..	..
3	**Total Manufacturing**	2 373	4 052	8 431	16 423	32 746	55 744	93 713	148 466	..	..
I	**Agric., Hunting, Forestry, Fishing**	..	..	..	..	..	..	..	..	..	..
2	**Mining & Quarrying**	310	481	988	1 931	..	..	..	..	..	..
21	Coal Mining	239	348	698	1 475	..	..	..	..	..	..
22	Crude Petroleum & Natural Gas	6	17	34	71	..	..	..	..	..	..
23.29	Other Mining	65	116	256	385	..	..	..	..	..	..
3	**Total Manufacturing**	2 373	4 052	8 431	16 423	32 746	55 744	93 713	148 466	..	..
4	**Electricity, Gas & Water**	64	111	214	644	..	..	..	..	..	..
5	**Construction**	..	..	..	..	..	..	..	..	..	..
6.9	**Services**	..	..	..	..	..	..	..	..	..	..
0000	**Grand Total**	..	..	..	..	..	..	..	..	..	..

Note: Break in series between 1991 and 1992, see Sources and Definitions.
Some data are not given for reasons of confidentiality.
ISIC 385 includes a figure for other professional goods (Turkish SIC 3854).

Billions of TL

(Current Prices)

ISIC2	Industry	WAGES & SALARIES + SUPPLEMENTS - EMPLOYEES									
		1987	1988	1989	1990	1991	1992	1993	1994	1995	1996
31	**Food, Beverages & Tobacco**	..	..	..	3 004	6 299	14 373	22 657	34 324	..	..
311.2	Food	..	..	..	2 167	4 380	10 784	16 260	23 746	..	..
313	Beverages	..	..	..	298	681	1 160	2 144	3 069	..	..
314	Tobacco	..	..	..	539	1 238	2 428	4 253	7 509	..	..
32	**Textiles, Apparel & Leather**	..	..	..	3 496	7 145	12 114	22 739	39 987	..	..
321	Textiles	..	..	..	2 654	5 661	9 288	17 552	30 311	..	..
3213	Knitting Mills	..	..	..	190	396	852	2 099	8 553	..	..
322	Wearing Apparel	..	..	..	694	1 233	2 346	4 314	8 191	..	..
323	Leather & Products	..	..	..	53	64	153	261	827	..	..
324	Footwear	..	..	..	96	186	327	613	658	..	..
33	**Wood Products & Furniture**	..	..	..	237	495	1 061	2 427	2 810	..	..
331	Wood Products	..	..	..	186	393	813	1 502	2 086	..	..
332	Furnitures & Fixtures	..	..	..	51	101	247	925	724	..	..
34	**Paper, Paper Products & Printing**	..	..	..	790	1 477	2 722	4 415	7 187	..	..
341	Paper & Products	..	..	..	494	947	1 647	2 786	4 521	..	..
3411	Pulp, Paper & Board	..	..	..	345	672	1 298	2 148	3 368	..	..
342	Printing & Publishing	..	..	..	297	530	1 075	1 628	2 666	..	..
35	**Chemical Products**	..	..	..	2 839	5 405	9 840	17 667	29 774	..	..
351	Industrial Chemicals	..	..	..	980	1 785	3 286	5 287	8 475	..	..
3511	Basic Industrial Chemicals	..	..	..	189	313	1 934	817	1 146	..	..
3512	Fertilizers & Pesticides	..	..	..	299	535	641	1 624	2 615	..	..
3513	Synthetic Resins	..	..	..	492	937	710	2 846	4 715	..	..
352	Other Chemicals	..	..	..	861	1 678	3 005	6 167	8 554	..	..
3521	Paints, Varnishes & Lacquers	..	..	..	115	327	346	1 375	1 032	..	..
3522	Drugs & Medicines	..	..	..	428	808	1 556	2 779	4 424	..	..
3523	Soap & Cleaning Preparations	..	..	..	189	278	640	1 188	1 741	..	..
3529	Chemical Products, nec	..	..	..	129	264	463	825	1 357	..	..
353	Petroleum Refineries	..	..	..	206	463	866	1 536	2 743	..	..
354	Petroleum & Coal Products	..	..	..	186	349	546	928	1 773	..	..
355	Rubber Products	..	..	..	366	698	1 342	2 341	4 489	..	..
356	Plastic Products, nec	..	..	..	240	433	796	1 407	3 739	..	..
36	**Non-Metallic Mineral Products**	..	..	..	1 674	2 733	5 461	9 090	15 182	..	..
361	Pottery, China etc	..	..	..	254	408	733	1 336	2 240	..	..
362	Glass & Products	..	..	..	452	793	1 606	2 022	3 457	..	..
369	Non-Metallic Products, nec	..	..	..	968	1 531	3 122	5 731	9 485	..	..
37	**Basic Metal Industries**	..	..	..	2 171	5 008	9 178	14 049	21 955	..	..
371	Iron & Steel	..	..	..	1 724	4 182	7 770	11 714	18 923	..	..
372	Non-Ferrous Metals	..	..	..	447	826	1 408	2 335	3 033	..	..
38	**Fabricated Metal Products**	..	..	..	4 389	8 780	16 333	28 921	51 945	..	..
381	Metal Products	..	..	..	675	1 278	2 333	4 220	11 309	..	..
3813	Structural Metal Products	..	..	..	128	255	468	922	1 327	..	..
382	Non-Electrical Machinery	..	..	..	1 032	2 018	3 759	6 413	12 168	..	..
3821	Engines & Turbines	..	..	..	45	86	143	287	264	..	..
3822	Agricultural Machinery	..	..	..	203	355	737	1 092	1 881	..	..
3823	Metal & Wood working Machinery	..	..	..	75	128	308	410	516	..	..
3824	Special Industrial Machinery	..	..	..	134	257	471	899	1 357	..	..
3825	Office & Computing Machinery	..	..	..	8	14	23	44	75	..	..
3829	Machinery & Equipment, nec	..	..	..	567	1 177	2 077	3 681	8 075	..	..
383	Electrical Machinery	..	..	..	1 037	2 110	3 888	6 634	9 194	..	..
3831	Electrical Industrial Machinery	..	..	..	272	477	731	1 502	2 253	..	..
3832	Radio, TV & Communication Equipment	..	..	..	461	1 017	2 059	3 458	4 470	..	..
3833	Electrical Appliances & Housewares	..	..	..	40	75	181	291	435	..	..
3839	Electrical Apparatus, nec	..	..	..	263	540	917	1 383	2 036	..	..
384	Transport Equipment	..	..	..	1 562	3 202	6 032	11 105	18 576	..	..
3841	Shipbuilding & Repairing	..	..	..	138	286	498	799	1 318	..	..
3842	Railroad Equipment	..	..	..	172	379	693	1 325	2 206	..	..
3843	Motor Vehicles	..	..	..	1 142	2 322	4 394	8 140	13 671	..	..
3844	Motorcycles & Bicycles	..	..	..	19	40	113	223	271	..	..
3845	Aircraft	..	..	..	90	174	334	615	1 105	..	..
3849	Transport Equipment, nec	..	..	..	0	0	1	3	5	..	..
385	Professional Goods	..	..	..	83	172	321	549	698	..	..
3851	Professional Equipment	..	..	..	62	133	228	378	438	..	..
3852	Photographic & Optical Goods	..	..	..	6	24	18	29	40	..	..
3853	Watches & Clocks	..	..	..	0	0	1	8	4	..	..
39	**Other Manufacturing, nes**	..	..	..	63	105	223	387	554	..	..
3901	Jewellery	..	..	..	5	9	49	76	130	..	..
3	**Total Manufacturing**	..	..	..	18 663	37 447	71 305	122 352	203 719	..	..
1	**Agric., Hunting, Forestry, Fishing**	..	..	..	..	..				..	..
2	**Mining & Quarrying**	..	..	..	..	..	..	..	..	..	..
21	Coal Mining	..	..	..	..	..	..	..	..	..	..
22	Crude Petroleum & Natural Gas	..	..	..	..	..	..	..	..	..	..
23.29	Other Mining	..	..	..	..	..	..	..	..	..	..
3	**Total Manufacturing**	..	..	..	18 663	37 447	71 305	122 352	203 719	..	..
4	**Electricity, Gas & Water**	..	..	..	..	..	..	..	..	..	..
5	**Construction**	..	..	..	..	..	..	..	..	..	..
6.9	**Services**	..	..	..	..	..	..	..	..	..	..
0000	**Grand Total**	..	..	..	..	..	..	..	..	..	..

Note: Break in series between 1991 and 1992, see Sources and Definitions.
Some data are not given for reasons of confidentiality.
ISIC 385 includes a figure for other professional goods (Turkish SIC 3854).

Thousands

ISIC2	Industry	HOURS WORKED									
		1987	1988	1989	1990	1991	1992	1993	1994	1995	1996
31	Food, Beverages & Tobacco	300 000	298 000	296 000	282 000	268 000	293 000	283 000	276 000	..	..
311.2	Food	209 000	214 000	210 000	200 000	189 000	218 000	212 000	213 000	..	..
313	Beverages	18 000	18 000	20 000	19 000	20 000	19 000	19 000	16 000	..	..
314	Tobacco	72 000	66 000	66 000	63 000	60 000	57 000	52 000	48 000	..	..
32	Textiles, Apparel & Leather	498 000	547 000	573 000	579 000	505 000	578 000	588 000	573 000	..	..
321	Textiles	387 000	402 000	410 000	411 000	348 000	380 000	385 000	369 000	..	..
3213	Knitting Mills	34 000	33 000	37 000	39 000	39 000	55 000	71 000	63 000	..	..
322	Wearing Apparel	91 000	127 000	144 000	147 000	137 000	171 000	177 000	179 000	..	..
323	Leather & Products	10 000	8 000	10 000	10 000	9 000	12 000	11 000	13 000	..	..
324	Footwear	11 000	10 000	10 000	12 000	12 000	14 000	15 000	12 000	..	..
33	Wood Products & Furniture	35 000	35 000	33 000	32 000	29 000	42 000	43 000	38 000	..	..
331	Wood Products	25 000	26 000	25 000	24 000	21 000	28 000	27 000	25 000	..	..
332	Furnitures & Fixtures	10 000	10 000	9 000	8 000	7 000	14 000	15 000	13 000	..	..
34	Paper, Paper Products & Printing	59 000	57 000	56 000	60 000	56 000	61 000	53 000	50 000	..	..
341	Paper & Products	40 000	35 000	35 000	39 000	39 000	38 000	31 000	30 000	..	..
3411	Pulp, Paper & Board	25 000	20 000	22 000	24 000	25 000	26 000	19 000	18 000	..	..
342	Printing & Publishing	19 000	23 000	21 000	21 000	18 000	23 000	22 000	20 000	..	..
35	Chemical Products	154 000	156 000	156 000	157 000	145 000	153 000	149 000	138 000	..	..
351	Industrial Chemicals	62 000	55 000	56 000	56 000	50 000	48 000	43 000	40 000	..	..
3511	Basic Industrial Chemicals	16 000	14 000	16 000	14 000	12 000	27 000	10 000	8 000	..	..
3512	Fertilizers & Pesticides	14 000	13 000	10 000	13 000	12 000	9 000	10 000	9 000	..	..
3513	Synthetic Resins	31 000	28 000	30 000	28 000	25 000	13 000	23 000	23 000	..	..
352	Other Chemicals	35 000	36 000	35 000	35 000	33 000	33 000	33 000	29 000	..	..
3521	Paints, Varnishes & Lacquers	6 000	5 000	5 000	6 000	5 000	5 000	5 000	5 000	..	..
3522	Drugs & Medicines	14 000	15 000	15 000	14 000	13 000	13 000	13 000	11 000	..	..
3523	Soap & Cleaning Preparations	8 000	7 000	9 000	8 000	8 000	7 000	7 000	6 000	..	..
3529	Chemical Products, nec	7 000	8 000	6 000	7 000	7 000	8 000	8 000	7 000	..	..
353	Petroleum Refineries	8 000	8 000	8 000	9 000	9 000	9 000	9 000	9 000	..	..
354	Petroleum & Coal Products	6 000	7 000	7 000	7 000	7 000	6 000	6 000	6 000	..	..
355	Rubber Products	22 000	27 000	25 000	22 000	20 000	23 000	25 000	23 000	..	..
356	Plastic Products, nec	21 000	23 000	25 000	28 000	26 000	32 000	33 000	31 000	..	..
36	Non-Metallic Mineral Products	147 000	157 000	158 000	142 000	124 000	133 000	126 000	121 000	..	..
361	Pottery, China etc	29 000	31 000	23 000	29 000	23 000	21 000	23 000	23 000	..	..
362	Glass & Products	30 000	32 000	34 000	32 000	26 000	25 000	23 000	21 000	..	..
369	Non-Metallic Products, nec	89 000	94 000	101 000	81 000	75 000	86 000	80 000	76 000	..	..
37	Basic Metal Industries	164 000	170 000	163 000	162 000	142 000	134 000	129 000	126 000	..	..
371	Iron & Steel	125 000	133 000	125 000	126 000	116 000	108 000	105 000	105 000	..	..
372	Non-Ferrous Metals	39 000	37 000	37 000	36 000	26 000	26 000	24 000	21 000	..	..
38	Fabricated Metal Products	353 000	355 000	331 000	364 000	332 000	371 000	380 000	335 000	..	..
381	Metal Products	79 000	78 000	71 000	77 000	68 000	80 000	81 000	75 000	..	..
3813	Structural Metal Products	14 000	14 000	13 000	14 000	13 000	18 000	20 000	18 000	..	..
382	Non-Electrical Machinery	100 000	95 000	86 000	90 000	74 000	86 000	85 000	80 000	..	..
3821	Engines & Turbines	3 000	3 000	3 000	3 000	2 000	2 000	2 000	1 000	..	..
3822	Agricultural Machinery	18 000	15 000	11 000	15 000	14 000	15 000	13 000	12 000	..	..
3823	Metal & Wood working Machinery	8 000	8 000	7 000	7 000	5 000	8 000	5 000	5 000	..	..
3824	Special Industrial Machinery	25 000	17 000	14 000	14 000	11 000	15 000	16 000	15 000	..	..
3825	Office & Computing Machinery	3 000	1 000	1 000	1 000	0	1 000	1 000	1 000	..	..
3829	Machinery & Equipment, nec	43 000	50 000	50 000	51 000	42 000	46 000	48 000	45 000	..	..
383	Electrical Machinery	71 000	72 000	68 000	79 000	72 000	78 000	75 000	64 000	..	..
3831	Electrical Industrial Machinery	22 000	19 000	19 000	20 000	17 000	15 000	19 000	16 000	..	..
3832	Radio, TV & Communication Equipment	23 000	25 000	24 000	30 000	28 000	31 000	27 000	22 000	..	..
3833	Electrical Appliances & Housewares	3 000	4 000	4 000	6 000	6 000	9 000	9 000	7 000	..	..
3839	Electrical Apparatus, nec	23 000	24 000	21 000	23 000	20 000	22 000	20 000	19 000	..	..
384	Transport Equipment	99 000	105 000	100 000	112 000	110 000	120 000	130 000	107 000	..	..
3841	Shipbuilding & Repairing	7 000	8 000	8 000	8 000	7 000	7 000	6 000	5 000	..	..
3842	Railroad Equipment	18 000	18 000	17 000	..	..	12 000	10 000	11 000	..	..
3843	Motor Vehicles	72 000	75 000	71 000	83 000	85 000	95 000	107 000	86 000	..	..
3844	Motorcycles & Bicycles	..	2 000	..	2 000	2 000	3 000	4 000	3 000	..	..
3845	Aircraft	..	2 000	2 000	..	..	3 000	3 000	3 000	..	..
3849	Transport Equipment, nec	..	..	..	..	..	0	0	0	..	..
385	Professional Goods	4 000	6 000	6 000	7 000	8 000	8 000	9 000	8 000	..	..
3851	Professional Equipment	2 000	4 000	4 000	5 000	5 000	5 000	5 000	4 000	..	..
3852	Photographic & Optical Goods	1 000	1 000	..	1 000	1 000	1 000	1 000	1 000	..	..
3853	Watches & Clocks	0	..	..	..	..	0	0	0	..	..
39	Other Manufacturing, nes	9 000	10 000	9 000	9 000	8 000	10 000	11 000	11 000	..	..
3901	Jewellery	1 000	1 000	1 000	..	1 000	2 000	3 000	3 000	..	..
3	Total Manufacturing	1 719 000	1 785 000	1 775 000	1 787 000	1 609 000	1 775 000	1 762 000	1 668 000	..	..
1	Agric., Hunting, Forestry, Fishing	..	..	..	..	..	..	..	..	..	..
2	Mining & Quarrying	..	218 000	253 000	187 000	172 000	..	..	..	..	..
21	Coal Mining	..	150 000	188 000	137 000	129 000	..	..	..	..	..
22	Crude Petroleum & Natural Gas	..	2 000	3 000	3 000	2 000	..	..	..	..	..
23.29	Other Mining	..	..	..	..	..	..	..	..	..	..
3	Total Manufacturing	1 719 000	1 785 000	1 775 000	1 787 000	1 609 000	1 775 000	1 762 000	1 668 000	..	..
4	Electricity, Gas & Water	..	50 000	53 000	68 000	69 000	..	..	..	..	..
5	Construction	..	..	..	..	..	..	..	..	..	..
6.9	Services	..	..	..	..	..	..	..	..	..	..
0000	Grand Total	..	..	..	..	..	..	..	..	..	..

Note: Break in series between 1991 and 1992, see Sources and Definitions.
Some data are not given for reasons of confidentiality.
ISIC 385 includes a figure for other professional goods (Turkish SIC 3854).

Units

ISIC2	Industry	ESTABLISHMENTS									
		1987	**1988**	**1989**	**1990**	**1991**	**1992**	**1993**	**1994**	**1995**	**1996**
31	**Food, Beverages & Tobacco**	979	989	1 034	980	945	2 163	1 966	1 860	..	..
311.2	Food	858	864	908	855	822	2 020	1 824	1 728	..	..
313	Beverages	73	77	79	75	75	96	96	91	..	..
314	Tobacco	48	48	47	50	48	47	46	41	..	..
32	**Textiles, Apparel & Leather**	1 262	1 403	1 523	1 572	1 536	3 316	3 133	2 976	..	..
321	Textiles	698	724	741	744	734	1 433	1 344	1 290	..	..
3213	Knitting Mills	155	156	168	169	180	380	358	328	..	..
322	Wearing Apparel	446	577	669	704	699	1 591	1 533	1 446	..	..
323	Leather & Products	79	62	67	72	57	151	136	128	..	..
324	Footwear	39	40	46	52	46	141	120	112	..	..
33	**Wood Products & Furniture**	175	176	171	167	163	477	443	418	..	..
331	Wood Products	119	118	123	120	115	285	262	246	..	..
332	Furnitures & Fixtures	56	58	48	47	48	192	181	172	..	..
34	**Paper, Paper Products & Printing**	208	215	212	217	205	395	365	355	..	..
341	Paper & Products	100	95	90	97	92	150	140	143	..	..
3411	Pulp, Paper & Board	24	25	23	22	23	60	56	45	..	..
342	Printing & Publishing	108	120	122	120	113	245	225	212	..	..
35	**Chemical Products**	539	529	529	548	525	947	918	905	..	..
351	Industrial Chemicals	88	77	75	72	67	92	86	89	..	..
3511	Basic Industrial Chemicals	48	39	40	37	34	50	42	39	..	..
3512	Fertilizers & Pesticides	18	19	15	19	18	16	19	18	..	..
3513	Synthetic Resins	22	19	20	16	15	26	25	31	..	..
352	Other Chemicals	179	173	167	174	170	265	265	255	..	..
3521	Paints, Varnishes & Lacquers	42	33	32	38	35	53	52	54	..	..
3522	Drugs & Medicines	57	56	59	54	53	65	67	61	..	..
3523	Soap & Cleaning Preparations	43	41	40	36	35	65	64	58	..	..
3529	Chemical Products, nec	37	43	36	46	47	82	82	82	..	..
353	Petroleum Refineries	5	5	5	5	5	5	5	5	..	..
354	Petroleum & Coal Products	28	25	25	26	27	32	32	33	..	..
355	Rubber Products	95	99	96	96	86	156	154	143	..	..
356	Plastic Products, nec	144	150	161	175	170	397	376	381	..	..
36	**Non-Metallic Mineral Products**	470	497	518	484	480	860	827	832	..	..
361	Pottery, China etc	33	29	27	29	25	46	46	55	..	..
362	Glass & Products	35	38	35	36	39	75	71	71	..	..
369	Non-Metallic Products, nec	402	430	456	419	416	739	710	706	..	..
37	**Basic Metal Industries**	296	315	296	266	259	421	376	345	..	..
371	Iron & Steel	209	220	204	185	176	297	262	239	..	..
372	Non-Ferrous Metals	87	95	92	81	83	124	114	106	..	..
38	**Fabricated Metal Products**	1 241	1 235	1 188	1 214	1 162	2 516	2 433	2 324	..	..
381	Metal Products	383	379	369	389	366	828	812	767	..	..
3813	Structural Metal Products	67	81	82	92	84	235	218	202	..	..
382	Non-Electrical Machinery	361	349	333	326	299	770	716	714	..	..
3821	Engines & Turbines	7	6	6	6	5	7	6	5	..	..
3822	Agricultural Machinery	56	53	48	48	44	115	106	109	..	..
3823	Metal & Wood working Machinery	38	38	37	45	34	98	85	89	..	..
3824	Special Industrial Machinery	82	84	77	70	66	180	177	177	..	..
3825	Office & Computing Machinery	14	7	6	6	6	18	19	22	..	..
3829	Machinery & Equipment, nec	164	161	159	151	144	352	323	312	..	..
383	Electrical Machinery	247	257	240	252	238	429	402	359	..	..
3831	Electrical Industrial Machinery	73	75	70	72	65	114	115	107	..	..
3832	Radio, TV & Communication Equipment	43	49	49	51	53	105	101	79	..	..
3833	Electrical Appliances & Housewares	27	31	31	36	35	53	50	39	..	..
3839	Electrical Apparatus, nec	104	102	90	93	85	157	136	134	..	..
384	Transport Equipment	221	214	209	209	215	414	418	395	..	..
3841	Shipbuilding & Repairing	14	14	19	19	19	37	35	36	..	..
3842	Railroad Equipment	4	4	4	4	4	4	3	4	..	..
3843	Motor Vehicles	195	188	178	179	184	352	349	327	..	..
3844	Motorcycles & Bicycles	7	6	5	5	6	17	24	20	..	..
3845	Aircraft	..	2	2	2	2	2	2	2	..	..
3849	Transport Equipment, nec	1	..	1	..	..	2	5	6	..	..
385	Professional Goods	29	36	37	38	44	75	85	89	..	..
3851	Professional Equipment	11	17	15	15	19	42	45	52	..	..
3852	Photographic & Optical Goods	8	9	9	12	13	16	17	14	..	..
3853	Watches & Clocks	3	2	2	..	..	1	5	3	..	..
39	**Other Manufacturing, nes**	62	63	60	60	55	106	106	112	..	..
3901	Jewellery	9	9	8	9	8	24	25	28	..	..
3	**Total Manufacturing**	5 232	5 422	5 531	5 508	5 330	11 201	10 567	10 127	..	..
1	**Agric., Hunting, Forestry, Fishing**	..	..	..	..				..	..	..
2	**Mining & Quarrying**	..	838	852	837	856	..	..	..	..	..
21	Coal Mining	..	249	247	256	231	..	..	..	..	..
22	Crude Petroleum & Natural Gas	..	57	63	67	37	..	..	..	..	..
23.29	Other Mining	..	..	..	..	..			..	..	..
3	**Total Manufacturing**	5 232	5 422	5 531	5 508	5 330	11 201	10 567	10 127	..	..
4	**Electricity, Gas & Water**	..	1 872	1 872	1 872	1 872	..	..	..	..	..
5	**Construction**	..	..	..	..	..	..	..	..	..	..
6.9	**Services**	..	..	..	..	..	..	..	..	..	..
0000	**Grand Total**	..	..	..	..	..	..	..	..	..	..

Note: Break in series between 1991 and 1992, see Sources and Definitions.
Some data are not given for reasons of confidentiality.
ISIC 385 includes a figure for other professional goods (Turkish SIC 3854).

Millions of £ (Current Prices)

ISIC2	Industry	1987	1988	1989	1990	1991	1992	1993	1994	1995	1996
						EXPORTS					
31	**Food, Beverages & Tobacco**	4 766	4 738	5 427	5 948	6 491	7 394	7 768	8 733	..	..
311.2	Food	2 837	2 585	3 018	3 080	3 350	3 878	4 394	4 908	..	..
313	Beverages	1 495	1 667	1 896	2 228	2 378	2 572	2 741	2 971	..	..
314	Tobacco	433	486	512	640	763	945	634	854	..	..
32	**Textiles, Apparel & Leather**	3 816	3 799	4 072	4 510	4 590	4 920	5 209	6 027	..	..
321	Textiles	2 189	2 250	2 445	2 639	2 604	2 798	2 891	3 305	..	..
3213	Knitting Mills	522	544	553	620	684	760	784	915	..	..
322	Wearing Apparel	955	916	943	1 154	1 300	1 391	1 479	1 745	..	..
323	Leather & Products	481	427	463	449	379	399	457	528	..	..
324	Footwear	191	205	222	267	307	331	382	453	..	..
33	**Wood Products & Furniture**	412	357	404	481	499	550	505	629	..	..
331	Wood Products	112	118	131	165	171	175	168	211	..	..
332	Furnitures & Fixtures	299	239	274	317	327	374	337	418	..	..
34	**Paper, Paper Products & Printing**	1 961	2 097	2 365	2 846	2 926	3 093	3 448	3 802	..	..
341	Paper & Products	1 064	1 147	1 318	1 620	1 683	1 784	1 851	2 014	..	..
3411	Pulp, Paper & Board	694	735	857	1 092	1 112	1 175	1 155	1 258	..	..
342	Printing & Publishing	897	950	1 047	1 226	1 243	1 309	1 597	1 788	..	..
35	**Chemical Products**	15 194	15 928	17 740	19 388	20 259	21 493	24 321	25 856	..	..
351	Industrial Chemicals	7 724	8 306	8 933	9 278	9 395	9 879	10 991	11 648	..	..
3511	Basic Industrial Chemicals	5 610	5 990	6 325	6 450	6 615	7 093	7 969	8 322	..	..
3512	Fertilizers & Pesticides	553	552	591	615	591	594	672	678	..	..
3513	Synthetic Resins	1 560	1 764	2 017	2 214	2 189	2 192	2 350	2 650	..	..
352	Other Chemicals	3 698	3 949	4 477	5 032	5 512	6 268	7 266	8 008	..	..
3521	Paints, Varnishes & Lacquers	289	286	336	394	392	447	470	535	..	..
3522	Drugs & Medicines	1 674	1 807	2 142	2 396	2 716	3 150	3 867	4 169	..	..
3523	Soap & Cleaning Preparations	579	618	663	788	884	1 015	1 148	1 376	..	..
3529	Chemical Products, nec	1 157	1 239	1 336	1 453	1 519	1 656	1 781	1 928	..	..
353	Petroleum Refineries	1 655	1 455	1 837	2 206	2 412	2 192	2 712	2 415	..	..
354	Petroleum & Coal Products	213	208	227	270	240	231	303	330	..	..
355	Rubber Products	732	765	862	941	962	1 044	1 120	1 239	..	..
356	Plastic Products, nec	1 172	1 243	1 404	1 662	1 738	1 879	1 932	2 216	..	..
36	**Non-Metallic Mineral Products**	988	1 239	1 377	1 512	1 563	1 539	1 668	1 854	..	..
361	Pottery, China etc	270	292	328	377	386	385	392	458	..	..
362	Glass & Products	327	317	358	396	441	422	449	512	..	..
369	Non-Metallic Products, nec	391	630	691	739	736	732	828	884	..	..
37	**Basic Metal Industries**	4 199	4 742	5 698	6 001	5 686	5 357	5 718	6 670	..	..
371	Iron & Steel	2 424	2 701	3 217	3 376	3 333	3 275	3 545	4 021	..	..
372	Non-Ferrous Metals	1 776	2 041	2 481	2 625	2 353	2 082	2 172	2 649	..	..
38	**Fabricated Metal Products**	34 101	37 357	43 954	48 663	50 415	51 345	55 515	63 162	..	..
381	Metal Products	1 646	1 682	2 032	2 431	2 486	2 471	2 496	2 848	..	..
3813	Structural Metal Products	517	544	580	703	683	723	793	897	..	..
382	Non-Electrical Machinery	12 734	13 672	15 504	17 109	16 648	16 789	18 921	21 398	..	..
3821	Engines & Turbines	601	673	729	836	849	904	1 077	1 046	..	..
3822	Agricultural Machinery	946	893	970	1 122	854	857	953	1 162	..	..
3823	Metal & Wood working Machinery	1 571	1 732	1 884	2 106	2 043	1 937	1 898	2 236	..	..
3824	Special Industrial Machinery	2 568	2 428	2 795	3 117	3 005	3 120	3 238	3 584	..	..
3825	Office & Computing Machinery	4 211	4 961	5 753	6 028	6 257	6 303	7 813	9 052	..	..
3829	Machinery & Equipment, nec	2 837	2 984	3 373	3 900	3 640	3 669	3 941	4 318	..	..
383	Electrical Machinery	7 945	8 431	9 787	11 159	11 472	12 333	15 056	18 116	..	..
3831	Electrical Industrial Machinery	2 682	2 433	2 653	2 991	3 054	3 265	3 800	4 239	..	..
3832	Radio, TV & Communication Equipment	4 076	4 898	5 815	6 631	6 944	7 581	9 629	11 919	..	..
3833	Electrical Appliances & Housewares	282	360	400	456	474	509	547	630	..	..
3839	Electrical Apparatus, nec	905	739	919	1 082	1 000	978	1 077	1 329	..	..
384	Transport Equipment	10 409	11 575	14 419	15 661	17 330	17 180	16 370	17 697	..	..
3841	Shipbuilding & Repairing	309	259	313	311	289	265	218	432	..	..
3842	Railroad Equipment	78	56	39	69	80	59	104	394	..	..
3843	Motor Vehicles	4 965	5 533	6 754	8 089	9 469	9 864	9 270	10 383	..	..
3844	Motorcycles & Bicycles	70	61	63	88	92	102	118	127	..	..
3845	Aircraft	4 972	5 641	7 223	7 074	7 368	6 855	6 624	6 320	..	..
3849	Transport Equipment, nec	15	25	26	31	33	35	33	41	..	..
385	Professional Goods	1 365	1 996	2 212	2 304	2 479	2 572	2 671	3 104	..	..
3851	Professional Equipment	704	1 276	1 380	1 498	1 589	1 589	1 768	2 015	..	..
3852	Photographic & Optical Goods	582	638	742	707	803	856	745	873	..	..
3853	Watches & Clocks	80	82	90	99	87	128	159	216	..	..
39	**Other Manufacturing, nes**	1 350	1 242	1 426	1 485	1 408	1 534	1 672	2 128	..	..
3901	Jewellery	717	597	730	735	651	762	905	1 249	..	..
3	**Total Manufacturing**	66 787	71 500	82 463	90 835	93 837	97 224	105 824	118 856	..	..
1	**Agric., Hunting, Forestry, Fishing**	1 551	1 277	1 581	1 592	1 638	1 707	1 467	1 536	..	..
2	**Mining & Quarrying**	8 721	6 541	6 175	7 332	6 430	6 182	7 874	8 934	..	..
21	Coal Mining	79	65	72	84	69	44	50	44	..	..
22	Crude Petroleum & Natural Gas	6 777	4 526	4 033	5 281	4 446	4 420	5 049	6 077	..	..
23.29	Other Mining	1 865	1 950	2 070	1 968	1 914	1 718	2 775	2 812	..	..
3	**Total Manufacturing**	66 787	71 500	82 463	90 835	93 837	97 224	105 824	118 856	..	..
4	**Electricity, Gas & Water**	5	7	5	30	4	4	3	5	..	..
5	**Construction**	0	0	0	0	0	0	0	0	..	..
6.9	**Services**	1 284	1 258	1 937	2 289	1 504	1 549	1 229	1 296	..	..
0000	**Grand Total**	79 848	82 097	93 761	103 692	104 817	108 506	117 313	133 877	..	..

Note: The Grand Total includes a figure for activities not adequately defined.

Millions of £

(Current Prices)

ISIC2	Industry	IMPORTS									
		1987	1988	1989	1990	1991	1992	1993	1994	1995	1996
31	Food, Beverages & Tobacco	7 920	8 252	9 000	9 639	9 693	10 675	10 895	11 492	..	..
311.2	Food	6 450	6 684	7 378	7 779	7 933	8 856	9 086	9 532	..	..
313	Beverages	1 355	1 459	1 514	1 733	1 612	1 671	1 658	1 782	..	..
314	Tobacco	115	109	107	126	148	148	151	177	..	..
32	Textiles, Apparel & Leather	7 434	7 993	8 616	9 305	9 237	9 757	9 943	10 823	..	..
321	Textiles	4 042	4 342	4 545	4 772	4 739	5 089	5 110	5 534	..	..
3213	Knitting Mills	834	985	1 111	1 215	1 372	1 563	1 664	1 648	..	..
322	Wearing Apparel	1 994	2 195	2 514	2 775	2 829	2 987	3 050	3 222	..	..
323	Leather & Products	574	558	595	602	509	539	589	659	..	..
324	Footwear	824	898	961	1 156	1 159	1 141	1 194	1 407	..	..
33	Wood Products & Furniture	2 711	3 045	3 190	3 158	2 605	2 632	2 618	3 108	..	..
331	Wood Products	2 062	2 330	2 405	2 369	1 874	1 883	1 974	2 385	..	..
332	Furnitures & Fixtures	649	715	785	788	731	749	644	723	..	..
34	Paper, Paper Products & Printing	4 499	5 135	5 778	5 725	5 411	5 432	5 161	5 805	..	..
341	Paper & Products	3 833	4 336	4 906	4 786	4 463	4 415	4 209	4 777	..	..
3411	Pulp, Paper & Board	3 290	3 737	4 180	3 944	3 645	3 611	3 465	3 956	..	..
342	Printing & Publishing	666	800	873	938	948	1 017	952	1 028	..	..
35	Chemical Products	13 509	14 430	16 289	17 485	17 136	17 792	19 042	20 884	..	..
351	Industrial Chemicals	6 578	7 204	8 108	8 313	8 164	8 334	9 002	9 939	..	..
3511	Basic Industrial Chemicals	4 085	4 340	4 918	4 956	4 989	5 179	5 674	6 052	..	..
3512	Fertilizers & Pesticides	319	361	452	451	463	435	470	553	..	..
3513	Synthetic Resins	2 174	2 503	2 737	2 907	2 712	2 719	2 857	3 333	..	..
352	Other Chemicals	2 597	2 800	3 169	3 442	3 669	4 201	4 765	5 155	..	..
3521	Paints, Varnishes & Lacquers	168	190	214	216	210	217	240	259	..	..
3522	Drugs & Medicines	853	942	1 134	1 224	1 434	1 723	2 079	2 324	..	..
3523	Soap & Cleaning Preparations	358	401	426	473	525	630	671	771	..	..
3529	Chemical Products, nec	1 218	1 267	1 394	1 529	1 500	1 631	1 775	1 800	..	..
353	Petroleum Refineries	1 593	1 370	1 652	2 224	1 837	1 507	1 563	1 552	..	..
354	Petroleum & Coal Products	254	181	242	187	221	194	174	155	..	..
355	Rubber Products	731	849	891	949	937	1 076	1 139	1 343	..	..
356	Plastic Products, nec	1 757	2 025	2 226	2 370	2 308	2 480	2 400	2 740	..	..
36	Non-Metallic Mineral Products	1 142	1 377	1 586	1 601	1 455	1 470	1 379	1 594	..	..
361	Pottery, China etc	232	274	311	310	289	308	292	377	..	..
362	Glass & Products	530	594	637	653	633	660	652	704	..	..
369	Non-Metallic Products, nec	380	508	638	638	533	502	435	513	..	..
37	Basic Metal Industries	4 314	5 511	6 580	6 275	5 643	5 560	5 774	6 299	..	..
371	Iron & Steel	1 901	2 384	2 786	2 708	2 631	2 542	2 476	2 837	..	..
372	Non-Ferrous Metals	2 413	3 127	3 794	3 566	3 012	3 018	3 298	3 462	..	..
38	Fabricated Metal Products	38 259	46 138	53 805	54 501	50 485	55 270	61 023	68 178	..	..
381	Metal Products	2 041	2 262	2 743	2 831	2 834	2 799	2 704	3 029	..	..
3813	Structural Metal Products	400	487	584	569	607	562	435	453	..	..
382	Non-Electrical Machinery	12 444	14 395	16 852	16 971	15 869	17 142	18 651	20 435	..	..
3821	Engines & Turbines	396	416	500	520	488	616	741	728	..	..
3822	Agricultural Machinery	779	606	674	663	573	627	761	859	..	..
3823	Metal & Wood working Machinery	1 665	2 202	2 589	2 661	2 350	2 433	2 055	2 487	..	..
3824	Special Industrial Machinery	2 154	2 450	2 743	2 462	2 115	2 152	2 195	2 396	..	..
3825	Office & Computing Machinery	5 099	5 877	7 094	7 247	7 122	7 867	9 521	10 026	..	..
3829	Machinery & Equipment, nec	2 351	2 844	3 251	3 418	3 220	3 446	3 380	3 940	..	..
383	Electrical Machinery	9 967	11 049	12 662	12 745	12 927	14 553	16 452	18 441	..	..
3831	Electrical Industrial Machinery	2 302	2 170	2 544	2 686	2 766	3 192	3 370	3 711	..	..
3832	Radio, TV & Communication Equipment	5 748	6 828	7 939	7 893	7 978	9 038	10 657	11 986	..	..
3833	Electrical Appliances & Housewares	945	1 052	1 007	942	984	991	943	963	..	..
3839	Electrical Apparatus, nec	972	1 000	1 172	1 225	1 199	1 332	1 482	1 782	..	..
384	Transport Equipment	12 108	16 132	18 935	19 268	16 153	17 932	20 007	22 950	..	..
3841	Shipbuilding & Repairing	197	183	186	138	298	230	58	56	..	..
3842	Railroad Equipment	33	48	60	64	84	138	231	714	..	..
3843	Motor Vehicles	8 967	11 699	13 486	13 009	10 673	12 696	14 740	16 749	..	..
3844	Motorcycles & Bicycles	181	224	286	356	310	309	342	372	..	..
3845	Aircraft	2 713	3 960	4 892	5 674	4 752	4 522	4 589	5 010	..	..
3849	Transport Equipment, nec	15	17	24	26	36	37	45	50	..	..
385	Professional Goods	1 699	2 301	2 614	2 686	2 702	2 843	3 209	3 322	..	..
3851	Professional Equipment	511	948	1 095	1 182	1 240	1 279	1 481	1 478	..	..
3852	Photographic & Optical Goods	900	1 018	1 171	1 146	1 145	1 208	1 285	1 383	..	..
3853	Watches & Clocks	288	335	347	358	316	356	443	461	..	..
39	Other Manufacturing, nes	1 729	1 973	2 462	2 456	2 265	2 481	2 925	3 437	..	..
3901	Jewellery	729	906	1 187	1 173	989	1 044	1 323	1 723	..	..
3	Total Manufacturing	81 519	93 854	107 306	110 144	103 931	111 069	118 761	131 607	..	..
1	Agric., Hunting, Forestry, Fishing	3 957	4 035	4 127	4 263	4 099	4 305	4 211	4 666	..	..
2	Mining & Quarrying	6 405	6 029	7 075	8 104	7 721	7 391	8 301	6 953	..	..
21	Coal Mining	369	418	470	607	703	703	616	562	..	..
22	Crude Petroleum & Natural Gas	3 598	2 754	3 700	4 574	4 359	4 156	4 412	3 263	..	..
23.29	Other Mining	2 437	2 857	2 904	2 923	2 660	2 532	3 272	3 129	..	..
3	Total Manufacturing	81 519	93 854	107 306	110 144	103 931	111 069	118 761	131 607	..	..
4	Electricity, Gas & Water	247	278	321	235	359	388	454	409	..	..
5	Construction	0	0	0	0	0	0	0	0	..	..
6.9	Services	1 023	1 194	1 806	1 982	1 234	1 399	1 086	1 288	..	..
0000	Grand Total	94 025	106 571	121 881	126 086	118 869	125 864	133 722	148 189	..	..

Note: The Grand Total includes a figure for activities not adequately defined.

Millions of $ (Current Prices)

ISIC2	Industry	PRODUCTION										
		1987	1988	1989	1990	1991	1992	1993	1994	1995	1996
31	**Food, Beverages & Tobacco**	350 482	375 344	390 207	413 931	419 632	442 131	451 641	461 015	481 389	..
311.2	Food	287 063	306 721	319 141	337 144	338 633	355 900	370 929	377 087	391 806	..
313	Beverages	42 662	44 791	45 263	46 865	48 968	51 034	52 328	53 907	56 600	..
314	Tobacco	20 757	23 832	25 803	29 923	32 032	35 198	28 384	30 021	32 984	..
32	**Textiles, Apparel & Leather**	137 422	140 841	141 971	141 630	141 613	153 612	159 502	166 424	168 621	..
321	Textiles	79 840	81 979	85 059	84 415	84 019	91 381	95 821	101 626	103 825	..
3213	Knitting Mills	13 531	13 224	15 019	14 596	15 449	16 990	18 150	19 128	19 216	..
322	Wearing Apparel	48 684	49 390	47 208	47 483	48 592	52 691	53 856	55 396	55 846	..
323	Leather & Products	4 501	4 892	5 082	5 087	4 844	5 324	5 548	5 160	4 971	..
324	Footwear	4 397	4 580	4 621	4 645	4 157	4 215	4 277	4 242	3 980	..
33	**Wood Products & Furniture**	80 911	83 561	87 061	87 484	83 956	95 001	106 706	116 256	119 641	..
331	Wood Products	51 168	52 579	54 736	54 339	52 233	59 540	68 147	75 183	74 894	..
332	Furnitures & Fixtures	29 744	30 982	32 325	33 144	31 723	35 461	38 559	41 073	44 747	..
34	**Paper, Paper Products & Printing**	240 606	261 517	275 632	283 010	280 425	293 836	300 711	314 124	354 164	..
341	Paper & Products	104 412	117 498	125 720	125 950	123 741	127 443	127 683	137 742	165 724	..
3411	Pulp, Paper & Board	46 961	54 900	58 123	57 480	53 687	54 392	52 669	58 244	76 573	..
342	Printing & Publishing	136 194	144 019	149 912	157 060	156 685	166 394	173 028	176 382	188 440	..
35	**Chemical Products**	453 185	492 139	527 614	569 546	558 800	577 597	590 460	618 931	667 609	..
351	Industrial Chemicals	126 051	146 546	157 893	159 114	155 700	159 388	158 944	170 750	189 292	..
3511	Basic Industrial Chemicals	70 932	82 081	90 151	92 386	90 943	91 934	90 567	94 536	103 261	..
3512	Fertilizers & Pesticides	14 267	16 077	17 212	18 307	18 522	18 850	18 903	20 899	22 525	..
3513	Synthetic Resins	40 851	48 388	50 530	48 420	46 235	48 605	49 473	55 314	63 506	..
352	Other Chemicals	107 889	117 666	124 799	133 947	142 184	151 938	161 588	168 689	179 235	..
3521	Paints, Varnishes & Lacquers	12 702	13 532	13 656	14 239	14 255	14 960	16 017	17 559	17 943	..
3522	Drugs & Medicines	39 263	43 986	49 114	53 720	60 836	67 663	70 823	76 238	80 884	..
3523	Soap & Cleaning Preparations	29 154	31 998	32 882	35 590	35 683	36 373	38 953	37 942	41 457	..
3529	Chemical Products, nec	26 769	28 149	29 147	30 398	31 411	32 942	35 795	36 951	38 951	..
353	Petroleum Refineries	118 186	118 829	131 192	159 411	145 392	136 579	129 856	128 157	136 023	..
354	Petroleum & Coal Products	12 228	12 585	12 510	13 177	12 685	13 642	14 916	14 916	15 238	..
355	Rubber Products	22 480	24 213	25 130	25 645	25 340	26 752	28 866	29 863	32 352	..
356	Plastic Products, nec	66 352	72 300	76 090	78 253	77 501	89 298	96 291	106 556	115 469	..
36	**Non-Metallic Mineral Products**	63 856	65 803	66 399	66 463	62 522	65 885	69 002	75 397	80 509	..
361	Pottery, China etc	2 416	2 550	2 607	2 613	2 558	2 817	2 933	3 301	3 532	..
362	Glass & Products	16 317	16 805	17 299	17 338	17 013	17 995	19 071	20 162	20 508	..
369	Non-Metallic Products, nec	45 123	46 448	46 493	46 512	42 950	45 073	46 998	51 935	56 469	..
37	**Basic Metal Industries**	110 099	136 887	140 309	134 281	121 717	125 530	128 644	145 259	164 065	..
371	Iron & Steel	63 514	77 147	78 105	75 737	68 862	71 296	75 617	84 710	91 515	..
372	Non-Ferrous Metals	46 585	59 740	62 204	58 544	52 855	54 233	53 027	60 549	72 550	..
38	**Fabricated Metal Products**	998 538	1 082 241	1 118 307	1 130 194	1 111 590	1 200 912	1 266 006	1 384 392	1 492 640	..
381	Metal Products	128 848	139 450	143 068	145 025	139 716	147 263	154 819	167 924	181 088	..
3813	Structural Metal Products	40 416	43 389	44 507	44 936	42 548	45 004	46 459	51 468	56 077	..
382	Non-Electrical Machinery	241 833	268 683	278 226	280 485	267 314	284 423	304 009	343 276	379 336	..
3821	Engines & Turbines	14 570	16 223	16 931	16 581	16 609	17 667	18 994	21 754	22 815	..
3822	Agricultural Machinery	11 474	13 560	14 996	16 456	15 166	14 781	17 028	20 037	20 716	..
3823	Metal & Wood working Machinery	20 783	22 788	25 305	25 288	23 617	24 594	26 507	29 423	33 237	..
3824	Special Industrial Machinery	35 416	39 777	42 779	44 654	41 823	42 573	47 291	52 367	60 631	..
3825	Office & Computing Machinery	61 260	68 370	66 074	64 753	59 453	67 388	69 869	80 278	90 892	..
3829	Machinery & Equipment, nec	98 330	107 965	112 141	112 753	110 647	117 422	124 321	139 417	151 045	..
383	Electrical Machinery	175 895	193 352	201 487	204 261	206 538	227 625	244 719	268 509	311 710	..
3831	Electrical Industrial Machinery	31 833	35 601	37 139	35 215	34 822	37 581	40 837	43 776	47 022	..
3832	Radio, TV & Communication Equipment	97 222	107 222	111 199	116 853	121 756	137 613	148 564	165 434	202 351	..
3833	Electrical Appliances & Housewares	6 548	6 613	8 121	8 041	7 875	8 123	9 064	9 219	9 629	..
3839	Electrical Apparatus, nec	40 292	43 917	45 028	44 153	42 086	44 309	46 255	50 081	52 708	..
384	Transport Equipment	349 768	371 998	383 787	384 827	379 617	417 117	436 149	477 004	490 133	..
3841	Shipbuilding & Repairing	13 857	14 728	15 380	15 854	14 524	15 232	14 912	15 289	15 226	..
3842	Railroad Equipment	2 471	3 286	4 429	4 694	4 450	4 718	5 365	6 569	7 317	..
3843	Motor Vehicles	228 788	245 181	249 132	237 610	227 383	263 986	297 250	347 720	362 226	..
3844	Motorcycles & Bicycles	1 063	1 057	1 370	1 476	1 914	1 878	2 159	2 632	2 833	..
3845	Aircraft	103 589	107 746	113 477	125 194	131 345	131 302	116 463	104 794	102 532	..
3849	Transport Equipment, nec	..	..	..	..	..	..	..	..	..	..
385	Professional Goods	102 194	108 758	111 739	115 596	118 405	124 483	126 310	127 679	130 374	..
3851	Professional Equipment	78 180	82 970	83 442	88 726	90 937	96 561	97 845	97 928	101 897	..
3852	Photographic & Optical Goods	22 794	24 493	26 849	25 511	26 091	27 111	27 653	28 929	27 696	..
3853	Watches & Clocks	1 221	1 295	1 448	1 360	1 377	812	812	823	781	..
39	**Other Manufacturing, nes**	29 862	32 604	33 496	34 734	34 519	37 037	39 745	41 353	43 977	..
3901	Jewellery	5 554	5 769	5 912	5 754	5 275	5 727	5 902	6 095	6 222	..
3	**Total Manufacturing**	2 464 961	2 670 936	2 780 996	2 861 273	2 814 774	2 991 541	3 112 415	3 323 151	3 572 617	..
1	**Agric., Hunting, Forestry, Fishing**	..	..	..	..	..	..	..	..	..	..
2	**Mining & Quarrying**	..	..	..	..	..	..	..	..	..	..
21	Coal Mining	..	..	..	..	..	..	..	..	..	..
22	Crude Petroleum & Natural Gas	..	..	..	..	..	..	..	..	..	..
23.29	Other Mining	..	..	..	..	..	..	..	..	..	..
3	**Total Manufacturing**	2 464 961	2 670 936	2 780 996	2 861 273	2 814 774	2 991 541	3 112 415	3 323 151	3 572 617	..
4	**Electricity, Gas & Water**	..	..	..	..	..	..	..	..	..	..
5	**Construction**	..	..	..	..	..	..	..	..	..	..
6.9	**Services**	..	..	..	..	..	..	..	..	..	..
0000	**Grand Total**	..	..	..	..	..	..	..	..	..	..

Note: Unless given separately, ISIC 3843 includes 3849.

Millions of $ (Current Prices)

ISIC2	Industry	VALUE ADDED									
		1987	1988	1989	1990	1991	1992	1993	1994	1995	1996
31	Food, Beverages & Tobacco	135 867	145 922	150 955	163 535	169 820	184 515	187 738	194 214	205 772	..
311.2	Food	102 312	108 266	111 160	119 837	122 620	133 324	141 719	146 311	154 465	..
313	Beverages	19 291	20 500	20 872	21 137	22 716	23 985	25 188	25 773	26 592	..
314	Tobacco	14 264	17 155	18 922	22 561	24 484	27 207	20 832	22 131	24 716	..
32	Textiles, Apparel & Leather	63 293	64 059	65 318	64 955	65 447	71 877	73 815	77 350	77 396	..
321	Textiles	33 355	33 967	35 462	34 954	35 349	39 543	41 143	43 949	43 964	..
3213	Knitting Mills	6 269	5 946	7 002	6 791	7 244	8 054	8 645	9 246	8 929	..
322	Wearing Apparel	25 635	25 638	25 258	25 475	25 863	27 885	28 100	28 877	29 402	..
323	Leather & Products	2 009	2 155	2 272	2 211	2 111	2 241	2 319	2 201	2 061	..
324	Footwear	2 294	2 300	2 327	2 317	2 124	2 209	2 253	2 323	1 969	..
33	Wood Products & Furniture	36 970	37 410	38 270	37 730	36 021	42 646	46 900	50 128	50 722	..
331	Wood Products	21 092	21 137	21 743	20 822	19 882	24 431	27 714	29 797	29 003	..
332	Furnitures & Fixtures	15 878	16 273	16 528	16 908	16 139	18 214	19 186	20 331	21 718	..
34	Paper, Paper Products & Printing	138 435	139 379	156 341	160 377	159 687	170 012	173 873	181 081	202 669	..
341	Paper & Products	48 274	55 006	58 525	57 198	55 916	57 315	56 741	60 478	76 657	..
3411	Pulp, Paper & Board	23 220	28 761	29 838	28 139	25 214	25 598	23 993	25 837	39 044	..
342	Printing & Publishing	90 161	84 373	97 816	103 179	103 771	112 697	117 132	120 603	126 012	..
35	Chemical Products	186 845	212 661	222 978	233 209	232 290	250 693	262 090	283 260	305 513	..
351	Industrial Chemicals	56 471	68 186	72 806	73 484	69 959	72 572	72 738	78 850	89 779	..
3511	Basic Industrial Chemicals	32 394	39 827	43 820	44 913	42 165	42 976	42 694	44 011	50 484	..
3512	Fertilizers & Pesticides	6 340	7 605	7 696	8 060	8 121	8 664	9 042	10 345	11 609	..
3513	Synthetic Resins	17 737	20 755	21 289	20 511	19 673	20 932	21 002	24 494	27 686	..
352	Other Chemicals	66 621	71 895	75 296	81 760	87 314	94 614	101 209	105 695	110 577	..
3521	Paints, Varnishes & Lacquers	6 221	6 489	6 453	6 766	6 784	7 148	7 718	8 504	8 409	..
3522	Drugs & Medicines	28 161	31 026	34 358	38 245	43 245	48 542	51 298	55 529	56 718	..
3523	Soap & Cleaning Preparations	17 998	19 838	19 721	21 316	21 480	22 062	23 471	22 307	25 227	..
3529	Chemical Products, nec	14 242	14 542	14 765	15 433	15 806	16 863	18 722	19 355	20 222	..
353	Petroleum Refineries	14 219	20 688	21 580	22 822	19 796	19 112	18 584	23 435	26 267	..
354	Petroleum & Coal Products	4 300	4 592	4 468	4 392	4 228	4 797	5 367	5 351	5 333	..
355	Rubber Products	11 931	12 529	12 856	13 433	13 508	14 311	15 731	16 309	17 043	..
356	Plastic Products, nec	33 305	34 772	35 973	37 318	37 486	45 287	48 462	53 620	56 515	..
36	Non-Metallic Mineral Products	34 799	35 869	36 082	35 904	33 505	36 613	37 788	42 188	45 155	..
361	Pottery, China etc	1 686	1 752	1 781	1 839	1 758	1 995	2 073	2 310	2 506	..
362	Glass & Products	9 521	9 792	9 955	10 079	9 696	10 963	11 085	12 120	12 417	..
369	Non-Metallic Products, nec	23 593	24 325	24 346	23 986	22 051	23 656	24 630	27 758	30 233	..
37	Basic Metal Industries	42 291	52 097	51 279	49 285	42 625	47 633	50 010	58 560	63 858	..
371	Iron & Steel	27 692	33 600	33 221	31 775	27 084	30 102	32 589	36 877	39 564	..
372	Non-Ferrous Metals	14 598	18 497	18 057	17 510	15 541	17 531	17 421	21 683	24 294	..
38	Fabricated Metal Products	506 922	543 148	564 085	558 335	551 778	593 614	627 693	683 370	728 457	..
381	Metal Products	65 240	69 800	69 959	70 352	67 686	73 336	77 562	84 560	90 270	..
3813	Structural Metal Products	18 683	19 681	20 022	19 935	19 313	21 302	21 725	24 328	26 517	..
382	Non-Electrical Machinery	131 157	142 555	147 716	145 054	136 924	146 512	154 480	176 928	187 698	..
3821	Engines & Turbines	7 040	7 711	7 637	7 159	7 560	7 746	8 965	10 211	9 384	..
3822	Agricultural Machinery	5 625	6 608	6 941	7 985	7 133	7 316	8 085	9 605	9 307	..
3823	Metal & Wood working Machinery	13 114	14 250	16 183	15 536	14 591	15 492	16 486	18 868	21 118	..
3824	Special Industrial Machinery	18 352	21 285	21 688	22 011	20 512	21 715	23 898	27 107	30 921	..
3825	Office & Computing Machinery	32 743	34 088	33 507	31 620	27 741	29 594	29 435	34 526	36 256	..
3829	Machinery & Equipment, nec	54 284	58 615	61 760	60 743	59 388	64 649	67 611	76 611	80 712	..
383	Electrical Machinery	98 521	107 239	111 048	112 395	111 767	127 536	135 466	151 481	180 077	..
3831	Electrical Industrial Machinery	17 328	19 079	19 780	19 050	18 624	20 698	22 307	23 529	24 811	..
3832	Radio, TV & Communication Equipment	57 049	62 617	65 216	67 925	68 703	80 872	85 917	98 480	124 841	..
3833	Electrical Appliances & Housewares	3 312	3 222	3 972	3 690	3 417	3 649	4 007	4 206	4 342	..
3839	Electrical Apparatus, nec	20 833	22 321	22 080	21 730	21 024	22 318	23 235	25 266	26 084	..
384	Transport Equipment	144 233	151 158	161 022	154 024	158 261	163 421	174 704	184 492	184 403	..
3841	Shipbuilding & Repairing	7 657	7 902	8 176	8 555	7 959	8 545	8 023	8 033	8 159	..
3842	Railroad Equipment	1 295	1 483	1 941	1 839	1 690	2 019	2 219	2 528	2 298	..
3843	Motor Vehicles	75 853	81 964	86 372	78 872	81 722	91 733	100 267	115 917	120 197	..
3844	Motorcycles & Bicycles	368	386	502	571	741	744	927	1 162	1 324	..
3845	Aircraft	59 059	59 424	64 032	64 187	66 149	60 380	63 268	56 853	52 426	..
3849	Transport Equipment, nec	..	..	..	..	..					
385	Professional Goods	67 771	72 396	74 340	76 510	77 139	82 810	85 482	85 909	86 009	..
3851	Professional Equipment	51 958	54 931	55 126	58 365	58 903	64 109	65 521	65 676	66 886	..
3852	Photographic & Optical Goods	15 229	16 820	18 533	17 480	17 591	18 277	19 530	19 783	18 736	..
3853	Watches & Clocks	585	645	681	665	646	424	431	449	388	..
39	Other Manufacturing, nes	16 241	17 736	18 285	18 723	18 558	20 466	21 747	22 840	24 038	..
3901	Jewellery	2 372	2 463	2 623	2 591	2 458	2 498	2 596	2 746	2 683	..
3	Total Manufacturing	1 161 663	1 248 280	1 303 593	1 322 052	1 309 732	1 418 070	1 481 654	1 592 989	1 703 579	..
1	Agric., Hunting, Forestry, Fishing	..	..	..	..	..	..	..	..	..	..
2	Mining & Quarrying	..	..	..	..	..	..	..	..	..	..
21	Coal Mining	..	..	..	..	..	..	..	..	..	..
22	Crude Petroleum & Natural Gas	..	..	..	..	..	..	..	..	..	..
23.29	Other Mining	..	..	..	..	..	..	..	..	..	..
3	Total Manufacturing	1 161 663	1 248 280	1 303 593	1 322 052	1 309 732	1 418 070	1 481 654	1 592 989	1 703 579	..
4	Electricity, Gas & Water	..	..	..	..	..	..	..	..	..	..
5	Construction	..	..	..	..	..	..	..	..	..	..
6.9	Services	..	..	..	..	..	..	..	..	..	..
0000	Grand Total	..	..	..	..	..	..	..	..	..	..

Note: Unless given separately, ISIC 3843 includes 3849.

Thousands

ISIC2	Industry	EMPLOYMENT - EMPLOYEES									
		1987	1988	1989	1990	1991	1992	1993	1994	1995	1996
31	**Food, Beverages & Tobacco**	1 494.0	1 510.0	1 502.0	1 511.0	1 515.0	1 541.0	1 558.0	1 546.0	1 557.0	..
311.2	Food	1 297.0	1 314.0	1 317.0	1 332.0	1 338.0	1 369.0	1 385.0	1 383.0	1 396.0	..
313	Beverages	152.0	151.0	142.0	138.0	137.0	134.0	136.0	128.0	130.0	..
314	Tobacco	45.0	45.0	43.0	41.0	40.0	38.0	37.0	35.0	31.0	..
32	**Textiles, Apparel & Leather**	1 890.0	1 870.0	1 798.0	1 751.0	1 671.0	1 706.0	1 696.0	1 676.0	1 650.0	..
321	Textiles	878.0	873.0	848.0	829.0	791.0	831.0	829.0	852.0	842.0	..
3213	Knitting Mills	203.0	197.0	200.0	198.0	181.0	193.0	193.0	195.0	180.0	..
322	Wearing Apparel	886.0	872.0	832.0	807.0	776.0	777.0	771.0	734.0	724.0	..
323	Leather & Products	50.0	50.0	48.0	48.0	45.0	46.0	44.0	39.0	36.0	..
324	Footwear	76.0	75.0	70.0	67.0	58.0	53.0	52.0	50.0	48.0	..
33	**Wood Products & Furniture**	958.0	962.0	952.0	946.0	876.0	895.0	925.0	961.0	995.0	..
331	Wood Products	514.0	518.0	511.0	508.0	470.0	481.0	500.0	522.0	535.0	..
332	Furnitures & Fixtures	444.0	444.0	441.0	438.0	406.0	414.0	425.0	439.0	460.0	..
34	**Paper, Paper Products & Printing**	2 068.0	2 082.0	2 094.0	2 129.0	2 073.0	2 082.0	2 088.0	2 085.0	2 122.0	..
341	Paper & Products	575.0	583.0	591.0	591.0	585.0	587.0	588.0	583.0	589.0	..
3411	Pulp, Paper & Board	196.0	198.0	197.0	199.0	198.0	198.0	194.0	190.0	189.0	..
342	Printing & Publishing	1 494.0	1 499.0	1 504.0	1 538.0	1 488.0	1 495.0	1 500.0	1 502.0	1 534.0	..
35	**Chemical Products**	1 804.0	1 843.0	1 877.0	1 872.0	1 836.0	1 908.0	1 929.0	1 943.0	2 003.0	..
351	Industrial Chemicals	382.0	386.0	393.0	401.0	401.0	397.0	382.0	370.0	365.0	..
3511	Basic Industrial Chemicals	219.0	219.0	221.0	227.0	231.0	228.0	218.0	202.0	199.0	..
3512	Fertilizers & Pesticides	40.0	41.0	42.0	43.0	41.0	40.0	39.0	40.0	39.0	..
3513	Synthetic Resins	123.0	126.0	131.0	132.0	129.0	128.0	126.0	128.0	126.0	..
352	Other Chemicals	467.0	478.0	489.0	485.0	479.0	483.0	489.0	485.0	506.0	..
3521	Paints, Varnishes & Lacquers	55.0	57.0	55.0	54.0	51.0	51.0	50.0	50.0	52.0	..
3522	Drugs & Medicines	172.0	175.0	184.0	183.0	184.0	194.0	202.0	206.0	218.0	..
3523	Soap & Cleaning Preparations	99.0	107.0	108.0	107.0	103.0	101.0	102.0	97.0	100.0	..
3529	Chemical Products, nec	141.0	139.0	143.0	141.0	141.0	137.0	135.0	132.0	137.0	..
353	Petroleum Refineries	75.0	73.0	72.0	72.0	74.0	75.0	73.0	72.0	70.0	..
354	Petroleum & Coal Products	41.0	42.0	39.0	40.0	39.0	40.0	41.0	41.0	40.0	..
355	Rubber Products	204.0	208.0	210.0	204.0	197.0	204.0	208.0	209.0	217.0	..
356	Plastic Products, nec	636.0	656.0	673.0	670.0	646.0	710.0	737.0	766.0	804.0	..
36	**Non-Metallic Mineral Products**	552.0	555.0	553.0	542.0	508.0	502.0	502.0	520.0	540.0	..
361	Pottery, China etc	38.0	39.0	38.0	38.0	37.0	37.0	37.0	40.0	44.0	..
362	Glass & Products	143.0	143.0	143.0	141.0	133.0	133.0	131.0	132.0	132.0	..
369	Non-Metallic Products, nec	371.0	373.0	373.0	364.0	339.0	333.0	334.0	347.0	364.0	..
37	**Basic Metal Industries**	645.0	668.0	672.0	660.0	628.0	609.0	599.0	605.0	628.0	..
371	Iron & Steel	402.0	422.0	420.0	413.0	392.0	379.0	367.0	364.0	373.0	..
372	Non-Ferrous Metals	243.0	246.0	251.0	247.0	236.0	230.0	232.0	241.0	255.0	..
38	**Fabricated Metal Products**	7 861.0	7 966.0	7 896.0	7 718.0	7 261.0	7 276.0	7 214.0	7 288.0	7 464.0	..
381	Metal Products	1 301.0	1 333.0	1 318.0	1 296.0	1 225.0	1 231.0	1 247.0	1 287.0	1 338.0	..
3813	Structural Metal Products	407.0	413.0	406.0	406.0	379.0	390.0	386.0	401.0	416.0	..
382	Non-Electrical Machinery	2 059.0	2 115.0	2 115.0	2 065.0	1 953.0	1 922.0	1 927.0	1 999.0	2 096.0	..
3821	Engines & Turbines	87.0	90.0	85.0	83.0	78.0	84.0	78.0	81.0	82.0	..
3822	Agricultural Machinery	82.0	89.0	94.0	94.0	90.0	86.0	89.0	95.0	94.0	..
3823	Metal & Wood working Machinery	258.0	263.0	276.0	270.0	253.0	242.0	249.0	254.0	275.0	..
3824	Special Industrial Machinery	302.0	311.0	318.0	321.0	306.0	297.0	295.0	304.0	326.0	..
3825	Office & Computing Machinery	334.0	337.0	311.0	294.0	272.0	256.0	249.0	256.0	256.0	..
3829	Machinery & Equipment, nec	996.0	1 025.0	1 030.0	1 004.0	955.0	957.0	967.0	1 009.0	1 064.0	..
383	Electrical Machinery	1 596.0	1 616.0	1 588.0	1 540.0	1 470.0	1 493.0	1 491.0	1 520.0	1 583.0	..
3831	Electrical Industrial Machinery	319.0	319.0	311.0	294.0	279.0	285.0	289.0	297.0	303.0	..
3832	Radio, TV & Communication Equipment	889.0	905.0	893.0	877.0	848.0	870.0	865.0	878.0	927.0	..
3833	Electrical Appliances & Housewares	52.0	52.0	53.0	52.0	50.0	44.0	45.0	47.0	48.0	..
3839	Electrical Apparatus, nec	337.0	339.0	332.0	318.0	293.0	293.0	292.0	297.0	306.0	..
384	Transport Equipment	1 960.0	1 958.0	1 949.0	1 914.0	1 760.0	1 777.0	1 725.0	1 707.0	1 690.0	..
3841	Shipbuilding & Repairing	177.0	183.0	180.0	175.0	162.0	163.0	158.0	150.0	143.0	..
3842	Railroad Equipment	22.0	26.0	27.0	30.0	26.0	28.0	29.0	30.0	32.0	..
3843	Motor Vehicles	944.0	921.0	910.0	884.0	815.0	880.0	912.0	977.0	1 016.0	..
3844	Motorcycles & Bicycles	7.0	8.0	8.0	9.0	11.0	12.0	12.0	16.0	16.0	..
3845	Aircraft	810.0	820.0	823.0	816.0	746.0	694.0	613.0	534.0	483.0	..
3849	Transport Equipment, nec	..	..	..	..	..	..	..	..	..	..
385	Professional Goods	944.0	945.0	926.0	902.0	855.0	853.0	825.0	776.0	757.0	..
3851	Professional Equipment	800.0	799.0	783.0	764.0	720.0	720.0	690.0	656.0	641.0	..
3852	Photographic & Optical Goods	132.0	134.0	133.0	129.0	127.0	126.0	127.0	112.0	109.0	..
3853	Watches & Clocks	12.0	12.0	11.0	9.0	8.0	8.0	7.0	7.0	7.0	..
39	**Other Manufacturing, nes**	358.0	376.0	370.0	369.0	346.0	351.0	365.0	368.0	383.0	..
3901	Jewellery	50.0	51.0	50.0	49.0	46.0	45.0	47.0	44.0	43.0	..
3	**Total Manufacturing**	17 631.0	17 831.0	17 714.0	17 496.0	16 715.0	16 870.0	16 875.0	16 992.0	17 343.0	..
1	**Agric., Hunting, Forestry, Fishing**	..	..	..	..	..	..	..	..	..	..
2	**Mining & Quarrying**	..	..	..	..	..	..	..	..	..	..
21	Coal Mining	..	..	..	..	..	..	..	..	..	..
22	Crude Petroleum & Natural Gas	..	..	..	..	..	..	..	..	..	..
23.29	Other Mining	..	..	..	..	..	..	..	..	..	..
3	**Total Manufacturing**	17 631.0	17 831.0	17 714.0	17 496.0	16 715.0	16 870.0	16 875.0	16 992.0	17 343.0	..
4	**Electricity, Gas & Water**	..	..	..	..	..	..	..	..	..	..
5	**Construction**	..	..	..	..	..	..	..	..	..	..
6.9	**Services**	..	..	..	..	..	..	..	..	..	..
0000	**Grand Total**	..	..	..	..	..	..	..	..	..	..

Note: Unless given separately, ISIC 3843 includes 3849.

Millions of $

(Current Prices)

ISIC2	Industry	INVESTMENT									
		1987	1988	1989	1990	1991	1992	1993	1994	1995	1996
31	**Food, Beverages & Tobacco**	7 662	7 902	8 729	9 136	9 672	10 289	9 777	10 481	12 340	..
311.2	Food	5 998	6 188	7 044	7 694	7 895	8 438	8 066	8 493	10 058	..
313	Beverages	1 200	1 304	1 286	1 165	1 372	1 462	1 323	1 602	1 872	..
314	Tobacco	464	410	399	278	405	389	388	387	411	..
32	**Textiles, Apparel & Leather**	2 916	3 083	3 307	3 292	2 999	3 373	3 607	4 242	4 257	..
321	Textiles	2 327	2 501	2 666	2 710	2 493	2 657	2 950	3 544	3 544	..
3213	Knitting Mills	388	394	446	483	435	526	576	608	476	..
322	Wearing Apparel	489	482	520	468	406	583	527	575	607	..
323	Leather & Products	59	58	79	68	66	78	88	64	72	..
324	Footwear	41	42	43	46	33	55	42	59	35	..
33	**Wood Products & Furniture**	1 999	2 057	2 206	1 997	1 742	1 884	2 189	2 645	3 074	..
331	Wood Products	1 361	1 404	1 490	1 377	1 232	1 275	1 444	1 860	2 165	..
332	Furnitures & Fixtures	638	653	716	620	510	609	745	785	908	..
34	**Paper, Paper Products & Printing**	10 462	12 017	15 609	16 408	13 872	13 145	12 007	12 752	13 557	..
341	Paper & Products	5 553	7 009	9 848	10 596	8 830	7 766	7 137	7 097	7 942	..
3411	Pulp, Paper & Board	3 764	5 126	7 587	8 308	6 781	5 725	4 925	4 829	5 299	..
342	Printing & Publishing	4 908	5 008	5 761	5 812	5 041	5 380	4 870	5 656	5 615	..
35	**Chemical Products**	14 820	17 424	21 691	24 141	26 555	28 239	27 487	27 579	31 037	..
351	Industrial Chemicals	5 456	7 138	9 243	11 007	11 099	10 186	9 274	9 026	10 826	..
3511	Basic Industrial Chemicals	3 194	4 040	5 431	6 480	6 648	6 354	5 242	4 868	6 647	..
3512	Fertilizers & Pesticides	361	530	785	826	925	989	726	671	779	..
3513	Synthetic Resins	1 901	2 568	3 027	3 701	3 527	2 843	3 306	3 486	3 400	..
352	Other Chemicals	3 498	4 009	4 469	4 511	5 239	6 629	6 768	6 789	7 220	..
3521	Paints, Varnishes & Lacquers	275	253	241	271	256	290	256	280	417	..
3522	Drugs & Medicines	1 749	2 058	2 392	2 280	2 669	3 882	4 043	4 140	4 526	..
3523	Soap & Cleaning Preparations	668	853	839	921	1 088	1 171	1 190	1 150	896	..
3529	Chemical Products, nec	807	846	997	1 039	1 226	1 285	1 279	1 220	1 381	..
353	Petroleum Refineries	2 035	2 327	2 987	3 819	5 601	6 140	5 986	5 518	5 876	..
354	Petroleum & Coal Products	306	287	344	340	295	399	315	409	337	..
355	Rubber Products	709	849	1 241	1 050	850	952	1 059	1 041	1 067	..
356	Plastic Products, nec	2 817	2 814	3 407	3 414	3 472	3 934	4 085	4 796	5 711	..
36	**Non-Metallic Mineral Products**	2 501	2 339	3 019	2 823	2 454	2 545	2 494	2 978	3 517	..
361	Pottery, China etc	83	82	122	108	138	85	111	120	149	..
362	Glass & Products	778	824	1 067	917	992	1 000	881	989	1 155	..
369	Non-Metallic Products, nec	1 640	1 432	1 830	1 799	1 324	1 460	1 503	1 869	2 212	..
37	**Basic Metal Industries**	3 672	4 462	5 363	5 468	5 650	5 024	4 454	5 999	6 177	..
371	Iron & Steel	2 219	2 782	3 537	3 537	3 895	3 126	2 777	3 740	4 038	..
372	Non-Ferrous Metals	1 453	1 680	1 826	1 931	1 756	1 897	1 677	2 260	2 139	..
38	**Fabricated Metal Products**	33 636	30 440	36 189	37 566	34 858	37 404	38 965	44 202	52 519	..
381	Metal Products	3 419	3 170	3 804	3 778	3 197	3 740	3 831	4 551	5 658	..
3813	Structural Metal Products	802	729	821	817	747	796	764	953	1 060	..
382	Non-Electrical Machinery	7 591	7 526	8 690	8 929	8 011	8 791	8 628	9 905	10 836	..
3821	Engines & Turbines	621	605	565	676	550	773	692	647	667	..
3822	Agricultural Machinery	311	277	310	292	296	322	321	385	416	..
3823	Metal & Wood working Machinery	691	592	825	866	741	784	962	1 080	1 411	..
3824	Special Industrial Machinery	916	984	1 392	1 388	1 161	1 193	1 127	1 443	1 650	..
3825	Office & Computing Machinery	2 196	2 382	2 355	2 258	1 955	2 294	2 197	2 080	2 139	..
3829	Machinery & Equipment, nec	2 856	2 686	3 243	3 449	3 309	3 426	3 329	4 270	4 553	..
383	Electrical Machinery	6 832	7 852	8 721	9 343	8 044	8 971	10 089	12 856	17 420	..
3831	Electrical Industrial Machinery	869	768	979	965	898	962	982	1 206	1 310	..
3832	Radio, TV & Communication Equipment	4 662	5 765	6 340	6 831	5 837	6 621	7 726	10 015	14 176	..
3833	Electrical Appliances & Housewares	177	150	190	149	150	192	185	165	193	..
3839	Electrical Apparatus, nec	1 124	1 170	1 213	1 398	1 160	1 195	1 196	1 470	1 741	..
384	Transport Equipment	12 068	8 098	10 778	11 490	11 364	11 601	12 313	13 068	14 624	..
3841	Shipbuilding & Repairing	407	379	313	310	211	192	238	240	320	..
3842	Railroad Equipment	59	61	67	95	96	95	102	112	129	..
3843	Motor Vehicles	7 960	4 254	6 450	7 572	7 589	7 410	9 209	10 224	11 900	..
3844	Motorcycles & Bicycles	31	17	26	24	62	46	39	92	118	..
3845	Aircraft	3 612	3 388	3 921	3 490	3 407	3 860	2 725	2 399	2 156	..
3849	Transport Equipment, nec										..
385	Professional Goods	3 726	3 793	4 197	4 026	4 243	4 302	4 104	3 823	3 982	..
3851	Professional Equipment	2 860	2 795	2 951	2 783	2 944	3 202	3 052	2 746	2 864	..
3852	Photographic & Optical Goods	841	982	1 227	1 223	1 287	1 077	1 037	1 061	1 102	..
3853	Watches & Clocks	24	17	19	20	12	22	15	17	16	..
39	**Other Manufacturing, nes**	632	616	722	716	727	953	841	927	1 165	..
3901	Jewellery	59	41	57	65	71	66	76	70	86	..
3	**Total Manufacturing**	78 299	80 340	96 834	101 548	98 529	102 855	101 822	111 805	127 642	..
1	**Agric., Hunting, Forestry, Fishing**	..	..	..	..	..	..	..	..	..	..
2	**Mining & Quarrying**	..	..	..	..	..	..	..	..	..	..
21	Coal Mining	..	..	..	..	..	..	..	..	..	..
22	Crude Petroleum & Natural Gas	..	..	..	..	..	..	..	..	..	..
23.29	Other Mining	..	..	..	..	..	..	..	..	..	..
3	**Total Manufacturing**	78 299	80 340	96 834	101 548	98 529	102 855	101 822	111 805	127 642	..
4	**Electricity, Gas & Water**	..	..	..	..	..	..	..	..	..	..
5	**Construction**	..	..	..	..	..	..	..	..	..	..
6.9	**Services**	..	..	..	..	..	..	..	..	..	..
0000	**Grand Total**	..	..	..	..	..	..	..	..	..	..

Note: Unless given separately, ISIC 3843 includes 3849.

Table US.5 **UNITED STATES**

Millions of $ (Current Prices)

ISIC2	Industry	INVESTMENT IN MACHINERY & EQUIPMENT									
		1987	1988	1989	1990	1991	1992	1993	1994	1995	1996
31	**Food, Beverages & Tobacco**	6 153	6 351	6 901	7 256	7 731	8 292	7 947	8 459	9 956	..
311.2	Food	4 801	4 881	5 530	6 066	6 240	6 768	6 471	6 769	8 007	..
313	Beverages	978	1 111	1 037	945	1 145	1 210	1 103	1 392	1 603	..
314	Tobacco	374	359	334	245	347	315	373	299	346	..
32	**Textiles, Apparel & Leather**	2 426	2 545	2 761	2 800	2 500	2 814	3 045	3 595	3 562	..
321	Textiles	2 000	2 103	2 310	2 331	2 105	2 267	2 509	3 052	2 991	..
3213	Knitting Mills	330	335	384	400	354	451	497	515	419	..
322	Wearing Apparel	349	368	360	380	321	447	429	447	496	..
323	Leather & Products	42	39	54	53	45	63	75	51	46	..
324	Footwear	36	35	36	36	29	37	32	45	30	..
33	**Wood Products & Furniture**	1 591	1 549	1 726	1 584	1 430	1 516	1 765	2 155	2 461	..
331	Wood Products	1 133	1 127	1 247	1 141	1 059	1 052	1 211	1 558	1 785	..
332	Furnitures & Fixtures	458	421	479	443	371	465	554	597	676	..
34	**Paper, Paper Products & Printing**	8 905	10 317	13 118	14 337	12 302	11 487	10 375	11 268	11 967	..
341	Paper & Products	4 845	6 280	8 758	9 567	8 129	7 011	6 293	6 417	7 195	..
3411	Pulp, Paper & Board	3 278	4 657	6 851	7 617	6 335	5 196	4 380	4 416	4 902	..
342	Printing & Publishing	4 061	4 037	4 359	4 770	4 173	4 476	4 082	4 851	4 772	..
35	**Chemical Products**	12 183	14 506	18 128	20 337	22 362	24 306	23 182	23 407	26 519	..
351	Industrial Chemicals	4 784	6 407	8 240	9 562	9 829	9 260	8 338	8 353	10 039	..
3511	Basic Industrial Chemicals	2 831	3 680	4 915	5 634	6 061	5 769	4 724	4 505	6 174	..
3512	Fertilizers & Pesticides	316	453	676	705	765	904	650	590	697	..
3513	Synthetic Resins	1 637	2 274	2 649	3 222	3 003	2 586	2 964	3 258	3 169	..
352	Other Chemicals	2 611	3 014	3 307	3 388	3 875	4 866	4 916	4 861	5 126	..
3521	Paints, Varnishes & Lacquers	190	165	175	200	183	222	193	215	299	..
3522	Drugs & Medicines	1 219	1 432	1 645	1 588	1 799	2 682	2 754	2 723	3 002	..
3523	Soap & Cleaning Preparations	544	709	703	768	855	902	958	931	749	..
3529	Chemical Products, nec	659	708	784	831	1 039	1 060	1 010	992	1 076	..
353	Petroleum Refineries	1 518	1 779	2 390	3 285	4 826	5 635	5 221	4 775	5 255	..
354	Petroleum & Coal Products	265	249	300	276	262	333	279	365	294	..
355	Rubber Products	623	739	1 086	922	772	837	914	909	922	..
356	Plastic Products, nec	2 382	2 319	2 805	2 904	2 798	3 376	3 514	4 144	4 882	..
36	**Non-Metallic Mineral Products**	2 219	1 965	2 644	2 436	2 137	2 237	2 136	2 611	3 036	..
361	Pottery, China etc	69	56	99	89	111	72	89	107	136	..
362	Glass & Products	691	693	954	802	877	886	765	890	1 023	..
369	Non-Metallic Products, nec	1 460	1 216	1 591	1 545	1 149	1 279	1 282	1 614	1 877	..
37	**Basic Metal Industries**	3 267	4 016	4 839	4 835	5 210	4 429	3 944	5 400	5 485	..
371	Iron & Steel	2 034	2 574	3 295	3 185	3 680	2 876	2 563	3 455	3 711	..
372	Non-Ferrous Metals	1 233	1 443	1 544	1 650	1 530	1 553	1 380	1 945	1 774	..
38	**Fabricated Metal Products**	28 118	24 733	29 483	31 142	29 270	30 786	33 150	37 033	43 453	..
381	Metal Products	2 793	2 523	3 071	3 116	2 740	3 183	3 218	3 766	4 585	..
3813	Structural Metal Products	635	534	642	624	612	647	608	731	821	..
382	Non-Electrical Machinery	6 441	6 286	7 249	7 414	6 766	7 590	7 346	8 305	9 125	..
3821	Engines & Turbines	587	541	499	612	487	665	629	584	583	..
3822	Agricultural Machinery	276	244	268	254	236	280	275	313	325	..
3823	Metal & Wood working Machinery	583	490	703	716	619	676	777	933	1 168	..
3824	Special Industrial Machinery	761	803	1 109	1 137	954	973	900	1 108	1 311	..
3825	Office & Computing Machinery	1 846	1 974	1 965	1 804	1 708	2 060	1 940	1 743	1 851	..
3829	Machinery & Equipment, nec	2 387	2 236	2 705	2 891	2 762	2 936	2 825	3 624	3 888	..
383	Electrical Machinery	5 898	6 379	7 167	7 810	6 857	7 792	8 802	10 665	13 603	..
3831	Electrical Industrial Machinery	743	658	799	846	795	846	874	1 032	1 139	..
3832	Radio, TV & Communication Equipment	4 049	4 632	5 193	5 651	4 935	5 733	6 703	8 196	10 814	..
3833	Electrical Appliances & Housewares	158	113	167	133	130	182	172	155	168	..
3839	Electrical Apparatus, nec	948	976	1 009	1 180	996	1 031	1 053	1 282	1 482	..
384	Transport Equipment	9 923	6 464	8 618	9 554	9 422	8 746	10 390	11 188	12 813	..
3841	Shipbuilding & Repairing	240	210	200	204	139	135	167	163	189	..
3842	Railroad Equipment	45	47	53	66	79	78	80	89	80	..
3843	Motor Vehicles	6 910	3 713	5 707	6 632	6 804	6 110	8 152	9 145	10 710	..
3844	Motorcycles & Bicycles	29	16	24	19	41	37	35	70	103	..
3845	Aircraft	2 701	2 479	2 634	2 633	2 359	2 387	1 955	1 722	1 731	..
3849	Transport Equipment, nec	..	..	..	..	..	..	..	..	..	..
385	Professional Goods	3 063	3 081	3 378	3 248	3 486	3 476	3 395	3 109	3 327	..
3851	Professional Equipment	2 301	2 216	2 361	2 225	2 346	2 526	2 489	2 239	2 342	..
3852	Photographic & Optical Goods	741	851	999	1 006	1 129	937	892	853	971	..
3853	Watches & Clocks	21	15	18	17	11	13	14	16	14	..
39	**Other Manufacturing, nes**	519	482	597	564	606	777	688	743	904	..
3901	Jewellery	53	35	49	54	59	51	52	45	66	..
3	**Total Manufacturing**	65 382	66 463	80 195	85 290	83 548	86 644	86 232	94 670	107 340	..
1	**Agric., Hunting, Forestry, Fishing**	..	..	..	..	..	..	..	..	..	..
2	**Mining & Quarrying**	..	..	..	..	..	..	..	..	..	..
21	Coal Mining	..	..	..	..	..	..	..	..	..	..
22	Crude Petroleum & Natural Gas	..	..	..	..	..	..	..	..	..	..
23.29	Other Mining	..	..	..	..	..	..	..	..	..	..
3	**Total Manufacturing**	65 382	66 463	80 195	85 290	83 548	86 644	86 232	94 670	107 340	..
4	**Electricity, Gas & Water**	..	..	..	..	..	..	..	..	..	..
5	**Construction**	..	..	..	..	..	..	..	..	..	..
6.9	**Services**	..	..	..	..	..	..	..	..	..	..
0000	**Grand Total**	..	..	..	..	..	..	..	..	..	..

Note: Unless given separately, ISIC 3843 includes 3849.

Millions of $ (Current Prices)

ISIC2	Industry	WAGES & SALARIES - EMPLOYEES									
		1987	1988	1989	1990	1991	1992	1993	1994	1995	1996
31	**Food, Beverages & Tobacco**	31 753	32 922	33 604	34 986	35 768	38 316	39 145	39 933	41 199	..
311.2	Food	26 004	27 089	27 897	29 231	29 931	32 348	33 172	33 992	35 139	..
313	Beverages	4 263	4 331	4 212	4 239	4 317	4 444	4 550	4 500	4 576	..
314	Tobacco	1 486	1 501	1 495	1 516	1 520	1 524	1 423	1 441	1 484	..
32	**Textiles, Apparel & Leather**	27 368	27 935	27 967	27 811	27 484	29 693	30 522	31 147	31 102	..
321	Textiles	14 776	15 028	15 291	15 135	14 969	16 511	17 093	18 138	18 225	..
3213	Knitting Mills	2 988	2 986	3 159	3 159	3 022	3 344	3 489	3 578	3 474	..
322	Wearing Apparel	10 795	11 059	10 842	10 821	10 795	11 422	11 649	11 333	11 286	..
323	Leather & Products	814	858	846	865	867	936	920	856	794	..
324	Footwear	983	990	988	990	853	825	860	821	797	..
33	**Wood Products & Furniture**	16 935	17 748	17 982	18 255	17 359	18 775	20 017	21 125	22 144	..
331	Wood Products	9 426	9 941	9 969	10 091	9 562	10 294	11 078	11 641	12 064	..
332	Furnitures & Fixtures	7 509	7 806	8 013	8 164	7 798	8 481	8 938	9 483	10 080	..
34	**Paper, Paper Products & Printing**	49 515	51 869	54 159	56 883	57 249	60 761	62 060	63 489	65 881	..
341	Paper & Products	16 076	16 835	17 515	18 076	18 508	19 495	19 902	20 500	21 136	..
3411	Pulp, Paper & Board	6 991	7 297	7 488	7 778	7 948	8 246	8 235	8 481	8 742	..
342	Printing & Publishing	33 440	35 034	36 644	38 807	38 742	41 266	42 158	42 989	44 744	..
35	**Chemical Products**	47 633	50 249	53 313	55 730	57 079	61 651	63 783	65 918	69 026	..
351	Industrial Chemicals	12 824	13 429	14 340	15 278	15 808	16 297	16 052	16 115	16 602	..
3511	Basic Industrial Chemicals	7 640	7 920	8 376	9 030	9 513	9 741	9 492	9 264	9 490	..
3512	Fertilizers & Pesticides	1 171	1 224	1 339	1 445	1 406	1 452	1 448	1 550	1 596	..
3513	Synthetic Resins	4 013	4 285	4 625	4 802	4 889	5 105	5 113	5 301	5 516	..
352	Other Chemicals	13 075	13 869	15 028	15 699	16 178	17 157	17 981	18 712	19 890	..
3521	Paints, Varnishes & Lacquers	1 492	1 565	1 608	1 628	1 568	1 709	1 696	1 913	1 981	..
3522	Drugs & Medicines	5 304	5 657	6 474	6 851	7 198	7 822	8 508	8 935	9 720	..
3523	Soap & Cleaning Preparations	2 599	2 860	3 020	3 150	3 177	3 280	3 373	3 311	3 447	..
3529	Chemical Products, nec	3 681	3 788	3 927	4 070	4 236	4 347	4 404	4 554	4 743	..
353	Petroleum Refineries	2 845	2 929	2 984	3 196	3 448	3 636	3 734	3 792	3 796	..
354	Petroleum & Coal Products	1 151	1 213	1 197	1 279	1 281	1 330	1 402	1 428	1 464	..
355	Rubber Products	5 000	5 312	5 506	5 357	5 314	5 858	6 120	6 209	6 494	..
356	Plastic Products, nec	12 738	13 496	14 257	14 922	15 051	17 372	18 494	19 662	20 779	..
36	**Non-Metallic Mineral Products**	12 976	13 467	13 735	13 996	13 422	13 991	14 321	15 168	16 041	..
361	Pottery, China etc	762	801	822	832	820	845	878	974	1 077	..
362	Glass & Products	3 526	3 667	3 765	3 817	3 744	3 893	3 960	4 089	4 180	..
369	Non-Metallic Products, nec	8 688	8 999	9 148	9 346	8 857	9 253	9 482	10 106	10 784	..
37	**Basic Metal Industries**	18 646	20 172	20 911	21 307	20 459	20 789	21 210	22 358	23 456	..
371	Iron & Steel	12 168	13 312	13 658	13 914	13 269	13 523	13 775	14 484	14 982	..
372	Non-Ferrous Metals	6 478	6 860	7 252	7 393	7 191	7 266	7 436	7 874	8 473	..
38	**Fabricated Metal Products**	215 609	227 809	232 681	234 658	229 038	240 691	243 291	253 583	264 445	..
381	Metal Products	29 071	31 032	31 236	31 872	31 092	33 109	34 010	35 876	38 057	..
3813	Structural Metal Products	9 042	9 549	9 647	9 991	9 643	10 456	10 500	11 068	11 766	..
382	Non-Electrical Machinery	56 197	60 062	61 857	61 920	60 351	62 923	64 093	68 431	72 964	..
3821	Engines & Turbines	2 906	3 121	2 997	2 976	2 871	3 178	3 112	3 382	3 297	..
3822	Agricultural Machinery	1 917	2 141	2 306	2 409	2 305	2 355	2 538	2 794	2 827	..
3823	Metal & Wood working Machinery	6 965	7 428	8 087	8 171	7 756	8 141	8 416	8 903	9 919	..
3824	Special Industrial Machinery	8 516	9 156	9 655	10 096	9 842	10 004	10 364	10 968	11 956	..
3825	Office & Computing Machinery	10 814	11 671	11 117	10 422	10 243	10 298	10 017	10 571	10 657	..
3829	Machinery & Equipment, nec	25 080	26 546	27 695	27 845	27 334	28 947	29 648	31 814	34 309	..
383	Electrical Machinery	39 661	42 280	43 514	43 766	43 386	46 489	47 635	49 886	53 458	..
3831	Electrical Industrial Machinery	7 671	8 015	8 081	7 750	7 693	8 107	8 398	8 926	9 249	..
3832	Radio, TV & Communication Equipment	23 117	24 984	26 026	26 582	26 632	29 138	29 794	30 959	33 733	..
3833	Electrical Appliances & Housewares	1 050	1 064	1 095	1 114	1 076	1 009	1 077	1 145	1 205	..
3839	Electrical Apparatus, nec	7 823	8 218	8 312	8 320	7 985	8 235	8 367	8 855	9 270	..
384	Transport Equipment	63 010	65 754	66 812	67 158	64 146	67 168	67 211	69 711	70 350	..
3841	Shipbuilding & Repairing	4 266	4 416	4 570	4 667	4 504	4 630	4 392	4 408	4 320	..
3842	Railroad Equipment	631	742	841	870	820	899	967	1 076	1 085	..
3843	Motor Vehicles	29 251	30 639	30 439	30 064	28 909	31 913	34 796	38 883	40 988	..
3844	Motorcycles & Bicycles	158	164	191	214	277	302	325	483	503	..
3845	Aircraft	28 705	29 794	30 773	31 344	29 636	29 425	26 731	24 861	23 454	..
3849	Transport Equipment, nec										..
385	Professional Goods	27 670	28 681	29 262	29 943	30 063	31 003	30 341	29 679	29 617	..
3851	Professional Equipment	23 513	24 357	24 780	25 480	25 356	26 353	25 788	25 323	25 181	..
3852	Photographic & Optical Goods	3 935	4 093	4 263	4 245	4 501	4 478	4 383	4 172	4 262	..
3853	Watches & Clocks	223	231	220	218	207	172	170	185	174	..
39	**Other Manufacturing, nes**	6 497	6 992	7 099	7 351	7 292	7 996	8 420	8 618	9 216	..
3901	Jewellery	941	997	1 027	1 040	982	1 066	1 121	1 070	1 053	..
3	**Total Manufacturing**	426 931	449 163	461 450	470 975	465 150	492 661	502 768	521 339	542 508	..
1	**Agric., Hunting, Forestry, Fishing**	..	..	..	..	..	..	..	..	..	..
2	**Mining & Quarrying**	..	..	..	..	..	..	..	..	..	..
21	Coal Mining	..	..	..	..	..	..	..	..	..	..
22	Crude Petroleum & Natural Gas	..	..	..	..	..	..	..	..	..	..
23.29	Other Mining	..	..	..	..	..	..	..	..	..	..
3	**Total Manufacturing**	426 931	449 163	461 450	470 975	465 150	492 661	502 768	521 339	542 508	..
4	**Electricity, Gas & Water**	..	..	..	..	..	..	..	..	..	..
5	**Construction**	..	..	..	..	..	..	..	..	..	..
6.9	**Services**	..	..	..	..	..	..	..	..	..	..
0000	**Grand Total**	..	..	..	..	..	..	..	..	..	..

Note: Unless given separately, ISIC 3843 includes 3849.

Millions of $ | (Current Prices)

ISIC2	Industry	SUPPLEMENTS TO WAGES & SALARIES									
		1987	1988	1989	1990	1991	1992	1993	1994	1995	1996
31	Food, Beverages & Tobacco	7 886	8 374	8 667	9 273	9 856	10 967	11 389	11 532	11 636	..
311.2	Food	6 435	6 843	7 136	7 679	8 096	9 082	9 481	9 694	9 807	..
313	Beverages	1 031	1 093	1 103	1 112	1 209	1 282	1 325	1 320	1 281	..
314	Tobacco	420	438	427	481	551	603	583	518	548	..
32	Textiles, Apparel & Leather	5 172	5 502	5 503	5 535	5 577	6 709	6 633	6 775	6 742	..
321	Textiles	2 911	3 036	3 123	3 139	3 146	3 975	3 833	4 084	4 134	..
3213	Knitting Mills	546	540	578	581	564	721	768	768	752	..
322	Wearing Apparel	1 894	2 077	2 002	2 011	2 056	2 318	2 371	2 291	2 241	..
323	Leather & Products	168	181	169	177	188	226	234	190	174	..
324	Footwear	198	208	209	208	187	190	195	210	194	..
33	Wood Products & Furniture	3 574	3 785	3 847	4 017	3 890	4 446	4 745	4 840	5 012	..
331	Wood Products	2 088	2 189	2 227	2 290	2 204	2 551	2 751	2 786	2 870	..
332	Furnitures & Fixtures	1 486	1 596	1 620	1 728	1 686	1 894	1 993	2 053	2 143	..
34	Paper, Paper Products & Printing	10 094	10 717	11 120	11 993	12 592	13 982	14 436	14 186	14 569	..
341	Paper & Products	3 588	3 828	4 125	4 408	4 753	5 083	5 309	5 361	5 519	..
3411	Pulp, Paper & Board	1 540	1 649	1 763	1 915	2 086	2 166	2 220	2 259	2 334	..
342	Printing & Publishing	6 506	6 889	6 996	7 585	7 839	8 899	9 127	8 825	9 050	..
35	Chemical Products	10 963	11 939	12 748	13 795	14 692	16 507	17 334	17 927	18 458	..
351	Industrial Chemicals	2 863	3 257	3 496	3 846	4 149	4 456	4 490	4 754	4 821	..
3511	Basic Industrial Chemicals	1 750	1 917	2 019	2 236	2 441	2 638	2 658	2 660	2 785	..
3512	Fertilizers & Pesticides	247	278	300	338	351	399	389	415	384	..
3513	Synthetic Resins	866	1 062	1 178	1 272	1 357	1 419	1 443	1 680	1 653	..
352	Other Chemicals	2 880	3 114	3 407	3 703	3 918	4 367	4 620	4 686	4 865	..
3521	Paints, Varnishes & Lacquers	325	347	378	376	386	427	445	471	458	..
3522	Drugs & Medicines	1 149	1 244	1 403	1 565	1 657	1 903	2 103	2 222	2 376	..
3523	Soap & Cleaning Preparations	611	678	721	812	861	880	896	841	866	..
3529	Chemical Products, nec	796	844	904	950	1 014	1 157	1 176	1 153	1 165	..
353	Petroleum Refineries	622	660	713	796	896	935	1 058	1 081	1 124	..
354	Petroleum & Coal Products	263	282	271	298	313	320	341	350	375	..
355	Rubber Products	1 420	1 477	1 569	1 625	1 712	1 939	2 038	2 136	2 172	..
356	Plastic Products, nec	2 914	3 149	3 294	3 526	3 703	4 491	4 788	4 919	5 102	..
36	Non-Metallic Mineral Products	3 121	3 238	3 339	3 515	3 542	3 830	4 016	4 160	4 320	..
361	Pottery, China etc	197	214	218	239	238	246	255	280	299	..
362	Glass & Products	944	939	974	1 043	1 060	1 197	1 279	1 295	1 306	..
369	Non-Metallic Products, nec	1 980	2 085	2 147	2 233	2 245	2 388	2 482	2 586	2 716	..
37	Basic Metal Industries	5 937	6 437	6 562	6 921	7 005	7 299	7 609	8 049	8 103	..
371	Iron & Steel	4 156	4 520	4 511	4 791	4 835	5 031	5 225	5 576	5 580	..
372	Non-Ferrous Metals	1 782	1 917	2 051	2 130	2 170	2 267	2 384	2 473	2 523	..
38	Fabricated Metal Products	51 242	55 005	56 804	59 863	62 363	67 197	69 109	70 009	70 163	..
381	Metal Products	6 868	7 397	7 446	7 830	8 016	8 723	9 070	9 018	9 321	..
3813	Structural Metal Products	2 073	2 233	2 226	2 385	2 410	2 665	2 658	2 689	2 742	..
382	Non-Electrical Machinery	12 875	13 524	14 216	14 805	15 059	16 304	16 989	17 545	17 990	..
3821	Engines & Turbines	781	806	772	807	850	944	920	1 071	1 060	..
3822	Agricultural Machinery	557	639	673	710	709	787	831	867	848	..
3823	Metal & Wood working Machinery	1 555	1 635	1 723	1 771	1 762	1 942	2 004	1 958	2 125	..
3824	Special Industrial Machinery	2 028	2 177	2 277	2 423	2 423	2 619	2 740	2 745	2 982	..
3825	Office & Computing Machinery	2 049	2 320	2 267	2 170	2 258	2 367	2 465	2 645	2 391	..
3829	Machinery & Equipment, nec	5 905	5 949	6 504	6 923	7 056	7 644	8 030	8 259	8 584	..
383	Electrical Machinery	9 130	10 440	10 031	10 454	11 007	11 842	12 391	12 649	13 265	..
3831	Electrical Industrial Machinery	1 941	2 016	2 037	2 052	2 184	2 334	2 396	2 477	2 520	..
3832	Radio, TV & Communication Equipment	5 048	6 121	5 654	5 953	6 309	6 948	7 329	7 348	7 872	..
3833	Electrical Appliances & Housewares	260	278	288	297	303	272	321	323	336	..
3839	Electrical Apparatus, nec	1 881	2 025	2 052	2 152	2 211	2 289	2 346	2 502	2 538	..
384	Transport Equipment	16 466	17 358	18 598	19 888	21 037	22 633	22 836	23 083	22 083	..
3841	Shipbuilding & Repairing	1 006	1 111	1 127	1 196	1 243	1 377	1 340	1 248	1 184	..
3842	Railroad Equipment	227	231	246	282	283	325	332	364	393	..
3843	Motor Vehicles	8 818	9 057	9 761	10 237	11 199	12 494	13 268	14 187	13 752	..
3844	Motorcycles & Bicycles	42	38	44	56	73	85	90	110	114	..
3845	Aircraft	6 372	6 922	7 421	8 116	8 239	8 353	7 806	7 174	6 639	..
3849	Transport Equipment, nec										..
385	Professional Goods	5 904	6 285	6 513	6 887	7 245	7 695	7 824	7 715	7 505	..
3851	Professional Equipment	5 081	5 440	5 682	6 036	6 295	6 672	6 693	6 633	6 401	..
3852	Photographic & Optical Goods	770	787	772	795	900	976	1 077	1 036	1 062	..
3853	Watches & Clocks	54	59	60	56	50	47	53	45	42	..
39	Other Manufacturing, nes	1 296	1 395	1 445	1 522	1 557	1 797	1 926	1 917	1 974	..
3901	Jewellery	177	191	194	199	198	229	239	208	197	..
3	Total Manufacturing	99 285	106 391	110 035	116 434	121 074	132 732	137 195	139 394	140 978	..
1	Agric., Hunting, Forestry, Fishing	..	..	..	..	..	..	..	..	..	..
2	Mining & Quarrying	..	..	..	..	..	..	..	..	..	..
21	Coal Mining	..	..	..	..	..	..	..	..	..	..
22	Crude Petroleum & Natural Gas	..	..	..	..	..	..	..	..	..	..
23.29	Other Mining	..	..	..	..	..	..	..	..	..	..
3	Total Manufacturing	99 285	106 391	110 035	116 434	121 074	132 732	137 195	139 394	140 978	..
4	Electricity, Gas & Water	..	..	..	..	..	..	..	..	..	..
5	Construction	..	..	..	..	..	..	..	..	..	..
6.9	Services	..	..	..	..	..	..	..	..	..	..
0000	Grand Total	..	..	..	..	..	..	..	..	..	..

Note: Unless given separately, ISIC 3843 includes 3849.

Millions of $ (Current Prices)

ISIC2	Industry	1987	1988	1989	1990	1991	1992	1993	1994	1995	1996
		WAGES & SALARIES + SUPPLEMENTS - EMPLOYEES									
31	**Food, Beverages & Tobacco**	39 639	41 295	42 270	44 259	45 624	49 283	50 534	51 465	52 834	..
311.2	Food	32 439	33 932	35 034	36 911	38 027	41 430	42 653	43 686	44 946	..
313	Beverages	5 294	5 425	5 315	5 351	5 526	5 726	5 875	5 820	5 857	..
314	Tobacco	1 905	1 939	1 922	1 998	2 071	2 127	2 006	1 959	2 032	..
32	**Textiles, Apparel & Leather**	32 539	33 437	33 470	33 346	33 061	36 401	37 155	37 922	37 844	..
321	Textiles	17 688	18 064	18 414	18 274	18 114	20 486	20 926	22 222	22 358	..
3213	Knitting Mills	3 534	3 526	3 737	3 740	3 586	4 065	4 257	4 346	4 225	..
322	Wearing Apparel	12 689	13 137	12 844	12 832	12 851	13 739	14 020	13 624	13 527	..
323	Leather & Products	982	1 039	1 015	1 042	1 055	1 161	1 153	1 046	968	..
324	Footwear	1 181	1 198	1 197	1 198	1 040	1 015	1 055	1 031	991	..
33	**Wood Products & Furniture**	20 509	21 532	21 829	22 272	21 250	23 220	24 761	25 964	27 156	..
331	Wood Products	11 515	12 130	12 196	12 381	11 766	12 846	13 830	14 428	14 933	..
332	Furnitures & Fixtures	8 994	9 402	9 633	9 891	9 484	10 375	10 931	11 536	12 223	..
34	**Paper, Paper Products & Printing**	59 609	62 586	65 279	68 876	69 841	74 743	76 495	77 675	80 450	..
341	Paper & Products	19 664	20 664	21 640	22 484	23 261	24 578	25 211	25 862	26 655	..
3411	Pulp, Paper & Board	8 531	8 946	9 251	9 693	10 034	10 412	10 455	10 741	11 076	..
342	Printing & Publishing	39 945	41 923	43 640	46 392	46 580	50 165	51 285	51 813	53 795	..
35	**Chemical Products**	58 596	62 188	66 061	69 524	71 771	78 158	81 116	83 845	87 484	..
351	Industrial Chemicals	15 687	16 686	17 836	19 124	19 957	20 753	20 542	20 870	21 423	..
3511	Basic Industrial Chemicals	9 390	9 837	10 395	11 266	11 954	12 378	12 150	11 924	12 275	..
3512	Fertilizers & Pesticides	1 418	1 503	1 639	1 784	1 757	1 851	1 836	1 965	1 980	..
3513	Synthetic Resins	4 879	5 347	5 802	6 074	6 246	6 524	6 556	6 981	7 169	..
352	Other Chemicals	15 955	16 983	18 435	19 402	20 096	21 524	22 601	23 399	24 755	..
3521	Paints, Varnishes & Lacquers	1 816	1 912	1 985	2 004	1 954	2 136	2 141	2 384	2 439	..
3522	Drugs & Medicines	6 453	6 901	7 877	8 416	8 854	9 725	10 611	11 157	12 096	..
3523	Soap & Cleaning Preparations	3 209	3 538	3 741	3 962	4 038	4 160	4 269	4 151	4 313	..
3529	Chemical Products, nec	4 477	4 632	4 831	5 020	5 250	5 504	5 580	5 707	5 907	..
353	Petroleum Refineries	3 467	3 589	3 697	3 991	4 344	4 571	4 792	4 873	4 920	..
354	Petroleum & Coal Products	1 414	1 495	1 468	1 577	1 594	1 650	1 742	1 777	1 839	..
355	Rubber Products	6 420	6 789	7 075	6 982	7 026	7 797	8 158	8 345	8 666	..
356	Plastic Products, nec	15 652	16 646	17 551	18 448	18 754	21 864	23 282	24 581	25 881	..
36	**Non-Metallic Mineral Products**	16 097	16 705	17 074	17 511	16 964	17 821	18 336	19 328	20 361	..
361	Pottery, China etc	960	1 015	1 040	1 072	1 058	1 090	1 133	1 253	1 375	..
362	Glass & Products	4 470	4 606	4 739	4 861	4 804	5 090	5 239	5 383	5 486	..
369	Non-Metallic Products, nec	10 668	11 084	11 295	11 579	11 102	11 641	11 964	12 692	13 500	..
37	**Basic Metal Industries**	24 583	26 609	27 473	28 228	27 464	28 088	28 819	30 407	31 558	..
371	Iron & Steel	16 323	17 832	18 170	18 705	18 103	18 554	19 000	20 060	20 562	..
372	Non-Ferrous Metals	8 259	8 777	9 303	9 523	9 360	9 533	9 820	10 347	10 996	..
38	**Fabricated Metal Products**	266 851	282 814	289 485	294 521	291 401	307 888	312 400	323 591	334 609	..
381	Metal Products	35 939	38 430	38 682	39 702	39 108	41 831	43 079	44 894	47 378	..
3813	Structural Metal Products	11 115	11 782	11 873	12 375	12 052	13 121	13 157	13 757	14 507	..
382	Non-Electrical Machinery	69 072	73 586	76 073	76 724	75 410	79 227	81 082	85 976	90 954	..
3821	Engines & Turbines	3 687	3 926	3 768	3 783	3 721	4 123	4 031	4 453	4 357	..
3822	Agricultural Machinery	2 474	2 780	2 979	3 120	3 014	3 142	3 368	3 661	3 675	..
3823	Metal & Wood working Machinery	8 520	9 062	9 810	9 943	9 518	10 083	10 420	10 861	12 044	..
3824	Special Industrial Machinery	10 544	11 333	11 932	12 519	12 265	12 623	13 104	13 713	14 938	..
3825	Office & Computing Machinery	12 863	13 990	13 384	12 592	12 501	12 666	12 481	13 215	13 048	..
3829	Machinery & Equipment, nec	30 984	32 494	34 200	34 768	34 390	36 591	37 678	40 072	42 893	..
383	Electrical Machinery	48 791	52 721	53 545	54 220	54 393	58 332	60 026	62 535	66 723	..
3831	Electrical Industrial Machinery	9 612	10 031	10 118	9 802	9 877	10 441	10 794	11 403	11 769	..
3832	Radio, TV & Communication Equipment	28 165	31 105	31 680	32 535	32 941	36 087	37 122	38 307	41 605	..
3833	Electrical Appliances & Housewares	1 310	1 342	1 383	1 411	1 379	1 281	1 398	1 468	1 541	..
3839	Electrical Apparatus, nec	9 704	10 243	10 363	10 472	10 196	10 524	10 713	11 357	11 808	..
384	Transport Equipment	79 475	83 113	85 410	87 045	85 183	89 801	90 047	92 794	92 432	..
3841	Shipbuilding & Repairing	5 272	5 527	5 697	5 863	5 747	6 007	5 732	5 656	5 504	..
3842	Railroad Equipment	858	973	1 086	1 152	1 103	1 224	1 299	1 440	1 478	..
3843	Motor Vehicles	38 069	39 695	40 199	40 301	40 108	44 406	48 064	53 070	54 740	..
3844	Motorcycles & Bicycles	200	202	234	269	349	387	415	592	616	..
3845	Aircraft	35 076	36 716	38 194	39 460	37 875	37 778	34 538	32 035	30 093	..
3849	Transport Equipment, nec	..	..	..	..	..	..	..	..	..	..
385	Professional Goods	33 574	34 966	35 775	36 830	37 308	38 698	38 165	37 394	37 121	..
3851	Professional Equipment	28 593	29 797	30 461	31 516	31 651	33 025	32 481	31 956	31 582	..
3852	Photographic & Optical Goods	4 705	4 880	5 034	5 040	5 401	5 454	5 460	5 208	5 324	..
3853	Watches & Clocks	277	290	280	274	257	219	223	230	216	..
39	**Other Manufacturing, nes**	7 793	8 387	8 544	8 872	8 849	9 792	10 346	10 535	11 190	..
3901	Jewellery	1 118	1 188	1 221	1 239	1 180	1 295	1 360	1 278	1 250	..
3	**Total Manufacturing**	526 215	555 554	571 484	587 409	586 224	625 393	639 963	660 733	683 486	..
1	**Agric., Hunting, Forestry, Fishing**	..	..	..	..	..	..	..	..	..	..
2	**Mining & Quarrying**	..	..	..	..	..	..	..	..	..	..
21	Coal Mining	..	..	..	..	..	..	..	..	..	..
22	Crude Petroleum & Natural Gas	..	..	..	..	..	..	..	..	..	..
23.29	Other Mining	..	..	..	..	..	..	..	..	..	..
3	**Total Manufacturing**	526 215	555 554	571 484	587 409	586 224	625 393	639 963	660 733	683 486	..
4	**Electricity, Gas & Water**	..	..	..	..	..	..	..	..	..	..
5	**Construction**	..	..	..	..	..	..	..	..	..	..
6.9	**Services**	..	..	..	..	..	..	..	..	..	..
0000	**Grand Total**	..	..	..	..	..	..	..	..	..	..

Note: Unless given separately, ISIC 3843 includes 3849.

Thousands

ISIC2	Industry	HOURS WORKED									
		1987	1988	1989	1990	1991	1992	1993	1994	1995	1996
31	**Food, Beverages & Tobacco**	2 081 000	2 118 000	2 137 000	2 196 000	2 209 000	2 295 000	2 326 000	2 346 000	2 364 000	..
311.2	Food	1 875 000	1 918 000	1 942 000	2 003 000	2 020 000	2 108 000	2 139 000	2 166 000	2 186 000	..
313	Beverages	144 000	142 000	138 000	136 000	135 000	136 000	140 000	134 000	134 000	..
314	Tobacco	61 000	58 000	58 000	57 000	53 000	51 000	48 000	46 000	45 000	..
32	**Textiles, Apparel & Leather**	3 010 000	2 954 000	2 904 000	2 844 000	2 731 000	2 761 000	2 762 000	2 745 000	2 674 000	..
321	Textiles	1 493 000	1 471 000	1 447 000	1 419 000	1 367 000	1 416 000	1 424 000	1 453 000	1 420 000	..
3213	Knitting Mills	342 000	333 000	343 000	349 000	327 000	334 000	332 000	334 000	311 000	..
322	Wearing Apparel	1 316 000	1 285 000	1 268 000	1 248 000	1 207 000	1 194 000	1 187 000	1 146 000	1 122 000	..
323	Leather & Products	76 000	76 000	73 000	70 000	66 000	70 000	68 000	64 000	60 000	..
324	Footwear	125 000	122 000	115 000	107 000	90 000	81 000	83 000	81 000	71 000	..
33	**Wood Products & Furniture**	1 578 000	1 581 000	1 562 000	1 555 000	1 431 000	1 477 000	1 543 000	1 621 000	1 663 000	..
331	Wood Products	863 000	872 000	861 000	856 000	796 000	812 000	863 000	901 000	911 000	..
332	Furnitures & Fixtures	715 000	709 000	701 000	699 000	635 000	666 000	679 000	720 000	752 000	..
34	**Paper, Paper Products & Printing**	2 450 000	2 503 000	2 508 000	2 542 000	2 481 000	2 510 000	2 509 000	2 521 000	2 565 000	..
341	Paper & Products	912 000	935 000	948 000	945 000	940 000	953 000	958 000	970 000	972 000	..
3411	Pulp, Paper & Board	323 000	330 000	329 000	329 000	326 000	330 000	326 000	325 000	321 000	..
342	Printing & Publishing	1 538 000	1 568 000	1 561 000	1 597 000	1 540 000	1 557 000	1 551 000	1 551 000	1 593 000	..
35	**Chemical Products**	2 453 000	2 533 000	2 573 000	2 566 000	2 509 000	2 649 000	2 700 000	2 770 000	2 884 000	..
351	Industrial Chemicals	483 000	503 000	509 000	517 000	519 000	518 000	502 000	491 000	491 000	..
3511	Basic Industrial Chemicals	256 000	270 000	268 000	274 000	281 000	279 000	268 000	251 000	252 000	..
3512	Fertilizers & Pesticides	51 000	53 000	55 000	58 000	56 000	56 000	54 000	55 000	55 000	..
3513	Synthetic Resins	177 000	181 000	187 000	185 000	182 000	183 000	180 000	186 000	184 000	..
352	Other Chemicals	509 000	521 000	522 000	519 000	514 000	535 000	541 000	541 000	580 000	..
3521	Paints, Varnishes & Lacquers	56 000	57 000	56 000	56 000	52 000	53 000	53 000	56 000	57 000	..
3522	Drugs & Medicines	155 000	158 000	161 000	161 000	163 000	187 000	191 000	198 000	226 000	..
3523	Soap & Cleaning Preparations	119 000	130 000	126 000	127 000	125 000	125 000	128 000	120 000	124 000	..
3529	Chemical Products, nec	178 000	176 000	180 000	175 000	174 000	170 000	168 000	167 000	174 000	..
353	Petroleum Refineries	103 000	103 000	105 000	106 000	107 000	109 000	107 000	110 000	107 000	..
354	Petroleum & Coal Products	55 000	55 000	55 000	56 000	54 000	56 000	58 000	56 000	57 000	..
355	Rubber Products	315 000	329 000	332 000	323 000	303 000	321 000	331 000	340 000	360 000	..
356	Plastic Products, nec	988 000	1 022 000	1 050 000	1 045 000	1 012 000	1 110 000	1 163 000	1 232 000	1 289 000	..
36	**Non-Metallic Mineral Products**	874 000	867 000	873 000	863 000	801 000	791 000	797 000	841 000	867 000	..
361	Pottery, China etc	60 000	62 000	60 000	60 000	59 000	57 000	58 000	64 000	68 000	..
362	Glass & Products	234 000	238 000	237 000	235 000	221 000	222 000	221 000	227 000	222 000	..
369	Non-Metallic Products, nec	579 000	567 000	577 000	569 000	521 000	513 000	518 000	550 000	576 000	..
37	**Basic Metal Industries**	1 024 000	1 087 000	1 117 000	1 066 000	989 000	982 000	987 000	1 027 000	1 063 000	..
371	Iron & Steel	646 000	698 000	721 000	676 000	620 000	614 000	619 000	631 000	636 000	..
372	Non-Ferrous Metals	378 000	389 000	396 000	390 000	369 000	368 000	368 000	396 000	427 000	..
38	**Fabricated Metal Products**	10 207 000	10 350 000	10 344 000	10 047 000	9 432 000	9 485 000	9 586 000	10 027 000	10 312 000	..
381	Metal Products	1 955 000	2 028 000	2 008 000	1 968 000	1 858 000	1 875 000	1 918 000	2 012 000	2 100 000	..
3813	Structural Metal Products	584 000	599 000	589 000	586 000	551 000	571 000	570 000	603 000	630 000	..
382	Non-Electrical Machinery	2 604 000	2 731 000	2 759 000	2 670 000	2 475 000	2 471 000	2 534 000	2 706 000	2 867 000	..
3821	Engines & Turbines	117 000	123 000	113 000	111 000	102 000	107 000	108 000	115 000	116 000	..
3822	Agricultural Machinery	111 000	126 000	134 000	134 000	123 000	119 000	134 000	144 000	145 000	..
3823	Metal & Wood working Machinery	377 000	395 000	413 000	406 000	375 000	366 000	380 000	395 000	432 000	..
3824	Special Industrial Machinery	359 000	380 000	395 000	391 000	358 000	349 000	351 000	371 000	397 000	..
3825	Office & Computing Machinery	253 000	254 000	238 000	223 000	193 000	188 000	185 000	192 000	199 000	..
3829	Machinery & Equipment, nec	1 388 000	1 453 000	1 466 000	1 405 000	1 323 000	1 343 000	1 376 000	1 489 000	1 579 000	..
383	Electrical Machinery	1 984 000	1 925 000	1 991 000	1 921 000	1 842 000	1 878 000	1 893 000	1 987 000	2 055 000	..
3831	Electrical Industrial Machinery	432 000	349 000	432 000	405 000	384 000	392 000	405 000	427 000	435 000	..
3832	Radio, TV & Communication Equipment	1 001 000	1 022 000	1 019 000	1 001 000	973 000	1 005 000	1 003 000	1 048 000	1 102 000	..
3833	Electrical Appliances & Housewares	77 000	76 000	78 000	76 000	73 000	67 000	70 000	78 000	77 000	..
3839	Electrical Apparatus, nec	474 000	478 000	462 000	439 000	411 000	413 000	414 000	435 000	442 000	..
384	Transport Equipment	2 697 000	2 705 000	2 644 000	2 540 000	2 354 000	2 396 000	2 410 000	2 507 000	2 504 000	..
3841	Shipbuilding & Repairing	272 000	280 000	277 000	269 000	246 000	245 000	231 000	231 000	214 000	..
3842	Railroad Equipment	29 000	36 000	40 000	41 000	38 000	40 000	43 000	46 000	50 000	..
3843	Motor Vehicles	1 557 000	1 565 000	1 518 000	1 431 000	1 318 000	1 452 000	1 565 000	1 732 000	1 770 000	..
3844	Motorcycles & Bicycles	12 000	12 000	14 000	15 000	17 000	17 000	18 000	21 000	23 000	..
3845	Aircraft	826 000	813 000	795 000	784 000	736 000	641 000	553 000	478 000	448 000	..
3849	Transport Equipment, nec	..	..	..					..		..
385	Professional Goods	967 000	960 000	943 000	948 000	904 000	866 000	832 000	815 000	787 000	..
3851	Professional Equipment	804 000	793 000	771 000	775 000	746 000	704 000	672 000	668 000	643 000	..
3852	Photographic & Optical Goods	145 000	149 000	156 000	158 000	145 000	150 000	149 000	136 000	134 000	..
3853	Watches & Clocks	18 000	18 000	16 000	15 000	13 000	11 000	11 000	11 000	10 000	..
39	**Other Manufacturing, nes**	495 000	521 000	511 000	504 000	487 000	487 000	506 000	519 000	532 000	..
3901	Jewellery	68 000	71 000	67 000	64 000	60 000	60 000	62 000	55 000	55 000	..
3	**Total Manufacturing**	24 170 000	24 513 000	24 530 000	24 183 000	23 069 000	23 436 000	23 715 000	24 415 000	24 924 000	..
1	**Agric., Hunting, Forestry, Fishing**	..	..	..	..	..	..	..	..	..	..
2	**Mining & Quarrying**	..	..	..	..	..	..	..	..	..	..
21	Coal Mining	..	..	..	..	..	..	..	..	..	..
22	Crude Petroleum & Natural Gas	..	..	..	..	..	..	..	..	..	..
23.29	Other Mining	..	..	..	..	..	..	..	..	..	..
3	**Total Manufacturing**	24 170 000	24 513 000	24 530 000	24 183 000	23 069 000	23 436 000	23 715 000	24 415 000	24 924 000	..
4	**Electricity, Gas & Water**	..	..	..	..	..	..	..	..	..	..
5	**Construction**	..	..	..	..	..	..	..	..	..	..
6.9	**Services**	..	..	..	..	..	..	..	..	..	..
0000	**Grand Total**	..	..	..	..	..	..	..	..	..	..

Note: Unless given separately, ISIC 3843 includes 3849.

Millions of $ (Current Prices)

ISIC2	Industry	EXPORTS									
		1987	1988	1989	1990	1991	1992	1993	1994	1995	1996
31	**Food, Beverages & Tobacco**	14 970	19 040	20 591	21 628	22 623	24 875	24 762	28 882	31 665	..
311.2	Food	12 317	15 699	16 231	15 820	17 144	19 338	19 484	22 077	24 747	..
313	Beverages	337	463	714	763	892	1 019	1 024	1 381	1 654	..
314	Tobacco	2 316	2 879	3 646	5 045	4 588	4 518	4 253	5 424	5 264	..
32	**Textiles, Apparel & Leather**	4 259	5 426	6 651	8 303	9 755	11 142	11 726	13 389	15 054	..
321	Textiles	2 502	3 082	3 555	4 494	5 200	5 642	5 769	6 536	7 176	..
3213	Knitting Mills	77	127	214	351	472	550	581	625	759	..
322	Wearing Apparel	1 039	1 396	1 922	2 329	3 022	3 846	4 434	5 188	6 178	..
323	Leather & Products	492	626	813	964	944	1 021	1 056	1 074	1 093	..
324	Footwear	226	322	361	516	589	632	466	591	607	..
33	**Wood Products & Furniture**	2 762	3 655	4 038	5 709	6 469	7 157	6 832	7 242	7 346	..
331	Wood Products	2 321	3 104	3 262	4 094	4 330	4 599	4 245	4 357	4 436	..
332	Furnitures & Fixtures	441	551	777	1 615	2 139	2 558	2 587	2 885	2 909	..
34	**Paper, Paper Products & Printing**	7 273	9 015	11 027	11 827	12 840	13 740	13 293	15 061	19 398	..
341	Paper & Products	5 727	7 105	8 293	8 545	9 122	9 832	9 236	10 868	14 828	..
3411	Pulp, Paper & Board	5 042	5 779	6 225	6 754	6 990	7 541	6 672	7 839	11 244	..
342	Printing & Publishing	1 545	1 910	2 734	3 282	3 718	3 908	4 057	4 194	4 570	..
35	**Chemical Products**	35 006	42 876	49 150	55 121	59 776	60 865	60 881	68 808	80 247	..
351	Industrial Chemicals	20 611	25 068	28 694	28 013	30 258	29 505	29 133	34 633	42 364	..
3511	Basic Industrial Chemicals	11 926	14 189	16 776	14 882	15 592	15 854	15 982	18 792	23 248	..
3512	Fertilizers & Pesticides	3 031	3 455	4 054	4 345	4 688	4 148	3 616	4 661	5 305	..
3513	Synthetic Resins	5 654	7 424	7 864	8 785	9 979	9 503	9 536	11 180	13 811	..
352	Other Chemicals	6 052	9 186	10 530	13 835	15 295	17 026	17 210	18 626	20 737	..
3521	Paints, Varnishes & Lacquers	304	323	433	583	700	710	811	943	1 021	..
3522	Drugs & Medicines	3 258	4 042	4 282	5 185	5 861	6 950	7 222	7 737	8 212	..
3523	Soap & Cleaning Preparations	851	914	1 062	1 774	2 169	2 455	2 684	3 287	3 609	..
3529	Chemical Products, nec	1 639	3 906	4 754	6 294	6 566	6 910	6 493	6 660	7 896	..
353	Petroleum Refineries	4 198	2 229	4 690	6 168	6 534	5 816	5 641	5 025	5 398	..
354	Petroleum & Coal Products	387	1 452	521	754	668	656	522	553	683	..
355	Rubber Products	1 096	1 496	1 691	2 371	2 633	2 792	3 017	3 535	4 000	..
356	Plastic Products, nec	2 661	3 444	3 024	3 979	4 388	5 071	5 357	6 435	7 065	..
36	**Non-Metallic Mineral Products**	2 096	2 574	2 774	3 658	3 967	4 305	4 244	4 852	5 454	..
361	Pottery, China etc	219	282	324	509	553	634	426	549	631	..
362	Glass & Products	820	994	1 161	1 566	1 696	1 775	1 867	2 105	2 372	..
369	Non-Metallic Products, nec	1 058	1 298	1 289	1 583	1 718	1 896	1 951	2 197	2 452	..
37	**Basic Metal Industries**	5 530	11 154	10 212	11 096	12 923	12 245	16 306	13 994	17 569	..
371	Iron & Steel	1 259	1 989	3 264	3 241	4 244	3 588	3 223	3 596	5 450	..
372	Non-Ferrous Metals	4 271	9 165	6 948	7 855	8 679	8 657	13 083	10 398	12 119	..
38	**Fabricated Metal Products**	130 031	161 095	180 983	209 659	230 708	248 264	242 648	292 163	325 440	..
381	Metal Products	4 237	4 341	6 165	7 419	8 448	9 292	9 678	11 388	12 779	..
3813	Structural Metal Products	755	924	1 105	1 174	1 382	1 533	1 731	1 844	2 114	..
382	Non-Electrical Machinery	44 057	57 216	61 459	66 476	71 713	75 706	74 693	92 067	106 389	..
3821	Engines & Turbines	2 378	3 818	4 378	3 668	4 256	4 738	6 552	8 133	9 303	..
3822	Agricultural Machinery	1 389	1 721	2 818	4 153	4 160	4 417	3 158	3 496	4 006	..
3823	Metal & Wood working Machinery	2 299	2 768	3 426	3 811	3 723	4 234	4 041	5 172	5 280	..
3824	Special Industrial Machinery	7 741	11 482	12 651	13 295	14 628	14 652	15 050	17 702	21 191	..
3825	Office & Computing Machinery	19 586	24 372	25 000	25 982	27 379	29 048	26 426	34 511	40 869	..
3829	Machinery & Equipment, nec	10 664	13 055	13 187	15 567	17 568	18 617	19 466	23 053	25 741	..
383	Electrical Machinery	27 173	32 063	37 710	47 041	51 766	57 089	55 806	77 675	94 954	..
3831	Electrical Industrial Machinery	3 598	3 888	6 077	4 356	5 116	5 744	7 161	8 057	8 900	..
3832	Radio, TV & Communication Equipment	19 438	22 601	26 978	32 854	35 490	39 031	38 018	56 921	71 518	..
3833	Electrical Appliances & Housewares	533	820	997	941	1 054	1 183	1 232	1 350	1 510	..
3839	Electrical Apparatus, nec	3 605	4 754	3 658	8 891	10 106	11 130	9 395	11 347	13 027	..
384	Transport Equipment	43 879	52 851	58 941	70 816	78 932	85 489	80 993	86 945	84 490	..
3841	Shipbuilding & Repairing	348	703	967	1 266	1 117	1 407	913	1 173	1 196	..
3842	Railroad Equipment	334	307	402	486	511	526	459	606	766	..
3843	Motor Vehicles	21 044	25 433	26 648	31 384	34 085	39 369	42 213	48 048	50 434	..
3844	Motorcycles & Bicycles	157	269	285	485	710	749	703	762	905	..
3845	Aircraft	21 816	26 140	30 639	37 196	42 509	43 438	36 704	36 357	31 190	..
3849	Transport Equipment, nec	180	..	..	..	..	..				..
385	Professional Goods	10 685	14 625	16 708	17 907	19 849	20 688	21 479	24 088	26 829	..
3851	Professional Equipment	6 679	10 322	11 503	12 944	14 276	15 074	16 488	18 132	20 116	..
3852	Photographic & Optical Goods	3 868	4 116	4 969	4 714	5 289	5 322	4 821	5 639	6 383	..
3853	Watches & Clocks	138	187	236	249	284	292	171	318	331	..
39	**Other Manufacturing, nes**	3 128	4 137	5 106	6 066	6 541	7 177	5 177	8 505	9 513	..
3901	Jewellery	1 348	1 791	2 205	2 561	2 522	2 504	712	3 074	3 488	..
3	**Total Manufacturing**	205 054	258 973	290 533	333 066	365 603	389 771	385 869	452 896	511 685	..
1	**Agric., Hunting, Forestry, Fishing**	..	..	..	..	..	..	..	..	..	..
2	**Mining & Quarrying**	..	..	..	..	..	..	..	..	..	..
21	Coal Mining	..	..	..	..	..	..	..	..	..	..
22	Crude Petroleum & Natural Gas	..	..	..	..	..	..	..	..	..	..
23.29	Other Mining	..	..	..	..	..	..	..	..	..	..
3	**Total Manufacturing**	205 054	258 973	290 533	333 066	365 603	389 771	385 869	452 896	511 685	..
4	**Electricity, Gas & Water**	..	..	..	..	..	..	..	..	..	..
5	**Construction**	..	..	..	..	..	..	..	..	..	..
6.9	**Services**	..	..	..	..	..	..	..	..	..	..
0000	**Grand Total**	..	..	..	..	..	..	..	..	..	..

Note: Unless given separately, ISIC 3843 includes 3849.

Millions of $ (Current Prices)

ISIC2	Industry	IMPORTS									
		1987	1988	1989	1990	1991	1992	1993	1994	1995	1996
31	**Food, Beverages & Tobacco**	13 729	14 434	15 650	17 374	16 983	18 459	18 429	17 961	18 897	..
311.2	Food	10 208	10 736	11 930	13 425	13 141	14 018	13 562	13 473	14 120	..
313	Beverages	3 419	3 597	3 608	3 827	3 621	4 080	4 248	4 326	4 593	..
314	Tobacco	103	101	112	121	221	360	618	163	184	..
32	**Textiles, Apparel & Leather**	36 396	37 900	40 342	42 860	43 789	50 284	56 638	58 528	62 218	..
321	Textiles	6 330	6 188	9 300	9 122	9 655	10 496	9 966	10 231	10 771	..
3213	Knitting Mills	152	299	2 996	2 477	2 444	2 575	560	644	715	..
322	Wearing Apparel	20 170	20 777	21 313	22 882	23 500	28 520	34 474	35 500	38 030	..
323	Leather & Products	2 775	3 070	3 040	3 100	3 105	3 353	3 845	4 196	4 652	..
324	Footwear	7 121	7 865	6 689	7 757	7 529	7 915	8 353	8 600	8 766	..
33	**Wood Products & Furniture**	10 549	10 625	10 727	10 392	10 092	12 020	15 039	16 779	17 286	..
331	Wood Products	5 896	5 851	5 844	5 436	5 230	6 658	9 197	10 145	9 938	..
332	Furnitures & Fixtures	4 653	4 774	4 883	4 956	4 862	5 362	5 842	6 634	7 349	..
34	**Paper, Paper Products & Printing**	11 047	12 734	13 357	13 159	11 981	12 087	13 423	13 744	19 093	..
341	Paper & Products	9 463	11 047	11 548	11 306	10 104	10 036	11 100	11 320	16 189	..
3411	Pulp, Paper & Board	8 482	9 454	10 412	10 274	9 093	8 865	9 629	9 656	13 980	..
342	Printing & Publishing	1 584	1 688	1 809	1 853	1 877	2 051	2 322	2 424	2 904	..
35	**Chemical Products**	34 727	41 010	43 995	48 200	46 387	50 385	56 265	58 604	65 241	..
351	Industrial Chemicals	9 858	15 150	15 216	15 859	16 018	17 351	19 529	21 786	25 559	..
3511	Basic Industrial Chemicals	7 365	12 180	10 797	11 102	11 269	11 932	12 831	14 317	16 783	..
3512	Fertilizers & Pesticides	734	857	1 727	1 707	1 695	1 889	2 291	2 251	2 603	..
3513	Synthetic Resins	1 760	2 113	2 692	3 050	3 055	3 531	4 407	5 218	6 172	..
352	Other Chemicals	4 842	7 109	6 880	7 593	9 047	10 777	11 851	12 565	14 759	..
3521	Paints, Varnishes & Lacquers	184	129	115	144	152	172	207	261	343	..
3522	Drugs & Medicines	2 822	3 666	3 524	3 802	4 849	5 991	6 407	6 935	8 555	..
3523	Soap & Cleaning Preparations	813	937	980	1 114	1 187	1 445	1 644	1 798	2 086	..
3529	Chemical Products, nec	1 023	2 376	2 260	2 534	2 860	3 169	3 594	3 570	3 775	..
353	Petroleum Refineries	13 528	10 866	12 244	14 823	11 326	10 904	10 999	9 789	8 816	..
354	Petroleum & Coal Products	107	70	144	156	150	161	177	230	206	..
355	Rubber Products	2 817	3 160	5 556	5 570	5 561	6 278	8 114	8 253	8 965	..
356	Plastic Products, nec	3 575	4 656	3 955	4 199	4 285	4 914	5 595	5 982	6 936	..
36	**Non-Metallic Mineral Products**	5 622	6 023	6 173	6 302	6 029	6 556	7 651	8 413	9 415	..
361	Pottery, China etc	1 506	1 562	1 613	1 586	1 609	1 844	1 955	2 021	2 211	..
362	Glass & Products	1 625	1 713	1 754	1 764	1 761	1 915	2 223	2 548	2 843	..
369	Non-Metallic Products, nec	2 491	2 748	2 806	2 953	2 660	2 797	3 473	3 844	4 361	..
37	**Basic Metal Industries**	18 593	23 045	22 287	19 981	19 047	19 211	21 657	27 600	30 523	..
371	Iron & Steel	9 253	11 546	10 134	9 356	8 837	8 888	10 447	13 868	13 909	..
372	Non-Ferrous Metals	9 340	11 499	12 154	10 625	10 211	10 323	11 210	13 733	16 614	..
38	**Fabricated Metal Products**	150 950	173 912	229 497	232 556	236 071	260 019	298 031	343 952	391 306	..
381	Metal Products	8 915	8 606	11 244	11 175	10 835	11 844	13 944	15 486	17 347	..
3813	Structural Metal Products	509	476	669	626	644	570	668	792	1 036	..
382	Non-Electrical Machinery	46 837	56 212	55 704	56 662	57 170	64 586	77 552	92 487	109 404	..
3821	Engines & Turbines	3 317	4 715	2 316	2 295	2 184	2 289	2 791	3 202	3 701	..
3822	Agricultural Machinery	1 993	2 463	2 620	2 742	2 097	2 242	2 391	3 097	3 268	..
3823	Metal & Wood working Machinery	4 281	5 018	5 940	5 589	5 717	5 308	6 131	7 810	9 374	..
3824	Special Industrial Machinery	7 725	9 003	9 221	9 491	8 096	8 831	10 845	12 625	14 304	..
3825	Office & Computing Machinery	17 383	20 563	22 535	23 797	26 759	32 478	40 096	47 827	58 152	..
3829	Machinery & Equipment, nec	12 137	14 450	13 071	12 747	12 316	13 438	15 299	17 928	20 606	..
383	Electrical Machinery	47 486	54 298	59 472	60 086	63 160	70 929	81 643	97 496	117 720	..
3831	Electrical Industrial Machinery	4 543	5 081	5 081	5 024	5 278	5 865	9 282	11 020	12 262	..
3832	Radio, TV & Communication Equipment	36 984	40 621	42 277	42 772	45 293	50 541	59 219	71 706	88 920	..
3833	Electrical Appliances & Housewares	1 312	2 009	2 017	1 997	2 261	2 562	2 913	3 048	3 286	..
3839	Electrical Apparatus, nec	4 647	6 587	10 097	10 293	10 329	11 961	10 229	11 721	13 252	..
384	Transport Equipment	36 113	40 755	89 145	89 525	88 178	94 105	104 204	115 783	121 262	..
3841	Shipbuilding & Repairing	556	684	551	296	217	274	937	750	765	..
3842	Railroad Equipment	573	407	731	633	550	625	597	969	1 088	..
3843	Motor Vehicles	27 601	32 060	76 576	76 146	73 570	78 429	89 246	100 536	106 271	..
3844	Motorcycles & Bicycles	1 361	1 327	1 325	1 216	1 371	1 574	1 826	1 801	2 179	..
3845	Aircraft	5 831	6 276	9 962	11 235	12 470	13 203	11 598	11 728	10 959	..
3849	Transport Equipment, nec	193	..	..	..	..	..	..	..	..	..
385	Professional Goods	11 599	14 042	13 931	15 109	16 728	18 556	20 689	22 700	25 573	..
3851	Professional Equipment	3 908	5 047	5 510	6 007	6 642	7 572	8 534	9 676	11 255	..
3852	Photographic & Optical Goods	6 024	7 090	7 539	7 389	7 863	8 724	9 664	10 507	11 687	..
3853	Watches & Clocks	1 668	1 905	882	1 713	2 223	2 259	2 490	2 518	2 631	..
39	**Other Manufacturing, nes**	14 642	16 703	19 779	20 087	20 004	22 975	26 093	26 756	28 599	..
3901	Jewellery	5 854	6 793	8 073	7 550	7 538	8 018	9 452	10 358	10 765	..
3	**Total Manufacturing**	296 257	336 386	401 807	410 911	410 384	451 997	513 225	572 336	642 577	..
1	**Agric., Hunting, Forestry, Fishing**	..	..	..	..	..	..	..	..	..	..
2	**Mining & Quarrying**	..	..	..	..	..	..	..	..	..	..
21	Coal Mining	..	..	..	..	..	..	..	..	..	..
22	Crude Petroleum & Natural Gas	..	..	..	..	..	..	..	..	..	..
23.29	Other Mining	..	..	..	..	..	..	..	..	..	..
3	**Total Manufacturing**	296 257	336 386	401 807	410 911	410 384	451 997	513 225	572 336	642 577	..
4	**Electricity, Gas & Water**	..	..	..	..	..	..	..	..	..	..
5	**Construction**	..	..	..	..	..	..	..	..	..	..
6.9	**Services**	..	..	..	..	..	..	..	..	..	..
0000	**Grand Total**	..	..	..	..	..	..	..	..	..	..

Note: Unless given separately, ISIC 3843 includes 3849.

Section II

Disaggregated national accounts by industry
Comptes nationaux désagrégés par industrie

List of countries
Liste des pays

Millions of BF

(Current Prices)

ISIC2	Industry	PRODUCTION									
		1987	1988	1989	1990	1991	1992	1993	1994	1995	1996
31	Food, Beverages & Tobacco	..	..	..	..	..	..	..	..	..	..
311.2	Food	..	..	..	..	..	..	..	..	..	..
313	Beverages	79 870	79 955	87 317	94 454	98 003	103 244	102 091	103 769	108 820	103 247
314	Tobacco	54 306	54 131	57 082	56 294	60 081	61 679	58 626	63 778	63 976	58 966
32	Textiles, Apparel & Leather	281 396	290 604	324 235	337 684	323 217	333 206	332 093	354 338	343 578	321 047
321	Textiles	211 306	215 614	240 516	242 300	230 360	237 328	227 797	246 108	234 505	228 433
3213	Knitting Mills	14 722	13 534	13 773	13 802	14 227	13 153	11 467	10 237	9 275	8 177
322	Wearing Apparel	64 984	69 708	78 413	90 377	88 031	90 930	100 356	104 853	105 991	89 646
323	Leather & Products	..	..	..	..	..	..	..	..	..	..
324	Footwear	5 106	5 282	5 306	5 007	4 826	4 948	3 940	3 377	3 082	2 968
33	Wood Products & Furniture	157 262	172 941	187 822	205 471	209 076	200 074	194 656	197 715	207 990	206 952
331	Wood Products	33 272	34 804	38 900	39 947	38 394	36 288	35 662	36 784	37 736	35 460
332	Furnitures & Fixtures	123 990	138 137	148 922	165 524	170 682	163 786	158 994	160 931	170 254	171 492
34	Paper, Paper Products & Printing	204 104	239 757	255 483	267 437	264 055	265 988	263 024	277 510	305 045	295 829
341	Paper & Products	108 799	123 529	131 298	132 822	128 065	126 497	111 347	119 128	130 796	127 686
3411	Pulp, Paper & Board	..	..	..	..	..	..	..	..	..	..
342	Printing & Publishing	95 305	116 228	124 185	134 615	135 990	139 491	151 677	158 382	174 249	168 143
35	Chemical Products	679 757	712 132	803 987	787 754	788 418	812 520	773 344	842 592	957 757	1 041 898
351	Industrial Chemicals	394 302	439 333	464 068	453 859	442 557	480 706	449 754	510 463	583 545	593 510
3511	Basic Industrial Chemicals	..	..	..	..	..	..	..	..	..	..
3512	Fertilizers & Pesticides	..	..	..	..	..	..	..	..	..	..
3513	Synthetic Resins	..	..	..	..	..	..	..	..	..	..
352	Other Chemicals	85 239	96 315	108 079	110 914	123 080	131 302	134 842	143 671	168 356	166 063
3521	Paints, Varnishes & Lacquers	..	..	..	..	..	..	..	..	..	..
3522	Drugs & Medicines	..	..	..	..	..	..	..	..	..	..
3523	Soap & Cleaning Preparations	..	..	..	..	..	..	..	..	..	..
3529	Chemical Products, nec	..	..	..	..	..	..	..	..	..	..
353	Petroleum Refineries	181 429	154 740	206 644	197 848	198 345	172 533	167 256	163 204	179 207	258 050
354	Petroleum & Coal Products	..	..	..	..	..	..	..	..	..	..
355	Rubber Products	18 787	21 744	25 196	25 133	24 436	27 979	21 492	25 254	26 649	24 275
356	Plastic Products, nec	..	..	..	..	..	..	..	..	..	..
36	Non-Metallic Mineral Products	108 227	123 878	137 182	142 675	136 568	153 154	154 174	163 930	170 965	165 034
361	Pottery, China etc	..	..	..	..	..	..	..	..	..	..
362	Glass & Products	..	..	..	..	..	..	..	..	..	..
369	Non-Metallic Products, nec	..	..	..	..	..	..	..	..	..	..
37	Basic Metal Industries	280 094	360 306	444 431	396 699	322 940	294 978	258 671	296 637	331 655	306 266
371	Iron & Steel	176 193	223 445	258 058	236 047	207 344	184 454	163 706	187 154	212 506	173 160
372	Non-Ferrous Metals	103 901	136 861	186 373	160 652	115 596	110 524	94 965	109 483	119 149	133 106
38	Fabricated Metal Products	1 068 270	1 176 413	1 320 859	1 408 048	1 378 760	1 385 299	1 362 845	1 451 769	1 477 289	1 484 505
381	Metal Products	..	..	..	..	..	..	..	..	..	..
3813	Structural Metal Products	..	..	..	..	..	..	..	..	..	..
382	Non-Electrical Machinery	..	..	..	..	..	..	..	..	..	..
3821	Engines & Turbines	..	..	..	..	..	..	..	..	..	..
3822	Agricultural Machinery	..	..	..	..	..	..	..	..	..	..
3823	Metal & Wood working Machinery	..	..	..	..	..	..	..	..	..	..
3824	Special Industrial Machinery	..	..	..	..	..	..	..	..	..	..
3825	Office & Computing Machinery	..	..	..	..	..	..	..	..	..	..
3829	Machinery & Equipment, nec	..	..	..	..	..	..	..	..	..	..
383	Electrical Machinery	..	..	..	..	..	..	..	..	..	..
3831	Electrical Industrial Machinery	..	..	..	..	..	..	..	..	..	..
3832	Radio, TV & Communication Equipment	..	..	..	..	..	..	..	..	..	..
3833	Electrical Appliances & Housewares	..	..	..	..	..	..	..	..	..	..
3839	Electrical Apparatus, nec	..	..	..	..	..	..	..	..	..	..
384	Transport Equipment	..	..	..	..	..	..	..	..	..	..
3841	Shipbuilding & Repairing	..	..	..	..	..	..	..	..	..	..
3842	Railroad Equipment	..	..	..	..	..	..	..	..	..	..
3843	Motor Vehicles	..	..	..	..	..	..	..	..	..	..
3844	Motorcycles & Bicycles	..	..	..	..	..	..	..	..	..	..
3845	Aircraft	..	..	..	..	..	..	..	..	..	..
3849	Transport Equipment, nec	..	..	..	..	..	..	..	..	..	..
385	Professional Goods	..	..	..	..	..	..	..	..	..	..
3851	Professional Equipment	..	..	..	..	..	..	..	..	..	..
3852	Photographic & Optical Goods	..	..	..	..	..	..	..	..	..	..
3853	Watches & Clocks	..	..	..	..	..	..	..	..	..	..
39	Other Manufacturing, nes	..	..	..	..	..	..	..	..	..	..
3901	Jewellery	..	..	..	..	..	..	..	..	..	..
3	Total Manufacturing	..	..	..	..	..	..	..	..	..	..
1	Agric., Hunting, Forestry, Fishing	260 391	269 030	306 300	289 948	305 491	302 505	297 307	301 349	283 770	296 712
2	Mining & Quarrying	37 650	37 099	39 593	39 197	37 360	43 241	38 849	42 886	48 123	48 878
21	Coal Mining	9 493	5 717	4 969	2 695	1 817	787	0	0	0	0
22	Crude Petroleum & Natural Gas	..	..	..	..	..	..	..	..	..	..
23.29	Other Mining	28 157	31 382	34 624	36 502	35 543	42 454	38 849	42 886	48 123	48 878
3	Total Manufacturing	..	..	..	..	..	..	..	..	..	..
4	Electricity, Gas & Water	..	..	..	..	..	..	..	..	..	..
5	Construction	570 497	665 349	729 021	793 306	816 428	873 611	857 318	901 424	929 425	918 170
6.9	Services	..	..	..	..	..	..	..	..	..	..
0000	Grand Total	..	..	..	..	..	..	..	..	..	..

Note: ISIC 324 includes 323; 353 includes 354.

Table BL.2 **BELGIUM**

Millions of BF

(Current Prices)

ISIC2	Industry	\multicolumn{10}{c}{VALUE ADDED (Market Prices)}
		1987	1988	1989	1990	1991	1992	1993	1994	1995	1996
31	Food, Beverages & Tobacco	227 664	222 753	242 100	253 316	267 232	272 966	274 854	287 957	302 769	315 268
311.2	Food	154 931	151 146	167 020	175 650	186 257	188 691	193 293	202 405	215 474	233 342
313	Beverages	34 616	33 415	34 678	36 268	37 636	39 783	39 271	39 588	41 188	39 449
314	Tobacco	38 117	38 192	40 402	41 398	43 339	44 492	42 290	45 964	46 107	42 477
32	Textiles, Apparel & Leather	87 344	77 642	87 807	96 078	92 782	95 483	94 700	99 118	96 630	89 504
321	Textiles	59 763	51 373	61 691	64 667	62 201	63 912	60 542	63 970	61 247	59 492
3213	Knitting Mills	6 280	5 711	5 537	5 360	5 742	5 309	4 629	4 119	3 732	3 285
322	Wearing Apparel	25 126	23 746	23 766	29 262	28 406	29 341	32 381	33 626	33 993	28 672
323	Leather & Products	..	..	..	..	..	..	..	..	..	..
324	Footwear	2 455	2 523	2 350	2 149	2 175	2 230	1 777	1 522	1 390	1 340
33	Wood Products & Furniture	49 930	52 950	58 442	64 306	67 806	64 956	63 193	63 670	67 145	66 698
331	Wood Products	9 406	9 860	9 981	11 021	10 619	10 068	9 910	10 001	10 346	9 583
332	Furnitures & Fixtures	40 524	43 090	48 461	53 285	57 187	54 888	53 283	53 669	56 799	57 115
34	Paper, Paper Products & Printing	67 932	77 649	79 990	88 207	87 764	88 941	90 761	95 111	104 692	101 290
341	Paper & Products	27 065	28 577	26 760	30 507	29 475	29 150	25 747	27 223	30 004	29 218
3411	Pulp, Paper & Board	11 736	12 626	11 025	12 784	11 903	11 502	9 489	10 440	10 693	9 932
342	Printing & Publishing	40 867	49 072	53 230	57 700	58 289	59 791	65 014	67 888	74 688	72 072
35	Chemical Products	158 798	180 484	196 481	194 714	194 866	200 019	189 960	209 055	239 876	247 253
351	Industrial Chemicals	114 255	128 933	136 192	133 197	129 879	133 634	125 030	140 737	160 886	162 949
3511	Basic Industrial Chemicals	..	..	..	..	..	..	..	..	..	..
3512	Fertilizers & Pesticides	..	..	..	..	..	..	..	..	..	..
3513	Synthetic Resins	..	..	..	..	..	..	..	..	..	..
352	Other Chemicals	28 443	32 742	37 588	36 005	37 247	39 772	41 071	43 687	52 450	51 108
3521	Paints, Varnishes & Lacquers	..	..	..	..	..	..	..	..	..	..
3522	Drugs & Medicines	20 430	23 645	27 411	25 742	27 453	29 377	30 716	32 880	41 516	39 632
3523	Soap & Cleaning Preparations	8 013	9 097	10 177	10 263	9 794	10 395	10 355	10 807	10 934	11 476
3529	Chemical Products, nec	..	..	..	..	..	..	..	..	..	..
353	Petroleum Refineries	9 257	11 429	14 011	17 379	19 373	17 033	16 500	16 044	17 495	24 962
354	Petroleum & Coal Products	..	..	..	..	..	..	..	..	..	..
355	Rubber Products	6 843	7 380	8 690	8 133	8 367	9 580	7 359	8 587	9 045	8 234
356	Plastic Products, nec	..	..	..	..	..	..	..	..	..	..
36	Non-Metallic Mineral Products	48 018	53 729	59 298	60 814	59 140	66 363	66 868	70 928	73 831	70 810
361	Pottery, China etc	..	..	..	..	..	..	..	..	..	..
362	Glass & Products	..	..	..	..	..	..	..	..	..	..
369	Non-Metallic Products, nec	..	..	..	..	..	..	..	..	..	..
37	Basic Metal Industries	71 283	100 850	125 940	101 927	77 360	83 380	73 342	83 659	93 902	83 842
371	Iron & Steel	50 186	72 718	87 097	68 479	53 282	60 065	53 309	60 547	68 749	55 839
372	Non-Ferrous Metals	21 097	28 132	38 843	33 448	24 078	23 315	20 033	23 112	25 153	28 003
38	Fabricated Metal Products	301 581	337 224	358 188	409 999	385 975	376 197	394 496	416 949	424 192	424 622
381	Metal Products	..	..	..	..	..	..	..	..	..	..
3813	Structural Metal Products	..	..	..	..	..	..	..	..	..	..
382	Non-Electrical Machinery	..	..	..	..	..	..	..	..	..	..
3821	Engines & Turbines	..	..	..	..	..	..	..	..	..	..
3822	Agricultural Machinery	..	..	..	..	..	..	..	..	..	..
3823	Metal & Wood working Machinery	..	..	..	..	..	..	..	..	..	..
3824	Special Industrial Machinery	..	..	..	..	..	..	..	..	..	..
3825	Office & Computing Machinery	..	..	..	..	..	..	..	..	..	..
3829	Machinery & Equipment, nec	..	..	..	..	..	..	..	..	..	..
383	Electrical Machinery	..	..	..	..	..	..	..	..	..	..
3831	Electrical Industrial Machinery	..	..	..	..	..	..	..	..	..	..
3832	Radio, TV & Communication Equipment	..	..	..	..	..	..	..	..	..	..
3833	Electrical Appliances & Housewares	..	..	..	..	..	..	..	..	..	..
3839	Electrical Apparatus, nec	..	..	..	..	..	..	..	..	..	..
384	Transport Equipment	..	..	..	..	..	..	..	..	..	..
3841	Shipbuilding & Repairing	..	..	..	..	..	..	..	..	..	..
3842	Railroad Equipment	..	..	..	..	..	..	..	..	..	..
3843	Motor Vehicles	..	..	..	..	..	..	..	..	..	..
3844	Motorcycles & Bicycles	..	..	..	..	..	..	..	..	..	..
3845	Aircraft	..	..	..	..	..	..	..	..	..	..
3849	Transport Equipment, nec	..	..	..	..	..	..	..	..	..	..
385	Professional Goods	..	..	..	..	..	..	..	..	..	..
3851	Professional Equipment	..	..	..	..	..	..	..	..	..	..
3852	Photographic & Optical Goods	..	..	..	..	..	..	..	..	..	..
3853	Watches & Clocks	..	..	..	..	..	..	..	..	..	..
39	Other Manufacturing, nes	61 755	72 247	66 730	77 359	87 598	92 014	85 514	87 219	99 039	95 140
3901	Jewellery	..	..	..	..	..	..	..	..	..	..
3	Total Manufacturing	1 074 305	1 175 528	1 274 976	1 346 720	1 320 523	1 340 319	1 333 688	1 413 666	1 502 076	1 494 427
1	Agric., Hunting, Forestry, Fishing	110 867	115 263	142 013	128 303	133 365	129 199	125 079	122 691	101 356	104 101
2	Mining & Quarrying	15 568	14 770	15 889	15 592	14 981	18 579	16 388	19 111	21 445	21 753
21	Coal Mining	3 302	807	578	-1 141	-900	-390	-970	0	0	0
22	Crude Petroleum & Natural Gas	..	..	..	..	..	..	..	..	..	..
23.29	Other Mining	12 266	13 963	15 311	16 733	15 881	18 969	17 358	19 111	21 445	21 753
3	Total Manufacturing	1 074 305	1 175 528	1 274 976	1 346 720	1 320 523	1 340 319	1 333 688	1 413 666	1 502 076	1 494 427
4	Electricity, Gas & Water	175 981	181 224	182 073	188 024	196 337	199 116	203 914	212 618	225 178	234 231
5	Construction	279 429	325 888	357 074	388 561	399 886	427 894	419 914	441 517	455 232	449 719
6.9	Services	3 918 136	4 153 136	4 461 654	4 766 021	5 096 951	5 424 220	5 611 449	5 922 168	6 124 488	6 418 933
0000	Grand Total	5 574 286	5 965 809	6 433 679	6 833 221	7 162 043	7 539 327	7 710 432	8 131 771	8 429 775	8 723 164

Note: ISIC 324 includes 323; 353 includes 354.
ISIC 39 excludes steam and heat (included in 4); 3 excludes garages, steam and heat; 21 - coal boards include their electric power stations. 6.9 includes garages. The Grand Total has deductible VAT on capital formation removed.

Millions of BF

(Current Prices)

ISIC2	Industry	VALUE ADDED (Factor Cost)									
		1987	**1988**	**1989**	**1990**	**1991**	**1992**	**1993**	**1994**	**1995**	**1996**
31	**Food, Beverages & Tobacco**	207 680	208 607	223 908	240 617	250 012	255 177	259 450	272 701	286 827	304 757
311.2	Food	177 166	179 395	193 464	201 986	210 232	213 248	218 571	230 414	243 648	263 382
313	Beverages	22 720	21 209	22 001	28 271	29 777	31 660	31 118	30 916	31 773	30 879
314	Tobacco	7 794	8 003	8 443	10 360	10 003	10 269	9 761	11 371	11 406	10 496
32	**Textiles, Apparel & Leather**	91 332	83 810	95 435	103 761	100 427	103 409	102 886	108 681	105 827	98 344
321	Textiles	64 496	57 312	68 268	71 231	68 295	70 233	66 871	71 441	68 316	66 524
3213	Knitting Mills	5 960	5 424	5 343	5 161	5 558	5 139	4 482	3 978	3 605	3 170
322	Wearing Apparel	24 696	24 298	25 082	30 671	30 222	31 217	34 456	35 907	36 297	30 655
323	Leather & Products	..	..	..	..	..	..	..	..	..	..
324	Footwear	2 140	2 200	2 085	1 859	1 910	1 959	1 559	1 333	1 214	1 165
33	**Wood Products & Furniture**	51 125	53 954	58 816	64 652	68 337	65 469	63 683	64 149	67 654	67 280
331	Wood Products	9 261	9 450	9 580	10 738	10 167	9 638	9 485	9 551	9 872	9 165
332	Furnitures & Fixtures	41 864	44 504	49 236	53 914	58 170	55 831	54 198	54 598	57 782	58 115
34	**Paper, Paper Products & Printing**	69 781	80 426	84 014	90 869	90 172	91 206	92 275	96 920	106 511	103 092
341	Paper & Products	30 242	32 714	32 314	34 828	33 559	33 134	29 130	31 068	34 063	33 181
3411	Pulp, Paper & Board	13 759	15 288	15 018	16 097	14 988	14 483	11 948	13 334	13 657	12 773
342	Printing & Publishing	39 539	47 712	51 700	56 041	56 613	58 072	63 145	65 852	72 448	69 911
35	**Chemical Products**	175 692	199 472	216 057	214 772	215 399	221 914	210 735	233 598	268 023	275 139
351	Industrial Chemicals	128 905	145 015	153 179	149 810	146 079	150 351	140 670	159 603	182 453	185 453
3511	Basic Industrial Chemicals	..	..	..	..	..	..	..	..	..	..
3512	Fertilizers & Pesticides	..	..	..	..	..	..	..	..	..	..
3513	Synthetic Resins	..	..	..	..	..	..	..	..	..	..
352	Other Chemicals	31 521	36 213	41 120	40 052	42 435	45 308	46 765	49 880	59 734	58 334
3521	Paints, Varnishes & Lacquers	..	..	..	..	..	..	..	..	..	..
3522	Drugs & Medicines	22 350	26 077	29 649	28 114	30 834	32 995	34 499	36 936	46 638	44 522
3523	Soap & Cleaning Preparations	9 171	10 136	11 471	11 938	11 601	12 313	12 266	12 944	13 096	13 812
3529	Chemical Products, nec	..	..	..	..	..	..	..	..	..	..
353	Petroleum Refineries	8 119	10 416	12 516	15 820	17 634	15 664	15 164	14 574	15 775	22 184
354	Petroleum & Coal Products	..	..	..	..	..	..	..	..	..	..
355	Rubber Products	7 147	7 828	9 242	9 090	9 251	10 591	8 136	9 541	10 061	9 168
356	Plastic Products, nec	..	..	..	..	..	..	..	..	..	..
36	**Non-Metallic Mineral Products**	47 438	52 600	58 038	59 565	57 526	64 543	65 029	68 837	72 031	69 185
361	Pottery, China etc	..	..	..	..	..	..	..	..	..	..
362	Glass & Products	..	..	..	..	..	..	..	..	..	..
369	Non-Metallic Products, nec	..	..	..	..	..	..	..	..	..	..
37	**Basic Metal Industries**	78 293	109 650	135 429	111 521	84 575	90 845	79 878	91 754	102 942	92 461
371	Iron & Steel	54 104	77 496	91 190	73 418	57 149	64 373	57 132	65 413	74 274	60 456
372	Non-Ferrous Metals	24 189	32 154	44 239	38 103	27 426	26 472	22 746	26 341	28 668	32 005
38	**Fabricated Metal Products**	345 645	380 072	412 201	452 152	425 684	414 870	430 919	459 036	467 080	468 894
381	Metal Products	..	..	..	..	..	..	..	..	..	..
3813	Structural Metal Products	..	..	..	..	..	..	..	..	..	..
382	Non-Electrical Machinery	..	..	..	..	..	..	..	..	..	..
3821	Engines & Turbines	..	..	..	..	..	..	..	..	..	..
3822	Agricultural Machinery	..	..	..	..	..	..	..	..	..	..
3823	Metal & Wood working Machinery	..	..	..	..	..	..	..	..	..	..
3824	Special Industrial Machinery	..	..	..	..	..	..	..	..	..	..
3825	Office & Computing Machinery	..	..	..	..	..	..	..	..	..	..
3829	Machinery & Equipment, nec	..	..	..	..	..	..	..	..	..	..
383	Electrical Machinery	..	..	..	..	..	..	..	..	..	..
3831	Electrical Industrial Machinery	..	..	..	..	..	..	..	..	..	..
3832	Radio, TV & Communication Equipment	..	..	..	..	..	..	..	..	..	..
3833	Electrical Appliances & Housewares	..	..	..	..	..	..	..	..	..	..
3839	Electrical Apparatus, nec	..	..	..	..	..	..	..	..	..	..
384	Transport Equipment	..	..	..	..	..	..	..	..	..	..
3841	Shipbuilding & Repairing	..	..	..	..	..	..	..	..	..	..
3842	Railroad Equipment	..	..	..	..	..	..	..	..	..	..
3843	Motor Vehicles	..	..	..	..	..	..	..	..	..	..
3844	Motorcycles & Bicycles	..	..	..	..	..	..	..	..	..	..
3845	Aircraft	..	..	..	..	..	..	..	..	..	..
3849	Transport Equipment, nec	..	..	..	..	..	..	..	..	..	..
385	Professional Goods	..	..	..	..	..	..	..	..	..	..
3851	Professional Equipment	..	..	..	..	..	..	..	..	..	..
3852	Photographic & Optical Goods	..	..	..	..	..	..	..	..	..	..
3853	Watches & Clocks	..	..	..	..	..	..	..	..	..	..
39	**Other Manufacturing, nes**	65 383	76 221	71 658	82 164	92 107	96 493	89 594	91 766	104 291	100 602
3901	Jewellery	..	..	..	..	..	..	..	..	..	..
3	**Total Manufacturing**	1 132 369	1 244 812	1 355 556	1 420 073	1 384 239	1 403 926	1 394 449	1 487 442	1 581 186	1 579 754
1	**Agric., Hunting, Forestry, Fishing**	107 503	112 229	138 493	130 780	131 370	126 693	126 250	130 143	106 879	112 185
2	**Mining & Quarrying**	16 105	14 691	16 387	15 854	14 825	18 000	15 846	18 193	19 812	20 071
21	Coal Mining	4 439	1 575	1 956	246	124	440	-223	0	0	0
22	Crude Petroleum & Natural Gas	..	..	..	..	..	..	..	..	..	..
23.29	Other Mining	11 666	13 116	14 431	15 608	14 701	17 560	16 069	18 193	19 812	20 071
3	**Total Manufacturing**	1 132 369	1 244 812	1 355 556	1 420 073	1 384 239	1 403 926	1 394 449	1 487 442	1 581 186	1 579 754
4	**Electricity, Gas & Water**	154 154	158 460	160 065	164 362	171 392	174 050	178 439	185 255	196 390	203 722
5	**Construction**	247 009	288 220	315 784	336 796	346 570	373 985	365 486	382 610	394 464	389 604
6.9	**Services**	3 234 583	3 411 249	3 625 611	3 898 668	4 213 795	4 480 295	4 613 530	4 843 121	5 027 402	5 220 580
0000	**Grand Total**	4 891 723	5 229 661	5 611 896	5 966 533	6 262 191	6 576 949	6 694 000	7 046 764	7 326 133	7 525 916

Note: ISIC 324 includes 323; 353 includes 354.
ISIC 39 excludes steam and heat (included in 4); 3 excludes garages, steam and heat; 21 - coal boards include their electric power stations. 6.9 includes garages and excludes duties and taxes on imports.

Millions of BF

(Current Prices)

ISIC2	Industry	INVESTMENT									
		1987	1988	1989	1990	1991	1992	1993	1994	1995	1996
31	**Food, Beverages & Tobacco**	25 841	33 410	37 048	45 392	50 344	52 148	44 158	39 692	38 824	41 916
311.2	Food	20 465	26 094	25 925	33 793	34 503	33 096	30 051	29 703	29 169	33 073
313	Beverages	4 514	6 594	9 783	10 146	14 854	17 629	13 314	8 871	9 010	7 961
314	Tobacco	862	722	1 340	1 453	987	1 423	793	1 118	645	882
32	**Textiles, Apparel & Leather**	19 603	20 462	20 601	21 601	19 512	18 656	17 542	20 681	16 858	15 258
321	Textiles	17 038	17 782	17 282	18 949	16 871	15 760	14 840	18 056	14 577	13 254
3213	Knitting Mills	751	976	654	953	935	722	735	637	563	716
322	Wearing Apparel	2 441	2 575	3 195	2 513	2 507	2 833	2 642	2 564	2 218	1 955
323	Leather & Products	15	5	14	58	28	8	8	14	9	5
324	Footwear	109	100	110	81	106	55	52	47	54	44
33	**Wood Products & Furniture**	8 582	9 716	11 115	12 607	10 891	8 024	7 309	8 528	7 609	9 164
331	Wood Products	1 505	1 647	2 171	2 500	1 149	957	801	852	1 032	955
332	Furnitures & Fixtures	7 077	8 069	8 944	10 107	9 742	7 067	6 508	7 676	6 577	8 209
34	**Paper, Paper Products & Printing**	18 801	21 194	26 445	27 217	36 388	35 191	23 946	31 401	29 142	28 052
341	Paper & Products	9 297	8 901	10 733	9 587	21 487	18 864	9 841	15 621	13 663	13 276
3411	Pulp, Paper & Board	5 838	4 718	5 244	4 163	14 523	14 609	6 427	11 759	9 620	8 691
342	Printing & Publishing	9 504	12 293	15 712	17 630	14 901	16 327	14 105	15 780	15 479	14 776
35	**Chemical Products**	39 859	67 702	90 357	135 250	108 929	101 637	105 144	89 008	108 154	132 474
351	Industrial Chemicals	24 168	46 174	61 264	86 927	75 955	66 118	58 667	54 269	79 275	99 577
3511	Basic Industrial Chemicals	..	..	..	..	..	..	..	..	..	..
3512	Fertilizers & Pesticides	..	..	..	..	..	..	..	..	..	..
3513	Synthetic Resins	..	..	..	..	..	..	..	..	..	..
352	Other Chemicals	..	..	..	..	..	..	..	..	..	..
3521	Paints, Varnishes & Lacquers	..	..	..	..	..	..	..	..	..	..
3522	Drugs & Medicines	3 959	4 759	5 666	6 653	6 608	8 270	7 501	9 596	11 190	11 647
3523	Soap & Cleaning Preparations	1 544	1 561	1 845	2 042	2 293	2 820	3 351	2 547	2 460	1 856
3529	Chemical Products, nec	..	..	..	..	..	..	..	..	..	..
353	Petroleum Refineries	1 730	1 737	4 779	16 436	9 379	11 097	25 715	13 517	6 620	7 133
354	Petroleum & Coal Products	..	..	..	..	..	..	..	..	..	..
355	Rubber Products	1 240	2 003	2 395	3 533	2 214	2 492	1 876	1 832	1 750	1 651
356	Plastic Products, nec	..	..	..	..	..	..	..	..	..	..
36	**Non-Metallic Mineral Products**	14 112	14 222	13 481	19 019	17 055	15 140	16 879	15 629	18 619	13 749
361	Pottery, China etc	..	..	..	..	..	..	..	..	..	..
362	Glass & Products	..	..	..	..	..	..	..	..	..	..
369	Non-Metallic Products, nec	..	..	..	..	..	..	..	..	..	..
37	**Basic Metal Industries**	12 185	16 574	22 255	21 930	27 771	26 511	20 260	21 821	22 312	22 557
371	Iron & Steel	7 871	13 133	18 227	17 641	23 134	22 841	17 453	19 740	18 627	17 055
372	Non-Ferrous Metals	4 314	3 441	4 028	4 289	4 637	3 670	2 807	2 081	3 685	5 502
38	**Fabricated Metal Products**	46 192	49 877	73 123	79 744	79 684	78 763	51 895	45 685	58 712	64 344
381	Metal Products	..	..	..	..	..	..	..	..	..	..
3813	Structural Metal Products	..	..	..	..	..	..	..	..	..	..
382	Non-Electrical Machinery	..	..	..	..	..	..	..	..	..	..
3821	Engines & Turbines	..	..	..	..	..	..	..	..	..	..
3822	Agricultural Machinery	..	..	..	..	..	..	..	..	..	..
3823	Metal & Wood working Machinery	..	..	..	..	..	..	..	..	..	..
3824	Special Industrial Machinery	..	..	..	..	..	..	..	..	..	..
3825	Office & Computing Machinery	..	..	..	..	..	..	..	..	..	..
3829	Machinery & Equipment, nec	..	..	..	..	..	..	..	..	..	..
383	Electrical Machinery	..	..	..	..	..	..	..	..	..	..
3831	Electrical Industrial Machinery	..	..	..	..	..	..	..	..	..	..
3832	Radio, TV & Communication Equipment	..	..	..	..	..	..	..	..	..	..
3833	Electrical Appliances & Housewares	..	..	..	..	..	..	..	..	..	..
3839	Electrical Apparatus, nec	..	..	..	..	..	..	..	..	..	..
384	Transport Equipment	..	..	..	..	..	..	..	..	..	..
3841	Shipbuilding & Repairing	..	..	..	..	..	..	..	..	..	..
3842	Railroad Equipment	..	..	..	..	..	..	..	..	..	..
3843	Motor Vehicles	..	..	..	..	..	..	..	..	..	..
3844	Motorcycles & Bicycles	..	..	..	..	..	..	..	..	..	..
3845	Aircraft	..	..	..	..	..	..	..	..	..	..
3849	Transport Equipment, nec	..	..	..	..	..	..	..	..	..	..
385	Professional Goods	..	..	..	..	..	..	..	..	..	..
3851	Professional Equipment	..	..	..	..	..	..	..	..	..	..
3852	Photographic & Optical Goods	..	..	..	..	..	..	..	..	..	..
3853	Watches & Clocks	..	..	..	..	..	..	..	..	..	..
39	**Other Manufacturing, nes**	4 369	2 192	1 964	1 720	1 636	1 463	1 360	1 835	1 804	2 190
3901	Jewellery	..	..	..	..	..	..	..	..	..	..
3	**Total Manufacturing**	189 544	235 349	296 389	364 480	352 210	337 533	288 493	274 280	302 034	329 704
1	**Agric., Hunting, Forestry, Fishing**	20 246	19 803	20 788	24 731	18 715	22 874	15 807	15 169	14 463	16 961
2	**Mining & Quarrying**	1 399	3 310	6 630	9 691	5 394	4 682	4 840	4 166	4 563	4 870
21	Coal Mining	..	..	..	..	..	..	..	..	..	..
22	Crude Petroleum & Natural Gas	..	..	..	..	..	..	..	..	..	..
23.29	Other Mining	..	..	..	..	..	..	..	..	..	..
3	**Total Manufacturing**	189 544	235 349	296 389	364 480	352 210	337 533	288 493	274 280	302 034	329 704
4	**Electricity, Gas & Water**	37 809	37 917	46 258	42 059	47 034	71 208	59 479	62 594	66 817	71 737
5	**Construction**	15 200	22 945	25 281	29 716	27 455	25 022	22 876	24 154	26 960	26 029
6.9	**Services**	589 529	694 342	783 305	857 305	841 843	886 641	929 590	968 510	1 001 714	988 610
0000	**Grand Total**	853 727	1 013 666	1 178 651	1 327 982	1 292 651	1 347 960	1 321 085	1 348 873	1 416 551	1 437 911

Note: ISIC 353 includes 354; 39 includes 356.

Table BL.7 **BELGIUM**

ISIC2	Industry	INVESTMENT IN MACHINERY & EQUIPMENT									
		1987	1988	1989	1990	1991	1992	1993	1994	1995	1996
31	**Food, Beverages & Tobacco**	20 766	25 916	28 258	34 988	38 360	40 399	34 385	29 823	29 934	31 353
311.2	Food	16 133	20 101	19 511	24 994	26 146	25 675	23 763	23 464	23 767	25 992
313	Beverages	3 898	5 263	7 999	8 790	11 326	13 481	10 078	5 425	5 628	4 624
314	Tobacco	735	552	748	1 204	888	1 243	544	934	539	737
32	**Textiles, Apparel & Leather**	16 595	16 773	16 926	17 825	15 901	15 058	14 997	17 100	14 279	12 917
321	Textiles	14 545	14 764	14 527	15 747	13 919	12 753	12 972	15 101	12 529	11 363
3213	Knitting Mills	642	738	489	831	924	609	700	615	543	691
322	Wearing Apparel	1 938	1 910	2 285	1 964	1 898	2 256	1 988	1 952	1 698	1 512
323	Leather & Products	14	4	8	33	10	6	0	5	4	3
324	Footwear	98	95	106	81	74	43	37	42	48	39
33	**Wood Products & Furniture**	6 687	7 474	7 831	9 425	8 447	6 134	5 640	6 404	5 754	6 982
331	Wood Products	1 007	1 140	1 198	1 586	952	768	636	727	879	812
332	Furnitures & Fixtures	5 680	6 334	6 633	7 839	7 495	5 366	5 004	5 677	4 875	6 170
34	**Paper, Paper Products & Printing**	15 469	17 903	21 644	21 095	28 286	29 132	19 960	26 085	24 275	24 696
341	Paper & Products	7 445	7 496	9 053	7 101	16 709	15 802	7 752	12 945	11 353	11 126
3411	Pulp, Paper & Board	4 928	4 216	4 684	2 810	10 987	12 209	4 738	9 594	7 845	7 147
342	Printing & Publishing	8 024	10 407	12 591	13 994	11 577	13 330	12 208	13 140	12 922	13 570
35	**Chemical Products**	33 059	55 522	76 558	117 104	94 934	90 451	91 547	76 353	94 033	115 482
351	Industrial Chemicals	20 932	38 601	53 949	77 947	67 885	62 949	51 748	48 252	71 940	90 324
3511	Basic Industrial Chemicals	..	..	..	..	..	..	..	..	..	..
3512	Fertilizers & Pesticides	..	..	..	..	..	..	..	..	..	..
3513	Synthetic Resins	..	..	..	..	..	..	..	..	..	..
352	Other Chemicals	..	..	..	..	..	..	..	..	..	..
3521	Paints, Varnishes & Lacquers	..	..	..	..	..	..	..	..	..	..
3522	Drugs & Medicines	2 377	2 904	3 444	4 100	4 966	5 745	5 257	5 824	6 791	7 068
3523	Soap & Cleaning Preparations	1 307	1 214	1 376	1 668	1 884	1 402	2 703	2 261	2 184	1 641
3529	Chemical Products, nec	..	..	..	..	..	..	..	..	..	..
353	Petroleum Refineries	1 547	1 689	4 455	16 097	8 588	9 483	23 818	12 779	6 258	6 745
354	Petroleum & Coal Products	..	..	..	..	..	..	..	..	..	..
355	Rubber Products	1 054	1 761	2 111	2 706	1 869	2 093	1 580	1 569	1 492	1 404
356	Plastic Products, nec	..	..	..	..	..	..	..	..	..	..
36	**Non-Metallic Mineral Products**	12 239	11 792	11 320	16 192	14 852	12 617	11 989	13 209	15 644	11 585
361	Pottery, China etc	..	..	..	..	..	..	..	..	..	..
362	Glass & Products	..	..	..	..	..	..	..	..	..	..
369	Non-Metallic Products, nec	..	..	..	..	..	..	..	..	..	..
37	**Basic Metal Industries**	10 825	14 122	19 526	19 333	23 847	22 850	18 647	21 093	21 518	21 697
371	Iron & Steel	6 965	11 266	16 511	15 817	20 419	19 978	16 328	19 142	18 063	16 538
372	Non-Ferrous Metals	3 860	2 856	3 015	3 516	3 428	2 872	2 319	1 951	3 455	5 159
38	**Fabricated Metal Products**	38 637	41 100	58 942	64 000	63 192	66 918	43 228	37 594	48 260	53 426
381	Metal Products	..	..	..	..	..	..	..	..	..	..
3813	Structural Metal Products	..	..	..	..	..	..	..	..	..	..
382	Non-Electrical Machinery	..	..	..	..	..	..	..	..	..	..
3821	Engines & Turbines	..	..	..	..	..	..	..	..	..	..
3822	Agricultural Machinery	..	..	..	..	..	..	..	..	..	..
3823	Metal & Wood working Machinery	..	..	..	..	..	..	..	..	..	..
3824	Special Industrial Machinery	..	..	..	..	..	..	..	..	..	..
3825	Office & Computing Machinery	..	..	..	..	..	..	..	..	..	..
3829	Machinery & Equipment, nec	..	..	..	..	..	..	..	..	..	..
383	Electrical Machinery	..	..	..	..	..	..	..	..	..	..
3831	Electrical Industrial Machinery	..	..	..	..	..	..	..	..	..	..
3832	Radio, TV & Communication Equipment	..	..	..	..	..	..	..	..	..	..
3833	Electrical Appliances & Housewares	..	..	..	..	..	..	..	..	..	..
3839	Electrical Apparatus, nec	..	..	..	..	..	..	..	..	..	..
384	Transport Equipment	..	..	..	..	..	..	..	..	..	..
3841	Shipbuilding & Repairing	..	..	..	..	..	..	..	..	..	..
3842	Railroad Equipment	..	..	..	..	..	..	..	..	..	..
3843	Motor Vehicles	..	..	..	..	..	..	..	..	..	..
3844	Motorcycles & Bicycles	..	..	..	..	..	..	..	..	..	..
3845	Aircraft	..	..	..	..	..	..	..	..	..	..
3849	Transport Equipment, nec	..	..	..	..	..	..	..	..	..	..
385	Professional Goods	..	..	..	..	..	..	..	..	..	..
3851	Professional Equipment	..	..	..	..	..	..	..	..	..	..
3852	Photographic & Optical Goods	..	..	..	..	..	..	..	..	..	..
3853	Watches & Clocks	..	..	..	..	..	..	..	..	..	..
39	**Other Manufacturing, nes**	3 205	2 030	1 386	1 347	1 179	1 173	478	1 261	618	1 493
3901	Jewellery	..	..	..	..	..	..	..	..	..	..
3	**Total Manufacturing**	157 482	192 632	242 391	301 309	288 998	284 732	240 871	228 922	254 315	279 631
1	**Agric., Hunting, Forestry, Fishing**	11 481	11 606	12 205	13 870	8 092	11 111	7 300	7 693	6 145	6 812
2	**Mining & Quarrying**	329	1 959	5 186	5 092	2 899	3 334	3 577	3 432	3 759	4 040
21	Coal Mining	..	..	..	..	..	..	..	..	..	..
22	Crude Petroleum & Natural Gas	..	..	..	..	..	..	..	..	..	..
23.29	Other Mining	..	..	..	..	..	..	..	..	..	..
3	**Total Manufacturing**	157 482	192 632	242 391	301 309	288 998	284 732	240 871	228 922	254 315	279 631
4	**Electricity, Gas & Water**	11 307	13 511	16 510	17 779	10 790	14 732	12 275	9 832	10 379	12 443
5	**Construction**	13 219	19 290	22 623	24 544	22 307	19 796	18 855	19 679	21 892	21 212
6.9	**Services**	168 008	188 616	221 258	247 734	237 699	232 830	244 647	245 509	260 361	269 110
0000	**Grand Total**	361 826	427 614	520 173	610 328	570 785	566 535	527 525	515 067	556 851	593 248

Note: ISIC 353 includes 354; 39 includes 356.

Millions of BF　　　　　　　　　　　　　　　　　　　　　　　　　　　　　　　　　　　　(Current Prices)

ISIC2	Industry	WAGES & SALARIES - EMPLOYEES									
		1987	1988	1989	1990	1991	1992	1993	1994	1995	1996
31	Food, Beverages & Tobacco	53 708	54 938	58 761	62 930	67 047	69 621	70 671	72 329	..	..
311.2	Food	40 617	41 857	45 074	48 558	52 172	54 399	55 432	56 576	..	..
313	Beverages	9 523	9 563	10 046	10 537	11 107	11 324	11 206	11 500	..	..
314	Tobacco	3 569	3 518	3 641	3 834	3 768	3 898	4 033	4 253	..	..
32	Textiles, Apparel & Leather	42 343	42 028	44 071	45 442	45 770	45 687	43 003	42 985	..	..
321	Textiles	26 698	26 739	28 209	29 056	29 433	28 789	30 082	31 233	..	..
3213	Knitting Mills	..	..	..	..	..	..	..	..	..	..
322	Wearing Apparel	13 592	13 352	13 916	14 475	14 460	14 700	10 881	9 853	..	..
323	Leather & Products	1 208	1 141	1 158	1 170	1 162	1 502	1 464	1 400	..	..
324	Footwear	846	795	788	741	715	696	576	499	..	..
33	Wood Products & Furniture	16 319	16 741	17 900	19 323	20 536	21 235	25 860	26 055	..	..
331	Wood Products	..	..	..	..	..	..	..	..	..	..
332	Furnitures & Fixtures	..	..	..	..	..	..	..	..	..	..
34	Paper, Paper Products & Printing	35 468	36 906	39 618	42 536	44 529	45 177	44 905	45 525	..	..
341	Paper & Products	12 649	12 526	13 336	14 229	15 252	15 373	14 250	14 557	..	..
3411	Pulp, Paper & Board	..	..	..	..	..	..	..	..	..	..
342	Printing & Publishing	22 820	24 380	26 283	28 306	29 277	29 804	30 655	30 968	..	..
35	Chemical Products	84 889	89 090	96 546	104 871	111 242	117 293	121 235	120 454	..	..
351	Industrial Chemicals	66 799	70 046	75 757	81 728	86 496	91 431	91 894	91 557	..	..
3511	Basic Industrial Chemicals	..	..	..	..	..	..	..	..	..	..
3512	Fertilizers & Pesticides	..	..	..	..	..	..	..	..	..	..
3513	Synthetic Resins	..	..	..	..	..	..	..	..	..	..
352	Other Chemicals	..	..	..	..	..	..	..	..	..	..
3521	Paints, Varnishes & Lacquers	..	..	..	..	..	..	..	..	..	..
3522	Drugs & Medicines	..	..	..	..	..	..	..	..	..	..
3523	Soap & Cleaning Preparations	..	..	..	..	..	..	..	..	..	..
3529	Chemical Products, nec	..	..	..	..	..	..	..	..	..	..
353	Petroleum Refineries	3 966	3 721	3 782	4 167	4 546	4 743	6 801	6 809	..	..
354	Petroleum & Coal Products	819	877	909	946	925	788	..	..	..	..
355	Rubber Products	3 215	3 337	3 732	3 947	4 055	4 180	4 087	4 316	..	..
356	Plastic Products, nec	10 089	11 110	12 366	14 083	15 220	16 151	18 453	17 772	..	..
36	Non-Metallic Mineral Products	21 487	22 528	25 113	26 951	27 959	29 209	29 348	30 021	..	..
361	Pottery, China etc	..	..	..	..	..	..	..	..	..	..
362	Glass & Products	8 515	8 789	9 738	10 155	10 462	10 966	11 102	11 229	..	..
369	Non-Metallic Products, nec	12 972	13 739	15 375	16 797	17 497	18 243	18 246	18 792	..	..
37	Basic Metal Industries	44 447	44 346	46 646	48 736	49 636	48 894	50 244	50 132	..	..
371	Iron & Steel	..	..	..	..	..	..	..	..	..	..
372	Non-Ferrous Metals	..	..	..	..	..	..	..	..	..	..
38	Fabricated Metal Products	176 778	177 811	191 532	203 554	207 161	209 204	197 444	199 046	..	..
381	Metal Products	40 939	40 459	44 405	48 830	51 953	52 692	43 274	43 657	..	..
3813	Structural Metal Products	..	..	..	..	..	..	..	..	..	..
382	Non-Electrical Machinery	32 224	33 825	36 902	38 231	37 911	37 017	38 324	39 756	..	..
3821	Engines & Turbines	..	..	..	..	..	..	..	..	..	..
3822	Agricultural Machinery	..	..	..	..	..	..	..	..	..	..
3823	Metal & Wood working Machinery	..	..	..	..	..	..	..	..	..	..
3824	Special Industrial Machinery	..	..	..	..	..	..	..	..	..	..
3825	Office & Computing Machinery	..	..	..	..	..	..	..	..	..	..
3829	Machinery & Equipment, nec	..	..	..	..	..	..	..	..	..	..
383	Electrical Machinery	51 438	49 455	50 774	52 015	52 617	51 364	46 710	46 927	..	..
3831	Electrical Industrial Machinery	..	..	..	..	..	..	..	..	..	..
3832	Radio, TV & Communication Equipment	..	..	..	..	..	..	..	..	..	..
3833	Electrical Appliances & Housewares	..	..	..	..	..	..	..	..	..	..
3839	Electrical Apparatus, nec	..	..	..	..	..	..	..	..	..	..
384	Transport Equipment	49 277	51 221	56 177	60 925	60 851	63 492	63 181	62 840	..	..
3841	Shipbuilding & Repairing	..	..	..	..	..	..	..	..	..	..
3842	Railroad Equipment	..	..	..	..	..	..	..	..	..	..
3843	Motor Vehicles	..	..	..	..	..	..	..	..	..	..
3844	Motorcycles & Bicycles	..	..	..	..	..	..	..	..	..	..
3845	Aircraft	..	..	..	..	..	..	..	..	..	..
3849	Transport Equipment, nec	..	..	..	..	..	..	..	..	..	..
385	Professional Goods	2 901	2 851	3 273	3 554	3 829	4 639	5 955	5 865	..	..
3851	Professional Equipment	..	..	..	..	..	..	..	..	..	..
3852	Photographic & Optical Goods	..	..	..	..	..	..	..	..	..	..
3853	Watches & Clocks	..	..	..	..	..	..	..	..	..	..
39	Other Manufacturing, nes	4 543	4 591	4 693	4 950	4 864	4 796	3 314	3 411	..	..
3901	Jewellery	..	..	..	..	..	..	..	..	..	..
3	Total Manufacturing	479 984	488 980	524 879	559 294	578 744	591 116	586 024	589 957	..	..
1	Agric., Hunting, Forestry, Fishing	4 339	4 847	5 288	5 800	6 078	6 544	6 728	7 296	..	..
2	Mining & Quarrying	13 171	9 386	8 172	6 618	6 142	6 051	5 870	5 535	..	..
21	Coal Mining	10 148	6 299	4 856	3 175	2 618	2 388	2 092	1 700	..	..
22	Crude Petroleum & Natural Gas	..	..	..	..	..	..	..	..	..	..
23.29	Other Mining	3 023	3 086	3 316	3 443	3 524	3 663	3 778	3 835	..	..
3	Total Manufacturing	479 984	488 980	524 879	559 294	578 744	591 116	586 024	589 957	..	..
4	Electricity, Gas & Water	27 898	28 204	29 351	30 318	31 570	32 242	31 974	32 551	..	..
5	Construction	70 219	77 587	86 629	98 711	104 484	112 550	111 143	116 519	..	..
6.9	Services	1 183 528	1 230 259	1 317 374	1 423 342	1 532 862	1 611 067	1 733 415	1 796 297	..	..
0000	Grand Total	1 779 138	1 839 262	1 971 694	2 124 082	2 259 880	2 359 570	2 475 154	2 548 155	..	..

Note: Break in series between 1992 and 1993. See Sources and Definitions. From 1993, ISIC 353 includes 354.
ISIC 351 includes 352; 369 includes 361.

Table BL.9 **BELGIUM**

ISIC2	Industry	ESTABLISHMENTS									
		1987	1988	1989	1990	1991	1992	1993	1994	1995	1996
31	**Food, Beverages & Tobacco**	7 039	7 388	7 348	7 264	7 233	7 112	7 054	7 029	..	..
311.2	Food	6 720	7 076	7 058	6 997	6 961	6 860	6 813	6 790	..	..
313	Beverages	261	254	233	212	217	197	198	200	..	..
314	Tobacco	58	58	57	55	55	55	43	39	..	..
32	**Textiles, Apparel & Leather**	3 525	3 559	3 533	3 480	3 384	3 273	3 039	2 824	..	..
321	Textiles	1 218	1 214	1 217	1 211	1 172	1 141	1 537	1 476	..	..
3213	Knitting Mills	..	..	..	..	..	..	..	..	..	..
322	Wearing Apparel	2 018	2 075	2 053	2 032	1 991	1 915	1 314	1 172	..	..
323	Leather & Products	180	162	153	139	128	126	108	95	..	..
324	Footwear	109	108	110	98	93	91	80	81	..	..
33	**Wood Products & Furniture**	2 248	2 367	2 444	2 520	2 542	2 550	3 139	3 087	..	..
331	Wood Products	..	..	..	..	..	..			..	..
332	Furnitures & Fixtures	..	..	..	..	..	..			..	..
34	**Paper, Paper Products & Printing**	2 581	2 725	2 797	2 865	2 961	2 924	2 850	2 811	..	..
341	Paper & Products	316	309	307	308	307	292	289	291	..	..
3411	Pulp, Paper & Board	..	..	..	..	..	..			..	..
342	Printing & Publishing	2 265	2 416	2 490	2 557	2 654	2 632	2 561	2 520	..	..
35	**Chemical Products**	1 336	1 373	1 446	1 497	1 482	1 490	1 501	1 475	..	..
351	Industrial Chemicals	738	741	769	807	784	780	778	772	..	..
3511	Basic Industrial Chemicals	..	..	..	..	..	..	..	..	..	..
3512	Fertilizers & Pesticides	..	..	..	..	..	..	..	..	..	..
3513	Synthetic Resins	..	..	..	..	..	..	..	..	..	..
352	Other Chemicals	..	..	..	..	..	..	..	..	..	..
3521	Paints, Varnishes & Lacquers	..	..	..	..	..	..	..	..	..	..
3522	Drugs & Medicines	..	..	..	..	..	..	..	..	..	..
3523	Soap & Cleaning Preparations	..	..	..	..	..	..	..	..	..	..
3529	Chemical Products, nec	..	..	..	..	..	..	..	..	..	..
353	Petroleum Refineries	23	22	22	21	21	21	40	35	..	..
354	Petroleum & Coal Products	4	4	4	4	4	4			..	..
355	Rubber Products	97	93	100	98	100	103	98	97	..	..
356	Plastic Products, nec	474	513	551	567	573	582	585	571	..	..
36	**Non-Metallic Mineral Products**	1 318	1 356	1 393	1 398	1 380	1 385	1 373	1 373	..	..
361	Pottery, China etc	..	..	..	..	..	..			..	..
362	Glass & Products	136	137	140	144	144	149	157	165	..	..
369	Non-Metallic Products, nec	1 182	1 219	1 253	1 254	1 236	1 236	1 216	1 208	..	..
37	**Basic Metal Industries**	149	147	152	153	159	154	290	284	..	..
371	Iron & Steel	..	..	..	..	..	..	..	..	..	..
372	Non-Ferrous Metals	..	..	..	..	..	..	..	..	..	..
38	**Fabricated Metal Products**	5 806	6 039	6 261	6 484	6 561	6 682	6 409	6 362	..	..
381	Metal Products	3 214	3 350	3 493	3 651	3 714	3 785	3 439	3 438	..	..
3813	Structural Metal Products	..	..	..	..	..	..	..	..	..	..
382	Non-Electrical Machinery	865	861	877	882	898	891	1 045	1 086	..	..
3821	Engines & Turbines	..	..	..	..	..	..	..	..	..	..
3822	Agricultural Machinery	..	..	..	..	..	..	..	..	..	..
3823	Metal & Wood working Machinery	..	..	..	..	..	..	..	..	..	..
3824	Special Industrial Machinery	..	..	..	..	..	..	..	..	..	..
3825	Office & Computing Machinery	..	..	..	..	..	..	..	..	..	..
3829	Machinery & Equipment, nec	..	..	..	..	..	..	..	..	..	..
383	Electrical Machinery	767	843	894	936	936	971	791	675	..	..
3831	Electrical Industrial Machinery	..	..	..	..	..	..	..	..	..	..
3832	Radio, TV & Communication Equipment	..	..	..	..	..	..	..	..	..	..
3833	Electrical Appliances & Housewares	..	..	..	..	..	..	..	..	..	..
3839	Electrical Apparatus, nec	..	..	..	..	..	..	..	..	..	..
384	Transport Equipment	497	502	516	531	537	549	528	528	..	..
3841	Shipbuilding & Repairing	..	..	..	..	..	..	..	..	..	..
3842	Railroad Equipment	..	..	..	..	..	..	..	..	..	..
3843	Motor Vehicles	..	..	..	..	..	..	..	..	..	..
3844	Motorcycles & Bicycles	..	..	..	..	..	..	..	..	..	..
3845	Aircraft	..	..	..	..	..	..	..	..	..	..
3849	Transport Equipment, nec	..	..	..	..	..	..	..	..	..	..
385	Professional Goods	463	483	481	484	476	486	606	635	..	..
3851	Professional Equipment	..	..	..	..	..	..	..	..	..	..
3852	Photographic & Optical Goods	..	..	..	..	..	..	..	..	..	..
3853	Watches & Clocks	..	..	..	..	..	..	..	..	..	..
39	**Other Manufacturing, nes**	1 006	1 032	1 033	986	951	895	556	564	..	..
3901	Jewellery	..	..	..	..	..	..	..	..	..	..
3	**Total Manufacturing**	25 008	25 986	26 407	26 647	26 653	26 465	26 211	25 809	..	..
1	**Agric., Hunting, Forestry, Fishing**	..	..	..	..	..	..	4 823	4 986	..	..
2	**Mining & Quarrying**	..	..	..	..	..	..	2 063	1 562	..	..
21	Coal Mining	..	..	..	..	..	..	1 831	1 338	..	..
22	Crude Petroleum & Natural Gas	..	..	..	..	..	..			..	..
23.29	Other Mining	..	..	..	..	..	..	232	224	..	..
3	**Total Manufacturing**	25 008	25 986	26 407	26 647	26 653	26 465	26 211	25 809	..	..
4	**Electricity, Gas & Water**	..	..	..	..	..	..	435	403	..	..
5	**Construction**	..	..	..	..	..	..	26 398	26 890	..	..
6.9	**Services**	..	..	..	..	..	..	431 926	434 641	..	..
0000	**Grand Total**	..	..	..	..	..	..	491 856	494 291	..	..

Note: Break in series between 1992 and 1993. See Sources and Definitions. From 1993, ISIC 353 includes 354.
ISIC 351 includes 352; 369 includes 361.

Millions of BF (1990 Prices)

ISIC2	Industry	VALUE ADDED (Market Prices)									
		1987	1988	1989	1990	1991	1992	1993	1994	1995	1996
31	**Food, Beverages & Tobacco**	244 779	246 772	257 607	253 316	261 382	258 465	257 092	263 230	274 500	281 245
311.2	Food	163 699	169 431	180 496	175 650	183 401	182 619	185 335	191 066	202 618	215 813
313	Beverages	37 373	36 518	37 458	36 268	34 497	35 515	33 575	32 811	33 828	32 093
314	Tobacco	43 707	40 823	39 653	41 398	43 484	40 331	38 182	39 353	38 054	33 339
32	**Textiles, Apparel & Leather**	82 385	80 245	90 215	96 078	92 275	93 987	93 825	94 388	89 332	85 053
321	Textiles	53 306	52 182	63 027	64 667	63 135	64 484	62 366	62 611	57 507	58 126
3213	Knitting Mills	7 454	6 231	5 905	5 360	5 818	5 180	4 670	4 103	3 660	3 249
322	Wearing Apparel	26 445	25 290	24 803	29 262	27 120	27 543	29 903	30 509	30 664	25 816
323	Leather & Products	..	..	..	..	..	..	..	..	..	..
324	Footwear	2 634	2 773	2 385	2 149	2 020	1 960	1 556	1 268	1 161	1 111
33	**Wood Products & Furniture**	54 491	57 802	62 501	64 306	65 891	61 903	59 032	59 101	60 778	59 787
331	Wood Products	9 599	9 085	12 405	11 021	12 326	11 578	11 269	11 421	11 574	10 720
332	Furnitures & Fixtures	44 892	48 717	50 096	53 285	53 565	50 325	47 763	47 680	49 204	49 067
34	**Paper, Paper Products & Printing**	69 064	78 949	86 224	88 207	85 883	86 562	91 227	95 078	96 069	94 556
341	Paper & Products	25 807	28 036	31 331	30 507	29 521	29 744	27 142	28 796	29 075	28 903
3411	Pulp, Paper & Board	11 206	11 373	12 619	12 784	12 124	12 649	11 299	12 633	10 803	10 474
342	Printing & Publishing	43 257	50 913	54 893	57 700	56 362	56 818	64 085	66 282	66 994	65 653
35	**Chemical Products**	170 520	182 956	192 891	194 714	201 767	210 281	202 131	217 174	233 152	243 787
351	Industrial Chemicals	127 056	131 651	130 203	133 197	137 549	144 425	138 656	153 051	161 216	168 900
3511	Basic Industrial Chemicals	..	..	..	..	..	..	..	..	..	..
3512	Fertilizers & Pesticides	..	..	..	..	..	..	..	..	..	..
3513	Synthetic Resins	..	..	..	..	..	..	..	..	..	..
352	Other Chemicals	24 342	29 512	36 537	36 005	39 344	39 825	39 811	39 908	44 925	45 265
3521	Paints, Varnishes & Lacquers	..	..	..	..	..	..	..	..	..	..
3522	Drugs & Medicines	20 767	23 772	27 732	25 742	26 355	26 988	27 506	27 284	32 412	32 196
3523	Soap & Cleaning Preparations	3 575	5 740	8 805	10 263	12 989	12 837	12 305	12 624	12 513	13 069
3529	Chemical Products, nec	..	..	..	..	..	..	..	..	..	..
353	Petroleum Refineries	13 800	16 108	18 681	17 379	17 549	18 064	16 910	16 295	18 740	22 236
354	Petroleum & Coal Products	..	..	..	..	..	..	..	..	..	..
355	Rubber Products	5 322	5 685	7 470	8 133	7 325	7 967	6 754	7 920	8 271	7 386
356	Plastic Products, nec	..	..	..	..	..	..	..	..	..	..
36	**Non-Metallic Mineral Products**	48 337	56 178	61 323	60 814	57 193	62 626	62 691	65 502	67 887	64 999
361	Pottery, China etc	..	..	..	..	..	..	..	..	..	..
362	Glass & Products	..	..	..	..	..	..	..	..	..	..
369	Non-Metallic Products, nec	..	..	..	..	..	..	..	..	..	..
37	**Basic Metal Industries**	90 226	99 958	101 226	101 927	98 672	92 340	88 045	94 809	100 181	96 279
371	Iron & Steel	63 005	69 671	68 753	68 479	67 842	61 960	59 052	63 032	64 885	60 356
372	Non-Ferrous Metals	27 221	30 287	32 473	33 448	30 830	30 380	28 993	31 777	35 296	35 923
38	**Fabricated Metal Products**	357 709	367 779	399 139	409 999	395 900	380 005	358 651	378 226	378 921	379 044
381	Metal Products	..	..	..	..	..	..	..	..	..	..
3813	Structural Metal Products	..	..	..	..	..	..	..	..	..	..
382	Non-Electrical Machinery	..	..	..	..	..	..	..	..	..	..
3821	Engines & Turbines	..	..	..	..	..	..	..	..	..	..
3822	Agricultural Machinery	..	..	..	..	..	..	..	..	..	..
3823	Metal & Wood working Machinery	..	..	..	..	..	..	..	..	..	..
3824	Special Industrial Machinery	..	..	..	..	..	..	..	..	..	..
3825	Office & Computing Machinery	..	..	..	..	..	..	..	..	..	..
3829	Machinery & Equipment, nec	..	..	..	..	..	..	..	..	..	..
383	Electrical Machinery	..	..	..	..	..	..	..	..	..	..
3831	Electrical Industrial Machinery	..	..	..	..	..	..	..	..	..	..
3832	Radio, TV & Communication Equipment	..	..	..	..	..	..	..	..	..	..
3833	Electrical Appliances & Housewares	..	..	..	..	..	..	..	..	..	..
3839	Electrical Apparatus, nec	..	..	..	..	..	..	..	..	..	..
384	Transport Equipment	..	..	..	..	..	..	..	..	..	..
3841	Shipbuilding & Repairing	..	..	..	..	..	..	..	..	..	..
3842	Railroad Equipment	..	..	..	..	..	..	..	..	..	..
3843	Motor Vehicles	..	..	..	..	..	..	..	..	..	..
3844	Motorcycles & Bicycles	..	..	..	..	..	..	..	..	..	..
3845	Aircraft	..	..	..	..	..	..	..	..	..	..
3849	Transport Equipment, nec	..	..	..	..	..	..	..	..	..	..
385	Professional Goods	..	..	..	..	..	..	..	..	..	..
3851	Professional Equipment	..	..	..	..	..	..	..	..	..	..
3852	Photographic & Optical Goods	..	..	..	..	..	..	..	..	..	..
3853	Watches & Clocks	..	..	..	..	..	..	..	..	..	..
39	**Other Manufacturing, nes**	64 158	71 502	69 775	77 359	82 820	85 029	78 568	80 214	89 549	86 463
3901	Jewellery	..	..	..	..	..	..	..	..	..	..
3	**Total Manufacturing**	1 181 669	1 242 141	1 320 901	1 346 720	1 341 783	1 331 198	1 291 262	1 347 722	1 390 369	1 391 213
1	**Agric., Hunting, Forestry, Fishing**	123 310	130 100	132 144	128 303	135 949	149 916	157 388	146 904	147 506	140 888
2	**Mining & Quarrying**	13 085	13 090	14 037	15 592	15 400	17 558	14 971	16 959	18 791	18 615
21	Coal Mining	2 762	1 152	770	-1 141	-789	-305	-852	0	0	0
22	Crude Petroleum & Natural Gas	..	..	..	..	..	..	..	..	..	..
23.29	Other Mining	10 323	11 938	13 267	16 733	16 189	17 863	15 823	16 959	18 791	18 615
3	**Total Manufacturing**	1 181 669	1 242 141	1 320 901	1 346 720	1 341 783	1 331 198	1 291 262	1 347 722	1 390 369	1 391 213
4	**Electricity, Gas & Water**	171 240	180 704	181 462	188 024	196 588	197 811	197 677	200 736	209 932	218 375
5	**Construction**	310 257	353 044	367 437	388 561	394 522	406 053	389 464	397 956	402 481	393 116
6.9	**Services**	4 313 600	4 485 144	4 646 757	4 766 021	4 891 294	4 998 274	4 967 321	5 067 706	5 151 442	5 278 198
0000	**Grand Total**	6 113 161	6 404 223	6 662 738	6 833 221	6 975 536	7 100 810	7 018 083	7 177 983	7 320 521	7 440 405

Note: ISIC 324 includes 323; 353 includes 354.
ISIC 39 excludes steam and heat (included in 4); 3 excludes garages, steam and heat; 21 - coal boards include their electric power stations. 6.9 includes garages. The Grand Total has deductible VAT on capital formation removed.

Millions of BF

(1990 Prices)

ISIC2	Industry	1987	1988	1989	1990	1991	1992	1993	1994	1995	1996
31	**Food, Beverages & Tobacco**	27 813	35 509	37 924	45 392	49 222	49 944	41 819	37 082	35 679	38 183
311.2	Food	22 056	27 775	26 550	33 793	33 739	31 676	28 456	27 789	26 846	30 164
313	Beverages	4 834	6 972	10 006	10 146	14 518	16 904	12 613	8 244	8 238	7 213
314	Tobacco	923	762	1 368	1 453	965	1 365	750	1 049	595	806
32	**Textiles, Apparel & Leather**	21 015	21 638	21 096	21 601	19 066	17 884	16 636	19 358	15 539	13 943
321	Textiles	18 247	18 786	17 684	18 949	16 493	15 111	14 082	16 925	13 451	12 116
3213	Knitting Mills	804	1 033	667	953	913	692	697	599	521	657
322	Wearing Apparel	2 634	2 741	3 283	2 513	2 443	2 712	2 498	2 376	2 030	1 782
323	Leather & Products	16	5	15	58	27	8	7	13	8	5
324	Footwear	118	105	114	81	104	53	49	44	50	40
33	**Wood Products & Furniture**	9 255	10 317	11 399	12 607	10 635	7 666	6 903	7 963	6 991	8 351
331	Wood Products	7 628	8 566	2 244	2 500	1 118	907	752	799	953	874
332	Furnitures & Fixtures	1 627	1 751	9 155	10 107	9 517	6 759	6 151	7 164	6 038	7 477
34	**Paper, Paper Products & Printing**	20 164	22 396	27 042	27 217	35 592	33 758	22 705	29 451	26 877	25 666
341	Paper & Products	9 971	9 410	10 982	9 587	21 023	18 097	9 329	14 650	12 601	12 130
3411	Pulp, Paper & Board	6 255	4 985	5 369	4 163	14 210	14 008	6 090	11 026	8 869	7 937
342	Printing & Publishing	10 193	12 986	16 060	17 630	14 569	15 661	13 376	14 801	14 276	13 536
35	**Chemical Products**	42 678	71 557	92 355	135 250	106 483	97 455	99 825	83 557	99 882	121 173
351	Industrial Chemicals	25 529	48 731	62 549	86 927	74 244	63 467	55 703	50 991	73 307	91 185
3511	Basic Industrial Chemicals	..	..	..	..	..	..	..	..	..	..
3512	Fertilizers & Pesticides	..	..	..	..	..	..	..	..	..	..
3513	Synthetic Resins	..	..	..	..	..	..	..	..	..	..
352	Other Chemicals	..	..	..	..	..	..	..	..	..	..
3521	Paints, Varnishes & Lacquers	..	..	..	..	..	..	..	..	..	..
3522	Drugs & Medicines	4 277	5 056	5 800	6 653	6 470	7 926	7 103	8 943	10 242	10 564
3523	Soap & Cleaning Preparations	1 653	1 651	1 889	2 042	2 242	2 704	3 178	2 395	2 274	1 698
3529	Chemical Products, nec	..	..	..	..	..	..	..	..	..	..
353	Petroleum Refineries	1 844	1 825	4 874	16 436	9 165	10 661	24 443	12 725	6 130	6 540
354	Petroleum & Coal Products	..	..	..	..	..	..	..	..	..	..
355	Rubber Products	1 760	2 123	2 460	3 533	2 164	2 388	1 780	1 721	1 615	1 509
356	Plastic Products, nec	..	..	..	..	..	..	..	..	..	..
36	**Non-Metallic Mineral Products**	15 152	15 081	13 808	19 019	16 646	14 504	15 971	14 640	17 147	12 551
361	Pottery, China etc	..	..	..	..	..	..	..	..	..	..
362	Glass & Products	..	..	..	..	..	..	..	..	..	..
369	Non-Metallic Products, nec	..	..	..	..	..	..	..	..	..	..
37	**Basic Metal Industries**	13 008	17 491	22 735	21 930	27 154	25 449	19 253	20 552	20 673	20 692
371	Iron & Steel	8 407	13 852	18 619	17 641	22 618	21 934	16 590	18 594	17 262	15 649
372	Non-Ferrous Metals	4 601	3 639	4 116	4 289	4 536	3 515	2 663	1 958	3 411	5 043
38	**Fabricated Metal Products**	49 505	52 732	74 756	79 744	77 920	75 572	49 207	42 801	54 110	58 773
381	Metal Products	..	..	..	..	..	..	..	..	..	..
3813	Structural Metal Products	..	..	..	..	..	..	..	..	..	..
382	Non-Electrical Machinery	..	..	..	..	..	..	..	..	..	..
3821	Engines & Turbines	..	..	..	..	..	..	..	..	..	..
3822	Agricultural Machinery	..	..	..	..	..	..	..	..	..	..
3823	Metal & Wood working Machinery	..	..	..	..	..	..	..	..	..	..
3824	Special Industrial Machinery	..	..	..	..	..	..	..	..	..	..
3825	Office & Computing Machinery	..	..	..	..	..	..	..	..	..	..
3829	Machinery & Equipment, nec	..	..	..	..	..	..	..	..	..	..
383	Electrical Machinery	..	..	..	..	..	..	..	..	..	..
3831	Electrical Industrial Machinery	..	..	..	..	..	..	..	..	..	..
3832	Radio, TV & Communication Equipment	..	..	..	..	..	..	..	..	..	..
3833	Electrical Appliances & Housewares	..	..	..	..	..	..	..	..	..	..
3839	Electrical Apparatus, nec	..	..	..	..	..	..	..	..	..	..
384	Transport Equipment	..	..	..	..	..	..	..	..	..	..
3841	Shipbuilding & Repairing	..	..	..	..	..	..	..	..	..	..
3842	Railroad Equipment	..	..	..	..	..	..	..	..	..	..
3843	Motor Vehicles	..	..	..	..	..	..	..	..	..	..
3844	Motorcycles & Bicycles	..	..	..	..	..	..	..	..	..	..
3845	Aircraft	..	..	..	..	..	..	..	..	..	..
3849	Transport Equipment, nec	..	..	..	..	..	..	..	..	..	..
385	Professional Goods	..	..	..	..	..	..	..	..	..	..
3851	Professional Equipment	..	..	..	..	..	..	..	..	..	..
3852	Photographic & Optical Goods	..	..	..	..	..	..	..	..	..	..
3853	Watches & Clocks	..	..	..	..	..	..	..	..	..	..
39	**Other Manufacturing, nes**	4 687	2 320	2 009	1 720	1 599	1 402	1 284	1 710	1 666	2 000
3901	Jewellery	..	..	..	..	..	..	..	..	..	..
3	**Total Manufacturing**	203 277	249 041	303 125	364 480	344 317	323 634	273 603	257 114	278 564	301 332
1	**Agric., Hunting, Forestry, Fishing**	22 580	21 569	21 587	24 731	18 500	22 421	15 445	14 096	13 227	15 092
2	**Mining & Quarrying**	1 546	3 532	6 800	9 691	5 276	4 470	4 569	3 902	4 205	4 448
21	Coal Mining	..	..	..	..	..	..	..	..	..	..
22	Crude Petroleum & Natural Gas	..	..	..	..	..	..	..	..	..	..
23.29	Other Mining	..	..	..	..	..	..	..	..	..	..
3	**Total Manufacturing**	203 277	249 041	303 125	364 480	344 317	323 634	273 603	257 114	278 564	301 332
4	**Electricity, Gas & Water**	41 391	40 632	47 481	42 059	46 161	68 055	55 865	57 549	60 200	64 160
5	**Construction**	16 604	24 528	26 020	29 716	26 722	23 756	21 538	22 457	24 734	23 746
6.9	**Services**	649 035	747 996	806 118	857 305	824 748	840 022	865 416	879 807	893 817	874 073
0000	**Grand Total**	934 433	1 087 298	1 211 131	1 327 982	1 265 724	1 282 358	1 236 436	1 234 925	1 274 747	1 282 851

Note: ISIC 353 includes 354; 39 includes 356.

Table BL.12 **BELGIUM**

Millions of BF (1990 Prices)

ISIC2	Industry	INVESTMENT IN MACHINERY & EQUIPMENT									
		1987	1988	1989	1990	1991	1992	1993	1994	1995	1996
31	Food, Beverages & Tobacco	22 195	27 398	28 877	34 988	37 442	38 719	32 668	28 049	27 174	28 789
311.2	Food	17 261	21 285	19 941	24 994	25 515	24 592	22 567	22 079	21 466	23 868
313	Beverages	4 153	5 535	8 174	8 790	11 060	12 934	9 584	5 090	5 208	4 244
314	Tobacco	781	579	762	1 204	867	1 193	517	880	500	677
32	Textiles, Apparel & Leather	17 681	17 649	17 312	17 825	15 518	14 445	14 254	16 080	13 226	11 861
321	Textiles	15 482	15 523	14 848	15 747	13 592	12 238	12 333	14 220	11 615	10 435
3213	Knitting Mills	683	776	497	831	901	584	665	579	503	634
322	Wearing Apparel	2 077	2 021	2 345	1 964	1 844	2 159	1 886	1 816	1 563	1 387
323	Leather & Products	15	4	9	33	10	6	0	5	4	3
324	Footwear	106	100	109	81	73	41	35	39	44	36
33	Wood Products & Furniture	7 157	7 890	8 019	9 425	8 233	5 860	5 340	6 019	5 328	6 410
331	Wood Products	1 083	1 209	1 243	1 586	925	727	597	686	814	745
332	Furnitures & Fixtures	6 074	6 681	6 776	7 839	7 308	5 133	4 743	5 333	4 514	5 665
34	Paper, Paper Products & Printing	16 475	18 834	22 101	21 095	27 628	27 969	18 411	24 585	22 515	22 680
341	Paper & Products	7 916	7 880	9 243	7 101	16 324	15 178	7 373	12 201	10 530	10 218
3411	Pulp, Paper & Board	5 181	4 429	4 780	2 810	10 727	11 719	4 508	9 045	7 277	6 563
342	Printing & Publishing	8 559	10 954	12 858	13 994	11 304	12 791	11 038	12 384	11 985	12 462
35	Chemical Products	35 150	58 374	78 153	117 104	92 726	86 769	87 094	71 973	87 226	106 061
351	Industrial Chemicals	21 956	40 567	57 160	77 947	66 315	60 460	49 225	45 483	66 734	82 956
3511	Basic Industrial Chemicals	..	..	..	..	..	..	..	..	..	..
3512	Fertilizers & Pesticides	..	..	..	..	..	..	..	..	..	..
3513	Synthetic Resins	..	..	..	..	..	..	..	..	..	..
352	Other Chemicals	..	..	..	..	..	..	..	..	..	..
3521	Paints, Varnishes & Lacquers	..	..	..	..	..	..	..	..	..	..
3522	Drugs & Medicines	2 527	3 050	3 515	4 100	4 850	5 518	5 002	5 491	6 300	6 492
3523	Soap & Cleaning Preparations	1 390	1 276	1 406	1 668	1 840	1 346	2 572	2 133	2 027	1 507
3529	Chemical Products, nec	..	..	..	..	..	..	..	..	..	..
353	Petroleum Refineries	1 643	1 773	4 544	16 097	8 391	9 111	22 667	12 049	5 806	6 195
354	Petroleum & Coal Products	..	..	..	..	..	..	..	..	..	..
355	Rubber Products	1 553	1 860	2 168	2 706	1 824	2 007	1 503	1 480	1 385	1 289
356	Plastic Products, nec	..	..	..	..	..	..	..	..	..	..
36	Non-Metallic Mineral Products	13 078	12 451	11 584	16 192	14 480	12 094	11 392	12 425	14 487	10 631
361	Pottery, China etc	..	..	..	..	..	..	..	..	..	..
362	Glass & Products	..	..	..	..	..	..	..	..	..	..
369	Non-Metallic Products, nec	..	..	..	..	..	..	..	..	..	..
37	Basic Metal Industries	11 503	14 838	19 926	19 333	23 297	21 951	17 743	19 885	19 962	19 927
371	Iron & Steel	7 406	11 838	16 850	15 817	19 951	19 195	15 537	18 047	16 757	15 189
372	Non-Ferrous Metals	4 097	3 000	3 076	3 516	3 346	2 756	2 206	1 838	3 205	4 738
38	Fabricated Metal Products	41 128	43 225	60 161	64 000	61 713	64 230	41 091	35 394	44 743	49 063
381	Metal Products	..	..	..	..	..	..	..	..	..	..
3813	Structural Metal Products	..	..	..	..	..	..	..	..	..	..
382	Non-Electrical Machinery	..	..	..	..	..	..	..	..	..	..
3821	Engines & Turbines	..	..	..	..	..	..	..	..	..	..
3822	Agricultural Machinery	..	..	..	..	..	..	..	..	..	..
3823	Metal & Wood working Machinery	..	..	..	..	..	..	..	..	..	..
3824	Special Industrial Machinery	..	..	..	..	..	..	..	..	..	..
3825	Office & Computing Machinery	..	..	..	..	..	..	..	..	..	..
3829	Machinery & Equipment, nec	..	..	..	..	..	..	..	..	..	..
383	Electrical Machinery	..	..	..	..	..	..	..	..	..	..
3831	Electrical Industrial Machinery	..	..	..	..	..	..	..	..	..	..
3832	Radio, TV & Communication Equipment	..	..	..	..	..	..	..	..	..	..
3833	Electrical Appliances & Housewares	..	..	..	..	..	..	..	..	..	..
3839	Electrical Apparatus, nec	..	..	..	..	..	..	..	..	..	..
384	Transport Equipment	..	..	..	..	..	..	..	..	..	..
3841	Shipbuilding & Repairing	..	..	..	..	..	..	..	..	..	..
3842	Railroad Equipment	..	..	..	..	..	..	..	..	..	..
3843	Motor Vehicles	..	..	..	..	..	..	..	..	..	..
3844	Motorcycles & Bicycles	..	..	..	..	..	..	..	..	..	..
3845	Aircraft	..	..	..	..	..	..	..	..	..	..
3849	Transport Equipment, nec	..	..	..	..	..	..	..	..	..	..
385	Professional Goods	..	..	..	..	..	..	..	..	..	..
3851	Professional Equipment	..	..	..	..	..	..	..	..	..	..
3852	Photographic & Optical Goods	..	..	..	..	..	..	..	..	..	..
3853	Watches & Clocks	..	..	..	..	..	..	..	..	..	..
39	Other Manufacturing, nes	3 416	2 138	1 416	1 347	1 151	1 125	1 021	1 187	1 137	1 375
3901	Jewellery	..	..	..	..	..	..	..	..	..	..
3	Total Manufacturing	167 783	202 796	247 548	301 309	282 188	273 162	229 014	215 597	235 798	256 797
1	Agric., Hunting, Forestry, Fishing	12 877	12 697	12 778	13 870	8 039	11 124	7 400	7 173	5 695	5 967
2	Mining & Quarrying	362	2 069	5 315	5 092	2 823	3 182	3 386	3 230	3 484	3 710
21	Coal Mining	..	..	..	..	..	..	..	..	..	..
22	Crude Petroleum & Natural Gas	..	..	..	..	..	..	..	..	..	..
23.29	Other Mining	..	..	..	..	..	..	..	..	..	..
3	Total Manufacturing	167 783	202 796	247 548	301 309	282 188	273 162	229 014	215 597	235 798	256 797
4	Electricity, Gas & Water	12 052	14 215	16 864	17 779	10 533	14 099	11 667	9 254	9 620	11 426
5	Construction	14 411	20 572	23 284	24 544	21 661	18 763	17 773	18 361	20 192	19 462
6.9	Services	183 296	201 618	227 873	247 734	230 396	219 259	229 488	227 811	239 291	246 253
0000	Grand Total	390 781	453 967	533 662	610 328	555 640	539 589	498 728	481 426	514 080	543 615

Note: ISIC 353 includes 354; 39 includes 356.

Millions of FF (Current Prices)

ISIC2	Industry	PRODUCTION									
		1987	1988	1989	1990	1991	1992	1993	1994	1995	1996
31	**Food, Beverages & Tobacco**	520 129	547 256	585 247	606 050	623 149	632 531	625 945	636 032	649 833	..
311.2	Food	455 817	477 675	508 690	520 841	532 382	544 168	532 230	540 681	553 029	..
313	Beverages	53 049	57 541	63 946	71 880	76 974	73 156	76 334	75 327	76 153	..
314	Tobacco	11 263	12 040	12 611	13 329	13 793	15 207	17 381	20 024	20 651	..
32	**Textiles, Apparel & Leather**	206 881	206 983	215 027	219 360	213 645	211 483	194 246	201 767	199 443	..
321	Textiles	109 025	110 579	114 435	115 718	111 577	111 278	100 729	107 803	108 871	..
3213	Knitting Mills	..	..	..	..	..	..	..	..	..	..
322	Wearing Apparel	69 918	68 571	71 504	74 190	73 202	72 186	67 860	67 908	64 080	..
323	Leather & Products	12 347	12 815	13 706	13 716	12 627	12 389	10 798	11 957	13 045	..
324	Footwear	15 591	15 018	15 382	15 736	16 239	15 630	14 859	14 099	13 447	..
33	**Wood Products & Furniture**	84 406	91 304	98 319	107 047	107 810	107 725	103 120	109 405	114 861	..
331	Wood Products	44 194	48 201	52 248	57 132	56 987	57 886	54 277	60 370	63 752	..
332	Furnitures & Fixtures	40 212	43 103	46 071	49 915	50 823	49 839	48 843	49 035	51 109	..
34	**Paper, Paper Products & Printing**	214 535	235 122	257 857	272 984	283 071	283 521	275 700	290 397	313 158	..
341	Paper & Products	84 931	93 458	103 234	108 983	107 852	107 600	96 791	105 018	121 852	..
3411	Pulp, Paper & Board	..	..	..	..	..	..	..	..	..	..
342	Printing & Publishing	129 604	141 664	154 623	164 001	175 219	175 921	178 909	185 379	191 306	..
35	**Chemical Products**	557 391	596 644	657 850	685 041	693 697	685 374	687 146	716 496	743 728	..
351	Industrial Chemicals	138 620	151 958	168 031	165 442	155 538	148 076	139 570	151 555	162 247	..
3511	Basic Industrial Chemicals	..	..	..	..	..	..	..	..	..	..
3512	Fertilizers & Pesticides	..	..	..	..	..	..	..	..	..	..
3513	Synthetic Resins	..	..	..	..	..	..	..	..	..	..
352	Other Chemicals	148 013	162 266	180 053	189 573	196 410	208 233	216 095	228 401	234 943	..
3521	Paints, Varnishes & Lacquers	..	..	..	..	..	..	..	..	..	..
3522	Drugs & Medicines	61 113	68 822	75 167	80 390	84 622	92 327	97 055	98 541	104 758	..
3523	Soap & Cleaning Preparations	..	..	..	..	..	..	..	..	..	..
3529	Chemical Products, nec	..	..	..	..	..	..	..	..	..	..
353	Petroleum Refineries	166 754	166 147	180 422	193 381	200 146	185 246	192 862	192 628	195 873	..
354	Petroleum & Coal Products	..	..	..	..	..	..	..	..	..	..
355	Rubber Products	32 215	34 997	38 356	37 775	38 160	39 480	36 219	37 769	38 985	..
356	Plastic Products, nec	71 789	81 276	90 988	98 870	103 443	104 339	102 400	106 143	111 680	..
36	**Non-Metallic Mineral Products**	100 338	109 696	118 268	123 624	127 850	125 195	118 061	125 255	130 583	..
361	Pottery, China etc	..	..	..	..	..	..	..	..	..	..
362	Glass & Products	25 269	27 094	29 728	31 241	31 432	31 534	29 615	31 495	34 241	..
369	Non-Metallic Products, nec	75 069	82 602	88 540	92 383	96 418	93 661	88 446	93 760	96 342	..
37	**Basic Metal Industries**	197 496	222 738	250 339	229 538	212 296	204 277	181 281	202 964	218 785	..
371	Iron & Steel	126 144	139 994	158 142	147 046	136 647	127 367	113 247	128 624	135 886	..
372	Non-Ferrous Metals	71 352	82 744	92 197	82 492	75 649	76 910	68 034	74 340	82 899	..
38	**Fabricated Metal Products**	1 078 892	1 190 267	1 322 177	1 406 344	1 427 753	1 435 953	1 334 953	1 424 838	1 506 632	..
381	Metal Products	166 161	185 909	208 933	226 975	230 247	225 197	204 480	223 239	239 795	..
3813	Structural Metal Products	..	..	..	..	..	..	..	..	..	..
382	Non-Electrical Machinery	266 255	286 864	315 755	337 968	343 691	330 968	303 730	312 384	333 933	..
3821	Engines & Turbines	..	..	..	..	..	..	..	..	..	..
3822	Agricultural Machinery	..	..	..	..	..	..	..	..	..	..
3823	Metal & Wood working Machinery	..	..	..	..	..	..	..	..	..	..
3824	Special Industrial Machinery	..	..	..	..	..	..	..	..	..	..
3825	Office & Computing Machinery	..	..	..	..	..	..	..	..	..	..
3829	Machinery & Equipment, nec	..	..	..	..	..	..	..	..	..	..
383	Electrical Machinery	239 511	261 920	284 569	300 239	316 494	317 983	309 917	324 171	342 641	..
3831	Electrical Industrial Machinery	..	..	..	..	..	..	..	..	..	..
3832	Radio, TV & Communication Equipment	..	..	..	..	..	..	..	..	..	..
3833	Electrical Appliances & Housewares	..	..	..	..	..	..	..	..	..	..
3839	Electrical Apparatus, nec	..	..	..	..	..	..	..	..	..	..
384	Transport Equipment	374 636	420 685	474 310	499 677	495 215	519 478	475 657	521 940	545 331	..
3841	Shipbuilding & Repairing	20 467	20 902	21 844	23 691	23 912	25 038	23 319	19 745	20 622	..
3842	Railroad Equipment	10 584	9 609	8 875	10 159	10 546	12 716	12 628	9 906	10 828	..
3843	Motor Vehicles	260 296	294 874	332 817	343 070	335 988	354 697	318 667	370 215	390 406	..
3844	Motorcycles & Bicycles	..	..	..	..	..	..	..	..	..	..
3845	Aircraft	83 289	95 300	110 774	122 757	124 769	127 027	121 043	122 074	123 475	..
3849	Transport Equipment, nec	..	..	..	..	..	..	..	..	..	..
385	Professional Goods	32 329	34 889	38 610	41 485	42 106	42 327	41 169	43 104	44 932	..
3851	Professional Equipment	..	..	..	..	..	..	..	..	..	..
3852	Photographic & Optical Goods	..	..	..	..	..	..	..	..	..	..
3853	Watches & Clocks	..	..	..	..	..	..	..	..	..	..
39	**Other Manufacturing, nes**	40 483	42 643	47 196	49 644	48 764	48 618	48 451	50 683	53 180	..
3901	Jewellery	..	..	..	..	..	..	..	..	..	..
3	**Total Manufacturing**	3 000 551	3 242 653	3 552 280	3 699 632	3 738 035	3 734 677	3 568 903	3 757 837	3 930 203	..
1	**Agric., Hunting, Forestry, Fishing**	402 021	411 093	433 517	438 612	433 369	423 513	375 085	391 436	399 471	..
2	**Mining & Quarrying**	72 040	67 414	70 433	71 056	78 573	76 984	74 329	73 898	75 230	..
21	Coal Mining	13 483	12 040	12 251	11 765	11 121	10 587	9 431	9 088	8 518	..
22	Crude Petroleum & Natural Gas	43 263	38 987	41 099	43 070	50 326	49 170	48 902	48 765	50 574	..
23.29	Other Mining	15 294	16 387	17 083	16 221	17 126	17 227	15 996	16 045	16 138	..
3	**Total Manufacturing**	3 000 551	3 242 653	3 552 280	3 699 632	3 738 035	3 734 677	3 568 903	3 757 837	3 930 203	..
4	**Electricity, Gas & Water**	189 552	194 290	207 722	219 706	241 222	253 280	262 248	267 094	277 129	..
5	**Construction**	611 643	679 142	736 023	781 288	822 528	821 590	787 310	789 675	801 165	..
6.9	**Services**	4 752 983	5 160 734	5 694 882	6 131 720	6 524 324	7 031 678	7 616 544	7 898 637	8 282 920	..
0000	**Grand Total**	9 028 790	9 755 326	10 694 857	11 342 014	11 838 051	12 341 722	12 684 419	13 178 577	13 766 118	..

Note: Figures for ISIC 3849 cannot be separately identified, and are distributed across the other categories in the 384 group.

Table FR.2 **FRANCE**

Millions of FF   (Current Prices)

ISIC2	Industry	VALUE ADDED									
		1987	1988	1989	1990	1991	1992	1993	1994	1995	1996
31	Food, Beverages & Tobacco	143 693	154 706	170 340	178 907	184 029	190 634	205 436	205 600	208 065	..
311.2	Food	114 000	123 391	134 647	139 150	143 470	149 901	156 657	153 756	156 589	..
313	Beverages	21 308	22 112	25 923	29 307	29 596	28 418	34 097	34 461	33 499	..
314	Tobacco	8 385	9 203	9 770	10 450	10 963	12 315	14 682	17 383	17 977	..
32	Textiles, Apparel & Leather	83 223	81 434	83 128	87 246	84 744	84 228	78 179	78 289	76 633	..
321	Textiles	39 886	39 139	39 740	41 744	38 971	38 467	33 942	35 901	36 255	..
3213	Knitting Mills	..	..	..	..	..	..	..	..	..	..
322	Wearing Apparel	30 381	29 499	30 279	31 620	31 532	31 756	31 208	29 656	27 408	..
323	Leather & Products	5 063	5 306	5 690	6 151	5 942	5 944	5 345	5 882	6 692	..
324	Footwear	7 893	7 490	7 419	7 731	8 299	8 061	7 684	6 850	6 278	..
33	Wood Products & Furniture	34 592	37 343	39 064	44 407	44 994	46 337	45 848	46 019	48 897	..
331	Wood Products	17 092	18 602	19 448	22 774	22 570	23 714	22 898	23 252	25 242	..
332	Furnitures & Fixtures	17 500	18 741	19 616	21 633	22 424	22 623	22 950	22 767	23 655	..
34	Paper, Paper Products & Printing	84 036	91 421	96 385	105 216	112 650	113 005	114 220	116 193	121 668	..
341	Paper & Products	28 157	30 703	33 677	37 151	37 457	36 099	32 843	33 193	38 585	..
3411	Pulp, Paper & Board	..	..	..	..	..	..	..	..	..	..
342	Printing & Publishing	55 879	60 718	62 708	68 065	75 193	76 906	81 377	83 000	83 083	..
35	Chemical Products	221 415	243 806	254 201	263 720	270 672	262 661	270 453	277 020	286 612	..
351	Industrial Chemicals	48 617	58 915	63 839	59 202	52 816	45 136	40 037	43 707	51 146	..
3511	Basic Industrial Chemicals	..	..	..	..	..	..	..	..	..	..
3512	Fertilizers & Pesticides	..	..	..	..	..	..	..	..	..	..
3513	Synthetic Resins	..	..	..	..	..	..	..	..	..	..
352	Other Chemicals	53 573	57 526	60 602	67 667	69 849	74 789	82 829	86 109	83 487	..
3521	Paints, Varnishes & Lacquers	..	..	..	..	..	..	..	..	..	..
3522	Drugs & Medicines	20 368	21 646	21 884	24 549	25 743	29 428	32 936	31 716	32 670	..
3523	Soap & Cleaning Preparations	..	..	..	..	..	..	..	..	..	..
3529	Chemical Products, nec	..	..	..	..	..	..	..	..	..	..
353	Petroleum Refineries	75 426	80 664	78 214	82 380	90 418	83 198	90 686	90 969	94 221	..
354	Petroleum & Coal Products	..	..	..	..	..	..	..	..	..	..
355	Rubber Products	16 465	17 307	18 596	18 192	19 119	20 169	18 417	18 184	17 602	..
356	Plastic Products, nec	27 334	29 394	32 950	36 279	38 470	39 369	38 484	38 051	40 156	..
36	Non-Metallic Mineral Products	48 081	53 124	55 333	57 788	59 217	57 485	54 424	56 756	60 390	..
361	Pottery, China etc	..	..	..	..	..	..	..	..	..	..
362	Glass & Products	13 535	14 905	15 981	16 824	16 764	16 069	14 970	15 523	16 638	..
369	Non-Metallic Products, nec	34 546	38 219	39 352	40 964	42 453	41 416	39 454	41 233	43 752	..
37	Basic Metal Industries	57 564	69 433	76 868	70 608	63 791	61 512	56 190	62 472	69 674	..
371	Iron & Steel	35 151	43 563	48 311	45 923	41 469	37 387	33 595	37 214	41 792	..
372	Non-Ferrous Metals	22 413	25 870	28 557	24 685	22 322	24 125	22 595	25 258	27 882	..
38	Fabricated Metal Products	450 478	490 656	527 806	563 095	567 155	563 958	531 464	555 510	580 352	..
381	Metal Products	82 140	89 164	97 698	109 426	114 154	113 430	104 738	111 576	118 930	..
3813	Structural Metal Products	..	..	..	..	..	..	..	..	..	..
382	Non-Electrical Machinery	111 560	117 575	125 147	135 148	134 414	126 696	112 861	111 819	116 132	..
3821	Engines & Turbines	..	..	..	..	..	..	..	..	..	..
3822	Agricultural Machinery	..	..	..	..	..	..	..	..	..	..
3823	Metal & Wood working Machinery	..	..	..	..	..	..	..	..	..	..
3824	Special Industrial Machinery	..	..	..	..	..	..	..	..	..	..
3825	Office & Computing Machinery	..	..	..	..	..	..	..	..	..	..
3829	Machinery & Equipment, nec	..	..	..	..	..	..	..	..	..	..
383	Electrical Machinery	115 463	124 747	132 554	140 323	145 698	147 439	145 711	149 112	156 850	..
3831	Electrical Industrial Machinery	..	..	..	..	..	..	..	..	..	..
3832	Radio, TV & Communication Equipment	..	..	..	..	..	..	..	..	..	..
3833	Electrical Appliances & Housewares	..	..	..	..	..	..	..	..	..	..
3839	Electrical Apparatus, nec	..	..	..	..	..	..	..	..	..	..
384	Transport Equipment	123 523	140 109	151 844	155 823	150 420	154 033	146 351	160 281	165 098	..
3841	Shipbuilding & Repairing	4 427	4 572	5 020	5 619	5 374	5 670	5 075	3 180	2 999	..
3842	Railroad Equipment	4 544	4 216	3 609	3 828	4 374	5 280	5 400	3 647	3 878	..
3843	Motor Vehicles	83 891	95 755	104 406	106 536	100 795	103 200	95 230	115 124	115 347	..
3844	Motorcycles & Bicycles	..	..	..	..	..	..	..	..	..	..
3845	Aircraft	30 661	35 566	38 809	39 840	39 877	39 883	40 646	38 330	42 874	..
3849	Transport Equipment, nec	..	..	..	..	..	..	..	..	..	..
385	Professional Goods	17 792	19 061	20 563	22 375	22 469	22 360	21 803	22 722	23 342	..
3851	Professional Equipment	..	..	..	..	..	..	..	..	..	..
3852	Photographic & Optical Goods	..	..	..	..	..	..	..	..	..	..
3853	Watches & Clocks	..	..	..	..	..	..	..	..	..	..
39	Other Manufacturing, nes	20 140	20 213	21 496	23 516	22 525	22 917	24 083	25 208	25 720	..
3901	Jewellery	..	..	..	..	..	..	..	..	..	..
3	Total Manufacturing	1 143 222	1 242 136	1 324 621	1 394 503	1 409 777	1 402 737	1 380 297	1 423 067	1 478 011	..
1	Agric., Hunting, Forestry, Fishing	189 002	191 278	215 282	221 865	204 699	197 741	165 859	177 863	183 444	..
2	Mining & Quarrying	34 723	30 772	31 738	29 754	31 200	32 945	31 662	31 943	31 938	..
21	Coal Mining	4 000	2 892	3 174	2 918	2 664	2 269	1 832	2 032	1 852	..
22	Crude Petroleum & Natural Gas	23 059	19 691	20 344	19 470	20 717	22 913	22 641	22 761	22 820	..
23.29	Other Mining	7 664	8 189	8 220	7 366	7 819	7 763	7 189	7 150	7 266	..
3	Total Manufacturing	1 143 222	1 242 136	1 324 621	1 394 503	1 409 777	1 402 737	1 380 297	1 423 067	1 478 011	..
4	Electricity, Gas & Water	122 784	126 454	128 259	138 739	153 795	165 111	171 619	173 396	178 069	..
5	Construction	278 086	309 643	320 643	335 812	357 518	363 316	357 982	342 298	342 836	..
6.9	Services	3 357 046	3 607 285	3 905 010	4 138 331	4 361 813	4 580 837	4 719 559	4 952 151	5 137 020	..
0000	Grand Total	4 878 358	5 245 078	5 646 130	5 980 984	6 249 466	6 468 024	6 551 751	6 837 586	7 088 408	..

Note: Figures for ISIC 3849 cannot be separately identified, and are distributed across the other categories in the 384 group.

Thousands

ISIC2	Industry	EMPLOYMENT									
		1987	**1988**	**1989**	**1990**	**1991**	**1992**	**1993**	**1994**	**1995**	**1996**
31	**Food, Beverages & Tobacco**	595.0	591.4	590.0	584.7	576.1	568.6	554.8	550.2	546.0	540.8
311.2	Food	542.9	541.0	539.5	534.3	526.9	521.0	508.2	504.1	499.9	495.1
313	Beverages	46.6	44.9	45.4	45.2	44.2	42.6	41.7	41.5	41.5	41.2
314	Tobacco	5.5	5.5	5.1	5.2	5.0	5.0	4.9	4.6	4.6	4.5
32	**Textiles, Apparel & Leather**	503.2	475.5	456.9	446.0	417.2	392.8	364.3	345.3	333.4	317.7
321	Textiles	242.2	229.0	221.7	214.3	200.3	185.7	172.3	163.5	157.6	149.8
3213	Knitting Mills	..	..	..	..	..	..	..	..	..	..
322	Wearing Apparel	177.3	168.4	159.8	156.6	147.7	142.9	132.5	126.1	120.8	115.0
323	Leather & Products	24.3	23.0	22.1	21.9	21.0	18.5	17.3	16.2	16.0	15.4
324	Footwear	59.4	55.1	53.3	53.2	48.2	45.7	42.2	39.5	39.0	37.5
33	**Wood Products & Furniture**	199.6	202.0	204.5	207.1	207.8	199.8	185.9	182.0	181.4	177.2
331	Wood Products	95.1	95.5	98.0	100.7	102.3	95.4	88.9	86.8	86.4	84.6
332	Furnitures & Fixtures	104.5	106.5	106.5	106.4	105.5	104.4	97.0	95.2	95.0	92.6
34	**Paper, Paper Products & Printing**	340.5	345.5	354.7	359.1	357.1	351.1	341.3	335.8	334.9	328.8
341	Paper & Products	105.9	104.9	106.9	108.1	106.8	105.8	102.6	101.5	101.0	98.7
3411	Pulp, Paper & Board	..	..	..	..	..	..	..	..	..	..
342	Printing & Publishing	234.6	240.6	247.8	251.0	250.3	245.3	238.7	234.3	233.9	230.1
35	**Chemical Products**	529.4	527.4	538.5	545.0	538.0	523.5	507.7	498.9	500.7	494.5
351	Industrial Chemicals	127.6	122.2	121.0	118.7	113.8	108.6	104.7	101.7	100.9	98.5
3511	Basic Industrial Chemicals	..	..	..	..	..	..	..	..	..	..
3512	Fertilizers & Pesticides	..	..	..	..	..	..	..	..	..	..
3513	Synthetic Resins	..	..	..	..	..	..	..	..	..	..
352	Other Chemicals	174.5	176.0	181.6	185.2	185.8	183.8	180.5	178.0	178.5	175.9
3521	Paints, Varnishes & Lacquers	..	..	..	..	..	..	..	..	..	..
3522	Drugs & Medicines	..	..	..	..	..	..	..	..	..	..
3523	Soap & Cleaning Preparations	..	..	..	..	..	..	..	..	..	..
3529	Chemical Products, nec	..	..	..	..	..	..	..	..	..	..
353	Petroleum Refineries	26.8	25.8	24.7	23.5	20.8	19.9	18.1	18.0	17.2	16.8
354	Petroleum & Coal Products	..	..	..	0.0	0.0	0.0	0.0	0.0	0.0	0.0
355	Rubber Products	89.8	88.2	93.1	94.4	91.9	85.8	83.2	82.0	83.2	83.0
356	Plastic Products, nec	110.7	115.2	118.1	123.2	125.7	125.4	121.2	119.2	120.9	120.3
36	**Non-Metallic Mineral Products**	145.7	146.4	149.2	150.0	148.5	142.6	135.2	130.5	129.9	127.0
361	Pottery, China etc	..	..	..	0.0	0.0	0.0	0.0	0.0	0.0	0.0
362	Glass & Products	55.2	54.7	56.3	57.1	56.5	56.1	54.0	52.3	52.1	51.0
369	Non-Metallic Products, nec	90.5	91.7	92.9	92.9	92.0	86.5	81.2	78.2	77.8	76.0
37	**Basic Metal Industries**	254.2	240.8	239.1	237.3	232.0	220.7	205.3	198.8	199.4	196.2
371	Iron & Steel	201.4	190.0	189.6	188.9	184.7	175.0	162.1	156.7	158.1	156.3
372	Non-Ferrous Metals	52.8	50.8	49.5	48.4	47.3	45.7	43.2	42.1	41.3	39.9
38	**Fabricated Metal Products**	1 891.4	1 864.9	1 884.0	1 916.8	1 901.2	1 838.2	1 745.1	1 686.2	1 697.1	1 685.5
381	Metal Products	337.7	343.7	357.0	370.1	366.5	350.0	326.4	313.6	318.1	318.7
3813	Structural Metal Products	..	..	..	..	..	..	..	..	..	..
382	Non-Electrical Machinery	443.6	435.2	444.9	455.1	451.4	433.1	408.1	392.1	396.0	393.7
3821	Engines & Turbines	..	..	..	..	..	..	..	..	..	..
3822	Agricultural Machinery	..	..	..	..	..	..	..	..	..	..
3823	Metal & Wood working Machinery	..	..	..	..	..	..	..	..	..	..
3824	Special Industrial Machinery	..	..	..	..	..	..	..	..	..	..
3825	Office & Computing Machinery	..	..	..	..	..	..	..	..	..	..
3829	Machinery & Equipment, nec	..	..	..	..	..	..	..	..	..	..
383	Electrical Machinery	477.6	471.9	471.8	479.8	478.3	461.4	436.4	425.9	430.3	425.4
3831	Electrical Industrial Machinery	..	..	..	..	..	..	..	..	..	..
3832	Radio, TV & Communication Equipment	..	..	..	..	..	..	..	..	..	..
3833	Electrical Appliances & Housewares	..	..	..	..	..	..	..	..	..	..
3839	Electrical Apparatus, nec	..	..	..	..	..	..	..	..	..	..
384	Transport Equipment	561.4	541.4	537.6	537.8	530.9	523.6	508.3	491.3	488.8	484.2
3841	Shipbuilding & Repairing	..	..	..	..	..	..	..	..	..	..
3842	Railroad Equipment	..	..	..	..	..	..	..	..	..	..
3843	Motor Vehicles	..	..	..	..	..	..	..	..	..	..
3844	Motorcycles & Bicycles	..	..	..	..	..	..	..	..	..	..
3845	Aircraft	..	..	..	..	..	..	..	..	..	..
3849	Transport Equipment, nec	..	..	..	..	..	..	..	..	..	..
385	Professional Goods	71.1	72.7	72.7	74.0	74.1	70.1	65.9	63.3	63.9	63.5
3851	Professional Equipment	..	..	..	..	..	..	..	..	..	..
3852	Photographic & Optical Goods	..	..	..	..	..	..	..	..	..	..
3853	Watches & Clocks	..	..	..	..	..	..	..	..	..	..
39	**Other Manufacturing, nes**	110.9	110.1	111.3	112.1	105.5	100.4	93.7	91.6	91.1	89.1
3901	Jewellery	..	..	..	..	..	..	..	..	..	..
3	**Total Manufacturing**	4 569.9	4 504.0	4 528.2	4 558.1	4 483.4	4 337.7	4 133.3	4 019.3	4 013.9	3 956.8
I	**Agric., Hunting, Forestry, Fishing**	1 438.5	1 382.1	1 322.7	1 262.1	1 208.6	1 158.2	1 107.7	1 062.7	1 029.6	997.5
2	**Mining & Quarrying**	130.8	123.7	118.8	112.9	106.2	99.3	93.8	91.0	89.9	87.6
21	Coal Mining	36.2	30.3	26.2	22.9	19.0	17.4	15.7	14.5	14.2	13.5
22	Crude Petroleum & Natural Gas	33.3	32.6	32.2	31.1	30.9	30.1	28.9	28.7	28.3	27.8
23.29	Other Mining	61.3	60.8	60.4	58.9	56.3	51.8	49.2	47.8	47.4	46.3
3	**Total Manufacturing**	4 569.9	4 504.0	4 528.2	4 558.1	4 483.4	4 337.7	4 133.3	4 019.3	4 013.9	3 956.8
4	**Electricity, Gas & Water**	164.7	164.6	163.4	162.0	162.5	161.2	161.8	163.1	163.6	163.2
5	**Construction**	1 588.4	1 612.3	1 649.5	1 662.2	1 651.4	1 597.3	1 517.8	1 472.3	1 473.9	1 426.5
6.9	**Services**	13 871.0	14 170.4	14 463.7	14 720.2	14 889.4	14 984.5	15 064.3	15 254.3	15 512.7	15 655.8
0000	**Grand Total**	21 763.3	21 957.1	22 246.3	22 477.5	22 501.5	22 338.2	22 078.7	22 062.7	22 283.6	22 287.4

Note: Figures for ISIC 3849 cannot be separately identified, and are distributed across the other categories in the 384 group.

Table FR.4 **FRANCE**

ISIC2	Industry	EMPLOYMENT - EMPLOYEES									
		1987	1988	1989	1990	1991	1992	1993	1994	1995	1996
31	**Food, Beverages & Tobacco**	513.8	512.1	512.8	511.4	507.3	503.5	495.3	490.9	488.4	485.6
311.2	Food	463.1	463.1	463.7	462.5	459.5	457.2	449.9	446.0	443.5	441.1
313	Beverages	45.2	43.5	44.0	43.8	42.9	41.4	40.6	40.4	40.4	40.1
314	Tobacco	5.5	5.5	5.1	5.1	4.9	4.9	4.8	4.5	4.5	4.4
32	**Textiles, Apparel & Leather**	481.3	454.6	437.1	427.0	399.1	375.2	347.8	329.0	318.9	303.5
321	Textiles	237.3	224.3	217.2	209.9	196.2	181.6	168.5	159.7	154.3	146.6
3213	Knitting Mills	..	..	..	..	..	..	..	..	..	..
322	Wearing Apparel	163.5	155.3	147.4	144.7	136.3	131.9	122.3	115.9	111.9	106.2
323	Leather & Products	21.9	20.7	19.9	19.9	19.1	16.7	15.5	14.5	14.3	13.8
324	Footwear	58.6	54.3	52.6	52.5	47.5	45.0	41.5	38.9	38.4	36.9
33	**Wood Products & Furniture**	167.3	170.3	173.6	176.7	177.4	170.2	158.8	154.8	153.8	151.1
331	Wood Products	87.3	87.9	90.6	93.2	94.8	88.1	82.2	80.1	79.6	78.2
332	Furnitures & Fixtures	80.0	82.4	83.0	83.5	82.6	82.1	76.6	74.7	74.2	72.9
34	**Paper, Paper Products & Printing**	321.9	327.0	336.5	341.0	339.1	333.7	324.2	319.9	319.3	313.9
341	Paper & Products	105.1	104.1	106.2	107.4	106.1	105.1	101.9	100.8	100.3	98.0
3411	Pulp, Paper & Board	..	..	..	..	..	..	..	..	..	..
342	Printing & Publishing	216.8	222.9	230.3	233.6	233.0	228.6	222.3	219.1	219.0	215.9
35	**Chemical Products**	525.3	523.4	534.7	541.2	534.2	519.9	504.2	495.7	497.5	491.5
351	Industrial Chemicals	127.1	121.8	120.6	118.3	113.4	108.2	104.3	101.3	100.5	98.1
3511	Basic Industrial Chemicals	..	..	..	..	..	..	..	..	..	..
3512	Fertilizers & Pesticides	..	..	..	..	..	..	..	..	..	..
3513	Synthetic Resins	..	..	..	..	..	..	..	..	..	..
352	Other Chemicals	173.5	175.0	180.7	184.3	184.8	182.8	179.5	177.1	177.6	175.0
3521	Paints, Varnishes & Lacquers	..	..	..	..	..	..	..	..	..	..
3522	Drugs & Medicines	..	..	..	..	..	..	..	..	..	..
3523	Soap & Cleaning Preparations	..	..	..	..	..	..	..	..	..	..
3529	Chemical Products, nec	..	..	..	..	..	..	..	..	..	..
353	Petroleum Refineries	26.7	25.7	24.6	23.4	20.7	19.8	18.0	18.0	17.2	16.8
354	Petroleum & Coal Products	..	..	..	0.0	0.0	0.0	0.0	0.0	0.0	0.0
355	Rubber Products	89.4	87.8	92.7	94.0	91.5	85.5	82.9	81.7	82.9	82.7
356	Plastic Products, nec	108.6	113.1	116.1	121.2	123.8	123.6	119.5	117.6	119.3	118.9
36	**Non-Metallic Mineral Products**	141.0	141.6	144.3	145.3	143.9	138.1	130.9	126.4	125.8	123.0
361	Pottery, China etc	..	..	..	0.0	0.0	0.0	0.0	0.0	0.0	0.0
362	Glass & Products	54.2	53.7	55.3	56.2	55.6	55.2	53.1	51.5	51.3	50.2
369	Non-Metallic Products, nec	86.8	87.9	89.0	89.1	88.3	82.9	77.8	74.9	74.5	72.8
37	**Basic Metal Industries**	253.6	240.2	238.5	236.7	231.4	220.1	204.7	198.2	198.8	195.6
371	Iron & Steel	200.9	189.5	189.1	188.4	184.2	174.5	161.6	156.2	157.6	155.8
372	Non-Ferrous Metals	52.7	50.7	49.4	48.3	47.2	45.6	43.1	42.0	41.2	39.8
38	**Fabricated Metal Products**	1 843.9	1 818.3	1 838.1	1 871.7	1 857.0	1 794.5	1 701.6	1 645.3	1 656.0	1 646.1
381	Metal Products	321.2	327.5	341.1	354.4	351.1	334.6	310.4	299.0	303.3	304.4
3813	Structural Metal Products	..	..	..	..	..	..	..	..	..	..
382	Non-Electrical Machinery	427.6	419.4	429.3	439.8	436.5	418.4	394.0	378.5	382.4	380.7
3821	Engines & Turbines	..	..	..	..	..	..	..	..	..	..
3822	Agricultural Machinery	..	..	..	..	..	..	..	..	..	..
3823	Metal & Wood working Machinery	..	..	..	..	..	..	..	..	..	..
3824	Special Industrial Machinery	..	..	..	..	..	..	..	..	..	..
3825	Office & Computing Machinery	..	..	..	..	..	..	..	..	..	..
3829	Machinery & Equipment, nec	..	..	..	..	..	..	..	..	..	..
383	Electrical Machinery	471.6	466.0	465.9	474.0	472.5	455.8	430.7	420.7	425.1	420.5
3831	Electrical Industrial Machinery	..	..	..	..	..	..	..	..	..	..
3832	Radio, TV & Communication Equipment	..	..	..	..	..	..	..	..	..	..
3833	Electrical Appliances & Housewares	..	..	..	..	..	..	..	..	..	..
3839	Electrical Apparatus, nec	..	..	..	..	..	..	..	..	..	..
384	Transport Equipment	559.0	539.1	535.4	535.6	528.7	521.4	506.1	489.2	486.7	482.2
3841	Shipbuilding & Repairing	..	..	..	..	..	..	..	..	..	..
3842	Railroad Equipment	..	..	..	..	..	..	..	..	..	..
3843	Motor Vehicles	..	..	..	..	..	..	..	..	..	..
3844	Motorcycles & Bicycles	..	..	..	..	..	..	..	..	..	..
3845	Aircraft	..	..	..	..	..	..	..	..	..	..
3849	Transport Equipment, nec	..	..	..	..	..	..	..	..	..	..
385	Professional Goods	64.5	66.3	66.4	67.9	68.2	64.3	60.4	57.9	58.5	58.3
3851	Professional Equipment	..	..	..	..	..	..	..	..	..	..
3852	Photographic & Optical Goods	..	..	..	..	..	..	..	..	..	..
3853	Watches & Clocks	..	..	..	..	..	..	..	..	..	..
39	**Other Manufacturing, nes**	98.9	98.2	99.7	100.2	93.6	88.9	83.1	81.0	80.3	78.9
3901	Jewellery	..	..	..	..	..	..	..	..	..	..
3	**Total Manufacturing**	4 347.0	4 285.7	4 315.3	4 351.2	4 283.0	4 144.1	3 950.6	3 841.2	3 838.8	3 789.2
1	**Agric., Hunting, Forestry, Fishing**	287.8	285.0	282.6	277.3	272.8	267.2	265.7	265.3	268.1	271.0
2	**Mining & Quarrying**	126.8	119.7	115.0	109.1	102.5	95.7	90.2	87.7	86.7	84.5
21	Coal Mining	36.2	30.3	26.2	22.9	19.0	17.4	15.7	14.5	14.2	13.5
22	Crude Petroleum & Natural Gas	33.3	32.6	32.2	31.1	30.9	30.1	28.9	28.7	28.3	27.8
23.29	Other Mining	57.3	56.8	56.6	55.1	52.6	48.2	45.6	44.5	44.2	43.2
3	**Total Manufacturing**	4 347.0	4 285.7	4 315.3	4 351.2	4 283.0	4 144.1	3 950.6	3 841.2	3 838.8	3 789.2
4	**Electricity, Gas & Water**	164.4	164.3	163.1	161.7	162.2	160.9	161.5	162.8	163.3	162.9
5	**Construction**	1 272.5	1 296.4	1 335.2	1 351.9	1 348.1	1 307.3	1 239.8	1 209.1	1 206.8	1 161.9
6.9	**Services**	12 482.0	12 764.4	13 052.5	13 309.1	13 483.3	13 607.7	13 713.0	13 903.0	14 174.0	14 332.2
0000	**Grand Total**	18 680.5	18 915.5	19 263.7	19 560.3	19 651.9	19 582.9	19 420.8	19 469.1	19 737.7	19 801.7

Note: Figures for ISIC 3849 cannot be separately identified, and are distributed across the other categories in the 384 group.

Millions of FF (Current Prices)

ISIC2	Industry	INVESTMENT									
		1987	**1988**	**1989**	**1990**	**1991**	**1992**	**1993**	**1994**	**1995**	**1996**
31	**Food, Beverages & Tobacco**	23 450	28 988	34 100	32 600	35 078	35 248	28 837	28 724	24 379	22 901
311.2	Food	..	..	..	..	..	..	..	..	..	..
313	Beverages	..	..	..	..	..	..	..	..	..	..
314	Tobacco	..	..	..	..	..	..	..	..	..	..
32	**Textiles, Apparel & Leather**	7 630	9 307	9 379	9 869	8 558	7 984	6 072	6 473	6 758	6 504
321	Textiles	6 815	7 619	8 212	8 670	8 046	7 555	5 263	5 520	6 344	6 173
3213	Knitting Mills	..	..	..	..	..	..	..	..	..	..
322	Wearing Apparel	..	..	..	..	..	..	..	..	..	..
323	Leather & Products	815	1 688	1 167	1 199	512	429	809	953	414	331
324	Footwear	..	..	..	..	..	..	..	..	..	..
33	**Wood Products & Furniture**	6 672	7 781	9 365	9 523	9 590	8 491	5 743	6 006	5 722	5 445
331	Wood Products	..	..	..	..	..	..	..	..	..	..
332	Furnitures & Fixtures	..	..	..	..	..	..	..	..	..	..
34	**Paper, Paper Products & Printing**	14 431	15 948	18 534	21 013	20 359	16 572	11 552	11 842	14 046	13 811
341	Paper & Products	7 928	7 089	7 490	10 513	10 439	8 460	4 562	4 449	6 006	6 005
3411	Pulp, Paper & Board	..	..	..	..	..	..	..	..	..	..
342	Printing & Publishing	6 503	8 859	11 044	10 500	9 920	8 112	6 990	7 393	8 040	7 806
35	**Chemical Products**	33 887	36 780	41 001	47 671	45 603	42 383	38 355	39 095	41 585	42 768
351	Industrial Chemicals	10 070	10 910	12 126	14 796	14 685	11 738	9 072	9 356	10 511	11 162
3511	Basic Industrial Chemicals	..	..	..	..	..	..	..	..	..	..
3512	Fertilizers & Pesticides	..	..	..	..	..	..	..	..	..	..
3513	Synthetic Resins	..	..	..	..	..	..	..	..	..	..
352	Other Chemicals	6 135	8 381	9 007	8 289	9 420	10 810	9 477	9 886	10 926	12 141
3521	Paints, Varnishes & Lacquers	..	..	..	..	..	..	..	..	..	..
3522	Drugs & Medicines	..	..	..	..	..	..	..	..	..	..
3523	Soap & Cleaning Preparations	..	..	..	..	..	..	..	..	..	..
3529	Chemical Products, nec	..	..	..	..	..	..	..	..	..	..
353	Petroleum Refineries	10 969	9 312	10 386	13 646	11 161	10 908	12 040	12 360	10 838	10 647
354	Petroleum & Coal Products	..	..	..	..	..	..	..	..	..	..
355	Rubber Products	6 713	8 177	9 482	10 940	10 337	8 927	7 766	7 493	9 310	8 818
356	Plastic Products, nec	..	..	..	..	..	..	..	..	..	..
36	**Non-Metallic Mineral Products**	8 863	11 534	13 177	11 063	9 706	6 575	8 882	10 136	12 848	13 190
361	Pottery, China etc	..	..	..	..	..	..	..	..	..	..
362	Glass & Products	1 782	2 678	2 763	2 448	1 152	2 038	1 918	2 357	2 770	3 365
369	Non-Metallic Products, nec	7 081	8 856	10 414	8 615	8 554	4 537	6 964	7 779	10 078	9 825
37	**Basic Metal Industries**	14 062	13 637	14 112	14 554	13 762	13 148	9 389	10 994	9 385	9 187
371	Iron & Steel	3 187	3 131	4 333	5 379	5 178	4 174	-1 111	-238	226	538
372	Non-Ferrous Metals	10 875	10 506	9 779	9 175	8 584	8 974	10 500	11 232	9 159	8 649
38	**Fabricated Metal Products**	62 441	71 182	76 954	92 108	91 212	80 846	61 367	66 626	69 144	69 755
381	Metal Products	12 396	14 752	18 171	20 520	20 884	16 521	11 846	12 116	13 457	12 759
3813	Structural Metal Products	..	..	..	..	..	..	..	..	..	..
382	Non-Electrical Machinery	9 749	11 684	12 119	15 059	13 970	11 993	11 021	11 338	13 989	14 148
3821	Engines & Turbines	..	..	..	..	..	..	..	..	..	..
3822	Agricultural Machinery	..	..	..	..	..	..	..	..	..	..
3823	Metal & Wood working Machinery	..	..	..	..	..	..	..	..	..	..
3824	Special Industrial Machinery	..	..	..	..	..	..	..	..	..	..
3825	Office & Computing Machinery	..	..	..	..	..	..	..	..	..	..
3829	Machinery & Equipment, nec	..	..	..	..	..	..	..	..	..	..
383	Electrical Machinery	19 091	19 560	19 480	24 461	22 622	19 132	13 641	14 354	14 427	14 148
3831	Electrical Industrial Machinery	..	..	..	..	..	..	..	..	..	..
3832	Radio, TV & Communication Equipment	..	..	..	..	..	..	..	..	..	..
3833	Electrical Appliances & Housewares	..	..	..	..	..	..	..	..	..	..
3839	Electrical Apparatus, nec	..	..	..	..	..	..	..	..	..	..
384	Transport Equipment	21 205	25 186	27 184	32 068	33 736	33 200	24 859	28 818	27 271	28 700
3841	Shipbuilding & Repairing	..	..	..	..	..	..	..	..	..	..
3842	Railroad Equipment	..	..	..	..	..	..	..	..	..	..
3843	Motor Vehicles	..	..	..	..	..	..	..	..	..	..
3844	Motorcycles & Bicycles	..	..	..	..	..	..	..	..	..	..
3845	Aircraft	..	..	..	..	..	..	..	..	..	..
3849	Transport Equipment, nec	..	..	..	..	..	..	..	..	..	..
385	Professional Goods	..	..	..	..	..	..	..	..	..	..
3851	Professional Equipment	..	..	..	..	..	..	..	..	..	..
3852	Photographic & Optical Goods	..	..	..	..	..	..	..	..	..	..
3853	Watches & Clocks	..	..	..	..	..	..	..	..	..	..
39	**Other Manufacturing, nes**	..	..	..	..	..	..	..	..	..	..
3901	Jewellery	..	..	..	..	..	..	..	..	..	..
3	**Total Manufacturing**	171 436	195 157	216 622	238 401	233 868	211 247	170 197	179 896	183 867	183 561
1	**Agric., Hunting, Forestry, Fishing**	29 536	34 784	39 778	41 729	38 743	35 475	32 757	36 836	41 073	43 018
2	**Mining & Quarrying**	941	1 146	1 058	788	627	573	41	-15	-7 017	427
21	Coal Mining	..	..	..	..	..	..	..	..	..	..
22	Crude Petroleum & Natural Gas	..	..	..	..	..	..	..	..	..	..
23.29	Other Mining	..	..	..	..	..	..	..	..	..	..
3	**Total Manufacturing**	171 436	195 157	216 622	238 401	233 868	211 247	170 197	179 896	183 867	183 561
4	**Electricity, Gas & Water**	46 834	45 594	45 492	43 797	44 872	52 200	52 819	48 440	49 264	53 383
5	**Construction**	25 505	29 777	36 033	32 432	35 509	30 564	28 701	28 173	26 443	24 290
6.9	**Services**	780 516	881 855	975 569	1 034 211	1 083 303	1 075 350	1 026 878	1 038 771	1 081 205	1 062 846
0000	**Grand Total**	1 054 768	1 188 313	1 314 552	1 391 358	1 436 922	1 405 409	1 311 393	1 332 101	1 374 835	1 367 525

Note: ISIC 321 includes 322; 323 includes 324; 353 includes 22; 355 includes 356.

Millions of FF (Current Prices)

ISIC2	Industry	INVESTMENT IN MACHINERY & EQUIPMENT									
		1987	1988	1989	1990	1991	1992	1993	1994	1995	1996
31	**Food, Beverages & Tobacco**	14 723	18 978	21 996	20 094	21 316	20 941	17 046	16 398	15 175	14 234
311.2	Food	..	..	..	..	..	..	..	..	..	..
313	Beverages	..	..	..	..	..	..	..	..	..	..
314	Tobacco	..	..	..	..	..	..	..	..	..	..
32	**Textiles, Apparel & Leather**	5 842	7 421	7 427	7 682	6 280	3 601	4 088	4 374	5 665	4 918
321	Textiles	5 257	6 121	6 542	6 794	5 909	3 446	3 844	4 013	4 797	4 716
3213	Knitting Mills	..	..	..	..	..	..	..	..	..	..
322	Wearing Apparel	..	..	..	..	..	..	..	..	..	..
323	Leather & Products	585	1 300	885	888	371	155	244	361	868	202
324	Footwear	..	..	..	..	..	..	..	..	..	..
33	**Wood Products & Furniture**	4 459	4 905	5 853	5 745	5 293	4 991	3 225	3 296	3 219	3 097
331	Wood Products	..	..	..	..	..	..	..	..	..	..
332	Furnitures & Fixtures	..	..	..	..	..	..	..	..	..	..
34	**Paper, Paper Products & Printing**	12 132	13 482	15 645	17 816	15 720	12 362	8 195	8 389	10 862	11 135
341	Paper & Products	6 719	5 734	6 033	8 804	7 953	6 438	3 356	3 212	4 687	4 782
3411	Pulp, Paper & Board	..	..	..	..	..	..	..	..	..	..
342	Printing & Publishing	5 413	7 748	9 612	9 012	7 767	5 924	4 839	5 177	6 175	6 353
35	**Chemical Products**	23 845	26 856	29 419	35 845	34 336	29 335	27 315	27 758	32 281	34 678
351	Industrial Chemicals	7 533	8 774	9 489	12 433	12 804	10 425	7 822	7 375	9 872	11 777
3511	Basic Industrial Chemicals	..	..	..	..	..	..	..	..	..	..
3512	Fertilizers & Pesticides	..	..	..	..	..	..	..	..	..	..
3513	Synthetic Resins	..	..	..	..	..	..	..	..	..	..
352	Other Chemicals	4 403	6 621	6 858	6 014	6 299	6 408	6 172	6 489	7 474	8 505
3521	Paints, Varnishes & Lacquers	..	..	..	..	..	..	..	..	..	..
3522	Drugs & Medicines	..	..	..	..	..	..	..	..	..	..
3523	Soap & Cleaning Preparations	..	..	..	..	..	..	..	..	..	..
3529	Chemical Products, nec	..	..	..	..	..	..	..	..	..	..
353	Petroleum Refineries	6 352	4 716	5 292	8 428	6 841	5 956	7 315	8 192	7 500	7 230
354	Petroleum & Coal Products	..	..	..	..	..	..	..	..	..	..
355	Rubber Products	5 557	6 745	7 780	8 970	8 392	6 546	6 006	5 702	7 435	7 166
356	Plastic Products, nec	..	..	..	..	..	..	..	..	..	..
36	**Non-Metallic Mineral Products**	6 612	8 753	9 749	7 770	6 436	4 379	6 033	6 944	8 595	8 920
361	Pottery, China etc	..	..	..	..	..	..	..	..	..	..
362	Glass & Products	1 466	2 221	2 279	1 954	492	1 547	1 414	1 804	2 046	2 520
369	Non-Metallic Products, nec	5 146	6 532	7 470	5 816	5 944	2 832	4 619	5 140	6 549	6 400
37	**Basic Metal Industries**	12 800	11 676	12 174	12 452	11 626	11 948	9 443	11 031	13 091	8 655
371	Iron & Steel	2 999	2 981	4 113	5 134	4 923	3 664	-106	799	4 687	702
372	Non-Ferrous Metals	9 801	8 695	8 061	7 318	6 703	8 284	9 549	10 232	8 404	7 953
38	**Fabricated Metal Products**	48 202	54 972	58 609	71 129	68 477	63 010	45 317	50 064	53 369	54 575
381	Metal Products	9 781	12 105	14 712	16 122	15 758	12 456	8 289	8 414	9 969	9 521
3813	Structural Metal Products	..	..	..	..	..	..	..	..	..	..
382	Non-Electrical Machinery	8 370	9 637	9 848	12 230	10 453	9 657	7 375	7 600	10 050	10 255
3821	Engines & Turbines	..	..	..	..	..	..	..	..	..	..
3822	Agricultural Machinery	..	..	..	..	..	..	..	..	..	..
3823	Metal & Wood working Machinery	..	..	..	..	..	..	..	..	..	..
3824	Special Industrial Machinery	..	..	..	..	..	..	..	..	..	..
3825	Office & Computing Machinery	..	..	..	..	..	..	..	..	..	..
3829	Machinery & Equipment, nec	..	..	..	..	..	..	..	..	..	..
383	Electrical Machinery	14 645	15 929	15 383	19 406	17 242	13 486	9 848	10 348	10 807	10 804
3831	Electrical Industrial Machinery	..	..	..	..	..	..	..	..	..	..
3832	Radio, TV & Communication Equipment	..	..	..	..	..	..	..	..	..	..
3833	Electrical Appliances & Housewares	..	..	..	..	..	..	..	..	..	..
3839	Electrical Apparatus, nec	..	..	..	..	..	..	..	..	..	..
384	Transport Equipment	15 406	17 301	18 666	23 371	25 024	27 411	19 805	23 702	22 543	23 995
3841	Shipbuilding & Repairing	..	..	..	..	..	..	..	..	..	..
3842	Railroad Equipment	..	..	..	..	..	..	..	..	..	..
3843	Motor Vehicles	..	..	..	..	..	..	..	..	..	..
3844	Motorcycles & Bicycles	..	..	..	..	..	..	..	..	..	..
3845	Aircraft	..	..	..	..	..	..	..	..	..	..
3849	Transport Equipment, nec	..	..	..	..	..	..	..	..	..	..
385	Professional Goods	..	..	..	..	..	..	..	..	..	..
3851	Professional Equipment	..	..	..	..	..	..	..	..	..	..
3852	Photographic & Optical Goods	..	..	..	..	..	..	..	..	..	..
3853	Watches & Clocks	..	..	..	..	..	..	..	..	..	..
39	**Other Manufacturing, nes**	..	..	..	..	..	..	..	..	..	..
3901	Jewellery	..	..	..	..	..	..	..	..	..	..
3	**Total Manufacturing**	128 615	147 043	160 872	178 533	169 484	150 567	120 662	128 254	142 257	140 212
1	**Agric., Hunting, Forestry, Fishing**	19 282	22 494	24 819	23 776	21 889	19 504	18 141	20 795	24 056	26 307
2	**Mining & Quarrying**	622	872	803	581	453	333	-14	-35	1 068	368
21	Coal Mining	..	..	..	..	..	..	..	..	..	..
22	Crude Petroleum & Natural Gas	..	..	..	..	..	..	..	..	..	..
23.29	Other Mining	..	..	..	..	..	..	..	..	..	..
3	**Total Manufacturing**	128 615	147 043	160 872	178 533	169 484	150 567	120 662	128 254	142 257	140 212
4	**Electricity, Gas & Water**	16 974	12 913	11 917	11 828	12 496	14 425	17 469	15 724	18 407	18 899
5	**Construction**	11 466	13 910	16 474	13 610	15 015	12 431	11 349	10 696	10 316	9 061
6.9	**Services**	149 759	168 448	189 459	199 587	219 843	221 133	211 511	217 821	217 924	215 627
0000	**Grand Total**	326 718	365 680	404 344	427 915	439 180	418 393	379 118	393 255	414 028	410 474

Note: ISIC 321 includes 322; 323 includes 324; 353 includes 22; 355 includes 356.

Table FR.8 **FRANCE**

Millions of FF

(1980 Prices)

ISIC2	Industry	PRODUCTION									
		1987	**1988**	**1989**	**1990**	**1991**	**1992**	**1993**	**1994**	**1995**	**1996**
31	**Food, Beverages & Tobacco**	348 754	358 993	366 707	379 387	388 569	389 836	391 007	397 293	405 335	..
311.2	Food	310 573	318 975	325 430	335 887	345 014	348 382	347 074	353 165	361 366	..
313	Beverages	32 313	34 285	35 692	37 813	37 956	36 056	38 222	38 459	38 483	..
314	Tobacco	5 868	5 733	5 585	5 687	5 599	5 398	5 711	5 669	5 486	..
32	**Textiles, Apparel & Leather**	125 500	122 795	125 137	126 192	121 976	120 963	112 827	117 242	115 762	..
321	Textiles	66 984	66 467	67 311	67 568	65 549	66 347	61 744	64 711	65 426	..
3213	Knitting Mills	..	..	..	..	..	..	..	..	..	..
322	Wearing Apparel	43 143	41 363	42 560	43 600	42 121	40 831	38 508	39 834	37 548	..
323	Leather & Products	6 248	6 306	6 544	6 356	5 835	5 515	4 717	5 010	5 219	..
324	Footwear	9 125	8 659	8 722	8 668	8 471	8 270	7 858	7 687	7 569	..
33	**Wood Products & Furniture**	55 572	58 673	61 054	63 965	62 447	60 986	57 935	61 050	62 291	..
331	Wood Products	30 471	32 605	34 173	35 821	34 724	34 587	32 519	35 817	36 461	..
332	Furnitures & Fixtures	25 101	26 068	26 881	28 144	27 723	26 399	25 416	25 233	25 830	..
34	**Paper, Paper Products & Printing**	126 318	135 283	141 389	146 310	148 301	148 685	148 277	156 269	156 865	..
341	Paper & Products	53 354	57 332	58 893	61 408	60 870	64 114	62 827	66 866	65 937	..
3411	Pulp, Paper & Board	..	..	..	..	..	..	..	..	..	..
342	Printing & Publishing	72 964	77 951	82 496	84 902	87 431	84 571	85 450	89 403	90 928	..
35	**Chemical Products**	386 979	410 386	431 260	442 805	448 965	455 074	460 527	474 426	483 537	..
351	Industrial Chemicals	100 177	102 745	109 413	111 750	108 800	111 686	110 292	117 732	119 237	..
3511	Basic Industrial Chemicals	..	..	..	..	..	..	..	..	..	..
3512	Fertilizers & Pesticides	..	..	..	..	..	..	..	..	..	..
3513	Synthetic Resins	..	..	..	..	..	..	..	..	..	..
352	Other Chemicals	95 778	103 233	112 199	115 486	119 869	124 803	128 356	134 355	139 154	..
3521	Paints, Varnishes & Lacquers	..	..	..	..	..	..	..	..	..	..
3522	Drugs & Medicines	42 493	47 523	51 912	54 384	57 729	61 317	64 067	65 265	69 332	..
3523	Soap & Cleaning Preparations	..	..	..	..	..	..	..	..	..	..
3529	Chemical Products, nec	..	..	..	..	..	..	..	..	..	..
353	Petroleum Refineries	124 241	132 572	132 759	135 332	138 375	134 472	141 315	137 621	139 629	..
354	Petroleum & Coal Products	..	..	..	..	..	..	..	..	..	..
355	Rubber Products	21 164	22 832	24 390	23 738	22 871	23 422	21 003	22 484	23 509	..
356	Plastic Products, nec	45 619	49 004	52 499	56 499	59 050	60 691	59 561	62 234	62 008	..
36	**Non-Metallic Mineral Products**	61 297	65 467	68 472	69 547	70 114	67 922	63 988	67 477	69 530	..
361	Pottery, China etc	..	..	..	..	..	..	..	..	..	..
362	Glass & Products	15 784	16 336	17 386	17 766	17 588	18 091	17 268	18 474	19 828	..
369	Non-Metallic Products, nec	45 513	49 131	51 086	51 781	52 526	49 831	46 720	49 003	49 702	..
37	**Basic Metal Industries**	136 677	145 967	151 351	146 894	144 099	143 147	130 925	138 639	143 212	..
371	Iron & Steel	85 005	91 995	95 077	90 427	88 738	84 209	76 586	83 963	84 850	..
372	Non-Ferrous Metals	51 672	53 972	56 274	56 467	55 361	58 938	54 339	54 676	58 362	..
38	**Fabricated Metal Products**	646 895	691 099	741 984	769 844	768 193	770 303	714 099	759 719	801 082	..
381	Metal Products	96 836	105 640	114 413	120 295	118 519	114 449	103 085	112 040	118 315	..
3813	Structural Metal Products	..	..	..	..	..	..	..	..	..	..
382	Non-Electrical Machinery	159 194	167 256	177 947	186 597	186 671	180 623	170 660	176 991	193 141	..
3821	Engines & Turbines	..	..	..	..	..	..	..	..	..	..
3822	Agricultural Machinery	..	..	..	..	..	..	..	..	..	..
3823	Metal & Wood working Machinery	..	..	..	..	..	..	..	..	..	..
3824	Special Industrial Machinery	..	..	..	..	..	..	..	..	..	..
3825	Office & Computing Machinery	..	..	..	..	..	..	..	..	..	..
3829	Machinery & Equipment, nec	..	..	..	..	..	..	..	..	..	..
383	Electrical Machinery	149 393	159 629	169 632	175 152	183 014	184 725	178 858	189 145	198 050	..
3831	Electrical Industrial Machinery	..	..	..	..	..	..	..	..	..	..
3832	Radio, TV & Communication Equipment	..	..	..	..	..	..	..	..	..	..
3833	Electrical Appliances & Housewares	..	..	..	..	..	..	..	..	..	..
3839	Electrical Apparatus, nec	..	..	..	..	..	..	..	..	..	..
384	Transport Equipment	222 286	238 615	258 541	265 362	257 589	268 140	239 798	259 007	268 019	..
3841	Shipbuilding & Repairing	12 707	12 717	14 383	14 334	14 032	14 605	12 314	10 481	11 124	..
3842	Railroad Equipment	6 683	5 977	5 285	6 202	6 111	7 080	7 396	5 877	6 288	..
3843	Motor Vehicles	153 165	165 495	179 326	179 490	172 776	179 945	158 742	179 840	187 561	..
3844	Motorcycles & Bicycles	..	..	..	..	..	..	..	..	..	..
3845	Aircraft	49 731	54 426	59 547	65 336	64 670	66 510	61 346	62 809	63 046	..
3849	Transport Equipment, nec	..	..	..	..	..	..	..	..	..	..
385	Professional Goods	19 186	19 959	21 451	22 438	22 400	22 366	21 698	22 536	23 557	..
3851	Professional Equipment	..	..	..	..	..	..	..	..	..	..
3852	Photographic & Optical Goods	..	..	..	..	..	..	..	..	..	..
3853	Watches & Clocks	..	..	..	..	..	..	..	..	..	..
39	**Other Manufacturing, nes**	23 530	25 438	27 864	28 343	28 334	27 880	26 665	26 876	27 974	..
3901	Jewellery	..	..	..	..	..	..	..	..	..	..
3	**Total Manufacturing**	1 911 522	2 014 101	2 115 218	2 173 287	2 180 998	2 184 796	2 106 250	2 198 991	2 265 588	..
1	**Agric., Hunting, Forestry, Fishing**	281 722	282 858	284 054	289 198	286 459	299 192	284 631	289 299	292 673	..
2	**Mining & Quarrying**	52 222	51 013	51 038	50 755	55 409	55 632	54 592	53 049	54 584	..
21	Coal Mining	9 642	9 377	8 813	8 281	8 311	8 101	7 542	7 287	6 902	..
22	Crude Petroleum & Natural Gas	33 096	31 477	31 954	32 555	37 006	37 312	37 608	36 620	38 617	..
23.29	Other Mining	9 484	10 159	10 271	9 919	10 092	10 219	9 442	9 142	9 065	..
3	**Total Manufacturing**	1 911 522	2 014 101	2 115 218	2 173 287	2 180 998	2 184 796	2 106 250	2 198 991	2 265 588	..
4	**Electricity, Gas & Water**	122 857	125 150	131 189	134 219	143 045	145 037	146 692	147 767	152 452	..
5	**Construction**	396 147	426 661	452 485	466 761	472 411	462 596	436 378	434 243	437 507	..
6.9	**Services**	2 784 729	2 930 377	3 107 223	3 244 501	3 345 165	3 505 861	3 681 744	3 734 360	3 846 113	..
0000	**Grand Total**	5 549 199	5 830 160	6 141 207	6 358 721	6 483 487	6 653 114	6 710 287	6 857 709	7 048 917	..

Note: Figures for ISIC 3849 cannot be separately identified, and are distributed across the other categories in the 384 group.

Millions of FF (1980 Prices)

ISIC2	Industry	VALUE ADDED									
		1987	1988	1989	1990	1991	1992	1993	1994	1995	1996
31	Food, Beverages & Tobacco	87 309	90 436	96 726	97 193	98 753	96 124	99 601	102 439	103 680	..
311.2	Food	70 947	74 511	79 796	79 614	81 237	79 669	80 859	82 941	85 003	..
313	Beverages	12 222	11 873	12 980	13 539	13 488	12 618	14 505	15 269	14 607	..
314	Tobacco	4 140	4 052	3 950	4 040	4 028	3 837	4 237	4 229	4 070	..
32	Textiles, Apparel & Leather	47 626	45 712	46 395	47 960	45 284	44 961	41 645	42 781	42 424	..
321	Textiles	22 607	22 108	22 087	22 914	21 382	21 894	19 823	20 220	20 938	..
3213	Knitting Mills	..	..	..	..	..	..	..	..	..	..
322	Wearing Apparel	18 196	17 043	17 609	18 298	17 654	17 024	16 210	17 031	15 884	..
323	Leather & Products	2 293	2 301	2 433	2 476	2 186	2 017	1 744	1 789	1 887	..
324	Footwear	4 530	4 260	4 266	4 272	4 062	4 026	3 868	3 741	3 715	..
33	Wood Products & Furniture	21 943	23 395	24 413	25 545	24 582	24 069	23 000	24 194	24 596	..
331	Wood Products	11 165	12 266	13 137	13 754	13 102	13 143	12 492	13 942	14 195	..
332	Furnitures & Fixtures	10 778	11 129	11 276	11 791	11 480	10 926	10 508	10 252	10 401	..
34	Paper, Paper Products & Printing	43 249	47 247	48 133	48 730	46 936	45 566	45 166	48 014	48 466	..
341	Paper & Products	15 029	17 044	17 281	17 440	15 300	15 852	15 029	16 314	15 967	..
3411	Pulp, Paper & Board	..	..	..	..	..	..	..	..	..	..
342	Printing & Publishing	28 220	30 203	30 852	31 290	31 636	29 714	30 137	31 700	32 499	..
35	Chemical Products	124 108	134 730	141 996	146 186	143 864	141 482	145 558	148 313	152 511	..
351	Industrial Chemicals	28 952	30 641	33 837	36 005	34 472	33 829	33 956	36 105	37 023	..
3511	Basic Industrial Chemicals	..	..	..	..	..	..	..	..	..	..
3512	Fertilizers & Pesticides	..	..	..	..	..	..	..	..	..	..
3513	Synthetic Resins	..	..	..	..	..	..	..	..	..	..
352	Other Chemicals	36 236	40 188	43 275	44 933	45 998	46 260	48 846	51 511	53 378	..
3521	Paints, Varnishes & Lacquers	..	..	..	..	..	..	..	..	..	..
3522	Drugs & Medicines	16 314	18 541	20 036	21 301	22 318	22 955	24 564	25 100	27 147	..
3523	Soap & Cleaning Preparations	..	..	..	..	..	..	..	..	..	..
3529	Chemical Products, nec	..	..	..	..	..	..	..	..	..	..
353	Petroleum Refineries	33 518	37 021	36 651	36 690	35 394	33 261	36 737	33 253	34 525	..
354	Petroleum & Coal Products	..	..	..	..	..	..	..	..	..	..
355	Rubber Products	10 743	11 615	12 376	11 861	11 197	11 353	9 816	10 499	10 956	..
356	Plastic Products, nec	14 659	15 265	15 857	16 697	16 803	16 779	16 203	16 945	16 629	..
36	Non-Metallic Mineral Products	29 040	31 040	31 661	31 818	31 619	30 527	28 535	30 164	31 694	..
361	Pottery, China etc	..	..	..	..	..	..	..	..	..	..
362	Glass & Products	8 436	8 824	9 340	9 379	9 145	9 226	8 809	9 462	10 137	..
369	Non-Metallic Products, nec	20 604	22 216	22 321	22 439	22 474	21 301	19 726	20 702	21 557	..
37	Basic Metal Industries	35 766	39 351	41 024	40 542	39 149	37 864	35 133	37 639	38 758	..
371	Iron & Steel	21 783	24 355	24 569	23 799	23 122	21 213	19 606	21 888	22 418	..
372	Non-Ferrous Metals	13 983	14 996	16 455	16 743	16 027	16 651	15 527	15 751	16 340	..
38	Fabricated Metal Products	261 964	277 621	294 439	300 404	294 156	290 219	270 233	287 712	302 725	..
381	Metal Products	44 585	47 757	51 178	53 382	51 989	50 126	45 373	49 233	51 793	..
3813	Structural Metal Products	..	..	..	..	..	..	..	..	..	..
382	Non-Electrical Machinery	64 594	67 437	70 383	73 433	71 273	67 729	64 581	67 390	73 611	..
3821	Engines & Turbines	..	..	..	..	..	..	..	..	..	..
3822	Agricultural Machinery	..	..	..	..	..	..	..	..	..	..
3823	Metal & Wood working Machinery	..	..	..	..	..	..	..	..	..	..
3824	Special Industrial Machinery	..	..	..	..	..	..	..	..	..	..
3825	Office & Computing Machinery	..	..	..	..	..	..	..	..	..	..
3829	Machinery & Equipment, nec	..	..	..	..	..	..	..	..	..	..
383	Electrical Machinery	71 763	77 485	82 668	84 040	86 474	87 265	84 772	90 921	95 352	..
3831	Electrical Industrial Machinery	..	..	..	..	..	..	..	..	..	..
3832	Radio, TV & Communication Equipment	..	..	..	..	..	..	..	..	..	..
3833	Electrical Appliances & Housewares	..	..	..	..	..	..	..	..	..	..
3839	Electrical Apparatus, nec	..	..	..	..	..	..	..	..	..	..
384	Transport Equipment	70 920	74 592	79 222	78 130	73 205	74 155	64 933	69 138	70 418	..
3841	Shipbuilding & Repairing	3 676	3 598	5 392	4 740	4 507	4 652	2 991	2 233	2 474	..
3842	Railroad Equipment	3 039	2 860	2 382	2 800	2 837	3 168	3 602	2 673	2 798	..
3843	Motor Vehicles	46 407	48 941	51 538	50 385	46 336	45 796	39 473	44 393	43 479	..
3844	Motorcycles & Bicycles	..	..	..	..	..	..	..	..	..	..
3845	Aircraft	17 798	19 193	19 910	20 205	19 525	20 539	18 867	19 839	21 667	..
3849	Transport Equipment, nec	..	..	..	..	..	..	..	..	..	..
385	Professional Goods	10 102	10 350	10 988	11 419	11 215	10 944	10 574	11 030	11 551	..
3851	Professional Equipment	..	..	..	..	..	..	..	..	..	..
3852	Photographic & Optical Goods	..	..	..	..	..	..	..	..	..	..
3853	Watches & Clocks	..	..	..	..	..	..	..	..	..	..
39	Other Manufacturing, nes	10 090	10 989	11 853	12 022	11 861	11 466	10 954	10 801	11 019	..
3901	Jewellery	..	..	..	..	..	..	..	..	..	..
3	Total Manufacturing	661 095	700 521	736 640	750 400	736 204	722 278	699 825	732 057	755 873	..
1	Agric., Hunting, Forestry, Fishing	141 354	140 801	145 962	148 989	143 700	159 587	146 795	147 338	150 156	..
2	Mining & Quarrying	21 054	20 275	19 729	18 338	20 771	21 357	21 842	20 865	21 193	..
21	Coal Mining	2 538	2 523	2 374	2 021	2 289	1 984	2 734	2 932	2 651	..
22	Crude Petroleum & Natural Gas	13 838	12 694	12 349	11 542	13 702	14 503	14 678	13 758	14 389	..
23.29	Other Mining	4 678	5 058	5 006	4 775	4 780	4 870	4 430	4 175	4 153	..
3	Total Manufacturing	661 095	700 521	736 640	750 400	736 204	722 278	699 825	732 057	755 873	..
4	Electricity, Gas & Water	81 682	83 221	82 712	84 444	88 838	91 573	92 224	93 092	95 350	..
5	Construction	187 684	202 688	212 123	217 515	218 195	213 137	201 497	195 817	193 448	..
6.9	Services	1 937 126	2 009 537	2 089 101	2 137 498	2 175 617	2 210 718	2 214 788	2 266 922	2 309 028	..
0000	Grand Total	2 889 880	3 013 482	3 140 440	3 218 373	3 253 635	3 291 754	3 254 069	3 343 625	3 413 964	..

Note: Figures for ISIC 3849 cannot be separately identified, and are distributed across the other categories in the 384 group.

Millions of FF (1980 Prices)

ISIC2	Industry	INVESTMENT									
		1987	1988	1989	1990	1991	1992	1993	1994	1995	1996
31	Food, Beverages & Tobacco	14 368	17 274	19 549	18 243	19 255	18 693	15 345	15 154	12 641	11 631
311.2	Food	..	..	..	..	..	..	..	..	..	..
313	Beverages	..	..	..	..	..	..	..	..	..	..
314	Tobacco	..	..	..	..	..	..	..	..	..	..
32	Textiles, Apparel & Leather	4 642	5 517	5 336	5 489	4 587	4 318	3 250	3 438	3 532	3 352
321	Textiles	4 142	4 512	4 667	4 817	4 308	4 082	2 806	2 919	3 318	3 176
3213	Knitting Mills	..	..	..	..	..	..	..	..	..	..
322	Wearing Apparel	..	..	..	..	..	..	..	..	..	..
323	Leather & Products	500	1 005	669	672	279	236	444	519	214	176
324	Footwear	..	..	..	..	..	..	..	..	..	..
33	Wood Products & Furniture	4 024	4 598	5 366	5 320	5 225	4 536	3 058	3 160	2 968	2 772
331	Wood Products	..	..	..	..	..	..	..	..	..	..
332	Furnitures & Fixtures	..	..	..	..	..	..	..	..	..	..
34	Paper, Paper Products & Printing	8 786	9 487	10 600	11 723	10 983	8 870	6 236	6 344	7 444	7 225
341	Paper & Products	4 819	4 218	4 289	5 865	5 629	4 515	2 454	2 382	3 183	3 147
3411	Pulp, Paper & Board	..	..	..	..	..	..	..	..	..	..
342	Printing & Publishing	3 967	5 269	6 311	5 858	5 354	4 355	3 782	3 962	4 261	4 078
35	Chemical Products	20 780	21 996	23 660	26 798	24 701	22 877	20 664	20 962	22 176	22 667
351	Industrial Chemicals	6 199	6 560	7 045	8 386	8 036	6 416	4 957	5 099	5 779	6 163
3511	Basic Industrial Chemicals	..	..	..	..	..	..	..	..	..	..
3512	Fertilizers & Pesticides	..	..	..	..	..	..	..	..	..	..
3513	Synthetic Resins	..	..	..	..	..	..	..	..	..	..
352	Other Chemicals	3 763	5 002	5 193	4 672	5 129	5 858	5 124	5 325	5 828	6 414
3521	Paints, Varnishes & Lacquers	..	..	..	..	..	..	..	..	..	..
3522	Drugs & Medicines	..	..	..	..	..	..	..	..	..	..
3523	Soap & Cleaning Preparations	..	..	..	..	..	..	..	..	..	..
3529	Chemical Products, nec	..	..	..	..	..	..	..	..	..	..
353	Petroleum Refineries	6 781	5 628	6 067	7 722	6 076	5 905	6 492	6 611	5 756	5 599
354	Petroleum & Coal Products	..	..	..	..	..	..	..	..	..	..
355	Rubber Products	4 037	4 806	5 355	6 018	5 460	4 698	4 091	3 927	4 813	4 491
356	Plastic Products, nec	..	..	..	..	..	..	..	..	..	..
36	Non-Metallic Mineral Products	5 456	6 939	7 635	6 260	5 297	3 550	4 806	5 471	6 813	7 018
361	Pottery, China etc	..	..	..	..	..	..	..	..	..	..
362	Glass & Products	1 099	1 617	1 606	1 391	640	1 108	1 048	1 289	1 495	1 831
369	Non-Metallic Products, nec	4 357	5 322	6 029	4 869	4 657	2 442	3 758	4 182	5 318	5 187
37	Basic Metal Industries	8 546	8 092	8 084	8 165	7 468	6 986	4 935	5 767	4 880	4 730
371	Iron & Steel	1 968	1 883	2 509	3 048	2 842	2 276	-613	-129	136	299
372	Non-Ferrous Metals	6 578	6 209	5 575	5 117	4 626	4 710	5 548	5 896	4 744	4 431
38	Fabricated Metal Products	37 885	42 225	44 052	51 508	49 311	43 136	32 975	35 563	36 646	36 652
381	Metal Products	7 444	8 625	10 238	11 281	11 080	8 631	6 226	6 325	6 914	6 448
3813	Structural Metal Products	..	..	..	..	..	..	..	..	..	..
382	Non-Electrical Machinery	5 876	6 898	6 914	8 381	7 544	6 363	5 909	6 049	7 374	7 402
3821	Engines & Turbines	..	..	..	..	..	..	..	..	..	..
3822	Agricultural Machinery	..	..	..	..	..	..	..	..	..	..
3823	Metal & Wood working Machinery	..	..	..	..	..	..	..	..	..	..
3824	Special Industrial Machinery	..	..	..	..	..	..	..	..	..	..
3825	Office & Computing Machinery	..	..	..	..	..	..	..	..	..	..
3829	Machinery & Equipment, nec	..	..	..	..	..	..	..	..	..	..
383	Electrical Machinery	11 669	11 708	11 254	13 905	12 531	10 593	7 625	7 969	8 069	7 936
3831	Electrical Industrial Machinery	..	..	..	..	..	..	..	..	..	..
3832	Radio, TV & Communication Equipment	..	..	..	..	..	..	..	..	..	..
3833	Electrical Appliances & Housewares	..	..	..	..	..	..	..	..	..	..
3839	Electrical Apparatus, nec	..	..	..	..	..	..	..	..	..	..
384	Transport Equipment	12 896	14 994	15 646	17 941	18 156	17 549	13 215	15 220	14 289	14 866
3841	Shipbuilding & Repairing	..	..	..	..	..	..	..	..	..	..
3842	Railroad Equipment	..	..	..	..	..	..	..	..	..	..
3843	Motor Vehicles	..	..	..	..	..	..	..	..	..	..
3844	Motorcycles & Bicycles	..	..	..	..	..	..	..	..	..	..
3845	Aircraft	..	..	..	..	..	..	..	..	..	..
3849	Transport Equipment, nec	..	..	..	..	..	..	..	..	..	..
385	Professional Goods	..	..	..	..	..	..	..	..	..	..
3851	Professional Equipment	..	..	..	..	..	..	..	..	..	..
3852	Photographic & Optical Goods	..	..	..	..	..	..	..	..	..	..
3853	Watches & Clocks	..	..	..	..	..	..	..	..	..	..
39	Other Manufacturing, nes	..	..	..	..	..	..	..	..	..	..
3901	Jewellery	..	..	..	..	..	..	..	..	..	..
3	Total Manufacturing	104 487	116 128	124 282	133 506	126 827	112 966	91 269	95 859	97 100	96 047
1	Agric., Hunting, Forestry, Fishing	17 311	19 781	22 202	22 636	20 116	18 475	17 179	19 098	20 467	20 960
2	Mining & Quarrying	592	696	620	455	357	322	23	-1	-3 797	233
21	Coal Mining	..	..	..	..	..	..	..	..	..	..
22	Crude Petroleum & Natural Gas	..	..	..	..	..	..	..	..	..	..
23.29	Other Mining	..	..	..	..	..	..	..	..	..	..
3	Total Manufacturing	104 487	116 128	124 282	133 506	126 827	112 966	91 269	95 859	97 100	96 047
4	Electricity, Gas & Water	29 556	28 072	27 299	25 570	25 290	28 911	29 008	26 413	26 419	28 266
5	Construction	15 903	18 163	21 122	18 562	19 612	16 545	15 621	15 158	13 907	12 852
6.9	Services	495 913	544 609	589 173	606 303	615 232	607 726	579 437	585 351	606 166	597 803
0000	Grand Total	663 762	727 449	784 698	807 032	807 434	784 945	732 537	741 878	760 262	756 161

Note: ISIC 321 includes 322; 323 includes 324; 353 includes 22; 355 includes 356.

Millions of FF

(1980 Prices)

ISIC2	Industry	INVESTMENT IN MACHINERY & EQUIPMENT									
		1987	1988	1989	1990	1991	1992	1993	1994	1995	1996
31	**Food, Beverages & Tobacco**	8 859	11 144	12 388	11 027	11 574	10 838	8 932	8 557	7 875	7 195
311.2	Food	..	..	..	..	..	..	..	..	..	..
313	Beverages	..	..	..	..	..	..	..	..	..	..
314	Tobacco	..	..	..	..	..	..	..	..	..	..
32	**Textiles, Apparel & Leather**	3 512	4 362	4 181	4 231	3 314	1 880	2 166	2 309	2 983	2 538
321	Textiles	3 157	3 594	3 679	3 737	3 113	1 796	2 033	2 112	2 515	2 430
3213	Knitting Mills	..	..	..	..	..	..	..	..	..	..
322	Wearing Apparel	..	..	..	..	..	..	..	..	..	..
323	Leather & Products	355	768	502	494	201	84	133	197	468	108
324	Footwear	..	..	..	..	..	..	..	..	..	..
33	**Wood Products & Furniture**	2 641	2 844	3 301	3 158	2 832	2 635	1 699	1 727	1 686	1 587
331	Wood Products	..	..	..	..	..	..	..	..	..	..
332	Furnitures & Fixtures	..	..	..	..	..	..	..	..	..	..
34	**Paper, Paper Products & Printing**	7 331	7 974	8 885	9 878	8 378	6 539	4 397	4 478	5 767	5 840
341	Paper & Products	4 053	3 384	3 419	4 874	4 231	3 395	1 793	1 712	2 486	2 508
3411	Pulp, Paper & Board	..	..	..	..	..	..	..	..	..	..
342	Printing & Publishing	3 278	4 590	5 466	5 004	4 147	3 144	2 604	2 766	3 281	3 332
35	**Chemical Products**	14 383	15 863	16 705	19 853	18 305	15 540	14 590	14 819	17 151	18 301
351	Industrial Chemicals	4 585	5 240	5 465	6 990	6 943	5 626	4 267	4 037	5 389	6 423
3511	Basic Industrial Chemicals	..	..	..	..	..	..	..	..	..	..
3512	Fertilizers & Pesticides	..	..	..	..	..	..	..	..	..	..
3513	Synthetic Resins	..	..	..	..	..	..	..	..	..	..
352	Other Chemicals	2 660	3 916	3 904	3 339	3 367	3 404	3 306	3 478	3 980	4 483
3521	Paints, Varnishes & Lacquers	..	..	..	..	..	..	..	..	..	..
3522	Drugs & Medicines	..	..	..	..	..	..	..	..	..	..
3523	Soap & Cleaning Preparations	..	..	..	..	..	..	..	..	..	..
3529	Chemical Products, nec	..	..	..	..	..	..	..	..	..	..
353	Petroleum Refineries	3 832	2 781	2 993	4 646	3 622	3 128	3 886	4 340	3 950	3 756
354	Petroleum & Coal Products	..	..	..	..	..	..	..	..	..	..
355	Rubber Products	3 306	3 926	4 343	4 878	4 373	3 382	3 131	2 964	3 832	3 639
356	Plastic Products, nec	..	..	..	..	..	..	..	..	..	..
36	**Non-Metallic Mineral Products**	4 042	5 242	5 618	4 367	3 478	2 348	3 265	3 782	4 620	4 844
361	Pottery, China etc	..	..	..	..	..	..	..	..	..	..
362	Glass & Products	899	1 337	1 319	1 104	267	837	773	993	1 114	1 391
369	Non-Metallic Products, nec	3 143	3 905	4 299	3 263	3 211	1 511	2 492	2 789	3 506	3 453
37	**Basic Metal Industries**	7 744	6 882	6 920	6 932	6 259	6 317	4 969	5 794	6 890	4 454
371	Iron & Steel	1 848	1 791	2 378	2 905	2 696	1 988	-58	438	2 545	387
372	Non-Ferrous Metals	5 896	5 091	4 542	4 027	3 563	4 329	5 027	5 356	4 345	4 067
38	**Fabricated Metal Products**	28 826	32 219	33 067	39 282	36 521	33 268	24 176	26 612	28 320	28 725
381	Metal Products	5 792	7 004	8 190	8 742	8 213	6 398	4 284	4 333	5 089	4 773
3813	Structural Metal Products	..	..	..	..	..	..	..	..	..	..
382	Non-Electrical Machinery	5 006	5 641	5 563	6 742	5 569	5 079	3 911	4 027	5 291	5 362
3821	Engines & Turbines	..	..	..	..	..	..	..	..	..	..
3822	Agricultural Machinery	..	..	..	..	..	..	..	..	..	..
3823	Metal & Wood working Machinery	..	..	..	..	..	..	..	..	..	..
3824	Special Industrial Machinery	..	..	..	..	..	..	..	..	..	..
3825	Office & Computing Machinery	..	..	..	..	..	..	..	..	..	..
3829	Machinery & Equipment, nec	..	..	..	..	..	..	..	..	..	..
383	Electrical Machinery	8 852	9 480	8 818	10 984	9 521	7 478	5 558	5 820	6 180	6 217
3831	Electrical Industrial Machinery	..	..	..	..	..	..	..	..	..	..
3832	Radio, TV & Communication Equipment	..	..	..	..	..	..	..	..	..	..
3833	Electrical Appliances & Housewares	..	..	..	..	..	..	..	..	..	..
3839	Electrical Apparatus, nec	..	..	..	..	..	..	..	..	..	..
384	Transport Equipment	9 176	10 094	10 496	12 814	13 218	14 313	10 423	12 432	11 760	12 373
3841	Shipbuilding & Repairing	..	..	..	..	..	..	..	..	..	..
3842	Railroad Equipment	..	..	..	..	..	..	..	..	..	..
3843	Motor Vehicles	..	..	..	..	..	..	..	..	..	..
3844	Motorcycles & Bicycles	..	..	..	..	..	..	..	..	..	..
3845	Aircraft	..	..	..	..	..	..	..	..	..	..
3849	Transport Equipment, nec	..	..	..	..	..	..	..	..	..	..
385	Professional Goods	..	..	..	..	..	..	..	..	..	..
3851	Professional Equipment	..	..	..	..	..	..	..	..	..	..
3852	Photographic & Optical Goods	..	..	..	..	..	..	..	..	..	..
3853	Watches & Clocks	..	..	..	..	..	..	..	..	..	..
39	**Other Manufacturing, nes**	..	..	..	..	..	..	..	..	..	..
3901	Jewellery	..	..	..	..	..	..	..	..	..	..
3	**Total Manufacturing**	77 338	86 530	91 065	98 728	90 661	79 365	64 194	68 078	75 292	73 484
1	**Agric., Hunting, Forestry, Fishing**	11 548	12 913	13 915	13 137	11 616	10 348	9 368	10 429	11 681	12 597
2	**Mining & Quarrying**	388	525	464	333	257	186	-7	-13	577	202
21	Coal Mining	..	..	..	..	..	..	..	..	..	..
22	Crude Petroleum & Natural Gas	..	..	..	..	..	..	..	..	..	..
23.29	Other Mining	..	..	..	..	..	..	..	..	..	..
3	**Total Manufacturing**	77 338	86 530	91 065	98 728	90 661	79 365	64 194	68 078	75 292	73 484
4	**Electricity, Gas & Water**	10 322	7 613	6 750	6 532	6 701	7 621	9 328	8 352	9 636	9 735
5	**Construction**	7 119	8 540	9 712	7 849	8 339	6 804	6 338	6 018	5 761	5 213
6.9	**Services**	93 359	104 470	114 559	120 696	131 402	134 481	132 892	139 149	143 420	147 284
0000	**Grand Total**	200 074	220 591	236 465	247 275	248 976	238 805	222 113	232 013	246 367	248 515

Note: ISIC 321 includes 322; 323 includes 324; 353 includes 22; 355 includes 356.

Table IC.1 **ICELAND**

Millions of IKr (Current Prices)

ISIC2	Industry	1987	1988	1989	1990	1991	1992	1993	1994	1995	1996
31	**Food, Beverages & Tobacco**	55 685	60 057	73 579	84 671	99 646	97 740	97 025	106 945	109 090	..
311.2	Food	53 967	57 894	70 596	80 987	95 391	93 924	93 401	102 930	105 120	..
313	Beverages	1 718	2 163	2 983	3 684	4 255	3 816	3 624	4 015	3 970	..
314	Tobacco	0	0	0	0	0	0	0	0	0	..
32	**Textiles, Apparel & Leather**	5 927	5 539	5 907	6 415	6 331	6 290	5 892	6 549	7 465	..
321	Textiles	3 494	3 136	3 425	3 497	3 346	3 156	3 013	3 145	3 852	..
3213	Knitting Mills	971	594	745	515	416	405	478	459	501	..
322	Wearing Apparel	1 579	1 742	1 590	1 728	1 837	1 963	1 940	2 087	2 114	..
323	Leather & Products	785	647	832	1 081	1 042	1 129	926	1 298	1 477	..
324	Footwear	69	14	60	110	105	43	12	19	22	..
33	**Wood Products & Furniture**	4 532	5 313	6 085	5 998	6 640	6 387	5 581	5 710	5 764	..
331	Wood Products	109	173	196	234	224	218	227	250	286	..
332	Furnitures & Fixtures	4 422	5 140	5 890	5 763	6 416	6 169	5 354	5 460	5 478	..
34	**Paper, Paper Products & Printing**	6 350	8 024	9 796	10 558	12 240	12 204	12 230	12 659	13 419	..
341	Paper & Products	885	1 034	1 253	1 422	1 601	1 532	1 616	1 948	2 062	..
3411	Pulp, Paper & Board	885	1 034	1 253	1 422	1 601	1 532	1 616	1 948	2 062	..
342	Printing & Publishing	5 465	6 990	8 543	9 137	10 639	10 672	10 614	10 711	11 357	..
35	**Chemical Products**	5 078	6 275	7 643	8 958	9 706	9 192	9 010	9 550	10 123	..
351	Industrial Chemicals	1 259	1 695	1 929	2 390	2 831	2 436	2 078	2 202	2 245	..
3511	Basic Industrial Chemicals	1 259	1 695	1 929	2 390	2 831	2 436	2 078	2 202	2 245	..
3512	Fertilizers & Pesticides	..	..	..	..	..	..	..	..	..	..
3513	Synthetic Resins	0	0	0	0	0	0	0	0	0	..
352	Other Chemicals	1 617	1 924	2 428	2 660	2 864	2 713	2 854	3 013	3 248	..
3521	Paints, Varnishes & Lacquers	755	918	1 112	1 215	1 310	1 323	1 394	1 460	1 525	..
3522	Drugs & Medicines	0	0	0	0	0	0	0	0	0	..
3523	Soap & Cleaning Preparations	862	1 007	1 317	1 445	1 555	1 391	1 459	1 553	1 723	..
3529	Chemical Products, nec	0	0	0	0	0	0	0	0	0	..
353	Petroleum Refineries	0	0	0	0	0	0	0	0	0	..
354	Petroleum & Coal Products	25	26	39	41	50	67	48	..	..	..
355	Rubber Products	0	0	0	0	0	0	0	0	0	..
356	Plastic Products, nec	2 178	2 630	3 247	3 866	3 961	3 976	4 030	4 336	4 631	..
36	**Non-Metallic Mineral Products**	3 890	4 706	5 197	5 528	6 174	5 729	5 363	5 866	5 922	..
361	Pottery, China etc	76	76	94	113	109	107	88	87	95	..
362	Glass & Products	412	480	586	579	639	605	549	545	550	..
369	Non-Metallic Products, nec	3 401	4 150	4 517	4 836	5 426	5 018	4 727	5 233	5 276	..
37	**Basic Metal Industries**	6 263	9 350	13 213	12 073	10 134	9 921	11 154	13 796	15 106	..
371	Iron & Steel	1 373	2 541	3 099	2 375	1 854	1 923	2 733	2 959	3 431	..
372	Non-Ferrous Metals	4 890	6 809	10 114	9 698	8 279	7 998	8 421	10 837	11 674	..
38	**Fabricated Metal Products**	9 240	9 963	12 104	12 141	13 154	12 572	12 267	13 111	14 973	..
381	Metal Products	7 078	7 729	10 110	10 130	10 896	10 045	9 717	11 086	12 698	..
3813	Structural Metal Products	..	..	..	..	..	..	..	..	..	..
382	Non-Electrical Machinery	0	0	0	0	0	0	0	0	0	..
3821	Engines & Turbines	..	..	..	..	..	..	..	..	..	..
3822	Agricultural Machinery	..	..	..	..	..	..	..	..	..	..
3823	Metal & Wood working Machinery	..	..	..	..	..	..	..	..	..	..
3824	Special Industrial Machinery	..	..	..	..	..	..	..	..	..	..
3825	Office & Computing Machinery	..	..	..	..	..	..	..	..	..	..
3829	Machinery & Equipment, nec	..	..	..	..	..	..	..	..	..	..
383	Electrical Machinery	0	0	0	0	0	0	0	0	0	..
3831	Electrical Industrial Machinery	..	..	..	..	..	..	..	..	..	..
3832	Radio, TV & Communication Equipment	..	..	..	..	..	..	..	..	..	..
3833	Electrical Appliances & Housewares	..	..	..	..	..	..	..	..	..	..
3839	Electrical Apparatus, nec	..	..	..	..	..	..	..	..	..	..
384	Transport Equipment	2 162	2 234	1 994	2 011	2 258	2 528	2 550	2 025	2 275	..
3841	Shipbuilding & Repairing	2 162	2 234	1 994	2 011	2 258	2 528	2 550	2 025	2 275	..
3842	Railroad Equipment	..	..	..	..	..	..	..	..	..	..
3843	Motor Vehicles	..	..	..	..	..	..	..	..	..	..
3844	Motorcycles & Bicycles	..	..	..	..	..	..	..	..	..	..
3845	Aircraft	..	..	..	..	..	..	..	..	..	..
3849	Transport Equipment, nec	..	..	..	..	..	..	..	..	..	..
385	Professional Goods	0	0	0	0	0	0	0	0	0	..
3851	Professional Equipment	..	..	..	..	..	..	..	..	..	..
3852	Photographic & Optical Goods	..	..	..	..	..	..	..	..	..	..
3853	Watches & Clocks	..	..	..	..	..	..	..	..	..	..
39	**Other Manufacturing, nes**	3 115	3 725	4 324	5 314	5 257	5 353	5 563	6 062	7 425	..
3901	Jewellery	188	218	243	235	260	245	229	239	255	..
3	**Total Manufacturing**	100 081	112 953	137 846	151 655	169 282	165 389	164 084	180 248	189 285	..
1	**Agric., Hunting, Forestry, Fishing**	35 107	43 080	50 779	62 768	67 639	65 121	67 792	70 150	72 375	
2	**Mining & Quarrying**	..	..	..	..	..	..	..	..	..	
21	Coal Mining	..	..	..	..	..	..	..	..	..	
22	Crude Petroleum & Natural Gas	..	..	..	..	..	..	..	..	..	
23.29	Other Mining	..	..	..	..	..	..	..	..	..	
3	**Total Manufacturing**	100 081	112 953	137 846	151 655	169 282	165 389	164 084	180 248	189 285	
4	**Electricity, Gas & Water**	11 809	15 887	18 666	19 849	20 926	22 470	23 612	24 464	25 587	
5	**Construction**	40 630	48 565	60 066	71 446	82 216	75 082	79 061	81 715	77 279	
6.9	**Services**	205 886	259 603	305 319	364 422	398 305	409 544	415 006	439 390	462 415	
0000	**Grand Total**	393 514	480 088	572 676	670 141	738 369	737 606	749 555	795 966	826 941	..

Note: National accounts figures for Iceland were revised in 1994. See Sources and Definitions.
ISIC 3511 includes 3512.

Table IC.2 **ICELAND**

Millions of IKr (Current Prices)

ISIC2	Industry	VALUE ADDED									
		1987	**1988**	**1989**	**1990**	**1991**	**1992**	**1993**	**1994**	**1995**	**1996**
31	**Food, Beverages & Tobacco**	15 043	14 109	17 626	17 847	27 581	27 258	27 917	31 523	29 851	..
311.2	Food	14 261	13 201	16 313	16 635	26 233	25 942	26 825	30 396	28 571	..
313	Beverages	781	908	1 313	1 212	1 348	1 316	1 092	1 127	1 281	..
314	Tobacco	0	0	0	0	0	0	0	0	0	..
32	**Textiles, Apparel & Leather**	2 168	2 049	1 967	2 128	2 309	2 442	2 259	2 598	2 916	..
321	Textiles	1 078	1 056	1 144	1 219	998	1 126	1 015	1 112	1 316	..
3213	Knitting Mills	315	197	259	155	154	190	210	158	214	..
322	Wearing Apparel	705	768	666	578	779	834	839	922	930	..
323	Leather & Products	356	231	137	292	512	482	402	562	664	..
324	Footwear	29	-6	20	38	21	2	3	2	5	..
33	**Wood Products & Furniture**	2 513	2 847	2 962	2 416	2 749	2 899	2 375	2 219	2 301	..
331	Wood Products	38	68	64	57	70	89	100	90	101	..
332	Furnitures & Fixtures	2 475	2 779	2 897	2 359	2 679	2 810	2 275	2 129	2 200	..
34	**Paper, Paper Products & Printing**	3 230	3 930	5 150	5 451	6 301	5 902	5 667	6 380	6 575	..
341	Paper & Products	334	404	456	547	634	566	647	745	738	..
3411	Pulp, Paper & Board	334	404	456	547	634	566	647	745	738	..
342	Printing & Publishing	2 897	3 526	4 694	4 904	5 667	5 337	5 020	5 634	5 837	..
35	**Chemical Products**	1 825	2 497	3 050	3 434	3 640	3 955	3 827	3 634	3 712	..
351	Industrial Chemicals	417	684	748	979	1 004	1 000	780	673	607	..
3511	Basic Industrial Chemicals	417	684	748	979	1 004	1 000	780	673	607	..
3512	Fertilizers & Pesticides	..	..	..	..	..	..	..	..	..	..
3513	Synthetic Resins	0	0	0	0	0	0	0	0	0	..
352	Other Chemicals	537	706	947	850	1 002	1 207	1 289	1 182	1 329	..
3521	Paints, Varnishes & Lacquers	252	350	485	455	515	548	577	580	523	..
3522	Drugs & Medicines	0	0	0	0	0	0	0	0	0	..
3523	Soap & Cleaning Preparations	286	356	462	396	486	660	712	602	806	..
3529	Chemical Products, nec	0	0	0	0	0	0	0	0	0	..
353	Petroleum Refineries	0	0	0	0	0	0	0	0	0	..
354	Petroleum & Coal Products	10	9	16	14	17	31	21	..	..	..
355	Rubber Products	0	0	0	0	0	0	0	0	0	..
356	Plastic Products, nec	861	1 098	1 339	1 591	1 617	1 717	1 738	1 779	1 776	..
36	**Non-Metallic Mineral Products**	1 859	2 171	2 543	2 423	2 535	2 568	2 312	2 684	2 552	..
361	Pottery, China etc	39	37	38	57	26	2	55	40	48	..
362	Glass & Products	198	228	292	212	248	277	238	235	236	..
369	Non-Metallic Products, nec	1 622	1 905	2 213	2 155	2 261	2 293	2 018	2 409	2 268	..
37	**Basic Metal Industries**	1 604	3 099	4 600	2 637	1 276	1 773	2 087	4 156	4 143	..
371	Iron & Steel	404	1 197	1 297	536	328	365	922	995	1 343	..
372	Non-Ferrous Metals	1 201	1 901	3 303	2 101	948	1 408	1 165	3 161	2 800	..
38	**Fabricated Metal Products**	5 303	6 031	6 165	6 077	6 430	5 560	5 319	5 178	5 940	..
381	Metal Products	4 098	4 696	5 072	4 927	5 149	4 118	3 996	4 110	4 738	..
3813	Structural Metal Products	..	..	..	..	..	..	..	..	..	..
382	Non-Electrical Machinery	0	0	0	0	0	0	0	0	0	..
3821	Engines & Turbines	..	..	..	..	..	..	..	..	..	..
3822	Agricultural Machinery	..	..	..	..	..	..	..	..	..	..
3823	Metal & Wood working Machinery	..	..	..	..	..	..	..	..	..	..
3824	Special Industrial Machinery	..	..	..	..	..	..	..	..	..	..
3825	Office & Computing Machinery	..	..	..	..	..	..	..	..	..	..
3829	Machinery & Equipment, nec	..	..	..	..	..	..	..	..	..	..
383	Electrical Machinery	0	0	0	0	0	0	0	0	0	..
3831	Electrical Industrial Machinery	..	..	..	..	..	..	..	..	..	..
3832	Radio, TV & Communication Equipment	..	..	..	..	..	..	..	..	..	..
3833	Electrical Appliances & Housewares	..	..	..	..	..	..	..	..	..	..
3839	Electrical Apparatus, nec	..	..	..	..	..	..	..	..	..	..
384	Transport Equipment	1 205	1 336	1 093	1 150	1 281	1 442	1 323	1 068	1 202	..
3841	Shipbuilding & Repairing	1 205	1 336	1 093	1 150	1 281	1 442	1 323	1 068	1 202	..
3842	Railroad Equipment	..	..	..	..	..	..	..	..	..	..
3843	Motor Vehicles	..	..	..	..	..	..	..	..	..	..
3844	Motorcycles & Bicycles	..	..	..	..	..	..	..	..	..	..
3845	Aircraft	..	..	..	..	..	..	..	..	..	..
3849	Transport Equipment, nec	..	..	..	..	..	..	..	..	..	..
385	Professional Goods	0	0	0	0	0	0	0	0	0	..
3851	Professional Equipment	..	..	..	..	..	..	..	..	..	..
3852	Photographic & Optical Goods	..	..	..	..	..	..	..	..	..	..
3853	Watches & Clocks	..	..	..	..	..	..	..	..	..	..
39	**Other Manufacturing, nes**	841	1 083	1 217	1 594	1 653	1 742	1 978	1 933	2 360	..
3901	Jewellery	106	116	131	118	126	124	109	108	113	..
3	**Total Manufacturing**	34 386	37 814	45 279	44 008	54 472	54 098	53 741	60 303	60 350	..
1	**Agric., Hunting, Forestry, Fishing**	21 211	25 367	29 254	35 311	39 452	38 181	39 483	39 799	42 655	..
2	**Mining & Quarrying**	..	..	..	..	..	..	..	..	..	..
21	Coal Mining	..	..	..	..	..	..	..	..	..	..
22	Crude Petroleum & Natural Gas	..	..	..	..	..	..	..	..	..	..
23.29	Other Mining	..	..	..	..	..	..	..	..	..	..
3	**Total Manufacturing**	34 386	37 814	45 279	44 008	54 472	54 098	53 741	60 303	60 350	..
4	**Electricity, Gas & Water**	6 872	9 981	11 860	11 784	11 967	12 710	13 491	13 526	14 824	..
5	**Construction**	15 847	17 990	21 792	24 305	24 891	25 273	24 389	23 413	23 851	..
6.9	**Services**	126 984	158 940	187 118	227 442	246 533	254 478	255 107	272 061	281 400	..
0000	**Grand Total**	205 301	250 092	295 302	342 848	377 315	384 740	386 211	409 103	423 080	..

Note: National accounts figures for Iceland were revised in 1994. See Sources and Definitions.
ISIC 3511 includes 3512.

Table IC.3 **ICELAND**

Person Years

ISIC2	Industry	EMPLOYMENT									
		1987	1988	1989	1990	1991	1992	1993	1994	1995	1996
31	**Food, Beverages & Tobacco**	14 628	12 871	12 436	11 707	11 440	10 524	10 463	10 898	11 005	..
311.2	Food	14 270	12 558	12 100	11 373	11 105	10 180	10 169	10 592	10 726	..
313	Beverages	356	311	334	333	325	334	294	306	273	..
314	Tobacco	2	2	2	1	10	10	0	0	6	..
32	**Textiles, Apparel & Leather**	2 566	2 046	1 711	1 603	1 450	1 293	1 190	1 205	1 266	..
321	Textiles	1 200	1 038	900	813	601	459	455	487	524	..
3213	Knitting Mills	308	361	269	227	60	72	67	72	85	..
322	Wearing Apparel	978	686	504	473	525	533	488	518	527	..
323	Leather & Products	341	289	269	276	283	285	235	188	207	..
324	Footwear	47	33	38	41	41	16	12	11	9	..
33	**Wood Products & Furniture**	1 504	1 277	1 102	1 104	1 354	1 239	1 110	1 092	1 090	..
331	Wood Products	56	55	54	54	42	36	44	37	43	..
332	Furnitures & Fixtures	1 448	1 222	1 048	1 050	1 312	1 203	1 066	1 055	1 047	..
34	**Paper, Paper Products & Printing**	2 426	2 421	2 312	2 375	2 395	2 276	2 153	2 080	2 210	..
341	Paper & Products	237	237	226	232	233	236	235	228	237	..
3411	Pulp, Paper & Board	237	237	226	232	233	236	235	228	237	..
342	Printing & Publishing	2 189	2 184	2 086	2 143	2 162	2 040	1 918	1 852	1 973	..
35	**Chemical Products**	1 280	1 199	1 146	1 102	1 196	1 128	1 067	1 058	1 088	..
351	Industrial Chemicals	280	265	246	259	250	248	236	217	197	..
3511	Basic Industrial Chemicals	280	265	246	259	250	248	236	217	197	..
3512	Fertilizers & Pesticides	..	..	..			..				
3513	Synthetic Resins	0	0	0	0	0	0	0	0	0	..
352	Other Chemicals	320	306	320	304	416	369	381	355	391	..
3521	Paints, Varnishes & Lacquers	116	110	113	109	181	161	169	172	169	..
3522	Drugs & Medicines	0	0	0	0	0	0	0	0	0	..
3523	Soap & Cleaning Preparations	204	196	207	195	235	208	212	183	222	..
3529	Chemical Products, nec	0	0	0	0	0	0	0	0	0	..
353	Petroleum Refineries	0	0	0	0	0	0	0	0	0	..
354	Petroleum & Coal Products	6	7	9	8	10	10	9	0	1	..
355	Rubber Products	0	0	0	0	0	0	0	0	0	..
356	Plastic Products, nec	674	621	571	531	520	501	441	486	499	..
36	**Non-Metallic Mineral Products**	983	973	929	922	975	928	852	790	817	..
361	Pottery, China etc	44	40	40	39	18	33	29	18	31	..
362	Glass & Products	124	118	118	101	122	112	108	104	97	..
369	Non-Metallic Products, nec	815	815	771	782	835	783	715	667	689	..
37	**Basic Metal Industries**	815	852	871	862	812	816	753	691	673	..
371	Iron & Steel	188	203	207	210	190	193	161	157	162	..
372	Non-Ferrous Metals	627	649	664	652	622	623	592	534	511	..
38	**Fabricated Metal Products**	3 708	3 456	3 268	3 009	2 826	2 672	2 540	2 356	2 513	..
381	Metal Products	2 697	2 574	2 540	2 349	2 196	2 097	1 978	1 974	2 095	..
3813	Structural Metal Products										
382	Non-Electrical Machinery	0	0	0	0	0	0	0	..	0	..
3821	Engines & Turbines	..	..	..	..	..	..	..	..	..	..
3822	Agricultural Machinery	..	..	..	..						
3823	Metal & Wood working Machinery	..									
3824	Special Industrial Machinery	1 003	1 055	1 698	..				..		
3825	Office & Computing Machinery	..	..	..							
3829	Machinery & Equipment, nec	..	..	..							
383	Electrical Machinery	0	0	0	0	0	0	0	0	0	..
3831	Electrical Industrial Machinery	..	..	..	..						
3832	Radio, TV & Communication Equipment	..	..	..	..						
3833	Electrical Appliances & Housewares	..	..	..	..						
3839	Electrical Apparatus, nec	..	..	..	..				..		
384	Transport Equipment	1 011	882	728	660	630	575	562	382	418	..
3841	Shipbuilding & Repairing	1 011	882	728	660	630	575	562	382	418	..
3842	Railroad Equipment	..	..	..	..						
3843	Motor Vehicles	..	..	..	..						
3844	Motorcycles & Bicycles	..	..	..	..						
3845	Aircraft	..	..	..	..						
3849	Transport Equipment, nec	..	..	..	..						
385	Professional Goods	0	0	0	0	0	0	0	0	0	..
3851	Professional Equipment	..	..	..	..						
3852	Photographic & Optical Goods	..	..	..	..						
3853	Watches & Clocks	..	..	..	..						
39	**Other Manufacturing, nes**	477	494	535	551	598	570	556	624	699	..
3901	Jewellery	55	53	57	63	60	62	58	63	65	..
3	**Total Manufacturing**	28 387	25 589	24 310	23 239	23 043	21 444	20 681	20 794	21 360	..
1	**Agric., Hunting, Forestry, Fishing**	13 986	13 083	13 177	13 253	13 554	12 868	12 771	12 177	11 992	..
2	**Mining & Quarrying**	..	..	..	..	..	..	..	..	..	..
21	Coal Mining	..	..	..	..	..	..	..	..	..	..
22	Crude Petroleum & Natural Gas	..	..	..	..	..	..	..	..	..	..
23.29	Other Mining	..	..	..	..	..	..	..	..	..	..
3	**Total Manufacturing**	28 387	25 589	24 310	23 239	23 043	21 444	20 681	20 794	21 360	..
4	**Electricity, Gas & Water**	1 145	1 199	1 108	1 110	1 269	1 259	1 243	1 297	1 364	..
5	**Construction**	12 339	11 837	12 354	12 382	10 972	10 743	10 570	10 364	9 783	..
6.9	**Services**	75 949	76 208	75 113	74 783	76 002	76 730	76 791	78 029	79 217	..
0000	**Grand Total**	131 806	127 916	126 062	124 763	124 840	123 044	122 056	122 660	123 715	..

Note: National accounts figures for Iceland were revised in 1994. See Sources and Definitions.
ISIC 3511 includes 3512.

Table IC.4 **ICELAND**

Person Years

ISIC2	Industry	EMPLOYMENT - EMPLOYEES									
		1987	1988	1989	1990	1991	1992	1993	1994	1995	1996
31	**Food, Beverages & Tobacco**	..	..	12 257	11 534	11 226	10 326	10 276	10 704	10 811	..
311.2	Food	..	..	11 921	11 200	10 891	9 982	9 982	10 399	10 532	..
313	Beverages	..	..	334	333	325	334	294	306	273	..
314	Tobacco	..	..	2	1	10	10	0	0	6	..
32	**Textiles, Apparel & Leather**	..	..	1 649	1 552	1 384	1 233	1 139	1 158	1 217	..
321	Textiles	..	..	882	796	579	440	436	468	506	..
3213	Knitting Mills	..	..	265	222	57	70	65	70	83	..
322	Wearing Apparel	..	..	472	447	493	502	464	495	501	..
323	Leather & Products	..	..	262	269	272	275	227	184	201	..
324	Footwear	..	..	33	40	40	16	12	11	9	..
33	**Wood Products & Furniture**	..	..	1 007	999	1 229	1 066	943	925	925	..
331	Wood Products	..	..	34	35	24	17	28	21	27	..
332	Furnitures & Fixtures	..	..	973	964	1 205	1 049	915	904	897	..
34	**Paper, Paper Products & Printing**	..	..	2 221	2 287	2 287	2 159	2 043	1 968	2 101	..
341	Paper & Products	..	..	224	231	231	233	231	224	234	..
3411	Pulp, Paper & Board	..	..	224	231	231	233	231	224	234	..
342	Printing & Publishing	..	..	1 997	2 056	2 056	1 926	1 812	1 745	1 867	..
35	**Chemical Products**	..	..	1 133	1 087	1 176	1 107	1 050	1 044	1 069	..
351	Industrial Chemicals	..	..	246	259	248	246	234	217	197	..
3511	Basic Industrial Chemicals	..	..	246	259	248	246	234	217	197	..
3512	Fertilizers & Pesticides	..	..	..	..	..	..	..	..	..	..
3513	Synthetic Resins	..	..	0	0	0	0	0	0	0	..
352	Other Chemicals	..	..	319	302	412	366	377	353	389	..
3521	Paints, Varnishes & Lacquers	..	..	113	109	181	161	169	172	169	..
3522	Drugs & Medicines	..	..	0	0	0	0	0	0	0	..
3523	Soap & Cleaning Preparations	..	..	206	193	231	205	208	181	219	..
3529	Chemical Products, nec	..	..	0	0	0	0	0	0	0	..
353	Petroleum Refineries	..	..	0	0	0	0	0	0	0	..
354	Petroleum & Coal Products	..	..	9	8	10	10	9	0	1	..
355	Rubber Products	..	..	0	0	0	0	0	0	0	..
356	Plastic Products, nec	..	..	559	518	506	485	429	474	482	..
36	**Non-Metallic Mineral Products**	..	..	895	894	936	892	820	749	776	..
361	Pottery, China etc	..	..	28	28	8	23	22	8	21	..
362	Glass & Products	..	..	111	96	113	102	98	91	82	..
369	Non-Metallic Products, nec	..	..	756	770	815	767	700	650	674	..
37	**Basic Metal Industries**	..	..	871	861	810	813	753	691	673	..
371	Iron & Steel	..	..	207	209	188	190	161	157	162	..
372	Non-Ferrous Metals	..	..	664	652	622	623	592	534	511	..
38	**Fabricated Metal Products**	..	..	3 046	2 780	2 559	2 403	2 278	2 090	2 228	..
381	Metal Products	..	..	2 343	2 146	1 960	1 857	1 740	1 730	1 834	..
3813	Structural Metal Products	..	..	..	..	..	..	..	..	..	..
382	Non-Electrical Machinery	..	..	0	0	0	0	0	0	0	..
3821	Engines & Turbines	..	..	..	..	..	..	..	..	..	..
3822	Agricultural Machinery	..	..	..	..	..	..	..	..	..	..
3823	Metal & Wood working Machinery	..	..	..	..	..	..	..	..	..	..
3824	Special Industrial Machinery	..	..	..	..	..	..	..	..	..	..
3825	Office & Computing Machinery	..	..	..	..	..	..	..	..	..	..
3829	Machinery & Equipment, nec	..	..	..	..	..	..	..	..	..	..
383	Electrical Machinery	..	..	0	0	0	0	0	0	0	..
3831	Electrical Industrial Machinery	..	..	..	..	..	..	..	..	..	..
3832	Radio, TV & Communication Equipment	..	..	..	..	..	..	..	..	..	..
3833	Electrical Appliances & Housewares	..	..	..	..	..	..	..	..	..	..
3839	Electrical Apparatus, nec	..	..	..	..	..	..	..	..	..	..
384	Transport Equipment	..	..	703	634	599	546	538	360	394	..
3841	Shipbuilding & Repairing	..	..	703	634	599	546	538	360	394	..
3842	Railroad Equipment	..	..	..	..	..	..	..	..	..	..
3843	Motor Vehicles	..	..	..	..	..	..	..	..	..	..
3844	Motorcycles & Bicycles	..	..	..	..	..	..	..	..	..	..
3845	Aircraft	..	..	..	..	..	..	..	..	..	..
3849	Transport Equipment, nec	..	..	..	..	..	..	..	..	..	..
385	Professional Goods	..	..	0	0	0	0	0	0	0	..
3851	Professional Equipment	..	..	..	..	..	..	..	..	..	..
3852	Photographic & Optical Goods	..	..	..	..	..	..	..	..	..	..
3853	Watches & Clocks	..	..	..	..	..	..	..	..	..	..
39	**Other Manufacturing, nes**	..	..	480	489	528	495	486	551	629	..
3901	Jewellery	..	..	34	38	36	41	38	39	42	..
3	**Total Manufacturing**	..	..	23 559	22 487	22 132	20 493	19 784	19 880	20 430	..
1	**Agric., Hunting, Forestry, Fishing**	..	..	7 637	8 006	7 314	6 832	7 438	7 015	6 962	..
2	**Mining & Quarrying**	..	..	..	..	..	..	..	..	..	..
21	Coal Mining	..	..	..	..	..	..	..	..	..	..
22	Crude Petroleum & Natural Gas	..	..	..	..	..	..	..	..	..	..
23.29	Other Mining	..	..	..	..	..	..	..	..	..	..
3	**Total Manufacturing**	..	..	23 559	22 487	22 132	20 493	19 784	19 880	20 430	..
4	**Electricity, Gas & Water**	..	..	1 108	1 110	1 269	1 259	1 243	1 297	1 364	..
5	**Construction**	..	..	9 556	9 780	8 248	8 089	8 040	7 907	7 331	..
6.9	**Services**	..	..	67 790	67 461	68 276	68 986	69 354	70 483	71 628	..
0000	**Grand Total**	..	..	109 650	108 840	107 242	105 659	105 859	106 581	107 715	..

Note: National accounts figures for Iceland were revised in 1994. See Sources and Definitions.
ISIC 3511 includes 3512.

Table IC.5 **ICELAND**

Millions of IKr (Current Prices)

ISIC2	Industry	WAGES & SALARIES + SUPPLEMENTS - EMPLOYEES									
		1987	1988	1989	1990	1991	1992	1993	1994	1995	1996
31	**Food, Beverages & Tobacco**	11 509	13 504	15 247	15 501	17 532	17 092	17 805	19 042	19 988	..
311.2	Food	11 179	13 088	14 777	14 870	16 740	16 354	17 095	18 355	19 233	..
313	Beverages	330	416	471	631	792	739	710	687	756	..
314	Tobacco	0	0	0	0	0	0	0	0	0	..
32	**Textiles, Apparel & Leather**	2 037	2 008	1 777	1 697	1 887	1 903	1 657	1 789	1 936	..
321	Textiles	1 221	1 195	1 177	1 076	794	705	683	685	802	..
3213	Knitting Mills	393	166	202	141	102	76	76	78	100	..
322	Wearing Apparel	482	495	437	479	657	770	640	705	733	..
323	Leather & Products	298	302	141	109	407	415	323	387	390	..
324	Footwear	36	17	22	33	30	13	11	12	11	..
33	**Wood Products & Furniture**	1 563	1 659	1 580	1 994	2 252	2 197	1 673	1 524	1 794	..
331	Wood Products	11	21	19	33	36	41	46	43	54	..
332	Furnitures & Fixtures	1 552	1 638	1 560	1 961	2 216	2 156	1 627	1 481	1 741	..
34	**Paper, Paper Products & Printing**	2 214	2 587	3 268	3 725	4 417	4 079	4 166	4 656	4 887	..
341	Paper & Products	253	300	330	385	468	434	406	462	488	..
3411	Pulp, Paper & Board	253	300	330	385	468	434	406	462	488	..
342	Printing & Publishing	1 961	2 287	2 938	3 340	3 949	3 646	3 760	4 194	4 399	..
35	**Chemical Products**	1 249	1 628	1 784	1 890	2 151	2 259	2 271	2 142	2 196	..
351	Industrial Chemicals	323	401	453	514	582	641	566	449	447	..
3511	Basic Industrial Chemicals	323	401	453	514	582	641	566	449	447	..
3512	Fertilizers & Pesticides	..	..	..	..	..	..	..	..	..	..
3513	Synthetic Resins	0	0	0	0	0	0	0	0	0	..
352	Other Chemicals	322	439	458	471	530	522	628	635	647	..
3521	Paints, Varnishes & Lacquers	134	183	200	216	249	282	327	334	327	..
3522	Drugs & Medicines	0	0	0	0	0	0	0	0	0	..
3523	Soap & Cleaning Preparations	188	256	258	255	281	240	300	301	320	..
3529	Chemical Products, nec	0	0	0	0	0	0	0	0	0	..
353	Petroleum Refineries	0	0	0	0	0	0	0	0	0	..
354	Petroleum & Coal Products	6	7	9	12	13	17	11			..
355	Rubber Products	0	0	0	0	0	0	0	0	0	..
356	Plastic Products, nec	599	781	864	893	1 026	1 079	1 066	1 059	1 101	..
36	**Non-Metallic Mineral Products**	915	1 199	1 288	1 560	1 846	1 772	1 411	1 474	1 472	..
361	Pottery, China etc	18	32	42	55	70	71	32	28	18	..
362	Glass & Products	99	125	121	151	188	186	160	140	138	..
369	Non-Metallic Products, nec	797	1 042	1 125	1 353	1 588	1 516	1 219	1 306	1 316	..
37	**Basic Metal Industries**	1 137	1 528	1 780	1 917	1 903	1 836	1 656	1 671	1 691	..
371	Iron & Steel	239	345	437	439	415	459	376	408	466	..
372	Non-Ferrous Metals	898	1 184	1 343	1 478	1 488	1 377	1 280	1 263	1 224	..
38	**Fabricated Metal Products**	4 328	4 820	4 528	4 451	4 905	4 491	3 978	3 671	4 432	..
381	Metal Products	3 163	3 622	3 499	3 475	3 786	3 214	2 802	2 803	3 424	..
3813	Structural Metal Products	..	..	..	..	..	..	..	..	..	..
382	Non-Electrical Machinery	0	0	0	..	0	0	0	0	0	..
3821	Engines & Turbines	..	..	..	..	..	..	..	..	..	..
3822	Agricultural Machinery	..	..	..	..	..	..	..	..	..	..
3823	Metal & Wood working Machinery	..	..	..	..	..	..	..	..	..	..
3824	Special Industrial Machinery	..	..	..	..	..	..	..	..	..	..
3825	Office & Computing Machinery	..	..	..	..	..	..	..	..	..	..
3829	Machinery & Equipment, nec	..	..	..	..	..	..	..	..	..	..
383	Electrical Machinery	0	0	0	0	0	0	0	0	0	..
3831	Electrical Industrial Machinery	..	..	..	..	..	..	..	..	..	..
3832	Radio, TV & Communication Equipment	..	..	..	..	..	..	..	..	..	..
3833	Electrical Appliances & Housewares	..	..	..	..	..	..	..	..	..	..
3839	Electrical Apparatus, nec	..	..	..	..	..	..	..	..	..	..
384	Transport Equipment	1 165	1 197	1 029	976	1 119	1 277	1 177	868	1 008	..
3841	Shipbuilding & Repairing	1 165	1 197	1 029	976	1 119	1 277	1 177	868	1 008	..
3842	Railroad Equipment	..	..	..	..	..	..	..	..	..	..
3843	Motor Vehicles	..	..	..	..	..	..	..	..	..	..
3844	Motorcycles & Bicycles	..	..	..	..	..	..	..	..	..	..
3845	Aircraft	..	..	..	..	..	..	..	..	..	..
3849	Transport Equipment, nec	..	..	..	..	..	..	..	..	..	..
385	Professional Goods	0	0	0	0	0	0	0	0	0	..
3851	Professional Equipment	..	..	..	..	..	..	..	..	..	..
3852	Photographic & Optical Goods	..	..	..	..	..	..	..	..	..	..
3853	Watches & Clocks	..	..	..	..	..	..	..	..	..	..
39	**Other Manufacturing, nes**	623	743	811	1 039	1 103	1 158	1 247	1 382	1 628	..
3901	Jewellery	41	42	46	40	58	67	55	44	55	..
3	**Total Manufacturing**	25 576	29 674	32 063	33 774	37 996	36 788	35 865	37 350	40 024	..
1	**Agric., Hunting, Forestry, Fishing**	11 840	14 339	16 958	21 116	22 249	22 208	23 028	23 417	24 116	..
2	**Mining & Quarrying**	..	..	..	..	..	..	..	..	..	..
21	Coal Mining	..	..	..	..	..	..	..	..	..	..
22	Crude Petroleum & Natural Gas	..	..	..	..	..	..	..	..	..	..
23.29	Other Mining	..	..	..	..	..	..	..	..	..	..
3	**Total Manufacturing**	25 576	29 674	32 063	33 774	37 996	36 788	35 865	37 350	40 024	..
4	**Electricity, Gas & Water**	1 360	1 806	2 271	2 730	2 935	3 091	3 139	3 286	3 529	..
5	**Construction**	8 814	10 514	12 528	14 103	16 397	15 408	14 581	13 945	13 912	..
6.9	**Services**	62 304	79 804	89 571	102 059	122 065	126 335	126 858	133 095	143 095	..
0000	**Grand Total**	109 893	136 137	153 392	173 781	201 642	203 831	203 471	211 092	224 677	..

Note: National accounts figures for Iceland were revised in 1994. See Sources and Definitions.
ISIC 3511 includes 3512.

Table IC.6 **ICELAND**

Units

ISIC2	Industry	ESTABLISHMENTS									
		1987	1988	1989	1990	1991	1992	1993	1994	1995	1996
31	**Food, Beverages & Tobacco**	909	869	814	801	711	686	722	763	747	..
311.2	Food	903	862	810	795	703	676	715	756	740	..
313	Beverages	6	5	3	5	7	9	7	7	6	..
314	Tobacco	0	2	1	1	1	1	0	0	1	..
32	**Textiles, Apparel & Leather**	258	211	205	189	193	184	171	190	190	..
321	Textiles	89	85	76	70	67	65	64	72	72	..
3213	Knitting Mills	32	28	21	20	21	21	19	21	20	..
322	Wearing Apparel	140	104	104	95	102	98	85	96	95	..
323	Leather & Products	24	19	18	21	21	19	20	19	20	..
324	Footwear	5	3	7	3	3	2	2	3	3	..
33	**Wood Products & Furniture**	359	333	275	280	313	372	382	388	383	..
331	Wood Products	46	43	41	40	36	37	38	41	39	..
332	Furnitures & Fixtures	313	290	234	240	277	335	344	347	344	..
34	**Paper, Paper Products & Printing**	318	319	317	320	342	353	369	390	414	..
341	Paper & Products	10	10	11	9	10	9	10	11	14	..
3411	Pulp, Paper & Board	10	10	11	9	10	9	10	11	14	..
342	Printing & Publishing	308	309	306	311	332	344	359	379	400	..
35	**Chemical Products**	92	92	85	92	93	91	83	85	97	..
351	Industrial Chemicals	6	8	7	6	6	6	7	7	7	..
3511	Basic Industrial Chemicals	6	8	7	6	6	6	7	7	7	..
3512	Fertilizers & Pesticides	..	..	..	..	..	..	..	..	..	..
3513	Synthetic Resins	0	0	0	0	0	0	0	0	0	..
352	Other Chemicals	24	24	21	25	26	25	22	25	25	..
3521	Paints, Varnishes & Lacquers	4	4	4	6	7	7	5	5	5	..
3522	Drugs & Medicines	0	0	0	0	0	0	0	0	0	..
3523	Soap & Cleaning Preparations	20	20	17	19	19	18	17	20	20	..
3529	Chemical Products, nec	0	0	0	0	0	0	0	0	0	..
353	Petroleum Refineries	0	0	0	0	0	0	0	0	0	..
354	Petroleum & Coal Products	3	3	3	2	2	2	2	0	2	..
355	Rubber Products	0	0	0	0	0	0	0	0	0	..
356	Plastic Products, nec	59	57	54	59	59	58	52	53	63	..
36	**Non-Metallic Mineral Products**	112	115	110	105	121	112	116	126	127	..
361	Pottery, China etc	22	23	24	23	24	24	21	24	24	..
362	Glass & Products	18	16	17	17	23	22	24	24	26	..
369	Non-Metallic Products, nec	72	76	69	65	74	66	71	78	77	..
37	**Basic Metal Industries**	2	2	2	2	2	2	2	2	2	..
371	Iron & Steel	1	1	1	1	1	1	1	1	1	..
372	Non-Ferrous Metals	1	1	1	1	1	1	1	1	1	..
38	**Fabricated Metal Products**	547	564	550	555	558	574	576	602	623	..
381	Metal Products	465	498	491	496	488	504	511	538	566	..
3813	Structural Metal Products	..	..	..	..	..	..	..	..	..	..
382	Non-Electrical Machinery	0	0	0	0	0	0	0	0	0	..
3821	Engines & Turbines	..	..	..	..	..	..	..	..	..	..
3822	Agricultural Machinery	..	..	..	..	..	..	..	..	..	..
3823	Metal & Wood working Machinery	..	..	..	..	..	..	..	..	..	..
3824	Special Industrial Machinery	3	3	..	..	..	..	..	..	..	..
3825	Office & Computing Machinery	..	..	..	..	..	..	..	..	..	..
3829	Machinery & Equipment, nec	..	..	..	..	..	..	..	..	..	..
383	Electrical Machinery	0	0	0	0	0	0	0	0	0	..
3831	Electrical Industrial Machinery	..	..	..	..	..	..	..	..	..	..
3832	Radio, TV & Communication Equipment	..	..	..	..	..	..	..	..	..	..
3833	Electrical Appliances & Housewares	..	..	..	..	..	..	..	..	..	..
3839	Electrical Apparatus, nec	..	..	..	..	..	..	..	..	..	..
384	Transport Equipment	82	66	59	59	70	70	65	64	57	..
3841	Shipbuilding & Repairing	82	66	59	59	70	70	65	64	57	..
3842	Railroad Equipment	..	..	..	..	..	..	..	..	..	..
3843	Motor Vehicles	..	..	..	..	..	..	..	..	..	..
3844	Motorcycles & Bicycles	..	..	..	..	..	..	..	..	..	..
3845	Aircraft	..	..	..	..	..	..	..	..	..	..
3849	Transport Equipment, nec	..	..	..	..	..	..	..	..	..	..
385	Professional Goods	0	0	0	0	0	0	0	0	0	..
3851	Professional Equipment	..	..	..	..	..	..	..	..	..	..
3852	Photographic & Optical Goods	..	..	..	..	..	..	..	..	..	..
3853	Watches & Clocks	..	..	..	..	..	..	..	..	..	..
39	**Other Manufacturing, nes**	130	137	129	145	144	158	157	174	153	..
3901	Jewellery	35	35	36	40	33	34	33	39	35	..
3	**Total Manufacturing**	2 727	2 642	2 487	2 489	2 477	2 532	2 578	2 720	2 736	..
1	**Agric., Hunting, Forestry, Fishing**	9 373	8 691	7 419	7 049	7 275	7 055	6 423	6 344	6 177	..
2	**Mining & Quarrying**	..	..	..	..	..	..	..	..	..	..
21	Coal Mining	..	..	..	..	..	..	..	..	..	..
22	Crude Petroleum & Natural Gas	..	..	..	..	..	..	..	..	..	..
23.29	Other Mining	..	..	..	..	..	..	..	..	..	..
3	**Total Manufacturing**	2 727	2 642	2 487	2 489	2 477	2 532	2 578	2 720	2 736	..
4	**Electricity, Gas & Water**	51	44	41	42	44	44	43	41	42	..
5	**Construction**	4 239	4 416	4 725	4 399	4 229	4 168	4 252	4 201	4 270	..
6.9	**Services**	15 138	16 275	19 043	19 015	17 831	18 598	19 005	20 368	21 083	..
0000	**Grand Total**	31 528	32 068	33 715	32 994	31 856	32 397	32 301	33 674	34 308	..

Note: National accounts figures for Iceland were revised in 1994. See Sources and Definitions.
ISIC 3511 includes 3512.

Table IC.7 **ICELAND**

Millions of IKr

(Current Prices)

ISIC2	Industry	EXPORTS									
		1987	1988	1989	1990	1991	1992	1993	1994	1995	1996
31	**Food, Beverages & Tobacco**	40 226	34 972	44 744	55 008	56 401	54 317	57 543	65 636	66 078	74 183
311.2	Food	40 226	34 972	44 729	54 907	56 229	54 133	57 320	65 155	65 888	74 004
313	Beverages	0	0	15	102	171	185	223	482	190	178
314	Tobacco	0	0	0	0	0	0	0	0	0	
32	**Textiles, Apparel & Leather**	2 084	1 808	2 355	2 227	1 885	1 576	1 409	1 652	2 055	2 295
321	Textiles	1 345	1 093	1 228	991	869	603	553	612	829	817
3213	Knitting Mills	926	796	909	685	644	383	293	310	276	251
322	Wearing Apparel	85	50	63	73	66	45	42	33	45	56
323	Leather & Products	654	665	1 062	1 162	950	926	814	1 006	1 179	1 420
324	Footwear	0	0	2	1	0	3	1	0	2	2
33	**Wood Products & Furniture**	11	25	18	4	5	3	15	174	107	18
331	Wood Products	0	0	0	0	1	1	1	2	3	3
332	Furnitures & Fixtures	11	25	18	4	4	2	13	172	104	15
34	**Paper, Paper Products & Printing**	42	58	99	111	97	100	156	184	223	296
341	Paper & Products	36	52	85	82	66	71	87	115	165	245
3411	Pulp, Paper & Board	36	52	85	82	66	71	87	115	165	245
342	Printing & Publishing	6	6	14	28	31	30	69	68	58	51
35	**Chemical Products**	400	513	563	722	615	609	688	865	1 655	1 532
351	Industrial Chemicals	296	357	394	486	421	392	421	560	722	620
3511	Basic Industrial Chemicals	296	357	394	486	421	392	421	560	722	620
3512	Fertilizers & Pesticides	..	..	..	..	..	..	..	..	..	..
3513	Synthetic Resins	0	0	0	0	0	0	0	0	0	
352	Other Chemicals	2	14	12	42	17	30	53	41	613	473
3521	Paints, Varnishes & Lacquers	1	2	3	3	3	1	2	1	1	3
3522	Drugs & Medicines	0	0	0	0	0	0	0	0	0	..
3523	Soap & Cleaning Preparations	1	13	9	39	14	29	51	40	613	470
3529	Chemical Products, nec	0	0	0	0	0	0	0	0	0	..
353	Petroleum Refineries	0	0	0	0	0	0	0	0	0	
354	Petroleum & Coal Products	0	0	0	0	0	0	0	0	0	..
355	Rubber Products	0	0	0	0	0	0	0	0	0	..
356	Plastic Products, nec	102	142	158	194	178	187	214	264	320	439
36	**Non-Metallic Mineral Products**	161	144	159	171	161	179	202	623	803	532
361	Pottery, China etc	4	3	3	2	1	1	1	1	0	1
362	Glass & Products	0	1	0	0		0	0		2	9
369	Non-Metallic Products, nec	157	140	155	169	160	178	201	622	801	521
37	**Basic Metal Industries**	6 602	9 149	13 515	12 306	10 127	10 037	10 947	13 905	15 946	16 266
371	Iron & Steel	1 473	2 418	3 027	2 430	1 765	1 659	2 361	2 689	3 213	3 814
372	Non-Ferrous Metals	5 129	6 731	10 489	9 875	8 363	8 378	8 587	11 216	12 733	12 452
38	**Fabricated Metal Products**	544	864	1 631	1 165	793	983	1 751	2 338	3 402	2 584
381	Metal Products	276	428	432	569	617	457	600	816	1 193	974
3813	Structural Metal Products	..	..	..	..	..	..	..	..	..	..
382	Non-Electrical Machinery	0	0	0	0	0	0	0	0	0	..
3821	Engines & Turbines	..	..	..	..	..	..	..	..	..	..
3822	Agricultural Machinery	..	..	..	..	..	..	..	..	..	..
3823	Metal & Wood working Machinery	..	..	..	..	..	..	..	..	..	..
3824	Special Industrial Machinery	..	..	..	..	..	..	..	..	..	..
3825	Office & Computing Machinery	..	..	..	..	..	..	..	..	..	..
3829	Machinery & Equipment, nec	..	..	..	..	..	..	..	..	..	..
383	Electrical Machinery	0	0	0	0	0	0	0	0	0	..
3831	Electrical Industrial Machinery	..	..	..	..	..	..	..	..	..	..
3832	Radio, TV & Communication Equipment	..	..	..	..	..	..	..	..	..	..
3833	Electrical Appliances & Housewares	..	..	..	..	..	..	..	..	..	..
3839	Electrical Apparatus, nec	..	..	..	..	..	..	..	..	..	..
384	Transport Equipment	269	435	1 199	596	176	526	1 151	1 523	2 209	1 610
3841	Shipbuilding & Repairing	269	435	1 199	596	176	526	1 151	1 523	2 209	1 610
3842	Railroad Equipment	..	..	..	..	..	..	..	..	..	..
3843	Motor Vehicles	..	..	..	..	..	..	..	..	..	..
3844	Motorcycles & Bicycles	..	..	..	..	..	..	..	..	..	..
3845	Aircraft	..	..	..	..	..	..	..	..	..	..
3849	Transport Equipment, nec	..	..	..	..	..	..	..	..	..	..
385	Professional Goods	0	0	0	0	0	0	0	0	0	..
3851	Professional Equipment	..	..	..	..	..	..	..	..	..	..
3852	Photographic & Optical Goods	..	..	..	..	..	..	..	..	..	..
3853	Watches & Clocks	..	..	..	..	..	..	..	..	..	..
39	**Other Manufacturing, nes**	349	2 110	458	810	129	202	279	2 257	2 262	3 002
3901	Jewellery	0	0	1	1	1	0	1	1	1	..
3	**Total Manufacturing**	50 418	49 642	63 543	72 522	70 214	68 006	72 989	87 633	92 531	100 708
1	**Agric., Hunting, Forestry, Fishing**	2 147	11 405	15 434	19 055	20 376	18 764	20 355	23 581	22 132	22 447
2	**Mining & Quarrying**	..	..	..	..	..	..	..	..	..	..
21	Coal Mining	..	..	..	..	..	..	..	..	..	..
22	Crude Petroleum & Natural Gas	..	..	..	..	..	..	..	..	..	..
23.29	Other Mining	..	..	..	..	..	..	..	..	..	..
3	**Total Manufacturing**	50 418	49 642	63 543	72 522	70 214	68 006	72 989	87 633	92 531	100 708
4	**Electricity, Gas & Water**	..	..	..	..	..	..	..	..	..	..
5	**Construction**	..	..	..	..	..	..	..	..	..	..
6.9	**Services**	413	620	1 094	1 048	971	1 076	1 226	1 439	1 945	2 535
0000	**Grand Total**	52 978	61 667	80 072	92 625	91 561	87 847	94 570	112 654	116 607	125 690

Note: National accounts figures for Iceland were revised in 1994. See Sources and Definitions.
ISIC 3511 includes 3512.
Data from 1988 onwards are not directly comparable with those for previous years due to a change in the tariff codification.

Millions of NZ$ (Current Prices)

ISIC2	Industry	PRODUCTION									
		1986-87	1987-88	1988-89	1989-90	1990-91	1991-92	1992-93	1993-94	1994-95	1995-96
31	**Food, Beverages & Tobacco**	9 984	11 094	12 283	13 147	13 582	14 664	15 571	16 635	..	..
311.2	Food	8 364	9 189	10 329	10 954	11 350	12 513	13 224	14 229	..	..
313	Beverages	1 620	1 905	1 954	2 193	2 232	2 151	2 347	2 406	..	..
314	Tobacco	..	..	..	..	..	..	..	..	..	..
32	**Textiles, Apparel & Leather**	2 944	2 979	2 804	2 783	2 419	2 475	2 527	2 583	..	..
321	Textiles	..	..	..	..	..	..	..	..	..	..
3213	Knitting Mills	..	..	..	..	..	..	..	..	..	..
322	Wearing Apparel	..	..	..	..	..	..	..	..	..	..
323	Leather & Products	..	..	..	..	..	..	..	..	..	..
324	Footwear	..	..	..	..	..	..	..	..	..	..
33	**Wood Products & Furniture**	2 160	2 109	2 041	2 069	2 099	2 196	2 476	3 284	..	..
331	Wood Products	..	..	..	..	..	..	..	..	..	..
332	Furnitures & Fixtures	..	..	..	..	..	..	..	..	..	..
34	**Paper, Paper Products & Printing**	3 663	4 352	4 406	4 712	4 848	4 731	4 675	5 031	..	..
341	Paper & Products	1 855	2 280	2 306	2 540	2 653	2 581	2 493	2 633	..	..
3411	Pulp, Paper & Board	..	..	..	..	..	..	..	..	..	..
342	Printing & Publishing	1 808	2 072	2 100	2 172	2 195	2 150	2 182	2 398	..	..
35	**Chemical Products**	4 274	3 975	4 178	4 492	4 187	4 164	4 501	5 017	..	..
351	Industrial Chemicals	2 006	1 639	1 744	1 982	1 676	1 660	1 875	2 145	..	..
3511	Basic Industrial Chemicals	..	..	..	..	..	..	..	..	..	..
3512	Fertilizers & Pesticides	..	..	..	..	..	..	..	..	..	..
3513	Synthetic Resins	..	..	..	..	..	..	..	..	..	..
352	Other Chemicals	2 268	2 336	2 434	2 510	2 511	2 504	2 626	2 872	..	..
3521	Paints, Varnishes & Lacquers	..	..	..	..	..	..	..	..	..	..
3522	Drugs & Medicines	..	..	..	..	..	..	..	..	..	..
3523	Soap & Cleaning Preparations	..	..	..	..	..	..	..	..	..	..
3529	Chemical Products, nec	..	..	..	..	..	..	..	..	..	..
353	Petroleum Refineries	..	..	..	..	..	..	..	..	..	..
354	Petroleum & Coal Products	..	..	..	..	..	..	..	..	..	..
355	Rubber Products	..	..	..	..	..	..	..	..	..	..
356	Plastic Products, nec	..	..	..	..	..	..	..	..	..	..
36	**Non-Metallic Mineral Products**	1 212	1 186	1 193	1 157	1 158	1 081	1 222	1 291	..	..
361	Pottery, China etc	..	..	..	..	..	..	..	..	..	..
362	Glass & Products	..	..	..	..	..	..	..	..	..	..
369	Non-Metallic Products, nec	..	..	..	..	..	..	..	..	..	..
37	**Basic Metal Industries**	1 266	1 110	1 259	1 449	1 405	1 450	1 587	1 640	..	..
371	Iron & Steel	..	..	..	..	..	..	..	..	..	..
372	Non-Ferrous Metals	..	..	..	..	..	..	..	..	..	..
38	**Fabricated Metal Products**	7 666	7 951	7 460	7 921	7 154	6 703	7 283	8 259	..	..
381	Metal Products	2 430	2 393	2 338	2 533	2 373	2 191	2 325	2 661	..	..
3813	Structural Metal Products	..	..	..	..	..	..	..	..	..	..
382	Non-Electrical Machinery	3 118	3 147	2 825	3 035	2 933	2 922	3 159	3 634	..	..
3821	Engines & Turbines	..	..	..	..	..	..	..	..	..	..
3822	Agricultural Machinery	..	..	..	..	..	..	..	..	..	..
3823	Metal & Wood working Machinery	..	..	..	..	..	..	..	..	..	..
3824	Special Industrial Machinery	..	..	..	..	..	..	..	..	..	..
3825	Office & Computing Machinery	..	..	..	..	..	..	..	..	..	..
3829	Machinery & Equipment, nec	..	..	..	..	..	..	..	..	..	..
383	Electrical Machinery	..	..	..	..	..	..	..	..	..	..
3831	Electrical Industrial Machinery	..	..	..	..	..	..	..	..	..	..
3832	Radio, TV & Communication Equipment	..	..	..	..	..	..	..	..	..	..
3833	Electrical Appliances & Housewares	..	..	..	..	..	..	..	..	..	..
3839	Electrical Apparatus, nec	..	..	..	..	..	..	..	..	..	..
384	Transport Equipment	2 118	2 411	2 297	2 353	1 848	1 590	1 799	1 964	..	..
3841	Shipbuilding & Repairing	..	..	..	..	..	..	..	..	..	..
3842	Railroad Equipment	..	..	..	..	..	..	..	..	..	..
3843	Motor Vehicles	..	..	..	..	..	..	..	..	..	..
3844	Motorcycles & Bicycles	..	..	..	..	..	..	..	..	..	..
3845	Aircraft	..	..	..	..	..	..	..	..	..	..
3849	Transport Equipment, nec	..	..	..	..	..	..	..	..	..	..
385	Professional Goods	..	..	..	..	..	..	..	..	..	..
3851	Professional Equipment	..	..	..	..	..	..	..	..	..	..
3852	Photographic & Optical Goods	..	..	..	..	..	..	..	..	..	..
3853	Watches & Clocks	..	..	..	..	..	..	..	..	..	..
39	**Other Manufacturing, nes**	339	348	365	364	356	334	360	404	..	..
3901	Jewellery	..	..	..	..	..	..	..	..	..	..
3	**Total Manufacturing**	33 508	35 104	35 989	38 094	37 208	37 798	40 202	44 144	..	..
1	**Agric., Hunting, Forestry, Fishing**	8 325	8 961	10 075	11 133	10 679	11 649	12 726	14 143	..	..
2	**Mining & Quarrying**	1 507	1 398	1 286	1 358	1 638	1 667	1 816	1 770	..	..
21	Coal Mining	..	..	..	..	..	..	..	..	..	..
22	Crude Petroleum & Natural Gas	1 032	976	869	829	1 111	1 089	1 207	1 111	..	..
23.29	Other Mining	475	422	417	529	527	578	609	659	..	..
3	**Total Manufacturing**	33 508	35 104	35 989	38 094	37 208	37 798	40 202	44 144	..	..
4	**Electricity, Gas & Water**	3 414	3 744	4 088	4 261	4 320	4 504	4 573	4 764	..	..
5	**Construction**	10 486	11 325	11 267	11 698	10 928	9 512	9 508	10 375	..	..
6.9	**Services**	48 693	53 419	56 504	58 381	59 329	59 154	62 134	66 949	..	..
0000	**Grand Total**	105 933	113 951	119 209	124 925	124 102	124 284	130 959	142 145	..	..

Millions of NZ$ (Current Prices)

ISIC2	Industry	VALUE ADDED									
		1986–87	1987–88	1988–89	1989–90	1990–91	1991–92	1992–93	1993–94	1994–95	1995–96
31	**Food, Beverages & Tobacco**	3 294	3 593	3 910	4 015	4 259	4 442	4 389	4 526	..	..
311.2	Food	2 446	2 391	2 675	2 627	2 862	3 048	2 957	3 063	..	..
313	Beverages	848	1 202	1 235	1 388	1 397	1 394	1 432	1 463	..	..
314	Tobacco	..	..	..	..	..	..	..	..	..	..
32	**Textiles, Apparel & Leather**	982	923	800	864	817	813	803	824	..	..
321	Textiles	..	..	..	..	..	..	..	..	..	..
3213	Knitting Mills	..	..	..	..	..	..	..	..	..	..
322	Wearing Apparel	..	..	..	..	..	..	..	..	..	..
323	Leather & Products	..	..	..	..	..	..	..	..	..	..
324	Footwear	..	..	..	..	..	..	..	..	..	..
33	**Wood Products & Furniture**	749	700	716	752	720	723	866	1 030	..	..
331	Wood Products	..	..	..	..	..	..	..	..	..	..
332	Furnitures & Fixtures	..	..	..	..	..	..	..	..	..	..
34	**Paper, Paper Products & Printing**	1 356	1 661	1 672	1 827	1 965	1 933	1 886	1 983	..	..
341	Paper & Products	540	757	733	842	959	932	869	875	..	..
3411	Pulp, Paper & Board	..	..	..	..	..	..	..	..	..	..
342	Printing & Publishing	816	904	939	985	1 006	1 001	1 017	1 108	..	..
35	**Chemical Products**	1 752	1 503	1 604	1 776	1 490	1 482	1 575	1 796	..	..
351	Industrial Chemicals	982	750	837	951	628	576	649	809	..	..
3511	Basic Industrial Chemicals	..	..	..	..	..	..	..	..	..	..
3512	Fertilizers & Pesticides	..	..	..	..	..	..	..	..	..	..
3513	Synthetic Resins	..	..	..	..	..	..	..	..	..	..
352	Other Chemicals	770	753	767	825	862	906	926	987	..	..
3521	Paints, Varnishes & Lacquers	..	..	..	..	..	..	..	..	..	..
3522	Drugs & Medicines	..	..	..	..	..	..	..	..	..	..
3523	Soap & Cleaning Preparations	..	..	..	..	..	..	..	..	..	..
3529	Chemical Products, nec	..	..	..	..	..	..	..	..	..	..
353	Petroleum Refineries	..	..	..	..	..	..	..	..	..	..
354	Petroleum & Coal Products	..	..	..	..	..	..	..	..	..	..
355	Rubber Products	..	..	..	..	..	..	..	..	..	..
356	Plastic Products, nec	..	..	..	..	..	..	..	..	..	..
36	**Non-Metallic Mineral Products**	418	405	427	413	424	381	417	491	..	..
361	Pottery, China etc	..	..	..	..	..	..	..	..	..	..
362	Glass & Products	..	..	..	..	..	..	..	..	..	..
369	Non-Metallic Products, nec	..	..	..	..	..	..	..	..	..	..
37	**Basic Metal Industries**	342	257	255	460	424	477	671	645	..	..
371	Iron & Steel	..	..	..	..	..	..	..	..	..	..
372	Non-Ferrous Metals	..	..	..	..	..	..	..	..	..	..
38	**Fabricated Metal Products**	2 670	2 792	2 694	2 840	2 606	2 535	2 653	3 049	..	..
381	Metal Products	848	844	829	967	891	808	884	1 085	..	..
3813	Structural Metal Products	..	..	..	..	..	..	..	..	..	..
382	Non-Electrical Machinery	1 163	1 155	1 098	1 152	1 061	1 151	1 230	1 455	..	..
3821	Engines & Turbines	..	..	..	..	..	..	..	..	..	..
3822	Agricultural Machinery	..	..	..	..	..	..	..	..	..	..
3823	Metal & Wood working Machinery	..	..	..	..	..	..	..	..	..	..
3824	Special Industrial Machinery	..	..	..	..	..	..	..	..	..	..
3825	Office & Computing Machinery	..	..	..	..	..	..	..	..	..	..
3829	Machinery & Equipment, nec	..	..	..	..	..	..	..	..	..	..
383	Electrical Machinery	..	..	..	..	..	..	..	..	..	..
3831	Electrical Industrial Machinery	..	..	..	..	..	..	..	..	..	..
3832	Radio, TV & Communication Equipment	..	..	..	..	..	..	..	..	..	..
3833	Electrical Appliances & Housewares	..	..	..	..	..	..	..	..	..	..
3839	Electrical Apparatus, nec	..	..	..	..	..	..	..	..	..	..
384	Transport Equipment	659	793	767	721	654	576	539	509	..	..
3841	Shipbuilding & Repairing	..	..	..	..	..	..	..	..	..	..
3842	Railroad Equipment	..	..	..	..	..	..	..	..	..	..
3843	Motor Vehicles	..	..	..	..	..	..	..	..	..	..
3844	Motorcycles & Bicycles	..	..	..	..	..	..	..	..	..	..
3845	Aircraft	..	..	..	..	..	..	..	..	..	..
3849	Transport Equipment, nec	..	..	..	..	..	..	..	..	..	..
385	Professional Goods	..	..	..	..	..	..	..	..	..	..
3851	Professional Equipment	..	..	..	..	..	..	..	..	..	..
3852	Photographic & Optical Goods	..	..	..	..	..	..	..	..	..	..
3853	Watches & Clocks	..	..	..	..	..	..	..	..	..	..
39	**Other Manufacturing, nes**	122	128	144	151	142	122	136	156	..	..
3901	Jewellery	..	..	..	..	..	..	..	..	..	..
3	**Total Manufacturing**	11 685	11 962	12 222	13 098	12 847	12 908	13 396	14 500	..	..
1	**Agric., Hunting, Forestry, Fishing**	3 694	4 271	4 890	5 355	4 922	5 598	5 667	6 673	..	..
2	**Mining & Quarrying**	621	597	643	837	1 004	1 082	1 107	1 121	..	..
21	Coal Mining	..	..	..	..	..	..	..	..	..	..
22	Crude Petroleum & Natural Gas	405	413	488	618	788	831	804	787	..	..
23.29	Other Mining	216	184	155	219	216	251	303	334	..	..
3	**Total Manufacturing**	11 685	11 962	12 222	13 098	12 847	12 908	13 396	14 500	..	..
4	**Electricity, Gas & Water**	1 723	1 757	1 991	2 133	2 086	2 107	2 125	2 228	..	..
5	**Construction**	2 806	2 943	2 997	3 217	2 802	2 389	2 324	2 289	..	..
6.9	**Services**	23 870	26 729	28 994	29 620	30 820	30 185	31 308	34 333	..	..
0000	**Grand Total**	44 399	48 259	51 737	54 260	54 481	54 269	55 927	61 144	..	..

Note: ISIC 313 includes 314. ISIC 351 includes 353 and 354; 352 includes 355 and 356. ISIC 382 includes 383 and 385.

Millions of NZ$ (Current Prices)

ISIC2	Industry	WAGES & SALARIES + SUPPLEMENTS									
		1986–87	1987–88	1988–89	1989–90	1990–91	1991–92	1992–93	1993–94	1994–95	1995–96
31	**Food, Beverages & Tobacco**	1 710	1 756	1 786	1 789	1 927	2 037	2 022	2 024	..	..
311.2	Food	1 583	1 610	1 647	1 646	1 767	1 881	1 866	1 864	..	..
313	Beverages	127	146	139	143	160	156	156	160	..	..
314	Tobacco	..	..	..	..	..	..	..	..	..	..
32	**Textiles, Apparel & Leather**	661	653	597	600	528	535	539	529	..	..
321	Textiles	..	..	..	..	..	..	..	..	..	..
3213	Knitting Mills	..	..	..	..	..	..	..	..	..	..
322	Wearing Apparel	..	..	..	..	..	..	..	..	..	..
323	Leather & Products	..	..	..	..	..	..	..	..	..	..
324	Footwear	..	..	..	..	..	..	..	..	..	..
33	**Wood Products & Furniture**	479	500	489	503	502	483	531	617	..	..
331	Wood Products	..	..	..	..	..	..	..	..	..	..
332	Furnitures & Fixtures	..	..	..	..	..	..	..	..	..	..
34	**Paper, Paper Products & Printing**	851	951	998	1 018	1 102	1 037	1 052	1 121	..	..
341	Paper & Products	348	402	359	387	428	418	410	433	..	..
3411	Pulp, Paper & Board	..	..	..	..	..	..	..	..	..	..
342	Printing & Publishing	503	549	639	631	674	619	642	688	..	..
35	**Chemical Products**	642	708	693	751	756	765	780	811	..	..
351	Industrial Chemicals	197	223	226	236	242	238	243	261	..	..
3511	Basic Industrial Chemicals	..	..	..	..	..	..	..	..	..	..
3512	Fertilizers & Pesticides	..	..	..	..	..	..	..	..	..	..
3513	Synthetic Resins	..	..	..	..	..	..	..	..	..	..
352	Other Chemicals	445	485	467	515	514	527	537	550	..	..
3521	Paints, Varnishes & Lacquers	..	..	..	..	..	..	..	..	..	..
3522	Drugs & Medicines	..	..	..	..	..	..	..	..	..	..
3523	Soap & Cleaning Preparations	..	..	..	..	..	..	..	..	..	..
3529	Chemical Products, nec	..	..	..	..	..	..	..	..	..	..
353	Petroleum Refineries	..	..	..	..	..	..	..	..	..	..
354	Petroleum & Coal Products	..	..	..	..	..	..	..	..	..	..
355	Rubber Products	..	..	..	..	..	..	..	..	..	..
356	Plastic Products, nec	..	..	..	..	..	..	..	..	..	..
36	**Non-Metallic Mineral Products**	236	245	240	227	231	206	229	238	..	..
361	Pottery, China etc	..	..	..	..	..	..	..	..	..	..
362	Glass & Products	..	..	..	..	..	..	..	..	..	..
369	Non-Metallic Products, nec	..	..	..	..	..	..	..	..	..	..
37	**Basic Metal Industries**	220	239	288	313	336	325	302	294	..	..
371	Iron & Steel	..	..	..	..	..	..	..	..	..	..
372	Non-Ferrous Metals	..	..	..	..	..	..	..	..	..	..
38	**Fabricated Metal Products**	1 692	1 823	1 697	1 696	1 628	1 536	1 535	1 721	..	..
381	Metal Products	535	611	594	601	573	523	557	631	..	..
3813	Structural Metal Products	..	..	..	..	..	..	..	..	..	..
382	Non-Electrical Machinery	729	757	677	664	647	644	658	741	..	..
3821	Engines & Turbines	..	..	..	..	..	..	..	..	..	..
3822	Agricultural Machinery	..	..	..	..	..	..	..	..	..	..
3823	Metal & Wood working Machinery	..	..	..	..	..	..	..	..	..	..
3824	Special Industrial Machinery	..	..	..	..	..	..	..	..	..	..
3825	Office & Computing Machinery	..	..	..	..	..	..	..	..	..	..
3829	Machinery & Equipment, nec	..	..	..	..	..	..	..	..	..	..
383	Electrical Machinery	..	..	..	..	..	..	..	..	..	..
3831	Electrical Industrial Machinery	..	..	..	..	..	..	..	..	..	..
3832	Radio, TV & Communication Equipment	..	..	..	..	..	..	..	..	..	..
3833	Electrical Appliances & Housewares	..	..	..	..	..	..	..	..	..	..
3839	Electrical Apparatus, nec	..	..	..	..	..	..	..	..	..	..
384	Transport Equipment	428	455	426	431	408	369	320	349	..	..
3841	Shipbuilding & Repairing	..	..	..	..	..	..	..	..	..	..
3842	Railroad Equipment	..	..	..	..	..	..	..	..	..	..
3843	Motor Vehicles	..	..	..	..	..	..	..	..	..	..
3844	Motorcycles & Bicycles	..	..	..	..	..	..	..	..	..	..
3845	Aircraft	..	..	..	..	..	..	..	..	..	..
3849	Transport Equipment, nec	..	..	..	..	..	..	..	..	..	..
385	Professional Goods	..	..	..	..	..	..	..	..	..	..
3851	Professional Equipment	..	..	..	..	..	..	..	..	..	..
3852	Photographic & Optical Goods	..	..	..	..	..	..	..	..	..	..
3853	Watches & Clocks	..	..	..	..	..	..	..	..	..	..
39	**Other Manufacturing, nes**	61	69	70	79	71	64	68	81	..	..
3901	Jewellery	..	..	..	..	..	..	..	..	..	..
3	**Total Manufacturing**	6 552	6 944	6 858	6 976	7 081	6 988	7 058	7 436	..	..
1	**Agric., Hunting, Forestry, Fishing**	805	814	901	1 037	1 051	1 066	1 148	1 221	..	..
2	**Mining & Quarrying**	183	174	167	158	170	154	192	179	..	..
21	Coal Mining	..	..	..	..	..	..	..	..	..	..
22	Crude Petroleum & Natural Gas	64	77	67	52	63	46	67	66	..	..
23.29	Other Mining	119	97	100	106	107	108	125	113	..	..
3	**Total Manufacturing**	6 552	6 944	6 858	6 976	7 081	6 988	7 058	7 436	..	..
4	**Electricity, Gas & Water**	479	558	564	549	543	511	499	467	..	..
5	**Construction**	1 535	1 614	1 656	1 705	1 591	1 559	1 469	1 493	..	..
6.9	**Services**	10 795	12 710	13 453	13 820	13 974	13 782	14 306	14 974	..	..
0000	**Grand Total**	20 349	22 814	23 599	24 245	24 410	24 060	24 672	25 770	..	..

Millions of SF (Current Prices)

ISIC2	Industry	PRODUCTION									
		1987	1988	1989	1990	1991	1992	1993	1994	1995	1996
31	**Food, Beverages & Tobacco**	24 532	24 551	25 197	26 421	27 310	26 935	27 300	28 395	29 162	28 851
311.2	Food	..	..	..	..	..	..	..	..	..	..
313	Beverages	..	..	..	..	..	..	..	..	..	..
314	Tobacco	..	..	..	..	..	..	..	..	..	..
32	**Textiles, Apparel & Leather**	7 127	7 112	6 956	7 073	6 755	6 579	5 919	5 746	6 800	6 809
321	Textiles	4 693	4 770	4 910	4 786	4 471	4 259	3 760	3 798	3 897	3 657
3213	Knitting Mills	..	..	..	..	..	..	..	..	..	..
322	Wearing Apparel	2 434	2 342	2 046	2 287	2 284	2 320	2 159	1 948	2 903	3 152
323	Leather & Products	..	..	..	..	..	..	..	..	..	..
324	Footwear	..	..	..	..	..	..	..	..	..	..
33	**Wood Products & Furniture**	11 511	12 125	12 434	14 233	14 048	13 540	13 290	14 224	14.939	13 946
331	Wood Products	..	..	..	..	..	..	..	..	..	..
332	Furnitures & Fixtures	..	..	..	..	..	..	..	..	..	..
34	**Paper, Paper Products & Printing**	13 725	14 384	14 760	15 595	15 148	14 583	13 822	13 881	15 070	14 649
341	Paper & Products	3 889	3 939	4 194	4 349	4 167	4 124	3 889	4 019	4 535	3 860
3411	Pulp, Paper & Board	..	..	..	..	..	..	..	..	..	..
342	Printing & Publishing	9 836	10 445	10 566	11 246	10 981	10 459	9 933	9 862	10 535	10 789
35	**Chemical Products**	24 451	28 125	31 886	33 442	34 229	35 443	36 574	40 405	44 746	46 717
351	Industrial Chemicals	20 080	23 057	26 523	27 564	28 475	29 527	31 099	34 442	37 910	40 319
3511	Basic Industrial Chemicals	..	..	..	..	..	..	..	..	..	..
3512	Fertilizers & Pesticides	..	..	..	..	..	..	..	..	..	..
3513	Synthetic Resins	..	..	..	..	..	..	..	..	..	..
352	Other Chemicals	..	..	..	..	..	..	..	..	..	..
3521	Paints, Varnishes & Lacquers	..	..	..	..	..	..	..	..	..	..
3522	Drugs & Medicines	..	..	..	..	..	..	..	..	..	..
3523	Soap & Cleaning Preparations	..	..	..	..	..	..	..	..	..	..
3529	Chemical Products, nec	..	..	..	..	..	..	..	..	..	..
353	Petroleum Refineries	..	..	..	..	..	..	..	..	..	..
354	Petroleum & Coal Products	..	..	..	..	..	..	..	..	..	..
355	Rubber Products	4 371	5 068	5 363	5 878	5 754	5 916	5 475	5 963	6 836	6 398
356	Plastic Products, nec	..	..	..	..	..	..	..	..	..	..
36	**Non-Metallic Mineral Products**	5 837	6 366	6 818	7 560	7 241	6 996	6 612	7 294	7 164	6 841
361	Pottery, China etc	..	..	..	..	..	..	..	..	..	..
362	Glass & Products	..	..	..	..	..	..	..	..	..	..
369	Non-Metallic Products, nec	..	..	..	..	..	..	..	..	..	..
37	**Basic Metal Industries**	17 501	21 303	23 066	22 636	21 525	20 560	20 547	21 069	23 482	21 127
371	Iron & Steel	..	..	..	..	..	..	..	..	..	..
372	Non-Ferrous Metals	..	..	..	..	..	..	..	..	..	..
38	**Fabricated Metal Products**	48 754	53 558	54 961	60 874	59 192	57 728	54 933	58 586	57 751	57 799
381	Metal Products	..	..	..	..	..	..	..	..	..	..
3813	Structural Metal Products	..	..	..	..	..	..	..	..	..	..
382	Non-Electrical Machinery	25 819	28 135	28 660	31 263	29 996	29 230	26 890	28 678	27 525	26 463
3821	Engines & Turbines	..	..	..	..	..	..	..	..	..	..
3822	Agricultural Machinery	..	..	..	..	..	..	..	..	..	..
3823	Metal & Wood working Machinery	..	..	..	..	..	..	..	..	..	..
3824	Special Industrial Machinery	..	..	..	..	..	..	..	..	..	..
3825	Office & Computing Machinery	..	..	..	..	..	..	..	..	..	..
3829	Machinery & Equipment, nec	..	..	..	..	..	..	..	..	..	..
383	Electrical Machinery	22 935	25 423	26 301	29 611	29 196	28 498	28 043	29 908	30 226	31 336
3831	Electrical Industrial Machinery	..	..	..	..	..	..	..	..	..	..
3832	Radio, TV & Communication Equipment	..	..	..	..	..	..	..	..	..	..
3833	Electrical Appliances & Housewares	..	..	..	..	..	..	..	..	..	..
3839	Electrical Apparatus, nec	..	..	..	..	..	..	..	..	..	..
384	Transport Equipment	..	..	..	..	..	..	..	..	..	..
3841	Shipbuilding & Repairing	..	..	..	..	..	..	..	..	..	..
3842	Railroad Equipment	..	..	..	..	..	..	..	..	..	..
3843	Motor Vehicles	..	..	..	..	..	..	..	..	..	..
3844	Motorcycles & Bicycles	..	..	..	..	..	..	..	..	..	..
3845	Aircraft	..	..	..	..	..	..	..	..	..	..
3849	Transport Equipment, nec	..	..	..	..	..	..	..	..	..	..
385	Professional Goods	..	..	..	..	..	..	..	..	..	..
3851	Professional Equipment	..	..	..	..	..	..	..	..	..	..
3852	Photographic & Optical Goods	..	..	..	..	..	..	..	..	..	..
3853	Watches & Clocks	..	..	..	..	..	..	..	..	..	..
39	**Other Manufacturing, nes**	..	..	..	..	..	..	..	..	..	..
3901	Jewellery	7 904	8 912	10 067	10 124	9 968	10 429	10 848	11 558	13 152	13 843
3	**Total Manufacturing**	161 342	176 436	186 145	197 958	195 416	192 793	189 845	201 158	212 266	210 582
1	**Agric., Hunting, Forestry, Fishing**	16 691	16 770	17 957	18 085	18 463	18 236	18 208	18 145	17 493	15 044
2	**Mining & Quarrying**	..	..	..	..	..	..	..	..	..	..
21	Coal Mining	..	..	..	..	..	..	..	..	..	..
22	Crude Petroleum & Natural Gas	..	..	..	..	..	..	..	..	..	..
23.29	Other Mining	..	..	..	..	..	..	..	..	..	..
3	**Total Manufacturing**	161 342	176 436	186 145	197 958	195 416	192 793	189 845	201 158	212 266	210 582
4	**Electricity, Gas & Water**	15 947	16 760	16 695	18 795	19 723	19 736	19 249	21 145	21 240	20 591
5	**Construction**	37 450	41 516	46 452	50 380	49 571	46 277	44 524	46 766	45 677	41 640
6.9	**Services**	274 429	286 308	309 752	337 499	352 938	366 273	378 845	381 019	395 433	400 491
0000	**Grand Total**	505 859	537 790	577 001	622 717	636 111	643 315	650 671	668 233	692 109	688 348

Note: Data have been retabulated according to a modified industrial classification. For details see Sources and Definitions.

Table SW.2 **SWITZERLAND**

Millions of SF (Current Prices)

ISIC2	Industry	VALUE ADDED									
		1987	**1988**	**1989**	**1990**	**1991**	**1992**	**1993**	**1994**	**1995**	**1996**
31	**Food, Beverages & Tobacco**	6 330	6 435	6 707	7 141	7 595	7 703	7 851	8 003	8 384	8 266
311.2	Food	..	..	..	..	..	..	..	..	..	..
313	Beverages	..	..	..	..	..	..	..	..	..	..
314	Tobacco	..	..	..	..	..	..	..	..	..	..
32	**Textiles, Apparel & Leather**	2 835	2 851	2 814	2 887	2 751	2 652	2 427	2 361	2 755	2 745
321	Textiles	1 821	1 890	1 987	1 976	1 818	1 769	1 602	1 579	1 623	1 516
3213	Knitting Mills	..	..	..	..	..	..	..	..	..	..
322	Wearing Apparel	1 014	961	827	911	933	883	825	782	1 132	1 229
323	Leather & Products	..	..	..	..	..	..	..	..	..	..
324	Footwear	..	..	..	..	..	..	..	..	..	..
33	**Wood Products & Furniture**	4 877	5 107	5 206	5 925	6 093	5 859	5 633	6 025	6 289	5 857
331	Wood Products	..	..	..	..	..	..	..	..	..	..
332	Furnitures & Fixtures	..	..	..	..	..	..	..	..	..	..
34	**Paper, Paper Products & Printing**	6 110	6 428	6 581	6 973	6 932	6 786	6 459	6 353	6 880	6 777
341	Paper & Products	1 335	1 359	1 454	1 516	1 574	1 581	1 454	1 437	1 692	1 447
3411	Pulp, Paper & Board	..	..	..	..	..	..	..	..	..	..
342	Printing & Publishing	4 775	5 069	5 127	5 457	5 358	5 205	5 005	4 916	5 188	5 330
35	**Chemical Products**	8 872	10 286	11 645	12 140	12 304	13 120	13 522	15 281	16 007	16 608
351	Industrial Chemicals	7 113	8 244	9 482	9 766	9 897	10 670	11 273	12 723	13 149	13 953
3511	Basic Industrial Chemicals	..	..	..	..	..	..	..	..	..	..
3512	Fertilizers & Pesticides	..	..	..	..	..	..	..	..	..	..
3513	Synthetic Resins	..	..	..	..	..	..	..	..	..	..
352	Other Chemicals	..	..	..	..	..	..	..	..	..	..
3521	Paints, Varnishes & Lacquers	..	..	..	..	..	..	..	..	..	..
3522	Drugs & Medicines	..	..	..	..	..	..	..	..	..	..
3523	Soap & Cleaning Preparations	..	..	..	..	..	..	..	..	..	..
3529	Chemical Products, nec	..	..	..	..	..	..	..	..	..	..
353	Petroleum Refineries	..	..	..	..	..	..	..	..	..	..
354	Petroleum & Coal Products	..	..	..	..	..	..	..	..	..	..
355	Rubber Products	1 759	2 042	2 163	2 374	2 407	2 450	2 249	2 558	2 858	2 655
356	Plastic Products, nec	..	..	..	..	..	..	..	..	..	..
36	**Non-Metallic Mineral Products**	2 627	2 852	3 042	3 358	3 321	3 293	3 101	3 317	3 353	3 215
361	Pottery, China etc	..	..	..	..	..	..	..	..	..	..
362	Glass & Products	..	..	..	..	..	..	..	..	..	..
369	Non-Metallic Products, nec	..	..	..	..	..	..	..	..	..	..
37	**Basic Metal Industries**	6 013	7 453	8 214	8 203	8 251	8 019	7 996	8 011	9 111	8 239
371	Iron & Steel	..	..	..	..	..	..	..	..	..	..
372	Non-Ferrous Metals	..	..	..	..	..	..	..	..	..	..
38	**Fabricated Metal Products**	20 809	22 579	22 880	25 013	24 557	24 259	23 252	25 155	24 161	23 868
381	Metal Products	..	..	..	..	..	..	..	..	..	..
3813	Structural Metal Products	..	..	..	..	..	..	..	..	..	..
382	Non-Electrical Machinery	11 047	11 960	12 103	13 115	13 159	13 133	12 242	13 192	12 373	11 710
3821	Engines & Turbines	..	..	..	..	..	..	..	..	..	..
3822	Agricultural Machinery	..	..	..	..	..	..	..	..	..	..
3823	Metal & Wood working Machinery	..	..	..	..	..	..	..	..	..	..
3824	Special Industrial Machinery	..	..	..	..	..	..	..	..	..	..
3825	Office & Computing Machinery	..	..	..	..	..	..	..	..	..	..
3829	Machinery & Equipment, nec	..	..	..	..	..	..	..	..	..	..
383	Electrical Machinery	9 762	10 619	10 777	11 898	11 398	11 126	11 010	11 963	11 788	12 158
3831	Electrical Industrial Machinery	..	..	..	..	..	..	..	..	..	..
3832	Radio, TV & Communication Equipment	..	..	..	..	..	..	..	..	..	..
3833	Electrical Appliances & Housewares	..	..	..	..	..	..	..	..	..	..
3839	Electrical Apparatus, nec	..	..	..	..	..	..	..	..	..	..
384	Transport Equipment	..	..	..	..	..	..	..	..	..	..
3841	Shipbuilding & Repairing	..	..	..	..	..	..	..	..	..	..
3842	Railroad Equipment	..	..	..	..	..	..	..	..	..	..
3843	Motor Vehicles	..	..	..	..	..	..	..	..	..	..
3844	Motorcycles & Bicycles	..	..	..	..	..	..	..	..	..	..
3845	Aircraft	..	..	..	..	..	..	..	..	..	..
3849	Transport Equipment, nec	..	..	..	..	..	..	..	..	..	..
385	Professional Goods	..	..	..	..	..	..	..	..	..	..
3851	Professional Equipment	..	..	..	..	..	..	..	..	..	..
3852	Photographic & Optical Goods	..	..	..	..	..	..	..	..	..	..
3853	Watches & Clocks	..	..	..	..	..	..	..	..	..	..
39	**Other Manufacturing, nes**	..	..	..	..	..	..	..	..	..	..
3901	Jewellery	2 753	3 075	3 441	3 428	3 489	3 772	3 927	4 233	4 840	5 108
3	**Total Manufacturing**	61 226	67 066	70 530	75 068	75 293	75 463	74 168	78 739	81 780	80 683
1	**Agric., Hunting, Forestry, Fishing**	8 629	8 703	9 353	9 456	9 613	9 488	9 285	8 973	9 062	7 635
2	**Mining & Quarrying**	..	..	..	..	..	..	..	..	..	..
21	Coal Mining	..	..	..	..	..	..	..	..	..	..
22	Crude Petroleum & Natural Gas	..	..	..	..	..	..	..	..	..	..
23.29	Other Mining	..	..	..	..	..	..	..	..	..	..
3	**Total Manufacturing**	61 226	67 066	70 530	75 068	75 293	75 463	74 168	78 739	81 780	80 683
4	**Electricity, Gas & Water**	5 201	5 558	5 479	6 179	6 499	6 716	6 768	7 935	7 156	6 901
5	**Construction**	19 338	21 339	23 767	25 659	25 787	24 170	22 577	24 059	23 524	21 653
6.9	**Services**	162 784	170 059	184 186	200 942	216 470	226 526	236 999	237 518	243 041	246 941
0000	**Grand Total**	257 178	272 725	293 315	317 304	333 662	342 363	349 797	357 224	364 563	363 813

Note: Data have been retabulated according to a modified industrial classification. For details see Sources and Definitions.

Thousands

ISIC2	Industry	EMPLOYMENT									
		1987	**1988**	**1989**	**1990**	**1991**	**1992**	**1993**	**1994**	**1995**	**1996**
31	**Food, Beverages & Tobacco**	72.0	72.8	73.7	75.1	74.3	70.8	69.1	70.7	70.3	68.2
311.2	Food	..	..	..	..	..	..	..	..	..	..
313	Beverages	..	..	..	..	..	..	..	..	..	..
314	Tobacco	..	..	..	..	..	..	..	..	..	..
32	**Textiles, Apparel & Leather**	59.4	56.8	55.1	53.0	49.0	43.8	40.2	40.2	37.6	34.1
321	Textiles	33.0	31.9	31.4	31.0	29.0	26.6	24.3	23.8	22.3	19.8
3213	Knitting Mills	..	..	..	..	..	..	..	..	..	..
322	Wearing Apparel	26.4	24.9	23.7	22.0	20.0	17.2	15.9	16.4	15.3	14.3
323	Leather & Products	..	..	..	..	..	..	..	..	..	..
324	Footwear	..	..	..	..	..	..	..	..	..	..
33	**Wood Products & Furniture**	91.0	92.0	93.4	95.2	92.0	83.8	78.1	79.5	79.0	75.3
331	Wood Products	..	..	..	..	..	..	..	..	..	..
332	Furnitures & Fixtures	..	..	..	..	..	..	..	..	..	..
34	**Paper, Paper Products & Printing**	83.0	85.3	87.8	89.5	88.3	81.0	77.7	77.6	76.9	73.9
341	Paper & Products	16.7	16.8	16.9	16.9	16.8	16.1	15.7	15.2	15.3	14.9
3411	Pulp, Paper & Board	..	..	..	..	..	..	..	..	..	..
342	Printing & Publishing	66.3	68.5	70.9	72.6	71.5	64.9	62.0	62.4	61.6	59.0
35	**Chemical Products**	101.9	103.6	106.3	108.5	107.0	102.7	100.8	103.1	102.7	99.4
351	Industrial Chemicals	70.6	72.0	73.7	74.9	74.1	72.5	72.9	74.6	74.5	73.0
3511	Basic Industrial Chemicals	..	..	..	..	..	..	..	..	..	..
3512	Fertilizers & Pesticides	..	..	..	..	..	..	..	..	..	..
3513	Synthetic Resins	..	..	..	..	..	..	..	..	..	..
352	Other Chemicals	..	..	..	..	..	..	..	..	..	..
3521	Paints, Varnishes & Lacquers	..	..	..	..	..	..	..	..	..	..
3522	Drugs & Medicines	..	..	..	..	..	..	..	..	..	..
3523	Soap & Cleaning Preparations	..	..	..	..	..	..	..	..	..	..
3529	Chemical Products, nec	..	..	..	..	..	..	..	..	..	..
353	Petroleum Refineries	..	..	..	..	..	..	..	..	..	..
354	Petroleum & Coal Products	..	..	..	..	..	..	..	..	..	..
355	Rubber Products	31.3	31.6	32.6	33.6	32.9	30.2	27.9	28.5	28.2	26.4
356	Plastic Products, nec	..	..	..	..	..	..	..	..	..	..
36	**Non-Metallic Mineral Products**	32.0	32.2	33.2	33.8	33.0	31.3	29.7	30.3	30.1	27.9
361	Pottery, China etc	..	..	..	..	..	..	..	..	..	..
362	Glass & Products	..	..	..	..	..	..	..	..	..	..
369	Non-Metallic Products, nec	..	..	..	..	..	..	..	..	..	..
37	**Basic Metal Industries**	100.1	101.0	103.7	106.6	105.3	99.5	94.4	94.4	93.8	88.6
371	Iron & Steel	..	..	..	..	..	..	..	..	..	..
372	Non-Ferrous Metals	..	..	..	..	..	..	..	..	..	..
38	**Fabricated Metal Products**	294.7	292.4	292.9	293.1	288.8	269.7	258.0	251.4	250.1	245.0
381	Metal Products	..	..	..	..	..	..	..	..	..	..
3813	Structural Metal Products	..	..	..	..	..	..	..	..	..	..
382	Non-Electrical Machinery	162.8	161.8	162.3	160.8	160.9	150.7	142.6	136.9	136.9	132.3
3821	Engines & Turbines	..	..	..	..	..	..	..	..	..	..
3822	Agricultural Machinery	..	..	..	..	..	..	..	..	..	..
3823	Metal & Wood working Machinery	..	..	..	..	..	..	..	..	..	..
3824	Special Industrial Machinery	..	..	..	..	..	..	..	..	..	..
3825	Office & Computing Machinery	..	..	..	..	..	..	..	..	..	..
3829	Machinery & Equipment, nec	..	..	..	..	..	..	..	..	..	..
383	Electrical Machinery	131.9	130.6	130.6	132.3	127.9	119.0	115.4	114.5	113.2	112.7
3831	Electrical Industrial Machinery	..	..	..	..	..	..	..	..	..	..
3832	Radio, TV & Communication Equipment	..	..	..	..	..	..	..	..	..	..
3833	Electrical Appliances & Housewares	..	..	..	..	..	..	..	..	..	..
3839	Electrical Apparatus, nec	..	..	..	..	..	..	..	..	..	..
384	Transport Equipment	..	..	..	..	..	..	..	..	..	..
3841	Shipbuilding & Repairing	..	..	..	..	..	..	..	..	..	..
3842	Railroad Equipment	..	..	..	..	..	..	..	..	..	..
3843	Motor Vehicles	..	..	..	..	..	..	..	..	..	..
3844	Motorcycles & Bicycles	..	..	..	..	..	..	..	..	..	..
3845	Aircraft	..	..	..	..	..	..	..	..	..	..
3849	Transport Equipment, nec	..	..	..	..	..	..	..	..	..	..
385	Professional Goods	..	..	..	..	..	..	..	..	..	..
3851	Professional Equipment	..	..	..	..	..	..	..	..	..	..
3852	Photographic & Optical Goods	..	..	..	..	..	..	..	..	..	..
3853	Watches & Clocks	..	..	..	..	..	..	..	..	..	..
39	**Other Manufacturing, nes**	..	..	..	..	..	..	..	..	..	..
3901	Jewellery	34.4	34.9	36.8	38.8	37.7	35.8	35.0	36.5	36.9	35.4
3	**Total Manufacturing**	868.5	871.0	882.9	893.6	875.4	818.4	783.0	783.7	777.4	747.8
1	**Agric., Hunting, Forestry, Fishing**	186.9	177.2	168.3	162.3	154.8	148.1	150.8	145.5	155.8	170.7
2	**Mining & Quarrying**	..	..	..	..	..	..	..	..	..	..
21	Coal Mining	..	..	..	..	..	..	..	..	..	..
22	Crude Petroleum & Natural Gas	..	..	..	..	..	..	..	..	..	..
23.29	Other Mining	..	..	..	..	..	..	..	..	..	..
3	**Total Manufacturing**	868.5	871.0	882.9	893.6	875.4	818.4	783.0	783.7	777.4	747.8
4	**Electricity, Gas & Water**	31.7	32.8	34.2	35.6	36.5	37.0	36.8	37.6	37.6	36.3
5	**Construction**	315.6	313.9	312.4	309.0	294.6	282.7	283.2	281.0	286.6	281.3
6.9	**Services**	2 112.3	2 211.5	2 305.9	2 420.4	2 504.3	2 518.3	2 529.7	2 528.3	2 526.1	2 553.2
0000	**Grand Total**	3 515.0	3 606.4	3 703.7	3 820.9	3 865.6	3 804.5	3 783.5	3 776.1	3 783.5	3 789.3

Note: Data have been retabulated according to a modified industrial classification. For details see Sources and Definitions.

Millions of SF (1990 Prices)

ISIC2	Industry	PRODUCTION									
		1987	1988	1989	1990	1991	1992	1993	1994	1995	1996
31	**Food, Beverages & Tobacco**	25 955	25 832	26 175	26 462	26 634	26 247	26 346	27 133	28 172	27 760
311.2	Food	..	..	..	..	..	..	..	..	..	..
313	Beverages	..	..	..	..	..	..	..	..	..	..
314	Tobacco	..	..	..	..	..	..	..	..	..	..
32	**Textiles, Apparel & Leather**	8 123	7 710	7 320	7 083	6 787	6 642	6 019	5 742	5 615	5 293
321	Textiles	5 360	5 262	5 043	4 793	4 606	4 485	4 054	4 000	3 847	3 505
3213	Knitting Mills	..	..	..	..	..	..	..	..	..	..
322	Wearing Apparel	2 763	2 448	2 277	2 290	2 181	2 157	1 965	1 742	1 768	1 788
323	Leather & Products	..	..	..	..	..	..	..	..	..	..
324	Footwear	..	..	..	..	..	..	..	..	..	..
33	**Wood Products & Furniture**	12 937	13 074	13 416	14 255	13 675	13 078	12 725	13 318	13 125	12 571
331	Wood Products	..	..	..	..	..	..	..	..	..	..
332	Furnitures & Fixtures	..	..	..	..	..	..	..	..	..	..
34	**Paper, Paper Products & Printing**	14 916	15 332	15 377	15 620	14 672	13 942	12 951	12 607	13 189	12 795
341	Paper & Products	4 204	4 259	4 339	4 356	4 167	4 246	4 191	4 294	4 492	4 153
3411	Pulp, Paper & Board	..	..	..	..	..	..	..	..	..	..
342	Printing & Publishing	10 712	11 073	11 038	11 264	10 505	9 696	8 760	8 313	8 697	8 642
35	**Chemical Products**	28 080	31 003	32 640	33 492	33 994	35 417	36 499	41 499	46 157	48 886
351	Industrial Chemicals	23 276	25 766	27 173	27 605	28 354	29 698	31 273	35 854	39 845	42 970
3511	Basic Industrial Chemicals	..	..	..	..	..	..	..	..	..	..
3512	Fertilizers & Pesticides	..	..	..	..	..	..	..	..	..	..
3513	Synthetic Resins	..	..	..	..	..	..	..	..	..	..
352	Other Chemicals	..	..	..	..	..	..	..	..	..	..
3521	Paints, Varnishes & Lacquers	..	..	..	..	..	..	..	..	..	..
3522	Drugs & Medicines	..	..	..	..	..	..	..	..	..	..
3523	Soap & Cleaning Preparations	..	..	..	..	..	..	..	..	..	..
3529	Chemical Products, nec	..	..	..	..	..	..	..	..	..	..
353	Petroleum Refineries	..	..	..	..	..	..	..	..	..	..
354	Petroleum & Coal Products	..	..	..	..	..	..	..	..	..	..
355	Rubber Products	4 804	5 237	5 467	5 887	5 640	5 719	5 226	5 645	6 312	5 916
356	Plastic Products, nec	..	..	..	..	..	..	..	..	..	..
36	**Non-Metallic Mineral Products**	6 804	7 174	7 472	7 572	6 757	6 310	5 873	6 333	6 167	5 920
361	Pottery, China etc	..	..	..	..	..	..	..	..	..	..
362	Glass & Products	..	..	..	..	..	..	..	..	..	..
369	Non-Metallic Products, nec	..	..	..	..	..	..	..	..	..	..
37	**Basic Metal Industries**	20 004	21 871	22 230	22 671	21 812	20 729	20 918	20 701	21 659	20 749
371	Iron & Steel	..	..	..	..	..	..	..	..	..	..
372	Non-Ferrous Metals	..	..	..	..	..	..	..	..	..	..
38	**Fabricated Metal Products**	52 058	55 925	55 743	60 967	57 352	55 590	52 533	57 861	61 788	61 804
381	Metal Products	..	..	..	..	..	..	..	..	..	..
3813	Structural Metal Products	..	..	..	..	..	..	..	..	..	..
382	Non-Electrical Machinery	27 485	29 333	28 986	31 311	29 063	28 149	25 715	28 323	29 483	28 620
3821	Engines & Turbines	..	..	..	..	..	..	..	..	..	..
3822	Agricultural Machinery	..	..	..	..	..	..	..	..	..	..
3823	Metal & Wood working Machinery	..	..	..	..	..	..	..	..	..	..
3824	Special Industrial Machinery	..	..	..	..	..	..	..	..	..	..
3825	Office & Computing Machinery	..	..	..	..	..	..	..	..	..	..
3829	Machinery & Equipment, nec	..	..	..	..	..	..	..	..	..	..
383	Electrical Machinery	24 573	26 592	26 757	29 656	28 289	27 441	26 818	29 538	32 305	33 184
3831	Electrical Industrial Machinery	..	..	..	..	..	..	..	..	..	..
3832	Radio, TV & Communication Equipment	..	..	..	..	..	..	..	..	..	..
3833	Electrical Appliances & Housewares	..	..	..	..	..	..	..	..	..	..
3839	Electrical Apparatus, nec	..	..	..	..	..	..	..	..	..	..
384	Transport Equipment	..	..	..	..	..	..	..	..	..	..
3841	Shipbuilding & Repairing	..	..	..	..	..	..	..	..	..	..
3842	Railroad Equipment	..	..	..	..	..	..	..	..	..	..
3843	Motor Vehicles	..	..	..	..	..	..	..	..	..	..
3844	Motorcycles & Bicycles	..	..	..	..	..	..	..	..	..	..
3845	Aircraft	..	..	..	..	..	..	..	..	..	..
3849	Transport Equipment, nec	..	..	..	..	..	..	..	..	..	..
385	Professional Goods	..	..	..	..	..	..	..	..	..	..
3851	Professional Equipment	..	..	..	..	..	..	..	..	..	..
3852	Photographic & Optical Goods	..	..	..	..	..	..	..	..	..	..
3853	Watches & Clocks	..	..	..	..	..	..	..	..	..	..
39	**Other Manufacturing, nes**	..	..	..	..	..	..	..	..	..	..
3901	Jewellery	9 142	9 339	10 058	10 140	9 889	11 364	11 948	11 608	12 083	11 730
3	**Total Manufacturing**	178 019	187 260	190 431	198 262	191 572	189 319	185 812	196 802	207 955	207 508
1	**Agric., Hunting, Forestry, Fishing**	18 671	18 303	18 972	18 112	18 533	19 133	19 230	18 770	19 730	18 048
2	**Mining & Quarrying**	..	..	..	..	..	..	..	..	..	..
21	Coal Mining	..	..	..	..	..	..	..	..	..	..
22	Crude Petroleum & Natural Gas	..	..	..	..	..	..	..	..	..	..
23.29	Other Mining	..	..	..	..	..	..	..	..	..	..
3	**Total Manufacturing**	178 019	187 260	190 431	198 262	191 572	189 319	185 812	196 802	207 955	207 508
4	**Electricity, Gas & Water**	17 012	18 107	17 275	18 821	19 270	19 650	18 471	19 963	19 318	18 481
5	**Construction**	43 307	45 921	49 226	50 458	48 448	46 809	46 504	48 127	47 510	43 907
6.9	**Services**	303 246	309 007	324 961	337 424	326 402	323 231	321 702	315 276	318 127	320 876
0000	**Grand Total**	560 255	578 598	600 865	623 077	604 225	598 142	591 719	598 938	612 640	608 820

Note: Data have been retabulated according to a modified industrial classification. For details see Sources and Definitions.

Millions of SF (1990 Prices)

ISIC2	Industry	VALUE ADDED									
		1987	1988	1989	1990	1991	1992	1993	1994	1995	1996
31	**Food, Beverages & Tobacco**	6 697	6 771	6 967	7 152	7 407	7 507	7 577	7 648	8 099	7 953
311.2	Food	..	..	..	..	..	..	..	..	..	..
313	Beverages	..	..	..	..	..	..	..	..	..	..
314	Tobacco	..	..	..	..	..	..	..	..	..	..
32	**Textiles, Apparel & Leather**	3 230	3 090	2 962	2 891	2 764	2 684	2 478	2 363	2 291	2 151
321	Textiles	2 079	2 085	2 041	1 979	1 873	1 863	1 727	1 663	1 602	1 453
3213	Knitting Mills	..	..	..	..	..	..	..	..	..	..
322	Wearing Apparel	1 151	1 005	921	912	891	821	751	700	689	698
323	Leather & Products	..	..	..	..	..	..	..	..	..	..
324	Footwear	..	..	..	..	..	..	..	..	..	..
33	**Wood Products & Furniture**	5 481	5 507	5 618	5 934	5 931	5 659	5 394	5 641	5 526	5 280
331	Wood Products	..	..	..	..	..	..	..	..	..	..
332	Furnitures & Fixtures	..	..	..	..	..	..	..	..	..	..
34	**Paper, Paper Products & Printing**	6 643	6 843	6 862	6 983	6 699	6 453	5 981	5 678	5 959	5 826
341	Paper & Products	1 443	1 469	1 505	1 518	1 574	1 627	1 567	1 535	1 676	1 557
3411	Pulp, Paper & Board	..	..	..	..	..	..	..	..	..	..
342	Printing & Publishing	5 200	5 374	5 357	5 465	5 125	4 826	4 414	4 143	4 283	4 269
35	**Chemical Products**	10 117	11 228	11 891	12 158	12 178	13 027	13 381	15 504	16 305	17 242
351	Industrial Chemicals	8 184	9 118	9 686	9 781	9 818	10 659	11 234	13 082	13 666	14 787
3511	Basic Industrial Chemicals	..	..	..	..	..	..	..	..	..	..
3512	Fertilizers & Pesticides	..	..	..	..	..	..	..	..	..	..
3513	Synthetic Resins	..	..	..	..	..	..	..	..	..	..
352	Other Chemicals	..	..	..	..	..	..	..	..	..	..
3521	Paints, Varnishes & Lacquers	..	..	..	..	..	..	..	..	..	..
3522	Drugs & Medicines	..	..	..	..	..	..	..	..	..	..
3523	Soap & Cleaning Preparations	..	..	..	..	..	..	..	..	..	..
3529	Chemical Products, nec	..	..	..	..	..	..	..	..	..	..
353	Petroleum Refineries	..	..	..	..	..	..	..	..	..	..
354	Petroleum & Coal Products	..	..	..	..	..	..	..	..	..	..
355	Rubber Products	1 933	2 110	2 205	2 377	2 360	2 368	2 147	2 422	2 639	2 455
356	Plastic Products, nec	..	..	..	..	..	..	..	..	..	..
36	**Non-Metallic Mineral Products**	3 062	3 215	3 334	3 363	3 099	2 970	2 754	2 880	2 886	2 782
361	Pottery, China etc	..	..	..	..	..	..	..	..	..	..
362	Glass & Products	..	..	..	..	..	..	..	..	..	..
369	Non-Metallic Products, nec	..	..	..	..	..	..	..	..	..	..
37	**Basic Metal Industries**	6 873	7 652	7 917	8 216	8 360	8 084	8 141	7 871	8 404	8 092
371	Iron & Steel	..	..	..	..	..	..	..	..	..	..
372	Non-Ferrous Metals	..	..	..	..	..	..	..	..	..	..
38	**Fabricated Metal Products**	22 219	23 576	23 205	25 051	23 794	23 360	22 236	24 844	25 852	25 539
381	Metal Products	..	..	..	..	..	..	..	..	..	..
3813	Structural Metal Products	..	..	..	..	..	..	..	..	..	..
382	Non-Electrical Machinery	11 760	12 469	12 241	13 135	12 750	12 647	11 707	13 029	13 253	12 664
3821	Engines & Turbines	..	..	..	..	..	..	..	..	..	..
3822	Agricultural Machinery	..	..	..	..	..	..	..	..	..	..
3823	Metal & Wood working Machinery	..	..	..	..	..	..	..	..	..	..
3824	Special Industrial Machinery	..	..	..	..	..	..	..	..	..	..
3825	Office & Computing Machinery	..	..	..	..	..	..	..	..	..	..
3829	Machinery & Equipment, nec	..	..	..	..	..	..	..	..	..	..
383	Electrical Machinery	10 459	11 107	10 964	11 916	11 044	10 713	10 529	11 815	12 599	12 875
3831	Electrical Industrial Machinery	..	..	..	..	..	..	..	..	..	..
3832	Radio, TV & Communication Equipment	..	..	..	..	..	..	..	..	..	..
3833	Electrical Appliances & Housewares	..	..	..	..	..	..	..	..	..	..
3839	Electrical Apparatus, nec	..	..	..	..	..	..	..	..	..	..
384	Transport Equipment	..	..	..	..	..	..	..	..	..	..
3841	Shipbuilding & Repairing	..	..	..	..	..	..	..	..	..	..
3842	Railroad Equipment	..	..	..	..	..	..	..	..	..	..
3843	Motor Vehicles	..	..	..	..	..	..	..	..	..	..
3844	Motorcycles & Bicycles	..	..	..	..	..	..	..	..	..	..
3845	Aircraft	..	..	..	..	..	..	..	..	..	..
3849	Transport Equipment, nec	..	..	..	..	..	..	..	..	..	..
385	Professional Goods	..	..	..	..	..	..	..	..	..	..
3851	Professional Equipment	..	..	..	..	..	..	..	..	..	..
3852	Photographic & Optical Goods	..	..	..	..	..	..	..	..	..	..
3853	Watches & Clocks	..	..	..	..	..	..	..	..	..	..
39	**Other Manufacturing, nes**	..	..	..	..	..	..	..	..	..	..
3901	Jewellery	3 184	3 222	3 439	3 434	3 461	4 110	4 325	4 251	4 447	4 328
3	**Total Manufacturing**	67 506	71 104	72 195	75 182	73 693	73 854	72 267	76 680	79 769	79 193
1	**Agric., Hunting, Forestry, Fishing**	9 652	9 498	9 882	9 470	9 650	9 955	9 807	9 282	10 220	9 159
2	**Mining & Quarrying**	..	..	..	..	..	..	..	..	..	..
21	Coal Mining	..	..	..	..	..	..	..	..	..	..
22	Crude Petroleum & Natural Gas	..	..	..	..	..	..	..	..	..	..
23.29	Other Mining	..	..	..	..	..	..	..	..	..	..
3	**Total Manufacturing**	67 506	71 104	72 195	75 182	73 693	73 854	72 267	76 680	79 769	79 193
4	**Electricity, Gas & Water**	5 494	5 893	5 649	6 188	6 358	6 635	6 444	7 364	6 382	6 117
5	**Construction**	22 361	23 603	25 187	25 698	25 203	24 448	23 582	24 759	24 468	22 832
6.9	**Services**	179 274	183 032	192 945	200 764	199 860	199 472	200 753	196 214	195 904	198 767
0000	**Grand Total**	284 287	293 130	305 858	317 302	314 764	314 364	312 853	314 299	316 743	316 068

Note: Data have been retabulated according to a modified industrial classification. For details see Sources and Definitions.

Millions of SF   (Current Prices)

ISIC2	Industry	EXPORTS									
		1987	1988	1989	1990	1991	1992	1993	1994	1995	1996
31	Food, Beverages & Tobacco	1 978	1 949	2 165	2 251	2 394	2 550	2 613	2 771	2 709	2 715
311.2	Food	..	..	..	..	..	..	..	..	..	..
313	Beverages	..	..	..	..	..	..	..	..	..	..
314	Tobacco	..	..	..	..	..	..	..	..	..	..
32	Textiles, Apparel & Leather	4 039	4 146	4 519	4 686	4 407	4 334	3 973	3 967	3 696	3 450
321	Textiles	3 221	3 390	3 666	3 713	3 395	3 364	3 023	3 029	2 823	2 564
3213	Knitting Mills	..	..	..	..	..	..	..	..	..	..
322	Wearing Apparel	818	756	853	973	1 012	970	950	938	873	886
323	Leather & Products	..	..	..	..	..	..	..	..	..	..
324	Footwear	..	..	..	..	..	..	..	..	..	..
33	Wood Products & Furniture	1 664	1 525	1 695	1 872	1 965	2 002	2 019	2 040	2 012	2 031
331	Wood Products	..	..	..	..	..	..	..	..	..	..
332	Furnitures & Fixtures	..	..	..	..	..	..	..	..	..	..
34	Paper, Paper Products & Printing	1 586	1 728	1 962	2 149	2 214	2 271	2 157	2 346	2 527	2 476
341	Paper & Products	1 014	1 138	1 327	1 455	1 479	1 538	1 407	1 585	1 855	1 821
3411	Pulp, Paper & Board	..	..	..	..	..	..	..	..	..	..
342	Printing & Publishing	572	590	635	694	735	733	750	761	672	655
35	Chemical Products	16 552	17 998	20 219	20 955	21 721	24 177	25 402	26 697	27 181	28 901
351	Industrial Chemicals	14 613	15 876	17 828	18 437	19 119	21 278	22 366	23 514	24 056	25 968
3511	Basic Industrial Chemicals	..	..	..	..	..	..	..	..	..	..
3512	Fertilizers & Pesticides	..	..	..	..	..	..	..	..	..	..
3513	Synthetic Resins	..	..	..	..	..	..	..	..	..	..
352	Other Chemicals	..	..	..	..	..	..	..	..	..	..
3521	Paints, Varnishes & Lacquers	..	..	..	..	..	..	..	..	..	..
3522	Drugs & Medicines	..	..	..	..	..	..	..	..	..	..
3523	Soap & Cleaning Preparations	..	..	..	..	..	..	..	..	..	..
3529	Chemical Products, nec	..	..	..	..	..	..	..	..	..	..
353	Petroleum Refineries	..	..	..	..	..	..	..	..	..	..
354	Petroleum & Coal Products	..	..	..	..	..	..	..	..	..	..
355	Rubber Products	1 939	2 122	2 391	2 518	2 602	2 899	3 036	3 183	3 125	2 933
356	Plastic Products, nec	..	..	..	..	..	..	..	..	..	..
36	Non-Metallic Mineral Products	430	467	536	604	630	653	670	712	733	705
361	Pottery, China etc	..	..	..	..	..	..	..	..	..	..
362	Glass & Products	..	..	..	..	..	..	..	..	..	..
369	Non-Metallic Products, nec	..	..	..	..	..	..	..	..	..	..
37	Basic Metal Industries	5 715	6 441	7 391	7 537	7 515	7 701	7 415	7 780	8 346	8 189
371	Iron & Steel	..	..	..	..	..	..	..	..	..	..
372	Non-Ferrous Metals	..	..	..	..	..	..	..	..	..	..
38	Fabricated Metal Products	25 315	27 449	29 856	31 673	31 816	32 424	31 484	32 831	34 364	35 683
381	Metal Products	..	..	..	..	..	..	..	..	..	..
3813	Structural Metal Products	..	..	..	..	..	..	..	..	..	..
382	Non-Electrical Machinery	14 944	16 833	18 305	19 400	19 112	19 274	18 314	19 247	20 435	21 051
3821	Engines & Turbines	..	..	..	..	..	..	..	..	..	..
3822	Agricultural Machinery	..	..	..	..	..	..	..	..	..	..
3823	Metal & Wood working Machinery	..	..	..	..	..	..	..	..	..	..
3824	Special Industrial Machinery	..	..	..	..	..	..	..	..	..	..
3825	Office & Computing Machinery	..	..	..	..	..	..	..	..	..	..
3829	Machinery & Equipment, nec	..	..	..	..	..	..	..	..	..	..
383	Electrical Machinery	10 371	10 616	11 551	12 273	12 704	13 150	13 170	13 584	13 929	14 632
3831	Electrical Industrial Machinery	..	..	..	..	..	..	..	..	..	..
3832	Radio, TV & Communication Equipment	..	..	..	..	..	..	..	..	..	..
3833	Electrical Appliances & Housewares	..	..	..	..	..	..	..	..	..	..
3839	Electrical Apparatus, nec	..	..	..	..	..	..	..	..	..	..
384	Transport Equipment	..	..	..	..	..	..	..	..	..	..
3841	Shipbuilding & Repairing	..	..	..	..	..	..	..	..	..	..
3842	Railroad Equipment	..	..	..	..	..	..	..	..	..	..
3843	Motor Vehicles	..	..	..	..	..	..	..	..	..	..
3844	Motorcycles & Bicycles	..	..	..	..	..	..	..	..	..	..
3845	Aircraft	..	..	..	..	..	..	..	..	..	..
3849	Transport Equipment, nec	..	..	..	..	..	..	..	..	..	..
385	Professional Goods	..	..	..	..	..	..	..	..	..	..
3851	Professional Equipment	..	..	..	..	..	..	..	..	..	..
3852	Photographic & Optical Goods	..	..	..	..	..	..	..	..	..	..
3853	Watches & Clocks	..	..	..	..	..	..	..	..	..	..
39	Other Manufacturing, nes	..	..	..	..	..	..	..	..	..	..
3901	Jewellery	5 420	6 394	7 925	8 669	8 808	9 518	10 390	10 528	9 913	9 490
3	Total Manufacturing	62 699	68 097	76 268	80 396	81 470	85 630	86 123	89 672	91 481	93 640
1	Agric., Hunting, Forestry, Fishing	279	318	374	437	439	446	439	448	455	436
2	Mining & Quarrying	..	..	..	..	..	..	..	..	..	..
21	Coal Mining	..	..	..	..	..	..	..	..	..	..
22	Crude Petroleum & Natural Gas	..	..	..	..	..	..	..	..	..	..
23.29	Other Mining	..	..	..	..	..	..	..	..	..	..
3	Total Manufacturing	62 699	68 097	76 268	80 396	81 470	85 630	86 123	89 672	91 481	93 640
4	Electricity, Gas & Water	787	864	846	860	924	897	1 068	1 189	1 248	1 184
5	Construction	..	..	..	..	..	..	..	..	..	..
6.9	Services	..	..	..	..	..	..	..	..	..	..
0000	Grand Total	..	..	..	..	..	..	..	..	..	..

Note: Data have been retabulated according to a modified industrial classification. For details see Sources and Definitions.

Millions of SF (Current Prices)

ISIC2	Industry	1987	1988	1989	1990	1991	1992	1993	1994	1995	1996
						IMPORTS					
31	Food, Beverages & Tobacco	4 999	5 121	5 502	5 599	5 829	5 724	5 649	5 941	5 661	5 953
311.2	Food	..	..	..	..	..	..	..	..	..	..
313	Beverages	..	..	..	..	..	..	..	..	..	..
314	Tobacco	..	..	..	..	..	..	..	..	..	..
32	Textiles, Apparel & Leather	6 683	6 846	7 655	7 844	7 908	7 792	7 512	7 381	6 981	6 890
321	Textiles	2 436	2 705	3 061	3 060	2 821	2 767	2 580	2 635	2 458	2 313
3213	Knitting Mills	..	..	..	..	..	..	..	..	..	..
322	Wearing Apparel	4 247	4 141	4 594	4 784	5 087	5 025	4 932	4 746	4 523	4 577
323	Leather & Products	..	..	..	..	..	..	..	..	..	..
324	Footwear	..	..	..	..	..	..	..	..	..	..
33	Wood Products & Furniture	3 787	4 209	4 846	4 966	4 807	4 664	4 425	4 670	4 833	4 759
331	Wood Products	..	..	..	..	..	..	..	..	..	..
332	Furnitures & Fixtures	..	..	..	..	..	..	..	..	..	..
34	Paper, Paper Products & Printing	2 983	3 274	3 715	3 818	3 810	3 819	3 668	3 873	4 175	4 040
341	Paper & Products	1 884	2 114	2 436	2 466	2 407	2 384	2 213	2 357	2 616	2 436
3411	Pulp, Paper & Board	..	..	..	..	..	..	..	..	..	..
342	Printing & Publishing	1 099	1 160	1 279	1 352	1 403	1 435	1 455	1 516	1 559	1 604
35	Chemical Products	12 991	14 132	15 973	16 039	16 341	17 062	17 388	18 085	18 427	19 111
351	Industrial Chemicals	9 341	10 246	11 579	11 601	11 966	12 558	12 973	13 501	13 853	14 702
3511	Basic Industrial Chemicals	..	..	..	..	..	..	..	..	..	..
3512	Fertilizers & Pesticides	..	..	..	..	..	..	..	..	..	..
3513	Synthetic Resins	..	..	..	..	..	..	..	..	..	..
352	Other Chemicals	..	..	..	..	..	..	..	..	..	..
3521	Paints, Varnishes & Lacquers	..	..	..	..	..	..	..	..	..	..
3522	Drugs & Medicines	..	..	..	..	..	..	..	..	..	..
3523	Soap & Cleaning Preparations	..	..	..	..	..	..	..	..	..	..
3529	Chemical Products, nec	..	..	..	..	..	..	..	..	..	..
353	Petroleum Refineries	..	..	..	..	..	..	..	..	..	..
354	Petroleum & Coal Products	..	..	..	..	..	..	..	..	..	..
355	Rubber Products	3 650	3 886	4 394	4 438	4 375	4 504	4 415	4 584	4 574	4 409
356	Plastic Products, nec	..	..	..	..	..	..	..	..	..	..
36	Non-Metallic Mineral Products	1 672	1 811	2 084	2 142	2 038	1 922	1 876	1 984	2 011	1 976
361	Pottery, China etc	..	..	..	..	..	..	..	..	..	..
362	Glass & Products	..	..	..	..	..	..	..	..	..	..
369	Non-Metallic Products, nec	..	..	..	..	..	..	..	..	..	..
37	Basic Metal Industries	6 665	7 610	9 334	9 025	8 062	7 731	7 299	7 936	8 912	8 042
371	Iron & Steel	..	..	..	..	..	..	..	..	..	..
372	Non-Ferrous Metals	..	..	..	..	..	..	..	..	..	..
38	Fabricated Metal Products	25 310	28 606	32 096	32 831	32 761	31 171	29 212	31 008	33 945	34 902
381	Metal Products	..	..	..	..	..	..	..	..	..	..
3813	Structural Metal Products	..	..	..	..	..	..	..	..	..	..
382	Non-Electrical Machinery	17 147	18 874	21 082	21 758	21 596	19 971	18 613	19 930	22 310	23 076
3821	Engines & Turbines	..	..	..	..	..	..	..	..	..	..
3822	Agricultural Machinery	..	..	..	..	..	..	..	..	..	..
3823	Metal & Wood working Machinery	..	..	..	..	..	..	..	..	..	..
3824	Special Industrial Machinery	..	..	..	..	..	..	..	..	..	..
3825	Office & Computing Machinery	..	..	..	..	..	..	..	..	..	..
3829	Machinery & Equipment, nec	..	..	..	..	..	..	..	..	..	..
383	Electrical Machinery	8 163	9 732	11 014	11 073	11 165	11 200	10 599	11 078	11 635	11 826
3831	Electrical Industrial Machinery	..	..	..	..	..	..	..	..	..	..
3832	Radio, TV & Communication Equipment	..	..	..	..	..	..	..	..	..	..
3833	Electrical Appliances & Housewares	..	..	..	..	..	..	..	..	..	..
3839	Electrical Apparatus, nec	..	..	..	..	..	..	..	..	..	..
384	Transport Equipment	..	..	..	..	..	..	..	..	..	..
3841	Shipbuilding & Repairing	..	..	..	..	..	..	..	..	..	..
3842	Railroad Equipment	..	..	..	..	..	..	..	..	..	..
3843	Motor Vehicles	..	..	..	..	..	..	..	..	..	..
3844	Motorcycles & Bicycles	..	..	..	..	..	..	..	..	..	..
3845	Aircraft	..	..	..	..	..	..	..	..	..	..
3849	Transport Equipment, nec	..	..	..	..	..	..	..	..	..	..
385	Professional Goods	..	..	..	..	..	..	..	..	..	..
3851	Professional Equipment	..	..	..	..	..	..	..	..	..	..
3852	Photographic & Optical Goods	..	..	..	..	..	..	..	..	..	..
3853	Watches & Clocks	..	..	..	..	..	..	..	..	..	..
39	Other Manufacturing, nes	..	..	..	..	..	..	..	..	..	..
3901	Jewellery	1 788	2 208	2 790	2 979	2 791	2 720	3 083	2 964	2 725	2 807
3	Total Manufacturing	66 878	73 817	83 995	85 243	84 347	82 605	80 112	83 842	87 670	88 480
1	Agric., Hunting, Forestry, Fishing	1 149	1 267	1 347	1 265	1 270	1 340	1 335	1 355	1 319	1 317
2	Mining & Quarrying	..	..	..	..	..	..	..	..	..	..
21	Coal Mining	..	..	..	..	..	..	..	..	..	..
22	Crude Petroleum & Natural Gas	..	..	..	..	..	..	..	..	..	..
23.29	Other Mining	..	..	..	..	..	..	..	..	..	..
3	Total Manufacturing	66 878	73 817	83 995	85 243	84 347	82 605	80 112	83 842	87 670	88 480
4	Electricity, Gas & Water	1 348	1 281	1 654	1 950	1 833	1 665	1 406	1 339	1 224	1 495
5	Construction	..	..	..	..	..	..	..	..	..	..
6.9	Services	..	..	..	..	..	..	..	..	..	..
0000	Grand Total	..	..	..	..	..	..	..	..	..	..

Note: Data have been retabulated according to a modified industrial classification. For details see Sources and Definitions.

Millions of SF   (1990 Prices)

ISIC2	Industry	EXPORTS									
		1987	1988	1989	1990	1991	1992	1993	1994	1995	1996
31	Food, Beverages & Tobacco	1 984	2 028	2 128	2 251	2 392	2 531	2 678	2 924	3 046	3 069
311.2	Food	..	..	..	..	..	..	..	..	..	..
313	Beverages	..	..	..	..	..	..	..	..	..	..
314	Tobacco	..	..	..	..	..	..	..	..	..	..
32	Textiles, Apparel & Leather	4 581	4 585	4 716	4 686	4 498	4 415	4 316	4 461	4 137	3 844
321	Textiles	3 601	3 728	3 794	3 713	3 477	3 465	3 359	3 511	3 245	2 966
3213	Knitting Mills	..	..	..	..	..	..	..	..	..	..
322	Wearing Apparel	980	857	922	973	1 021	950	957	950	892	878
323	Leather & Products	..	..	..	..	..	..	..	..	..	..
324	Footwear	..	..	..	..	..	..	..	..	..	..
33	Wood Products & Furniture	1 940	1 612	1 767	1 872	1 899	1 801	1 718	1 843	1 866	1 993
331	Wood Products	..	..	..	..	..	..	..	..	..	..
332	Furnitures & Fixtures	..	..	..	..	..	..	..	..	..	..
34	Paper, Paper Products & Printing	1 691	1 830	1 988	2 149	2 193	2 332	2 424	2 628	2 608	2 772
341	Paper & Products	1 117	1 227	1 334	1 455	1 492	1 613	1 638	1 857	1 883	2 107
3411	Pulp, Paper & Board	..	..	..	..	..	..	..	..	..	..
342	Printing & Publishing	574	603	654	694	701	719	786	771	725	665
35	Chemical Products	19 753	20 811	20 824	20 955	20 867	22 059	22 586	23 872	25 581	26 780
351	Industrial Chemicals	17 631	18 551	18 405	18 437	18 291	19 250	19 570	20 590	22 343	23 641
3511	Basic Industrial Chemicals	..	..	..	..	..	..	..	..	..	..
3512	Fertilizers & Pesticides	..	..	..	..	..	..	..	..	..	..
3513	Synthetic Resins	..	..	..	..	..	..	..	..	..	..
352	Other Chemicals	..	..	..	..	..	..	..	..	..	..
3521	Paints, Varnishes & Lacquers	..	..	..	..	..	..	..	..	..	..
3522	Drugs & Medicines	..	..	..	..	..	..	..	..	..	..
3523	Soap & Cleaning Preparations	..	..	..	..	..	..	..	..	..	..
3529	Chemical Products, nec	..	..	..	..	..	..	..	..	..	..
353	Petroleum Refineries	..	..	..	..	..	..	..	..	..	..
354	Petroleum & Coal Products	..	..	..	..	..	..	..	..	..	..
355	Rubber Products	2 122	2 260	2 419	2 518	2 576	2 809	3 016	3 282	3 238	3 139
356	Plastic Products, nec	..	..	..	..	..	..	..	..	..	..
36	Non-Metallic Mineral Products	455	479	547	604	626	629	615	654	655	636
361	Pottery, China etc	..	..	..	..	..	..	..	..	..	..
362	Glass & Products	..	..	..	..	..	..	..	..	..	..
369	Non-Metallic Products, nec	..	..	..	..	..	..	..	..	..	..
37	Basic Metal Industries	6 289	6 940	7 364	7 537	7 665	7 938	7 755	8 382	8 806	8 814
371	Iron & Steel	..	..	..	..	..	..	..	..	..	..
372	Non-Ferrous Metals	..	..	..	..	..	..	..	..	..	..
38	Fabricated Metal Products	26 488	27 991	29 768	31 673	30 858	30 892	29 825	31 982	33 777	34 647
381	Metal Products	..	..	..	..	..	..	..	..	..	..
3813	Structural Metal Products	..	..	..	..	..	..	..	..	..	..
382	Non-Electrical Machinery	15 912	17 477	18 338	19 400	18 426	18 199	17 234	18 479	19 959	20 568
3821	Engines & Turbines	..	..	..	..	..	..	..	..	..	..
3822	Agricultural Machinery	..	..	..	..	..	..	..	..	..	..
3823	Metal & Wood working Machinery	..	..	..	..	..	..	..	..	..	..
3824	Special Industrial Machinery	..	..	..	..	..	..	..	..	..	..
3825	Office & Computing Machinery	..	..	..	..	..	..	..	..	..	..
3829	Machinery & Equipment, nec	..	..	..	..	..	..	..	..	..	..
383	Electrical Machinery	10 576	10 514	11 430	12 273	12 432	12 693	12 591	13 503	13 818	14 079
3831	Electrical Industrial Machinery	..	..	..	..	..	..	..	..	..	..
3832	Radio, TV & Communication Equipment	..	..	..	..	..	..	..	..	..	..
3833	Electrical Appliances & Housewares	..	..	..	..	..	..	..	..	..	..
3839	Electrical Apparatus, nec	..	..	..	..	..	..	..	..	..	..
384	Transport Equipment	..	..	..	..	..	..	..	..	..	..
3841	Shipbuilding & Repairing	..	..	..	..	..	..	..	..	..	..
3842	Railroad Equipment	..	..	..	..	..	..	..	..	..	..
3843	Motor Vehicles	..	..	..	..	..	..	..	..	..	..
3844	Motorcycles & Bicycles	..	..	..	..	..	..	..	..	..	..
3845	Aircraft	..	..	..	..	..	..	..	..	..	..
3849	Transport Equipment, nec	..	..	..	..	..	..	..	..	..	..
385	Professional Goods	..	..	..	..	..	..	..	..	..	..
3851	Professional Equipment	..	..	..	..	..	..	..	..	..	..
3852	Photographic & Optical Goods	..	..	..	..	..	..	..	..	..	..
3853	Watches & Clocks	..	..	..	..	..	..	..	..	..	..
39	Other Manufacturing, nes	..	..	..	..	..	..	..	..	..	..
3901	Jewellery	6 340	7 030	8 080	8 669	8 808	10 373	11 426	10 715	9 563	8 643
3	Total Manufacturing	69 521	73 306	77 182	80 396	79 806	82 970	83 343	87 461	90 039	91 198
1	Agric., Hunting, Forestry, Fishing	298	333	372	437	439	440	447	466	492	480
2	Mining & Quarrying	..	..	..	..	..	..	..	..	..	..
21	Coal Mining	..	..	..	..	..	..	..	..	..	..
22	Crude Petroleum & Natural Gas	..	..	..	..	..	..	..	..	..	..
23.29	Other Mining	..	..	..	..	..	..	..	..	..	..
3	Total Manufacturing	69 521	73 306	77 182	80 396	79 806	82 970	83 343	87 461	90 039	91 198
4	Electricity, Gas & Water	847	953	874	860	911	903	1 062	1 170	1 208	1 140
5	Construction	..	..	..	..	..	..	..	..	..	..
6.9	Services	..	..	..	..	..	..	..	..	..	..
0000	Grand Total	..	..	..	..	..	..	..	..	..	..

Note: Data have been retabulated according to a modified industrial classification. For details see Sources and Definitions.

Millions of SF

(1990 Prices)

ISIC2	Industry	IMPORTS									
		1987	**1988**	**1989**	**1990**	**1991**	**1992**	**1993**	**1994**	**1995**	**1996**
31	**Food, Beverages & Tobacco**	5 376	5 377	5 456	5 599	5 845	5 751	5 809	6 263	6 331	6 485
311.2	Food	..	..	..	..	..	..	..	..	..	..
313	Beverages	..	..	..	..	..	..	..	..	..	..
314	Tobacco	..	..	..	..	..	..	..	..	..	..
32	**Textiles, Apparel & Leather**	7 198	7 369	7 715	7 844	8 144	8 041	8 190	8 462	8 290	8 412
321	Textiles	2 635	2 876	3 052	3 060	2 990	2 979	2 918	3 171	3 169	3 102
3213	Knitting Mills	..	..	..	..	..	..	..	..	..	..
322	Wearing Apparel	4 563	4 493	4 663	4 784	5 154	5 062	5 272	5 291	5 121	5 310
323	Leather & Products	..	..	..	..	..	..	..	..	..	..
324	Footwear	..	..	..	..	..	..	..	..	..	..
33	**Wood Products & Furniture**	3 841	4 580	4 864	4 966	4 755	4 455	4 341	4 788	5 155	4 988
331	Wood Products	..	..	..	..	..	..	..	..	..	..
332	Furnitures & Fixtures	..	..	..	..	..	..	..	..	..	..
34	**Paper, Paper Products & Printing**	3 235	3 467	3 740	3 818	3 839	3 913	3 980	4 334	4 470	4 462
341	Paper & Products	2 052	2 247	2 452	2 466	2 465	2 515	2 530	2 839	2 874	2 835
3411	Pulp, Paper & Board	..	..	..	..	..	..	..	..	..	..
342	Printing & Publishing	1 183	1 220	1 288	1 352	1 374	1 398	1 450	1 495	1 596	1 627
35	**Chemical Products**	14 385	15 589	16 261	16 039	16 124	16 526	16 833	17 667	17 300	17 148
351	Industrial Chemicals	10 495	11 449	11 849	11 601	11 845	12 242	12 417	12 853	12 422	12 479
3511	Basic Industrial Chemicals	..	..	..	..	..	..	..	..	..	..
3512	Fertilizers & Pesticides	..	..	..	..	..	..	..	..	..	..
3513	Synthetic Resins	..	..	..	..	..	..	..	..	..	..
352	Other Chemicals	..	..	..	..	..	..	..	..	..	..
3521	Paints, Varnishes & Lacquers	..	..	..	..	..	..	..	..	..	..
3522	Drugs & Medicines	..	..	..	..	..	..	..	..	..	..
3523	Soap & Cleaning Preparations	..	..	..	..	..	..	..	..	..	..
3529	Chemical Products, nec	..	..	..	..	..	..	..	..	..	..
353	Petroleum Refineries	..	..	..	..	..	..	..	..	..	..
354	Petroleum & Coal Products	..	..	..	..	..	..	..	..	..	..
355	Rubber Products	3 890	4 140	4 412	4 438	4 279	4 284	4 416	4 814	4 878	4 669
356	Plastic Products, nec	..	..	..	..	..	..	..	..	..	..
36	**Non-Metallic Mineral Products**	1 693	1 771	1 949	2 142	2 053	1 863	1 794	1 896	1 889	1 876
361	Pottery, China etc	..	..	..	..	..	..	..	..	..	..
362	Glass & Products	..	..	..	..	..	..	..	..	..	..
369	Non-Metallic Products, nec	..	..	..	..	..	..	..	..	..	..
37	**Basic Metal Industries**	7 611	8 889	9 589	9 025	7 887	7 528	7 670	9 298	10 607	9 425
371	Iron & Steel	..	..	..	..	..	..	..	..	..	..
372	Non-Ferrous Metals	..	..	..	..	..	..	..	..	..	..
38	**Fabricated Metal Products**	27 380	29 445	31 294	32 831	31 993	29 165	27 268	30 357	33 946	34 872
381	Metal Products	..	..	..	..	..	..	..	..	..	..
3813	Structural Metal Products	..	..	..	..	..	..	..	..	..	..
382	Non-Electrical Machinery	18 846	19 784	20 819	21 758	21 166	18 789	17 473	19 575	22 249	22 980
3821	Engines & Turbines	..	..	..	..	..	..	..	..	..	..
3822	Agricultural Machinery	..	..	..	..	..	..	..	..	..	..
3823	Metal & Wood working Machinery	..	..	..	..	..	..	..	..	..	..
3824	Special Industrial Machinery	..	..	..	..	..	..	..	..	..	..
3825	Office & Computing Machinery	..	..	..	..	..	..	..	..	..	..
3829	Machinery & Equipment, nec	..	..	..	..	..	..	..	..	..	..
383	Electrical Machinery	8 534	9 661	10 475	11 073	10 827	10 376	9 795	10 782	11 697	11 892
3831	Electrical Industrial Machinery	..	..	..	..	..	..	..	..	..	..
3832	Radio, TV & Communication Equipment	..	..	..	..	..	..	..	..	..	..
3833	Electrical Appliances & Housewares	..	..	..	..	..	..	..	..	..	..
3839	Electrical Apparatus, nec	..	..	..	..	..	..	..	..	..	..
384	Transport Equipment	..	..	..	..	..	..	..	..	..	..
3841	Shipbuilding & Repairing	..	..	..	..	..	..	..	..	..	..
3842	Railroad Equipment	..	..	..	..	..	..	..	..	..	..
3843	Motor Vehicles	..	..	..	..	..	..	..	..	..	..
3844	Motorcycles & Bicycles	..	..	..	..	..	..	..	..	..	..
3845	Aircraft	..	..	..	..	..	..	..	..	..	..
3849	Transport Equipment, nec	..	..	..	..	..	..	..	..	..	..
385	Professional Goods	..	..	..	..	..	..	..	..	..	..
3851	Professional Equipment	..	..	..	..	..	..	..	..	..	..
3852	Photographic & Optical Goods	..	..	..	..	..	..	..	..	..	..
3853	Watches & Clocks	..	..	..	..	..	..	..	..	..	..
39	**Other Manufacturing, nes**	..	..	..	..	..	..	..	..	..	..
3901	Jewellery	2 253	2 912	3 095	2 979	3 093	2 574	3 025	3 140	3 226	3 243
3	**Total Manufacturing**	72 972	79 399	83 963	85 243	83 733	79 816	78 910	86 205	91 214	90 911
1	**Agric., Hunting, Forestry, Fishing**	1 165	1 349	1 351	1 265	1 276	1 339	1 367	1 432	1 464	1 436
2	**Mining & Quarrying**	..	..	..	..	..	..	..	..	..	..
21	Coal Mining	..	..	..	..	..	..	..	..	..	..
22	Crude Petroleum & Natural Gas	..	..	..	..	..	..	..	..	..	..
23.29	Other Mining	..	..	..	..	..	..	..	..	..	..
3	**Total Manufacturing**	72 972	79 399	83 963	85 243	83 733	79 816	78 910	86 205	91 214	90 911
4	**Electricity, Gas & Water**	1 598	1 711	1 767	1 950	1 772	1 805	1 508	1 614	1 516	1 612
5	**Construction**	..	..	..	..	..	..	..	..	..	..
6.9	**Services**	..	..	..	..	..	..	..	..	..	..
0000	**Grand Total**	..	..	..	..	..	..	..	..	..	..

Note: Data have been retabulated according to a modified industrial classification. For details see Sources and Definitions.

Detailed ISIC Rev. 2 industry listing, 4 digit level

Extract from ISIC Revision 2

Division	Major group	Group	Detailed description
Major Division 1			**AGRICULTURE, HUNTING, FORESTRY AND FISHING**
Major Division 2			**MINING AND QUARRYING**
21	210		**Coal Mining**
22	220		**Crude Petroleum and Natural Gas Production**
23	230		**Metal Ore Mining**
		2301	Iron ore mining
		2302	Non-ferrous metal ore mining
29	290		**Other Mining**
		2901	Stone quarrying, clay and sand pits
		2902	Chemical and fertilizer mineral mining
		2903	Salt mining
		2909	Mining and quarrying not elsewhere classified
Major Division 3			**MANUFACTURING**
31			**Manufacture of Food, Beverages and Tobacco**
	311/312		Food manufacturing
		3111	Slaughtering, preparing and preserving meat
		3112	Manufacture of dairy products
		3113	Canning and preserving of fruits and vegetables
		3114	Canning, preserving and processing of fish, crustacea and similar foods
		3115	Manufacture of vegetable and animal oils and fats
		3116	Grain mill products
		3117	Manufacture of bakery products
		3118	Sugar factories and refineries
		3119	Manufacture of cocoa, chocolate and sugar confectionery
		3121	Manufacture of food products not elsewhere classified
		3122	Manufacture of prepared animal feeds
	313		Beverage industries
		3131	Distilling, rectifying and blending spirits
		3132	Wine industries
		3133	Malt liquors and malt
		3134	Soft drinks and carbonated waters industries
	314		Tobacco manufactures
32			**Textile, Wearing Apparel and Leather Industries**
	321		Manufacture of textiles
		3211	Spinning, weaving and finishing textiles
		3212	Manufacture of made-up textile goods except wearing apparel
		3213	Knitting mills
		3214	Manufacture of carpets and rugs
		3215	Cordage, rope and twine industries
		3219	Manufacture of textiles not elsewhere classified
	322		Manufacture of wearing apparel, except footwear

		323	Manufacture of leather and products of leather, leather substitutes and fur, except footwear and wearing apparel
		3231	Tanneries and leather finishing
		3232	Fur dressing and dyeing industries
		3233	Manufacture of products of leather and leather substitutes, except footwear and wearing apparel
		324	Manufacture of footwear, except vulcanised or moulded rubber or plastic footwear

33   **Manufacture of Wood and Wood Products, including Furniture**

		331	Manufacture of wood and wood and cork products, except furniture
		3311	Sawmills, planing and other wood mills
		3312	Manufacture of wooden and cane containers and small cane ware
		3319	Manufacture of wood and cork products not elsewhere classified
		332	Manufacture of furniture and fixtures, except primarily of metal

34   **Manufacture of Paper and Paper Products; Printing and Publishing**

		341	Manufacture of paper and paper products
		3411	Manufacture of pulp, paper and paperboard
		3412	Manufacture of containers and boxes of paper and paperboard
		3419	Manufacture of pulp, paper and paperboard articles not elsewhere classified
		342	Printing, publishing and allied industries

35   **Manufacture of Chemicals and Chemical, Petroleum, Coal, Rubber and Plastic Products**

		351	Manufacture of industrial chemicals
		3511	Manufacture of basic industrial chemicals except fertilizer
		3512	Manufacture of fertilizers and pesticides
		3513	Manufacture of synthetic resins, plastic materials and man-made fibres except glass
		352	Manufacture of other chemical products
		3521	Manufacture of paints, varnishes and lacquers
		3522	Manufacture of drugs and medicines
		3523	Manufacture of soap and cleaning preparations, perfumes, cosmetics and other toilet preparations
		3529	Manufacture of chemical products not elsewhere classified
		353	Petroleum refineries
		354	Manufacture of miscellaneous products of petroleum and coal
		355	Manufacture of rubber products
		3551	Tyre and tube industries
		3559	Manufacture of rubber products not elsewhere classified
		356	Manufacture of plastic products not elsewhere classified

36   **Manufacture of Non-Metallic Mineral Products, except Products of Petroleum and Coal**

		361	Manufacture of pottery, china and earthenware
		362	Manufacture of glass and glass products
		369	Manufacture of other non-metallic mineral products
		3691	Manufacture of structural clay products
		3692	Manufacture of cement, lime and plaster
		3699	Manufacture of non-metallic mineral products not elsewhere classified

37   **Basic Metal Industries**

| | | 371 | Iron and steel basic industries |
| | | 372 | Non-ferrous metal basic industries |

38   **Manufacture of Fabricated Metal Products, Machinery and Equipment**

		381	Manufacture of fabricated metal products, except machinery and equipment
		3811	Manufacture of cutlery, hand tools and general hardware
		3812	Manufacture of furniture and fixtures primarily of metal

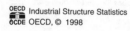

		3813	Manufacture of structural metal products
		3819	Manufacture of fabricated metal products except machinery and equipment not elsewhere classified
	382		Manufacture of machinery except electrical
		3821	Manufacture of engines and turbines
		3822	Manufacture of agriculture machinery and equipment
		3823	Manufacture of metal and wood working machinery
		3824	Manufacture of special industrial machinery and equipment except metal and wood working machinery
		3825	Manufacture of office, computing and accounting machinery
		3829	Machinery and equipment, except electrical not elsewhere classified
	383		Manufacture of electrical machinery apparatus, appliance and supplies
		3831	Manufacture of electrical industrial machinery and apparatus
		3832	Manufacture of radio, television and communication equipment and apparatus
		3833	Manufacture of electrical appliances and housewares
		3839	Manufacture of electrical apparatus and supplies not elsewhere classified
	384		Manufacture of transport equipment
		3841	Shipbuilding and repairing
		3842	Manufacture of railroad equipment
		3843	Manufacture of motor vehicles
		3844	Manufacture of motorcycles and bicycles
		3845	Manufacture of aircraft
		3849	Manufacture of transport equipment not elsewhere classified
	385		Manufacture of professional and scientific and measuring and controlling equipment not elsewhere classified, and of photographic and optical goods
		3851	Manufacture of professional and scientific, and measuring and controlling equipment not elsewhere classified
		3852	Manufacture of photographic and optical goods
		3853	Manufacture of watches and clocks
39	**390**		**Other Manufacturing Industries**
		3901	Manufacture of jewellery and related articles
		3902	Manufacture of musical instruments
		3903	Manufacture of sporting and athletic goods
		3909	Manufacturing industries not elsewhere classified

Major Division 4   **ELECTRICITY, GAS AND WATER**

Major Division 5   **CONSTRUCTION**

Major Division 6   **WHOLESALE AND RETAIL TRADE AND RESTAURANTS AND HOTELS**

Major Division 7   **TRANSPORT, STORAGE AND COMMUNICATION**

Major Division 8   **FINANCING, INSURANCE, REAL ESTATE AND BUSINESS SERVICES**

Major Division 9   **COMMUNITY, SOCIAL AND PERSONAL SERVICES**

Statistiques des Structures Industrielles
OCDE, © 1998   OECD OCDE

Liste industrielle détaillée de la CITI Rév. 2, au niveau 4-chiffres

Extrait de la CITI révision 2

Division	Classe	Groupe	Description détaillée

Branche 1 — AGRICULTURE, CHASSE, SYLVICULTURE ET PÊCHE

Branche 2 — INDUSTRIES EXTRACTIVES

21	210		**Extraction du charbon**
22	220		**Production de pétrole brut et de gaz naturel**
23	230		**Extraction des minerais métalliques**
		2301	Extraction du minerai de fer
		2302	Extraction des minerais autres que le minerai de fer
29	290		**Extraction d'autres métaux**
		2901	Extraction de la pierre à bâtir, de l'argile et du sable
		2902	Extraction de minéraux pour l'industrie chimique et la fabrication d'engrais
		2903	Extraction du sel
		2909	Extraction des matières minérales non classées ailleurs

Branche 3 — INDUSTRIES MANUFACTURIÈRES

31			**Fabrication de produits alimentaires, boissons et tabacs**
	311/312		Industries alimentaires
		3111	Abattage du bétail ; fabrication des préparations et conserves de viande
		3112	Industrie du lait
		3113	Fabrication des conserves de fruits et de légumes
		3114	Mise en conserve et préparation de poissons, crustacés et produits analogues
		3115	Fabrication des corps gras d'origine végétale et animale
		3116	Travail des grains
		3117	Boulangerie et pâtisserie
		3118	Industrie du sucre
		3119	Fabrication de cacao et de chocolat et confiserie
		3121	Fabrication de produits alimentaires non classés ailleurs
		3122	Fabrication de produits pour l'alimentation des animaux
	313		Fabrication des boissons
		3131	Distillation, rectification et mélange des spiritueux
		3132	Industries du vin et des boissons alcoolisées non maltées
		3133	Bière et malt
		3134	Industries des boissons hygiéniques et eaux gazeuses
	314		Industrie du tabac
32			**Industries des textiles, de l'habillement et du cuir**
	321		Industrie textile
		3211	Filature, tissage et finissage des textiles
		3212	Confection d'ouvrages en tissu, à l'exception des articles d'habillement
		3213	Bonneterie
		3214	Fabrication de tapis et carpettes
		3215	Corderie, câblerie, ficellerie
		3219	Fabrication des articles textiles non classés ailleurs
	322		Fabrication d'articles d'habillement, à l'exclusion des chaussures
	323		Industrie du cuir, des articles en cuir et en succédanés du cuir et de la fourrure, à l'exclusion des chaussures et des articles d'habillement

Division	Classe	Groupe	Description détaillée
		3231	Tannerie-mégisserie
		3232	Préparation et teinture des fourrures
		3233	Fabrication d'articles en cuir et en succédanés du cuir, à l'exclusion des chaussures et des articles d'habillement
	324		Fabrication des chaussures, à l'exclusion des chaussures en caoutchouc vulcanisé ou moulé et des chaussures en matière plastique
33			**Industrie du bois et fabrication d'ouvrages en bois, y compris les meubles**
	331		Industrie du bois et fabrication d'ouvrages en bois et en liège, à l'exclusion des meubles
		3311	Scieries et travail mécanique du bois
		3312	Fabrication des emballages en bois et en vannerie et des petits articles en vannerie
		3319	Fabrication des ouvrages en bois et des ouvrages en liège non classés ailleurs
	332		Fabrication de meubles et d'accessoires, à l'exclusion des meubles et accessoires faits principalement en métal
34			**Fabrication de papier et d'articles en papier ; imprimerie et édition**
	341		Fabrication de papier et d'articles en papier
		3411	Fabrication de la pâte à papier, du papier et du carton
		3412	Fabrication d'emballages et de boîtes en papier et en carton
		3419	Fabrication d'articles en pâte à papier et en carton non classés ailleurs
	342		Imprimerie, édition et industries annexes
35			**Industrie chimique et fabrication de produits chimiques, de dérivés du pétrole et du charbon et d'ouvrages en caoutchouc et en matière plastique**
	351		Industrie chimique
		3511	Industrie chimique de base, à l'exception des engrais
		3512	Fabrication d'engrais et de pesticides
		3513	Fabrication des résines synthétiques, matières plastiques et fibres artificielles à l'exclusion du verre
	352		Fabrication d'autres produits chimiques
		3521	Fabrication de peintures, vernis et laques
		3522	Fabrication de produits pharmaceutiques et médicaments
		3523	Fabrication de savons et produits de nettoyage, de parfums, de produits de beauté et autres préparations pour la toilette
		3529	Fabrication de produits chimiques non classés ailleurs
	353		Raffineries de pétrole
	354		Fabrication de divers dérivés du pétrole et du charbon
	355		Industrie du caoutchouc
		3551	Industries des pneumatiques et chambres à air
		3559	Fabrication d'ouvrages en caoutchouc non classés ailleurs
	356		Fabrication d'ouvrages en matière plastique non classés ailleurs
36			**Fabrication de produits minéraux non métalliques, à l'exclusion des dérivés du pétrole et du charbon**
	361		Fabrication des grès, porcelaines et faïences
	362		Industrie du verre
	369		Fabrication d'autres produits minéraux non métalliques
		3691	Fabrication de matériaux de construction en terre cuite
		3692	Fabrication de ciment, de chaux et de plâtre
		3699	Fabrication de produits minéraux non métalliques non classés ailleurs
37			**Industrie métallurgique de base**
	371		Sidérurgie et première transformation de la fonte, du fer et de l'acier
	372		Production et première transformation des métaux non ferreux
38			**Fabrication d'ouvrages en métaux, de machines et de matériel**
	381		Fabrication d'ouvrages en métaux, à l'exclusion des machines et du matériel
		3811	Fabrication de coutellerie, d'outils à main et de quincaillerie

		3812	Fabrication de meubles et d'accessoires faits principalement en métal
		3813	Fabrication d'éléments de construction en métal
		3819	Fabrication d'ouvrages en métaux, à l'exclusion des machines et du matériel, non classés ailleurs
	382		Construction de machines, à l'exclusion des machines électriques
		3821	Construction de moteurs et de turbines
		3822	Fabrication de machines et de matériel agricoles
		3823	Construction de machines pour le travail du métal et du bois
		3824	Fabrication de machines et matériel spéciaux pour l'industrie, à l'exclusion des machines à travailler le métal et le bois
		3825	Fabrication de machines de bureau, de machines à calculer et de machines comptables
		3829	Machines et matériel, à l'exclusion des machines électriques, non classés ailleurs
	383		Fabrication de machines, appareils et fournitures électriques
		3831	Fabrication de machines et appareils électriques industriels
		3832	Fabrication de matériel et d'appareils de radio, de télévision et de télécommunications
		3833	Fabrication d'appareils électro-ménagers
		3839	Fabrication d'appareils et de fournitures électriques non classés ailleurs
	384		Construction de matériel de transport
		3841	Construction navale et réparation des navires
		3842	Construction de matériel ferroviaire
		3843	Construction de véhicules automobiles
		3844	Fabrication de motocycles et cycles
		3845	Construction aéronautique
		3849	Construction de matériel de transport non classé ailleurs
	385		Fabrication de matériel médico-chirurgical, d'instruments de précision, d'appareils de mesure et de contrôle non classés ailleurs, de matériel photographique et d'instruments d'optique
		3851	Fabrication de matériel médico-chirurgical, d'instruments de précision, d'appareils de mesure et de contrôle non classés ailleurs
		3852	Fabrication de matériel photographique et d'instruments d'optique
		3853	Fabrication des montres et des horloges
39	**390**		**Autres industries manufacturières**
		3901	Bijouterie et orfèvrerie en métaux précieux ; joaillerie fine
		3902	Fabrication d'instruments de musique
		3903	Fabrication d'articles de sport et d'athlétisme
		3909	Industries manufacturières non classées ailleurs

Branche 4   **ÉLECTRICITÉ, GAZ ET EAU**

Branche 5   **BÂTIMENT ET TRAVAUX PUBLICS**

Branche 6   **COMMERCE DE GROS ET DE DÉTAIL ; RESTAURANTS ET HÔTELS**

Branche 7   **TRANSPORTS, ENTREPÔTS ET COMMUNICATIONS**

Branche 8   **BANQUE, ASSURANCES, AFFAIRES IMMOBILIÈRES ET SERVICES FOURNIS AUX ENTREPRISES**

Branche 9   **SERVICES FOURNIS À LA COLLECTIVITÉ, SERVICES SOCIAUX ET SERVICES PERSONNELS**

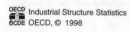

ISIC REVISION 3

CITI REVISION 3

Section I

Industrial survey and foreign trade statistics
Statistiques des enquêtes industrielles et du commerce extérieur

List of countries
Liste des pays

AUSTRALIA

Table AS.1 PRODUCTION - PRODUCTION

Millions of A$ (Current Prices)

ISIC revision 3				1988-89	1989-90	1990-91	1991-92	1992-93	1993-94	1994-95	1995-96
A	01-02		Agriculture, hunting and forestry	..	..	..	..	20 068	21 565	..	..
B	05		Fishing	..	..	..	..	..	..	..	..
C	10-14		Mining and quarrying	..	..	..	..	38 224	36 807	..	..
	10		Mining of coal and lignite; extraction of peat	..	..	..	..	9 218	9 855	..	..
	11		Crude petroleum & natural gas; related service activ.	..	..	..	..	8 481	7 805	..	..
	13		Mining of metal ores	..	..	..	..	..	..	..	..
	14		Other mining and quarrying	..	..	..	..	2 545	..	..	..
D	15-37		Total manufacturing	..	..	..	..	173 638	183 855	191 372	202 162
	15		Food products and beverages	..	..	..	..	36 641	39 059	40 334	42 408
		155	Beverages	..	..	..	..	5 666	5 953	6 195	6 396
	16	160	Tobacco products	..	..	..	..	848	899	935	879
	17		Textiles	..	..	..	..	4 511	4 802	4 691	5 092
		171	Spinning, weaving and finishing of textiles	..	..	..	..	2 070	2 106	2 144	2 499
		172	Other textiles	..	..	..	..	1 538	1 684	1 575	1 628
		173	Knitted and crocheted fabrics and articles	..	..	..	..	903	1 012	972	965
	18		Wearing apparel dressing & dyeing of fur	..	..	..	..	3 885	3 934	4 129	4 532
		181	Wearing apparel, except fur apparel	..	..	..	..	3 270	3 267	3 312	3 635
		182	Dressing and dyeing of fur; articles of fur	..	..	..	..	615	667	817	897
	19		Tanning, dressing leather; leather artic.; footwear	..	..	..	..	..	..	..	..
		191	Tanning, dressing leather; manuf. of leather articles	..	..	..	..	..	..	..	..
		192	Footwear	..	..	..	..	611	630	590	583
	20		Wood and cork products, ex. furniture	..	..	..	..	5 375	5 918	6 368	6 030
		201	Sawmilling and planing of wood	..	..	..	..	4 023	4 233	4 184	..
		202	Products of wood, cork, straw & plaiting material	..	..	..	..	1 352	1 685	2 189	..
	21		Paper and paper products	..	..	..	..	..	..	..	..
	22		Publishing, printing & reprod. of recorded media	..	..	..	..	..	..	..	..
		221	Publishing	..	..	..	..	..	..	..	..
		222	Printing and related service activities	..	..	..	..	..	..	..	..
		223	Reproduction of recorded media	..	..	..	..	..	..	..	..
	23		Coke, refined petroleum products & nuclear fuel	..	..	..	..	8 227	8 082	7 347	6 998
	24		Chemicals and chemical products	..	..	..	..	13 632	14 264	15 212	16 607
		241	Basic chemicals	..	..	..	..	8 672	8 940	9 244	10 078
		242	Other chemical products	..	..	..	..	4 960	5 324	5 968	6 529
		243	Man-made fibres	..	..	..	..	..	..	..	..
	25		Rubber and plastic products	..	..	..	..	6 461	6 810	7 147	7 852
		251	Rubber products	..	..	..	..	1 380	1 406	1 447	1 527
		252	Plastic products	..	..	..	..	5 081	5 405	5 700	6 325
	26		Other non-metallic mineral products	..	..	..	..	8 333	8 609	7 969	8 384
		261	Glass and glass products	..	..	..	..	1 068	1 173	1 149	1 160
		269	Non-metallic mineral products, nec	..	..	..	..	7 266	7 436	6 820	7 224
	27		Basic metals	..	..	..	..	21 986	22 516	23 902	..
		271	Basic iron and steel	..	..	..	..	21 758	22 328	23 732	..
		272	Basic precious and non-ferrous metals	..	..	..	..	..	..	..	..
		273	Casting of metals	..	..	..	..	228	188	170	101
	28		Fabricated metal products, ex. machin. & equip.	..	..	..	..	..	..	..	..
		281	Structural metal prod., tanks, reservoirs, generators	..	..	..	..	8 086	8 586	8 628	..
		289	Other fabricated metal products & service activities	..	..	..	..	4 617	4 731	4 420	..
	29		Machinery and equipment, nec	..	..	..	..	5 697	6 494	6 743	..
		291	General purpose machinery	..	..	..	..	1 623	1 752	1 610	1 893
		292	Special purpose machinery	..	..	..	..	2 109	2 517	3 100	..
		293	Domestic appliances, nec	..	..	..	..	1 965	2 225	2 033	2 273
	30		Office, accounting and computing machinery	..	..	..	..	914	989	1 501	1 434
	31		Electrical machinery and apparatus, nec	..	..	..	..	3 748	3 985	3 125	4 415
		311	Electric motors, generators and transformers	..	..	..	..	1 933	2 074	1 643	2 198
		312	Electricity distribution and control apparatus	..	..	..	..	..	..	..	..
		313	Insulated wire and cable	..	..	..	..	1 128	1 221	1 418	1 455
		314	Accumulators, primary cells and primary batteries	..	..	..	..	248	226	333	286
		315	Electric lamps and lighting equipment	..	..	..	..	439	463	592	476
		319	Other electrical equipment, nec	..	..	..	..	..	..	..	..
	32		Radio, TV, communication equip. & apparatus	..	..	..	..	2 902	2 684	3 648	3 762
		321	Electronic valves, tubes & other electronic compon.	..	..	..	..	1 300	852	1 263	1 638
		322	TV, radio transmitters & appar. for line teleph., telegr.	..	..	..	..	1 602	1 832	2 005	2 124
		323	TV, radio receivers and associated goods	..	..	..	..	..	..	..	..
	33		Medical, precision, optical instr.; watches, clocks	..	..	..	..	1 377	1 638	1 640	2 198
		331	Medical equip.; precision instruments and appliances	..	..	..	..	..	..	..	..
		332	Optical instruments and photographic equipment	..	..	..	..	..	..	..	..
		333	Watches and clocks	..	..	..	..	..	..	..	..
	34		Motor vehicles, trailers, and semi-trailers	..	..	..	..	10 738	12 881	14 220	14 545
	35		Other transport equipment	..	..	..	..	4 002	4 122	3 926	4 274
		351	Building and repairing of ships and boats	..	..	..	..	1 909	1 763	1 675	2 097
		352	Railway, tramway locomotives and rolling stock	..	..	..	..	555	914	934	738
		353	Aircraft and spacecraft	..	..	..	..	1 487	1 392	1 317	1 374
		359	Transport equipment, nec	..	..	..	..	51	53	28	65
	36		Furniture; manufacturing, nec	..	..	..	..	4 669	5 025	5 129	5 388
		361	Furniture	..	..	..	..	3 449	3 845	3 938	4 130
		369	Manufacturing, nec	..	..	..	..	1 220	1 181	1 191	1 258
	37		Recycling	..	..	..	..	..	..	..	..
E	40-41		Electricity, gas and water supply	..	..	..	..	..	..	..	..
	40		Electricity, gas, steam and hot water supply	..	..	..	..	..	..	..	..
		401	Production, collection and distribution of electricity	..	..	..	..	18 395	21 441	..	..
	41	410	Collection, purification, distribution of water	..	..	..	..	..	..	..	..
F	45		Construction	..	..	..	..	45 398	47 638	..	..
G	50-52		Wholesale and retail trade; repairs etc	..	..	..	..	269 264	296 731	..	..
H	55		Hotels and restaurants	..	..	..	..	22 594	21 975	..	..
I	60-64		Transport, storage and communications	..	..	..	..	..	..	..	..
J	65-67		Financial intermediation	..	..	..	..	16 557	17 432	..	..
K	70-74		Real estate, renting and business activities	..	..	..	..	42 406	39 261	..	..
L-Q	75-99		Public admin.; education; health; other services	..	..	..	..	34 847	37 617	..	..
A-Q	01-99		Grand total	..	..	..	..	..	..	..	..

Note: Data cover the fiscal year ending 30 June. Recycling activities are included with the industry of original manufacture. ISIC 1530 includes 1544; 1711 include 2430; 182 includes 191; 201 includes 2022; 2023 includes 2029; 2211 includes 2219; 2213 includes 223; 2411 include 2412 and 2423; 2694 includes 2695; 2696 includes 2699; 271 includes 272, 2731, 2891, and 371; 2813 includes 2911, 2913, 2914, 2919, 2926, and 2929; 2899 includes 2927; 291 includes 2912 and 2915; 2922 includes 2923; 311 includes 312 and 319; and 321 includes 323. ISIC 154 excludes 1544; 24 excludes 2430; 242 excludes 2423; 273 excludes 2731; 289 excludes 2891; ISIC 292 excludes 2926, 2927, 2929

Industrial Structure Statistics
OECD, © 1998

Table AS.2 VALEUR AJOUTÉE - VALUE ADDED

Millions de A$ (Prix courants)

1988-89	1989-90	1990-91	1991-92	1992-93	1993-94	1994-95	1995-96			CITI révision 3	
..	..	..	..	..	..	..	..	**Agriculture, chasse et sylviculture**	A	01-02	
..	..	..	..	..	..	..	..	**Pêche**	B	05	
..	..	..	..	27 448	..	..	..	**Activités extractives**	C	10-14	
..	..	..	..	5 118	..	..	..	Extraction de charbon, de lignite et de tourbe		10	
..	..	..	..	7 762	..	..	..	Extraction de pétrole brut et de gaz naturel		11	
..	..	..	..	2 244	..	..	..	Extraction de minerais métalliques		13	
..	..	..	..	1 597	..	..	..	Autres activités extractives		14	
..	..	..	..	67 965	..	..	..	**Activités de fabrication**	D	15-37	
..	..	..	..	13 065	..	..	..	**Produits alimentaires et boissons**		15	
..	..	..	..	2 474	..	..	..	Boissons			155
..	..	..	..	486	..	..	..	**Produits à base de tabac**		16	160
..	..	..	..	1 081	..	..	..	**Textiles**		17	
..	..	..	..	869	..	..	..	Filature, tissage et achèvement des textiles			171
..	..	..	..	654	..	..	..	Autres articles textiles			172
..	..	..	..	427	..	..	..	Etoffes et articles de bonneterie			173
..	..	..	..	1 650	..	..	..	**Habillement; préparation, teinture des fourrures**		18	
..	..	..	..	1 494	..	..	..	Articles d'habillement autres qu'en fourrure			181
..	..	..	..	156	..	..	..	Préparation, teinture des fourrures; art. en fourrure			182
..	..	..	..	..	..	..	..	**Travail des cuirs; articles en cuir; chaussures**		19	
..	..	..	..	..	..	..	..	Apprêt et tannage des cuirs et articles en cuirs			191
..	..	..	..	308	..	..	..	Chaussures			192
..	..	..	..	2 161	..	..	..	**Bois et articles en bois et liège (sauf meubles)**		20	
..	..	..	..	1 687	..	..	..	Sciage et rabotage du bois			201
..	..	..	..	475	..	..	..	Articles en bois, liège, vannerie, sparterie			202
..	..	..	..	..	..	..	..	**Papier et carton; articles en papier et en carton**		21	
..	..	..	..	..	..	..	..	**Edition, imprimerie et reproduction**		22	
..	..	..	..	..	..	..	..	Edition			221
..	..	..	..	..	..	..	..	Imprimerie et activités annexes			222
..	..	..	..	..	..	..	..	Reproduction de supports enregistrés			223
..	..	..	..	1 721	..	..	..	**Cokéfaction; prod. pétroliers; comb. nucléaires**		23	
..	..	..	..	..	..	..	..	**Produits chimiques**		24	
..	..	..	..	..	..	..	..	Produits chimiques de base			241
..	..	..	..	..	..	..	..	Autres produits chimiques			242
..	..	..	..	..	..	..	..	Fibres synthétiques ou artificielles			243
..	..	..	..	2 951	..	..	..	**Articles en caoutchouc et en matières plastiques**		25	
..	..	..	..	606	..	..	..	Articles en caoutchouc			251
..	..	..	..	2 345	..	..	..	Articles en matières plastiques			252
..	..	..	..	3 581	..	..	..	**Autres produits minéraux non métalliques**		26	
..	..	..	..	587	..	..	..	Verre et articles en verre			261
..	..	..	..	2 993	..	..	..	Produits minéraux non métalliques, nca			269
..	..	..	..	..	..	..	..	**Produits métallurgiques de base**		27	
..	..	..	..	6 668	..	..	..	Sidérurgie et première transformation de l'acier			271
..	..	..	..	..	..	..	..	Métallurgie; métaux précieux et non ferreux			272
..	..	..	..	..	..	..	..	Fonderie			273
..	..	..	..	..	..	..	..	**Ouvrages en métaux, sauf machines et matériel**		28	
..	..	..	..	..	..	..	..	Constr. et menuiserie métal.; réservoirs; générateurs			281
..	..	..	..	..	..	..	..	Autres ouvrages en métaux			289
..	..	..	..	..	..	..	..	**Machines et matériel, nca**		29	
..	..	..	..	..	..	..	..	Machines d'usage général			291
..	..	..	..	..	..	..	..	Machines d'usage spécifique			292
..	..	..	..	845	..	..	..	Appareils domestiques, nca			293
..	..	..	..	385	..	..	..	**Mach. de bureau, comptables, matériel inform.**		30	
..	..	..	..	1 696	..	..	..	**Machines et appareils électriques, nca**		31	
..	..	..	..	894	..	..	..	Moteurs, génératrices et transformateurs électriques			311
..	..	..	..	..	..	..	..	Matériel électrique de distribution et de commande			312
..	..	..	..	488	..	..	..	Fils et câbles électriques isolés			313
..	..	..	..	118	..	..	..	Accumulateurs, piles électriques			314
..	..	..	..	196	..	..	..	Lampes électriques et appareils d'éclairage			315
..	..	..	..	..	..	..	..	Autres matériels électriques, nca			319
..	..	..	..	1 310	..	..	..	**Equip. et appar. de radio, TV, communication**		32	
..	..	..	..	557	..	..	..	Tubes et valves électroniques; autres composants			321
..	..	..	..	753	..	..	..	Emetteurs radio et TV; app. téléphonie, télégraphie			322
..	..	..	..	..	..	..	..	Récepteurs radio et TV et articles associés			323
..	..	..	..	783	..	..	..	**Instruments médicaux, de précision, d'optique**		33	
..	..	..	..	..	..	..	..	Appareils médicaux et de précision			331
..	..	..	..	..	..	..	..	Instruments d'optique ; matériel photographique			332
..	..	..	..	..	..	..	..	Horlogerie			333
..	..	..	..	3 206	..	..	..	**Véhicules automobiles et nemorques**		34	
..	..	..	..	1 707	..	..	..	**Autres matériels de transport**		35	
..	..	..	..	631	..	..	..	Construction et réparation de navires			351
..	..	..	..	226	..	..	..	Construction de matériel ferroviaire roulant			352
..	..	..	..	827	..	..	..	Construction aéronautique et spatiale			353
..	..	..	..	24	..	..	..	Autres équipements de transport			359
..	..	..	..	2 087	..	..	..	**Meubles; activités de fabrication, nca**		36	
..	..	..	..	1 497	..	..	..	Meubles			361
..	..	..	..	590	..	..	..	Activités de fabrication, nca			369
..	..	..	..	..	..	..	..	**Récupération**		37	
..	..	..	..	..	..	..	..	**Production et distrib. d'électricité, de gaz, d'eau**	E	40-41	
..	..	..	..	..	..	..	..	**Electricité, gaz, vapeur et eau chaude**		40	
..	..	..	..	9 965	..	..	..	Production, collecte et distribution d'électricité			401
..	..	..	..	..	..	..	..	**Captage, épuration et distribution d'eau**		41	410
..	..	..	..	..	..	..	..	**Construction**	F	45	
..	..	..	..	..	..	..	..	**Commerce de gros et de détail; réparation**	G	50-52	
..	..	..	..	..	..	..	..	**Hôtels et restaurants**	H	55	
..	..	..	..	..	..	..	..	**Transports, entreposage et communications**	I	60-64	
..	..	..	..	..	..	..	..	**Intermédiation financière**	J	65-67	
..	..	..	..	..	..	..	..	**Immobilier, locations, services aux entreprises**	K	70-74	
..	..	..	..	..	..	..	..	**Admin. publique; éducation; santé; autres**	L-Q	75-99	
..	..	..	..	..	..	..	..	**Grand total**	A-Q	01-99	

Note: Data cover the fiscal year ending 30 June. Recycling activities are included with the industry of original manufacture. ISIC 1530 includes 1544; 1711 include 2430; 182 includes 19 201 includes 2022; 2023 includes 2029; 2211 includes 2219; 2213 includes 223; 2411 include 2412 and 2423; 2694 includes 2695; 2696 includes 2699; 271 includes 272, 2731, 2891, and 371; 2813 includes 2911, 2913, 2914, 2919, 2926, and 2929; 2899 includes 2927; 291 includes 2912 and 2915; 2922 includes 2923; 311 includes 312 and 319; and 321 includes 323. ISIC 154 excludes 1544; 24 excludes 2430; 242 excludes 2423; 273 excludes 2731; 289 excludes 2891; ISIC 292 excludes 2926, 2927, 2929

AUSTRALIA

Table AS.3 ESTABLISHMENTS - ETABLISSEMENTS

Units

ISIC revision 3			1988-89	1989-90	1990-91	1991-92	1992-93	1993-94	1994-95	1995-96
A	01-02	Agriculture, hunting and forestry	..	..	..	..	106 057	107 538	..	..
B	05	Fishing	..	..	..	..	..	..	..	..
C	10-14	Mining and quarrying	..	..	..	..	1 217	641	..	..
10		Mining of coal and lignite; extraction of peat	..	..	..	..	156	159	..	..
11		Crude petroleum & natural gas; related service activ.	..	..	..	..	103	102	..	..
13		Mining of metal ores	..	..	..	..	..	..	..	..
14		Other mining and quarrying	..	..	..	..	613			
D	15-37	Total manufacturing	..	..	..	..	42 707	44 585	47 332	54 340
15		Food products and beverages	..	..	..	..	3 567	3 507	3 521	3 907
	155	Beverages	..	..	..	..	367	417	443	521
16	160	Tobacco products	..	..	..	..	6	6	5	5
17		Textiles	..	..	..	..	1 334	1 394	1 540	1 641
	171	Spinning, weaving and finishing of textiles	..	..	..	..	302	273	314	287
	172	Other textiles	..	..	..	..	756	921	1 000	1 131
	173	Knitted and crocheted fabrics and articles	..	..	..	..	276	200	226	223
18		Wearing apparel dressing & dyeing of fur	..	..	..	..	2 585	2 708	3 642	4 646
	181	Wearing apparel, except fur apparel	..	..	..	..	2 464	2 607	3 531	4 345
	182	Dressing and dyeing of fur; articles of fur	..	..	..	..	121	101	111	301
19		Tanning, dressing leather; leather artic.; footwear	..	..	..	..	..	..	..	..
	191	Tanning, dressing leather; manuf. of leather articles	..	..	..	..	..	..	..	..
	192	Footwear	..	..	..	..	235	222	163	258
20		Wood and cork products, ex. furniture	..	..	..	..	3 475	3 700	4 095	4 794
	201	Sawmilling and planing of wood	..	..	..	..	2 553	2 609	2 685	..
	202	Products of wood, cork, straw & plaiting material	..	..	..	..	922	1 091	1 410	..
21		Paper and paper products	..	..	..	..	..	..	..	..
22		Publishing, printing & reprod. of recorded media	..	..	..	..	..	..	..	..
	221	Publishing	..	..	..	..	..	..	..	..
	222	Printing and related service activities	..	..	..	..	..	..	..	..
	223	Reproduction of recorded media	..	..	..	..	..	..	..	..
23		Coke, refined petroleum products & nuclear fuel	..	..	..	..	67	70	49	65
24		Chemicals and chemical products	..	..	..	..	1 162	1 190	1 200	..
	241	Basic chemicals	..	..	..	..	512	524	528	..
	242	Other chemical products	..	..	..	..	650	666	672	789
	243	Man-made fibres	..	..	..	..	..	..	..	..
25		Rubber and plastic products	..	..	..	..	1 636	1 745	1 797	2 053
	251	Rubber products	..	..	..	..	271	277	260	278
	252	Plastic products	..	..	..	..	1 365	1 468	1 537	1 775
26		Other non-metallic mineral products	..	..	..	..	1 787	1 908	1 924	2 138
	261	Glass and glass products	..	..	..	..	174	275	305	318
	269	Non-metallic mineral products, nec	..	..	..	..	1 613	1 633	1 619	1 820
27		Basic metals	..	..	..	..	1 947	1 772	1 672	..
	271	Basic iron and steel	..	..	..	..	1 849	1 683	1 590	..
	272	Basic precious and non-ferrous metals	..	..	..	..	..	..	..	..
	273	Casting of metals	..	..	..	..	98	89	82	92
28		Fabricated metal products, ex. machin. & equip.	..	..	..	..	7 057	7 242	7 676	..
	281	Structural metal prod., tanks, reservoirs, generators	..	..	..	..	4 074	4 142	4 422	..
	289	Other fabricated metal products & service activities	..	..	..	..	2 983	3 100	3 254	..
29		Machinery and equipment, nec	..	..	..	..	2 159	2 412	2 386	..
	291	General purpose machinery	..	..	..	..	482	521	465	661
	292	Special purpose machinery	..	..	..	..	1 381	1 537	1 658	..
	293	Domestic appliances, nec	..	..	..	..	296	354	263	363
30		Office, accounting and computing machinery	..	..	..	..	124	160	153	150
31		Electrical machinery and apparatus, nec	..	..	..	..	915	1 131	1 313	1 237
	311	Electric motors, generators and transformers	..	..	..	..	637	729	665	660
	312	Electricity distribution and control apparatus	..	..	..	..	..	..	..	..
	313	Insulated wire and cable	..	..	..	..	53	51	61	53
	314	Accumulators, primary cells and primary batteries	..	..	..	..	16	18	19	18
	315	Electric lamps and lighting equipment	..	..	..	..	209	333	401	506
	319	Other electrical equipment, nec	..	..	..	..	..	..	..	..
32		Radio, TV, communication equip. & apparatus	..	..	..	..	526	607	776	593
	321	Electronic valves, tubes & other electronic compon.	..	..	..	..	398	477	518	463
	322	TV, radio transmitters & appar. for line teleph., telegr.	..	..	..	..	128	130	111	130
	323	TV, radio receivers and associated goods	..	..	..	..	..	..	..	..
33		Medical, precision, optical instr.; watches, clocks	..	..	..	..	1 022	1 069	1 094	1 259
	331	Medical equip.; precision instruments and appliances	..	..	..	..	..	..	..	..
	332	Optical instruments and photographic equipment	..	..	..	..	..	..	..	..
	333	Watches and clocks	..	..	..	..	..	..	..	..
34		Motor vehicles, trailers, and semi-trailers	..	..	..	..	1 410	1 390	1 256	1 562
35		Other transport equipment	..	..	..	..	852	904	983	1 035
	351	Building and repairing of ships and boats	..	..	..	..	541	538	604	667
	352	Railway, tramway locomotives and rolling stock	..	..	..	..	32	35	105	24
	353	Aircraft and spacecraft	..	..	..	..	218	268	274	271
	359	Transport equipment, nec	..	..	..	..	62	63	61	73
36		Furniture; manufacturing, nec	..	..	..	..	5 351	5 729	6 383	7 134
	361	Furniture	..	..	..	..	3 738	4 039	4 606	5 165
	369	Manufacturing, nec	..	..	..	..	1 613	1 690	1 777	1 969
37		Recycling	..	..	..	..	..	..	..	..
E	40-41	Electricity, gas and water supply	..	..	..	..	..	..	..	..
40		Electricity, gas, steam and hot water supply	..	..	..	..	..	..	..	..
	401	Production, collection and distribution of electricity	..	..	..	..	63	81	..	..
41	410	Collection, purification, distribution of water	..	..	..	..	..	..	..	..
F	45	Construction	..	..	..	..	60 744	68 750	..	..
G	50-52	Wholesale and retail trade; repairs etc	..	..	..	..	135 437	141 532	..	..
H	55	Hotels and restaurants	..	..	..	..	26 944	28 150	..	..
I	60-64	Transport, storage and communications	..	..	..	..	..	..	..	..
J	65-67	Financial intermediation	..	..	..	..	20 171	20 498	..	..
K	70-74	Real estate, renting and business activities	..	..	..	..	95 882	102 007	..	..
L-Q	75-99	Public admin.; education; health; other services	..	..	..	..	81 881	85 521	..	..
A-Q	01-99	Grand total	..	..	..	..	..	..	..	..

Note: Data cover the fiscal year ending 30 June. Recycling activities are included with the industry of original manufacture. ISIC 1530 includes 1544; 1711 include 2430; 182 includes 191; 201 includes 2022; 2023 includes 2029; 2211 includes 2219; 2213 includes 223; 2411 include 2412 and 2423; 2694 includes 2695; 2696 includes 2699; 271 includes 272, 2731, 2891, and 371; 2813 includes 2911, 2913, 2914, 2919, 2926, and 2929; 2899 includes 2927; 291 includes 2912 and 2915; 2922 includes 2923; 311 includes 312 and 319; and 321 includes 323. ISIC 154 excludes 1544; 24 excludes 2430; 242 excludes 2423; 273 excludes 2731; 289 excludes 2891; ISIC 292 excludes 2926, 2927, 2929

Table AS.4 EMPLOI - EMPLOYMENT

Thousands

1988-89	1989-90	1990-91	1991-92	1992-93	1993-94	1994-95	1995-96			CITI révision 3	
..	..	..	..	336.0	342.0	339.0	347.0	**Agriculture, chasse et sylviculture**	A	01-02	
..	..	..	..	11.0	9.0	12.0	13.0	**Pêche**	B	05	
..	..	..	..	64.6	60.9	..	..	**Activités extractives**	C	10-14	
..	..	..	..	26.8	26.3	..	..	Extraction de charbon, de lignite et de tourbe		10	
..	..	..	..	..	4.4	..	..	Extraction de pétrole brut et de gaz naturel		11	
..	..	..	..	..	..	..	..	Extraction de minerais métalliques		13	
..	..	..	..	7.5	..	..	..	Autres activités extractives		14	
..	..	..	..	914.8	911.1	924.3	944.8	**Activités de fabrication**	D	15-37	
..	..	..	..	160.1	161.8	161.3	161.3	**Produits alimentaires et boissons**		15	
..	..	..	..	17.1	17.0	16.7	16.8	Boissons			155
..	..	..	..	2.9	2.3	1.8	1.6	**Produits à base de tabac**		16	160
..	..	..	..	33.2	33.0	32.6	32.3	**Textiles**		17	
..	..	..	..	14.1	14.4	14.2	13.7	Filature, tissage et achèvement des textiles			171
..	..	..	..	11.3	12.0	12.0	12.2	Autres articles textiles			172
..	..	..	..	7.7	6.6	6.4	6.4	Etoffes et articles de bonneterie			173
..	..	..	..	..	..	..	..	**Habillement; préparation, teinture des fourrures**		18	
..	..	..	..	35.2	31.8	34.0	35.7	Articles d'habillement autres qu'en fourrure			181
..	..	..	..	2.7	2.9	3.1	4.3	Préparation, teinture des fourrures; art. en fourrure			182
..	..	..	..	..	..	..	..	**Travail des cuirs; articles en cuir; chaussures**		19	
..	..	..	..	..	..	..	..	Apprêt et tannage des cuirs et articles en cuirs			191
..	..	..	..	7.3	7.1	5.9	5.7	Chaussures			192
..	..	..	..	42.3	44.7	42.5	46.3	**Bois et articles en bois et liège (sauf meubles)**		20	
..	..	..	..	32.4	32.2	33.4	..	Sciage et rabotage du bois			201
..	..	..	..	9.9	12.5	13.5	..	Articles en bois, liège, vannerie, sparterie			202
..	..	..	..	..	..	..	..	**Papier et carton; articles en papier et en carton**		21	
..	..	..	..	..	..	..	..	**Edition, imprimerie et reproduction**		22	
..	..	..	..	..	..	..	..	Edition			221
..	..	..	..	..	..	..	..	Imprimerie et activités annexes			222
..	..	..	..	..	..	..	..	Reproduction de supports enregistrés			223
..	..	..	..	4.4	4.5	4.2	4.4	**Cokéfaction; prod. pétroliers; comb. nucléaires**		23	
..	..	..	..	45.3	43.4	43.9	46.0	**Produits chimiques**		24	
..	..	..	..	26.3	25.2	24.8	25.9	Produits chimiques de base			241
..	..	..	..	19.0	18.2	19.1	20.1	Autres produits chimiques			242
..	..	..	..	..	..	..	..	Fibres synthétiques ou artificielles			243
..	..	..	..	39.6	40.5	..	43.9	**Articles en caoutchouc et en matières plastiques**		25	
..	..	..	..	8.1	7.9	8.0	7.8	Articles en caoutchouc			251
..	..	..	..	31.5	32.6	..	36.1	Articles en matières plastiques			252
..	..	..	..	39.6	38.2	34.2	36.4	**Autres produits minéraux non métalliques**		26	
..	..	..	..	5.7	5.6	5.7	5.2	Verre et articles en verre			261
..	..	..	..	33.9	32.6	28.5	31.1	Produits minéraux non métalliques, nca			269
..	..	..	..	74.8	69.3	67.4	..	**Produits métallurgiques de base**		27	
..	..	..	..	72.8	67.6	65.9	..	Sidérurgie et première transformation de l'acier			271
..	..	..	..	..	..	..	..	Métallurgie; métaux précieux et non ferreux			272
..	..	..	..	2.0	1.7	1.5	1.0	Fonderie			273
..	..	..	..	..	..	..	..	**Ouvrages en métaux, sauf machines et matériel**		28	
..	..	..	..	54.4	55.9	58.5	..	Constr. et menuiserie métal.; réservoirs; générateurs			281
..	..	..	..	38.4	39.5	39.4	..	Autres ouvrages en métaux			289
..	..	..	..	30.1	31.7	33.4	..	**Machines et matériel, nca**		29	
..	..	..	..	10.7	11.0	10.8	12.2	Machines d'usage général			291
..	..	..	..	19.4	20.7	22.6	..	Machines d'usage spécifique			292
..	..	..	..	12.4	14.3	13.1	13.1	Appareils domestiques, nca			293
..	..	..	..	2.1	2.5	3.5	3.2	**Mach. de bureau, comptables, matériel inform.**		30	
..	..	..	..	24.5	25.3	25.8	38.7	**Machines et appareils électriques, nca**		31	
..	..	..	..	15.4	16.0	15.5	15.6	Moteurs, génératrices et transformateurs électriques			311
..	..	..	..	..	..	..	..	Matériel électrique de distribution et de commande			312
..	..	..	..	4.3	4.3	4.6	4.4	Fils et câbles électriques isolés			313
..	..	..	..	1.3	1.0	1.1	0.7	Accumulateurs, piles électriques			314
..	..	..	..	3.5	4.0	4.6	4.8	Lampes électriques et appareils d'éclairage			315
..	..	..	..	..	..	..	..	Autres matériels électriques, nca			319
..	..	..	..	15.7	12.8	23.1	18.1	**Equip. et appar. de radio, TV, communication**		32	
..	..	..	..	8.1	6.1	6.5	10.5	Tubes et valves électroniques; autres composants			321
..	..	..	..	7.6	6.8	7.6	7.6	Emetteurs radio et TV; app. téléphonie, télégraphie			322
..	..	..	..	..	..	..	..	Récepteurs radio et TV et articles associés			323
..	..	..	..	11.7	12.1	12.4	11.4	**Instruments médicaux, de précision, d'optique**		33	
..	..	..	..	..	..	..	..	Appareils médicaux et de précision			331
..	..	..	..	..	..	..	..	Instruments d'optique ; matériel photographique			332
..	..	..	..	..	..	..	..	Horlogerie			333
..	..	..	..	53.8	52.8	54.5	55.9	**Véhicules automobiles et nemorques**		34	
..	..	..	..	27.8	27.1	26.9	28.4	**Autres matériels de transport**		35	
..	..	..	..	9.1	9.2	9.4	10.8	Construction et réparation de navires			351
..	..	..	..	4.6	4.9	5.3	5.1	Construction de matériel ferroviaire roulant			352
..	..	..	..	13.6	12.4	12.1	11.9	Construction aéronautique et spatiale			353
..	..	..	..	0.5	0.6	0.6	0.6	Autres équipements de transport			359
..	..	..	..	49.6	51.3	51.4	52.6	**Meubles; activités de fabrication, nca**		36	
..	..	..	..	36.8	39.6	39.3	40.7	Meubles			361
..	..	..	..	12.8	11.7	12.1	11.9	Activités de fabrication, nca			369
..	..	..	..	..	..	..	..	**Récupération**		37	
..	..	..	..	..	..	..	..	**Production et distrib. d'électricité, de gaz, d'eau**	E	40-41	
..	..	..	..	..	..	..	..	**Electricité, gaz, vapeur et eau chaude**		40	
..	..	..	..	53.1	44.3	..	..	Production, collecte et distribution d'électricité			401
..	..	..	..	..	..	..	..	**Captage, épuration et distribution d'eau**		41	410
..	..	..	..	257.0	273.0	306.0	342.0	**Construction**	F	45	
..	..	..	..	1 243.0	1 310.0	1 384.0	1 463.0	**Commerce de gros et de détail; réparation**	G	50-52	
..	..	..	..	344.0	385.0	393.0	407.0	**Hôtels et restaurants**	H	55	
..	..	..	..	407.0	410.0	433.0	444.0	**Transports, entreposage et communications**	I	60-64	
..	..	..	..	294.0	298.0	291.0	291.0	**Intermédiation financière**	J	65-67	
..	..	..	..	568.0	566.0	651.0	780.0	**Immobilier, locations, services aux entreprises**	K	70-74	
..	..	..	..	..	..	..	..	**Admin. publique; éducation; santé; autres**	L-Q	75-99	
..	..	..	..	..	..	..	..	**Grand total**	A-Q	01-99	

Note: Data cover the fiscal year ending 30 June. Recycling activities are included with the industry of original manufacture. ISIC 1530 includes 1544; 1711 includes 2430; 182 includes 19 201 includes 2022; 2023 includes 2029; 2211 includes 2219; 2213 includes 223; 2411 include 2412 and 2423; 2694 includes 2695; 2696 includes 2699; 271 includes 272, 2731, 2891, and 371; 2813 includes 2911, 2913, 2914, 2919, 2926, and 2929; 2899 includes 2927; 291 includes 2912 and 2915; 2922 includes 2923; 311 includes 312 and 319; and 321 includes 323. ISIC 154 excludes 1544; 24 excludes 2430; 242 excludes 2423; 273 excludes 2731; 289 excludes 2891; ISIC 292 excludes 2926, 2927, 2929

Statistiques des Structures Industrielles
OCDE, © 1998

AUSTRALIA

Table AS.5 WAGES AND SALARIES, EMPLOYEES - SALAIRES ET TRAITEMENTS, SALARIÉS

Millions of A$ *(Current Prices)*

ISIC revision 3			1988-89	1989-90	1990-91	1991-92	1992-93	1993-94	1994-95	1995-96
A	01-02	**Agriculture, hunting and forestry**	..	..	..	..	2 167	2 343	2 701	2 627
B	05	**Fishing**	..	..	..	..	181	194	242	284
C	10-14	**Mining and quarrying**	..	..	..	..	3 889	3 946	..	..
	10	Mining of coal and lignite; extraction of peat	..	..	..	..	1 779	1 950	..	..
	11	Crude petroleum & natural gas; related service activ.	..	..	..	..	329	322	..	..
	13	Mining of metal ores	..	..	..	..	..	..	..	..
	14	Other mining and quarrying	..	..	..	..	292	..	..	..
D	15-37	**Total manufacturing**	..	..	..	..	27 809	28 107	29 653	30 515
	15	**Food products and beverages**	..	..	..	..	4 692	4 850	4 928	5 053
	155	Beverages	..	..	..	..	608	579	601	600
	16	**Tobacco products**	..	..	..	..	127	119	112	95
	160									
	17	**Textiles**	..	..	..	..	904	887	961	916
	171	Spinning, weaving and finishing of textiles	..	..	..	..	431	440	471	442
	172	Other textiles	..	..	..	..	276	276	312	305
	173	Knitted and crocheted fabrics and articles	..	..	..	..	197	171	178	169
	18	**Wearing apparel dressing & dyeing of fur**	..	..	..	..	..	..	..	..
	181	Wearing apparel, except fur apparel	..	..	..	..	743	663	705	721
	182	Dressing and dyeing of fur; articles of fur	..	..	..	..	75	82	88	117
	19	**Tanning, dressing leather; leather artic.; footwear**	..	..	..	..	..	..	..	..
	191	Tanning, dressing leather; manuf. of leather articles	..	..	..	..	..	..	..	..
	192	Footwear	..	..	..	..	163	160	146	141
	20	**Wood and cork products, ex. furniture**	..	..	..	..	1 039	1 081	1 371	1 191
	201	Sawmilling and planing of wood	..	..	..	..	788	761	850	..
	202	Products of wood, cork, straw & plaiting material	..	..	..	..	251	320	368	..
	21	**Paper and paper products**	..	..	..	..	..	..	..	..
	22	**Publishing, printing & reprod. of recorded media**	..	..	..	..	..	..	..	..
	221	Publishing	..	..	..	..	..	..	..	..
	222	Printing and related service activities	..	..	..	..	..	..	..	..
	223	Reproduction of recorded media	..	..	..	..	..	..	..	..
	23	**Coke, refined petroleum products & nuclear fuel**	..	..	..	..	249	262	263	247
	24	**Chemicals and chemical products**	..	..	..	..	1 687	1 723	1 781	1 922
	241	Basic chemicals	..	..	..	..	1 049	1 069	1 054	1 159
	242	Other chemical products	..	..	..	..	638	654	727	763
	243	Man-made fibres	..	..	..	..	..	..	..	..
	25	**Rubber and plastic products**	..	..	..	..	1 209	1 249	..	1 419
	251	Rubber products	..	..	..	..	273	293	298	308
	252	Plastic products	..	..	..	..	935	956	..	1 111
	26	**Other non-metallic mineral products**	..	..	..	..	1 300	1 289	1 177	1 251
	261	Glass and glass products	..	..	..	..	207	213	210	200
	269	Non-metallic mineral products, nec	..	..	..	..	1 093	1 076	967	1 050
	27	**Basic metals**	..	..	..	..	2 807	2 751	2 868	..
	271	Basic iron and steel	..	..	..	..	2 747	2 701	2 820	..
	272	Basic precious and non-ferrous metals	..	..	..	..	..	..	..	..
	273	Casting of metals	..	..	..	..	60	50	48	27
	28	**Fabricated metal products, ex. machin. & equip.**	..	..	..	..	2 420	..	..	..
	281	Structural metal prod., tanks, reservoirs, generators	..	..	..	..	1 523	1 578	1 701	..
	289	Other fabricated metal products & service activities	..	..	..	..	1 050	1 069	894	..
	29	**Machinery and equipment, nec**	..	..	..	..	1 280	1 334	1 418	..
	291	General purpose machinery	..	..	..	..	382	360	380	392
	292	Special purpose machinery	..	..	..	..	556	588	656	..
	293	Domestic appliances, nec	..	..	..	..	342	386	382	414
	30	**Office, accounting and computing machinery**	..	..	..	..	68	82	123	119
	31	**Electrical machinery and apparatus, nec**	..	..	..	..	734	768	571	832
	311	Electric motors, generators and transformers	..	..	..	..	448	465	472	490
	312	Electricity distribution and control apparatus	..	..	..	..	..	..	..	..
	313	Insulated wire and cable	..	..	..	..	150	164	183	182
	314	Accumulators, primary cells and primary batteries	..	..	..	..	37	31	40	38
	315	Electric lamps and lighting equipment	..	..	..	..	100	108	118	123
	319	Other electrical equipment, nec	..	..	..	..	..	..	..	..
	32	**Radio, TV, communication equip. & apparatus**	..	..	..	..	567	425	765	653
	321	Electronic valves, tubes & other electronic compon.	..	..	..	..	255	172	..	333
	322	TV, radio transmitters & appar. for line teleph., telegr.	..	..	..	..	313	252	293	320
	323	TV, radio receivers and associated goods	..	..	..	..	..	..	..	..
	33	**Medical, precision, optical instr.; watches, clocks**	..	..	..	..	359	374	211	367
	331	Medical equip.; precision instruments and appliances	..	..	..	..	..	..	..	..
	332	Optical instruments and photographic equipment	..	..	..	..	..	..	..	..
	333	Watches and clocks	..	..	..	..	..	..	..	..
	34	**Motor vehicles, trailers, and semi-trailers**	..	..	..	..	1 549	1 633	1 828	1 865
	35	**Other transport equipment**	..	..	..	..	1 064	1 062	1 032	1 065
	351	Building and repairing of ships and boats	..	..	..	..	311	322	337	354
	352	Railway, tramway locomotives and rolling stock	..	..	..	..	142	169	164	174
	353	Aircraft and spacecraft	..	..	..	..	602	558	531	522
	359	Transport equipment, nec	..	..	..	..	10	13	16	15
	36	**Furniture; manufacturing, nec**	..	..	..	..	1 110	1 139	1 166	1 246
	361	Furniture	..	..	..	..	836	878	904	965
	369	Manufacturing, nec	..	..	..	..	274	261	262	281
	37	**Recycling**	..	..	..	..	..	..	..	..
E	40-41	**Electricity, gas and water supply**	..	..	..	..	..	..	..	..
	40	**Electricity, gas, steam and hot water supply**	..	..	..	..	..	..	..	..
	401	Production, collection and distribution of electricity	..	..	..	..	2 290	2 013	..	..
	41	410	**Collection, purification, distribution of water**	..	..	..	..	..	..	..	..
F	45	**Construction**	..	..	..	..	6 187	7 095	7 874	8 991
G	50-52	**Wholesale and retail trade; repairs etc**	..	..	..	..	23 573	26 568	28 724	30 623
H	55	**Hotels and restaurants**	..	..	..	..	4 832	5 518	5 919	6 301
I	60-64	**Transport, storage and communications**	..	..	..	..	14 053	14 582	15 679	15 774
J	65-67	**Financial intermediation**	..	..	..	..	10 218	10 958	11 464	11 970
K	70-74	**Real estate, renting and business activities**	..	..	..	..	14 331	12 916	16 761	22 261
L-Q	75-99	**Public admin.; education; health; other services**	..	..	..	..	..	..	..	..
A-Q	01-99	**Grand total**	..	..	..	..	..	..	..	..

Note: Data cover the fiscal year ending 30 June. Recycling activities are included with the industry of original manufacture. ISIC 1530 includes 1544; 1711 include 2430; 182 includes 191;
201 includes 2022; 2023 includes 2029; 2211 includes 2219; 2213 includes 223; 2411 include 2412 and 2423; 2694 includes 2695; 2696 includes 2699; 271 includes 272, 2731, 2891, and
371; 2813 includes 2911, 2913, 2914, 2919, 2926, and 2929; 2899 includes 2927; 291 includes 2912 and 2915; 2922 includes 2923; 311 includes 312 and 319; and 321 includes 323. ISIC
154 excludes 1544; 24 excludes 2430; 242 excludes 2423; 273 excludes 2731; 289 excludes 2891; ISIC 292 excludes 2926, 2927, 2929

OECD Industrial Structure Statistics
OCDE OECD, © 1998

Table AU.1 PRODUCTION - PRODUCTION

Millions de Sch (Prix courants) — CITI révision 3

1989	1990	1991	1992	1993	1994	1995	1996		A–Q	CITI	Grp
..	..	..	..	..	..	..	..	**Agriculture, chasse et sylviculture**	A	01-02	
..	..	..	..	..	..	..	..	**Pêche**	B	05	
..	20 032	20 665	19 999	20 338	18 906	11 473	..	**Activités extractives**	C	10-14	
..	1 648	1 630	1 628	1 431	1 134	1 027	..	Extraction de charbon, de lignite et de tourbe		10	
..	12 352	13 115	11 998				..	Extraction de pétrole brut et de gaz naturel		11	
..	906	705	641				..	Extraction de minerais métalliques		13	
..	5 126	5 215	5 732	5 787	6 042	9 096	..	Autres activités extractives		14	
..	1 028 691	1 072 598	1 058 828	1 020 148	1 073 536	1 100 497	..	**Activités de fabrication**	D	15-37	
..	142 168	149 697	155 810	158 323	156 777	154 958	..	**Produits alimentaires et boissons**		15	
..	25 999	28 140	31 795	31 972	33 696	26 141	..	Boissons			155
..	18 999	19 782	20 086	19 921	20 849		..	**Produits à base de tabac**		16	160
..	40 897	40 812	41 053	38 216	37 395	39 377	..	**Textiles**		17	
..	18 994	18 209	17 819	16 147	15 818	21 479	..	Filature, tissage et achèvement des textiles			171
..	13 731	14 038	14 309	13 779	13 579	11 804	..	Autres articles textiles			172
..	8 172	8 564	8 924	8 290	7 998	6 095	..	Etoffes et articles de bonneterie			173
..	15 785	15 343	14 682	13 459	12 188	14 298	..	**Habillement; préparation, teinture des fourrures**		18	
..	15 498	15 113	14 450	13 298	12 014	13 992	..	Articles d'habillement autres qu'en fourrure			181
..	288	230	232	161	173	307	..	Préparation, teinture des fourrures; art. en fourrure			182
..	11 595	10 970	10 166	9 407	9 024	9 409	..	**Travail des cuirs; articles en cuir; chaussures**		19	
..	3 546	3 283	3 346	3 112	3 001	3 360	..	Apprêt et tannage des cuirs et articles en cuirs			191
..	8 049	7 687	6 820	6 294	6 023	6 048	..	Chaussures			192
..	64 503	67 512	68 963	65 885	71 603	54 689	..	**Bois et articles en bois et liège (sauf meubles)**		20	
..	24 334	23 456	22 495	19 653	21 789	20 993	..	Sciage et rabotage du bois			201
..	40 169	44 056	46 468	46 232	49 814	33 696	..	Articles en bois, liège, vannerie, sparterie			202
..	47 452	47 909	47 126	43 232	48 478	56 697	..	**Papier et carton; articles en papier et en carton**		21	
..	32 184	34 926	34 954	33 225	34 144	43 341	..	**Edition, imprimerie et reproduction**		22	
..	8 793	10 198	10 483	9 945	11 216	16 143	..	Edition			221
..	22 356	23 742	23 478	22 333	22 034	25 098	..	Imprimerie et activités annexes			222
..	1 034	986	993	947	894	2 101	..	Reproduction de supports enregistrés			223
..	38 371	37 748	32 910	32 796	33 047		..	**Cokéfaction; prod. pétroliers; comb. nucléaires**		23	
..	91 003	93 172	89 468	85 440	90 238	62 046	..	**Produits chimiques**		24	
..	52 517	51 915	48 076	42 555	47 051	26 972	..	Produits chimiques de base			241
..	38 486	41 257	41 392	42 885	43 187		..	Autres produits chimiques			242
..	..	..	..	..	..	..	..	Fibres synthétiques ou artificielles			243
..	27 740	29 626	29 967	29 296	30 375	42 213	..	**Articles en caoutchouc et en matières plastiques**		25	
..	10 733	10 902	10 936	9 679	10 258	7 853	..	Articles en caoutchouc			251
..	17 007	18 723	19 032	19 617	20 117	34 360	..	Articles en matières plastiques			252
..	56 400	60 186	61 104	61 281	65 735	61 763	..	**Autres produits minéraux non métalliques**		26	
..	11 115	11 593	12 126	11 732	12 139	11 170	..	Verre et articles en verre			261
..	45 286	48 593	48 977	49 549	53 596	50 593	..	Produits minéraux non métalliques, nca			269
..	84 186	78 719	75 239	66 782	71 839	78 865	..	**Produits métallurgiques de base**		27	
..	45 456	42 531	40 116	36 851	40 652	50 301	..	Sidérurgie et première transformation de l'acier			271
..	29 148	26 433	25 575	21 372	21 880	21 628	..	Métallurgie; métaux précieux et non ferreux			272
..	9 582	9 756	9 548	8 559	9 307	6 936	..	Fonderie			273
..	67 253	69 192	72 052	70 224	74 868	86 967	..	**Ouvrages en métaux, sauf machines et matériel**		28	
..	26 650	27 407	28 923	29 354	31 203	43 822	..	Constr. et menuiserie métal.; réservoirs; générateurs			281
..	40 603	41 784	43 128	40 871	43 664	43 146	..	Autres ouvrages en métaux			289
..	110 171	118 406	104 294	98 250	108 040	108 890	..	**Machines et matériel, nca**		29	
..	27 660	31 877	18 974	19 911	22 268	42 108	..	Machines d'usage général			291
..	76 075	79 774	78 262	71 724	78 872	59 253	..	Machines d'usage spécifique			292
..	6 436	6 755	7 057	6 615	6 900	7 528	..	Appareils domestiques, nca			293
..						565	..	**Mach. de bureau, comptables, matériel inform.**		30	
..	66 605	72 165	70 992	71 862	71 569	45 437	..	**Machines et appareils électriques, nca**		31	
..	13 419	14 787	12 832	16 700	14 751	13 240	..	Moteurs, génératrices et transformateurs électriques			311
..						10 965	..	Matériel électrique de distribution et de commande			312
..	5 371	5 658	5 730	6 021	6 041	7 083	..	Fils et câbles électriques isolés			313
..	47 815	51 720	52 430	49 141	50 778	1 907	..	Accumulateurs, piles électriques			314
..						4 230	..	Lampes électriques et appareils d'éclairage			315
..						8 013	..	Autres matériels électriques, nca			319
..	41 529	43 971	41 498	39 838	50 004	61 965	..	**Equip. et appar. de radio, TV, communication**		32	
..	32 545	33 350	27 926	28 380	35 061	11 468	..	Tubes et valves électroniques; autres composants			321
..	8 985	10 621	13 572	11 457	14 943	34 943	..	Emetteurs radio et TV; app. téléphonie, télégraphie			322
..						15 553	..	Récepteurs radio et TV et articles associés			323
..	10 561	11 945	12 901	12 593	12 561	14 110	..	**Instruments médicaux, de précision, d'optique**		33	
..	7 058	7 681	8 116	8 396	8 912	11 604	..	Appareils médicaux et de précision			331
..	2 980	3 683	4 174	3 550	2 995	2 452	..	Instruments d'optique ; matériel photographique			332
..	524	582	611	647	654	54	..	Horlogerie			333
..	46 557	55 576	60 381	54 931	60 415	64 751	..	**Véhicules automobiles et nemorques**		34	
..	7 399	7 594	6 808	7 173	6 049	12 253	..	**Autres matériels de transport**		35	
..	1 473	1 371	714	931	405	365	..	Construction et réparation de navires			351
..	4 690	4 467	4 303	4 580	3 885	10 368	..	Construction de matériel ferroviaire roulant			352
..						214	..	Construction aéronautique et spatiale			353
..						1 305	..	Autres équipements de transport			359
..	7 332	7 346	8 374	8 013	8 339	52 702	..	**Meubles; activités de fabrication, nca**		36	
..	349	367	445	410	419	33 762	..	Meubles			361
..	6 983	6 980	7 930	7 603	7 920	18 940	..	Activités de fabrication, nca			369
..						1 461	..	**Récupération**		37	
..	108 741	117 575	121 262	125 801	124 681	134 961	..	**Production et distrib. d'électricité, de gaz, d'eau**	E	40-41	
..	105 102	113 673	117 031	120 953	119 671	130 750	..	**Electricité, gaz, vapeur et eau chaude**		40	
..	86 533	91 460	94 942	96 993	94 693	110 750	..	Production, collecte et distribution d'électricité			401
..	3 639	3 902	4 231	4 848	5 009	4 210	..	**Captage, épuration et distribution d'eau**		41	410
..			180 728	187 669	202 143	277 540		..	**Construction**	F	45	
..	..	..	..	..	..	478 247	..	**Commerce de gros et de détail; réparation**	G	50-52	
..	..	..	..	..	..	111 403	..	**Hôtels et restaurants**	H	55	
..	..	..	..	..	..	204 040	..	**Transports, entreposage et communications**	I	60-64	
..	..	..	..	..	..	228 556	..	**Intermédiation financière**	J	65-67	
..	..	..	..	..	..	211 941	..	**Immobilier, locations, services aux entreprises**	K	70-74	
..	..	..	..	..	..	122 927	..	**Admin. publique; éducation; santé; autres**	L-Q	75-99	
..	..	..	..	..	..	..	..	**Grand total**	A-Q	01-99	

Note: Data for 1990-94 are not comparable with 1995 due to changes in statistical concepts, sources and methods. For more detail see "sources and definitions" section of this publication.

Statistiques des Structures Industrielles
OCDE, © 1998

Table AU.2 VALUE ADDED - VALEUR AJOUTÉE

Millions of Sch (Current Prices)

ISIC revision 3			1989	1990	1991	1992	1993	1994	1995	1996
A	01-02	**Agriculture, hunting and forestry**	..	..	..	..	..	..	..	..
B	05	**Fishing**	..	..	..	..	..	..	..	..
C	10-14	**Mining and quarrying**	..	8 134	7 982	7 595	7 494	6 756	6 653	..
	10	Mining of coal and lignite; extraction of peat	..	998	966	903	842	600	1 004	..
	11	Crude petroleum & natural gas; related service activ.	..	4 217	4 145	3 754	..	..	..	..
	13	Mining of metal ores	..	425	222	207	..	..	..	..
	14	Other mining and quarrying	..	2 494	2 649	2 731	2 809	2 940	4 674	..
D	15-37	**Total manufacturing**	..	356 078	372 142	369 703	359 832	381 165	420 731	..
	15	**Food products and beverages**	..	35 734	38 162	42 325	43 810	42 886	46 233	..
	155	Beverages	..	9 558	9 940	12 505	12 761	13 588	9 699	..
	16 160	**Tobacco products**	..	16 115	16 635	17 204	16 853	17 948		..
	17	**Textiles**	..	14 680	14 788	15 293	14 562	14 137	16 148	..
	171	Spinning, weaving and finishing of textiles	..	6 812	6 492	6 452	5 840	5 893	8 895	..
	172	Other textiles	..	4 672	4 849	5 141	5 130	4 875	4 790	..
	173	Knitted and crocheted fabrics and articles	..	3 196	3 448	3 700	3 592	3 368	2 463	..
	18	**Wearing apparel dressing & dyeing of fur**	..	6 220	6 059	5 667	5 096	4 537	5 796	..
	181	Wearing apparel, except fur apparel	..	6 133	5 994	5 607	5 037	4 480	5 658	..
	182	Dressing and dyeing of fur; articles of fur	..	87	65	61	59	57	139	..
	19	**Tanning, dressing leather; leather artic.; footwear**	..	3 358	3 448	3 264	3 073	2 579	3 020	..
	191	Tanning, dressing leather; manuf. of leather articles	..	934	979	947	907	733	799	..
	192	Footwear	..	2 423	2 469	2 317	2 166	1 846	2 221	..
	20	**Wood and cork products, ex. furniture**	..	21 174	23 741	24 563	23 579	24 950	19 497	..
	201	Sawmilling and planing of wood	..	5 961	6 111	5 786	5 221	5 702	5 677	..
	202	Products of wood, cork, straw & plaiting material	..	15 213	17 630	18 777	18 358	19 248	13 820	..
	21	**Paper and paper products**	..	15 159	15 255	14 319	13 100	15 441	19 690	..
	22	**Publishing, printing & reprod. of recorded media**	..	13 222	14 330	13 843	13 675	14 045	19 187	..
	221	Publishing	..	2 298	2 763	2 260	2 765	3 267	5 110	..
	222	Printing and related service activities	..	10 412	11 075	11 155	10 415	10 326	12 770	..
	223	Reproduction of recorded media	..	513	492	428	495	452	1 306	..
	23	**Coke, refined petroleum products & nuclear fuel**	..	6 292	6 130	5 453	5 756	6 900	..	..
	24	**Chemicals and chemical products**	..	26 679	27 757	27 070	27 257	28 523	21 724	..
	241	Basic chemicals	..	14 519	14 186	13 389	12 456	14 156	7 170	..
	242	Other chemical products	..	12 161	13 571	13 681	14 801	14 367		..
	243	Man-made fibres	..	..	..	..	..	..	..	..
	25	**Rubber and plastic products**	..	9 727	11 011	11 602	11 750	12 214	17 420	..
	251	Rubber products	..	3 536	3 824	3 926	3 543	3 980	3 357	..
	252	Plastic products	..	6 192	7 187	7 676	8 207	8 234	14 063	..
	26	**Other non-metallic mineral products**	..	23 900	26 163	26 320	25 612	28 071	28 793	..
	261	Glass and glass products	..	5 885	6 074	6 702	6 630	6 941	6 324	..
	269	Non-metallic mineral products, nec	..	18 015	20 090	19 618	18 983	21 131	22 470	..
	27	**Basic metals**	..	28 683	26 152	22 413	19 982	22 029	27 767	..
	271	Basic iron and steel	..	19 011	16 633	12 989	11 888	13 381	20 113	..
	272	Basic precious and non-ferrous metals	..	4 939	5 031	4 662	3 858	4 259	4 464	..
	273	Casting of metals	..	4 734	4 489	4 762	4 236	4 390	3 190	..
	28	**Fabricated metal products, ex. machin. & equip.**	..	28 808	28 957	30 477	29 392	32 310	38 850	..
	281	Structural metal prod., tanks, reservoirs, generators	..	11 156	10 486	11 476	10 881	12 475	17 347	..
	289	Other fabricated metal products & service activities	..	17 652	18 472	19 001	18 511	19 834	21 503	..
	29	**Machinery and equipment, nec**	..	39 790	42 443	36 933	35 447	40 211	44 300	..
	291	General purpose machinery	..	11 400	12 745	6 585	8 146	9 167	17 809	..
	292	Special purpose machinery	..	26 032	27 306	27 479	24 657	28 385	23 293	..
	293	Domestic appliances, nec	..	2 358	2 392	2 868	2 644	2 659	3 199	..
	30	**Office, accounting and computing machinery**	..	..	..	..	..	..	212	..
	31	**Electrical machinery and apparatus, nec**	..	25 598	27 451	27 300	28 214	27 734	20 708	..
	311	Electric motors, generators and transformers	..	5 552	5 885	5 870	7 161	6 349	6 201	..
	312	Electricity distribution and control apparatus	..	..	..	..	..	..	5 048	..
	313	Insulated wire and cable	..	1 890	2 280	2 373	2 594	2 640	2 831	..
	314	Accumulators, primary cells and primary batteries	..	18 156	19 286	19 057	18 459	18 745	733	..
	315	Electric lamps and lighting equipment	..	..	..	..	..	..	2 015	..
	319	Other electrical equipment, nec	..	..	..	..	..	..	3 879	..
	32	**Radio, TV, communication equip. & apparatus**	..	14 129	13 855	14 250	14 100	16 409	25 970	..
	321	Electronic valves, tubes & other electronic compon.	..	9 910	9 247	8 721	9 107	10 398	5 747	..
	322	TV, radio transmitters & appar. for line teleph., telegr.	..	4 220	4 608	5 529	4 993	6 012	16 629	..
	323	TV, radio receivers and associated goods	..	..	..	..	..	..	3 593	..
	33	**Medical, precision, optical instr.; watches, clocks**	..	5 077	5 609	5 989	5 973	5 867	7 371	..
	331	Medical equip.; precision instruments and appliances	..	3 262	3 513	3 688	3 907	4 138	6 114	..
	332	Optical instruments and photographic equipment	..	1 606	1 863	2 053	1 814	1 454	1 226	..
	333	Watches and clocks	..	209	232	249	252	275	32	..
	34	**Motor vehicles, trailers, and semi-trailers**	..	15 583	17 843	19 199	16 198	18 465	19 334	..
	35	**Other transport equipment**	..	3 199	3 333	2 929	3 215	2 753	3 964	..
	351	Building and repairing of ships and boats	..	525	481	266	472	210	185	..
	352	Railway, tramway locomotives and rolling stock	..	2 393	2 132	2 053	2 103	1 883	3 317	..
	353	Aircraft and spacecraft	..	..	..	..	..	..	90	..
	359	Transport equipment, nec	..	..	..	..	..	..	372	..
	36	**Furniture; manufacturing, nec**	..	2 952	3 018	3 290	3 188	3 155	22 386	..
	361	Furniture	..	122	126	156	140	150	16 191	..
	369	Manufacturing, nec	..	2 830	2 892	3 134	3 047	3 005	6 195	..
	37	**Recycling**	..	..	..	..	..	..	631	..
E	40-41	**Electricity, gas and water supply**	..	48 423	51 528	55 342	58 609	58 548	62 268	..
	40	**Electricity, gas, steam and hot water supply**	..	46 064	48 999	52 565	55 404	55 245	59 463	..
	401	Production, collection and distribution of electricity	..	39 666	41 502	44 470	46 493	45 344	52 345	..
	41 410	**Collection, purification, distribution of water**	..	2 359	2 529	2 776	3 205	3 303	2 805	..
F	45	**Construction**	..	..	..	82 904	88 204	95 979	130 184	..
G	50-52	**Wholesale and retail trade; repairs etc**	..	..	..	..	..	..	254 460	..
H	55	**Hotels and restaurants**	..	..	..	..	..	..	52 552	..
I	60-64	**Transport, storage and communications**	..	..	..	..	..	..	139 130	..
J	65-67	**Financial intermediation**	..	..	..	..	..	..	142 120	..
K	70-74	**Real estate, renting and business activities**	..	..	..	..	..	..	129 264	..
L-Q	75-99	**Public admin.; education; health; other services**	..	..	..	..	..	..	74 777	..
A-Q	01-99	**Grand total**	..	..	..	..	..	..	..	..

Note: Data for 1990-94 are not comparable with 1995 due to changes in statistical concepts, sources and methods. For more detail see "sources and definitions" section of this publication.

Table AU.3 INVESTISSEMENT - INVESTMENT

Millions de Sch (Prix courants) CITI révision 3

1989	1990	1991	1992	1993	1994	1995	1996				
..						..		**Agriculture, chasse et sylviculture**	A	01-02	
								Pêche	B	05	
..	1 640	1 802	1 774	1 932	1 941	2 364	..	**Activités extractives**	C	10-14	
..	131	63	55	69	46	111		Extraction de charbon, de lignite et de tourbe		10	
..	547	856	964	..	..	..		Extraction de pétrole brut et de gaz naturel		11	
..	205	48	41					Extraction de minerais métalliques		13	
..	757	835	714	838	903	1 807		Autres activités extractives		14	
..	66 959	69 911	70 599	59 098	57 422	64 346		**Activités de fabrication**	D	15-37	
..	7 530	8 418	8 622	9 484	9 515	9 313		**Produits alimentaires et boissons**		15	
..	2 512	3 104	3 344	3 347	3 302	2 689		Boissons			155
..	293	252	338	383	290	..		**Produits à base de tabac**		16	160
..	3 071	3 298	2 196	1 649	1 743	2 028		**Textiles**		17	
..	1 795	2 127	1 258	682	714	1 145		Filature, tissage et achèvement des textiles			171
..	967	893	645	692	649	597		Autres articles textiles			172
..	308	279	294	274	380	286		Etoffes et articles de bonneterie			173
..	459	373	405	433	289	370		**Habillement; préparation, teinture des fourrures**		18	
..	457	368	405	431	282	362		Articles d'habillement autres qu'en fourrure			181
..	3	5	1	2	6	8		Préparation, teinture des fourrures; art. en fourrure			182
..	351	370	337	404	250	261		**Travail des cuirs; articles en cuir; chaussures**		19	
..	120	167	121	168	75	55		Apprêt et tannage des cuirs et articles en cuirs			191
..	231	203	216	237	175	206		Chaussures			192
..	4 559	4 869	4 574	4 115	4 153	4 386		**Bois et articles en bois et liège (sauf meubles)**		20	
..	1 660	1 818	1 477	1 238	1 344	1 691		Sciage et rabotage du bois			201
..	2 899	3 051	3 097	2 878	2 810	2 695		Articles en bois, liège, vannerie, sparterie			202
..	9 547	6 098	5 351	3 709	3 042	3 205		**Papier et carton; articles en papier et en carton**		21	
..	2 009	3 519	2 281	2 390	1 936	2 746		**Edition, imprimerie et reproduction**		22	
..	312	1 408	627	466	543	652		Edition			221
..	1 588	2 022	1 563	1 866	1 354	1 912		Imprimerie et activités annexes			222
..	109	89	92	58	38	183		Reproduction de supports enregistrés			223
..	1 430	1 265	1 504	863	828	..		**Cokéfaction; prod. pétroliers; comb. nucléaires**		23	
..	6 391	6 842	7 709	6 519	5 391	3 957		**Produits chimiques**		24	
..	3 670	4 235	4 778	3 157	2 333	1 237		Produits chimiques de base			241
..	2 722	2 607	2 931	3 362	3 058	..		Autres produits chimiques			242
..	..	..	..	..	..			Fibres synthétiques ou artificielles			243
..	2 247	2 234	2 270	1 906	2 095	2 767		**Articles en caoutchouc et en matières plastiques**		25	
..	543	547	629	381	354	388		Articles en caoutchouc			251
..	1 704	1 687	1 642	1 524	1 741	2 379		Articles en matières plastiques			252
..	5 562	5 673	5 981	4 654	5 521	5 479		**Autres produits minéraux non métalliques**		26	
..	1 936	1 556	1 694	1 046	1 197	1 490		Verre et articles en verre			261
..	3 626	4 118	4 287	3 607	4 324	3 989		Produits minéraux non métalliques, nca			269
..	4 985	5 307	5 732	3 670	3 841	4 474		**Produits métallurgiques de base**		27	
..	2 801	2 620	2 725	1 825	2 048	3 444		Sidérurgie et première transformation de l'acier			271
..	1 340	1 730	1 898	1 182	993	493		Métallurgie; métaux précieux et non ferreux			272
..	843	957	1 109	662	800	537		Fonderie			273
..	4 186	4 601	4 462	4 220	4 478	5 542		**Ouvrages en métaux, sauf machines et matériel**		28	
..	1 272	1 224	1 342	1 277	1 595	2 219		Constr. et menuiserie métal.; réservoirs; générateurs			281
..	2 915	3 377	3 120	2 943	2 884	3 322		Autres ouvrages en métaux			289
..	5 036	5 404	4 573	3 838	4 542	4 459		**Machines et matériel, nca**		29	
..	1 399	1 405	1 065	1 149	1 710	1 708		Machines d'usage général			291
..	3 287	3 447	3 035	2 348	2 472	2 351		Machines d'usage spécifique			292
..	350	552	472	341	360	401		Appareils domestiques, nca			293
..	..	..	..	..	..	30		**Mach. de bureau, comptables, matériel inform.**		30	
..	3 367	3 264	3 128	2 952	2 165	2 066		**Machines et appareils électriques, nca**		31	
..	855	768	511	679	511	465		Moteurs, génératrices et transformateurs électriques			311
..	..	..	..	..	..	590		Matériel électrique de distribution et de commande			312
..	219	217	410	373	340	219		Fils et câbles électriques isolés			313
..	2 294	2 279	2 207	1 899	1 313	70		Accumulateurs, piles électriques			314
..	..	..	..	..	..	167		Lampes électriques et appareils d'éclairage			315
..	..	..	..	..	..	555		Autres matériels électriques, nca			319
..	2 636	2 726	3 411	2 319	3 096	3 785		**Equip. et appar. de radio, TV, communication**		32	
..	2 127	2 263	2 669	1 671	2 484	1 364		Tubes et valves électroniques; autres composants			321
..	509	463	743	648	612	1 895		Emetteurs radio et TV; app. téléphonie, télégraphie			322
..	..	..	..	..	..	526		Récepteurs radio et TV et articles associés			323
..	647	710	545	715	832	769		**Instruments médicaux, de précision, d'optique**		33	
..	461	471	333	413	642	673		Appareils médicaux et de précision			331
..	176	230	204	283	170	95		Instruments d'optique ; matériel photographique			332
..	10	10	8	20	21	1		Horlogerie			333
..	2 160	4 200	6 245	4 227	2 847	3 586		**Véhicules automobiles et nemorques**		34	
..	249	238	311	265	227	390		**Autres matériels de transport**		35	
..	54	39	14	7	14	34		Construction et réparation de navires			351
..	187	182	188	208	171	294		Construction de matériel ferroviaire roulant			352
..	..	..	..	..	..	39		Construction aéronautique et spatiale			353
..	..	..	..	..	..	24		Autres équipements de transport			359
..	241	250	622	382	340	3 034		**Meubles; activités de fabrication, nca**		36	
..	7	6	15	15	10	2 276		Meubles			361
..	234	243	607	367	331	758		Activités de fabrication, nca			369
..	..	..	..	..	..	162		**Récupération**		37	
..	19 502	18 999	21 812	21 098	21 459	23 980		**Production et distrib. d'électricité, de gaz, d'eau**	E	40-41	
..	18 174	17 684	20 561	19 747	20 149	22 606		**Electricité, gaz, vapeur et eau chaude**		40	
..	14 123	13 933	15 590	14 203	14 436	19 174		Production, collecte et distribution d'électricité			401
..	1 327	1 315	1 251	1 350	1 310	1 374		**Captage, épuration et distribution d'eau**		41	410
..	..	..	7 295	8 025	7 698	11 487		**Construction**	F	45	
..	..	..	..	..	..	43 414		**Commerce de gros et de détail; réparation**	G	50-52	
..	..	..	..	..	..	12 917		**Hôtels et restaurants**	H	55	
..	..	..	..	..	..	48 854		**Transports, entreposage et communications**	I	60-64	
..	..	..	..	..	..	20 846		**Intermédiation financière**	J	65-67	
..	..	..	..	..	..	82 042		**Immobilier, locations, services aux entreprises**	K	70-74	
..	..	..	..	..	..	14 545		**Admin. publique; éducation; santé; autres**	L-Q	75-99	
								Grand total	A-Q	01-99	

Note: Data for 1990-94 are not comparable with 1995 due to changes in statistical concepts, sources and methods. For more detail see "sources and definitions" section of this publication.

Statistiques des Structures Industrielles
OCDE, © 1998

Table AU.4 **INVESTMENT IN MACHINERY AND EQUIPMENT - DÉPENSES EN MACHINES ET ÉQUIPEMENT**

Millions of Sch (Current Prices)

ISIC revision 3				1989	1990	1991	1992	1993	1994	1995	1996
A	01-02		**Agriculture, hunting and forestry**	..	..	..	..	..	..	..	..
B	05		**Fishing**	..	..	..	..	..	..	..	..
C	10-14		**Mining and quarrying**	..	1 033	1 148	1 294	1 300	1 439	1 593	..
	10		Mining of coal and lignite; extraction of peat	..	53	17	36	26	24	94	..
	11		Crude petroleum & natural gas; related service activ.	..	457	749	905				..
	13		Mining of metal ores	..	103	15	6	..	..	..	..
	14		Other mining and quarrying	..	421	366	347	316	503	1 092	..
D	15-37		**Total manufacturing**	..	43 946	46 673	46 402	37 977	37 289	44 189	..
	15		**Food products and beverages**	..	4 205	4 613	4 722	5 265	4 926	5 588	..
		155	Beverages	..	1 101	1 554	1 505	1 600	1 457	1 507	..
	16	160	**Tobacco products**	..	163	180	250	143	104		..
	17		**Textiles**	..	2 056	2 176	1 487	1 058	1 119	1 519	..
		171	Spinning, weaving and finishing of textiles	..	1 308	1 351	844	467	517	930	..
		172	Other textiles	..	543	646	424	415	419	384	..
		173	Knitted and crocheted fabrics and articles	..	205	180	219	176	183	204	..
	18		**Wearing apparel dressing & dyeing of fur**	..	260	223	256	199	166	270	..
		181	Wearing apparel, except fur apparel	..	259	221	255	199	162	265	..
		182	Dressing and dyeing of fur; articles of fur	..	2	2	1	1	4	5	..
	19		**Tanning, dressing leather; leather artic.; footwear**	..	238	224	211	202	199	207	..
		191	Tanning, dressing leather; manuf. of leather articles	..	79	91	78	58	54	46	..
		192	Footwear	..	159	133	133	143	145	161	..
	20		**Wood and cork products, ex. furniture**	..	2 596	2 846	2 772	2 408	2 203	2 852	..
		201	Sawmilling and planing of wood	..	944	1 108	872	778	761	1 174	..
		202	Products of wood, cork, straw & plaiting material	..	1 653	1 738	1 900	1 630	1 442	1 678	..
	21		**Paper and paper products**	..	6 310	4 513	3 927	2 677	2 451	2 550	..
	22		**Publishing, printing & reprod. of recorded media**	..	1 483	2 760	1 716	1 789	1 475	2 011	..
		221	Publishing	..	215	1 109	523	326	417	428	..
		222	Printing and related service activities	..	1 170	1 572	1 128	1 408	1 029	1 453	..
		223	Reproduction of recorded media	..	98	79	65	56	29	131	..
	23		**Coke, refined petroleum products & nuclear fuel**	..	942	876	984	588	611		..
	24		**Chemicals and chemical products**	..	4 276	4 546	4 683	3 735	3 714	2 717	..
		241	Basic chemicals	..	2 753	3 101	3 304	1 760	1 676	930	..
		242	Other chemical products	..	1 523	1 445	1 379	1 974	2 037	..	..
		243	Man-made fibres	..	..	..	..	..	..	..	..
	25		**Rubber and plastic products**	..	1 577	1 654	1 498	1 304	1 608	2 073	..
		251	Rubber products	..	450	501	467	328	284	347	..
		252	Plastic products	..	1 127	1 153	1 031	976	1 324	1 726	..
	26		**Other non-metallic mineral products**	..	3 777	3 677	3 622	2 915	3 159	3 813	..
		261	Glass and glass products	..	1 570	1 198	1 268	892	714	1 015	..
		269	Non-metallic mineral products, nec	..	2 207	2 479	2 353	2 023	2 445	2 798	..
	27		**Basic metals**	..	3 917	4 115	4 270	2 881	3 119	3 860	..
		271	Basic iron and steel	..	2 250	2 065	2 284	1 543	1 741	2 998	..
		272	Basic precious and non-ferrous metals	..	1 003	1 461	1 194	795	791	421	..
		273	Casting of metals	..	664	589	792	543	588	441	..
	28		**Fabricated metal products, ex. machin. & equip.**	..	2 496	2 895	2 853	2 553	2 615	3 715	..
		281	Structural metal prod., tanks, reservoirs, generators	..	609	660	747	712	782	1 246	..
		289	Other fabricated metal products & service activities	..	1 887	2 235	2 107	1 841	1 833	2 469	..
	29		**Machinery and equipment, nec**	..	3 272	3 309	2 788	2 393	2 668	2 996	..
		291	General purpose machinery	..	957	859	745	595	883	1 143	..
		292	Special purpose machinery	..	2 034	2 057	1 697	1 513	1 509	1 545	..
		293	Domestic appliances, nec	..	281	393	346	284	276	308	..
	30		**Office, accounting and computing machinery**	..	..	..	..	..	..	12	..
	31		**Electrical machinery and apparatus, nec**	..	1 924	2 125	1 854	1 987	1 562	1 529	..
		311	Electric motors, generators and transformers	..	448	553	350	525	350	323	..
		312	Electricity distribution and control apparatus	..	..	..	..	..	..	467	..
		313	Insulated wire and cable	..	174	148	272	353	255	161	..
		314	Accumulators, primary cells and primary batteries	..	1 303	1 423	1 231	1 110	957	55	..
		315	Electric lamps and lighting equipment	..	..	..	..	..	..	108	..
		319	Other electrical equipment, nec	..	..	..	..	..	..	416	..
	32		**Radio, TV, communication equip. & apparatus**	..	2 215	2 344	2 784	1 652	2 549	3 093	..
		321	Electronic valves, tubes & other electronic compon.	..	1 845	1 983	2 298	1 249	2 093	1 153	..
		322	TV, radio transmitters & appar. for line teleph., telegr.	..	369	362	486	403	457	1 443	..
		323	TV, radio receivers and associated goods	..	..	..	..	..	..	496	..
	33		**Medical, precision, optical instr.; watches, clocks**	..	457	470	431	556	383	436	..
		331	Medical equip.; precision instruments and appliances	..	318	318	252	286	241	365	..
		332	Optical instruments and photographic equipment	..	133	148	175	262	125	71	..
		333	Watches and clocks	..	6	5	4	8	17		..
	34		**Motor vehicles, trailers, and semi-trailers**	..	1 426	2 792	4 874	3 169	2 270	1 768	..
	35		**Other transport equipment**	..	181	130	162	207	101	211	..
		351	Building and repairing of ships and boats	..	33	15	8	4	9	16	..
		352	Railway, tramway locomotives and rolling stock	..	142	112	104	158	66	167	..
		353	Aircraft and spacecraft	..	..	..	..	..	..	13	..
		359	Transport equipment, nec	..	..	..	..	..	..	15	..
	36		**Furniture; manufacturing, nec**	..	174	204	258	298	287	1 753	..
		361	Furniture	..	2	2	6	5	4	1 217	..
		369	Manufacturing, nec	..	172	202	252	293	283	537	..
	37		**Recycling**	..	..	..	..	..	..	126	..
E	40-41		**Electricity, gas and water supply**	..	12 638	12 885	14 284	12 678	13 510	15 117	..
	40		**Electricity, gas, steam and hot water supply**	..	12 403	12 632	13 997	12 456	13 217	14 945	..
		401	Production, collection and distribution of electricity	..	9 569	9 814	10 503	9 307	9 280	12 740	..
	41	410	**Collection, purification, distribution of water**	..	235	253	287	222	294	173	..
F	45		**Construction**	..	..	..	3 685	3 855	3 631	6 798	..
G	50-52		**Wholesale and retail trade; repairs etc**	..	..	..	..	..	..	22 565	..
H	55		**Hotels and restaurants**	..	..	..	..	..	..	4 563	..
I	60-64		**Transport, storage and communications**	..	..	..	..	..	..	32 638	..
J	65-67		**Financial intermediation**	..	..	..	..	..	..	898	..
K	70-74		**Real estate, renting and business activities**	..	..	..	..	..	..	20 013	..
L-Q	75-99		**Public admin.; education; health; other services**	..	..	..	..	..	..	6 771	..
A-Q	01-99		**Grand total**	..	..	..	..	..	..	..	..

Note: Data for 1990-94 are not comparable with 1995 due to changes in statistical concepts, sources and methods. For more detail see "sources and definitions" section of this publication.

AUTRICHE

Table AU.5 ETABLISSEMENTS - ESTABLISHMENTS

Unités

1989	1990	1991	1992	1993	1994	1995	1996			CITI révision 3
..	..	..	..	..	..	..	..	**Agriculture, chasse et sylviculture**	A	01-02
..	..	..	..	..	..	..	..	**Pêche**	B	05
..	166	159	156	156	154	..	..	**Activités extractives**	C	10-14
..	12	10	12	10	10	..	..	Extraction de charbon, de lignite et de tourbe		10
..	8	8	6	7	7	..	..	Extraction de pétrole brut et de gaz naturel		11
..	6	6	5	4	3	..	..	Extraction de minerais métalliques		13
..	140	135	133	135	134	..	..	Autres activités extractives		14
..	9 144	8 920	8 598	8 385	8 185	..	..	**Activités de fabrication**	D	15-37
..	1 105	1 047	1 034	1 018	986	..	..	**Produits alimentaires et boissons**		15
..	242	234	226	222	225	..	..	Boissons		155
..	15	14	14	14	13	..	..	**Produits à base de tabac**		16 160
..	448	432	410	400	387	..	..	**Textiles**		17
..	113	112	104	101	99	..	..	Filature, tissage et achèvement des textiles		171
..	233	222	210	200	200	..	..	Autres articles textiles		172
..	102	98	96	99	88	..	..	Etoffes et articles de bonneterie		173
..	403	369	342	308	280	..	..	**Habillement; préparation, teinture des fourrures**		18
..	393	361	336	303	275	..	..	Articles d'habillement autres qu'en fourrure		181
..	10	8	6	5	5	..	..	Préparation, teinture des fourrures; art. en fourrure		182
..	106	97	92	90	82	..	..	**Travail des cuirs; articles en cuir; chaussures**		19
..	43	40	41	41	35	..	..	Apprêt et tannage des cuirs et articles en cuirs		191
..	63	57	51	49	47	..	..	Chaussures		192
..	2 592	2 528	2 465	2 367	2 306	..	..	**Bois et articles en bois et liège (sauf meubles)**		20
..	1 850	1 807	1 737	1 672	1 638	..	..	Sciage et rabotage du bois		201
..	742	721	728	695	668	..	..	Articles en bois, liège, vannerie, sparterie		202
..	148	147	141	141	136	..	..	**Papier et carton; articles en papier et en carton**		21
..	333	324	329	324	313	..	..	**Edition, imprimerie et reproduction**		22
..	52	50	55	55	58	..	..	Edition		221
..	264	257	257	253	239	..	..	Imprimerie et activités annexes		222
..	17	17	17	16	16	..	..	Reproduction de supports enregistrés		223
..	62	58	54	56	59	..	..	**Cokéfaction; prod. pétroliers; comb. nucléaires**		23
..	426	426	400	396	378	..	..	**Produits chimiques**		24
..	143	145	143	143	136	..	..	Produits chimiques de base		241
..	283	281	257	253	242	..	..	Autres produits chimiques		242
..	..	..	..	..	..	..	..	Fibres synthétiques ou artificielles		243
..	284	286	291	290	285	..	..	**Articles en caoutchouc et en matières plastiques**		25
..	39	37	35	33	33	..	..	Articles en caoutchouc		251
..	245	249	256	257	252	..	..	Articles en matières plastiques		252
..	548	535	537	526	523	..	..	**Autres produits minéraux non métalliques**		26
..	74	73	73	72	75	..	..	Verre et articles en verre		261
..	474	462	464	454	448	..	..	Produits minéraux non métalliques, nca		269
..	168	172	163	154	154	..	..	**Produits métallurgiques de base**		27
..	35	41	39	37	37	..	..	Sidérurgie et première transformation de l'acier		271
..	57	57	54	51	49	..	..	Métallurgie; métaux précieux et non ferreux		272
..	76	74	70	66	68	..	..	Fonderie		273
..	896	869	888	878	883	..	..	**Ouvrages en métaux, sauf machines et matériel**		28
..	305	318	323	322	328	..	..	Constr. et menuiserie métal.; réservoirs; générateurs		281
..	591	551	565	556	555	..	..	Autres ouvrages en métaux		289
..	866	889	694	697	677	..	..	**Machines et matériel, nca**		29
..	311	338	144	143	146	..	..	Machines d'usage général		291
..	522	518	521	525	503	..	..	Machines d'usage spécifique		292
..	33	33	29	29	28	..	..	Appareils domestiques, nca		293
..	..	..	..	..	..	..	..	**Mach. de bureau, comptables, matériel inform.**		30
..	276	271	291	293	290	..	..	**Machines et appareils électriques, nca**		31
..	71	74	85	87	85	..	..	Moteurs, génératrices et transformateurs électriques		311
..	..	..	..	..	..	..	..	Matériel électrique de distribution et de commande		312
..	22	22	23	22	21	..	..	Fils et câbles électriques isolés		313
..	183	175	183	184	184	..	..	Accumulateurs, piles électriques		314
..	..	..	..	..	..	..	..	Lampes électriques et appareils d'éclairage		315
..	..	..	..	..	..	..	..	Autres matériels électriques, nca		319
..	130	127	118	114	114	..	..	**Equip. et appar. de radio, TV, communication**		32
..	63	63	58	59	53	..	..	Tubes et valves électroniques; autres composants		321
..	67	64	60	55	61	..	..	Emetteurs radio et TV; app. téléphonie, télégraphie		322
..	..	..	..	..	..	..	..	Récepteurs radio et TV et articles associés		323
..	138	136	134	134	132	..	..	**Instruments médicaux, de précision, d'optique**		33
..	98	98	96	98	100	..	..	Appareils médicaux et de précision		331
..	22	22	21	21	20	..	..	Instruments d'optique ; matériel photographique		332
..	18	16	17	15	12	..	..	Horlogerie		333
..	116	117	119	109	113	..	..	**Véhicules automobiles et nemorques**		34
..	18	18	21	21	21	..	..	**Autres matériels de transport**		35
..	5	5	5	5	5	..	..	Construction et réparation de navires		351
..	7	7	8	8	8	..	..	Construction de matériel ferroviaire roulant		352
..	3	4	4	4	5	..	..	Construction aéronautique et spatiale		353
..	3	2	4	4	3	..	..	Autres équipements de transport		359
..	66	58	61	55	53	..	..	**Meubles; activités de fabrication, nca**		36
..	11	9	9	9	9	..	..	Meubles		361
..	55	49	52	46	44	..	..	Activités de fabrication, nca		369
..	..	..	..	..	..	..	..	**Récupération**		37
..	592	589	606	603	609	..	..	**Production et distrib. d'électricité, de gaz, d'eau**	E	40-41
..	403	402	418	415	419	..	..	**Electricité, gaz, vapeur et eau chaude**		40
..	278	278	278	275	275	..	..	Production, collecte et distribution d'électricité		401
..	189	187	188	188	190	..	..	**Captage, épuration et distribution d'eau**		41 410
..	..	..	4 033	3 955	4 006	..	..	**Construction**	F	45
..	..	..	..	..	..	..	..	**Commerce de gros et de détail; réparation**	G	50-52
..	..	..	..	..	..	..	..	**Hôtels et restaurants**	H	55
..	..	..	..	..	..	..	..	**Transports, entreposage et communications**	I	60-64
..	..	..	..	..	..	..	..	**Intermédiation financière**	J	65-67
..	..	..	..	..	..	..	..	**Immobilier, locations, services aux entreprises**	K	70-74
..	..	..	..	..	..	..	..	**Admin. publique; éducation; santé; autres**	L-Q	75-99
..	..	..	..	..	..	..	..	**Grand total**	A-Q	01-99

Statistiques des Structures Industrielles
OCDE, © 1998

AUSTRIA

Table AU.6 ENTERPRISES - ENTREPRISES

Units

ISIC revision 3			1989	1990	1991	1992	1993	1994	1995	1996
A	01-02	Agriculture, hunting and forestry	..	..	..	..	..	..	..	..
B	05	Fishing	..	..	..	..	..	..	..	..
C	10-14	Mining and quarrying	..	..	..	..	..	..	303	..
	10	Mining of coal and lignite; extraction of peat	..	..	..	..	..	..	11	..
	11	Crude petroleum & natural gas; related service activ.	..	..	..	..	..	..	3	..
	13	Mining of metal ores	..	..	..	..	..	..	1	..
	14	Other mining and quarrying	..	..	..	..	..	..	288	..
D	15-37	Total manufacturing	..	..	..	..	..	..	25 509	..
	15	Food products and beverages	..	..	..	..	..	..	4 736	..
	155	Beverages	..	..	..	..	..	..	262	..
	16 160	Tobacco products	..	..	..	..	..	..	1	..
	17	Textiles	..	..	..	..	..	..	962	..
	171	Spinning, weaving and finishing of textiles	..	..	..	..	..	..	176	..
	172	Other textiles	..	..	..	..	..	..	662	..
	173	Knitted and crocheted fabrics and articles	..	..	..	..	..	..	124	..
	18	Wearing apparel dressing & dyeing of fur	..	..	..	..	..	..	1 354	..
	181	Wearing apparel, except fur apparel	..	..	..	..	..	..	1 232	..
	182	Dressing and dyeing of fur; articles of fur	..	..	..	..	..	..	122	..
	19	Tanning, dressing leather; leather artic.; footwear	..	..	..	..	..	..	243	..
	191	Tanning, dressing leather; manuf. of leather articles	..	..	..	..	..	..	140	..
	192	Footwear	..	..	..	..	..	..	103	..
	20	Wood and cork products, ex. furniture	..	..	..	..	..	..	3 487	..
	201	Sawmilling and planing of wood	..	..	..	..	..	..	1 311	..
	202	Products of wood, cork, straw & plaiting material	..	..	..	..	..	..	2 176	..
	21	Paper and paper products	..	..	..	..	..	..	143	..
	22	Publishing, printing & reprod. of recorded media	..	..	..	..	..	..	1 436	..
	221	Publishing	..	..	..	..	..	..	364	..
	222	Printing and related service activities	..	..	..	..	..	..	1 065	..
	223	Reproduction of recorded media	..	..	..	..	..	..	7	..
	23	Coke, refined petroleum products & nuclear fuel	..	..	..	..	..	..	8	..
	24	Chemicals and chemical products	..	..	..	..	..	..	378	..
	241	Basic chemicals	..	..	..	..	..	..	66	..
	242	Other chemical products	..	..	..	..	..	..	308	..
	243	Man-made fibres	..	..	..	..	..	..	4	..
	25	Rubber and plastic products	..	..	..	..	..	..	605	..
	251	Rubber products	..	..	..	..	..	..	45	..
	252	Plastic products	..	..	..	..	..	..	560	..
	26	Other non-metallic mineral products	..	..	..	..	..	..	1 198	..
	261	Glass and glass products	..	..	..	..	..	..	181	..
	269	Non-metallic mineral products, nec	..	..	..	..	..	..	1 017	..
	27	Basic metals	..	..	..	..	..	..	152	..
	271	Basic iron and steel	..	..	..	..	..	..	41	..
	272	Basic precious and non-ferrous metals	..	..	..	..	..	..	41	..
	273	Casting of metals	..	..	..	..	..	..	70	..
	28	Fabricated metal products, ex. machin. & equip.	..	..	..	..	..	..	2 968	..
	281	Structural metal prod., tanks, reservoirs, generators	..	..	..	..	..	..	832	..
	289	Other fabricated metal products & service activities	..	..	..	..	..	..	2 136	..
	29	Machinery and equipment, nec	..	..	..	..	..	..	1 727	..
	291	General purpose machinery	..	..	..	..	..	..	589	..
	292	Special purpose machinery	..	..	..	..	..	..	1 058	..
	293	Domestic appliances, nec	..	..	..	..	..	..	80	..
	30	Office, accounting and computing machinery	..	..	..	..	..	..	49	..
	31	Electrical machinery and apparatus, nec	..	..	..	..	..	..	385	..
	311	Electric motors, generators and transformers	..	..	..	..	..	..	87	..
	312	Electricity distribution and control apparatus	..	..	..	..	..	..	114	..
	313	Insulated wire and cable	..	..	..	..	..	..	23	..
	314	Accumulators, primary cells and primary batteries	..	..	..	..	..	..	9	..
	315	Electric lamps and lighting equipment	..	..	..	..	..	..	74	..
	319	Other electrical equipment, nec	..	..	..	..	..	..	78	..
	32	Radio, TV, communication equip. & apparatus	..	..	..	..	..	..	129	..
	321	Electronic valves, tubes & other electronic compon.	..	..	..	..	..	..	58	..
	322	TV, radio transmitters & appar. for line teleph., telegr.	..	..	..	..	..	..	24	..
	323	TV, radio receivers and associated goods	..	..	..	..	..	..	47	..
	33	Medical, precision, optical instr.; watches, clocks	..	..	..	..	..	..	954	..
	331	Medical equip.; precision instruments and appliances	..	..	..	..	..	..	855	..
	332	Optical instruments and photographic equipment	..	..	..	..	..	..	89	..
	333	Watches and clocks	..	..	..	..	..	..	10	..
	34	Motor vehicles, trailers, and semi-trailers	..	..	..	..	..	..	201	..
	35	Other transport equipment	..	..	..	..	..	..	79	..
	351	Building and repairing of ships and boats	..	..	..	..	..	..	34	..
	352	Railway, tramway locomotives and rolling stock	..	..	..	..	..	..	11	..
	353	Aircraft and spacecraft	..	..	..	..	..	..	23	..
	359	Transport equipment, nec	..	..	..	..	..	..	11	..
	36	Furniture; manufacturing, nec	..	..	..	..	..	..	4 223	..
	361	Furniture	..	..	..	..	..	..	3 191	..
	369	Manufacturing, nec	..	..	..	..	..	..	1 032	..
	37	Recycling	..	..	..	..	..	..	91	..
E	40-41	Electricity, gas and water supply	..	..	..	..	..	..	613	..
	40	Electricity, gas, steam and hot water supply	..	..	..	..	..	..	422	..
	401	Production, collection and distribution of electricity	..	..	..	..	..	..	248	..
	41 410	Collection, purification, distribution of water	..	..	..	..	..	..	191	..
F	45	Construction	..	..	..	..	..	..	15 817	..
G	50-52	Wholesale and retail trade; repairs etc	..	..	..	..	..	..	64 531	..
H	55	Hotels and restaurants	..	..	..	..	..	..	38 768	..
I	60-64	Transport, storage and communications	..	..	..	..	..	..	11 271	..
J	65-67	Financial intermediation	..	..	..	..	..	..	2 709	..
K	70-74	Real estate, renting and business activities	..	..	..	..	..	..	30 900	..
L-Q	75-99	Public admin.; education; health; other services	..	..	..	..	..	..	28 894	..
A-Q	01-99	Grand total	..	..	..	..	..	..	219 315	..

Table AU.7 EMPLOI - EMPLOYMENT

Milliers

1989	1990	1991	1992	1993	1994	1995	1996			CITI révision 3
..	..	..	..	..	..	..	..	**Agriculture, chasse et sylviculture**	A	01-02
..	..	..	..	..	..	..	..	**Pêche**	B	05
..	8.7	7.5	6.9	6.8	6.1	6.3	..	**Activités extractives**	C	10-14
..	1.5	1.2	1.0	0.9	0.6	1.2	..	Extraction de charbon, de lignite et de tourbe		10
..	2.5	2.3	2.0	..	..	..	..	Extraction de pétrole brut et de gaz naturel		11
..	1.1	0.7	0.6	..	..	..	..	Extraction de minerais métalliques		13
..	3.6	3.3	3.3	3.2	3.2	4.6	..	Autres activités extractives		14
..	646.5	633.5	600.4	564.1	557.8	650.9	..	**Activités de fabrication**	D	15-37
..	66.0	65.3	64.1	62.8	61.4	86.5	..	**Produits alimentaires et boissons**		15
..	12.7	12.8	12.5	12.4	12.0	11.4	..	Boissons		155
..	1.4	1.3	1.3	1.2	1.2	..	..	**Produits à base de tabac**	16	160
..	37.3	35.6	33.1	28.8	28.3	27.4	..	**Textiles**	17	
..	15.8	14.5	13.5	10.8	11.1	12.4	..	Filature, tissage et achèvement des textiles		171
..	11.1	10.9	10.0	9.5	9.4	9.4	..	Autres articles textiles		172
..	10.4	10.2	9.5	8.5	7.9	5.6	..	Etoffes et articles de bonneterie		173
..	24.3	22.1	19.1	16.0	13.6	17.1	..	**Habillement; préparation, teinture des fourrures**	18	
..	24.1	21.9	18.9	15.9	13.5	16.6	..	Articles d'habillement autres qu'en fourrure		181
..	0.2	0.2	0.2	0.1	0.1	0.5	..	Préparation, teinture des fourrures; art. en fourrure		182
..	11.2	10.0	8.6	7.9	7.6	7.8	..	**Travail des cuirs; articles en cuir; chaussures**	19	
..	2.8	2.6	2.6	2.3	2.4	2.5	..	Apprêt et tannage des cuirs et articles en cuirs		191
..	8.4	7.4	6.0	5.6	5.2	5.3	..	Chaussures		192
..	52.2	52.6	51.7	50.2	49.9	39.3	..	**Bois et articles en bois et liège (sauf meubles)**	20	
..	13.2	12.7	12.2	11.6	11.2	10.2	..	Sciage et rabotage du bois		201
..	39.0	39.9	39.4	38.6	38.6	29.1	..	Articles en bois, liège, vannerie, sparterie		202
..	20.0	20.4	19.8	18.9	18.3	17.9	..	**Papier et carton; articles en papier et en carton**	21	
..	24.7	24.3	23.5	21.9	21.1	27.3	..	**Edition, imprimerie et reproduction**	22	
..	4.8	4.8	5.3	4.8	4.9	7.3	..	Edition		221
..	18.9	18.5	17.3	16.3	15.4	19.2	..	Imprimerie et activités annexes		222
..	1.0	1.0	0.9	0.7	0.8	0.8	..	Reproduction de supports enregistrés		223
..	4.8	4.8	4.4	4.2	4.5	..	..	**Cokéfaction; prod. pétroliers; comb. nucléaires**	23	
..	39.1	38.9	37.5	35.6	34.4	23.9	..	**Produits chimiques**	24	
..	20.3	19.9	19.4	17.9	17.1	7.6	..	Produits chimiques de base		241
..	18.8	19.0	18.1	17.6	17.3	..	..	Autres produits chimiques		242
..	..	..	..	..	..	..	..	Fibres synthétiques ou artificielles		243
..	20.8	20.6	20.5	20.0	20.1	27.1	..	**Articles en caoutchouc et en matières plastiques**	25	
..	7.1	6.3	5.9	5.3	5.1	5.1	..	Articles en caoutchouc		251
..	13.7	14.2	14.5	14.7	14.9	22.0	..	Articles en matières plastiques		252
..	38.0	37.7	36.4	34.4	34.6	36.4	..	**Autres produits minéraux non métalliques**	26	
..	9.1	9.3	9.0	8.4	8.7	8.1	..	Verre et articles en verre		261
..	28.9	28.4	27.4	26.0	25.9	28.3	..	Produits minéraux non métalliques, nca		269
..	46.1	42.0	38.7	34.9	34.5	33.2	..	**Produits métallurgiques de base**	27	
..	27.9	24.4	23.2	20.8	20.5	21.8	..	Sidérurgie et première transformation de l'acier		271
..	9.6	9.2	7.6	7.0	6.8	6.1	..	Métallurgie; métaux précieux et non ferreux		272
..	8.7	8.3	7.9	7.1	7.3	5.3	..	Fonderie		273
..	58.2	57.8	56.1	53.9	55.5	66.1	..	**Ouvrages en métaux, sauf machines et matériel**	28	
..	20.9	21.3	21.4	20.7	21.3	30.0	..	Constr. et menuiserie métal.; réservoirs; générateurs		281
..	37.3	36.4	34.7	33.2	34.2	36.1	..	Autres ouvrages en métaux		289
..	78.3	78.9	66.9	62.7	62.1	71.9	..	**Machines et matériel, nca**	29	
..	23.1	24.5	13.8	14.2	14.6	28.1	..	Machines d'usage général		291
..	50.1	49.5	48.2	44.1	43.1	38.4	..	Machines d'usage spécifique		292
..	5.2	5.0	4.8	4.4	4.5	5.5	..	Appareils domestiques, nca		293
..	..	..	..	..	..	0.4	..	**Mach. de bureau, comptables, matériel inform.**	30	
..	46.0	45.7	44.6	41.8	40.9	32.2	..	**Machines et appareils électriques, nca**	31	
..	12.1	12.1	11.7	11.3	10.9	8.5	..	Moteurs, génératrices et transformateurs électriques		311
..	..	..	..	..	..	8.5	..	Matériel électrique de distribution et de commande		312
..	3.5	3.4	3.4	3.3	3.4	4.6	..	Fils et câbles électriques isolés		313
..	30.3	30.2	29.5	27.2	26.5	1.2	..	Accumulateurs, piles électriques		314
..	..	..	..	..	..	3.2	..	Lampes électriques et appareils d'éclairage		315
..	..	..	..	..	..	6.4	..	Autres matériels électriques, nca		319
..	27.0	25.5	24.7	22.9	23.3	32.8	..	**Equip. et appar. de radio, TV, communication**	32	
..	19.6	17.9	16.9	15.9	16.0	6.7	..	Tubes et valves électroniques; autres composants		321
..	7.4	7.6	7.8	7.0	7.3	20.3	..	Emetteurs radio et TV; app. téléphonie, télégraphie		322
..	..	..	..	..	..	5.8	..	Récepteurs radio et TV et articles associés		323
..	11.8	11.8	12.0	11.0	10.9	13.9	..	**Instruments médicaux, de précision, d'optique**	33	
..	6.9	7.2	7.2	6.9	7.2	11.4	..	Appareils médicaux et de précision		331
..	4.3	3.9	4.1	3.5	3.1	2.4	..	Instruments d'optique ; matériel photographique		332
..	0.7	0.7	0.6	0.5	0.5	0.0	..	Horlogerie		333
..	25.2	25.3	25.0	23.6	24.3	24.0	..	**Véhicules automobiles et nemorques**	34	
..	6.6	5.9	5.2	4.7	4.5	5.1	..	**Autres matériels de transport**	35	
..	1.4	1.0	0.6	0.4	0.4	0.4	..	Construction et réparation de navires		351
..	4.2	3.5	3.3	3.0	2.9	3.9	..	Construction de matériel ferroviaire roulant		352
..	..	..	..	..	..	0.2	..	Construction aéronautique et spatiale		353
..	..	..	..	..	..	0.6	..	Autres équipements de transport		359
..	7.5	7.1	7.4	6.7	6.8	53.8	..	**Meubles; activités de fabrication, nca**	36	
..	0.3	0.4	0.4	0.3	0.4	41.2	..	Meubles		361
..	7.1	6.8	7.0	6.3	6.4	12.6	..	Activités de fabrication, nca		369
..	..	..	..	..	..	1.0	..	**Récupération**	37	
..	37.3	37.1	36.9	36.2	35.3	38.2	..	**Production et distrib. d'électricité, de gaz, d'eau**	E	40-41
..	35.0	34.8	34.5	33.8	33.0	36.2	..	**Electricité, gaz, vapeur et eau chaude**	40	
..	29.9	29.6	29.1	28.4	27.5	31.4	..	Production, collecte et distribution d'électricité		401
..	2.3	2.3	2.4	2.4	2.4	2.0	..	**Captage, épuration et distribution d'eau**	41	410
..	..	..	174.0	174.2	175.9	236.0	..	**Construction**	F	45
..	..	..	..	..	..	523.5	..	**Commerce de gros et de détail; réparation**	G	50-52
..	..	..	..	..	..	184.7	..	**Hôtels et restaurants**	H	55
..	..	..	..	..	..	225.8	..	**Transports, entreposage et communications**	I	60-64
..	..	..	..	..	..	116.7	..	**Intermédiation financière**	J	65-67
..	..	..	..	..	..	185.3	..	**Immobilier, locations, services aux entreprises**	K	70-74
..	..	..	..	..	..	156.3	..	**Admin. publique; éducation; santé; autres**	L-Q	75-99
..	..	..	..	..	..	..	..	**Grand total**	A-Q	01-99

Note: Data for 1990-94 are not comparable with 1995 due to changes in statistical concepts, sources and methods. For more detail see "sources and definitions" section of this publication.

Statistiques des Structures Industrielles
OCDE, © 1998
OECD / OCDE

Table AU.8 EMPLOYMENT, EMPLOYEES - EMPLOI, SALARIÉS

Thousands

ISIC revision 3			1989	1990	1991	1992	1993	1994	1995	1996
A	01-02	**Agriculture, hunting and forestry**	..	..	..	..	..	..	..	..
B	05	**Fishing**	..	..	..	..	..	..	..	..
C	10-14	**Mining and quarrying**	..	8.6	7.5	6.9	6.8	6.1	6.1	..
	10	Mining of coal and lignite; extraction of peat	..	1.5	1.2	1.0	0.9	0.6	1.2	..
	11	Crude petroleum & natural gas; related service activ.	..	2.5	2.3	2.0	..	..	..	..
	13	Mining of metal ores	..	1.1	0.7	0.6	..	..	..	..
	14	Other mining and quarrying	..	3.6	3.2	3.2	3.2	3.2	4.4	..
D	15-37	**Total manufacturing**	..	641.7	629.0	596.1	560.0	553.8	629.7	..
	15	**Food products and beverages**	..	65.4	64.8	63.6	62.3	61.0	81.4	..
	155	Beverages	..	12.7	12.7	12.5	12.3	11.9	11.2	..
	16 160	**Tobacco products**	..	1.4	1.3	1.3	1.2	1.2	..	..
	17	**Textiles**	..	37.1	35.3	32.9	28.6	28.1	26.6	..
	171	Spinning, weaving and finishing of textiles	..	15.8	14.5	13.5	10.8	11.1	12.2	..
	172	Other textiles	..	10.9	10.7	9.9	9.3	9.2	8.9	..
	173	Knitted and crocheted fabrics and articles	..	10.3	10.2	9.5	8.5	7.8	5.5	..
	18	**Wearing apparel dressing & dyeing of fur**	..	24.1	21.9	18.9	15.9	13.4	15.9	..
	181	Wearing apparel, except fur apparel	..	23.9	21.8	18.8	15.7	13.3	15.6	..
	182	Dressing and dyeing of fur; articles of fur	..	0.2	0.2	0.2	0.1	0.1	0.4	..
	19	**Tanning, dressing leather; leather artic.; footwear**	..	11.2	10.0	8.5	7.8	7.5	7.6	..
	191	Tanning, dressing leather; manuf. of leather articles	..	2.8	2.6	2.6	2.2	2.4	2.4	..
	192	Footwear	..	8.4	7.4	6.0	5.6	5.2	5.3	..
	20	**Wood and cork products, ex. furniture**	..	49.8	50.3	49.4	48.0	47.7	36.0	..
	201	Sawmilling and planing of wood	..	11.2	10.8	10.4	9.8	9.4	8.9	..
	202	Products of wood, cork, straw & plaiting material	..	38.6	39.5	39.0	38.2	38.3	27.1	..
	21	**Paper and paper products**	..	20.0	20.3	19.7	18.9	18.3	17.9	..
	22	**Publishing, printing & reprod. of recorded media**	..	24.6	24.1	23.4	21.8	21.0	26.4	..
	221	Publishing	..	4.8	4.8	5.3	4.8	4.9	7.2	..
	222	Printing and related service activities	..	18.8	18.4	17.2	16.3	15.4	18.5	..
	223	Reproduction of recorded media	..	1.0	1.0	0.9	0.7	0.8	0.8	..
	23	**Coke, refined petroleum products & nuclear fuel**	..	4.8	4.8	4.4	4.2	4.5	..	..
	24	**Chemicals and chemical products**	..	39.0	38.8	37.5	35.5	34.3	23.7	..
	241	Basic chemicals	..	20.3	19.9	19.4	17.9	17.1	7.5	..
	242	Other chemical products	..	18.7	18.9	18.1	17.6	17.2	..	..
	243	Man-made fibres	..	..	..	..	..	..	..	..
	25	**Rubber and plastic products**	..	20.8	20.5	20.4	20.0	20.0	26.8	..
	251	Rubber products	..	7.1	6.3	5.9	5.3	5.1	5.1	..
	252	Plastic products	..	13.7	14.2	14.5	14.6	14.9	21.7	..
	26	**Other non-metallic mineral products**	..	37.8	37.5	36.2	34.2	34.5	35.6	..
	261	Glass and glass products	..	9.0	9.2	8.9	8.4	8.6	8.0	..
	269	Non-metallic mineral products, nec	..	28.8	28.3	27.3	25.9	25.8	27.6	..
	27	**Basic metals**	..	46.1	42.0	38.7	34.9	34.5	33.1	..
	271	Basic iron and steel	..	27.9	24.4	23.2	20.8	20.5	21.8	..
	272	Basic precious and non-ferrous metals	..	9.6	9.2	7.6	7.0	6.7	6.1	..
	273	Casting of metals	..	8.7	8.3	7.9	7.1	7.3	5.2	..
	28	**Fabricated metal products, ex. machin. & equip.**	..	57.9	57.4	55.8	53.6	55.2	63.9	..
	281	Structural metal prod., tanks, reservoirs, generators	..	20.8	21.2	21.3	20.6	21.2	29.5	..
	289	Other fabricated metal products & service activities	..	37.0	36.3	34.5	33.0	34.1	34.4	..
	29	**Machinery and equipment, nec**	..	78.1	78.7	66.7	62.5	62.0	70.9	..
	291	General purpose machinery	..	23.0	24.4	13.8	14.2	14.5	27.8	..
	292	Special purpose machinery	..	49.9	49.3	48.1	44.0	42.9	37.7	..
	293	Domestic appliances, nec	..	5.2	5.0	4.8	4.4	4.5	5.4	..
	30	**Office, accounting and computing machinery**	..	..	..	..	..	..	0.3	..
	31	**Electrical machinery and apparatus, nec**	..	45.9	45.6	44.5	41.8	40.8	32.0	..
	311	Electric motors, generators and transformers	..	12.1	12.1	11.7	11.3	10.9	8.4	..
	312	Electricity distribution and control apparatus	..	..	..	..	..	..	8.4	..
	313	Insulated wire and cable	..	3.5	3.4	3.4	3.3	3.4	4.5	..
	314	Accumulators, primary cells and primary batteries	..	30.3	30.1	29.4	27.2	26.5	1.2	..
	315	Electric lamps and lighting equipment	..	..	..	..	..	..	3.1	..
	319	Other electrical equipment, nec	..	..	..	..	..	..	6.3	..
	32	**Radio, TV, communication equip. & apparatus**	..	27.0	25.5	24.7	22.9	23.3	32.8	..
	321	Electronic valves, tubes & other electronic compon.	..	19.6	17.9	16.9	15.9	16.0	6.7	..
	322	TV, radio transmitters & appar. for line teleph., telegr.	..	7.4	7.6	7.8	7.0	7.3	20.3	..
	323	TV, radio receivers and associated goods	..	..	..	..	..	..	5.8	..
	33	**Medical, precision, optical instr.; watches, clocks**	..	11.7	11.7	11.9	10.9	10.8	13.3	..
	331	Medical equip.; precision instruments and appliances	..	6.8	7.2	7.2	6.9	7.2	10.9	..
	332	Optical instruments and photographic equipment	..	4.3	3.9	4.1	3.5	3.1	2.3	..
	333	Watches and clocks	..	0.7	0.7	0.6	0.5	0.5	0.0	..
	34	**Motor vehicles, trailers, and semi-trailers**	..	25.2	25.2	25.0	23.5	24.3	23.9	..
	35	**Other transport equipment**	..	6.6	5.9	5.2	4.7	4.5	5.0	..
	351	Building and repairing of ships and boats	..	1.4	1.0	0.6	0.4	0.4	0.3	..
	352	Railway, tramway locomotives and rolling stock	..	4.2	3.5	3.3	3.0	2.9	3.9	..
	353	Aircraft and spacecraft	..	..	..	..	..	..	0.2	..
	359	Transport equipment, nec	..	..	..	..	..	..	0.6	..
	36	**Furniture; manufacturing, nec**	..	7.4	7.1	7.4	6.6	6.8	49.9	..
	361	Furniture	..	0.3	0.4	0.4	0.3	0.4	38.3	..
	369	Manufacturing, nec	..	7.1	6.7	7.0	6.3	6.4	11.6	..
	37	**Recycling**	..	..	..	..	..	..	1.0	..
E	40-41	**Electricity, gas and water supply**	..	37.2	37.0	36.8	36.1	35.3	38.0	..
	40	**Electricity, gas, steam and hot water supply**	..	34.9	34.7	34.4	33.7	33.0	36.0	..
	401	Production, collection and distribution of electricity	..	29.8	29.5	29.0	28.3	27.5	31.2	..
	41 410	**Collection, purification, distribution of water**	..	2.3	2.3	2.4	2.4	2.4	1.9	..
F	45	**Construction**	..	..	..	171.4	171.7	173.5	224.7	..
G	50-52	**Wholesale and retail trade; repairs etc**	..	..	..	..	..	..	472.3	..
H	55	**Hotels and restaurants**	..	..	..	..	..	..	145.0	..
I	60-64	**Transport, storage and communications**	..	..	..	..	..	..	218.1	..
J	65-67	**Financial intermediation**	..	..	..	..	..	..	115.6	..
K	70-74	**Real estate, renting and business activities**	..	..	..	..	..	..	160.4	..
L-Q	75-99	**Public admin.; education; health; other services**	..	..	..	..	..	..	129.4	..
A-Q	01-99	**Grand total**	..	..	..	..	..	..	..	..

Note: Data for 1990-94 are not comparable with 1995 due to changes in statistical concepts, sources and methods. For more detail see "sources and definitions" section of this publication.

Table AU.9 SALAIRES ET CHARGES SOCIALES - COMPENSATION OF LABOUR

Millions de Sch (Prix courants)

1989	1990	1991	1992	1993	1994	1995	1996			CITI révision 3
..	..	..	..	..	..	..		**Agriculture, chasse et sylviculture**	A	01-02
..	..	..	..	..	..	..		**Pêche**	B	05
..	4 251 346	4 246 163	4 080 864	4 347 623	4 295 202	3 478 288		**Activités extractives**	C	10-14
..	715 642	672 447	533 508	510 546	347 246	692 388		Extraction de charbon, de lignite et de tourbe		10
..	1 553 565	1 606 532	1 613 200					Extraction de pétrole brut et de gaz naturel		11
..	507 689	484 336	361 363					Extraction de minerais métalliques		13
..	1 474 450	1 482 848	1 572 793	1 619 267	1 685 108	2 307 736		Autres activités extractives		14
..	241 102 023	255 315 568	259 286 745	256 899 471	261 543 019	297 250 204		**Activités de fabrication**	D	15-37
..	22 988 550	24 566 121	25 643 131	26 423 806	26 760 841	32 857 687		**Produits alimentaires et boissons**		15
..	5 359 119	5 824 242	6 083 066	6 324 465	6 522 517	6 069 451		Boissons		155
..	867 432	951 350	946 139	1 036 439	799 367			**Produits à base de tabac**	16	160
..	10 826 738	11 203 426	11 343 347	10 670 000	10 408 490	11 037 655		**Textiles**	17	
..	5 036 677	5 162 041	5 130 734	4 544 845	4 419 571	5 874 826		Filature, tissage et achèvement des textiles		171
..	3 120 946	3 336 690	3 389 192	3 376 390	3 412 418	3 272 439		Autres articles textiles		172
..	2 669 115	2 704 695	2 823 421	2 748 765	2 576 501	1 890 390		Etoffes et articles de bonneterie		173
..	5 060 297	4 927 688	4 626 962	4 240 146	3 766 088	4 626 020		**Habillement; préparation, teinture des fourrures**	18	
..	5 000 360	4 880 132	4 581 660	4 202 622	3 728 183	4 541 597		Articles d'habillement autres qu'en fourrure		181
..	59 937	47 556	45 302	37 524	37 905	84 423		Préparation, teinture des fourrures; art. en fourrure		182
..	2 598 291	2 558 906	2 427 844	2 314 892	2 173 381	2 341 949		**Travail des cuirs; articles en cuir; chaussures**	19	
..	709 410	696 238	716 606	682 938	680 838	663 995		Apprêt et tannage des cuirs et articles en cuirs		191
..	1 888 881	1 862 668	1 711 238	1 631 954	1 492 543	1 677 954		Chaussures		192
..	13 764 731	15 166 847	16 281 953	16 614 758	17 195 002	12 713 176		**Bois et articles en bois et liège (sauf meubles)**	20	
..	2 994 387	3 191 762	3 157 514	3 119 196	3 141 552	3 138 148		Sciage et rabotage du bois		201
..	10 770 344	11 975 085	13 124 439	13 495 562	14 053 450	9 575 028		Articles en bois, liège, vannerie, sparterie		202
..	8 944 190	9 726 828	10 085 445	9 763 593	9 954 412	9 785 655		**Papier et carton; articles en papier et en carton**	21	
..	10 686 045	11 532 589	12 021 131	11 757 227	11 672 530	14 094 085		**Edition, imprimerie et reproduction**	22	
..	2 079 523	2 464 910	2 722 037	2 641 969	2 828 698	3 964 633		Edition		221
..	8 284 999	8 705 531	8 848 295	8 801 821	8 537 993	9 754 403		Imprimerie et activités annexes		222
..	321 523	362 148	450 799	313 437	305 839	375 049		Reproduction de supports enregistrés		223
..	3 176 447	3 420 543	3 748 278	3 816 302	4 576 905	..		**Cokéfaction; prod. pétroliers; comb. nucléaires**	23	
..	17 846 226	19 104 293	19 395 435	19 366 793	19 404 690	13 951 266		**Produits chimiques**	24	
..	9 764 316	10 351 109	10 400 424	10 085 224	10 052 183	4 957 423		Produits chimiques de base		241
..	8 081 910	8 753 184	8 995 011	9 281 569	9 352 507			Autres produits chimiques		242
..	..	..	..	..	..	..		Fibres synthétiques ou artificielles		243
..	7 303 426	7 568 622	8 177 156	8 263 537	8 560 520	12 155 574		**Articles en caoutchouc et en matières plastiques**	25	
..	3 129 010	2 919 792	2 979 872	2 708 339	2 749 089	2 695 357		Articles en caoutchouc		251
..	4 174 416	4 648 830	5 197 284	5 555 198	5 811 431	9 460 217		Articles en matières plastiques		252
..	15 770 992	16 445 053	17 440 013	17 184 135	17 791 697	19 168 880		**Autres produits minéraux non métalliques**	26	
..	3 384 849	3 603 285	3 922 669	3 880 187	4 025 229	3 868 467		Verre et articles en verre		261
..	12 386 143	12 841 768	13 517 344	13 303 948	13 766 468	15 300 413		Produits minéraux non métalliques, nca		269
..	20 276 937	19 287 747	18 954 859	17 725 626	17 786 915	18 432 675		**Produits métallurgiques de base**	27	
..	13 144 920	11 960 875	11 871 817	11 061 764	11 133 537	12 857 840		Sidérurgie et première transformation de l'acier		271
..	3 887 384	4 011 401	3 712 402	3 502 729	3 448 290	3 172 516		Métallurgie; métaux précieux et non ferreux		272
..	3 244 633	3 315 471	3 370 640	3 161 133	3 205 088	2 402 319		Fonderie		273
..	20 663 391	21 781 418	23 110 617	22 862 752	23 808 064	28 648 776		**Ouvrages en métaux, sauf machines et matériel**	28	
..	8 035 680	8 511 804	9 142 386	9 147 909	9 472 702	13 845 934		Constr. et menuiserie métal.; réservoirs; générateurs		281
..	12 627 711	13 269 614	13 968 231	13 714 843	14 335 362	14 802 842		Autres ouvrages en métaux		289
..	31 291 798	34 665 491	30 738 683	30 238 448	30 797 922	35 331 941		**Machines et matériel, nca**	29	
..	9 266 025	10 715 821	6 058 634	6 542 974	6 881 586	14 004 085		Machines d'usage général		291
..	20 422 074	22 199 840	22 897 311	21 947 951	22 112 773	19 023 637		Machines d'usage spécifique		292
..	1 603 699	1 749 830	1 782 738	1 747 523	1 803 563	2 304 219		Appareils domestiques, nca		293
..	..	..	..	..	..	154 648		**Mach. de bureau, comptables, matériel inform.**	30	
..	20 552 152	21 232 820	21 988 676	22 622 523	22 620 316	15 991 767		**Machines et appareils électriques, nca**	31	
..	4 263 035	4 794 260	4 815 413	5 013 197	5 001 950	4 420 679		Moteurs, génératrices et transformateurs électriques		311
..	..	..	..	..	..	4 309 026		Matériel électrique de distribution et de commande		312
..	1 471 697	1 552 510	1 663 913	1 777 053	1 840 414	2 478 761		Fils et câbles électriques isolés		313
..	14 817 420	14 886 050	15 509 350	15 832 273	15 777 952	667 103		Accumulateurs, piles électriques		314
..	..	..	..	..	..	1 462 711		Lampes électriques et appareils d'éclairage		315
..	..	..	..	..	..	2 653 487		Autres matériels électriques, nca		319
..	10 219 182	10 850 835	11 026 607	11 052 531	11 726 295	11 255 631		**Equip. et appar. de radio, TV, communication**	32	
..	6 940 690	7 249 105	7 011 426	7 114 195	7 375 421	3 360 546		Tubes et valves électroniques; autres composants		321
..	3 278 492	3 601 730	4 015 181	3 938 336	4 350 874	14 763 692		Emetteurs radio et TV; app. téléphonie, télégraphie		322
..	..	..	..	..	..	3 131 393		Récepteurs radio et TV et articles associés		323
..	4 062 271	4 614 627	4 991 212	4 934 504	5 063 799	5 659 688		**Instruments médicaux, de précision, d'optique**	33	
..	2 654 694	2 905 173	3 027 609	3 139 670	3 456 250	4 560 158		Appareils médicaux et de précision		331
..	1 240 367	1 511 397	1 731 528	1 604 989	1 413 220	1 073 040		Instruments d'optique ; matériel photographique		332
..	167 210	198 057	232 075	189 845	194 329	26 490		Horlogerie		333
..	9 071 346	10 440 850	11 253 065	10 908 742	11 856 893	11 633 341		**Véhicules automobiles et nemorques**	34	
..	2 713 240	2 884 897	2 430 837	2 476 410	2 194 112	3 091 686		**Autres matériels de transport**	35	
..	590 916	613 454	328 249	340 491	187 024	139 427		Construction et réparation de navires		351
..	1 859 896	1 658 649	1 530 090	1 519 701	1 362 704	2 623 529		Construction de matériel ferroviaire roulant		352
..	..	..	..	..	..	86 101		Construction aéronautique et spatiale		353
..	..	..	..	..	..	242 629		Autres équipements de transport		359
..	2 418 341	2 384 617	2 655 355	2 626 307	2 624 780	17 011 833		**Meubles; activités de fabrication, nca**	36	
..	101 293	106 617	122 582	129 464	131 978	12 355 953		Meubles		361
..	2 317 048	2 278 000	2 532 773	2 496 843	2 492 802	4 655 980		Activités de fabrication, nca		369
..	..	..	..	..	..	434 311		**Récupération**	37	
..	23 158 124	25 375 801	27 669 395	27 893 334	28 508 318	29 412 980		**Production et distrib. d'électricité, de gaz, d'eau**	E	40-41
..	22 080 606	24 229 429	26 455 825	26 639 911	27 231 239	28 376 869		**Electricité, gaz, vapeur et eau chaude**	40	
..	19 099 798	20 945 154	22 831 024	22 718 199	23 140 863	25 536 544		Production, collecte et distribution d'électricité		401
..	1 077 518	1 146 372	1 213 570	1 253 423	1 277 079	1 036 111		**Captage, épuration et distribution d'eau**	41	410
..	..	..	64 360 820	67 304 773	72 468 516	102 204 682		**Construction**	F	45
..	..	..	..	..	..	174 391 339		**Commerce de gros et de détail; réparation**	G	50-52
..	..	..	..	..	..	35 027 214		**Hôtels et restaurants**	H	55
..	..	..	..	..	..	102 184 010		**Transports, entreposage et communications**	I	60-64
..	..	..	..	..	..	76 935 594		**Intermédiation financière**	J	65-67
..	..	..	..	..	..	64 035 188		**Immobilier, locations, services aux entreprises**	K	70-74
..	..	..	..	..	..	44 215 793		**Admin. publique; éducation; santé; autres**	L-Q	75-99
..	..	..	..	..	..	..		**Grand total**	A-Q	01-99

Note: Data for 1990-94 are not comparable with 1995 due to changes in statistical concepts, sources and methods. For more detail see "sources and definitions" section of this publication.

Statistiques des Structures Industrielles
OCDE, © 1998

OECD
OCDE

AUSTRIA

Table AU.10 TOTAL WAGES AND SALARIES - SALAIRES ET TRAITEMENTS, TOTAL

Millions of Sch (Current Prices)

ISIC revision 3				1989	1990	1991	1992	1993	1994	1995	1996
A	01-02		Agriculture, hunting and forestry	..	..	..	..	..	..	..	..
B	05		Fishing	..	..	..	..	..	..	..	..
C	10-14		**Mining and quarrying**	..	3 250	3 272	3 149	3 327	3 022	2 629	..
	10		Mining of coal and lignite; extraction of peat	..	550	517	415	410	276	533	
	11		Crude petroleum & natural gas; related service activ.	..	1 164	1 226	1 231				
	13		Mining of metal ores	..	384	368	262	..	..	..	
	14		Other mining and quarrying	..	1 151	1 162	1 241	1 265	1 307	1 771	
D	15-37		**Total manufacturing**	..	187 424	199 419	201 581	199 411	201 470	228 712	
	15		**Food products and beverages**	..	17 892	19 092	19 827	20 384	20 524	25 396	..
		155	Beverages	..	4 161	4 480	4 643	4 866	4 928	4 670	
	16	160	**Tobacco products**	..	547	585	584	626	627		
	17		**Textiles**	..	8 513	8 826	8 897	8 303	8 090	8 510	
		171	Spinning, weaving and finishing of textiles	..	3 977	4 075	4 020	3 556	3 449	4 538	
		172	Other textiles	..	2 444	2 619	2 642	2 598	2 626	2 510	
		173	Knitted and crocheted fabrics and articles	..	2 091	2 132	2 236	2 149	2 014	1 462	
	18		**Wearing apparel dressing & dyeing of fur**	..	3 936	3 871	3 590	3 302	2 921	3 549	
		181	Wearing apparel, except fur apparel	..	3 887	3 833	3 553	3 271	2 892	3 482	
		182	Dressing and dyeing of fur; articles of fur	..	49	38	37	31	29	67	
	19		**Tanning, dressing leather; leather artic.; footwear**	..	2 058	2 026	1 911	1 798	1 681	1 819	
		191	Tanning, dressing leather; manuf. of leather articles	..	556	538	558	529	531	514	
		192	Footwear	..	1 502	1 488	1 354	1 269	1 151	1 305	
	20		**Wood and cork products, ex. furniture**	..	10 878	11 995	12 796	13 025	13 385	9 823	
		201	Sawmilling and planing of wood	..	2 395	2 550	2 494	2 448	2 451	2 422	
		202	Products of wood, cork, straw & plaiting material	..	8 483	9 445	10 302	10 577	10 934	7 401	
	21		**Paper and paper products**	..	7 011	7 562	7 887	7 562	7 621	7 490	
	22		**Publishing, printing & reprod. of recorded media**	..	8 650	9 348	9 796	9 489	9 308	11 120	
		221	Publishing	..	1 683	2 001	2 233	2 178	2 276	3 128	
		222	Printing and related service activities	..	6 714	7 056	7 189	7 062	6 791	7 698	
		223	Reproduction of recorded media	..	252	290	374	250	241	294	
	23		**Coke, refined petroleum products & nuclear fuel**	..	2 434	2 611	2 928	2 929	2 993	..	
	24		**Chemicals and chemical products**	..	13 544	14 484	14 659	14 698	14 695	10 748	
		241	Basic chemicals	..	7 311	7 843	7 817	7 606	7 494	3 832	
		242	Other chemical products	..	6 233	6 641	6 842	7 092	7 201		
		243	Man-made fibres	..	..	..	..	..	..	..	
	25		**Rubber and plastic products**	..	5 827	6 009	6 437	6 489	6 699	9 401	
		251	Rubber products	..	2 510	2 325	2 346	2 136	2 168	2 094	
		252	Plastic products	..	3 318	3 683	4 091	4 353	4 531	7 307	
	26		**Other non-metallic mineral products**	..	12 139	12 718	13 393	13 128	13 431	14 624	
		261	Glass and glass products	..	2 635	2 815	3 030	2 955	3 056	2 922	
		269	Non-metallic mineral products, nec	..	9 504	9 903	10 363	10 173	10 375	11 702	
	27		**Basic metals**	..	15 228	14 586	14 196	13 362	13 540	14 057	
		271	Basic iron and steel	..	9 678	8 902	8 681	8 217	8 389	9 834	
		272	Basic precious and non-ferrous metals	..	3 029	3 099	2 907	2 719	2 690	2 394	
		273	Casting of metals	..	2 522	2 586	2 608	2 426	2 461	1 828	
	28		**Fabricated metal products, ex. machin. & equip.**	..	16 240	17 128	18 108	17 858	18 491	22 316	
		281	Structural metal prod., tanks, reservoirs, generators	..	6 250	6 603	7 115	7 116	7 363	10 807	
		289	Other fabricated metal products & service activities	..	9 991	10 524	10 993	10 742	11 128	11 509	
	29		**Machinery and equipment, nec**	..	24 754	27 332	24 066	23 722	23 935	27 373	
		291	General purpose machinery	..	7 291	8 389	4 756	5 117	5 348	10 814	
		292	Special purpose machinery	..	16 205	17 564	17 914	17 248	17 198	14 781	
		293	Domestic appliances, nec	..	1 259	1 379	1 396	1 358	1 389	1 778	
	30		**Office, accounting and computing machinery**	..	..	..	..	..	..	123	
	31		**Electrical machinery and apparatus, nec**	..	15 378	16 612	17 109	17 749	17 579	12 338	
		311	Electric motors, generators and transformers	..	3 371	3 781	3 774	3 907	3 864	3 420	
		312	Electricity distribution and control apparatus	..						3 334	
		313	Insulated wire and cable	..	1 140	1 232	1 304	1 380	1 400	1 895	
		314	Accumulators, primary cells and primary batteries	..	10 866	11 599	12 031	12 462	12 315	513	
		315	Electric lamps and lighting equipment	..	..	..	..	..	..	1 135	
		319	Other electrical equipment, nec	..	..	..	..	..	..	2 043	
	32		**Radio, TV, communication equip. & apparatus**	..	8 021	8 638	8 686	8 674	9 167	16 464	
		321	Electronic valves, tubes & other electronic compon.	..	5 502	5 765	5 529	5 566	5 718	2 600	
		322	TV, radio transmitters & appar. for line teleph., telegr.	..	2 519	2 873	3 157	3 108	3 448	11 443	
		323	TV, radio receivers and associated goods	..						2 422	
	33		**Medical, precision, optical instr.; watches, clocks**	..	3 236	3 679	3 947	3 864	3 917	4 391	
		331	Medical equip.; precision instruments and appliances	..	2 138	2 331	2 413	2 490	2 700	3 550	
		332	Optical instruments and photographic equipment	..	964	1 188	1 355	1 223	1 066	821	
		333	Watches and clocks	..	134	160	178	151	150	21	
	34		**Motor vehicles, trailers, and semi-trailers**	..	7 080	8 136	8 758	8 417	9 102	8 930	
	35		**Other transport equipment**	..	2 152	2 288	1 923	1 970	1 723	2 414	
		351	Building and repairing of ships and boats	..	472	491	269	289	144	110	
		352	Railway, tramway locomotives and rolling stock	..	1 474	1 336	1 203	1 189	1 066	2 048	
		353	Aircraft and spacecraft	..	..	..	..	..	..	67	
		359	Transport equipment, nec	..	..	..	..	..	..	189	
	36		**Furniture; manufacturing, nec**	..	1 906	1 891	2 082	2 062	2 040	13 170	
		361	Furniture	..	81	82	95	100	101	9 563	
		369	Manufacturing, nec	..	1 825	1 809	1 987	1 962	1 939	3 607	
	37		**Recycling**	..	..	..	..	..	..	334	
E	40-41		**Electricity, gas and water supply**	..	15 047	16 014	16 966	17 448	17 556	19 921	
	40		**Electricity, gas, steam and hot water supply**	..	14 295	15 206	16 112	16 563	16 646	19 165	
		401	Production, collection and distribution of electricity	..	12 477	13 180	13 916	14 211	14 132	17 206	
	41	410	**Collection, purification, distribution of water**	..	752	808	854	885	910	756	
F	45		**Construction**	..	..	..	51 010	53 115	57 127	79 787	..
G	50-52		**Wholesale and retail trade; repairs etc**	..	..	..	..	..	..	135 668	..
H	55		**Hotels and restaurants**	..	..	..	..	..	..	26 699	..
I	60-64		**Transport, storage and communications**	..	..	..	..	..	..	73 153	..
J	65-67		**Financial intermediation**	..	..	..	..	..	..	55 120	..
K	70-74		**Real estate, renting and business activities**	..	..	..	..	..	..	50 160	..
L-Q	75-99		**Public admin.; education; health; other services**	..	..	..	..	..	..	33 604	..
A-Q	01-99		**Grand total**	..	..	..	..	..	..	..	..

Note: Data for 1990-94 are not comparable with 1995 due to changes in statistical concepts, sources and methods. For more detail see "sources and definitions" section of this publication.

Table AU.11 **SALAIRES ET TRAITEMENTS, SALARIÉS - WAGES AND SALARIES, EMPLOYEES**

Millions de Sch (Prix courants)

1989	1990	1991	1992	1993	1994	1995	1996			CITI révision 3	
..	..	..	..	..	..	..	..	**Agriculture, chasse et sylviculture**	A	01-02	
								Pêche	B	05	
..	1 072	1 152	1 259	1 182	1 133	1 110	..	**Activités extractives**	C	10-14	
..	124	126	199	98	84	316	..	Extraction de charbon, de lignite et de tourbe		10	
..	445	495	508	..	..	..	..	Extraction de pétrole brut et de gaz naturel		11	
..	134	141	113					Extraction de minerais métalliques		13	
..	369	391	439	428	444	580	..	Autres activités extractives		14	
..	83 072	90 131	92 778	93 886	95 420	104 272	..	**Activités de fabrication**	D	15-37	
..	7 706	8 220	8 555	8 839	8 959	10 301	..	**Produits alimentaires et boissons**		15	
..	1 823	1 995	2 119	2 204	2 242	2 094	..	Boissons			155
..	295	305	312	336	344	..		**Produits à base de tabac**		16	160
..	3 914	4 076	4 205	4 022	3 865	3 969	..	**Textiles**		17	
..	1 867	1 965	1 950	1 766	1 625	2 090	..	Filature, tissage et achèvement des textiles			171
..	1 169	1 218	1 274	1 304	1 292	1 169	..	Autres articles textiles			172
..	878	892	981	951	948	710	..	Etoffes et articles de bonneterie			173
..	1 243	1 260	1 242	1 184	1 104	1 359	..	**Habillement; préparation, teinture des fourrures**		18	
..	1 208	1 235	1 216	1 164	1 087	1 325	..	Articles d'habillement autres qu'en fourrure			181
..	35	25	26	20	17	34	..	Préparation, teinture des fourrures; art. en fourrure			182
..	650	645	608	597	586	619	..	**Travail des cuirs; articles en cuir; chaussures**		19	
..	212	217	220	217	212	198	..	Apprêt et tannage des cuirs et articles en cuirs			191
..	438	428	388	380	375	420	..	Chaussures			192
..	3 142	3 536	3 786	3 967	4 065	2 398	..	**Bois et articles en bois et liège (sauf meubles)**		20	
..	548	596	544	547	551	540	..	Sciage et rabotage du bois			201
..	2 594	2 940	3 241	3 419	3 514	1 858	..	Articles en bois, liège, vannerie, sparterie			202
..	2 754	3 006	3 141	2 994	3 050	2 963	..	**Papier et carton; articles en papier et en carton**		21	
..	4 590	5 075	5 353	5 352	5 330	6 121	..	**Edition, imprimerie et reproduction**		22	
..	1 537	1 834	2 042	2 032	2 130	2 622	..	Edition			221
..	2 897	3 112	3 169	3 184	3 059	3 208	..	Imprimerie et activités annexes			222
..	156	129	143	136	141	291	..	Reproduction de supports enregistrés			223
..	1 442	1 562	1 829	1 887	1 965		..	**Cokéfaction; prod. pétroliers; comb. nucléaires**		23	
..	7 780	8 357	8 620	8 799	8 867	7 343	..	**Produits chimiques**		24	
..	3 465	3 800	3 894	3 809	3 775	2 237	..	Produits chimiques de base			241
..	4 314	4 557	4 726	4 989	5 092	..	..	Autres produits chimiques			242
..	..	..	..	..	..	..	..	Fibres synthétiques ou artificielles			243
..	2 354	2 394	2 639	2 681	2 716	3 944	..	**Articles en caoutchouc et en matières plastiques**		25	
..	978	884	941	855	849	761	..	Articles en caoutchouc			251
..	1 376	1 510	1 697	1 827	1 867	3 182	..	Articles en matières plastiques			252
..	4 602	4 915	5 195	5 129	5 407	5 769	..	**Autres produits minéraux non métalliques**		26	
..	898	976	1 053	1 040	1 133	1 026	..	Verre et articles en verre			261
..	3 704	3 939	4 142	4 088	4 274	4 743	..	Produits minéraux non métalliques, nca			269
..	5 084	5 005	5 006	4 818	4 853	4 989	..	**Produits métallurgiques de base**		27	
..	3 250	3 062	3 048	2 825	2 882	3 426	..	Sidérurgie et première transformation de l'acier			271
..	1 171	1 251	1 208	1 277	1 253	1 026	..	Métallurgie; métaux précieux et non ferreux			272
..	662	692	749	716	718	537	..	Fonderie			273
..	6 401	6 888	7 379	7 308	7 741	9 435	..	**Ouvrages en métaux, sauf machines et matériel**		28	
..	2 422	2 613	2 874	2 895	3 106	4 973	..	Constr. et menuiserie métal.; réservoirs; générateurs			281
..	3 978	4 275	4 505	4 413	4 634	4 462	..	Autres ouvrages en métaux			289
..	11 871	13 487	12 292	12 386	12 499	13 378	..	**Machines et matériel, nca**		29	
..	3 226	3 920	2 401	2 644	2 740	5 411	..	Machines d'usage général			291
..	8 211	9 103	9 408	9 249	9 264	7 275	..	Machines d'usage spécifique			292
..	434	464	483	493	496	692	..	Appareils domestiques, nca			293
..	..	..	..	..	..	92	..	**Mach. de bureau, comptables, matériel inform.**		30	
..	9 303	10 063	10 651	11 331	11 243	6 289	..	**Machines et appareils électriques, nca**		31	
..	1 525	1 784	1 882	1 963	1 967	1 747	..	Moteurs, génératrices et transformateurs électriques			311
..	..	..	..	..	..	1 806	..	Matériel électrique de distribution et de commande			312
..	456	498	530	574	569	865	..	Fils et câbles électriques isolés			313
..	7 321	7 781	8 239	8 793	8 707	252	..	Accumulateurs, piles électriques			314
..	..	..	..	..	..	653	..	Lampes électriques et appareils d'éclairage			315
..	..	..	..	..	..	966	..	Autres matériels électriques, nca			319
..	4 231	4 621	4 882	5 113	5 373	11 380	..	**Equip. et appar. de radio, TV, communication**		32	
..	2 477	2 574	2 597	2 707	2 704	1 039	..	Tubes et valves électroniques; autres composants			321
..	1 754	2 047	2 285	2 407	2 669	8 972	..	Emetteurs radio et TV; app. téléphonie, télégraphie			322
..	..	..	..	..	..	1 369	..	Récepteurs radio et TV et articles associés			323
..	1 861	2 159	2 283	2 312	2 412	2 753	..	**Instruments médicaux, de précision, d'optique**		33	
..	1 407	1 579	1 653	1 736	1 870	2 312	..	Appareils médicaux et de précision			331
..	399	513	556	510	476	422	..	Instruments d'optique ; matériel photographique			332
..	55	67	74	66	66	19	..	Horlogerie			333
..	2 394	2 828	3 121	3 115	3 404	3 043	..	**Véhicules automobiles et nemorques**		34	
..	833	1 094	975	1 003	931	1 100	..	**Autres matériels de transport**		35	
..	162	171	85	85	40	41	..	Construction et réparation de navires			351
..	605	564	536	514	468	944	..	Construction de matériel ferroviaire roulant			352
..	..	..	..	..	..	46	..	Construction aéronautique et spatiale			353
..	..	..	..	..	..	69	..	Autres équipements de transport			359
..	621	636	704	716	706	4 256	..	**Meubles; activités de fabrication, nca**		36	
..	30	30	36	38	40	2 873	..	Meubles			361
..	591	606	668	678	665	1 383	..	Activités de fabrication, nca			369
..	..	..	..	..	..	103	..	**Récupération**		37	
..	10 891	11 627	12 339	12 721	13 159	14 979	..	**Production et distrib. d'électricité, de gaz, d'eau**	E	40-41	
..	10 462	11 168	11 951	12 320	12 659	14 631	..	**Electricité, gaz, vapeur et eau chaude**		40	
..	9 426	10 041	10 711	10 979	11 183	13 528	..	Production, collecte et distribution d'électricité			401
..	752	808	854	885	910	348	..	**Captage, épuration et distribution d'eau**		41	410
..			14 990	15 600	16 811	22 996	..	**Construction**	F	45	
..						106 522	..	**Commerce de gros et de détail; réparation**	G	50-52	
..						5 361	..	**Hôtels et restaurants**	H	55	
..						53 184	..	**Transports, entreposage et communications**	I	60-64	
..						54 341	..	**Intermédiation financière**	J	65-67	
..						39 800	..	**Immobilier, locations, services aux entreprises**	K	70-74	
..						14 111	..	**Admin. publique; éducation; santé; autres**	L-Q	75-99	
..						..	..	**Grand total**	A-Q	01-99	

Note: Data for 1990-94 are not comparable with 1995 due to changes in statistical concepts, sources and methods. For more detail see "sources and definitions" section of this publication.

AUSTRIA

Table AU.12 EMPLOYERS' SOCIAL COSTS – CHARGES SOCIALES DES EMPLOYEURS

Millions of Sch (Current Prices)

ISIC revision 3				1989	1990	1991	1992	1993	1994	1995	1996
A	01-02		Agriculture, hunting and forestry	..	..	..	..	..	..	..	..
B	05		Fishing	..	..	..	..	..	..	..	..
C	10-14		Mining and quarrying	..	1 002	974	932	1 021	1 273	849	..
	10		Mining of coal and lignite; extraction of peat	..	165	156	118	101	71	160	..
	11		Crude petroleum & natural gas; related service activ.	..	390	381	382	..	..		..
	13		Mining of metal ores	..	123	117	100				..
	14		Other mining and quarrying	..	324	321	332	355	378	537	..
D	15-37		**Total manufacturing**	..	53 678	55 897	57 706	57 488	60 073	68 538	..
	15		**Food products and beverages**	..	5 096	5 474	5 816	6 040	6 236	7 462	..
		155	Beverages	..	1 198	1 344	1 440	1 458	1 594	1 399	..
	16	160	**Tobacco products**	..	320	366	362	411	172		..
	17		**Textiles**	..	2 314	2 378	2 446	2 367	2 319	2 528	..
		171	Spinning, weaving and finishing of textiles	..	1 059	1 088	1 111	989	970	1 337	..
		172	Other textiles	..	677	718	747	778	786	762	..
		173	Knitted and crocheted fabrics and articles	..	578	572	588	600	562	429	..
	18		**Wearing apparel dressing & dyeing of fur**	..	1 124	1 056	1 037	939	845	1 077	..
		181	Wearing apparel, except fur apparel	..	1 113	1 047	1 029	932	836	1 060	..
		182	Dressing and dyeing of fur; articles of fur	..	11	9	8	7	9	18	..
	19		**Tanning, dressing leather; leather artic.; footwear**	..	541	533	516	517	492	523	..
		191	Tanning, dressing leather; manuf. of leather articles	..	153	158	159	154	150	150	..
		192	Footwear	..	387	375	357	363	342	373	..
	20		**Wood and cork products, ex. furniture**	..	2 886	3 172	3 486	3 590	3 810	2 890	..
		201	Sawmilling and planing of wood	..	599	642	663	671	691	716	..
		202	Products of wood, cork, straw & plaiting material	..	2 288	2 530	2 822	2 919	3 119	2 174	..
	21		**Paper and paper products**	..	1 933	2 164	2 198	2 202	2 333	2 296	..
	22		**Publishing, printing & reprod. of recorded media**	..	2 036	2 185	2 226	2 268	2 365	2 974	..
		221	Publishing	..	397	464	489	464	553	837	..
		222	Printing and related service activities	..	1 571	1 650	1 659	1 740	1 747	2 056	..
		223	Reproduction of recorded media	..	69	72	77	64	65	81	..
	23		**Coke, refined petroleum products & nuclear fuel**	..	742	809	820	887	1 584	..	..
	24		**Chemicals and chemical products**	..	4 303	4 621	4 737	4 669	4 710	3 203	..
		241	Basic chemicals	..	2 453	2 508	2 583	2 479	2 559	1 125	..
		242	Other chemical products	..	1 849	2 113	2 153	2 190	2 151		..
		243	Man-made fibres	..	..	..	..	..	..	..	..
	25		**Rubber and plastic products**	..	1 476	1 560	1 741	1 774	1 861	2 754	..
		251	Rubber products	..	619	595	634	572	581	601	..
		252	Plastic products	..	857	965	1 106	1 202	1 281	2 153	..
	26		**Other non-metallic mineral products**	..	3 632	3 727	4 047	4 056	4 360	4 545	..
		261	Glass and glass products	..	750	788	893	925	969	947	..
		269	Non-metallic mineral products, nec	..	2 882	2 939	3 154	3 131	3 392	3 598	..
	27		**Basic metals**	..	5 049	4 701	4 758	4 363	4 247	4 376	..
		271	Basic iron and steel	..	3 467	3 059	3 191	2 845	2 744	3 023	..
		272	Basic precious and non-ferrous metals	..	858	913	805	783	758	778	..
		273	Casting of metals	..	723	730	762	735	745	574	..
	28		**Fabricated metal products, ex. machin. & equip.**	..	4 423	4 654	5 003	5 005	5 317	6 333	..
		281	Structural metal prod., tanks, reservoirs, generators	..	1 786	1 908	2 028	2 032	2 110	3 039	..
		289	Other fabricated metal products & service activities	..	2 637	2 745	2 975	2 973	3 207	3 294	..
	29		**Machinery and equipment, nec**	..	6 538	7 333	6 672	6 516	6 863	7 959	..
		291	General purpose machinery	..	1 975	2 327	1 302	1 426	1 534	3 190	..
		292	Special purpose machinery	..	4 217	4 636	4 983	4 700	4 915	4 243	..
		293	Domestic appliances, nec	..	345	371	387	390	415	526	..
	30		**Office, accounting and computing machinery**	..	..	..	..	..	..	32	..
	31		**Electrical machinery and apparatus, nec**	..	5 174	4 620	4 879	4 874	5 041	3 653	..
		311	Electric motors, generators and transformers	..	892	1 014	1 041	1 106	1 138	1 001	..
		312	Electricity distribution and control apparatus	..	..	..	..	..	..	975	..
		313	Insulated wire and cable	..	331	320	360	397	440	584	..
		314	Accumulators, primary cells and primary batteries	..	3 951	3 287	3 478	3 371	3 463	154	..
		315	Electric lamps and lighting equipment	..	..	..	..	..	..	328	..
		319	Other electrical equipment, nec	..	..	..	..	..	..	611	..
	32		**Radio, TV, communication equip. & apparatus**	..	2 198	2 213	2 340	2 378	2 560	4 791	..
		321	Electronic valves, tubes & other electronic compon.	..	1 439	1 484	1 483	1 548	1 657	761	..
		322	TV, radio transmitters & appar. for line teleph., telegr.	..	759	729	858	830	903	3 321	..
		323	TV, radio receivers and associated goods	..	..	..	..	..	..	710	..
	33		**Medical, precision, optical instr.; watches, clocks**	..	826	935	1 044	1 070	1 147	1 269	..
		331	Medical equip.; precision instruments and appliances	..	516	574	615	650	756	1 011	..
		332	Optical instruments and photographic equipment	..	277	323	376	382	347	252	..
		333	Watches and clocks	..	33	38	54	39	44	6	..
	34		**Motor vehicles, trailers, and semi-trailers**	..	1 991	2 305	2 496	2 492	2 755	2 703	..
	35		**Other transport equipment**	..	561	597	507	507	471	678	..
		351	Building and repairing of ships and boats	..	119	122	60	52	43	30	..
		352	Railway, tramway locomotives and rolling stock	..	386	323	327	331	297	575	..
		353	Aircraft and spacecraft	..	..	..	..	..	..	19	..
		359	Transport equipment, nec	..	..	..	..	..	..	54	..
	36		**Furniture; manufacturing, nec**	..	512	493	573	565	585	3 842	..
		361	Furniture	..	20	24	28	30	31	2 793	..
		369	Manufacturing, nec	..	492	469	545	535	554	1 049	..
	37		**Recycling**	..	..	..	..	..	..	100	..
E	40-41		**Electricity, gas and water supply**	..	8 111	9 362	10 703	10 446	10 952	9 492	..
	40		**Electricity, gas, steam and hot water supply**	..	7 786	9 024	10 344	10 077	10 585	9 211	..
		401	Production, collection and distribution of electricity	..	6 623	7 766	8 915	8 507	9 009	8 330	..
	41	410	**Collection, purification, distribution of water**	..	325	338	360	368	368	280	..
F	45		**Construction**	..	..	..	13 350	14 190	15 342	22 418	..
G	50-52		**Wholesale and retail trade; repairs etc**	..	..	..	..	..	..	38 723	..
H	55		**Hotels and restaurants**	..	..	..	..	..	..	8 329	..
I	60-64		**Transport, storage and communications**	..	..	..	..	..	..	29 031	..
J	65-67		**Financial intermediation**	..	..	..	..	..	..	21 815	..
K	70-74		**Real estate, renting and business activities**	..	..	..	..	..	..	13 875	..
L-Q	75-99		**Public admin.; education; health; other services**	..	..	..	..	..	..	10 611	..
A-Q	01-99		**Grand total**	..	..	..	..	..	..		

Note: Data for 1990-94 are not comparable with 1995 due to changes in statistical concepts, sources and methods. For more detail see "sources and definitions" section of this publication.

Table AU.13 HEURES OUVRÉES - HOURS WORKED

Milliers

1989	1990	1991	1992	1993	1994	1995	1996			CITI révision 3
..	..	..	..	..	..	..		**Agriculture, chasse et sylviculture**	A	01-02
..	..	..	..	..	..	..		**Pêche**	B	05
..	..	..	..	..	..	10 791	..	**Activités extractives**	C	10-14
..	..	..	..	..	..	2 072		Extraction de charbon, de lignite et de tourbe		10
..	..	..	..	..	..	..		Extraction de pétrole brut et de gaz naturel		11
..	..	..	..	..	..			Extraction de minerais métalliques		13
..	..	..	..	..	..	7 909		Autres activités extractives		14
..	..	..	..	..	..	1 057 207		**Activités de fabrication**	D	15-37
..	..	..	..	..	..	139 536		**Produits alimentaires et boissons**		15
..	..	..	..	..	..	19 469		Boissons		155
..	..	..	..	..	..	..		**Produits à base de tabac**		16 160
..	..	..	..	..	..	43 392		**Textiles**		17
..	..	..	..	..	..	20 986		Filature, tissage et achèvement des textiles		171
..	..	..	..	..	..	13 640	..	Autres articles textiles		172
..	..	..	..	..	..	8 765		Etoffes et articles de bonneterie		173
..	..	..	..	..	..	25 874		**Habillement; préparation, teinture des fourrures**		18
..	..	..	..	..	..	25 354		Articles d'habillement autres qu'en fourrure		181
..	..	..	..	..	..	520		Préparation, teinture des fourrures; art. en fourrure		182
..	..	..	..	..	..	11 668		**Travail des cuirs; articles en cuir; chaussures**		19
..	..	..	..	..	..	3 831		Apprêt et tannage des cuirs et articles en cuirs		191
..	..	..	..	..	..	7 837		Chaussures		192
..	..	..	..	..	..	61 479		**Bois et articles en bois et liège (sauf meubles)**		20
..	..	..	..	..	..	15 319		Sciage et rabotage du bois		201
..	..	..	..	..	..	46 160	..	Articles en bois, liège, vannerie, sparterie		202
..	..	..	..	..	..	30 003		**Papier et carton; articles en papier et en carton**		21
..	..	..	..	..	..	42 250		**Edition, imprimerie et reproduction**		22
..	..	..	..	..	..	10 496	..	Edition		221
..	..	..	..	..	..	30 445		Imprimerie et activités annexes		222
..	..	..	..	..	..	1 309		Reproduction de supports enregistrés		223
..	..	..	..	..	..	..		**Cokéfaction; prod. pétroliers; comb. nucléaires**		23
..	..	..	..	..	..	39 594		**Produits chimiques**		24
..	..	..	..	..	..	12 618		Produits chimiques de base		241
..	..	..	..	..	..	..	..	Autres produits chimiques		242
..	..	..	..	..	..			Fibres synthétiques ou artificielles		243
..	..	..	..	..	..	45 041		**Articles en caoutchouc et en matières plastiques**		25
..	..	..	..	..	..	8 141		Articles en caoutchouc		251
..	..	..	..	..	..	36 901		Articles en matières plastiques		252
..	..	..	..	..	..	60 892		**Autres produits minéraux non métalliques**		26
..	..	..	..	..	..	12 998		Verre et articles en verre		261
..	..	..	..	..	..	47 893	..	Produits minéraux non métalliques, nca		269
..	..	..	..	..	..	55 883		**Produits métallurgiques de base**		27
..	..	..	..	..	..	36 612		Sidérurgie et première transformation de l'acier		271
..	..	..	..	..	..	10 316		Métallurgie; métaux précieux et non ferreux		272
..	..	..	..	..	..	8 956		Fonderie		273
..	..	..	..	..	..	108 118		**Ouvrages en métaux, sauf machines et matériel**		28
..	..	..	..	..	..	50 410		Constr. et menuiserie métal.; réservoirs; générateurs		281
..	..	..	..	..	..	57 709		Autres ouvrages en métaux		289
..	..	..	..	..	..	119 782		**Machines et matériel, nca**		29
..	..	..	..	..	..	47 129		Machines d'usage général		291
..	..	..	..	..	..	63 789		Machines d'usage spécifique		292
..	..	..	..	..	..	8 864		Appareils domestiques, nca		293
..	..	..	..	..	..	549		**Mach. de bureau, comptables, matériel inform.**		30
..	..	..	..	..	..	52 896		**Machines et appareils électriques, nca**		31
..	..	..	..	..	..	13 835		Moteurs, génératrices et transformateurs électriques		311
..	..	..	..	..	..	13 870		Matériel électrique de distribution et de commande		312
..	..	..	..	..	..	7 520		Fils et câbles électriques isolés		313
..	..	..	..	..	..	2 037		Accumulateurs, piles électriques		314
..	..	..	..	..	..	4 934		Lampes électriques et appareils d'éclairage		315
..	..	..	..	..	..	10 699		Autres matériels électriques, nca		319
..	..	..	..	..	..	55 921		**Equip. et appar. de radio, TV, communication**		32
..	..	..	..	..	..	11 267		Tubes et valves électroniques; autres composants		321
..	..	..	..	..	..	34 793		Emetteurs radio et TV; app. téléphonie, télégraphie		322
..	..	..	..	..	..	9 862		Récepteurs radio et TV et articles associés		323
..	..	..	..	..	..	21 858		**Instruments médicaux, de précision, d'optique**		33
..	..	..	..	..	..	18 012		Appareils médicaux et de précision		331
..	..	..	..	..	..	3 779		Instruments d'optique ; matériel photographique		332
..	..	..	..	..	..	67		Horlogerie		333
..	..	..	..	..	..	39 837		**Véhicules automobiles et nemorques**		34
..	..	..	..	..	..	8 704		**Autres matériels de transport**		35
..	..	..	..	..	..	545		Construction et réparation de navires		351
..	..	..	..	..	..	6 815		Construction de matériel ferroviaire roulant		352
..	..	..	..	..	..	291		Construction aéronautique et spatiale		353
..	..	..	..	..	..	1 054		Autres équipements de transport		359
..	..	..	..	..	..	82 539		**Meubles; activités de fabrication, nca**		36
..	..	..	..	..	..	63 831		Meubles		361
..	..	..	..	..	..	18 708		Activités de fabrication, nca		369
..	..	..	..	..	..	1 709		**Récupération**		37
..	..	..	..	..	..	64 599		**Production et distrib. d'électricité, de gaz, d'eau**	E	40-41
..	..	..	..	..	..	61 470		**Electricité, gaz, vapeur et eau chaude**		40
..	..	..	..	..	..	53 229		Production, collecte et distribution d'électricité		401
..	..	..	..	..	..	..		**Captage, épuration et distribution d'eau**		41 410
..	..	..	..	..	..	..		**Construction**	F	45
..	..	..	..	..	..	..		**Commerce de gros et de détail; réparation**	G	50-52
..	..	..	..	..	..	..		**Hôtels et restaurants**	H	55
..	..	..	..	..	..	..		**Transports, entreposage et communications**	I	60-64
..	..	..	..	..	..	..		**Intermédiation financière**	J	65-67
..	..	..	..	..	..	..		**Immobilier, locations, services aux entreprises**	K	70-74
..	..	..	..	..	..	..		**Admin. publique; éducation; santé; autres**	L-Q	75-99
..	..	..	..	..	..	..		**Grand total**	A-Q	01-99

Statistiques des Structures Industrielles
OCDE, © 1998
OECD OCDE

BELGIUM

Table BE.1 EXPORTS - EXPORTATIONS

Millions of BF (Current Prices)

ISIC revision 3		Description	1989	1990	1991	1992	1993	1994	1995	1996
A	01-02	Agriculture, hunting and forestry	81 350	75 618	81 384	78 442	79 601	92 452	..	..
B	05	Fishing	2 320	2 214	2 381	2 012	1 798	1 955	..	..
C	10-14	Mining and quarrying	179 556	156 470	153 634	152 084	179 746	188 043	..	..
	10	Mining of coal and lignite; extraction of peat	2 434	2 179	2 363	1 827	2 707	3 323	..	..
	11	Crude petroleum & natural gas; related service activ.	41	19	23	42	1 646	622	..	..
	13	Mining of metal ores	5 765	4 485	3 142	3 231	3 236	5 026	..	..
	14	Other mining and quarrying	171 316	149 787	148 106	146 984	172 158	179 072	..	..
D	15-37	Total manufacturing	3 669 348	3 697 387	3 775 296	3 726 525	3 907 920	4 299 308	..	..
	15	Food products and beverages	317 966	314 284	350 276	368 826	382 133	405 199	..	..
	155	Beverages	22 607	21 676	22 823	23 433	29 811	32 230	..	..
	16 160	Tobacco products	10 652	10 925	10 941	10 787	13 711	13 734	..	..
	17	Textiles	212 184	215 835	216 125	208 290	211 977	225 752	..	..
	171	Spinning, weaving and finishing of textiles	90 140	89 428	85 145	78 673	78 673	85 749	..	..
	172	Other textiles	111 543	114 876	118 436	117 354	119 794	125 484	..	..
	173	Knitted and crocheted fabrics and articles	10 501	11 532	12 543	12 262	13 510	14 519	..	..
	18	Wearing apparel dressing & dyeing of fur	48 898	58 300	63 321	66 731	62 956	59 973	..	..
	181	Wearing apparel, except fur apparel	47 884	57 269	62 313	65 791	62 221	59 046	..	..
	182	Dressing and dyeing of fur; articles of fur	1 014	1 031	1 008	940	735	927	..	..
	19	Tanning, dressing leather; leather artic.; footwear	13 269	14 207	13 673	14 392	16 738	17 819	..	..
	191	Tanning, dressing leather; manuf. of leather articles	9 313	10 217	9 035	9 633	10 718	11 577	..	..
	192	Footwear	3 955	3 989	4 638	4 759	6 019	6 243	..	..
	20	Wood and cork products, ex. furniture	29 828	30 930	31 859	31 371	30 781	34 621	..	..
	201	Sawmilling and planing of wood	6 093	6 379	6 065	6 143	6 359	7 775	..	..
	202	Products of wood, cork, straw & plaiting material	23 735	24 550	25 794	25 229	24 421	26 845	..	..
	21	Paper and paper products	87 603	87 834	87 188	81 517	84 245	87 067	..	..
	22	Publishing, printing & reprod. of recorded media	33 384	35 747	37 349	37 177	34 510	38 365	..	..
	221	Publishing	22 573	23 857	24 172	24 553	22 782	24 864	..	..
	222	Printing and related service activities	10 811	11 891	13 176	12 624	11 728	13 501	..	..
	223	Reproduction of recorded media	..	..	..	..	..	..	..	..
	23	Coke, refined petroleum products & nuclear fuel	143 703	143 609	167 142	151 182	144 056	140 820	..	..
	24	Chemicals and chemical products	596 284	597 810	620 481	639 407	729 214	837 000	..	..
	241	Basic chemicals	370 026	359 803	361 606	355 119	405 825	483 920	..	..
	242	Other chemical products	214 686	225 558	244 930	270 179	304 357	332 326	..	..
	243	Man-made fibres	11 572	12 449	13 945	14 109	19 032	20 754	..	..
	25	Rubber and plastic products	133 952	142 396	148 259	153 906	158 047	167 159	..	..
	251	Rubber products	33 771	33 543	33 675	37 395	36 137	38 780	..	..
	252	Plastic products	100 181	108 853	114 585	116 511	121 910	128 379	..	..
	26	Other non-metallic mineral products	97 849	101 102	97 356	100 625	105 377	113 858	..	..
	261	Glass and glass products	55 794	55 976	51 414	52 344	56 664	59 960	..	..
	269	Non-metallic mineral products, nec	42 055	45 125	45 941	48 280	48 713	53 898	..	..
	27	Basic metals	533 083	462 399	419 996	374 054	351 151	405 498	..	..
	271	Basic iron and steel	342 033	317 136	289 174	250 973	230 460	269 025	..	..
	272	Basic precious and non-ferrous metals	191 050	145 263	130 822	123 081	120 691	136 473	..	..
	273	Casting of metals	..	..	..	..	..	..	..	..
	28	Fabricated metal products, ex. machin. & equip.	102 786	109 071	110 942	111 211	105 520	103 985	..	..
	281	Structural metal prod., tanks, reservoirs, generators	31 506	36 403	38 392	40 197	38 142	33 947	..	..
	289	Other fabricated metal products & service activities	71 280	72 669	72 549	71 014	67 378	70 038	..	..
	29	Machinery and equipment, nec	254 349	264 339	253 375	261 503	263 905	304 028	..	..
	291	General purpose machinery	86 078	88 026	90 208	99 093	107 317	119 657	..	..
	292	Special purpose machinery	157 472	165 631	152 034	150 718	143 987	170 776	..	..
	293	Domestic appliances, nec	10 799	10 683	11 132	11 692	12 602	13 596	..	..
	30	Office, accounting and computing machinery	39 798	41 226	41 126	38 210	43 095	52 939	..	..
	31	Electrical machinery and apparatus, nec	84 461	90 922	93 963	96 188	95 611	103 749	..	..
	311	Electric motors, generators and transformers	11 823	14 032	13 632	14 189	14 914	13 550	..	..
	312	Electricity distribution and control apparatus	12 163	13 211	13 143	15 111	16 984	18 956	..	..
	313	Insulated wire and cable	11 967	11 631	11 933	11 287	7 980	10 603	..	..
	314	Accumulators, primary cells and primary batteries	13 114	14 398	16 372	15 960	18 023	19 325	..	..
	315	Electric lamps and lighting equipment	14 098	14 640	15 027	15 723	13 713	16 499	..	..
	319	Other electrical equipment, nec	21 297	23 009	23 855	23 918	23 997	24 815	..	..
	32	Radio, TV, communication equip. & apparatus	76 996	81 832	80 585	74 680	107 198	118 153	..	..
	321	Electronic valves, tubes & other electronic compon.	12 691	12 826	12 943	10 722	18 879	22 020	..	..
	322	TV, radio transmitters & appar. for line teleph., telegr.	18 148	17 779	20 947	22 986	27 153	36 963	..	..
	323	TV, radio receivers and associated goods	46 157	51 226	46 694	40 972	61 166	59 171	..	..
	33	Medical, precision, optical instr.; watches, clocks	34 499	35 713	36 826	37 812	48 891	52 055	..	..
	331	Medical equip.; precision instruments and appliances	28 008	29 281	30 731	32 389	40 276	42 443	..	..
	332	Optical instruments and photographic equipment	4 385	4 344	4 091	3 782	6 646	7 534	..	..
	333	Watches and clocks	2 106	2 089	2 004	1 640	1 969	2 078	..	..
	34	Motor vehicles, trailers, and semi-trailers	555 340	606 940	622 820	610 379	630 732	732 848	..	..
	35	Other transport equipment	34 776	37 536	46 325	43 753	44 157	31 181	..	..
	351	Building and repairing of ships and boats	2 514	2 068	2 127	2 686	1 930	2 012	..	..
	352	Railway, tramway locomotives and rolling stock	1 719	3 650	3 886	4 581	10 926	9 747	..	..
	353	Aircraft and spacecraft	26 227	26 095	34 316	31 477	27 048	15 496	..	..
	359	Transport equipment, nec	4 316	5 723	5 996	5 009	4 252	3 926	..	..
	36	Furniture; manufacturing, nec	227 690	214 430	225 371	214 523	243 916	253 503	..	..
	361	Furniture	39 854	43 693	46 705	48 286	47 127	48 098	..	..
	369	Manufacturing, nec	187 836	170 737	178 666	166 237	196 790	205 405	..	..
	37	Recycling	..	..	..	..	..	..	..	..
E	40-41	Electricity, gas and water supply	6 871	6 680	4 414	3 544	4 070	3 826	..	..
	40	Electricity, gas, steam and hot water supply	6 871	6 680	4 414	3 544	4 070	3 826	..	..
	401	Production, collection and distribution of electricity	6 871	6 680	4 414	3 544	4 070	3 826	..	..
	41 410	Collection, purification, distribution of water	..	..	..	..	..	..	..	..
F	45	Construction	..	..	..	..	..	..	..	..
G	50-52	Wholesale and retail trade; repairs etc	..	..	..	..	..	..	..	..
H	55	Hotels and restaurants	..	..	..	..	..	..	..	..
I	60-64	Transport, storage and communications	..	..	..	..	..	..	..	..
J	65-67	Financial intermediation	..	..	..	..	..	..	..	..
K	70-74	Real estate, renting and business activities	..	..	..	..	..	..	..	..
L-Q	75-99	Public admin.; education; health; other services	..	..	..	..	..	..	..	..
A-Q	01-99	Grand total	3 943 071	3 944 461	4 023 361	3 969 811	4 175 428	4 588 184	..	..

Table BE.2 **IMPORTATIONS - IMPORTS**

Millions de BF (Prix courants)   CITI révision 3

1989	1990	1991	1992	1993	1994	1995	1996				
175 285	164 083	171 921	165 264	144 914	164 888	..	..	**Agriculture, chasse et sylviculture**	A	01-02	
8 212	9 115	9 360	9 917	8 850	9 443	..	..	**Pêche**	B	05	
433 636	424 957	427 125	391 031	390 470	400 554	..	..	**Activités extractives**	C	10-14	
30 279	32 543	32 486	30 340	25 022	25 717	..	..	Extraction de charbon, de lignite et de tourbe		10	
156 050	168 235	184 926	163 346	146 789	140 279	..	..	Extraction de pétrole brut et de gaz naturel		11	
43 630	37 890	33 377	27 784	21 570	26 800	..	..	Extraction de minerais métalliques		13	
203 677	186 289	176 336	169 562	197 087	207 758	..	..	Autres activités extractives		14	
3 255 062	3 400 269	3 494 330	3 446 743	3 282 259	3 617 680	..	..	**Activités de fabrication**	D	15-37	
239 179	244 340	268 025	280 808	288 784	322 246	..	..	**Produits alimentaires et boissons**		15	
32 467	36 638	38 397	40 943	46 446	46 493	..	..	Boissons			155
4 972	4 981	5 414	6 034	6 660	7 925	..	..	**Produits à base de tabac**		16	160
121 080	126 284	128 471	123 515	117 353	129 754	..	..	**Textiles**		17	
63 320	64 873	61 998	56 282	54 492	62 435	..	..	Filature, tissage et achèvement des textiles			171
33 797	35 636	37 714	37 907	32 120	36 179	..	..	Autres articles textiles			172
23 963	25 775	28 760	29 325	30 741	31 140	..	..	Etoffes et articles de bonneterie			173
83 485	96 938	104 764	107 778	105 313	100 297	..	..	**Habillement; préparation, teinture des fourrures**		18	
82 691	96 167	104 060	107 051	104 863	99 632	..	..	Articles d'habillement autres qu'en fourrure			181
795	772	704	727	451	665	..	..	Préparation, teinture des fourrures; art. en fourrure			182
35 141	37 985	39 843	39 409	36 532	38 583	..	..	**Travail des cuirs; articles en cuir; chaussures**		19	
10 966	12 157	11 914	11 903	11 653	12 678	..	..	Apprêt et tannage des cuirs et articles en cuirs			191
24 175	25 829	27 929	27 506	24 878	25 906	..	..	Chaussures			192
40 800	43 232	42 743	41 964	41 109	44 039	..	..	**Bois et articles en bois et liège (sauf meubles)**		20	
21 813	22 055	20 693	19 316	19 010	20 721	..	..	Sciage et rabotage du bois			201
18 987	21 177	22 050	22 648	22 099	23 318	..	..	Articles en bois, liège, vannerie, sparterie			202
102 830	106 025	104 966	99 952	94 626	108 104	..	..	**Papier et carton; articles en papier et en carton**		21	
41 152	44 171	47 215	47 942	42 303	45 593	..	..	**Edition, imprimerie et reproduction**		22	
32 858	35 584	38 216	38 500	35 507	37 765	..	..	Edition			221
8 293	8 587	8 999	9 442	6 796	7 828	..	..	Imprimerie et activités annexes			222
..	..	..	..	..	..	..	..	Reproduction de supports enregistrés			223
120 053	144 989	142 760	130 544	121 044	128 050	..	..	**Cokéfaction; prod. pétroliers; comb. nucléaires**		23	
477 291	486 481	501 365	505 443	520 973	577 508	..	..	**Produits chimiques**		24	
297 847	289 463	288 132	280 993	295 446	329 353	..	..	Produits chimiques de base			241
150 150	167 313	184 023	196 164	200 598	218 330	..	..	Autres produits chimiques			242
29 294	29 705	29 210	28 287	24 929	29 824	..	..	Fibres synthétiques ou artificielles			243
100 324	108 638	113 372	115 377	113 190	122 894	..	..	**Articles en caoutchouc et en matières plastiques**		25	
31 608	32 998	33 254	34 968	33 642	38 336	..	..	Articles en caoutchouc			251
68 716	75 640	80 118	80 410	79 548	84 558	..	..	Articles en matières plastiques			252
61 765	65 533	67 195	69 474	63 323	67 025	..	..	**Autres produits minéraux non métalliques**		26	
21 771	21 746	22 649	23 731	23 746	25 196	..	..	Verre et articles en verre			261
39 994	43 788	44 545	45 743	39 576	41 830	..	..	Produits minéraux non métalliques, nca			269
286 140	255 210	236 158	223 023	186 936	224 188	..	..	**Produits métallurgiques de base**		27	
134 349	128 314	121 166	109 773	97 560	121 093	..	..	Sidérurgie et première transformation de l'acier			271
151 791	126 896	114 992	113 249	89 376	103 095	..	..	Métallurgie; métaux précieux et non ferreux			272
..	..	..	..	..	..	..	..	Fonderie			273
94 519	105 316	104 611	108 153	83 961	93 553	..	..	**Ouvrages en métaux, sauf machines et matériel**		28	
21 165	28 495	27 979	28 004	17 649	19 625	..	..	Constr. et menuiserie métal.; réservoirs; générateurs			281
73 354	76 822	76 631	80 149	66 312	73 928	..	..	Autres ouvrages en métaux			289
298 352	330 868	334 461	333 975	258 551	295 071	..	..	**Machines et matériel, nca**		29	
118 643	137 888	134 907	137 541	110 374	124 886	..	..	Machines d'usage général			291
149 868	161 201	164 508	159 007	112 644	134 335	..	..	Machines d'usage spécifique			292
29 841	31 779	35 046	37 426	35 533	35 849	..	..	Appareils domestiques, nca			293
78 086	84 371	83 884	83 419	73 139	84 099	..	..	**Mach. de bureau, comptables, matériel inform.**		30	
85 575	91 302	95 911	96 902	89 618	100 818	..	..	**Machines et appareils électriques, nca**		31	
15 453	17 400	18 420	18 097	14 278	14 765	..	..	Moteurs, génératrices et transformateurs électriques			311
24 554	26 653	26 372	27 575	24 596	27 650	..	..	Matériel électrique de distribution et de commande			312
9 495	9 659	9 888	10 120	6 961	9 444	..	..	Fils et câbles électriques isolés			313
6 058	6 713	7 670	6 196	7 266	7 018	..	..	Accumulateurs, piles électriques			314
10 873	11 465	11 986	12 808	11 969	12 768	..	..	Lampes électriques et appareils d'éclairage			315
19 143	19 410	21 576	22 106	24 548	29 173	..	..	Autres matériels électriques, nca			319
72 783	77 105	76 945	76 535	92 807	99 768	..	..	**Equip. et appar. de radio, TV, communication**		32	
22 149	20 924	19 382	18 799	22 682	29 534	..	..	Tubes et valves électroniques; autres composants			321
15 142	17 068	18 612	18 994	19 392	21 286	..	..	Emetteurs radio et TV; app. téléphonie, télégraphie			322
35 492	39 113	38 951	38 742	50 733	48 948	..	..	Récepteurs radio et TV et articles associés			323
61 166	63 977	65 061	68 473	67 156	73 275	..	..	**Instruments médicaux, de précision, d'optique**		33	
46 537	49 028	50 598	53 655	51 991	57 190	..	..	Appareils médicaux et de précision			331
9 803	9 882	9 619	10 107	10 823	11 433	..	..	Instruments d'optique ; matériel photographique			332
4 826	5 067	4 844	4 711	4 342	4 652	..	..	Horlogerie			333
551 024	586 670	618 530	593 856	568 679	644 512	..	..	**Véhicules automobiles et nemorques**		34	
50 895	54 816	65 303	50 843	66 386	41 507	..	..	**Autres matériels de transport**		35	
2 296	2 642	2 782	2 842	2 907	5 038	..	..	Construction et réparation de navires			351
2 097	3 175	4 493	4 581	7 451	8 175	..	..	Construction de matériel ferroviaire roulant			352
39 966	40 829	47 826	33 626	44 733	17 192	..	..	Construction aéronautique et spatiale			353
6 536	8 170	10 201	9 795	11 294	11 101	..	..	Autres équipements de transport			359
248 449	241 037	247 333	243 323	243 817	268 871	..	..	**Meubles; activités de fabrication, nca**		36	
41 082	47 458	51 408	54 559	43 629	49 042	..	..	Meubles			361
207 366	193 578	195 925	188 764	200 188	219 830	..	..	Activités de fabrication, nca			369
..	..	..	..	..	..	..	..	**Récupération**		37	
7 107	5 856	7 201	5 756	12 849	15 095	..	..	**Production et distrib. d'électricité, de gaz, d'eau**	E	40-41	
7 107	5 856	7 201	5 756	12 849	15 095	..	..	**Electricité, gaz, vapeur et eau chaude**		40	
6 539	5 805	7 201	5 756	12 833	14 946	..	..	Production, collecte et distribution d'électricité			401
								Captage, épuration et distribution d'eau		41	410
..	..	..	..	..	..	..	..	**Construction**	F	45	
..	..	..	..	..	..	..	..	**Commerce de gros et de détail; réparation**	G	50-52	
..	..	..	..	..	..	..	..	**Hôtels et restaurants**	H	55	
..	..	..	..	..	..	..	..	**Transports, entreposage et communications**	I	60-64	
..	..	..	..	..	..	..	..	**Intermédiation financière**	J	65-67	
..	..	..	..	..	..	..	..	**Immobilier, locations, services aux entreprises**	K	70-74	
..	..	..	..	..	..	..	..	**Admin. publique; éducation; santé; autres**	L-Q	75-99	
3 883 880	4 011 589	4 116 262	4 023 293	3 842 506	4 211 570	..	..	**Grand total**	A-Q	01-99	

Statistiques des Structures Industrielles
OCDE, © 1998

CANADA

Table CA.1 PRODUCTION - PRODUCTION

Millions of C$ (Current Prices)

ISIC revision 3			1989	1990	1991	1992	1993	1994	1995	1996
A	01-02	Agriculture, hunting and forestry	..	..	..	..	..	..	..	..
B	05	Fishing	..	..	..	..	..	..	..	..
C	10-14	Mining and quarrying	..	..	..	..	..	..	..	..
	10	Mining of coal and lignite; extraction of peat	..	..	..	..	..	1 590	1 790	..
	11	Crude petroleum & natural gas; related service activ.	..	..	..	..	..	21 870	24 100	..
	13	Mining of metal ores	..	..	..	..	..			..
	14	Other mining and quarrying	..	..	..	..	..			..
D	15-37	Total manufacturing	..	..	..	..	..	418 630	465 170	..
	15	Food products and beverages	..	..	..	..	..	58 350	61 500	..
	155	Beverages	..	..	..	..	..	7 290	8 200	..
	16 160	Tobacco products	..	..	..	..	..	3 870	3 880	..
	17	Textiles	..	..	..	..	..	6 070	6 440	..
	171	Spinning, weaving and finishing of textiles	..	..	..	..	..	1 800	1 990	..
	172	Other textiles	..	..	..	..	..	3 140	3 280	..
	173	Knitted and crocheted fabrics and articles	..	..	..	..	..	1 130	1 170	..
	18	Wearing apparel dressing & dyeing of fur	..	..	..	..	..	6 370	6 590	..
	181	Wearing apparel, except fur apparel	..	..	..	..	..	6 280	6 500	..
	182	Dressing and dyeing of fur; articles of fur	..	..	..	..	..	90	90	..
	19	Tanning, dressing leather; leather artic.; footwear	..	..	..	..	..	1 200	1 160	..
	191	Tanning, dressing leather; manuf. of leather articles	..	..	..	..	..	270	280	..
	192	Footwear	..	..	..	..	..	930	880	..
	20	Wood and cork products, ex. furniture	..	..	..	..	..	23 150	23 150	..
	201	Sawmilling and planing of wood	..	..	..	..	..	15 500	15 350	..
	202	Products of wood, cork, straw & plaiting material	..	..	..	..	..	7 650	7 800	..
	21	Paper and paper products	..	..	..	..	..	26 740	39 070	..
	22	Publishing, printing & reprod. of recorded media	..	..	..	..	..	14 700	16 060	..
	221	Publishing	..	..	..	..	..	6 240	6 550	..
	222	Printing and related service activities	..	..	..	..	..	8 000	8 900	..
	223	Reproduction of recorded media	..	..	..	..	..	460	610	..
	23	Coke, refined petroleum products & nuclear fuel	..	..	..	..	..	17 900	18 170	..
	24	Chemicals and chemical products	..	..	..	..	..	34 090	37 730	..
	241	Basic chemicals	..	..	..	..	..	16 480	18 250	..
	242	Other chemical products	..	..	..	..	..	16 300	17 640	..
	243	Man-made fibres	..	..	..	..	..	1 310	1 840	..
	25	Rubber and plastic products	..	..	..	..	..	14 810	16 450	..
	251	Rubber products	..	..	..	..	..	6 880	7 570	..
	252	Plastic products	..	..	..	..	..	7 930	8 880	..
	26	Other non-metallic mineral products	..	..	..	..	..	8 230	8 770	..
	261	Glass and glass products	..	..	..	..	..	2 110	2 260	..
	269	Non-metallic mineral products, nec	..	..	..	..	..	6 120	6 510	..
	27	Basic metals	..	..	..	..	..	24 630	28 570	..
	271	Basic iron and steel	..	..	..	..	..	12 280	13 560	..
	272	Basic precious and non-ferrous metals	..	..	..	..	..	9 950	12 240	..
	273	Casting of metals	..	..	..	..	..	2 400	2 770	..
	28	Fabricated metal products, ex. machin. & equip.	..	..	..	..	..	17 460	19 800	..
	281	Structural metal prod., tanks, reservoirs, generators	..	..	..	..	..	7 360	8 330	..
	289	Other fabricated metal products & service activities	..	..	..	..	..	10 100	11 470	..
	29	Machinery and equipment, nec	..	..	..	..	..	17 000	19 770	..
	291	General purpose machinery	..	..	..	..	..	7 270	8 340	..
	292	Special purpose machinery	..	..	..	..	..	7 230	8 950	..
	293	Domestic appliances, nec	..	..	..	..	..	2 500	2 480	..
	30	Office, accounting and computing machinery	..	..	..	..	..	5 990	7 930	..
	31	Electrical machinery and apparatus, nec	..	..	..	..	..	7 910	8 530	..
	311	Electric motors, generators and transformers	..	..	..	..	..	1 580	1 810	..
	312	Electricity distribution and control apparatus	..	..	..	..	..	1 340	1 390	..
	313	Insulated wire and cable	..	..	..	..	..	1 890	2 030	..
	314	Accumulators, primary cells and primary batteries	..	..	..	..	..	340	350	..
	315	Electric lamps and lighting equipment	..	..	..	..	..	910	990	..
	319	Other electrical equipment, nec	..	..	..	..	..	1 850	1 960	..
	32	Radio, TV, communication equip. & apparatus	..	..	..	..	..	12 480	14 960	..
	321	Electronic valves, tubes & other electronic compon.	..	..	..	..	..	3 930	5 000	..
	322	TV, radio transmitters & appar. for line teleph., telegr.	..	..	..	..	..	7 710	9 140	..
	323	TV, radio receivers and associated goods	..	..	..	..	..	840	820	..
	33	Medical, precision, optical instr.; watches, clocks	..	..	..	..	..	1 730	1 740	..
	331	Medical equip.; precision instruments and appliances	..	..	..	..	..	1 400	1 510	..
	332	Optical instruments and photographic equipment	..	..	..	..	..	290	200	..
	333	Watches and clocks	..	..	..	..	..	40	30	..
	34	Motor vehicles, trailers, and semi-trailers	..	..	..	..	..	93 980	100 050	..
	35	Other transport equipment	..	..	..	..	..	9 540	11 590	..
	351	Building and repairing of ships and boats	..	..	..	..	..	1 300	1 460	..
	352	Railway, tramway locomotives and rolling stock	..	..	..	..	..	2 310	2 520	..
	353	Aircraft and spacecraft	..	..	..	..	..	5 930	7 610	..
	359	Transport equipment, nec	..	..	..	..	..			..
	36	Furniture; manufacturing, nec	..	..	..	..	..	12 400	13 230	..
	361	Furniture	..	..	..	..	..	7 830	8 430	..
	369	Manufacturing, nec	..	..	..	..	..	4 570	4 800	..
	37	Recycling	..	..	..	..	..			..
E	40-41	Electricity, gas and water supply	..	..	..	..	..	46 170		..
	40	Electricity, gas, steam and hot water supply	..	..	..	..	..	44 200	41 800	..
	401	Production, collection and distribution of electricity	..	..	..	..	..	36 600	34 600	..
	41 410	Collection, purification, distribution of water	..	..	..	..	..	1 970	..	..
F	45	Construction	..	..	..	..	..	..	..	..
G	50-52	Wholesale and retail trade; repairs etc	..	..	..	..	..	..	..	..
H	55	Hotels and restaurants	..	..	..	..	..	..	..	..
I	60-64	Transport, storage and communications	..	..	..	..	..	..	..	..
J	65-67	Financial intermediation	..	..	..	..	..	..	..	..
K	70-74	Real estate, renting and business activities	..	..	..	..	..	..	..	..
L-Q	75-99	Public admin.; education; health; other services	..	..	..	..	..	..	..	..
A-Q	01-99	Grand total	..	..	..	..	..	..	..	..

Note: ISIC 1549 includes 1532; 1721 includes 1723; 2230 includes 2213 and 3692; 2411 includes 2330; 2429 includes 3311; 2699 includes 2310; 2720 includes 2891; 2915 includes 2924; 2929 includes 2913 and 2923; 2925 and 2926; 2930 includes 2914; 3220 includes 3313; 3410 includes 3591; 3693 includes 3592.

OECD OCDE Industrial Structure Statistics
OECD, © 1998

Table CA.2 VALEUR AJOUTÉE - VALUE ADDED

Millions de C$ (Prix courants)

1989	1990	1991	1992	1993	1994	1995	1996			CITI révision 3	
..	..	..	..	..	..	..	..	**Agriculture, chasse et sylviculture**	A	01-02	
..	..	..	..	..	..	..	..	**Pêche**	B	05	
..	..	..	..	..	30 920	28 830	..	**Activités extractives**	C	10-14	
..	..	..	..	..	1 270	1 420	..	Extraction de charbon, de lignite et de tourbe		10	
..	..	..	..	..	22 000	18 580	..	Extraction de pétrole brut et de gaz naturel		11	
..	..	..	..	..	5 260	6 820	..	Extraction de minerais métalliques		13	
..	..	..	..	..	1 940	1 610	..	Autres activités extractives		14	
..	..	..	..	..	153 790	173 560	..	**Activités de fabrication**	D	15-37	
..	..	..	..	..	21 030	21 000	..	**Produits alimentaires et boissons**		15	
..	..	..	..	..	4 290	4 280	..	Boissons			155
..	..	..	..	..	1 630	1 660	..	**Produits à base de tabac**		16	160
..	..	..	..	..	2 740	2 830	..	**Textiles**		17	
..	..	..	..	..	850	930	..	Filature, tissage et achèvement des textiles			171
..	..	..	..	..	1 370	1 380	..	Autres articles textiles			172
..	..	..	..	..	520	520	..	Etoffes et articles de bonneterie			173
..	..	..	..	..	2 950	3 120	..	**Habillement; préparation, teinture des fourrures**		18	
..	..	..	..	..	2 910	3 080	..	Articles d'habillement autres qu'en fourrure			181
..	..	..	..	..	40	40	..	Préparation, teinture des fourrures; art. en fourrure			182
..	..	..	..	..	550	510	..	**Travail des cuirs; articles en cuir; chaussures**		19	
..	..	..	..	..	110	110	..	Apprêt et tannage des cuirs et articles en cuirs			191
..	..	..	..	..	440	400	..	Chaussures			192
..	..	..	..	..	9 720	8 490	..	**Bois et articles en bois et liège (sauf meubles)**		20	
..	..	..	..	..	6 360	5 220	..	Sciage et rabotage du bois			201
..	..	..	..	..	3 360	3 270	..	Articles en bois, liège, vannerie, sparterie			202
..	..	..	..	..	10 790	18 160	..	**Papier et carton; articles en papier et en carton**		21	
..	..	..	..	..	9 270	9 740	..	**Edition, imprimerie et reproduction**		22	
..	..	..	..	..	4 440	4 560	..	Edition			221
..	..	..	..	..	4 520	4 770	..	Imprimerie et activités annexes			222
..	..	..	..	..	310	410	..	Reproduction de supports enregistrés			223
..	..	..	..	..	2 620	2 740	..	**Cokéfaction; prod. pétroliers; comb. nucléaires**		23	
..	..	..	..	..	15 310	17 820	..	**Produits chimiques**		24	
..	..	..	..	..	6 450	8 310	..	Produits chimiques de base			241
..	..	..	..	..	8 290	8 870	..	Autres produits chimiques			242
..	..	..	..	..	570	640	..	Fibres synthétiques ou artificielles			243
..	..	..	..	..	5 890	6 170	..	**Articles en caoutchouc et en matières plastiques**		25	
..	..	..	..	..	2 370	2 350	..	Articles en caoutchouc			251
..	..	..	..	..	3 520	3 820	..	Articles en matières plastiques			252
..	..	..	..	..	4 000	4 350	..	**Autres produits minéraux non métalliques**		26	
..	..	..	..	..	1 110	1 210	..	Verre et articles en verre			261
..	..	..	..	..	2 890	3 140	..	Produits minéraux non métalliques, nca			269
..	..	..	..	..	9 680	11 700	..	**Produits métallurgiques de base**		27	
..	..	..	..	..	4 400	5 160	..	Sidérurgie et première transformation de l'acier			271
..	..	..	..	..	4 050	5 130	..	Métallurgie; métaux précieux et non ferreux			272
..	..	..	..	..	1 230	1 410	..	Fonderie			273
..	..	..	..	..	8 380	9 630	..	**Ouvrages en métaux, sauf machines et matériel**		28	
..	..	..	..	..	3 120	3 790	..	Constr. et menuiserie métal.; réservoirs; générateurs			281
..	..	..	..	..	5 260	5 840	..	Autres ouvrages en métaux			289
..	..	..	..	..	7 750	9 160	..	**Machines et matériel, nca**		29	
..	..	..	..	..	3 300	3 870	..	Machines d'usage général			291
..	..	..	..	..	3 430	4 290	..	Machines d'usage spécifique			292
..	..	..	..	..	1 020	1 000	..	Appareils domestiques, nca			293
..	..	..	..	..	1 280	1 170	..	**Mach. de bureau, comptables, matériel inform.**		30	
..	..	..	..	..	3 650	3 560	..	**Machines et appareils électriques, nca**		31	
..	..	..	..	..	760	790	..	Moteurs, génératrices et transformateurs électriques			311
..	..	..	..	..	700	670	..	Matériel électrique de distribution et de commande			312
..	..	..	..	..	740	710	..	Fils et câbles électriques isolés			313
..	..	..	..	..	180	170	..	Accumulateurs, piles électriques			314
..	..	..	..	..	390	390	..	Lampes électriques et appareils d'éclairage			315
..	..	..	..	..	880	830	..	Autres matériels électriques, nca			319
..	..	..	..	..	5 500	6 820	..	**Equip. et appar. de radio, TV, communication**		32	
..	..	..	..	..	1 120	1 540	..	Tubes et valves électroniques; autres composants			321
..	..	..	..	..	4 220	5 140	..	Emetteurs radio et TV; app. téléphonie, télégraphie			322
..	..	..	..	..	160	140	..	Récepteurs radio et TV et articles associés			323
..	..	..	..	..	980	940	..	**Instruments médicaux, de précision, d'optique**		33	
..	..	..	..	..	810	840	..	Appareils médicaux et de précision			331
..	..	..	..	..	150	90	..	Instruments d'optique ; matériel photographique			332
..	..	..	..	..	20	10	..	Horlogerie			333
..	..	..	..	..	18 730	21 230	..	**Véhicules automobiles et nemorques**		34	
..	..	..	..	..	5 240	6 190	..	**Autres matériels de transport**		35	
..	..	..	..	..	780	910	..	Construction et réparation de navires			351
..	..	..	..	..	930	940	..	Construction de matériel ferroviaire roulant			352
..	..	..	..	..	3 530	4 340	..	Construction aéronautique et spatiale			353
..	..	..	..	..	..	..	..	Autres équipements de transport			359
..	..	..	..	..	6 080	6 560	..	**Meubles; activités de fabrication, nca**		36	
..	..	..	..	..	3 660	4 000	..	Meubles			361
..	..	..	..	..	2 420	2 560	..	Activités de fabrication, nca			369
..	..	..	..	..	..	..	..	**Récupération**		37	
..	..	..	..	..	22 190	..	..	**Production et distrib. d'électricité, de gaz, d'eau**	E	40-41	
..	..	..	..	..	21 430	21 770	..	Electricité, gaz, vapeur et eau chaude		40	
..	..	..	..	..	19 150	19 670	..	Production, collecte et distribution d'électricité			401
..	..	..	..	..	760	..	..	**Captage, épuration et distribution d'eau**		41	410
..	..	..	..	..	..	..	..	**Construction**	F	45	
..	..	..	..	..	..	..	..	**Commerce de gros et de détail; réparation**	G	50-52	
..	..	..	..	..	..	..	..	**Hôtels et restaurants**	H	55	
..	..	..	..	..	..	..	..	**Transports, entreposage et communications**	I	60-64	
..	..	..	..	..	..	..	..	**Intermédiation financière**	J	65-67	
..	..	..	..	..	..	..	..	**Immobilier, locations, services aux entreprises**	K	70-74	
..	..	..	..	..	..	..	..	**Admin. publique; éducation; santé; autres**	L-Q	75-99	
..	..	..	..	..	..	..	..	**Grand total**	A-Q	01-99	

Note: ISIC 1549 includes 1532; 1721 includes 1723; 2230 includes 2213 and 3692; 2411 includes 2330; 2429 includes 3311; 2699 includes 2310; 2720 includes 2891; 2915 includes 2924; 2929 includes 2913 and 2923, 2925 and 2926; 2930 includes 2914; 3220 includes 3313; 3410 includes 3591; 3693 includes 3592.

Statistiques des Structures Industrielles
OCDE, © 1998

CANADA

Table CA.3 ESTABLISHMENTS - ETABLISSEMENTS

Units

ISIC revision 3			1989	1990	1991	1992	1993	1994	1995	1996
A	01-02	**Agriculture, hunting and forestry**	..	..	..	..	..	..	..	..
B	05	**Fishing**	..	..	..	..	..	..	..	..
C	10-14	**Mining and quarrying**	..	..	..	..	..	1 238	1 395	..
	10	Mining of coal and lignite; extraction of peat	..	..	..	..	..	94	98	..
	11	Crude petroleum & natural gas; related service activ.	..	..	..	..	..	686	686	..
	13	Mining of metal ores	..	..	..	..	..	84	89	..
	14	Other mining and quarrying	..	..	..	..	..	370	518	..
D	15-37	**Total manufacturing**	..	..	..	..	..	31 974	32 718	..
	15	**Food products and beverages**	..	..	..	..	..	3 146	3 190	..
	155	Beverages	..	..	..	..	..	197	233	..
	16	**Tobacco products**		160	..	..	..	..	17	16	..
	17	**Textiles**	..	..	..	..	..	918	1 005	..
	171	Spinning, weaving and finishing of textiles	..	..	..	..	..	227	251	..
	172	Other textiles	..	..	..	..	..	545	606	..
	173	Knitted and crocheted fabrics and articles	..	..	..	..	..	146	148	..
	18	**Wearing apparel dressing & dyeing of fur**	..	..	..	..	..	1 674	1 641	..
	181	Wearing apparel, except fur apparel	..	..	..	..	..	1 549	1 524	..
	182	Dressing and dyeing of fur; articles of fur	..	..	..	..	..	125	117	..
	19	**Tanning, dressing leather; leather artic.; footwear**	..	..	..	..	..	216	229	..
	191	Tanning, dressing leather; manuf. of leather articles	..	..	..	..	..	70	73	..
	192	Footwear	..	..	..	..	..	146	156	..
	20	**Wood and cork products, ex. furniture**	..	..	..	..	..	2 189	2 213	..
	201	Sawmilling and planing of wood	..	..	..	..	..	837	883	..
	202	Products of wood, cork, straw & plaiting material	..	..	..	..	..	1 352	1 330	..
	21	**Paper and paper products**	..	..	..	..	..	649	668	..
	22	**Publishing, printing & reprod. of recorded media**	..	..	..	..	..	4 514	4 468	..
	221	Publishing	..	..	..	..	..	1 300	1 269	..
	222	Printing and related service activities	..	..	..	..	..	3 172	3 153	..
	223	Reproduction of recorded media	..	..	..	..	..	42	46	..
	23	**Coke, refined petroleum products & nuclear fuel**	..	..	..	..	..	61	64	..
	24	**Chemicals and chemical products**	..	..	..	..	..	1 429	1 459	..
	241	Basic chemicals	..	..	..	..	..	434	450	..
	242	Other chemical products	..	..	..	..	..	971	982	..
	243	Man-made fibres	..	..	..	..	..	24	27	..
	25	**Rubber and plastic products**	..	..	..	..	..	1 307	1 474	..
	251	Rubber products	..	..	..	..	..	175	200	..
	252	Plastic products	..	..	..	..	..	1 132	1 274	..
	26	**Other non-metallic mineral products**	..	..	..	..	..	1 641	1 663	..
	261	Glass and glass products	..	..	..	..	..	182	191	..
	269	Non-metallic mineral products, nec	..	..	..	..	..	1 459	1 472	..
	27	**Basic metals**	..	..	..	..	..	447	456	..
	271	Basic iron and steel	..	..	..	..	..	121	123	..
	272	Basic precious and non-ferrous metals	..	..	..	..	..	140	144	..
	273	Casting of metals	..	..	..	..	..	186	189	..
	28	**Fabricated metal products, ex. machin. & equip.**	..	..	..	..	..	4 806	4 813	..
	281	Structural metal prod., tanks, reservoirs, generators	..	..	..	..	..	1 672	1 656	..
	289	Other fabricated metal products & service activities	..	..	..	..	..	3 134	3 157	..
	29	**Machinery and equipment, nec**	..	..	..	..	..	2 057	2 148	..
	291	General purpose machinery	..	..	..	..	..	900	937	..
	292	Special purpose machinery	..	..	..	..	..	971	1 018	..
	293	Domestic appliances, nec	..	..	..	..	..	186	193	..
	30	**Office, accounting and computing machinery**	..	..	..	..	..	147	157	..
	31	**Electrical machinery and apparatus, nec**	..	..	..	..	..	623	657	..
	311	Electric motors, generators and transformers	..	..	..	..	..	168	186	..
	312	Electricity distribution and control apparatus	..	..	..	..	..	136	132	..
	313	Insulated wire and cable	..	..	..	..	..	58	59	..
	314	Accumulators, primary cells and primary batteries	..	..	..	..	..	16	20	..
	315	Electric lamps and lighting equipment	..	..	..	..	..	150	151	..
	319	Other electrical equipment, nec	..	..	..	..	..	95	109	..
	32	**Radio, TV, communication equip. & apparatus**	..	..	..	..	..	474	528	..
	321	Electronic valves, tubes & other electronic compon.	..	..	..	..	..	209	239	..
	322	TV, radio transmitters & appar. for line teleph., telegr.	..	..	..	..	..	249	272	..
	323	TV, radio receivers and associated goods	..	..	..	..	..	16	17	..
	33	**Medical, precision, optical instr.; watches, clocks**	..	..	..	..	..	370	352	..
	331	Medical equip.; precision instruments and appliances	..	..	..	..	..	216	212	..
	332	Optical instruments and photographic equipment	..	..	..	..	..	139	127	..
	333	Watches and clocks	..	..	..	..	..	15	13	..
	34	**Motor vehicles, trailers, and semi-trailers**	..	..	..	..	..	838	873	..
	35	**Other transport equipment**	..	..	..	..	..	438	487	..
	351	Building and repairing of ships and boats	..	..	..	..	..	240	276	..
	352	Railway, tramway locomotives and rolling stock	..	..	..	..	..	21	18	..
	353	Aircraft and spacecraft	..	..	..	..	..	177	193	..
	359	Transport equipment, nec	..	..	..	..	..	..	..	..
	36	**Furniture; manufacturing, nec**	..	..	..	..	..	4 013	4 157	..
	361	Furniture	..	..	..	..	..	1 927	2 016	..
	369	Manufacturing, nec	..	..	..	..	..	2 086	2 141	..
	37	**Recycling**	..	..	..	..	..	..	..	..
E	40-41	**Electricity, gas and water supply**	..	..	..	..	..	..	..	..
	40	**Electricity, gas, steam and hot water supply**	..	..	..	..	..	136	136	..
	401	Production, collection and distribution of electricity	..	..	..	..	..	53	53	..
	41	410	**Collection, purification, distribution of water**	..	..	..	..	..	..	..	..
F	45	**Construction**	..	..	..	..	..	..	..	..
G	50-52	**Wholesale and retail trade; repairs etc**	..	..	..	..	..	..	..	..
H	55	**Hotels and restaurants**	..	..	..	..	..	..	..	..
I	60-64	**Transport, storage and communications**	..	..	..	..	..	..	..	..
J	65-67	**Financial intermediation**	..	..	..	..	..	..	..	..
K	70-74	**Real estate, renting and business activities**	..	..	..	..	..	..	..	..
L-Q	75-99	**Public admin.; education; health; other services**	..	..	..	..	..	..	..	..
A-Q	01-99	**Grand total**	..	..	..	..	..	..	..	..

Note: ISIC 1549 includes 1532; 1721 includes 1723; 2230 includes 2213 and 3692; 2411 includes 2330; 2429 includes 3311; 2699 includes 2310; 2720 includes 2891; 2915 includes 2924; 2929 includes 2913 and 2923; 2925 and 2926; 2930 includes 2914; 3220 includes 3313; 3410 includes 3591; 3693 includes 3592.

CANADA

Table CA.4 EMPLOI, SALARIÉS - EMPLOYMENT, EMPLOYEES

Milliers

CITI révision 3

1989	1990	1991	1992	1993	1994	1995	1996				
..	..	..	..	..				**Agriculture, chasse et sylviculture**	A	01-02	
..	..	..	..	..	..	..		**Pêche**	B	05	
..	..	..	..	..	91.0	91.0	..	**Activités extractives**	C	10-14	
..	..	..	..	..	11.0	11.0	..	Extraction de charbon, de lignite et de tourbe		10	
..	..	..	..	..	35.0	33.0	..	Extraction de pétrole brut et de gaz naturel		11	
..	..	..	..	..	31.0	33.0	..	Extraction de minerais métalliques		13	
..	..	..	..	..	12.0	12.0	..	Autres activités extractives		14	
..	..	..	..	..	1 670.0	1 715.0	..	**Activités de fabrication**	D	15-37	
..	..	..	..	..	215.0	214.0	..	**Produits alimentaires et boissons**		15	
..	..	..	..	..	26.0	24.0	..	Boissons			155
..	..	..	..	..	5.0	4.0	..	**Produits à base de tabac**		16	160
..	..	..	..	..	50.0	51.0	..	**Textiles**		17	
..	..	..	..	..	15.0	16.0	..	Filature, tissage et achèvement des textiles			171
..	..	..	..	..	24.0	24.0	..	Autres articles textiles			172
..	..	..	..	..	11.0	11.0	..	Etoffes et articles de bonneterie			173
..	..	..	..	..	73.0	72.0	..	**Habillement; préparation, teinture des fourrures**		18	
..	..	..	..	..	72.0	71.0	..	Articles d'habillement autres qu'en fourrure			181
..	..	..	..	..	1.0	1.0	..	Préparation, teinture des fourrures; art. en fourrure			182
..	..	..	..	..	13.0	12.0	..	**Travail des cuirs; articles en cuir; chaussures**		19	
..	..	..	..	..	2.0	2.0	..	Apprêt et tannage des cuirs et articles en cuirs			191
..	..	..	..	..	11.0	10.0	..	Chaussures			192
..	..	..	..	..	106.0	109.0	..	**Bois et articles en bois et liège (sauf meubles)**		20	
..	..	..	..	..	62.0	63.0	..	Sciage et rabotage du bois			201
..	..	..	..	..	44.0	46.0	..	Articles en bois, liège, vannerie, sparterie			202
..	..	..	..	..	100.0	103.0	..	**Papier et carton; articles en papier et en carton**		21	
..	..	..	..	..	125.0	128.0	..	**Edition, imprimerie et reproduction**		22	
..	..	..	..	..	50.0	50.0	..	Edition			221
..	..	..	..	..	72.0	74.0	..	Imprimerie et activités annexes			222
..	..	..	..	..	3.0	4.0	..	Reproduction de supports enregistrés			223
..	..	..	..	..	12.0	11.0	..	**Cokéfaction; prod. pétroliers; comb. nucléaires**		23	
..	..	..	..	..	97.0	98.0	..	**Produits chimiques**		24	
..	..	..	..	..	27.0	27.0	..	Produits chimiques de base			241
..	..	..	..	..	65.0	66.0	..	Autres produits chimiques			242
..	..	..	..	..	5.0	5.0	..	Fibres synthétiques ou artificielles			243
..	..	..	..	..	77.0	80.0	..	**Articles en caoutchouc et en matières plastiques**		25	
..	..	..	..	..	24.0	24.0	..	Articles en caoutchouc			251
..	..	..	..	..	53.0	56.0	..	Articles en matières plastiques			252
..	..	..	..	..	46.0	47.0	..	**Autres produits minéraux non métalliques**		26	
..	..	..	..	..	12.0	12.0	..	Verre et articles en verre			261
..	..	..	..	..	34.0	35.0	..	Produits minéraux non métalliques, nca			269
..	..	..	..	..	86.0	90.0	..	**Produits métallurgiques de base**		27	
..	..	..	..	..	39.0	39.0	..	Sidérurgie et première transformation de l'acier			271
..	..	..	..	..	32.0	34.0	..	Métallurgie; métaux précieux et non ferreux			272
..	..	..	..	..	15.0	17.0	..	Fonderie			273
..	..	..	..	..	130.0	140.0	..	**Ouvrages en métaux, sauf machines et matériel**		28	
..	..	..	..	..	49.0	52.0	..	Constr. et menuiserie métal.; réservoirs; générateurs			281
..	..	..	..	..	81.0	88.0	..	Autres ouvrages en métaux			289
..	..	..	..	..	99.0	107.0	..	**Machines et matériel, nca**		29	
..	..	..	..	..	41.0	44.0	..	Machines d'usage général			291
..	..	..	..	..	43.0	49.0	..	Machines d'usage spécifique			292
..	..	..	..	..	15.0	14.0	..	Appareils domestiques, nca			293
..	..	..	..	..	15.0	15.0	..	**Mach. de bureau, comptables, matériel inform.**		30	
..	..	..	..	..	42.0	43.0	..	**Machines et appareils électriques, nca**		31	
..	..	..	..	..	11.0	11.0	..	Moteurs, génératrices et transformateurs électriques			311
..	..	..	..	..	8.0	8.0	..	Matériel électrique de distribution et de commande			312
..	..	..	..	..	7.0	7.0	..	Fils et câbles électriques isolés			313
..	..	..	..	..	1.0	1.0	..	Accumulateurs, piles électriques			314
..	..	..	..	..	5.0	6.0	..	Lampes électriques et appareils d'éclairage			315
..	..	..	..	..	10.0	10.0	..	Autres matériels électriques, nca			319
..	..	..	..	..	54.0	58.0	..	**Equip. et appar. de radio, TV, communication**		32	
..	..	..	..	..	14.0	18.0	..	Tubes et valves électroniques; autres composants			321
..	..	..	..	..	38.0	39.0	..	Emetteurs radio et TV; app. téléphonie, télégraphie			322
..	..	..	..	..	2.0	1.0	..	Récepteurs radio et TV et articles associés			323
..	..	..	..	..	12.0	12.0	..	**Instruments médicaux, de précision, d'optique**		33	
..	..	..	..	..	9.0	10.0	..	Appareils médicaux et de précision			331
..	..	..	..	..	3.0	2.0	..	Instruments d'optique ; matériel photographique			332
..	..	..	..	..	..	..	..	Horlogerie			333
..	..	..	..	..	149.0	158.0	..	**Véhicules automobiles et nemorques**		34	
..	..	..	..	..	54.0	58.0	..	**Autres matériels de transport**		35	
..	..	..	..	..	10.0	11.0	..	Construction et réparation de navires			351
..	..	..	..	..	8.0	8.0	..	Construction de matériel ferroviaire roulant			352
..	..	..	..	..	36.0	39.0	..	Construction aéronautique et spatiale			353
..	..	..	..	..	..	..	..	Autres équipements de transport			359
..	..	..	..	..	108.0	110.0	..	**Meubles; activités de fabrication, nca**		36	
..	..	..	..	..	65.0	67.0	..	Meubles			361
..	..	..	..	..	43.0	43.0	..	Activités de fabrication, nca			369
..	..	..	..	..	..	..	..	**Récupération**		37	
..	..	..	..	..	91.0	92.0	..	**Production et distrib. d'électricité, de gaz, d'eau**	E	40-41	
..	..	..	..	..	91.0	92.0	..	**Electricité, gaz, vapeur et eau chaude**		40	
..	..	..	..	..	76.0	77.0	..	Production, collecte et distribution d'électricité			401
..	..	..	..	..	..	..	..	**Captage, épuration et distribution d'eau**		41	410
..	..	..	..	..	..	..	..	**Construction**	F	45	
..	..	..	..	..	..	..	..	**Commerce de gros et de détail; réparation**	G	50-52	
..	..	..	..	..	..	..	..	**Hôtels et restaurants**	H	55	
..	..	..	..	..	..	..	..	**Transports, entreposage et communications**	I	60-64	
..	..	..	..	..	..	..	..	**Intermédiation financière**	J	65-67	
..	..	..	..	..	..	..	..	**Immobilier, locations, services aux entreprises**	K	70-74	
..	..	..	..	..	..	..	..	**Admin. publique; éducation; santé; autres**	L-Q	75-99	
..	..	..	..	..	..	..	..	Grand total	A-Q	01-99	

Note: ISIC 1549 includes 1532; 1721 includes 1723; 2230 includes 2213 and 3692; 2411 includes 2330; 2429 includes 3311; 2699 includes 2310; 2720 includes 2891; 2915 includes 2924; 2929 includes 2913 and 2923, 2925 and 2926; 2930 includes 2914; 3220 includes 3313; 3410 includes 3591; 3693 includes 3592.

Statistiques des Structures Industrielles
OCDE, © 1998

CANADA

Table CA.5 WAGES AND SALARIES, EMPLOYEES - SALAIRES ET TRAITEMENTS, SALARIÉS

ISIC revision 3

Millions of C$ (Current Prices)

			1989	1990	1991	1992	1993	1994	1995	1996
A	01-02	**Agriculture, hunting and forestry**	..	..	..	..	..	..	..	..
B	05	**Fishing**	..	..	..	..	..	..	..	..
C	10-14	**Mining and quarrying**	..	..	..	..	..	5 361	5 602	..
	10	Mining of coal and lignite; extraction of peat	..	..	..	..	..	503	521	..
	11	Crude petroleum & natural gas; related service activ.	..	..	..	..	..	2 440	2 462	..
	13	Mining of metal ores	..	..	..	..	..	1 449	1 974	..
	14	Other mining and quarrying	..	..	..	..	..	516	560	..
D	15-37	**Total manufacturing**	..	..	..	..	..	61 638	64 936	..
	15	**Food products and beverages**	..	..	..	..	..	7 086	7 166	..
		155	Beverages	..	..	..	..	..	1 182	1 163	..
	16	160	**Tobacco products**	..	..	..	..	..	271	261	..
	17	**Textiles**	..	..	..	..	..	1 330	1 380	..
		171	Spinning, weaving and finishing of textiles	..	..	..	..	..	437	472	..
		172	Other textiles	..	..	..	..	..	629	638	..
		173	Knitted and crocheted fabrics and articles	..	..	..	..	..	264	270	..
	18	**Wearing apparel dressing & dyeing of fur**	..	..	..	..	..	1 554	1 571	..
		181	Wearing apparel, except fur apparel	..	..	..	..	..	1 538	1 553	..
		182	Dressing and dyeing of fur; articles of fur	..	..	..	..	..	16	18	..
	19	**Tanning, dressing leather; leather artic.; footwear**	..	..	..	..	..	298	280	..
		191	Tanning, dressing leather; manuf. of leather articles	..	..	..	..	..	55	56	..
		192	Footwear	..	..	..	..	..	243	224	..
	20	**Wood and cork products, ex. furniture**	..	..	..	..	..	3 844	4 036	..
		201	Sawmilling and planing of wood	..	..	..	..	..	2 405	2 541	..
		202	Products of wood, cork, straw & plaiting material	..	..	..	..	..	1 439	1 495	..
	21	**Paper and paper products**	..	..	..	..	..	4 691	4 987	..
	22	**Publishing, printing & reprod. of recorded media**	..	..	..	..	..	4 568	4 726	..
		221	Publishing	..	..	..	..	..	1 975	2 000	..
		222	Printing and related service activities	..	..	..	..	..	2 501	2 600	..
		223	Reproduction of recorded media	..	..	..	..	..	92	126	..
	23	**Coke, refined petroleum products & nuclear fuel**	..	..	..	..	..	690	653	..
	24	**Chemicals and chemical products**	..	..	..	..	..	4 305	4 319	..
		241	Basic chemicals	..	..	..	..	..	1 464	1 447	..
		242	Other chemical products	..	..	..	..	..	2 647	2 661	..
		243	Man-made fibres	..	..	..	..	..	194	211	..
	25	**Rubber and plastic products**	..	..	..	..	..	2 450	2 681	..
		251	Rubber products	..	..	..	..	..	903	974	..
		252	Plastic products	..	..	..	..	..	1 547	1 707	..
	26	**Other non-metallic mineral products**	..	..	..	..	..	1 616	1 699	..
		261	Glass and glass products	..	..	..	..	..	426	440	..
		269	Non-metallic mineral products, nec	..	..	..	..	..	1 190	1 259	..
	27	**Basic metals**	..	..	..	..	..	4 209	4 462	..
		271	Basic iron and steel	..	..	..	..	..	1 971	2 062	..
		272	Basic precious and non-ferrous metals	..	..	..	..	..	1 605	1 727	..
		273	Casting of metals	..	..	..	..	..	633	673	..
	28	**Fabricated metal products, ex. machin. & equip.**	..	..	..	..	..	4 344	4 820	..
		281	Structural metal prod., tanks, reservoirs, generators	..	..	..	..	..	1 631	1 790	..
		289	Other fabricated metal products & service activities	..	..	..	..	..	2 713	3 030	..
	29	**Machinery and equipment, nec**	..	..	..	..	..	3 553	3 984	..
		291	General purpose machinery	..	..	..	..	..	1 517	1 704	..
		292	Special purpose machinery	..	..	..	..	..	1 554	1 839	..
		293	Domestic appliances, nec	..	..	..	..	..	482	441	..
	30	**Office, accounting and computing machinery**	..	..	..	..	..	599	631	..
	31	**Electrical machinery and apparatus, nec**	..	..	..	..	..	1 516	1 585	..
		311	Electric motors, generators and transformers	..	..	..	..	..	418	428	..
		312	Electricity distribution and control apparatus	..	..	..	..	..	292	300	..
		313	Insulated wire and cable	..	..	..	..	..	288	296	..
		314	Accumulators, primary cells and primary batteries	..	..	..	..	..	47	43	..
		315	Electric lamps and lighting equipment	..	..	..	..	..	162	174	..
		319	Other electrical equipment, nec	..	..	..	..	..	309	344	..
	32	**Radio, TV, communication equip. & apparatus**	..	..	..	..	..	2 229	2 340	..
		321	Electronic valves, tubes & other electronic compon.	..	..	..	..	..	456	560	..
		322	TV, radio transmitters & appar. for line teleph., telegr.	..	..	..	..	..	1 727	1 747	..
		323	TV, radio receivers and associated goods	..	..	..	..	..	46	33	..
	33	**Medical, precision, optical instr.; watches, clocks**	..	..	..	..	..	425	437	..
		331	Medical equip.; precision instruments and appliances	..	..	..	..	..	343	381	..
		332	Optical instruments and photographic equipment	..	..	..	..	..	73	49	..
		333	Watches and clocks	..	..	..	..	..	9	7	..
	34	**Motor vehicles, trailers, and semi-trailers**	..	..	..	..	..	6 652	7 140	..
	35	**Other transport equipment**	..	..	..	..	..	2 438	2 656	..
		351	Building and repairing of ships and boats	..	..	..	..	..	419	397	..
		352	Railway, tramway locomotives and rolling stock	..	..	..	..	..	370	386	..
		353	Aircraft and spacecraft	..	..	..	..	..	1 649	1 873	..
		359	Transport equipment, nec	..	..	..	..	..	..	..	..
	36	**Furniture; manufacturing, nec**	..	..	..	..	..	2 978	3 118	..
		361	Furniture	..	..	..	..	..	1 831	1 940	..
		369	Manufacturing, nec	..	..	..	..	..	1 147	1 178	..
	37	**Recycling**	..	..	..	..	..	..	..	..
E	40-41	**Electricity, gas and water supply**	..	..	..	..	..	..	..	..
	40	**Electricity, gas, steam and hot water supply**	..	..	..	..	..	4 733	4 958	..
		401	Production, collection and distribution of electricity	..	..	..	..	..	4 017	4 229	..
	41	410	**Collection, purification, distribution of water**	..	..	..	..	..	..	..	..
F	45	**Construction**	..	..	..	..	..	..	..	..
G	50-52	**Wholesale and retail trade; repairs etc**	..	..	..	..	..	..	..	..
H	55	**Hotels and restaurants**	..	..	..	..	..	..	..	..
I	60-64	**Transport, storage and communications**	..	..	..	..	..	..	..	..
J	65-67	**Financial intermediation**	..	..	..	..	..	..	..	..
K	70-74	**Real estate, renting and business activities**	..	..	..	..	..	..	..	..
L-Q	75-99	**Public admin.; education; health; other services**	..	..	..	..	..	..	..	..
A-Q	01-99	**Grand total**	..	..	..	..	..	..	..	..

Note: ISIC 1549 includes 1532; 1721 includes 1723; 2230 includes 2213 and 3692; 2411 includes 2330; 2429 includes 3311; 2699 includes 2310; 2720 includes 2891; 2915 includes 2924; 2929 includes 2913 and 2923, 2925 and 2926; 2930 includes 2914; 3220 includes 3313; 3410 includes 3591; 3693 includes 3592.

Table CA.6 HEURES OUVRÉES - HOURS WORKED

Milliers

1989	1990	1991	1992	1993	1994	1995	1996			CITI révision 3	
..	..	..	..	..	..	..		**Agriculture, chasse et sylviculture**	A	01-02	
..	..	..	..	..	..	..		**Pêche**	B	05	
..	..	..	..	..	..	..		**Activités extractives**	C	10-14	
..	..	..	..	..	16 000	16 000		Extraction de charbon, de lignite et de tourbe		10	
..	..	..	..	..	25 000	25 000		Extraction de pétrole brut et de gaz naturel		11	
..	..	..	..	..	..	..		Extraction de minerais métalliques		13	
..	..	..	..	..	..	..		Autres activités extractives		14	
..	..	..	..	..	2 374 000	2 458 000		**Activités de fabrication**	D	15-37	
..	..	..	..	..	281 000	285 000		**Produits alimentaires et boissons**		15	
..	..	..	..	..	24 000	24 000		Boissons			155
..	..	..	..	..	4 000	4 000		**Produits à base de tabac**		16	160
..	..	..	..	..	78 000	80 000		**Textiles**		17	
..	..	..	..	..	24 000	26 000		Filature, tissage et achèvement des textiles			171
..	..	..	..	..	35 000	36 000		Autres articles textiles			172
..	..	..	..	..	19 000	18 000		Etoffes et articles de bonneterie			173
..	..	..	..	..	113 000	110 000		**Habillement; préparation, teinture des fourrures**		18	
..	..	..	..	..	112 000	109 000		Articles d'habillement autres qu'en fourrure			181
..	..	..	..	..	1 000	1 000		Préparation, teinture des fourrures; art. en fourrure			182
..	..	..	..	..	20 000	17 000		**Travail des cuirs; articles en cuir; chaussures**		19	
..	..	..	..	..	3 000	3 000		Apprêt et tannage des cuirs et articles en cuirs			191
..	..	..	..	..	17 000	14 000		Chaussures			192
..	..	..	..	..	172 000	181 000		**Bois et articles en bois et liège (sauf meubles)**		20	
..	..	..	..	..	102 000	108 000		Sciage et rabotage du bois			201
..	..	..	..	..	70 000	73 000		Articles en bois, liège, vannerie, sparterie			202
..	..	..	..	..	143 000	150 000		**Papier et carton; articles en papier et en carton**		21	
..	..	..	..	..	132 000	135 000		**Edition, imprimerie et reproduction**		22	
..	..	..	..	..	27 000	28 000		Edition			221
..	..	..	..	..	100 000	102 000		Imprimerie et activités annexes			222
..	..	..	..	..	5 000	5 000		Reproduction de supports enregistrés			223
..	..	..	..	..	11 000	10 000		**Cokéfaction; prod. pétroliers; comb. nucléaires**		23	
..	..	..	..	..	110 000	113 000		**Produits chimiques**		24	
..	..	..	..	..	35 000	35 000		Produits chimiques de base			241
..	..	..	..	..	67 000	70 000		Autres produits chimiques			242
..	..	..	..	..	8 000	8 000		Fibres synthétiques ou artificielles			243
..	..	..	..	..	117 000	122 000		**Articles en caoutchouc et en matières plastiques**		25	
..	..	..	..	..	34 000	35 000		Articles en caoutchouc			251
..	..	..	..	..	83 000	87 000		Articles en matières plastiques			252
..	..	..	..	..	65 000	67 000		**Autres produits minéraux non métalliques**		26	
..	..	..	..	..	18 000	18 000		Verre et articles en verre			261
..	..	..	..	..	47 000	49 000		Produits minéraux non métalliques, nca			269
..	..	..	..	..	135 000	140 000		**Produits métallurgiques de base**		27	
..	..	..	..	..	61 000	62 000		Sidérurgie et première transformation de l'acier			271
..	..	..	..	..	47 000	50 000		Métallurgie; métaux précieux et non ferreux			272
..	..	..	..	..	27 000	28 000		Fonderie			273
..	..	..	..	..	199 000	217 000		**Ouvrages en métaux, sauf machines et matériel**		28	
..	..	..	..	..	70 000	76 000		Constr. et menuiserie métal.; réservoirs; générateurs			281
..	..	..	..	..	129 000	141 000		Autres ouvrages en métaux			289
..	..	..	..	..	139 000	150 000		**Machines et matériel, nca**		29	
..	..	..	..	..	57 000	61 000		Machines d'usage général			291
..	..	..	..	..	62 000	70 000		Machines d'usage spécifique			292
..	..	..	..	..	20 000	19 000		Appareils domestiques, nca			293
..	..	..	..	..	16 000	16 000		**Mach. de bureau, comptables, matériel inform.**		30	
..	..	..	..	..	63 000	64 000		**Machines et appareils électriques, nca**		31	
..	..	..	..	..	17 000	17 000		Moteurs, génératrices et transformateurs électriques			311
..	..	..	..	..	11 000	11 000		Matériel électrique de distribution et de commande			312
..	..	..	..	..	10 000	11 000		Fils et câbles électriques isolés			313
..	..	..	..	..	2 000	1 000		Accumulateurs, piles électriques			314
..	..	..	..	..	8 000	8 000		Lampes électriques et appareils d'éclairage			315
..	..	..	..	..	15 000	16 000		Autres matériels électriques, nca			319
..	..	..	..	..	73 000	78 000		**Equip. et appar. de radio, TV, communication**		32	
..	..	..	..	..	22 000	27 000		Tubes et valves électroniques; autres composants			321
..	..	..	..	..	49 000	49 000		Emetteurs radio et TV; app. téléphonie, télégraphie			322
..	..	..	..	..	2 000	2 000		Récepteurs radio et TV et articles associés			323
..	..	..	..	..	15 000	14 000		**Instruments médicaux, de précision, d'optique**		33	
..	..	..	..	..	10 000	11 000		Appareils médicaux et de précision			331
..	..	..	..	..	5 000	3 000		Instruments d'optique ; matériel photographique			332
..	..	..	..	..	..	..		Horlogerie			333
..	..	..	..	..	248 000	260 000		**Véhicules automobiles et nemorques**		34	
..	..	..	..	..	74 000	78 000		**Autres matériels de transport**		35	
..	..	..	..	..	16 000	17 000		Construction et réparation de navires			351
..	..	..	..	..	12 000	12 000		Construction de matériel ferroviaire roulant			352
..	..	..	..	..	46 000	49 000		Construction aéronautique et spatiale			353
..	..	..	..	..	..	..		Autres équipements de transport			359
..	..	..	..	..	163 000	166 000		**Meubles; activités de fabrication, nca**		36	
..	..	..	..	..	103 000	106 000		Meubles			361
..	..	..	..	..	60 000	60 000		Activités de fabrication, nca			369
..	..	..	..	..	..	..		**Récupération**		37	
..	..	..	..	..	..	..		**Production et distrib. d'électricité, de gaz, d'eau**	E	40-41	
..	..	..	..	..	..	..		**Electricité, gaz, vapeur et eau chaude**		40	
..	..	..	..	..	..	..		Production, collecte et distribution d'électricité			401
..	..	..	..	..	..	..		**Captage, épuration et distribution d'eau**		41	410
..	..	..	..	..	..	..		**Construction**	F	45	
..	..	..	..	..	..	..		**Commerce de gros et de détail; réparation**	G	50-52	
..	..	..	..	..	..	..		**Hôtels et restaurants**	H	55	
..	..	..	..	..	..	..		**Transports, entreposage et communications**	I	60-64	
..	..	..	..	..	..	..		**Intermédiation financière**	J	65-67	
..	..	..	..	..	..	..		**Immobilier, locations, services aux entreprises**	K	70-74	
..	..	..	..	..	..	..		**Admin. publique; éducation; santé; autres**	L-Q	75-99	
..	..	..	..	..	..	..		**Grand total**	A-Q	01-99	

Note: ISIC 1549 includes 1532; 1721 includes 1723; 2230 includes 2213 and 3692; 2411 includes 2330; 2429 includes 3311; 2699 includes 2310; 2720 includes 2891; 2915 includes 2924; 2929 includes 2913 and 2923; 2925 and 2926; 2930 includes 2914; 3220 includes 3313; 3410 includes 3591; 3693 includes 3592.

Statistiques des Structures Industrielles
OCDE, © 1998

Table CZ.1 **PRODUCTION - PRODUCTION**

Millions of CK (Current Prices)

ISIC revision 3			1989	1990	1991	1992	1993	1994	1995	1996
A	01-02	Agriculture, hunting and forestry	..	..	..	..	..	..	137 140	163 889
B	05	Fishing	..	..	..	..	..	..	1 250	1 640
C	10-14	Mining and quarrying	..	..	..	..	..	..	86 391	88 273
	10	Mining of coal and lignite; extraction of peat	..	..	..	..	..	..	73 154	72 317
	11	Crude petroleum & natural gas; related service activ.	..	..	..	..	..	..	1 860	1 905
	13	Mining of metal ores	..	..	..	..	..	..	..	..
	14	Other mining and quarrying	..	..	..	..	..	..	7 723	9 993
D	15-37	Total manufacturing	..	..	..	..	..	..	1 296 686	1 419 906
	15	Food products and beverages	..	..	..	..	..	..	194 309	232 056
	155	Beverages	..	..	..	..	..	..	..	..
	16 160	Tobacco products	..	..	..	..	..	..	..	..
	17	Textiles	..	..	..	..	..	..	55 374	55 590
	171	Spinning, weaving and finishing of textiles	..	..	..	..	..	..	..	..
	172	Other textiles	..	..	..	..	..	..	..	..
	173	Knitted and crocheted fabrics and articles	..	..	..	..	..	..	..	..
	18	Wearing apparel dressing & dyeing of fur	..	..	..	..	..	..	16 878	16 528
	181	Wearing apparel, except fur apparel	..	..	..	..	..	..	..	..
	182	Dressing and dyeing of fur; articles of fur	..	..	..	..	..	..	..	..
	19	Tanning, dressing leather; leather artic.; footwear	..	..	..	..	..	..	17 203	16 380
	191	Tanning, dressing leather; manuf. of leather articles	..	..	..	..	..	..	..	..
	192	Footwear	..	..	..	..	..	..	..	..
	20	Wood and cork products, ex. furniture	..	..	..	..	..	..	36 331	40 349
	201	Sawmilling and planing of wood	..	..	..	..	..	..	..	..
	202	Products of wood, cork, straw & plaiting material	..	..	..	..	..	..	..	..
	21	Paper and paper products	..	..	..	..	..	..	36 797	33 693
	22	Publishing, printing & reprod. of recorded media	..	..	..	..	..	..	32 198	37 599
	221	Publishing	..	..	..	..	..	..	..	..
	222	Printing and related service activities	..	..	..	..	..	..	..	..
	223	Reproduction of recorded media	..	..	..	..	..	..	..	..
	23	Coke, refined petroleum products & nuclear fuel	..	..	..	..	..	..	..	..
	24	Chemicals and chemical products	..	..	..	..	..	..	72 696	100 559
	241	Basic chemicals	..	..	..	..	..	..	..	..
	242	Other chemical products	..	..	..	..	..	..	..	..
	243	Man-made fibres	..	..	..	..	..	..	..	..
	25	Rubber and plastic products	..	..	..	..	..	..	37 966	48 027
	251	Rubber products	..	..	..	..	..	..	..	..
	252	Plastic products	..	..	..	..	..	..	..	..
	26	Other non-metallic mineral products	..	..	..	..	..	..	64 207	75 712
	261	Glass and glass products	..	..	..	..	..	..	..	..
	269	Non-metallic mineral products, nec	..	..	..	..	..	..	..	..
	27	Basic metals	..	..	..	..	..	..	219 590	179 985
	271	Basic iron and steel	..	..	..	..	..	..	..	..
	272	Basic precious and non-ferrous metals	..	..	..	..	..	..	..	..
	273	Casting of metals	..	..	..	..	..	..	..	..
	28	Fabricated metal products, ex. machin. & equip.	..	..	..	..	..	..	93 512	108 352
	281	Structural metal prod., tanks, reservoirs, generators	..	..	..	..	..	..	..	..
	289	Other fabricated metal products & service activities	..	..	..	..	..	..	..	..
	29	Machinery and equipment, nec	..	..	..	..	..	..	112 000	127 827
	291	General purpose machinery	..	..	..	..	..	..	..	..
	292	Special purpose machinery	..	..	..	..	..	..	..	..
	293	Domestic appliances, nec	..	..	..	..	..	..	..	..
	30	Office, accounting and computing machinery	..	..	..	..	..	..	2 270	2 280
	31	Electrical machinery and apparatus, nec	..	..	..	..	..	..	53 688	61 849
	311	Electric motors, generators and transformers	..	..	..	..	..	..	..	..
	312	Electricity distribution and control apparatus	..	..	..	..	..	..	..	..
	313	Insulated wire and cable	..	..	..	..	..	..	..	..
	314	Accumulators, primary cells and primary batteries	..	..	..	..	..	..	..	..
	315	Electric lamps and lighting equipment	..	..	..	..	..	..	..	..
	319	Other electrical equipment, nec	..	..	..	..	..	..	..	..
	32	Radio, TV, communication equip. & apparatus	..	..	..	..	..	..	14 037	18 849
	321	Electronic valves, tubes & other electronic compon.	..	..	..	..	..	..	..	..
	322	TV, radio transmitters & appar. for line teleph., telegr.	..	..	..	..	..	..	..	..
	323	TV, radio receivers and associated goods	..	..	..	..	..	..	..	..
	33	Medical, precision, optical instr.; watches, clocks	..	..	..	..	..	..	15 263	18 655
	331	Medical equip.; precision instruments and appliances	..	..	..	..	..	..	..	..
	332	Optical instruments and photographic equipment	..	..	..	..	..	..	..	..
	333	Watches and clocks	..	..	..	..	..	..	..	..
	34	Motor vehicles, trailers, and semi-trailers	..	..	..	..	..	..	76 444	98 407
	35	Other transport equipment	..	..	..	..	..	..	22 487	27 000
	351	Building and repairing of ships and boats	..	..	..	..	..	..	..	..
	352	Railway, tramway locomotives and rolling stock	..	..	..	..	..	..	..	..
	353	Aircraft and spacecraft	..	..	..	..	..	..	..	..
	359	Transport equipment, nec	..	..	..	..	..	..	..	..
	36	Furniture; manufacturing, nec	..	..	..	..	..	..	39 948	48 177
	361	Furniture	..	..	..	..	..	..	..	..
	369	Manufacturing, nec	..	..	..	..	..	..	..	..
	37	Recycling	..	..	..	..	..	..	11 116	9 450
E	40-41	Electricity, gas and water supply	..	..	..	..	..	..	231 723	225 518
	40	Electricity, gas, steam and hot water supply	..	..	..	..	..	..	218 506	210 389
	401	Production, collection and distribution of electricity	..	..	..	..	..	..	..	..
	41 410	Collection, purification, distribution of water	..	..	..	..	..	..	13 217	15 129
F	45	Construction	..	..	..	..	..	..	322 994	360 886
G	50-52	Wholesale and retail trade; repairs etc	..	..	..	..	..	..	349 226	434 076
H	55	Hotels and restaurants	..	..	..	..	..	..	47 562	63 382
I	60-64	Transport, storage and communications	..	..	..	..	..	..	181 433	224 424
J	65-67	Financial intermediation	..	..	..	..	..	..	279 628	103 123
K	70-74	Real estate, renting and business activities	..	..	..	..	..	..	202 374	236 956
L-Q	75-99	Public admin.; education; health; other services	..	..	..	..	..	..	68 935	75 344
A-Q	01-99	Grand total	..	..	..	..	..	..	3 205 342	3 397 417

Table CZ.2 **VALEUR AJOUTÉE - VALUE ADDED**

Millions de CK (Prix courants)

1989	1990	1991	1992	1993	1994	1995	1996			CITI révision 3
..	..	..	..	..	..	59 264	52 291	**Agriculture, chasse et sylviculture**	**A**	**01-02**
..	..	..	..	..	..	482	470	**Pêche**	**B**	**05**
..	..	..	..	..	..	28 648	29 493	**Activités extractives**	**C**	**10-14**
..	..	..	..	..	..	23 675	24 625	Extraction de charbon, de lignite et de tourbe		10
..	..	..	..	..	..	880	821	Extraction de pétrole brut et de gaz naturel		11
..	..	..	..	..	..	..	..	Extraction de minerais métalliques		13
..	..	..	..	..	..	3 093	4 074	Autres activités extractives		14
..	..	..	..	..	..	337 157	362 696	**Activités de fabrication**	**D**	**15-37**
..	..	..	..	..	..	41 918	44 588	**Produits alimentaires et boissons**		**15**
..	..	..	..	..	..	..	..	Boissons		155
..	..	..	..	..	..	..	..	**Produits à base de tabac**		**16** 160
..	..	..	..	..	..	14 149	15 136	**Textiles**		**17**
..	..	..	..	..	..	..	..	Filature, tissage et achèvement des textiles		171
..	..	..	..	..	..	..	..	Autres articles textiles		172
..	..	..	..	..	..	..	..	Etoffes et articles de bonneterie		173
..	..	..	..	..	..	7 485	6 035	**Habillement; préparation, teinture des fourrures**		**18**
..	..	..	..	..	..	..	..	Articles d'habillement autres qu'en fourrure		181
..	..	..	..	..	..	..	..	Préparation, teinture des fourrures; art. en fourrure		182
..	..	..	..	..	..	5 225	5 118	**Travail des cuirs; articles en cuir; chaussures**		**19**
..	..	..	..	..	..	..	..	Apprêt et tannage des cuirs et articles en cuirs		191
..	..	..	..	..	..	..	..	Chaussures		192
..	..	..	..	..	..	11 133	12 183	**Bois et articles en bois et liège (sauf meubles)**		**20**
..	..	..	..	..	..	..	..	Sciage et rabotage du bois		201
..	..	..	..	..	..	..	..	Articles en bois, liège, vannerie, sparterie		202
..	..	..	..	..	..	9 745	7 676	**Papier et carton; articles en papier et en carton**		**21**
..	..	..	..	..	..	9 078	11 804	**Edition, imprimerie et reproduction**		**22**
..	..	..	..	..	..	..	..	Edition		221
..	..	..	..	..	..	..	..	Imprimerie et activités annexes		222
..	..	..	..	..	..	..	..	Reproduction de supports enregistrés		223
..	..	..	..	..	..	..	..	**Cokéfaction; prod. pétroliers; comb. nucléaires**		**23**
..	..	..	..	..	..	20 303	25 156	**Produits chimiques**		**24**
..	..	..	..	..	..	..	..	Produits chimiques de base		241
..	..	..	..	..	..	..	..	Autres produits chimiques		242
..	..	..	..	..	..	..	..	Fibres synthétiques ou artificielles		243
..	..	..	..	..	..	10 689	14 188	**Articles en caoutchouc et en matières plastiques**		**25**
..	..	..	..	..	..	..	..	Articles en caoutchouc		251
..	..	..	..	..	..	..	..	Articles en matières plastiques		252
..	..	..	..	..	..	23 374	27 605	**Autres produits minéraux non métalliques**		**26**
..	..	..	..	..	..	..	..	Verre et articles en verre		261
..	..	..	..	..	..	..	..	Produits minéraux non métalliques, nca		269
..	..	..	..	..	..	30 445	29 369	**Produits métallurgiques de base**		**27**
..	..	..	..	..	..	..	..	Sidérurgie et première transformation de l'acier		271
..	..	..	..	..	..	..	..	Métallurgie; métaux précieux et non ferreux		272
..	..	..	..	..	..	..	..	Fonderie		273
..	..	..	..	..	..	32 832	35 918	**Ouvrages en métaux, sauf machines et matériel**		**28**
..	..	..	..	..	..	..	..	Constr. et menuiserie métal.; réservoirs; générateurs		281
..	..	..	..	..	..	..	..	Autres ouvrages en métaux		289
..	..	..	..	..	..	37 868	40 862	**Machines et matériel, nca**		**29**
..	..	..	..	..	..	..	..	Machines d'usage général		291
..	..	..	..	..	..	..	..	Machines d'usage spécifique		292
..	..	..	..	..	..	..	..	Appareils domestiques, nca		293
..	..	..	..	..	..	618	743	**Mach. de bureau, comptables, matériel inform.**		**30**
..	..	..	..	..	..	16 254	19 284	**Machines et appareils électriques, nca**		**31**
..	..	..	..	..	..	..	..	Moteurs, génératrices et transformateurs électriques		311
..	..	..	..	..	..	..	..	Matériel électrique de distribution et de commande		312
..	..	..	..	..	..	..	..	Fils et câbles électriques isolés		313
..	..	..	..	..	..	..	..	Accumulateurs, piles électriques		314
..	..	..	..	..	..	..	..	Lampes électriques et appareils d'éclairage		315
..	..	..	..	..	..	..	..	Autres matériels électriques, nca		319
..	..	..	..	..	..	5 315	6 100	**Equip. et appar. de radio, TV, communication**		**32**
..	..	..	..	..	..	..	..	Tubes et valves électroniques; autres composants		321
..	..	..	..	..	..	..	..	Emetteurs radio et TV; app. téléphonie, télégraphie		322
..	..	..	..	..	..	..	..	Récepteurs radio et TV et articles associés		323
..	..	..	..	..	..	6 256	7 354	**Instruments médicaux, de précision, d'optique**		**33**
..	..	..	..	..	..	..	..	Appareils médicaux et de précision		331
..	..	..	..	..	..	..	..	Instruments d'optique ; matériel photographique		332
..	..	..	..	..	..	..	..	Horlogerie		333
..	..	..	..	..	..	15 928	21 018	**Véhicules automobiles et nemorques**		**34**
..	..	..	..	..	..	6 766	7 308	**Autres matériels de transport**		**35**
..	..	..	..	..	..	..	..	Construction et réparation de navires		351
..	..	..	..	..	..	..	..	Construction de matériel ferroviaire roulant		352
..	..	..	..	..	..	..	..	Construction aéronautique et spatiale		353
..	..	..	..	..	..	..	..	Autres équipements de transport		359
..	..	..	..	..	..	14 166	16 326	**Meubles; activités de fabrication, nca**		**36**
..	..	..	..	..	..	..	..	Meubles		361
..	..	..	..	..	..	..	..	Activités de fabrication, nca		369
..	..	..	..	..	..	2 119	1 788	**Récupération**		**37**
..	..	..	..	..	..	68 521	65 366	**Production et distrib. d'électricité, de gaz, d'eau**	**E**	**40-41**
..	..	..	..	..	..	62 883	59 018	**Electricité, gaz, vapeur et eau chaude**		**40**
..	..	..	..	..	..	..	..	Production, collecte et distribution d'électricité		401
..	..	..	..	..	..	5 638	6 348	**Captage, épuration et distribution d'eau**		**41** 410
..	..	..	..	..	..	91 069	91 362	**Construction**	**F**	**45**
..	..	..	..	..	..	157 036	189 372	**Commerce de gros et de détail; réparation**	**G**	**50-52**
..	..	..	..	..	..	15 133	23 892	**Hôtels et restaurants**	**H**	**55**
..	..	..	..	..	..	64 645	79 723	**Transports, entreposage et communications**	**I**	**60-64**
..	..	..	..	..	..	80 951	62 994	**Intermédiation financière**	**J**	**65-67**
..	..	..	..	..	..	84 247	102 629	**Immobilier, locations, services aux entreprises**	**K**	**70-74**
..	..	..	..	..	..	27 372	32 511	**Admin. publique; éducation; santé; autres**	**L-Q**	**75-99**
..	..	..	..	..	..	1 014 525	1 092 799	**Grand total**	**A-Q**	**01-99**

Table CZ.3 ESTABLISHMENTS - ETABLISSEMENTS

Units

ISIC revision 3			1989	1990	1991	1992	1993	1994	1995	1996
A	01-02	Agriculture, hunting and forestry	..	..	..	..	..	..	48 951	50 826
B	05	Fishing	..	..	..	..	..	..	142	218
C	10-14	Mining and quarrying	..	..	..	..	..	..	287	290
	10	Mining of coal and lignite; extraction of peat	..	..	..	..	..	..	30	29
	11	Crude petroleum & natural gas; related service activ.	..	..	..	..	..	..	19	10
	13	Mining of metal ores	..	..	..	..	..	..	..	..
	14	Other mining and quarrying	..	..	..	..	..	..	228	244
D	15-37	Total manufacturing	..	..	..	..	..	..	100 889	110 163
	15	Food products and beverages	..	..	..	..	..	..	5 595	5 623
	155	Beverages	..	..	..	..	..	..	..	..
	16 160	Tobacco products	..	..	..	..	..	..	..	..
	17	Textiles	..	..	..	..	..	..	3 525	3 195
	171	Spinning, weaving and finishing of textiles	..	..	..	..	..	..	..	..
	172	Other textiles	..	..	..	..	..	..	..	..
	173	Knitted and crocheted fabrics and articles	..	..	..	..	..	..	..	..
	18	Wearing apparel dressing & dyeing of fur	..	..	..	..	..	..	11 383	8 768
	181	Wearing apparel, except fur apparel	..	..	..	..	..	..	..	..
	182	Dressing and dyeing of fur; articles of fur	..	..	..	..	..	..	..	..
	19	Tanning, dressing leather; leather artic.; footwear	..	..	..	..	..	..	1 064	1 107
	191	Tanning, dressing leather; manuf. of leather articles	..	..	..	..	..	..	..	..
	192	Footwear	..	..	..	..	..	..	..	..
	20	Wood and cork products, ex. furniture	..	..	..	..	..	..	15 093	17 370
	201	Sawmilling and planing of wood	..	..	..	..	..	..	..	..
	202	Products of wood, cork, straw & plaiting material	..	..	..	..	..	..	..	..
	21	Paper and paper products	..	..	..	..	..	..	366	391
	22	Publishing, printing & reprod. of recorded media	..	..	..	..	..	..	4 166	4 202
	221	Publishing	..	..	..	..	..	..	..	..
	222	Printing and related service activities	..	..	..	..	..	..	..	..
	223	Reproduction of recorded media	..	..	..	..	..	..	..	..
	23	Coke, refined petroleum products & nuclear fuel	..	..	..	..	..	..	..	..
	24	Chemicals and chemical products	..	..	..	..	..	..	1 024	893
	241	Basic chemicals	..	..	..	..	..	..	..	..
	242	Other chemical products	..	..	..	..	..	..	..	..
	243	Man-made fibres	..	..	..	..	..	..	..	..
	25	Rubber and plastic products	..	..	..	..	..	..	1 637	1 988
	251	Rubber products	..	..	..	..	..	..	..	..
	252	Plastic products	..	..	..	..	..	..	..	..
	26	Other non-metallic mineral products	..	..	..	..	..	..	4 573	5 587
	261	Glass and glass products	..	..	..	..	..	..	..	..
	269	Non-metallic mineral products, nec	..	..	..	..	..	..	..	..
	27	Basic metals	..	..	..	..	..	..	364	310
	271	Basic iron and steel	..	..	..	..	..	..	..	..
	272	Basic precious and non-ferrous metals	..	..	..	..	..	..	..	..
	273	Casting of metals	..	..	..	..	..	..	..	..
	28	Fabricated metal products, ex. machin. & equip.	..	..	..	..	..	..	21 562	28 181
	281	Structural metal prod., tanks, reservoirs, generators	..	..	..	..	..	..	..	..
	289	Other fabricated metal products & service activities	..	..	..	..	..	..	..	..
	29	Machinery and equipment, nec	..	..	..	..	..	..	5 858	6 351
	291	General purpose machinery	..	..	..	..	..	..	..	..
	292	Special purpose machinery	..	..	..	..	..	..	..	..
	293	Domestic appliances, nec	..	..	..	..	..	..	..	..
	30	Office, accounting and computing machinery	..	..	..	..	..	..	160	152
	31	Electrical machinery and apparatus, nec	..	..	..	..	..	..	9 936	9 641
	311	Electric motors, generators and transformers	..	..	..	..	..	..	..	..
	312	Electricity distribution and control apparatus	..	..	..	..	..	..	..	..
	313	Insulated wire and cable	..	..	..	..	..	..	..	..
	314	Accumulators, primary cells and primary batteries	..	..	..	..	..	..	..	..
	315	Electric lamps and lighting equipment	..	..	..	..	..	..	..	..
	319	Other electrical equipment, nec	..	..	..	..	..	..	..	..
	32	Radio, TV, communication equip. & apparatus	..	..	..	..	..	..	2 548	1 796
	321	Electronic valves, tubes & other electronic compon.	..	..	..	..	..	..	..	..
	322	TV, radio transmitters & appar. for line teleph., telegr.	..	..	..	..	..	..	..	..
	323	TV, radio receivers and associated goods	..	..	..	..	..	..	..	..
	33	Medical, precision, optical instr.; watches, clocks	..	..	..	..	..	..	2 740	3 422
	331	Medical equip.; precision instruments and appliances	..	..	..	..	..	..	..	..
	332	Optical instruments and photographic equipment	..	..	..	..	..	..	..	..
	333	Watches and clocks	..	..	..	..	..	..	..	..
	34	Motor vehicles, trailers, and semi-trailers	..	..	..	..	..	..	548	311
	35	Other transport equipment	..	..	..	..	..	..	305	422
	351	Building and repairing of ships and boats	..	..	..	..	..	..	..	..
	352	Railway, tramway locomotives and rolling stock	..	..	..	..	..	..	..	..
	353	Aircraft and spacecraft	..	..	..	..	..	..	..	..
	359	Transport equipment, nec	..	..	..	..	..	..	..	..
	36	Furniture; manufacturing, nec	..	..	..	..	..	..	7 992	10 058
	361	Furniture	..	..	..	..	..	..	..	..
	369	Manufacturing, nec	..	..	..	..	..	..	..	..
	37	Recycling	..	..	..	..	..	..	437	386
E	40-41	Electricity, gas and water supply	..	..	..	..	..	..	890	810
	40	Electricity, gas, steam and hot water supply	..	..	..	..	..	..	706	671
	401	Production, collection and distribution of electricity	..	..	..	..	..	..	..	..
	41 410	Collection, purification, distribution of water	..	..	..	..	..	..	184	138
F	45	Construction	..	..	..	..	..	..	76 713	90 527
G	50-52	Wholesale and retail trade; repairs etc	..	..	..	..	..	..	290 148	216 993
H	55	Hotels and restaurants	..	..	..	..	..	..	33 370	31 822
I	60-64	Transport, storage and communications	..	..	..	..	..	..	27 986	33 538
J	65-67	Financial intermediation	..	..	..	..	..	..	5 050	4 706
K	70-74	Real estate, renting and business activities	..	..	..	..	..	..	113 250	121 503
L-Q	75-99	Public admin.; education; health; other services	..	..	..	..	..	..	53 733	52 124
A-Q	01-99	Grand total	..	..	..	..	..	..	751 409	713 520

Table CZ.4 **EMPLOI - EMPLOYMENT**

Milliers

1989	1990	1991	1992	1993	1994	1995	1996			CITI révision 3
..	..	..	..	..	..	306.0	291.0	**Agriculture, chasse et sylviculture**	A	01-02
..	..	..	..	..	..	2.0	2.0	**Pêche**	B	05
..	..	..	..	..	..	96.0	85.0	**Activités extractives**	C	10-14
..	..	..	..	..	..	72.0	68.0	Extraction de charbon, de lignite et de tourbe		10
..	..	..	..	..	..	2.0	2.0	Extraction de pétrole brut et de gaz naturel		11
..	..	..	..	..	..	..	..	Extraction de minerais métalliques		13
..	..	..	..	..	..	18.0	12.0	Autres activités extractives		14
..	..	..	..	..	..	1 439.0	1 446.0	**Activités de fabrication**	D	15-37
..	..	..	..	..	..	144.0	157.0	**Produits alimentaires et boissons**		15
..	..	..	..	..	..	..	..	Boissons		155
..	..	..	..	..	..	..	..	**Produits à base de tabac**		16 160
..	..	..	..	..	..	95.0	91.0	**Textiles**		17
..	..	..	..	..	..	..	..	Filature, tissage et achèvement des textiles		171
..	..	..	..	..	..	..	..	Autres articles textiles		172
..	..	..	..	..	..	..	..	Etoffes et articles de bonneterie		173
..	..	..	..	..	..	67.0	61.0	**Habillement; préparation, teinture des fourrures**		18
..	..	..	..	..	..	..	..	Articles d'habillement autres qu'en fourrure		181
..	..	..	..	..	..	..	..	Préparation, teinture des fourrures; art. en fourrure		182
..	..	..	..	..	..	44.0	33.0	**Travail des cuirs; articles en cuir; chaussures**		19
..	..	..	..	..	..	..	..	Apprêt et tannage des cuirs et articles en cuirs		191
..	..	..	..	..	..	..	..	Chaussures		192
..	..	..	..	..	..	67.0	65.0	**Bois et articles en bois et liège (sauf meubles)**		20
..	..	..	..	..	..	..	..	Sciage et rabotage du bois		201
..	..	..	..	..	..	..	..	Articles en bois, liège, vannerie, sparterie		202
..	..	..	..	..	..	31.0	25.0	**Papier et carton; articles en papier et en carton**		21
..	..	..	..	..	..	29.0	38.0	**Edition, imprimerie et reproduction**		22
..	..	..	..	..	..	..	..	Edition		221
..	..	..	..	..	..	..	..	Imprimerie et activités annexes		222
..	..	..	..	..	..	..	..	Reproduction de supports enregistrés		223
..	..	..	..	..	..	..	..	**Cokéfaction; prod. pétroliers; comb. nucléaires**		23
..	..	..	..	..	..	50.0	55.0	**Produits chimiques**		24
..	..	..	..	..	..	..	..	Produits chimiques de base		241
..	..	..	..	..	..	..	..	Autres produits chimiques		242
..	..	..	..	..	..	..	..	Fibres synthétiques ou artificielles		243
..	..	..	..	..	..	41.0	46.0	**Articles en caoutchouc et en matières plastiques**		25
..	..	..	..	..	..	..	..	Articles en caoutchouc		251
..	..	..	..	..	..	..	..	Articles en matières plastiques		252
..	..	..	..	..	..	80.0	85.0	**Autres produits minéraux non métalliques**		26
..	..	..	..	..	..	..	..	Verre et articles en verre		261
..	..	..	..	..	..	..	..	Produits minéraux non métalliques, nca		269
..	..	..	..	..	..	122.0	107.0	**Produits métallurgiques de base**		27
..	..	..	..	..	..	..	..	Sidérurgie et première transformation de l'acier		271
..	..	..	..	..	..	..	..	Métallurgie; métaux précieux et non ferreux		272
..	..	..	..	..	..	..	..	Fonderie		273
..	..	..	..	..	..	141.0	161.0	**Ouvrages en métaux, sauf machines et matériel**		28
..	..	..	..	..	..	..	..	Constr. et menuiserie métal.; réservoirs; générateurs		281
..	..	..	..	..	..	..	..	Autres ouvrages en métaux		289
..	..	..	..	..	..	189.0	188.0	**Machines et matériel, nca**		29
..	..	..	..	..	..	..	..	Machines d'usage général		291
..	..	..	..	..	..	..	..	Machines d'usage spécifique		292
..	..	..	..	..	..	..	..	Appareils domestiques, nca		293
..	..	..	..	..	..	9.0	4.0	**Mach. de bureau, comptables, matériel inform.**		30
..	..	..	..	..	..	76.0	83.0	**Machines et appareils électriques, nca**		31
..	..	..	..	..	..	..	..	Moteurs, génératrices et transformateurs électriques		311
..	..	..	..	..	..	..	..	Matériel électrique de distribution et de commande		312
..	..	..	..	..	..	..	..	Fils et câbles électriques isolés		313
..	..	..	..	..	..	..	..	Accumulateurs, piles électriques		314
..	..	..	..	..	..	..	..	Lampes électriques et appareils d'éclairage		315
..	..	..	..	..	..	..	..	Autres matériels électriques, nca		319
..	..	..	..	..	..	26.0	24.0	**Equip. et appar. de radio, TV, communication**		32
..	..	..	..	..	..	..	..	Tubes et valves électroniques; autres composants		321
..	..	..	..	..	..	..	..	Emetteurs radio et TV; app. téléphonie, télégraphie		322
..	..	..	..	..	..	..	..	Récepteurs radio et TV et articles associés		323
..	..	..	..	..	..	28.0	33.0	**Instruments médicaux, de précision, d'optique**		33
..	..	..	..	..	..	..	..	Appareils médicaux et de précision		331
..	..	..	..	..	..	..	..	Instruments d'optique ; matériel photographique		332
..	..	..	..	..	..	..	..	Horlogerie		333
..	..	..	..	..	..	56.0	57.0	**Véhicules automobiles et nemorques**		34
..	..	..	..	..	..	43.0	36.0	**Autres matériels de transport**		35
..	..	..	..	..	..	..	..	Construction et réparation de navires		351
..	..	..	..	..	..	..	..	Construction de matériel ferroviaire roulant		352
..	..	..	..	..	..	..	..	Construction aéronautique et spatiale		353
..	..	..	..	..	..	..	..	Autres équipements de transport		359
..	..	..	..	..	..	74.0	83.0	**Meubles; activités de fabrication, nca**		36
..	..	..	..	..	..	..	..	Meubles		361
..	..	..	..	..	..	..	..	Activités de fabrication, nca		369
..	..	..	..	..	..	8.0	7.0	**Récupération**		37
..	..	..	..	..	..	87.0	84.0	**Production et distrib. d'électricité, de gaz, d'eau**	E	40-41
..	..	..	..	..	..	65.0	63.0	**Electricité, gaz, vapeur et eau chaude**		40
..	..	..	..	..	..	..	..	Production, collecte et distribution d'électricité		401
..	..	..	..	..	..	22.0	21.0	**Captage, épuration et distribution d'eau**		41 410
..	..	..	..	..	..	392.0	444.0	**Construction**	F	45
..	..	..	..	..	..	710.0	752.0	**Commerce de gros et de détail; réparation**	G	50-52
..	..	..	..	..	..	136.0	149.0	**Hôtels et restaurants**	H	55
..	..	..	..	..	..	331.0	348.0	**Transports, entreposage et communications**	I	60-64
..	..	..	..	..	..	85.0	88.0	**Intermédiation financière**	J	65-67
..	..	..	..	..	..	351.0	336.0	**Immobilier, locations, services aux entreprises**	K	70-74
..	..	..	..	..	..	152.0	159.0	**Admin. publique; éducation; santé; autres**	L-Q	75-99
..	..	..	..	..	..	4 087.0	4 184.0	**Grand total**	A-Q	01-99

Statistiques des Structures Industrielles
OCDE, © 1998
OECD OCDE

Table CZ.5 EMPLOYMENT, EMPLOYEES - EMPLOI, SALARIÉS

Thousands

ISIC revision 3			1989	1990	1991	1992	1993	1994	1995	1996
A	01-02	Agriculture, hunting and forestry	..	..	..	..	..	..	257.0	244.0
B	05	Fishing	..	..	..	..	..	..	2.0	2.0
C	10-14	Mining and quarrying	..	..	..	..	..	..	96.0	84.0
	10	Mining of coal and lignite; extraction of peat	..	..	..	..	..	..	72.0	67.0
	11	Crude petroleum & natural gas; related service activ.	..	..	..	..	..	..	2.0	2.0
	13	Mining of metal ores	..	..	..	..	..	..	..	..
	14	Other mining and quarrying	..	..	..	..	..	..	18.0	12.0
D	15-37	Total manufacturing	..	..	..	..	..	..	1 347.0	1 341.0
	15	Food products and beverages	..	..	..	..	..	..	139.0	152.0
	155	Beverages	..	..	..	..	..	..	..	..
	16 160	Tobacco products	..	..	..	..	..	..	..	..
	17	Textiles	..	..	..	..	..	..	92.0	88.0
	171	Spinning, weaving and finishing of textiles	..	..	..	..	..	..	..	..
	172	Other textiles	..	..	..	..	..	..	..	..
	173	Knitted and crocheted fabrics and articles	..	..	..	..	..	..	..	..
	18	Wearing apparel dressing & dyeing of fur	..	..	..	..	..	..	56.0	53.0
	181	Wearing apparel, except fur apparel	..	..	..	..	..	..	..	..
	182	Dressing and dyeing of fur; articles of fur	..	..	..	..	..	..	..	..
	19	Tanning, dressing leather; leather artic.; footwear	..	..	..	..	..	..	43.0	31.0
	191	Tanning, dressing leather; manuf. of leather articles	..	..	..	..	..	..	..	..
	192	Footwear	..	..	..	..	..	..	..	..
	20	Wood and cork products, ex. furniture	..	..	..	..	..	..	53.0	49.0
	201	Sawmilling and planing of wood	..	..	..	..	..	..	..	..
	202	Products of wood, cork, straw & plaiting material	..	..	..	..	..	..	..	..
	21	Paper and paper products	..	..	..	..	..	..	31.0	25.0
	22	Publishing, printing & reprod. of recorded media	..	..	..	..	..	..	26.0	34.0
	221	Publishing	..	..	..	..	..	..	..	..
	222	Printing and related service activities	..	..	..	..	..	..	..	..
	223	Reproduction of recorded media	..	..	..	..	..	..	..	..
	23	Coke, refined petroleum products & nuclear fuel	..	..	..	..	..	..	..	..
	24	Chemicals and chemical products	..	..	..	..	..	..	49.0	54.0
	241	Basic chemicals	..	..	..	..	..	..	..	..
	242	Other chemical products	..	..	..	..	..	..	..	..
	243	Man-made fibres	..	..	..	..	..	..	..	..
	25	Rubber and plastic products	..	..	..	..	..	..	40.0	44.0
	251	Rubber products	..	..	..	..	..	..	..	..
	252	Plastic products	..	..	..	..	..	..	..	..
	26	Other non-metallic mineral products	..	..	..	..	..	..	76.0	80.0
	261	Glass and glass products	..	..	..	..	..	..	..	..
	269	Non-metallic mineral products, nec	..	..	..	..	..	..	..	..
	27	Basic metals	..	..	..	..	..	..	122.0	107.0
	271	Basic iron and steel	..	..	..	..	..	..	..	..
	272	Basic precious and non-ferrous metals	..	..	..	..	..	..	..	..
	273	Casting of metals	..	..	..	..	..	..	..	..
	28	Fabricated metal products, ex. machin. & equip.	..	..	..	..	..	..	121.0	132.0
	281	Structural metal prod., tanks, reservoirs, generators	..	..	..	..	..	..	..	..
	289	Other fabricated metal products & service activities	..	..	..	..	..	..	..	..
	29	Machinery and equipment, nec	..	..	..	..	..	..	184.0	182.0
	291	General purpose machinery	..	..	..	..	..	..	..	..
	292	Special purpose machinery	..	..	..	..	..	..	..	..
	293	Domestic appliances, nec	..	..	..	..	..	..	..	..
	30	Office, accounting and computing machinery	..	..	..	..	..	..	8.0	4.0
	31	Electrical machinery and apparatus, nec	..	..	..	..	..	..	67.0	73.0
	311	Electric motors, generators and transformers	..	..	..	..	..	..	..	..
	312	Electricity distribution and control apparatus	..	..	..	..	..	..	..	..
	313	Insulated wire and cable	..	..	..	..	..	..	..	..
	314	Accumulators, primary cells and primary batteries	..	..	..	..	..	..	..	..
	315	Electric lamps and lighting equipment	..	..	..	..	..	..	..	..
	319	Other electrical equipment, nec	..	..	..	..	..	..	..	..
	32	Radio, TV, communication equip. & apparatus	..	..	..	..	..	..	24.0	23.0
	321	Electronic valves, tubes & other electronic compon.	..	..	..	..	..	..	..	..
	322	TV, radio transmitters & appar. for line teleph., telegr.	..	..	..	..	..	..	..	..
	323	TV, radio receivers and associated goods	..	..	..	..	..	..	..	..
	33	Medical, precision, optical instr.; watches, clocks	..	..	..	..	..	..	25.0	29.0
	331	Medical equip.; precision instruments and appliances	..	..	..	..	..	..	..	..
	332	Optical instruments and photographic equipment	..	..	..	..	..	..	..	..
	333	Watches and clocks	..	..	..	..	..	..	..	..
	34	Motor vehicles, trailers, and semi-trailers	..	..	..	..	..	..	56.0	57.0
	35	Other transport equipment	..	..	..	..	..	..	42.0	36.0
	351	Building and repairing of ships and boats	..	..	..	..	..	..	..	..
	352	Railway, tramway locomotives and rolling stock	..	..	..	..	..	..	..	..
	353	Aircraft and spacecraft	..	..	..	..	..	..	..	..
	359	Transport equipment, nec	..	..	..	..	..	..	..	..
	36	Furniture; manufacturing, nec	..	..	..	..	..	..	67.0	74.0
	361	Furniture	..	..	..	..	..	..	..	..
	369	Manufacturing, nec	..	..	..	..	..	..	..	..
	37	Recycling	..	..	..	..	..	..	7.0	7.0
E	40-41	Electricity, gas and water supply	..	..	..	..	..	..	87.0	84.0
	40	Electricity, gas, steam and hot water supply	..	..	..	..	..	..	65.0	63.0
	401	Production, collection and distribution of electricity	..	..	..	..	..	..	..	..
	41 410	Collection, purification, distribution of water	..	..	..	..	..	..	22.0	21.0
F	45	Construction	..	..	..	..	..	..	464.0	359.0
G	50-52	Wholesale and retail trade; repairs etc	..	..	..	..	..	..	551.0	572.0
H	55	Hotels and restaurants	..	..	..	..	..	..	110.0	119.0
I	60-64	Transport, storage and communications	..	..	..	..	..	..	304.0	317.0
J	65-67	Financial intermediation	..	..	..	..	..	..	82.0	84.0
K	70-74	Real estate, renting and business activities	..	..	..	..	..	..	253.0	235.0
L-Q	75-99	Public admin.; education; health; other services	..	..	..	..	..	..	101.0	110.0
A-Q	01-99	Grand total	..	..	..	..	..	..	3 654.0	3 551.0

Table CZ.6 **SALAIRES ET TRAITEMENTS, TOTAL - TOTAL WAGES AND SALARIES**

Millions de CK (Prix courants)

1989	1990	1991	1992	1993	1994	1995	1996			CITI révision 3	
..	..	..	..	..	..	20 929	23 228	**Agriculture, chasse et sylviculture**	A	01-02	
..	..	..	..	..	..	197	240	**Pêche**	B	05	
..	..	..	..	..	..	10 642	11 657	**Activités extractives**	C	10-14	
..	..	..	..	..	..	8 913	9 571	Extraction de charbon, de lignite et de tourbe		10	
..	..	..	..	..	..	285	320	Extraction de pétrole brut et de gaz naturel		11	
..	..	..	..	..	..	..	..	Extraction de minerais métalliques		13	
..	..	..	..	..	..	1 088	1 378	Autres activités extractives		14	
..	..	..	..	..	..	125 039	144 650	**Activités de fabrication**	D	15-37	
..	..	..	..	..	..	12 661	15 381	**Produits alimentaires et boissons**		15	
..	..	..	..	..	..	..	..	Boissons			155
..	..	..	..	..	..	..	..	**Produits à base de tabac**		16	160
..	..	..	..	..	..	6 452	7 102	**Textiles**		17	
..	..	..	..	..	..	..	..	Filature, tissage et achèvement des textiles			171
..	..	..	..	..	..	..	..	Autres articles textiles			172
..	..	..	..	..	..	..	..	Etoffes et articles de bonneterie			173
..	..	..	..	..	..	3 685	3 523	**Habillement; préparation, teinture des fourrures**		18	
..	..	..	..	..	..	..	..	Articles d'habillement autres qu'en fourrure			181
..	..	..	..	..	..	..	..	Préparation, teinture des fourrures; art. en fourrure			182
..	..	..	..	..	..	2 562	2 582	**Travail des cuirs; articles en cuir; chaussures**		19	
..	..	..	..	..	..	..	..	Apprêt et tannage des cuirs et articles en cuirs			191
..	..	..	..	..	..	..	..	Chaussures			192
..	..	..	..	..	..	4 919	4 668	**Bois et articles en bois et liège (sauf meubles)**		20	
..	..	..	..	..	..	..	..	Sciage et rabotage du bois			201
..	..	..	..	..	..	..	..	Articles en bois, liège, vannerie, sparterie			202
..	..	..	..	..	..	2 244	2 674	**Papier et carton; articles en papier et en carton**		21	
..	..	..	..	..	..	3 701	4 376	**Edition, imprimerie et reproduction**		22	
..	..	..	..	..	..	..	..	Edition			221
..	..	..	..	..	..	..	..	Imprimerie et activités annexes			222
..	..	..	..	..	..	..	..	Reproduction de supports enregistrés			223
..	..	..	..	..	..	..	..	**Cokéfaction; prod. pétroliers; comb. nucléaires**		23	
..	..	..	..	..	..	5 064	6 945	**Produits chimiques**		24	
..	..	..	..	..	..	..	..	Produits chimiques de base			241
..	..	..	..	..	..	..	..	Autres produits chimiques			242
..	..	..	..	..	..	..	..	Fibres synthétiques ou artificielles			243
..	..	..	..	..	..	3 878	5 061	**Articles en caoutchouc et en matières plastiques**		25	
..	..	..	..	..	..	..	..	Articles en caoutchouc			251
..	..	..	..	..	..	..	..	Articles en matières plastiques			252
..	..	..	..	..	..	7 769	9 029	**Autres produits minéraux non métalliques**		26	
..	..	..	..	..	..	..	..	Verre et articles en verre			261
..	..	..	..	..	..	..	..	Produits minéraux non métalliques, nca			269
..	..	..	..	..	..	12 089	13 773	**Produits métallurgiques de base**		27	
..	..	..	..	..	..	..	..	Sidérurgie et première transformation de l'acier			271
..	..	..	..	..	..	..	..	Métallurgie; métaux précieux et non ferreux			272
..	..	..	..	..	..	..	..	Fonderie			273
..	..	..	..	..	..	12 259	14 675	**Ouvrages en métaux, sauf machines et matériel**		28	
..	..	..	..	..	..	..	..	Constr. et menuiserie métal.; réservoirs; générateurs			281
..	..	..	..	..	..	..	..	Autres ouvrages en métaux			289
..	..	..	..	..	..	18 259	20 447	**Machines et matériel, nca**		29	
..	..	..	..	..	..	..	..	Machines d'usage général			291
..	..	..	..	..	..	..	..	Machines d'usage spécifique			292
..	..	..	..	..	..	..	..	Appareils domestiques, nca			293
..	..	..	..	..	..	306	361	**Mach. de bureau, comptables, matériel inform.**		30	
..	..	..	..	..	..	6 710	8 339	**Machines et appareils électriques, nca**		31	
..	..	..	..	..	..	..	..	Moteurs, génératrices et transformateurs électriques			311
..	..	..	..	..	..	..	..	Matériel électrique de distribution et de commande			312
..	..	..	..	..	..	..	..	Fils et câbles électriques isolés			313
..	..	..	..	..	..	..	..	Accumulateurs, piles électriques			314
..	..	..	..	..	..	..	..	Lampes électriques et appareils d'éclairage			315
..	..	..	..	..	..	..	..	Autres matériels électriques, nca			319
..	..	..	..	..	..	2 179	2 451	**Equip. et appar. de radio, TV, communication**		32	
..	..	..	..	..	..	..	..	Tubes et valves électroniques; autres composants			321
..	..	..	..	..	..	..	..	Emetteurs radio et TV; app. téléphonie, télégraphie			322
..	..	..	..	..	..	..	..	Récepteurs radio et TV et articles associés			323
..	..	..	..	..	..	2 686	3 261	**Instruments médicaux, de précision, d'optique**		33	
..	..	..	..	..	..	..	..	Appareils médicaux et de précision			331
..	..	..	..	..	..	..	..	Instruments d'optique ; matériel photographique			332
..	..	..	..	..	..	..	..	Horlogerie			333
..	..	..	..	..	..	5 839	7 412	**Véhicules automobiles et nemorques**		34	
..	..	..	..	..	..	3 478	4 114	**Autres matériels de transport**		35	
..	..	..	..	..	..	..	..	Construction et réparation de navires			351
..	..	..	..	..	..	..	..	Construction de matériel ferroviaire roulant			352
..	..	..	..	..	..	..	..	Construction aéronautique et spatiale			353
..	..	..	..	..	..	..	..	Autres équipements de transport			359
..	..	..	..	..	..	5 650	6 617	**Meubles; activités de fabrication, nca**		36	
..	..	..	..	..	..	..	..	Meubles			361
..	..	..	..	..	..	..	..	Activités de fabrication, nca			369
..	..	..	..	..	..	697	704	**Récupération**		37	
..	..	..	..	..	..	10 391	11 703	**Production et distrib. d'électricité, de gaz, d'eau**	E	40-41	
..	..	..	..	..	..	8 284	9 373	**Electricité, gaz, vapeur et eau chaude**		40	
..	..	..	..	..	..	..	..	Production, collecte et distribution d'électricité			401
..	..	..	..	..	..	2 107	2 330	**Captage, épuration et distribution d'eau**		41	410
..	..	..	..	..	..	41 395	42 272	**Construction**	F	45	
..	..	..	..	..	..	48 135	61 577	**Commerce de gros et de détail; réparation**	G	50-52	
..	..	..	..	..	..	6 856	8 933	**Hôtels et restaurants**	H	55	
..	..	..	..	..	..	29 409	36 913	**Transports, entreposage et communications**	I	60-64	
..	..	..	..	..	..	13 692	16 515	**Intermédiation financière**	J	65-67	
..	..	..	..	..	..	24 969	30 236	**Immobilier, locations, services aux entreprises**	K	70-74	
..	..	..	..	..	..	8 608	10 450	**Admin. publique; éducation; santé; autres**	L-Q	75-99	
..	..	..	..	..	..	340 262	398 374	**Grand total**	A-Q	01-99	

Statistiques des Structures Industrielles
OCDE, © 1998

OECD
OCDE

Table CZ.7 HOURS WORKED - HEURES OUVRÉES

Thousands

ISIC revision 3			1989	1990	1991	1992	1993	1994	1995	1996
A	01-02	**Agriculture, hunting and forestry**	..	..	..	..	..	..	..	..
B	05	**Fishing**	..	..	..	..	..	..	..	..
C	10-14	**Mining and quarrying**	..	..	..	..	..	..	117 000	110 000
	10	Mining of coal and lignite; extraction of peat	..	..	..	..	..	..	101 000	94 000
	11	Crude petroleum & natural gas; related service activ.	..	..	..	..	..	..	3 000	3 000
	13	Mining of metal ores	..	..	..	..	..	..		
	14	Other mining and quarrying	..	..	..	..	..	..	10 000	10 000
D	15-37	**Total manufacturing**	..	..	..	..	..	..	1 252 000	1 192 000
	15	**Food products and beverages**	..	..	..	..	..	..	135 834	134 000
	155	Beverages	..	..	..	..	..	..		
	16 160	**Tobacco products**	..	..	..	..	..	..	..	..
	17	**Textiles**	..	..	..	..	..	..	100 003	90 000
	171	Spinning, weaving and finishing of textiles	..	..	..	..	..	..		
	172	Other textiles	..	..	..	..	..	..		
	173	Knitted and crocheted fabrics and articles	..	..	..	..	..	..		
	18	**Wearing apparel dressing & dyeing of fur**	..	..	..	..	..	..	39 189	34 000
	181	Wearing apparel, except fur apparel	..	..	..	..	..	..		
	182	Dressing and dyeing of fur; articles of fur	..	..	..	..	..	..		
	19	**Tanning, dressing leather; leather artic.; footwear**	..	..	..	..	..	..	37 941	32 000
	191	Tanning, dressing leather; manuf. of leather articles	..	..	..	..	..	..		
	192	Footwear	..	..	..	..	..	..		
	20	**Wood and cork products, ex. furniture**	..	..	..	..	..	..	29 266	26 000
	201	Sawmilling and planing of wood	..	..	..	..	..	..		
	202	Products of wood, cork, straw & plaiting material	..	..	..	..	..	..		
	21	**Paper and paper products**	..	..	..	..	..	..	27 417	27 000
	22	**Publishing, printing & reprod. of recorded media**	..	..	..	..	..	..	15 772	15 000
	221	Publishing	..	..	..	..	..	..		
	222	Printing and related service activities	..	..	..	..	..	..		
	223	Reproduction of recorded media	..	..	..	..	..	..		
	23	**Coke, refined petroleum products & nuclear fuel**	..	..	..	..	..	..		
	24	**Chemicals and chemical products**	..	..	..	..	..	..	46 332	52 000
	241	Basic chemicals	..	..	..	..	..	..		
	242	Other chemical products	..	..	..	..	..	..		
	243	Man-made fibres	..	..	..	..	..	..		
	25	**Rubber and plastic products**	..	..	..	..	..	..	36 087	38 000
	251	Rubber products	..	..	..	..	..	..		
	252	Plastic products	..	..	..	..	..	..		
	26	**Other non-metallic mineral products**	..	..	..	..	..	..	85 658	80 000
	261	Glass and glass products	..	..	..	..	..	..		
	269	Non-metallic mineral products, nec	..	..	..	..	..	..		
	27	**Basic metals**	..	..	..	..	..	..	132 945	129 000
	271	Basic iron and steel	..	..	..	..	..	..		
	272	Basic precious and non-ferrous metals	..	..	..	..	..	..		
	273	Casting of metals	..	..	..	..	..	..		
	28	**Fabricated metal products, ex. machin. & equip.**	..	..	..	..	..	..	91 678	88 000
	281	Structural metal prod., tanks, reservoirs, generators	..	..	..	..	..	..		
	289	Other fabricated metal products & service activities	..	..	..	..	..	..		
	29	**Machinery and equipment, nec**	..	..	..	..	..	..	186 126	170 000
	291	General purpose machinery	..	..	..	..	..	..		
	292	Special purpose machinery	..	..	..	..	..	..		
	293	Domestic appliances, nec	..	..	..	..	..	..		
	30	**Office, accounting and computing machinery**	..	..	..	..	..	..	3 335	3 000
	31	**Electrical machinery and apparatus, nec**	..	..	..	..	..	..	62 756	62 000
	311	Electric motors, generators and transformers	..	..	..	..	..	..		
	312	Electricity distribution and control apparatus	..	..	..	..	..	..		
	313	Insulated wire and cable	..	..	..	..	..	..		
	314	Accumulators, primary cells and primary batteries	..	..	..	..	..	..		
	315	Electric lamps and lighting equipment	..	..	..	..	..	..		
	319	Other electrical equipment, nec	..	..	..	..	..	..		
	32	**Radio, TV, communication equip. & apparatus**	..	..	..	..	..	..	18 004	19 000
	321	Electronic valves, tubes & other electronic compon.	..	..	..	..	..	..		
	322	TV, radio transmitters & appar. for line teleph., telegr.	..	..	..	..	..	..		
	323	TV, radio receivers and associated goods	..	..	..	..	..	..		
	33	**Medical, precision, optical instr.; watches, clocks**	..	..	..	..	..	..	21 314	22 000
	331	Medical equip.; precision instruments and appliances	..	..	..	..	..	..		
	332	Optical instruments and photographic equipment	..	..	..	..	..	..		
	333	Watches and clocks	..	..	..	..	..	..		
	34	**Motor vehicles, trailers, and semi-trailers**	..	..	..	..	..	..	63 631	67 000
	35	**Other transport equipment**	..	..	..	..	..	..	38 165	37 000
	351	Building and repairing of ships and boats	..	..	..	..	..	..		
	352	Railway, tramway locomotives and rolling stock	..	..	..	..	..	..		
	353	Aircraft and spacecraft	..	..	..	..	..	..		
	359	Transport equipment, nec	..	..	..	..	..	..		
	36	**Furniture; manufacturing, nec**	..	..	..	..	..	..	58 218	54 000
	361	Furniture	..	..	..	..	..	..		
	369	Manufacturing, nec	..	..	..	..	..	..		
	37	**Recycling**	..	..	..	..	..	..	4 778	4 000
E	40-41	**Electricity, gas and water supply**	..	..	..	..	..	..	91 000	85 000
	40	**Electricity, gas, steam and hot water supply**	..	..	..	..	..	..	68 000	63 000
	401	Production, collection and distribution of electricity	..	..	..	..	..	..		
	41 410	**Collection, purification, distribution of water**	..	..	..	..	..	..	23 000	22 000
F	45	**Construction**	..	..	..	..	..	..	379 000	..
G	50-52	**Wholesale and retail trade; repairs etc**	..	..	..	..	..	..	..	..
H	55	**Hotels and restaurants**	..	..	..	..	..	..	..	..
I	60-64	**Transport, storage and communications**	..	..	..	..	..	..	..	..
J	65-67	**Financial intermediation**	..	..	..	..	..	..	..	..
K	70-74	**Real estate, renting and business activities**	..	..	..	..	..	..	..	..
L-Q	75-99	**Public admin.; education; health; other services**	..	..	..	..	..	..	..	..
A-Q	01-99	**Grand total**	..	..	..	..	..	..	..	..

Table DN.1 PRODUCTION - PRODUCTION

Millions de DKr (Prix courants)

CITI révision 3

1989	1990	1991	1992	1993	1994	1995	1996				
..	..	..	..	..	..	..	..	**Agriculture, chasse et sylviculture**	A	01-02	
..	..	..	..	..	..	..	..	**Pêche**	B	05	
..	..	..	..	..	..	..	..	**Activités extractives**	C	10-14	
..	..	..	..	..	..	..	..	Extraction de charbon, de lignite et de tourbe		10	
..	..	..	..	..	..	..	..	Extraction de pétrole brut et de gaz naturel		11	
..	..	..	..	..	..	..	..	Extraction de minerais métalliques		13	
..	..	..	1 331	1 356	1 460	..	..	Autres activités extractives		14	
..	..	..	345 756	331 814	357 546	..	..	**Activités de fabrication**	D	15-37	
..	..	..	109 578	107 028	113 221	..	..	**Produits alimentaires et boissons**		15	
..	..	..	9 722	9 718	9 973	..	..	Boissons			155
..	..	..	2 852	2 762	2 916	..	..	**Produits à base de tabac**		16	160
..	..	..	7 184	6 503	6 632	..	..	**Textiles**		17	
..	..	..	1 554	1 304	1 333	..	..	Filature, tissage et achèvement des textiles			171
..	..	..	3 560	3 176	3 297	..	..	Autres articles textiles			172
..	..	..	2 071	2 022	2 003	..	..	Etoffes et articles de bonneterie			173
..	..	..	4 469	4 088	4 294	..	..	**Habillement; préparation, teinture des fourrures**		18	
..	..	..	..	..	..	..	..	Articles d'habillement autres qu'en fourrure			181
..	..	..	..	..	..	..	..	Préparation, teinture des fourrures; art. en fourrure			182
..	..	..	1 652	1 830	1 976	..	..	**Travail des cuirs; articles en cuir; chaussures**		19	
..	..	..	278	368	397	..	..	Apprêt et tannage des cuirs et articles en cuirs			191
..	..	..	1 374	1 463	1 579	..	..	Chaussures			192
..	..	..	6 695	6 996	8 124	..	..	**Bois et articles en bois et liège (sauf meubles)**		20	
..	..	..	786	809	893	..	..	Sciage et rabotage du bois			201
..	..	..	5 909	6 187	7 231	..	..	Articles en bois, liège, vannerie, sparterie			202
..	..	..	9 053	7 473	8 024	..	..	**Papier et carton; articles en papier et en carton**		21	
..	..	..	14 477	14 382	14 375	..	..	**Edition, imprimerie et reproduction**		22	
..	..	..	7 854	7 950	7 706	..	..	Edition			221
..	..	..	6 622	6 433	6 669	..	..	Imprimerie et activités annexes			222
..	..	..	..	..	..	..	..	Reproduction de supports enregistrés			223
..	..	..	10 648	10 149	9 790	..	..	**Cokéfaction; prod. pétroliers; comb. nucléaires**		23	
..	..	..	31 465	28 541	31 363	..	..	**Produits chimiques**		24	
..	..	..	10 227	7 362	8 260	..	..	Produits chimiques de base			241
..	..	..	21 237	21 179	23 103	..	..	Autres produits chimiques			242
..	..	..	..	..	..	..	..	Fibres synthétiques ou artificielles			243
..	..	..	12 527	11 790	12 791	..	..	**Articles en caoutchouc et en matières plastiques**		25	
..	..	..	1 156	1 099	1 270	..	..	Articles en caoutchouc			251
..	..	..	11 371	10 691	11 520	..	..	Articles en matières plastiques			252
..	..	..	12 124	11 573	12 948	..	..	**Autres produits minéraux non métalliques**		26	
..	..	..	1 940	2 300	2 299	..	..	Verre et articles en verre			261
..	..	..	10 183	9 273	10 649	..	..	Produits minéraux non métalliques, nca			269
..	..	..	7 367	7 545	8 637	..	..	**Produits métallurgiques de base**		27	
..	..	..	4 854	4 605	5 385	..	..	Sidérurgie et première transformation de l'acier			271
..	..	..	2 513	2 941	3 252	..	..	Métallurgie; métaux précieux et non ferreux			272
..	..	..	..	..	..	..	..	Fonderie			273
..	..	..	18 428	16 716	17 235	..	..	**Ouvrages en métaux, sauf machines et matériel**		28	
..	..	..	..	..	..	..	..	Constr. et menuiserie métal.; réservoirs; générateurs			281
..	..	..	..	..	..	..	..	Autres ouvrages en métaux			289
..	..	..	40 294	38 992	43 205	..	..	**Machines et matériel, nca**		29	
..	..	..	23 185	24 159	26 139	..	..	Machines d'usage général			291
..	..	..	12 014	10 138	11 390	..	..	Machines d'usage spécifique			292
..	..	..	5 094	4 695	5 676	..	..	Appareils domestiques, nca			293
..	..	..	1 512	1 228	1 603	..	..	**Mach. de bureau, comptables, matériel inform.**		30	
..	..	..	7 180	7 305	9 474	..	..	**Machines et appareils électriques, nca**		31	
..	..	..	2 392	1 827	3 139	..	..	Moteurs, génératrices et transformateurs électriques			311
..	..	..	2 136	2 059	2 293	..	..	Matériel électrique de distribution et de commande			312
..	..	..	907	1 114	1 560	..	..	Fils et câbles électriques isolés			313
..	..	..	..	..	..	..	..	Accumulateurs, piles électriques			314
..	..	..	1 213	1 467	1 638	..	..	Lampes électriques et appareils d'éclairage			315
..	..	..	532	837	844	..	..	Autres matériels électriques, nca			319
..	..	..	7 474	7 085	7 843	..	..	**Equip. et appar. de radio, TV, communication**		32	
..	..	..	2 128	2 149	2 351	..	..	Tubes et valves électroniques; autres composants			321
..	..	..	1 564	1 237	1 518	..	..	Emetteurs radio et TV; app. téléphonie, télégraphie			322
..	..	..	3 782	3 700	3 973	..	..	Récepteurs radio et TV et articles associés			323
..	..	..	6 999	7 463	8 827	..	..	**Instruments médicaux, de précision, d'optique**		33	
..	..	..	6 162	6 506	7 637	..	..	Appareils médicaux et de précision			331
..	..	..	838	956	1 189	..	..	Instruments d'optique ; matériel photographique			332
..	..	..	..	..	..	..	..	Horlogerie			333
..	..	..	4 357	4 212	4 562	..	..	**Véhicules automobiles et nemorques**		34	
..	..	..	12 121	10 793	9 975	..	..	**Autres matériels de transport**		35	
..	..	..	10 132	9 256	8 489	..	..	Construction et réparation de navires			351
..	..	..	..	..	..	..	..	Construction de matériel ferroviaire roulant			352
..	..	..	..	..	..	..	..	Construction aéronautique et spatiale			353
..	..	..	801	706	..	..	..	Autres équipements de transport			359
..	..	..	17 301	17 359	19 731	..	..	**Meubles; activités de fabrication, nca**		36	
..	..	..	11 642	11 218	13 435	..	..	Meubles			361
..	..	..	5 659	6 140	6 296	..	..	Activités de fabrication, nca			369
..	..	..	..	..	..	..	..	**Récupération**		37	
..	..	..	..	..	..	..	..	**Production et distrib. d'électricité, de gaz, d'eau**	E	40-41	
..	..	..	..	..	..	..	..	**Electricité, gaz, vapeur et eau chaude**		40	
..	..	..	..	..	..	..	..	Production, collecte et distribution d'électricité			401
..	..	..	..	..	..	..	..	**Captage, épuration et distribution d'eau**		41	410
..	..	..	..	..	..	..	..	**Construction**	F	45	
..	..	..	..	..	..	..	..	**Commerce de gros et de détail; réparation**	G	50-52	
..	..	..	..	..	..	..	..	**Hôtels et restaurants**	H	55	
..	..	..	..	..	..	..	..	**Transports, entreposage et communications**	I	60-64	
..	..	..	..	..	..	..	..	**Intermédiation financière**	J	65-67	
..	..	..	..	..	..	..	..	**Immobilier, locations, services aux entreprises**	K	70-74	
..	..	..	..	..	..	..	..	**Admin. publique; éducation; santé; autres**	L-Q	75-99	
..	..	..	347 176	333 255	359 100	..	..	**Grand total**	A-Q	01-99	

Note: ISIC 2222 includes 2230; 2422 includes 2421 and 2430; 3150 includes 3140.

Statistiques des Structures Industrielles
OCDE, © 1998

DENMARK

Table DN.2 VALUE ADDED - VALEUR AJOUTÉE

Millions of DKr (Current Prices)

ISIC revision 3			1989	1990	1991	1992	1993	1994	1995	1996
A	01-02	Agriculture, hunting and forestry	..	..	..	..	..	..	..	..
B	05	Fishing	..	..	..	..	..	..	..	..
C	10-14	Mining and quarrying	..	..	..	..	..	..	..	..
	10	Mining of coal and lignite; extraction of peat	..	..	..	..	..	..	..	..
	11	Crude petroleum & natural gas; related service activ.	..	..	..	..	..	..	..	..
	13	Mining of metal ores	..	..	..	..	..	..	..	..
	14	Other mining and quarrying	..	..	..	988	1 019	1 047	..	..
D	15-37	Total manufacturing	..	..	..	155 315	154 141	164 923	..	..
	15	Food products and beverages	..	..	..	33 232	34 954	36 918	..	..
	155	Beverages	..	..	..	5 811	5 616	5 833	..	..
	16 160	Tobacco products	..	..	..	1 801	1 781	1 894	..	..
	17	Textiles	..	..	..	3 375	3 129	3 218	..	..
	171	Spinning, weaving and finishing of textiles	..	..	..	839	684	742	..	..
	172	Other textiles	..	..	..	1 602	1 518	1 616	..	..
	173	Knitted and crocheted fabrics and articles	..	..	..	934	927	860	..	..
	18	Wearing apparel dressing & dyeing of fur	..	..	..	2 171	2 004	1 973	..	..
	181	Wearing apparel, except fur apparel	..	..	..	..	..	..	..	..
	182	Dressing and dyeing of fur; articles of fur	..	..	..	..	..	..	..	..
	19	Tanning, dressing leather; leather artic.; footwear	..	..	..	582	613	641	..	..
	191	Tanning, dressing leather; manuf. of leather articles	..	..	..	127	143	129	..	..
	192	Footwear	..	..	..	455	470	513	..	..
	20	Wood and cork products, ex. furniture	..	..	..	3 189	3 429	3 967	..	..
	201	Sawmilling and planing of wood	..	..	..	363	383	404	..	..
	202	Products of wood, cork, straw & plaiting material	..	..	..	2 825	3 046	3 563	..	..
	21	Paper and paper products	..	..	..	4 543	3 877	4 168	..	..
	22	Publishing, printing & reprod. of recorded media	..	..	..	9 565	9 643	9 644	..	..
	221	Publishing	..	..	..	5 712	5 904	5 773	..	..
	222	Printing and related service activities	..	..	..	3 853	3 740	3 871	..	..
	223	Reproduction of recorded media	..	..	..	..	..	..	..	..
	23	Coke, refined petroleum products & nuclear fuel	..	..	..	1 005	1 277	1 124	..	..
	24	Chemicals and chemical products	..	..	..	18 025	16 955	18 362	..	..
	241	Basic chemicals	..	..	..	5 498	4 165	4 566	..	..
	242	Other chemical products	..	..	..	12 526	12 790	13 796	..	..
	243	Man-made fibres	..	..	..	..	..	..	..	..
	25	Rubber and plastic products	..	..	..	7 030	6 699	7 254	..	..
	251	Rubber products	..	..	..	708	678	764	..	..
	252	Plastic products	..	..	..	6 322	6 021	6 490	..	..
	26	Other non-metallic mineral products	..	..	..	7 172	7 165	7 831	..	..
	261	Glass and glass products	..	..	..	1 160	1 561	1 422	..	..
	269	Non-metallic mineral products, nec	..	..	..	6 012	5 604	6 409	..	..
	27	Basic metals	..	..	..	3 420	3 597	3 818	..	..
	271	Basic iron and steel	..	..	..	2 370	2 136	2 307	..	..
	272	Basic precious and non-ferrous metals	..	..	..	1 050	1 462	1 510	..	..
	273	Casting of metals	..	..	..	..	..	..	..	..
	28	Fabricated metal products, ex. machin. & equip.	..	..	..	9 703	9 191	9 422	..	..
	281	Structural metal prod., tanks, reservoirs, generators	..	..	..	..	..	..	..	..
	289	Other fabricated metal products & service activities	..	..	..	..	..	..	..	..
	29	Machinery and equipment, nec	..	..	..	21 799	21 280	23 298	..	..
	291	General purpose machinery	..	..	..	12 913	13 328	14 329	..	..
	292	Special purpose machinery	..	..	..	6 514	5 725	6 296	..	..
	293	Domestic appliances, nec	..	..	..	2 372	2 228	2 673	..	..
	30	Office, accounting and computing machinery	..	..	..	914	691	827	..	..
	31	Electrical machinery and apparatus, nec	..	..	..	3 643	3 607	4 508	..	..
	311	Electric motors, generators and transformers	..	..	..	1 021	777	1 188	..	..
	312	Electricity distribution and control apparatus	..	..	..	1 164	991	1 191	..	..
	313	Insulated wire and cable	..	..	..	449	510	707	..	..
	314	Accumulators, primary cells and primary batteries	..	..	..	..	..	..	..	..
	315	Electric lamps and lighting equipment	..	..	..	706	942	1 027	..	..
	319	Other electrical equipment, nec	..	..	..	304	388	395	..	..
	32	Radio, TV, communication equip. & apparatus	..	..	..	3 683	3 438	3 828	..	..
	321	Electronic valves, tubes & other electronic compon.	..	..	..	1 174	1 149	1 210	..	..
	322	TV, radio transmitters & appar. for line teleph., telegr.	..	..	..	740	604	763	..	..
	323	TV, radio receivers and associated goods	..	..	..	1 769	1 685	1 854	..	..
	33	Medical, precision, optical instr.; watches, clocks	..	..	..	4 307	4 553	5 378	..	..
	331	Medical equip.; precision instruments and appliances	..	..	..	3 905	4 080	4 780	..	..
	332	Optical instruments and photographic equipment	..	..	..	402	473	598	..	..
	333	Watches and clocks	..	..	..	..	..	..	..	..
	34	Motor vehicles, trailers, and semi-trailers	..	..	..	1 970	1 946	2 098	..	..
	35	Other transport equipment	..	..	..	5 003	4 794	4 150	..	..
	351	Building and repairing of ships and boats	..	..	..	4 251	4 172	3 466	..	..
	352	Railway, tramway locomotives and rolling stock	..	..	..	..	..	..	..	..
	353	Aircraft and spacecraft	..	..	..	..	..	..	..	..
	359	Transport equipment, nec	..	..	..	335	316	..	..	..
	36	Furniture; manufacturing, nec	..	..	..	9 187	9 518	10 601	..	..
	361	Furniture	..	..	..	5 978	5 947	6 998	..	..
	369	Manufacturing, nec	..	..	..	3 208	3 571	3 602	..	..
	37	Recycling	..	..	..	..	..	..	..	..
E	40-41	Electricity, gas and water supply	..	..	..			..	..	..
	40	Electricity, gas, steam and hot water supply	..	..	..			..	..	..
	401	Production, collection and distribution of electricity	..	..	..			..	..	..
	41 410	Collection, purification, distribution of water	..	..	..			..	..	..
F	45	Construction	..	..	..			..	..	..
G	50-52	Wholesale and retail trade; repairs etc	..	..	..			..	..	..
H	55	Hotels and restaurants	..	..	..			..	..	..
I	60-64	Transport, storage and communications	..	..	..			..	..	..
J	65-67	Financial intermediation	..	..	..			..	..	..
K	70-74	Real estate, renting and business activities	..	..	..			..	..	..
L-Q	75-99	Public admin.; education; health; other services	..	..	..			..	..	..
A-Q	01-99	Grand total	..	..	..	156 361	155 221	166 037	..	..

Note: ISIC 2222 includes 2230; 2422 includes 2421 and 2430; 3150 includes 3140.

Table DN.3 INVESTISSEMENT - INVESTMENT

Millions de DKr (Prix courants)　　　　　　　　　　　　　　　　　　　　　　　　　　　　CITI révision 3

1989	1990	1991	1992	1993	1994	1995	1996			
..	..	..	..	..	..	..	..	**Agriculture, chasse et sylviculture**	A	01-02
..	..	..	..	..	..	..	..	**Pêche**	B	05
..	..	..	..	..	..	..	..	**Activités extractives**	C	10-14
..	..	..	..	..	..	..	..	Extraction de charbon, de lignite et de tourbe		10
..	..	..	..	..	..	..	..	Extraction de pétrole brut et de gaz naturel		11
..	..	..	..	..	..	..	..	Extraction de minerais métalliques		13
..	..	..	220	162	239	..	..	Autres activités extractives		14
..	..	..	14 652	13 880	15 387	..	..	**Activités de fabrication**	D	15-37
..	..	..	3 348	3 625	3 146	..	..	**Produits alimentaires et boissons**		15
..	..	..	472	512	442	..	..	Boissons		155
..	..	..	37	93	99	..	..	**Produits à base de tabac**	16	160
..	..	..	275	264	242	..	..	**Textiles**		17
..	..	..	53	47	97	..	..	Filature, tissage et achèvement des textiles		171
..	..	..	134	112	89	..	..	Autres articles textiles		172
..	..	..	88	106	55	..	..	Etoffes et articles de bonneterie		173
..	..	..	115	134	89	..	..	**Habillement; préparation, teinture des fourrures**		18
..	..	..	..	..	..	..	..	Articles d'habillement autres qu'en fourrure		181
..	..	..	..	..	..	..	..	Préparation, teinture des fourrures; art. en fourrure		182
..	..	..	32	44	38	..	..	**Travail des cuirs; articles en cuir; chaussures**		19
..	..	..	5	16		..	..	Apprêt et tannage des cuirs et articles en cuirs		191
..	..	..	26	28	38	..	..	Chaussures		192
..	..	..	496	257	358	..	..	**Bois et articles en bois et liège (sauf meubles)**		20
..	..	..	40	41	21	..	..	Sciage et rabotage du bois		201
..	..	..	457	216	337	..	..	Articles en bois, liège, vannerie, sparterie		202
..	..	..	480	618	493	..	..	**Papier et carton; articles en papier et en carton**		21
..	..	..	609	477	675	..	..	**Edition, imprimerie et reproduction**		22
..	..	..	270	218	231	..	..	Edition		221
..	..	..	339	259	444	..	..	Imprimerie et activités annexes		222
..	..	..	..	..	..	..	..	Reproduction de supports enregistrés		223
..	..	..	181	267	1 713	..	..	**Cokéfaction; prod. pétroliers; comb. nucléaires**		23
..	..	..	2 471	2 749	2 452	..	..	**Produits chimiques**		24
..	..	..	716	694	624	..	..	Produits chimiques de base		241
..	..	..	1 754	2 054	1 828	..	..	Autres produits chimiques		242
..	..	..	..	..	..	..	..	Fibres synthétiques ou artificielles		243
..	..	..	750	522	556	..	..	**Articles en caoutchouc et en matières plastiques**		25
..	..	..	163	49	36	..	..	Articles en caoutchouc		251
..	..	..	587	473	520	..	..	Articles en matières plastiques		252
..	..	..	575	495	460	..	..	**Autres produits minéraux non métalliques**		26
..	..	..	116	59	79	..	..	Verre et articles en verre		261
..	..	..	459	436	381	..	..	Produits minéraux non métalliques, nca		269
..	..	..	317	244	200	..	..	**Produits métallurgiques de base**		27
..	..	..	241	125	149	..	..	Sidérurgie et première transformation de l'acier		271
..	..	..	76	119	51	..	..	Métallurgie; métaux précieux et non ferreux		272
..	..	..	..	..	..	..	..	Fonderie		273
..	..	..	828	674	748	..	..	**Ouvrages en métaux, sauf machines et matériel**		28
..	..	..	..	..	..	..	..	Constr. et menuiserie métal.; réservoirs; générateurs		281
..	..	..	..	..	..	..	..	Autres ouvrages en métaux		289
..	..	..	1 618	1 565	1 611	..	..	**Machines et matériel, nca**		29
..	..	..	1 075	1 192	1 128	..	..	Machines d'usage général		291
..	..	..	342	228	339	..	..	Machines d'usage spécifique		292
..	..	..	201	145	144	..	..	Appareils domestiques, nca		293
..	..	..	41	8	26	..	..	**Mach. de bureau, comptables, matériel inform.**		30
..	..	..	317	214	388	..	..	**Machines et appareils électriques, nca**		31
..	..	..	107	47	146	..	..	Moteurs, génératrices et transformateurs électriques		311
..	..	..	83	55	75	..	..	Matériel électrique de distribution et de commande		312
..	..	..	70	55	91	..	..	Fils et câbles électriques isolés		313
..	..	..	..	..	..	..	..	Accumulateurs, piles électriques		314
..	..	..	45	41	64	..	..	Lampes électriques et appareils d'éclairage		315
..	..	..	13	16	12	..	..	Autres matériels électriques, nca		319
..	..	..	420	310	298	..	..	**Equip. et appar. de radio, TV, communication**		32
..	..	..	73	93	58	..	..	Tubes et valves électroniques; autres composants		321
..	..	..	71	15	60	..	..	Emetteurs radio et TV; app. téléphonie, télégraphie		322
..	..	..	277	202	181	..	..	Récepteurs radio et TV et articles associés		323
..	..	..	209	257	323	..	..	**Instruments médicaux, de précision, d'optique**		33
..	..	..	167	235	289	..	..	Appareils médicaux et de précision		331
..	..	..	42	22	34	..	..	Instruments d'optique ; matériel photographique		332
..	..	..	..	..	..	..	..	Horlogerie		333
..	..	..	133	86	101	..	..	**Véhicules automobiles et nemorques**		34
..	..	..	558	155	323	..	..	**Autres matériels de transport**		35
..	..	..	508	146	300	..	..	Construction et réparation de navires		351
..	..	..	..	..	..	..	..	Construction de matériel ferroviaire roulant		352
..	..	..	..	..	..	..	..	Construction aéronautique et spatiale		353
..	..	..	22	12	..	..	..	Autres équipements de transport		359
..	..	..	842	821	1 049	..	..	**Meubles; activités de fabrication, nca**		36
..	..	..	469	592	564	..	..	Meubles		361
..	..	..	374	229	485	..	..	Activités de fabrication, nca		369
..	..	..	..	..	..	..	..	**Récupération**		37
..	..	..	..	..	..	..	..	**Production et distrib. d'électricité, de gaz, d'eau**	E	40-41
..	..	..	..	..	..	..	..	**Electricité, gaz, vapeur et eau chaude**		40
..	..	..	..	..	..	..	..	Production, collecte et distribution d'électricité		401
..	..	..	..	..	..	..	..	**Captage, épuration et distribution d'eau**	41	410
..	..	..	..	..	..	..	..	**Construction**	F	45
..	..	..	..	..	..	..	..	**Commerce de gros et de détail; réparation**	G	50-52
..	..	..	..	..	..	..	..	**Hôtels et restaurants**	H	55
..	..	..	..	..	..	..	..	**Transports, entreposage et communications**	I	60-64
..	..	..	..	..	..	..	..	**Intermédiation financière**	J	65-67
..	..	..	..	..	..	..	..	**Immobilier, locations, services aux entreprises**	K	70-74
..	..	..	..	..	..	..	..	**Admin. publique; éducation; santé; autres**	L-Q	75-99
..	..	..	14 883	14 069	15 633	..	..	**Grand total**	A-Q	01-99

Note: ISIC 2222 includes 2230; 2422 includes 2421 and 2430; 3150 includes 3140.

Statistiques des Structures Industrielles
OCDE, © 1998
OECD OCDE

DENMARK

Table DN.4 INVESTMENT IN MACHINERY AND EQUIPMENT - DÉPENSES EN MACHINES ET ÉQUIPEMENT

Millions of DKr (Current Prices)

ISIC revision 3			1989	1990	1991	1992	1993	1994	1995	1996
A	01-02	Agriculture, hunting and forestry	..	..	..	..	..	..	..	..
B	05	Fishing	..	..	..	..	..	..	..	..
C	10-14	Mining and quarrying	..	..	..	..	..	..	..	..
	10	Mining of coal and lignite; extraction of peat	..	..	..	..	..	..	..	..
	11	Crude petroleum & natural gas; related service activ.	..	..	..	..	..	..	..	..
	13	Mining of metal ores	..	..	..	..	..	..	..	..
	14	Other mining and quarrying	..	..	..	135	85	175	..	..
D	15-37	Total manufacturing	..	..	..	8 620	8 626	9 637	..	..
	15	Food products and beverages	..	..	..	1 958	2 329	2 125	..	..
	155	Beverages	..	..	..	330	310	257	..	..
	16 160	Tobacco products	..	..	..	19	83	89	..	..
	17	Textiles	..	..	..	143	148	146	..	..
	171	Spinning, weaving and finishing of textiles	..	..	..	39	27	46	..	..
	172	Other textiles	..	..	..	59	63	51	..	..
	173	Knitted and crocheted fabrics and articles	..	..	..	45	58	48	..	..
	18	Wearing apparel dressing & dyeing of fur	..	..	..	55	68	36	..	..
	181	Wearing apparel, except fur apparel	..	..	..	..	..	..	..	..
	182	Dressing and dyeing of fur; articles of fur	..	..	..	..	..	..	..	..
	19	Tanning, dressing leather; leather artic.; footwear	..	..	..	11	15	7	..	..
	191	Tanning, dressing leather; manuf. of leather articles	..	..	..	2	6	3	..	..
	192	Footwear	..	..	..	10	9	4	..	..
	20	Wood and cork products, ex. furniture	..	..	..	357	141	221	..	..
	201	Sawmilling and planing of wood	..	..	..	8	21	17	..	..
	202	Products of wood, cork, straw & plaiting material	..	..	..	348	120	204	..	..
	21	Paper and paper products	..	..	..	385	502	381	..	..
	22	Publishing, printing & reprod. of recorded media	..	..	..	436	327	433	..	..
	221	Publishing	..	..	..	187	114	76	..	..
	222	Printing and related service activities	..	..	..	249	213	357	..	..
	223	Reproduction of recorded media	..	..	..	..	..		..	..
	23	Coke, refined petroleum products & nuclear fuel	..	..	..	154	214	1 541	..	..
	24	Chemicals and chemical products	..	..	..	1 214	1 357	1 020	..	..
	241	Basic chemicals	..	..	..	483	396	345	..	..
	242	Other chemical products	..	..	..	731	961	675	..	..
	243	Man-made fibres	..	..	..	..	..		..	..
	25	Rubber and plastic products	..	..	..	483	357	381	..	..
	251	Rubber products	..	..	..	53	32	21	..	..
	252	Plastic products	..	..	..	431	324	360	..	..
	26	Other non-metallic mineral products	..	..	..	400	362	305	..	..
	261	Glass and glass products	..	..	..	62	39	52	..	..
	269	Non-metallic mineral products, nec	..	..	..	338	323	253	..	..
	27	Basic metals	..	..	..	221	211	156	..	..
	271	Basic iron and steel	..	..	..	231	80	140	..	..
	272	Basic precious and non-ferrous metals	..	..	..	- 10	131	16	..	..
	273	Casting of metals	..	..	..	..	..		..	..
	28	Fabricated metal products, ex. machin. & equip.	..	..	..	472	467	501	..	..
	281	Structural metal prod., tanks, reservoirs, generators	..	..	..	..	..		..	..
	289	Other fabricated metal products & service activities	..	..	..	..	..		..	..
	29	Machinery and equipment, nec	..	..	..	907	999	1 003	..	..
	291	General purpose machinery	..	..	..	623	791	743	..	..
	292	Special purpose machinery	..	..	..	173	95	144	..	..
	293	Domestic appliances, nec	..	..	..	111	113	116	..	..
	30	Office, accounting and computing machinery	..	..	..	13	7	17	..	..
	31	Electrical machinery and apparatus, nec	..	..	..	161	145	228	..	..
	311	Electric motors, generators and transformers	..	..	..	44	27	60	..	..
	312	Electricity distribution and control apparatus	..	..	..	41	40	66	..	..
	313	Insulated wire and cable	..	..	..	36	47	57	..	..
	314	Accumulators, primary cells and primary batteries	..	..	..	..	..		..	..
	315	Electric lamps and lighting equipment	..	..	..	34	22	39	..	..
	319	Other electrical equipment, nec	..	..	..	6	8	5	..	..
	32	Radio, TV, communication equip. & apparatus	..	..	..	271	239	182	..	..
	321	Electronic valves, tubes & other electronic compon.	..	..	..	23	71	27	..	..
	322	TV, radio transmitters & appar. for line teleph., telegr.	..	..	..	40	8	42	..	..
	323	TV, radio receivers and associated goods	..	..	..	207	160	113	..	..
	33	Medical, precision, optical instr.; watches, clocks	..	..	..	109	131	129	..	..
	331	Medical equip.; precision instruments and appliances	..	..	..	75	120	112	..	..
	332	Optical instruments and photographic equipment	..	..	..	35	11	18	..	..
	333	Watches and clocks	..	..	..	..	..		..	..
	34	Motor vehicles, trailers, and semi-trailers	..	..	..	77	47	64	..	..
	35	Other transport equipment	..	..	..	370	73	194	..	..
	351	Building and repairing of ships and boats	..	..	..	351	71	178	..	..
	352	Railway, tramway locomotives and rolling stock	..	..	..	..	..		..	..
	353	Aircraft and spacecraft	..	..	..	..	..		..	..
	359	Transport equipment, nec	..	..	..	16	10		..	..
	36	Furniture; manufacturing, nec	..	..	..	402	402	478	..	..
	361	Furniture	..	..	..	257	238	294	..	..
	369	Manufacturing, nec	..	..	..	145	164	184	..	..
	37	Recycling	..	..	..	..	..		..	..
E	40-41	Electricity, gas and water supply	..	..	..	..	..	..	..	..
	40	Electricity, gas, steam and hot water supply	..	..	..	..	..	..	..	..
	401	Production, collection and distribution of electricity	..	..	..	..	..	..	..	..
	41 410	Collection, purification, distribution of water	..	..	..	..	..	..	..	..
F	45	Construction	..	..	..				..	..
G	50-52	Wholesale and retail trade; repairs etc	..	..	..				..	..
H	55	Hotels and restaurants	..	..	..				..	..
I	60-64	Transport, storage and communications	..	..	..	..	..	..	..	..
J	65-67	Financial intermediation	..	..	..	..	..		..	..
K	70-74	Real estate, renting and business activities	..	..	..	..	..	..	..	..
L-Q	75-99	Public admin.; education; health; other services	..	..	..	..	..	..	..	..
A-Q	01-99	Grand total	..	..	..	8 759	8 724	9 637	..	..

Note: ISIC 2222 includes 2230; 2422 includes 2421 and 2430; 3150 includes 3140.

Table DN.5 ETABLISSEMENTS - ESTABLISHMENTS

Unités

1989	1990	1991	1992	1993	1994	1995	1996			CITI révision 3	
..	..	..	..	62 504	58 878	56 380	..	**Agriculture, chasse et sylviculture**	A	01-02	
..	..	..	..	3 049	2 828	2 845	..	**Pêche**	B	05	
..	..	..	..	327	341	312	..	**Activités extractives**	C	10-14	
..	..	..	..	16	13	12	..	Extraction de charbon, de lignite et de tourbe		10	
..	..	..	..	13	17	17	..	Extraction de pétrole brut et de gaz naturel		11	
..	..	..	..	..	..	..	..	Extraction de minerais métalliques		13	
..	..	..	..	..	..	..	..	Autres activités extractives		14	
..	..	..	..	25 477	24 603	24 024	..	**Activités de fabrication**	D	15-37	
..	..	..	..	2 747	2 663	2 595	..	**Produits alimentaires et boissons**		15	
..	..	..	..	69	65	65	..	Boissons			155
..	..	..	..	17	15	13	..	**Produits à base de tabac**		16	160
..	..	..	..	961	924	876	..	**Textiles**		17	
..	..	..	..	178	173	156	..	Filature, tissage et achèvement des textiles			171
..	..	..	..	579	558	535	..	Autres articles textiles			172
..	..	..	..	204	193	185	..	Etoffes et articles de bonneterie			173
..	..	..	..	1 400	1 217	1 149	..	**Habillement; préparation, teinture des fourrures**		18	
..	..	..	..	1 311	1 131	1 069	..	Articles d'habillement autres qu'en fourrure			181
..	..	..	..	89	86	80	..	Préparation, teinture des fourrures; art. en fourrure			182
..	..	..	..	205	196	189	..	**Travail des cuirs; articles en cuir; chaussures**		19	
..	..	..	..	97	92	83	..	Apprêt et tannage des cuirs et articles en cuirs			191
..	..	..	..	108	104	106	..	Chaussures			192
..	..	..	..	997	964	938	..	**Bois et articles en bois et liège (sauf meubles)**		20	
..	..	..	..	218	217	196	..	Sciage et rabotage du bois			201
..	..	..	..	779	747	742	..	Articles en bois, liège, vannerie, sparterie			202
..	..	..	..	269	260	252	..	**Papier et carton; articles en papier et en carton**		21	
..	..	..	..	3 605	3 484	3 409	..	**Edition, imprimerie et reproduction**		22	
..	..	..	..	1 418	1 393	1 391	..	Edition			221
..	..	..	..	2 168	2 071	1 991	..	Imprimerie et activités annexes			222
..	..	..	..	19	20	27	..	Reproduction de supports enregistrés			223
..	..	..	..	17	17	18	..	**Cokéfaction; prod. pétroliers; comb. nucléaires**		23	
..	..	..	..	478	475	460	..	**Produits chimiques**		24	
..	..	..	..	95	92	94	..	Produits chimiques de base			241
..	..	..	..	383	383	366	..	Autres produits chimiques			242
..	..	..	..	..	..	..	..	Fibres synthétiques ou artificielles			243
..	..	..	..	778	755	730	..	**Articles en caoutchouc et en matières plastiques**		25	
..	..	..	..	134	124	118	..	Articles en caoutchouc			251
..	..	..	..	644	631	612	..	Articles en matières plastiques			252
..	..	..	..	1 429	1 382	1 318	..	**Autres produits minéraux non métalliques**		26	
..	..	..	..	176	192	191	..	Verre et articles en verre			261
..	..	..	..	1 253	1 190	1 127	..	Produits minéraux non métalliques, nca			269
..	..	..	..	191	190	189	..	**Produits métallurgiques de base**		27	
..	..	..	..	85	93	101	..	Sidérurgie et première transformation de l'acier			271
..	..	..	..	39	45	46	..	Métallurgie; métaux précieux et non ferreux			272
..	..	..	..	67	52	42	..	Fonderie			273
..	..	..	..	4 250	4 115	4 017	..	**Ouvrages en métaux, sauf machines et matériel**		28	
..	..	..	..	524	528	502	..	Constr. et menuiserie métal.; réservoirs; générateurs			281
..	..	..	..	3 726	3 587	3 515	..	Autres ouvrages en métaux			289
..	..	..	..	2 299	2 296	2 328	..	**Machines et matériel, nca**		29	
..	..	..	..	1 014	1 003	1 029	..	Machines d'usage général			291
..	..	..	..	1 182	1 202	1 210	..	Machines d'usage spécifique			292
..	..	..	..	103	91	89	..	Appareils domestiques, nca			293
..	..	..	..	138	145	140	..	**Mach. de bureau, comptables, matériel inform.**		30	
..	..	..	..	1 097	1 083	1 063	..	**Machines et appareils électriques, nca**		31	
..	..	..	..	75	77	79	..	Moteurs, génératrices et transformateurs électriques			311
..	..	..	..	172	167	150	..	Matériel électrique de distribution et de commande			312
..	..	..	..	30	30	31	..	Fils et câbles électriques isolés			313
..	..	..	..	19	18	20	..	Accumulateurs, piles électriques			314
..	..	..	..	221	205	201	..	Lampes électriques et appareils d'éclairage			315
..	..	..	..	580	586	582	..	Autres matériels électriques, nca			319
..	..	..	..	297	272	262	..	**Equip. et appar. de radio, TV, communication**		32	
..	..	..	..	123	104	104	..	Tubes et valves électroniques; autres composants			321
..	..	..	..	57	55	51	..	Emetteurs radio et TV; app. téléphonie, télégraphie			322
..	..	..	..	117	113	107	..	Récepteurs radio et TV et articles associés			323
..	..	..	..	678	682	673	..	**Instruments médicaux, de précision, d'optique**		33	
..	..	..	..	624	628	621	..	Appareils médicaux et de précision			331
..	..	..	..	51	49	49	..	Instruments d'optique ; matériel photographique			332
..	..	..	..	3	5	3	..	Horlogerie			333
..	..	..	..	216	221	214	..	**Véhicules automobiles et nemorques**		34	
..	..	..	..	549	524	511	..	**Autres matériels de transport**		35	
..	..	..	..	437	415	396	..	Construction et réparation de navires			351
..	..	..	..	4	5	7	..	Construction de matériel ferroviaire roulant			352
..	..	..	..	45	42	44	..	Construction aéronautique et spatiale			353
..	..	..	..	63	62	64	..	Autres équipements de transport			359
..	..	..	..	2 832	2 696	2 650	..	**Meubles; activités de fabrication, nca**		36	
..	..	..	..	1 670	1 603	1 583	..	Meubles			361
..	..	..	..	1 162	1 093	1 067	..	Activités de fabrication, nca			369
..	..	..	..	27	27	30	..	**Récupération**		37	
..	..	..	..	1 664	1 869	1 896	..	**Production et distrib. d'électricité, de gaz, d'eau**	E	40-41	
..	..	..	..	835	866	877	..	**Electricité, gaz, vapeur et eau chaude**		40	
..	..	..	..	439	486	501	..	Production, collecte et distribution d'électricité			401
..	..	..	..	829	1 003	1 019	..	**Captage, épuration et distribution d'eau**		41	410
..	..	..	..	23 352	23 135	23 273	..	**Construction**	F	45	
..	..	..	..	63 891	62 483	62 248	..	**Commerce de gros et de détail; réparation**	G	50-52	
..	..	..	..	11 535	11 473	11 755	..	**Hôtels et restaurants**	H	55	
..	..	..	..	16 065	15 674	15 629	..	**Transports, entreposage et communications**	I	60-64	
..	..	..	..	4 920	4 873	4 698	..	**Intermédiation financière**	J	65-67	
..	..	..	..	44 352	44 859	45 690	..	**Immobilier, locations, services aux entreprises**	K	70-74	
..	..	..	..	53 393	52 899	53 103	..	**Admin. publique; éducation; santé; autres**	L-Q	75-99	
..	..	..	..	310 529	303 915	301 853	..	**Grand total**	A-Q	01-99	

Note: ISIC 2429 includes 2430; 2691 includes 2692.

Statistiques des Structures Industrielles
OCDE, © 1998

Table DN.6 EMPLOYMENT - EMPLOI

Thousands

ISIC revision 3			1989	1990	1991	1992	1993	1994	1995	1996
A	01-02	**Agriculture, hunting and forestry**	..	..	..	..	129.0	122.9	119.3	..
B	05	**Fishing**	..	..	..	..	7.2	7.2	7.2	..
C	10-14	**Mining and quarrying**	..	..	..	..	3.8	3.9	3.9	..
	10	Mining of coal and lignite; extraction of peat	..	..	..	..	0.2	0.1	0.1	..
	11	Crude petroleum & natural gas; related service activ.	..	..	..	..	1.3	1.2	1.4	..
	13	Mining of metal ores	..	..	..	..	..	..	..	..
	14	Other mining and quarrying	..	..	..	..	..	..	..	..
D	15-37	**Total manufacturing**	..	..	..	..	480.9	500.1	505.4	..
	15	**Food products and beverages**	..	..	..	..	92.5	92.9	91.6	..
	155	Beverages	..	..	..	..	6.8	6.8	6.9	..
	16 160	**Tobacco products**	..	..	..	..	1.5	1.5	1.5	..
	17	**Textiles**	..	..	..	..	12.9	12.8	11.7	..
	171	Spinning, weaving and finishing of textiles	..	..	..	..	3.2	3.1	2.3	..
	172	Other textiles	..	..	..	..	6.0	6.4	6.3	..
	173	Knitted and crocheted fabrics and articles	..	..	..	..	3.7	3.3	3.1	..
	18	**Wearing apparel dressing & dyeing of fur**	..	..	..	..	11.0	10.1	8.7	..
	181	Wearing apparel, except fur apparel	..	..	..	..	10.7	9.8	8.4	..
	182	Dressing and dyeing of fur; articles of fur	..	..	..	..	0.3	0.3	0.3	..
	19	**Tanning, dressing leather; leather artic.; footwear**	..	..	..	..	2.1	2.2	2.0	..
	191	Tanning, dressing leather; manuf. of leather articles	..	..	..	..	0.7	0.7	0.6	..
	192	Footwear	..	..	..	..	1.4	1.5	1.4	..
	20	**Wood and cork products, ex. furniture**	..	..	..	..	14.4	16.4	16.3	..
	201	Sawmilling and planing of wood	..	..	..	..	2.1	2.3	2.1	..
	202	Products of wood, cork, straw & plaiting material	..	..	..	..	12.3	14.2	14.2	..
	21	**Paper and paper products**	..	..	..	..	9.7	10.1	10.4	..
	22	**Publishing, printing & reprod. of recorded media**	..	..	..	..	51.3	50.8	52.6	..
	221	Publishing	..	..	..	..	31.8	31.5	34.2	..
	222	Printing and related service activities	..	..	..	..	19.4	19.1	18.2	..
	223	Reproduction of recorded media	..	..	..	..	0.1	0.1	0.2	..
	23	**Coke, refined petroleum products & nuclear fuel**	..	..	..	..	0.9	1.0	1.0	..
	24	**Chemicals and chemical products**	..	..	..	..	25.3	27.1	28.1	..
	241	Basic chemicals	..	..	..	..	6.4	5.8	6.0	..
	242	Other chemical products	..	..	..	..	18.9	21.3	22.1	..
	243	Man-made fibres	..	..	..	..	..	..	..	..
	25	**Rubber and plastic products**	..	..	..	..	20.9	21.3	21.4	..
	251	Rubber products	..	..	..	..	2.9	2.8	2.6	..
	252	Plastic products	..	..	..	..	18.0	18.5	18.7	..
	26	**Other non-metallic mineral products**	..	..	..	..	19.2	20.6	20.9	..
	261	Glass and glass products	..	..	..	..	3.5	4.3	4.7	..
	269	Non-metallic mineral products, nec	..	..	..	..	15.7	16.3	16.2	..
	27	**Basic metals**	..	..	..	..	7.7	7.3	7.8	..
	271	Basic iron and steel	..	..	..	..	4.5	4.9	5.5	..
	272	Basic precious and non-ferrous metals	..	..	..	..	2.1	1.9	2.2	..
	273	Casting of metals	..	..	..	..	1.1	0.5	0.1	..
	28	**Fabricated metal products, ex. machin. & equip.**	..	..	..	..	45.8	49.4	50.2	..
	281	Structural metal prod., tanks, reservoirs, generators	..	..	..	..	14.2	15.2	15.7	..
	289	Other fabricated metal products & service activities	..	..	..	..	31.6	34.2	34.5	..
	29	**Machinery and equipment, nec**	..	..	..	..	68.0	73.3	76.3	..
	291	General purpose machinery	..	..	..	..	37.9	42.1	45.0	..
	292	Special purpose machinery	..	..	..	..	22.7	23.8	24.4	..
	293	Domestic appliances, nec	..	..	..	..	7.4	7.3	6.9	..
	30	**Office, accounting and computing machinery**	..	..	..	..	2.1	2.2	2.1	..
	31	**Electrical machinery and apparatus, nec**	..	..	..	..	15.3	15.9	16.7	..
	311	Electric motors, generators and transformers	..	..	..	..	3.1	3.4	4.4	..
	312	Electricity distribution and control apparatus	..	..	..	..	4.2	4.2	3.9	..
	313	Insulated wire and cable	..	..	..	..	1.5	1.5	1.4	..
	314	Accumulators, primary cells and primary batteries	..	..	..	..	0.3	0.3	0.3	..
	315	Electric lamps and lighting equipment	..	..	..	..	2.4	2.8	2.8	..
	319	Other electrical equipment, nec	..	..	..	..	3.7	3.6	3.9	..
	32	**Radio, TV, communication equip. & apparatus**	..	..	..	..	11.0	11.2	11.5	..
	321	Electronic valves, tubes & other electronic compon.	..	..	..	..	3.1	2.7	2.9	..
	322	TV, radio transmitters & appar. for line teleph., telegr.	..	..	..	..	2.8	3.1	3.0	..
	323	TV, radio receivers and associated goods	..	..	..	..	5.1	5.4	5.7	..
	33	**Medical, precision, optical instr.; watches, clocks**	..	..	..	..	14.6	14.8	15.9	..
	331	Medical equip.; precision instruments and appliances	..	..	..	..	13.5	13.3	14.4	..
	332	Optical instruments and photographic equipment	..	..	..	..	1.1	1.4	1.4	..
	333	Watches and clocks	..	..	..	..	0.0	0.0	0.0	..
	34	**Motor vehicles, trailers, and semi-trailers**	..	..	..	..	5.6	7.1	7.9	..
	35	**Other transport equipment**	..	..	..	..	14.5	16.0	15.2	..
	351	Building and repairing of ships and boats	..	..	..	..	11.9	13.4	12.4	..
	352	Railway, tramway locomotives and rolling stock	..	..	..	..	0.9	0.8	0.7	..
	353	Aircraft and spacecraft	..	..	..	..	0.6	0.7	0.8	..
	359	Transport equipment, nec	..	..	..	..	1.1	1.2	1.3	..
	36	**Furniture; manufacturing, nec**	..	..	..	..	34.1	35.7	35.3	..
	361	Furniture	..	..	..	..	25.1	26.8	26.1	..
	369	Manufacturing, nec	..	..	..	..	9.0	9.0	9.2	..
	37	**Recycling**	..	..	..	..	0.5	0.4	0.4	..
E	40-41	**Electricity, gas and water supply**	..	..	..	..	19.4	20.8	20.7	..
	40	**Electricity, gas, steam and hot water supply**	..	..	..	..	16.3	17.0	17.1	..
	401	Production, collection and distribution of electricity	..	..	..	..	12.1	12.4	12.7	..
	41 410	**Collection, purification, distribution of water**	..	..	..	..	3.1	3.8	3.7	..
F	45	**Construction**	..	..	..	..	149.5	162.6	165.4	..
G	50-52	**Wholesale and retail trade; repairs etc**	..	..	..	..	393.3	403.6	419.3	..
H	55	**Hotels and restaurants**	..	..	..	..	77.4	81.7	86.4	..
I	60-64	**Transport, storage and communications**	..	..	..	..	183.6	184.8	185.5	..
J	65-67	**Financial intermediation**	..	..	..	..	85.3	83.1	82.8	..
K	70-74	**Real estate, renting and business activities**	..	..	..	..	221.0	238.2	244.6	..
L-Q	75-99	**Public admin.; education; health; other services**	..	..	..	..	1 025.7	1 003.3	1 017.0	..
A-Q	01-99	**Grand total**	..	..	..	..	2 776.1	2 812.1	2 857.5	..

Note: ISIC 2429 includes 2430; 2691 includes 2692.

Table DN.7 EMPLOI, SALARIÉS - EMPLOYMENT, EMPLOYEES

Milliers

1989	1990	1991	1992	1993	1994	1995	1996			CITI révision 3	
..	..	..	..	50.9	51.5	51.7	..	**Agriculture, chasse et sylviculture**	A	01-02	
..	..	..	..	4.1	4.3	4.3	..	**Pêche**	B	05	
..	..	..	..	3.6	3.7	3.8	..	**Activités extractives**	C	10-14	
..	..	..	..	0.2	0.1	0.1	..	Extraction de charbon, de lignite et de tourbe		10	
..	..	..	..	1.3	1.2	1.4	..	Extraction de pétrole brut et de gaz naturel		11	
..	..	..	..	..	..	..	..	Extraction de minerais métalliques		13	
..	..	..	..	..	..	..	..	Autres activités extractives		14	
..	..	..	..	464.7	484.9	490.6	..	**Activités de fabrication**	D	15-37	
..	..	..	..	90.3	90.8	89.6	..	**Produits alimentaires et boissons**		15	
..	..	..	..	6.8	6.8	6.9	..	Boissons			155
..	..	..	..	1.5	1.5	1.5	..	**Produits à base de tabac**		16	160
..	..	..	..	12.2	12.2	11.2	..	**Textiles**		17	
..	..	..	..	3.1	3.0	2.2	..	Filature, tissage et achèvement des textiles			171
..	..	..	..	5.6	6.0	5.9	..	Autres articles textiles			172
..	..	..	..	3.5	3.2	3.0	..	Etoffes et articles de bonneterie			173
..	..	..	..	9.9	9.1	7.7	..	**Habillement; préparation, teinture des fourrures**		18	
..	..	..	..	9.6	8.9	7.5	..	Articles d'habillement autres qu'en fourrure			181
..	..	..	..	0.2	0.2	0.2	..	Préparation, teinture des fourrures; art. en fourrure			182
..	..	..	..	2.0	2.0	1.9	..	**Travail des cuirs; articles en cuir; chaussures**		19	
..	..	..	..	0.6	0.6	0.5	..	Apprêt et tannage des cuirs et articles en cuirs			191
..	..	..	..	1.4	1.4	1.3	..	Chaussures			192
..	..	..	..	13.8	15.9	15.7	..	**Bois et articles en bois et liège (sauf meubles)**		20	
..	..	..	..	1.9	2.2	2.0	..	Sciage et rabotage du bois			201
..	..	..	..	11.8	13.7	13.7	..	Articles en bois, liège, vannerie, sparterie			202
..	..	..	..	9.6	10.0	10.3	..	**Papier et carton; articles en papier et en carton**		21	
..	..	..	..	49.3	48.9	50.7	..	**Edition, imprimerie et reproduction**		22	
..	..	..	..	31.2	30.9	33.5	..	Edition			221
..	..	..	..	18.0	17.9	17.0	..	Imprimerie et activités annexes			222
..	..	..	..	0.1	0.1	0.2	..	Reproduction de supports enregistrés			223
..	..	..	..	0.9	1.0	1.0	..	**Cokéfaction; prod. pétroliers; comb. nucléaires**		23	
..	..	..	..	25.2	27.0	28.0	..	**Produits chimiques**		24	
..	..	..	..	6.4	5.8	6.0	..	Produits chimiques de base			241
..	..	..	..	18.8	21.3	22.0	..	Autres produits chimiques			242
..	..	..	..	..	..	..	..	Fibres synthétiques ou artificielles			243
..	..	..	..	20.6	21.0	21.1	..	**Articles en caoutchouc et en matières plastiques**		25	
..	..	..	..	2.8	2.7	2.5	..	Articles en caoutchouc			251
..	..	..	..	17.8	18.3	18.6	..	Articles en matières plastiques			252
..	..	..	..	18.3	19.7	20.1	..	**Autres produits minéraux non métalliques**		26	
..	..	..	..	3.4	4.1	4.6	..	Verre et articles en verre			261
..	..	..	..	14.9	15.6	15.5	..	Produits minéraux non métalliques, nca			269
..	..	..	..	7.7	7.2	7.8	..	**Produits métallurgiques de base**		27	
..	..	..	..	4.4	4.9	5.5	..	Sidérurgie et première transformation de l'acier			271
..	..	..	..	2.1	1.9	2.2	..	Métallurgie; métaux précieux et non ferreux			272
..	..	..	..	1.1	0.4	0.1	..	Fonderie			273
..	..	..	..	42.8	46.4	47.3	..	**Ouvrages en métaux, sauf machines et matériel**		28	
..	..	..	..	14.0	15.1	15.5	..	Constr. et menuiserie métal.; réservoirs; générateurs			281
..	..	..	..	28.8	31.4	31.8	..	Autres ouvrages en métaux			289
..	..	..	..	67.1	72.3	75.3	..	**Machines et matériel, nca**		29	
..	..	..	..	37.5	41.7	44.6	..	Machines d'usage général			291
..	..	..	..	22.2	23.2	23.8	..	Machines d'usage spécifique			292
..	..	..	..	7.4	7.3	6.9	..	Appareils domestiques, nca			293
..	..	..	..	2.0	2.1	2.0	..	**Mach. de bureau, comptables, matériel inform.**		30	
..	..	..	..	14.6	15.3	16.1	..	**Machines et appareils électriques, nca**		31	
..	..	..	..	3.1	3.4	4.4	..	Moteurs, génératrices et transformateurs électriques			311
..	..	..	..	4.2	4.2	3.9	..	Matériel électrique de distribution et de commande			312
..	..	..	..	1.5	1.4	1.4	..	Fils et câbles électriques isolés			313
..	..	..	..	0.3	0.3	0.3	..	Accumulateurs, piles électriques			314
..	..	..	..	2.3	2.7	2.7	..	Lampes électriques et appareils d'éclairage			315
..	..	..	..	3.3	3.2	3.5	..	Autres matériels électriques, nca			319
..	..	..	..	10.9	11.1	11.5	..	**Equip. et appar. de radio, TV, communication**		32	
..	..	..	..	3.1	2.7	2.8	..	Tubes et valves électroniques; autres composants			321
..	..	..	..	2.7	3.1	3.0	..	Emetteurs radio et TV; app. téléphonie, télégraphie			322
..	..	..	..	5.1	5.4	5.7	..	Récepteurs radio et TV et articles associés			323
..	..	..	..	14.3	14.5	15.6	..	**Instruments médicaux, de précision, d'optique**		33	
..	..	..	..	13.2	13.1	14.2	..	Appareils médicaux et de précision			331
..	..	..	..	1.0	1.4	1.4	..	Instruments d'optique ; matériel photographique			332
..	..	..	..	0.0	0.0	0.0	..	Horlogerie			333
..	..	..	..	5.5	7.1	7.8	..	**Véhicules automobiles et nemorques**		34	
..	..	..	..	14.1	15.7	14.8	..	**Autres matériels de transport**		35	
..	..	..	..	11.6	13.1	12.1	..	Construction et réparation de navires			351
..	..	..	..	0.9	0.8	0.7	..	Construction de matériel ferroviaire roulant			352
..	..	..	..	0.6	0.7	0.7	..	Construction aéronautique et spatiale			353
..	..	..	..	1.1	1.1	1.3	..	Autres équipements de transport			359
..	..	..	..	31.9	33.7	33.3	..	**Meubles; activités de fabrication, nca**		36	
..	..	..	..	24.0	25.7	25.0	..	Meubles			361
..	..	..	..	7.9	8.0	8.2	..	Activités de fabrication, nca			369
..	..	..	..	0.5	0.4	0.4	..	**Récupération**		37	
..	..	..	..	19.0	20.4	20.4	..	**Production et distrib. d'électricité, de gaz, d'eau**	E	40-41	
..	..	..	..	16.1	16.7	16.8	..	**Electricité, gaz, vapeur et eau chaude**		40	
..	..	..	..	11.8	12.1	12.4	..	Production, collecte et distribution d'électricité			401
..	..	..	..	2.9	3.7	3.5	..	**Captage, épuration et distribution d'eau**		41	410
..	..	..	..	130.5	143.9	146.8	..	**Construction**	F	45	
..	..	..	..	344.5	357.0	373.8	..	**Commerce de gros et de détail; réparation**	G	50-52	
..	..	..	..	67.0	71.4	75.9	..	**Hôtels et restaurants**	H	55	
..	..	..	..	171.8	173.1	173.9	..	**Transports, entreposage et communications**	I	60-64	
..	..	..	..	84.8	82.6	82.3	..	**Intermédiation financière**	J	65-67	
..	..	..	..	189.4	207.3	213.0	..	**Immobilier, locations, services aux entreprises**	K	70-74	
..	..	..	..	1 004.4	983.0	996.9	..	**Admin. publique; éducation; santé; autres**	L-Q	75-99	
..	..	..	..	2 534.8	2 583.1	2 633.2	..	**Grand total**	A-Q	01-99	

Note: ISIC 2429 includes 2430; 2691 includes 2692.

Statistiques des Structures Industrielles
OCDE, © 1998

DENMARK

Table DN.8 WAGES AND SALARIES, EMPLOYEES - SALAIRES ET TRAITEMENTS, SALARIÉS

Millions of DKr (Current Prices)

ISIC revision 3				1989	1990	1991	1992	1993	1994	1995	1996
A	01-02		Agriculture, hunting and forestry	..	..	..	..	5 940	6 074	6 300	..
B	05		Fishing	..	..	..	..	812	873	899	..
C	10-14		Mining and quarrying	..	..	..	..	977	993	1 019	..
	10		Mining of coal and lignite; extraction of peat	..	..	..	..	36	34	34	..
	11		Crude petroleum & natural gas; related service activ.	..	..	..	..	482	459	495	..
	13		Mining of metal ores	..	..	..	..	..	..	..	..
	14		Other mining and quarrying	..	..	..	..	..	..	..	..
D	15-37		Total manufacturing	..	..	..	..	91 258	96 073	101 688	..
	15		Food products and beverages	..	..	..	..	16 662	17 097	17 496	..
		155	Beverages	..	..	..	..	1 676	1 685	1 751	..
	16	160	Tobacco products	..	..	..	..	316	312	324	..
	17		Textiles	..	..	..	..	2 061	2 122	2 047	..
		171	Spinning, weaving and finishing of textiles	..	..	..	..	561	554	447	..
		172	Other textiles	..	..	..	..	974	1 042	1 065	..
		173	Knitted and crocheted fabrics and articles	..	..	..	..	526	527	535	..
	18		Wearing apparel dressing & dyeing of fur	..	..	..	..	1 392	1 324	1 206	..
		181	Wearing apparel, except fur apparel	..	..	..	..	1 370	1 301	1 188	..
		182	Dressing and dyeing of fur; articles of fur	..	..	..	..	22	23	18	..
	19		Tanning, dressing leather; leather artic.; footwear	..	..	..	..	341	372	350	..
		191	Tanning, dressing leather; manuf. of leather articles	..	..	..	..	104	101	91	..
		192	Footwear	..	..	..	..	237	272	259	..
	20		Wood and cork products, ex. furniture	..	..	..	..	2 363	2 803	2 998	..
		201	Sawmilling and planing of wood	..	..	..	..	295	354	343	..
		202	Products of wood, cork, straw & plaiting material	..	..	..	..	2 068	2 449	2 654	..
	21		Paper and paper products	..	..	..	..	2 162	2 286	2 457	..
	22		Publishing, printing & reprod. of recorded media	..	..	..	..	8 731	8 885	9 110	..
		221	Publishing	..	..	..	..	4 805	4 979	5 245	..
		222	Printing and related service activities	..	..	..	..	3 912	3 888	3 822	..
		223	Reproduction of recorded media	..	..	..	..	14	18	43	..
	23		Coke, refined petroleum products & nuclear fuel	..	..	..	..	257	283	302	..
	24		Chemicals and chemical products	..	..	..	..	6 288	6 831	7 391	..
		241	Basic chemicals	..	..	..	..	1 653	1 512	1 622	..
		242	Other chemical products	..	..	..	..	4 634	5 319	5 769	..
		243	Man-made fibres	..	..	..	..	..	..	..	..
	25		Rubber and plastic products	..	..	..	..	4 109	4 237	4 350	..
		251	Rubber products	..	..	..	..	569	552	543	..
		252	Plastic products	..	..	..	..	3 540	3 686	3 807	..
	26		Other non-metallic mineral products	..	..	..	..	3 791	4 104	4 485	..
		261	Glass and glass products	..	..	..	..	648	772	918	..
		269	Non-metallic mineral products, nec	..	..	..	..	3 144	3 333	3 567	..
	27		Basic metals	..	..	..	..	1 643	1 557	1 744	..
		271	Basic iron and steel	..	..	..	..	958	1 058	1 210	..
		272	Basic precious and non-ferrous metals	..	..	..	..	501	430	516	..
		273	Casting of metals	..	..	..	..	184	69	18	..
	28		Fabricated metal products, ex. machin. & equip.	..	..	..	..	8 151	8 867	9 557	..
		281	Structural metal prod., tanks, reservoirs, generators	..	..	..	..	2 939	3 147	3 414	..
		289	Other fabricated metal products & service activities	..	..	..	..	5 212	5 719	6 143	..
	29		Machinery and equipment, nec	..	..	..	..	14 328	15 212	16 724	..
		291	General purpose machinery	..	..	..	..	8 115	8 849	9 969	..
		292	Special purpose machinery	..	..	..	..	4 724	4 884	5 260	..
		293	Domestic appliances, nec	..	..	..	..	1 488	1 479	1 495	..
	30		Office, accounting and computing machinery	..	..	..	..	536	586	551	..
	31		Electrical machinery and apparatus, nec	..	..	..	..	2 921	3 015	3 332	..
		311	Electric motors, generators and transformers	..	..	..	..	617	706	936	..
		312	Electricity distribution and control apparatus	..	..	..	..	893	882	835	..
		313	Insulated wire and cable	..	..	..	..	319	296	320	..
		314	Accumulators, primary cells and primary batteries	..	..	..	..	61	56	58	..
		315	Electric lamps and lighting equipment	..	..	..	..	385	473	524	..
		319	Other electrical equipment, nec	..	..	..	..	645	603	659	..
	32		Radio, TV, communication equip. & apparatus	..	..	..	..	2 304	2 263	2 408	..
		321	Electronic valves, tubes & other electronic compon.	..	..	..	..	647	560	592	..
		322	TV, radio transmitters & appar. for line teleph., telegr.	..	..	..	..	744	736	717	..
		323	TV, radio receivers and associated goods	..	..	..	..	914	967	1 098	..
	33		Medical, precision, optical instr.; watches, clocks	..	..	..	..	3 154	3 223	3 569	..
		331	Medical equip.; precision instruments and appliances	..	..	..	..	2 898	2 924	3 237	..
		332	Optical instruments and photographic equipment	..	..	..	..	255	297	330	..
		333	Watches and clocks	..	..	..	..	2	2	2	..
	34		Motor vehicles, trailers, and semi-trailers	..	..	..	..	1 045	1 303	1 543	..
	35		Other transport equipment	..	..	..	..	3 300	3 466	3 558	..
		351	Building and repairing of ships and boats	..	..	..	..	2 781	2 940	2 983	..
		352	Railway, tramway locomotives and rolling stock	..	..	..	..	217	180	165	..
		353	Aircraft and spacecraft	..	..	..	..	116	138	166	..
		359	Transport equipment, nec	..	..	..	..	186	208	243	..
	36		Furniture; manufacturing, nec	..	..	..	..	5 313	5 846	6 099	..
		361	Furniture	..	..	..	..	3 919	4 420	4 584	..
		369	Manufacturing, nec	..	..	..	..	1 394	1 427	1 514	..
	37		Recycling	..	..	..	..	90	77	86	..
E	40-41		Electricity, gas and water supply	..	..	..	..	4 236	4 430	4 536	..
	40		Electricity, gas, steam and hot water supply	..	..	..	..	3 805	3 926	4 047	..
		401	Production, collection and distribution of electricity	..	..	..	..	2 840	2 876	3 041	..
	41	410	Collection, purification, distribution of water	..	..	..	..	431	504	489	..
F	45		Construction	..	..	..	..	24 120	26 586	28 619	..
G	50-52		Wholesale and retail trade; repairs etc	..	..	..	..	57 254	60 165	64 279	..
H	55		Hotels and restaurants	..	..	..	..	6 677	7 020	7 416	..
I	60-64		Transport, storage and communications	..	..	..	..	33 825	35 123	36 025	..
J	65-67		Financial intermediation	..	..	..	..	21 595	21 337	21 746	..
K	70-74		Real estate, renting and business activities	..	..	..	..	36 149	39 355	40 990	..
L-Q	75-99		Public admin.; education; health; other services	..	..	..	..	163 890	167 965	172 797	..
A-Q	01-99		Grand total	..	..	..	..	446 728	465 995	486 315	..

Note: ISIC 2429 includes 2430; 2691 includes 2692.

Table FN.1 PRODUCTION - PRODUCTION

Millions de Mk (Prix courants) — CITI révision 3

1989	1990	1991	1992	1993	1994	1995	1996			CITI	
..	..	..	..	..	..	..		Agriculture, chasse et sylviculture	A	01-02	
..	..	..	..	..	..	..		Pêche	B	05	
..	..	..	..	..	..	4 115	4 286	**Activités extractives**	C	10-14	
..	..	..	..	..	..	1 364	1 406	Extraction de charbon, de lignite et de tourbe		10	
..	..	..	..	..	..	..	..	Extraction de pétrole brut et de gaz naturel		11	
..	..	..	..	..	..	560	580	Extraction de minerais métalliques		13	
..	..	..	..	..	..	2 190	2 299	Autres activités extractives		14	
..	..	..	..	..	..	388 708	395 249	**Activités de fabrication**	D	15-37	
..	..	..	..	..	..	46 314	48 714	**Produits alimentaires et boissons**		15	
..	..	..	..	..	..	4 124	4 542	Boissons			155
..	..	..	..	..	..	914	687	**Produits à base de tabac**		16	160
..	..	..	..	..	..	3 512	3 602	**Textiles**		17	
..	..	..	..	..	..	815	709	Filature, tissage et achèvement des textiles			171
..	..	..	..	..	..	2 091	2 257	Autres articles textiles			172
..	..	..	..	..	..	606	635	Etoffes et articles de bonneterie			173
..	..	..	..	..	..	3 177	3 093	**Habillement; préparation, teinture des fourrures**		18	
..	..	..	..	..	..	3 023	2 939	Articles d'habillement autres qu'en fourrure			181
..	..	..	..	..	..	153	154	Préparation, teinture des fourrures; art. en fourrure			182
..	..	..	..	..	..	1 363	1 317	**Travail des cuirs; articles en cuir; chaussures**		19	
..	..	..	..	..	..	453	420	Apprêt et tannage des cuirs et articles en cuirs			191
..	..	..	..	..	..	910	897	Chaussures			192
..	..	..	..	..	..	21 470	20 486	**Bois et articles en bois et liège (sauf meubles)**		20	
..	..	..	..	..	..	12 488	11 357	Sciage et rabotage du bois			201
..	..	..	..	..	..	8 982	9 129	Articles en bois, liège, vannerie, sparterie			202
..	..	..	..	..	..	77 931	67 236	**Papier et carton; articles en papier et en carton**		21	
..	..	..	..	..	..	19 572	20 458	**Edition, imprimerie et reproduction**		22	
..	..	..	..	..	..	10 507	11 048	Edition			221
..	..	..	..	..	..	8 981	9 347	Imprimerie et activités annexes			222
..	..	..	..	..	..	83	64	Reproduction de supports enregistrés			223
..	..	..	..	..	..	11 321	14 137	**Cokéfaction; prod. pétroliers; comb. nucléaires**		23	
..	..	..	..	..	..	23 042	23 356	**Produits chimiques**		24	
..	..	..	..	..	..	15 649	15 761	Produits chimiques de base			241
..	..	..	..	..	..	..	..	Autres produits chimiques			242
..	..	..	..	..	..	..	..	Fibres synthétiques ou artificielles			243
..	..	..	..	..	..	8 912	9 477	**Articles en caoutchouc et en matières plastiques**		25	
..	..	..	..	..	..	1 663	1 555	Articles en caoutchouc			251
..	..	..	..	..	..	7 249	7 922	Articles en matières plastiques			252
..	..	..	..	..	..	7 999	8 769	**Autres produits minéraux non métalliques**		26	
..	..	..	..	..	..	1 949	2 102	Verre et articles en verre			261
..	..	..	..	..	..	..	..	Produits minéraux non métalliques, nca			269
..	..	..	..	..	..	31 102	30 451	**Produits métallurgiques de base**		27	
..	..	..	..	..	..	20 286	18 505	Sidérurgie et première transformation de l'acier			271
..	..	..	..	..	..	9 354	10 629	Métallurgie; métaux précieux et non ferreux			272
..	..	..	..	..	..	1 462	1 317	Fonderie			273
..	..	..	..	..	..	17 156	17 677	**Ouvrages en métaux, sauf machines et matériel**		28	
..	..	..	..	..	..	9 851	9 808	Constr. et menuiserie métal.; réservoirs; générateurs			281
..	..	..	..	..	..	7 305	7 870	Autres ouvrages en métaux			289
..	..	..	..	..	..	41 253	47 634	**Machines et matériel, nca**		29	
..	..	..	..	..	..	17 702	19 923	Machines d'usage général			291
..	..	..	..	..	..	22 523	26 611	Machines d'usage spécifique			292
..	..	..	..	..	..	1 029	1 100	Appareils domestiques, nca			293
..	..	..	..	..	..	5 598	5 134	**Mach. de bureau, comptables, matériel inform.**		30	
..	..	..	..	..	..	11 748	12 980	**Machines et appareils électriques, nca**		31	
..	..	..	..	..	..	5 143	6 062	Moteurs, génératrices et transformateurs électriques			311
..	..	..	..	..	..	2 755	2 859	Matériel électrique de distribution et de commande			312
..	..	..	..	..	..	1 685	1 891	Fils et câbles électriques isolés			313
..	..	..	..	..	..	65	15	Accumulateurs, piles électriques			314
..	..	..	..	..	..	847	873	Lampes électriques et appareils d'éclairage			315
..	..	..	..	..	..	1 252	1 280	Autres matériels électriques, nca			319
..	..	..	..	..	..	28 347	32 308	**Equip. et appar. de radio, TV, communication**		32	
..	..	..	..	..	..	2 186	2 577	Tubes et valves électroniques; autres composants			321
..	..	..	..	..	..	24 907	28 636	Emetteurs radio et TV; app. téléphonie, télégraphie			322
..	..	..	..	..	..	1 253	1 094	Récepteurs radio et TV et articles associés			323
..	..	..	..	..	..	5 494	6 143	**Instruments médicaux, de précision, d'optique**		33	
..	..	..	..	..	..	5 341	5 970	Appareils médicaux et de précision			331
..	..	..	..	..	..	146	164	Instruments d'optique ; matériel photographique			332
..	..	..	..	..	..	7	9	Horlogerie			333
..	..	..	..	..	..	4 099	4 076	**Véhicules automobiles et nemorques**		34	
..	..	..	..	..	..	11 077	10 418	**Autres matériels de transport**		35	
..	..	..	..	..	..	8 809	8 014	Construction et réparation de navires			351
..	..	..	..	..	..	796	935	Construction de matériel ferroviaire roulant			352
..	..	..	..	..	..	1 170	1 192	Construction aéronautique et spatiale			353
..	..	..	..	..	..	301	277	Autres équipements de transport			359
..	..	..	..	..	..	6 777	6 594	**Meubles; activités de fabrication, nca**		36	
..	..	..	..	..	..	4 755	4 558	Meubles			361
..	..	..	..	..	..	2 022	2 036	Activités de fabrication, nca			369
..	..	..	..	..	..	538	502	**Récupération**		37	
..	..	..	..	..	..	29 556	35 544	**Production et distrib. d'électricité, de gaz, d'eau**	E	40-41	
..	..	..	..	..	..	28 133	34 154	**Electricité, gaz, vapeur et eau chaude**		40	
..	..	..	..	..	..	27 346	32 888	Production, collecte et distribution d'électricité			401
..	..	..	..	..	..	1 423	1 390	**Captage, épuration et distribution d'eau**		41	410
..	..	..	..	..	..	51 448	50 487	**Construction**	F	45	
..	..	..	..	..	..	..	..	**Commerce de gros et de détail; réparation**	G	50-52	
..	..	..	..	..	..	..	..	**Hôtels et restaurants**	H	55	
..	..	..	..	..	..	..	..	**Transports, entreposage et communications**	I	60-64	
..	..	..	..	..	..	..	..	**Intermédiation financière**	J	65-67	
..	..	..	..	..	..	..	..	**Immobilier, locations, services aux entreprises**	K	70-74	
..	..	..	..	..	..	..	..	**Admin. publique; éducation; santé; autres**	L-Q	75-99	
..	..	..	..	..	..	..	..	**Grand total**	A-Q	01-99	

Note: Unless given separately, ISIC 1711 excludes Nace 17.13, 17.14, 17.16, 17.17, 17.22 and 17.23; ISIC 2230 excludes Nace 22.32 and 22.32; ISIC 2429 excludes Nace 24.63 and 24.65; ISIC 2710 excludes Nace 27.31 and 27.34; ISIC 272 excludes Nace 27.41 and 27.43; ISIC 1514 excludes Nace 15.41 and 15.42. ISIC 2690 is not available.

Statistiques des Structures Industrielles
OCDE, © 1998

171

FINLAND

Table FN.2 VALUE ADDED - VALEUR AJOUTÉE

Millions of Mk (Current Prices)

ISIC revision 3		Description	1989	1990	1991	1992	1993	1994	1995	1996
A	01-02	Agriculture, hunting and forestry	..	..	..	..	..	..	..	..
B	05	Fishing	..	..	..	..	..	..	..	..
C	10-14	Mining and quarrying	..	..	..	..	..	..	..	..
	10	Mining of coal and lignite; extraction of peat	..	..	..	..	..	..	1 599	1 562
	11	Crude petroleum & natural gas; related service activ.	..	..	..	..	..	..	576	580
	13	Mining of metal ores	..	..	..	..	..	..	175	170
	14	Other mining and quarrying	..	..	..	..	..	..	848	812
D	15-37	Total manufacturing	..	..	..	..	..	..	121 236	119 390
	15	Food products and beverages	..	..	..	..	..	..	10 607	11 347
	155	Beverages	..	..	..	..	..	..	1 115	1 510
	16 / 160	Tobacco products	..	..	..	..	..	..	224	215
	17	Textiles	..	..	..	..	..	..	1 373	1 477
	171	Spinning, weaving and finishing of textiles	..	..	..	..	..	..	231	238
	172	Other textiles	..	..	..	..	..	..	867	938
	173	Knitted and crocheted fabrics and articles	..	..	..	..	..	..	275	300
	18	Wearing apparel dressing & dyeing of fur	..	..	..	..	..	..	1 318	1 266
	181	Wearing apparel, except fur apparel	..	..	..	..	..	..	1 272	1 207
	182	Dressing and dyeing of fur; articles of fur	..	..	..	..	..	..	46	59
	19	Tanning, dressing leather; leather artic.; footwear	..	..	..	..	..	..	542	499
	191	Tanning, dressing leather; manuf. of leather articles	..	..	..	..	..	..	166	145
	192	Footwear	..	..	..	..	..	..	376	354
	20	Wood and cork products, ex. furniture	..	..	..	..	..	..	6 234	5 389
	201	Sawmilling and planing of wood	..	..	..	..	..	..	3 057	2 108
	202	Products of wood, cork, straw & plaiting material	..	..	..	..	..	..	3 177	3 282
	21	Paper and paper products	..	..	..	..	..	..	25 311	18 708
	22	Publishing, printing & reprod. of recorded media	..	..	..	..	..	..	7 793	8 140
	221	Publishing	..	..	..	..	..	..	3 820	4 044
	222	Printing and related service activities	..	..	..	..	..	..	3 941	4 073
	223	Reproduction of recorded media	..	..	..	..	..	..	32	23
	23	Coke, refined petroleum products & nuclear fuel	..	..	..	..	..	..	1 396	1 726
	24	Chemicals and chemical products	..	..	..	..	..	..	8 002	7 783
	241	Basic chemicals	..	..	..	..	..	..	4 958	4 652
	242	Other chemical products	..	..	..	..	..	..	..	..
	243	Man-made fibres	..	..	..	..	..	..	..	..
	25	Rubber and plastic products	..	..	..	..	..	..	3 325	3 890
	251	Rubber products	..	..	..	..	..	..	706	715
	252	Plastic products	..	..	..	..	..	..	2 619	3 176
	26	Other non-metallic mineral products	..	..	..	..	..	..	3 295	3 449
	261	Glass and glass products	..	..	..	..	..	..	840	873
	269	Non-metallic mineral products, nec	..	..	..	..	..	..	..	..
	27	Basic metals	..	..	..	..	..	..	7 483	6 153
	271	Basic iron and steel	..	..	..	..	..	..	5 743	4 166
	272	Basic precious and non-ferrous metals	..	..	..	..	..	..	1 019	1 319
	273	Casting of metals	..	..	..	..	..	..	721	668
	28	Fabricated metal products, ex. machin. & equip.	..	..	..	..	..	..	6 243	6 922
	281	Structural metal prod., tanks, reservoirs, generators	..	..	..	..	..	..	3 103	3 438
	289	Other fabricated metal products & service activities	..	..	..	..	..	..	3 141	3 485
	29	Machinery and equipment, nec	..	..	..	..	..	..	14 344	16 486
	291	General purpose machinery	..	..	..	..	..	..	6 364	7 089
	292	Special purpose machinery	..	..	..	..	..	..	7 674	9 039
	293	Domestic appliances, nec	..	..	..	..	..	..	306	358
	30	Office, accounting and computing machinery	..	..	..	..	..	..	732	669
	31	Electrical machinery and apparatus, nec	..	..	..	..	..	..	4 089	4 655
	311	Electric motors, generators and transformers	..	..	..	..	..	..	1 676	2 095
	312	Electricity distribution and control apparatus	..	..	..	..	..	..	1 090	1 127
	313	Insulated wire and cable	..	..	..	..	..	..	458	541
	314	Accumulators, primary cells and primary batteries	..	..	..	..	..	..	26	5
	315	Electric lamps and lighting equipment	..	..	..	..	..	..	323	341
	319	Other electrical equipment, nec	..	..	..	..	..	..	516	547
	32	Radio, TV, communication equip. & apparatus	..	..	..	..	..	..	8 450	9 758
	321	Electronic valves, tubes & other electronic compon.	..	..	..	..	..	..	822	925
	322	TV, radio transmitters & appar. for line teleph., telegr.	..	..	..	..	..	..	7 374	8 597
	323	TV, radio receivers and associated goods	..	..	..	..	..	..	255	236
	33	Medical, precision, optical instr.; watches, clocks	..	..	..	..	..	..	2 300	2 632
	331	Medical equip.; precision instruments and appliances	..	..	..	..	..	..	2 227	2 550
	332	Optical instruments and photographic equipment	..	..	..	..	..	..	70	78
	333	Watches and clocks	..	..	..	..	..	..	3	4
	34	Motor vehicles, trailers, and semi-trailers	..	..	..	..	..	..	1 461	1 555
	35	Other transport equipment	..	..	..	..	..	..	3 713	3 801
	351	Building and repairing of ships and boats	..	..	..	..	..	..	2 662	2 643
	352	Railway, tramway locomotives and rolling stock	..	..	..	..	..	..	259	339
	353	Aircraft and spacecraft	..	..	..	..	..	..	670	709
	359	Transport equipment, nec	..	..	..	..	..	..	123	111
	36	Furniture; manufacturing, nec	..	..	..	..	..	..	2 889	2 795
	361	Furniture	..	..	..	..	..	..	2 016	1 911
	369	Manufacturing, nec	..	..	..	..	..	..	873	884
	37	Recycling	..	..	..	..	..	..	111	76
E	40-41	Electricity, gas and water supply	..	..	..	..	..	..	11 966	12 912
	40	Electricity, gas, steam and hot water supply	..	..	..	..	..	..	10 948	11 913
	401	Production, collection and distribution of electricity	..	..	..	..	..	..	10 594	11 469
	41 / 410	Collection, purification, distribution of water	..	..	..	..	..	..	1 018	999
F	45	Construction	..	..	..	..	..	..	16 939	17 272
G	50-52	Wholesale and retail trade; repairs etc	..	..	..	..	..	..	..	..
H	55	Hotels and restaurants	..	..	..	..	..	..	..	..
I	60-64	Transport, storage and communications	..	..	..	..	..	..	..	..
J	65-67	Financial intermediation	..	..	..	..	..	..	..	..
K	70-74	Real estate, renting and business activities	..	..	..	..	..	..	..	..
L-Q	75-99	Public admin.; education; health; other services	..	..	..	..	..	..	..	..
A-Q	01-99	Grand total	..	..	..	..	..	..	..	..

Note: Unless given separately, ISIC 1711 excludes Nace 17.13, 17.14, 17.16, 17.17, 17.22 and 17.23; ISIC 2230 excludes Nace 22.32 and 22.32; ISIC 2429 excludes Nace 24.63 and 24.65; ISIC 2710 excludes Nace 27.31 and 27.34; ISIC 272 excludes Nace 27.41 and 27.43; ISIC 1514 excludes Nace 15.41 and 15.42. ISIC 2690 is not available.

OECD / OCDE Industrial Structure Statistics
OECD, © 1998

Table FN.3 **INVESTISSEMENT - INVESTMENT**

Millions de Mk (Prix courants)

1989	1990	1991	1992	1993	1994	1995	1996			CITI révision 3	
..	..	..	..	..	..	..	..	**Agriculture, chasse et sylviculture**	A	01-02	
..	..	..	..	..	..	..	..	**Pêche**	B	05	
..	..	..	..	..	..	470	400	**Activités extractives**	C	10-14	
..	..	..	..	..	..	242	176	Extraction de charbon, de lignite et de tourbe		10	
..	..	..	..	..	..	..	..	Extraction de pétrole brut et de gaz naturel		11	
..	..	..	..	..	..	57	62	Extraction de minerais métalliques		13	
..	..	..	..	..	..	171	162	Autres activités extractives		14	
..	..	..	..	..	..	20 649	23 426	**Activités de fabrication**	D	15-37	
..	..	..	..	..	..	2 022	1 963	**Produits alimentaires et boissons**		15	
..	..	..	..	..	..	329	295	Boissons			155
..	..	..	..	..	..	95	64	**Produits à base de tabac**		16	160
..	..	..	..	..	..	265	132	**Textiles**		17	
..	..	..	..	..	..	21	19	Filature, tissage et achèvement des textiles			171
..	..	..	..	..	..	218	93	Autres articles textiles			172
..	..	..	..	..	..	26	20	Etoffes et articles de bonneterie			173
..	..	..	..	..	..	71	86	**Habillement; préparation, teinture des fourrures**		18	
..	..	..	..	..	..	69	82	Articles d'habillement autres qu'en fourrure			181
..	..	..	..	..	..	2	4	Préparation, teinture des fourrures; art. en fourrure			182
..	..	..	..	..	..	47	50	**Travail des cuirs; articles en cuir; chaussures**		19	
..	..	..	..	..	..	22	17	Apprêt et tannage des cuirs et articles en cuirs			191
..	..	..	..	..	..	26	33	Chaussures			192
..	..	..	..	..	..	1 374	931	**Bois et articles en bois et liège (sauf meubles)**		20	
..	..	..	..	..	..	817	568	Sciage et rabotage du bois			201
..	..	..	..	..	..	556	363	Articles en bois, liège, vannerie, sparterie			202
..	..	..	..	..	..	4 156	9 015	**Papier et carton; articles en papier et en carton**		21	
..	..	..	..	..	..	980	897	**Edition, imprimerie et reproduction**		22	
..	..	..	..	..	..	300	251	Edition			221
..	..	..	..	..	..	673	640	Imprimerie et activités annexes			222
..	..	..	..	..	..	6	5	Reproduction de supports enregistrés			223
..	..	..	..	..	..	244	272	**Cokéfaction; prod. pétroliers; comb. nucléaires**		23	
..	..	..	..	..	..	2 225	1 231	**Produits chimiques**		24	
..	..	..	..	..	..	1 829	857	Produits chimiques de base			241
..	..	..	..	..	..	..	..	Autres produits chimiques			242
..	..	..	..	..	..	..	..	Fibres synthétiques ou artificielles			243
..	..	..	..	..	..	634	618	**Articles en caoutchouc et en matières plastiques**		25	
..	..	..	..	..	..	85	137	Articles en caoutchouc			251
..	..	..	..	..	..	548	481	Articles en matières plastiques			252
..	..	..	..	..	..	490	441	**Autres produits minéraux non métalliques**		26	
..	..	..	..	..	..	188	185	Verre et articles en verre			261
..	..	..	..	..	..	..	..	Produits minéraux non métalliques, nca			269
..	..	..	..	..	..	2 165	2 401	**Produits métallurgiques de base**		27	
..	..	..	..	..	..	1 045	1 693	Sidérurgie et première transformation de l'acier			271
..	..	..	..	..	..	1 025	611	Métallurgie; métaux précieux et non ferreux			272
..	..	..	..	..	..	95	97	Fonderie			273
..	..	..	..	..	..	775	822	**Ouvrages en métaux, sauf machines et matériel**		28	
..	..	..	..	..	..	293	327	Constr. et menuiserie métal.; réservoirs; générateurs			281
..	..	..	..	..	..	482	494	Autres ouvrages en métaux			289
..	..	..	..	..	..	1 672	1 811	**Machines et matériel, nca**		29	
..	..	..	..	..	..	865	838	Machines d'usage général			291
..	..	..	..	..	..	770	944	Machines d'usage spécifique			292
..	..	..	..	..	..	37	29	Appareils domestiques, nca			293
..	..	..	..	..	..	116	68	**Mach. de bureau, comptables, matériel inform.**		30	
..	..	..	..	..	..	535	505	**Machines et appareils électriques, nca**		31	
..	..	..	..	..	..	229	214	Moteurs, génératrices et transformateurs électriques			311
..	..	..	..	..	..	107	122	Matériel électrique de distribution et de commande			312
..	..	..	..	..	..	59	63	Fils et câbles électriques isolés			313
..	..	..	..	..	..	1	0	Accumulateurs, piles électriques			314
..	..	..	..	..	..	59	30	Lampes électriques et appareils d'éclairage			315
..	..	..	..	..	..	80	75	Autres matériels électriques, nca			319
..	..	..	..	..	..	1 796	1 123	**Equip. et appar. de radio, TV, communication**		32	
..	..	..	..	..	..	259	174	Tubes et valves électroniques; autres composants			321
..	..	..	..	..	..	1 459	921	Emetteurs radio et TV; app. téléphonie, télégraphie			322
..	..	..	..	..	..	77	28	Récepteurs radio et TV et articles associés			323
..	..	..	..	..	..	167	183	**Instruments médicaux, de précision, d'optique**		33	
..	..	..	..	..	..	161	174	Appareils médicaux et de précision			331
..	..	..	..	..	..	6	9	Instruments d'optique ; matériel photographique			332
..	..	..	..	..	..	0	0	Horlogerie			333
..	..	..	..	..	..	162	213	**Véhicules automobiles et nemorques**		34	
..	..	..	..	..	..	374	331	**Autres matériels de transport**		35	
..	..	..	..	..	..	209	151	Construction et réparation de navires			351
..	..	..	..	..	..	9	20	Construction de matériel ferroviaire roulant			352
..	..	..	..	..	..	145	152	Construction aéronautique et spatiale			353
..	..	..	..	..	..	11	8	Autres équipements de transport			359
..	..	..	..	..	..	261	234	**Meubles; activités de fabrication, nca**		36	
..	..	..	..	..	..	174	169	Meubles			361
..	..	..	..	..	..	87	65	Activités de fabrication, nca			369
..	..	..	..	..	..	26	36	**Récupération**		37	
..	..	..	..	..	..	4 609	4 085	**Production et distrib. d'électricité, de gaz, d'eau**	E	40-41	
..	..	..	..	..	..	4 192	3 692	**Electricité, gaz, vapeur et eau chaude**		40	
..	..	..	..	..	..	4 058	3 450	Production, collecte et distribution d'électricité			401
..	..	..	..	..	..	418	393	**Captage, épuration et distribution d'eau**		41	410
..	..	..	..	..	..	2 327	1 969	**Construction**	F	45	
..	..	..	..	..	..	..	..	**Commerce de gros et de détail; réparation**	G	50-52	
..	..	..	..	..	..	..	..	**Hôtels et restaurants**	H	55	
..	..	..	..	..	..	..	..	**Transports, entreposage et communications**	I	60-64	
..	..	..	..	..	..	..	..	**Intermédiation financière**	J	65-67	
..	..	..	..	..	..	..	..	**Immobilier, locations, services aux entreprises**	K	70-74	
..	..	..	..	..	..	..	..	**Admin. publique; éducation; santé; autres**	L-Q	75-99	
..	..	..	..	..	..	..	..	**Grand total**	A-Q	01-99	

Note: Unless given separately, ISIC 1711 excludes Nace 17.13, 17.14, 17.16, 17.17, 17.22 and 17.23; ISIC 2230 excludes Nace 22.32 and 22.32; ISIC 2429 excludes Nace 24.63 and 24.65; ISIC 2710 excludes Nace 27.31 and 27.34; ISIC 272 excludes Nace 27.41 and 27.43; ISIC 1514 excludes Nace 15.41 and 15.42. ISIC 2690 is not available.

Statistiques des Structures Industrielles
OCDE, © 1998

Table FN.4 **INVESTMENT IN MACHINERY AND EQUIPMENT - DÉPENSES EN MACHINES ET ÉQUIPEMENT**

Millions of Mk (Current Prices)

ISIC revision 3				1989	1990	1991	1992	1993	1994	1995	1996
A	01-02		Agriculture, hunting and forestry	..	..	..	..	..	..	..	..
B	05		Fishing	..	..	..	..	..	..	..	..
C	10-14		Mining and quarrying	..	..	..	..	..	..	364	334
	10		Mining of coal and lignite; extraction of peat	..	..	..	..	..	..	183	138
	11		Crude petroleum & natural gas; related service activ.	..	..	..	..	..	..	..	..
	13		Mining of metal ores	..	..	..	..	..	..	23	52
	14		Other mining and quarrying	..	..	..	..	..	..	157	144
D	15-37		Total manufacturing	..	..	..	..	..	..	16 333	18 765
	15		Food products and beverages	..	..	..	..	..	..	1 543	1 465
		155	Beverages	..	..	..	..	..	..	242	223
	16	160	Tobacco products	..	..	..	..	..	..	73	22
	17		Textiles	..	..	..	..	..	..	210	125
		171	Spinning, weaving and finishing of textiles	..	..	..	..	..	..	20	19
		172	Other textiles	..	..	..	..	..	..	165	86
		173	Knitted and crocheted fabrics and articles	..	..	..	..	..	..	25	20
	18		Wearing apparel dressing & dyeing of fur	..	..	..	..	..	..	54	59
		181	Wearing apparel, except fur apparel	..	..	..	..	..	..	52	56
		182	Dressing and dyeing of fur; articles of fur	..	..	..	..	..	..	2	4
	19		Tanning, dressing leather; leather artic.; footwear	..	..	..	..	..	..	39	46
		191	Tanning, dressing leather; manuf. of leather articles	..	..	..	..	..	..	18	15
		192	Footwear	..	..	..	..	..	..	21	31
	20		Wood and cork products, ex. furniture	..	..	..	..	..	..	1 101	737
		201	Sawmilling and planing of wood	..	..	..	..	..	..	646	416
		202	Products of wood, cork, straw & plaiting material	..	..	..	..	..	..	455	321
	21		Paper and paper products	..	..	..	..	..	..	3 208	7 499
	22		Publishing, printing & reprod. of recorded media	..	..	..	..	..	..	847	792
		221	Publishing	..	..	..	..	..	..	213	211
		222	Printing and related service activities	..	..	..	..	..	..	627	576
		223	Reproduction of recorded media	..	..	..	..	..	..	6	5
	23		Coke, refined petroleum products & nuclear fuel	..	..	..	..	..	..	196	195
	24		Chemicals and chemical products	..	..	..	..	..	..	1 762	971
		241	Basic chemicals	..	..	..	..	..	..	1 478	698
		242	Other chemical products	..	..	..	..	..	..	..	..
		243	Man-made fibres	..	..	..	..	..	..	..	..
	25		Rubber and plastic products	..	..	..	..	..	..	534	536
		251	Rubber products	..	..	..	..	..	..	82	106
		252	Plastic products	..	..	..	..	..	..	451	430
	26		Other non-metallic mineral products	..	..	..	..	..	..	387	344
		261	Glass and glass products	..	..	..	..	..	..	151	154
		269	Non-metallic mineral products, nec	..	..	..	..	..	..	..	..
	27		Basic metals	..	..	..	..	..	..	1 762	1 686
		271	Basic iron and steel	..	..	..	..	..	..	897	1 241
		272	Basic precious and non-ferrous metals	..	..	..	..	..	..	785	384
		273	Casting of metals	..	..	..	..	..	..	80	61
	28		Fabricated metal products, ex. machin. & equip.	..	..	..	..	..	..	649	710
		281	Structural metal prod., tanks, reservoirs, generators	..	..	..	..	..	..	254	282
		289	Other fabricated metal products & service activities	..	..	..	..	..	..	394	428
	29		Machinery and equipment, nec	..	..	..	..	..	..	1 139	1 374
		291	General purpose machinery	..	..	..	..	..	..	596	624
		292	Special purpose machinery	..	..	..	..	..	..	511	725
		293	Domestic appliances, nec	..	..	..	..	..	..	32	25
	30		Office, accounting and computing machinery	..	..	..	..	..	..	95	64
	31		Electrical machinery and apparatus, nec	..	..	..	..	..	..	443	428
		311	Electric motors, generators and transformers	..	..	..	..	..	..	210	176
		312	Electricity distribution and control apparatus	..	..	..	..	..	..	100	110
		313	Insulated wire and cable	..	..	..	..	..	..	37	58
		314	Accumulators, primary cells and primary batteries	..	..	..	..	..	..	1	0
		315	Electric lamps and lighting equipment	..	..	..	..	..	..	30	21
		319	Other electrical equipment, nec	..	..	..	..	..	..	66	62
	32		Radio, TV, communication equip. & apparatus	..	..	..	..	..	..	1 510	873
		321	Electronic valves, tubes & other electronic compon.	..	..	..	..	..	..	211	152
		322	TV, radio transmitters & appar. for line teleph., telegr.	..	..	..	..	..	..	1 230	693
		323	TV, radio receivers and associated goods	..	..	..	..	..	..	69	27
	33		Medical, precision, optical instr.; watches, clocks	..	..	..	..	..	..	155	168
		331	Medical equip.; precision instruments and appliances	..	..	..	..	..	..	150	159
		332	Optical instruments and photographic equipment	..	..	..	..	..	..	6	9
		333	Watches and clocks	..	..	..	..	..	..	0	0
	34		Motor vehicles, trailers, and semi-trailers	..	..	..	..	..	..	114	177
	35		Other transport equipment	..	..	..	..	..	..	282	247
		351	Building and repairing of ships and boats	..	..	..	..	..	..	128	92
		352	Railway, tramway locomotives and rolling stock	..	..	..	..	..	..	8	15
		353	Aircraft and spacecraft	..	..	..	..	..	..	136	135
		359	Transport equipment, nec	..	..	..	..	..	..	11	6
	36		Furniture; manufacturing, nec	..	..	..	..	..	..	210	215
		361	Furniture	..	..	..	..	..	..	137	157
		369	Manufacturing, nec	..	..	..	..	..	..	73	59
	37		Recycling	..	..	..	..	..	..	22	32
E	40-41		Electricity, gas and water supply	..	..	..	..	..	..	1 773	1 689
	40		Electricity, gas, steam and hot water supply	..	..	..	..	..	..	1 731	1 639
		401	Production, collection and distribution of electricity	..	..	..	..	..	..	1 680	1 440
	41	410	Collection, purification, distribution of water	..	..	..	..	..	..	42	50
F	45		Construction	..	..	..	..	..	..	1 947	1 869
G	50-52		Wholesale and retail trade; repairs etc	..	..	..	..	..	..	..	..
H	55		Hotels and restaurants	..	..	..	..	..	..	..	..
I	60-64		Transport, storage and communications	..	..	..	..	..	..	..	..
J	65-67		Financial intermediation	..	..	..	..	..	..	..	..
K	70-74		Real estate, renting and business activities	..	..	..	..	..	..	..	..
L-Q	75-99		Public admin.; education; health; other services	..	..	..	..	..	..	..	..
A-Q	01-99		Grand total	..	..	..	..	..	..	..	..

Note: Unless given separately, ISIC 1711 excludes Nace 17.13, 17.14, 17.16, 17.17, 17.22 and 17.23; ISIC 2230 excludes Nace 22.32 and 22.32; ISIC 2429 excludes Nace 24.63 and 24.65; ISIC 2710 excludes Nace 27.31 and 27.34; ISIC 272 excludes Nace 27.41 and 27.43; ISIC 1514 excludes Nace 15.41 and 15.42. ISIC 2690 is not available.

Table FN.5 ETABLISSEMENTS - ESTABLISHMENTS

Unités

1989	1990	1991	1992	1993	1994	1995	1996			CITI révision 3	
..	..	..	..	..	..	..	..	**Agriculture, chasse et sylviculture**	A	01-02	
..	..	..	..	..	..	..	..	**Pêche**	B	05	
..	..	..	..	..	..	1 250	1 090	**Activités extractives**	C	10-14	
..	..	..	..	..	..	776	663	Extraction de charbon, de lignite et de tourbe		10	
..	..	..	..	..	..	..	..	Extraction de pétrole brut et de gaz naturel		11	
..	..	..	..	..	..	8	9	Extraction de minerais métalliques		13	
..	..	..	..	..	..	466	418	Autres activités extractives		14	
..	..	..	..	..	..	25 036	23 093	**Activités de fabrication**	D	15-37	
..	..	..	..	..	..	2 031	1 810	**Produits alimentaires et boissons**		15	
..	..	..	..	..	..	65	67	Boissons			155
..	..	..	..	..	..	5	3	**Produits à base de tabac**		16	160
..	..	..	..	..	..	991	952	**Textiles**		17	
..	..	..	..	..	..	176	170	Filature, tissage et achèvement des textiles			171
..	..	..	..	..	..	646	622	Autres articles textiles			172
..	..	..	..	..	..	169	160	Etoffes et articles de bonneterie			173
..	..	..	..	..	..	1 332	1 216	**Habillement; préparation, teinture des fourrures**		18	
..	..	..	..	..	..	1 186	1 096	Articles d'habillement autres qu'en fourrure			181
..	..	..	..	..	..	146	120	Préparation, teinture des fourrures; art. en fourrure			182
..	..	..	..	..	..	381	350	**Travail des cuirs; articles en cuir; chaussures**		19	
..	..	..	..	..	..	283	258	Apprêt et tannage des cuirs et articles en cuirs			191
..	..	..	..	..	..	98	92	Chaussures			192
..	..	..	..	..	..	2 922	2 636	**Bois et articles en bois et liège (sauf meubles)**		20	
..	..	..	..	..	..	1 233	1 057	Sciage et rabotage du bois			201
..	..	..	..	..	..	1 689	1 579	Articles en bois, liège, vannerie, sparterie			202
..	..	..	..	..	..	331	286	**Papier et carton; articles en papier et en carton**		21	
..	..	..	..	..	..	2 627	2 387	**Edition, imprimerie et reproduction**		22	
..	..	..	..	..	..	1 151	1 036	Edition			221
..	..	..	..	..	..	1 427	1 313	Imprimerie et activités annexes			222
..	..	..	..	..	..	49	38	Reproduction de supports enregistrés			223
..	..	..	..	..	..	14	19	**Cokéfaction; prod. pétroliers; comb. nucléaires**		23	
..	..	..	..	..	..	347	345	**Produits chimiques**		24	
..	..	..	..	..	..	153	151	Produits chimiques de base			241
..	..	..	..	..	..	192	192	Autres produits chimiques			242
..	..	..	..	..	..	2	2	Fibres synthétiques ou artificielles			243
..	..	..	..	..	..	655	621	**Articles en caoutchouc et en matières plastiques**		25	
..	..	..	..	..	..	73	55	Articles en caoutchouc			251
..	..	..	..	..	..	582	566	Articles en matières plastiques			252
..	..	..	..	..	..	985	961	**Autres produits minéraux non métalliques**		26	
..	..	..	..	..	..	124	122	Verre et articles en verre			261
..	..	..	..	..	..	861	839	Produits minéraux non métalliques, nca			269
..	..	..	..	..	..	164	175	**Produits métallurgiques de base**		27	
..	..	..	..	..	..	84	82	Sidérurgie et première transformation de l'acier			271
..	..	..	..	..	..	24	34	Métallurgie; métaux précieux et non ferreux			272
..	..	..	..	..	..	56	59	Fonderie			273
..	..	..	..	..	..	3 888	3 735	**Ouvrages en métaux, sauf machines et matériel**		28	
..	..	..	..	..	..	1 372	1 313	Constr. et menuiserie métal.; réservoirs; générateurs			281
..	..	..	..	..	..	2 516	2 422	Autres ouvrages en métaux			289
..	..	..	..	..	..	3 494	3 155	**Machines et matériel, nca**		29	
..	..	..	..	..	..	1 694	1 517	Machines d'usage général			291
..	..	..	..	..	..	1 754	1 599	Machines d'usage spécifique			292
..	..	..	..	..	..	46	39	Appareils domestiques, nca			293
..	..	..	..	..	..	61	49	**Mach. de bureau, comptables, matériel inform.**		30	
..	..	..	..	..	..	491	446	**Machines et appareils électriques, nca**		31	
..	..	..	..	..	..	102	99	Moteurs, génératrices et transformateurs électriques			311
..	..	..	..	..	..	112	103	Matériel électrique de distribution et de commande			312
..	..	..	..	..	..	35	31	Fils et câbles électriques isolés			313
..	..	..	..	..	..	5	4	Accumulateurs, piles électriques			314
..	..	..	..	..	..	91	80	Lampes électriques et appareils d'éclairage			315
..	..	..	..	..	..	146	129	Autres matériels électriques, nca			319
..	..	..	..	..	..	307	293	**Equip. et appar. de radio, TV, communication**		32	
..	..	..	..	..	..	171	169	Tubes et valves électroniques; autres composants			321
..	..	..	..	..	..	89	85	Emetteurs radio et TV; app. téléphonie, télégraphie			322
..	..	..	..	..	..	47	39	Récepteurs radio et TV et articles associés			323
..	..	..	..	..	..	799	706	**Instruments médicaux, de précision, d'optique**		33	
..	..	..	..	..	..	757	673	Appareils médicaux et de précision			331
..	..	..	..	..	..	35	28	Instruments d'optique ; matériel photographique			332
..	..	..	..	..	..	7	5	Horlogerie			333
..	..	..	..	..	..	278	256	**Véhicules automobiles et nemorques**		34	
..	..	..	..	..	..	510	482	**Autres matériels de transport**		35	
..	..	..	..	..	..	463	437	Construction et réparation de navires			351
..	..	..	..	..	..	6	12	Construction de matériel ferroviaire roulant			352
..	..	..	..	..	..	13	9	Construction aéronautique et spatiale			353
..	..	..	..	..	..	28	24	Autres équipements de transport			359
..	..	..	..	..	..	2 334	2 150	**Meubles; activités de fabrication, nca**		36	
..	..	..	..	..	..	1 466	1 376	Meubles			361
..	..	..	..	..	..	868	774	Activités de fabrication, nca			369
..	..	..	..	..	..	89	60	**Récupération**		37	
..	..	..	..	..	..	859	795	**Production et distrib. d'électricité, de gaz, d'eau**	E	40-41	
..	..	..	..	..	..	615	607	**Electricité, gaz, vapeur et eau chaude**		40	
..	..	..	..	..	..	315	338	Production, collecte et distribution d'électricité			401
..	..	..	..	..	..	244	188	**Captage, épuration et distribution d'eau**		41	410
..	..	..	..	..	..	23 786	22 011	**Construction**	F	45	
..	..	..	..	..	..	..	..	**Commerce de gros et de détail; réparation**	G	50-52	
..	..	..	..	..	..	..	..	**Hôtels et restaurants**	H	55	
..	..	..	..	..	..	..	..	**Transports, entreposage et communications**	I	60-64	
..	..	..	..	..	..	..	..	**Intermédiation financière**	J	65-67	
..	..	..	..	..	..	..	..	**Immobilier, locations, services aux entreprises**	K	70-74	
..	..	..	..	..	..	..	..	**Admin. publique; éducation; santé; autres**	L-Q	75-99	
..	..	..	..	..	..	..	..	**Grand total**	A-Q	01-99	

Note: Unless given separately, ISIC 1711 excludes Nace 17.13, 17.14, 17.16, 17.17, 17.22 and 17.23; ISIC 2230 excludes Nace 22.32 and 22.32; ISIC 2429 excludes Nace 24.63 and 24.65; ISIC 2710 excludes Nace 27.31 and 27.34; ISIC 272 excludes Nace 27.41 and 27.43; ISIC 1514 excludes Nace 15.41 and 15.42. ISIC 2690 is not available.

Statistiques des Structures Industrielles
OCDE, © 1998

FINLAND

Table FN.6 EMPLOYMENT - EMPLOI

Thousands

ISIC revision 3			1989	1990	1991	1992	1993	1994	1995	1996
A	01-02	**Agriculture, hunting and forestry**	..	..	..	..	..	..	..	..
B	05	**Fishing**	..	..	..	..	..	..	..	..
C	10-14	**Mining and quarrying**	..	..	..	..	..	..	4.3	4.2
	10	Mining of coal and lignite; extraction of peat	..	..	..	..	..	..	1.2	1.2
	11	Crude petroleum & natural gas; related service activ.	..	..	..	..	..	..	..	..
	13	Mining of metal ores	..	..	..	..	..	..	0.6	0.6
	14	Other mining and quarrying	..	..	..	..	..	..	2.5	2.4
D	15-37	**Total manufacturing**	..	..	..	..	..	..	395.5	388.2
	15	**Food products and beverages**	..	..	..	..	..	..	44.0	42.0
		155 Beverages	..	..	..	..	..	..	3.9	3.6
	16	160 **Tobacco products**	..	..	..	..	..	..	0.9	0.8
	17	**Textiles**	..	..	..	..	..	..	6.9	6.8
		171 Spinning, weaving and finishing of textiles	..	..	..	..	..	..	1.3	1.2
		172 Other textiles	..	..	..	..	..	..	3.7	3.6
		173 Knitted and crocheted fabrics and articles	..	..	..	..	..	..	1.9	1.9
	18	**Wearing apparel dressing & dyeing of fur**	..	..	..	..	..	..	8.9	7.7
		181 Wearing apparel, except fur apparel	..	..	..	..	..	..	8.5	7.3
		182 Dressing and dyeing of fur; articles of fur	..	..	..	..	..	..	0.4	0.3
	19	**Tanning, dressing leather; leather artic.; footwear**	..	..	..	..	..	..	3.6	3.1
		191 Tanning, dressing leather; manuf. of leather articles	..	..	..	..	..	..	1.1	0.9
		192 Footwear	..	..	..	..	..	..	2.5	2.3
	20	**Wood and cork products, ex. furniture**	..	..	..	..	..	..	27.8	25.7
		201 Sawmilling and planing of wood	..	..	..	..	..	..	10.8	9.5
		202 Products of wood, cork, straw & plaiting material	..	..	..	..	..	..	17.0	16.2
	21	**Paper and paper products**	..	..	..	..	..	..	39.2	38.4
	22	**Publishing, printing & reprod. of recorded media**	..	..	..	..	..	..	31.6	29.2
		221 Publishing	..	..	..	..	..	..	16.5	14.9
		222 Printing and related service activities	..	..	..	..	..	..	15.1	14.3
		223 Reproduction of recorded media	..	..	..	..	..	..	0.1	0.1
	23	**Coke, refined petroleum products & nuclear fuel**	..	..	..	..	..	..	3.3	3.4
	24	**Chemicals and chemical products**	..	..	..	..	..	..	18.6	18.2
		241 Basic chemicals	..	..	..	..	..	..	8.6	8.4
		242 Other chemical products	..	..	..	..	..	..	9.3	9.3
		243 Man-made fibres	..	..	..	..	..	..	..	..
	25	**Rubber and plastic products**	..	..	..	..	..	..	13.4	13.4
		251 Rubber products	..	..	..	..	..	..	2.6	2.3
		252 Plastic products	..	..	..	..	..	..	10.9	11.1
	26	**Other non-metallic mineral products**	..	..	..	..	..	..	12.9	12.5
		261 Glass and glass products	..	..	..	..	..	..	3.3	3.3
		269 Non-metallic mineral products, nec	..	..	..	..	..	..	..	..
	27	**Basic metals**	..	..	..	..	..	..	16.3	16.9
		271 Basic iron and steel	..	..	..	..	..	..	10.2	10.3
		272 Basic precious and non-ferrous metals	..	..	..	..	..	..	3.3	4.0
		273 Casting of metals	..	..	..	..	..	..	2.7	2.7
	28	**Fabricated metal products, ex. machin. & equip.**	..	..	..	..	..	..	26.4	27.0
		281 Structural metal prod., tanks, reservoirs, generators	..	..	..	..	..	..	13.1	13.4
		289 Other fabricated metal products & service activities	..	..	..	..	..	..	13.3	13.6
	29	**Machinery and equipment, nec**	..	..	..	..	..	..	53.4	55.0
		291 General purpose machinery	..	..	..	..	..	..	23.3	23.5
		292 Special purpose machinery	..	..	..	..	..	..	28.4	29.9
		293 Domestic appliances, nec	..	..	..	..	..	..	1.7	1.6
	30	**Office, accounting and computing machinery**	..	..	..	..	..	..	3.5	3.2
	31	**Electrical machinery and apparatus, nec**	..	..	..	..	..	..	15.7	15.9
		311 Electric motors, generators and transformers	..	..	..	..	..	..	5.7	6.4
		312 Electricity distribution and control apparatus	..	..	..	..	..	..	4.5	4.1
		313 Insulated wire and cable	..	..	..	..	..	..	1.7	1.7
		314 Accumulators, primary cells and primary batteries	..	..	..	..	..	..	0.1	0.0
		315 Electric lamps and lighting equipment	..	..	..	..	..	..	1.4	1.4
		319 Other electrical equipment, nec	..	..	..	..	..	..	2.3	2.3
	32	**Radio, TV, communication equip. & apparatus**	..	..	..	..	..	..	22.4	24.5
		321 Electronic valves, tubes & other electronic compon.	..	..	..	..	..	..	3.6	4.0
		322 TV, radio transmitters & appar. for line teleph., telegr.	..	..	..	..	..	..	17.4	19.2
		323 TV, radio receivers and associated goods	..	..	..	..	..	..	1.5	1.4
	33	**Medical, precision, optical instr.; watches, clocks**	..	..	..	..	..	..	8.2	8.2
		331 Medical equip.; precision instruments and appliances	..	..	..	..	..	..	7.9	7.9
		332 Optical instruments and photographic equipment	..	..	..	..	..	..	0.3	0.3
		333 Watches and clocks	..	..	..	..	..	..	0.0	0.0
	34	**Motor vehicles, trailers, and semi-trailers**	..	..	..	..	..	..	6.6	6.5
	35	**Other transport equipment**	..	..	..	..	..	..	16.8	16.2
		351 Building and repairing of ships and boats	..	..	..	..	..	..	10.9	10.6
		352 Railway, tramway locomotives and rolling stock	..	..	..	..	..	..	2.4	2.1
		353 Aircraft and spacecraft	..	..	..	..	..	..	3.0	3.0
		359 Transport equipment, nec	..	..	..	..	..	..	0.5	0.4
	36	**Furniture; manufacturing, nec**	..	..	..	..	..	..	14.9	13.5
		361 Furniture	..	..	..	..	..	..	10.5	9.6
		369 Manufacturing, nec	..	..	..	..	..	..	4.4	3.9
	37	**Recycling**	..	..	..	..	..	..	0.3	0.2
E	40-41	**Electricity, gas and water supply**	..	..	..	..	..	..	19.6	19.3
	40	**Electricity, gas, steam and hot water supply**	..	..	..	..	..	..	17.3	17.1
		401 Production, collection and distribution of electricity	..	..	..	..	..	..	16.6	16.4
	41	410 **Collection, purification, distribution of water**	..	..	..	..	..	..	2.3	2.2
F	45	**Construction**	..	..	..	..	..	..	83.3	78.4
G	50-52	**Wholesale and retail trade; repairs etc**	..	..	..	..	..	..	..	..
H	55	**Hotels and restaurants**	..	..	..	..	..	..	..	..
I	60-64	**Transport, storage and communications**	..	..	..	..	..	..	..	..
J	65-67	**Financial intermediation**	..	..	..	..	..	..	..	..
K	70-74	**Real estate, renting and business activities**	..	..	..	..	..	..	..	..
L-Q	75-99	**Public admin.; education; health; other services**	..	..	..	..	..	..	..	..
A-Q	01-99	**Grand total**	..	..	..	..	..	..	..	..

Note: Unless given separately, ISIC 1711 excludes Nace 17.13, 17.14, 17.16, 17.17, 17.22 and 17.23; ISIC 2230 excludes Nace 22.32 and 22.32; ISIC 2429 excludes Nace 24.63 and 24.65; ISIC 2710 excludes Nace 27.31 and 27.34; ISIC 272 excludes Nace 27.41 and 27.43; ISIC 1514 excludes Nace 15.41 and 15.42. ISIC 2690 is not available.

Table FN.7 **EMPLOI, SALARIÉS - EMPLOYMENT, EMPLOYEES**

Milliers

1989	1990	1991	1992	1993	1994	1995	1996			CITI révision 3	
..	..	..	..	..	..	..	..	**Agriculture, chasse et sylviculture**	A	01-02	
..	..	..	..	..	..	..	..	**Pêche**	B	05	
..	..	..	..	..	..	3.9	3.8	**Activités extractives**	C	10-14	
..	..	..	..	..	..	0.9	1.0	Extraction de charbon, de lignite et de tourbe		10	
..	..	..	..	..	..	..	..	Extraction de pétrole brut et de gaz naturel		11	
..	..	..	..	..	..	0.6	0.6	Extraction de minerais métalliques		13	
..	..	..	..	..	..	2.3	2.3	Autres activités extractives		14	
..	..	..	..	..	..	386.6	380.8	**Activités de fabrication**	D	15-37	
..	..	..	..	..	..	43.2	41.4	**Produits alimentaires et boissons**		15	
..	..	..	..	..	..	3.8	3.6	Boissons			155
..	..	..	..	..	..	0.9	0.8	**Produits à base de tabac**		16	160
..	..	..	..	..	..	6.5	6.4	**Textiles**		17	
..	..	..	..	..	..	1.3	1.1	Filature, tissage et achèvement des textiles			171
..	..	..	..	..	..	3.4	3.4	Autres articles textiles			172
..	..	..	..	..	..	1.8	1.9	Etoffes et articles de bonneterie			173
..	..	..	..	..	..	8.4	7.3	**Habillement; préparation, teinture des fourrures**		18	
..	..	..	..	..	..	8.1	7.0	Articles d'habillement autres qu'en fourrure			181
..	..	..	..	..	..	0.3	0.3	Préparation, teinture des fourrures; art. en fourrure			182
..	..	..	..	..	..	3.4	3.0	**Travail des cuirs; articles en cuir; chaussures**		19	
..	..	..	..	..	..	0.9	0.8	Apprêt et tannage des cuirs et articles en cuirs			191
..	..	..	..	..	..	2.4	2.2	Chaussures			192
..	..	..	..	..	..	26.8	24.8	**Bois et articles en bois et liège (sauf meubles)**		20	
..	..	..	..	..	..	10.4	9.1	Sciage et rabotage du bois			201
..	..	..	..	..	..	16.3	15.6	Articles en bois, liège, vannerie, sparterie			202
..	..	..	..	..	..	39.1	38.3	**Papier et carton; articles en papier et en carton**		21	
..	..	..	..	..	..	30.8	28.6	**Edition, imprimerie et reproduction**		22	
..	..	..	..	..	..	16.1	14.6	Edition			221
..	..	..	..	..	..	14.6	13.9	Imprimerie et activités annexes			222
..	..	..	..	..	..	0.1	0.1	Reproduction de supports enregistrés			223
..	..	..	..	..	..	3.3	3.4	**Cokéfaction; prod. pétroliers; comb. nucléaires**		23	
..	..	..	..	..	..	18.5	18.1	**Produits chimiques**		24	
..	..	..	..	..	..	8.5	8.3	Produits chimiques de base			241
..	..	..	..	..	..	..	,.	Autres produits chimiques			242
..	..	..	..	..	..	..	..	Fibres synthétiques ou artificielles			243
..	..	..	..	..	..	13.2	13.3	**Articles en caoutchouc et en matières plastiques**		25	
..	..	..	..	..	..	2.5	2.3	Articles en caoutchouc			251
..	..	..	..	..	..	10.7	11.0	Articles en matières plastiques			252
..	..	..	..	..	..	12.6	12.2	**Autres produits minéraux non métalliques**		26	
..	..	..	..	..	..	3.3	3.2	Verre et articles en verre			261
..	..	..	..	..	..	..	..	Produits minéraux non métalliques, nca			269
..	..	..	..	..	..	16.2	16.9	**Produits métallurgiques de base**		27	
..	..	..	..	..	..	10.2	10.2	Sidérurgie et première transformation de l'acier			271
..	..	..	..	..	..	3.3	4.0	Métallurgie; métaux précieux et non ferreux			272
..	..	..	..	..	..	2.7	2.7	Fonderie			273
..	..	..	..	..	..	25.0	25.8	**Ouvrages en métaux, sauf machines et matériel**		28	
..	..	..	..	..	..	12.7	13.0	Constr. et menuiserie métal.; réservoirs; générateurs			281
..	..	..	..	..	..	12.3	12.7	Autres ouvrages en métaux			289
..	..	..	..	..	..	52.1	53.9	**Machines et matériel, nca**		29	
..	..	..	..	..	..	22.6	22.9	Machines d'usage général			291
..	..	..	..	..	..	27.8	29.4	Machines d'usage spécifique			292
..	..	..	..	..	..	1.7	1.6	Appareils domestiques, nca			293
..	..	..	..	..	..	3.4	3.2	**Mach. de bureau, comptables, matériel inform.**		30	
..	..	..	..	..	..	15.5	15.8	**Machines et appareils électriques, nca**		31	
..	..	..	..	..	..	5.6	6.4	Moteurs, génératrices et transformateurs électriques			311
..	..	..	..	..	..	4.5	4.0	Matériel électrique de distribution et de commande			312
..	..	..	..	..	..	1.7	1.7	Fils et câbles électriques isolés			313
..	..	..	..	..	..	0.1	0.0	Accumulateurs, piles électriques			314
..	..	..	..	..	..	1.4	1.4	Lampes électriques et appareils d'éclairage			315
..	..	..	..	..	..	2.3	2.3	Autres matériels électriques, nca			319
..	..	..	..	..	..	22.4	24.4	**Equip. et appar. de radio, TV, communication**		32	
..	..	..	..	..	..	3.5	3.9	Tubes et valves électroniques; autres composants			321
..	..	..	..	..	..	17.4	19.2	Emetteurs radio et TV; app. téléphonie, télégraphie			322
..	..	..	..	..	..	1.5	1.4	Récepteurs radio et TV et articles associés			323
..	..	..	..	..	..	8.0	8.0	**Instruments médicaux, de précision, d'optique**		33	
..	..	..	..	..	..	7.7	7.7	Appareils médicaux et de précision			331
..	..	..	..	..	..	0.3	0.3	Instruments d'optique ; matériel photographique			332
..	..	..	..	..	..	0.0	0.0	Horlogerie			333
..	..	..	..	..	..	6.5	6.4	**Véhicules automobiles et nemorques**		34	
..	..	..	..	..	..	16.7	16.1	**Autres matériels de transport**		35	
..	..	..	..	..	..	10.8	10.5	Construction et réparation de navires			351
..	..	..	..	..	..	2.4	2.1	Construction de matériel ferroviaire roulant			352
..	..	..	..	..	..	3.0	3.0	Construction aéronautique et spatiale			353
..	..	..	..	..	..	0.5	0.4	Autres équipements de transport			359
..	..	..	..	..	..	13.9	12.7	**Meubles; activités de fabrication, nca**		36	
..	..	..	..	..	..	9.9	9.1	Meubles			361
..	..	..	..	..	..	4.0	3.6	Activités de fabrication, nca			369
..	..	..	..	..	..	0.3	0.2	**Récupération**		37	
..	..	..	..	..	..	19.5	19.2	**Production et distrib. d'électricité, de gaz, d'eau**	E	40-41	
..	..	..	..	..	..	17.2	17.1	**Electricité, gaz, vapeur et eau chaude**		40	
..	..	..	..	..	..	16.6	16.4	Production, collecte et distribution d'électricité			401
..	..	..	..	..	..	2.3	2.1	**Captage, épuration et distribution d'eau**		41	410
..	..	..	..	..	..	74.0	70.2	**Construction**	F	45	
..	..	..	..	..	..	..	..	**Commerce de gros et de détail; réparation**	G	50-52	
..	..	..	..	..	..	..	..	**Hôtels et restaurants**	H	55	
..	..	..	..	..	..	..	..	**Transports, entreposage et communications**	I	60-64	
..	..	..	..	..	..	..	..	**Intermédiation financière**	J	65-67	
..	..	..	..	..	..	..	..	**Immobilier, locations, services aux entreprises**	K	70-74	
..	..	..	..	..	..	..	..	**Admin. publique; éducation; santé; autres**	L-Q	75-99	
..	..	..	..	..	..	..	..	**Grand total**	A-Q	01-99	

Note: Unless given separately, ISIC 1711 excludes Nace 17.13, 17.14, 17.16, 17.17, 17.22 and 17.23; ISIC 2230 excludes Nace 22.32 and 32.32; ISIC 2429 excludes Nace 24.63 and 24.65; ISIC 2710 excludes Nace 27.31 and 27.34; ISIC 272 excludes Nace 27.41 and 27.43; ISIC 1514 excludes Nace 15.41 and 15.42. ISIC 2690 is not available.

Statistiques des Structures Industrielles
OCDE, © 1998

FINLAND

Table FN.8 COMPENSATION OF LABOUR, EMPLOYEES - SALAIRES ET CHARGES SOCIALES, SALARIÉS

Millions of Mk (Current Prices)

ISIC revision 3			1989	1990	1991	1992	1993	1994	1995	1996
A	01-02	Agriculture, hunting and forestry	..	..	..	..	..	..	..	..
B	05	Fishing	..	..	..	..	..	..	..	..
C	10-14	Mining and quarrying	..	..	..	..	..	..	..	..
	10	Mining of coal and lignite; extraction of peat	..	..	..	..	..	..	701	700
	11	Crude petroleum & natural gas; related service activ.	..	..	..	..	..	..	157	162
	13	Mining of metal ores	..	..	..	..	..	..	..	..
	14	Other mining and quarrying	..	..	..	..	..	..	140	134
									404	404
D	15-37	Total manufacturing	..	..	..	..	..	..	69 717	71 046
	15	Food products and beverages	..	..	..	..	..	..	7 140	7 073
	155	Beverages	..	..	..	..	..	..	784	764
	16 160	Tobacco products	..	..	..	..	..	..	178	151
	17	Textiles	..	..	..	..	..	..	921	940
	171	Spinning, weaving and finishing of textiles	..	..	..	..	..	..	169	156
	172	Other textiles	..	..	..	..	..	..	520	555
	173	Knitted and crocheted fabrics and articles	..	..	..	..	..	..	233	230
	18	Wearing apparel dressing & dyeing of fur	..	..	..	..	..	..	977	898
	181	Wearing apparel, except fur apparel	..	..	..	..	..	..	931	853
	182	Dressing and dyeing of fur; articles of fur	..	..	..	..	..	..	46	44
	19	Tanning, dressing leather; leather artic.; footwear	..	..	..	..	..	..	404	374
	191	Tanning, dressing leather; manuf. of leather articles	..	..	..	..	..	..	116	96
	192	Footwear	..	..	..	..	..	..	288	277
	20	Wood and cork products, ex. furniture	..	..	..	..	..	..	4 134	3 903
	201	Sawmilling and planing of wood	..	..	..	..	..	..	1 678	1 514
	202	Products of wood, cork, straw & plaiting material	..	..	..	..	..	..	2 456	2 389
	21	Paper and paper products	..	..	..	..	..	..	8 831	8 952
	22	Publishing, printing & reprod. of recorded media	..	..	..	..	..	..	5 475	5 409
	221	Publishing	..	..	..	..	..	..	2 892	2 811
	222	Printing and related service activities	..	..	..	..	..	..	2 566	2 586
	223	Reproduction of recorded media	..	..	..	..	..	..	17	12
	23	Coke, refined petroleum products & nuclear fuel	..	..	..	..	..	..	763	808
	24	Chemicals and chemical products	..	..	..	..	..	..	3 677	3 651
	241	Basic chemicals	..	..	..	..	..	..	1 902	1 896
	242	Other chemical products	..	..	..	..	..	..	..	..
	243	Man-made fibres	..	..	..	..	..	..	..	..
	25	Rubber and plastic products	..	..	..	..	..	..	2 196	2 288
	251	Rubber products	..	..	..	..	..	..	445	431
	252	Plastic products	..	..	..	..	..	..	1 752	1 857
	26	Other non-metallic mineral products	..	..	..	..	..	..	2 128	2 172
	261	Glass and glass products	..	..	..	..	..	..	586	624
	269	Non-metallic mineral products, nec	..	..	..	..	..	..	..	..
	27	Basic metals	..	..	..	..	..	..	3 266	3 457
	271	Basic iron and steel	..	..	..	..	..	..	2 080	2 145
	272	Basic precious and non-ferrous metals	..	..	..	..	..	..	688	832
	273	Casting of metals	..	..	..	..	..	..	498	480
	28	Fabricated metal products, ex. machin. & equip.	..	..	..	..	..	..	4 215	4 535
	281	Structural metal prod., tanks, reservoirs, generators	..	..	..	..	..	..	2 233	2 404
	289	Other fabricated metal products & service activities	..	..	..	..	..	..	1 982	2 130
	29	Machinery and equipment, nec	..	..	..	..	..	..	10 091	10 834
	291	General purpose machinery	..	..	..	..	..	..	4 389	4 609
	292	Special purpose machinery	..	..	..	..	..	..	5 445	5 980
	293	Domestic appliances, nec	..	..	..	..	..	..	257	245
	30	Office, accounting and computing machinery	..	..	..	..	..	..	608	534
	31	Electrical machinery and apparatus, nec	..	..	..	..	..	..	2 742	2 875
	311	Electric motors, generators and transformers	..	..	..	..	..	..	1 068	1 253
	312	Electricity distribution and control apparatus	..	..	..	..	..	..	744	712
	313	Insulated wire and cable	..	..	..	..	..	..	322	321
	314	Accumulators, primary cells and primary batteries	..	..	..	..	..	..	20	3
	315	Electric lamps and lighting equipment	..	..	..	..	..	..	226	211
	319	Other electrical equipment, nec	..	..	..	..	..	..	362	374
	32	Radio, TV, communication equip. & apparatus	..	..	..	..	..	..	4 079	4 589
	321	Electronic valves, tubes & other electronic compon.	..	..	..	..	..	..	535	626
	322	TV, radio transmitters & appar. for line teleph., telegr.	..	..	..	..	..	..	3 297	3 734
	323	TV, radio receivers and associated goods	..	..	..	..	..	..	247	229
	33	Medical, precision, optical instr.; watches, clocks	..	..	..	..	..	..	1 522	1 572
	331	Medical equip.; precision instruments and appliances	..	..	..	..	..	..	1 472	1 522
	332	Optical instruments and photographic equipment	..	..	..	..	..	..	48	50
	333	Watches and clocks	..	..	..	..	..	..	2	0
	34	Motor vehicles, trailers, and semi-trailers	..	..	..	..	..	..	1 111	1 113
	35	Other transport equipment	..	..	..	..	..	..	3 201	2 969
	351	Building and repairing of ships and boats	..	..	..	..	..	..	2 014	1 855
	352	Railway, tramway locomotives and rolling stock	..	..	..	..	..	..	455	364
	353	Aircraft and spacecraft	..	..	..	..	..	..	647	676
	359	Transport equipment, nec	..	..	..	..	..	..	85	73
	36	Furniture; manufacturing, nec	..	..	..	..	..	..	2 010	1 913
	361	Furniture	..	..	..	..	..	..	1 415	1 347
	369	Manufacturing, nec	..	..	..	..	..	..	595	566
	37	Recycling	..	..	..	..	..	..	48	37
E	40-41	Electricity, gas and water supply	..	..	..	..	..	..	3 782	3 947
	40	Electricity, gas, steam and hot water supply	..	..	..	..	..	..	3 441	3 601
	401	Production, collection and distribution of electricity	..	..	..	..	..	..	3 324	3 465
	41 410	Collection, purification, distribution of water	..	..	..	..	..	..	342	346
F	45	Construction	..	..	..	..	..	..	12 257	11 996
G	50-52	Wholesale and retail trade; repairs etc	..	..	..	..	..	..	..	..
H	55	Hotels and restaurants	..	..	..	..	..	..	..	..
I	60-64	Transport, storage and communications	..	..	..	..	..	..	..	..
J	65-67	Financial intermediation	..	..	..	..	..	..	..	..
K	70-74	Real estate, renting and business activities	..	..	..	..	..	..	..	..
L-Q	75-99	Public admin.; education; health; other services	..	..	..	..	..	..	..	..
A-Q	01-99	Grand total	..	..	..	..	..	..	..	..

Note: Unless given separately, ISIC 1711 excludes Nace 17.13, 17.14, 17.16, 17.17, 17.22 and 17.23; ISIC 2230 excludes Nace 22.32 and 22.32; ISIC 2429 excludes Nace 24.63 and 24.65; ISIC 2710 excludes Nace 27.31 and 27.34; ISIC 272 excludes Nace 27.41 and 27.43; ISIC 1514 excludes Nace 15.41 and 15.42. ISIC 2690 is not available.

OECD OCDE Industrial Structure Statistics OECD, © 1998

Table FN.9 **SALAIRES ET TRAITEMENTS, SALARIÉS - WAGES AND SALARIES, EMPLOYEES**

Millions de Mk (Prix courants)

1989	1990	1991	1992	1993	1994	1995	1996			CITI révision 3	
..	..	..	..	..	..	..	..	**Agriculture, chasse et sylviculture**	A	01-02	
..	..	..	..	..	..	..	..	**Pêche**	B	05	
..	..	..	..	..	..	532	535	**Activités extractives**	C	10-14	
..	..	..	..	..	..	120	125	Extraction de charbon, de lignite et de tourbe		10	
..	..	..	..	..	..	..	..	Extraction de pétrole brut et de gaz naturel		11	
..	..	..	..	..	..	105	104	Extraction de minerais métalliques		13	
..	..	..	..	..	..	307	305	Autres activités extractives		14	
..	..	..	..	..	..	53 696	55 350	**Activités de fabrication**	D	15-37	
..	..	..	..	..	..	5 477	5 463	**Produits alimentaires et boissons**		15	
..	..	..	..	..	..	605	574	Boissons			155
..	..	..	..	..	..	135	120	**Produits à base de tabac**		16	160
..	..	..	..	..	..	711	737	**Textiles**		17	
..	..	..	..	..	..	132	123	Filature, tissage et achèvement des textiles			171
..	..	..	..	..	..	399	433	Autres articles textiles			172
..	..	..	..	..	..	181	181	Etoffes et articles de bonneterie			173
..	..	..	..	..	..	769	709	**Habillement; préparation, teinture des fourrures**		18	
..	..	..	..	..	..	733	675	Articles d'habillement autres qu'en fourrure			181
..	..	..	..	..	..	36	35	Préparation, teinture des fourrures; art. en fourrure			182
..	..	..	..	..	..	314	292	**Travail des cuirs; articles en cuir; chaussures**		19	
..	..	..	..	..	..	90	75	Apprêt et tannage des cuirs et articles en cuirs			191
..	..	..	..	..	..	224	217	Chaussures			192
..	..	..	..	..	..	3 164	3 029	**Bois et articles en bois et liège (sauf meubles)**		20	
..	..	..	..	..	..	1 279	1 159	Sciage et rabotage du bois			201
..	..	..	..	..	..	1 885	1 870	Articles en bois, liège, vannerie, sparterie			202
..	..	..	..	..	..	6 751	6 940	**Papier et carton; articles en papier et en carton**		21	
..	..	..	..	..	..	4 247	4 251	**Edition, imprimerie et reproduction**		22	
..	..	..	..	..	..	2 240	2 216	Edition			221
..	..	..	..	..	..	1 994	2 026	Imprimerie et activités annexes			222
..	..	..	..	..	..	13	9	Reproduction de supports enregistrés			223
..	..	..	..	..	..	588	637	**Cokéfaction; prod. pétroliers; comb. nucléaires**		23	
..	..	..	..	..	..	2 827	2 851	**Produits chimiques**		24	
..	..	..	..	..	..	1 463	1 476	Produits chimiques de base			241
..	..	..	..	..	..	..	..	Autres produits chimiques			242
..	..	..	..	..	..	..	..	Fibres synthétiques ou artificielles			243
..	..	..	..	..	..	1 704	1 786	**Articles en caoutchouc et en matières plastiques**		25	
..	..	..	..	..	..	346	331	Articles en caoutchouc			251
..	..	..	..	..	..	1 358	1 455	Articles en matières plastiques			252
..	..	..	..	..	..	1 635	1 667	**Autres produits minéraux non métalliques**		26	
..	..	..	..	..	..	457	486	Verre et articles en verre			261
..	..	..	..	..	..	..	..	Produits minéraux non métalliques, nca			269
..	..	..	..	..	..	2 525	2 724	**Produits métallurgiques de base**		27	
..	..	..	..	..	..	1 620	1 695	Sidérurgie et première transformation de l'acier			271
..	..	..	..	..	..	524	654	Métallurgie; métaux précieux et non ferreux			272
..	..	..	..	..	..	381	375	Fonderie			273
..	..	..	..	..	..	3 250	3 515	**Ouvrages en métaux, sauf machines et matériel**		28	
..	..	..	..	..	..	1 723	1 863	Constr. et menuiserie métal.; réservoirs; générateurs			281
..	..	..	..	..	..	1 527	1 651	Autres ouvrages en métaux			289
..	..	..	..	..	..	7 704	8 383	**Machines et matériel, nca**		29	
..	..	..	..	..	..	3 362	3 588	Machines d'usage général			291
..	..	..	..	..	..	4 145	4 603	Machines d'usage spécifique			292
..	..	..	..	..	..	197	193	Appareils domestiques, nca			293
..	..	..	..	..	..	481	431	**Mach. de bureau, comptables, matériel inform.**		30	
..	..	..	..	..	..	2 126	2 229	**Machines et appareils électriques, nca**		31	
..	..	..	..	..	..	809	953	Moteurs, génératrices et transformateurs électriques			311
..	..	..	..	..	..	588	568	Matériel électrique de distribution et de commande			312
..	..	..	..	..	..	248	250	Fils et câbles électriques isolés			313
..	..	..	..	..	..	15	3	Accumulateurs, piles électriques			314
..	..	..	..	..	..	175	163	Lampes électriques et appareils d'éclairage			315
..	..	..	..	..	..	290	294	Autres matériels électriques, nca			319
..	..	..	..	..	..	3 184	3 612	**Equip. et appar. de radio, TV, communication**		32	
..	..	..	..	..	..	419	489	Tubes et valves électroniques; autres composants			321
..	..	..	..	..	..	2 578	2 942	Emetteurs radio et TV; app. téléphonie, télégraphie			322
..	..	..	..	..	..	188	181	Récepteurs radio et TV et articles associés			323
..	..	..	..	..	..	1 172	1 232	**Instruments médicaux, de précision, d'optique**		33	
..	..	..	..	..	..	1 133	1 193	Appareils médicaux et de précision			331
..	..	..	..	..	..	37	39	Instruments d'optique ; matériel photographique			332
..	..	..	..	..	..	1	0	Horlogerie			333
..	..	..	..	..	..	861	870	**Véhicules automobiles et nemorques**		34	
..	..	..	..	..	..	2 473	2 354	**Autres matériels de transport**		35	
..	..	..	..	..	..	1 554	1 474	Construction et réparation de navires			351
..	..	..	..	..	..	352	292	Construction de matériel ferroviaire roulant			352
..	..	..	..	..	..	503	529	Construction aéronautique et spatiale			353
..	..	..	..	..	..	64	58	Autres équipements de transport			359
..	..	..	..	..	..	1 560	1 490	**Meubles; activités de fabrication, nca**		36	
..	..	..	..	..	..	1 098	1 051	Meubles			361
..	..	..	..	..	..	462	439	Activités de fabrication, nca			369
..	..	..	..	..	..	37	29	**Récupération**		37	
..	..	..	..	..	..	2 845	3 012	**Production et distrib. d'électricité, de gaz, d'eau**	E	40-41	
..	..	..	..	..	..	2 601	2 750	**Electricité, gaz, vapeur et eau chaude**		40	
..	..	..	..	..	..	2 512	2 645	Production, collecte et distribution d'électricité			401
..	..	..	..	..	..	245	262	**Captage, épuration et distribution d'eau**		41	410
..	..	..	..	..	..	9 362	9 181	**Construction**	F	45	
..	..	..	..	..	..	..	..	**Commerce de gros et de détail; réparation**	G	50-52	
..	..	..	..	..	..	..	..	**Hôtels et restaurants**	H	55	
..	..	..	..	..	..	..	..	**Transports, entreposage et communications**	I	60-64	
..	..	..	..	..	..	..	..	**Intermédiation financière**	J	65-67	
..	..	..	..	..	..	..	..	**Immobilier, locations, services aux entreprises**	K	70-74	
..	..	..	..	..	..	..	..	**Admin. publique; éducation; santé; autres**	L-Q	75-99	
..	..	..	..	..	..	..	..	**Grand total**	A-Q	01-99	

Note: Unless given separately, ISIC 1711 excludes Nace 17.13, 17.14, 17.16, 17.17, 17.22 and 17.23; ISIC 2230 excludes Nace 22.32 and 23.32; ISIC 2429 excludes Nace 24.63 and 24.65; ISIC 2710 excludes Nace 27.31 and 27.34; ISIC 272 excludes Nace 27.41 and 27.43; ISIC 1514 excludes Nace 15.41 and 15.42. ISIC 2690 is not available.

Statistiques des Structures Industrielles
OCDE, © 1998

FINLAND

Table FN.10 EMPLOYERS' SOCIAL COSTS – CHARGES SOCIALES DES EMPLOYEURS

Millions of Mk (Current Prices)

	ISIC revision 3		1989	1990	1991	1992	1993	1994	1995	1996
A	01-02	Agriculture, hunting and forestry	..	..	..	..	..	..	..	..
B	05	Fishing	..	..	..	..	..	..	..	..
C	10-14	Mining and quarrying	..	..	..	..	..	..	169	166
	10	Mining of coal and lignite; extraction of peat	..	..	..	..	..	..	37	37
	11	Crude petroleum & natural gas; related service activ.	..	..	..	..	..	..	..	..
	13	Mining of metal ores	..	..	..	..	..	..	36	29
	14	Other mining and quarrying	..	..	..	..	..	..	97	99
D	15-37	**Total manufacturing**	..	..	..	..	..	..	16 021	15 696
	15	Food products and beverages	..	..	..	..	..	..	1 663	1 609
		155	Beverages	..	..	..	..	..	..	180	191
	16	160	Tobacco products	..	..	..	..	..	..	43	31
	17	Textiles	..	..	..	..	..	..	209	203
		171	Spinning, weaving and finishing of textiles	..	..	..	..	..	..	37	33
		172	Other textiles	..	..	..	..	..	..	121	121
		173	Knitted and crocheted fabrics and articles	..	..	..	..	..	..	52	49
	18	Wearing apparel dressing & dyeing of fur	..	..	..	..	..	..	208	188
		181	Wearing apparel, except fur apparel	..	..	..	..	..	..	197	179
		182	Dressing and dyeing of fur; articles of fur	..	..	..	..	..	..	10	10
	19	Tanning, dressing leather; leather artic.; footwear	..	..	..	..	..	..	90	82
		191	Tanning, dressing leather; manuf. of leather articles	..	..	..	..	..	..	26	21
		192	Footwear	..	..	..	..	..	..	64	61
	20	Wood and cork products, ex. furniture	..	..	..	..	..	..	970	874
		201	Sawmilling and planing of wood	..	..	..	..	..	..	400	355
		202	Products of wood, cork, straw & plaiting material	..	..	..	..	..	..	570	520
	21	Paper and paper products	..	..	..	..	..	..	2 080	2 012
	22	Publishing, printing & reprod. of recorded media	..	..	..	..	..	..	1 227	1 158
		221	Publishing	..	..	..	..	..	..	651	595
		222	Printing and related service activities	..	..	..	..	..	..	572	560
		223	Reproduction of recorded media	..	..	..	..	..	..	3	3
	23	Coke, refined petroleum products & nuclear fuel	..	..	..	..	..	..	175	172
	24	Chemicals and chemical products	..	..	..	..	..	..	849	800
		241	Basic chemicals	..	..	..	..	..	..	439	420
		242	Other chemical products	..	..	..	..	..	..	..	..
		243	Man-made fibres	..	..	..	..	..	..	..	..
	25	Rubber and plastic products	..	..	..	..	..	..	492	502
		251	Rubber products	..	..	..	..	..	..	98	100
		252	Plastic products	..	..	..	..	..	..	394	402
	26	Other non-metallic mineral products	..	..	..	..	..	..	493	506
		261	Glass and glass products	..	..	..	..	..	..	129	138
		269	Non-metallic mineral products, nec	..	..	..	..	..	..	..	..
	27	Basic metals	..	..	..	..	..	..	741	1 046
		271	Basic iron and steel	..	..	..	..	..	..	460	762
		272	Basic precious and non-ferrous metals	..	..	..	..	..	..	164	178
		273	Casting of metals	..	..	..	..	..	..	117	105
	28	Fabricated metal products, ex. machin. & equip.	..	..	..	..	..	..	965	1 020
		281	Structural metal prod., tanks, reservoirs, generators	..	..	..	..	..	..	510	541
		289	Other fabricated metal products & service activities	..	..	..	..	..	..	455	479
	29	Machinery and equipment, nec	..	..	..	..	..	..	2 387	2 450
		291	General purpose machinery	..	..	..	..	..	..	1 027	1 021
		292	Special purpose machinery	..	..	..	..	..	..	1 300	1 378
		293	Domestic appliances, nec	..	..	..	..	..	..	61	52
	30	Office, accounting and computing machinery	..	..	..	..	..	..	127	102
	31	Electrical machinery and apparatus, nec	..	..	..	..	..	..	616	645
		311	Electric motors, generators and transformers	..	..	..	..	..	..	259	300
		312	Electricity distribution and control apparatus	..	..	..	..	..	..	156	145
		313	Insulated wire and cable	..	..	..	..	..	..	74	72
		314	Accumulators, primary cells and primary batteries	..	..	..	..	..	..	5	1
		315	Electric lamps and lighting equipment	..	..	..	..	..	..	50	48
		319	Other electrical equipment, nec	..	..	..	..	..	..	72	81
	32	Radio, TV, communication equip. & apparatus	..	..	..	..	..	..	894	978
		321	Electronic valves, tubes & other electronic compon.	..	..	..	..	..	..	116	137
		322	TV, radio transmitters & appar. for line teleph., telegr.	..	..	..	..	..	..	719	792
		323	TV, radio receivers and associated goods	..	..	..	..	..	..	59	48
	33	Medical, precision, optical instr.; watches, clocks	..	..	..	..	..	..	350	339
		331	Medical equip.; precision instruments and appliances	..	..	..	..	..	..	339	328
		332	Optical instruments and photographic equipment	..	..	..	..	..	..	11	11
		333	Watches and clocks	..	..	..	..	..	..	0	0
	34	Motor vehicles, trailers, and semi-trailers	..	..	..	..	..	..	250	243
	35	Other transport equipment	..	..	..	..	..	..	727	615
		351	Building and repairing of ships and boats	..	..	..	..	..	..	461	381
		352	Railway, tramway locomotives and rolling stock	..	..	..	..	..	..	103	72
		353	Aircraft and spacecraft	..	..	..	..	..	..	144	147
		359	Transport equipment, nec	..	..	..	..	..	..	20	15
	36	Furniture; manufacturing, nec	..	..	..	..	..	..	450	423
		361	Furniture	..	..	..	..	..	..	317	296
		369	Manufacturing, nec	..	..	..	..	..	..	133	127
	37	Recycling	..	..	..	..	..	..	11	9
E	40-41	Electricity, gas and water supply	..	..	..	..	..	..	922	935
	40	Electricity, gas, steam and hot water supply	..	..	..	..	..	..	840	851
		401	Production, collection and distribution of electricity	..	..	..	..	..	..	813	820
	41	410	Collection, purification, distribution of water	..	..	..	..	..	..	82	83
F	45	Construction	..	..	..	..	..	..	2 894	2 815
G	50-52	Wholesale and retail trade; repairs etc	..	..	..	..	..	..	..	..
H	55	Hotels and restaurants	..	..	..	..	..	..	..	..
I	60-64	Transport, storage and communications	..	..	..	..	..	..	..	..
J	65-67	Financial intermediation	..	..	..	..	..	..	..	..
K	70-74	Real estate, renting and business activities	..	..	..	..	..	..	..	..
L-Q	75-99	Public admin.; education; health; other services	..	..	..	..	..	..	..	..
A-Q	01-99	Grand total	..	..	..	..	..	..	..	..

Note: Unless given separately, ISIC 1711 excludes Nace 17.13, 17.14, 17.16, 17.17, 17.22 and 17.23; ISIC 2230 excludes Nace 22.32 and 22.32; ISIC 2429 excludes Nace 24.63 and 24.65; ISIC 2710 excludes Nace 27.31 and 27.34; ISIC 272 excludes Nace 27.41 and 27.43; ISIC 1514 excludes Nace 15.41 and 15.42. ISIC 2690 is not available.

Table FN.11 HEURES OUVRÉES - HOURS WORKED

Milliers

1989	1990	1991	1992	1993	1994	1995	1996			CITI révision 3	
..	..	..	..	..	..	..	..	Agriculture, chasse et sylviculture	A	01-02	
..	..	..	..	..	..	..	..	Pêche	B	05	
..	..	..	..	..	..	4 087	3 875	Activités extractives	C	10-14	
..	..	..	..	..	..	591	612	Extraction de charbon, de lignite et de tourbe		10	
..	..	..	..	..	..	..	..	Extraction de pétrole brut et de gaz naturel		11	
..	..	..	..	..	..	729	692	Extraction de minerais métalliques		13	
..	..	..	..	..	..	2 767	2 571	Autres activités extractives		14	
..	..	..	..	..	..	418 928	405 848	Activités de fabrication	D	15-37	
..	..	..	..	..	..	49 159	47 448	Produits alimentaires et boissons		15	
..	..	..	..	..	..	3 726	3 568	Boissons			155
..	..	..	..	..	..	763	737	Produits à base de tabac		16	160
..	..	..	..	..	..	7 949	7 963	Textiles		17	
..	..	..	..	..	..	1 592	1 435	Filature, tissage et achèvement des textiles			171
..	..	..	..	..	..	4 058	4 212	Autres articles textiles			172
..	..	..	..	..	..	2 299	2 316	Etoffes et articles de bonneterie			173
..	..	..	..	..	..	9 877	8 424	Habillement; préparation, teinture des fourrures		18	
..	..	..	..	..	..	9 476	8 066	Articles d'habillement autres qu'en fourrure			181
..	..	..	..	..	..	401	358	Préparation, teinture des fourrures; art. en fourrure			182
..	..	..	..	..	..	4 486	3 872	Travail des cuirs; articles en cuir; chaussures		19	
..	..	..	..	..	..	1 262	1 008	Apprêt et tannage des cuirs et articles en cuirs			191
..	..	..	..	..	..	3 224	2 864	Chaussures			192
..	..	..	..	..	..	35 023	31 993	Bois et articles en bois et liège (sauf meubles)		20	
..	..	..	..	..	..	14 160	12 394	Sciage et rabotage du bois			201
..	..	..	..	..	..	20 863	19 599	Articles en bois, liège, vannerie, sparterie			202
..	..	..	..	..	..	46 016	44 813	Papier et carton; articles en papier et en carton		21	
..	..	..	..	..	..	25 473	23 247	Edition, imprimerie et reproduction		22	
..	..	..	..	..	..	7 092	5 959	Edition			221
..	..	..	..	..	..	18 309	17 252	Imprimerie et activités annexes			222
..	..	..	..	..	..	72	36	Reproduction de supports enregistrés			223
..	..	..	..	..	..	2 228	2 202	Cokéfaction; prod. pétroliers; comb. nucléaires		23	
..	..	..	..	..	..	14 978	14 594	Produits chimiques		24	
..	..	..	..	..	..	7 854	7 571	Produits chimiques de base			241
..	..	..	..	..	..	..	..	Autres produits chimiques			242
..	..	..	..	..	..	..	..	Fibres synthétiques ou artificielles			243
..	..	..	..	..	..	16 020	15 519	Articles en caoutchouc et en matières plastiques		25	
..	..	..	..	..	..	3 075	2 717	Articles en caoutchouc			251
..	..	..	..	..	..	12 945	12 802	Articles en matières plastiques			252
..	..	..	..	..	..	15 095	14 336	Autres produits minéraux non métalliques		26	
..	..	..	..	..	..	3 995	4 096	Verre et articles en verre			261
..	..	..	..	..	..	..	..	Produits minéraux non métalliques, nca			269
..	..	..	..	..	..	18 983	19 314	Produits métallurgiques de base		27	
..	..	..	..	..	..	11 371	11 282	Sidérurgie et première transformation de l'acier			271
..	..	..	..	..	..	3 826	4 444	Métallurgie; métaux précieux et non ferreux			272
..	..	..	..	..	..	3 786	3 588	Fonderie			273
..	..	..	..	..	..	30 580	31 361	Ouvrages en métaux, sauf machines et matériel		28	
..	..	..	..	..	..	14 996	15 500	Constr. et menuiserie métal.; réservoirs; générateurs			281
..	..	..	..	..	..	15 584	15 861	Autres ouvrages en métaux			289
..	..	..	..	..	..	54 822	54 981	Machines et matériel, nca		29	
..	..	..	..	..	..	23 428	23 272	Machines d'usage général			291
..	..	..	..	..	..	29 425	29 800	Machines d'usage spécifique			292
..	..	..	..	..	..	1 969	1 909	Appareils domestiques, nca			293
..	..	..	..	..	..	3 308	2 831	Mach. de bureau, comptables, matériel inform.		30	
..	..	..	..	..	..	16 563	16 232	Machines et appareils électriques, nca		31	
..	..	..	..	..	..	5 629	6 017	Moteurs, génératrices et transformateurs électriques			311
..	..	..	..	..	..	4 817	4 340	Matériel électrique de distribution et de commande			312
..	..	..	..	..	..	1 910	1 847	Fils et câbles électriques isolés			313
..	..	..	..	..	..	88	23	Accumulateurs, piles électriques			314
..	..	..	..	..	..	1 740	1 627	Lampes électriques et appareils d'éclairage			315
..	..	..	..	..	..	2 379	2 378	Autres matériels électriques, nca			319
..	..	..	..	..	..	17 426	18 574	Equip. et appar. de radio, TV, communication		32	
..	..	..	..	..	..	4 495	4 791	Tubes et valves électroniques; autres composants			321
..	..	..	..	..	..	11 396	12 448	Emetteurs radio et TV; app. téléphonie, télégraphie			322
..	..	..	..	..	..	1 535	1 335	Récepteurs radio et TV et articles associés			323
..	..	..	..	..	..	5 479	5 119	Instruments médicaux, de précision, d'optique		33	
..	..	..	..	..	..	5 173	4 832	Appareils médicaux et de précision			331
..	..	..	..	..	..	299	280	Instruments d'optique ; matériel photographique			332
..	..	..	..	..	..	7	7	Horlogerie			333
..	..	..	..	..	..	7 674	8 259	Véhicules automobiles et nemorques		34	
..	..	..	..	..	..	19 825	18 199	Autres matériels de transport		35	
..	..	..	..	..	..	13 567	12 235	Construction et réparation de navires			351
..	..	..	..	..	..	2 836	2 363	Construction de matériel ferroviaire roulant			352
..	..	..	..	..	..	2 814	3 067	Construction aéronautique et spatiale			353
..	..	..	..	..	..	608	534	Autres équipements de transport			359
..	..	..	..	..	..	17 057	15 692	Meubles; activités de fabrication, nca		36	
..	..	..	..	..	..	12 252	11 410	Meubles			361
..	..	..	..	..	..	4 805	4 282	Activités de fabrication, nca			369
..	..	..	..	..	..	144	138	Récupération		37	
..	..	..	..	..	..	15 769	15 327	Production et distrib. d'électricité, de gaz, d'eau	E	40-41	
..	..	..	..	..	..	13 446	13 117	Electricité, gaz, vapeur et eau chaude		40	
..	..	..	..	..	..	12 867	12 499	Production, collecte et distribution d'électricité			401
..	..	..	..	..	..	2 323	2 210	Captage, épuration et distribution d'eau		41	410
..	..	..	..	..	..	88 870	85 430	Construction	F	45	
..	..	..	..	..	..	..	..	Commerce de gros et de détail; réparation	G	50-52	
..	..	..	..	..	..	..	..	Hôtels et restaurants	H	55	
..	..	..	..	..	..	..	..	Transports, entreposage et communications	I	60-64	
..	..	..	..	..	..	..	..	Intermédiation financière	J	65-67	
..	..	..	..	..	..	..	..	Immobilier, locations, services aux entreprises	K	70-74	
..	..	..	..	..	..	..	..	Admin. publique; éducation; santé; autres	L-Q	75-99	
..	..	..	..	..	..	..	..	Grand total	A-Q	01-99	

Note: Unless given separately, ISIC 1711 excludes Nace 17.13, 17.14, 17.16, 17.17, 17.22 and 17.23; ISIC 2230 excludes Nace 22.32 and 22.32; ISIC 2429 excludes Nace 24.63 and 24.65; ISIC 2710 excludes Nace 27.31 and 27.34; ISIC 272 excludes Nace 27.41 and 27.43; ISIC 1514 excludes Nace 15.41 and 15.42. ISIC 2690 is not available.

Statistiques des Structures Industrielles
OCDE, © 1998

FINLAND

Table FN.12 EXPORTS - EXPORTATIONS

Millions of Mk (Current Prices)

ISIC revision 3			1989	1990	1991	1992	1993	1994	1995	1996
A	01-02	**Agriculture, hunting and forestry**	..	..	..	..	..	..	..	..
B	05	**Fishing**	..	..	..	..	..	..	..	..
C	10-14	**Mining and quarrying**	..	..	..	..	..	..	448	512
	10	Mining of coal and lignite; extraction of peat	..	..	..	..	..	..	21	56
	11	Crude petroleum & natural gas; related service activ.	..	..	..	..	..	..	..	..
	13	Mining of metal ores	..	..	..	..	..	..	98	122
	14	Other mining and quarrying	..	..	..	..	..	..	329	334
D	15-37	**Total manufacturing**	..	..	..	..	..	..	171 126	179 087
	15	**Food products and beverages**	..	..	..	..	..	..	4 490	5 249
	155	Beverages	..	..	..	..	..	..	788	803
	16	**Tobacco products**	..	..	..	..	..	..	145	33
	160									
	17	**Textiles**	..	..	..	..	..	..	1 255	1 351
	171	Spinning, weaving and finishing of textiles	..	..	..	..	..	..	178	180
	172	Other textiles	..	..	..	..	..	..	970	1 050
	173	Knitted and crocheted fabrics and articles	..	..	..	..	..	..	107	121
	18	**Wearing apparel dressing & dyeing of fur**	..	..	..	..	..	..	983	903
	181	Wearing apparel, except fur apparel	..	..	..	..	..	..	943	864
	182	Dressing and dyeing of fur; articles of fur	..	..	..	..	..	..	40	39
	19	**Tanning, dressing leather; leather artic.; footwear**	..	..	..	..	..	..	436	372
	191	Tanning, dressing leather; manuf. of leather articles	..	..	..	..	..	..	82	27
	192	Footwear	..	..	..	..	..	..	354	345
	20	**Wood and cork products, ex. furniture**	..	..	..	..	..	..	10 969	11 049
	201	Sawmilling and planing of wood	..	..	..	..	..	..	6 869	6 827
	202	Products of wood, cork, straw & plaiting material	..	..	..	..	..	..	4 100	4 222
	21	**Paper and paper products**	..	..	..	..	..	..	50 968	45 230
	22	**Publishing, printing & reprod. of recorded media**	..	..	..	..	..	..	1 519	1 615
	221	Publishing	..	..	..	..	..	..	91	136
	222	Printing and related service activities	..	..	..	..	..	..	1 428	1 478
	223	Reproduction of recorded media	..	..	..	..	..	..	0	1
	23	**Coke, refined petroleum products & nuclear fuel**	..	..	..	..	..	..	3 308	4 901
	24	**Chemicals and chemical products**	..	..	..	..	..	..	9 797	9 997
	241	Basic chemicals	..	..	..	..	..	..	7 142	7 035
	242	Other chemical products	..	..	..	..	..	..	..	..
	243	Man-made fibres	..	..	..	..	..	..	..	..
	25	**Rubber and plastic products**	..	..	..	..	..	..	3 103	3 279
	251	Rubber products	..	..	..	..	..	..	777	766
	252	Plastic products	..	..	..	..	..	..	2 326	2 513
	26	**Other non-metallic mineral products**	..	..	..	..	..	..	1 911	2 101
	261	Glass and glass products	..	..	..	..	..	..	960	989
	269	Non-metallic mineral products, nec	..	..	..	..	..	..	..	..
	27	**Basic metals**	..	..	..	..	..	..	12 867	12 813
	271	Basic iron and steel	..	..	..	..	..	..	9 177	8 932
	272	Basic precious and non-ferrous metals	..	..	..	..	..	..	3 305	3 538
	273	Casting of metals	..	..	..	..	..	..	386	343
	28	**Fabricated metal products, ex. machin. & equip.**	..	..	..	..	..	..	4 819	4 839
	281	Structural metal prod., tanks, reservoirs, generators	..	..	..	..	..	..	3 059	3 006
	289	Other fabricated metal products & service activities	..	..	..	..	..	..	1 760	1 833
	29	**Machinery and equipment, nec**	..	..	..	..	..	..	22 534	24 595
	291	General purpose machinery	..	..	..	..	..	..	10 357	11 131
	292	Special purpose machinery	..	..	..	..	..	..	11 755	12 929
	293	Domestic appliances, nec	..	..	..	..	..	..	423	535
	30	**Office, accounting and computing machinery**	..	..	..	..	..	..	4 274	3 893
	31	**Electrical machinery and apparatus, nec**	..	..	..	..	..	..	5 853	6 781
	311	Electric motors, generators and transformers	..	..	..	..	..	..	3 013	3 562
	312	Electricity distribution and control apparatus	..	..	..	..	..	..	1 084	1 161
	313	Insulated wire and cable	..	..	..	..	..	..	643	925
	314	Accumulators, primary cells and primary batteries	..	..	..	..	..	..	16	0
	315	Electric lamps and lighting equipment	..	..	..	..	..	..	408	434
	319	Other electrical equipment, nec	..	..	..	..	..	..	689	699
	32	**Radio, TV, communication equip. & apparatus**	..	..	..	..	..	..	19 873	24 141
	321	Electronic valves, tubes & other electronic compon.	..	..	..	..	..	..	876	989
	322	TV, radio transmitters & appar. for line teleph., telegr.	..	..	..	..	..	..	17 951	22 321
	323	TV, radio receivers and associated goods	..	..	..	..	..	..	1 046	831
	33	**Medical, precision, optical instr.; watches, clocks**	..	..	..	..	..	..	2 865	3 391
	331	Medical equip.; precision instruments and appliances	..	..	..	..	..	..	2 856	3 390
	332	Optical instruments and photographic equipment	..	..	..	..	..	..	8	1
	333	Watches and clocks	..	..	..	..	..	..	0	0
	34	**Motor vehicles, trailers, and semi-trailers**	..	..	..	..	..	..	1 728	1 905
	35	**Other transport equipment**	..	..	..	..	..	..	5 509	8 929
	351	Building and repairing of ships and boats	..	..	..	..	..	..	4 924	8 332
	352	Railway, tramway locomotives and rolling stock	..	..	..	..	..	..	126	149
	353	Aircraft and spacecraft	..	..	..	..	..	..	399	400
	359	Transport equipment, nec	..	..	..	..	..	..	60	48
	36	**Furniture; manufacturing, nec**	..	..	..	..	..	..	1 736	1 627
	361	Furniture	..	..	..	..	..	..	964	855
	369	Manufacturing, nec	..	..	..	..	..	..	772	772
	37	**Recycling**	..	..	..	..	..	..	186	93
E	40-41	**Electricity, gas and water supply**	..	..	..	..	..	..	143	944
	40	**Electricity, gas, steam and hot water supply**	..	..	..	..	..	..	143	944
	401	Production, collection and distribution of electricity	..	..	..	..	..	..	143	944
	41 410	**Collection, purification, distribution of water**	..	..	..	..	..	..	0	0
F	45	**Construction**	..	..	..	..	..	..	1 953	2 321
G	50-52	**Wholesale and retail trade; repairs etc**	..	..	..	..	..	..	..	..
H	55	**Hotels and restaurants**	..	..	..	..	..	..	..	..
I	60-64	**Transport, storage and communications**	..	..	..	..	..	..	..	..
J	65-67	**Financial intermediation**	..	..	..	..	..	..	..	..
K	70-74	**Real estate, renting and business activities**	..	..	..	..	..	..	..	..
L-Q	75-99	**Public admin.; education; health; other services**	..	..	..	..	..	..	..	..
A-Q	01-99	**Grand total**	..	..	..	..	..	..	..	..

Note: Unless given separately, ISIC 1711 excludes Nace 17.13, 17.14, 17.16, 17.17, 17.22 and 17.23; ISIC 2230 excludes Nace 22.32 and 22.32; ISIC 2429 excludes Nace 24.63 and 24.65; ISIC 2710 excludes Nace 27.31 and 27.34; ISIC 272 excludes Nace 27.41 and 27.43; ISIC 1514 excludes Nace 15.41 and 15.42. ISIC 2690 is not available.

Table FN.13 **IMPORTATIONS - IMPORTS**

Millions de Mk (Prix courants)

1989	1990	1991	1992	1993	1994	1995	1996		CITI révision 3	
..	..	..	..	..	..	..	..	**Agriculture, chasse et sylviculture**	**A**	**01-02**
..	..	..	..	..	..	..	..	**Pêche**	**B**	**05**
..	..	..	..	..	..	45	62	**Activités extractives**	**C**	**10-14**
..	..	..	..	..	..	..	9	Extraction de charbon, de lignite et de tourbe	10	
..	..	..	..	..	..	..	..	Extraction de pétrole brut et de gaz naturel	11	
..	..	..	..	..	..	8	11	Extraction de minerais métalliques	13	
..	..	..	..	..	..	37	42	Autres activités extractives	14	
..	..	..	..	..	..	55 951	59 382	**Activités de fabrication**	**D**	**15-37**
..	..	..	..	..	..	3 976	4 746	**Produits alimentaires et boissons**	**15**	
..	..	..	..	..	..	217	440	Boissons		155
..	..	..	..	..	..	90	163	**Produits à base de tabac**	**16**	160
..	..	..	..	..	..	825	665	**Textiles**	**17**	
..	..	..	..	..	..	137	99	Filature, tissage et achèvement des textiles		171
..	..	..	..	..	..	574	446	Autres articles textiles		172
..	..	..	..	..	..	114	121	Etoffes et articles de bonneterie		173
..	..	..	..	..	..	797	480	**Habillement; préparation, teinture des fourrures**	**18**	
..	..	..	..	..	..	783	463	Articles d'habillement autres qu'en fourrure		181
..	..	..	..	..	..	13	17	Préparation, teinture des fourrures; art. en fourrure		182
..	..	..	..	..	..	218	184	**Travail des cuirs; articles en cuir; chaussures**	**19**	
..	..	..	..	..	..	67	25	Apprêt et tannage des cuirs et articles en cuirs		191
..	..	..	..	..	..	151	160	Chaussures		192
..	..	..	..	..	..	291	282	**Bois et articles en bois et liège (sauf meubles)**	**20**	
..	..	..	..	..	..	14	17	Sciage et rabotage du bois		201
..	..	..	..	..	..	278	264	Articles en bois, liège, vannerie, sparterie		202
..	..	..	..	..	..	2 720	2 679	**Papier et carton; articles en papier et en carton**	**21**	
..	..	..	..	..	..	159	181	**Edition, imprimerie et reproduction**	**22**	
..	..	..	..	..	..	55	42	Edition		221
..	..	..	..	..	..	101	139	Imprimerie et activités annexes		222
..	..	..	..	..	..	3		Reproduction de supports enregistrés		223
..	..	..	..	..	..	6 871	9 731	**Cokéfaction; prod. pétroliers; comb. nucléaires**	**23**	
..	..	..	..	..	..	4 268	3 924	**Produits chimiques**	**24**	
..	..	..	..	..	..	2 479	2 307	Produits chimiques de base		241
..	..	..	..	..	..	..	..	Autres produits chimiques		242
..	..	..	..	..	..	..	..	Fibres synthétiques ou artificielles		243
..	..	..	..	..	..	1 991	1 949	**Articles en caoutchouc et en matières plastiques**	**25**	
..	..	..	..	..	..	581	555	Articles en caoutchouc		251
..	..	..	..	..	..	1 410	1 394	Articles en matières plastiques		252
..	..	..	..	..	..	654	694	**Autres produits minéraux non métalliques**	**26**	
..	..	..	..	..	..	316	303	Verre et articles en verre		261
..	..	..	..	..	..	..	..	Produits minéraux non métalliques, nca		269
..	..	..	..	..	..	4 883	6 592	**Produits métallurgiques de base**	**27**	
..	..	..	..	..	..	2 954	2 931	Sidérurgie et première transformation de l'acier		271
..	..	..	..	..	..	1 858	3 598	Métallurgie; métaux précieux et non ferreux		272
..	..	..	..	..	..	71	63	Fonderie		273
..	..	..	..	..	..	834	874	**Ouvrages en métaux, sauf machines et matériel**	**28**	
..	..	..	..	..	..	335	398	Constr. et menuiserie métal.; réservoirs; générateurs		281
..	..	..	..	..	..	499	476	Autres ouvrages en métaux		289
..	..	..	..	..	..	4 786	5 054	**Machines et matériel, nca**	**29**	
..	..	..	..	..	..	2 149	2 632	Machines d'usage général		291
..	..	..	..	..	..	2 374	2 128	Machines d'usage spécifique		292
..	..	..	..	..	..	263	294	Appareils domestiques, nca		293
..	..	..	..	..	..	3 671	2 723	**Mach. de bureau, comptables, matériel inform.**	**30**	
..	..	..	..	..	..	2 813	3 007	**Machines et appareils électriques, nca**	**31**	
..	..	..	..	..	..	1 447	1 324	Moteurs, génératrices et transformateurs électriques		311
..	..	..	..	..	..	348	503	Matériel électrique de distribution et de commande		312
..	..	..	..	..	..	556	694	Fils et câbles électriques isolés		313
..	..	..	..	..	..	35		Accumulateurs, piles électriques		314
..	..	..	..	..	..	214	216	Lampes électriques et appareils d'éclairage		315
..	..	..	..	..	..	212	270	Autres matériels électriques, nca		319
..	..	..	..	..	..	12 548	11 953	**Equip. et appar. de radio, TV, communication**	**32**	
..	..	..	..	..	..	491	546	Tubes et valves électroniques; autres composants		321
..	..	..	..	..	..	11 305	10 851	Emetteurs radio et TV; app. téléphonie, télégraphie		322
..	..	..	..	..	..	752	556	Récepteurs radio et TV et articles associés		323
..	..	..	..	..	..	452	538	**Instruments médicaux, de précision, d'optique**	**33**	
..	..	..	..	..	..	401	499	Appareils médicaux et de précision		331
..	..	..	..	..	..	51	39	Instruments d'optique ; matériel photographique		332
..	..	..	..	..	..			Horlogerie		333
..	..	..	..	..	..	569	660	**Véhicules automobiles et nemorques**	**34**	
..	..	..	..	..	..	1 840	1 705	**Autres matériels de transport**	**35**	
..	..	..	..	..	..	1 310	1 047	Construction et réparation de navires		351
..	..	..	..	..	..	78	85	Construction de matériel ferroviaire roulant		352
..	..	..	..	..	..	407	505	Construction aéronautique et spatiale		353
..	..	..	..	..	..	45	68	Autres équipements de transport		359
..	..	..	..	..	..	634	563	**Meubles; activités de fabrication, nca**	**36**	
..	..	..	..	..	..	294	277	Meubles		361
..	..	..	..	..	..	340	286	Activités de fabrication, nca		369
..	..	..	..	..	..	62	35	**Récupération**	**37**	
..	..	..	..	..	..	639	2 112	**Production et distrib. d'électricité, de gaz, d'eau**	**E**	**40-41**
..	..	..	..	..	..	639	2 111	**Electricité, gaz, vapeur et eau chaude**	**40**	
..	..	..	..	..	..	639	2 111	Production, collecte et distribution d'électricité		401
..	..	..	..	..	..		1	**Captage, épuration et distribution d'eau**	**41**	410
..	..	..	..	..	..	210	226	**Construction**	**F**	**45**
..	..	..	..	..	..	..	..	**Commerce de gros et de détail; réparation**	**G**	**50-52**
..	..	..	..	..	..	..	..	**Hôtels et restaurants**	**H**	**55**
..	..	..	..	..	..	..	..	**Transports, entreposage et communications**	**I**	**60-64**
..	..	..	..	..	..	..	..	**Intermédiation financière**	**J**	**65-67**
..	..	..	..	..	..	..	..	**Immobilier, locations, services aux entreprises**	**K**	**70-74**
..	..	..	..	..	..	..	..	**Admin. publique; éducation; santé; autres**	**L-Q**	**75-99**
..	..	..	..	..	..	..	..	**Grand total**	**A-Q**	**01-99**

Note: Unless given separately, ISIC 1711 excludes Nace 17.13, 17.14, 17.16, 17.17, 17.22 and 17.23; ISIC 2230 excludes Nace 22.32 and 22.32; ISIC 2429 excludes Nace 24.63 and 24.65; ISIC 2710 excludes Nace 27.31 and 27.34; ISIC 272 excludes Nace 27.41 and 27.43; ISIC 1514 excludes Nace 15.41 and 15.42. ISIC 2690 is not available.

Statistiques des Structures Industrielles
OCDE, © 1998

FRANCE

Table FR.1 PRODUCTION - PRODUCTION

Millions of FF (Current Prices)

ISIC revision 3				1989	1990	1991	1992	1993	1994	1995	1996
A	01-02		Agriculture, hunting and forestry	..	..	..	..	..	..	..	..
B	05		Fishing	..	..	..	..	..	..	..	..
C	10-14		Mining and quarrying	..	..	..	..	..	..	..	..
	10		Mining of coal and lignite; extraction of peat	..	21 870	23 333	21 938	22 014	20 522	18 021	17 960
	11		Crude petroleum & natural gas; related service activ.	..	..	..	..	..	..	..	..
	13		Mining of metal ores	..	680	709	612	620	416	431	411
	14		Other mining and quarrying	..	21 395	23 164	21 007	19 907	20 449	21 124	19 569
D	15-37		Total manufacturing	..	2 743 400	2 784 593	2 754 794	3 285 968	2 815 444	2 994 536	3 048 550
	15		Food products and beverages	..	..	..	..	..	..	..	..
		155	Beverages	..	..	..	..	..	..	..	..
	16	160	Tobacco products	..	..	..	..	..	..	..	..
	17		Textiles	..	91 645	90 633	91 823	82 264	87 901	90 238	87 260
		171	Spinning, weaving and finishing of textiles	..	52 921	50 272	48 667	42 625	46 472	47 082	45 330
		172	Other textiles	..	22 465	23 838	25 936	24 280	26 650	28 720	28 242
		173	Knitted and crocheted fabrics and articles	..	16 259	16 523	17 221	15 359	14 779	14 436	13 689
	18		Wearing apparel dressing & dyeing of fur	..	63 803	62 331	62 015	59 420	59 799	62 335	62 890
		181	Wearing apparel, except fur apparel	..	63 000	61 624	61 304	58 968	59 349	61 805	62 323
		182	Dressing and dyeing of fur; articles of fur	..	803	708	710	452	450	530	567
	19		Tanning, dressing leather; leather artic.; footwear	..	27 061	26 191	24 633	24 312	23 054	23 001	21 172
		191	Tanning, dressing leather; manuf. of leather articles	..	9 807	8 467	8 399	7 226	8 693	8 409	7 851
		192	Footwear	..	17 253	17 724	16 234	17 086	14 361	14 592	13 321
	20		Wood and cork products, ex. furniture	..	31 130	31 909	31 534	29 514	31 707	33 124	31 919
		201	Sawmilling and planing of wood	..	292	299	334	411	439	526	349
		202	Products of wood, cork, straw & plaiting material	..	30 838	31 610	31 200	29 103	31 268	32 598	31 570
	21		Paper and paper products	..	95 959	96 200	95 171	89 983	96 634	111 661	101 023
	22		Publishing, printing & reprod. of recorded media	..	129 320	132 236	131 965	131 019	136 253	141 368	144 550
		221	Publishing	..	75 798	77 196	76 390	78 039	81 550	83 963	88 149
		222	Printing and related service activities	..	52 061	53 296	53 591	51 229	52 873	55 320	53 974
		223	Reproduction of recorded media	..	1 461	1 744	1 984	1 751	1 830	2 085	2 428
	23		Coke, refined petroleum products & nuclear fuel	..	238 063	223 052	201 773	220 117	222 724	234 245	263 675
	24		Chemicals and chemical products	..	392 396	389 892	399 416	398 844	422 907	455 275	463 193
		241	Basic chemicals	..	145 136	134 181	130 233	122 724	135 161	156 316	160 900
		242	Other chemical products	..	243 536	252 599	266 165	273 381	284 864	295 666	299 179
		243	Man-made fibres	..	3 724	3 111	3 017	2 739	2 882	3 293	3 115
	25		Rubber and plastic products	..	118 218	122 666	124 550	119 144	128 359	138 386	138 676
		251	Rubber products	..	41 408	42 014	42 550	39 653	40 671	44 730	44 937
		252	Plastic products	..	76 810	80 651	82 000	79 491	87 688	93 655	93 739
	26		Other non-metallic mineral products	..	105 514	107 002	104 188	99 145	104 389	107 781	105 130
		261	Glass and glass products	..	34 143	34 762	35 264	33 486	35 903	38 336	37 473
		269	Non-metallic mineral products, nec	..	71 371	72 240	68 924	65 659	68 486	69 446	67 658
	27		Basic metals	..	165 720	153 321	143 854	129 544	146 727	167 447	164 757
		271	Basic iron and steel	..	101 362	93 896	87 495	79 891	90 604	103 845	103 993
		272	Basic precious and non-ferrous metals	..	43 556	39 976	37 826	33 893	38 483	43 882	41 399
		273	Casting of metals	..	20 802	19 448	18 533	15 760	17 639	19 720	19 365
	28		Fabricated metal products, ex. machin. & equip.	..	190 358	193 574	188 255	173 844	183 802	196 485	198 391
		281	Structural metal prod., tanks, reservoirs, generators	..	75 618	79 521	76 598	72 058	71 940	71 395	69 193
		289	Other fabricated metal products & service activities	..	114 740	114 053	111 657	101 787	111 862	125 090	129 197
	29		Machinery and equipment, nec	..	206 798	201 173	204 050	189 630	197 633	211 888	218 710
		291	General purpose machinery	..	107 402	107 822	112 159	105 608	108 874	112 673	117 005
		292	Special purpose machinery	..	80 291	72 828	70 238	63 389	67 753	76 914	78 896
		293	Domestic appliances, nec	..	19 106	20 523	21 653	20 633	21 006	22 302	22 808
	30		Office, accounting and computing machinery	..	62 580	63 898	56 911	60 433	63 555	71 768	69 563
	31		Electrical machinery and apparatus, nec	..	116 831	121 978	108 787	114 542	122 493	131 043	131 006
		311	Electric motors, generators and transformers	..	17 819	18 050	17 025	16 120	16 004	18 136	17 818
		312	Electricity distribution and control apparatus	..	50 861	53 339	38 789	47 009	49 431	52 162	51 534
		313	Insulated wire and cable	..	22 569	21 768	22 421	21 853	22 697	23 306	20 012
		314	Accumulators, primary cells and primary batteries	..	4 578	6 535	6 447	6 648	6 976	7 295	7 329
		315	Electric lamps and lighting equipment	..	7 527	7 743	7 859	7 226	7 870	8 314	7 868
		319	Other electrical equipment, nec	..	13 479	14 543	16 246	15 685	19 514	21 829	26 445
	32		Radio, TV, communication equip. & apparatus	..	82 054	131 520	126 171	123 174	131 030	147 476	166 588
		321	Electronic valves, tubes & other electronic compon.	..	21 885	65 838	62 263	56 928	59 565	64 838	73 108
		322	TV, radio transmitters & appar. for line teleph., telegr.	..	47 312	50 600	48 016	51 742	56 666	66 297	73 159
		323	TV, radio receivers and associated goods	..	12 857	15 082	15 891	14 503	14 799	16 341	20 320
	33		Medical, precision, optical instr.; watches, clocks	..	50 818	53 930	53 759	51 628	53 256	56 403	60 541
		331	Medical equip.; precision instruments and appliances	..	40 227	42 976	43 218	41 666	43 008	45 387	49 967
		332	Optical instruments and photographic equipment	..	7 020	7 498	7 336	7 061	7 439	7 956	7 595
		333	Watches and clocks	..	3 571	3 456	3 204	2 902	2 809	3 059	2 980
	34		Motor vehicles, trailers, and semi-trailers	..	387 626	386 431	405 533	363 608	416 172	426 833	424 945
	35		Other transport equipment	..	120 156	123 287	126 513	110 035	112 697	118 438	119 204
		351	Building and repairing of ships and boats	..	12 148	11 904	10 897	8 925	12 390	11 613	10 313
		352	Railway, tramway locomotives and rolling stock	..	4 966	5 755	14 495	13 155	11 870	11 880	13 152
		353	Aircraft and spacecraft	..	96 330	99 542	95 161	82 501	82 549	82 509	89 312
		359	Transport equipment, nec	..	6 711	6 086	5 959	5 453	5 889	6 855	6 427
	36		Furniture; manufacturing, nec	..	67 347	73 370	73 893	72 489	74 352	74 923	75 358
		361	Furniture	..	42 173	48 394	48 711	46 075	48 134	48 737	49 685
		369	Manufacturing, nec	..	25 174	24 977	25 182	26 414	26 218	26 186	25 674
	37		Recycling	..	..	..	..	..	..	..	..
E	40-41		Electricity, gas and water supply	..	261 823	288 260	298 428	311 990	312 719	328 440	340 212
	40		Electricity, gas, steam and hot water supply	..	228 880	252 467	258 923	269 280	266 757	280 359	290 797
		401	Production, collection and distribution of electricity	..	177 278	193 309	199 609	204 876	204 411	212 229	215 997
	41	410	Collection, purification, distribution of water	..	32 944	35 793	39 505	42 710	45 962	48 082	49 415
F	45		Construction	..	..	..	..	..	..	..	..
G	50-52		Wholesale and retail trade; repairs etc	..	..	..	..	..	..	..	..
H	55		Hotels and restaurants	..	..	..	..	..	..	..	..
I	60-64		Transport, storage and communications	..	..	..	..	..	..	..	..
J	65-67		Financial intermediation	..	..	..	..	..	..	..	..
K	70-74		Real estate, renting and business activities	..	..	..	..	..	..	..	..
L-Q	75-99		Public admin.; education; health; other services	..	..	..	..	..	..	..	..
A-Q	01-99		Grand total	..	3 094 186	3 120 060	3 096 779	3 653 360	3 169 550	3 362 553	3 426 703

Note: ISIC 15 and 16 are not covered by the inquiry and do not figure in the subtotals and totals. ISIC 10 includes 11 and 12; ISIC 131 includes 132; ISIC 1421 includes1422;
ISIC 231 includes 233; ISIC 2694 includes 2695.

Table FR.2 **VALEUR AJOUTÉE AU COÛT DES FACTEURS - VALUE ADDED AT FACTOR COSTS**

Millions de FF (Prix courants)

1989	1990	1991	1992	1993	1994	1995	1996			CITI révision 3	
..	..	..	..	..	..	..	..	**Agriculture, chasse et sylviculture**	A	01-02	
..	..	..	..	..	..	..	..	**Pêche**	B	05	
..	..	..	..	..	..	..	..	**Activités extractives**	C	10-14	
..	10 256	10 176	8 843	9 707	9 325	6 804	6 808	Extraction de charbon, de lignite et de tourbe		10	
..	..	..	..	..	..	..	..	Extraction de pétrole brut et de gaz naturel		11	
..	313	340	275	137	176	180	175	Extraction de minerais métalliques		13	
..	8 798	9 485	8 693	7 862	8 160	8 354	7 642	Autres activités extractives		14	
..	889 785	903 034	882 429	831 946	889 206	920 018	908 693	**Activités de fabrication**	D	15-37	
..	..	..	..	..	..	..	..	**Produits alimentaires et boissons**		15	
..	..	..	..	..	..	..	..	Boissons			155
..	..	..	..	..	..	..	..	**Produits à base de tabac**		16	160
..	30 243	30 263	30 207	27 293	29 345	28 450	26 400	**Textiles**		17	
..	15 495	15 115	14 629	12 991	14 486	13 630	12 459	Filature, tissage et achèvement des textiles			171
..	8 598	9 029	9 520	8 909	9 442	9 623	9 084	Autres articles textiles			172
..	6 150	6 119	6 058	5 393	5 417	5 197	4 857	Etoffes et articles de bonneterie			173
..	23 744	23 390	22 725	21 690	20 501	19 723	19 099	**Habillement; préparation, teinture des fourrures**		18	
..	23 460	23 137	22 509	21 562	20 369	19 572	18 946	Articles d'habillement autres qu'en fourrure			181
..	284	253	216	128	133	151	154	Préparation, teinture des fourrures; art. en fourrure			182
..	11 150	11 014	10 234	9 832	9 798	9 425	8 841	**Travail des cuirs; articles en cuir; chaussures**		19	
..	4 031	3 628	3 599	3 222	3 840	3 574	3 487	Apprêt et tannage des cuirs et articles en cuirs			191
..	7 119	7 386	6 635	6 610	5 958	5 851	5 355	Chaussures			192
..	10 186	10 344	10 295	9 521	9 768	9 852	9 537	**Bois et articles en bois et liège (sauf meubles)**		20	
..	147	152	170	225	254	290	211	Sciage et rabotage du bois			201
..	10 039	10 193	10 125	9 297	9 514	9 562	9 326	Articles en bois, liège, vannerie, sparterie			202
..	29 744	29 871	28 320	26 831	28 467	31 811	28 519	**Papier et carton; articles en papier et en carton**		21	
..	49 488	51 570	51 371	50 917	53 232	54 016	55 193	**Edition, imprimerie et reproduction**		22	
..	27 444	28 753	28 247	29 081	30 853	31 282	32 975	Edition			221
..	21 532	22 235	22 439	21 202	21 764	22 026	21 476	Imprimerie et activités annexes			222
..	513	582	685	634	614	708	742	Reproduction de supports enregistrés			223
..	30 708	24 761	21 637	24 490	23 861	25 060	31 133	**Cokéfaction; prod. pétroliers; comb. nucléaires**		23	
..	121 303	118 316	119 544	120 197	131 982	145 357	141 831	**Produits chimiques**		24	
..	40 374	34 467	33 256	30 704	39 478	47 882	42 791	Produits chimiques de base			241
..	79 801	82 995	85 506	88 904	91 866	96 851	98 376	Autres produits chimiques			242
..	1 128	855	782	589	638	625	664	Fibres synthétiques ou artificielles			243
..	44 310	47 745	48 980	47 437	50 287	51 076	51 940	**Articles en caoutchouc et en matières plastiques**		25	
..	16 993	18 558	18 746	17 817	18 268	18 888	19 343	Articles en caoutchouc			251
..	27 317	29 187	30 233	29 620	32 019	32 188	32 596	Articles en matières plastiques			252
..	45 176	45 329	43 129	41 537	43 759	44 707	42 767	**Autres produits minéraux non métalliques**		26	
..	15 555	15 790	15 176	14 406	15 302	16 061	15 651	Verre et articles en verre			261
..	29 621	29 539	27 953	27 131	28 457	28 646	27.115	Produits minéraux non métalliques, nca			269
..	46 668	41 648	38 148	32 926	39 487	45 094	40 438	**Produits métallurgiques de base**		27	
..	29 338	24 984	22 959	19 518	24 498	28 984	24 878	Sidérurgie et première transformation de l'acier			271
..	8 824	8 481	7 523	6 725	7 792	8 700	8 109	Métallurgie; métaux précieux et non ferreux			272
..	8 506	8 183	7 665	6 683	7 198	7 411	7 451	Fonderie			273
..	77 823	79 630	77 573	70 645	74 634	77 236	76 351	**Ouvrages en métaux, sauf machines et matériel**		28	
..	28 143	29 918	29 646	27 498	27 750	26 114	24 451	Constr. et menuiserie métal.; réservoirs; générateurs			281
..	49 680	49 712	47 926	43 147	46 884	51 122	51 900	Autres ouvrages en métaux			289
..	75 544	75 508	75 490	71 508	73 461	75 364	75 949	**Machines et matériel, nca**		29	
..	40 157	41 161	41 722	39 853	40 738	41 470	42 462	Machines d'usage général			291
..	28 309	26 693	25 644	23 699	24 641	25 821	25 698	Machines d'usage spécifique			292
..	7 078	7 654	8 125	7 956	8 081	8 074	7 789	Appareils domestiques, nca			293
..	33 091	31 688	27 891	20 778	22 726	23 778	22 408	**Mach. de bureau, comptables, matériel inform.**		30	
..	43 364	46 588	42 042	43 213	46 051	46 890	46 198	**Machines et appareils électriques, nca**		31	
..	6 754	7 025	6 608	6 207	6 091	6 621	6 357	Moteurs, génératrices et transformateurs électriques			311
..	20 207	21 926	16 871	18 747	19 898	20 095	19 423	Matériel électrique de distribution et de commande			312
..	6 379	6 105	6 513	6 456	6 680	6 309	5 803	Fils et câbles électriques isolés			313
..	1 749	2 669	2 543	2 640	2 518	2 555	2 376	Accumulateurs, piles électriques			314
..	3 347	3 403	3 273	2 916	3 171	3 313	3 055	Lampes électriques et appareils d'éclairage			315
..	4 928	5 461	6 233	6 246	7 693	7 997	9 184	Autres matériels électriques, nca			319
..	32 094	51 202	47 719	45 619	47 518	50 651	53 276	**Equip. et appar. de radio, TV, communication**		32	
..	9 815	26 665	23 980	22 225	24 137	24 171	25 759	Tubes et valves électroniques; autres composants			321
..	18 613	20 329	19 866	19 420	19 551	22 614	23 254	Emetteurs radio et TV; app. téléphonie, télégraphie			322
..	3 666	4 208	3 873	3 973	3 830	3 866	4 264	Récepteurs radio et TV et articles associés			323
..	21 791	23 080	22 833	23 319	23 827	24 822	24 349	**Instruments médicaux, de précision, d'optique**		33	
..	17 064	18 192	18 029	18 660	19 131	19 982	19 823	Appareils médicaux et de précision			331
..	3 229	3 461	3 385	3 308	3 436	3 501	3 342	Instruments d'optique ; matériel photographique			332
..	1 498	1 427	1 419	1 351	1 259	1 339	1 184	Horlogerie			333
..	97 073	92 010	94 333	78 965	92 653	91 873	89 344	**Véhicules automobiles et nemorques**		34	
..	39 580	40 287	41 465	37 924	40 272	37 823	38 227	**Autres matériels de transport**		35	
..	3 711	3 547	3 829	2 998	3 710	3 424	2 910	Construction et réparation de navires			351
..	1 822	2 130	5 483	4 784	4 773	4 762	4 748	Construction de matériel ferroviaire roulant			352
..	31 749	32 572	30 271	28 442	29 857	27 486	28 548	Construction aéronautique et spatiale			353
..	2 299	2 037	1 882	1 699	1 932	2 150	2 021	Autres équipements de transport			359
..	26 706	28 789	28 493	27 305	27 579	27 009	26 894	**Meubles; activités de fabrication, nca**		36	
..	16 395	18 303	18 074	17 029	17 201	16 849	16 740	Meubles			361
..	10 311	10 487	10 419	10 276	10 378	10 160	10 153	Activités de fabrication, nca			369
..	..	..	..	..	..	..	..	**Récupération**		37	
..	132 726	146 742	156 421	157 891	150 819	153 771	153 823	**Production et distrib. d'électricité, de gaz, d'eau**	E	40-41	
..	122 104	135 305	144 660	145 261	137 765	140 271	140 405	**Electricité, gaz, vapeur et eau chaude**		40	
..	103 450	114 291	121 232	119 964	113 712	113 379	111 943	Production, collecte et distribution d'électricité			401
..	10 622	11 437	11 761	12 630	13 054	13 500	13 417	**Captage, épuration et distribution d'eau**		41	410
..	..	..	..	..	..	..	..	**Construction**	F	45	
..	..	..	..	..	..	..	..	**Commerce de gros et de détail; réparation**	G	50-52	
..	..	..	..	..	..	..	..	**Hôtels et restaurants**	H	55	
..	..	..	..	..	..	..	..	**Transports, entreposage et communications**	I	60-64	
..	..	..	..	..	..	..	..	**Intermédiation financière**	J	65-67	
..	..	..	..	..	..	..	..	**Immobilier, locations, services aux entreprises**	K	70-74	
..	..	..	..	..	..	..	..	**Admin. publique; éducation; santé; autres**	L-Q	75-99	
..	1 061 579	1 069 777	1 056 660	1 007 543	1 057 685	1 089 126	1 077 141	**Grand total**	A-Q	01-99	

Note: ISIC 15 and 16 are not covered by the inquiry and do not figure in the subtotals and totals. ISIC 10 includes 11 and 12; ISIC 131 includes 132; ISIC 1421 includes1422; ISIC 231 includes 233; ISIC 2694 includes 2695.

Statistiques des Structures Industrielles
OCDE, © 1998
OECD OCDE

FRANCE

Table FR.3 INVESTMENT - INVESTISSEMENT

Millions of FF (Current Prices)

ISIC revision 3			1989	1990	1991	1992	1993	1994	1995	1996
A	01-02	Agriculture, hunting and forestry	..	..	..	..	..	..	..	..
B	05	Fishing	..	..	..	..	..	..	..	..
C	10-14	Mining and quarrying	..	..	..	..	..	..	..	..
	10	Mining of coal and lignite; extraction of peat	..	1 648	1 717	1 548	1 257	1 162	1 020	906
	11	Crude petroleum & natural gas; related service activ.	..	..	..	..	..	..	..	..
	13	Mining of metal ores	..	67	77	46	80	147	60	41
	14	Other mining and quarrying	..	2 378	2 303	1 945	1 585	1 636	1 991	1 846
D	15-37	Total manufacturing	..	153 718	147 107	135 133	131 065	110 476	121 403	128 785
	15	Food products and beverages	..	..	..	..	..	..	..	..
	155	Beverages	..	..	..	..	..	..	..	..
	16 160	Tobacco products	..	..	..	..	..	..	..	..
	17	Textiles	..	4 455	4 040	3 879	3 015	3 081	3 519	3 383
	171	Spinning, weaving and finishing of textiles	..	2 784	2 234	2 037	1 413	1 560	1 855	1 714
	172	Other textiles	..	1 107	1 345	1 337	1 180	1 123	1 233	1 192
	173	Knitted and crocheted fabrics and articles	..	564	461	506	422	398	431	476
	18	Wearing apparel dressing & dyeing of fur	..	1 376	1 294	1 448	1 256	1 031	1 216	1 105
	181	Wearing apparel, except fur apparel	..	1 367	1 278	1 431	1 252	1 030	1 211	1 095
	182	Dressing and dyeing of fur; articles of fur	..	10	16	17	3	2	4	9
	19	Tanning, dressing leather; leather artic.; footwear	..	890	739	674	625	527	623	543
	191	Tanning, dressing leather; manuf. of leather articles	..	312	302	269	184	182	210	172
	192	Footwear	..	578	437	406	441	345	413	371
	20	Wood and cork products, ex. furniture	..	2 233	1 655	1 493	1 001	1 534	1 327	1 375
	201	Sawmilling and planing of wood	..	11	10	8	8	11	10	6
	202	Products of wood, cork, straw & plaiting material	..	2 222	1 645	1 485	993	1 522	1 317	1 369
	21	Paper and paper products	..	8 390	7 625	7 641	4 265	3 770	4 706	5 245
	22	Publishing, printing & reprod. of recorded media	..	4 788	4 189	3 721	3 261	3 774	4 009	4 667
	221	Publishing	..	1 801	1 684	1 346	1 150	1 488	1 322	1 461
	222	Printing and related service activities	..	2 866	2 339	2 269	1 988	2 175	2 483	3 031
	223	Reproduction of recorded media	..	122	166	106	122	111	204	175
	23	Coke, refined petroleum products & nuclear fuel	..	10 446	11 480	11 907	12 342	11 817	9 140	7 720
	24	Chemicals and chemical products	..	25 154	22 592	21 485	18 600	16 229	17 879	20 525
	241	Basic chemicals	..	14 065	11 257	9 176	6 988	6 139	7 321	9 156
	242	Other chemical products	..	10 760	11 046	12 006	11 328	9 866	10 173	11 239
	243	Man-made fibres	..	329	289	303	284	224	386	130
	25	Rubber and plastic products	..	8 077	6 852	6 827	5 874	5 629	7 096	7 760
	251	Rubber products	..	2 825	1 947	1 968	1 571	1 332	2 001	2 442
	252	Plastic products	..	5 251	4 904	4 859	4 303	4 297	5 094	5 318
	26	Other non-metallic mineral products	..	7 527	6 163	5 931	4 770	4 982	6 135	6 429
	261	Glass and glass products	..	2 177	1 853	1 858	1 659	2 032	2 227	2 314
	269	Non-metallic mineral products, nec	..	5 350	4 310	4 073	3 112	2 950	3 908	4 115
	27	Basic metals	..	9 972	10 496	6 563	5 234	4 505	5 213	6 423
	271	Basic iron and steel	..	5 766	5 168	4 293	3 534	2 740	3 176	4 152
	272	Basic precious and non-ferrous metals	..	2 966	4 292	1 437	1 149	1 094	1 166	1 282
	273	Casting of metals	..	1 239	1 036	833	551	671	871	988
	28	Fabricated metal products, ex. machin. & equip.	..	9 503	8 793	8 556	6 862	6 322	7 207	7 531
	281	Structural metal prod., tanks, reservoirs, generators	..	2 366	2 397	2 453	2 055	1 628	1 422	1 561
	289	Other fabricated metal products & service activities	..	7 138	6 396	6 102	4 807	4 694	5 785	5 970
	29	Machinery and equipment, nec	..	8 426	7 977	6 549	5 370	5 062	6 579	6 992
	291	General purpose machinery	..	4 086	3 864	3 586	2 707	2 543	3 078	3 494
	292	Special purpose machinery	..	3 305	2 843	1 884	1 489	1 544	2 187	2 365
	293	Domestic appliances, nec	..	1 035	1 270	1 078	1 174	975	1 315	1 133
	30	Office, accounting and computing machinery	..	4 222	4 358	3 745	3 077	2 754	2 598	2 758
	31	Electrical machinery and apparatus, nec	..	6 298	6 685	5 673	4 749	4 486	4 919	5 507
	311	Electric motors, generators and transformers	..	691	642	635	454	455	673	581
	312	Electricity distribution and control apparatus	..	2 593	2 730	2 228	1 729	1 852	1 826	2 100
	313	Insulated wire and cable	..	1 187	1 429	814	723	641	647	639
	314	Accumulators, primary cells and primary batteries	..	289	439	328	491	328	332	349
	315	Electric lamps and lighting equipment	..	475	383	369	274	292	329	341
	319	Other electrical equipment, nec	..	1 063	1 062	1 299	1 078	919	1 112	1 498
	32	Radio, TV, communication equip. & apparatus	..	4 580	6 588	5 557	5 516	6 882	7 770	8 020
	321	Electronic valves, tubes & other electronic compon.	..	1 784	3 363	2 826	3 205	4 445	4 550	4 962
	322	TV, radio transmitters & appar. for line teleph., telegr.	..	2 217	2 242	1 684	1 786	1 804	2 267	1 990
	323	TV, radio receivers and associated goods	..	579	983	1 046	525	633	954	1 068
	33	Medical, precision, optical instr.; watches, clocks	..	2 239	2 186	1 938	1 807	1 780	1 976	2 109
	331	Medical equip.; precision instruments and appliances	..	1 711	1 725	1 543	1 434	1 415	1 516	1 766
	332	Optical instruments and photographic equipment	..	360	278	240	240	265	289	235
	333	Watches and clocks	..	168	183	155	133	100	171	108
	34	Motor vehicles, trailers, and semi-trailers	..	26 480	24 022	23 716	18 849	21 211	23 818	24 489
	35	Other transport equipment	..	5 660	6 280	5 032	3 228	2 870	3 192	3 591
	351	Building and repairing of ships and boats	..	305	300	384	293	302	290	445
	352	Railway, tramway locomotives and rolling stock	..	241	263	497	397	376	334	383
	353	Aircraft and spacecraft	..	4 809	5 462	3 905	2 317	2 004	2 334	2 515
	359	Transport equipment, nec	..	305	255	245	221	188	234	247
	36	Furniture; manufacturing, nec	..	3 002	3 092	2 798	2 288	2 230	2 482	2 613
	361	Furniture	..	1 845	1 892	1 742	1 427	1 328	1 529	1 504
	369	Manufacturing, nec	..	1 157	1 200	1 055	861	902	953	1 109
	37	Recycling	..	..	..	..	..	..	..	..
E	40-41	Electricity, gas and water supply	..	43 696	43 262	44 396	45 989	44 806	45 766	45 131
	40	Electricity, gas, steam and hot water supply	..	41 385	41 551	42 277	43 671	41 387	41 988	41 732
	401	Production, collection and distribution of electricity	..	36 243	36 231	35 964	37 044	34 962	35 348	34 883
	41 410	Collection, purification, distribution of water	..	2 311	1 710	2 120	2 318	3 419	3 778	3 399
F	45	Construction	..	..	..	..	..	..	..	..
G	50-52	Wholesale and retail trade; repairs etc	..	..	..	..	..	..	..	..
H	55	Hotels and restaurants	..	..	..	..	..	..	..	..
I	60-64	Transport, storage and communications	..	..	..	..	..	..	..	..
J	65-67	Financial intermediation	..	..	..	..	..	..	..	..
K	70-74	Real estate, renting and business activities	..	..	..	..	..	..	..	..
L-Q	75-99	Public admin.; education; health; other services	..	..	..	..	..	..	..	..
A-Q	01-99	Grand total	..	203 357	194 466	183 069	160 900	158 226	170 242	176 710

Note: ISIC 15 and 16 are not covered by the inquiry and do not figure in the subtotals and totals. ISIC 10 includes 11 and 12; ISIC 131 includes 132; ISIC 1421 includes1422; ISIC 231 includes 233; ISIC 2694 includes 2695.

Table FR.4 ENTREPRISES – ENTERPRISES

Unités

1989	1990	1991	1992	1993	1994	1995	1996			CITI révision 3
..	..	..	..	..	..	..	..	**Agriculture, chasse et sylviculture**	A	01-02
..	..	..	..	..	..	..	..	**Pêche**	B	05
..	..	..	..	..	..	..	..	**Activités extractives**	C	10-14
..	18	19	19	20	19	19	20	Extraction de charbon, de lignite et de tourbe		10
..	..	..	..	..	..	..	..	Extraction de pétrole brut et de gaz naturel		11
..	5	5	6	6	5	5	5	Extraction de minerais métalliques		13
..	400	423	363	346	347	354	321	Autres activités extractives		14
..	23 431	24 484	23 880	22 438	22 332	22 066	21 803	**Activités de fabrication**	D	15-37
..	..	..	..	..	..	..	..	**Produits alimentaires et boissons**		15
..	..	..	..	..	..	..	..	Boissons		155
..	..	..	..	..	..	..	..	**Produits à base de tabac**	16	160
..	1 647	1 691	1 646	1 546	1 567	1 528	1 427	**Textiles**	17	
..	825	826	773	732	729	730	702	Filature, tissage et achèvement des textiles		171
..	498	533	547	519	537	525	489	Autres articles textiles		172
..	324	332	326	295	301	273	236	Etoffes et articles de bonneterie		173
..	2 135	2 160	2 091	1 913	1 829	1 715	1 669	**Habillement; préparation, teinture des fourrures**	18	
..	2 105	2 131	2 064	1 891	1 809	1 694	1 649	Articles d'habillement autres qu'en fourrure		181
..	30	29	27	22	20	21	20	Préparation, teinture des fourrures; art. en fourrure		182
..	595	602	559	517	492	470	441	**Travail des cuirs; articles en cuir; chaussures**	19	
..	279	284	253	223	217	203	191	Apprêt et tannage des cuirs et articles en cuirs		191
..	316	318	306	294	275	267	250	Chaussures		192
..	731	755	741	686	675	668	656	**Bois et articles en bois et liège (sauf meubles)**	20	
..	12	12	13	17	18	23	18	Sciage et rabotage du bois		201
..	719	743	728	669	657	645	638	Articles en bois, liège, vannerie, sparterie		202
..	665	711	688	655	667	658	648	**Papier et carton; articles en papier et en carton**	21	
..	2 022	2 112	2 044	1 931	2 002	2 012	1 980	**Edition, imprimerie et reproduction**	22	
..	542	596	569	554	601	622	650	Edition		221
..	1 466	1 502	1 458	1 362	1 384	1 371	1 312	Imprimerie et activités annexes		222
..	14	14	17	15	17	19	18	Reproduction de supports enregistrés		223
..	51	57	57	54	53	64	60	**Cokéfaction; prod. pétroliers; comb. nucléaires**	23	
..	1 183	1 201	1 205	1 188	1 225	1 196	1 184	**Produits chimiques**	24	
..	238	241	256	243	256	272	281	Produits chimiques de base		241
..	936	954	942	935	956	911	891	Autres produits chimiques		242
..	9	6	7	10	13	13	12	Fibres synthétiques ou artificielles		243
..	1 319	1 380	1 401	1 364	1 382	1 412	1 419	**Articles en caoutchouc et en matières plastiques**	25	
..	163	168	169	165	154	168	163	Articles en caoutchouc		251
..	1 156	1 212	1 232	1 199	1 228	1 244	1 256	Articles en matières plastiques		252
..	962	990	984	990	986	939	918	**Autres produits minéraux non métalliques**	26	
..	170	195	210	207	193	197	198	Verre et articles en verre		261
..	792	795	774	783	793	742	720	Produits minéraux non métalliques, nca		269
..	513	526	503	477	484	489	481	**Produits métallurgiques de base**	27	
..	125	132	132	125	143	147	150	Sidérurgie et première transformation de l'acier		271
..	104	107	100	98	94	94	96	Métallurgie; métaux précieux et non ferreux		272
..	284	287	271	254	247	248	235	Fonderie		273
..	4 665	4 884	4 774	4 396	4 398	4 410	4 458	**Ouvrages en métaux, sauf machines et matériel**	28	
..	1 568	1 692	1 701	1 616	1 567	1 477	1 443	Constr. et menuiserie métal.; réservoirs; générateurs		281
..	3 097	3 192	3 073	2 780	2 831	2 933	3 015	Autres ouvrages en métaux		289
..	2 434	2 578	2 562	2 419	2 198	2 146	2 196	**Machines et matériel, nca**	29	
..	1 187	1 256	1 257	1 198	1 040	1 012	1 079	Machines d'usage général		291
..	1 168	1 240	1 221	1 144	1 083	1 056	1 043	Machines d'usage spécifique		292
..	79	82	84	77	75	78	74	Appareils domestiques, nca		293
..	104	117	110	74	81	88	73	**Mach. de bureau, comptables, matériel inform.**	30	
..	776	795	809	763	761	756	735	**Machines et appareils électriques, nca**	31	
..	190	200	205	181	170	182	157	Moteurs, génératrices et transformateurs électriques		311
..	305	300	283	264	269	251	247	Matériel électrique de distribution et de commande		312
..	65	64	69	65	63	63	61	Fils et câbles électriques isolés		313
..	11	12	13	12	14	15	13	Accumulateurs, piles électriques		314
..	104	109	108	99	112	108	102	Lampes électriques et appareils d'éclairage		315
..	101	110	131	142	133	137	155	Autres matériels électriques, nca		319
..	503	641	583	540	558	606	601	**Equip. et appar. de radio, TV, communication**	32	
..	257	391	327	319	315	332	340	Tubes et valves électroniques; autres composants		321
..	194	191	199	174	189	221	208	Emetteurs radio et TV; app. téléphonie, télégraphie		322
..	52	59	57	47	54	53	53	Récepteurs radio et TV et articles associés		323
..	882	942	897	856	891	870	863	**Instruments médicaux, de précision, d'optique**	33	
..	685	729	694	666	708	700	700	Appareils médicaux et de précision		331
..	117	131	125	115	112	106	100	Instruments d'optique ; matériel photographique		332
..	80	82	78	75	71	64	63	Horlogerie		333
..	567	604	569	540	545	541	522	**Véhicules automobiles et nemorques**	34	
..	324	328	320	297	291	289	273	**Autres matériels de transport**	35	
..	135	135	130	108	101	97	87	Construction et réparation de navires		351
..	37	38	43	41	39	38	40	Construction de matériel ferroviaire roulant		352
..	91	93	92	92	92	93	91	Construction aéronautique et spatiale		353
..	61	62	55	56	59	61	55	Autres équipements de transport		359
..	1 353	1 410	1 337	1 232	1 247	1 209	1 199	**Meubles; activités de fabrication, nca**	36	
..	840	862	813	759	765	750	743	Meubles		361
..	513	548	524	473	482	459	456	Activités de fabrication, nca		369
..	..	..	..	..	..	..	..	**Récupération**		37
..	139	154	144	164	180	178	170	**Production et distrib. d'électricité, de gaz, d'eau**	E	40-41
..	74	81	74	86	98	104	105	**Electricité, gaz, vapeur et eau chaude**		40
..	37	37	33	32	32	33	32	Production, collecte et distribution d'électricité		401
..	65	73	70	78	82	74	65	**Captage, épuration et distribution d'eau**	41	410
..	..	..	..	..	..	..	..	**Construction**	F	45
..	..	..	..	..	..	..	..	**Commerce de gros et de détail; réparation**	G	50-52
..	..	..	..	..	..	..	..	**Hôtels et restaurants**	H	55
..	..	..	..	..	..	..	..	**Transports, entreposage et communications**	I	60-64
..	..	..	..	..	..	..	..	**Intermédiation financière**	J	65-67
..	..	..	..	..	..	..	..	**Immobilier, locations, services aux entreprises**	K	70-74
..	..	..	..	..	..	..	..	**Admin. publique; éducation; santé; autres**	L-Q	75-99
..	24 123	25 085	24 412	22 974	22 883	22 622	22 319	**Grand total**	A-Q	01-99

Note: ISIC 15 and 16 are not covered by the inquiry and do not figure in the subtotals and totals. ISIC 10 includes 11 and 12; ISIC 131 includes 132; ISIC 1421 includes1422; ISIC 231 includes 233; ISIC 2694 includes 2695.

Statistiques des Structures Industrielles
OCDE, © 1998

FRANCE

Table FR.5 EMPLOYMENT - EMPLOI

Thousands

ISIC revision 3				1989	1990	1991	1992	1993	1994	1995	1996
A	01-02		Agriculture, hunting and forestry	..	..	..	..	..	..	..	..
B	05		Fishing	..	..	..	..	..	..	..	..
C	10-14		Mining and quarrying	..	..	..	..	..	..	..	..
	10		Mining of coal and lignite; extraction of peat	..	27.9	27.0	25.9	24.6	23.3	21.0	19.9
	11		Crude petroleum & natural gas; related service activ.	..	..	..	..	..	..	..	..
	13		Mining of metal ores	..	1.3	1.2	1.1	0.8	0.6	0.5	0.5
	14		Other mining and quarrying	..	28.8	29.6	26.8	25.3	24.4	24.3	23.5
D	15-37		Total manufacturing	..	3 119.2	3 166.5	3 062.0	2 907.8	2 857.0	2 863.9	2 883.6
	15		Food products and beverages	..	..	..	..	..	..	..	..
		155	Beverages	..	..	..	..	..	..	..	..
	16	160	Tobacco products	..	..	..	..	..	..	..	..
	17		Textiles	..	150.9	148.8	141.3	128.7	129.4	128.1	121.1
		171	Spinning, weaving and finishing of textiles	..	76.4	73.5	66.8	60.4	59.9	58.9	56.3
		172	Other textiles	..	40.6	42.5	42.2	40.0	41.0	42.2	40.0
		173	Knitted and crocheted fabrics and articles	..	33.9	32.8	32.3	28.4	28.5	27.0	24.7
	18		Wearing apparel dressing & dyeing of fur	..	143.3	139.2	132.5	121.4	113.9	108.3	104.2
		181	Wearing apparel, except fur apparel	..	142.0	138.1	131.4	120.6	113.2	107.6	103.4
		182	Dressing and dyeing of fur; articles of fur	..	1.3	1.1	1.1	0.8	0.7	0.7	0.8
	19		Tanning, dressing leather; leather artic.; footwear	..	60.8	59.2	54.3	51.6	49.0	46.9	45.0
		191	Tanning, dressing leather; manuf. of leather articles	..	19.2	18.8	17.2	15.5	16.0	14.9	14.8
		192	Footwear	..	41.6	40.4	37.1	36.1	33.1	32.0	30.2
	20		Wood and cork products, ex. furniture	..	47.7	48.0	46.8	43.2	43.0	42.9	42.2
		201	Sawmilling and planing of wood	..	0.7	0.8	0.8	1.0	1.0	1.3	0.9
		202	Products of wood, cork, straw & plaiting material	..	47.0	47.3	46.0	42.2	42.0	41.6	41.3
	21		Paper and paper products	..	99.0	99.5	98.5	95.2	93.7	92.5	91.7
	22		Publishing, printing & reprod. of recorded media	..	158.7	161.0	153.9	148.5	149.0	149.7	149.6
		221	Publishing	..	72.1	74.1	69.6	68.8	69.2	69.7	69.2
		222	Printing and related service activities	..	84.8	85.1	82.2	77.9	77.8	77.6	78.0
		223	Reproduction of recorded media	..	1.8	1.9	2.1	1.9	2.0	2.4	2.4
	23		Coke, refined petroleum products & nuclear fuel	..	36.3	34.8	34.4	33.2	32.3	31.5	31.6
	24		Chemicals and chemical products	..	292.2	289.8	288.5	279.8	278.1	275.8	280.3
		241	Basic chemicals	..	81.2	79.5	79.0	75.5	74.8	75.8	76.8
		242	Other chemical products	..	206.6	206.6	206.0	200.9	200.1	197.0	200.8
		243	Man-made fibres	..	4.3	3.7	3.5	3.4	3.2	3.0	2.7
	25		Rubber and plastic products	..	190.3	192.7	190.8	186.4	186.9	190.6	195.2
		251	Rubber products	..	80.7	77.8	73.9	71.3	68.7	69.9	69.8
		252	Plastic products	..	109.6	114.9	116.8	115.0	118.2	120.7	125.4
	26		Other non-metallic mineral products	..	144.3	145.2	141.0	135.1	131.8	131.0	132.2
		261	Glass and glass products	..	51.1	51.9	52.7	50.6	50.2	51.0	50.4
		269	Non-metallic mineral products, nec	..	93.2	93.3	88.3	84.5	81.6	80.0	81.9
	27		Basic metals	..	149.5	146.5	142.7	133.9	130.8	132.9	131.4
		271	Basic iron and steel	..	81.1	77.5	76.1	72.4	70.2	70.6	70.3
		272	Basic precious and non-ferrous metals	..	28.1	29.2	27.9	26.7	26.3	26.1	25.7
		273	Casting of metals	..	40.2	39.9	38.7	34.8	34.3	36.2	35.5
	28		Fabricated metal products, ex. machin. & equip.	..	328.4	332.8	322.7	301.8	299.2	304.3	318.0
		281	Structural metal prod., tanks, reservoirs, generators	..	116.7	119.8	119.3	114.0	107.9	101.6	105.8
		289	Other fabricated metal products & service activities	..	211.7	213.0	203.5	187.8	191.3	202.8	212.3
	29		Machinery and equipment, nec	..	291.5	293.9	288.2	271.3	255.1	258.1	266.6
		291	General purpose machinery	..	151.5	154.1	153.6	147.4	137.7	138.5	145.2
		292	Special purpose machinery	..	106.8	105.7	100.1	91.4	86.5	87.8	89.5
		293	Domestic appliances, nec	..	33.2	34.1	34.5	32.4	30.9	31.8	31.8
	30		Office, accounting and computing machinery	..	55.5	59.8	52.6	46.2	43.2	41.7	39.6
	31		Electrical machinery and apparatus, nec	..	167.2	170.1	151.4	153.5	154.6	155.9	158.1
		311	Electric motors, generators and transformers	..	27.6	28.1	27.3	25.4	23.6	24.7	23.7
		312	Electricity distribution and control apparatus	..	77.8	77.5	59.0	65.5	64.1	64.0	64.6
		313	Insulated wire and cable	..	22.1	20.2	20.2	19.0	21.0	19.1	17.2
		314	Accumulators, primary cells and primary batteries	..	6.7	9.7	9.2	9.1	8.5	8.5	8.3
		315	Electric lamps and lighting equipment	..	12.9	13.1	12.9	11.8	12.0	11.7	11.5
		319	Other electrical equipment, nec	..	20.0	21.6	22.9	22.7	25.3	28.0	32.7
	32		Radio, TV, communication equip. & apparatus	..	116.9	164.4	153.9	144.1	144.0	149.8	160.0
		321	Electronic valves, tubes & other electronic compon.	..	40.4	87.8	82.9	77.1	73.9	71.2	72.9
		322	TV, radio transmitters & appar. for line teleph., telegr.	..	62.8	61.3	56.9	53.1	54.8	62.7	69.2
		323	TV, radio receivers and associated goods	..	13.7	15.3	14.1	13.9	15.3	15.9	17.9
	33		Medical, precision, optical instr.; watches, clocks	..	86.7	89.3	87.6	83.8	84.5	85.1	83.8
		331	Medical equip.; precision instruments and appliances	..	63.5	66.6	65.9	64.0	65.5	65.9	65.5
		332	Optical instruments and photographic equipment	..	15.7	15.5	14.8	13.7	13.3	13.7	13.4
		333	Watches and clocks	..	7.5	7.2	6.9	6.2	5.6	5.5	4.9
	34		Motor vehicles, trailers, and semi-trailers	..	341.9	326.3	317.6	302.3	295.8	302.2	295.0
	35		Other transport equipment	..	137.3	135.4	137.9	130.8	125.8	122.5	120.5
		351	Building and repairing of ships and boats	..	18.9	17.8	16.3	15.0	15.7	14.9	15.1
		352	Railway, tramway locomotives and rolling stock	..	8.6	9.2	19.0	18.3	16.8	16.0	16.3
		353	Aircraft and spacecraft	..	98.9	98.5	93.2	88.9	84.5	82.5	80.5
		359	Transport equipment, nec	..	10.8	10.0	9.4	8.7	8.7	9.1	8.6
	36		Furniture; manufacturing, nec	..	120.9	129.6	125.4	116.9	116.9	114.0	117.4
		361	Furniture	..	77.0	84.3	82.4	76.9	77.1	76.2	78.0
		369	Manufacturing, nec	..	43.9	45.3	43.0	40.0	39.8	37.9	39.4
	37		Recycling	..	..	..	..	..	..	..	..
E	40-41		Electricity, gas and water supply	..	193.0	192.3	191.7	196.0	197.0	200.1	201.0
	40		Electricity, gas, steam and hot water supply	..	163.9	161.1	159.4	164.1	164.9	167.7	169.1
		401	Production, collection and distribution of electricity	..	129.2	126.3	124.7	124.3	124.2	124.6	124.9
	41	410	Collection, purification, distribution of water	..	29.1	31.2	32.2	31.9	32.1	32.4	31.9
F	45		Construction	..	..	..	..	..	..	..	..
G	50-52		Wholesale and retail trade; repairs etc	..	..	..	..	..	..	..	..
H	55		Hotels and restaurants	..	..	..	..	..	..	..	..
I	60-64		Transport, storage and communications	..	..	..	..	..	..	..	..
J	65-67		Financial intermediation	..	..	..	..	..	..	..	..
K	70-74		Real estate, renting and business activities	..	..	..	..	..	..	..	..
L-Q	75-99		Public admin.; education; health; other services	..	..	..	..	..	..	..	..
A-Q	01-99		Grand total	..	3 422.5	3 416.5	3 307.5	3 154.5	3 102.2	3 109.8	3 128.6

Note: ISIC 15 and 16 are not covered by the inquiry and do not figure in the subtotals and totals. ISIC 10 includes 11 and 12; ISIC 131 includes 132; ISIC 1421 includes1422; ISIC 231 includes 233; ISIC 2694 includes 2695.

Table FR.6 **EMPLOI, SALARIÉS - EMPLOYMENT, EMPLOYEES**

Milliers

1989	1990	1991	1992	1993	1994	1995	1996			CITI révision 3	
..	..	..	..	..	..	..	..	**Agriculture, chasse et sylviculture**	A	01-02	
..	..	..	..	..	..	..	..	**Pêche**	B	05	
..	..	..	..	..	..	..	..	**Activités extractives**	C	10-14	
..	29.2	28.3	27.3	26.0	24.5	23.4	22.0	Extraction de charbon, de lignite et de tourbe		10	
..	..	..	..	..	..	..	..	Extraction de pétrole brut et de gaz naturel		11	
..	1.3	1.2	1.1	0.8	0.6	0.5	0.5	Extraction de minerais métalliques		13	
..	28.8	29.6	26.7	25.1	24.2	24.1	22.7	Autres activités extractives		14	
..	3 104.2	3 135.1	3 024.2	3 255.1	2 811.1	2 802.6	2 762.3	**Activités de fabrication**	D	15-37	
..	..	..	..	..	..	..	..	**Produits alimentaires et boissons**		15	
..	..	..	..	..	..	..	..	Boissons			155
..	..	..	..	..	..	..	..	**Produits à base de tabac**		16	160
..	150.3	147.7	139.5	127.5	127.4	126.1	117.2	**Textiles**		17	
..	75.8	72.7	65.7	59.6	59.0	58.0	54.4	Filature, tissage et achèvement des textiles			171
..	40.7	42.2	41.7	39.5	40.2	41.3	38.5	Autres articles textiles			172
..	33.9	32.8	32.1	28.3	28.2	26.8	24.3	Etoffes et articles de bonneterie			173
..	143.1	138.9	131.8	120.8	112.7	107.1	102.0	**Habillement; préparation, teinture des fourrures**		18	
..	141.9	137.8	130.7	120.0	112.0	106.4	101.3	Articles d'habillement autres qu'en fourrure			181
..	1.3	1.1	1.1	0.8	0.7	0.7	0.8	Préparation, teinture des fourrures; art. en fourrure			182
..	60.4	58.8	53.8	51.5	49.0	46.7	44.5	**Travail des cuirs; articles en cuir; chaussures**		19	
..	19.2	18.8	17.2	15.5	15.9	14.8	14.5	Apprêt et tannage des cuirs et articles en cuirs			191
..	41.2	40.0	36.6	36.0	33.1	31.9	30.0	Chaussures			192
..	47.7	47.9	46.5	43.0	42.8	42.5	40.7	**Bois et articles en bois et liège (sauf meubles)**		20	
..	0.7	0.8	0.8	1.0	1.0	1.3	0.9	Sciage et rabotage du bois			201
..	47.0	47.1	45.7	42.0	41.8	41.2	39.8	Articles en bois, liège, vannerie, sparterie			202
..	99.1	98.7	97.4	94.2	92.2	90.8	88.6	**Papier et carton; articles en papier et en carton**		21	
..	157.5	159.4	152.3	146.8	147.1	147.7	143.0	**Edition, imprimerie et reproduction**		22	
..	71.0	73.0	68.5	67.6	68.1	68.6	65.3	Edition			221
..	84.7	84.6	81.7	77.4	77.2	76.9	75.5	Imprimerie et activités annexes			222
..	1.9	1.9	2.0	1.8	1.8	2.2	2.1	Reproduction de supports enregistrés			223
..	36.9	35.4	35.4	35.0	33.7	33.3	31.3	**Cokéfaction; prod. pétroliers; comb. nucléaires**		23	
..	291.9	287.8	284.1	275.7	272.9	270.8	267.3	**Produits chimiques**		24	
..	81.9	80.1	79.4	76.0	74.7	75.2	74.0	Produits chimiques de base			241
..	205.8	204.1	201.4	196.4	195.2	192.8	190.9	Autres produits chimiques			242
..	4.2	3.6	3.4	3.3	3.0	2.8	2.4	Fibres synthétiques ou artificielles			243
..	190.4	190.6	187.9	184.0	182.5	185.8	186.0	**Articles en caoutchouc et en matières plastiques**		25	
..	80.7	77.6	73.1	70.7	67.3	68.1	67.5	Articles en caoutchouc			251
..	109.6	113.0	114.8	113.4	115.2	117.7	118.5	Articles en matières plastiques			252
..	144.2	144.7	140.4	134.3	130.8	129.3	128.4	**Autres produits minéraux non métalliques**		26	
..	51.1	51.9	52.5	50.5	49.8	50.4	49.1	Verre et articles en verre			261
..	93.1	92.9	87.9	83.9	81.0	79.0	79.3	Produits minéraux non métalliques, nca			269
..	149.3	144.5	140.6	132.6	127.8	127.6	126.0	**Produits métallurgiques de base**		27	
..	81.0	76.6	75.7	71.8	69.1	68.1	67.9	Sidérurgie et première transformation de l'acier			271
..	28.1	28.7	27.4	26.4	25.6	25.2	24.7	Métallurgie; métaux précieux et non ferreux			272
..	40.2	39.3	37.6	34.4	33.1	34.2	33.5	Fonderie			273
..	328.1	329.1	319.1	297.6	294.0	297.2	299.2	**Ouvrages en métaux, sauf machines et matériel**		28	
..	116.6	118.5	118.0	112.1	106.3	99.3	98.0	Constr. et menuiserie métal.; réservoirs; générateurs			281
..	211.5	210.6	201.1	185.4	187.7	197.9	201.2	Autres ouvrages en métaux			289
..	289.4	290.9	284.6	268.6	251.1	252.3	254.8	**Machines et matériel, nca**		29	
..	150.5	153.2	152.6	146.9	136.7	136.3	140.0	Machines d'usage général			291
..	105.8	104.1	98.6	90.1	84.4	85.2	85.0	Machines d'usage spécifique			292
..	33.0	33.5	33.4	31.7	30.1	30.8	29.8	Appareils domestiques, nca			293
..	55.6	59.5	52.2	45.7	42.4	40.6	36.2	**Mach. de bureau, comptables, matériel inform.**		30	
..	167.1	168.0	149.7	151.4	151.7	152.3	151.2	**Machines et appareils électriques, nca**		31	
..	27.5	27.5	26.9	24.9	23.1	23.8	22.7	Moteurs, génératrices et transformateurs électriques			311
..	77.8	76.9	58.5	64.6	62.7	62.5	62.3	Matériel électrique de distribution et de commande			312
..	22.1	20.0	20.1	19.0	20.9	18.8	16.4	Fils et câbles électriques isolés			313
..	6.7	9.4	9.1	9.0	8.5	8.4	7.9	Accumulateurs, piles électriques			314
..	12.9	13.0	12.6	11.6	11.6	11.5	11.1	Lampes électriques et appareils d'éclairage			315
..	20.1	21.2	22.5	22.4	24.9	27.3	30.7	Autres matériels électriques, nca			319
..	116.5	162.7	152.5	143.3	141.7	145.6	152.7	**Equip. et appar. de radio, TV, communication**		32	
..	40.3	87.0	82.5	76.9	73.2	70.0	70.4	Tubes et valves électroniques; autres composants			321
..	62.5	60.5	56.1	52.8	53.8	60.8	66.1	Emetteurs radio et TV; app. téléphonie, télégraphie			322
..	13.7	15.1	13.8	13.6	14.7	14.9	16.2	Récepteurs radio et TV et articles associés			323
..	86.6	88.9	87.0	83.1	83.8	84.3	81.6	**Instruments médicaux, de précision, d'optique**		33	
..	63.4	66.3	65.3	63.4	65.0	65.3	63.6	Appareils médicaux et de précision			331
..	15.7	15.4	14.8	13.6	13.2	13.5	13.1	Instruments d'optique ; matériel photographique			332
..	7.4	7.2	6.9	6.2	5.6	5.4	4.9	Horlogerie			333
..	333.7	319.4	310.0	297.6	288.3	290.4	283.0	**Véhicules automobiles et nemorques**		34	
..	135.2	133.4	135.9	129.2	124.6	120.7	117.3	**Autres matériels de transport**		35	
..	18.2	17.4	15.9	14.4	14.9	14.2	14.1	Construction et réparation de navires			351
..	8.4	8.7	18.1	17.7	16.7	15.6	15.6	Construction de matériel ferroviaire roulant			352
..	98.2	97.5	92.7	88.4	84.7	82.3	79.3	Construction aéronautique et spatiale			353
..	10.4	9.8	9.1	8.6	8.4	8.6	8.3	Autres équipements de transport			359
..	121.0	128.8	123.7	115.4	114.4	111.6	111.3	**Meubles; activités de fabrication, nca**		36	
..	77.0	83.5	81.0	75.6	75.1	74.0	73.6	Meubles			361
..	44.1	45.3	42.7	39.8	39.3	37.6	37.7	Activités de fabrication, nca			369
..	..	..	..	..	..	..	..	**Récupération**		37	
..	192.1	191.7	190.9	195.7	196.5	198.2	196.7	**Production et distrib. d'électricité, de gaz, d'eau**	E	40-41	
..	163.3	161.0	159.2	163.8	164.8	166.2	165.5	**Electricité, gaz, vapeur et eau chaude**		40	
..	128.6	126.2	124.6	124.1	124.0	123.2	122.6	Production, collecte et distribution d'électricité			401
..	28.9	30.7	31.7	31.9	31.8	32.0	31.2	**Captage, épuration et distribution d'eau**		41	410
..	..	..	..	..	..	..	..	**Construction**	F	45	
..	..	..	..	..	..	..	..	**Commerce de gros et de détail; réparation**	G	50-52	
..	..	..	..	..	..	..	..	**Hôtels et restaurants**	H	55	
..	..	..	..	..	..	..	..	**Transports, entreposage et communications**	I	60-64	
..	..	..	..	..	..	..	..	**Intermédiation financière**	J	65-67	
..	..	..	..	..	..	..	..	**Immobilier, locations, services aux entreprises**	K	70-74	
..	..	..	..	..	..	..	..	**Admin. publique; éducation; santé; autres**	L-Q	75-99	
..	3 407.9	3 385.9	3 270.2	3 125.0	3 056.9	3 048.7	3 004.3	**Grand total**	A-Q	01-99	

Note: ISIC 15 and 16 are not covered by the inquiry and do not figure in the subtotals and totals. ISIC 10 includes 11 and 12; ISIC 131 includes 132; ISIC 1421 includes1422; ISIC 231 includes 233; ISIC 2694 includes 2695.

Statistiques des Structures Industrielles
OCDE, © 1998

FRANCE

Table FR.7 WAGES AND SALARIES, EMPLOYEES - SALAIRES ET TRAITEMENTS, SALARIÉS

Millions of FF (Current Prices)

ISIC revision 3			1989	1990	1991	1992	1993	1994	1995	1996
A	01-02	Agriculture, hunting and forestry	..	..	..	..	..	..	..	..
B	05	Fishing	..	..	..	..	..	..	..	..
C	10-14	Mining and quarrying	..	..	..	..	..	..	..	..
	10	Mining of coal and lignite; extraction of peat	..	5 738	5 717	5 845	5 697	5 525	5 307	5 190
	11	Crude petroleum & natural gas; related service activ.	..	..	..	..	..	..	..	..
	13	Mining of metal ores	..	193	182	165	131	89	83	83
	14	Other mining and quarrying	..	3 846	4 128	3 886	3 718	3 634	3 702	3 622
D	15-37	Total manufacturing	..	551 999	459 492	461 367	449 106	450 186	458 287	463 188
	15	Food products and beverages	..	..	..	..	..	..	..	..
	155	Beverages	..	..	..	..	..	..	..	..
	16 160	Tobacco products	..	..	..	..	..	..	..	..
	17	Textiles	..	16 246	16 686	16 289	15 056	15 306	15 583	14 830
	171	Spinning, weaving and finishing of textiles	..	8 484	8 518	7 951	7 309	7 374	7 326	6 975
	172	Other textiles	..	4 402	4 768	4 883	4 627	4 850	5 204	4 973
	173	Knitted and crocheted fabrics and articles	..	3 360	3 400	3 454	3 119	3 081	3 053	2 882
	18	Wearing apparel dressing & dyeing of fur	..	13 906	13 936	13 700	12 889	12 218	11 968	11 661
	181	Wearing apparel, except fur apparel	..	13 739	13 796	13 566	12 792	12 138	11 879	11 562
	182	Dressing and dyeing of fur; articles of fur	..	167	140	134	97	80	89	100
	19	Tanning, dressing leather; leather artic.; footwear	..	5 997	6 078	5 711	5 548	5 328	5 182	4 948
	191	Tanning, dressing leather; manuf. of leather articles	..	2 052	2 039	1 946	1 796	1 915	1 797	1 757
	192	Footwear	..	3 945	4 039	3 765	3 752	3 413	3 386	3 191
	20	Wood and cork products, ex. furniture	..	5 113	5 259	5 326	4 996	5 031	5 099	5 013
	201	Sawmilling and planing of wood	..	92	102	105	129	152	178	139
	202	Products of wood, cork, straw & plaiting material	..	5 021	5 157	5 221	4 867	4 879	4 922	4 874
	21	Paper and paper products	..	13 660	14 177	14 405	14 590	14 453	14 569	14 579
	22	Publishing, printing & reprod. of recorded media	..	26 494	27 800	27 064	26 681	27 187	27 588	27 722
	221	Publishing	..	13 922	14 743	14 204	14 268	14 824	15 023	15 237
	222	Printing and related service activities	..	12 369	12 830	12 600	12 179	12 121	12 270	12 200
	223	Reproduction of recorded media	..	202	227	259	234	241	294	285
	23	Coke, refined petroleum products & nuclear fuel	..	8 426	8 363	8 431	8 473	8 513	8 444	8 181
	24	Chemicals and chemical products	..	50 286	52 082	53 475	54 405	54 740	56 406	56 694
	241	Basic chemicals	..	14 447	14 963	15 208	15 152	15 110	15 706	15 998
	242	Other chemical products	..	35 132	36 552	37 699	38 684	39 083	40 242	40 287
	243	Man-made fibres	..	707	567	569	570	548	457	409
	25	Rubber and plastic products	..	23 249	24 338	24 812	25 122	25 383	26 311	26 751
	251	Rubber products	..	10 258	10 401	10 205	10 244	9 867	10 197	10 337
	252	Plastic products	..	12 991	13 937	14 606	14 877	15 516	16 114	16 414
	26	Other non-metallic mineral products	..	19 262	19 991	20 045	19 834	19 836	20 160	20 326
	261	Glass and glass products	..	6 951	7 290	7 549	7 519	7 702	8 012	8 030
	269	Non-metallic mineral products, nec	..	12 311	12 701	12 496	12 315	12 133	12 148	12 296
	27	Basic metals	..	23 258	23 091	22 713	21 609	21 330	22 068	21 751
	271	Basic iron and steel	..	14 505	13 983	13 694	13 071	12 781	13 155	12 757
	272	Basic precious and non-ferrous metals	..	4 151	4 474	4 480	4 350	4 367	4 456	4 531
	273	Casting of metals	..	4 602	4 634	4 538	4 187	4 181	4 457	4 463
	28	Fabricated metal products, ex. machin. & equip.	..	41 557	43 454	43 606	41 204	41 134	42 669	43 706
	281	Structural metal prod., tanks, reservoirs, generators	..	15 327	16 270	16 762	16 118	15 413	14 860	14 832
	289	Other fabricated metal products & service activities	..	26 230	27 184	26 844	25 087	25 721	27 810	28 874
	29	Machinery and equipment, nec	..	39 953	41 857	42 671	41 408	39 239	40 450	41 715
	291	General purpose machinery	..	20 932	22 304	23 266	22 841	21 738	22 382	23 383
	292	Special purpose machinery	..	15 267	15 564	15 241	14 372	13 556	14 002	14 276
	293	Domestic appliances, nec	..	3 754	3 989	4 164	4 196	3 945	4 066	4 056
	30	Office, accounting and computing machinery	..	132 297	13 816	12 896	11 545	12 029	10 852	10 493
	31	Electrical machinery and apparatus, nec	..	22 452	23 667	21 347	22 911	23 789	24 488	24 985
	311	Electric motors, generators and transformers	..	3 639	3 786	3 782	3 606	3 414	3 607	3 505
	312	Electricity distribution and control apparatus	..	10 908	11 292	8 556	10 268	10 438	10 630	10 940
	313	Insulated wire and cable	..	2 876	2 782	2 872	2 901	3 214	3 123	2 776
	314	Accumulators, primary cells and primary batteries	..	874	1 346	1 358	1 359	1 350	1 356	1 352
	315	Electric lamps and lighting equipment	..	1 596	1 682	1 676	1 577	1 623	1 674	1 644
	319	Other electrical equipment, nec	..	2 559	2 779	3 103	3 199	3 751	4 099	4 766
	32	Radio, TV, communication equip. & apparatus	..	17 294	28 286	30 018	26 927	27 085	28 366	31 042
	321	Electronic valves, tubes & other electronic compon.	..	5 292	15 016	17 316	14 275	13 860	13 284	13 936
	322	TV, radio transmitters & appar. for line teleph., telegr.	..	10 389	11 268	10 887	10 847	11 138	12 948	14 640
	323	TV, radio receivers and associated goods	..	1 613	2 002	1 815	1 806	2 088	2 134	2 466
	33	Medical, precision, optical instr.; watches, clocks	..	12 164	13 358	13 730	13 474	13 837	14 337	14 041
	331	Medical equip.; precision instruments and appliances	..	9 436	10 519	10 838	10 746	11 222	11 613	11 422
	332	Optical instruments and photographic equipment	..	1 898	1 999	2 051	1 953	1 896	2 001	1 952
	333	Watches and clocks	..	829	840	841	774	719	724	666
	34	Motor vehicles, trailers, and semi-trailers	..	43 478	43 712	44 363	43 908	44 667	45 514	45 932
	35	Other transport equipment	..	23 020	24 226	25 572	24 038	24 445	23 628	23 966
	351	Building and repairing of ships and boats	..	2 354	2 295	2 182	1 990	2 213	2 013	2 001
	352	Railway, tramway locomotives and rolling stock	..	1 109	1 191	2 760	2 763	2 719	2 628	2 709
	353	Aircraft and spacecraft	..	18 436	19 644	19 557	18 245	18 423	17 822	18 105
	359	Transport equipment, nec	..	1 121	1 095	1 073	1 041	1 090	1 166	1 151
	36	Furniture; manufacturing, nec	..	13 889	15 313	15 192	14 488	14 635	14 604	14 853
	361	Furniture	..	8 504	9 601	9 651	9 235	9 358	9 439	9 531
	369	Manufacturing, nec	..	5 385	5 712	5 540	5 253	5 278	5 164	5 322
	37	Recycling	..	..	..	..	..	..	..	..
E	40-41	Electricity, gas and water supply	..	32 580	33 298	34 531	36 055	37 950	38 423	40 074
	40	Electricity, gas, steam and hot water supply	..	28 048	28 382	29 290	30 497	32 296	32 583	34 127
	401	Production, collection and distribution of electricity	..	22 451	22 520	23 301	23 555	25 115	24 740	25 985
	41 410	Collection, purification, distribution of water	..	4 532	4 916	5 241	5 558	5 653	5 840	5 947
F	45	Construction	..	..	..	..	..	..	..	..
G	50-52	Wholesale and retail trade; repairs etc	..	..	..	..	..	..	..	..
H	55	Hotels and restaurants	..	..	..	..	..	..	..	..
I	60-64	Transport, storage and communications	..	..	..	..	..	..	..	..
J	65-67	Financial intermediation	..	..	..	..	..	..	..	..
K	70-74	Real estate, renting and business activities	..	..	..	..	..	..	..	..
L-Q	75-99	Public admin.; education; health; other services	..	..	..	..	..	..	..	..
A-Q	01-99	Grand total	..	485 557	502 817	505 794	494 707	497 384	505 801	512 157

Note: ISIC 15 and 16 are not covered by the inquiry and do not figure in the subtotals and totals. ISIC 10 includes 11 and 12; ISIC 131 includes 132; ISIC 1421 includes1422; ISIC 231 includes 233; ISIC 2694 includes 2695.

Table FR.8 **CHARGES SOCIALES DES EMPLOYEURS - EMPLOYERS' SOCIAL COSTS**

Millions de FF (Prix courants)

1989	1990	1991	1992	1993	1994	1995	1996			CITI révision 3
..	..	..	..	..	..	..	..	Agriculture, chasse et sylviculture	A	01-02
..	..	..	..	..	..	..	..	Pêche	B	05
..	..	..	..	4 348	..	..	..	Activités extractives	C	10-14
..	2 505	2 476	2 533	2 405	2 372	2 365	2 358	Extraction de charbon, de lignite et de tourbe		10
..				1 301				Extraction de pétrole brut et de gaz naturel		11
..	133	126	117	121	48	46	45	Extraction de minerais métalliques		13
..	1 856	1 998	1 904	1 837	1 818	1 837	1 792	Autres activités extractives		14
..	183 007	194 824	195 379	195 726	197 854	199 972	200 503	Activités de fabrication	D	15-37
..	..	..	..	..	..	..	..	Produits alimentaires et boissons		15
..	..	..	..	..	..	..	..	Boissons		155
..	..	..	..	..	..	..	..	Produits à base de tabac	16	160
..	6 483	6 668	6 566	6 166	6 279	6 245	5 566	Textiles	17	
..	3 403	3 442	3 201	3 017	3 050	2 959	2 662	Filature, tissage et achèvement des textiles		171
..	1 755	1 910	1 994	1 901	2 000	2 086	1 894	Autres articles textiles		172
..	1 325	1 316	1 371	1 248	1 229	1 200	1 010	Etoffes et articles de bonneterie		173
..	5 335	5 372	5 373	5 076	4 730	4 499	4 003	Habillement; préparation, teinture des fourrures	18	
..	5 272	5 317	5 321	5 037	4 698	4 463	3 966	Articles d'habillement autres qu'en fourrure		181
..	63	55	52	38	32	35	37	Préparation, teinture des fourrures; art. en fourrure		182
..	2 372	2 375	2 285	2 223	2 129	2 018	1 773	Travail des cuirs; articles en cuir; chaussures	19	
..	815	808	786	732	784	725	668	Apprêt et tannage des cuirs et articles en cuirs		191
..	1 557	1 568	1 499	1 490	1 345	1 294	1 105	Chaussures		192
..	2 197	2 250	2 307	2 169	2 184	2 170	2 079	Bois et articles en bois et liège (sauf meubles)	20	
..	35	40	42	49	56	68	51	Sciage et rabotage du bois		201
..	2 162	2 211	2 264	2 119	2 128	2 102	2 028	Articles en bois, liège, vannerie, sparterie		202
..	5 695	5 956	6 142	6 044	6 201	6 225	6 212	Papier et carton; articles en papier et en carton	21	
..	10 627	11 276	11 232	11 296	11 569	11 703	11 682	Edition, imprimerie et reproduction	22	
..	5 475	5 870	5 813	5 953	6 257	6 307	6 348	Edition		221
..	5 069	5 313	5 312	5 244	5 210	5 276	5 218	Imprimerie et activités annexes		222
..	83	93	107	99	103	120	116	Reproduction de supports enregistrés		223
..	4 315	4 665	4 850	5 020	5 180	5 162	5 070	Cokéfaction; prod. pétroliers; comb. nucléaires	23	
..	22 299	23 136	24 230	24 818	25 280	25 859	26 112	Produits chimiques	24	
..	6 899	7 262	7 623	7 592	7 605	7 919	8 094	Produits chimiques de base		241
..	14 967	15 550	16 264	16 853	17 297	17 689	17 795	Autres produits chimiques		242
..	433	324	343	372	378	251	223	Fibres synthétiques ou artificielles		243
..	9 520	9 998	10 356	10 621	10 775	11 114	11 172	Articles en caoutchouc et en matières plastiques	25	
..	4 234	4 306	4 300	4 357	4 227	4 345	4 382	Articles en caoutchouc		251
..	5 286	5 691	6 056	6 264	6 549	6 769	6 790	Articles en matières plastiques		252
..	8 250	8 583	8 690	8 640	8 721	8 736	8 779	Autres produits minéraux non métalliques	26	
..	2 814	2 966	3 127	3 135	3 209	3 291	3 314	Verre et articles en verre		261
..	5 435	5 616	5 563	5 505	5 512	5 446	5 465	Produits minéraux non métalliques, nca		269
..	9 927	10 049	10 137	9 854	9 723	9 868	9 831	Produits métallurgiques de base	27	
..	6 072	6 063	6 135	5 966	5 813	5 825	5 818	Sidérurgie et première transformation de l'acier		271
..	1 868	2 016	2 066	2 089	2 089	2 116	2 111	Métallurgie; métaux précieux et non ferreux		272
..	1 987	1 970	1 935	1 799	1 821	1 927	1 901	Fonderie		273
..	17 400	18 224	18 422	17 659	17 787	18 297	18 573	Ouvrages en métaux, sauf machines et matériel	28	
..	6 599	7 048	7 270	7 120	6 916	6 617	6 539	Constr. et menuiserie métal.; réservoirs; générateurs		281
..	10 802	11 177	11 152	10 539	10 871	11 681	12 035	Autres ouvrages en métaux		289
..	16 581	17 430	18 038	17 653	17 177	17 580	18 075	Machines et matériel, nca	29	
..	8 693	9 294	9 869	9 802	9 589	9 817	10 240	Machines d'usage général		291
..	6 365	6 514	6 443	6 137	5 914	6 048	6 125	Machines d'usage spécifique		292
..	1 523	1 623	1 726	1 713	1 674	1 715	1 710	Appareils domestiques, nca		293
..	5 866	6 078	5 731	5 249	5 154	4 801	4 481	Mach. de bureau, comptables, matériel inform.	30	
..	9 446	9 881	9 072	9 864	10 352	10 555	10 764	Machines et appareils électriques, nca	31	
..	1 463	1 545	1 550	1 499	1 454	1 509	1 456	Moteurs, génératrices et transformateurs électriques		311
..	4 679	4 718	3 663	4 465	4 541	4 599	4 750	Matériel électrique de distribution et de commande		312
..	1 203	1 184	1 260	1 249	1 433	1 378	1 242	Fils et câbles électriques isolés		313
..	358	553	569	585	589	590	572	Accumulateurs, piles électriques		314
..	664	697	709	674	698	716	708	Lampes électriques et appareils d'éclairage		315
..	1 079	1 184	1 321	1 392	1 639	1 763	2 035	Autres matériels électriques, nca		319
..	7 323	12 201	9 875	11 825	11 873	12 503	13 484	Equip. et appar. de radio, TV, communication	32	
..	2 190	6 685	4 420	6 302	6 192	5 813	5 993	Tubes et valves électroniques; autres composants		321
..	4 456	4 727	4 680	4 739	4 784	5 782	6 458	Emetteurs radio et TV; app. téléphonie, télégraphie		322
..	677	789	775	784	897	908	1 034	Récepteurs radio et TV et articles associés		323
..	5 076	5 564	5 769	5 753	5 997	6 170	6 051	Instruments médicaux, de précision, d'optique	33	
..	3 960	4 411	4 589	4 614	4 865	5 017	4 938	Appareils médicaux et de précision		331
..	791	823	847	832	837	865	855	Instruments d'optique ; matériel photographique		332
..	325	330	332	307	295	288	257	Horlogerie		333
..	18 508	18 489	18 981	18 977	19 817	19 677	19 921	Véhicules automobiles et nemorques	34	
..	10 154	10 459	11 071	10 801	10 800	10 721	10 827	Autres matériels de transport	35	
..	1 004	973	930	877	985	899	880	Construction et réparation de navires		351
..	467	506	1 206	1 212	1 195	1 152	1 190	Construction de matériel ferroviaire roulant		352
..	8 228	8 533	8 488	8 275	8 161	8 192	8 286	Construction aéronautique et spatiale		353
..	455	448	447	438	458	477	471	Autres équipements de transport		359
..	5 633	6 170	6 253	6 018	6 126	6 069	6 046	Meubles; activités de fabrication, nca	36	
..	3 466	3 868	3 983	3 852	3 921	3 929	3 892	Meubles		361
..	2 167	2 302	2 270	2 166	2 206	2 141	2 155	Activités de fabrication, nca		369
..	..	..	..	..	..	..	..	Récupération		37
..	19 962	21 157	22 278	23 317	24 093	24 660	25 439	Production et distrib. d'électricité, de gaz, d'eau	E	40-41
..	17 685	18 727	19 661	20 518	21 219	21 657	22 340	Electricité, gaz, vapeur et eau chaude		40
..	14 174	14 929	15 717	16 122	16 662	16 780	17 310	Production, collecte et distribution d'électricité		401
..	2 277	2 430	2 617	2 798	2 873	3 003	3 100	Captage, épuration et distribution d'eau	41	410
..	..	..	..	..	..	..	..	Construction	F	45
..	..	..	..	..	..	..	..	Commerce de gros et de détail; réparation	G	50-52
..	..	..	..	..	..	..	..	Hôtels et restaurants	H	55
..	..	..	..	..	..	..	..	Transports, entreposage et communications	I	60-64
..	..	..	..	..	..	..	..	Intermédiation financière	J	65-67
..	..	..	..	..	..	..	..	Immobilier, locations, services aux entreprises	K	70-74
..	..	..	..	..	..	..	..	Admin. publique; éducation; santé; autres	L-Q	75-99
..	211 797	220 581	222 211	223 390	226 184	228 880	230 137	Grand total	A-Q	01-99

Note: ISIC 15 and 16 are not covered by the inquiry and do not figure in the subtotals and totals. ISIC 10 includes 11 and 12; ISIC 131 includes 132; ISIC 1421 includes1422; ISIC 231 includes 233; ISIC 2694 includes 2695.

Statistiques des Structures Industrielles
OCDE, © 1998

Table FR.9 EXPORTS - EXPORTATIONS

Millions of FF (Current Prices)

ISIC revision 3			1989	1990	1991	1992	1993	1994	1995	1996
A	01-02	Agriculture, hunting and forestry	..	..	..	..	..	..	..	..
B	05	Fishing	..	..	..	..	..	..	..	..
C	10-14	Mining and quarrying	..	..	..	..	..	..	..	..
	10	Mining of coal and lignite; extraction of peat	..	3 854	4 411	4 799	5 007	4 908	4 582	4 116
	11	Crude petroleum & natural gas; related service activ.	..	..	..	..	..	..	..	..
	13	Mining of metal ores	..	170	167	156	162	160	248	248
	14	Other mining and quarrying	..	1 967	2 290	2 170	2 197	2 383	2 528	2 324
D	15-37	Total manufacturing	..	807 190	852 783	871 485	933 883	926 814	1 007 520	1 064 025
	15	Food products and beverages	..	..	..	..	..	..	..	..
	155	Beverages	..	..	..	..	..	..	..	..
	16 / 160	Tobacco products	..	..	..	..	..	..	..	..
	17	Textiles	..	28 637	28 399	28 494	25 124	28 054	30 101	29 560
	171	Spinning, weaving and finishing of textiles	..	19 471	18 523	17 409	15 431	17 351	18 031	17 879
	172	Other textiles	..	5 798	6 568	7 434	6 805	7 855	9 257	8 874
	173	Knitted and crocheted fabrics and articles	..	3 368	3 307	3 651	2 889	2 848	2 813	2 807
	18	Wearing apparel dressing & dyeing of fur	..	14 369	14 699	15 235	14 396	15 013	16 545	16 872
	181	Wearing apparel, except fur apparel	..	14 098	14 446	14 989	14 225	14 847	16 263	16 547
	182	Dressing and dyeing of fur; articles of fur	..	271	253	246	170	166	281	324
	19	Tanning, dressing leather; leather artic.; footwear	..	7 716	7 871	7 442	7 176	7 845	7 399	7 453
	191	Tanning, dressing leather; manuf. of leather articles	..	3 151	2 929	3 038	2 870	4 328	3 774	3 855
	192	Footwear	..	4 565	4 942	4 405	4 305	3 517	3 625	3 598
	20	Wood and cork products, ex. furniture	..	3 570	3 960	4 443	4 265	5 267	5 751	5 420
	201	Sawmilling and planing of wood	..	13	1	13	2	1	12	2
	202	Products of wood, cork, straw & plaiting material	..	3 557	3 959	4 431	4 263	5 266	5 739	5 418
	21	Paper and paper products	..	22 061	22 964	24 821	24 512	27 032	32 993	29 926
	22	Publishing, printing & reprod. of recorded media	..	7 838	8 237	8 542	9 002	9 757	9 960	10 602
	221	Publishing	..	4 852	5 210	4 915	5 318	5 579	5 683	6 275
	222	Printing and related service activities	..	2 768	2 816	3 260	3 325	3 780	3 798	3 722
	223	Reproduction of recorded media	..	218	210	366	359	398	480	605
	23	Coke, refined petroleum products & nuclear fuel	..	31 562	32 873	28 339	26 137	25 695	26 619	36 130
	24	Chemicals and chemical products	..	133 331	135 843	138 830	140 774	156 373	172 886	179 078
	241	Basic chemicals	..	64 979	63 174	61 318	61 374	70 896	77 838	76 914
	242	Other chemical products	..	66 365	70 834	75 741	77 622	83 836	93 136	100 385
	243	Man-made fibres	..	1 988	1 835	1 772	1 778	1 640	1 912	1 779
	25	Rubber and plastic products	..	31 249	33 279	34 189	33 466	35 951	38 851	41 830
	251	Rubber products	..	18 445	19 130	19 292	18 429	18 995	20 339	22 375
	252	Plastic products	..	12 804	14 149	14 897	15 037	16 956	18 512	19 455
	26	Other non-metallic mineral products	..	21 215	21 871	21 603	22 095	23 472	25 281	25 880
	261	Glass and glass products	..	11 081	11 581	11 374	11 710	12 822	13 646	13 601
	269	Non-metallic mineral products, nec	..	10 134	10 290	10 229	10 385	10 650	11 636	12 279
	27	Basic metals	..	69 269	69 439	66 002	61 358	67 778	80 554	77 655
	271	Basic iron and steel	..	42 507	43 951	40 623	38 663	42 709	49 997	48 265
	272	Basic precious and non-ferrous metals	..	22 524	21 423	21 404	18 990	20 993	25 515	24 031
	273	Casting of metals	..	4 239	4 065	3 976	3 705	4 077	5 042	5 358
	28	Fabricated metal products, ex. machin. & equip.	..	26 287	29 084	30 424	29 103	39 731	35 870	36 708
	281	Structural metal prod., tanks, reservoirs, generators	..	8 701	11 131	12 316	11 751	19 490	12 295	11 091
	289	Other fabricated metal products & service activities	..	17 587	17 953	18 108	17 352	20 241	23 575	25 617
	29	Machinery and equipment, nec	..	77 096	76 283	82 576	78 252	90 222	98 576	101 770
	291	General purpose machinery	..	37 179	38 663	43 714	40 218	47 603	49 236	50 793
	292	Special purpose machinery	..	33 691	29 634	29 973	29 344	33 859	39 665	40 437
	293	Domestic appliances, nec	..	6 226	7 985	8 889	8 690	8 759	9 676	10 539
	30	Office, accounting and computing machinery	..	28 903	30 341	29 666	28 538	28 394	35 115	37 528
	31	Electrical machinery and apparatus, nec	..	33 988	37 629	34 276	38 723	41 163	46 754	50 429
	311	Electric motors, generators and transformers	..	5 736	5 921	5 434	5 473	5 282	5 928	6 297
	312	Electricity distribution and control apparatus	..	15 696	16 812	12 715	16 171	17 526	18 985	19 947
	313	Insulated wire and cable	..	5 307	5 357	6 002	6 673	6 182	7 291	7 202
	314	Accumulators, primary cells and primary batteries	..	1 006	2 206	2 083	2 322	2 455	2 764	2 821
	315	Electric lamps and lighting equipment	..	1 950	2 194	2 407	2 628	3 089	3 412	3 762
	319	Other electrical equipment, nec	..	4 292	5 139	5 634	5 455	6 629	8 374	10 401
	32	Radio, TV, communication equip. & apparatus	..	27 609	46 018	49 143	43 610	52 008	59 629	76 042
	321	Electronic valves, tubes & other electronic compon.	..	13 798	26 626	27 479	21 605	25 011	28 242	36 688
	322	TV, radio transmitters & appar. for line teleph., telegr.	..	7 881	9 978	11 550	13 293	18 020	20 363	24 469
	323	TV, radio receivers and associated goods	..	5 930	9 415	10 113	8 712	8 977	11 023	14 885
	33	Medical, precision, optical instr.; watches, clocks	..	17 389	19 086	19 351	20 199	22 214	23 941	25 232
	331	Medical equip.; precision instruments and appliances	..	12 825	14 549	15 010	16 416	18 182	19 438	20 813
	332	Optical instruments and photographic equipment	..	2 703	2 835	2 743	2 361	2 614	2 969	2 986
	333	Watches and clocks	..	1 861	1 703	1 599	1 423	1 418	1 534	1 433
	34	Motor vehicles, trailers, and semi-trailers	..	152 612	158 990	169 384	156 424	177 062	189 323	200 132
	35	Other transport equipment	..	56 890	59 461	61 822	51 490	56 081	52 611	56 032
	351	Building and repairing of ships and boats	..	5 242	7 329	5 713	4 167	7 812	6 923	4 673
	352	Railway, tramway locomotives and rolling stock	..	929	1 453	3 798	3 406	3 738	3 462	3 870
	353	Aircraft and spacecraft	..	47 983	48 093	49 759	41 562	41 748	39 111	44 319
	359	Transport equipment, nec	..	2 736	2 586	2 552	2 354	2 783	3 116	3 170
	36	Furniture; manufacturing, nec	..	15 598	16 456	16 900	16 687	17 701	18 761	19 747
	361	Furniture	..	5 333	6 558	6 924	6 664	7 119	7 591	8 058
	369	Manufacturing, nec	..	10 265	9 898	9 976	10 023	10 582	11 170	11 689
	37	Recycling	..	..	..	..	..	..	..	..
E	40-41	Electricity, gas and water supply	..	13 612	15 861	16 452	17 944	19 363	21 551	20 802
	40	Electricity, gas, steam and hot water supply	..	13 418	15 604	16 112	17 572	18 936	21 238	20 481
	401	Production, collection and distribution of electricity	..	13 132	14 909	15 176	16 811	17 901	20 038	19 206
	41 / 410	Collection, purification, distribution of water	..	194	258	340	373	427	313	321
F	45	Construction	..	..	..	..	..	..	..	..
G	50-52	Wholesale and retail trade; repairs etc	..	..	..	..	..	..	..	..
H	55	Hotels and restaurants	..	..	..	..	..	..	..	..
I	60-64	Transport, storage and communications	..	..	..	..	..	..	..	..
J	65-67	Financial intermediation	..	..	..	..	..	..	..	..
K	70-74	Real estate, renting and business activities	..	..	..	..	..	..	..	..
L-Q	75-99	Public admin.; education; health; other services	..	..	..	..	..	..	..	..
A-Q	01-99	Grand total	..	847 304	875 512	895 062	856 639	953 627	1 036 429	1 091 515

Note: ISIC 15 and 16 are not covered by the inquiry and do not figure in the subtotals and totals. ISIC 10 includes 11 and 12; ISIC 131 includes 132; ISIC 1421 includes1422;
ISIC 231 includes 233; ISIC 2694 includes 2695.

Table GE.1 PRODUCTION - PRODUCTION

Millions de DM *(Prix courants)*

1989	1990	1991	1992	1993	1994	1995	1996			CITI révision 3
..	..					..	..	**Agriculture, chasse et sylviculture**	A	01-02
..	..					..	..	**Pêche**	B	05
..	..	44 308	41 748	40 660	41 105	40 507	..	**Activités extractives**	C	10-14
..	..	29 978	26 477	26 311	24 872	23 861	13 630	Extraction de charbon, de lignite et de tourbe		10
..	..	5 054	5 375	4 953	5 223	5 675	5 788	Extraction de pétrole brut et de gaz naturel		11
..	..	494	503	552	608	653	..	Extraction de minerais métalliques		13
..	..	8 783	9 393	8 844	10 402	10 318	9 917	Autres activités extractives		14
..	..	1 970 348	1 971 602	1 849 078	1 914 710	2 033 160	2 049 960	**Activités de fabrication**	D	15-37
..	..	214 621	218 736	216 817	218 645	221 006	222 521	**Produits alimentaires et boissons**		15
..	..					43 321	41 890	Boissons		155
..	..	29 327	28 007	29 340	29 343	29 918	29 633	**Produits à base de tabac**	16	160
..	..	39 969	38 238	34 272	33 067	32 098	31 512	**Textiles**		17
..	..					15 915	14 947	Filature, tissage et achèvement des textiles		171
..	..					11 639	12 094	Autres articles textiles		172
..	..					4 544	4 471	Etoffes et articles de bonneterie		173
..	..	30 163	28 259	26 911	24 737	23 504	22 449	**Habillement; préparation, teinture des fourrures**		18
..	..					23 442	22 387	Articles d'habillement autres qu'en fourrure		181
..	..					61	62	Préparation, teinture des fourrures; art. en fourrure		182
..	..	9 748	9 132	8 771	8 584	8 359	8 541	**Travail des cuirs; articles en cuir; chaussures**		19
..	..					2 411	2 309	Apprêt et tannage des cuirs et articles en cuirs		191
..	..					5 948	6 232	Chaussures		192
..	..	25 060	26 274	25 646	28 586	32 108	30 373	**Bois et articles en bois et liège (sauf meubles)**		20
..	..					7 970	7 309	Sciage et rabotage du bois		201
..	..					24 137	23 064	Articles en bois, liège, vannerie, sparterie		202
..	..	50 091	48 743	44 519	46 908	54 030	50 315	**Papier et carton; articles en papier et en carton**		21
..	..					68 623	71 593	**Edition, imprimerie et reproduction**		22
..	..					35 109	38 565	Edition		221
..	..					32 215	31 722	Imprimerie et activités annexes		222
..	..					1 299	1 307	Reproduction de supports enregistrés		223
..	..					111 145	120 445	**Cokéfaction; prod. pétroliers; comb. nucléaires**		23
..	..	206 923	204 706	194 523	223 112	219 654	215 655	**Produits chimiques**		24
..	..					111 159	107 900	Produits chimiques de base		241
..	..					101 251	100 706	Autres produits chimiques		242
..	..					7 244	7 050	Fibres synthétiques ou artificielles		243
..	..	79 701	81 983	77 669	82 076	88 404	86 090	**Articles en caoutchouc et en matières plastiques**		25
..	..					21 476	20 455	Articles en caoutchouc		251
..	..					66 928	65 635	Articles en matières plastiques		252
..	..	59 669	64 375	65 939	72 680	73 523	70 102	**Autres produits minéraux non métalliques**		26
..	..					15 390	15 087	Verre et articles en verre		261
..	..					58 133	55 015	Produits minéraux non métalliques, nca		269
..	..	104 196	97 812	84 061	93 438	101 558	92 386	**Produits métallurgiques de base**		27
..	..						51 553	Sidérurgie et première transformation de l'acier		271
..	..					31 429	29 087	Métallurgie; métaux précieux et non ferreux		272
..	..						11 746	Fonderie		273
..	..	117 705	123 171	115 326	116 386	125 354	123 883	**Ouvrages en métaux, sauf machines et matériel**		28
..	..					46 578	46 667	Constr. et menuiserie métal.; réservoirs; générateurs		281
..	..					78 776	77 216	Autres ouvrages en métaux		289
..	..	259 554	263 939	241 687	245 310	250 806	258 174	**Machines et matériel, nca**		29
..	..					119 794	122 472	Machines d'usage général		291
..	..					108 090	112 506	Machines d'usage spécifique		292
..	..					22 921	23 196	Appareils domestiques, nca		293
..	..	25 782	25 313	23 188	27 041	28 140	26 426	**Mach. de bureau, comptables, matériel inform.**		30
..	..	106 225	102 091	97 216	118 904	123 227	126 518	**Machines et appareils électriques, nca**		31
..	..					15 613	14 536	Moteurs, génératrices et transformateurs électriques		311
..	..					68 161	72 164	Matériel électrique de distribution et de commande		312
..	..					6 847	6 220	Fils et câbles électriques isolés		313
..	..					3 145	2 462	Accumulateurs, piles électriques		314
..	..					9 093	8 965	Lampes électriques et appareils d'éclairage		315
..	..					20 369	22 171	Autres matériels électriques, nca		319
..	..	55 021	57 488	40 478	40 709	39 498	39 221	**Equip. et appar. de radio, TV, communication**		32
..	..					10 479	11 220	Tubes et valves électroniques; autres composants		321
..	..					11 956	15 255	Emetteurs radio et TV; app. téléphonie, télégraphie		322
..	..					17 063	12 746	Récepteurs radio et TV et articles associés		323
..	..	52 178	54 416	66 793	49 018	48 921	50 418	**Instruments médicaux, de précision, d'optique**		33
..	..					40 894	41 420	Appareils médicaux et de précision		331
..	..					6 576	7 663	Instruments d'optique ; matériel photographique		332
..	..					1 451	1 335	Horlogerie		333
..	..	260 833	258 778	218 487	234 179	262 343	283 175	**Véhicules automobiles et nemorques**		34
..	..	37 985	35 451	35 161	34 456	33 345	33 138	**Autres matériels de transport**		35
..	..					10 085	8 420	Construction et réparation de navires		351
..	..					6 071	5 575	Construction de matériel ferroviaire roulant		352
..	..					13 781	16 025	Construction aéronautique et spatiale		353
..	..					3 408	3 118	Autres équipements de transport		359
..	..	55 428	56 153	55 338	54 723	55 481	55 208	**Meubles; activités de fabrication, nca**		36
..	..					42 823	42 445	Meubles		361
..	..					12 658	12 763	Activités de fabrication, nca		369
..	..					2 113	2 185	**Récupération**		37
..	..					..	..	**Production et distrib. d'électricité, de gaz, d'eau**	E	40-41
..	..					..	..	**Electricité, gaz, vapeur et eau chaude**		40
..	..					..	..	Production, collecte et distribution d'électricité		401
..	..					..	..	**Captage, épuration et distribution d'eau**	41	410
..	..					..	..	**Construction**	F	45
..	..					..	..	**Commerce de gros et de détail; réparation**	G	50-52
..	..					..	..	**Hôtels et restaurants**	H	55
..	..					..	..	**Transports, entreposage et communications**	I	60-64
..	..					..	..	**Intermédiation financière**	J	65-67
..	..					..	..	**Immobilier, locations, services aux entreprises**	K	70-74
..	..					..	..	**Admin. publique; éducation; santé; autres**	L-Q	75-99
..	..					..	..	**Grand total**	A-Q	01-99

Statistiques des Structures Industrielles
OCDE, © 1998

Table GE.2 ESTABLISHMENTS - ETABLISSEMENTS

Units

ISIC revision 3			1989	1990	1991	1992	1993	1994	1995	1996
A	01-02	Agriculture, hunting and forestry	..	..	..	..	..	..	..	..
B	05	Fishing	..	..	..	..	..	..	..	..
C	10-14	Mining and quarrying	..	..	1 484	1 460	1 440	1 474	1 520	..
	10	Mining of coal and lignite; extraction of peat	..	..	169	160	151	146	150	143
	11	Crude petroleum & natural gas; related service activ.	..	..	49	50	48	47	49	48
	13	Mining of metal ores	..	..	14	9	6	6	5	..
	14	Other mining and quarrying	..	..	1 252	1 241	1 235	1 275	1 316	1 331
D	15-37	Total manufacturing	..	..	50 090	49 592	47 893	46 768	46 398	45 800
	15	Food products and beverages	..	..	5 602	5 418	5 263	5 210	5 085	5 037
	155	Beverages	..	..	..	..	..	..	910	871
	16 160	Tobacco products	..	..	57	53	46	44	41	36
	17	Textiles	..	..	1 831	1 689	1 582	1 506	1 449	1 394
	171	Spinning, weaving and finishing of textiles	..	..	..	..	..	..	533	508
	172	Other textiles	..	..	..	..	..	..	639	632
	173	Knitted and crocheted fabrics and articles	..	..	..	..	..	..	277	254
	18	Wearing apparel dressing & dyeing of fur	..	..	2 245	1 951	1 669	1 429	1 252	1 100
	181	Wearing apparel, except fur apparel	..	..	..	..	..	..	1 240	1 090
	182	Dressing and dyeing of fur; articles of fur	..	..	..	..	..	..	12	10
	19	Tanning, dressing leather; leather artic.; footwear	..	..	631	566	501	453	384	344
	191	Tanning, dressing leather; manuf. of leather articles	..	..	..	..	..	..	186	166
	192	Footwear	..	..	..	..	..	..	198	179
	20	Wood and cork products, ex. furniture	..	..	3 212	3 200	2 287	2 201	2 188	2 130
	201	Sawmilling and planing of wood	..	..	..	..	..	..	921	887
	202	Products of wood, cork, straw & plaiting material	..	..	..	..	..	..	..	1 242
	21	Paper and paper products	..	..	1 146	1 142	1 104	1 075	1 072	1 058
	22	Publishing, printing & reprod. of recorded media	..	..	..	..	..	..	2 939	2 870
	221	Publishing	..	..	..	..	..	..	822	831
	222	Printing and related service activities	..	..	..	..	..	..	2 096	2 019
	223	Reproduction of recorded media	..	..	..	..	..	..	22	20
	23	Coke, refined petroleum products & nuclear fuel	..	..	..	..	..	..	86	83
	24	Chemicals and chemical products	..	..	1 774	1 768	1 744	1 740	1 717	1 716
	241	Basic chemicals	..	..	..	..	..	..	434	436
	242	Other chemical products	..	..	..	..	..	..	1 237	1 236
	243	Man-made fibres	..	..	..	..	..	..	45	44
	25	Rubber and plastic products	..	..	2 745	2 838	2 873	2 916	2 956	2 949
	251	Rubber products	..	..	..	..	..	..	292	290
	252	Plastic products	..	..	..	..	..	..	2 664	2 660
	26	Other non-metallic mineral products	..	..	3 403	3 459	3 542	3 668	3 742	3 793
	261	Glass and glass products	..	..	..	..	..	..	416	422
	269	Non-metallic mineral products, nec	..	..	..	..	..	..	3 327	3 371
	27	Basic metals	..	..	1 301	1 305	1 258	1 205	1 128	1 110
	271	Basic iron and steel	..	..	..	..	..	..	..	425
	272	Basic precious and non-ferrous metals	..	..	..	..	..	..	222	221
	273	Casting of metals	..	..	..	..	..	..	..	463
	28	Fabricated metal products, ex. machin. & equip.	..	..	6 397	6 512	6 544	6 408	6 498	6 531
	281	Structural metal prod., tanks, reservoirs, generators	..	..	..	..	..	..	2 368	2 326
	289	Other fabricated metal products & service activities	..	..	..	..	..	..	4 130	4 206
	29	Machinery and equipment, nec	..	..	7 528	7 431	7 236	6 946	6 667	6 596
	291	General purpose machinery	..	..	..	..	..	..	3 133	3 085
	292	Special purpose machinery	..	..	..	..	..	..	3 319	3 310
	293	Domestic appliances, nec	..	..	..	..	..	..	215	202
	30	Office, accounting and computing machinery	..	..	217	219	208	214	204	201
	31	Electrical machinery and apparatus, nec	..	..	2 318	2 315	2 297	2 282	2 341	2 306
	311	Electric motors, generators and transformers	..	..	..	..	..	..	505	504
	312	Electricity distribution and control apparatus	..	..	..	..	..	..	998	988
	313	Insulated wire and cable	..	..	..	..	..	..	111	111
	314	Accumulators, primary cells and primary batteries	..	..	..	..	..	..	34	31
	315	Electric lamps and lighting equipment	..	..	..	..	..	..	289	271
	319	Other electrical equipment, nec	..	..	..	..	..	..	404	401
	32	Radio, TV, communication equip. & apparatus	..	..	747	740	728	702	594	592
	321	Electronic valves, tubes & other electronic compon.	..	..	..	..	..	..	260	277
	322	TV, radio transmitters & appar. for line teleph., telegr.	..	..	..	..	..	..	156	138
	323	TV, radio receivers and associated goods	..	..	..	..	..	..	179	178
	33	Medical, precision, optical instr.; watches, clocks	..	..	2 176	2 208	2 276	2 235	2 018	2 012
	331	Medical equip.; precision instruments and appliances	..	..	..	..	..	..	1 761	1 760
	332	Optical instruments and photographic equipment	..	..	..	..	..	..	187	181
	333	Watches and clocks	..	..	..	..	..	..	71	72
	34	Motor vehicles, trailers, and semi-trailers	..	..	959	1 000	1 021	1 035	1 047	1 013
	35	Other transport equipment	..	..	432	437	447	438	430	410
	351	Building and repairing of ships and boats	..	..	..	..	..	..	112	106
	352	Railway, tramway locomotives and rolling stock	..	..	..	..	..	..	158	144
	353	Aircraft and spacecraft	..	..	..	..	..	..	82	82
	359	Transport equipment, nec	..	..	..	..	..	..	78	78
	36	Furniture; manufacturing, nec	..	..	2 812	2 752	2 696	2 586	2 450	2 385
	361	Furniture	..	..	..	..	..	..	1 647	1 609
	369	Manufacturing, nec	..	..	..	..	..	..	803	776
	37	Recycling	..	..	..	..	..	..	111	134
E	40-41	Electricity, gas and water supply	..	..	..	..	..	..	..	..
	40	Electricity, gas, steam and hot water supply	..	..	..	..	..	..	..	..
	401	Production, collection and distribution of electricity	..	..	..	..	..	..	..	..
	41 410	Collection, purification, distribution of water	..	..	..	..	..	..	..	..
F	45	Construction	..	..	..	..	..	..	..	..
G	50-52	Wholesale and retail trade; repairs etc	..	..	..	..	..	..	..	..
H	55	Hotels and restaurants	..	..	..	..	..	..	..	..
I	60-64	Transport, storage and communications	..	..	..	..	..	..	..	..
J	65-67	Financial intermediation	..	..	..	..	..	..	..	..
K	70-74	Real estate, renting and business activities	..	..	..	..	..	..	..	..
L-Q	75-99	Public admin.; education; health; other services	..	..	..	..	..	..	..	..
A-Q	01-99	Grand total	..	..	..	..	..	..	..	..

Table GE.3 EMPLOI - EMPLOYMENT

Milliers

1989	1990	1991	1992	1993	1994	1995	1996			CITI révision 3	
..	..						..	**Agriculture, chasse et sylviculture**	A	01-02	
..	..						..	**Pêche**	B	05	
..	..	308.7	252.7	220.1	197.6	185.7	..	**Activités extractives**	C	10-14	
..	..	241.3	199.8	173.0	151.0	139.6	123.0	Extraction de charbon, de lignite et de tourbe		10	
..	..	7.7	7.0	6.7	6.4	6.3	6.0	Extraction de pétrole brut et de gaz naturel		11	
..	..	3.0	1.2	0.4	0.4	0.4	..	Extraction de minerais métalliques		13	
..	..	56.8	44.8	40.0	39.8	39.4	37.7	Autres activités extractives		14	
..	..	8 796.4	7 866.7	7 168.1	6 694.0	6 592.8	6 353.1	**Activités de fabrication**	D	15-37	
..	..	624.2	574.9	547.3	533.2	524.5	518.2	**Produits alimentaires et boissons**		15	
..	..					85.4	82.1	Boissons			155
..	..	19.3	17.1	15.9	15.5	14.6	13.8	**Produits à base de tabac**		16	160
..	..	274.7	208.6	179.7	163.7	150.7	139.1	**Textiles**		17	
..	..					71.2	63.8	Filature, tissage et achèvement des textiles			171
..	..					54.8	53.3	Autres articles textiles			172
..	..					24.8	22.0	Etoffes et articles de bonneterie			173
..	..	216.6	167.7	139.0	121.4	105.9	93.6	**Habillement; préparation, teinture des fourrures**		18	
..	..					105.3	93.2	Articles d'habillement autres qu'en fourrure			181
..	..					0.5	0.4	Préparation, teinture des fourrures; art. en fourrure			182
..	..	76.6	52.4	42.8	38.4	34.5	31.4	**Travail des cuirs; articles en cuir; chaussures**		19	
..	..					12.6	11.2	Apprêt et tannage des cuirs et articles en cuirs			191
..	..					21.9	20.2	Chaussures			192
..	..	131.3	125.0	116.1	116.2	126.4	120.2	**Bois et articles en bois et liège (sauf meubles)**		20	
..	..					26.6	25.0	Sciage et rabotage du bois			201
..	..					99.8	95.3	Articles en bois, liège, vannerie, sparterie			202
..	..	181.9	171.3	159.4	153.1	154.7	152.1	**Papier et carton; articles en papier et en carton**		21	
..	..					267.0	262.2	**Edition, imprimerie et reproduction**		22	
..	..					107.6	112.4	Edition			221
..	..					154.3	145.1	Imprimerie et activités annexes			222
..	..					5.1	4.7	Reproduction de supports enregistrés			223
..	..					26.8	24.5	**Cokéfaction; prod. pétroliers; comb. nucléaires**		23	
..	..	709.3	649.8	595.7	561.1	535.9	517.5	**Produits chimiques**		24	
..	..					246.9	239.7	Produits chimiques de base			241
..	..					264.7	255.2	Autres produits chimiques			242
..	..					24.3	22.7	Fibres synthétiques ou artificielles			243
..	..	412.6	397.5	370.1	357.7	362.0	347.7	**Articles en caoutchouc et en matières plastiques**		25	
..	..					84.1	78.1	Articles en caoutchouc			251
..	..					277.9	269.6	Articles en matières plastiques			252
..	..	341.7	306.3	292.1	285.9	283.8	269.2	**Autres produits minéraux non métalliques**		26	
..	..					68.8	66.8	Verre et articles en verre			261
..	..					215.0	202.3	Produits minéraux non métalliques, nca			269
..	..	476.3	408.5	353.5	318.7	294.6	279.2	**Produits métallurgiques de base**		27	
..	..						149.7	Sidérurgie et première transformation de l'acier			271
..	..					65.0	62.2	Métallurgie; métaux précieux et non ferreux			272
..	..						67.3	Fonderie			273
..	..	705.9	670.4	625.7	585.9	596.5	574.0	**Ouvrages en métaux, sauf machines et matériel**		28	
..	..					207.7	197.1	Constr. et menuiserie métal.; réservoirs; générateurs			281
..	..					388.9	376.9	Autres ouvrages en métaux			289
..	..	1 555.2	1 367.8	1 211.6	1 106.7	1 044.4	1 020.6	**Machines et matériel, nca**		29	
..	..					500.3	489.2	Machines d'usage général			291
..	..					465.3	456.1	Machines d'usage spécifique			292
..	..					78.9	75.3	Appareils domestiques, nca			293
..	..	108.3	86.7	62.3	55.4	49.6	45.0	**Mach. de bureau, comptables, matériel inform.**		30	
..	..	652.6	565.2	511.2	496.8	495.1	470.0	**Machines et appareils électriques, nca**		31	
..	..					82.8	75.4	Moteurs, génératrices et transformateurs électriques			311
..	..					247.8	239.0	Matériel électrique de distribution et de commande			312
..	..					26.0	23.0	Fils et câbles électriques isolés			313
..	..					10.6	9.4	Accumulateurs, piles électriques			314
..	..					36.7	34.5	Lampes électriques et appareils d'éclairage			315
..	..					91.2	88.6	Autres matériels électriques, nca			319
..	..	279.3	234.4	191.7	175.3	158.4	152.1	**Equip. et appar. de radio, TV, communication**		32	
..	..					59.2	61.5	Tubes et valves électroniques; autres composants			321
..	..					55.3	53.3	Emetteurs radio et TV; app. téléphonie, télégraphie			322
..	..					43.9	37.3	Récepteurs radio et TV et articles associés			323
..	..	346.5	305.1	305.4	257.2	233.9	225.5	**Instruments médicaux, de précision, d'optique**		33	
..	..					195.6	186.6	Appareils médicaux et de précision			331
..	..					31.4	32.6	Instruments d'optique ; matériel photographique			332
..	..					7.0	6.3	Horlogerie			333
..	..	821.0	766.3	703.7	659.2	689.3	682.0	**Véhicules automobiles et nemorques**		34	
..	..	256.1	228.8	218.4	197.3	182.2	164.2	**Autres matériels de transport**		35	
..	..					36.7	31.9	Construction et réparation de navires			351
..	..					69.7	61.2	Construction de matériel ferroviaire roulant			352
..	..					62.8	59.0	Construction aéronautique et spatiale			353
..	..					13.0	12.1	Autres équipements de transport			359
..	..	330.3	298.6	278.7	264.8	255.3	243.4	**Meubles; activités de fabrication, nca**		36	
..	..					185.7	177.0	Meubles			361
..	..					69.6	66.5	Activités de fabrication, nca			369
..	..					6.5	7.5	**Récupération**		37	
..	..	..	..	..	..	..	..	**Production et distrib. d'électricité, de gaz, d'eau**	E	40-41	
..	..	..	..	..	..	..	..	**Electricité, gaz, vapeur et eau chaude**		40	
..	..	..	..	..	..	..	..	Production, collecte et distribution d'électricité			401
..	..	..	..	..	..	..	..	**Captage, épuration et distribution d'eau**		41	410
..	..	..	..	..	..	..	..	**Construction**	F	45	
..	..	..	..	..	..	..	..	**Commerce de gros et de détail; réparation**	G	50-52	
..	..	..	..	..	..	..	..	**Hôtels et restaurants**	H	55	
..	..	..	..	..	..	..	..	**Transports, entreposage et communications**	I	60-64	
..	..	..	..	..	..	..	..	**Intermédiation financière**	J	65-67	
..	..	..	..	..	..	..	..	**Immobilier, locations, services aux entreprises**	K	70-74	
..	..	..	..	..	..	..	..	**Admin. publique; éducation; santé; autres**	L-Q	75-99	
..	..	..	..	..	..	..	..	**Grand total**	A-Q	01-99	

Statistiques des Structures Industrielles
OCDE, © 1998

GERMANY

Table GE.4 TOTAL WAGES AND SALARIES - SALAIRES ET TRAITEMENTS, TOTAL

Millions of DM (Current Prices)

ISIC revision 3			1989	1990	1991	1992	1993	1994	1995	1996
A	01-02	Agriculture, hunting and forestry	..	..	..	..	..	..	..	..
B	05	Fishing	..	..	..	..	..	..	..	..
C	10-14	Mining and quarrying	..	..	13 575	13 698	12 916	11 538	11 434	..
	10	Mining of coal and lignite; extraction of peat	..	..	10 750	10 872	10 219	8 747	8 567	7 973
	11	Crude petroleum & natural gas; related service activ.	..	..	520	541	551	562	566	568
	13	Mining of metal ores	..	..	100	62	26	27	25	..
	14	Other mining and quarrying	..	..	2 206	2 223	2 119	2 203	2 276	2 207
D	15-37	Total manufacturing	..	..	410 675	420 036	401 036	391 119	402 832	400 582
	15	Food products and beverages	..	..	23 768	24 684	24 981	24 970	24 906	25 074
		155	Beverages	..	..	..	..	..	..	5 111	5 065
	16	160	Tobacco products	..	..	1 049	1 012	1 072	1 121	1 115	1 076
	17	Textiles	..	..	8 863	8 353	7 645	7 232	6 897	6 559
		171	Spinning, weaving and finishing of textiles	..	..	..	..	..	..	3 437	3 155
		172	Other textiles	..	..	..	..	..	..	2 467	2 497
		173	Knitted and crocheted fabrics and articles	..	..	..	..	..	..	993	907
	18	Wearing apparel dressing & dyeing of fur	..	..	5 961	5 481	4 936	4 450	4 077	3 778
		181	Wearing apparel, except fur apparel	..	..	..	..	..	..	4 056	3 759
		182	Dressing and dyeing of fur; articles of fur	..	..	..	..	..	..	20	19
	19	Tanning, dressing leather; leather artic.; footwear	..	..	2 073	1 868	1 661	1 568	1 478	1 405
		191	Tanning, dressing leather; manuf. of leather articles	..	..	..	..	..	..	499	460
		192	Footwear	..	..	..	..	..	..	980	945
	20	Wood and cork products, ex. furniture	..	..	5 209	5 574	5 519	5 667	6 454	6 221
		201	Sawmilling and planing of wood	..	..	..	..	..	..	1 248	1 189
		202	Products of wood, cork, straw & plaiting material	..	..	..	..	..	..	5 205	5 032
	21	Paper and paper products	..	..	8 543	8 867	8 625	8 533	8 914	8 961
	22	Publishing, printing & reprod. of recorded media	..	..	..	..	..	..	17 240	17 566
		221	Publishing	..	..	..	..	..	..	7 434	8 116
		222	Printing and related service activities	..	..	..	..	..	..	9 523	9 184
		223	Reproduction of recorded media	..	..	..	..	..	..	283	267
	23	Coke, refined petroleum products & nuclear fuel	..	..	..	..	..	..	2 064	1 980
	24	Chemicals and chemical products	..	..	40 800	42 283	40 835	39 874	39 908	39 645
		241	Basic chemicals	..	..	..	..	..	..	19 625	19 647
		242	Other chemical products	..	..	..	..	..	..	18 761	18 545
		243	Man-made fibres	..	..	..	..	..	..	1 521	1 453
	25	Rubber and plastic products	..	..	18 745	19 665	18 991	19 050	19 633	19 183
		251	Rubber products	..	..	..	..	..	..	4 989	4 703
		252	Plastic products	..	..	..	..	..	..	14 644	14 480
	26	Other non-metallic mineral products	..	..	14 268	14 881	15 053	15 546	15 832	15 367
		261	Glass and glass products	..	..	..	..	..	..	3 798	3 819
		269	Non-metallic mineral products, nec	..	..	..	..	..	..	12 034	11 549
	27	Basic metals	..	..	21 997	21 642	19 245	18 557	18 152	17 400
		271	Basic iron and steel	..	..	..	..	..	..	..	9 256
		272	Basic precious and non-ferrous metals	..	..	..	..	..	..	4 272	4 184
		273	Casting of metals	..	..	..	..	..	..	..	3 961
	28	Fabricated metal products, ex. machin. & equip.	..	..	32 140	33 528	32 172	31 268	33 400	32 852
		281	Structural metal prod., tanks, reservoirs, generators	..	..	..	..	..	..	11 919	11 553
		289	Other fabricated metal products & service activities	..	..	..	..	..	..	21 481	21 299
	29	Machinery and equipment, nec	..	..	73 651	74 836	70 171	67 909	67 759	68 125
		291	General purpose machinery	..	..	..	..	..	..	32 756	32 992
		292	Special purpose machinery	..	..	..	..	..	..	30 304	30 488
		293	Domestic appliances, nec	..	..	..	..	..	..	4 699	4 645
	30	Office, accounting and computing machinery	..	..	6 157	6 060	4 683	4 324	3 904	3 794
	31	Electrical machinery and apparatus, nec	..	..	30 421	30 353	29 299	30 209	31 442	31 374
		311	Electric motors, generators and transformers	..	..	..	..	..	..	4 845	4 694
		312	Electricity distribution and control apparatus	..	..	..	..	..	..	17 005	17 201
		313	Insulated wire and cable	..	..	..	..	..	..	1 615	1 481
		314	Accumulators, primary cells and primary batteries	..	..	..	..	..	..	645	607
		315	Electric lamps and lighting equipment	..	..	..	..	..	..	2 006	1 978
		319	Other electrical equipment, nec	..	..	..	..	..	..	5 325	5 413
	32	Radio, TV, communication equip. & apparatus	..	..	13 397	13 951	11 962	11 582	10 891	10 747
		321	Electronic valves, tubes & other electronic compon.	..	..	..	..	..	..	3 965	4 228
		322	TV, radio transmitters & appar. for line teleph., telegr.	..	..	..	..	..	..	4 293	4 207
		323	TV, radio receivers and associated goods	..	..	..	..	..	..	2 633	2 312
	33	Medical, precision, optical instr.; watches, clocks	..	..	16 056	16 896	17 740	15 117	14 481	14 576
		331	Medical equip.; precision instruments and appliances	..	..	..	..	..	..	12 294	12 177
		332	Optical instruments and photographic equipment	..	..	..	..	..	..	1 805	2 046
		333	Watches and clocks	..	..	..	..	..	..	381	354
	34	Motor vehicles, trailers, and semi-trailers	..	..	48 461	49 744	46 047	45 206	49 526	51 132
	35	Other transport equipment	..	..	11 630	11 914	12 290	11 803	11 515	10 786
		351	Building and repairing of ships and boats	..	..	..	..	..	..	2 232	1 895
		352	Railway, tramway locomotives and rolling stock	..	..	..	..	..	..	3 592	3 419
		353	Aircraft and spacecraft	..	..	..	..	..	..	5 001	4 810
		359	Transport equipment, nec	..	..	..	..	..	..	690	662
	36	Furniture; manufacturing, nec	..	..	13 144	13 422	13 212	12 957	12 922	12 612
		361	Furniture	..	..	..	..	..	..	9 716	9 453
		369	Manufacturing, nec	..	..	..	..	..	..	3 206	3 159
	37	Recycling	..	..	..	..	..	..	322	369
E	40-41	Electricity, gas and water supply	..	..	..	..	..	..	..	..
	40	Electricity, gas, steam and hot water supply	..	..	..	..	..	..	..	..
		401	Production, collection and distribution of electricity	..	..	..	..	..	..	..	..
	41	410	Collection, purification, distribution of water	..	..	..	..	..	..	..	..
F	45	Construction	..	..	..	..	..	..	..	..
G	50-52	Wholesale and retail trade; repairs etc	..	..	..	..	..	..	..	..
H	55	Hotels and restaurants	..	..	..	..	..	..	..	..
I	60-64	Transport, storage and communications	..	..	..	..	..	..	..	..
J	65-67	Financial intermediation	..	..	..	..	..	..	..	..
K	70-74	Real estate, renting and business activities	..	..	..	..	..	..	..	..
L-Q	75-99	Public admin.; education; health; other services	..	..	..	..	..	..	..	..
A-Q	01-99	Grand total	..	..	..	..	..	..	..	..

Table GE.5 **HEURES OUVRÉES - HOURS WORKED**

Milliers / CITI révision 3

1989	1990	1991	1992	1993	1994	1995	1996			CITI	
..	..	..	..	..	..	..	..	**Agriculture, chasse et sylviculture**	A	01-02	
..	..	..	..	..	..	..	..	**Pêche**	B	05	
..	..	336 876	291 090	244 225	212 335	200 773	..	**Activités extractives**	C	10-14	
..	..	261 969	225 745	186 269	153 923	143 906	123 106	Extraction de charbon, de lignite et de tourbe		10	
..	..	5 457	4 314	4 253	4 083	3 908	3 553	Extraction de pétrole brut et de gaz naturel		11	
..	..	3 016	1 408	526	521	439	..	Extraction de minerais métalliques		13	
..	..	66 434	59 623	53 177	53 808	52 520	49 096	Autres activités extractives		14	
..	..	8 872 737	8 172 828	7 179 897	6 821 740	6 683 591	6 307 652	**Activités de fabrication**	D	15-37	
..	..	720 347	672 141	627 047	605 488	588 185	572 655	**Produits alimentaires et boissons**		15	
						95 786	88 220	Boissons			155
..	..	19 114	17 221	15 260	14 673	13 588	12 685	**Produits à base de tabac**		16	160
..	..	280 264	232 170	196 988	179 633	162 129	149 723	**Textiles**		17	
						76 964	68 908	Filature, tissage et achèvement des textiles			171
						59 071	57 234	Autres articles textiles			172
						26 094	23 581	Etoffes et articles de bonneterie			173
..	..	221 930	176 430	144 006	119 165	99 015	84 901	**Habillement; préparation, teinture des fourrures**		18	
						98 524	84 446	Articles d'habillement autres qu'en fourrure			181
						491	455	Préparation, teinture des fourrures; art. en fourrure			182
..	..	74 631	56 814	45 823	40 817	36 930	32 564	**Travail des cuirs; articles en cuir; chaussures**		19	
						13 326	11 638	Apprêt et tannage des cuirs et articles en cuirs			191
						23 604	20 926	Chaussures			192
..	..	169 309	163 865	151 479	153 385	163 072	151 039	**Bois et articles en bois et liège (sauf meubles)**		20	
						36 141	33 343	Sciage et rabotage du bois			201
						126 931	117 696	Articles en bois, liège, vannerie, sparterie			202
..	..	210 780	198 018	183 736	177 644	177 498	171 656	**Papier et carton; articles en papier et en carton**		21	
						199 190	187 144	**Edition, imprimerie et reproduction**		22	
						32 433	31 029	Edition			221
						162 045	151 638	Imprimerie et activités annexes			222
						4 712	4 477	Reproduction de supports enregistrés			223
						19 814	18 208	**Cokéfaction; prod. pétroliers; comb. nucléaires**		23	
..	..	562 548	520 358	453 156	420 377	403 998	380 542	**Produits chimiques**		24	
						199 575	186 922	Produits chimiques de base			241
						175 526	166 942	Autres produits chimiques			242
						28 897	26 678	Fibres synthétiques ou artificielles			243
..	..	478 803	467 524	421 217	416 827	421 570	400 863	**Articles en caoutchouc et en matières plastiques**		25	
						95 796	87 413	Articles en caoutchouc			251
						325 774	313 450	Articles en matières plastiques			252
..	..	403 297	378 956	358 400	355 175	347 206	319 086	**Autres produits minéraux non métalliques**		26	
						83 168	80 101	Verre et articles en verre			261
						264 038	238 985	Produits minéraux non métalliques, nca			269
..	..	518 828	459 873	379 974	359 969	340 318	310 153	**Produits métallurgiques de base**		27	
							163 623	Sidérurgie et première transformation de l'acier			271
						71 156	64 911	Métallurgie; métaux précieux et non ferreux			272
							81 619	Fonderie			273
..	..	810 703	786 120	704 214	677 811	688 606	649 297	**Ouvrages en métaux, sauf machines et matériel**		28	
						234 347	218 846	Constr. et menuiserie métal.; réservoirs; générateurs			281
						454 259	430 451	Autres ouvrages en métaux			289
..	..	1 441 030	1 315 384	1 112 758	1 040 349	993 183	943 605	**Machines et matériel, nca**		29	
						473 080	448 582	Machines d'usage général			291
						442 096	422 048	Machines d'usage spécifique			292
						78 007	72 975	Appareils domestiques, nca			293
..	..	53 977	42 195	29 309	26 431	23 714	20 932	**Mach. de bureau, comptables, matériel inform.**		30	
..	..	585 734	531 542	459 038	445 157	448 404	412 719	**Machines et appareils électriques, nca**		31	
						84 449	73 974	Moteurs, génératrices et transformateurs électriques			311
						197 344	183 470	Matériel électrique de distribution et de commande			312
						27 774	26 674	Fils et câbles électriques isolés			313
						10 296	9 092	Accumulateurs, piles électriques			314
						37 646	34 808	Lampes électriques et appareils d'éclairage			315
						90 895	84 701	Autres matériels électriques, nca			319
..	..	214 753	184 674	149 034	136 389	126 536	118 651	**Equip. et appar. de radio, TV, communication**		32	
						53 624	53 845	Tubes et valves électroniques; autres composants			321
						34 903	34 095	Emetteurs radio et TV; app. téléphonie, télégraphie			322
						38 009	30 711	Récepteurs radio et TV et articles associés			323
..	..	273 306	250 807	231 734	208 235	186 015	177 089	**Instruments médicaux, de précision, d'optique**		33	
						153 927	144 819	Appareils médicaux et de précision			331
						24 992	25 900	Instruments d'optique ; matériel photographique			332
						7 096	6 370	Horlogerie			333
..	..	936 459	882 051	741 810	725 032	772 446	755 028	**Véhicules automobiles et nemorques**		34	
..	..	232 723	217 441	202 376	185 127	173 537	156 825	**Autres matériels de transport**		35	
						39 757	34 306	Construction et réparation de navires			351
						80 309	69 383	Construction de matériel ferroviaire roulant			352
						39 013	40 166	Construction aéronautique et spatiale			353
						14 458	12 970	Autres équipements de transport			359
..	..	379 242	350 148	323 298	303 859	289 272	271 733	**Meubles; activités de fabrication, nca**		36	
						216 170	203 095	Meubles			361
						73 102	68 638	Activités de fabrication, nca			369
						9 365	10 554	**Récupération**		37	
..	..	..	..	..	..	..	..	**Production et distrib. d'électricité, de gaz, d'eau**	E	40-41	
..	..	..	..	..	..	..	..	**Electricité, gaz, vapeur et eau chaude**		40	
..	..	..	..	..	..	..	..	Production, collecte et distribution d'électricité			401
..	..	..	..	..	..	..	..	**Captage, épuration et distribution d'eau**		41	410
..	..	..	..	..	..	..	..	**Construction**	F	45	
..	..	..	..	..	..	..	..	**Commerce de gros et de détail; réparation**	G	50-52	
..	..	..	..	..	..	..	..	**Hôtels et restaurants**	H	55	
..	..	..	..	..	..	..	..	**Transports, entreposage et communications**	I	60-64	
..	..	..	..	..	..	..	..	**Intermédiation financière**	J	65-67	
..	..	..	..	..	..	..	..	**Immobilier, locations, services aux entreprises**	K	70-74	
..	..	..	..	..	..	..	..	**Admin. publique; éducation; santé; autres**	L-Q	75-99	
..	..	..	..	..	..	..	..	**Grand total**	A-Q	01-99	

Statistiques des Structures Industrielles
OCDE, © 1998

Table GR.1 PRODUCTION - PRODUCTION

Millions of Dr (Current Prices)

ISIC revision 3			1989	1990	1991	1992	1993	1994	1995	1996
A	01-02	Agriculture, hunting and forestry	..	..	..	..	..	..	..	..
B	05	Fishing	..	..	..	..	..	..	..	..
C	10-14	Mining and quarrying	..	..	..	..	208	225	..	..
	10	Mining of coal and lignite; extraction of peat	..	..	..	..	80	88	..	..
	11	Crude petroleum & natural gas; related service activ.	..	..	..	..	13	14	..	..
	13	Mining of metal ores	..	..	..	..	25	29	..	..
	14	Other mining and quarrying	..	..	..	..	89	94	..	..
D	15-37	Total manufacturing	..	..	..	..	5 734 980	6 292 839	7 026 424	..
	15	Food products and beverages	..	..	..	..	1 499 763	1 653 302	1 785 575	..
	155	Beverages	..	..	..	..	314 586	352 009	375 664	..
16	160	Tobacco products	..	..	..	..	93 769	113 629	129 878	..
17		Textiles	..	..	..	..	384 903	413 311	439 973	..
	171	Spinning, weaving and finishing of textiles	..	..	..	..	221 813	243 266	270 362	..
	172	Other textiles	..	..	..	..	59 394	64 677	68 762	..
	173	Knitted and crocheted fabrics and articles	..	..	..	..	103 697	105 367	100 850	..
18		Wearing apparel dressing & dyeing of fur	..	..	..	..	321 704	319 539	345 668	..
	181	Wearing apparel, except fur apparel	..	..	..	..	310 040	306 320	333 047	..
	182	Dressing and dyeing of fur; articles of fur	..	..	..	..	11 664	13 219	12 621	..
19		Tanning, dressing leather; leather artic.; footwear	..	..	..	..	82 547	84 747	88 260	..
	191	Tanning, dressing leather; manuf. of leather articles	..	..	..	..	26 530	23 860	23 507	..
	192	Footwear	..	..	..	..	56 017	60 887	64 753	..
20		Wood and cork products, ex. furniture	..	..	..	..	107 459	97 197	111 832	..
	201	Sawmilling and planing of wood	..	..	..	..	14 692	14 970	14 328	..
	202	Products of wood, cork, straw & plaiting material	..	..	..	..	92 767	82 228	97 504	..
21		Paper and paper products	..	..	..	..	155 032	177 871	228 518	..
22		Publishing, printing & reprod. of recorded media	..	..	..	..	132 061	150 669	175 868	..
	221	Publishing	..	..	..	..	88 071	98 939	120 290	..
	222	Printing and related service activities	..	..	..	..	43 990	51 730	55 578	..
	223	Reproduction of recorded media	..	..	..	..	0	0	0	..
23		Coke, refined petroleum products & nuclear fuel	..	..	..	..	567 731	658 902	735 162	..
24		Chemicals and chemical products	..	..	..	..	548 544	635 786	689 507	..
	241	Basic chemicals	..	..	..	..	124 741	143 781	174 527	..
	242	Other chemical products	..	..	..	..	411 013	476 010	496 377	..
	243	Man-made fibres	..	..	..	..	12 790	15 995	18 604	..
25		Rubber and plastic products	..	..	..	..	178 935	208 853	260 864	..
	251	Rubber products	..	..	..	..	32 744	35 784	40 473	..
	252	Plastic products	..	..	..	..	146 191	173 069	220 391	..
26		Other non-metallic mineral products	..	..	..	..	339 298	353 009	380 034	..
	261	Glass and glass products	..	..	..	..	17 111	17 665	18 908	..
	269	Non-metallic mineral products, nec	..	..	..	..	322 187	335 344	361 125	..
27		Basic metals	..	..	..	..	397 759	478 112	634 066	..
	271	Basic iron and steel	..	..	..	..	207 461	235 380	309 038	..
	272	Basic precious and non-ferrous metals	..	..	..	..	188 707	240 795	321 765	..
	273	Casting of metals	..	..	..	..	1 590	1 937	3 263	..
28		Fabricated metal products, ex. machin. & equip.	..	..	..	..	189 700	207 014	232 780	..
	281	Structural metal prod., tanks, reservoirs, generators	..	..	..	..	67 710	64 245	75 163	..
	289	Other fabricated metal products & service activities	..	..	..	..	121 990	142 769	157 618	..
29		Machinery and equipment, nec	..	..	..	..	157 786	175 337	196 952	..
	291	General purpose machinery	..	..	..	..	51 518	59 115	65 547	..
	292	Special purpose machinery	..	..	..	..	58 071	59 813	71 535	..
	293	Domestic appliances, nec	..	..	..	..	48 197	56 408	59 870	..
30		Office, accounting and computing machinery	..	..	..	..	1 106	909	1 473	..
31		Electrical machinery and apparatus, nec	..	..	..	..	146 340	146 447	177 639	..
	311	Electric motors, generators and transformers	..	..	..	..	19 293	20 118	23 389	..
	312	Electricity distribution and control apparatus	..	..	..	..	24 285	26 504	25 258	..
	313	Insulated wire and cable	..	..	..	..	82 114	77 236	108 287	..
	314	Accumulators, primary cells and primary batteries	..	..	..	..	10 714	11 298	7 980	..
	315	Electric lamps and lighting equipment	..	..	..	..	7 804	8 826	10 294	..
	319	Other electrical equipment, nec	..	..	..	..	2 130	2 464	2 430	..
32		Radio, TV, communication equip. & apparatus	..	..	..	..	131 100	108 395	91 186	..
	321	Electronic valves, tubes & other electronic compon.	..	..	..	..	3 242	5 000	4 365	..
	322	TV, radio transmitters & appar. for line teleph., telegr.	..	..	..	..	126 218	101 823	85 267	..
	323	TV, radio receivers and associated goods	..	..	..	..	1 640	1 572	1 553	..
33		Medical, precision, optical instr.; watches, clocks	..	..	..	..	12 445	14 225	18 756	..
	331	Medical equip.; precision instruments and appliances	..	..	..	..	10 395	11 788	15 124	..
	332	Optical instruments and photographic equipment	..	..	..	..	2 007	2 400	3 596	..
	333	Watches and clocks	..	..	..	..	43	38	36	..
34		Motor vehicles, trailers, and semi-trailers	..	..	..	..	62 203	52 282	48 203	..
35		Other transport equipment	..	..	..	..	127 083	139 686	138 927	..
	351	Building and repairing of ships and boats	..	..	..	..	66 907	71 978	69 301	..
	352	Railway, tramway locomotives and rolling stock	..	..	..	..	14 828	16 982	17 198	..
	353	Aircraft and spacecraft	..	..	..	..	42 735	47 906	49 246	..
	359	Transport equipment, nec	..	..	..	..	2 613	2 821	3 183	..
36		Furniture; manufacturing, nec	..	..	..	..	92 894	97 992	107 661	..
	361	Furniture	..	..	..	..	70 762	75 030	79 599	..
	369	Manufacturing, nec	..	..	..	..	22 133	22 962	28 062	..
37		Recycling	..	..	..	..	4 819	5 624	7 641	..
E	40-41	Electricity, gas and water supply	..	..	..	..	679 884	734 446	..	..
	40	Electricity, gas, steam and hot water supply	..	..	..	..	623 673	671 402	..	..
	401	Production, collection and distribution of electricity	..	..	..	..	621 769	671 402	..	..
	41	410 Collection, purification, distribution of water	..	..	..	..	56 212	63 043	..	..
F	45	Construction	..	..	..	..	..	..	..	..
G	50-52	Wholesale and retail trade; repairs etc	..	..	..	..	..	..	..	..
H	55	Hotels and restaurants	..	..	..	..	..	..	..	..
I	60-64	Transport, storage and communications	..	..	..	..	..	..	..	..
J	65-67	Financial intermediation	..	..	..	..	..	..	..	..
K	70-74	Real estate, renting and business activities	..	..	..	..	..	..	..	..
L-Q	75-99	Public admin.; education; health; other services	..	..	..	..	..	..	..	..
A-Q	01-99	Grand total	..	..	..	..	..	..	..	..

Table GR.2 VALEUR AJOUTÉE - VALUE ADDED

Millions de Dr (Prix courants)   CITI révision 3

1989	1990	1991	1992	1993	1994	1995	1996			
..	..	..	..	..	..	..	..	**Agriculture, chasse et sylviculture**	**A**	**01-02**
..	..	..	..	..	..	..	..	**Pêche**	**B**	**05**
..	..	..	..	118	138	..	..	**Activités extractives**	**C**	**10-14**
..	..	..	..	45	55	..	..	Extraction de charbon, de lignite et de tourbe		10
..	..	..	..	10	11	..	..	Extraction de pétrole brut et de gaz naturel		11
..	..	..	..	17	21	..	..	Extraction de minerais métalliques		13
..	..	..	..	46	51		..	Autres activités extractives		14
..	..	..	..	2 100 613	2 278 580	2 488 186	..	**Activités de fabrication**	**D**	**15-37**
..	..	..	..	507 817	569 956	611 712	..	**Produits alimentaires et boissons**		**15**
..	..	..	..	137 992	156 414	156 552	..	Boissons		155
..	..	..	..	38 381	44 908	48 358	..	**Produits à base de tabac**	**16**	160
..	..	..	..	162 707	171 950	174 958	..	**Textiles**	**17**	
..	..	..	..	97 602	105 206	109 641	..	Filature, tissage et achèvement des textiles		171
..	..	..	..	24 779	26 509	26 283	..	Autres articles textiles		172
..	..	..	..	40 325	40 234	39 035	..	Etoffes et articles de bonneterie		173
..	..	..	..	141 847	136 583	143 799	..	**Habillement; préparation, teinture des fourrures**	**18**	
..	..	..	..	138 128	132 799	140 595	..	Articles d'habillement autres qu'en fourrure		181
..	..	..	..	3 719	3 784	3 204	..	Préparation, teinture des fourrures; art. en fourrure		182
..	..	..	..	35 446	33 418	34 560	..	**Travail des cuirs; articles en cuir; chaussures**	**19**	
..	..	..	..	12 127	8 056	7 595	..	Apprêt et tannage des cuirs et articles en cuirs		191
..	..	..	..	23 319	25 362	26 964	..	Chaussures		192
..	..	..	..	39 305	33 261	38 854	..	**Bois et articles en bois et liège (sauf meubles)**	**20**	
..	..	..	..	3 878	4 611	4 576	..	Sciage et rabotage du bois		201
..	..	..	..	35 427	28 650	34 278	..	Articles en bois, liège, vannerie, sparterie		202
..	..	..	..	60 873	66 986	79 246	..	**Papier et carton; articles en papier et en carton**	**21**	
..	..	..	..	74 634	82 293	92 300	..	**Edition, imprimerie et reproduction**	**22**	
..	..	..	..	51 604	55 966	64 733	..	Edition		221
..	..	..	..	23 030	26 327	27 566	..	Imprimerie et activités annexes		222
..	..	..	..	0	0	0	..	Reproduction de supports enregistrés		223
..	..	..	..	105 191	105 745	129 570	..	**Cokéfaction; prod. pétroliers; comb. nucléaires**	**23**	
..	..	..	..	221 893	258 414	280 154	..	**Produits chimiques**	**24**	
..	..	..	..	47 252	50 897	61 018	..	Produits chimiques de base		241
..	..	..	..	168 937	200 739	211 370	..	Autres produits chimiques		242
..	..	..	..	5 703	6 778	7 766	..	Fibres synthétiques ou artificielles		243
..	..	..	..	71 631	80 875	93 079	..	**Articles en caoutchouc et en matières plastiques**	**25**	
..	..	..	..	12 314	13 527	14 042	..	Articles en caoutchouc		251
..	..	..	..	59 317	67 347	79 037	..	Articles en matières plastiques		252
..	..	..	..	142 544	149 696	155 809	..	**Autres produits minéraux non métalliques**	**26**	
..	..	..	..	7 937	8 706	9 203	..	Verre et articles en verre		261
..	..	..	..	134 607	140 990	146 606	..	Produits minéraux non métalliques, nca		269
..	..	..	..	98 675	118 137	165 363	..	**Produits métallurgiques de base**	**27**	
..	..	..	..	45 256	46 251	69 525	..	Sidérurgie et première transformation de l'acier		271
..	..	..	..	52 697	70 945	94 171	..	Métallurgie; métaux précieux et non ferreux		272
..	..	..	..	722	941	1 667	..	Fonderie		273
..	..	..	..	74 028	81 758	89 617	..	**Ouvrages en métaux, sauf machines et matériel**	**28**	
..	..	..	..	26 488	25 222	28 631	..	Constr. et menuiserie métal.; réservoirs; générateurs		281
..	..	..	..	47 540	56 535	60 986	..	Autres ouvrages en métaux		289
..	..	..	..	63 608	73 376	80 216	..	**Machines et matériel, nca**	**29**	
..	..	..	..	23 532	27 287	29 232	..	Machines d'usage général		291
..	..	..	..	21 069	23 843	27 825	..	Machines d'usage spécifique		292
..	..	..	..	19 007	22 246	23 158	..	Appareils domestiques, nca		293
..	..	..	..	484	473	932	..	**Mach. de bureau, comptables, matériel inform.**	**30**	
..	..	..	..	50 053	50 187	54 452	..	**Machines et appareils électriques, nca**	**31**	
..	..	..	..	8 785	9 126	9 763	..	Moteurs, génératrices et transformateurs électriques		311
..	..	..	..	10 495	12 332	11 262	..	Matériel électrique de distribution et de commande		312
..	..	..	..	21 405	19 205	23 892	..	Fils et câbles électriques isolés		313
..	..	..	..	5 061	4 409	4 034	..	Accumulateurs, piles électriques		314
..	..	..	..	3 429	3 989	4 468	..	Lampes électriques et appareils d'éclairage		315
..	..	..	..	878	1 125	1 033	..	Autres matériels électriques, nca		319
..	..	..	..	52 520	51 281	42 035	..	**Equip. et appar. de radio, TV, communication**	**32**	
..	..	..	..	1 514	2 010	1 895	..	Tubes et valves électroniques; autres composants		321
..	..	..	..	50 125	48 392	39 205	..	Emetteurs radio et TV; app. téléphonie, télégraphie		322
..	..	..	..	881	879	935	..	Récepteurs radio et TV et articles associés		323
..	..	..	..	5 932	6 560	7 994	..	**Instruments médicaux, de précision, d'optique**	**33**	
..	..	..	..	4 972	5 287	6 299	..	Appareils médicaux et de précision		331
..	..	..	..	935	1 256	1 673	..	Instruments d'optique ; matériel photographique		332
..	..	..	..	24	16	22	..	Horlogerie		333
..	..	..	..	16 723	13 871	15 267	..	**Véhicules automobiles et nemorques**	**34**	
..	..	..	..	91 323	102 850	100 458	..	**Autres matériels de transport**	**35**	
..	..	..	..	47 425	51 805	47 786	..	Construction et réparation de navires		351
..	..	..	..	11 247	12 888	13 097	..	Construction de matériel ferroviaire roulant		352
..	..	..	..	31 810	37 191	38 530	..	Construction aéronautique et spatiale		353
..	..	..	..	841	966	1 044	..	Autres équipements de transport		359
..	..	..	..	43 583	44 954	48 296	..	**Meubles; activités de fabrication, nca**	**36**	
..	..	..	..	32 692	34 638	36 044	..	Meubles		361
..	..	..	..	10 891	10 316	12 252	..	Activités de fabrication, nca		369
..	..	..	..	1 414	1 051	1 157	..	**Récupération**	**37**	
..	..	..	..	233 468	284 713	..	..	**Production et distrib. d'électricité, de gaz, d'eau**	**E**	**40-41**
..	..	..	..	193 157	245 646	..	..	**Electricité, gaz, vapeur et eau chaude**		**40**
..	..	..	..	192 290	245 646	..	..	Production, collecte et distribution d'électricité		401
..	..	..	..	40 311	39 066	..	..	**Captage, épuration et distribution d'eau**	**41**	410
..	..	..	..	..	..	..	..	**Construction**	**F**	**45**
..	..	..	..	..	..	..	..	**Commerce de gros et de détail; réparation**	**G**	**50-52**
..	..	..	..	..	..	..	..	**Hôtels et restaurants**	**H**	**55**
..	..	..	..	..	..	..	..	**Transports, entreposage et communications**	**I**	**60-64**
..	..	..	..	..	..	..	..	**Intermédiation financière**	**J**	**65-67**
..	..	..	..	..	..	..	..	**Immobilier, locations, services aux entreprises**	**K**	**70-74**
..	..	..	..	..	..	..	..	**Admin. publique; éducation; santé; autres**	**L-Q**	**75-99**
..	..	..	..	..	..	..	..	**Grand total**	**A-Q**	**01-99**

Statistiques des Structures Industrielles
OCDE, © 1998

Table GR.3 INVESTMENT - INVESTISSEMENT

Millions of Dr (Current Prices)

ISIC revision 3			1989	1990	1991	1992	1993	1994	1995	1996
A	01-02	Agriculture, hunting and forestry	..	..	..	..	..	..	..	..
B	05	Fishing	..	..	..	..	..	..	..	..
C	10-14	Mining and quarrying	..	..	..	..	..	..	..	..
	10	Mining of coal and lignite; extraction of peat	..	..	..	..	23	31	..	..
	11	Crude petroleum & natural gas; related service activ.	..	..	..	..	8	13	..	..
	13	Mining of metal ores	..	..	..	..	6	8	..	..
	14	Other mining and quarrying	..	..	..	..	2	3	..	..
			..	..	..	..	7	7	..	..
D	15-37	Total manufacturing	..	..	..	..	302 020	286 936	344 414	..
	15	Food products and beverages	..	..	..	..	99 330	90 021	111 305	..
	155	Beverages	..	..	..	..	16 454	19 403	23 544	..
16	160	Tobacco products	..	..	..	..	2 705	5 567	4 859	..
17		Textiles	..	..	..	..	23 906	28 919	27 060	..
	171	Spinning, weaving and finishing of textiles	..	..	..	..	16 562	17 066	16 623	..
	172	Other textiles	..	..	..	..	2 349	7 206	5 050	..
	173	Knitted and crocheted fabrics and articles	..	..	..	..	4 995	4 647	5 387	..
18		Wearing apparel dressing & dyeing of fur	..	..	..	..	9 169	11 218	12 406	..
	181	Wearing apparel, except fur apparel	..	..	..	..	9 022	10 999	12 231	..
	182	Dressing and dyeing of fur; articles of fur	..	..	..	..	147	219	175	..
19		Tanning, dressing leather; leather artic.; footwear	..	..	..	..	2 682	1 516	2 721	..
	191	Tanning, dressing leather; manuf. of leather articles	..	..	..	..	1 260	328	581	..
	192	Footwear	..	..	..	..	1 422	1 187	2 140	..
20		Wood and cork products, ex. furniture	..	..	..	..	3 870	4 790	3 637	..
	201	Sawmilling and planing of wood	..	..	..	..	303	306	470	..
	202	Products of wood, cork, straw & plaiting material	..	..	..	..	3 567	4 484	3 167	..
21		Paper and paper products	..	..	..	..	6 843	9 734	16 448	..
22		Publishing, printing & reprod. of recorded media	..	..	..	..	12 836	11 135	8 541	..
	221	Publishing	..	..	..	..	8 351	8 749	5 557	..
	222	Printing and related service activities	..	..	..	..	4 485	2 387	2 984	..
	223	Reproduction of recorded media	..	..	..	..	0	0	0	..
23		Coke, refined petroleum products & nuclear fuel	..	..	..	..	10 073	8 968	16 973	..
24		Chemicals and chemical products	..	..	..	..	19 838	20 357	27 942	..
	241	Basic chemicals	..	..	..	..	5 544	5 446	8 843	..
	242	Other chemical products	..	..	..	..	12 427	13 186	17 445	..
	243	Man-made fibres	..	..	..	..	1 867	1 725	1 654	..
25		Rubber and plastic products	..	..	..	..	10 498	12 389	18 656	..
	251	Rubber products	..	..	..	..	619	819	1 480	..
	252	Plastic products	..	..	..	..	9 879	11 570	17 176	..
26		Other non-metallic mineral products	..	..	..	..	18 227	17 848	16 406	..
	261	Glass and glass products	..	..	..	..	1 667	721	896	..
	269	Non-metallic mineral products, nec	..	..	..	..	16 560	17 127	15 510	..
27		Basic metals	..	..	..	..	22 947	15 747	20 962	..
	271	Basic iron and steel	..	..	..	..	10 894	5 099	10 813	..
	272	Basic precious and non-ferrous metals	..	..	..	..	11 983	10 548	10 059	..
	273	Casting of metals	..	..	..	..	70	100	90	..
28		Fabricated metal products, ex. machin. & equip.	..	..	..	..	8 345	8 687	10 832	..
	281	Structural metal prod., tanks, reservoirs, generators	..	..	..	..	3 504	4 306	3 707	..
	289	Other fabricated metal products & service activities	..	..	..	..	4 841	4 381	7 125	..
29		Machinery and equipment, nec	..	..	..	..	7 794	9 727	9 608	..
	291	General purpose machinery	..	..	..	..	3 924	3 605	3 841	..
	292	Special purpose machinery	..	..	..	..	2 126	2 712	2 863	..
	293	Domestic appliances, nec	..	..	..	..	1 743	3 410	2 904	..
30		Office, accounting and computing machinery	..	..	..	..	27	27	59	..
31		Electrical machinery and apparatus, nec	..	..	..	..	7 192	10 143	8 468	..
	311	Electric motors, generators and transformers	..	..	..	..	337	697	714	..
	312	Electricity distribution and control apparatus	..	..	..	..	1 247	2 592	2 746	..
	313	Insulated wire and cable	..	..	..	..	4 956	3 718	2 680	..
	314	Accumulators, primary cells and primary batteries	..	..	..	..	175	2 768	1 447	..
	315	Electric lamps and lighting equipment	..	..	..	..	314	227	520	..
	319	Other electrical equipment, nec	..	..	..	..	163	141	361	..
32		Radio, TV, communication equip. & apparatus	..	..	..	..	8 547	5 031	4 512	..
	321	Electronic valves, tubes & other electronic compon.	..	..	..	..	407	742	395	..
	322	TV, radio transmitters & appar. for line teleph., telegr.	..	..	..	..	8 110	4 276	4 044	..
	323	TV, radio receivers and associated goods	..	..	..	..	30	13	73	..
33		Medical, precision, optical instr.; watches, clocks	..	..	..	..	590	2 009	1 194	..
	331	Medical equip.; precision instruments and appliances	..	..	..	..	555	460	661	..
	332	Optical instruments and photographic equipment	..	..	..	..	34	1 549	533	..
	333	Watches and clocks	..	..	..	..	1	0	..	..
34		Motor vehicles, trailers, and semi-trailers	..	..	..	..	1 994	1 231	502	..
35		Other transport equipment	..	..	..	..	19 874	7 438	16 170	..
	351	Building and repairing of ships and boats	..	..	..	..	3 126	353	1 165	..
	352	Railway, tramway locomotives and rolling stock	..	..	..	..	12	2	12	..
	353	Aircraft and spacecraft	..	..	..	..	16 649	7 049	13 803	..
	359	Transport equipment, nec	..	..	..	..	88	35	1 189	..
36		Furniture; manufacturing, nec	..	..	..	..	4 441	4 364	4 672	..
	361	Furniture	..	..	..	..	2 603	2 830	3 548	..
	369	Manufacturing, nec	..	..	..	..	1 837	1 534	1 124	..
37		Recycling	..	..	..	..	293	69	484	..
E	40-41	Electricity, gas and water supply	..	..	..	..	160 850	163 934	..	..
	40	Electricity, gas, steam and hot water supply	..	..	..	..	142 715	151 489	..	..
	401	Production, collection and distribution of electricity	..	..	..	..	142 715	151 489	..	..
41	410	Collection, purification, distribution of water	..	..	..	..	18 135	12 445	..	..
F	45	Construction	..	..	..	..	..	..	..	..
G	50-52	Wholesale and retail trade; repairs etc	..	..	..	..	..	..	..	..
H	55	Hotels and restaurants	..	..	..	..	..	..	..	..
I	60-64	Transport, storage and communications	..	..	..	..	..	..	..	..
J	65-67	Financial intermediation	..	..	..	..	..	..	..	..
K	70-74	Real estate, renting and business activities	..	..	..	..	..	..	..	..
L-Q	75-99	Public admin.; education; health; other services	..	..	..	..	..	..	..	..
A-Q	01-99	Grand total	..	..	..	..	..	..	..	..

Note:

Table GR.4 DÉPENSES EN MACHINES ET ÉQUIPEMENT - INVESTMENT IN MACHINERY AND EQUIPMENT

Millions de Dr (Prix courants)

1989	1990	1991	1992	1993	1994	1995	1996			CITI révision 3	
..	..	..	..	..	..	..	..	**Agriculture, chasse et sylviculture**	A	01-02	
..	..	..	..	..	..	..	..	**Pêche**	B	05	
..	..	..	..	12	13	..	..	**Activités extractives**	C	10-14	
..	..	..	..	6	8	..	..	Extraction de charbon, de lignite et de tourbe		10	
..	..	..	..	0	1	..	..	Extraction de pétrole brut et de gaz naturel		11	
..	..	..	..	0	0	..	..	Extraction de minerais métalliques		13	
..	..	..	..	5	4	..	..	Autres activités extractives		14	
..	..	..	..	183 428	181 973	222 105	..	**Activités de fabrication**	D	15-37	
..	..	..	..	62 667	55 757	78 151	..	**Produits alimentaires et boissons**		15	
..	..	..	..	12 216	16 049	19 473	..	Boissons			155
..	..	..	..	2 397	3 604	3 623	..	**Produits à base de tabac**		16	160
..	..	..	..	13 901	19 427	19 136	..	**Textiles**		17	
..	..	..	..	8 144	10 009	11 120	..	Filature, tissage et achèvement des textiles			171
..	..	..	..	1 883	5 534	3 595	..	Autres articles textiles			172
..	..	..	..	3 874	3 885	4 421	..	Etoffes et articles de bonneterie			173
..	..	..	..	5 726	6 228	6 820	..	**Habillement; préparation, teinture des fourrures**		18	
..	..	..	..	5 655	6 137	6 721	..	Articles d'habillement autres qu'en fourrure			181
..	..	..	..	72	90	99	..	Préparation, teinture des fourrures; art. en fourrure			182
..	..	..	..	1 098	1 268	1 814	..	**Travail des cuirs; articles en cuir; chaussures**		19	
..	..	..	..	354	195	407	..	Apprêt et tannage des cuirs et articles en cuirs			191
..	..	..	..	743	1 073	1 407	..	Chaussures			192
..	..	..	..	2 046	1 337	1 826	..	**Bois et articles en bois et liège (sauf meubles)**		20	
..	..	..	..	153	235	214	..	Sciage et rabotage du bois			201
..	..	..	..	1 893	1 101	1 611	..	Articles en bois, liège, vannerie, sparterie			202
..	..	..	..	5 494	5 916	8 282	..	**Papier et carton; articles en papier et en carton**		21	
..	..	..	..	7 712	9 286	4 751	..	**Edition, imprimerie et reproduction**		22	
..	..	..	..	4 355	5 993	2 508	..	Edition			221
..	..	..	..	3 357	3 293	2 243	..	Imprimerie et activités annexes			222
..	..	..	..	0	0	0	..	Reproduction de supports enregistrés			223
..	..	..	..	5 482	7 271	10 705	..	**Cokéfaction; prod. pétroliers; comb. nucléaires**		23	
..	..	..	..	13 164	15 552	18 743	..	**Produits chimiques**		24	
..	..	..	..	4 027	5 030	7 671	..	Produits chimiques de base			241
..	..	..	..	7 425	8 945	9 460	..	Autres produits chimiques			242
..	..	..	..	1 712	1 577	1 612	..	Fibres synthétiques ou artificielles			243
..	..	..	..	8 184	9 476	14 804	..	**Articles en caoutchouc et en matières plastiques**		25	
..	..	..	..	497	700	1 422	..	Articles en caoutchouc			251
..	..	..	..	7 687	8 776	13 383	..	Articles en matières plastiques			252
..	..	..	..	13 583	11 847	11 718	..	**Autres produits minéraux non métalliques**		26	
..	..	..	..	975	394	737	..	Verre et articles en verre			261
..	..	..	..	12 608	11 453	10 981	..	Produits minéraux non métalliques, nca			269
..	..	..	..	15 410	10 279	15 701	..	**Produits métallurgiques de base**		27	
..	..	..	..	7 138	3 225	7 981	..	Sidérurgie et première transformation de l'acier			271
..	..	..	..	8 218	6 963	7 661	..	Métallurgie; métaux précieux et non ferreux			272
..	..	..	..	53	90	59	..	Fonderie			273
..	..	..	..	5 762	5 915	7 499	..	**Ouvrages en métaux, sauf machines et matériel**		28	
..	..	..	..	1 989	2 352	2 009	..	Constr. et menuiserie métal.; réservoirs; générateurs			281
..	..	..	..	3 773	3 563	5 490	..	Autres ouvrages en métaux			289
..	..	..	..	4 826	5 087	5 398	..	**Machines et matériel, nca**		29	
..	..	..	..	2 003	1 602	2 241	..	Machines d'usage général			291
..	..	..	..	1 078	1 406	1 386	..	Machines d'usage spécifique			292
..	..	..	..	1 744	2 079	1 771	..	Appareils domestiques, nca			293
..	..	..	..	5	27	49	..	**Mach. de bureau, comptables, matériel inform.**		30	
..	..	..	..	5 803	6 634	5 804	..	**Machines et appareils électriques, nca**		31	
..	..	..	..	241	591	666	..	Moteurs, génératrices et transformateurs électriques			311
..	..	..	..	1 100	1 042	1 587	..	Matériel électrique de distribution et de commande			312
..	..	..	..	3 976	2 165	2 065	..	Fils et câbles électriques isolés			313
..	..	..	..	149	2 550	1 077	..	Accumulateurs, piles électriques			314
..	..	..	..	273	163	299	..	Lampes électriques et appareils d'éclairage			315
..	..	..	..	64	123	110	..	Autres matériels électriques, nca			319
..	..	..	..	2 866	1 721	1 872	..	**Equip. et appar. de radio, TV, communication**		32	
..	..	..	..	336	316	315	..	Tubes et valves électroniques; autres composants			321
..	..	..	..	2 501	1 400	1 485	..	Emetteurs radio et TV; app. téléphonie, télégraphie			322
..	..	..	..	29	4	73	..	Récepteurs radio et TV et articles associés			323
..	..	..	..	519	554	766	..	**Instruments médicaux, de précision, d'optique**		33	
..	..	..	..	484	270	497	..	Appareils médicaux et de précision			331
..	..	..	..	34	283	269	..	Instruments d'optique ; matériel photographique			332
..	..	..	..	1	0	0	..	Horlogerie			333
..	..	..	..	810	525	213	..	**Véhicules automobiles et nemorques**		34	
..	..	..	..	2 957	1 700	1 462	..	**Autres matériels de transport**		35	
..	..	..	..	2 023	1 216	834	..	Construction et réparation de navires			351
..	..	..	..	12	2	12	..	Construction de matériel ferroviaire roulant			352
..	..	..	..	845	458	319	..	Construction aéronautique et spatiale			353
..	..	..	..	78	24	297	..	Autres équipements de transport			359
..	..	..	..	2 738	2 511	2 614	..	**Meubles; activités de fabrication, nca**		36	
..	..	..	..	1 855	1 526	2 016	..	Meubles			361
..	..	..	..	883	985	598	..	Activités de fabrication, nca			369
..	..	..	..	280	51	356	..	**Récupération**		37	
..	..	..	..	..	..	..	..	**Production et distrib. d'électricité, de gaz, d'eau**	E	40-41	
..	..	..	..	..	..	..	..	**Electricité, gaz, vapeur et eau chaude**		40	
..	..	..	..	..	..	..	..	Production, collecte et distribution d'électricité			401
..	..	..	..	63 821	71 129	..	..	**Captage, épuration et distribution d'eau**		41	410
..	..	..	..	..	..	..	..	**Construction**	F	45	
..	..	..	..	..	..	..	..	**Commerce de gros et de détail; réparation**	G	50-52	
..	..	..	..	..	..	..	..	**Hôtels et restaurants**	H	55	
..	..	..	..	..	..	..	..	**Transports, entreposage et communications**	I	60-64	
..	..	..	..	..	..	..	..	**Intermédiation financière**	J	65-67	
..	..	..	..	..	..	..	..	**Immobilier, locations, services aux entreprises**	K	70-74	
..	..	..	..	..	..	..	..	**Admin. publique; éducation; santé; autres**	L-Q	75-99	
..	..	..	..	..	..	..	..	**Grand total**	A-Q	01-99	

Statistiques des Structures Industrielles
OCDE, © 1998

Table GR.5 ESTABLISHMENTS - ETABLISSEMENTS

Units

ISIC revision 3			1989	1990	1991	1992	1993	1994	1995	1996
A	01-02	**Agriculture, hunting and forestry**	..	..	..	..	..	..	..	..
B	05	**Fishing**	..	..	..	..	..	..	..	..
C	10-14	**Mining and quarrying**	..	..	..	..	866	861	..	..
	10	Mining of coal and lignite; extraction of peat	..	..	..	..	26	26	..	..
	11	Crude petroleum & natural gas; related service activ.	..	..	..	..	15	15	..	..
	13	Mining of metal ores	..	..	..	..	56	55	..	..
	14	Other mining and quarrying	..	..	..	..	769	765	..	..
D	15-37	**Total manufacturing**	..	..	..	..	6 119	5 945	5 813	..
	15	**Food products and beverages**	..	..	..	..	1 126	1 106	1 091	..
	155	Beverages	..	..	..	..	158	158	154	..
	16 160	**Tobacco products**	..	..	..	..	14	14	14	..
	17	**Textiles**	..	..	..	..	525	499	480	..
	171	Spinning, weaving and finishing of textiles	..	..	..	..	220	201	194	..
	172	Other textiles	..	..	..	..	133	126	124	..
	173	Knitted and crocheted fabrics and articles	..	..	..	..	172	172	162	..
	18	**Wearing apparel dressing & dyeing of fur**	..	..	..	..	903	843	797	..
	181	Wearing apparel, except fur apparel	..	..	..	..	863	805	759	..
	182	Dressing and dyeing of fur; articles of fur	..	..	..	..	40	38	38	..
	19	**Tanning, dressing leather; leather artic.; footwear**	..	..	..	..	245	235	228	..
	191	Tanning, dressing leather; manuf. of leather articles	..	..	..	..	57	50	47	..
	192	Footwear	..	..	..	..	188	185	181	..
	20	**Wood and cork products, ex. furniture**	..	..	..	..	177	166	160	..
	201	Sawmilling and planing of wood	..	..	..	..	36	32	32	..
	202	Products of wood, cork, straw & plaiting material	..	..	..	..	141	134	128	..
	21	**Paper and paper products**	..	..	..	..	138	138	139	..
	22	**Publishing, printing & reprod. of recorded media**	..	..	..	..	238	234	236	..
	221	Publishing	..	..	..	..	112	112	111	..
	222	Printing and related service activities	..	..	..	..	126	122	125	..
	223	Reproduction of recorded media	..	..	..	..	0	0	0	..
	23	**Coke, refined petroleum products & nuclear fuel**	..	..	..	..	18	17	17	..
	24	**Chemicals and chemical products**	..	..	..	..	337	327	323	..
	241	Basic chemicals	..	..	..	..	66	65	65	..
	242	Other chemical products	..	..	..	..	266	257	253	..
	243	Man-made fibres	..	..	..	..	5	5	5	..
	25	**Rubber and plastic products**	..	..	..	..	257	263	268	..
	251	Rubber products	..	..	..	..	25	25	25	..
	252	Plastic products	..	..	..	..	232	238	243	..
	26	**Other non-metallic mineral products**	..	..	..	..	514	505	496	..
	261	Glass and glass products	..	..	..	..	25	22	20	..
	269	Non-metallic mineral products, nec	..	..	..	..	489	483	476	..
	27	**Basic metals**	..	..	..	..	129	126	125	..
	271	Basic iron and steel	..	..	..	..	75	70	69	..
	272	Basic precious and non-ferrous metals	..	..	..	..	48	51	50	..
	273	Casting of metals	..	..	..	..	6	5	6	..
	28	**Fabricated metal products, ex. machin. & equip.**	..	..	..	..	379	362	361	..
	281	Structural metal prod., tanks, reservoirs, generators	..	..	..	..	156	140	139	..
	289	Other fabricated metal products & service activities	..	..	..	..	223	222	222	..
	29	**Machinery and equipment, nec**	..	..	..	..	342	339	332	..
	291	General purpose machinery	..	..	..	..	150	149	140	..
	292	Special purpose machinery	..	..	..	..	127	127	129	..
	293	Domestic appliances, nec	..	..	..	..	65	63	63	..
	30	**Office, accounting and computing machinery**	..	..	..	..	5	4	4	..
	31	**Electrical machinery and apparatus, nec**	..	..	..	..	118	117	114	..
	311	Electric motors, generators and transformers	..	..	..	..	17	16	15	..
	312	Electricity distribution and control apparatus	..	..	..	..	35	37	35	..
	313	Insulated wire and cable	..	..	..	..	21	21	22	..
	314	Accumulators, primary cells and primary batteries	..	..	..	..	10	8	8	..
	315	Electric lamps and lighting equipment	..	..	..	..	29	28	28	..
	319	Other electrical equipment, nec	..	..	..	..	6	7	6	..
	32	**Radio, TV, communication equip. & apparatus**	..	..	..	..	31	31	29	..
	321	Electronic valves, tubes & other electronic componen.	..	..	..	..	11	13	11	..
	322	TV, radio transmitters & appar. for line teleph., telegr.	..	..	..	..	6	6	6	..
	323	TV, radio receivers and associated goods	..	..	..	..	14	12	12	..
	33	**Medical, precision, optical instr.; watches, clocks**	..	..	..	..	36	31	31	..
	331	Medical equip.; precision instruments and appliances	..	..	..	..	27	23	23	..
	332	Optical instruments and photographic equipment	..	..	..	..	8	7	7	..
	333	Watches and clocks	..	..	..	..	1	1	1	..
	34	**Motor vehicles, trailers, and semi-trailers**	..	..	..	..	47	47	47	..
	35	**Other transport equipment**	..	..	..	..	114	126	127	..
	351	Building and repairing of ships and boats	..	..	..	..	92	101	101	..
	352	Railway, tramway locomotives and rolling stock	..	..	..	..	12	13	13	..
	353	Aircraft and spacecraft	..	..	..	..	5	6	6	..
	359	Transport equipment, nec	..	..	..	..	5	6	7	..
	36	**Furniture; manufacturing, nec**	..	..	..	..	413	405	384	..
	361	Furniture	..	..	..	..	319	313	295	..
	369	Manufacturing, nec	..	..	..	..	94	92	89	..
	37	**Recycling**	..	..	..	..	13	10	10	..
E	40-41	**Electricity, gas and water supply**	..	..	..	..	49	49	..	..
	40	**Electricity, gas, steam and hot water supply**	..	..	..	..	2	1	..	..
	401	Production, collection and distribution of electricity	..	..	..	..	1	1	..	..
	41 410	**Collection, purification, distribution of water**	..	..	..	..	47	48	..	..
F	45	**Construction**	..	..	..	..	..	..	..	..
G	50-52	**Wholesale and retail trade; repairs etc**	..	..	..	..	..	..	..	..
H	55	**Hotels and restaurants**	..	..	..	..	..	..	..	..
I	60-64	**Transport, storage and communications**	..	..	..	..	..	..	..	..
J	65-67	**Financial intermediation**	..	..	..	..	..	..	..	..
K	70-74	**Real estate, renting and business activities**	..	..	..	..	..	..	..	..
L-Q	75-99	**Public admin.; education; health; other services**	..	..	..	..	..	..	..	..
A-Q	01-99	**Grand total**	..	..	..	..	..	..	..	..

Table GR.6 EMPLOI - EMPLOYMENT

Milliers

1989	1990	1991	1992	1993	1994	1995	1996			CITI révision 3
..	..	..	..				..	**Agriculture, chasse et sylviculture**	A	01-02
..	..	..	..	..	..	..	..	**Pêche**	B	05
..	..	..	..	18.7	17.1	..	..	**Activités extractives**	C	10-14
..	..	..	..	7.9	6.8	..		Extraction de charbon, de lignite et de tourbe		10
..	..	..	..	0.7	0.7	..		Extraction de pétrole brut et de gaz naturel		11
..	..	..	..	2.7	2.6	..		Extraction de minerais métalliques		13
..	..	..	..	7.4	7.1	..	..	Autres activités extractives		14
..	..	..	..	274.6	261.9	255.0	..	**Activités de fabrication**	D	15-37
..	..	..	..	52.2	52.1	51.4		**Produits alimentaires et boissons**		15
..	..	..	..	9.1	9.0	8.6		Boissons		155
..	..	..	..	3.3	3.0	2.9	..	**Produits à base de tabac**		16 160
..	..	..	..	28.0	24.9	24.0		**Textiles**		17
..	..	..	..	16.0	14.2	14.1		Filature, tissage et achèvement des textiles		171
..	..	..	..	4.6	4.1	4.2		Autres articles textiles		172
..	..	..	..	7.4	6.6	5.7		Etoffes et articles de bonneterie		173
..	..	..	..	36.3	31.8	29.6	..	**Habillement; préparation, teinture des fourrures**		18
..	..	..	..	35.4	31.0	28.9		Articles d'habillement autres qu'en fourrure		181
..	..	..	..	0.9	0.8	0.7		Préparation, teinture des fourrures; art. en fourrure		182
..	..	..	..	6.5	6.0	5.6	..	**Travail des cuirs; articles en cuir; chaussures**		19
..	..	..	..	1.2	1.0	0.9		Apprêt et tannage des cuirs et articles en cuirs		191
..	..	..	..	5.3	5.0	4.7		Chaussures		192
..	..	..	..	5.8	5.2	4.9	..	**Bois et articles en bois et liège (sauf meubles)**		20
..	..	..	..	0.9	0.8	0.8		Sciage et rabotage du bois		201
..	..	..	..	4.9	4.4	4.1		Articles en bois, liège, vannerie, sparterie		202
..	..	..	..	7.9	8.1	8.3	..	**Papier et carton; articles en papier et en carton**		21
..	..	..	..	10.3	10.4	10.3	..	**Edition, imprimerie et reproduction**		22
..	..	..	..	6.8	6.9	7.0		Edition		221
..	..	..	..	3.5	3.5	3.4		Imprimerie et activités annexes		222
..	..	..	..	0.0	0.0	0.0		Reproduction de supports enregistrés		223
..	..	..	..	4.2	4.3	4.1	..	**Cokéfaction; prod. pétroliers; comb. nucléaires**		23
..	..	..	..	20.7	20.2	19.3	..	**Produits chimiques**		24
..	..	..	..	4.6	4.4	4.4		Produits chimiques de base		241
..	..	..	..	15.0	14.8	14.0		Autres produits chimiques		242
..	..	..	..	1.1	1.0	0.9		Fibres synthétiques ou artificielles		243
..	..	..	..	9.1	9.2	9.5	..	**Articles en caoutchouc et en matières plastiques**		25
..	..	..	..	1.0	1.0	1.0		Articles en caoutchouc		251
..	..	..	..	8.1	8.2	8.5		Articles en matières plastiques		252
..	..	..	..	19.3	17.9	17.3	..	**Autres produits minéraux non métalliques**		26
..	..	..	..	1.1	1.0	0.9		Verre et articles en verre		261
..	..	..	..	18.2	16.9	16.4		Produits minéraux non métalliques, nca		269
..	..	..	..	11.0	10.7	10.6	..	**Produits métallurgiques de base**		27
..	..	..	..	6.1	5.7	5.5		Sidérurgie et première transformation de l'acier		271
..	..	..	..	4.8	4.8	4.9		Métallurgie; métaux précieux et non ferreux		272
..	..	..	..	0.1	0.2	0.3		Fonderie		273
..	..	..	..	11.4	10.9	10.7	..	**Ouvrages en métaux, sauf machines et matériel**		28
..	..	..	..	4.4	3.8	3.8		Constr. et menuiserie métal.; réservoirs; générateurs		281
..	..	..	..	7.0	7.1	6.9		Autres ouvrages en métaux		289
..	..	..	..	11.6	11.4	11.4	..	**Machines et matériel, nca**		29
..	..	..	..	4.5	4.4	4.2		Machines d'usage général		291
..	..	..	..	4.8	4.7	5.0		Machines d'usage spécifique		292
..	..	..	..	2.3	2.3	2.2		Appareils domestiques, nca		293
..	..	..	..	0.1	0.1	0.1	..	**Mach. de bureau, comptables, matériel inform.**		30
..	..	..	..	5.6	5.4	5.3	..	**Machines et appareils électriques, nca**		31
..	..	..	..	1.2	1.1	1.1		Moteurs, génératrices et transformateurs électriques		311
..	..	..	..	1.5	1.5	1.5		Matériel électrique de distribution et de commande		312
..	..	..	..	1.6	1.5	1.5		Fils et câbles électriques isolés		313
..	..	..	..	0.6	0.4	0.4		Accumulateurs, piles électriques		314
..	..	..	..	0.6	0.6	0.6		Lampes électriques et appareils d'éclairage		315
..	..	..	..	0.1	0.2	0.1		Autres matériels électriques, nca		319
..	..	..	..	2.6	2.6	2.5	..	**Equip. et appar. de radio, TV, communication**		32
..	..	..	..	0.3	0.4	0.3		Tubes et valves électroniques; autres composants		321
..	..	..	..	2.1	2.0	2.0		Emetteurs radio et TV; app. téléphonie, télégraphie		322
..	..	..	..	0.2	0.2	0.2		Récepteurs radio et TV et articles associés		323
..	..	..	..	1.1	1.2	1.3	..	**Instruments médicaux, de précision, d'optique**		33
..	..	..	..	0.9	0.9	0.9		Appareils médicaux et de précision		331
..	..	..	..	0.2	0.2	0.3		Instruments d'optique ; matériel photographique		332
..	..	..	..	0.0	0.0	0.0		Horlogerie		333
..	..	..	..	2.4	2.3	2.2	..	**Véhicules automobiles et nemorques**		34
..	..	..	..	16.2	15.9	15.5	..	**Autres matériels de transport**		35
..	..	..	..	8.8	8.6	8.6		Construction et réparation de navires		351
..	..	..	..	2.4	2.4	2.2		Construction de matériel ferroviaire roulant		352
..	..	..	..	4.9	4.8	4.6		Construction aéronautique et spatiale		353
..	..	..	..	0.1	0.1	0.2		Autres équipements de transport		359
..	..	..	..	8.9	8.4	7.9	..	**Meubles; activités de fabrication, nca**		36
..	..	..	..	6.8	6.4	6.0		Meubles		361
..	..	..	..	2.0	2.0	1.9		Activités de fabrication, nca		369
..	..	..	..	0.2	0.1	0.1		**Récupération**		37
..	..	..	..	..	..	..	..	**Production et distrib. d'électricité, de gaz, d'eau**	E	40-41
..	..	..	..	..	..	..	..	**Electricité, gaz, vapeur et eau chaude**		40
..	..	..	..	..	..	..	..	Production, collecte et distribution d'électricité		401
..	..	..	..	..	..	..	..	**Captage, épuration et distribution d'eau**		41 410
..	..	..	..	..	..	..	..	**Construction**	F	45
..	..	..	..	..	..	..	..	**Commerce de gros et de détail; réparation**	G	50-52
..	..	..	..	..	..	..	..	**Hôtels et restaurants**	H	55
..	..	..	..	..	..	..	..	**Transports, entreposage et communications**	I	60-64
..	..	..	..	..	..	..	..	**Intermédiation financière**	J	65-67
..	..	..	..	..	..	..	..	**Immobilier, locations, services aux entreprises**	K	70-74
..	..	..	..	..	..	..	..	**Admin. publique; éducation; santé; autres**	L-Q	75-99
..	..	..	..	..	..	..	..	**Grand total**	A-Q	01-99

Statistiques des Structures Industrielles
OCDE, © 1998

Table GR.7 EMPLOYMENT, EMPLOYEES - EMPLOI, SALARIÉS

Thousands

ISIC revision 3				1989	1990	1991	1992	1993	1994	1995	1996
A	01-02		Agriculture, hunting and forestry	..	..	..	..	..	..	..	..
B	05		Fishing	..	..	..	..	..	..	..	..
C	10-14		Mining and quarrying	..	..	..	..	17.8	16.3	..	..
	10		Mining of coal and lignite; extraction of peat	..	..	..	..	7.9	6.8	..	..
	11		Crude petroleum & natural gas; related service activ.	..	..	..	..	0.7	0.7	..	..
	13		Mining of metal ores	..	..	..	..	2.7	2.6	..	..
	14		Other mining and quarrying	..	..	..	..	6.5	6.2	..	..
D	15-37		Total manufacturing	..	..	..	..	269.4	257.1	250.5	..
	15		Food products and beverages	..	..	..	..	51.3	51.3	50.6	..
		155	Beverages	..	..	..	..	9.1	8.9	8.6	..
	16	160	Tobacco products	..	..	..	..	3.3	3.0	2.9	..
	17		Textiles	..	..	..	..	27.7	24.6	23.7	..
		171	Spinning, weaving and finishing of textiles	..	..	..	..	15.9	14.2	14.0	..
		172	Other textiles	..	..	..	..	4.5	4.0	4.1	..
		173	Knitted and crocheted fabrics and articles	..	..	..	..	7.3	6.4	5.6	..
	18		Wearing apparel dressing & dyeing of fur	..	..	..	..	35.3	30.8	28.8	..
		181	Wearing apparel, except fur apparel	..	..	..	..	34.5	30.1	28.1	..
		182	Dressing and dyeing of fur; articles of fur	..	..	..	..	0.8	0.8	0.7	..
	19		Tanning, dressing leather; leather artic.; footwear	..	..	..	..	6.2	5.7	5.4	..
		191	Tanning, dressing leather; manuf. of leather articles	..	..	..	..	1.1	1.0	0.9	..
		192	Footwear	..	..	..	..	5.1	4.7	4.5	..
	20		Wood and cork products, ex. furniture	..	..	..	..	5.6	5.0	4.7	..
		201	Sawmilling and planing of wood	..	..	..	..	0.8	0.8	0.8	..
		202	Products of wood, cork, straw & plaiting material	..	..	..	..	4.8	4.3	4.0	..
	21		Paper and paper products	..	..	..	..	7.9	8.0	8.3	..
	22		Publishing, printing & reprod. of recorded media	..	..	..	..	10.0	10.2	10.1	..
		221	Publishing	..	..	..	..	6.7	6.8	6.9	..
		222	Printing and related service activities	..	..	..	..	3.4	3.4	3.2	..
		223	Reproduction of recorded media	..	..	..	..	0.0	0.0	0.0	..
	23		Coke, refined petroleum products & nuclear fuel	..	..	..	..	4.2	4.3	4.1	..
	24		Chemicals and chemical products	..	..	..	..	20.6	20.1	19.2	..
		241	Basic chemicals	..	..	..	..	4.6	4.4	4.3	..
		242	Other chemical products	..	..	..	..	14.9	14.8	13.9	..
		243	Man-made fibres	..	..	..	..	1.1	1.0	0.9	..
	25		Rubber and plastic products	..	..	..	..	9.0	9.1	9.4	..
		251	Rubber products	..	..	..	..	1.0	1.0	1.0	..
		252	Plastic products	..	..	..	..	8.0	8.1	8.4	..
	26		Other non-metallic mineral products	..	..	..	..	18.7	17.6	17.0	..
		261	Glass and glass products	..	..	..	..	1.1	1.0	0.9	..
		269	Non-metallic mineral products, nec	..	..	..	..	17.6	16.6	16.1	..
	27		Basic metals	..	..	..	..	11.0	10.6	10.6	..
		271	Basic iron and steel	..	..	..	..	6.1	5.6	5.4	..
		272	Basic precious and non-ferrous metals	..	..	..	..	4.8	4.8	4.9	..
		273	Casting of metals	..	..	..	..	0.1	0.2	0.3	..
	28		Fabricated metal products, ex. machin. & equip.	..	..	..	..	11.1	10.6	10.4	..
		281	Structural metal prod., tanks, reservoirs, generators	..	..	..	..	4.3	3.7	3.7	..
		289	Other fabricated metal products & service activities	..	..	..	..	6.8	6.9	6.7	..
	29		Machinery and equipment, nec	..	..	..	..	11.3	11.1	11.2	..
		291	General purpose machinery	..	..	..	..	4.3	4.3	4.1	..
		292	Special purpose machinery	..	..	..	..	4.7	4.6	4.9	..
		293	Domestic appliances, nec	..	..	..	..	2.3	2.2	2.2	..
	30		Office, accounting and computing machinery	..	..	..	..	0.1	0.1	0.1	..
	31		Electrical machinery and apparatus, nec	..	..	..	..	5.5	5.3	5.2	..
		311	Electric motors, generators and transformers	..	..	..	..	1.2	1.1	1.1	..
		312	Electricity distribution and control apparatus	..	..	..	..	1.5	1.5	1.5	..
		313	Insulated wire and cable	..	..	..	..	1.6	1.5	1.5	..
		314	Accumulators, primary cells and primary batteries	..	..	..	..	0.6	0.4	0.4	..
		315	Electric lamps and lighting equipment	..	..	..	..	0.6	0.5	0.5	..
		319	Other electrical equipment, nec	..	..	..	..	0.1	0.2	0.1	..
	32		Radio, TV, communication equip. & apparatus	..	..	..	..	2.6	2.6	2.5	..
		321	Electronic valves, tubes & other electronic compon.	..	..	..	..	0.3	0.4	0.3	..
		322	TV, radio transmitters & appar. for line teleph., telegr.	..	..	..	..	2.1	2.0	2.0	..
		323	TV, radio receivers and associated goods	..	..	..	..	0.2	0.2	0.1	..
	33		Medical, precision, optical instr.; watches, clocks	..	..	..	..	1.1	1.1	1.3	..
		331	Medical equip.; precision instruments and appliances	..	..	..	..	0.9	0.9	0.9	..
		332	Optical instruments and photographic equipment	..	..	..	..	0.2	0.2	0.3	..
		333	Watches and clocks	..	..	..	..	0.0	0.0	0.0	..
	34		Motor vehicles, trailers, and semi-trailers	..	..	..	..	2.3	2.2	2.1	..
	35		Other transport equipment	..	..	..	..	16.2	15.9	15.5	..
		351	Building and repairing of ships and boats	..	..	..	..	8.8	8.6	8.5	..
		352	Railway, tramway locomotives and rolling stock	..	..	..	..	2.4	2.4	2.2	..
		353	Aircraft and spacecraft	..	..	..	..	4.9	4.8	4.6	..
		359	Transport equipment, nec	..	..	..	..	0.1	0.1	0.2	..
	36		Furniture; manufacturing, nec	..	..	..	..	8.3	7.8	7.3	..
		361	Furniture	..	..	..	..	6.4	6.0	5.6	..
		369	Manufacturing, nec	..	..	..	..	1.9	1.8	1.8	..
	37		Recycling	..	..	..	..	0.2	0.1	0.1	..
E	40-41		Electricity, gas and water supply	..	..	..	..	29.1	29.5	..	..
	40		Electricity, gas, steam and hot water supply	..	..	..	..	22.5	22.8	..	..
		401	Production, collection and distribution of electricity	..	..	..	..	22.4	22.8	..	..
	41	410	Collection, purification, distribution of water	..	..	..	..	6.6	6.7	..	..
F	45		Construction	..	..	..	..	..	..	..	..
G	50-52		Wholesale and retail trade; repairs etc	..	..	..	..	..	..	..	..
H	55		Hotels and restaurants	..	..	..	..	..	..	..	..
I	60-64		Transport, storage and communications	..	..	..	..	..	..	..	..
J	65-67		Financial intermediation	..	..	..	..	..	..	..	..
K	70-74		Real estate, renting and business activities	..	..	..	..	..	..	..	..
L-Q	75-99		Public admin.; education; health; other services	..	..	..	..	..	..	..	..
A-Q	01-99		Grand total	..	..	..	..	..	..	..	..

Table GR.8 **SALAIRES ET CHARGES SOCIALES , SALARIÉS - COMPENSATION OF LABOUR, EMPLOYEES**

Millions de Dr (Prix courants)

1989	1990	1991	1992	1993	1994	1995	1996		CITI révision 3	
..	..	..	..	..	..	..	..	**Agriculture, chasse et sylviculture**	A	01-02
..	..	..	..	..	..	..	..	**Pêche**	B	05
..	..	..	..	76	87	..	..	**Activités extractives**	C	10-14
..	..	..	..	33	41	..		Extraction de charbon, de lignite et de tourbe		10
..	..	..	..	7	7	..		Extraction de pétrole brut et de gaz naturel		11
..	..	..	..	14	15	..		Extraction de minerais métalliques		13
..	..	..	..	23	25	..		Autres activités extractives		14
..	..	..	..	1 034 794	1 130 253	1 238 658	..	**Activités de fabrication**	D	15-37
..	..	..	..	193 941	225 832	245 536	..	**Produits alimentaires et boissons**		15
..	..	..	..	45 225	51 751	56 079		Boissons		155
..	..	..	..	13 972	18 138	19 435	..	**Produits à base de tabac**	16	160
..	..	..	..	87 628	89 416	95 601	..	**Textiles**	17	
..	..	..	..	56 341	57 763	63 270		Filature, tissage et achèvement des textiles		171
..	..	..	..	12 323	12 861	14 084		Autres articles textiles		172
..	..	..	..	18 963	18 792	18 247		Etoffes et articles de bonneterie		173
..	..	..	..	84 979	83 760	88 451	..	**Habillement; préparation, teinture des fourrures**	18	
..	..	..	..	83 242	81 972	86 665		Articles d'habillement autres qu'en fourrure		181
..	..	..	..	1 737	1 788	1 786		Préparation, teinture des fourrures; art. en fourrure		182
..	..	..	..	16 549	17 977	19 343	..	**Travail des cuirs; articles en cuir; chaussures**	19	
..	..	..	..	3 650	3 608	3 599		Apprêt et tannage des cuirs et articles en cuirs		191
..	..	..	..	12 899	14 369	15 744		Chaussures		192
..	..	..	..	19 899	19 085	20 694	..	**Bois et articles en bois et liège (sauf meubles)**	20	
..	..	..	..	2 569	2 605	2 691		Sciage et rabotage du bois		201
..	..	..	..	17 330	16 480	18 003		Articles en bois, liège, vannerie, sparterie		202
..	..	..	..	32 645	35 590	41 210	..	**Papier et carton; articles en papier et en carton**	21	
..	..	..	..	41 295	47 571	50 940	..	**Edition, imprimerie et reproduction**	22	
..	..	..	..	28 947	32 815	35 821		Edition		221
..	..	..	..	12 347	14 756	15 119		Imprimerie et activités annexes		222
..	..	..	..	0	0	0		Reproduction de supports enregistrés		223
..	..	..	..	26 333	32 809	38 214	..	**Cokéfaction; prod. pétroliers; comb. nucléaires**	23	
..	..	..	..	102 652	114 283	124 141	..	**Produits chimiques**	24	
..	..	..	..	28 650	31 491	35 553		Produits chimiques de base		241
..	..	..	..	70 439	78 469	84 074		Autres produits chimiques		242
..	..	..	..	3 563	4 323	4 514		Fibres synthétiques ou artificielles		243
..	..	..	..	32 878	37 098	42 345	..	**Articles en caoutchouc et en matières plastiques**	25	
..	..	..	..	5 578	6 158	6 970	..	Articles en caoutchouc		251
..	..	..	..	27 300	30 940	35 375		Articles en matières plastiques		252
..	..	..	..	81 782	87 322	95 370	..	**Autres produits minéraux non métalliques**	26	
..	..	..	..	3 715	3 858	4 139		Verre et articles en verre		261
..	..	..	..	78 068	83 464	91 231		Produits minéraux non métalliques, nca		269
..	..	..	..	63 806	63 874	74 164	..	**Produits métallurgiques de base**	27	
..	..	..	..	32 193	32 671	36 509		Sidérurgie et première transformation de l'acier		271
..	..	..	..	31 245	30 545	36 577		Métallurgie; métaux précieux et non ferreux		272
..	..	..	..	368	659	1 078		Fonderie		273
..	..	..	..	38 833	41 786	46 262	..	**Ouvrages en métaux, sauf machines et matériel**	28	
..	..	..	..	14 459	13 742	15 788		Constr. et menuiserie métal.; réservoirs; générateurs		281
..	..	..	..	24 373	28 044	30 474		Autres ouvrages en métaux		289
..	..	..	..	42 394	47 962	54 624	..	**Machines et matériel, nca**	29	
..	..	..	..	14 584	16 145	17 940		Machines d'usage général		291
..	..	..	..	18 815	21 723	25 875		Machines d'usage spécifique		292
..	..	..	..	8 994	10 094	10 810		Appareils domestiques, nca		293
..	..	..	..	304	242	638	..	**Mach. de bureau, comptables, matériel inform.**	30	
..	..	..	..	24 426	23 654	26 580	..	**Machines et appareils électriques, nca**	31	
..	..	..	..	5 497	5 703	6 502		Moteurs, génératrices et transformateurs électriques		311
..	..	..	..	5 468	6 086	6 364		Matériel électrique de distribution et de commande		312
..	..	..	..	7 863	7 695	8 993		Fils et câbles électriques isolés		313
..	..	..	..	3 800	1 994	2 278		Accumulateurs, piles électriques		314
..	..	..	..	1 434	1 631	1 896		Lampes électriques et appareils d'éclairage		315
..	..	..	..	365	545	547		Autres matériels électriques, nca		319
..	..	..	..	12 380	13 202	14 695	..	**Equip. et appar. de radio, TV, communication**	32	
..	..	..	..	1 006	1 240	1 253		Tubes et valves électroniques; autres composants		321
..	..	..	..	10 799	11 383	12 894		Emetteurs radio et TV; app. téléphonie, télégraphie		322
..	..	..	..	575	578	548		Récepteurs radio et TV et articles associés		323
..	..	..	..	3 283	3 747	4 798	..	**Instruments médicaux, de précision, d'optique**	33	
..	..	..	..	2 822	3 050	3 647		Appareils médicaux et de précision		331
..	..	..	..	446	682	1 137		Instruments d'optique ; matériel photographique		332
..	..	..	..	15	16	14		Horlogerie		333
..	..	..	..	9 897	10 237	10 863	..	**Véhicules automobiles et nemorques**	34	
..	..	..	..	81 881	92 664	99 373	..	**Autres matériels de transport**	35	
..	..	..	..	44 454	47 455	52 398		Construction et réparation de navires		351
..	..	..	..	9 696	11 085	11 301		Construction de matériel ferroviaire roulant		352
..	..	..	..	27 421	33 761	35 104		Construction aéronautique et spatiale		353
..	..	..	..	310	364	569		Autres équipements de transport		359
..	..	..	..	22 410	23 719	24 932	..	**Meubles; activités de fabrication, nca**	36	
..	..	..	..	17 289	18 166	18 838		Meubles		361
..	..	..	..	5 121	5 553	6 094		Activités de fabrication, nca		369
..	..	..	..	629	287	449	..	**Récupération**		37
..	..	..	..	143 441	172 839		..	**Production et distrib. d'électricité, de gaz, d'eau**	E	40-41
..	..	..	..	110 146	133 895		..	**Electricité, gaz, vapeur et eau chaude**		40
..	..	..	..	109 712	133 895			Production, collecte et distribution d'électricité		401
..	..	..	..	33 295	38 943		..	**Captage, épuration et distribution d'eau**	41	410
..	..	..	..	..	..	..	..	**Construction**	F	45
..	..	..	..	..	..	..	..	**Commerce de gros et de détail; réparation**	G	50-52
..	..	..	..	..	..	..	..	**Hôtels et restaurants**	H	55
..	..	..	..	..	..	..	..	**Transports, entreposage et communications**	I	60-64
..	..	..	..	..	..	..	..	**Intermédiation financière**	J	65-67
..	..	..	..	..	..	..	..	**Immobilier, locations, services aux entreprises**	K	70-74
..	..	..	..	..	..	..	..	**Admin. publique; éducation; santé; autres**	L-Q	75-99
..	..	..	..	..	..	..		**Grand total**	A-Q	01-99

Statistiques des Structures Industrielles
OCDE, © 1998

Table GR.9 WAGES AND SALARIES, EMPLOYEES - SALAIRES ET TRAITEMENTS, SALARIÉS

Millions of Dr (Current Prices)

ISIC revision 3			1989	1990	1991	1992	1993	1994	1995	1996
A	01-02	Agriculture, hunting and forestry	..	..	..	..	..	..	..	..
B	05	Fishing	..	..	..	..	..	..	..	..
C	10-14	Mining and quarrying	..	..	..	..	57	65	..	..
	10	Mining of coal and lignite; extraction of peat	..	..	..	..	24	29	..	..
	11	Crude petroleum & natural gas; related service activ.	..	..	..	..	5	5	..	..
	13	Mining of metal ores	..	..	..	..	10	11	..	..
	14	Other mining and quarrying	..	..	..	..	17	19	..	..
D	15-37	Total manufacturing	..	..	..	..	791 644	865 853	947 536	..
	15	Food products and beverages	..	..	..	..	148 713	173 365	188 161	..
	155	Beverages	..	..	..	..	34 431	39 308	42 443	..
	16 160	Tobacco products	..	..	..	..	10 289	13 475	14 663	..
	17	Textiles	..	..	..	..	67 005	68 374	72 806	..
	171	Spinning, weaving and finishing of textiles	..	..	..	..	42 749	43 851	47 871	..
	172	Other textiles	..	..	..	..	9 499	9 943	10 813	..
	173	Knitted and crocheted fabrics and articles	..	..	..	..	14 757	14 580	14 121	..
	18	Wearing apparel dressing & dyeing of fur	..	..	..	..	66 200	65 271	68 478	..
	181	Wearing apparel, except fur apparel	..	..	..	..	64 840	63 876	67 077	..
	182	Dressing and dyeing of fur; articles of fur	..	..	..	..	1 361	1 395	1 400	..
	19	Tanning, dressing leather; leather artic.; footwear	..	..	..	..	12 748	13 814	14 742	..
	191	Tanning, dressing leather; manuf. of leather articles	..	..	..	..	2 816	2 791	2 776	..
	192	Footwear	..	..	..	..	9 932	11 023	11 966	..
	20	Wood and cork products, ex. furniture	..	..	..	..	15 445	14 705	15 882	..
	201	Sawmilling and planing of wood	..	..	..	..	1 972	1 975	2 029	..
	202	Products of wood, cork, straw & plaiting material	..	..	..	..	13 472	12 730	13 852	..
	21	Paper and paper products	..	..	..	..	24 874	27 001	31 116	..
	22	Publishing, printing & reprod. of recorded media	..	..	..	..	31 940	37 600	40 117	..
	221	Publishing	..	..	..	..	22 518	26 301	28 683	..
	222	Printing and related service activities	..	..	..	..	9 422	11 299	11 434	..
	223	Reproduction of recorded media	..	..	..	..	0	0	0	..
	23	Coke, refined petroleum products & nuclear fuel	..	..	..	..	18 783	23 716	28 334	..
	24	Chemicals and chemical products	..	..	..	..	78 686	87 368	94 741	..
	241	Basic chemicals	..	..	..	..	21 990	23 997	26 932	..
	242	Other chemical products	..	..	..	..	54 009	60 058	64 344	..
	243	Man-made fibres	..	..	..	..	2 687	3 313	3 465	..
	25	Rubber and plastic products	..	..	..	..	25 303	28 820	32 806	..
	251	Rubber products	..	..	..	..	4 185	4 805	5 492	..
	252	Plastic products	..	..	..	..	21 118	24 015	27 314	..
	26	Other non-metallic mineral products	..	..	..	..	62 410	66 685	72 548	..
	261	Glass and glass products	..	..	..	..	2 859	2 973	3 089	..
	269	Non-metallic mineral products, nec	..	..	..	..	59 551	63 712	69 460	..
	27	Basic metals	..	..	..	..	47 385	48 413	56 256	..
	271	Basic iron and steel	..	..	..	..	24 035	24 618	27 433	..
	272	Basic precious and non-ferrous metals	..	..	..	..	23 068	23 287	28 005	..
	273	Casting of metals	..	..	..	..	281	508	817	..
	28	Fabricated metal products, ex. machin. & equip.	..	..	..	..	29 950	32 075	35 438	..
	281	Structural metal prod., tanks, reservoirs, generators	..	..	..	..	11 190	10 516	12 078	..
	289	Other fabricated metal products & service activities	..	..	..	..	18 760	21 559	23 361	..
	29	Machinery and equipment, nec	..	..	..	..	32 342	36 515	41 712	..
	291	General purpose machinery	..	..	..	..	11 244	12 406	13 733	..
	292	Special purpose machinery	..	..	..	..	14 084	16 243	19 545	..
	293	Domestic appliances, nec	..	..	..	..	7 014	7 865	8 434	..
	30	Office, accounting and computing machinery	..	..	..	..	239	186	498	..
	31	Electrical machinery and apparatus, nec	..	..	..	..	19 152	18 306	20 502	..
	311	Electric motors, generators and transformers	..	..	..	..	4 208	4 355	4 949	..
	312	Electricity distribution and control apparatus	..	..	..	..	4 276	4 763	4 926	..
	313	Insulated wire and cable	..	..	..	..	6 135	5 977	6 996	..
	314	Accumulators, primary cells and primary batteries	..	..	..	..	3 133	1 530	1 728	..
	315	Electric lamps and lighting equipment	..	..	..	..	1 113	1 265	1 474	..
	319	Other electrical equipment, nec	..	..	..	..	286	417	429	..
	32	Radio, TV, communication equip. & apparatus	..	..	..	..	9 311	10 357	11 610	..
	321	Electronic valves, tubes & other electronic compon.	..	..	..	..	787	957	969	..
	322	TV, radio transmitters & appar. for line teleph., telegr.	..	..	..	..	8 073	8 943	10 207	..
	323	TV, radio receivers and associated goods	..	..	..	..	450	457	434	..
	33	Medical, precision, optical instr.; watches, clocks	..	..	..	..	2 528	2 856	3 681	..
	331	Medical equip.; precision instruments and appliances	..	..	..	..	2 171	2 324	2 767	..
	332	Optical instruments and photographic equipment	..	..	..	..	346	519	902	..
	333	Watches and clocks	..	..	..	..	11	12	11	..
	34	Motor vehicles, trailers, and semi-trailers	..	..	..	..	7 323	7 704	8 252	..
	35	Other transport equipment	..	..	..	..	63 156	70 711	75 633	..
	351	Building and repairing of ships and boats	..	..	..	..	34 344	36 414	40 175	..
	352	Railway, tramway locomotives and rolling stock	..	..	..	..	7 554	8 634	8 815	..
	353	Aircraft and spacecraft	..	..	..	..	21 016	25 385	26 200	..
	359	Transport equipment, nec	..	..	..	..	242	278	443	..
	36	Furniture; manufacturing, nec	..	..	..	..	17 365	18 314	19 212	..
	361	Furniture	..	..	..	..	13 402	14 027	14 513	..
	369	Manufacturing, nec	..	..	..	..	3 963	4 287	4 699	..
	37	Recycling	..	..	..	..	496	222	348	..
E	40-41	Electricity, gas and water supply	..	..	..	..	111 078	128 937	..	..
	40	Electricity, gas, steam and hot water supply	..	..	..	..	86 438	99 875	..	..
	401	Production, collection and distribution of electricity	..	..	..	..	86 131	99 875	..	..
	41 410	Collection, purification, distribution of water	..	..	..	..	24 640	29 063	..	..
F	45	Construction	..	..	..	..	..	..	..	..
G	50-52	Wholesale and retail trade; repairs etc	..	..	..	..	..	..	..	..
H	55	Hotels and restaurants	..	..	..	..	..	..	..	..
I	60-64	Transport, storage and communications	..	..	..	..	..	..	..	..
J	65-67	Financial intermediation	..	..	..	..	..	..	..	..
K	70-74	Real estate, renting and business activities	..	..	..	..	..	..	..	..
L-Q	75-99	Public admin.; education; health; other services	..	..	..	..	..	..	..	..
A-Q	01-99	Grand total	..	..	..	..	..	..	..	..

Table GR.10 CHARGES SOCIALES DES EMPLOYEURS - EMPLOYERS' SOCIAL COSTS

Millions de Dr (Prix courants)

1989	1990	1991	1992	1993	1994	1995	1996			CITI révision 3	
..	..	..	..	..	..	..	..	**Agriculture, chasse et sylviculture**	**A**	**01-02**	
..	..	..	..	..	..	..	..	**Pêche**	**B**	**05**	
..	..	..	..	19	23	..	..	**Activités extractives**	**C**	**10-14**	
..	..	..	..	9	11	..		Extraction de charbon, de lignite et de tourbe		10	
..	..	..	..	2	2	..		Extraction de pétrole brut et de gaz naturel		11	
..	..	..	..	4	4	..		Extraction de minerais métalliques		13	
..	..	..	..	5	6	..		Autres activités extractives		14	
..	..	..	..	243 150	264 400	291 122	..	**Activités de fabrication**	**D**	**15-37**	
..	..	..	..	45 227	52 467	57 375	..	**Produits alimentaires et boissons**		**15**	
..	..	..	..	10 795	12 443	13 636		Boissons			155
..	..	..	..	3 683	4 663	4 772		**Produits à base de tabac**		**16**	160
..	..	..	..	20 622	21 041	22 795		**Textiles**		**17**	
..	..	..	..	13 592	13 912	15 399		Filature, tissage et achèvement des textiles			171
..	..	..	..	2 824	2 917	3 270		Autres articles textiles			172
..	..	..	..	4 206	4 212	4 126		Etoffes et articles de bonneterie			173
..	..	..	..	18 779	18 490	19 973		**Habillement; préparation, teinture des fourrures**		**18**	
..	..	..	..	18 402	18 096	19 588		Articles d'habillement autres qu'en fourrure			181
..	..	..	..	376	394	385		Préparation, teinture des fourrures; art. en fourrure			182
..	..	..	..	3 800	4 163	4 601		**Travail des cuirs; articles en cuir; chaussures**		**19**	
..	..	..	..	834	817	823		Apprêt et tannage des cuirs et articles en cuirs			191
..	..	..	..	2 966	3 346	3 778		Chaussures			192
..	..	..	..	4 455	4 380	4 812		**Bois et articles en bois et liège (sauf meubles)**		**20**	
..	..	..	..	597	630	661		Sciage et rabotage du bois			201
..	..	..	..	3 858	3 750	4 150		Articles en bois, liège, vannerie, sparterie			202
..	..	..	..	7 771	8 588	10 094		**Papier et carton; articles en papier et en carton**		**21**	
..	..	..	..	9 355	9 971	10 822		**Edition, imprimerie et reproduction**		**22**	
..	..	..	..	6 429	6 514	7 138		Edition			221
..	..	..	..	2 925	3 457	3 684		Imprimerie et activités annexes			222
..	..	..	..	0	0	0		Reproduction de supports enregistrés			223
..	..	..	..	7 550	9 093	9 880		**Cokéfaction; prod. pétroliers; comb. nucléaires**		**23**	
..	..	..	..	23 966	26 914	29 400		**Produits chimiques**		**24**	
..	..	..	..	6 659	7 493	8 621		Produits chimiques de base			241
..	..	..	..	16 431	18 411	19 731		Autres produits chimiques			242
..	..	..	..	876	1 010	1 049		Fibres synthétiques ou artificielles			243
..	..	..	..	7 575	8 278	9 539		**Articles en caoutchouc et en matières plastiques**		**25**	
..	..	..	..	1 393	1 353	1 478		Articles en caoutchouc			251
..	..	..	..	6 183	6 925	8 061		Articles en matières plastiques			252
..	..	..	..	19 372	20 637	22 821		**Autres produits minéraux non métalliques**		**26**	
..	..	..	..	856	885	1 050		Verre et articles en verre			261
..	..	..	..	18 517	19 752	21 771		Produits minéraux non métalliques, nca			269
..	..	..	..	16 421	15 461	17 908		**Produits métallurgiques de base**		**27**	
..	..	..	..	8 158	8 053	9 076		Sidérurgie et première transformation de l'acier			271
..	..	..	..	8 177	7 257	8 572		Métallurgie; métaux précieux et non ferreux			272
..	..	..	..	86	151	260		Fonderie			273
..	..	..	..	8 883	9 712	10 823		**Ouvrages en métaux, sauf machines et matériel**		**28**	
..	..	..	..	3 270	3 226	3 710		Constr. et menuiserie métal.; réservoirs; générateurs			281
..	..	..	..	5 613	6 485	7 113		Autres ouvrages en métaux			289
..	..	..	..	10 052	11 447	12 912		**Machines et matériel, nca**		**29**	
..	..	..	..	3 341	3 739	4 207		Machines d'usage général			291
..	..	..	..	4 731	5 480	6 330		Machines d'usage spécifique			292
..	..	..	..	1 980	2 229	2 376		Appareils domestiques, nca			293
..	..	..	..	64	55	140		**Mach. de bureau, comptables, matériel inform.**		**30**	
..	..	..	..	5 274	5 348	6 079		**Machines et appareils électriques, nca**		**31**	
..	..	..	..	1 289	1 348	1 552		Moteurs, génératrices et transformateurs électriques			311
..	..	..	..	1 191	1 323	1 438		Matériel électrique de distribution et de commande			312
..	..	..	..	1 727	1 718	1 998		Fils et câbles électriques isolés			313
..	..	..	..	667	464	550		Accumulateurs, piles électriques			314
..	..	..	..	321	366	423		Lampes électriques et appareils d'éclairage			315
..	..	..	..	79	128	118		Autres matériels électriques, nca			319
..	..	..	..	3 069	2 845	3 085		**Equip. et appar. de radio, TV, communication**		**32**	
..	..	..	..	219	284	283		Tubes et valves électroniques; autres composants			321
..	..	..	..	2 725	2 440	2 687		Emetteurs radio et TV; app. téléphonie, télégraphie			322
..	..	..	..	125	121	114		Récepteurs radio et TV et articles associés			323
..	..	..	..	754	892	1 117		**Instruments médicaux, de précision, d'optique**		**33**	
..	..	..	..	651	725	880		Appareils médicaux et de précision			331
..	..	..	..	100	163	234		Instruments d'optique ; matériel photographique			332
..	..	..	..	3	3	3		Horlogerie			333
..	..	..	..	2 574	2 533	2 610		**Véhicules automobiles et nemorques**		**34**	
..	..	..	..	18 725	21 953	23 740		**Autres matériels de transport**		**35**	
..	..	..	..	10 110	11 040	12 223		Construction et réparation de navires			351
..	..	..	..	2 142	2 451	2 486		Construction de matériel ferroviaire roulant			352
..	..	..	..	6 406	8 376	8 905		Construction aéronautique et spatiale			353
..	..	..	..	68	86	126		Autres équipements de transport			359
..	..	..	..	5 045	5 405	5 721		**Meubles; activités de fabrication, nca**		**36**	
..	..	..	..	3 887	4 139	4 325		Meubles			361
..	..	..	..	1 158	1 266	1 396		Activités de fabrication, nca			369
..	..	..	..	133	65	101		**Récupération**		**37**	
..	..	..	..	30 160	41 611	..		**Production et distrib. d'électricité, de gaz, d'eau**	**E**	**40-41**	
..	..	..	..	23 708	34 821	..		**Electricité, gaz, vapeur et eau chaude**		**40**	
..	..	..	..	23 581	34 021	..		Production, collecte et distribution d'électricité			401
..	..	..	..	6 452	7 590	..		**Captage, épuration et distribution d'eau**		**41**	410
..	..	..	..	..	..	..	..	**Construction**	**F**	**45**	
..	..	..	..	..	..	..	..	**Commerce de gros et de détail; réparation**	**G**	**50-52**	
..	..	..	..	..	..	..	..	**Hôtels et restaurants**	**H**	**55**	
..	..	..	..	..	..	..	..	**Transports, entreposage et communications**	**I**	**60-64**	
..	..	..	..	..	..	..	..	**Intermédiation financière**	**J**	**65-67**	
..	..	..	..	..	..	..	..	**Immobilier, locations, services aux entreprises**	**K**	**70-74**	
..	..	..	..	..	..	..	..	**Admin. publique; éducation; santé; autres**	**L-Q**	**75-99**	
..	..	..	..	..	..	..	..	**Grand total**	**A-Q**	**01-99**	

Statistiques des Structures Industrielles
OCDE, © 1998

Table GR.11 HOURS WORKED - HEURES OUVRÉES

Thousands

ISIC revision 3			1989	1990	1991	1992	1993	1994	1995	1996
A	01-02	Agriculture, hunting and forestry	..	..	..	..	..	..	..	..
B	05	Fishing	..	..	..	..	..	..	..	..
C	10-14	Mining and quarrying	..	..	..	..	1 255	1 181	..	..
	10	Mining of coal and lignite; extraction of peat	..	..	..	..	71	58	..	..
	11	Crude petroleum & natural gas; related service activ.	..	..	..	..	9	9	..	..
	13	Mining of metal ores	..	..	..	..	239	231	..	..
	14	Other mining and quarrying	..	..	..	..	936	883	..	..
D	15-37	Total manufacturing	..	..	..	..	47 149	44 986	42 471	..
	15	Food products and beverages	..	..	..	..	8 228	8 179	7 776	..
	155	Beverages	..	..	..	..	791	753	638	..
	16 160	Tobacco products	..	..	..	..	579	464	390	..
	17	Textiles	..	..	..	..	6 669	6 178	5 810	..
	171	Spinning, weaving and finishing of textiles	..	..	..	..	3 717	3 624	3 484	..
	172	Other textiles	..	..	..	..	1 076	933	980	..
	173	Knitted and crocheted fabrics and articles	..	..	..	..	1 876	1 621	1 346	..
	18	Wearing apparel dressing & dyeing of fur	..	..	..	..	8 776	8 012	7 153	..
	181	Wearing apparel, except fur apparel	..	..	..	..	8 555	7 820	6 980	..
	182	Dressing and dyeing of fur; articles of fur	..	..	..	..	221	192	173	..
	19	Tanning, dressing leather; leather artic.; footwear	..	..	..	..	1 509	1 372	1 297	..
	191	Tanning, dressing leather; manuf. of leather articles	..	..	..	..	267	217	190	..
	192	Footwear	..	..	..	..	1 242	1 155	1 106	..
	20	Wood and cork products, ex. furniture	..	..	..	..	1 078	921	884	..
	201	Sawmilling and planing of wood	..	..	..	..	171	150	153	..
	202	Products of wood, cork, straw & plaiting material	..	..	..	..	906	771	731	..
	21	Paper and paper products	..	..	..	..	1 036	1 061	1 086	..
	22	Publishing, printing & reprod. of recorded media	..	..	..	..	982	991	959	..
	221	Publishing	..	..	..	..	366	369	338	..
	222	Printing and related service activities	..	..	..	..	616	622	621	..
	223	Reproduction of recorded media	..	..	..	..	0	0	0	..
	23	Coke, refined petroleum products & nuclear fuel	..	..	..	..	133	91	54	..
	24	Chemicals and chemical products	..	..	..	..	1 917	1 944	1 843	..
	241	Basic chemicals	..	..	..	..	284	314	294	..
	242	Other chemical products	..	..	..	..	1 393	1 397	1 328	..
	243	Man-made fibres	..	..	..	..	240	232	222	..
	25	Rubber and plastic products	..	..	..	..	1 734	1 773	1 829	..
	251	Rubber products	..	..	..	..	203	203	204	..
	252	Plastic products	..	..	..	..	1 531	1 570	1 625	..
	26	Other non-metallic mineral products	..	..	..	..	2 620	2 472	2 189	..
	261	Glass and glass products	..	..	..	..	268	257	205	..
	269	Non-metallic mineral products, nec	..	..	..	..	2 352	2 215	1 984	..
	27	Basic metals	..	..	..	..	2 079	1 807	1 857	..
	271	Basic iron and steel	..	..	..	..	1 169	914	912	..
	272	Basic precious and non-ferrous metals	..	..	..	..	883	854	879	..
	273	Casting of metals	..	..	..	..	27	39	66	..
	28	Fabricated metal products, ex. machin. & equip.	..	..	..	..	2 180	2 117	2 147	..
	281	Structural metal prod., tanks, reservoirs, generators	..	..	..	..	879	773	811	..
	289	Other fabricated metal products & service activities	..	..	..	..	1 301	1 344	1 336	..
	29	Machinery and equipment, nec	..	..	..	..	1 932	1 851	1 910	..
	291	General purpose machinery	..	..	..	..	755	669	676	..
	292	Special purpose machinery	..	..	..	..	742	721	799	..
	293	Domestic appliances, nec	..	..	..	..	436	461	435	..
	30	Office, accounting and computing machinery	..	..	..	..	8	4	2	..
	31	Electrical machinery and apparatus, nec	..	..	..	..	868	827	833	..
	311	Electric motors, generators and transformers	..	..	..	..	102	86	81	..
	312	Electricity distribution and control apparatus	..	..	..	..	277	284	291	..
	313	Insulated wire and cable	..	..	..	..	289	274	275	..
	314	Accumulators, primary cells and primary batteries	..	..	..	..	67	51	52	..
	315	Electric lamps and lighting equipment	..	..	..	..	115	112	112	..
	319	Other electrical equipment, nec	..	..	..	..	17	20	22	..
	32	Radio, TV, communication equip. & apparatus	..	..	..	..	293	274	245	..
	321	Electronic valves, tubes & other electronic compon.	..	..	..	..	64	67	67	..
	322	TV, radio transmitters & appar. for line teleph., telegr.	..	..	..	..	195	183	155	..
	323	TV, radio receivers and associated goods	..	..	..	..	33	24	24	..
	33	Medical, precision, optical instr.; watches, clocks	..	..	..	..	170	199	190	..
	331	Medical equip.; precision instruments and appliances	..	..	..	..	136	152	142	..
	332	Optical instruments and photographic equipment	..	..	..	..	32	45	48	..
	333	Watches and clocks	..	..	..	..	1	1	1	..
	34	Motor vehicles, trailers, and semi-trailers	..	..	..	..	495	456	439	..
	35	Other transport equipment	..	..	..	..	1 978	2 048	1 850	..
	351	Building and repairing of ships and boats	..	..	..	..	1 961	2 009	1 809	..
	352	Railway, tramway locomotives and rolling stock	..	..	..	..	0	3	2	..
	353	Aircraft and spacecraft	..	..	..	..	9	11	13	..
	359	Transport equipment, nec	..	..	..	..	8	24	25	..
	36	Furniture; manufacturing, nec	..	..	..	..	1 850	1 931	1 710	..
	361	Furniture	..	..	..	..	1 436	1 409	1 302	..
	369	Manufacturing, nec	..	..	..	..	414	523	408	..
	37	Recycling	..	..	..	..	35	14	19	..
E	40-41	Electricity, gas and water supply	..	..	..	..	..	..	..	..
	40	Electricity, gas, steam and hot water supply	..	..	..	..	..	..	..	..
	401	Production, collection and distribution of electricity	..	..	..	..	..	..	..	..
	41 410	Collection, purification, distribution of water	..	..	..	..	..	..	..	..
F	45	Construction	..	..	..	..	..	..	..	..
G	50-52	Wholesale and retail trade; repairs etc	..	..	..	..	..	..	..	..
H	55	Hotels and restaurants	..	..	..	..	..	..	..	..
I	60-64	Transport, storage and communications	..	..	..	..	..	..	..	..
J	65-67	Financial intermediation	..	..	..	..	..	..	..	..
K	70-74	Real estate, renting and business activities	..	..	..	..	..	..	..	..
L-Q	75-99	Public admin.; education; health; other services	..	..	..	..	..	..	..	..
A-Q	01-99	Grand total	..	..	..	..	..	..	..	..

Table HU.1 **PRODUCTION - PRODUCTION**

Millions de Ft *(Prix courants)*   CITI révision 3

1989	1990	1991	1992	1993	1994	1995	1996			
..	..	..	282 712	284 240	347 228	436 226	..	**Agriculture, chasse et sylviculture**	A	01-02
..	..	..	1 702	1 584	2 186	2 812	..	**Pêche**	B	05
..	..	..	57 943	48 236	42 156	48 473	..	**Activités extractives**	C	10-14
..	..	..	40 595	22 516	15 313	15 096	..	Extraction de charbon, de lignite et de tourbe		10
..	..	..	6 260	12 322	11 088	15 330	..	Extraction de pétrole brut et de gaz naturel		11
..	..	..	3 513	3 590	2 458	3 539	..	Extraction de minerais métalliques		13
..	..	..	5 466	7 232	10 388	12 216	..	Autres activités extractives		14
..	..	..	1 665 207	1 898 976	2 401 544	3 305 368	..	**Activités de fabrication**	D	15-37
..	..	..	437 178	505 656	668 364	862 549	..	**Produits alimentaires et boissons**		15
..	..	..	52 748	72 449	87 632	115 455	..	Boissons		155
..	..	..	14 462	18 402	23 756	26 634	..	**Produits à base de tabac**	16	160
..	..	..	50 041	58 065	66 407	86 137	..	**Textiles**		17
..	..	..	25 340	29 196	30 714	36 366	..	Filature, tissage et achèvement des textiles		171
..	..	..	16 302	21 256	26 352	38 210	..	Autres articles textiles		172
..	..	..	8 399	7 613	9 341	11 561	..	Etoffes et articles de bonneterie		173
..	..	..	35 888	39 808	47 958	60 586	..	**Habillement; préparation, teinture des fourrures**		18
..	..	..	..	..	..	..	..	Articles d'habillement autres qu'en fourrure		181
..	..	..	..	..	..	..	..	Préparation, teinture des fourrures; art. en fourrure		182
..	..	..	23 876	26 960	26 345	32 179	..	**Travail des cuirs; articles en cuir; chaussures**		19
..	..	..	9 357	10 778	8 801	11 240	..	Apprêt et tannage des cuirs et articles en cuirs		191
..	..	..	14 519	16 182	17 544	20 939	..	Chaussures		192
..	..	..	30 702	34 381	42 358	60 240	..	**Bois et articles en bois et liège (sauf meubles)**		20
..	..	..	15 452	16 249	20 035	29 321	..	Sciage et rabotage du bois		201
..	..	..	15 250	18 132	22 323	30 919	..	Articles en bois, liège, vannerie, sparterie		202
..	..	..	39 125	35 974	50 159	77 805	..	**Papier et carton; articles en papier et en carton**		21
..	..	..	70 449	80 748	100 191	130 751	..	**Edition, imprimerie et reproduction**		22
..	..	..	37 932	41 265	48 444	60 188	..	Edition		221
..	..	..	30 602	36 782	48 069	65 319	..	Imprimerie et activités annexes		222
..	..	..	1 915	2 701	3 678	5 244	..	Reproduction de supports enregistrés		223
..	..	..	174 905	193 586	198 787	249 414	..	**Cokéfaction; prod. pétroliers; comb. nucléaires**		23
..	..	..	176 081	202 601	255 433	357 412	..	**Produits chimiques**		24
..	..	..	68 060	80 073	100 074	161 886	..	Produits chimiques de base		241
..	..	..	103 528	119 654	149 404	187 578	..	Autres produits chimiques		242
..	..	..	4 493	2 874	5 955	7 948	..	Fibres synthétiques ou artificielles		243
..	..	..	48 345	56 666	86 492	128 335	..	**Articles en caoutchouc et en matières plastiques**		25
..	..	..	12 864	7 957	15 885	23 432	..	Articles en caoutchouc		251
..	..	..	35 481	48 709	70 607	104 903	..	Articles en matières plastiques		252
..	..	..	60 249	71 503	91 753	125 191	..	**Autres produits minéraux non métalliques**		26
..	..	..	..	..	..	..	..	Verre et articles en verre		261
..	..	..	..	..	..	..	..	Produits minéraux non métalliques, nca		269
..	..	..	83 885	79 644	110 988	195 398	..	**Produits métallurgiques de base**		27
..	..	..	50 667	51 331	76 136	120 012	..	Sidérurgie et première transformation de l'acier		271
..	..	..	27 742	22 098	27 449	45 880	..	Métallurgie; métaux précieux et non ferreux		272
..	..	..	5 476	6 215	7 403	29 506	..	Fonderie		273
..	..	..	85 363	102 248	139 990	198 322	..	**Ouvrages en métaux, sauf machines et matériel**		28
..	..	..	16 776	21 795	31 542	47 960	..	Constr. et menuiserie métal.; réservoirs; générateurs		281
..	..	..	68 587	80 453	108 448	150 362	..	Autres ouvrages en métaux		289
..	..	..	114 234	121 865	148 644	200 848	..	**Machines et matériel, nca**		29
..	..	..	..	..	..	..	..	Machines d'usage général		291
..	..	..	..	..	..	..	..	Machines d'usage spécifique		292
..	..	..	..	..	..	..	..	Appareils domestiques, nca		293
..	..	..	6 688	12 725	10 032	12 103	..	**Mach. de bureau, comptables, matériel inform.**		30
..	..	..	52 160	66 258	92 979	139 493	..	**Machines et appareils électriques, nca**		31
..	..	..	7 044	8 846	10 163	20 095	..	Moteurs, génératrices et transformateurs électriques		311
..	..	..	3 487	4 331	4 908	9 107	..	Matériel électrique de distribution et de commande		312
..	..	..	11 859	9 736	16 958	27 930	..	Fils et câbles électriques isolés		313
..	..	..	1 593	3 309	3 305	3 667	..	Accumulateurs, piles électriques		314
..	..	..	19 032	27 786	36 652	49 379	..	Lampes électriques et appareils d'éclairage		315
..	..	..	9 145	12 250	20 993	29 315	..	Autres matériels électriques, nca		319
..	..	..	32 503	40 444	53 585	85 064	..	**Equip. et appar. de radio, TV, communication**		32
..	..	..	4 674	6 177	9 053	15 497	..	Tubes et valves électroniques; autres composants		321
..	..	..	17 726	21 373	25 151	44 061	..	Emetteurs radio et TV; app. téléphonie, télégraphie		322
..	..	..	10 103	12 894	19 381	25 506	..	Récepteurs radio et TV et articles associés		323
..	..	..	27 840	29 945	38 356	53 109	..	**Instruments médicaux, de précision, d'optique**		33
..	..	..	..	..	..	..	..	Appareils médicaux et de précision		331
..	..	..	..	..	..	..	..	Instruments d'optique ; matériel photographique		332
..	..	..	..	..	..	..	..	Horlogerie		333
..	..	..	60 175	75 010	94 623	158 296	..	**Véhicules automobiles et nemorques**		34
..	..	..	7 907	8 965	11 441	13 051	..	**Autres matériels de transport**		35
..	..	..	1 537	403	275	386	..	Construction et réparation de navires		351
..	..	..	2 741	1 828	4 228	4 153	..	Construction de matériel ferroviaire roulant		352
..	..	..	2 009	1 800	1 395	1 639	..	Construction aéronautique et spatiale		353
..	..	..	1 620	4 934	5 543	6 873	..	Autres équipements de transport		359
..	..	..	32 468	36 816	41 809	50 177	..	**Meubles; activités de fabrication, nca**		36
..	..	..	25 240	28 308	31 212	36 837	..	Meubles		361
..	..	..	7 228	8 508	10 597	13 340	..	Activités de fabrication, nca		369
..	..	..	683	706	1 094	2 274	..	**Récupération**		37
..	..	..	297 965	287 059	327 899	429 665	..	**Production et distrib. d'électricité, de gaz, d'eau**	E	40-41
..	..	..	260 102	248 060	283 602	381 051	..	**Electricité, gaz, vapeur et eau chaude**		40
..	..	..	139 512	145 238	148 353	196 888	..	Production, collecte et distribution d'électricité		401
..	..	..	37 863	38 999	44 297	48 614	..	**Captage, épuration et distribution d'eau**	41	410
..	..	..	223 789	258 128	340 418	386 113	..	**Construction**	F	45
..	..	..	470 160	565 122	691 908	888 885	..	**Commerce de gros et de détail; réparation**	G	50-52
..	..	..	50 042	57 123	69 342	83 178	..	**Hôtels et restaurants**	H	55
..	..	..	170 916	146 696	206 207	263 124	..	**Transports, entreposage et communications**	I	60-64
..	..	..	140 875	188 551	242 422	325 513	..	**Intermédiation financière**	J	65-67
..	..	..	208 986	259 957	333 846	422 244	..	**Immobilier, locations, services aux entreprises**	K	70-74
..	..	..	74 909	88 874	113 759	145 336	..	**Admin. publique; éducation; santé; autres**	L-Q	75-99
..	..	..	3 645 206	4 084 546	5 118 915	6 736 937	..	**Grand total**	A-Q	01-99

Statistiques des Structures Industrielles
OCDE, © 1998

Table HU.2 VALUE ADDED - VALEUR AJOUTÉE

Millions of Ft (Current Prices)

ISIC revision 3			1989	1990	1991	1992	1993	1994	1995	1996
A	01-02	Agriculture, hunting and forestry	..	..	..	92 329	91 412	128 765	154 293	..
B	05	Fishing	..	..	..	588	445	787	1 166	..
C	10-14	Mining and quarrying	..	..	..	29 883	20 053	18 007	22 115	..
	10	Mining of coal and lignite; extraction of peat	..	..	..	22 746	7 870	5 130	6 140	..
	11	Crude petroleum & natural gas; related service activ.	..	..	..	2 402	5 960	6 045	7 135	..
	13	Mining of metal ores	..	..	..	1 988	2 162	1 398	2 345	..
	14	Other mining and quarrying	..	..	..	1 907	2 709	4 159	5 340	..
D	15-37	Total manufacturing	..	..	..	490 418	597 674	759 956	993 200	..
	15	Food products and beverages	..	..	..	105 001	122 163	154 541	180 721	..
		155 Beverages	..	..	..	16 304	23 083	24 129	24 855	..
	16	160 Tobacco products	..	..	..	3 325	3 817	6 285	4 854	..
	17	Textiles	..	..	..	15 205	18 924	22 403	29 800	..
		171 Spinning, weaving and finishing of textiles	..	..	..	7 102	8 974	9 692	10 475	..
		172 Other textiles	..	..	..	5 805	7 268	8 946	14 667	..
		173 Knitted and crocheted fabrics and articles	..	..	..	2 298	2 682	3 765	4 658	..
	18	Wearing apparel dressing & dyeing of fur	..	..	..	18 386	21 008	26 126	32 056	..
		181 Wearing apparel, except fur apparel	..	..	..	..	..	..	..	..
		182 Dressing and dyeing of fur; articles of fur	..	..	..	..	..	..	..	..
	19	Tanning, dressing leather; leather artic.; footwear	..	..	..	8 077	9 689	12 254	15 221	..
		191 Tanning, dressing leather; manuf. of leather articles	..	..	..	1 934	2 275	3 933	4 780	..
		192 Footwear	..	..	..	6 143	7 414	8 321	10 441	..
	20	Wood and cork products, ex. furniture	..	..	..	8 064	9 854	12 436	16 406	..
		201 Sawmilling and planing of wood	..	..	..	3 602	4 034	5 248	7 422	..
		202 Products of wood, cork, straw & plaiting material	..	..	..	4 462	5 820	7 188	8 984	..
	21	Paper and paper products	..	..	..	9 243	10 199	14 520	21 473	..
	22	Publishing, printing & reprod. of recorded media	..	..	..	20 647	27 425	35 552	37 677	..
		221 Publishing	..	..	..	9 311	12 343	16 419	16 673	..
		222 Printing and related service activities	..	..	..	10 596	14 043	17 343	19 920	..
		223 Reproduction of recorded media	..	..	..	740	1 039	1 790	1 084	..
	23	Coke, refined petroleum products & nuclear fuel	..	..	..	79 694	91 636	83 141	98 110	..
	24	Chemicals and chemical products	..	..	..	46 300	61 157	87 832	127 307	..
		241 Basic chemicals	..	..	..	10 848	15 904	28 664	56 903	..
		242 Other chemical products	..	..	..	34 935	44 497	58 305	70 202	..
		243 Man-made fibres	..	..	..	517	756	863	202	..
	25	Rubber and plastic products	..	..	..	13 298	17 806	25 697	36 428	..
		251 Rubber products	..	..	..	2 972	2 745	5 143	7 349	..
		252 Plastic products	..	..	..	10 326	15 061	20 554	29 079	..
	26	Other non-metallic mineral products	..	..	..	19 922	26 682	36 177	49 769	..
		261 Glass and glass products	..	..	..	..	..	..	..	..
		269 Non-metallic mineral products, nec	..	..	..	..	..	..	..	..
	27	Basic metals	..	..	..	10 219	11 566	20 713	37 455	..
		271 Basic iron and steel	..	..	..	5 973	6 446	12 616	25 498	..
		272 Basic precious and non-ferrous metals	..	..	..	2 909	3 373	5 499	8 245	..
		273 Casting of metals	..	..	..	1 337	1 747	2 598	3 712	..
	28	Fabricated metal products, ex. machin. & equip.	..	..	..	23 092	30 064	41 974	58 574	..
		281 Structural metal prod., tanks, reservoirs, generators	..	..	..	5 331	7 341	10 744	17 031	..
		289 Other fabricated metal products & service activities	..	..	..	17 761	22 723	31 230	41 543	..
	29	Machinery and equipment, nec	..	..	..	46 288	46 522	53 731	75 032	..
		291 General purpose machinery	..	..	..	..	..	..	..	..
		292 Special purpose machinery	..	..	..	..	..	..	..	..
		293 Domestic appliances, nec	..	..	..	..	..	..	..	..
	30	Office, accounting and computing machinery	..	..	..	1 675	2 818	2 079	2 083	..
	31	Electrical machinery and apparatus, nec	..	..	..	13 367	19 253	36 574	42 247	..
		311 Electric motors, generators and transformers	..	..	..	1 610	2 305	3 146	7 199	..
		312 Electricity distribution and control apparatus	..	..	..	756	1 494	1 342	2 762	..
		313 Insulated wire and cable	..	..	..	3 326	3 890	5 071	6 591	..
		314 Accumulators, primary cells and primary batteries	..	..	..	587	1 404	1 417	1 421	..
		315 Electric lamps and lighting equipment	..	..	..	3 550	5 104	18 223	14 037	..
		319 Other electrical equipment, nec	..	..	..	3 538	5 056	7 375	10 237	..
	32	Radio, TV, communication equip. & apparatus	..	..	..	8 420	13 169	18 752	28 092	..
		321 Electronic valves, tubes & other electronic compon.	..	..	..	1 708	2 540	3 908	7 470	..
		322 TV, radio transmitters & appar. for line teleph., telegr.	..	..	..	4 858	7 712	8 914	15 113	..
		323 TV, radio receivers and associated goods	..	..	..	1 854	2 917	5 930	5 509	..
	33	Medical, precision, optical instr.; watches, clocks	..	..	..	11 509	13 135	16 673	22 031	..
		331 Medical equip.; precision instruments and appliances	..	..	..	..	..	..	..	..
		332 Optical instruments and photographic equipment	..	..	..	..	..	..	..	..
		333 Watches and clocks	..	..	..	..	..	..	..	..
	34	Motor vehicles, trailers, and semi-trailers	..	..	..	15 057	24 815	32 251	54 700	..
	35	Other transport equipment	..	..	..	2 368	2 927	5 004	5 274	..
		351 Building and repairing of ships and boats	..	..	..	218	- 290	19	83	..
		352 Railway, tramway locomotives and rolling stock	..	..	..	892	- 4	1 005	1 320	..
		353 Aircraft and spacecraft	..	..	..	432	433	394	304	..
		359 Transport equipment, nec	..	..	..	826	2 788	3 586	3 567	..
	36	Furniture; manufacturing, nec	..	..	..	11 093	12 945	15 015	17 187	..
		361 Furniture	..	..	..	8 231	9 471	10 451	11 489	..
		369 Manufacturing, nec	..	..	..	2 862	3 474	4 564	5 698	..
	37	Recycling	..	..	..	168	100	226	703	..
E	40-41	Electricity, gas and water supply	..	..	..	102 874	108 429	123 607	161 631	..
	40	Electricity, gas, steam and hot water supply	..	..	..	81 944	87 198	98 612	134 494	..
		401 Production, collection and distribution of electricity	..	..	..	59 667	66 477	69 111	93 899	..
	41	410 Collection, purification, distribution of water	..	..	..	20 930	21 231	24 995	27 137	..
F	45	Construction	..	..	..	90 649	102 837	126 224	131 206	..
G	50-52	Wholesale and retail trade; repairs etc	..	..	..	184 754	229 437	277 407	351 453	..
H	55	Hotels and restaurants	..	..	..	24 685	27 754	32 268	39 853	..
I	60-64	Transport, storage and communications	..	..	..	88 528	70 515	99 817	133 471	..
J	65-67	Financial intermediation	..	..	..	71 809	99 625	120 982	169 785	..
K	70-74	Real estate, renting and business activities	..	..	..	105 353	137 467	173 908	212 173	..
L-Q	75-99	Public admin.; education; health; other services	..	..	..	33 139	35 325	46 390	56 902	..
A-Q	01-99	Grand total	..	..	..	1 315 009	1 520 973	1 908 118	2 427 248	..

Table HU.3 INVESTISSEMENT - INVESTMENT

Millions de Ft (Prix courants)

1989	1990	1991	1992	1993	1994	1995	1996		CITI révision 3
..	..	21 117	16 200	19 686	24 476	29 711	..	**Agriculture, chasse et sylviculture**	A 01-02
..	..	73	59	85	114	290	..	**Pêche**	B 05
..	..	4 298	3 605	3 413	4 345	4 221	..	**Activités extractives**	C 10-14
..	..	2 950	1 643	917	1 372	1 461	..	Extraction de charbon, de lignite et de tourbe	10
..	..	498	1 033	1 098	1 333	1 206	..	Extraction de pétrole brut et de gaz naturel	11
..	..	37	76	65	37	44	..	Extraction de minerais métalliques	13
..	..	431	640	1 227	1 361	1 385	..	Autres activités extractives	14
..	..	100 547	132 174	124 512	155 903	213 485	..	**Activités de fabrication**	D 15-37
..	..	15 390	18 018	26 191	37 388	47 207	..	**Produits alimentaires et boissons**	15
..	..	..	4 073	7 786	13 172	13 937	..	Boissons	155
..	..	906	1 910	3 903	2 094	2 351	..	**Produits à base de tabac**	16 160
..	..	1 457	2 020	3 393	3 071	3 201	..	**Textiles**	17
..	..	..	716	1 570	1 460	1 504	..	Filature, tissage et achèvement des textiles	171
..	..	..	852	929	1 151	1 331	..	Autres articles textiles	172
..	..	..	452	894	460	366	..	Etoffes et articles de bonneterie	173
..	..	1 584	1 785	1 949	1 550	2 127	..	**Habillement; préparation, teinture des fourrures**	18
..	..	..	1 765	1 938	1 538	2 116	..	Articles d'habillement autres qu'en fourrure	181
..	..	..	20	11	12	11	..	Préparation, teinture des fourrures; art. en fourrure	182
..	..	627	689	647	647	828	..	**Travail des cuirs; articles en cuir; chaussures**	19
..	..	..	346	177	274	363	..	Apprêt et tannage des cuirs et articles en cuirs	191
..	..	..	343	470	373	465	..	Chaussures	192
..	..	1 217	1 408	1 696	1 444	3 046	..	**Bois et articles en bois et liège (sauf meubles)**	20
..	..	..	194	252	222	145	..	Sciage et rabotage du bois	201
..	..	..	1 214	1 444	1 222	2 901	..	Articles en bois, liège, vannerie, sparterie	202
..	..	3 159	5 033	2 503	3 557	3 118	..	**Papier et carton; articles en papier et en carton**	21
..	..	3 821	3 310	3 740	4 036	4 032	..	**Edition, imprimerie et reproduction**	22
..	..	..	1 297	783	720	958	..	Edition	221
..	..	..	1 776	2 840	3 195	2 918	..	Imprimerie et activités annexes	222
..	..	..	237	117	121	156	..	Reproduction de supports enregistrés	223
..	..	12 281	23 151	20 642	29 918	39 532	..	**Cokéfaction; prod. pétroliers; comb. nucléaires**	23
..	..	9 832	11 008	16 101	19 307	26 091	..	**Produits chimiques**	24
..	..	..	2 936	6 772	6 918	10 586	..	Produits chimiques de base	241
..	..	..	8 030	9 238	12 284	15 452	..	Autres produits chimiques	242
..	..	..	42	91	105	53	..	Fibres synthétiques ou artificielles	243
..	..	1 829	2 404	6 340	4 206	5 827	..	**Articles en caoutchouc et en matières plastiques**	25
..	..	..	196	399	494	1 087	..	Articles en caoutchouc	251
..	..	..	2 208	5 941	3 712	4 740	..	Articles en matières plastiques	252
..	..	2 886	4 094	4 881	6 751	10 365	..	**Autres produits minéraux non métalliques**	26
..	..	..	423	373	1 319	1 417	..	Verre et articles en verre	261
..	..	..	3 671	4 508	5 432	8 948	..	Produits minéraux non métalliques, nca	269
..	..	2 185	2 719	2 030	3 105	7 070	..	**Produits métallurgiques de base**	27
..	..	..	1 928	1 404	2 244	3 770	..	Sidérurgie et première transformation de l'acier	271
..	..	..	637	422	748	2 945	..	Métallurgie; métaux précieux et non ferreux	272
..	..	..	154	204	113	355	..	Fonderie	273
..	..	15 269	13 988	6 340	9 084	8 540	..	**Ouvrages en métaux, sauf machines et matériel**	28
..	..	..	3 539	1 622	1 725	1 838	..	Constr. et menuiserie métal.; réservoirs; générateurs	281
..	..	..	10 449	4 718	7 359	6 702	..	Autres ouvrages en métaux	289
..	..	3 755	4 620	4 841	13 517	8 477	..	**Machines et matériel, nca**	29
..	..	..	1 255	802	8 672	1 555	..	Machines d'usage général	291
..	..	..	2 556	2 596	3 002	4 897	..	Machines d'usage spécifique	292
..	..	..	809	1 443	1 843	2 025	..	Appareils domestiques, nca	293
..	..	44	48	2 696	248	2 198	..	**Mach. de bureau, comptables, matériel inform.**	30
..	..	9 277	5 905	4 381	5 693	9 161	..	**Machines et appareils électriques, nca**	31
..	..	..	1 036	789	612	801	..	Moteurs, génératrices et transformateurs électriques	311
..	..	..	115	157	135	409	..	Matériel électrique de distribution et de commande	312
..	..	..	383	890	575	1 968	..	Fils et câbles électriques isolés	313
..	..	..	109	112	108	40	..	Accumulateurs, piles électriques	314
..	..	..	3 449	1 953	3 197	4 801	..	Lampes électriques et appareils d'éclairage	315
..	..	..	813	480	1 066	1 142	..	Autres matériels électriques, nca	319
..	..	1 147	1 915	2 738	2 724	4 947	..	**Equip. et appar. de radio, TV, communication**	32
..	..	..	86	132	367	1 170	..	Tubes et valves électroniques; autres composants	321
..	..	..	834	955	1 339	3 032	..	Emetteurs radio et TV; app. téléphonie, télégraphie	322
..	..	..	995	1 651	1 018	745	..	Récepteurs radio et TV et articles associés	323
..	..	613	909	1 155	2 188	3 011	..	**Instruments médicaux, de précision, d'optique**	33
..	..	..	660	798	1 211	1 448	..	Appareils médicaux et de précision	331
..	..	..	249	357	977	1 563	..	Instruments d'optique ; matériel photographique	332
..	..	..	0	0	0	0	..	Horlogerie	333
..	..	12 036	25 894	5 661	3 643	20 658	..	**Véhicules automobiles et nemorques**	34
..	..	84	91	213	93	141	..	**Autres matériels de transport**	35
..	..	..	2	0	1	4	..	Construction et réparation de navires	351
..	..	..	25	18	12	13	..	Construction de matériel ferroviaire roulant	352
..	..	..	0	0	0	0	..	Construction aéronautique et spatiale	353
..	..	..	64	195	80	124	..	Autres équipements de transport	359
..	..	1 133	1 226	2 439	1 567	1 444	..	**Meubles; activités de fabrication, nca**	36
..	..	..	769	1 799	1 000	980	..	Meubles	361
..	..	..	457	640	567	464	..	Activités de fabrication, nca	369
..	..	15	29	32	72	113	..	**Récupération**	37
..	..	41 018	39 899	53 493	74 819	90 215	..	**Production et distrib. d'électricité, de gaz, d'eau**	E 40-41
..	..	27 314	30 735	44 765	63 252	77 928	..	**Electricité, gaz, vapeur et eau chaude**	40
..	..	..	19 776	24 724	36 303	48 647	..	Production, collecte et distribution d'électricité	401
..	..	13 704	9 164	8 728	11 567	12 287	..	Captage, épuration et distribution d'eau	41 410
..	..	8 261	10 105	11 221	17 972	24 235	..	**Construction**	F 45
..	..	24 564	29 387	36 929	43 813	47 052	..	**Commerce de gros et de détail; réparation**	G 50-52
..	..	7 519	11 732	7 340	7 192	8 185	..	**Hôtels et restaurants**	H 55
..	..	91 384	88 223	117 007	175 988	193 423	..	**Transports, entreposage et communications**	I 60-64
..	..	19 209	25 056	29 750	33 888	38 605	..	**Intermédiation financière**	J 65-67
..	..	113 696	114 600	134 597	167 141	226 908	..	**Immobilier, locations, services aux entreprises**	K 70-74
..	..	55 875	78 677	94 345	130 136	118 271	..	**Admin. publique; éducation; santé; autres**	L-Q 75-99
..	..	487 561	549 717	632 378	835 787	994 601	..	**Grand total**	A-Q 01-99

Statistiques des Structures Industrielles
OCDE, © 1998

Table HU.4 ESTABLISHMENTS - ETABLISSEMENTS

Units

ISIC revision 3				1989	1990	1991	1992	1993	1994	1995	1996
A	01-02		Agriculture, hunting and forestry	..	..	..	4 657	5 940	6 921	7 781	..
B	05		Fishing	..	..	..	57	75	86	97	..
C	10-14		Mining and quarrying	..	..	..	177	209	214	250	..
	10		Mining of coal and lignite; extraction of peat	..	..	..	30	35	31	32	..
	11		Crude petroleum & natural gas; related service activ.	..	..	..	8	10	12	17	..
	13		Mining of metal ores	..	..	..	4	6	7	8	..
	14		Other mining and quarrying	..	..	..	133	156	162	191	..
D	15-37		Total manufacturing	..	..	..	22 226	25 713	28 143	30 263	..
	15		Food products and beverages	..	..	..	2 416	3 122	3 475	3 678	..
		155	Beverages	..	..	..	462	677	769	800	..
	16	160	Tobacco products	..	..	..	13	13	14	9	..
	17		Textiles	..	..	..	910	1 135	1 280	1 405	..
		171	Spinning, weaving and finishing of textiles	..	..	..	146	164	176	176	..
		172	Other textiles	..	..	..	542	722	851	951	..
		173	Knitted and crocheted fabrics and articles	..	..	..	222	249	253	278	..
	18		Wearing apparel dressing & dyeing of fur	..	..	..	1 411	1 485	1 546	1 655	..
		181	Wearing apparel, except fur apparel	..	..	..	..	..	..	..	..
		182	Dressing and dyeing of fur; articles of fur	..	..	..	..	..	..	..	..
	19		Tanning, dressing leather; leather artic.; footwear	..	..	..	421	469	510	529	..
		191	Tanning, dressing leather; manuf. of leather articles	..	..	..	139	165	185	192	..
		192	Footwear	..	..	..	282	304	325	337	..
	20		Wood and cork products, ex. furniture	..	..	..	1 258	1 488	1 666	1 842	..
		201	Sawmilling and planing of wood	..	..	..	351	449	520	599	..
		202	Products of wood, cork, straw & plaiting material	..	..	..	907	1 039	1 146	1 243	..
	21		Paper and paper products	..	..	..	207	248	292	311	..
	22		Publishing, printing & reprod. of recorded media	..	..	..	2 579	3 219	3 687	4 186	..
		221	Publishing	..	..	..	990	1 339	1 591	1 859	..
		222	Printing and related service activities	..	..	..	1 334	1 604	1 833	2 039	..
		223	Reproduction of recorded media	..	..	..	255	276	263	288	..
	23		Coke, refined petroleum products & nuclear fuel	..	..	..	10	15	13	13	..
	24		Chemicals and chemical products	..	..	..	576	614	622	656	..
		241	Basic chemicals	..	..	..	180	190	209	228	..
		242	Other chemical products	..	..	..	386	415	405	419	..
		243	Man-made fibres	..	..	..	10	9	8	9	..
	25		Rubber and plastic products	..	..	..	1 107	1 256	1 351	1 421	..
		251	Rubber products	..	..	..	135	157	167	167	..
		252	Plastic products	..	..	..	972	1 099	1 184	1 254	..
	26		Other non-metallic mineral products	..	..	..	660	785	873	926	..
		261	Glass and glass products	..	..	..	..	..	..	..	..
		269	Non-metallic mineral products, nec	..	..	..	..	..	..	..	..
	27		Basic metals	..	..	..	237	259	261	277	..
		271	Basic iron and steel	..	..	..	78	86	81	81	..
		272	Basic precious and non-ferrous metals	..	..	..	41	42	44	49	..
		273	Casting of metals	..	..	..	118	131	136	147	..
	28		Fabricated metal products, ex. machin. & equip.	..	..	..	2 900	3 226	3 500	3 752	..
		281	Structural metal prod., tanks, reservoirs, generators	..	..	..	601	829	988	1 129	..
		289	Other fabricated metal products & service activities	..	..	..	2 299	2 397	2 512	2 623	..
	29		Machinery and equipment, nec	..	..	..	3 191	3 483	3 619	3 791	..
		291	General purpose machinery	..	..	..	..	..	..	..	..
		292	Special purpose machinery	..	..	..	..	..	..	..	..
		293	Domestic appliances, nec	..	..	..	..	..	..	..	..
	30		Office, accounting and computing machinery	..	..	..	159	187	208	218	..
	31		Electrical machinery and apparatus, nec	..	..	..	871	1 039	1 101	1 171	..
		311	Electric motors, generators and transformers	..	..	..	72	91	86	98	..
		312	Electricity distribution and control apparatus	..	..	..	80	93	88	98	..
		313	Insulated wire and cable	..	..	..	20	24	24	30	..
		314	Accumulators, primary cells and primary batteries	..	..	..	20	24	19	21	..
		315	Electric lamps and lighting equipment	..	..	..	86	102	106	119	..
		319	Other electrical equipment, nec	..	..	..	593	705	778	805	..
	32		Radio, TV, communication equip. & apparatus	..	..	..	728	771	817	882	..
		321	Electronic valves, tubes & other electronic compon.	..	..	..	214	220	224	239	..
		322	TV, radio transmitters & appar. for line teleph., telegr.	..	..	..	404	442	482	529	..
		323	TV, radio receivers and associated goods	..	..	..	110	109	111	114	..
	33		Medical, precision, optical instr.; watches, clocks	..	..	..	1 067	1 162	1 358	1 428	..
		331	Medical equip.; precision instruments and appliances	..	..	..	..	..	..	..	..
		332	Optical instruments and photographic equipment	..	..	..	..	..	..	..	..
		333	Watches and clocks	..	..	..	..	..	..	..	..
	34		Motor vehicles, trailers, and semi-trailers	..	..	..	203	232	236	250	..
	35		Other transport equipment	..	..	..	139	162	184	204	..
		351	Building and repairing of ships and boats	..	..	..	45	52	57	63	..
		352	Railway, tramway locomotives and rolling stock	..	..	..	8	6	9	10	..
		353	Aircraft and spacecraft	..	..	..	5	10	14	15	..
		359	Transport equipment, nec	..	..	..	81	94	104	116	..
	36		Furniture; manufacturing, nec	..	..	..	1 099	1 269	1 455	1 573	..
		361	Furniture	..	..	..	534	668	776	876	..
		369	Manufacturing, nec	..	..	..	565	601	679	697	..
	37		Recycling	..	..	..	64	74	75	86	..
E	40-41		Electricity, gas and water supply	..	..	..	255	339	366	399	..
	40		Electricity, gas, steam and hot water supply	..	..	..	163	200	202	210	..
		401	Production, collection and distribution of electricity	..	..	..	55	58	58	56	..
	41	410	Collection, purification, distribution of water	..	..	..	92	139	164	189	..
F	45		Construction	..	..	..	10 854	12 674	14 574	15 846	..
G	50-52		Wholesale and retail trade; repairs etc	..	..	..	39 818	48 978	58 550	64 463	..
H	55		Hotels and restaurants	..	..	..	4 984	5 943	6 826	7 531	..
I	60-64		Transport, storage and communications	..	..	..	2 180	2 776	3 591	4 018	..
J	65-67		Financial intermediation	..	..	..	2 221	2 491	1 829	3 060	..
K	70-74		Real estate, renting and business activities	..	..	..	23 320	28 378	37 170	41 779	..
L-Q	75-99		Public admin.; education; health; other services	..	..	..	6 222	8 268	12 807	14 736	..
A-Q	01-99		Grand total	..	..	..	116 971	141 784	171 077	190 223	..

Table HU.5 EMPLOI, SALARIÉS - EMPLOYMENT, EMPLOYEES

Milliers

1989	1990	1991	1992	1993	1994	1995	1996			CITI révision 3	
..	..	..	290.0	228.0	187.1	162.3	150.5	**Agriculture, chasse et sylviculture**	A	01-02	
..	..	..	1.5	1.3	1.1	1.1	1.1	**Pêche**	B	05	
..	..	..	47.0	30.9	20.0	17.0	15.4	**Activités extractives**	C	10-14	
..	..	..	35.1	19.1	9.7	8.1	7.5	Extraction de charbon, de lignite et de tourbe		10	
..	..	..	2.7	3.9	3.5	3.3	2.9	Extraction de pétrole brut et de gaz naturel		11	
..	..	..	2.8	2.2	1.8	1.4	1.4	Extraction de minerais métalliques		13	
..	..	..	4.4	3.7	3.1	2.9	2.5	Autres activités extractives		14	
..	..	..	835.1	726.7	679.3	625.4	605.1	**Activités de fabrication**	D	15-37	
..	..	..	180.2	151.6	139.0	124.7	117.4	**Produits alimentaires et boissons**		15	
..	..	..	..	..	16.1	13.7	11.2	Boissons			155
..	..	..	3.4	3.0	2.7	2.4	2.2	**Produits à base de tabac**		16	160
..	..	..	55.8	49.2	44.4	38.3	35.4	**Textiles**		17	
..	..	..	..	..	20.0	15.8	13.9	Filature, tissage et achèvement des textiles			171
..	..	..	..	..	14.7	13.7	13.5	Autres articles textiles			172
..	..	..	..	..	9.7	8.8	8.0	Etoffes et articles de bonneterie			173
..	..	..	62.1	58.5	57.4	49.6	50.3	**Habillement; préparation, teinture des fourrures**		18	
..	..	..	..	..	56.7	49.0	49.8	Articles d'habillement autres qu'en fourrure			181
..	..	..	..	..	0.7	0.6	0.5	Préparation, teinture des fourrures; art. en fourrure			182
..	..	..	33.6	30.4	23.7	21.5	21.0	**Travail des cuirs; articles en cuir; chaussures**		19	
..	..	..	..	..	5.1	4.0	3.8	Apprêt et tannage des cuirs et articles en cuirs			191
..	..	..	..	..	18.6	17.5	17.2	Chaussures			192
..	..	..	21.9	18.1	17.5	16.7	15.2	**Bois et articles en bois et liège (sauf meubles)**		20	
..	..	..	..	..	3.7	3.6	3.3	Sciage et rabotage du bois			201
..	..	..	..	..	13.8	13.1	11.9	Articles en bois, liège, vannerie, sparterie			202
..	..	..	13.5	10.7	10.3	8.5	8.0	**Papier et carton; articles en papier et en carton**		21	
..	..	..	24.4	24.4	21.7	18.6	16.2	**Edition, imprimerie et reproduction**		22	
..	..	..	..	..	7.0	6.2	5.2	Edition			221
..	..	..	..	..	14.1	11.9	10.5	Imprimerie et activités annexes			222
..	..	..	..	..	0.6	0.5	0.5	Reproduction de supports enregistrés			223
..	..	..	22.2	21.0	18.5	17.3	16.3	**Cokéfaction; prod. pétroliers; comb. nucléaires**		23	
..	..	..	52.3	49.3	46.2	43.8	42.2	**Produits chimiques**		24	
..	..	..	..	..	14.9	14.9	13.8	Produits chimiques de base			241
..	..	..	..	..	29.4	27.1	26.8	Autres produits chimiques			242
..	..	..	..	..	1.9	1.8	1.6	Fibres synthétiques ou artificielles			243
..	..	..	22.4	20.1	19.6	19.4	20.5	**Articles en caoutchouc et en matières plastiques**		25	
..	..	..	..	..	4.9	5.1	5.5	Articles en caoutchouc			251
..	..	..	..	..	14.8	14.3	15.0	Articles en matières plastiques			252
..	..	..	39.7	35.2	31.6	30.5	29.6	**Autres produits minéraux non métalliques**		26	
..	..	..	..	..	9.2	8.7	8.2	Verre et articles en verre			261
..	..	..	..	..	22.5	21.8	21.4	Produits minéraux non métalliques, nca			269
..	..	..	38.5	30.4	29.0	28.3	28.1	**Produits métallurgiques de base**		27	
..	..	..	..	..	13.5	13.2	16.7	Sidérurgie et première transformation de l'acier			271
..	..	..	..	..	6.5	6.2	8.0	Métallurgie; métaux précieux et non ferreux			272
..	..	..	..	..	9.0	8.8	3.3	Fonderie			273
..	..	..	49.8	49.0	42.2	40.4	35.6	**Ouvrages en métaux, sauf machines et matériel**		28	
..	..	..	..	..	18.5	18.8	18.0	Constr. et menuiserie métal.; réservoirs; générateurs			281
..	..	..	..	..	23.7	21.6	17.6	Autres ouvrages en métaux			289
..	..	..	86.5	65.8	56.6	52.0	50.8	**Machines et matériel, nca**		29	
..	..	..	..	..	13.6	11.6	11.1	Machines d'usage général			291
..	..	..	..	..	34.3	32.1	30.7	Machines d'usage spécifique			292
..	..	..	..	..	8.7	8.3	9.1	Appareils domestiques, nca			293
..	..	..	2.5	2.9	2.3	1.8	3.8	**Mach. de bureau, comptables, matériel inform.**		30	
..	..	..	33.4	29.6	30.3	30.4	32.4	**Machines et appareils électriques, nca**		31	
..	..	..	..	..	5.9	5.7	6.4	Moteurs, génératrices et transformateurs électriques			311
..	..	..	..	..	1.7	1.4	1.9	Matériel électrique de distribution et de commande			312
..	..	..	..	..	3.5	4.3	5.3	Fils et câbles électriques isolés			313
..	..	..	..	..	0.9	0.7	0.6	Accumulateurs, piles électriques			314
..	..	..	..	..	12.4	11.6	11.6	Lampes électriques et appareils d'éclairage			315
..	..	..	..	..	6.0	6.6	6.7	Autres matériels électriques, nca			319
..	..	..	26.1	21.5	18.7	20.2	20.7	**Equip. et appar. de radio, TV, communication**		32	
..	..	..	..	..	5.6	6.9	8.3	Tubes et valves électroniques; autres composants			321
..	..	..	..	..	9.2	9.2	8.5	Emetteurs radio et TV; app. téléphonie, télégraphie			322
..	..	..	..	..	4.0	4.2	3.9	Récepteurs radio et TV et articles associés			323
..	..	..	21.9	16.3	15.1	14.1	13.1	**Instruments médicaux, de précision, d'optique**		33	
..	..	..	..	..	13.7	12.6	11.7	Appareils médicaux et de précision			331
..	..	..	..	..	1.4	1.5	1.4	Instruments d'optique ; matériel photographique			332
..	..	..	..	..	0.0	0.0	0.0	Horlogerie			333
..	..	..	31.8	27.5	24.5	23.1	24.4	**Véhicules automobiles et nemorques**		34	
..	..	..	4.9	5.8	4.7	3.6	3.3	**Autres matériels de transport**		35	
..	..	..	..	..	0.4	0.1	0.1	Construction et réparation de navires			351
..	..	..	..	..	0.8	0.7	0.7	Construction de matériel ferroviaire roulant			352
..	..	..	..	..	..	..	..	Construction aéronautique et spatiale			353
..	..	..	..	..	3.5	2.8	2.5	Autres équipements de transport			359
..	..	..	8.1	6.2	23.1	19.8	18.0	**Meubles; activités de fabrication, nca**		36	
..	..	..	..	..	17.7	15.2	13.0	Meubles			361
..	..	..	..	..	5.4	4.6	5.0	Activités de fabrication, nca			369
..	..	..	0.0	0.1	0.1	0.3	0.5	**Récupération**		37	
..	..	..	92.8	93.5	98.8	91.2	86.5	**Production et distrib. d'électricité, de gaz, d'eau**	E	40-41	
..	..	..	59.1	63.0	70.4	65.9	62.9	**Electricité, gaz, vapeur et eau chaude**		40	
..	..	..	..	..	..	43.7	41.5	Production, collecte et distribution d'électricité			401
..	..	..	33.7	30.5	28.5	25.3	23.6	**Captage, épuration et distribution d'eau**		41	410
..	..	..	140.6	125.9	104.6	88.4	75.5	**Construction**	F	45	
..	..	..	251.5	227.9	189.0	165.1	152.6	**Commerce de gros et de détail; réparation**	G	50-52	
..	..	..	57.4	57.7	52.9	45.7	43.7	**Hôtels et restaurants**	H	55	
..	..	..	258.2	266.0	248.2	227.4	215.7	**Transports, entreposage et communications**	I	60-64	
..	..	..	53.3	61.2	63.8	61.7	58.9	**Intermédiation financière**	J	65-67	
..	..	..	91.5	90.1	79.6	70.2	70.3	**Immobilier, locations, services aux entreprises**	K	70-74	
..	..	..	800.3	906.5	894.6	809.2	776.9	**Admin. publique; éducation; santé; autres**	L-Q	75-99	
..	..	..	2 919.3	2 815.6	2 619.1	2 364.9	2 252.2	**Grand total**	A-Q	01-99	

Statistiques des Structures Industrielles
OCDE, © 1998

Table HU.6 WAGES AND SALARIES, EMPLOYEES - SALAIRES ET TRAITEMENTS, SALARIÉS

Millions of Ft (Current Prices)

ISIC revision 3			1989	1990	1991	1992	1993	1994	1995	1996
A	01-02	**Agriculture, hunting and forestry**	..	..	..	..	..	..	58 215	63 169
B	05	**Fishing**	..	..	..	..	..	..	420	477
C	10-14	**Mining and quarrying**	..	..	..	..	..	..	10 398	11 147
	10	Mining of coal and lignite; extraction of peat	..	..	..	..	..	..	4 332	4 869
	11	Crude petroleum & natural gas; related service activ.	..	..	..	..	..	..	2 818	2 671
	13	Mining of metal ores	..	..	..	..	..	..	872	1 099
	14	Other mining and quarrying	..	..	..	..	..	..	1 565	1 638
D	15-37	**Total manufacturing**	..	..	..	..	..	264 429	296 852	349 927
	15	**Food products and beverages**	..	..	..	..	..	54 974	58 703	66 574
	155	Beverages	..	..	..	..	..	7 439	8 024	8 388
	16 160	**Tobacco products**	..	..	..	..	..	1 805	2 142	2 128
	17	**Textiles**	..	..	..	..	..	12 133	12 617	14 221
	171	Spinning, weaving and finishing of textiles	..	..	..	..	..	5 912	5 461	6 013
	172	Other textiles	..	..	..	..	..	3 949	4 618	5 472
	173	Knitted and crocheted fabrics and articles	..	..	..	..	..	2 272	2 538	2 736
	18	**Wearing apparel dressing & dyeing of fur**	..	..	..	..	..	13 054	14 244	17 705
	181	Wearing apparel, except fur apparel	..	..	..	..	..	12 872	14 073	17 538
	182	Dressing and dyeing of fur; articles of fur	..	..	..	..	..	182	171	167
	19	**Tanning, dressing leather; leather artic.; footwear**	..	..	..	..	..	5 787	6 318	7 512
	191	Tanning, dressing leather; manuf. of leather articles	..	..	..	..	..	1 342	1 279	1 397
	192	Footwear	..	..	..	..	..	4 445	5 040	6 115
	20	**Wood and cork products, ex. furniture**	..	..	..	..	..	5 226	6 066	6 515
	201	Sawmilling and planing of wood	..	..	..	..	..	1 010	1 202	1 375
	202	Products of wood, cork, straw & plaiting material	..	..	..	..	..	4 216	4 865	5 140
	21	**Paper and paper products**	..	..	..	..	..	4 611	5 454	6 114
	22	**Publishing, printing & reprod. of recorded media**	..	..	..	..	..	11 057	10 724	10 802
	221	Publishing	..	..	..	..	..	4 725	4 400	4 179
	222	Printing and related service activities	..	..	..	..	..	6 010	6 021	6 279
	223	Reproduction of recorded media	..	..	..	..	..	322	303	344
	23	**Coke, refined petroleum products & nuclear fuel**	..	..	..	..	..	13 248	15 112	17 698
	24	**Chemicals and chemical products**	..	..	..	..	..	24 964	29 104	35 438
	241	Basic chemicals	..	..	..	..	..	7 512	9 420	10 923
	242	Other chemical products	..	..	..	..	..	16 772	18 993	23 563
	243	Man-made fibres	..	..	..	..	..	680	692	953
	25	**Rubber and plastic products**	..	..	..	..	..	7 670	9 349	11 875
	251	Rubber products	..	..	..	..	..	2 082	2 519	3 414
	252	Plastic products	..	..	..	..	..	5 588	6 830	8 461
	26	**Other non-metallic mineral products**	..	..	..	..	..	12 678	14 847	17 557
	261	Glass and glass products	..	..	..	..	..	3 290	3 705	4 353
	269	Non-metallic mineral products, nec	..	..	..	..	..	9 388	11 142	13 204
	27	**Basic metals**	..	..	..	..	..	13 315	15 838	19 573
	271	Basic iron and steel	..	..	..	..	..	6 434	8 006	11 748
	272	Basic precious and non-ferrous metals	..	..	..	..	..	3 024	3 491	6 078
	273	Casting of metals	..	..	..	..	..	3 857	4 341	1 747
	28	**Fabricated metal products, ex. machin. & equip.**	..	..	..	..	..	16 041	18 595	18 577
	281	Structural metal prod., tanks, reservoirs, generators	..	..	..	..	..	7 195	8 467	9 335
	289	Other fabricated metal products & service activities	..	..	..	..	..	8 846	10 128	9 242
	29	**Machinery and equipment, nec**	..	..	..	..	..	21 779	24 185	28 718
	291	General purpose machinery	..	..	..	..	..	5 328	5 622	6 520
	292	Special purpose machinery	..	..	..	..	..	13 490	15 126	17 646
	293	Domestic appliances, nec	..	..	..	..	..	2 961	3 438	4 551
	30	**Office, accounting and computing machinery**	..	..	..	..	..	821	865	2 180
	31	**Electrical machinery and apparatus, nec**	..	..	..	..	..	12 865	15 607	20 700
	311	Electric motors, generators and transformers	..	..	..	..	..	2 456	2 927	4 077
	312	Electricity distribution and control apparatus	..	..	..	..	..	851	956	1 446
	313	Insulated wire and cable	..	..	..	..	..	1 499	2 153	3 358
	314	Accumulators, primary cells and primary batteries	..	..	..	..	..	504	464	440
	315	Electric lamps and lighting equipment	..	..	..	..	..	5 349	6 136	7 610
	319	Other electrical equipment, nec	..	..	..	..	..	2 206	2 971	3 770
	32	**Radio, TV, communication equip. & apparatus**	..	..	..	..	..	6 899	8 905	11 288
	321	Electronic valves, tubes & other electronic compon.	..	..	..	..	..	1 746	2 665	4 017
	322	TV, radio transmitters & appar. for line teleph., telegr.	..	..	..	..	..	3 450	4 381	4 985
	323	TV, radio receivers and associated goods	..	..	..	..	..	1 703	1 860	2 285
	33	**Medical, precision, optical instr.; watches, clocks**	..	..	..	..	..	6 124	6 878	7 645
	331	Medical equip.; precision instruments and appliances	..	..	..	..	..	5 578	6 141	6 854
	332	Optical instruments and photographic equipment	..	..	..	..	..	546	736	791
	333	Watches and clocks	..	..	..	..	..	0	0	0
	34	**Motor vehicles, trailers, and semi-trailers**	..	..	..	..	..	10 375	12 117	16 745
	35	**Other transport equipment**	..	..	..	..	..	2 380	2 371	2 696
	351	Building and repairing of ships and boats	..	..	..	..	..	126	61	25
	352	Railway, tramway locomotives and rolling stock	..	..	..	..	..	464	427	560
	353	Aircraft and spacecraft	..	..	..	..	..	..	..	..
	359	Transport equipment, nec	..	..	..	..	..	1 790	1 883	2 111
	36	**Furniture; manufacturing, nec**	..	..	..	..	..	6 595	6 665	7 366
	361	Furniture	..	..	..	..	..	5 040	5 016	5 329
	369	Manufacturing, nec	..	..	..	..	..	1 555	1 650	2 037
	37	**Recycling**	..	..	..	..	..	28	145	298
E	40-41	**Electricity, gas and water supply**	..	..	..	..	..	..	55 598	65 000
	40	**Electricity, gas, steam and hot water supply**	..	..	..	..	..	..	43 399	51 069
	401	Production, collection and distribution of electricity	..	..	..	..	..	..	29 529	34 546
	41 410	**Collection, purification, distribution of water**	..	..	..	..	..	..	12 199	13 930
F	45	**Construction**	..	..	..	..	..	..	37 046	37 141
G	50-52	**Wholesale and retail trade; repairs etc**	..	..	..	..	..	..	77 605	85 021
H	55	**Hotels and restaurants**	..	..	..	..	..	..	17 618	19 558
I	60-64	**Transport, storage and communications**	..	..	..	..	..	..	114 965	134 355
J	65-67	**Financial intermediation**	..	..	..	..	..	..	53 202	62 959
K	70-74	**Real estate, renting and business activities**	..	..	..	..	..	..	38 267	44 714
L-Q	75-99	**Public admin.; education; health; other services**	..	..	..	..	..	..	370 819	410 028
A-Q	01-99	**Grand total**	..	..	..	..	..	..	1 131 003	1 283 495

Table IR.1 PRODUCTION - PRODUCTION

Millions de Ir £ (Prix courants)

1989	1990	1991	1992	1993	1994	1995	1996			CITI révision 3
..	..	..	..	..	..	..	..	Agriculture, chasse et sylviculture	A	01-02
..	..	..	..	..	..	..	..	Pêche	B	05
..	..	389	365	362	434	512	..	Activités extractives	C	10-14
..	..	..	..	..	..	..	..	Extraction de charbon, de lignite et de tourbe		10
..	..	..	..	..	..	..	..	Extraction de pétrole brut et de gaz naturel		11
..	..	..	..	..	..	..	..	Extraction de minerais métalliques		13
..	..	..	..	..	..	..	..	Autres activités extractives		14
..	..	20 898	22 361	24 904	27 787	33 583	..	Activités de fabrication	D	15-37
..	..	7 664	8 017	8 559	8 768	9 631	..	Produits alimentaires et boissons		15
..	..	895	950	937	955	1 128	..	Boissons		155
..	..	143	155	148	165	173	..	Produits à base de tabac		16 160
..	..	452	421	423	445	442	..	Textiles		17
..	..	240	211	223	233	229	..	Filature, tissage et achèvement des textiles		171
..	..	137	133	120	131	138	..	Autres articles textiles		172
..	..	75	77	80	81	76	..	Etoffes et articles de bonneterie		173
..	..	291	294	301	320	336	..	Habillement; préparation, teinture des fourrures		18
..	..	289	293	299	317	333	..	Articles d'habillement autres qu'en fourrure		181
..	..	2	1	2	3	3	..	Préparation, teinture des fourrures; art. en fourrure		182
..	..	65	66	65	88	83	..	Travail des cuirs; articles en cuir; chaussures		19
..	..	44	50	50	70	67	..	Apprêt et tannage des cuirs et articles en cuirs		191
..	..	21	16	15	18	16	..	Chaussures		192
..	..	230	237	241	282	322	..	Bois et articles en bois et liège (sauf meubles)		20
..	..	120	125	131	158	180	..	Sciage et rabotage du bois		201
..	..	110	112	109	124	142	..	Articles en bois, liège, vannerie, sparterie		202
..	..	335	343	347	369	467	..	Papier et carton; articles en papier et en carton		21
..	..	1 311	1 497	1 715	2 235	2 573	..	Edition, imprimerie et reproduction		22
..	..	530	598	644	678	702	..	Edition		221
..	..	..	..	..	..	..	..	Imprimerie et activités annexes		222
..	..	781	899	1 071	1 557	1 871	..	Reproduction de supports enregistrés		223
..	..	..	..	..	..	..	..	Cokéfaction; prod. pétroliers; comb. nucléaires		23
..	..	2 685	3 229	3 809	4 614	5 446	..	Produits chimiques		24
..	..	1 407	1 627	1 969	2 282	2 792	..	Produits chimiques de base		241
..	..	1 159	1 471	1 704	2 181	2 467	..	Autres produits chimiques		242
..	..	119	131	136	150	187	..	Fibres synthétiques ou artificielles		243
..	..	515	546	559	628	734	..	Articles en caoutchouc et en matières plastiques		25
..	..	133	141	134	165	186	..	Articles en caoutchouc		251
..	..	382	405	425	463	548	..	Articles en matières plastiques		252
..	..	582	556	584	653	716	..	Autres produits minéraux non métalliques		26
..	..	152	141	150	171	194	..	Verre et articles en verre		261
..	..	430	415	434	482	523	..	Produits minéraux non métalliques, nca		269
..	..	278	222	253	272	303	..	Produits métallurgiques de base		27
..	..	89	74	81	92	97	..	Sidérurgie et première transformation de l'acier		271
..	..	189	148	172	180	206	..	Métallurgie; métaux précieux et non ferreux		272
..	..	..	..	..	..	..	..	Fonderie		273
..	..	591	584	585	633	690	..	Ouvrages en métaux, sauf machines et matériel		28
..	..	252	243	242	274	304	..	Constr. et menuiserie métal.; réservoirs; générateurs		281
..	..	339	341	343	359	387	..	Autres ouvrages en métaux		289
..	..	732	756	769	923	1 072	..	Machines et matériel, nca		29
..	..	388	393	396	481	588	..	Machines d'usage général		291
..	..	150	173	173	207	246	..	Machines d'usage spécifique		292
..	..	193	190	200	235	239	..	Appareils domestiques, nca		293
..	..	2 177	2 471	3 136	3 559	5 994	..	Mach. de bureau, comptables, matériel inform.		30
..	..	543	587	611	680	1 010	..	Machines et appareils électriques, nca		31
..	..	110	124	151	186	230	..	Moteurs, génératrices et transformateurs électriques		311
..	..	124	132	139	153	209	..	Matériel électrique de distribution et de commande		312
..	..	109	122	117	134	230	..	Fils et câbles électriques isolés		313
..	..	74	76	82	94	234	..	Accumulateurs, piles électriques		314
..	..	12	14	13	12	13	..	Lampes électriques et appareils d'éclairage		315
..	..	115	118	109	101	95	..	Autres matériels électriques, nca		319
..	..	470	489	737	978	1 151	..	Equip. et appar. de radio, TV, communication		32
..	..	160	204	337	475	681	..	Tubes et valves électroniques; autres composants		321
..	..	273	240	337	436	405	..	Emetteurs radio et TV; app. téléphonie, télégraphie		322
..	..	37	45	63	68	66	..	Récepteurs radio et TV et articles associés		323
..	..	658	699	837	904	1 005	..	Instruments médicaux, de précision, d'optique		33
..	..	535	561	639	682	765	..	Appareils médicaux et de précision		331
..	..	123	138	198	222	240	..	Instruments d'optique ; matériel photographique		332
..	..	..	..	..	..	..	..	Horlogerie		333
..	..	167	178	187	232	280	..	Véhicules automobiles et nemorques		34
..	..	239	233	229	221	245	..	Autres matériels de transport		35
..	..	27	25	23	23	29	..	Construction et réparation de navires		351
..	..	210	207	205	197	213	..	Construction de matériel ferroviaire roulant		352
..	..	..	..	..	..	..	..	Construction aéronautique et spatiale		353
..	..	1	1	1	1	3	..	Autres équipements de transport		359
..	..	771	781	809	818	907	..	Meubles; activités de fabrication, nca		36
..	..	152	159	166	173	191	..	Meubles		361
..	..	619	622	643	645	717	..	Activités de fabrication, nca		369
..	..	..	..	..	..	..	..	Récupération		37
..	..	1 256	1 330	1 396	1 402	1 472	..	Production et distrib. d'électricité, de gaz, d'eau	E	40-41
..	..	1 188	1 258	1 315	1 319	1 387	..	Electricité, gaz, vapeur et eau chaude		40
..	..	945	1 018	1 051	1 042	1 090	..	Production, collecte et distribution d'électricité		401
..	..	68	72	81	83	84	..	Captage, épuration et distribution d'eau		41 410
..	..	..	..	..	..	..	..	Construction	F	45
..	..	..	..	..	..	..	..	Commerce de gros et de détail; réparation	G	50-52
..	..	..	..	..	..	..	..	Hôtels et restaurants	H	55
..	..	..	..	..	..	..	..	Transports, entreposage et communications	I	60-64
..	..	..	..	..	..	..	..	Intermédiation financière	J	65-67
..	..	..	..	..	..	..	..	Immobilier, locations, services aux entreprises	K	70-74
..	..	..	..	..	..	..	..	Admin. publique; éducation; santé; autres	L-Q	75-99
..	..	22 543	24 055	26 662	29 623	35 566	..	Grand total	A-Q	01-99

Note: ISIC 1542 includes 1543; 1544 includes part of 1549; 1551 includes 1552 and 1554; 1712 includes 1721. Part of ISIC 1711, 1729 and 1730 is not covered. ISIC 2010 includes 2021; ISIC 2102 includes part of 2109. Part of ISIC 2029, 2101 and 2109 are not covered. ISIC 2210, 2330 and part of 2413 are not covered. ISIC 2693 includes part of 2691 and 269 2695. ISIC 2720 includes 2730; 2812 includes 2813. ISIC 2891 includes part of 2892. ISIC 2923 and 2927 are not covered. ISIC 2914 includes part of 2919; 2926 includes 2929; 3312 includes 3313; 3320 includes 3330. ISIC 3691 includes part of 3699. ISIC 3699 includes 2320 and 37. ISIC 4020 includes 4030.

Statistiques des Structures Industrielles
OCDE, © 1998

Table IR.2 VALUE ADDED - VALEUR AJOUTÉE

Millions of Ir £ (Current Prices)

ISIC revision 3			1989	1990	1991	1992	1993	1994	1995	1996
A	01-02	**Agriculture, hunting and forestry**	..	..	..	..	..	..	..	..
B	05	**Fishing**	..	..	..	..	..	..	..	..
C	10-14	**Mining and quarrying**	..	..	262	246	239	314	371	..
	10	Mining of coal and lignite; extraction of peat	..	..	..	..	..	..	..	..
	11	Crude petroleum & natural gas; related service activ.	..	..	..	..	..	..	..	..
	13	Mining of metal ores	..	..	..	..	..	..	..	..
	14	Other mining and quarrying	..	..	..	..	..	..	..	..
D	15-37	**Total manufacturing**	..	..	9 664	10 485	11 722	13 325	16 237	..
	15	**Food products and beverages**	..	..	2 624	2 852	3 155	3 378	3 663	..
	155	Beverages	..	..	565	626	578	646	735	..
	16 160	**Tobacco products**	..	..	99	104	102	113	126	..
	17	**Textiles**	..	..	195	185	199	203	189	..
	171	Spinning, weaving and finishing of textiles	..	..	88	76	91	95	84	..
	172	Other textiles	..	..	68	68	64	65	63	..
	173	Knitted and crocheted fabrics and articles	..	..	39	40	43	43	42	..
	18	**Wearing apparel dressing & dyeing of fur**	..	..	136	134	148	151	159	..
	181	Wearing apparel, except fur apparel	..	..	136	134	147	150	158	..
	182	Dressing and dyeing of fur; articles of fur	..	..	1	1	1	1	2	..
	19	**Tanning, dressing leather; leather artic.; footwear**	..	..	20	18	21	26	26	..
	191	Tanning, dressing leather; manuf. of leather articles	..	..	10	12	14	17	16	..
	192	Footwear	..	..	10	7	7	9	9	..
	20	**Wood and cork products, ex. furniture**	..	..	87	96	95	108	115	..
	201	Sawmilling and planing of wood	..	..	41	46	49	63	62	..
	202	Products of wood, cork, straw & plaiting material	..	..	46	50	45	45	53	..
	21	**Paper and paper products**	..	..	144	158	170	174	222	..
	22	**Publishing, printing & reprod. of recorded media**	..	..	928	1 043	1 198	1 617	1 960	..
	221	Publishing	..	..	341	371	399	419	430	..
	222	Printing and related service activities	..	..	..	..	..	..	..	..
	223	Reproduction of recorded media	..	..	586	672	799	1 198	1 531	..
	23	**Coke, refined petroleum products & nuclear fuel**	..	..	..	..	..	..	..	..
	24	**Chemicals and chemical products**	..	..	1 741	2 190	2 652	3 253	3 857	..
	241	Basic chemicals	..	..	952	1 152	1 453	1 733	2 112	..
	242	Other chemical products	..	..	737	987	1 142	1 456	1 664	..
	243	Man-made fibres	..	..	52	51	57	64	81	..
	25	**Rubber and plastic products**	..	..	252	277	281	323	349	..
	251	Rubber products	..	..	75	80	75	93	107	..
	252	Plastic products	..	..	177	197	206	231	242	..
	26	**Other non-metallic mineral products**	..	..	325	317	351	380	402	..
	261	Glass and glass products	..	..	88	88	97	115	120	..
	269	Non-metallic mineral products, nec	..	..	237	229	253	266	282	..
	27	**Basic metals**	..	..	101	52	87	63	82	..
	271	Basic iron and steel	..	..	32	26	36	18	21	..
	272	Basic precious and non-ferrous metals	..	..	68	26	52	46	61	..
	273	Casting of metals	..	..	..	..	..	..	..	..
	28	**Fabricated metal products, ex. machin. & equip.**	..	..	258	264	269	284	307	..
	281	Structural metal prod., tanks, reservoirs, generators	..	..	106	102	103	116	119	..
	289	Other fabricated metal products & service activities	..	..	153	162	166	168	188	..
	29	**Machinery and equipment, nec**	..	..	372	387	401	457	519	..
	291	General purpose machinery	..	..	199	204	201	225	283	..
	292	Special purpose machinery	..	..	87	94	100	114	124	..
	293	Domestic appliances, nec	..	..	86	89	100	118	112	..
	30	**Office, accounting and computing machinery**	..	..	998	933	923	1 001	2 163	..
	31	**Electrical machinery and apparatus, nec**	..	..	275	304	303	355	524	..
	311	Electric motors, generators and transformers	..	..	67	77	97	121	147	..
	312	Electricity distribution and control apparatus	..	..	67	67	74	83	116	..
	313	Insulated wire and cable	..	..	34	42	37	44	103	..
	314	Accumulators, primary cells and primary batteries	..	..	40	44	34	49	104	..
	315	Electric lamps and lighting equipment	..	..	6	7	6	5	6	..
	319	Other electrical equipment, nec	..	..	61	66	55	54	48	..
	32	**Radio, TV, communication equip. & apparatus**	..	..	214	191	267	312	341	..
	321	Electronic valves, tubes & other electronic compon.	..	..	77	86	106	113	152	..
	322	TV, radio transmitters & appar. for line teleph., telegr.	..	..	120	91	136	168	167	..
	323	TV, radio receivers and associated goods	..	..	17	14	25	30	22	..
	33	**Medical, precision, optical instr.; watches, clocks**	..	..	419	461	559	572	618	..
	331	Medical equip.; precision instruments and appliances	..	..	342	366	412	430	480	..
	332	Optical instruments and photographic equipment	..	..	77	94	147	142	138	..
	333	Watches and clocks	..	..	..	..	..	..	..	..
	34	**Motor vehicles, trailers, and semi-trailers**	..	..	72	83	84	96	116	..
	35	**Other transport equipment**	..	..	112	130	125	115	133	..
	351	Building and repairing of ships and boats	..	..	12	11	10	10	16	..
	352	Railway, tramway locomotives and rolling stock	..	..	99	118	114	104	116	..
	353	Aircraft and spacecraft	..	..	..	..	..	..	..	..
	359	Transport equipment, nec	..	..	1			1	2	..
	36	**Furniture; manufacturing, nec**	..	..	293	306	333	344	364	..
	361	Furniture	..	..	71	74	78	81	86	..
	369	Manufacturing, nec	..	..	222	233	255	262	278	..
	37	**Recycling**	..	..	..	..	..	..	..	..
E	40-41	**Electricity, gas and water supply**	..	..	775	798	853	825	836	..
	40	**Electricity, gas, steam and hot water supply**	..	..	728	749	795	765	776	..
	401	Production, collection and distribution of electricity	..	..	608	624	663	617	622	..
	41 410	**Collection, purification, distribution of water**	..	..	47	49	59	60	60	..
F	45	**Construction**	..	..	..	..	..	..	..	..
G	50-52	**Wholesale and retail trade; repairs etc**	..	..	..	..	..	..	..	..
H	55	**Hotels and restaurants**	..	..	..	..	..	..	..	..
I	60-64	**Transport, storage and communications**	..	..	..	..	..	..	..	..
J	65-67	**Financial intermediation**	..	..	..	..	..	..	..	..
K	70-74	**Real estate, renting and business activities**	..	..	..	..	..	..	..	..
L-Q	75-99	**Public admin.; education; health; other services**	..	..	..	..	..	..	..	..
A-Q	01-99	**Grand total**	..	..	10 700	11 529	12 814	14 464	17 444	..

Note: ISIC 1542 includes 1543; 1544 includes part of 1549; 1551 includes 1552 and 1554; 1712 includes 1721. Part of ISIC 1711, 1729 and 1730 is not covered. ISIC 2010 includes 2021; ISIC 2102 includes part of 2109. Part of ISIC 2029, 2101 and 2109 are not covered. ISIC 2210 includes 2220. ISIC 2310, 2330 and part of 2413 are not covered. ISIC 2693 includes part of 2691 and 2692. 2695. ISIC 2720 includes 2730; 2812 includes 2813. ISIC 2891 includes part of 2892. ISIC 2923 and 2927 are not covered. ISIC 2914 includes part of 2919; 2926 includes 2929; 3312 includes 3313; 3320 includes 3330. ISIC 3691 includes part of 3699. ISIC 3699 includes 2320 and 37. ISIC 4020 includes 4030.

Industrial Structure Statistics
OECD, © 1998

Table IR.3 INVESTISSEMENT - INVESTMENT

Millions de Ir £ (Prix courants)

1989	1990	1991	1992	1993	1994	1995	1996			CITI révision 3
..	..	..	..	..	..	..	..	**Agriculture, chasse et sylviculture**	A	01-02
..	..	..	..	..	..	..	..	**Pêche**	B	05
..	..	41	44	29	15	39	..	**Activités extractives**	C	10-14
..	..	..	..	..	..	..	..	Extraction de charbon, de lignite et de tourbe		10
..	..	..	..	..	..	..	..	Extraction de pétrole brut et de gaz naturel		11
..	..	..	..	..	..	..	..	Extraction de minerais métalliques		13
..	..	..	..	..	..	..	..	Autres activités extractives		14
..	..	1 024	1 109	1 163	1 084	1 283	..	**Activités de fabrication**	D	15-37
..	..	244	223	247	283	229	..	**Produits alimentaires et boissons**		15
..	..	70	52	59	57	37	..	Boissons		155
..	..	2	5	1	- 1	5	..	**Produits à base de tabac**	16	160
..	..	9	10	19	12	25	..	**Textiles**	17	
..	..	3	3	11	5	12	..	Filature, tissage et achèvement des textiles		171
..	..	4	3	4	3	8	..	Autres articles textiles		172
..	..	3	4	4	4	5	..	Etoffes et articles de bonneterie		173
..	..	13	11	20	11	14	..	**Habillement; préparation, teinture des fourrures**	18	
..	..	13	11	20	11	14	..	Articles d'habillement autres qu'en fourrure		181
..	..	0	0	0	0	0	..	Préparation, teinture des fourrures; art. en fourrure		182
..	..	1	0	0	4	2	..	**Travail des cuirs; articles en cuir; chaussures**	19	
..	..	1	0	0	4	2	..	Apprêt et tannage des cuirs et articles en cuirs		191
..	..	0	0	0	0	0	..	Chaussures		192
..	..	10	12	17	26	12	..	**Bois et articles en bois et liège (sauf meubles)**	20	
..	..	7	7	12	23	6	..	Sciage et rabotage du bois		201
..	..	4	5	5	3	6	..	Articles en bois, liège, vannerie, sparterie		202
..	..	16	14	12	17	18	..	**Papier et carton; articles en papier et en carton**	21	
..	..	45	47	58	42	75	..	**Edition, imprimerie et reproduction**	22	
..	..	30	32	32	20	26	..	Edition		221
..	..	..	..	..	..	..	..	Imprimerie et activités annexes		222
..	..	15	15	25	22	48	..	Reproduction de supports enregistrés		223
..	..	..	..	..	..	..	..	**Cokéfaction; prod. pétroliers; comb. nucléaires**	23	
..	..	233	376	295	259	272	..	**Produits chimiques**	24	
..	..	53	101	121	118	100	..	Produits chimiques de base		241
..	..	178	251	164	137	150	..	Autres produits chimiques		242
..	..	3	23	9	4	22	..	Fibres synthétiques ou artificielles		243
..	..	56	25	27	37	49	..	**Articles en caoutchouc et en matières plastiques**	25	
..	..	33	7	8	7	16	..	Articles en caoutchouc		251
..	..	23	18	19	30	33	..	Articles en matières plastiques		252
..	..	31	16	24	26	42	..	**Autres produits minéraux non métalliques**	26	
..	..	10	6	9	10	17	..	Verre et articles en verre		261
..	..	21	10	15	16	25	..	Produits minéraux non métalliques, nca		269
..	..	13	12	9	9	11	..	**Produits métallurgiques de base**	27	
..	..	2	5	5	1	2	..	Sidérurgie et première transformation de l'acier		271
..	..	10	8	5	8	10	..	Métallurgie; métaux précieux et non ferreux		272
..	..	..	..	..	..	..	..	Fonderie		273
..	..	25	13	13	25	28	..	**Ouvrages en métaux, sauf machines et matériel**	28	
..	..	8	6	5	9	9	..	Constr. et menuiserie métal.; réservoirs; générateurs		281
..	..	17	7	8	15	18	..	Autres ouvrages en métaux		289
..	..	32	28	26	30	41	..	**Machines et matériel, nca**	29	
..	..	11	9	11	12	16	..	Machines d'usage général		291
..	..	9	5	7	10	11	..	Machines d'usage spécifique		292
..	..	12	14	8	9	14	..	Appareils domestiques, nca		293
..	..	79	147	254	117	144	..	**Mach. de bureau, comptables, matériel inform.**	30	
..	..	31	28	24	43	125	..	**Machines et appareils électriques, nca**	31	
..	..	11	15	13	27	62	..	Moteurs, génératrices et transformateurs électriques		311
..	..	8	4	6	9	14	..	Matériel électrique de distribution et de commande		312
..	..	2	3	4	2	30	..	Fils et câbles électriques isolés		313
..	..	7	3	- 2	4	15	..	Accumulateurs, piles électriques		314
..	..	0	0	0	0	0	..	Lampes électriques et appareils d'éclairage		315
..	..	3	2	3	1	4	..	Autres matériels électriques, nca		319
..	..	17	32	24	57	67	..	**Equip. et appar. de radio, TV, communication**	32	
..	..	7	7	9	35	46	..	Tubes et valves électroniques; autres composants		321
..	..	8	19	12	21	18	..	Emetteurs radio et TV; app. téléphonie, télégraphie		322
..	..	2	6	2	1	3	..	Récepteurs radio et TV et articles associés		323
..	..	47	41	45	43	61	..	**Instruments médicaux, de précision, d'optique**	33	
..	..	26	27	38	30	55	..	Appareils médicaux et de précision		331
..	..	20	14	7	12	6	..	Instruments d'optique ; matériel photographique		332
..	..	..	..	..	..	..	..	Horlogerie		333
..	..	6	6	6	10	14	..	**Véhicules automobiles et nemorques**	34	
..	..	79	33	11	0	10	..	**Autres matériels de transport**	35	
..	..	4	0	0	1	1	..	Construction et réparation de navires		351
..	..	76	32	10	- 1	6	..	Construction de matériel ferroviaire roulant		352
..	..	..	..	..	..	..	..	Construction aéronautique et spatiale		353
..	..	0	0	0	0	4	..	Autres équipements de transport		359
..	..	34	31	31	32	39	..	**Meubles; activités de fabrication, nca**	36	
..	..	8	9	7	9	8	..	Meubles		361
..	..	26	22	24	24	31	..	Activités de fabrication, nca		369
..	..	..	..	..	..	..	..	**Récupération**	37	
..	..	153	252	346	199	161	..	**Production et distrib. d'électricité, de gaz, d'eau**	E	40-41
..	..	138	236	329	186	154	..	**Electricité, gaz, vapeur et eau chaude**		40
..	..	99	126	139	136	108	..	Production, collecte et distribution d'électricité		401
..	..	15	16	18	13	8	..	**Captage, épuration et distribution d'eau**	41	410
..	..	..	..	..	..	..	..	**Construction**	F	45
..	..	..	..	..	..	..	..	**Commerce de gros et de détail; réparation**	G	50-52
..	..	..	..	..	..	..	..	**Hôtels et restaurants**	H	55
..	..	..	..	..	..	..	..	**Transports, entreposage et communications**	I	60-64
..	..	..	..	..	..	..	..	**Intermédiation financière**	J	65-67
..	..	..	..	..	..	..	..	**Immobilier, locations, services aux entreprises**	K	70-74
..	..	..	..	..	..	..	..	**Admin. publique; éducation; santé; autres**	L-Q	75-99
..	..	1 218	1 406	1 537	1 298	1 483	..	**Grand total**	A-Q	01-99

Note: ISIC 1542 includes 1543; 1544 includes part of 1549; 1551 includes 1552 and 1554; 1712 includes 1721. Part of ISIC 1711, 1729 and 1730 is not covered. ISIC 2010 includes 2021
ISIC 2102 includes part of 2109. Part of ISIC 2029, 2101 and 2109 are not covered. ISIC 2210, 2330 and part of 2413 are not covered. ISIC 2693 includes part of 2691 and 269
2695. ISIC 2720 includes 2730; 2812 includes 2813. ISIC 2891 includes part of 2892. ISIC 2923 and 2927 are not covered. ISIC 2914 includes part of 2919; 2926 includes 2929; 3312
includes 3313; 3320 includes 3330. ISIC 3691 includes part of 3699. ISIC 3699 includes 2320 and 37. ISIC 4020 includes 4030.

Statistiques des Structures Industrielles
OCDE, © 1998

IRELAND

Table IR.4 INVESTMENT IN MACHINERY AND EQUIPMENT - DÉPENSES EN MACHINES ET ÉQUIPEMENT

Millions of Ir £ (Current Prices)

ISIC revision 3			1989	1990	1991	1992	1993	1994	1995	1996
A	01-02	Agriculture, hunting and forestry	..	..	..	..	..	..	..	..
B	05	Fishing	..	..	..	..	..	..	..	..
C	10-14	Mining and quarrying	..	..	16	15	14	11	23	..
	10	Mining of coal and lignite; extraction of peat	..	..	..	..	..	..	..	..
	11	Crude petroleum & natural gas; related service activ.	..	..	..	..	..	..	..	..
	13	Mining of metal ores	..	..	..	..	..	..	..	..
	14	Other mining and quarrying	..	..	..	..	..	..	..	..
D	15-37	Total manufacturing	..	..	708	698	884	793	943	..
	15	Food products and beverages	..	..	173	161	166	195	157	..
	155	Beverages	..	..	43	44	39	43	25	..
16	160	Tobacco products	..	..	1	3	1	- 1	5	..
17		Textiles	..	..	7	8	16	9	21	..
	171	Spinning, weaving and finishing of textiles	..	..	1	2	9	4	10	..
	172	Other textiles	..	..	3	2	4	2	7	..
	173	Knitted and crocheted fabrics and articles	..	..	2	3	2	3	4	..
18		Wearing apparel dressing & dyeing of fur	..	..	7	8	10	8	8	..
	181	Wearing apparel, except fur apparel	..	..	7	8	10	7	8	..
	182	Dressing and dyeing of fur; articles of fur	..	..	0	0	0	0	0	..
19		Tanning, dressing leather; leather artic.; footwear	..	..	1	0	0	3	1	..
	191	Tanning, dressing leather; manuf. of leather articles	..	..	0	0	0	3	1	..
	192	Footwear	..	..	0	0	0	0	0	..
20		Wood and cork products, ex. furniture	..	..	6	10	14	24	9	..
	201	Sawmilling and planing of wood	..	..	4	6	10	22	4	..
	202	Products of wood, cork, straw & plaiting material	..	..	2	3	4	3	5	..
21		Paper and paper products	..	..	12	12	11	13	15	..
22		Publishing, printing & reprod. of recorded media	..	..	30	32	40	31	51	..
	221	Publishing	..	..	25	28	28	16	23	..
	222	Printing and related service activities	..	..	..	..	..	..	..	..
	223	Reproduction of recorded media	..	..	5	5	12	15	29	..
23		Coke, refined petroleum products & nuclear fuel	..	..	..	..	..	..	..	..
24		Chemicals and chemical products	..	..	167	222	196	195	185	..
	241	Basic chemicals	..	..	43	50	94	97	76	..
	242	Other chemical products	..	..	121	152	96	94	95	..
	243	Man-made fibres	..	..	3	20	7	4	14	..
25		Rubber and plastic products	..	..	46	20	22	28	39	..
	251	Rubber products	..	..	28	6	7	5	13	..
	252	Plastic products	..	..	18	14	16	23	25	..
26		Other non-metallic mineral products	..	..	27	12	18	21	34	..
	261	Glass and glass products	..	..	9	5	7	9	14	..
	269	Non-metallic mineral products, nec	..	..	18	7	11	12	21	..
27		Basic metals	..	..	11	12	9	8	11	..
	271	Basic iron and steel	..	..	1	4	5	0	2	..
	272	Basic precious and non-ferrous metals	..	..	9	7	5	8	9	..
	273	Casting of metals	..	..	..	..	..	..	..	..
28		Fabricated metal products, ex. machin. & equip.	..	..	22	9	10	17	22	..
	281	Structural metal prod., tanks, reservoirs, generators	..	..	6	4	4	5	7	..
	289	Other fabricated metal products & service activities	..	..	15	5	7	12	15	..
29		Machinery and equipment, nec	..	..	22	22	21	22	33	..
	291	General purpose machinery	..	..	6	7	8	7	13	..
	292	Special purpose machinery	..	..	5	3	6	8	9	..
	293	Domestic appliances, nec	..	..	11	13	7	7	11	..
30		Office, accounting and computing machinery	..	..	59	56	245	87	99	..
31		Electrical machinery and apparatus, nec	..	..	29	26	21	23	93	..
	311	Electric motors, generators and transformers	..	..	11	15	12	9	50	..
	312	Electricity distribution and control apparatus	..	..	7	4	5	8	11	..
	313	Insulated wire and cable	..	..	2	3	4	2	14	..
	314	Accumulators, primary cells and primary batteries	..	..	6	2	- 2	3	14	..
	315	Electric lamps and lighting equipment	..	..	0	0	0	0	0	..
	319	Other electrical equipment, nec	..	..	3	2	2	1	3	..
32		Radio, TV, communication equip. & apparatus	..	..	11	17	22	44	61	..
	321	Electronic valves, tubes & other electronic compon.	..	..	5	5	9	31	42	..
	322	TV, radio transmitters & appar. for line teleph., telegr.	..	..	5	8	11	13	16	..
	323	TV, radio receivers and associated goods	..	..	2	4	2	1	3	..
33		Medical, precision, optical instr.; watches, clocks	..	..	33	27	30	31	49	..
	331	Medical equip.; precision instruments and appliances	..	..	20	15	24	22	45	..
	332	Optical instruments and photographic equipment	..	..	13	12	6	9	4	..
	333	Watches and clocks	..	..	..	..	..	..	..	..
34		Motor vehicles, trailers, and semi-trailers	..	..	4	5	5	7	9	..
35		Other transport equipment	..	..	13	12	3	1	8	..
	351	Building and repairing of ships and boats	..	..	2	0	0	0	0	..
	352	Railway, tramway locomotives and rolling stock	..	..	11	12	3	0	6	..
	353	Aircraft and spacecraft	..	..	..	..	..	..	..	..
	359	Transport equipment, nec	..	..	0	0	0	0	2	..
36		Furniture; manufacturing, nec	..	..	28	22	22	26	33	..
	361	Furniture	..	..	5	7	5	6	5	..
	369	Manufacturing, nec	..	..	23	16	17	20	28	..
37		Recycling	..	..	..	..	..	..	..	..
E	40-41	Electricity, gas and water supply	..	..	110	131	152	129	108	..
	40	Electricity, gas, steam and hot water supply	..	..	104	124	150	129	105	..
	401	Production, collection and distribution of electricity	..	..	93	118	133	125	104	..
41	410	Collection, purification, distribution of water	..	..	6	7	2	1	3	..
F	45	Construction	..	..	..	..	..	..	..	..
G	50-52	Wholesale and retail trade; repairs etc	..	..	..	..	..	..	..	..
H	55	Hotels and restaurants	..	..	..	..	..	..	..	..
I	60-64	Transport, storage and communications	..	..	..	..	..	..	..	..
J	65-67	Financial intermediation	..	..	..	..	..	..	..	..
K	70-74	Real estate, renting and business activities	..	..	..	..	..	..	..	..
L-Q	75-99	Public admin.; education; health; other services	..	..	..	..	..	..	..	..
A-Q	01-99	Grand total	..	..	834	844	1 049	933	1 073	..

Note: ISIC 1542 includes 1543; 1544 includes part of 1549; 1551 includes 1552 and 1554; 1712 includes 1721. Part of ISIC 1711, 1729 and 1730 is not covered. ISIC 2010 includes 2021; 2102 includes part of 2109. Part of ISIC 2029, 2101 and 2109 are not covered. Part of ISIC 2210 includes 2220. ISIC 2310, 2330 and part of 2413 are not covered. ISIC 2693 includes part of 2691 and 2692. 2695. ISIC 2720 includes 2730; 2812 includes 2813. ISIC 2891 includes part of 2892. ISIC 2923 and 2927 are not covered. ISIC 2914 includes part of 2919; 2926 includes 2929; 3312 includes 3313; 3320 includes 3330. ISIC 3691 includes part of 3699. ISIC 3699 includes 2320 and 37. ISIC 4020 includes 4030.

Industrial Structure Statistics
OECD, © 1998

Table IR.5 **ETABLISSEMENTS - ESTABLISHMENTS**

Unités

1989	1990	1991	1992	1993	1994	1995	1996			CITI révision 3	
..	..						..	Agriculture, chasse et sylviculture	A	01-02	
..	..						..	Pêche	B	05	
..	..	102	108	99	106	117	..	Activités extractives	C	10-14	
..	..	..	..	..	..	..	..	Extraction de charbon, de lignite et de tourbe		10	
..	..	..	..	..	..	..	..	Extraction de pétrole brut et de gaz naturel		11	
..	..	..	..	..	..	..	..	Extraction de minerais métalliques		13	
..	..	..	..	..	..	..	..	Autres activités extractives		14	
..	..	4 546	4 542	4 544	4 603	4 604	..	Activités de fabrication	D	15-37	
..	..	790	796	775	799	830	..	Produits alimentaires et boissons		15	
..	..	63	65	61	63	65	..	Boissons			155
..	..	6	6	6	6	6	..	Produits à base de tabac		16	160
..	..	200	195	195	198	190	..	Textiles		17	
..	..	96	90	88	94	92	..	Filature, tissage et achèvement des textiles			171
..	..	49	49	45	44	41	..	Autres articles textiles			172
..	..	55	56	62	60	57	..	Etoffes et articles de bonneterie			173
..	..	246	232	222	209	199	..	Habillement; préparation, teinture des fourrures		18	
..	..	238	226	215	202	192	..	Articles d'habillement autres qu'en fourrure			181
..	..	8	6	7	7	7	..	Préparation, teinture des fourrures; art. en fourrure			182
..	..	42	40	41	39	33	..	Travail des cuirs; articles en cuir; chaussures		19	
..	..	24	25	26	24	19	..	Apprêt et tannage des cuirs et articles en cuirs			191
..	..	18	15	15	15	14	..	Chaussures			192
..	..	225	229	220	214	208	..	Bois et articles en bois et liège (sauf meubles)		20	
..	..	49	48	48	45	43	..	Sciage et rabotage du bois			201
..	..	176	181	172	169	165	..	Articles en bois, liège, vannerie, sparterie			202
..	..	100	106	110	104	102	..	Papier et carton; articles en papier et en carton		21	
..	..	384	396	427	440	443	..	Edition, imprimerie et reproduction		22	
..	..	362	371	392	401	400	..	Edition			221
..	..	..	..	..	..	..	..	Imprimerie et activités annexes			222
..	..	22	25	35	39	43	..	Reproduction de supports enregistrés			223
..	..	..	..	..	..	..	..	Cokéfaction; prod. pétroliers; comb. nucléaires		23	
..	..	239	232	239	245	243	..	Produits chimiques		24	
..	..	74	70	72	73	73	..	Produits chimiques de base			241
..	..	160	157	162	167	165	..	Autres produits chimiques			242
..	..	5	5	5	5	5	..	Fibres synthétiques ou artificielles			243
..	..	242	238	238	238	231	..	Articles en caoutchouc et en matières plastiques		25	
..	..	44	41	41	43	42	..	Articles en caoutchouc			251
..	..	198	197	197	195	189	..	Articles en matières plastiques			252
..	..	280	275	280	292	283	..	Autres produits minéraux non métalliques		26	
..	..	49	49	50	50	52	..	Verre et articles en verre			261
..	..	231	226	230	242	231	..	Produits minéraux non métalliques, nca			269
..	..	42	40	46	52	51	..	Produits métallurgiques de base		27	
..	..	19	18	20	22	20	..	Sidérurgie et première transformation de l'acier			271
..	..	23	22	26	30	31	..	Métallurgie; métaux précieux et non ferreux			272
..	..	..	..	..	..	..	..	Fonderie			273
..	..	518	502	496	503	485	..	Ouvrages en métaux, sauf machines et matériel		28	
..	..	260	251	240	245	237	..	Constr. et menuiserie métal.; réservoirs; générateurs			281
..	..	258	251	256	258	248	..	Autres ouvrages en métaux			289
..	..	316	325	324	335	337	..	Machines et matériel, nca		29	
..	..	157	161	161	164	163	..	Machines d'usage général			291
..	..	144	148	148	155	157	..	Machines d'usage spécifique			292
..	..	15	16	15	16	17	..	Appareils domestiques, nca			293
..	..	67	66	69	71	71	..	Mach. de bureau, comptables, matériel inform.		30	
..	..	153	150	150	148	155	..	Machines et appareils électriques, nca		31	
..	..	28	27	25	26	28	..	Moteurs, génératrices et transformateurs électriques			311
..	..	47	48	50	48	49	..	Matériel électrique de distribution et de commande			312
..	..	22	23	22	21	22	..	Fils et câbles électriques isolés			313
..	..	25	22	23	24	25	..	Accumulateurs, piles électriques			314
..	..	20	19	20	19	20	..	Lampes électriques et appareils d'éclairage			315
..	..	11	11	10	10	11	..	Autres matériels électriques, nca			319
..	..	52	54	53	53	53	..	Equip. et appar. de radio, TV, communication		32	
..	..	21	24	24	23	24	..	Tubes et valves électroniques; autres composants			321
..	..	20	17	17	18	17	..	Emetteurs radio et TV; app. téléphonie, télégraphie			322
..	..	11	13	12	12	12	..	Récepteurs radio et TV et articles associés			323
..	..	133	137	129	131	135	..	Instruments médicaux, de précision, d'optique		33	
..	..	111	115	108	109	112	..	Appareils médicaux et de précision			331
..	..	22	22	21	22	23	..	Instruments d'optique ; matériel photographique			332
..	..	..	..	..	..	..	..	Horlogerie			333
..	..	104	103	94	92	99	..	Véhicules automobiles et nemorques		34	
..	..	47	46	48	47	48	..	Autres matériels de transport		35	
..	..	29	26	27	27	26	..	Construction et réparation de navires			351
..	..	14	16	17	16	16	..	Construction de matériel ferroviaire roulant			352
..	..	..	..	..	..	..	..	Construction aéronautique et spatiale			353
..	..	4	4	4	4	6	..	Autres équipements de transport			359
..	..	360	374	382	387	402	..	Meubles; activités de fabrication, nca		36	
..	..	245	255	259	269	282	..	Meubles			361
..	..	115	119	123	118	120	..	Activités de fabrication, nca			369
..	..	..	..	..	..	..	..	Récupération		37	
..	..	96	94	95	96	96	..	Production et distrib. d'électricité, de gaz, d'eau	E	40-41	
..	..	41	41	41	41	41	..	Electricité, gaz, vapeur et eau chaude		40	
..	..	28	28	28	28	28	..	Production, collecte et distribution d'électricité			401
..	..	55	53	54	55	55	..	Captage, épuration et distribution d'eau		41	410
..	..	..	..	..	..	..	..	Construction	F	45	
..	..	..	..	..	..	..	..	Commerce de gros et de détail; réparation	G	50-52	
..	..	..	..	..	..	..	..	Hôtels et restaurants	H	55	
..	..	..	..	..	..	..	..	Transports, entreposage et communications	I	60-64	
..	..	..	..	..	..	..	..	Intermédiation financière	J	65-67	
..	..	..	..	..	..	..	..	Immobilier, locations, services aux entreprises	K	70-74	
..	..	..	..	..	..	..	..	Admin. publique; éducation; santé; autres	L-Q	75-99	
..	..	4 744	4 744	4 738	4 805	4 817	..	Grand total	A-Q	01-99	

Note: ISIC 1542 includes 1543; 1544 includes part of 1549; 1551 includes 1552 and 1554; 1712 includes 1721. Part of ISIC 1711, 1729 and 1730 is not covered. ISIC 2010 includes 2021 ISIC 2102 includes part of 2109. Part of ISIC 2029, 2101 and 2109 are not covered. ISIC 2210 includes 2220. ISIC 2310, 2330 and part of 2413 are not covered. ISIC 2693 includes part of 2691 and 269 2695. ISIC 2720 includes 2730; 2812 includes 2813. ISIC 2891 includes part of 2892. ISIC 2923 and 2927 are not covered. ISIC 2914 includes part of 2919; 2926 includes 2929; 3312 includes 3313; 3320 includes 3330. ISIC 3691 includes part of 3699. ISIC 3699 includes 2320 and 37. ISIC 4020 includes 4030.

Statistiques des Structures Industrielles
OCDE, © 1998

IRELAND

Table IR.6 EMPLOYMENT - EMPLOI

Thousands

ISIC revision 3			1989	1990	1991	1992	1993	1994	1995	1996
A	**01-02**	**Agriculture, hunting and forestry**	..	..	..	..	..	..	..	..
B	**05**	**Fishing**	..	..	..	..	..	..	..	..
C	**10-14**	**Mining and quarrying**	..	..	5.4	5.0	5.3	5.3	5.0	..
	10	Mining of coal and lignite; extraction of peat	..	..	..	..	..	..	..	..
	11	Crude petroleum & natural gas; related service activ.	..	..	..	..	..	..	..	..
	13	Mining of metal ores	..	..	..	..	..	..	..	..
	14	Other mining and quarrying	..	..	..	..	..	..	..	..
D	**15-37**	**Total manufacturing**	..	..	196.9	199.0	200.0	205.4	220.6	..
	15	**Food products and beverages**	..	..	43.4	43.5	43.4	43.3	44.6	..
	155	Beverages	..	..	5.4	5.2	5.1	5.2	4.9	..
	16 160	**Tobacco products**	..	..	1.3	1.3	1.2	1.0	1.0	..
	17	**Textiles**	..	..	9.4	8.8	8.5	8.3	8.0	..
	171	Spinning, weaving and finishing of textiles	..	..	4.2	3.8	3.6	3.7	3.5	..
	172	Other textiles	..	..	2.8	2.6	2.4	2.3	2.4	..
	173	Knitted and crocheted fabrics and articles	..	..	2.4	2.4	2.5	2.3	2.1	..
	18	**Wearing apparel dressing & dyeing of fur**	..	..	11.7	11.8	11.1	11.4	11.3	..
	181	Wearing apparel, except fur apparel	..	..	11.6	11.8	11.0	11.4	11.2	..
	182	Dressing and dyeing of fur; articles of fur	..	..	0.1	0.0	0.1	0.1	0.1	..
	19	**Tanning, dressing leather; leather artic.; footwear**	..	..	1.3	1.2	1.2	1.2	1.2	..
	191	Tanning, dressing leather; manuf. of leather articles	..	..	0.5	0.5	0.6	0.7	0.7	..
	192	Footwear	..	..	0.7	0.6	0.6	0.5	0.5	..
	20	**Wood and cork products, ex. furniture**	..	..	4.3	4.2	4.1	4.1	4.5	..
	201	Sawmilling and planing of wood	..	..	1.5	1.5	1.5	1.6	1.7	..
	202	Products of wood, cork, straw & plaiting material	..	..	2.8	2.7	2.6	2.5	2.8	..
	21	**Paper and paper products**	..	..	4.2	4.1	4.1	4.1	4.4	..
	22	**Publishing, printing & reprod. of recorded media**	..	..	12.5	13.2	14.1	14.9	15.7	..
	221	Publishing	..	..	10.8	11.2	11.5	11.8	11.7	..
	222	Printing and related service activities	..	..	..	..	..	..	..	..
	223	Reproduction of recorded media	..	..	1.7	2.0	2.6	3.1	4.0	..
	23	**Coke, refined petroleum products & nuclear fuel**	..	..	..	..	..	..	..	..
	24	**Chemicals and chemical products**	..	..	14.7	15.3	16.3	17.5	18.2	..
	241	Basic chemicals	..	..	4.3	4.4	4.5	4.7	4.9	..
	242	Other chemical products	..	..	9.0	9.6	10.5	11.4	11.9	..
	243	Man-made fibres	..	..	1.3	1.4	1.3	1.4	1.4	..
	25	**Rubber and plastic products**	..	..	8.1	8.4	8.5	8.8	9.5	..
	251	Rubber products	..	..	2.2	2.2	2.2	2.3	2.4	..
	252	Plastic products	..	..	6.0	6.2	6.3	6.6	7.1	..
	26	**Other non-metallic mineral products**	..	..	10.1	9.6	9.2	9.3	9.4	..
	261	Glass and glass products	..	..	4.1	3.8	3.3	3.4	3.6	..
	269	Non-metallic mineral products, nec	..	..	6.0	5.8	5.9	5.9	5.8	..
	27	**Basic metals**	..	..	2.5	2.4	2.4	2.3	2.2	..
	271	Basic iron and steel	..	..	1.0	1.0	1.1	1.1	0.9	..
	272	Basic precious and non-ferrous metals	..	..	1.4	1.3	1.3	1.2	1.3	..
	273	Casting of metals	..	..	..	..	..	..	..	..
	28	**Fabricated metal products, ex. machin. & equip.**	..	..	10.4	10.2	9.9	10.2	10.6	..
	281	Structural metal prod., tanks, reservoirs, generators	..	..	4.6	4.5	4.4	4.5	4.7	..
	289	Other fabricated metal products & service activities	..	..	5.8	5.7	5.5	5.6	5.9	..
	29	**Machinery and equipment, nec**	..	..	12.4	12.6	12.5	13.6	14.2	..
	291	General purpose machinery	..	..	5.7	5.8	5.7	6.2	6.8	..
	292	Special purpose machinery	..	..	3.3	3.5	3.5	3.9	3.8	..
	293	Domestic appliances, nec	..	..	3.4	3.2	3.3	3.5	3.7	..
	30	**Office, accounting and computing machinery**	..	..	8.0	7.9	8.9	10.2	14.4	..
	31	**Electrical machinery and apparatus, nec**	..	..	10.3	10.6	10.2	10.1	12.4	..
	311	Electric motors, generators and transformers	..	..	2.0	2.1	2.1	2.3	2.7	..
	312	Electricity distribution and control apparatus	..	..	2.3	2.4	2.4	2.4	3.3	..
	313	Insulated wire and cable	..	..	1.3	1.5	1.5	1.4	2.1	..
	314	Accumulators, primary cells and primary batteries	..	..	1.5	1.4	1.2	1.4	2.1	..
	315	Electric lamps and lighting equipment	..	..	0.3	0.4	0.3	0.3	0.4	..
	319	Other electrical equipment, nec	..	..	2.8	2.9	2.7	2.2	1.9	..
	32	**Radio, TV, communication equip. & apparatus**	..	..	4.9	5.2	6.1	7.2	7.2	..
	321	Electronic valves, tubes & other electronic compon.	..	..	2.5	2.7	3.3	3.7	4.1	..
	322	TV, radio transmitters & appar. for line teleph., telegr.	..	..	1.8	1.8	2.1	2.5	2.1	..
	323	TV, radio receivers and associated goods	..	..	0.6	0.6	0.7	0.9	1.0	..
	33	**Medical, precision, optical instr.; watches, clocks**	..	..	9.3	9.7	10.2	10.6	11.8	..
	331	Medical equip.; precision instruments and appliances	..	..	7.4	7.5	7.9	8.4	9.3	..
	332	Optical instruments and photographic equipment	..	..	1.9	2.1	2.3	2.2	2.5	..
	333	Watches and clocks	..	..	..	..	..	..	..	..
	34	**Motor vehicles, trailers, and semi-trailers**	..	..	3.8	3.9	3.3	3.7	4.4	..
	35	**Other transport equipment**	..	..	5.1	5.8	5.5	4.0	5.2	..
	351	Building and repairing of ships and boats	..	..	0.6	0.6	0.5	0.5	0.5	..
	352	Railway, tramway locomotives and rolling stock	..	..	4.5	5.1	5.0	3.5	4.5	..
	353	Aircraft and spacecraft	..	..	..	..	..	..	..	..
	359	Transport equipment, nec	..	..	0.0	0.0	0.0	0.0	0.1	..
	36	**Furniture; manufacturing, nec**	..	..	9.2	9.3	9.4	9.6	10.2	..
	361	Furniture	..	..	3.8	3.8	3.9	4.0	4.2	..
	369	Manufacturing, nec	..	..	5.5	5.5	5.5	5.6	6.0	..
	37	**Recycling**	..	..	..	..	..	..	..	..
E	**40-41**	**Electricity, gas and water supply**	..	..	14.3	14.4	14.3	14.0	13.3	..
	40	**Electricity, gas, steam and hot water supply**	..	..	12.1	12.2	12.0	11.8	11.2	..
	401	Production, collection and distribution of electricity	..	..	10.8	10.9	10.9	10.7	10.1	..
	41 410	**Collection, purification, distribution of water**	..	..	2.2	2.3	2.2	2.2	2.1	..
F	**45**	**Construction**	..	..	..	..	..	..	..	..
G	**50-52**	**Wholesale and retail trade; repairs etc**	..	..	..	..	..	..	..	..
H	**55**	**Hotels and restaurants**	..	..	..	..	..	..	..	..
I	**60-64**	**Transport, storage and communications**	..	..	..	..	..	..	..	..
J	**65-67**	**Financial intermediation**	..	..	..	..	..	..	..	..
K	**70-74**	**Real estate, renting and business activities**	..	..	..	..	..	..	..	..
L-Q	**75-99**	**Public admin.; education; health; other services**	..	..	..	..	..	..	..	..
A-Q	**01-99**	**Grand total**	..	..	216.6	218.4	219.6	224.7	238.9	..

Note: ISIC 1542 includes 1543; 1544 includes part of 1549; 1551 includes 1552 and 1554; 1712 includes 1721. Part of ISIC 1711, 1729 and 1730 is not covered. ISIC 2010 includes 2021; ISIC 2102 includes part of 2109. Part of ISIC 2029, 2101 and 2109 are not covered. ISIC 2210 includes 2220. ISIC 2310, 2330 and part of 2413 are not covered. ISIC 2693 includes part of 2691 and 2692. 2695. ISIC 2720 includes 2730; 2812 includes 2813. ISIC 2891 includes part of 2892. ISIC 2923 and 2927 are not covered. ISIC 2914 includes part of 2919; 2926 includes 2929; 3312 includes 3313; 3320 includes 3330. ISIC 3691 includes part of 3699. ISIC 3699 includes 2320 and 37. ISIC 4020 includes 4030.

Industrial Structure Statistics
OECD, © 1998

Table IR.7 **EMPLOI, SALARIÉS - EMPLOYMENT, EMPLOYEES**

Milliers

1989	1990	1991	1992	1993	1994	1995	1996			CITI révision 3
..	..	..	..	..	..	..	..	**Agriculture, chasse et sylviculture**	A	01-02
..	..	..	..	..	..	..	..	**Pêche**	B	05
..	..	5.4	5.0	5.3	5.3	5.0	..	**Activités extractives**	C	10-14
..	..	..	..	..	..	..	..	Extraction de charbon, de lignite et de tourbe		10
..	..	..	..	..	..	..	..	Extraction de pétrole brut et de gaz naturel		11
..	..	..	..	..	..	..	..	Extraction de minerais métalliques		13
..	..	..	..	..	..	..	..	Autres activités extractives		14
..	..	195.6	197.7	198.8	203.9	219.0	..	**Activités de fabrication**	D	15-37
..	..	43.2	43.2	43.2	43.0	44.3	..	**Produits alimentaires et boissons**		15
..	..	5.4	5.2	5.1	5.2	4.9	..	Boissons		155
..	..	1.3	1.3	1.2	1.0	1.0	..	**Produits à base de tabac**		16 160
..	..	9.3	8.8	8.4	8.2	8.0	..	**Textiles**		17
..	..	4.2	3.7	3.6	3.6	3.5	..	Filature, tissage et achèvement des textiles		171
..	..	2.8	2.6	2.4	2.3	2.3	..	Autres articles textiles		172
..	..	2.3	2.4	2.4	2.3	2.1	..	Etoffes et articles de bonneterie		173
..	..	11.6	11.7	11.0	11.3	11.2	..	**Habillement; préparation, teinture des fourrures**		18
..	..	11.5	11.7	11.0	11.3	11.1	..	Articles d'habillement autres qu'en fourrure		181
..	..	0.1	0.0	0.1	0.1	0.1	..	Préparation, teinture des fourrures; art. en fourrure		182
..	..	1.3	1.2	1.2	1.2	1.2	..	**Travail des cuirs; articles en cuir; chaussures**		19
..	..	0.5	0.5	0.5	0.7	0.7	..	Apprêt et tannage des cuirs et articles en cuirs		191
..	..	0.7	0.6	0.6	0.5	0.5	..	Chaussures		192
..	..	4.2	4.2	4.0	4.0	4.4	..	**Bois et articles en bois et liège (sauf meubles)**		20
..	..	1.5	1.5	1.5	1.6	1.7	..	Sciage et rabotage du bois		201
..	..	2.7	2.7	2.5	2.4	2.7	..	Articles en bois, liège, vannerie, sparterie		202
..	..	4.2	4.1	4.1	4.1	4.4	..	**Papier et carton; articles en papier et en carton**		21
..	..	12.4	13.1	14.0	14.7	15.6	..	**Edition, imprimerie et reproduction**		22
..	..	10.7	11.1	11.4	11.7	11.6	..	Edition		221
..	..	..	..	..	..	..	..	Imprimerie et activités annexes		222
..	..	1.7	2.0	2.6	3.0	4.0	..	Reproduction de supports enregistrés		223
..	..	..	..	..	..	..	..	**Cokéfaction; prod. pétroliers; comb. nucléaires**		23
..	..	14.6	15.3	16.2	17.4	18.1	..	**Produits chimiques**		24
..	..	4.3	4.4	4.5	4.7	4.8	..	Produits chimiques de base		241
..	..	9.0	9.5	10.4	11.4	11.8	..	Autres produits chimiques		242
..	..	1.3	1.4	1.3	1.4	1.4	..	Fibres synthétiques ou artificielles		243
..	..	8.1	8.4	8.5	8.8	9.5	..	**Articles en caoutchouc et en matières plastiques**		25
..	..	2.1	2.2	2.2	2.3	2.4	..	Articles en caoutchouc		251
..	..	5.9	6.2	6.3	6.5	7.1	..	Articles en matières plastiques		252
..	..	10.0	9.5	9.1	9.2	9.3	..	**Autres produits minéraux non métalliques**		26
..	..	4.1	3.8	3.3	3.3	3.6	..	Verre et articles en verre		261
..	..	5.9	5.7	5.9	5.8	5.7	..	Produits minéraux non métalliques, nca		269
..	..	2.5	2.3	2.4	2.3	2.2	..	**Produits métallurgiques de base**		27
..	..	1.0	1.0	1.1	1.1	0.9	..	Sidérurgie et première transformation de l'acier		271
..	..	1.4	1.3	1.3	1.2	1.2	..	Métallurgie; métaux précieux et non ferreux		272
..	..	..	..	..	..	..	..	Fonderie		273
..	..	10.2	10.0	9.7	9.9	10.4	..	**Ouvrages en métaux, sauf machines et matériel**		28
..	..	4.5	4.4	4.3	4.4	4.6	..	Constr. et menuiserie métal.; réservoirs; générateurs		281
..	..	5.7	5.6	5.4	5.6	5.8	..	Autres ouvrages en métaux		289
..	..	12.3	12.5	12.4	13.5	14.1	..	**Machines et matériel, nca**		29
..	..	5.6	5.8	5.7	6.1	6.7	..	Machines d'usage général		291
..	..	3.3	3.5	3.4	3.9	3.7	..	Machines d'usage spécifique		292
..	..	3.4	3.2	3.3	3.5	3.7	..	Appareils domestiques, nca		293
..	..	8.0	7.9	8.9	10.2	14.4	..	**Mach. de bureau, comptables, matériel inform.**		30
..	..	10.2	10.6	10.2	10.1	12.4	..	**Machines et appareils électriques, nca**		31
..	..	2.0	2.1	2.1	2.3	2.7	..	Moteurs, génératrices et transformateurs électriques		311
..	..	2.3	2.4	2.4	2.4	3.3	..	Matériel électrique de distribution et de commande		312
..	..	1.3	1.5	1.5	1.4	2.1	..	Fils et câbles électriques isolés		313
..	..	1.5	1.4	1.2	1.4	2.1	..	Accumulateurs, piles électriques		314
..	..	0.3	0.4	0.3	0.3	0.4	..	Lampes électriques et appareils d'éclairage		315
..	..	2.8	2.9	2.7	2.2	1.9	..	Autres matériels électriques, nca		319
..	..	4.9	5.2	6.1	7.2	7.2	..	**Equip. et appar. de radio, TV, communication**		32
..	..	2.5	2.7	3.3	3.7	4.1	..	Tubes et valves électroniques; autres composants		321
..	..	1.8	1.8	2.1	2.5	2.1	..	Emetteurs radio et TV; app. téléphonie, télégraphie		322
..	..	0.6	0.6	0.7	0.9	1.0	..	Récepteurs radio et TV et articles associés		323
..	..	9.3	9.6	10.2	10.6	11.8	..	**Instruments médicaux, de précision, d'optique**		33
..	..	7.4	7.5	7.9	8.4	9.3	..	Appareils médicaux et de précision		331
..	..	1.9	2.1	2.3	2.2	2.5	..	Instruments d'optique ; matériel photographique		332
..	..	..	..	..	..	..	..	Horlogerie		333
..	..	3.8	3.9	3.3	3.6	4.4	..	**Véhicules automobiles et nemorques**		34
..	..	5.1	5.7	5.5	4.0	5.1	..	**Autres matériels de transport**		35
..	..	0.6	0.6	0.5	0.5	0.5	..	Construction et réparation de navires		351
..	..	4.5	5.1	5.0	3.5	4.5	..	Construction de matériel ferroviaire roulant		352
..	..	..	..	..	..	..	..	Construction aéronautique et spatiale		353
..	..	0.0	0.0	0.0	0.0	0.1	..	Autres équipements de transport		359
..	..	9.1	9.2	9.3	9.4	10.0	..	**Meubles; activités de fabrication, nca**		36
..	..	3.7	3.7	3.8	3.9	4.1	..	Meubles		361
..	..	5.4	5.4	5.4	5.5	6.0	..	Activités de fabrication, nca		369
..	..	..	..	..	..	..	..	**Récupération**		37
..	..	14.3	14.4	14.3	14.0	13.3	..	**Production et distrib. d'électricité, de gaz, d'eau**	E	40-41
..	..	12.1	12.2	12.0	11.8	11.2	..	**Electricité, gaz, vapeur et eau chaude**		40
..	..	10.8	10.9	10.9	10.7	10.1	..	Production, collecte et distribution d'électricité		401
..	..	2.2	2.3	2.2	2.2	2.1	..	**Captage, épuration et distribution d'eau**		41 410
..	..	..	..	..	..	..	..	**Construction**	F	45
..	..	..	..	..	..	..	..	**Commerce de gros et de détail; réparation**	G	50-52
..	..	..	..	..	..	..	..	**Hôtels et restaurants**	H	55
..	..	..	..	..	..	..	..	**Transports, entreposage et communications**	I	60-64
..	..	..	..	..	..	..	..	**Intermédiation financière**	J	65-67
..	..	..	..	..	..	..	..	**Immobilier, locations, services aux entreprises**	K	70-74
..	..	..	..	..	..	..	..	**Admin. publique; éducation; santé; autres**	L-Q	75-99
..	..	215.3	217.1	218.3	223.2	237.3	..	**Grand total**	A-Q	01-99

Note: ISIC 1542 includes 1543; 1544 includes part of 1549; 1551 includes 1552 and 1554; 1712 includes 1721. Part of ISIC 1711, 1729 and 1730 is not covered. ISIC 2010 includes 2021
ISIC 2102 includes part of 2109. Part of ISIC 2029, 2101 and 2109 are not covered. ISIC 2310, 2330 and part of 2413 are not covered. ISIC 2693 includes part of 2691 and 269
2695. ISIC 2720 includes 2730; 2812 includes 2813. ISIC 2891 includes part of 2892. ISIC 2923 and 2927 are not covered. ISIC 2914 includes part of 2919; 2926 includes 2929; 3312
includes 3313; 3320 includes 3330. ISIC 3691 includes part of 3699. ISIC 3699 includes 2320 and 37. ISIC 4020 includes 4030.

Statistiques des Structures Industrielles
OCDE, © 1998

Table IR.8 **WAGES AND SALARIES, EMPLOYEES - SALAIRES ET TRAITEMENTS, SALARIÉS**

Millions of Ir £ (Current Prices)

ISIC revision 3				1989	1990	1991	1992	1993	1994	1995	1996
A	01-02		**Agriculture, hunting and forestry**	..	..	..	..	..	..	..	..
B	05		**Fishing**	..	..	..	..	..	..	..	..
C	10-14		**Mining and quarrying**	..	..	95	95	99	106	114	..
	10		Mining of coal and lignite; extraction of peat	..	..	..	..	..	..	..	..
	11		Crude petroleum & natural gas; related service activ.	..	..	..	..	..	..	..	..
	13		Mining of metal ores	..	..	..	..	..	..	..	..
	14		Other mining and quarrying	..	..	..	..	..	..	..	..
D	15-37		**Total manufacturing**	..	..	2 598	2 760	2 883	3 051	3 335	..
	15		**Food products and beverages**	..	..	585	616	639	655	694	..
		155	Beverages	..	..	109	111	116	119	123	..
	16	160	**Tobacco products**	..	..	25	26	24	23	24	..
	17		**Textiles**	..	..	98	96	95	98	99	..
		171	Spinning, weaving and finishing of textiles	..	..	45	41	42	43	43	..
		172	Other textiles	..	..	34	34	31	33	34	..
		173	Knitted and crocheted fabrics and articles	..	..	20	21	22	22	22	..
	18		**Wearing apparel dressing & dyeing of fur**	..	..	89	95	94	98	103	..
		181	Wearing apparel, except fur apparel	..	..	89	94	93	98	103	..
		182	Dressing and dyeing of fur; articles of fur	..	..	..	..	..	1	1	..
	19		**Tanning, dressing leather; leather artic.; footwear**	..	..	12	10	11	13	11	..
		191	Tanning, dressing leather; manuf. of leather articles	..	..	5	5	6	8	6	..
		192	Footwear	..	..	7	5	5	6	5	..
	20		**Wood and cork products, ex. furniture**	..	..	42	43	43	44	50	..
		201	Sawmilling and planing of wood	..	..	18	19	20	21	23	..
		202	Products of wood, cork, straw & plaiting material	..	..	25	24	24	23	27	..
	21		**Paper and paper products**	..	..	63	65	68	70	78	..
	22		**Publishing, printing & reprod. of recorded media**	..	..	199	224	250	266	284	..
		221	Publishing	..	..	173	189	201	208	210	..
		222	Printing and related service activities	..	..	..	..	..	..	..	..
		223	Reproduction of recorded media	..	..	26	35	49	58	74	..
	23		**Coke, refined petroleum products & nuclear fuel**	..	..	..	..	..	..	..	..
	24		**Chemicals and chemical products**	..	..	253	279	308	339	369	..
		241	Basic chemicals	..	..	99	105	108	115	128	..
		242	Other chemical products	..	..	135	151	177	198	215	..
		243	Man-made fibres	..	..	19	23	23	25	26	..
	25		**Rubber and plastic products**	..	..	103	112	116	126	139	..
		251	Rubber products	..	..	33	36	34	37	42	..
		252	Plastic products	..	..	70	77	82	88	97	..
	26		**Other non-metallic mineral products**	..	..	140	139	146	151	153	..
		261	Glass and glass products	..	..	58	57	61	65	63	..
		269	Non-metallic mineral products, nec	..	..	82	82	86	86	90	..
	27		**Basic metals**	..	..	42	38	43	41	38	..
		271	Basic iron and steel	..	..	17	16	20	20	16	..
		272	Basic precious and non-ferrous metals	..	..	25	22	23	21	22	..
		273	Casting of metals	..	..	..	..	..	..	..	..
	28		**Fabricated metal products, ex. machin. & equip.**	..	..	117	119	117	128	139	..
		281	Structural metal prod., tanks, reservoirs, generators	..	..	50	51	49	54	57	..
		289	Other fabricated metal products & service activities	..	..	67	69	68	74	82	..
	29		**Machinery and equipment, nec**	..	..	150	164	165	190	206	..
		291	General purpose machinery	..	..	74	81	81	93	108	..
		292	Special purpose machinery	..	..	38	44	44	53	53	..
		293	Domestic appliances, nec	..	..	38	39	40	44	46	..
	30		**Office, accounting and computing machinery**	..	..	131	136	153	175	211	..
	31		**Electrical machinery and apparatus, nec**	..	..	125	137	134	139	177	..
		311	Electric motors, generators and transformers	..	..	28	30	32	36	43	..
		312	Electricity distribution and control apparatus	..	..	26	27	30	32	44	..
		313	Insulated wire and cable	..	..	18	20	19	22	31	..
		314	Accumulators, primary cells and primary batteries	..	..	19	21	17	18	29	..
		315	Electric lamps and lighting equipment	..	..	3	3	4	3	4	..
		319	Other electrical equipment, nec	..	..	31	35	32	28	26	..
	32		**Radio, TV, communication equip. & apparatus**	..	..	66	72	84	104	112	..
		321	Electronic valves, tubes & other electronic compon.	..	..	33	35	40	50	57	..
		322	TV, radio transmitters & appar. for line teleph., telegr.	..	..	27	31	35	43	44	..
		323	TV, radio receivers and associated goods	..	..	6	7	9	11	11	..
	33		**Medical, precision, optical instr.; watches, clocks**	..	..	121	132	143	155	172	..
		331	Medical equip.; precision instruments and appliances	..	..	98	104	113	121	135	..
		332	Optical instruments and photographic equipment	..	..	23	28	31	34	37	..
		333	Watches and clocks	..	..	..	..	..	..	..	..
	34		**Motor vehicles, trailers, and semi-trailers**	..	..	45	47	38	47	60	..
	35		**Other transport equipment**	..	..	86	99	91	71	92	..
		351	Building and repairing of ships and boats	..	..	7	6	7	6	7	..
		352	Railway, tramway locomotives and rolling stock	..	..	79	92	84	64	84	..
		353	Aircraft and spacecraft	..	..	..	..	..	..	..	..
		359	Transport equipment, nec	..	..	..	..	..	..	1	..
	36		**Furniture; manufacturing, nec**	..	..	104	112	118	118	124	..
		361	Furniture	..	..	31	33	37	38	39	..
		369	Manufacturing, nec	..	..	74	78	81	80	86	..
	37		**Recycling**	..	..	..	..	..	..	..	..
E	40-41		**Electricity, gas and water supply**	..	..	252	270	274	287	288	..
	40		**Electricity, gas, steam and hot water supply**	..	..	228	244	246	259	259	..
		401	Production, collection and distribution of electricity	..	..	200	215	219	231	232	..
	41	410	**Collection, purification, distribution of water**	..	..	24	26	28	28	29	..
F	45		**Construction**	..	..	..	..	..	..	..	..
G	50-52		**Wholesale and retail trade; repairs etc**	..	..	..	..	..	..	..	..
H	55		**Hotels and restaurants**	..	..	..	..	..	..	..	..
I	60-64		**Transport, storage and communications**	..	..	..	..	..	..	..	..
J	65-67		**Financial intermediation**	..	..	..	..	..	..	..	..
K	70-74		**Real estate, renting and business activities**	..	..	..	..	..	..	..	..
L-Q	75-99		**Public admin.; education; health; other services**	..	..	..	..	..	..	..	..
A-Q	01-99		**Grand total**	..	..	2 945	3 126	3 255	3 444	3 737	..

Note: ISIC 1542 includes 1543; 1544 includes part of 1549; 1551 includes 1552 and 1554; 1712 includes 1721. Part of ISIC 1711, 1729 and 1730 is not covered. ISIC 2010 includes 2021;
ISIC 2102 includes part of 2109. Part of ISIC 2029, 2101 and 2109 are not covered. ISIC 2210 includes 2220. ISIC 2310, 2330 and part of 2413 are not covered. ISIC 2693 includes part of 2691 and 2692
2695. ISIC 2720 includes 2730; 2812 includes 2813. ISIC 2891 includes part of 2892. ISIC 2923 and 2927 are not covered. ISIC 2914 includes part of 2919; 2926 includes 2929; 3312
includes 3313; 3320 includes 3330. ISIC 3691 includes part of 3699. ISIC 3699 includes 2320 and 37. ISIC 4020 includes 4030.

Industrial Structure Statistics
OECD, © 1998

Table IT.1 PRODUCTION - PRODUCTION

Milliards de L *(Prix courants)*

1989	1990	1991	1992	1993	1994	1995	1996			CITI révision 3
..	..	..	..	..	..	..	..	**Agriculture, chasse et sylviculture**	A	01-02
..	..	..	..	..	..	..	..	**Pêche**	B	05
..	..	..	13 676	7 487	8 061	..	..	**Activités extractives**	C	10-14
..	..	..	..	..	..	..	..	Extraction de charbon, de lignite et de tourbe		10
..	..	..	11 352	5 279	5 636	..	..	Extraction de pétrole brut et de gaz naturel		11
..	..	..	39	53	32	..	..	Extraction de minerais métalliques		13
..	..	..	2 286	2 155	2 393	..	..	Autres activités extractives		14
..	..	..	677 387	691 196	812 281	..	..	**Activités de fabrication**	D	15-37
..	..	..	92 684	95 335	99 797	..	..	**Produits alimentaires et boissons**	15	
..	..	..	12 170	13 479	14 887	..	..	Boissons		155
..	..	..	6 224	6 424	6 750	..	..	**Produits à base de tabac**	16	160
..	..	..	40 981	42 818	50 184	..	..	**Textiles**	17	
..	..	..	24 987	26 254	32 170	..	..	Filature, tissage et achèvement des textiles		171
..	..	..	5 479	5 540	6 155	..	..	Autres articles textiles		172
..	..	..	10 515	11 024	11 859	..	..	Etoffes et articles de bonneterie		173
..	..	..	26 459	26 949	29 636	..	..	**Habillement; préparation, teinture des fourrures**	18	
..	..	..	26 259	26 758	29 495	..	..	Articles d'habillement autres qu'en fourrure		181
..	..	..	200	192	141	..	..	Préparation, teinture des fourrures; art. en fourrure		182
..	..	..	20 507	22 974	27 942	..	..	**Travail des cuirs; articles en cuir; chaussures**	19	
..	..	..	8 510	9 392	11 696	..	..	Apprêt et tannage des cuirs et articles en cuirs		191
..	..	..	11 997	13 582	16 245	..	..	Chaussures		192
..	..	..	8 107	8 546	9 756	..	..	**Bois et articles en bois et liège (sauf meubles)**	20	
..	..	..	1 011	966	1 078	..	..	Sciage et rabotage du bois		201
..	..	..	7 096	7 579	8 678	..	..	Articles en bois, liège, vannerie, sparterie		202
..	..	..	16 128	16 989	20 898	..	..	**Papier et carton; articles en papier et en carton**	21	
..	..	..	19 381	19 806	20 981	..	..	**Edition, imprimerie et reproduction**	22	
..	..	..	10 800	11 138	11 686	..	..	Edition		221
..	..	..	8 142	8 292	9 024	..	..	Imprimerie et activités annexes		222
..	..	..	439	377	271	..	..	Reproduction de supports enregistrés		223
..	..	..	26 802	34 177	66 329	..	..	**Cokéfaction; prod. pétroliers; comb. nucléaires**	23	
..	..	..	64 272	67 265	72 832	..	..	**Produits chimiques**	24	
..	..	..	20 205	22 063	25 949	..	..	Produits chimiques de base		241
..	..	..	40 724	41 527	43 274	..	..	Autres produits chimiques		242
..	..	..	3 343	3 675	3 609	..	..	Fibres synthétiques ou artificielles		243
..	..	..	22 242	24 423	29 119	..	..	**Articles en caoutchouc et en matières plastiques**	25	
..	..	..	5 752	6 028	7 458	..	..	Articles en caoutchouc		251
..	..	..	16 490	18 395	21 662	..	..	Articles en matières plastiques		252
..	..	..	32 953	31 742	33 340	..	..	**Autres produits minéraux non métalliques**	26	
..	..	..	5 350	5 321	5 919	..	..	Verre et articles en verre		261
..	..	..	27 603	26 421	27 421	..	..	Produits minéraux non métalliques, nca		269
..	..	..	38 985	35 068	48 605	..	..	**Produits métallurgiques de base**	27	
..	..	..	26 232	22 217	33 105	..	..	Sidérurgie et première transformation de l'acier		271
..	..	..	8 207	8 278	9 354	..	..	Métallurgie; métaux précieux et non ferreux		272
..	..	..	4 547	4 573	6 146	..	..	Fonderie		273
..	..	..	41 296	41 734	46 291	..	..	**Ouvrages en métaux, sauf machines et matériel**	28	
..	..	..	15 622	14 982	14 574	..	..	Constr. et menuiserie métal.; réservoirs; générateurs		281
..	..	..	25 674	26 752	31 718	..	..	Autres ouvrages en métaux		289
..	..	..	75 287	78 414	90 820	..	..	**Machines et matériel, nca**	29	
..	..	..	28 581	29 040	35 174	..	..	Machines d'usage général		291
..	..	..	35 312	36 971	39 862	..	..	Machines d'usage spécifique		292
..	..	..	11 395	12 403	15 784	..	..	Appareils domestiques, nca		293
..	..	..	6 797	7 351	8 046	..	..	**Mach. de bureau, comptables, matériel inform.**	30	
..	..	..	32 060	28 811	31 405	..	..	**Machines et appareils électriques, nca**	31	
..	..	..	6 226	6 704	6 470	..	..	Moteurs, génératrices et transformateurs électriques		311
..	..	..	4 576	4 362	5 417	..	..	Matériel électrique de distribution et de commande		312
..	..	..	4 758	4 040	4 370	..	..	Fils et câbles électriques isolés		313
..	..	..	918	824	1 015	..	..	Accumulateurs, piles électriques		314
..	..	..	2 166	2 441	2 680	..	..	Lampes électriques et appareils d'éclairage		315
..	..	..	13 415	10 440	11 454	..	..	Autres matériels électriques, nca		319
..	..	..	15 274	15 858	17 873	..	..	**Equip. et appar. de radio, TV, communication**	32	
..	..	..	3 658	4 420	5 380	..	..	Tubes et valves électroniques; autres composants		321
..	..	..	10 076	9 964	10 475	..	..	Emetteurs radio et TV; app. téléphonie, télégraphie		322
..	..	..	1 540	1 474	2 018	..	..	Récepteurs radio et TV et articles associés		323
..	..	..	9 308	10 654	11 127	..	..	**Instruments médicaux, de précision, d'optique**	33	
..	..	..	7 185	8 466	8 620	..	..	Appareils médicaux et de précision		331
..	..	..	1 838	1 950	2 243	..	..	Instruments d'optique ; matériel photographique		332
..	..	..	284	238	264	..	..	Horlogerie		333
..	..	..	39 197	31 729	41 531	..	..	**Véhicules automobiles et nemorques**	34	
..	..	..	17 051	17 303	18 190	..	..	**Autres matériels de transport**	35	
..	..	..	4 333	4 109	4 424	..	..	Construction et réparation de navires		351
..	..	..	2 818	3 498	3 263	..	..	Construction de matériel ferroviaire roulant		352
..	..	..	6 266	5 860	5 981	..	..	Construction aéronautique et spatiale		353
..	..	..	3 634	3 836	4 521	..	..	Autres équipements de transport		359
..	..	..	24 943	26 326	30 210	..	..	**Meubles; activités de fabrication, nca**	36	
..	..	..	17 161	17 136	19 959	..	..	Meubles		361
..	..	..	7 782	9 190	10 251	..	..	Activités de fabrication, nca		369
..	..	..	446	497	616	..	..	**Récupération**	37	
..	..	..	64 081	67 804	73 562	..	..	**Production et distrib. d'électricité, de gaz, d'eau**	E	40-41
..	..	..	60 923	64 533	70 124	..	..	**Electricité, gaz, vapeur et eau chaude**	40	
..	..	..	39 117	41 085	44 654	..	..	Production, collecte et distribution d'électricité		401
..	..	..	3 158	3 272	3 438	..	..	**Captage, épuration et distribution d'eau**	41	410
..	..	..	82 951	76 870	64 738	..	..	**Construction**	F	45
..	..	..	..	..	..	..	..	**Commerce de gros et de détail; réparation**	G	50-52
..	..	..	..	..	..	..	..	**Hôtels et restaurants**	H	55
..	..	..	..	..	..	..	..	**Transports, entreposage et communications**	I	60-64
..	..	..	..	..	..	..	..	**Intermédiation financière**	J	65-67
..	..	..	..	..	..	..	..	**Immobilier, locations, services aux entreprises**	K	70-74
..	..	..	..	..	..	..	..	**Admin. publique; éducation; santé; autres**	L-Q	75-99
..	..	..	838 096	843 357	958 642	..	..	**Grand total**	A-Q	01-99

Statistiques des Structures Industrielles
OCDE, © 1998

ITALY

Table IT.2 VALUE ADDED - VALEUR AJOUTÉE

Billions of L (Current Prices)

ISIC revision 3				1989	1990	1991	1992	1993	1994	1995	1996
A	01-02		Agriculture, hunting and forestry	..	..	..	..	..	..	..	..
B	05		Fishing	..	..	..	..	..	..	..	..
C	10-14		Mining and quarrying	..	..	..	4 664	4 977	5 529	..	..
	10		Mining of coal and lignite; extraction of peat	..	..	..	..	..	..	..	..
	11		Crude petroleum & natural gas; related service activ.	..	..	..	3 556	3 937	4 514	..	..
	13		Mining of metal ores	..	..	..	14	16	5	..	..
	14		Other mining and quarrying	..	..	..	1 093	1 024	1 010	..	..
D	15-37		Total manufacturing	..	..	..	209 926	214 355	233 824	..	..
	15		Food products and beverages	..	..	..	19 546	20 704	20 377	..	..
		155	Beverages	..	..	..	2 963	3 567	3 538	..	..
	16	160	Tobacco products	..	..	..	829	643	1 147	..	..
	17		Textiles	..	..	..	13 125	13 901	15 506	..	..
		171	Spinning, weaving and finishing of textiles	..	..	..	8 408	8 865	10 412	..	..
		172	Other textiles	..	..	..	1 798	1 845	1 901	..	..
		173	Knitted and crocheted fabrics and articles	..	..	..	2 919	3 191	3 194	..	..
	18		Wearing apparel dressing & dyeing of fur	..	..	..	8 535	8 496	9 134	..	..
		181	Wearing apparel, except fur apparel	..	..	..	8 446	8 410	9 065	..	..
		182	Dressing and dyeing of fur; articles of fur	..	..	..	89	86	70	..	..
	19		Tanning, dressing leather; leather artic.; footwear	..	..	..	5 708	6 216	6 869	..	..
		191	Tanning, dressing leather; manuf. of leather articles	..	..	..	2 205	2 257	2 536	..	..
		192	Footwear	..	..	..	3 502	3 959	4 332	..	..
	20		Wood and cork products, ex. furniture	..	..	..	2 544	2 673	2 866	..	..
		201	Sawmilling and planing of wood	..	..	..	279	291	323	..	..
		202	Products of wood, cork, straw & plaiting material	..	..	..	2 266	2 383	2 543	..	..
	21		Paper and paper products	..	..	..	4 980	5 241	6 163	..	..
	22		Publishing, printing & reprod. of recorded media	..	..	..	8 570	8 689	8 307	..	..
		221	Publishing	..	..	..	4 863	4 884	4 466	..	..
		222	Printing and related service activities	..	..	..	3 476	3 638	3 762	..	..
		223	Reproduction of recorded media	..	..	..	231	167	79	..	..
	23		Coke, refined petroleum products & nuclear fuel	..	..	..	3 273	5 002	5 794	..	..
	24		Chemicals and chemical products	..	..	..	20 687	21 840	23 653	..	..
		241	Basic chemicals	..	..	..	5 245	5 799	6 871	..	..
		242	Other chemical products	..	..	..	14 368	14 822	15 574	..	..
		243	Man-made fibres	..	..	..	1 075	1 219	1 209	..	..
	25		Rubber and plastic products	..	..	..	8 359	9 125	10 735	..	..
		251	Rubber products	..	..	..	2 794	2 954	3 826	..	..
		252	Plastic products	..	..	..	5 565	6 171	6 909	..	..
	26		Other non-metallic mineral products	..	..	..	13 319	12 895	13 441	..	..
		261	Glass and glass products	..	..	..	2 184	2 150	2 586	..	..
		269	Non-metallic mineral products, nec	..	..	..	11 136	10 745	10 854	..	..
	27		Basic metals	..	..	..	9 290	8 209	11 823	..	..
		271	Basic iron and steel	..	..	..	5 976	4 884	7 799	..	..
		272	Basic precious and non-ferrous metals	..	..	..	1 510	1 597	1 961	..	..
		273	Casting of metals	..	..	..	1 803	1 728	2 062	..	..
	28		Fabricated metal products, ex. machin. & equip.	..	..	..	15 425	15 689	16 820	..	..
		281	Structural metal prod., tanks, reservoirs, generators	..	..	..	5 491	5 344	5 014	..	..
		289	Other fabricated metal products & service activities	..	..	..	9 934	10 346	11 806	..	..
	29		Machinery and equipment, nec	..	..	..	26 496	27 722	30 951	..	..
		291	General purpose machinery	..	..	..	10 360	10 594	12 997	..	..
		292	Special purpose machinery	..	..	..	12 458	13 040	13 199	..	..
		293	Domestic appliances, nec	..	..	..	3 678	4 087	4 755	..	..
	30		Office, accounting and computing machinery	..	..	..	1 588	1 234	765	..	..
	31		Electrical machinery and apparatus, nec	..	..	..	12 860	11 078	11 046	..	..
		311	Electric motors, generators and transformers	..	..	..	2 554	2 324	2 135	..	..
		312	Electricity distribution and control apparatus	..	..	..	2 092	2 094	2 329	..	..
		313	Insulated wire and cable	..	..	..	1 331	1 179	1 141	..	..
		314	Accumulators, primary cells and primary batteries	..	..	..	291	215	245	..	..
		315	Electric lamps and lighting equipment	..	..	..	788	878	867	..	..
		319	Other electrical equipment, nec	..	..	..	5 803	4 387	4 329	..	..
	32		Radio, TV, communication equip. & apparatus	..	..	..	6 261	6 965	7 361	..	..
		321	Electronic valves, tubes & other electronic compon.	..	..	..	1 495	1 925	2 130	..	..
		322	TV, radio transmitters & appar. for line teleph., telegr.	..	..	..	4 388	4 662	4 678	..	..
		323	TV, radio receivers and associated goods	..	..	..	378	377	554	..	..
	33		Medical, precision, optical instr.; watches, clocks	..	..	..	4 385	4 943	5 124	..	..
		331	Medical equip.; precision instruments and appliances	..	..	..	3 459	3 990	4 075	..	..
		332	Optical instruments and photographic equipment	..	..	..	848	886	974	..	..
		333	Watches and clocks	..	..	..	78	68	75	..	..
	34		Motor vehicles, trailers, and semi-trailers	..	..	..	10 873	8 562	11 210	..	..
	35		Other transport equipment	..	..	..	5 914	6 698	6 466	..	..
		351	Building and repairing of ships and boats	..	..	..	962	985	751	..	..
		352	Railway, tramway locomotives and rolling stock	..	..	..	1 228	1 885	1 713	..	..
		353	Aircraft and spacecraft	..	..	..	2 577	2 687	2 618	..	..
		359	Transport equipment, nec	..	..	..	1 147	1 140	1 384	..	..
	36		Furniture; manufacturing, nec	..	..	..	7 280	7 713	8 066	..	..
		361	Furniture	..	..	..	5 111	5 354	5 586	..	..
		369	Manufacturing, nec	..	..	..	2 169	2 359	2 480	..	..
	37		Recycling	..	..	..	78	116	201	..	..
E	40-41		Electricity, gas and water supply	..	..	..	28 291	28 945	33 433	..	..
	40		Electricity, gas, steam and hot water supply	..	..	..	27 021	27 567	31 993	..	..
		401	Production, collection and distribution of electricity	..	..	..	20 537	20 992	24 643	..	..
	41	410	Collection, purification, distribution of water	..	..	..	1 270	1 378	1 440	..	..
F	45		Construction	..	..	..	25 816	24 285	20 951	..	..
G	50-52		Wholesale and retail trade; repairs etc	..	..	..	..	..	..	..	..
H	55		Hotels and restaurants	..	..	..	..	..	..	..	..
I	60-64		Transport, storage and communications	..	..	..	..	..	..	..	..
J	65-67		Financial intermediation	..	..	..	..	..	..	..	..
K	70-74		Real estate, renting and business activities	..	..	..	..	..	..	..	..
L-Q	75-99		Public admin.; education; health; other services	..	..	..	..	..	..	..	..
A-Q	01-99		Grand total	..	..	..	268 696	272 562	293 737	..	..

Table IT.3 INVESTISSEMENT - INVESTMENT

Milliards de L *(Prix courants)*

1989	1990	1991	1992	1993	1994	1995	1996			CITI révision 3	
..	..	..	..	..	..	..	..	**Agriculture, chasse et sylviculture**	A	01-02	
..	..	..	..	..	..	..	..	**Pêche**	B	05	
..	..	..	1 667	2 177	1 719	..	..	**Activités extractives**	C	10-14	
..	..	..	..	..	..	..	..	Extraction de charbon, de lignite et de tourbe		10	
..	..	..	1 384	1 947	1 558	..	..	Extraction de pétrole brut et de gaz naturel		11	
..	..	..	8	11	2	..	..	Extraction de minerais métalliques		13	
..	..	..	274	219	159	..	..	Autres activités extractives		14	
..	..	..	35 287	32 828	34 369	..	..	**Activités de fabrication**	D	15-37	
..	..	..	4 065	3 827	3 935	..	..	**Produits alimentaires et boissons**		15	
..	..	..	763	685	678	..	..	Boissons			155
..	..	..	222	84	68	..	..	**Produits à base de tabac**		16	160
..	..	..	1 735	1 723	2 066	..	..	**Textiles**		17	
..	..	..	1 148	1 162	1 473	..	..	Filature, tissage et achèvement des textiles			171
..	..	..	273	294	263	..	..	Autres articles textiles			172
..	..	..	314	267	330	..	..	Etoffes et articles de bonneterie			173
..	..	..	538	502	606	..	..	**Habillement; préparation, teinture des fourrures**		18	
..	..	..	536	499	603	..	..	Articles d'habillement autres qu'en fourrure			181
..	..	..	2	3	2	..	..	Préparation, teinture des fourrures; art. en fourrure			182
..	..	..	486	470	615	..	..	**Travail des cuirs; articles en cuir; chaussures**		19	
..	..	..	204	156	222	..	..	Apprêt et tannage des cuirs et articles en cuirs			191
..	..	..	282	314	393	..	..	Chaussures			192
..	..	..	473	376	372	..	..	**Bois et articles en bois et liège (sauf meubles)**		20	
..	..	..	45	28	32	..	..	Sciage et rabotage du bois			201
..	..	..	428	348	340	..	..	Articles en bois, liège, vannerie, sparterie			202
..	..	..	1 097	1 185	1 063	..	..	**Papier et carton; articles en papier et en carton**		21	
..	..	..	702	822	842	..	..	**Edition, imprimerie et reproduction**		22	
..	..	..	305	400	281	..	..	Edition			221
..	..	..	390	414	550	..	..	Imprimerie et activités annexes			222
..	..	..	6	8	10	..	..	Reproduction de supports enregistrés			223
..	..	..	1 584	1 761	1 227	..	..	**Cokéfaction; prod. pétroliers; comb. nucléaires**		23	
..	..	..	3 900	3 236	3 191	..	..	**Produits chimiques**		24	
..	..	..	1 696	1 142	933	..	..	Produits chimiques de base			241
..	..	..	1 944	1 859	1 990	..	..	Autres produits chimiques			242
..	..	..	260	235	268	..	..	Fibres synthétiques ou artificielles			243
..	..	..	1 360	1 434	1 535	..	..	**Articles en caoutchouc et en matières plastiques**		25	
..	..	..	288	339	385	..	..	Articles en caoutchouc			251
..	..	..	1 072	1 096	1 151	..	..	Articles en matières plastiques			252
..	..	..	2 588	2 299	2 387	..	..	**Autres produits minéraux non métalliques**		26	
..	..	..	462	361	410	..	..	Verre et articles en verre			261
..	..	..	2 126	1 939	1 976	..	..	Produits minéraux non métalliques, nca			269
..	..	..	2 870	1 458	2 027	..	..	**Produits métallurgiques de base**		27	
..	..	..	2 208	867	1 357	..	..	Sidérurgie et première transformation de l'acier			271
..	..	..	348	307	314	..	..	Métallurgie; métaux précieux et non ferreux			272
..	..	..	314	284	356	..	..	Fonderie			273
..	..	..	2 139	1 972	2 318	..	..	**Ouvrages en métaux, sauf machines et matériel**		28	
..	..	..	674	497	466	..	..	Constr. et menuiserie métal.; réservoirs; générateurs			281
..	..	..	1 465	1 475	1 853	..	..	Autres ouvrages en métaux			289
..	..	..	2 528	2 544	3 086	..	..	**Machines et matériel, nca**		29	
..	..	..	1 047	959	1 314	..	..	Machines d'usage général			291
..	..	..	998	930	1 081	..	..	Machines d'usage spécifique			292
..	..	..	484	654	690	..	..	Appareils domestiques, nca			293
..	..	..	247	214	195	..	..	**Mach. de bureau, comptables, matériel inform.**		30	
..	..	..	1 361	1 205	1 195	..	..	**Machines et appareils électriques, nca**		31	
..	..	..	287	217	210	..	..	Moteurs, génératrices et transformateurs électriques			311
..	..	..	200	198	224	..	..	Matériel électrique de distribution et de commande			312
..	..	..	179	153	117	..	..	Fils et câbles électriques isolés			313
..	..	..	52	51	38	..	..	Accumulateurs, piles électriques			314
..	..	..	104	96	120	..	..	Lampes électriques et appareils d'éclairage			315
..	..	..	541	490	486	..	..	Autres matériels électriques, nca			319
..	..	..	936	1 012	1 109	..	..	**Equip. et appar. de radio, TV, communication**		32	
..	..	..	371	563	710	..	..	Tubes et valves électroniques; autres composants			321
..	..	..	512	390	353	..	..	Emetteurs radio et TV; app. téléphonie, télégraphie			322
..	..	..	53	60	46	..	..	Récepteurs radio et TV et articles associés			323
..	..	..	405	385	418	..	..	**Instruments médicaux, de précision, d'optique**		33	
..	..	..	315	299	314	..	..	Appareils médicaux et de précision			331
..	..	..	84	83	99	..	..	Instruments d'optique ; matériel photographique			332
..	..	..	5	3	5	..	..	Horlogerie			333
..	..	..	3 599	3 726	4 019	..	..	**Véhicules automobiles et nemorques**		34	
..	..	..	1 606	1 755	1 157	..	..	**Autres matériels de transport**		35	
..	..	..	181	95	100	..	..	Construction et réparation de navires			351
..	..	..	677	1 030	563	..	..	Construction de matériel ferroviaire roulant			352
..	..	..	538	394	307	..	..	Construction aéronautique et spatiale			353
..	..	..	210	236	188	..	..	Autres équipements de transport			359
..	..	..	825	805	905	..	..	**Meubles; activités de fabrication, nca**		36	
..	..	..	583	570	637	..	..	Meubles			361
..	..	..	242	236	268	..	..	Activités de fabrication, nca			369
..	..	..	21	32	31	..	..	**Récupération**		37	
..	..	..	15 340	13 668	11 680	..	..	**Production et distrib. d'électricité, de gaz, d'eau**	E	40-41	
..	..	..	14 864	13 159	11 231	..	..	**Electricité, gaz, vapeur et eau chaude**		40	
..	..	..	11 092	9 498	8 433	..	..	Production, collecte et distribution d'électricité			401
..	..	..	476	509	448	..	..	**Captage, épuration et distribution d'eau**		41	410
..	..	..	2 088	1 941	2 056	..	..	**Construction**	F	45	
..	..	..	..	..	..	..	..	**Commerce de gros et de détail; réparation**	G	50-52	
..	..	..	..	..	..	..	..	**Hôtels et restaurants**	H	55	
..	..	..	..	..	..	..	..	**Transports, entreposage et communications**	I	60-64	
..	..	..	..	..	..	..	..	**Intermédiation financière**	J	65-67	
..	..	..	..	..	..	..	..	**Immobilier, locations, services aux entreprises**	K	70-74	
..	..	..	..	..	..	..	..	**Admin. publique; éducation; santé; autres**	L-Q	75-99	
..	..	..	54 382	50 615	49 824	..	..	**Grand total**	A-Q	01-99	

Statistiques des Structures Industrielles
OCDE, © 1998

ITALY

Table IT.4 INVESTMENT IN MACHINERY AND EQUIPMENT - DÉPENSES EN MACHINES ET ÉQUIPEMENT

Billions of L (Current Prices)

ISIC revision 3			1989	1990	1991	1992	1993	1994	1995	1996
A	01-02	Agriculture, hunting and forestry	..	..	..	..	..	..	..	..
B	05	Fishing				..	..	..		
C	10-14	Mining and quarrying	..	..	..	1 604	2 100	1 691	..	..
	10	Mining of coal and lignite; extraction of peat	..	..	..	..	..	..	..	..
	11	Crude petroleum & natural gas; related service activ.	..	..	..	1 376	1 930	1 535	..	..
	13	Mining of metal ores	..	..	..	6	10	2	..	..
	14	Other mining and quarrying	..	..	..	222	159	154	..	..
D	15-37	Total manufacturing	..	..	..	28 378	26 188	29 230	..	..
	15	Food products and beverages	..	..	..	3 146	2 960	3 205	..	..
	155	Beverages	..	..	..	605	536	579	..	..
	16 160	Tobacco products	..	..	..	153	39	48	..	..
	17	Textiles	..	..	..	1 400	1 380	1 768	..	..
	171	Spinning, weaving and finishing of textiles	..	..	..	966	943	1 272	..	..
	172	Other textiles	..	..	..	201	237	222	..	..
	173	Knitted and crocheted fabrics and articles	..	..	..	233	200	275	..	..
	18	Wearing apparel dressing & dyeing of fur	..	..	..	362	349	439	..	..
	181	Wearing apparel, except fur apparel	..	..	..	360	347	436	..	..
	182	Dressing and dyeing of fur; articles of fur	..	..	..	2	2	2	..	..
	19	Tanning, dressing leather; leather artic.; footwear	..	..	..	375	370	523	..	..
	191	Tanning, dressing leather; manuf. of leather articles	..	..	..	140	114	169	..	..
	192	Footwear	..	..	..	234	256	354	..	..
	20	Wood and cork products, ex. furniture	..	..	..	354	292	330	..	..
	201	Sawmilling and planing of wood	..	..	..	34	23	34	..	..
	202	Products of wood, cork, straw & plaiting material	..	..	..	320	270	296	..	..
	21	Paper and paper products	..	..	..	922	1 059	943	..	..
	22	Publishing, printing & reprod. of recorded media	..	..	..	522	572	670	..	..
	221	Publishing	..	..	..	217	220	213	..	..
	222	Printing and related service activities	..	..	..	299	345	450	..	..
	223	Reproduction of recorded media	..	..	..	6	7	7	..	..
	23	Coke, refined petroleum products & nuclear fuel	..	..	..	1 439	1 703	1 125	..	..
	24	Chemicals and chemical products	..	..	..	3 216	2 668	2 725	..	..
	241	Basic chemicals	..	..	..	1 513	1 018	841	..	..
	242	Other chemical products	..	..	..	1 472	1 446	1 639	..	..
	243	Man-made fibres	..	..	..	231	204	245	..	..
	25	Rubber and plastic products	..	..	..	1 168	1 209	1 355	..	..
	251	Rubber products	..	..	..	262	292	364	..	..
	252	Plastic products	..	..	..	906	917	991	..	..
	26	Other non-metallic mineral products	..	..	..	2 093	1 872	2 128	..	..
	261	Glass and glass products	..	..	..	397	328	360	..	..
	269	Non-metallic mineral products, nec	..	..	..	1 696	1 545	1 767	..	..
	27	Basic metals	..	..	..	2 453	1 289	1 833	..	..
	271	Basic iron and steel	..	..	..	1 876	750	1 159	..	..
	272	Basic precious and non-ferrous metals	..	..	..	311	282	266	..	..
	273	Casting of metals	..	..	..	267	257	408	..	..
	28	Fabricated metal products, ex. machin. & equip.	..	..	..	1 639	1 588	2 055	..	..
	281	Structural metal prod., tanks, reservoirs, generators	..	..	..	454	372	408	..	..
	289	Other fabricated metal products & service activities	..	..	..	1 185	1 216	1 647	..	..
	29	Machinery and equipment, nec	..	..	..	2 015	2 001	2 575	..	..
	291	General purpose machinery	..	..	..	849	778	1 108	..	..
	292	Special purpose machinery	..	..	..	741	721	866	..	..
	293	Domestic appliances, nec	..	..	..	425	502	601	..	..
	30	Office, accounting and computing machinery	..	..	..	222	194	182	..	..
	31	Electrical machinery and apparatus, nec	..	..	..	1 085	956	1 031	..	..
	311	Electric motors, generators and transformers	..	..	..	217	196	195	..	..
	312	Electricity distribution and control apparatus	..	..	..	167	152	203	..	..
	313	Insulated wire and cable	..	..	..	159	130	106	..	..
	314	Accumulators, primary cells and primary batteries	..	..	..	45	29	33	..	..
	315	Electric lamps and lighting equipment	..	..	..	87	74	95	..	..
	319	Other electrical equipment, nec	..	..	..	409	376	399	..	..
	32	Radio, TV, communication equip. & apparatus	..	..	..	801	903	1 008	..	..
	321	Electronic valves, tubes & other electronic compon.	..	..	..	356	530	648	..	..
	322	TV, radio transmitters & appar. for line teleph., telegr.	..	..	..	402	342	325	..	..
	323	TV, radio receivers and associated goods	..	..	..	43	31	35	..	..
	33	Medical, precision, optical instr.; watches, clocks	..	..	..	340	317	359	..	..
	331	Medical equip.; precision instruments and appliances	..	..	..	262	253	269	..	..
	332	Optical instruments and photographic equipment	..	..	..	73	61	85	..	..
	333	Watches and clocks	..	..	..	5	3	5	..	..
	34	Motor vehicles, trailers, and semi-trailers	..	..	..	3 349	3 245	3 661	..	..
	35	Other transport equipment	..	..	..	680	595	531	..	..
	351	Building and repairing of ships and boats	..	..	..	121	77	81	..	..
	352	Railway, tramway locomotives and rolling stock	..	..	..	90	91	53	..	..
	353	Aircraft and spacecraft	..	..	..	316	217	231	..	..
	359	Transport equipment, nec	..	..	..	153	209	165	..	..
	36	Furniture; manufacturing, nec	..	..	..	626	605	705	..	..
	361	Furniture	..	..	..	436	417	481	..	..
	369	Manufacturing, nec	..	..	..	190	188	223	..	..
	37	Recycling	..	..	..	17	19	32	..	..
E	40-41	Electricity, gas and water supply	..	..	..	9 656	8 743	7 390	..	..
	40	Electricity, gas, steam and hot water supply	..	..	..	9 240	8 392	7 037	..	..
	401	Production, collection and distribution of electricity	..	..	..	6 121	5 160	4 579	..	..
	41 410	Collection, purification, distribution of water	..	..	..	416	351	353	..	..
F	45	Construction	..	..	..	1 556	1 119	1 681	..	..
G	50-52	Wholesale and retail trade; repairs etc	..	..	..	..	..	..	..	..
H	55	Hotels and restaurants	..	..	..	..	..	..	..	..
I	60-64	Transport, storage and communications	..	..	..	..	..	..	..	..
J	65-67	Financial intermediation	..	..	..	..	..	..	..	..
K	70-74	Real estate, renting and business activities	..	..	..	..	..	..	..	..
L-Q	75-99	Public admin.; education; health; other services	..	..	..	..	..	..	..	..
A-Q	01-99	Grand total	..	..	..	41 194	38 150	39 991	..	..

Table IT.5 **ETABLISSEMENTS - ESTABLISHMENTS**

Unités

1989	1990	1991	1992	1993	1994	1995	1996			CITI révision 3
..	..	..				..	..	**Agriculture, chasse et sylviculture**	A	01-02
..	..	..				..	..	**Pêche**	B	05
..	..	..	386	384	367	..	..	**Activités extractives**	C	10-14
..	..	..	2	2	..	..	..	Extraction de charbon, de lignite et de tourbe		10
..	..	..	17	21	18	..	..	Extraction de pétrole brut et de gaz naturel		11
..	..	..	4	6	7	..	..	Extraction de minerais métalliques		13
..	..	..	362	355	342	..	..	Autres activités extractives		14
..	..	..	38 708	39 118	38 983	..	..	**Activités de fabrication**	D	15-37
..	..	..	2 696	2 734	2 698	..	..	**Produits alimentaires et boissons**		15
..	..	..	388	386	376	..	..	Boissons		155
..	..	..	42	40	32	..	..	**Produits à base de tabac**	16	160
..	..	..	3 465	3 514	3 511	..	..	**Textiles**	17	
..	..	..	1 778	1 804	1 812	..	..	Filature, tissage et achèvement des textiles		171
..	..	..	600	611	584	..	..	Autres articles textiles		172
..	..	..	1 087	1 099	1 115	..	..	Etoffes et articles de bonneterie		173
..	..	..	3 946	4 063	3 888	..	..	**Habillement; préparation, teinture des fourrures**	18	
..	..	..	3 899	4 020	3 852	..	..	Articles d'habillement autres qu'en fourrure		181
..	..	..	47	43	36	..	..	Préparation, teinture des fourrures; art. en fourrure		182
..	..	..	2 721	2 747	2 740	..	..	**Travail des cuirs; articles en cuir; chaussures**	19	
..	..	..	835	784	778	..	..	Apprêt et tannage des cuirs et articles en cuirs		191
..	..	..	1 886	1 963	1 962	..	..	Chaussures		192
..	..	..	979	983	1 018	..	..	**Bois et articles en bois et liège (sauf meubles)**	20	
..	..	..	105	113	124	..	..	Sciage et rabotage du bois		201
..	..	..	874	870	894	..	..	Articles en bois, liège, vannerie, sparterie		202
..	..	..	782	793	806	..	..	**Papier et carton; articles en papier et en carton**	21	
..	..	..	1 370	1 383	1 344	..	..	**Edition, imprimerie et reproduction**	22	
..	..	..	298	306	289	..	..	Edition		221
..	..	..	1 056	1 058	1 037	..	..	Imprimerie et activités annexes		222
..	..	..	16	19	18	..	..	Reproduction de supports enregistrés		223
..	..	..	117	119	113	..	..	**Cokéfaction; prod. pétroliers; comb. nucléaires**	23	
..	..	..	1 220	1 215	1 214	..	..	**Produits chimiques**	24	
..	..	..	284	297	297	..	..	Produits chimiques de base		241
..	..	..	895	873	876	..	..	Autres produits chimiques		242
..	..	..	41	45	41	..	..	Fibres synthétiques ou artificielles		243
..	..	..	1 592	1 677	1 742	..	..	**Articles en caoutchouc et en matières plastiques**	25	
..	..	..	258	266	272	..	..	Articles en caoutchouc		251
..	..	..	1 334	1 411	1 470	..	..	Articles en matières plastiques		252
..	..	..	2 330	2 312	2 222	..	..	**Autres produits minéraux non métalliques**	26	
..	..	..	320	318	307	..	..	Verre et articles en verre		261
..	..	..	2 010	1 994	1 915	..	..	Produits minéraux non métalliques, nca		269
..	..	..	1 008	993	995	..	..	**Produits métallurgiques de base**	27	
..	..	..	521	510	495	..	..	Sidérurgie et première transformation de l'acier		271
..	..	..	128	135	139	..	..	Métallurgie; métaux précieux et non ferreux		272
..	..	..	359	348	361	..	..	Fonderie		273
..	..	..	4 879	4 948	5 084	..	..	**Ouvrages en métaux, sauf machines et matériel**	28	
..	..	..	1 641	1 645	1 624	..	..	Constr. et menuiserie métal.; réservoirs; générateurs		281
..	..	..	3 238	3 303	3 460	..	..	Autres ouvrages en métaux		289
..	..	..	4 511	4 560	4 605	..	..	**Machines et matériel, nca**	29	
..	..	..	1 784	1 852	1 972	..	..	Machines d'usage général		291
..	..	..	2 493	2 467	2 398	..	..	Machines d'usage spécifique		292
..	..	..	234	241	235	..	..	Appareils domestiques, nca		293
..	..	..	116	126	112	..	..	**Mach. de bureau, comptables, matériel inform.**	30	
..	..	..	1 672	1 647	1 632	..	..	**Machines et appareils électriques, nca**	31	
..	..	..	426	407	396	..	..	Moteurs, génératrices et transformateurs électriques		311
..	..	..	345	341	331	..	..	Matériel électrique de distribution et de commande		312
..	..	..	126	121	116	..	..	Fils et câbles électriques isolés		313
..	..	..	25	25	24	..	..	Accumulateurs, piles électriques		314
..	..	..	171	168	175	..	..	Lampes électriques et appareils d'éclairage		315
..	..	..	579	585	590	..	..	Autres matériels électriques, nca		319
..	..	..	497	514	504	..	..	**Equip. et appar. de radio, TV, communication**	32	
..	..	..	208	216	223	..	..	Tubes et valves électroniques; autres composants		321
..	..	..	238	251	232	..	..	Emetteurs radio et TV; app. téléphonie, télégraphie		322
..	..	..	51	47	49	..	..	Récepteurs radio et TV et articles associés		323
..	..	..	802	802	789	..	..	**Instruments médicaux, de précision, d'optique**	33	
..	..	..	609	609	609	..	..	Appareils médicaux et de précision		331
..	..	..	174	173	166	..	..	Instruments d'optique ; matériel photographique		332
..	..	..	19	20	14	..	..	Horlogerie		333
..	..	..	736	695	686	..	..	**Véhicules automobiles et nemorques**	34	
..	..	..	489	485	466	..	..	**Autres matériels de transport**	35	
..	..	..	218	217	208	..	..	Construction et réparation de navires		351
..	..	..	51	45	32	..	..	Construction de matériel ferroviaire roulant		352
..	..	..	45	43	41	..	..	Construction aéronautique et spatiale		353
..	..	..	175	180	185	..	..	Autres équipements de transport		359
..	..	..	2 705	2 729	2 740	..	..	**Meubles; activités de fabrication, nca**	36	
..	..	..	1 924	1 927	1 952	..	..	Meubles		361
..	..	..	781	802	788	..	..	Activités de fabrication, nca		369
..	..	..	33	39	42	..	..	**Récupération**	37	
..	..	..	311	325	315	..	..	**Production et distrib. d'électricité, de gaz, d'eau**	E	40-41
..	..	..	200	209	208	..	..	**Electricité, gaz, vapeur et eau chaude**	40	
..	..	..	51	52	51	..	..	Production, collecte et distribution d'électricité		401
..	..	..	111	116	107	..	..	**Captage, épuration et distribution d'eau**	41	410
..	..	..	7 436	7 659	6 994	..	..	**Construction**	F	45
..	..	..	..	..	..	..	..	**Commerce de gros et de détail; réparation**	G	50-52
..	..	..	..	..	..	..	..	**Hôtels et restaurants**	H	55
..	..	..	..	..	..	..	..	**Transports, entreposage et communications**	I	60-64
..	..	..	..	..	..	..	..	**Intermédiation financière**	J	65-67
..	..	..	..	..	..	..	..	**Immobilier, locations, services aux entreprises**	K	70-74
..	..	..	..	..	..	..	..	**Admin. publique; éducation; santé; autres**	L-Q	75-99
..	..	..	46 841	47 486	46 659	..	..	**Grand total**	A-Q	01-99

Statistiques des Structures Industrielles
OCDE, © 1998

ITALY

Table IT.6 EMPLOYMENT - EMPLOI

Thousands

ISIC revision 3			1989	1990	1991	1992	1993	1994	1995	1996
A	01-02	**Agriculture, hunting and forestry**	..	..	..	..	..	..	..	..
B	05	**Fishing**	..	..	..	..	..	..	..	..
C	10-14	**Mining and quarrying**	..	..	..	24.1	23.8	22.1	..	..
	10	Mining of coal and lignite; extraction of peat	..	..	..	..	..	..	..	..
	11	Crude petroleum & natural gas; related service activ.	..	..	..	9.1	8.4	8.0	..	..
	13	Mining of metal ores	..	..	..	0.5	0.8	0.7	..	..
	14	Other mining and quarrying	..	..	..	14.5	14.7	13.4	..	..
D	15-37	**Total manufacturing**	..	..	..	3 043.8	2 920.6	2 887.6	..	..
	15	**Food products and beverages**	..	..	..	222.7	220.0	217.1	..	..
	155	Beverages	..	..	..	28.2	29.8	29.2	..	..
	16 160	**Tobacco products**	..	..	..	17.0	16.2	14.1	..	..
	17	**Textiles**	..	..	..	221.5	215.4	216.3	..	..
	171	Spinning, weaving and finishing of textiles	..	..	..	135.6	131.5	132.8	..	..
	172	Other textiles	..	..	..	30.3	30.0	28.9	..	..
	173	Knitted and crocheted fabrics and articles	..	..	..	55.5	53.9	54.6	..	..
	18	**Wearing apparel dressing & dyeing of fur**	..	..	..	191.8	185.1	174.7	..	..
	181	Wearing apparel, except fur apparel	..	..	..	190.0	183.4	173.3	..	..
	182	Dressing and dyeing of fur; articles of fur	..	..	..	1.8	1.7	1.5	..	..
	19	**Tanning, dressing leather; leather artic.; footwear**	..	..	..	126.3	121.5	121.2	..	..
	191	Tanning, dressing leather; manuf. of leather articles	..	..	..	36.9	32.6	32.2	..	..
	192	Footwear	..	..	..	89.4	88.9	89.0	..	..
	20	**Wood and cork products, ex. furniture**	..	..	..	42.8	42.2	43.2	..	..
	201	Sawmilling and planing of wood	..	..	..	4.1	4.2	4.5	..	..
	202	Products of wood, cork, straw & plaiting material	..	..	..	38.7	38.0	38.7	..	..
	21	**Paper and paper products**	..	..	..	64.3	63.3	63.8	..	..
	22	**Publishing, printing & reprod. of recorded media**	..	..	..	91.7	91.0	87.4	..	..
	221	Publishing	..	..	..	38.8	37.6	35.8	..	..
	222	Printing and related service activities	..	..	..	51.9	52.4	50.7	..	..
	223	Reproduction of recorded media	..	..	..	1.0	1.0	0.9	..	..
	23	**Coke, refined petroleum products & nuclear fuel**	..	..	..	23.3	21.3	25.2	..	..
	24	**Chemicals and chemical products**	..	..	..	206.9	199.3	189.6	..	..
	241	Basic chemicals	..	..	..	62.3	60.9	56.9	..	..
	242	Other chemical products	..	..	..	130.1	124.2	120.4	..	..
	243	Man-made fibres	..	..	..	14.4	14.2	12.3	..	..
	25	**Rubber and plastic products**	..	..	..	112.4	112.8	117.1	..	..
	251	Rubber products	..	..	..	34.9	32.3	33.8	..	..
	252	Plastic products	..	..	..	77.5	80.6	83.3	..	..
	26	**Other non-metallic mineral products**	..	..	..	166.3	159.1	152.6	..	..
	261	Glass and glass products	..	..	..	31.3	29.9	28.1	..	..
	269	Non-metallic mineral products, nec	..	..	..	135.0	129.2	124.5	..	..
	27	**Basic metals**	..	..	..	148.0	114.3	126.9	..	..
	271	Basic iron and steel	..	..	..	95.3	64.7	77.3	..	..
	272	Basic precious and non-ferrous metals	..	..	..	22.9	22.4	22.0	..	..
	273	Casting of metals	..	..	..	29.8	27.2	27.5	..	..
	28	**Fabricated metal products, ex. machin. & equip.**	..	..	..	246.3	241.5	242.0	..	..
	281	Structural metal prod., tanks, reservoirs, generators	..	..	..	90.8	86.8	81.9	..	..
	289	Other fabricated metal products & service activities	..	..	..	155.5	154.6	160.1	..	..
	29	**Machinery and equipment, nec**	..	..	..	375.2	368.0	371.2	..	..
	291	General purpose machinery	..	..	..	142.2	141.8	151.4	..	..
	292	Special purpose machinery	..	..	..	182.4	174.5	165.0	..	..
	293	Domestic appliances, nec	..	..	..	50.6	51.7	54.9	..	..
	30	**Office, accounting and computing machinery**	..	..	..	23.2	19.7	16.5	..	..
	31	**Electrical machinery and apparatus, nec**	..	..	..	173.7	150.8	139.8	..	..
	311	Electric motors, generators and transformers	..	..	..	38.4	33.9	28.8	..	..
	312	Electricity distribution and control apparatus	..	..	..	28.1	27.5	28.7	..	..
	313	Insulated wire and cable	..	..	..	15.8	14.4	12.8	..	..
	314	Accumulators, primary cells and primary batteries	..	..	..	3.4	3.1	3.1	..	..
	315	Electric lamps and lighting equipment	..	..	..	11.5	10.9	9.9	..	..
	319	Other electrical equipment, nec	..	..	..	76.5	61.0	56.5	..	..
	32	**Radio, TV, communication equip. & apparatus**	..	..	..	83.7	85.2	89.2	..	..
	321	Electronic valves, tubes & other electronic compon.	..	..	..	23.6	23.7	24.8	..	..
	322	TV, radio transmitters & appar. for line teleph., telegr.	..	..	..	52.4	55.4	57.3	..	..
	323	TV, radio receivers and associated goods	..	..	..	7.7	6.1	7.2	..	..
	33	**Medical, precision, optical instr.; watches, clocks**	..	..	..	58.1	61.0	60.8	..	..
	331	Medical equip.; precision instruments and appliances	..	..	..	43.9	47.0	46.5	..	..
	332	Optical instruments and photographic equipment	..	..	..	12.9	13.2	13.6	..	..
	333	Watches and clocks	..	..	..	1.2	0.9	0.7	..	..
	34	**Motor vehicles, trailers, and semi-trailers**	..	..	..	201.2	185.6	181.2	..	..
	35	**Other transport equipment**	..	..	..	113.4	116.3	103.6	..	..
	351	Building and repairing of ships and boats	..	..	..	25.1	23.3	22.1	..	..
	352	Railway, tramway locomotives and rolling stock	..	..	..	27.9	28.1	23.1	..	..
	353	Aircraft and spacecraft	..	..	..	42.0	46.8	41.2	..	..
	359	Transport equipment, nec	..	..	..	18.4	18.1	17.2	..	..
	36	**Furniture; manufacturing, nec**	..	..	..	132.8	129.8	131.3	..	..
	361	Furniture	..	..	..	95.0	91.3	92.8	..	..
	369	Manufacturing, nec	..	..	..	37.8	38.5	38.5	..	..
	37	**Recycling**	..	..	..	1.1	1.2	2.7	..	..
E	40-41	**Electricity, gas and water supply**	..	..	..	168.2	167.2	161.7	..	..
	40	**Electricity, gas, steam and hot water supply**	..	..	..	151.3	150.2	144.7	..	..
	401	Production, collection and distribution of electricity	..	..	..	122.2	120.6	115.6	..	..
	41 410	**Collection, purification, distribution of water**	..	..	..	16.9	17.0	17.0	..	..
F	45	**Construction**	..	..	..	394.6	368.3	320.2	..	..
G	50-52	**Wholesale and retail trade; repairs etc**	..	..	..	..	..	..	..	..
H	55	**Hotels and restaurants**	..	..	..	..	..	..	..	..
I	60-64	**Transport, storage and communications**	..	..	..	..	..	..	..	..
J	65-67	**Financial intermediation**	..	..	..	..	..	..	..	..
K	70-74	**Real estate, renting and business activities**	..	..	..	..	..	..	..	..
L-Q	75-99	**Public admin.; education; health; other services**	..	..	..	..	..	..	..	..
A-Q	01-99	**Grand total**	..	..	..	3 630.7	3 479.9	3 391.6	..	..

Table IT.7 EMPLOI, SALARIÉS - EMPLOYMENT, EMPLOYEES

Milliers

1989	1990	1991	1992	1993	1994	1995	1996			CITI révision 3	
..	..	..	..	..	..	..	..	**Agriculture, chasse et sylviculture**	A	01-02	
..	..	..	..	..	..	..	..	**Pêche**	B	05	
..	..	..	23.5	23.2	21.6	..	..	**Activités extractives**	C	10-14	
..	..	..	..	..	..	..	..	Extraction de charbon, de lignite et de tourbe		10	
..	..	..	9.1	8.3	8.0	..	..	Extraction de pétrole brut et de gaz naturel		11	
..	..	..	0.5	0.8	0.7	..	..	Extraction de minerais métalliques		13	
..	..	..	13.9	14.1	12.9	..	..	Autres activités extractives		14	
..	..	..	2 981.5	2 858.6	2 825.5	..	..	**Activités de fabrication**	D	15-37	
..	..	..	218.6	215.7	212.8	..	..	**Produits alimentaires et boissons**		15	
..	..	..	27.7	29.2	28.7	..	..	Boissons			155
..	..	..	16.9	16.2	14.1	..	..	**Produits à base de tabac**		16	160
..	..	..	215.7	209.7	210.4	..	..	**Textiles**		17	
..	..	..	132.9	128.8	130.0	..	..	Filature, tissage et achèvement des textiles			171
..	..	..	29.3	28.9	27.9	..	..	Autres articles textiles			172
..	..	..	53.5	51.9	52.5	..	..	Etoffes et articles de bonneterie			173
..	..	..	185.8	178.9	168.8	..	..	**Habillement; préparation, teinture des fourrures**		18	
..	..	..	184.1	177.4	167.5	..	..	Articles d'habillement autres qu'en fourrure			181
..	..	..	1.7	1.5	1.4	..	..	Préparation, teinture des fourrures; art. en fourrure			182
..	..	..	121.5	116.7	116.3	..	..	**Travail des cuirs; articles en cuir; chaussures**		19	
..	..	..	35.4	31.3	30.9	..	..	Apprêt et tannage des cuirs et articles en cuirs			191
..	..	..	86.1	85.4	85.4	..	..	Chaussures			192
..	..	..	41.0	40.3	41.3	..	..	**Bois et articles en bois et liège (sauf meubles)**		20	
..	..	..	3.9	3.9	4.3	..	..	Sciage et rabotage du bois			201
..	..	..	37.1	36.3	37.0	..	..	Articles en bois, liège, vannerie, sparterie			202
..	..	..	63.1	62.2	62.6	..	..	**Papier et carton; articles en papier et en carton**		21	
..	..	..	89.4	88.7	85.2	..	..	**Edition, imprimerie et reproduction**		22	
..	..	..	38.4	37.2	35.4	..	..	Edition			221
..	..	..	50.1	50.5	49.0	..	..	Imprimerie et activités annexes			222
..	..	..	1.0	1.0	0.9	..	..	Reproduction de supports enregistrés			223
..	..	..	23.1	21.2	25.1	..	..	**Cokéfaction; prod. pétroliers; comb. nucléaires**		23	
..	..	..	205.3	197.7	188.0	..	..	**Produits chimiques**		24	
..	..	..	62.0	60.5	56.5	..	..	Produits chimiques de base			241
..	..	..	129.0	123.0	119.3	..	..	Autres produits chimiques			242
..	..	..	14.4	14.2	12.2	..	..	Fibres synthétiques ou artificielles			243
..	..	..	110.1	110.4	114.6	..	..	**Articles en caoutchouc et en matières plastiques**		25	
..	..	..	34.6	31.9	33.4	..	..	Articles en caoutchouc			251
..	..	..	75.5	78.5	81.1	..	..	Articles en matières plastiques			252
..	..	..	162.9	155.7	149.2	..	..	**Autres produits minéraux non métalliques**		26	
..	..	..	30.8	29.4	27.5	..	..	Verre et articles en verre			261
..	..	..	132.1	126.3	121.7	..	..	Produits minéraux non métalliques, nca			269
..	..	..	146.6	112.9	125.4	..	..	**Produits métallurgiques de base**		27	
..	..	..	94.6	64.0	76.6	..	..	Sidérurgie et première transformation de l'acier			271
..	..	..	22.7	22.2	21.8	..	..	Métallurgie; métaux précieux et non ferreux			272
..	..	..	29.3	26.6	27.0	..	..	Fonderie			273
..	..	..	238.0	233.3	233.6	..	..	**Ouvrages en métaux, sauf machines et matériel**		28	
..	..	..	88.1	84.1	79.4	..	..	Constr. et menuiserie métal.; réservoirs; générateurs			281
..	..	..	150.0	149.1	154.3	..	..	Autres ouvrages en métaux			289
..	..	..	368.1	360.8	364.2	..	..	**Machines et matériel, nca**		29	
..	..	..	139.5	138.9	148.4	..	..	Machines d'usage général			291
..	..	..	178.2	170.6	161.2	..	..	Machines d'usage spécifique			292
..	..	..	50.3	51.3	54.6	..	..	Appareils domestiques, nca			293
..	..	..	23.1	19.4	16.3	..	..	**Mach. de bureau, comptables, matériel inform.**		30	
..	..	..	170.7	148.4	137.3	..	..	**Machines et appareils électriques, nca**		31	
..	..	..	37.3	33.2	28.2	..	..	Moteurs, génératrices et transformateurs électriques			311
..	..	..	27.6	27.0	28.2	..	..	Matériel électrique de distribution et de commande			312
..	..	..	15.7	14.3	12.6	..	..	Fils et câbles électriques isolés			313
..	..	..	3.4	3.1	3.1	..	..	Accumulateurs, piles électriques			314
..	..	..	11.2	10.6	9.6	..	..	Lampes électriques et appareils d'éclairage			315
..	..	..	75.6	60.2	55.7	..	..	Autres matériels électriques, nca			319
..	..	..	82.9	84.5	88.5	..	..	**Equip. et appar. de radio, TV, communication**		32	
..	..	..	23.3	23.4	24.4	..	..	Tubes et valves électroniques; autres composants			321
..	..	..	52.0	55.1	56.9	..	..	Emetteurs radio et TV; app. téléphonie, télégraphie			322
..	..	..	7.6	6.0	7.1	..	..	Récepteurs radio et TV et articles associés			323
..	..	..	56.8	59.8	59.6	..	..	**Instruments médicaux, de précision, d'optique**		33	
..	..	..	43.0	46.0	45.6	..	..	Appareils médicaux et de précision			331
..	..	..	12.7	12.9	13.3	..	..	Instruments d'optique ; matériel photographique			332
..	..	..	1.2	0.9	0.7	..	..	Horlogerie			333
..	..	..	200.0	184.5	180.1	..	..	**Véhicules automobiles et nemorques**		34	
..	..	..	112.7	115.6	102.9	..	..	**Autres matériels de transport**		35	
..	..	..	24.7	22.9	21.8	..	..	Construction et réparation de navires			351
..	..	..	27.8	28.0	23.0	..	..	Construction de matériel ferroviaire roulant			352
..	..	..	42.0	46.8	41.2	..	..	Construction aéronautique et spatiale			353
..	..	..	18.2	17.8	16.9	..	..	Autres équipements de transport			359
..	..	..	128.0	124.9	126.4	..	..	**Meubles; activités de fabrication, nca**		36	
..	..	..	91.5	87.9	89.3	..	..	Meubles			361
..	..	..	36.5	37.1	37.1	..	..	Activités de fabrication, nca			369
..	..	..	1.1	1.1	2.6	..	..	**Récupération**		37	
..	..	..	167.9	166.8	161.4	..	..	**Production et distrib. d'électricité, de gaz, d'eau**	E	40-41	
..	..	..	151.1	150.0	144.5	..	..	**Electricité, gaz, vapeur et eau chaude**		40	
..	..	..	122.1	120.6	115.6	..	..	Production, collecte et distribution d'électricité			401
..	..	..	16.8	16.9	16.9	..	..	**Captage, épuration et distribution d'eau**		41	410
..	..	..	382.4	355.7	308.5	..	..	**Construction**	F	45	
..	..	..	..	..	..	..	..	**Commerce de gros et de détail; réparation**	G	50-52	
..	..	..	..	..	..	..	..	**Hôtels et restaurants**	H	55	
..	..	..	..	..	..	..	..	**Transports, entreposage et communications**	I	60-64	
..	..	..	..	..	..	..	..	**Intermédiation financière**	J	65-67	
..	..	..	..	..	..	..	..	**Immobilier, locations, services aux entreprises**	K	70-74	
..	..	..	..	..	..	..	..	**Admin. publique; éducation; santé; autres**	L-Q	75-99	
..	..	..	3 555.2	3 404.3	3 317.0	..	..	**Grand total**	A-Q	01-99	

Statistiques des Structures Industrielles
OCDE, © 1998
OECD / OCDE

ITALY

Table IT.8 COMPENSATION OF LABOUR – SALAIRES ET CHARGES SOCIALES

Billions of L (Current Prices)

ISIC revision 3			1989	1990	1991	1992	1993	1994	1995	1996
A	01-02	Agriculture, hunting and forestry	..	..	..	..	..	..	..	..
B	05	Fishing	..	..	..	..	..	..	..	..
C	10-14	Mining and quarrying	..	..	..	1 282	1 285	1 359	..	..
	10	Mining of coal and lignite; extraction of peat	..	..	..	..	..	..	..	..
	11	Crude petroleum & natural gas; related service activ.	..	..	..	..	..	..	..	..
	13	Mining of metal ores	..	..	..	592	586	652	..	..
	14	Other mining and quarrying	..	..	..	22	31	32	..	..
			..	..	..	668	668	675	..	..
D	15-37	Total manufacturing	..	..	..	143 821	142 119	148 035	..	..
	15	Food products and beverages	..	..	..	11 438	11 868	12 200	..	..
	155	Beverages	..	..	..	1 613	1 834	1 929	..	..
	16 160	Tobacco products	..	..	..	660	623	561	..	..
	17	Textiles	..	..	..	8 569	8 590	9 113	..	..
	171	Spinning, weaving and finishing of textiles	..	..	..	5 682	5 646	6 067	..	..
	172	Other textiles	..	..	..	1 109	1 132	1 155	..	..
	173	Knitted and crocheted fabrics and articles	..	..	..	1 779	1 812	1 891	..	..
	18	Wearing apparel dressing & dyeing of fur	..	..	..	5 663	5 512	5 619	..	..
	181	Wearing apparel, except fur apparel	..	..	..	5 606	5 456	5 568	..	..
	182	Dressing and dyeing of fur; articles of fur	..	..	..	58	55	51	..	..
	19	Tanning, dressing leather; leather artic.; footwear	..	..	..	3 835	3 868	4 128	..	..
	191	Tanning, dressing leather; manuf. of leather articles	..	..	..	1 343	1 216	1 286	..	..
	192	Footwear	..	..	..	2 492	2 652	2 841	..	..
	20	Wood and cork products, ex. furniture	..	..	..	1 588	1 626	1 724	..	..
	201	Sawmilling and planing of wood	..	..	..	153	152	181	..	..
	202	Products of wood, cork, straw & plaiting material	..	..	..	1 436	1 474	1 543	..	..
	21	Paper and paper products	..	..	..	3 166	3 212	3 446	..	..
	22	Publishing, printing & reprod. of recorded media	..	..	..	5 728	6 020	6 021	..	..
	221	Publishing	..	..	..	3 103	3 246	3 162	..	..
	222	Printing and related service activities	..	..	..	2 571	2 712	2 810	..	..
	223	Reproduction of recorded media	..	..	..	54	62	48	..	..
	23	Coke, refined petroleum products & nuclear fuel	..	..	..	1 647	1 533	1 966	..	..
	24	Chemicals and chemical products	..	..	..	13 518	13 555	13 464	..	..
	241	Basic chemicals	..	..	..	3 913	4 007	3 875	..	..
	242	Other chemical products	..	..	..	8 820	8 792	8 882	..	..
	243	Man-made fibres	..	..	..	786	756	708	..	..
	25	Rubber and plastic products	..	..	..	5 201	5 421	5 879	..	..
	251	Rubber products	..	..	..	1 725	1 666	1 843	..	..
	252	Plastic products	..	..	..	3 476	3 755	4 035	..	..
	26	Other non-metallic mineral products	..	..	..	7 958	7 954	7 955	..	..
	261	Glass and glass products	..	..	..	1 523	1 540	1 526	..	..
	269	Non-metallic mineral products, nec	..	..	..	6 434	6 414	6 429	..	..
	27	Basic metals	..	..	..	7 640	5 995	7 253	..	..
	271	Basic iron and steel	..	..	..	4 978	3 399	4 510	..	..
	272	Basic precious and non-ferrous metals	..	..	..	1 280	1 252	1 286	..	..
	273	Casting of metals	..	..	..	1 383	1 343	1 457	..	..
	28	Fabricated metal products, ex. machin. & equip.	..	..	..	10 644	10 815	11 269	..	..
	281	Structural metal prod., tanks, reservoirs, generators	..	..	..	3 920	3 881	3 727	..	..
	289	Other fabricated metal products & service activities	..	..	..	6 724	6 934	7 542	..	..
	29	Machinery and equipment, nec	..	..	..	18 907	19 133	20 405	..	..
	291	General purpose machinery	..	..	..	7 192	7 314	8 287	..	..
	292	Special purpose machinery	..	..	..	9 341	9 326	9 332	..	..
	293	Domestic appliances, nec	..	..	..	2 374	2 493	2 787	..	..
	30	Office, accounting and computing machinery	..	..	..	1 455	1 218	1 010	..	..
	31	Electrical machinery and apparatus, nec	..	..	..	8 749	7 493	7 287	..	..
	311	Electric motors, generators and transformers	..	..	..	1 890	1 716	1 506	..	..
	312	Electricity distribution and control apparatus	..	..	..	1 348	1 358	1 478	..	..
	313	Insulated wire and cable	..	..	..	827	734	696	..	..
	314	Accumulators, primary cells and primary batteries	..	..	..	170	153	169	..	..
	315	Electric lamps and lighting equipment	..	..	..	501	499	474	..	..
	319	Other electrical equipment, nec	..	..	..	4 013	3 034	2 964	..	..
	32	Radio, TV, communication equip. & apparatus	..	..	..	4 446	4 764	5 114	..	..
	321	Electronic valves, tubes & other electronic compon.	..	..	..	1 125	1 228	1 315	..	..
	322	TV, radio transmitters & appar. for line teleph., telegr.	..	..	..	2 985	3 224	3 483	..	..
	323	TV, radio receivers and associated goods	..	..	..	337	311	315	..	..
	33	Medical, precision, optical instr.; watches, clocks	..	..	..	2 870	3 301	3 358	..	..
	331	Medical equip.; precision instruments and appliances	..	..	..	2 296	2 725	2 765	..	..
	332	Optical instruments and photographic equipment	..	..	..	518	538	560	..	..
	333	Watches and clocks	..	..	..	55	38	33	..	..
	34	Motor vehicles, trailers, and semi-trailers	..	..	..	9 272	8 377	9 009	..	..
	35	Other transport equipment	..	..	..	5 791	6 068	5 812	..	..
	351	Building and repairing of ships and boats	..	..	..	1 166	1 128	1 069	..	..
	352	Railway, tramway locomotives and rolling stock	..	..	..	1 411	1 554	1 403	..	..
	353	Aircraft and spacecraft	..	..	..	2 414	2 574	2 521	..	..
	359	Transport equipment, nec	..	..	..	800	812	820	..	..
	36	Furniture; manufacturing, nec	..	..	..	5 029	5 113	5 311	..	..
	361	Furniture	..	..	..	3 600	3 613	3 742	..	..
	369	Manufacturing, nec	..	..	..	1 429	1 500	1 569	..	..
	37	Recycling	..	..	..	45	61	132	..	..
E	40-41	Electricity, gas and water supply	..	..	..	12 896	12 826	13 306	..	..
	40	Electricity, gas, steam and hot water supply	..	..	..	11 725	11 662	12 146	..	..
	401	Production, collection and distribution of electricity	..	..	..	9 839	9 710	10 063	..	..
	41 410	Collection, purification, distribution of water	..	..	..	1 171	1 164	1 161	..	..
F	45	Construction	..	..	..	18 666	17 556	15 775	..	..
G	50-52	Wholesale and retail trade; repairs etc	..	..	..	..	..	..	..	..
H	55	Hotels and restaurants	..	..	..	..	..	..	..	..
I	60-64	Transport, storage and communications	..	..	..	..	..	..	..	..
J	65-67	Financial intermediation	..	..	..	..	..	..	..	..
K	70-74	Real estate, renting and business activities	..	..	..	..	..	..	..	..
L-Q	75-99	Public admin.; education; health; other services	..	..	..	..	..	..	..	..
A-Q	01-99	Grand total	..	..	..	176 665	173 785	178 476	..	..

ITALIE

Table IT.9 SALAIRES ET CHARGES SOCIALES , SALARIÉS - COMPENSATION OF LABOUR, EMPLOYEES

Milliards de L (Prix courants) — CITI révision 3

1989	1990	1991	1992	1993	1994	1995	1996			
..	..	..	..	..	..	..	..	**Agriculture, chasse et sylviculture**	A	01-02
..	..	..	..	..	..	..	..	**Pêche**	B	05
..	..	..	1 267	1 253	1 325	..	..	**Activités extractives**	C	10-14
..	..	..	..	..	..	..	..	Extraction de charbon, de lignite et de tourbe		10
..	..	..	582	563	629	..	..	Extraction de pétrole brut et de gaz naturel		11
..	..	..	22	30	31	..	..	Extraction de minerais métalliques		13
..	..	..	664	660	665	..	..	Autres activités extractives		14
..	..	..	142 527	140 577	146 454	..	..	**Activités de fabrication**	D	15-37
..	..	..	11 348	11 748	12 085	..	..	**Produits alimentaires et boissons**		15
..	..	..	1 592	1 789	1 894	..	..	Boissons		155
..	..	..	653	609	550	..	..	**Produits à base de tabac**	16	160
..	..	..	8 536	8 548	9 093	..	..	**Textiles**		17
..	..	..	5 657	5 616	6 059	..	..	Filature, tissage et achèvement des textiles		171
..	..	..	1 105	1 125	1 148	..	..	Autres articles textiles		172
..	..	..	1 774	1 807	1 886	..	..	Etoffes et articles de bonneterie		173
..	..	..	5 638	5 501	5 598	..	..	**Habillement; préparation, teinture des fourrures**		18
..	..	..	5 580	5 446	5 547	..	..	Articles d'habillement autres qu'en fourrure		181
..	..	..	58	55	50	..	..	Préparation, teinture des fourrures; art. en fourrure		182
..	..	..	3 822	3 854	4 113	..	..	**Travail des cuirs; articles en cuir; chaussures**		19
..	..	..	1 338	1 212	1 280	..	..	Apprêt et tannage des cuirs et articles en cuirs		191
..	..	..	2 484	2 642	2 833	..	..	Chaussures		192
..	..	..	1 580	1 619	1 715	..	..	**Bois et articles en bois et liège (sauf meubles)**		20
..	..	..	152	152	180	..	..	Sciage et rabotage du bois		201
..	..	..	1 428	1 468	1 535	..	..	Articles en bois, liège, vannerie, sparterie		202
..	..	..	3 153	3 198	3 421	..	..	**Papier et carton; articles en papier et en carton**		21
..	..	..	5 676	5 945	5 970	..	..	**Edition, imprimerie et reproduction**		22
..	..	..	3 065	3 189	3 131	..	..	Edition		221
..	..	..	2 557	2 695	2 791	..	..	Imprimerie et activités annexes		222
..	..	..	54	61	48	..	..	Reproduction de supports enregistrés		223
..	..	..	1 567	1 465	1 900	..	..	**Cokéfaction; prod. pétroliers; comb. nucléaires**		23
..	..	..	13 315	13 329	13 201	..	..	**Produits chimiques**		24
..	..	..	3 858	3 909	3 773	..	..	Produits chimiques de base		241
..	..	..	8 690	8 680	8 733	..	..	Autres produits chimiques		242
..	..	..	767	739	695	..	..	Fibres synthétiques ou artificielles		243
..	..	..	5 167	5 374	5 834	..	..	**Articles en caoutchouc et en matières plastiques**		25
..	..	..	1 710	1 645	1 824	..	..	Articles en caoutchouc		251
..	..	..	3 457	3 728	4 010	..	..	Articles en matières plastiques		252
..	..	..	7 906	7 871	7 879	..	..	**Autres produits minéraux non métalliques**		26
..	..	..	1 512	1 526	1 511	..	..	Verre et articles en verre		261
..	..	..	6 394	6 345	6 368	..	..	Produits minéraux non métalliques, nca		269
..	..	..	7 575	5 920	7 174	..	..	**Produits métallurgiques de base**		27
..	..	..	4 943	3 370	4 470	..	..	Sidérurgie et première transformation de l'acier		271
..	..	..	1 265	1 224	1 265	..	..	Métallurgie; métaux précieux et non ferreux		272
..	..	..	1 367	1 327	1 439	..	..	Fonderie		273
..	..	..	10 556	10 699	11 144	..	..	**Ouvrages en métaux, sauf machines et matériel**		28
..	..	..	3 877	3 819	3 659	..	..	Constr. et menuiserie métal.; réservoirs; générateurs		281
..	..	..	6 678	6 880	7 485	..	..	Autres ouvrages en métaux		289
..	..	..	18 696	18 821	20 101	..	..	**Machines et matériel, nca**		29
..	..	..	7 086	7 180	8 148	..	..	Machines d'usage général		291
..	..	..	9 259	9 179	9 205	..	..	Machines d'usage spécifique		292
..	..	..	2 351	2 462	2 747	..	..	Appareils domestiques, nca		293
..	..	..	1 615	1 374	1 100	..	..	**Mach. de bureau, comptables, matériel inform.**		30
..	..	..	8 638	7 393	7 213	..	..	**Machines et appareils électriques, nca**		31
..	..	..	1 868	1 697	1 489	..	..	Moteurs, génératrices et transformateurs électriques		311
..	..	..	1 316	1 326	1 469	..	..	Matériel électrique de distribution et de commande		312
..	..	..	824	730	692	..	..	Fils et câbles électriques isolés		313
..	..	..	167	151	167	..	..	Accumulateurs, piles électriques		314
..	..	..	496	491	470	..	..	Lampes électriques et appareils d'éclairage		315
..	..	..	3 967	2 999	2 927	..	..	Autres matériels électriques, nca		319
..	..	..	4 394	4 695	5 044	..	..	**Equip. et appar. de radio, TV, communication**		32
..	..	..	1 111	1 203	1 292	..	..	Tubes et valves électroniques; autres composants		321
..	..	..	2 957	3 192	3 441	..	..	Emetteurs radio et TV; app. téléphonie, télégraphie		322
..	..	..	327	301	311	..	..	Récepteurs radio et TV et articles associés		323
..	..	..	2 842	3 257	3 314	..	..	**Instruments médicaux, de précision, d'optique**		33
..	..	..	2 275	2 687	2 728	..	..	Appareils médicaux et de précision		331
..	..	..	513	533	554	..	..	Instruments d'optique ; matériel photographique		332
..	..	..	54	37	33	..	..	Horlogerie		333
..	..	..	9 127	8 255	8 892	..	..	**Véhicules automobiles et nemorques**		34
..	..	..	5 680	5 961	5 706	..	..	**Autres matériels de transport**		35
..	..	..	1 143	1 103	1 048	..	..	Construction et réparation de navires		351
..	..	..	1 380	1 525	1 368	..	..	Construction de matériel ferroviaire roulant		352
..	..	..	2 368	2 534	2 481	..	..	Construction aéronautique et spatiale		353
..	..	..	789	799	808	..	..	Autres équipements de transport		359
..	..	..	5 000	5 079	5 274	..	..	**Meubles; activités de fabrication, nca**		36
..	..	..	3 579	3 588	3 720	..	..	Meubles		361
..	..	..	1 421	1 491	1 554	..	..	Activités de fabrication, nca		369
..	..	..	44	61	132	..	..	**Récupération**		37
..	..	..	12 498	12 462	12 895	..	..	**Production et distrib. d'électricité, de gaz, d'eau**	E	40-41
..	..	..	11 338	11 306	11 747	..	..	**Electricité, gaz, vapeur et eau chaude**		40
..	..	..	9 529	9 363	9 705	..	..	Production, collecte et distribution d'électricité		401
..	..	..	1 160	1 156	1 148	..	..	**Captage, épuration et distribution d'eau**	41	410
..	..	..	18 358	17 258	15 503	..	..	**Construction**	F	45
..	..	..	..	..	..	..	..	**Commerce de gros et de détail; réparation**	G	50-52
..	..	..	..	..	..	..	..	**Hôtels et restaurants**	H	55
..	..	..	..	..	..	..	..	**Transports, entreposage et communications**	I	60-64
..	..	..	..	..	..	..	..	**Intermédiation financière**	J	65-67
..	..	..	..	..	..	..	..	**Immobilier, locations, services aux entreprises**	K	70-74
..	..	..	..	..	..	..	..	**Admin. publique; éducation; santé; autres**	L-Q	75-99
..	..	..	174 650	171 550	176 176	..	..	**Grand total**	A-Q	01-99

Statistiques des Structures Industrielles
OCDE, © 1998

Table IT.10 EMPLOYERS' SOCIAL COSTS – CHARGES SOCIALES DES EMPLOYEURS

Billions of L (Current Prices)

ISIC revision 3				1989	1990	1991	1992	1993	1994	1995	1996
A	01-02		Agriculture, hunting and forestry	..	..	..	..	..	..	..	..
B	05		Fishing	..	..	..	..	..	..	..	..
C	10-14		Mining and quarrying	..	..	..	405	388	396	..	..
	10		Mining of coal and lignite; extraction of peat	..	..	..	..	..	..	..	..
	11		Crude petroleum & natural gas; related service activ.	..	..	..	180	168	170	..	..
	13		Mining of metal ores	..	..	..	7	9	9	..	..
	14		Other mining and quarrying	..	..	..	218	210	217	..	..
D	15-37		Total manufacturing	..	..	..	45 692	45 026	46 766	..	..
	15		Food products and beverages	..	..	..	3 580	3 675	3 734	..	..
		155	Beverages	..	..	..	498	553	586	..	..
	16	160	Tobacco products	..	..	..	92	96	78	..	..
	17		Textiles	..	..	..	2 785	2 800	2 965	..	..
		171	Spinning, weaving and finishing of textiles	..	..	..	1 859	1 848	1 986	..	..
		172	Other textiles	..	..	..	361	367	375	..	..
		173	Knitted and crocheted fabrics and articles	..	..	..	565	585	604	..	..
	18		Wearing apparel dressing & dyeing of fur	..	..	..	1 771	1 742	1 759	..	..
		181	Wearing apparel, except fur apparel	..	..	..	1 752	1 724	1 743	..	..
		182	Dressing and dyeing of fur; articles of fur	..	..	..	19	18	16	..	..
	19		Tanning, dressing leather; leather artic.; footwear	..	..	..	1 217	1 212	1 302	..	..
		191	Tanning, dressing leather; manuf. of leather articles	..	..	..	429	385	407	..	..
		192	Footwear	..	..	..	789	827	895	..	..
	20		Wood and cork products, ex. furniture	..	..	..	526	544	566	..	..
		201	Sawmilling and planing of wood	..	..	..	51	52	60	..	..
		202	Products of wood, cork, straw & plaiting material	..	..	..	475	493	506	..	..
	21		Paper and paper products	..	..	..	1 035	1 036	1 116	..	..
	22		Publishing, printing & reprod. of recorded media	..	..	..	1 818	1 890	1 898	..	..
		221	Publishing	..	..	..	970	1 009	989	..	..
		222	Printing and related service activities	..	..	..	831	863	895	..	..
		223	Reproduction of recorded media	..	..	..	16	18	14	..	..
	23		Coke, refined petroleum products & nuclear fuel	..	..	..	476	436	575	..	..
	24		Chemicals and chemical products	..	..	..	4 104	4 172	4 167	..	..
		241	Basic chemicals	..	..	..	1 183	1 214	1 185	..	..
		242	Other chemical products	..	..	..	2 677	2 721	2 758	..	..
		243	Man-made fibres	..	..	..	243	237	224	..	..
	25		Rubber and plastic products	..	..	..	1 706	1 779	1 909	..	..
		251	Rubber products	..	..	..	570	553	593	..	..
		252	Plastic products	..	..	..	1 136	1 227	1 316	..	..
	26		Other non-metallic mineral products	..	..	..	2 650	2 638	2 626	..	..
		261	Glass and glass products	..	..	..	503	510	498	..	..
		269	Non-metallic mineral products, nec	..	..	..	2 147	2 128	2 129	..	..
	27		Basic metals	..	..	..	2 481	1 936	2 330	..	..
		271	Basic iron and steel	..	..	..	1 599	1 103	1 453	..	..
		272	Basic precious and non-ferrous metals	..	..	..	404	383	390	..	..
		273	Casting of metals	..	..	..	478	451	487	..	..
	28		Fabricated metal products, ex. machin. & equip.	..	..	..	3 391	3 485	3 588	..	..
		281	Structural metal prod., tanks, reservoirs, generators	..	..	..	1 187	1 239	1 143	..	..
		289	Other fabricated metal products & service activities	..	..	..	2 203	2 246	2 445	..	..
	29		Machinery and equipment, nec	..	..	..	6 171	6 175	6 527	..	..
		291	General purpose machinery	..	..	..	2 304	2 353	2 647	..	..
		292	Special purpose machinery	..	..	..	3 072	3 010	2 990	..	..
		293	Domestic appliances, nec	..	..	..	795	812	890	..	..
	30		Office, accounting and computing machinery	..	..	..	505	442	368	..	..
	31		Electrical machinery and apparatus, nec	..	..	..	2 698	2 263	2 244	..	..
		311	Electric motors, generators and transformers	..	..	..	580	521	478	..	..
		312	Electricity distribution and control apparatus	..	..	..	416	413	464	..	..
		313	Insulated wire and cable	..	..	..	251	217	213	..	..
		314	Accumulators, primary cells and primary batteries	..	..	..	52	48	51	..	..
		315	Electric lamps and lighting equipment	..	..	..	162	161	154	..	..
		319	Other electrical equipment, nec	..	..	..	1 237	903	883	..	..
	32		Radio, TV, communication equip. & apparatus	..	..	..	1 349	1 405	1 499	..	..
		321	Electronic valves, tubes & other electronic compon.	..	..	..	341	365	387	..	..
		322	TV, radio transmitters & appar. for line teleph., telegr.	..	..	..	900	933	1 013	..	..
		323	TV, radio receivers and associated goods	..	..	..	108	107	99	..	..
	33		Medical, precision, optical instr.; watches, clocks	..	..	..	906	1 022	1 043	..	..
		331	Medical equip.; precision instruments and appliances	..	..	..	722	844	859	..	..
		332	Optical instruments and photographic equipment	..	..	..	168	167	174	..	..
		333	Watches and clocks	..	..	..	17	12	11	..	..
	34		Motor vehicles, trailers, and semi-trailers	..	..	..	2 999	2 729	2 929	..	..
	35		Other transport equipment	..	..	..	1 773	1 872	1 791	..	..
		351	Building and repairing of ships and boats	..	..	..	397	381	361	..	..
		352	Railway, tramway locomotives and rolling stock	..	..	..	419	468	415	..	..
		353	Aircraft and spacecraft	..	..	..	698	759	748	..	..
		359	Transport equipment, nec	..	..	..	260	264	266	..	..
	36		Furniture; manufacturing, nec	..	..	..	1 643	1 655	1 712	..	..
		361	Furniture	..	..	..	1 183	1 172	1 207	..	..
		369	Manufacturing, nec	..	..	..	460	483	505	..	..
	37		Recycling	..	..	..	15	20	39	..	..
E	40-41		Electricity, gas and water supply	..	..	..	4 078	4 157	4 406	..	..
	40		Electricity, gas, steam and hot water supply	..	..	..	3 724	3 796	4 053	..	..
		401	Production, collection and distribution of electricity	..	..	..	3 134	3 164	3 382	..	..
	41	410	Collection, purification, distribution of water	..	..	..	354	360	353	..	..
F	45		Construction	..	..	..	6 396	5 920	5 355	..	..
G	50-52		Wholesale and retail trade; repairs etc	..	..	..	..	..	..	..	..
H	55		Hotels and restaurants	..	..	..	..	..	..	..	..
I	60-64		Transport, storage and communications	..	..	..	..	..	..	..	..
J	65-67		Financial intermediation	..	..	..	..	..	..	..	..
K	70-74		Real estate, renting and business activities	..	..	..	..	..	..	..	..
L-Q	75-99		Public admin.; education; health; other services	..	..	..	..	..	..	..	..
A-Q	01-99		Grand total	..	..	..	56 571	55 490	56 923	..	..

Table IT.11 HEURES OUVRÉES - HOURS WORKED

Milliers

CITI révision 3

1989	1990	1991	1992	1993	1994	1995	1996			
..	..	..	..	..	..	..	..	Agriculture, chasse et sylviculture	A	01-02
..	..	..	..	..	..	..	..	Pêche	B	05
..	..	..	25 267	24 495	23 724	..	..	Activités extractives	C	10-14
..	..	..	..	..	..	..	..	Extraction de charbon, de lignite et de tourbe		10
..	..	..	5 375	4 873	5 309	..	..	Extraction de pétrole brut et de gaz naturel		11
..	..	..	568	886	872	..	..	Extraction de minerais métalliques		13
..	..	..	19 324	18 736	17 543	..	..	Autres activités extractives		14
..	..	..	3 402 887	3 218 757	3 380 003	..	..	Activités de fabrication	D	15-37
..	..	..	271 216	266 595	261 424	..	..	Produits alimentaires et boissons		15
..	..	..	30 474	31 309	30 802	..	..	Boissons		155
..	..	..	20 135	19 379	15 631	..	..	Produits à base de tabac	16	160
..	..	..	275 250	266 591	274 374	..	..	Textiles	17	
..	..	..	170 212	165 287	171 361	..	..	Filature, tissage et achèvement des textiles		171
..	..	..	36 349	35 412	35 215	..	..	Autres articles textiles		172
..	..	..	68 689	65 892	67 798	..	..	Etoffes et articles de bonneterie		173
..	..	..	233 039	221 157	215 095	..	..	Habillement; préparation, teinture des fourrures	18	
..	..	..	230 902	219 232	213 285	..	..	Articles d'habillement autres qu'en fourrure		181
..	..	..	2 137	1 925	1 810	..	..	Préparation, teinture des fourrures; art. en fourrure		182
..	..	..	159 988	152 864	157 811	..	..	Travail des cuirs; articles en cuir; chaussures	19	
..	..	..	46 330	40 094	42 811	..	..	Apprêt et tannage des cuirs et articles en cuirs		191
..	..	..	113 658	112 770	115 000	..	..	Chaussures		192
..	..	..	57 777	55 843	58 269	..	..	Bois et articles en bois et liège (sauf meubles)	20	
..	..	..	5 346	5 391	6 002	..	..	Sciage et rabotage du bois		201
..	..	..	52 431	50 452	52 267	..	..	Articles en bois, liège, vannerie, sparterie		202
..	..	..	82 341	83 093	82 713	..	..	Papier et carton; articles en papier et en carton	21	
..	..	..	82 318	82 683	80 763	..	..	Edition, imprimerie et reproduction	22	
..	..	..	16 910	16 416	14 494	..	..	Edition		221
..	..	..	64 635	65 322	65 353	..	..	Imprimerie et activités annexes		222
..	..	..	773	945	916	..	..	Reproduction de supports enregistrés		223
..	..	..	19 463	17 447	19 100	..	..	Cokéfaction; prod. pétroliers; comb. nucléaires	23	
..	..	..	153 124	142 387	139 137	..	..	Produits chimiques	24	
..	..	..	54 904	50 708	49 445	..	..	Produits chimiques de base		241
..	..	..	82 994	75 990	74 568	..	..	Autres produits chimiques		242
..	..	..	15 226	15 689	15 124	..	..	Fibres synthétiques ou artificielles		243
..	..	..	138 618	139 587	146 237	..	..	Articles en caoutchouc et en matières plastiques	25	
..	..	..	42 944	38 624	40 212	..	..	Articles en caoutchouc		251
..	..	..	95 674	100 963	106 025	..	..	Articles en matières plastiques		252
..	..	..	215 806	202 964	194 455	..	..	Autres produits minéraux non métalliques	26	
..	..	..	38 599	37 874	35 551	..	..	Verre et articles en verre		261
..	..	..	177 207	165 090	158 904	..	..	Produits minéraux non métalliques, nca		269
..	..	..	176 527	142 394	159 668	..	..	Produits métallurgiques de base	27	
..	..	..	113 492	80 495	96 197	..	..	Sidérurgie et première transformation de l'acier		271
..	..	..	25 519	27 440	26 126	..	..	Métallurgie; métaux précieux et non ferreux		272
..	..	..	37 516	34 459	37 345	..	..	Fonderie		273
..	..	..	310 236	301 498	417 819	..	..	Ouvrages en métaux, sauf machines et matériel	28	
..	..	..	114 227	104 366	101 820	..	..	Constr. et menuiserie métal.; réservoirs; générateurs		281
..	..	..	196 009	197 132	315 999	..	..	Autres ouvrages en métaux		289
..	..	..	396 792	385 835	405 378	..	..	Machines et matériel, nca	29	
..	..	..	147 672	145 488	161 440	..	..	Machines d'usage général		291
..	..	..	181 409	173 068	170 303	..	..	Machines d'usage spécifique		292
..	..	..	67 711	67 279	73 635	..	..	Appareils domestiques, nca		293
..	..	..	9 778	9 610	9 679	..	..	Mach. de bureau, comptables, matériel inform.	30	
..	..	..	177 050	155 832	149 972	..	..	Machines et appareils électriques, nca	31	
..	..	..	38 871	33 585	30 756	..	..	Moteurs, génératrices et transformateurs électriques		311
..	..	..	28 431	27 506	27 253	..	..	Matériel de distribution et de commande		312
..	..	..	19 027	16 302	14 997	..	..	Fils et câbles électriques isolés		313
..	..	..	4 272	3 352	3 816	..	..	Accumulateurs, piles électriques		314
..	..	..	12 501	11 746	11 014	..	..	Lampes électriques et appareils d'éclairage		315
..	..	..	73 948	63 341	62 136	..	..	Autres matériels électriques, nca		319
..	..	..	66 936	64 644	66 997	..	..	Equip. et appar. de radio, TV, communication	32	
..	..	..	22 022	21 092	24 393	..	..	Tubes et valves électroniques; autres composants		321
..	..	..	38 094	37 820	34 842	..	..	Emetteurs radio et TV; app. téléphonie, télégraphie		322
..	..	..	6 820	5 732	7 762	..	..	Récepteurs radio et TV et articles associés		323
..	..	..	51 173	51 909	49 362	..	..	Instruments médicaux, de précision, d'optique	33	
..	..	..	34 057	33 696	30 479	..	..	Appareils médicaux et de précision		331
..	..	..	15 852	17 039	17 939	..	..	Instruments d'optique ; matériel photographique		332
..	..	..	1 264	1 174	944	..	..	Horlogerie		333
..	..	..	220 921	188 215	208 426	..	..	Véhicules automobiles et nemorques	34	
..	..	..	118 906	107 388	100 718	..	..	Autres matériels de transport	35	
..	..	..	27 497	24 735	21 571	..	..	Construction et réparation de navires		351
..	..	..	35 466	32 573	30 201	..	..	Construction de matériel ferroviaire roulant		352
..	..	..	33 524	28 870	27 565	..	..	Construction aéronautique et spatiale		353
..	..	..	22 419	21 210	21 381	..	..	Autres équipements de transport		359
..	..	..	164 019	159 335	163 826	..	..	Meubles; activités de fabrication, nca	36	
..	..	..	118 282	114 505	118 645	..	..	Meubles		361
..	..	..	45 737	44 830	45 181	..	..	Activités de fabrication, nca		369
..	..	..	1 474	1 507	3 149	..	..	Récupération	37	
..	..	..	121 966	118 232	112 401	..	..	Production et distrib. d'électricité, de gaz, d'eau	E	40-41
..	..	..	109 510	105 489	99 732	..	..	Electricité, gaz, vapeur et eau chaude		40
..	..	..	88 277	84 647	78 742	..	..	Production, collecte et distribution d'électricité		401
..	..	..	12 456	12 743	12 669	..	..	Captage, épuration et distribution d'eau	41	410
..	..	..	482 194	528 841	382 000	..	..	Construction	F	45
..	..	..	..	..	..	..	..	Commerce de gros et de détail; réparation	G	50-52
..	..	..	..	..	..	..	..	Hôtels et restaurants	H	55
..	..	..	..	..	..	..	..	Transports, entreposage et communications	I	60-64
..	..	..	..	..	..	..	..	Intermédiation financière	J	65-67
..	..	..	..	..	..	..	..	Immobilier, locations, services aux entreprises	K	70-74
..	..	..	..	..	..	..	..	Admin. publique; éducation; santé; autres	L-Q	75-99
..	..	..	4 032 314	3 890 325	3 898 128	..	..	Grand total	A-Q	01-99

Statistiques des Structures Industrielles
OCDE, © 1998

Table JN.1 PRODUCTION - PRODUCTION

Billions of ¥ (Current Prices)

ISIC revision 3			1989	1990	1991	1992	1993	1994	1995	1996
A	01-02	**Agriculture, hunting and forestry**	..	..	..	..	..	..	..	..
B	05	**Fishing**	..	..	..	..	..	..	..	..
C	10-14	**Mining and quarrying**	..	..	..	..	..	..	..	..
	10	Mining of coal and lignite; extraction of peat	..	..	..	..	..	424	..	..
	11	Crude petroleum & natural gas; related service activ.	..	..	..	..	..	94	..	..
	13	Mining of metal ores	..	..	..	..	..	91	..	..
	14	Other mining and quarrying	..	..	..	..	..	238	..	..
D	15-37	**Total manufacturing**	..	..	..	..	..	..	..	..
	15	**Food products and beverages**	..	..	..	..	..	298 112	306 731	..
	155	Beverages	..	..	..	..	..	32 108	32 198	..
	16	**Tobacco products**	..	..	..	..	..	6 722	6 702	..
	160		..	..	..	..	..	2 290	2 252	..
	17	**Textiles**	..	..	..	..	..	7 311	6 953	..
	171	Spinning, weaving and finishing of textiles	..	..	..	..	..	3 298	3 047	..
	172	Other textiles	..	..	..	..	..	2 223	2 199	..
	173	Knitted and crocheted fabrics and articles	..	..	..	..	..	1 789	1 707	..
	18	**Wearing apparel dressing & dyeing of fur**	..	..	..	..	..	2 718	2 581	..
	181	Wearing apparel, except fur apparel	..	..	..	..	..	2 704	2 568	..
	182	Dressing and dyeing of fur; articles of fur	..	..	..	..	..	14	13	..
	19	**Tanning, dressing leather; leather artic.; footwear**	..	..	..	..	..	1 253	1 310	..
	191	Tanning, dressing leather; manuf. of leather articles	..	..	..	..	..	615	601	..
	192	Footwear	..	..	..	..	..	638	709	..
	20	**Wood and cork products, ex. furniture**	..	..	..	..	..	5 099	4 976	..
	201	Sawmilling and planing of wood	..	..	..	..	..	2 094	1 973	..
	202	Products of wood, cork, straw & plaiting material	..	..	..	..	..	3 005	3 003	..
	21	**Paper and paper products**	..	..	..	..	..	8 068	8 468	..
	22	**Publishing, printing & reprod. of recorded media**	..	..	..	..	..	12 715	13 323	..
	221	Publishing	..	..	..	..	..	4 620	4 825	..
	222	Printing and related service activities	..	..	..	..	..	7 869	8 232	..
	223	Reproduction of recorded media	..	..	..	..	..	225	266	..
	23	**Coke, refined petroleum products & nuclear fuel**	..	..	..	..	..	7 868	7 688	..
	24	**Chemicals and chemical products**	..	..	..	..	..	22 413	23 389	..
	241	Basic chemicals	..	..	..	..	..	8 390	8 995	..
	242	Other chemical products	..	..	..	..	..	13 143	13 511	..
	243	Man-made fibres	..	..	..	..	..	880	884	..
	25	**Rubber and plastic products**	..	..	..	..	..	13 103	13 401	..
	251	Rubber products	..	..	..	..	..	2 841	3 002	..
	252	Plastic products	..	..	..	..	..	10 263	10 400	..
	26	**Other non-metallic mineral products**	..	..	..	..	..	10 230	10 126	..
	261	Glass and glass products	..	..	..	..	..	1 687	1 593	..
	269	Non-metallic mineral products, nec	..	..	..	..	..	8 544	8 533	..
	27	**Basic metals**	..	..	..	..	..	16 758	17 678	..
	271	Basic iron and steel	..	..	..	..	..	11 693	12 057	..
	272	Basic precious and non-ferrous metals	..	..	..	..	..	3 176	3 624	..
	273	Casting of metals	..	..	..	..	..	1 889	1 996	..
	28	**Fabricated metal products, ex. machin. & equip.**	..	..	..	..	..	19 643	19 931	..
	281	Structural metal prod., tanks, reservoirs, generators	..	..	..	..	..	10 052	10 149	..
	289	Other fabricated metal products & service activities	..	..	..	..	..	9 591	9 782	..
	29	**Machinery and equipment, nec**	..	..	..	..	..	29 232	31 696	..
	291	General purpose machinery	..	..	..	..	..	12 056	12 515	..
	292	Special purpose machinery	..	..	..	..	..	12 193	13 828	..
	293	Domestic appliances, nec	..	..	..	..	..	4 984	5 354	..
	30	**Office, accounting and computing machinery**	..	..	..	..	..	10 565	11 010	..
	31	**Electrical machinery and apparatus, nec**	..	..	..	..	..	15 026	15 407	..
	311	Electric motors, generators and transformers	..	..	..	..	..	2 207	2 369	..
	312	Electricity distribution and control apparatus	..	..	..	..	..	4 316	4 325	..
	313	Insulated wire and cable	..	..	..	..	..	1 719	1 848	..
	314	Accumulators, primary cells and primary batteries	..	..	..	..	..	750	730	..
	315	Electric lamps and lighting equipment	..	..	..	..	..	1 327	1 276	..
	319	Other electrical equipment, nec	..	..	..	..	..	4 708	4 858	..
	32	**Radio, TV, communication equip. & apparatus**	..	..	..	..	..	24 779	27 209	..
	321	Electronic valves, tubes & other electronic compon.	..	..	..	..	..	10 533	11 841	..
	322	TV, radio transmitters & appar. for line teleph., telegr.	..	..	..	..	..	3 576	4 160	..
	323	TV, radio receivers and associated goods	..	..	..	..	..	10 669	11 209	..
	33	**Medical, precision, optical instr.; watches, clocks**	..	..	..	..	..	5 333	5 470	..
	331	Medical equip.; precision instruments and appliances	..	..	..	..	..	3 417	3 710	..
	332	Optical instruments and photographic equipment	..	..	..	..	..	1 188	1 091	..
	333	Watches and clocks	..	..	..	..	..	727	669	..
	34	**Motor vehicles, trailers, and semi-trailers**	..	..	..	..	..	39 507	39 556	..
	35	**Other transport equipment**	..	..	..	..	..	3 828	3 819	..
	351	Building and repairing of ships and boats	..	..	..	..	..	2 162	2 110	..
	352	Railway, tramway locomotives and rolling stock	..	..	..	..	..	366	428	..
	353	Aircraft and spacecraft	..	..	..	..	..	837	839	..
	359	Transport equipment, nec	..	..	..	..	..	463	441	..
	36	**Furniture; manufacturing, nec**	..	..	..	..	..	7 879	7 840	..
	361	Furniture	..	..	..	..	..	2 919	2 909	..
	369	Manufacturing, nec	..	..	..	..	..	4 960	4 931	..
	37	**Recycling**	..	..	..	..	..	385	451	..
E	40-41	**Electricity, gas and water supply**	..	..	..	..	..	..	..	..
	40	**Electricity, gas, steam and hot water supply**	..	..	..	..	..	..	..	..
	401	Production, collection and distribution of electricity	..	..	..	..	..	..	..	..
	41	410	**Collection, purification, distribution of water**	..	..	..	..	..	..	..
F	45	**Construction**	..	..	..	..	..	..	..	..
G	50-52	**Wholesale and retail trade; repairs etc**	..	..	..	..	..	..	..	..
H	55	**Hotels and restaurants**	..	..	..	..	..	..	..	..
I	60-64	**Transport, storage and communications**	..	..	..	..	..	..	..	..
J	65-67	**Financial intermediation**	..	..	..	..	..	..	..	..
K	70-74	**Real estate, renting and business activities**	..	..	..	..	..	..	..	..
L-Q	75-99	**Public admin.; education; health; other services**	..	..	..	..	..	..	..	..
A-Q	01-99	**Grand total**	..	..	..	..	..	..	..	..

Table JN.2 VALEUR AJOUTÉE - VALUE ADDED

Milliards de ¥ *(Prix courants)*

1989	1990	1991	1992	1993	1994	1995	1996		CITI révision 3		
..	..	..	..	..	..	..	..	**Agriculture, chasse et sylviculture**	A	01-02	
..	..	..	..	..	..	..	..	**Pêche**	B	05	
..	..	..	..	..	197	..	..	**Activités extractives**	C	10-14	
..	..	..	..	..	46	..	..	Extraction de charbon, de lignite et de tourbe		10	
..	..	..	..	..	50	..	..	Extraction de pétrole brut et de gaz naturel		11	
..	..	..	..	..	100	..	..	Extraction de minerais métalliques		13	
..	..	..	..	..	..	..	..	Autres activités extractives		14	
..	..	..	..	..	123 750	128 296	..	**Activités de fabrication**	D	15-37	
..	..	..	..	..	12 499	12 859	..	**Produits alimentaires et boissons**		15	
..	..	..	..	..	2 480	2 529	..	Boissons			155
..	..	..	..	..	377	404	..	**Produits à base de tabac**		16	160
..	..	..	..	..	3 288	3 158	..	**Textiles**		17	
..	..	..	..	..	1 550	1 442	..	Filature, tissage et achèvement des textiles			171
..	..	..	..	..	972	981	..	Autres articles textiles			172
..	..	..	..	..	765	735	..	Etoffes et articles de bonneterie			173
..	..	..	..	..	1 477	1 405	..	**Habillement; préparation, teinture des fourrures**		18	
..	..	..	..	..	1 471	1 399	..	Articles d'habillement autres qu'en fourrure			181
..	..	..	..	..	6	6	..	Préparation, teinture des fourrures; art. en fourrure			182
..	..	..	..	..	529	559	..	**Travail des cuirs; articles en cuir; chaussures**		19	
..	..	..	..	..	242	242	..	Apprêt et tannage des cuirs et articles en cuirs			191
..	..	..	..	..	287	317	..	Chaussures			192
..	..	..	..	..	1 999	1 977	..	**Bois et articles en bois et liège (sauf meubles)**		20	
..	..	..	..	..	774	731	..	Sciage et rabotage du bois			201
..	..	..	..	..	1 225	1 246	..	Articles en bois, liège, vannerie, sparterie			202
..	..	..	..	..	3 465	3 629	..	**Papier et carton; articles en papier et en carton**		21	
..	..	..	..	..	7 011	7 295	..	**Edition, imprimerie et reproduction**		22	
..	..	..	..	..	2 913	3 032	..	Edition			221
..	..	..	..	..	3 935	4 094	..	Imprimerie et activités annexes			222
..	..	..	..	..	163	168	..	Reproduction de supports enregistrés			223
..	..	..	..	..	2 030	1 691	..	**Cokéfaction; prod. pétroliers; comb. nucléaires**		23	
..	..	..	..	..	12 555	13 125	..	**Produits chimiques**		24	
..	..	..	..	..	4 268	4 597	..	Produits chimiques de base			241
..	..	..	..	..	7 838	8 089	..	Autres produits chimiques			242
..	..	..	..	..	448	440	..	Fibres synthétiques ou artificielles			243
..	..	..	..	..	6 052	6 147	..	**Articles en caoutchouc et en matières plastiques**		25	
..	..	..	..	..	1 499	1 530	..	Articles en caoutchouc			251
..	..	..	..	..	4 553	4 617	..	Articles en matières plastiques			252
..	..	..	..	..	5 530	5 434	..	**Autres produits minéraux non métalliques**		26	
..	..	..	..	..	1 033	940	..	Verre et articles en verre			261
..	..	..	..	..	4 496	4 495	..	Produits minéraux non métalliques, nca			269
..	..	..	..	..	6 695	7 036	..	**Produits métallurgiques de base**		27	
..	..	..	..	..	4 684	4 899	..	Sidérurgie et première transformation de l'acier			271
..	..	..	..	..	1 030	1 118	..	Métallurgie; métaux précieux et non ferreux			272
..	..	..	..	..	980	1 019	..	Fonderie			273
..	..	..	..	..	9 496	9 681	..	**Ouvrages en métaux, sauf machines et matériel**		28	
..	..	..	..	..	4 680	4 737	..	Constr. et menuiserie métal.; réservoirs; générateurs			281
..	..	..	..	..	4 817	4 944	..	Autres ouvrages en métaux			289
..	..	..	..	..	12 961	13 945	..	**Machines et matériel, nca**		29	
..	..	..	..	..	5 387	5 545	..	Machines d'usage général			291
..	..	..	..	..	5 300	6 005	..	Machines d'usage spécifique			292
..	..	..	..	..	2 273	2 394	..	Appareils domestiques, nca			293
..	..	..	..	..	3 315	3 059	..	**Mach. de bureau, comptables, matériel inform.**		30	
..	..	..	..	..	6 164	6 391	..	**Machines et appareils électriques, nca**		31	
..	..	..	..	..	887	966	..	Moteurs, génératrices et transformateurs électriques			311
..	..	..	..	..	1 893	1 887	..	Matériel électrique de distribution et de commande			312
..	..	..	..	..	498	593	..	Fils et câbles électriques isolés			313
..	..	..	..	..	370	349	..	Accumulateurs, piles électriques			314
..	..	..	..	..	562	536	..	Lampes électriques et appareils d'éclairage			315
..	..	..	..	..	1 953	2 060	..	Autres matériels électriques, nca			319
..	..	..	..	..	9 572	10 868	..	**Equip. et appar. de radio, TV, communication**		32	
..	..	..	..	..	4 531	5 242	..	Tubes et valves électroniques; autres composants			321
..	..	..	..	..	1 312	1 547	..	Emetteurs radio et TV; app. téléphonie, télégraphie			322
..	..	..	..	..	3 729	4 079	..	Récepteurs radio et TV et articles associés			323
..	..	..	..	..	2 328	2 453	..	**Instruments médicaux, de précision, d'optique**		33	
..	..	..	..	..	1 647	1 808	..	Appareils médicaux et de précision			331
..	..	..	..	..	500	453	..	Instruments d'optique ; matériel photographique			332
..	..	..	..	..	181	191	..	Horlogerie			333
..	..	..	..	..	11 260	12 049	..	**Véhicules automobiles et nemorques**		34	
..	..	..	..	..	1 577	1 587	..	**Autres matériels de transport**		35	
..	..	..	..	..	842	811	..	Construction et réparation de navires			351
..	..	..	..	..	164	195	..	Construction de matériel ferroviaire roulant			352
..	..	..	..	..	342	366	..	Construction aéronautique et spatiale			353
..	..	..	..	..	229	215	..	Autres équipements de transport			359
..	..	..	..	..	3 422	3 357	..	**Meubles; activités de fabrication, nca**		36	
..	..	..	..	..	1 312	1 308	..	Meubles			361
..	..	..	..	..	2 110	2 048	..	Activités de fabrication, nca			369
..	..	..	..	..	149	188	..	**Récupération**		37	
..	..	..	..	..	..	..	..	**Production et distrib. d'électricité, de gaz, d'eau**	E	40-41	
..	..	..	..	..	..	..	..	**Electricité, gaz, vapeur et eau chaude**		40	
..	..	..	..	..	..	..	..	Production, collecte et distribution d'électricité			401
..	..	..	..	..	..	..	..	**Captage, épuration et distribution d'eau**		41	410
..	..	..	..	..	..	..	..	**Construction**	F	45	
..	..	..	..	..	..	..	..	**Commerce de gros et de détail; réparation**	G	50-52	
..	..	..	..	..	..	..	..	**Hôtels et restaurants**	H	55	
..	..	..	..	..	..	..	..	**Transports, entreposage et communications**	I	60-64	
..	..	..	..	..	..	..	..	**Intermédiation financière**	J	65-67	
..	..	..	..	..	..	..	..	**Immobilier, locations, services aux entreprises**	K	70-74	
..	..	..	..	..	..	..	..	**Admin. publique; éducation; santé; autres**	L-Q	75-99	
..	..	..	..	..	..	..	..	**Grand total**	A-Q	01-99	

Statistiques des Structures Industrielles
OCDE, © 1998

JAPAN

Table JN.3 INVESTMENT - INVESTISSEMENT

Billions of ¥ (Current Prices)

ISIC revision 3			1989	1990	1991	1992	1993	1994	1995	1996
A	01-02	Agriculture, hunting and forestry	..	..	..	..	..	..	..	..
B	05	Fishing	..	..	..	..	..	..	..	..
C	10-14	Mining and quarrying	..	..	..	..	..	..	..	..
	10	Mining of coal and lignite; extraction of peat	..	..	..	..	..	..	..	..
	11	Crude petroleum & natural gas; related service activ.	..	..	..	..	..	..	..	..
	13	Mining of metal ores	..	..	..	..	..	..	..	..
	14	Other mining and quarrying	..	..	..	..	..	..	..	..
D	15-37	Total manufacturing	..	..	..	..	..	11 316	..	..
	15	Food products and beverages	..	..	..	..	..	1 039	..	..
	155	Beverages	..	..	..	..	..	229	..	..
	16 160	Tobacco products	..	..	..	..	..	30	..	..
	17	Textiles	..	..	..	..	..	176	..	..
	171	Spinning, weaving and finishing of textiles	..	..	..	..	..	105	..	..
	172	Other textiles	..	..	..	..	..	42	..	..
	173	Knitted and crocheted fabrics and articles	..	..	..	..	..	29	..	..
	18	Wearing apparel dressing & dyeing of fur	..	..	..	..	..	33	..	..
	181	Wearing apparel, except fur apparel	..	..	..	..	..	33	..	..
	182	Dressing and dyeing of fur; articles of fur	..	..	..	..	..	..	..	..
	19	Tanning, dressing leather; leather artic.; footwear	..	..	..	..	..	22	..	..
	191	Tanning, dressing leather; manuf. of leather articles	..	..	..	..	..	14	..	..
	192	Footwear	..	..	..	..	..	7	..	..
	20	Wood and cork products, ex. furniture	..	..	..	..	..	76	..	..
	201	Sawmilling and planing of wood	..	..	..	..	..	18	..	..
	202	Products of wood, cork, straw & plaiting material	..	..	..	..	..	58	..	..
	21	Paper and paper products	..	..	..	..	..	381	..	..
	22	Publishing, printing & reprod. of recorded media	..	..	..	..	..	403	..	..
	221	Publishing	..	..	..	..	..	151	..	..
	222	Printing and related service activities	..	..	..	..	..	244	..	..
	223	Reproduction of recorded media	..	..	..	..	..	8	..	..
	23	Coke, refined petroleum products & nuclear fuel	..	..	..	..	..	373	..	..
	24	Chemicals and chemical products	..	..	..	..	..	1 212	..	..
	241	Basic chemicals	..	..	..	..	..	605	..	..
	242	Other chemical products	..	..	..	..	..	524	..	..
	243	Man-made fibres	..	..	..	..	..	83	..	..
	25	Rubber and plastic products	..	..	..	..	..	551	..	..
	251	Rubber products	..	..	..	..	..	137	..	..
	252	Plastic products	..	..	..	..	..	414	..	..
	26	Other non-metallic mineral products	..	..	..	..	..	442	..	..
	261	Glass and glass products	..	..	..	..	..	101	..	..
	269	Non-metallic mineral products, nec	..	..	..	..	..	341	..	..
	27	Basic metals	..	..	..	..	..	1 119	..	..
	271	Basic iron and steel	..	..	..	..	..	858	..	..
	272	Basic precious and non-ferrous metals	..	..	..	..	..	162	..	..
	273	Casting of metals	..	..	..	..	..	100	..	..
	28	Fabricated metal products, ex. machin. & equip.	..	..	..	..	..	580	..	..
	281	Structural metal prod., tanks, reservoirs, generators	..	..	..	..	..	262	..	..
	289	Other fabricated metal products & service activities	..	..	..	..	..	318	..	..
	29	Machinery and equipment, nec	..	..	..	..	..	850	..	..
	291	General purpose machinery	..	..	..	..	..	356	..	..
	292	Special purpose machinery	..	..	..	..	..	308	..	..
	293	Domestic appliances, nec	..	..	..	..	..	186	..	..
	30	Office, accounting and computing machinery	..	..	..	..	..	404	..	..
	31	Electrical machinery and apparatus, nec	..	..	..	..	..	524	..	..
	311	Electric motors, generators and transformers	..	..	..	..	..	48	..	..
	312	Electricity distribution and control apparatus	..	..	..	..	..	105	..	..
	313	Insulated wire and cable	..	..	..	..	..	72	..	..
	314	Accumulators, primary cells and primary batteries	..	..	..	..	..	55	..	..
	315	Electric lamps and lighting equipment	..	..	..	..	..	36	..	..
	319	Other electrical equipment, nec	..	..	..	..	..	208	..	..
	32	Radio, TV, communication equip. & apparatus	..	..	..	..	..	1 242	..	..
	321	Electronic valves, tubes & other electronic compon.	..	..	..	..	..	780	..	..
	322	TV, radio transmitters & appar. for line teleph., telegr.	..	..	..	..	..	83	..	..
	323	TV, radio receivers and associated goods	..	..	..	..	..	379	..	..
	33	Medical, precision, optical instr.; watches, clocks	..	..	..	..	..	159	..	..
	331	Medical equip.; precision instruments and appliances	..	..	..	..	..	92	..	..
	332	Optical instruments and photographic equipment	..	..	..	..	..	37	..	..
	333	Watches and clocks	..	..	..	..	..	30	..	..
	34	Motor vehicles, trailers, and semi-trailers	..	..	..	..	..	1 356	..	..
	35	Other transport equipment	..	..	..	..	..	148	..	..
	351	Building and repairing of ships and boats	..	..	..	..	..	95	..	..
	352	Railway, tramway locomotives and rolling stock	..	..	..	..	..	10	..	..
	353	Aircraft and spacecraft	..	..	..	..	..	30	..	..
	359	Transport equipment, nec	..	..	..	..	..	13	..	..
	36	Furniture; manufacturing, nec	..	..	..	..	..	193	..	..
	361	Furniture	..	..	..	..	..	60	..	..
	369	Manufacturing, nec	..	..	..	..	..	133	..	..
	37	Recycling	..	..	..	..	..	3	..	..
E	40-41	Electricity, gas and water supply	..	..	..	..	..	..	..	..
	40	Electricity, gas, steam and hot water supply	..	..	..	..	..	..	..	..
	401	Production, collection and distribution of electricity	..	..	..	..	..	..	..	..
	41 410	Collection, purification, distribution of water	..	..	..	..	..	..	..	..
F	45	Construction	..	..	..	..	..	..	..	..
G	50-52	Wholesale and retail trade; repairs etc	..	..	..	..	..	..	..	..
H	55	Hotels and restaurants	..	..	..	..	..	..	..	..
I	60-64	Transport, storage and communications	..	..	..	..	..	..	..	..
J	65-67	Financial intermediation	..	..	..	..	..	..	..	..
K	70-74	Real estate, renting and business activities	..	..	..	..	..	..	..	..
L-Q	75-99	Public admin.; education; health; other services	..	..	..	..	..	..	..	..
A-Q	01-99	Grand total	..	..	..	..	..	..	..	..

Table JN.4 ETABLISSEMENTS - ESTABLISHMENTS

Unités

1989	1990	1991	1992	1993	1994	1995	1996		CITI révision 3	
..	..	..	..	..	..	..	..	**Agriculture, chasse et sylviculture**	A	01-02
..	..	..	..	..	..	..	..	**Pêche**	B	05
..	..	..	..	..	683	..	..	**Activités extractives**	C	10-14
..	..	..	..	..	19	..	..	Extraction de charbon, de lignite et de tourbe	10	
..	..	..	..	..	53	..	..	Extraction de pétrole brut et de gaz naturel	11	
..	..	..	..	..	611	..	..	Extraction de minerais métalliques	13	
..	..	..	..	..			..	Autres activités extractives	14	
..	..	..	..	..	382 825	387 726	..	**Activités de fabrication**	D	15-37
..	..	..	..	..	46 225	47 245	..	**Produits alimentaires et boissons**	15	
..	..	..	..	..	3 387	3 410	..	Boissons		155
..	..	..	..	..	26	26	..	**Produits à base de tabac**	16	160
..	..	..	..	..	31 279	30 450	..	**Textiles**	17	
..	..	..	..	..	12 326	11 735	..	Filature, tissage et achèvement des textiles		171
..	..	..	..	..	10 055	10 031	..	Autres articles textiles		172
..	..	..	..	..	8 898	8 684	..	Etoffes et articles de bonneterie		173
..	..	..	..	..	20 242	19 283	..	**Habillement; préparation, teinture des fourrures**	18	
..	..	..	..	..	20 166	19 205	..	Articles d'habillement autres qu'en fourrure		181
..	..	..	..	..	76	78	..	Préparation, teinture des fourrures; art. en fourrure		182
..	..	..	..	..	5 412	5 800	..	**Travail des cuirs; articles en cuir; chaussures**	19	
..	..	..	..	..	2 985	2 851	..	Apprêt et tannage des cuirs et articles en cuirs		191
..	..	..	..	..	2 427	2 949	..	Chaussures		192
..	..	..	..	..	23 970	23 844	..	**Bois et articles en bois et liège (sauf meubles)**	20	
..	..	..	..	..	9 887	9 628	..	Sciage et rabotage du bois		201
..	..	..	..	..	14 083	14 216	..	Articles en bois, liège, vannerie, sparterie		202
..	..	..	..	..	10 392	10 538	..	**Papier et carton; articles en papier et en carton**	21	
..	..	..	..	..	26 536	27 235	..	**Edition, imprimerie et reproduction**	22	
..	..	..	..	..	2 307	2 308	..	Edition		221
..	..	..	..	..	24 154	24 837	..	Imprimerie et activités annexes		222
..	..	..	..	..	75	90	..	Reproduction de supports enregistrés		223
..	..	..	..	..	1 076	1 094	..	**Cokéfaction; prod. pétroliers; comb. nucléaires**	23	
..	..	..	..	..	5 232	5 302	..	**Produits chimiques**	24	
..	..	..	..	..	1 217	1 231	..	Produits chimiques de base		241
..	..	..	..	..	3 928	3 979	..	Autres produits chimiques		242
..	..	..	..	..	87	92	..	Fibres synthétiques ou artificielles		243
..	..	..	..	..	22 171	22 909	..	**Articles en caoutchouc et en matières plastiques**	25	
..	..	..	..	..	3 339	3 505	..	Articles en caoutchouc		251
..	..	..	..	..	18 832	19 404	..	Articles en matières plastiques		252
..	..	..	..	..	19 199	19 297	..	**Autres produits minéraux non métalliques**	26	
..	..	..	..	..	1 094	1 104	..	Verre et articles en verre		261
..	..	..	..	..	18 105	18 193	..	Produits minéraux non métalliques, nca		269
..	..	..	..	..	7 658	7 693	..	**Produits métallurgiques de base**	27	
..	..	..	..	..	3 143	3 156	..	Sidérurgie et première transformation de l'acier		271
..	..	..	..	..	1 131	1 155	..	Métallurgie; métaux précieux et non ferreux		272
..	..	..	..	..	3 384	3 382	..	Fonderie		273
..	..	..	..	..	48 450	49 830	..	**Ouvrages en métaux, sauf machines et matériel**	28	
..	..	..	..	..	21 681	22 505	..	Constr. et menuiserie métal.; réservoirs; générateurs		281
..	..	..	..	..	26 769	27 325	..	Autres ouvrages en métaux		289
..	..	..	..	..	41 101	42 990	..	**Machines et matériel, nca**	29	
..	..	..	..	..	15 060	15 801	..	Machines d'usage général		291
..	..	..	..	..	22 705	23 841	..	Machines d'usage spécifique		292
..	..	..	..	..	3 336	3 348	..	Appareils domestiques, nca		293
..	..	..	..	..	3 124	3 075	..	**Mach. de bureau, comptables, matériel inform.**	30	
..	..	..	..	..	14 473	14 608	..	**Machines et appareils électriques, nca**	31	
..	..	..	..	..	2 665	2 708	..	Moteurs, génératrices et transformateurs électriques		311
..	..	..	..	..	5 162	5 189	..	Matériel électrique de distribution et de commande		312
..	..	..	..	..	598	625	..	Fils et câbles électriques isolés		313
..	..	..	..	..	197	212	..	Accumulateurs, piles électriques		314
..	..	..	..	..	1 374	1 386	..	Lampes électriques et appareils d'éclairage		315
..	..	..	..	..	4 477	4 488	..	Autres matériels électriques, nca		319
..	..	..	..	..	11 961	11 832	..	**Equip. et appar. de radio, TV, communication**	32	
..	..	..	..	..	2 592	2 697	..	Tubes et valves électroniques; autres composants		321
..	..	..	..	..	482	507	..	Emetteurs radio et TV; app. téléphonie, télégraphie		322
..	..	..	..	..	8 887	8 628	..	Récepteurs radio et TV et articles associés		323
..	..	..	..	..	7 051	7 064	..	**Instruments médicaux, de précision, d'optique**	33	
..	..	..	..	..	4 525	4 608	..	Appareils médicaux et de précision		331
..	..	..	..	..	2 018	1 984	..	Instruments d'optique ; matériel photographique		332
..	..	..	..	..	508	472	..	Horlogerie		333
..	..	..	..	..	10 467	10 648	..	**Véhicules automobiles et nemorques**	34	
..	..	..	..	..	2 756	2 805	..	**Autres matériels de transport**	35	
..	..	..	..	..	1 334	1 365	..	Construction et réparation de navires		351
..	..	..	..	..	406	436	..	Construction de matériel ferroviaire roulant		352
..	..	..	..	..	217	221	..	Construction aéronautique et spatiale		353
..	..	..	..	..	799	783	..	Autres équipements de transport		359
..	..	..	..	..	23 332	23 444	..	**Meubles; activités de fabrication, nca**	36	
..	..	..	..	..	9 537	9 433	..	Meubles		361
..	..	..	..	..	13 795	14 011	..	Activités de fabrication, nca		369
..	..	..	..	..	692	714	..	**Récupération**	37	
..	..	..	..	..	..	..	..	**Production et distrib. d'électricité, de gaz, d'eau**	E	40-41
..	..	..	..	..	..	..	..	**Electricité, gaz, vapeur et eau chaude**	40	
..	..	..	..	..			..	Production, collecte et distribution d'électricité		401
..	..	..	..	..	16 121	15 980	..	**Captage, épuration et distribution d'eau**	41	410
..	..	..	..	..	..	..	..	**Construction**	F	45
..	..	..	..	..	..	..	..	**Commerce de gros et de détail; réparation**	G	50-52
..	..	..	..	..	..	..	..	**Hôtels et restaurants**	H	55
..	..	..	..	..	..	..	..	**Transports, entreposage et communications**	I	60-64
..	..	..	..	..	..	..	..	**Intermédiation financière**	J	65-67
..	..	..	..	..	..	..	..	**Immobilier, locations, services aux entreprises**	K	70-74
..	..	..	..	..	..	..	..	**Admin. publique; éducation; santé; autres**	L-Q	75-99
..	..	..	..	..	..	..	..	**Grand total**	A-Q	01-99

Statistiques des Structures Industrielles
OCDE, © 1998

Table JN.5 EMPLOYMENT - EMPLOI

Thousands

ISIC revision 3			1989	1990	1991	1992	1993	1994	1995	1996
A	01-02	Agriculture, hunting and forestry	..	..	..	..	..	..	..	..
B	05	Fishing	..	..	..	..	..	..	..	..
C	10-14	Mining and quarrying	..	..	..	..	..	19.0	..	..
	10	Mining of coal and lignite; extraction of peat	..	..	..	..	..	6.0	..	..
	11	Crude petroleum & natural gas; related service activ.	..	..	..	..	..	2.0	..	..
	13	Mining of metal ores	..	..	..	..	..	..	..	..
	14	Other mining and quarrying	..	..	..	..	..	12.0	..	..
D	15-37	Total manufacturing	..	..	..	..	..	10 416.0	10 321.0	..
	15	Food products and beverages	..	..	..	..	..	1 225.0	1 249.0	..
		155 Beverages	..	..	..	..	..	89.0	89.0	..
	16	160 Tobacco products	..	..	..	..	..	8.0	8.0	..
	17	Textiles	..	..	..	..	..	518.0	491.0	..
		171 Spinning, weaving and finishing of textiles	..	..	..	..	..	218.0	200.0	..
		172 Other textiles	..	..	..	..	..	139.0	137.0	..
		173 Knitted and crocheted fabrics and articles	..	..	..	..	..	161.0	154.0	..
	18	Wearing apparel dressing & dyeing of fur	..	..	..	..	..	407.0	374.0	..
		181 Wearing apparel, except fur apparel	..	..	..	..	..	406.0	373.0	..
		182 Dressing and dyeing of fur; articles of fur	..	..	..	..	..	1.0	1.0	..
	19	Tanning, dressing leather; leather artic.; footwear	..	..	..	..	..	83.0	86.0	..
		191 Tanning, dressing leather; manuf. of leather articles	..	..	..	..	..	36.0	34.0	..
		192 Footwear	..	..	..	..	..	47.0	52.0	..
	20	Wood and cork products, ex. furniture	..	..	..	..	..	275.0	270.0	..
		201 Sawmilling and planing of wood	..	..	..	..	..	108.0	104.0	..
		202 Products of wood, cork, straw & plaiting material	..	..	..	..	..	167.0	167.0	..
	21	Paper and paper products	..	..	..	..	..	269.0	268.0	..
	22	Publishing, printing & reprod. of recorded media	..	..	..	..	..	542.0	548.0	..
		221 Publishing	..	..	..	..	..	115.0	114.0	..
		222 Printing and related service activities	..	..	..	..	..	421.0	427.0	..
		223 Reproduction of recorded media	..	..	..	..	..	6.0	6.0	..
	23	Coke, refined petroleum products & nuclear fuel	..	..	..	..	..	37.0	37.0	..
	24	Chemicals and chemical products	..	..	..	..	..	398.0	392.0	..
		241 Basic chemicals	..	..	..	..	..	124.0	120.0	..
		242 Other chemical products	..	..	..	..	..	249.0	248.0	..
		243 Man-made fibres	..	..	..	..	..	25.0	23.0	..
	25	Rubber and plastic products	..	..	..	..	..	567.0	572.0	..
		251 Rubber products	..	..	..	..	..	128.0	128.0	..
		252 Plastic products	..	..	..	..	..	439.0	445.0	..
	26	Other non-metallic mineral products	..	..	..	..	..	430.0	426.0	..
		261 Glass and glass products	..	..	..	..	..	56.0	55.0	..
		269 Non-metallic mineral products, nec	..	..	..	..	..	374.0	371.0	..
	27	Basic metals	..	..	..	..	..	390.0	379.0	..
		271 Basic iron and steel	..	..	..	..	..	231.0	218.0	..
		272 Basic precious and non-ferrous metals	..	..	..	..	..	67.0	69.0	..
		273 Casting of metals	..	..	..	..	..	92.0	92.0	..
	28	Fabricated metal products, ex. machin. & equip.	..	..	..	..	..	882.0	882.0	..
		281 Structural metal prod., tanks, reservoirs, generators	..	..	..	..	..	382.0	383.0	..
		289 Other fabricated metal products & service activities	..	..	..	..	..	500.0	498.0	..
	29	Machinery and equipment, nec	..	..	..	..	..	1 127.0	1 135.0	..
		291 General purpose machinery	..	..	..	..	..	456.0	455.0	..
		292 Special purpose machinery	..	..	..	..	..	515.0	525.0	..
		293 Domestic appliances, nec	..	..	..	..	..	156.0	156.0	..
	30	Office, accounting and computing machinery	..	..	..	..	..	225.0	220.0	..
	31	Electrical machinery and apparatus, nec	..	..	..	..	..	613.0	598.0	..
		311 Electric motors, generators and transformers	..	..	..	..	..	108.0	108.0	..
		312 Electricity distribution and control apparatus	..	..	..	..	..	182.0	177.0	..
		313 Insulated wire and cable	..	..	..	..	..	46.0	46.0	..
		314 Accumulators, primary cells and primary batteries	..	..	..	..	..	23.0	22.0	..
		315 Electric lamps and lighting equipment	..	..	..	..	..	51.0	50.0	..
		319 Other electrical equipment, nec	..	..	..	..	..	202.0	195.0	..
	32	Radio, TV, communication equip. & apparatus	..	..	..	..	..	871.0	871.0	..
		321 Electronic valves, tubes & other electronic compon.	..	..	..	..	..	350.0	351.0	..
		322 TV, radio transmitters & appar. for line teleph., telegr.	..	..	..	..	..	87.0	90.0	..
		323 TV, radio receivers and associated goods	..	..	..	..	..	434.0	429.0	..
	33	Medical, precision, optical instr.; watches, clocks	..	..	..	..	..	255.0	247.0	..
		331 Medical equip.; precision instruments and appliances	..	..	..	..	..	156.0	157.0	..
		332 Optical instruments and photographic equipment	..	..	..	..	..	69.0	63.0	..
		333 Watches and clocks	..	..	..	..	..	30.0	27.0	..
	34	Motor vehicles, trailers, and semi-trailers	..	..	..	..	..	789.0	770.0	..
	35	Other transport equipment	..	..	..	..	..	115.0	116.0	..
		351 Building and repairing of ships and boats	..	..	..	..	..	57.0	57.0	..
		352 Railway, tramway locomotives and rolling stock	..	..	..	..	..	15.0	17.0	..
		353 Aircraft and spacecraft	..	..	..	..	..	27.0	26.0	..
		359 Transport equipment, nec	..	..	..	..	..	17.0	16.0	..
	36	Furniture; manufacturing, nec	..	..	..	..	..	380.0	370.0	..
		361 Furniture	..	..	..	..	..	160.0	155.0	..
		369 Manufacturing, nec	..	..	..	..	..	219.0	215.0	..
	37	Recycling	..	..	..	..	..	10.0	11.0	..
E	40-41	Electricity, gas and water supply	..	..	..	..	..	..	..	..
	40	Electricity, gas, steam and hot water supply	..	..	..	..	..	..	..	..
		401 Production, collection and distribution of electricity	..	..	..	..	..	..	..	..
	41	410 Collection, purification, distribution of water	..	..	..	..	..	..	..	..
F	45	Construction	..	..	..	..	..	..	..	..
G	50-52	Wholesale and retail trade; repairs etc	..	..	..	..	..	..	..	..
H	55	Hotels and restaurants	..	..	..	..	..	..	..	..
I	60-64	Transport, storage and communications	..	..	..	..	..	..	..	..
J	65-67	Financial intermediation	..	..	..	..	..	..	..	..
K	70-74	Real estate, renting and business activities	..	..	..	..	..	..	..	..
L-Q	75-99	Public admin.; education; health; other services	..	..	..	..	..	..	..	..
A-Q	01-99	Grand total	..	..	..	..	..	..	..	..

Table JN.6 SALAIRES ET TRAITEMENTS, SALARIÉS - WAGES AND SALARIES, EMPLOYEES

Milliards de ¥ *(Prix courants)*

1989	1990	1991	1992	1993	1994	1995	1996		Description		CITI révision 3	
..	..	..	..	..	..	..	..		Agriculture, chasse et sylviculture	A	01-02	
..	..	..	..	..	..	..	..		Pêche	B	05	
..	..	..	..	..	105	..	..		Activités extractives	C	10-14	
..	..	..	..	..	36	..	..		Extraction de charbon, de lignite et de tourbe		10	
..	..	..	..	..	11	..	..		Extraction de pétrole brut et de gaz naturel		11	
..	..	..	..	..	58	..	..		Extraction de minerais métalliques		13	
..	..	..	..	..	..	..	..		Autres activités extractives		14	
..	..	..	..	..	44 603	44 931	..		Activités de fabrication	D	15-37	
..	..	..	..	..	3 798	3 901	..		Produits alimentaires et boissons		15	
..	..	..	..	..	397	405	..		Boissons			155
..	..	..	..	..	55	58	..		Produits à base de tabac		16	160
..	..	..	..	..	1 567	1 511	..		Textiles		17	
..	..	..	..	..	760	712	..		Filature, tissage et achèvement des textiles			171
..	..	..	..	..	426	428	..		Autres articles textiles			172
..	..	..	..	..	381	370	..		Etoffes et articles de bonneterie			173
..	..	..	..	..	857	795	..		Habillement; préparation, teinture des fourrures		18	
..	..	..	..	..	854	792	..		Articles d'habillement autres qu'en fourrure			181
..	..	..	..	..	3	3	..		Préparation, teinture des fourrures; art. en fourrure			182
..	..	..	..	..	258	265	..		Travail des cuirs; articles en cuir; chaussures		19	
..	..	..	..	..	116	110	..		Apprêt et tannage des cuirs et articles en cuirs			191
..	..	..	..	..	142	155	..		Chaussures			192
..	..	..	..	..	912	909	..		Bois et articles en bois et liège (sauf meubles)		20	
..	..	..	..	..	347	340	..		Sciage et rabotage du bois			201
..	..	..	..	..	565	568	..		Articles en bois, liège, vannerie, sparterie			202
..	..	..	..	..	1 166	1 175	..		Papier et carton; articles en papier et en carton		21	
..	..	..	..	..	2 810	2 862	..		Edition, imprimerie et reproduction		22	
..	..	..	..	..	948	964	..		Edition			221
..	..	..	..	..	1 833	1 869	..		Imprimerie et activités annexes			222
..	..	..	..	..	29	29	..		Reproduction de supports enregistrés			223
..	..	..	..	..	259	259	..		Cokéfaction; prod. pétroliers; comb. nucléaires		23	
..	..	..	..	..	2 320	2 315	..		Produits chimiques		24	
..	..	..	..	..	783	768	..		Produits chimiques de base			241
..	..	..	..	..	1 398	1 412	..		Autres produits chimiques			242
..	..	..	..	..	139	136	..		Fibres synthétiques ou artificielles			243
..	..	..	..	..	2 336	2 393	..		Articles en caoutchouc et en matières plastiques		25	
..	..	..	..	..	598	608	..		Articles en caoutchouc			251
..	..	..	..	..	1 739	1 785	..		Articles en matières plastiques			252
..	..	..	..	..	1 853	1 862	..		Autres produits minéraux non métalliques		26	
..	..	..	..	..	282	273	..		Verre et articles en verre			261
..	..	..	..	..	1 571	1 589	..		Produits minéraux non métalliques, nca			269
..	..	..	..	..	2 293	2 247	..		Produits métallurgiques de base		27	
..	..	..	..	..	1 501	1 436	..		Sidérurgie et première transformation de l'acier			271
..	..	..	..	..	380	383	..		Métallurgie; métaux précieux et non ferreux			272
..	..	..	..	..	412	428	..		Fonderie			273
..	..	..	..	..	3 940	3 956	..		Ouvrages en métaux, sauf machines et matériel		28	
..	..	..	..	..	1 798	1 810	..		Constr. et menuiserie métal.; réservoirs; générateurs			281
..	..	..	..	..	2 142	2 146	..		Autres ouvrages en métaux			289
..	..	..	..	..	5 528	5 631	..		Machines et matériel, nca		29	
..	..	..	..	..	2 304	2 322	..		Machines d'usage général			291
..	..	..	..	..	2 559	2 624	..		Machines d'usage spécifique			292
..	..	..	..	..	665	685	..		Appareils domestiques, nca			293
..	..	..	..	..	1 005	1 022	..		Mach. de bureau, comptables, matériel inform.		30	
..	..	..	..	..	2 664	2 657	..		Machines et appareils électriques, nca		31	
..	..	..	..	..	475	493	..		Moteurs, génératrices et transformateurs électriques			311
..	..	..	..	..	836	819	..		Matériel électrique de distribution et de commande			312
..	..	..	..	..	239	248	..		Fils et câbles électriques isolés			313
..	..	..	..	..	114	113	..		Accumulateurs, piles électriques			314
..	..	..	..	..	214	212	..		Lampes électriques et appareils d'éclairage			315
..	..	..	..	..	786	772	..		Autres matériels électriques, nca			319
..	..	..	..	..	3 629	3 776	..		Equip. et appar. de radio, TV, communication		32	
..	..	..	..	..	1 586	1 628	..		Tubes et valves électroniques; autres composants			321
..	..	..	..	..	428	466	..		Emetteurs radio et TV; app. téléphonie, télégraphie			322
..	..	..	..	..	1 614	1 682	..		Récepteurs radio et TV et articles associés			323
..	..	..	..	..	1 144	1 121	..		Instruments médicaux, de précision, d'optique		33	
..	..	..	..	..	745	759	..		Appareils médicaux et de précision			331
..	..	..	..	..	273	254	..		Instruments d'optique ; matériel photographique			332
..	..	..	..	..	126	109	..		Horlogerie			333
..	..	..	..	..	4 113	4 137	..		Véhicules automobiles et nemorques		34	
..	..	..	..	..	633	636	..		Autres matériels de transport		35	
..	..	..	..	..	322	311	..		Construction et réparation de navires			351
..	..	..	..	..	84	98	..		Construction de matériel ferroviaire roulant			352
..	..	..	..	..	157	159	..		Construction aéronautique et spatiale			353
..	..	..	..	..	69	67	..		Autres équipements de transport			359
..	..	..	..	..	1 416	1 389	..		Meubles; activités de fabrication, nca		36	
..	..	..	..	..	591	583	..		Meubles			361
..	..	..	..	..	825	806	..		Activités de fabrication, nca			369
..	..	..	..	..	48	54	..		Récupération		37	
..	..	..	..	..	..	..	..		Production et distrib. d'électricité, de gaz, d'eau	E	40-41	
..	..	..	..	..	..	..	..		Electricité, gaz, vapeur et eau chaude		40	
..	..	..	..	..	..	..	..		Production, collecte et distribution d'électricité			401
..	..	..	..	..	..	..	..		Captage, épuration et distribution d'eau		41	410
..	..	..	..	..	..	..	..		Construction	F	45	
..	..	..	..	..	..	..	..		Commerce de gros et de détail; réparation	G	50-52	
..	..	..	..	..	..	..	..		Hôtels et restaurants	H	55	
..	..	..	..	..	..	..	..		Transports, entreposage et communications	I	60-64	
..	..	..	..	..	..	..	..		Intermédiation financière	J	65-67	
..	..	..	..	..	..	..	..		Immobilier, locations, services aux entreprises	K	70-74	
..	..	..	..	..	..	..	..		Admin. publique; éducation; santé; autres	L-Q	75-99	
..	..	..	..	..	..	..	..		Grand total	A-Q	01-99	

Statistiques des Structures Industrielles
OCDE, © 1998

KOREA

Table KR.1 PRODUCTION - PRODUCTION

Millions of Won (Current Prices)

ISIC revision 3		Description	1989	1990	1991	1992	1993	1994	1995	1996
A	01-02	Agriculture, hunting and forestry	..	..	..	..	..	..	..	..
B	05	Fishing	..	..	..	..	..	..	..	..
C	10-14	Mining and quarrying	..	2 178 371	2 206 188	1 979 918	1 849 908	1 767 686	1 740 513	..
	10	Mining of coal and lignite; extraction of peat	..	1 549 847	1 284 128	1 012 542	756 991	595 910	424 301	..
	11	Crude petroleum & natural gas; related service activ.	..	..	..	..	..	..	..	..
	13	Mining of metal ores	..	56 486	62 219	54 781	37 498	35 431	34 398	..
	14	Other mining and quarrying	..	572 038	859 841	912 595	1 055 419	1 136 345	1 281 814	..
D	15-37	Total manufacturing	..	176 439 723	205 699 006	226 816 626	255 926 066	299 246 191	364 821 270	..
	15	Food products and beverages	..	14 808 011	17 167 280	19 000 744	20 904 331	23 545 088	26 429 987	..
	155	Beverages	..	2 234 786	3 062 422	3 253 450	3 363 504	4 278 626	4 294 701	..
	16 160	Tobacco products	..	2 580 739	2 974 982	3 037 239	3 223 976	3 254 118	3 379 356	..
	17	Textiles	..	12 488 123	14 311 117	15 885 288	17 284 429	18 174 008	19 765 258	..
	171	Spinning, weaving and finishing of textiles	..	9 352 907	11 024 834	11 987 611	11 900 792	13 038 662	14 757 763	..
	172	Other textiles	..	1 629 264	1 785 600	2 064 389	2 747 012	3 043 129	3 272 369	..
	173	Knitted and crocheted fabrics and articles	..	1 505 952	1 500 683	1 833 288	2 636 625	2 092 217	1 735 126	..
	18	Wearing apparel dressing & dyeing of fur	..	5 633 347	5 921 649	6 047 414	7 767 903	8 813 922	10 812 604	..
	181	Wearing apparel, except fur apparel	..	5 382 272	5 603 214	5 759 637	7 478 540	8 440 956	10 391 772	..
	182	Dressing and dyeing of fur; articles of fur	..	251 075	318 435	287 777	289 363	372 966	420 832	..
	19	Tanning, dressing leather; leather artic.; footwear	..	6 802 118	6 642 851	6 368 120	5 585 091	5 553 985	5 441 433	..
	191	Tanning, dressing leather; manuf. of leather articles	..	2 506 370	2 510 717	2 621 000	2 658 225	2 910 750	2 883 132	..
	192	Footwear	..	4 295 748	4 132 134	3 747 120	2 926 866	2 643 235	2 558 301	..
	20	Wood and cork products, ex. furniture	..	1 756 689	2 150 883	2 171 009	2 731 767	2 913 500	3 121 322	..
	201	Sawmilling and planing of wood	..	768 012	832 971	814 404	1 065 618	1 165 350	1 185 360	..
	202	Products of wood, cork, straw & plaiting material	..	988 677	1 317 912	1 356 605	1 666 149	1 748 150	1 935 962	..
	21	Paper and paper products	..	4 603 203	5 193 134	5 811 911	6 115 412	7 508 571	9 614 828	..
	22	Publishing, printing & reprod. of recorded media	..	3 196 143	3 190 461	3 874 895	4 942 764	5 683 990	6 874 598	..
	221	Publishing	..	1 866 825	2 056 885	2 506 493	3 376 007	3 783 006	4 673 304	..
	222	Printing and related service activities	..	985 333	1 064 755	1 236 087	1 423 996	1 727 937	2 012 311	..
	223	Reproduction of recorded media	..	343 985	68 821	132 315	142 761	173 047	188 983	..
	23	Coke, refined petroleum products & nuclear fuel	..	7 421 834	9 567 178	11 938 107	12 766 450	13 230 778	16 415 970	..
	24	Chemicals and chemical products	..	15 722 324	18 122 323	21 105 790	23 592 873	27 738 282	33 518 623	..
	241	Basic chemicals	..	7 152 007	8 105 575	10 402 930	10 794 566	13 094 946	17 387 167	..
	242	Other chemical products	..	7 114 595	8 135 476	8 912 446	10 258 410	11 336 508	11 649 041	..
	243	Man-made fibres	..	1 455 722	1 881 272	1 790 414	2 539 897	3 306 828	4 482 415	..
	25	Rubber and plastic products	..	6 903 885	7 707 767	8 243 781	9 708 630	11 174 981	14 069 213	..
	251	Rubber products	..	1 840 440	2 143 157	2 378 890	2 742 489	3 060 868	3 508 206	..
	252	Plastic products	..	5 063 445	5 564 610	5 864 891	6 966 141	8 114 113	10 561 007	..
	26	Other non-metallic mineral products	..	7 600 538	10 081 216	11 165 830	12 015 022	13 062 244	15 290 894	..
	261	Glass and glass products	..	1 207 791	1 496 252	1 754 011	1 948 761	2 242 890	2 744 959	..
	269	Non-metallic mineral products, nec	..	6 392 747	8 584 964	9 411 819	10 066 261	10 819 354	12 545 935	..
	27	Basic metals	..	15 577 032	18 168 098	19 136 516	21 435 077	24 911 038	31 007 526	..
	271	Basic iron and steel	..	11 818 664	13 791 537	14 735 772	16 917 007	19 234 063	22 875 681	..
	272	Basic precious and non-ferrous metals	..	3 163 459	3 575 952	3 636 521	3 749 571	4 713 810	7 015 842	..
	273	Casting of metals	..	594 909	800 609	764 223	768 499	963 165	1 116 003	..
	28	Fabricated metal products, ex. machin. & equip.	..	6 286 154	8 574 259	9 206 270	10 801 665	14 008 030	16 957 734	..
	281	Structural metal prod., tanks, reservoirs, generators	..	2 463 644	3 537 337	4 080 900	5 158 260	6 983 935	8 681 388	..
	289	Other fabricated metal products & service activities	..	3 822 510	5 036 922	5 125 370	5 643 405	7 024 095	8 276 346	..
	29	Machinery and equipment, nec	..	13 906 626	17 689 163	17 866 339	20 078 513	24 582 100	30 924 278	..
	291	General purpose machinery	..	3 857 304	5 533 592	6 612 789	7 376 159	9 425 332	13 455 047	..
	292	Special purpose machinery	..	7 264 715	8 475 000	7 623 271	8 547 687	10 338 662	13 282 147	..
	293	Domestic appliances, nec	..	2 784 607	3 680 571	3 630 279	4 154 667	4 818 106	4 187 084	..
	30	Office, accounting and computing machinery	..	1 309 913	1 485 854	1 576 276	3 087 347	3 720 556	5 263 691	..
	31	Electrical machinery and apparatus, nec	..	5 709 151	6 584 394	7 866 935	8 546 351	9 880 754	12 554 570	..
	311	Electric motors, generators and transformers	..	1 607 196	1 565 385	1 959 179	2 362 984	2 547 672	3 113 386	..
	312	Electricity distribution and control apparatus	..	1 427 546	1 914 127	2 210 169	2 334 483	2 789 599	3 618 851	..
	313	Insulated wire and cable	..	1 559 041	1 795 563	2 040 861	2 049 946	2 582 198	3 001 767	..
	314	Accumulators, primary cells and primary batteries	..	269 585	328 705	474 215	367 386	401 982	539 514	..
	315	Electric lamps and lighting equipment	..	323 155	389 983	474 425	612 094	759 908	955 621	..
	319	Other electrical equipment, nec	..	522 608	590 631	708 086	819 104	799 395	1 325 431	..
	32	Radio, TV, communication equip. & apparatus	..	17 738 566	19 732 279	21 523 566	25 811 970	32 923 365	45 890 917	..
	321	Electronic valves, tubes & other electronic compon.	..	5 970 979	6 775 519	7 459 524	10 957 791	14 790 701	24 897 450	..
	322	TV, radio transmitters & appar. for line teleph., telegr.	..	2 432 830	2 421 019	2 861 252	2 727 629	4 176 478	4 627 686	..
	323	TV, radio receivers and associated goods	..	9 334 757	10 535 741	11 202 790	12 126 550	13 956 186	16 365 781	..
	33	Medical, precision, optical instr.; watches, clocks	..	1 666 224	2 054 848	2 158 663	2 610 832	3 220 095	3 807 622	..
	331	Medical equip.; precision instruments and appliances	..	752 231	1 010 104	1 088 416	1 321 317	1 756 280	2 375 880	..
	332	Optical instruments and photographic equipment	..	497 042	493 400	514 020	740 857	923 324	939 496	..
	333	Watches and clocks	..	416 951	551 344	556 227	548 658	540 491	492 246	..
	34	Motor vehicles, trailers, and semi-trailers	..	16 239 285	17 745 997	20 248 773	23 457 427	28 788 727	35 089 516	..
	35	Other transport equipment	..	4 101 904	5 530 912	7 104 406	7 480 792	9 900 494	11 032 792	..
	351	Building and repairing of ships and boats	..	3 282 337	4 372 836	5 887 570	5 918 061	7 534 843	9 199 091	..
	352	Railway, tramway locomotives and rolling stock	..	242 431	193 017	384 912	759 885	1 141 533	616 982	..
	353	Aircraft and spacecraft	..	..	440 669	341 668	330 341	594 804	564 503	..
	359	Transport equipment, nec	..	..	524 390	490 256	472 505	629 314	652 216	..
	36	Furniture; manufacturing, nec	..	4 336 978	5 069 761	5 436 716	5 858 246	6 453 851	7 104 511	..
	361	Furniture	..	1 667 534	2 268 107	2 693 877	2 955 946	3 345 800	3 636 358	..
	369	Manufacturing, nec	..	2 669 444	2 801 654	2 742 839	2 902 300	3 108 051	3 468 153	..
	37	Recycling	..	50 936	32 600	42 038	119 198	203 714	454 027	..
E	40-41	Electricity, gas and water supply	..	..	..	..	..	..	..	..
	40	Electricity, gas, steam and hot water supply	..	..	..	..	..	..	..	..
	401	Production, collection and distribution of electricity	..	..	..	..	..	..	..	..
	41 410	Collection, purification, distribution of water	..	..	..	..	..	..	..	..
F	45	Construction	..	..	..	..	..	..	..	..
G	50-52	Wholesale and retail trade; repairs etc	..	..	..	..	..	..	..	..
H	55	Hotels and restaurants	..	..	..	..	..	..	..	..
I	60-64	Transport, storage and communications	..	..	..	..	..	..	..	..
J	65-67	Financial intermediation	..	..	..	..	..	..	..	..
K	70-74	Real estate, renting and business activities	..	..	..	..	..	..	..	..
L-Q	75-99	Public admin.; education; health; other services	..	..	..	..	..	..	..	..
A-Q	01-99	Grand total	..	..	..	..	..	..	..	..

Table KR.2 VALEUR AJOUTÉE - VALUE ADDED

Millions de Won (Prix courants)

1989	1990	1991	1992	1993	1994	1995	1996			CITI révision 3
..	..	..	..	..	..	..	..	Agriculture, chasse et sylviculture	A	01-02
..	..	..	..	..	..	..	..	Pêche	B	05
..	1 109 386	1 265 130	1 237 648	1 193 393	1 208 790	1 244 548	..	**Activités extractives**	C	10-14
..	675 359	575 528	510 105	348 935	306 464	236 495	..	Extraction de charbon, de lignite et de tourbe		10
..	..	..	..	..	..	..	..	Extraction de pétrole brut et de gaz naturel		11
..	37 467	45 156	44 187	30 270	30 057	29 583	..	Extraction de minerais métalliques		13
..	396 560	644 446	683 356	814 188	872 269	978 470	..	Autres activités extractives		14
..	70 775 119	86 366 481	96 018 026	108 521 742	129 610 868	159 448 345	..	**Activités de fabrication**	D	15-37
..	5 597 254	6 925 216	8 005 391	8 746 335	9 948 876	10 884 639	..	**Produits alimentaires et boissons**		15
..	1 099 545	1 593 100	1 779 520	1 762 938	2 321 474	2 212 097	..	Boissons		155
..	1 977 459	2 210 145	2 134 273	2 176 722	2 225 032	2 527 308	..	**Produits à base de tabac**		16 160
..	4 814 818	6 143 505	7 219 959	7 726 945	8 216 740	8 820 887	..	**Textiles**		17
..	3 534 897	4 781 156	5 437 592	5 364 497	5 913 416	6 683 152	..	Filature, tissage et achèvement des textiles		171
..	671 952	743 941	935 557	1 260 276	1 385 307	1 415 985	..	Autres articles textiles		172
..	607 969	618 408	846 810	1 102 172	918 017	721 750	..	Etoffes et articles de bonneterie		173
..	2 441 295	2 833 333	2 945 354	3 855 188	4 296 242	5 250 871	..	**Habillement; préparation, teinture des fourrures**		18
..	2 348 627	2 688 735	2 811 758	3 758 431	4 157 425	5 104 408	..	Articles d'habillement autres qu'en fourrure		181
..	92 668	144 598	133 596	96 757	138 817	146 463	..	Préparation, teinture des fourrures; art. en fourrure		182
..	2 521 569	2 616 980	2 613 670	2 293 992	2 337 979	2 160 517	..	**Travail des cuirs; articles en cuir; chaussures**		19
..	737 714	764 981	877 831	904 197	1 062 075	964 915	..	Apprêt et tannage des cuirs et articles en cuirs		191
..	1 783 855	1 851 999	1 735 839	1 389 795	1 275 904	1 195 602	..	Chaussures		192
..	626 675	901 561	860 537	1 065 791	1 176 435	1 298 164	..	**Bois et articles en bois et liège (sauf meubles)**		20
..	252 470	316 933	317 811	383 084	461 796	491 680	..	Sciage et rabotage du bois		201
..	374 205	584 628	542 726	682 707	714 639	806 484	..	Articles en bois, liège, vannerie, sparterie		202
..	1 585 740	2 015 431	2 339 049	2 529 781	3 107 959	3 669 364	..	**Papier et carton; articles en papier et en carton**		21
..	1 893 573	1 919 130	2 325 740	3 119 794	3 509 289	4 161 717	..	**Edition, imprimerie et reproduction**		22
..	1 091 850	1 328 326	1 588 284	2 229 319	2 480 297	2 964 912	..	Edition		221
..	633 491	556 273	656 273	806 936	951 041	1 089 757	..	Imprimerie et activités annexes		222
..	168 232	34 531	81 183	83 539	77 951	107 048	..	Reproduction de supports enregistrés		223
..	2 126 840	2 589 889	3 231 117	3 285 770	4 028 940	5 383 395	..	**Cokéfaction; prod. pétroliers; comb. nucléaires**		23
..	6 510 146	7 855 822	9 242 148	10 719 576	12 657 456	14 853 890	..	**Produits chimiques**		24
..	2 376 076	2 753 225	3 721 922	4 033 078	5 175 956	6 939 026	..	Produits chimiques de base		241
..	3 628 445	4 195 964	4 652 703	5 491 707	6 049 922	6 099 412	..	Autres produits chimiques		242
..	505 625	906 633	867 523	1 194 791	1 431 578	1 815 452	..	Fibres synthétiques ou artificielles		243
..	2 749 631	3 203 730	3 685 331	4 241 116	4 897 704	6 282 508	..	**Articles en caoutchouc et en matières plastiques**		25
..	823 441	1 000 438	1 148 346	1 250 449	1 434 948	1 672 485	..	Articles en caoutchouc		251
..	1 926 190	2 203 292	2 536 985	2 990 667	3 462 756	4 610 023	..	Articles en matières plastiques		252
..	3 627 457	5 067 890	5 444 796	6 026 923	6 460 618	7 706 751	..	**Autres produits minéraux non métalliques**		26
..	701 615	894 011	1 027 066	1 044 496	1 330 481	1 653 141	..	Verre et articles en verre		261
..	2 925 842	4 173 879	4 417 730	4 982 427	5 130 137	6 053 610	..	Produits minéraux non métalliques, nca		269
..	5 230 643	6 667 396	7 059 148	7 436 022	8 798 750	10 920 647	..	**Produits métallurgiques de base**		27
..	4 132 180	5 231 812	5 637 117	5 936 175	6 934 928	8 340 739	..	Sidérurgie et première transformation de l'acier		271
..	809 616	1 041 251	1 032 544	1 105 432	1 373 565	2 038 064	..	Métallurgie; métaux précieux et non ferreux		272
..	288 847	394 333	389 487	394 415	490 257	541 844	..	Fonderie		273
..	2 813 592	3 650 636	4 205 286	5 135 666	6 689 555	7 453 567	..	**Ouvrages en métaux, sauf machines et matériel**		28
..	998 628	1 270 690	1 717 457	2 273 578	3 147 924	3 388 840	..	Constr. et menuiserie métal.; réservoirs; générateurs		281
..	1 814 964	2 379 946	2 487 829	2 862 088	3 541 631	4 064 727	..	Autres ouvrages en métaux		289
..	5 950 856	7 330 608	7 568 090	8 610 322	10 354 247	12 890 390	..	**Machines et matériel, nca**		29
..	1 654 834	2 360 620	2 807 020	3 349 053	4 110 250	5 793 785	..	Machines d'usage général		291
..	3 088 095	3 545 954	3 372 785	3 716 057	4 483 249	5 576 386	..	Machines d'usage spécifique		292
..	1 207 927	1 424 034	1 388 285	1 545 212	1 760 748	1 520 219	..	Appareils domestiques, nca		293
..	523 380	578 088	593 465	994 599	1 273 915	1 634 955	..	**Mach. de bureau, comptables, matériel inform.**		30
..	2 110 297	2 501 941	3 152 200	3 427 822	4 006 084	5 082 025	..	**Machines et appareils électriques, nca**		31
..	619 252	595 227	799 261	961 848	1 050 143	1 255 826	..	Moteurs, génératrices et transformateurs électriques		311
..	548 512	762 547	942 702	943 066	1 149 861	1 536 892	..	Matériel électrique de distribution et de commande		312
..	455 672	542 130	600 448	676 454	917 897	1 034 115	..	Fils et câbles électriques isolés		313
..	113 553	147 591	261 342	190 131	169 879	232 370	..	Accumulateurs, piles électriques		314
..	150 233	186 110	224 715	293 707	365 794	462 628	..	Lampes électriques et appareils d'éclairage		315
..	223 435	268 336	323 732	362 616	352 510	560 194	..	Autres matériels électriques, nca		319
..	7 446 955	8 549 805	8 848 544	11 431 469	16 029 479	24 993 880	..	**Equip. et appar. de radio, TV, communication**		32
..	3 270 631	3 515 331	3 712 301	6 666 354	9 348 707	17 090 457	..	Tubes et valves électroniques; autres composants		321
..	1 063 938	951 779	1 228 591	1 041 415	1 900 779	1 848 407	..	Emetteurs radio et TV; app. téléphonie, télégraphie		322
..	3 112 386	4 082 695	3 907 652	3 723 700	4 779 993	6 055 016	..	Récepteurs radio et TV et articles associés		323
..	746 112	929 893	983 913	1 177 389	1 434 516	1 749 224	..	**Instruments médicaux, de précision, d'optique**		33
..	324 501	462 268	494 793	603 062	715 706	1 052 964	..	Appareils médicaux et de précision		331
..	228 289	233 095	242 103	332 976	489 240	475 263	..	Instruments d'optique ; matériel photographique		332
..	193 322	234 530	247 017	241 351	229 570	220 997	..	Horlogerie		333
..	5 839 211	6 637 398	7 358 174	8 414 378	10 054 689	13 081 433	..	**Véhicules automobiles et nemorques**		34
..	1 579 978	2 719 908	3 494 616	3 176 821	4 740 094	4 940 410	..	**Autres matériels de transport**		35
..	1 252 582	2 124 909	3 029 205	2 657 396	3 677 076	4 093 883	..	Construction et réparation de navires		351
..	81 269	99 754	148 104	224 112	441 400	244 395	..	Construction de matériel ferroviaire roulant		352
..	..	291 720	139 454	137 674	386 256	339 334	..	Construction aéronautique et spatiale		353
..	..	203 525	177 853	157 639	235 362	262 798	..	Autres équipements de transport		359
..	2 046 367	2 501 231	2 685 064	2 883 946	3 292 537	3 581 417	..	**Meubles; activités de fabrication, nca**		36
..	797 026	1 179 547	1 355 529	1 462 449	1 741 095	1 798 022	..	Meubles		361
..	1 249 341	1 321 684	1 329 535	1 421 497	1 551 442	1 783 395	..	Activités de fabrication, nca		369
..	15 211	16 945	22 161	45 375	73 732	120 386	..	**Récupération**		37
..	..	..	..	..	..	..	..	**Production et distrib. d'électricité, de gaz, d'eau**	E	40-41
..	..	..	..	..	..	..	..	**Electricité, gaz, vapeur et eau chaude**		40
..	..	..	..	..	..	..	..	Production, collecte et distribution d'électricité		401
..	..	..	..	..	..	..	..	**Captage, épuration et distribution d'eau**		41 410
..	..	..	..	..	..	..	..	**Construction**	F	45
..	..	..	..	..	..	..	..	**Commerce de gros et de détail; réparation**	G	50-52
..	..	..	..	..	..	..	..	**Hôtels et restaurants**	H	55
..	..	..	..	..	..	..	..	**Transports, entreposage et communications**	I	60-64
..	..	..	..	..	..	..	..	**Intermédiation financière**	J	65-67
..	..	..	..	..	..	..	..	**Immobilier, locations, services aux entreprises**	K	70-74
..	..	..	..	..	..	..	..	**Admin. publique; éducation; santé; autres**	L-Q	75-99
..	..	..	..	..	..	..	..	**Grand total**	A-Q	01-99

KOREA

Table KR.3 INVESTMENT - INVESTISSEMENT

Millions of Won (Current Prices)

ISIC revision 3			1989	1990	1991	1992	1993	1994	1995	1996
A	01-02	Agriculture, hunting and forestry	..	..	..	..	..	..	..	..
B	05	Fishing	..	..	..	..	..	..	..	..
C	10-14	Mining and quarrying	..	314 340	300 719	357 142	336 720	236 127	280 726	..
	10	Mining of coal and lignite; extraction of peat	..	171 710	102 565	138 917	117 266	79 818	61 486	..
	11	Crude petroleum & natural gas; related service activ.	..	..	..	..	..	..	..	..
	13	Mining of metal ores	..	13 300	10 582	8 434	6 449	8 071	4 253	..
	14	Other mining and quarrying	..	129 330	187 572	209 791	213 005	148 238	214 987	..
D	15-37	Total manufacturing	..	22 027 583	32 365 767	26 192 079	28 738 026	31 855 089	43 312 249	..
	15	Food products and beverages	..	1 315 754	1 571 621	1 636 749	1 801 477	2 241 527	2 645 663	..
	155	Beverages	..	260 070	328 848	378 957	362 157	819 177	755 760	..
	16 160	Tobacco products	..	13 675	49 877	45 292	32 670	32 472	37 865	..
	17	Textiles	..	1 398 421	2 276 665	2 327 977	1 926 502	2 072 077	2 209 131	..
	171	Spinning, weaving and finishing of textiles	..	1 151 003	1 963 302	2 028 625	1 518 907	1 612 467	1 824 858	..
	172	Other textiles	..	153 489	196 285	159 315	300 724	359 178	311 407	..
	173	Knitted and crocheted fabrics and articles	..	93 929	117 078	140 037	106 871	100 432	72 866	..
	18	Wearing apparel dressing & dyeing of fur	..	241 136	231 535	181 588	241 229	255 404	317 345	..
	181	Wearing apparel, except fur apparel	..	221 444	218 190	171 300	211 508	248 562	288 992	..
	182	Dressing and dyeing of fur; articles of fur	..	19 692	13 345	10 288	29 721	6 842	28 353	..
	19	Tanning, dressing leather; leather artic.; footwear	..	313 893	402 998	303 713	216 092	273 159	211 410	..
	191	Tanning, dressing leather; manuf. of leather articles	..	96 295	103 638	93 742	80 761	145 435	85 575	..
	192	Footwear	..	217 598	299 360	209 971	135 331	127 724	125 835	..
	20	Wood and cork products, ex. furniture	..	123 881	172 906	176 953	178 055	156 954	326 251	..
	201	Sawmilling and planing of wood	..	35 069	56 512	59 736	47 845	58 689	77 674	..
	202	Products of wood, cork, straw & plaiting material	..	88 812	116 394	117 217	130 210	98 265	248 577	..
	21	Paper and paper products	..	603 077	901 709	866 482	775 321	846 086	1 250 761	..
	22	Publishing, printing & reprod. of recorded media	..	283 121	285 794	362 178	410 137	424 745	542 645	..
	221	Publishing	..	143 688	174 442	268 147	307 089	315 495	378 999	..
	222	Printing and related service activities	..	101 642	103 807	84 740	93 671	98 997	141 188	..
	223	Reproduction of recorded media	..	37 791	7 545	9 291	9 377	10 253	22 458	..
	23	Coke, refined petroleum products & nuclear fuel	..	1 174 495	1 441 529	823 161	604 541	886 916	1 929 341	..
	24	Chemicals and chemical products	..	2 641 031	5 416 119	3 783 799	3 542 437	3 822 553	4 878 961	..
	241	Basic chemicals	..	1 681 649	4 104 548	2 396 645	1 782 741	1 949 098	2 750 441	..
	242	Other chemical products	..	618 212	859 544	737 748	1 186 278	1 116 450	1 502 294	..
	243	Man-made fibres	..	341 170	452 027	649 406	573 418	757 005	626 226	..
	25	Rubber and plastic products	..	910 420	1 163 460	1 124 792	1 305 158	1 323 576	1 737 650	..
	251	Rubber products	..	317 229	323 911	411 469	355 734	364 416	477 521	..
	252	Plastic products	..	593 191	839 549	713 323	949 424	959 160	1 260 129	..
	26	Other non-metallic mineral products	..	1 540 631	1 936 831	2 112 971	1 826 272	1 905 489	2 061 801	..
	261	Glass and glass products	..	281 833	367 065	308 472	299 646	403 738	691 167	..
	269	Non-metallic mineral products, nec	..	1 258 798	1 569 766	1 804 499	1 526 626	1 501 751	1 370 634	..
	27	Basic metals	..	3 170 216	3 215 471	2 958 595	2 302 204	2 996 560	6 020 974	..
	271	Basic iron and steel	..	2 796 664	2 745 949	2 145 523	1 168 850	2 436 245	5 259 362	..
	272	Basic precious and non-ferrous metals	..	287 892	377 906	694 480	1 014 722	442 278	650 249	..
	273	Casting of metals	..	85 660	91 616	118 592	118 632	118 037	111 363	..
	28	Fabricated metal products, ex. machin. & equip.	..	644 443	817 901	916 986	1 001 693	1 353 528	1 425 596	..
	281	Structural metal prod., tanks, reservoirs, generators	..	241 970	293 310	333 919	426 284	622 182	632 766	..
	289	Other fabricated metal products & service activities	..	402 473	524 591	583 067	575 409	731 346	792 830	..
	29	Machinery and equipment, nec	..	1 398 717	1 708 511	1 856 638	2 437 306	2 123 387	2 597 647	..
	291	General purpose machinery	..	378 025	552 224	808 970	690 124	731 904	1 241 684	..
	292	Special purpose machinery	..	810 431	896 336	794 030	1 273 592	1 035 867	1 013 425	..
	293	Domestic appliances, nec	..	210 261	259 951	253 638	473 590	355 616	342 538	..
	30	Office, accounting and computing machinery	..	49 887	136 546	87 390	260 522	210 727	343 779	..
	31	Electrical machinery and apparatus, nec	..	492 345	511 503	601 961	835 452	744 728	947 872	..
	311	Electric motors, generators and transformers	..	119 857	91 243	129 672	237 778	159 160	183 667	..
	312	Electricity distribution and control apparatus	..	110 759	137 400	140 503	261 288	185 066	199 666	..
	313	Insulated wire and cable	..	132 112	111 409	111 264	174 431	201 950	223 375	..
	314	Accumulators, primary cells and primary batteries	..	48 114	44 763	60 786	63 924	51 668	59 600	..
	315	Electric lamps and lighting equipment	..	29 071	53 619	79 613	40 429	45 703	100 992	..
	319	Other electrical equipment, nec	..	52 432	73 069	80 123	57 602	101 181	180 572	..
	32	Radio, TV, communication equip. & apparatus	..	2 478 937	2 727 261	2 456 979	3 240 714	4 817 443	7 317 454	..
	321	Electronic valves, tubes & other electronic compon.	..	1 304 273	1 770 182	1 505 398	2 376 288	3 989 767	6 130 582	..
	322	TV, radio transmitters & appar. for line teleph., telegr.	..	220 188	177 202	147 543	175 956	263 246	366 028	..
	323	TV, radio receivers and associated goods	..	954 476	779 877	804 038	688 470	564 430	820 844	..
	33	Medical, precision, optical instr.; watches, clocks	..	123 879	178 761	185 644	186 185	209 698	289 205	..
	331	Medical equip.; precision instruments and appliances	..	57 175	72 589	129 022	90 971	109 192	148 443	..
	332	Optical instruments and photographic equipment	..	41 236	85 095	46 283	61 860	90 371	126 374	..
	333	Watches and clocks	..	25 468	21 077	10 339	33 354	10 135	14 388	..
	34	Motor vehicles, trailers, and semi-trailers	..	2 273 395	2 984 493	2 214 268	3 058 428	3 118 907	3 975 915	..
	35	Other transport equipment	..	508 121	836 256	807 672	2 119 939	1 626 070	1 759 610	..
	351	Building and repairing of ships and boats	..	422 379	635 992	696 843	1 819 463	1 375 048	1 494 103	..
	352	Railway, tramway locomotives and rolling stock	..	28 302	54 135	25 774	158 525	69 242	131 097	..
	353	Aircraft and spacecraft	..	..	99 593	54 312	119 105	153 593	73 156	..
	359	Transport equipment, nec	..	..	46 536	30 743	22 846	28 187	61 254	..
	36	Furniture; manufacturing, nec	..	323 842	3 386 584	347 312	416 521	383 735	433 869	..
	361	Furniture	..	135 066	3 192 316	209 926	192 307	205 747	252 817	..
	369	Manufacturing, nec	..	188 776	194 268	137 386	224 214	177 988	181 052	..
	37	Recycling	..	4 266	11 436	12 979	19 171	29 348	51 504	..
E	40-41	Electricity, gas and water supply	..	..	..	..	..	..	..	..
	40	Electricity, gas, steam and hot water supply	..	..	..	..	..	..	..	..
	401	Production, collection and distribution of electricity	..	..	..	..	..	..	..	..
	41 410	Collection, purification, distribution of water	..	..	..	..	..	..	..	..
F	45	Construction	..	..	..	..	..	..	..	..
G	50-52	Wholesale and retail trade; repairs etc	..	..	..	..	..	..	..	..
H	55	Hotels and restaurants	..	..	..	..	..	..	..	..
I	60-64	Transport, storage and communications	..	..	..	..	..	..	..	..
J	65-67	Financial intermediation	..	..	..	..	..	..	..	..
K	70-74	Real estate, renting and business activities	..	..	..	..	..	..	..	..
L-Q	75-99	Public admin.; education; health; other services	..	..	..	..	..	..	..	..
A-Q	01-99	Grand total	..	..	..	..	..	..	..	..

Table KR.4 **DÉPENSES EN MACHINES ET ÉQUIPEMENT - INVESTMENT IN MACHINERY AND EQUIPMENT**

Millions de Won (Prix courants)

1989	1990	1991	1992	1993	1994	1995	1996				CITI révision 3
..	..	..	..	..	..	..	..	..	**Agriculture, chasse et sylviculture**	A	01-02
	..	..	..	..	..	..		..	**Pêche**	B	05
..	108 603	115 888	124 435	72 399	87 779	83 125		..	**Activités extractives**	C	10-14
..	54 105	26 789	49 483	14 591	17 367	12 847		..	Extraction de charbon, de lignite et de tourbe		10
								..	Extraction de pétrole brut et de gaz naturel		11
..	6 025	4 074	2 883	1 733	2 924	418		..	Extraction de minerais métalliques		13
..	48 473	85 025	72 069	56 075	67 488	69 860		..	Autres activités extractives		14
..	13 480 289	17 820 795	17 181 351	13 889 159	14 793 274	21 672 766		..	**Activités de fabrication**	D	15-37
..	689 128	802 532	698 250	808 023	928 825	1 105 202		..	**Produits alimentaires et boissons**		15
..	131 283	162 087	114 778	165 780	258 299	269 903		..	Boissons		155
..	11 224	35 840	18 597	43 382	22 845	20 032		..	**Produits à base de tabac**	16	160
..	860 815	1 179 221	1 358 357	963 410	1 172 248	1 254 310		..	**Textiles**	17	
..	742 446	1 019 706	1 243 331	770 560	929 528	1 073 574		..	Filature, tissage et achèvement des textiles		171
..	79 634	108 147	71 363	151 224	199 128	141 814		..	Autres articles textiles		172
..	38 735	51 368	43 663	41 626	43 592	38 922		..	Etoffes et articles de bonneterie		173
..	96 071	97 079	76 384	62 377	72 553	82 684		..	**Habillement; préparation, teinture des fourrures**	18	
..	91 424	91 729	74 799	60 174	70 247	75 789		..	Articles d'habillement autres qu'en fourrure		181
..	4 647	5 350	1 585	2 203	2 306	6 895		..	Préparation, teinture des fourrures; art. en fourrure		182
..	158 158	164 366	83 737	82 130	97 598	69 941		..	**Travail des cuirs; articles en cuir; chaussures**	19	
..	42 122	41 634	34 137	30 475	57 928	34 602		..	Apprêt et tannage des cuirs et articles en cuirs		191
..	116 036	122 732	49 600	51 655	39 670	35 339		..	Chaussures		192
..	44 749	61 516	54 725	71 647	53 862	136 918		..	**Bois et articles en bois et liège (sauf meubles)**	20	
..	9 131	14 850	15 533	15 338	15 955	24 939		..	Sciage et rabotage du bois		201
..	35 618	46 666	39 192	56 309	37 907	111 979		..	Articles en bois, liège, vannerie, sparterie		202
..	284 356	509 066	445 139	655 415	549 498	653 908		..	**Papier et carton; articles en papier et en carton**	21	
..	180 838	181 569	142 562	172 622	131 120	286 408		..	**Edition, imprimerie et reproduction**	22	
..	78 047	103 767	88 623	113 022	73 999	189 911		..	Edition		221
..	70 990	72 270	49 909	55 009	53 814	88 394		..	Imprimerie et activités annexes		222
..	31 801	5 532	4 030	4 591	3 307	8 103		..	Reproduction de supports enregistrés		223
..	641 714	681 003	731 291	396 515	136 745	1 278 701		..	**Cokéfaction; prod. pétroliers; comb. nucléaires**	23	
..	1 582 329	3 552 742	4 171 703	1 913 988	1 914 264	2 329 088		..	**Produits chimiques**	24	
..	981 363	2 763 469	3 420 006	985 580	1 000 570	1 333 845		..	Produits chimiques de base		241
..	301 666	359 211	277 953	493 562	330 812	534 940		..	Autres produits chimiques		242
..	299 300	430 062	473 744	434 846	582 882	460 303		..	Fibres synthétiques ou artificielles		243
..	447 714	796 192	578 677	631 578	661 157	873 971		..	**Articles en caoutchouc et en matières plastiques**	25	
..	126 242	269 882	206 668	156 917	144 367	222 399		..	Articles en caoutchouc		251
..	321 472	526 310	372 009	474 661	516 790	651 572		..	Articles en matières plastiques		252
..	638 007	926 157	1 207 800	745 633	879 876	945 788		..	**Autres produits minéraux non métalliques**	26	
..	139 097	300 450	204 266	169 293	152 373	416 768		..	Verre et articles en verre		261
..	498 910	625 707	1 003 534	576 340	727 503	529 020		..	Produits minéraux non métalliques, nca		269
..	3 025 904	994 000	3 323 037	1 573 106	1 505 701	2 664 698		..	**Produits métallurgiques de base**	27	
..	2 833 539	767 059	2 970 876	829 791	1 018 869	2 319 628		..	Sidérurgie et première transformation de l'acier		271
..	137 870	177 069	309 493	704 592	436 358	303 371		..	Métallurgie; métaux précieux et non ferreux		272
..	54 495	49 872	42 668	38 723	50 474	41 699		..	Fonderie		273
..	354 868	462 185	385 245	397 809	500 998	583 673		..	**Ouvrages en métaux, sauf machines et matériel**	28	
..	109 682	122 628	140 443	124 822	172 056	210 739		..	Constr. et menuiserie métal.; réservoirs; générateurs		281
..	245 186	339 557	244 802	272 987	328 942	372 934		..	Autres ouvrages en métaux		289
..	710 629	818 843	697 000	696 748	739 545	891 223		..	**Machines et matériel, nca**	29	
..	192 142	281 987	262 143	245 183	272 609	380 869		..	Machines d'usage général		291
..	388 422	378 350	353 487	332 485	342 730	380 246		..	Machines d'usage spécifique		292
..	130 065	158 506	81 370	119 080	124 206	130 108		..	Appareils domestiques, nca		293
..	30 713	57 923	35 772	85 477	97 023	126 386		..	**Mach. de bureau, comptables, matériel inform.**	30	
..	285 504	313 355	289 285	279 900	368 817	398 919		..	**Machines et appareils électriques, nca**	31	
..	63 704	52 298	67 296	59 782	76 238	61 661		..	Moteurs, génératrices et transformateurs électriques		311
..	69 698	92 994	52 666	70 362	55 639	84 383		..	Matériel électrique de distribution et de commande		312
..	72 043	67 962	62 286	72 076	146 056	113 202		..	Fils et câbles électriques isolés		313
..	31 592	28 598	32 459	25 686	24 373	26 569		..	Accumulateurs, piles électriques		314
..	15 798	29 022	29 963	24 910	22 932	34 098		..	Lampes électriques et appareils d'éclairage		315
..	32 669	42 481	44 615	27 084	43 579	79 006		..	Autres matériels électriques, nca		319
..	1 253 794	2 074 979	1 207 270	2 416 611	2 831 711	5 449 743		..	**Equip. et appar. de radio, TV, communication**	32	
..	704 172	1 573 231	758 100	2 058 710	2 507 600	4 838 614		..	Tubes et valves électroniques; autres composants		321
..	103 385	105 151	69 355	60 147	103 447	160 727		..	Emetteurs radio et TV; app. téléphonie, télégraphie		322
..	446 237	396 597	379 815	297 754	220 664	450 402		..	Récepteurs radio et TV et articles associés		323
..	76 839	98 262	56 758	74 874	67 897	87 743		..	**Instruments médicaux, de précision, d'optique**	33	
..	28 694	37 043	37 463	36 196	31 464	37 926		..	Appareils médicaux et de précision		331
..	28 005	45 787	15 054	32 162	32 567	45 650		..	Instruments d'optique ; matériel photographique		332
..	20 140	15 432	4 241	6 516	3 866	4 167		..	Horlogerie		333
..	1 678 633	1 477 968	1 155 238	1 334 422	1 561 529	1 969 343		..	**Véhicules automobiles et nemorques**	34	
..	295 827	352 212	343 896	356 687	360 058	311 301		..	**Autres matériels de transport**	35	
..	256 825	262 622	311 274	282 147	268 189	212 065		..	Construction et réparation de navires		351
..	5 476	13 632	6 610	23 859	30 613	31 850		..	Construction de matériel ferroviaire roulant		352
..	..	45 153	13 583	40 317	49 934	43 787		..	Construction aéronautique et spatiale		353
..		30 805	12 429	10 364	11 322	23 599		..	Autres équipements de transport		359
..	130 391	2 176 956	115 411	119 468	126 137	138 000		..	**Meubles; activités de fabrication, nca**	36	
..	43 154	2 076 202	63 513	66 558	73 920	83 174		..	Meubles		361
..	87 237	100 754	51 898	52 910	52 217	54 826		..	Activités de fabrication, nca		369
..	2 084	6 829	5 217	7 337	13 267	14 786		..	**Récupération**	37	
..	..	..	..	..	..	..		..	**Production et distrib. d'électricité, de gaz, d'eau**	E	40-41
..	..	..	..	..	..	..		..	**Electricité, gaz, vapeur et eau chaude**	40	
								..	Production, collecte et distribution d'électricité		401
..	..	..	..	..	..	..		..	**Captage, épuration et distribution d'eau**	41	410
								..	**Construction**	F	45
								..	**Commerce de gros et de détail; réparation**	G	50-52
								..	**Hôtels et restaurants**	H	55
								..	**Transports, entreposage et communications**	I	60-64
								..	**Intermédiation financière**	J	65-67
								..	**Immobilier, locations, services aux entreprises**	K	70-74
								..	**Admin. publique; éducation; santé; autres**	L-Q	75-99
..	13 588 892	17 936 683	17 305 786	13 961 558	14 881 053	21 755 891		..	**Grand total**	A-Q	01-99

Statistiques des Structures Industrielles
OCDE, © 1998

Table KR.5 ESTABLISHMENTS - ETABLISSEMENTS

Units

ISIC revision 3				1989	1990	1991	1992	1993	1994	1995	1996
A	01-02		Agriculture, hunting and forestry	..	..	..	..	..	..	..	..
B	05		Fishing	..	..	..	..	..	..	..	..
C	10-14		Mining and quarrying	..	1 765	1 788	1 678	1 642	1 206	1 082	..
	10		Mining of coal and lignite; extraction of peat	..	353	307	261	204	168	130	..
	11		Crude petroleum & natural gas; related service activ.	..	..	..	..	..	..	..	..
	13		Mining of metal ores	..	23	20	12	10	13	9	..
	14		Other mining and quarrying	..	1 389	1 461	1 405	1 428	1 025	943	..
D	15-37		Total manufacturing	..	68 690	72 213	74 679	88 864	91 372	96 202	..
	15		Food products and beverages	..	4 638	4 753	5 044	5 792	5 858	6 248	..
		155	Beverages	..	694	650	570	531	508	513	..
	16	160	Tobacco products	..	20	20	20	16	16	16	..
	17		Textiles	..	7 621	7 982	8 106	9 617	9 838	9 740	..
		171	Spinning, weaving and finishing of textiles	..	4 362	4 502	4 556	5 228	5 436	5 314	..
		172	Other textiles	..	1 704	1 815	1 932	2 337	2 417	2 572	..
		173	Knitted and crocheted fabrics and articles	..	1 555	1 665	1 618	2 052	1 985	1 854	..
	18		Wearing apparel dressing & dyeing of fur	..	6 607	6 638	6 573	8 141	8 460	8 732	..
		181	Wearing apparel, except fur apparel	..	6 501	6 507	6 468	7 987	8 293	8 545	..
		182	Dressing and dyeing of fur; articles of fur	..	106	131	105	154	167	187	..
	19		Tanning, dressing leather; leather artic.; footwear	..	3 038	2 924	2 721	3 130	3 085	3 027	..
		191	Tanning, dressing leather; manuf. of leather articles	..	1 178	1 176	1 101	1 245	1 231	1 218	..
		192	Footwear	..	1 860	1 748	1 620	1 885	1 854	1 809	..
	20		Wood and cork products, ex. furniture	..	2 050	2 194	2 150	2 556	2 505	2 490	..
		201	Sawmilling and planing of wood	..	1 088	1 149	1 121	1 254	1 229	1 202	..
		202	Products of wood, cork, straw & plaiting material	..	962	1 045	1 029	1 302	1 276	1 288	..
	21		Paper and paper products	..	2 128	2 236	2 309	2 496	2 600	2 671	..
	22		Publishing, printing & reprod. of recorded media	..	2 900	3 189	3 406	4 192	4 366	4 819	..
		221	Publishing	..	1 955	1 105	1 014	1 274	1 276	1 320	..
		222	Printing and related service activities	..	833	2 036	2 341	2 841	3 011	3 423	..
		223	Reproduction of recorded media	..	112	48	51	77	79	76	..
	23		Coke, refined petroleum products & nuclear fuel	..	70	65	77	77	76	70	..
	24		Chemicals and chemical products	..	1 804	2 168	2 353	2 553	2 644	2 796	..
		241	Basic chemicals	..	606	925	1 023	1 091	1 112	1 197	..
		242	Other chemical products	..	1 148	1 158	1 228	1 388	1 417	1 488	..
		243	Man-made fibres	..	50	85	102	74	115	111	..
	25		Rubber and plastic products	..	4 365	4 057	4 313	5 251	5 416	5 671	..
		251	Rubber products	..	652	650	686	772	801	858	..
		252	Plastic products	..	3 713	3 407	3 627	4 479	4 615	4 813	..
	26		Other non-metallic mineral products	..	3 764	4 204	4 405	4 708	4 657	4 709	..
		261	Glass and glass products	..	356	389	431	534	573	599	..
		269	Non-metallic mineral products, nec	..	3 408	3 815	3 974	4 174	4 084	4 110	..
	27		Basic metals	..	1 821	1 798	1 835	1 988	1 921	2 075	..
		271	Basic iron and steel	..	794	713	757	847	832	911	..
		272	Basic precious and non-ferrous metals	..	609	645	668	685	640	708	..
		273	Casting of metals	..	418	440	410	456	449	456	..
	28		Fabricated metal products, ex. machin. & equip.	..	4 955	5 636	6 129	8 229	8 790	9 616	..
		281	Structural metal prod., tanks, reservoirs, generators	..	1 425	1 704	1 884	2 865	3 134	3 365	..
		289	Other fabricated metal products & service activities	..	3 530	3 932	4 245	5 364	5 656	6 251	..
	29		Machinery and equipment, nec	..	7 858	8 759	9 302	11 246	11 582	12 408	..
		291	General purpose machinery	..	2 230	2 879	3 169	4 251	4 437	4 857	..
		292	Special purpose machinery	..	4 631	4 754	4 959	5 854	5 988	6 389	..
		293	Domestic appliances, nec	..	997	1 126	1 174	1 141	1 157	1 162	..
	30		Office, accounting and computing machinery	..	302	400	428	530	599	657	..
	31		Electrical machinery and apparatus, nec	..	2 590	2 706	2 993	3 780	4 043	4 542	..
		311	Electric motors, generators and transformers	..	782	768	798	987	1 074	1 157	..
		312	Electricity distribution and control apparatus	..	812	874	1 018	1 311	1 404	1 556	..
		313	Insulated wire and cable	..	214	247	273	375	410	451	..
		314	Accumulators, primary cells and primary batteries	..	31	45	45	41	34	41	..
		315	Electric lamps and lighting equipment	..	344	424	466	605	639	749	..
		319	Other electrical equipment, nec	..	407	348	393	461	482	588	..
	32		Radio, TV, communication equip. & apparatus	..	3 208	3 181	3 132	3 393	3 434	3 546	..
		321	Electronic valves, tubes & other electronic componen.	..	980	936	963	1 186	1 251	1 383	..
		322	TV, radio transmitters & appar. for line teleph., telegr.	..	528	578	581	618	620	667	..
		323	TV, radio receivers and associated goods	..	1 700	1 667	1 588	1 589	1 563	1 496	..
	33		Medical, precision, optical instr.; watches, clocks	..	1 104	1 248	1 345	1 668	1 801	1 982	..
		331	Medical equip.; precision instruments and appliances	..	536	639	717	904	1 002	1 121	..
		332	Optical instruments and photographic equipment	..	350	367	383	487	517	581	..
		333	Watches and clocks	..	218	242	245	277	282	280	..
	34		Motor vehicles, trailers, and semi-trailers	..	2 138	2 291	2 392	2 655	2 815	3 070	..
	35		Other transport equipment	..	538	656	638	767	808	954	..
		351	Building and repairing of ships and boats	..	255	365	346	459	503	609	..
		352	Railway, tramway locomotives and rolling stock	..	56	61	85	97	98	143	..
		353	Aircraft and spacecraft	..	..	15	29	31	39	39	..
		359	Transport equipment, nec	..	..	215	178	180	168	163	..
	36		Furniture; manufacturing, nec	..	5 103	5 010	4 917	5 947	5 896	6 183	..
		361	Furniture	..	2 215	2 360	2 445	3 061	3 080	3 314	..
		369	Manufacturing, nec	..	2 888	2 650	2 472	2 886	2 816	2 869	..
	37		Recycling	..	68	98	91	132	162	180	..
E	40-41		Electricity, gas and water supply	..	..	..	..	..	..	..	..
	40		Electricity, gas, steam and hot water supply	..	..	..	..	..	..	..	..
		401	Production, collection and distribution of electricity	..	..	..	..	..	..	..	..
	41	410	Collection, purification, distribution of water	..	..	..	..	..	..	..	..
F	45		Construction	..	..	..	..	..	..	..	..
G	50-52		Wholesale and retail trade; repairs etc	..	..	..	..	..	..	..	..
H	55		Hotels and restaurants	..	..	..	..	..	..	..	..
I	60-64		Transport, storage and communications	..	..	..	..	..	..	..	..
J	65-67		Financial intermediation	..	..	..	..	..	..	..	..
K	70-74		Real estate, renting and business activities	..	..	..	..	..	..	..	..
L-Q	75-99		Public admin.; education; health; other services	..	..	..	..	..	..	..	..
A-Q	01-99		Grand total	..	..	..	..	..	..	..	..

Table KR.6 EMPLOI - EMPLOYMENT

Milliers — CITI révision 3

1989	1990	1991	1992	1993	1994	1995	1996			
..	..	..	..	..	..	..	..	**Agriculture, chasse et sylviculture**	A	01-02
..	..	..	..	..	..	..	..	**Pêche**	B	05
..	66.7	61.0	51.0	45.5	35.3	29.9	..	**Activités extractives**	C	10-14
..	44.4	37.8	29.5	24.6	16.7	12.7	..	Extraction de charbon, de lignite et de tourbe		10
..	..	..	..	..	..	..	..	Extraction de pétrole brut et de gaz naturel		11
..	2.5	2.1	1.6	1.0	0.7	0.6	..	Extraction de minerais métalliques		13
..	19.8	21.1	19.9	19.9	17.8	16.6	..	Autres activités extractives		14
..	3 013.5	2 918.0	2 801.4	2 885.3	2 929.9	2 951.9	..	**Activités de fabrication**	D	15-37
..	206.6	200.2	196.6	198.5	200.6	206.5	..	**Produits alimentaires et boissons**		15
..	22.4	21.0	19.7	19.5	19.4	21.9	..	Boissons		155
..	7.2	6.9	6.5	5.8	5.5	5.0	..	**Produits à base de tabac**		16 160
..	355.2	339.7	323.3	316.8	304.6	280.6	..	**Textiles**		17
..	269.3	255.3	239.7	223.6	220.5	204.5	..	Filature, tissage et achèvement des textiles		171
..	46.1	45.1	45.9	50.7	49.0	47.4	..	Autres articles textiles		172
..	39.8	39.4	37.7	42.5	35.1	28.6	..	Etoffes et articles de bonneterie		173
..	240.4	211.3	198.4	209.6	203.1	199.8	..	**Habillement; préparation, teinture des fourrures**		18
..	234.6	205.2	194.2	206.1	199.9	195.9	..	Articles d'habillement autres qu'en fourrure		181
..	5.8	6.1	4.2	3.5	3.3	3.9	..	Préparation, teinture des fourrures; art. en fourrure		182
..	217.1	179.7	142.2	111.9	96.1	81.5	..	**Travail des cuirs; articles en cuir; chaussures**		19
..	37.5	34.5	30.9	29.6	28.6	26.0	..	Apprêt et tannage des cuirs et articles en cuirs		191
..	179.6	145.2	111.3	82.4	67.4	55.5	..	Chaussures		192
..	43.3	42.7	39.4	42.9	42.0	40.5	..	**Bois et articles en bois et liège (sauf meubles)**		20
..	16.2	16.0	14.9	15.2	16.0	14.5	..	Sciage et rabotage du bois		201
..	27.1	26.6	24.6	27.8	26.0	26.0	..	Articles en bois, liège, vannerie, sparterie		202
..	66.2	65.2	64.4	65.3	68.7	69.1	..	**Papier et carton; articles en papier et en carton**		21
..	75.0	74.3	79.3	90.2	92.3	94.1	..	**Edition, imprimerie et reproduction**		22
..	42.7	40.1	43.8	49.6	50.9	51.0	..	Edition		221
..	26.8	32.9	33.9	38.6	39.6	41.1	..	Imprimerie et activités annexes		222
..	5.5	1.3	1.7	2.0	1.9	2.0	..	Reproduction de supports enregistrés		223
..	9.1	9.8	9.9	10.0	10.6	12.4	..	**Cokéfaction; prod. pétroliers; comb. nucléaires**		23
..	129.1	143.0	145.7	149.8	154.4	153.3	..	**Produits chimiques**		24
..	39.3	49.2	51.0	50.1	51.3	53.2	..	Produits chimiques de base		241
..	80.0	81.4	82.3	80.1	80.8	78.6	..	Autres produits chimiques		242
..	9.9	12.4	12.4	19.6	22.3	21.5	..	Fibres synthétiques ou artificielles		243
..	136.0	125.3	122.7	135.8	137.8	141.9	..	**Articles en caoutchouc et en matières plastiques**		25
..	34.8	31.8	32.0	33.5	34.1	35.6	..	Articles en caoutchouc		251
..	101.2	93.5	90.7	102.3	103.7	106.3	..	Articles en matières plastiques		252
..	130.8	138.0	138.2	139.1	135.9	132.4	..	**Autres produits minéraux non métalliques**		26
..	25.8	24.9	25.6	25.3	25.8	26.1	..	Verre et articles en verre		261
..	105.0	113.1	112.5	113.8	110.2	106.3	..	Produits minéraux non métalliques, nca		269
..	123.7	120.6	116.0	117.0	117.1	122.4	..	**Produits métallurgiques de base**		27
..	76.4	73.3	71.7	74.3	74.0	76.6	..	Sidérurgie et première transformation de l'acier		271
..	30.9	30.3	28.7	27.7	27.6	31.6	..	Métallurgie; métaux précieux et non ferreux		272
..	16.5	17.0	15.5	14.9	15.5	14.2	..	Fonderie		273
..	145.5	154.0	151.7	172.5	186.8	196.4	..	**Ouvrages en métaux, sauf machines et matériel**		28
..	44.9	48.6	51.0	62.1	69.1	75.2	..	Constr. et menuiserie métal.; réservoirs; générateurs		281
..	100.6	105.4	100.7	110.4	117.7	121.3	..	Autres ouvrages en métaux		289
..	257.5	268.4	259.6	278.5	293.6	301.1	..	**Machines et matériel, nca**		29
..	72.5	87.1	90.9	102.7	114.7	125.9	..	Machines d'usage général		291
..	136.8	132.2	123.2	131.5	133.2	135.8	..	Machines d'usage spécifique		292
..	48.3	49.1	45.5	44.3	45.8	39.5	..	Appareils domestiques, nca		293
..	19.1	25.4	21.3	28.0	30.3	32.2	..	**Mach. de bureau, comptables, matériel inform.**		30
..	110.7	107.8	112.1	124.1	125.4	133.8	..	**Machines et appareils électriques, nca**		31
..	36.7	31.9	32.7	37.1	36.2	37.0	..	Moteurs, génératrices et transformateurs électriques		311
..	30.1	31.3	32.7	38.0	37.9	41.2	..	Matériel électrique de distribution et de commande		312
..	14.1	16.1	16.1	16.8	18.3	17.3	..	Fils et câbles électriques isolés		313
..	4.7	4.9	5.6	4.4	4.7	5.1	..	Accumulateurs, piles électriques		314
..	11.9	12.1	12.2	13.8	14.6	15.0	..	Lampes électriques et appareils d'éclairage		315
..	13.2	11.5	12.8	14.1	13.6	18.0	..	Autres matériels électriques, nca		319
..	298.8	273.9	260.7	251.1	264.2	272.1	..	**Equip. et appar. de radio, TV, communication**		32
..	115.8	105.1	103.0	109.1	118.6	136.0	..	Tubes et valves électroniques; autres composants		321
..	37.9	37.8	34.1	30.5	35.3	32.3	..	Emetteurs radio et TV; app. téléphonie, télégraphie		322
..	145.1	131.0	123.5	111.5	110.3	103.8	..	Récepteurs radio et TV et articles associés		323
..	45.7	45.4	42.2	46.6	48.9	50.2	..	**Instruments médicaux, de précision, d'optique**		33
..	18.7	22.0	20.8	23.9	27.4	29.0	..	Appareils médicaux et de précision		331
..	17.0	13.3	12.0	13.2	13.6	14.6	..	Instruments d'optique ; matériel photographique		332
..	9.9	10.1	9.4	9.6	7.9	6.7	..	Horlogerie		333
..	186.3	183.0	183.9	192.7	209.7	220.6	..	**Véhicules automobiles et nemorques**		34
..	62.8	68.5	65.6	74.1	83.6	90.3	..	**Autres matériels de transport**		35
..	47.7	53.0	50.3	55.4	64.4	73.6	..	Construction et réparation de navires		351
..	3.8	3.3	4.4	8.1	8.2	6.6	..	Construction de matériel ferroviaire roulant		352
..	..	5.2	4.6	4.9	5.2	5.0	..	Construction aéronautique et spatiale		353
..	..	7.0	6.2	5.8	5.8	5.2	..	Autres équipements de transport		359
..	146.5	134.1	120.6	123.0	116.7	113.4	..	**Meubles; activités de fabrication, nca**		36
..	51.8	54.7	53.6	58.7	57.2	56.6	..	Meubles		361
..	94.7	79.5	67.1	64.3	59.5	56.8	..	Activités de fabrication, nca		369
..	0.8	1.2	1.2	1.8	2.1	2.3	..	**Récupération**		37
..	..	..	..	..	..	..	..	**Production et distrib. d'électricité, de gaz, d'eau**	E	40-41
..	..	..	..	..	..	..	..	**Electricité, gaz, vapeur et eau chaude**		40
..	..	..	..	..	..	..	..	Production, collecte et distribution d'électricité		401
..	..	..	..	..	..	..	..	**Captage, épuration et distribution d'eau**		41 410
..	..	..	..	..	..	..	..	**Construction**	F	45
..	..	..	..	..	..	..	..	**Commerce de gros et de détail; réparation**	G	50-52
..	..	..	..	..	..	..	..	**Hôtels et restaurants**	H	55
..	..	..	..	..	..	..	..	**Transports, entreposage et communications**	I	60-64
..	..	..	..	..	..	..	..	**Intermédiation financière**	J	65-67
..	..	..	..	..	..	..	..	**Immobilier, locations, services aux entreprises**	K	70-74
..	..	..	..	..	..	..	..	**Admin. publique; éducation; santé; autres**	L-Q	75-99
..	..	..	..	..	..	..	..	**Grand total**	A-Q	01-99

Statistiques des Structures Industrielles
OCDE, © 1998

KOREA

Table KR.7 EMPLOYMENT, EMPLOYEES - EMPLOI, SALARIÉS

Thousands

ISIC revision 3			1989	1990	1991	1992	1993	1994	1995	1996
A	01-02	**Agriculture, hunting and forestry**	..	..	..	..	..	..	..	..
B	05	**Fishing**	..	..	..	..	..	..	..	..
C	10-14	**Mining and quarrying**	..	64.9	59.3	49.4	44.1	34.6	29.3	..
	10	Mining of coal and lignite; extraction of peat	..	44.1	37.6	29.3	24.5	16.7	12.6	..
	11	Crude petroleum & natural gas; related service activ.	..	..	..	..	..	..	..	..
	13	Mining of metal ores	..	2.5	2.1	1.6	1.0	0.7	0.6	..
	14	Other mining and quarrying	..	18.2	19.6	18.5	18.6	17.2	16.1	..
D	15-37	**Total manufacturing**	..	2 951.9	2 853.6	2 734.2	2 804.6	2 848.8	2 865.2	..
	15	**Food products and beverages**	..	201.3	194.8	190.9	191.9	194.2	199.6	..
	155	Beverages	..	21.5	20.2	19.0	18.9	18.9	21.5	..
	16	160 **Tobacco products**	..	7.2	6.9	6.5	5.8	5.5	5.0	..
	17	**Textiles**	..	347.5	331.8	315.2	307.1	294.9	270.9	..
	171	Spinning, weaving and finishing of textiles	..	265.1	251.1	235.4	218.8	215.7	199.7	..
	172	Other textiles	..	44.4	43.2	43.9	48.3	46.4	44.7	..
	173	Knitted and crocheted fabrics and articles	..	38.0	37.5	35.9	40.1	32.9	26.4	..
	18	**Wearing apparel dressing & dyeing of fur**	..	233.6	204.1	191.0	200.1	193.3	189.4	..
	181	Wearing apparel, except fur apparel	..	227.8	198.1	187.0	196.7	190.2	185.6	..
	182	Dressing and dyeing of fur; articles of fur	..	5.8	6.0	4.1	3.4	3.1	3.8	..
	19	**Tanning, dressing leather; leather artic.; footwear**	..	214.4	177.1	139.7	108.9	93.1	78.4	..
	191	Tanning, dressing leather; manuf. of leather articles	..	36.5	33.5	30.0	28.5	27.6	24.9	..
	192	Footwear	..	177.9	143.5	109.7	80.5	65.5	53.5	..
	20	**Wood and cork products, ex. furniture**	..	41.2	40.5	37.3	40.5	39.6	38.1	..
	201	Sawmilling and planing of wood	..	15.1	15.0	13.8	14.0	14.8	13.4	..
	202	Products of wood, cork, straw & plaiting material	..	26.1	25.6	23.5	26.5	24.8	24.7	..
	21	**Paper and paper products**	..	64.4	63.3	62.4	63.2	66.5	66.9	..
	22	**Publishing, printing & reprod. of recorded media**	..	72.4	71.3	76.0	86.3	88.2	89.5	..
	221	Publishing	..	40.9	39.2	43.0	48.7	50.0	50.1	..
	222	Printing and related service activities	..	26.0	30.8	31.3	35.6	36.4	37.4	..
	223	Reproduction of recorded media	..	5.5	1.3	1.7	2.0	1.8	2.0	..
	23	**Coke, refined petroleum products & nuclear fuel**	..	9.1	9.8	9.9	10.0	10.6	12.4	..
	24	**Chemicals and chemical products**	..	128.4	141.9	144.6	148.5	153.1	152.0	..
	241	Basic chemicals	..	39.1	48.7	50.5	49.5	50.7	52.5	..
	242	Other chemical products	..	79.5	81.0	81.8	79.5	80.2	78.0	..
	243	Man-made fibres	..	9.8	12.3	12.3	19.6	22.2	21.5	..
	25	**Rubber and plastic products**	..	132.3	121.9	119.1	131.2	133.3	137.0	..
	251	Rubber products	..	34.3	31.3	31.4	32.9	33.4	34.9	..
	252	Plastic products	..	98.0	90.7	87.6	98.4	99.8	102.1	..
	26	**Other non-metallic mineral products**	..	127.3	134.2	134.3	135.2	132.3	128.6	..
	261	Glass and glass products	..	25.5	24.6	25.3	24.8	25.4	25.6	..
	269	Non-metallic mineral products, nec	..	101.8	109.6	108.9	110.4	106.9	103.0	..
	27	**Basic metals**	..	122.5	119.5	114.9	115.8	116.0	121.2	..
	271	Basic iron and steel	..	75.9	72.9	71.3	73.9	73.7	76.2	..
	272	Basic precious and non-ferrous metals	..	30.5	30.0	28.3	27.3	27.2	31.2	..
	273	Casting of metals	..	16.1	16.7	15.2	14.6	15.2	13.8	..
	28	**Fabricated metal products, ex. machin. & equip.**	..	141.3	149.1	146.4	165.3	179.2	188.1	..
	281	Structural metal prod., tanks, reservoirs, generators	..	43.9	47.3	49.6	60.0	66.8	72.7	..
	289	Other fabricated metal products & service activities	..	97.4	101.8	96.8	105.3	112.4	115.4	..
	29	**Machinery and equipment, nec**	..	251.1	261.3	252.0	269.4	284.5	291.3	..
	291	General purpose machinery	..	70.8	84.9	88.6	99.5	111.5	122.4	..
	292	Special purpose machinery	..	132.8	128.2	119.0	126.5	128.1	130.3	..
	293	Domestic appliances, nec	..	47.5	48.2	44.5	43.4	44.9	38.5	..
	30	**Office, accounting and computing machinery**	..	18.9	25.1	21.1	27.7	29.9	31.8	..
	31	**Electrical machinery and apparatus, nec**	..	108.8	105.7	109.8	121.2	122.4	130.3	..
	311	Electric motors, generators and transformers	..	36.1	31.3	32.1	36.3	35.4	36.2	..
	312	Electricity distribution and control apparatus	..	29.5	30.6	31.9	37.0	36.9	40.0	..
	313	Insulated wire and cable	..	13.9	15.9	15.9	16.5	18.0	17.0	..
	314	Accumulators, primary cells and primary batteries	..	4.7	4.9	5.6	4.4	4.7	5.1	..
	315	Electric lamps and lighting equipment	..	11.6	11.7	11.8	13.2	14.1	14.4	..
	319	Other electrical equipment, nec	..	12.9	11.3	12.5	13.8	13.3	17.6	..
	32	**Radio, TV, communication equip. & apparatus**	..	296.4	271.4	258.3	248.5	261.6	269.4	..
	321	Electronic valves, tubes & other electronic compon.	..	115.2	104.5	102.3	108.2	117.6	135.0	..
	322	TV, radio transmitters & appar. for line teleph., telegr.	..	37.5	37.4	33.7	30.1	34.9	31.8	..
	323	TV, radio receivers and associated goods	..	143.7	129.6	122.2	110.2	109.0	102.6	..
	33	**Medical, precision, optical instr.; watches, clocks**	..	44.8	44.5	41.1	45.3	47.4	48.6	..
	331	Medical equip.; precision instruments and appliances	..	18.4	21.6	20.3	23.2	26.7	28.2	..
	332	Optical instruments and photographic equipment	..	16.7	12.9	11.7	12.7	13.1	14.0	..
	333	Watches and clocks	..	9.7	9.9	9.1	9.3	7.6	6.4	..
	34	**Motor vehicles, trailers, and semi-trailers**	..	184.6	181.3	182.0	190.7	207.6	218.2	..
	35	**Other transport equipment**	..	62.3	68.0	65.1	73.5	83.0	89.6	..
	351	Building and repairing of ships and boats	..	47.4	52.7	50.0	55.0	64.0	73.1	..
	352	Railway, tramway locomotives and rolling stock	..	3.8	3.3	4.4	8.0	8.1	6.5	..
	353	Aircraft and spacecraft	..	..	5.2	4.6	4.9	5.2	5.0	..
	359	Transport equipment, nec	..	..	6.8	6.1	5.6	5.7	5.1	..
	36	**Furniture; manufacturing, nec**	..	141.4	129.0	115.5	116.7	110.7	106.9	..
	361	Furniture	..	49.4	52.0	50.7	55.2	53.8	52.9	..
	369	Manufacturing, nec	..	92.0	77.0	64.7	61.5	56.9	54.0	..
	37	**Recycling**	..	0.7	1.1	1.1	1.7	2.0	2.2	..
E	40-41	**Electricity, gas and water supply**	..	..	..	..	..	..	..	..
	40	**Electricity, gas, steam and hot water supply**	..	..	..	..	..	..	..	..
	401	Production, collection and distribution of electricity	..	..	..	..	..	..	..	..
	41	410 **Collection, purification, distribution of water**	..	..	..	..	..	..	..	..
F	45	**Construction**	..	..	..	..	..	..	..	..
G	50-52	**Wholesale and retail trade; repairs etc**	..	..	..	..	..	..	..	..
H	55	**Hotels and restaurants**	..	..	..	..	..	..	..	..
I	60-64	**Transport, storage and communications**	..	..	..	..	..	..	..	..
J	65-67	**Financial intermediation**	..	..	..	..	..	..	..	..
K	70-74	**Real estate, renting and business activities**	..	..	..	..	..	..	..	..
L-Q	75-99	**Public admin.; education; health; other services**	..	..	..	..	..	..	..	..
A-Q	01-99	**Grand total**	..	..	..	..	..	..	..	..

Table KR.8 SALAIRES ET CHARGES SOCIALES - COMPENSATION OF LABOUR

Millions de Won (Prix courants) — CITI révision 3

1989	1990	1991	1992	1993	1994	1995	1996				
..	..	..	..	..	..	..	..	**Agriculture, chasse et sylviculture**	A	01-02	
..	..	..	..	..	..	..	..	**Pêche**	B	05	
..	..	..	..	..	..	..	..	**Activités extractives**	C	10-14	
..	..	..	..	..	..	..	..	Extraction de charbon, de lignite et de tourbe		10	
..	..	..	..	..	..	..	..	Extraction de pétrole brut et de gaz naturel		11	
..	..	..	..	..	..	..	..	Extraction de minerais métalliques		13	
..	..	..	..	..	..	..	..	Autres activités extractives		14	
..	..	29 034 229	31 545 528	35 045 612	..	..	..	**Activités de fabrication**	D	15-37	
..	..	1 701 047	1 891 112	2 101 106	..	..	..	**Produits alimentaires et boissons**		15	
..	..	249 178	281 490	271 440	..	..	..	Boissons			155
..	..	134 589	137 856	145 147	..	..	..	**Produits à base de tabac**		16	160
..	..	2 643 185	2 971 831	3 083 033	..	..	..	**Textiles**		17	
..	..	2 057 742	2 278 758	2 245 189	..	..	..	Filature, tissage et achèvement des textiles			171
..	..	316 237	384 823	463 535	..	..	..	Autres articles textiles			172
..	..	269 206	308 250	374 309	..	..	..	Etoffes et articles de bonneterie			173
..	..	1 336 451	1 425 426	1 680 814	..	..	..	**Habillement; préparation, teinture des fourrures**		18	
..	..	1 282 938	1 384 412	1 644 955	..	..	..	Articles d'habillement autres qu'en fourrure			181
..	..	53 513	41 014	35 859	..	..	..	Préparation, teinture des fourrures; art. en fourrure			182
..	..	1 329 522	1 162 472	1 013 532	..	..	..	**Travail des cuirs; articles en cuir; chaussures**		19	
..	..	287 611	311 223	308 731	..	..	..	Apprêt et tannage des cuirs et articles en cuirs			191
..	..	1 041 911	851 249	704 801	..	..	..	Chaussures			192
..	..	367 892	381 618	435 333	..	..	..	**Bois et articles en bois et liège (sauf meubles)**		20	
..	..	128 491	131 633	143 420	..	..	..	Sciage et rabotage du bois			201
..	..	239 401	249 985	291 913	..	..	..	Articles en bois, liège, vannerie, sparterie			202
..	..	654 782	741 907	783 338	..	..	..	**Papier et carton; articles en papier et en carton**		21	
..	..	838 043	1 000 598	1 236 933	..	..	..	**Edition, imprimerie et reproduction**		22	
..	..	571 535	677 165	850 885	..	..	..	Edition			221
..	..	252 492	302 628	363 758	..	..	..	Imprimerie et activités annexes			222
..	..	14 016	20 805	22 290	..	..	..	Reproduction de supports enregistrés			223
..	..	203 994	214 408	222 112	..	..	..	**Cokéfaction; prod. pétroliers; comb. nucléaires**		23	
..	..	1 830 922	2 119 750	2 352 519	..	..	..	**Produits chimiques**		24	
..	..	714 688	848 700	899 633	..	..	..	Produits chimiques de base			241
..	..	942 569	1 068 823	1 118 800	..	..	..	Autres produits chimiques			242
..	..	173 665	202 227	334 086	..	..	..	Fibres synthétiques ou artificielles			243
..	..	1 156 272	1 282 638	1 529 739	..	..	..	**Articles en caoutchouc et en matières plastiques**		25	
..	..	324 063	367 950	412 218	..	..	..	Articles en caoutchouc			251
..	..	832 209	914 688	1 117 521	..	..	..	Articles en matières plastiques			252
..	..	1 444 048	1 664 018	1 794 840	..	..	..	**Autres produits minéraux non métalliques**		26	
..	..	304 204	365 195	391 093	..	..	..	Verre et articles en verre			261
..	..	1 139 844	1 298 823	1 403 747	..	..	..	Produits minéraux non métalliques, nca			269
..	..	1 781 477	1 861 887	1 991 655	..	..	..	**Produits métallurgiques de base**		27	
..	..	1 259 713	1 303 124	1 435 926	..	..	..	Sidérurgie et première transformation de l'acier			271
..	..	340 843	370 731	367 011	..	..	..	Métallurgie; métaux précieux et non ferreux			272
..	..	180 921	188 032	188 718	..	..	..	Fonderie			273
..	..	1 522 685	1 613 352	2 020 238	..	..	..	**Ouvrages en métaux, sauf machines et matériel**		28	
..	..	555 277	615 040	824 769	..	..	..	Constr. et menuiserie métal.; réservoirs; générateurs			281
..	..	967 408	998 312	1 195 469	..	..	..	Autres ouvrages en métaux			289
..	..	2 833 842	3 073 820	3 508 083	..	..	..	**Machines et matériel, nca**		29	
..	..	880 611	1 136 706	1 280 894	..	..	..	Machines d'usage général			291
..	..	1 488 137	1 466 741	1 704 480	..	..	..	Machines d'usage spécifique			292
..	..	465 094	470 373	522 709	..	..	..	Appareils domestiques, nca			293
..	..	222 550	219 111	332 724	..	..	..	**Mach. de bureau, comptables, matériel inform.**		30	
..	..	1 027 376	1 192 207	1 405 236	..	..	..	**Machines et appareils électriques, nca**		31	
..	..	278 064	307 220	417 360	..	..	..	Moteurs, génératrices et transformateurs électriques			311
..	..	308 619	369 135	417 474	..	..	..	Matériel électrique de distribution et de commande			312
..	..	195 162	225 347	233 150	..	..	..	Fils et câbles électriques isolés			313
..	..	58 528	70 689	64 521	..	..	..	Accumulateurs, piles électriques			314
..	..	87 722	103 162	124 816	..	..	..	Lampes électriques et appareils d'éclairage			315
..	..	99 281	116 654	147 915	..	..	..	Autres matériels électriques, nca			319
..	..	2 792 581	3 026 232	3 000 397	..	..	..	**Equip. et appar. de radio, TV, communication**		32	
..	..	1 189 250	1 221 776	1 424 038	..	..	..	Tubes et valves électroniques; autres composants			321
..	..	374 751	405 067	362 458	..	..	..	Emetteurs radio et TV; app. téléphonie, télégraphie			322
..	..	1 228 580	1 399 389	1 213 901	..	..	..	Récepteurs radio et TV et articles associés			323
..	..	390 902	405 207	483 779	..	..	..	**Instruments médicaux, de précision, d'optique**		33	
..	..	191 428	197 012	246 363	..	..	..	Appareils médicaux et de précision			331
..	..	110 277	109 470	132 269	..	..	..	Instruments d'optique ; matériel photographique			332
..	..	89 197	98 725	105 147	..	..	..	Horlogerie			333
..	..	2 528 763	2 750 565	3 156 084	..	..	..	**Véhicules automobiles et nemorques**		34	
..	..	1 217 292	1 288 638	1 531 385	..	..	..	**Autres matériels de transport**		35	
..	..	1 027 378	1 080 353	1 214 438	..	..	..	Construction et réparation de navires			351
..	..	40 663	71 086	162 679	..	..	..	Construction de matériel ferroviaire roulant			352
..	..	82 206	69 160	88 096	..	..	..	Construction aéronautique et spatiale			353
..	..	67 045	68 039	66 172	..	..	..	Autres équipements de transport			359
..	..	1 068 703	1 111 371	1 220 109	..	..	..	**Meubles; activités de fabrication, nca**		36	
..	..	456 890	508 982	592 352	..	..	..	Meubles			361
..	..	611 813	602 389	627 757	..	..	..	Activités de fabrication, nca			369
..	..	7 311	9 504	17 476	..	..	..	**Récupération**		37	
..	..	..	..	..	..	..	..	**Production et distrib. d'électricité, de gaz, d'eau**	E	40-41	
..	..	..	..	..	..	..	..	**Electricité, gaz, vapeur et eau chaude**		40	
..	..	..	..	..	..	..	..	Production, collecte et distribution d'électricité			401
..	..	..	..	..	..	..	..	**Captage, épuration et distribution d'eau**		41	410
..	..	..	..	..	..	..	..	**Construction**	F	45	
..	..	..	..	..	..	..	..	**Commerce de gros et de détail; réparation**	G	50-52	
..	..	..	..	..	..	..	..	**Hôtels et restaurants**	H	55	
..	..	..	..	..	..	..	..	**Transports, entreposage et communications**	I	60-64	
..	..	..	..	..	..	..	..	**Intermédiation financière**	J	65-67	
..	..	..	..	..	..	..	..	**Immobilier, locations, services aux entreprises**	K	70-74	
..	..	..	..	..	..	..	..	**Admin. publique; éducation; santé; autres**	L-Q	75-99	
..	..	..	..	..	..	..	..	**Grand total**	A-Q	01-99	

Statistiques des Structures Industrielles
OCDE, © 1998   OECD / OCDE

KOREA

Table KR.9 WAGES AND SALARIES, EMPLOYEES - SALAIRES ET TRAITEMENTS, SALARIÉS

Millions of Won (Current Prices)

ISIC revision 3			1989	1990	1991	1992	1993	1994	1995	1996
A	01-02	Agriculture, hunting and forestry	..	..	..	..	..	..	..	..
B	05	Fishing		..	..	..	..	..	..	..
C	10-14	Mining and quarrying	..	441 165	474 466	486 208	474 717	409 712	412 822	..
	10	Mining of coal and lignite; extraction of peat		316 229	307 185	300 994	274 751	200 795	185 464	
	11	Crude petroleum & natural gas; related service activ.		..	..	..	..	..	..	
	13	Mining of metal ores		20 189	19 416	15 695	9 528	6 892	7 427	
	14	Other mining and quarrying		104 747	147 865	169 519	190 438	202 025	219 931	..
D	15-37	Total manufacturing	..	19 532 300	22 830 419	25 234 409	28 834 306	32 791 213	37 844 431	
	15	Food products and beverages		1 161 695	1 338 969	1 471 187	1 700 148	1 876 719	2 150 178	
	155	Beverages		166 478	188 259	194 748	212 192	239 676	288 606	
	16 160	Tobacco products		75 449	90 407	96 805	98 072	94 832	104 475	
	17	Textiles		1 925 994	2 180 703	2 445 466	2 620 686	2 780 040	2 963 269	
	171	Spinning, weaving and finishing of textiles		1 490 765	1 683 964	1 864 057	1 904 537	2 057 129	2 229 133	
	172	Other textiles		239 462	267 825	317 215	393 667	433 121	472 614	
	173	Knitted and crocheted fabrics and articles		195 767	228 914	264 194	322 482	289 790	261 522	
	18	Wearing apparel dressing & dyeing of fur		1 072 190	1 135 558	1 223 068	1 474 682	1 619 693	1 841 478	
	181	Wearing apparel, except fur apparel		1 041 175	1 090 314	1 188 623	1 444 705	1 584 729	1 792 961	
	182	Dressing and dyeing of fur; articles of fur		31 015	45 244	34 445	29 977	34 964	48 517	
	19	Tanning, dressing leather; leather artic.; footwear		1 086 348	1 120 506	976 683	873 497	819 654	781 635	
	191	Tanning, dressing leather; manuf. of leather articles		219 318	242 282	257 780	265 275	281 040	285 511	
	192	Footwear		867 030	878 224	718 903	608 222	538 614	496 124	
	20	Wood and cork products, ex. furniture		247 023	310 888	323 807	378 054	418 383	447 587	
	201	Sawmilling and planing of wood		92 987	111 867	115 526	129 074	152 448	153 559	
	202	Products of wood, cork, straw & plaiting material		154 036	199 021	208 281	248 980	265 935	294 028	
	21	Paper and paper products		433 741	515 855	590 942	650 678	760 377	885 549	
	22	Publishing, printing & reprod. of recorded media		582 252	633 442	786 902	1 021 646	1 141 758	1 254 869	
	221	Publishing		314 002	404 675	508 980	678 107	747 287	797 423	
	222	Printing and related service activities		233 127	217 911	261 255	324 891	372 471	433 659	
	223	Reproduction of recorded media		35 123	10 856	16 667	18 648	22 000	23 787	
	23	Coke, refined petroleum products & nuclear fuel		120 716	130 856	145 191	164 920	205 785	258 217	
	24	Chemicals and chemical products		1 088 211	1 398 365	1 606 516	1 870 388	2 161 919	2 454 942	
	241	Basic chemicals		397 665	561 480	652 026	706 332	830 054	969 223	
	242	Other chemical products		595 108	710 472	810 653	902 112	1 013 489	1 086 735	
	243	Man-made fibres		95 438	126 413	143 837	261 944	318 376	398 984	
	25	Rubber and plastic products		822 332	935 579	1 037 187	1 288 092	1 432 077	1 697 547	
	251	Rubber products		230 993	256 601	288 031	344 389	381 113	467 494	
	252	Plastic products		591 339	678 978	749 156	943 703	1 050 964	1 230 053	
	26	Other non-metallic mineral products		911 658	1 154 925	1 352 672	1 475 461	1 596 684	1 795 101	
	261	Glass and glass products		218 992	245 865	294 979	313 209	346 566	408 489	
	269	Non-metallic mineral products, nec		692 666	909 060	1 057 693	1 162 252	1 250 118	1 386 612	
	27	Basic metals		1 081 070	1 294 699	1 385 232	1 487 621	1 694 347	1 954 375	
	271	Basic iron and steel		734 385	880 507	935 220	1 027 759	1 162 650	1 303 006	
	272	Basic precious and non-ferrous metals		230 121	266 118	294 348	301 226	343 034	457 866	
	273	Casting of metals		116 564	148 074	155 664	158 636	188 663	193 503	
	28	Fabricated metal products, ex. machin. & equip.		928 346	1 217 818	1 349 374	1 704 624	2 078 683	2 471 457	
	281	Structural metal prod., tanks, reservoirs, generators		322 170	430 552	515 194	690 851	857 374	1 079 857	
	289	Other fabricated metal products & service activities		606 176	787 266	834 180	1 013 773	1 221 309	1 391 600	
	29	Machinery and equipment, nec		1 825 987	2 264 371	2 523 626	2 928 188	3 392 294	3 992 799	
	291	General purpose machinery		507 580	714 396	923 039	1 078 204	1 305 256	1 690 466	
	292	Special purpose machinery		1 012 951	1 183 834	1 213 386	1 423 946	1 590 357	1 837 912	
	293	Domestic appliances, nec		305 456	366 141	387 201	426 038	496 681	464 421	
	30	Office, accounting and computing machinery		116 296	176 941	178 267	273 709	329 176	394 563	
	31	Electrical machinery and apparatus, nec		697 206	814 283	944 461	1 167 762	1 261 723	1 583 479	
	311	Electric motors, generators and transformers		225 057	225 003	244 639	351 386	344 198	420 760	
	312	Electricity distribution and control apparatus		186 377	243 915	285 690	350 041	386 871	501 601	
	313	Insulated wire and cable		111 973	144 039	174 185	182 777	221 156	241 518	
	314	Accumulators, primary cells and primary batteries		37 031	45 604	55 550	50 538	57 671	71 380	
	315	Electric lamps and lighting equipment		59 025	73 620	86 505	108 032	129 203	159 819	
	319	Other electrical equipment, nec		77 743	82 102	97 892	124 988	122 624	188 401	
	32	Radio, TV, communication equip. & apparatus		1 921 581	2 202 877	2 343 643	2 401 830	2 816 779	3 518 523	
	321	Electronic valves, tubes & other electronic compon.		754 651	887 776	983 381	1 135 995	1 366 718	1 930 224	
	322	TV, radio transmitters & appar. for line teleph., telegr.		233 674	291 103	306 791	286 029	395 207	430 707	
	323	TV, radio receivers and associated goods		933 256	1 023 998	1 053 471	979 806	1 054 854	1 157 592	
	33	Medical, precision, optical instr.; watches, clocks		266 587	318 879	338 453	406 723	464 745	567 681	
	331	Medical equip.; precision instruments and appliances		109 112	153 460	163 480	207 432	264 500	339 164	
	332	Optical instruments and photographic equipment		100 414	92 239	92 629	112 483	125 454	156 393	
	333	Watches and clocks		57 061	73 180	82 344	86 808	74 791	72 124	
	34	Motor vehicles, trailers, and semi-trailers		1 668 286	1 884 215	2 179 582	2 538 401	3 227 348	3 729 235	
	35	Other transport equipment		711 916	808 617	1 004 875	1 243 807	1 511 754	1 786 238	
	351	Building and repairing of ships and boats		579 260	661 357	835 356	989 810	1 231 569	1 512 008	
	352	Railway, tramway locomotives and rolling stock		37 998	30 488	55 708	129 278	128 101	101 776	
	353	Aircraft and spacecraft		64 450	58 757	70 125	91 140	111 056		
	359	Transport equipment, nec		52 322	55 054	54 594	60 944	61 398		
	36	Furniture; manufacturing, nec		782 951	895 201	922 137	1 050 085	1 086 963	1 187 269	
	361	Furniture		285 361	388 538	422 938	512 908	536 865	605 862	
	369	Manufacturing, nec		497 590	506 663	499 199	537 177	550 098	581 407	
	37	Recycling		4 465	6 465	8 333	15 232	19 480	23 965	
E	40-41	Electricity, gas and water supply	..	..	..	..	..	..	..	..
	40	Electricity, gas, steam and hot water supply	..	..	..	..	..	..	..	..
	401	Production, collection and distribution of electricity		..	..	..	..	..	..	
	41 410	Collection, purification, distribution of water	..	..	..	..	..	..	..	..
F	45	Construction	..	..	..	..	..	..	..	..
G	50-52	Wholesale and retail trade; repairs etc	..	..	..	..	..	..	..	..
H	55	Hotels and restaurants	..	..	..	..	..	..	..	..
I	60-64	Transport, storage and communications	..	..	..	..	..	..	..	..
J	65-67	Financial intermediation	..	..	..	..	..	..	..	..
K	70-74	Real estate, renting and business activities	..	..	..	..	..	..	..	..
L-Q	75-99	Public admin.; education; health; other services	..	..	..	..	..	..	..	..
A-Q	01-99	Grand total	..	..	..	..	..	..	..	..

Table KR.10 CHARGES SOCIALES DES EMPLOYEURS - EMPLOYERS' SOCIAL COSTS

Millions de Won (Prix courants) · CITI révision 3

1989	1990	1991	1992	1993	1994	1995	1996	Branche	Sect.	Div.	Grp.
..	..	..	..	..	..	..	..	Agriculture, chasse et sylviculture	A	01-02	
..	..	..	..	..	..	..	..	Pêche	B	05	
..	50 196	54 914	60 005	49 334	56 788	56 311	..	Activités extractives	C	10-14	
..	36 452	35 056	38 828	28 359	30 900	27 438	..	Extraction de charbon, de lignite et de tourbe		10	
..	..	..	..	..	..	..	..	Extraction de pétrole brut et de gaz naturel		11	
..	1 833	1 802	1 419	639	488	550	..	Extraction de minerais métalliques		13	
..	11 911	18 056	19 758	20 336	25 400	28 323	..	Autres activités extractives		14	
..	2 309 062	2 825 841	3 069 635	3 482 552	4 087 818	4 894 136	..	Activités de fabrication	D	15-37	
..	144 250	174 651	195 952	220 379	247 679	297 791	..	Produits alimentaires et boissons		15	
..	23 076	31 684	33 357	30 470	40 394	51 990	..	Boissons			155
..	16 483	21 174	28 162	26 767	27 897	29 284	..	Produits à base de tabac		16	160
..	176 249	210 047	247 077	250 265	268 278	286 665	..	Textiles		17	
..	136 358	162 591	187 907	179 500	198 568	218 260	..	Filature, tissage et achèvement des textiles			171
..	22 914	27 224	35 854	41 315	44 488	47 729	..	Autres articles textiles			172
..	16 977	20 232	23 316	29 450	25 222	20 676	..	Etoffes et articles de bonneterie			173
..	89 380	100 359	101 323	123 312	138 825	151 869	..	Habillement; préparation, teinture des fourrures		18	
..	86 084	96 766	98 623	119 661	135 463	147 079	..	Articles d'habillement autres qu'en fourrure			181
..	3 296	3 593	2 700	3 651	3 362	4 790	..	Préparation, teinture des fourrures; art. en fourrure			182
..	91 653	101 745	88 894	79 994	76 520	72 357	..	Travail des cuirs; articles en cuir; chaussures		19	
..	23 888	25 248	27 370	28 135	30 754	29 599	..	Apprêt et tannage des cuirs et articles en cuirs			191
..	67 765	76 497	61 524	51 859	45 766	42 758	..	Chaussures			192
..	21 782	27 996	29 080	33 722	37 920	41 249	..	Bois et articles en bois et liège (sauf meubles)		20	
..	6 471	8 990	8 993	9 251	11 966	11 321	..	Sciage et rabotage du bois			201
..	15 311	19 006	20 087	24 471	25 954	29 928	..	Articles en bois, liège, vannerie, sparterie			202
..	53 241	69 313	76 921	78 207	99 167	116 956	..	Papier et carton; articles en papier et en carton		21	
..	62 589	66 880	85 705	110 173	134 061	147 373	..	Edition, imprimerie et reproduction		22	
..	33 832	47 489	61 879	84 018	101 503	112 272	..	Edition			221
..	23 729	18 095	21 820	23 720	29 771	32 257	..	Imprimerie et activités annexes			222
..	5 028	1 296	2 006	2 435	2 787	2 844	..	Reproduction de supports enregistrés			223
..	36 987	45 942	16 947	24 581	30 737	42 655	..	Cokéfaction; prod. pétroliers; comb. nucléaires		23	
..	151 392	187 238	220 947	250 638	293 237	350 161	..	Produits chimiques		24	
..	50 537	69 083	85 427	97 819	117 541	144 718	..	Produits chimiques de base			241
..	87 258	100 677	116 035	118 700	133 643	154 449	..	Autres produits chimiques			242
..	13 597	17 478	19 485	34 119	42 053	50 994	..	Fibres synthétiques ou artificielles			243
..	97 106	112 329	119 572	141 970	162 860	206 970	..	Articles en caoutchouc et en matières plastiques		25	
..	25 050	30 589	32 430	35 915	45 155	55 514	..	Articles en caoutchouc			251
..	72 056	81 740	87 142	106 055	117 705	151 456	..	Articles en matières plastiques			252
..	113 706	143 823	166 714	184 428	203 686	248 576	..	Autres produits minéraux non métalliques		26	
..	23 856	27 217	32 566	40 227	41 077	50 471	..	Verre et articles en verre			261
..	89 850	116 606	134 148	144 201	162 609	198 105	..	Produits minéraux non métalliques, nca			269
..	170 683	224 691	250 213	298 329	385 144	455 120	..	Produits métallurgiques de base		27	
..	132 958	172 123	198 440	244 307	318 715	370 196	..	Sidérurgie et première transformation de l'acier			271
..	24 936	34 642	34 369	36 510	44 369	62 528	..	Métallurgie; métaux précieux et non ferreux			272
..	12 789	17 926	17 404	17 512	22 060	22 396	..	Fonderie			273
..	106 626	146 366	145 977	187 681	234 500	270 950	..	Ouvrages en métaux, sauf machines et matériel		28	
..	36 429	51 583	50 559	79 327	95 314	118 660	..	Constr. et menuiserie métal.; réservoirs; générateurs			281
..	70 197	94 783	95 418	108 354	139 186	152 290	..	Autres ouvrages en métaux			289
..	220 739	286 141	308 386	348 974	437 465	521 071	..	Machines et matériel, nca		29	
..	61 058	84 780	116 925	126 464	171 111	213 252	..	Machines d'usage général			291
..	121 231	151 639	141 295	164 305	190 654	245 468	..	Machines d'usage spécifique			292
..	38 450	49 722	50 166	58 205	75 700	62 351	..	Appareils domestiques, nca			293
..	12 540	19 936	20 677	32 291	38 159	57 875	..	Mach. de bureau, comptables, matériel inform.		30	
..	87 904	100 978	124 053	133 193	149 523	192 952	..	Machines et appareils électriques, nca		31	
..	30 365	23 990	31 149	37 509	37 765	46 033	..	Moteurs, génératrices et transformateurs électriques			311
..	24 229	31 818	42 931	39 539	47 614	62 257	..	Matériel électrique de distribution et de commande			312
..	14 807	24 537	24 839	25 896	29 209	35 042	..	Fils et câbles électriques isolés			313
..	4 038	5 179	6 328	6 363	7 453	9 496	..	Accumulateurs, piles électriques			314
..	5 501	7 367	8 407	9 900	13 220	16 170	..	Lampes électriques et appareils d'éclairage			315
..	8 964	8 087	10 399	13 986	14 262	23 954	..	Autres matériels électriques, nca			319
..	253 455	284 657	354 584	354 398	437 102	595 280	..	Equip. et appar. de radio, TV, communication		32	
..	98 054	122 348	140 215	173 842	222 784	316 371	..	Tubes et valves électroniques; autres composants			321
..	38 823	44 038	52 190	46 345	57 717	77 092	..	Emetteurs radio et TV; app. téléphonie, télégraphie			322
..	116 578	118 271	162 179	134 211	156 601	201 817	..	Récepteurs radio et TV et articles associés			323
..	29 762	34 955	36 807	45 537	59 801	69 355	..	Instruments médicaux, de précision, d'optique		33	
..	12 736	17 635	19 610	23 561	36 400	46 099	..	Appareils médicaux et de précision			331
..	9 629	9 625	8 775	11 555	13 165	16 217	..	Instruments d'optique ; matériel photographique			332
..	7 397	7 695	8 422	10 421	10 236	7 039	..	Horlogerie			333
..	215 072	265 942	221 368	294 471	320 969	390 326	..	Véhicules automobiles et nemorques		34	
..	83 201	113 850	132 281	163 176	199 980	227 120	..	Autres matériels de transport		35	
..	65 863	94 565	109 014	124 949	152 589	179 078	..	Construction et réparation de navires			351
..	5 121	4 009	7 416	20 620	25 385	19 496	..	Construction de matériel ferroviaire roulant			352
..	..	8 564	8 246	10 821	14 990	19 319	..	Construction aéronautique et spatiale			353
..	..	6 712	7 605	6 786	7 016	9 227	..	Autres équipements de transport			359
..	73 977	86 227	97 231	98 466	102 243	119 811	..	Meubles; activités de fabrication, nca		36	
..	26 787	35 280	44 848	46 925	51 975	62 852	..	Meubles			361
..	47 190	50 947	52 383	51 541	50 268	56 959	..	Activités de fabrication, nca			369
..	449	601	764	1 600	2 065	2 370	..	Récupération		37	
..	..	..	..	..	..	..	..	Production et distrib. d'électricité, de gaz, d'eau	E	40-41	
..	..	..	..	..	..	..	..	Electricité, gaz, vapeur et eau chaude		40	
..	..	..	..	..	..	..	..	Production, collecte et distribution d'électricité			401
..	..	..	..	..	..	..	..	Captage, épuration et distribution d'eau		41	410
..	..	..	..	..	..	..	..	Construction	F	45	
..	..	..	..	..	..	..	..	Commerce de gros et de détail; réparation	G	50-52	
..	..	..	..	..	..	..	..	Hôtels et restaurants	H	55	
..	..	..	..	..	..	..	..	Transports, entreposage et communications	I	60-64	
..	..	..	..	..	..	..	..	Intermédiation financière	J	65-67	
..	..	..	..	..	..	..	..	Immobilier, locations, services aux entreprises	K	70-74	
..	..	..	..	..	..	..	..	Admin. publique; éducation; santé; autres	L-Q	75-99	
..	..	..	..	..	..	..	..	Grand total	A-Q	01-99	

Statistiques des Structures Industrielles
OCDE, © 1998

Table ME.1 PRODUCTION - PRODUCTION

Millions of NM$ (Current Prices)

ISIC revision 3			1989	1990	1991	1992	1993	1994	1995	1996
A	01-02	Agriculture, hunting and forestry	..	..	..	..	..	..	..	..
B	05	Fishing	..	..	..	..	..	..	..	..
C	10-14	Mining and quarrying	..	..	..	..	..	..	..	..
	10	Mining of coal and lignite; extraction of peat	..	..	..	..	..	..	..	..
	11	Crude petroleum & natural gas; related service activ.	..	..	..	..	..	..	..	..
	13	Mining of metal ores	3 627	..	..	..	..	4 256	..	..
	14	Other mining and quarrying	2 071	..	..	..	..	2 972	..	..
D	15-37	Total manufacturing	192 276	..	..	..	..	522 731	..	..
	15	Food products and beverages	36 951	..	..	..	..	117 340	..	..
	155	Beverages	8 284	..	..	..	..	29 894	..	..
	16 160	Tobacco products	2 063	..	..	..	..	6 040	..	..
	17	Textiles	9 210	..	..	..	..	21 895	..	..
	171	Spinning, weaving and finishing of textiles	5 840	..	..	..	..	9 692	..	..
	172	Other textiles	1 837	..	..	..	..	7 621	..	..
	173	Knitted and crocheted fabrics and articles	1 533	..	..	..	..	4 582	..	..
	18	Wearing apparel dressing & dyeing of fur	2 865	..	..	..	..	10 277	..	..
	181	Wearing apparel, except fur apparel	2 490	..	..	..	..	9 343	..	..
	182	Dressing and dyeing of fur; articles of fur	375	..	..	..	..	933	..	..
	19	Tanning, dressing leather; leather artic.; footwear	2 640	..	..	..	..	6 938	..	..
	191	Tanning, dressing leather; manuf. of leather articles	682	..	..	..	..	1 393	..	..
	192	Footwear	1 958	..	..	..	..	5 545	..	..
	20	Wood and cork products, ex. furniture	6 119	..	..	..	..	15 827	..	..
	201	Sawmilling and planing of wood	797	..	..	..	..	1 152	..	..
	202	Products of wood, cork, straw & plaiting material	5 322	..	..	..	..	14 675	..	..
	21	Paper and paper products	6 512	..	..	..	..	13 727	..	..
	22	Publishing, printing & reprod. of recorded media	6 876	..	..	..	..	23 627	..	..
	221	Publishing	6 400	..	..	..	..	23 038	..	..
	222	Printing and related service activities	476	..	..	..	..	589	..	..
	223	Reproduction of recorded media	..	..	..	..	..	..	..	..
	23	Coke, refined petroleum products & nuclear fuel	12 375	..	..	..	..	33 694	..	..
	24	Chemicals and chemical products	27 925	..	..	..	..	65 383	..	..
	241	Basic chemicals	22 064	..	..	..	..	48 286	..	..
	242	Other chemical products	4 771	..	..	..	..	13 257	..	..
	243	Man-made fibres	1 090	..	..	..	..	3 840	..	..
	25	Rubber and plastic products	2 654	..	..	..	..	4 779	..	..
	251	Rubber products	2 654	..	..	..	..	4 779	..	..
	252	Plastic products	..	..	..	..	..	..	..	..
	26	Other non-metallic mineral products	8 794	..	..	..	..	25 717	..	..
	261	Glass and glass products	2 713	..	..	..	..	5 938	..	..
	269	Non-metallic mineral products, nec	6 081	..	..	..	..	19 780	..	..
	27	Basic metals	15 194	..	..	..	..	32 554	..	..
	271	Basic iron and steel	9 441	..	..	..	..	21 709	..	..
	272	Basic precious and non-ferrous metals	4 841	..	..	..	..	9 648	..	..
	273	Casting of metals	912	..	..	..	..	1 197	..	..
	28	Fabricated metal products, ex. machin. & equip.	6 798	..	..	..	..	20 992	..	..
	281	Structural metal prod., tanks, reservoirs, generators	1 713	..	..	..	..	6 313	..	..
	289	Other fabricated metal products & service activities	5 085	..	..	..	..	14 679	..	..
	29	Machinery and equipment, nec	7 742	..	..	..	..	19 946	..	..
	291	General purpose machinery	5 183	..	..	..	..	13 533	..	..
	292	Special purpose machinery	2 559	..	..	..	..	6 413	..	..
	293	Domestic appliances, nec	..	..	..	..	..	..	..	..
	30	Office, accounting and computing machinery	1 918	..	..	..	..	4 162	..	..
	31	Electrical machinery and apparatus, nec	8 021	..	..	..	..	18 723	..	..
	311	Electric motors, generators and transformers	4 155	..	..	..	..	6 834	..	..
	312	Electricity distribution and control apparatus	..	..	..	..	..	..	..	..
	313	Insulated wire and cable	..	..	..	..	..	..	..	..
	314	Accumulators, primary cells and primary batteries	499	..	..	..	..	1 597	..	..
	315	Electric lamps and lighting equipment	431	..	..	..	..	1 255	..	..
	319	Other electrical equipment, nec	2 937	..	..	..	..	9 036	..	..
	32	Radio, TV, communication equip. & apparatus	1 962	..	..	..	..	5 391	..	..
	321	Electronic valves, tubes & other electronic compon.	1 007	..	..	..	..	3 334	..	..
	322	TV, radio transmitters & appar. for line teleph., telegr.	..	..	..	..	..	..	..	..
	323	TV, radio receivers and associated goods	955	..	..	..	..	2 057	..	..
	33	Medical, precision, optical instr.; watches, clocks	590	..	..	..	..	1 860	..	..
	331	Medical equip.; precision instruments and appliances	470	..	..	..	..	1 453	..	..
	332	Optical instruments and photographic equipment	70	..	..	..	..	296	..	..
	333	Watches and clocks	50	..	..	..	..	111	..	..
	34	Motor vehicles, trailers, and semi-trailers	23 950	..	..	..	..	71 567	..	..
	35	Other transport equipment	691	..	..	..	..	1 339	..	..
	351	Building and repairing of ships and boats	142	..	..	..	..	191	..	..
	352	Railway, tramway locomotives and rolling stock	213	..	..	..	..	265	..	..
	353	Aircraft and spacecraft	32	..	..	..	..	52	..	..
	359	Transport equipment, nec	304	..	..	..	..	830	..	..
	36	Furniture; manufacturing, nec	424	..	..	..	..	953	..	..
	361	Furniture	..	..	..	..	..	..	..	..
	369	Manufacturing, nec	424	..	..	..	..	953	..	..
	37	Recycling	..	..	..	..	..	..	..	..
E	40-41	Electricity, gas and water supply	..	..	..	..	..	..	..	..
	40	Electricity, gas, steam and hot water supply	..	..	..	..	..	..	..	..
	401	Production, collection and distribution of electricity	..	..	..	..	..	..	..	..
	41 410	Collection, purification, distribution of water	..	..	..	..	..	..	..	..
F	45	Construction	..	..	..	..	..	..	..	..
G	50-52	Wholesale and retail trade; repairs etc	..	..	..	..	..	..	..	..
H	55	Hotels and restaurants	8 893	..	..	..	..	33 423	..	..
I	60-64	Transport, storage and communications	..	..	..	..	..	..	..	..
J	65-67	Financial intermediation	..	..	..	..	..	..	..	..
K	70-74	Real estate, renting and business activities	7 527	..	..	..	..	56 880	..	..
L-Q	75-99	Public admin.; education; health; other services	5 429	..	..	..	..	27 859	..	..
A-Q	01-99	Grand total	..	..	..	..	..	..	..	..

Note: ISIC 1531 includes 1532 and 1549; 1541 includes 1544; 1721 includes 1723 and 1729; 1820 includes 1912; 2029 includes 2520; 2211 includes 2212, 2219, 2221 and 3691.
ISIC 2213 includes 2230, 2422 and 2429; 2411 includes 2423; 2899 includes 3699; 2912 includes 2913 and 2919; 2914 includes 2930; 2922 includes 2923; 2929 includes part of 70_74.
ISIC 3110 includes 3120, 3130; 3190 includes 3220; 3430 includes 3610; 3511 includes 3512; 3591 includes 3592; 55 includes part of 75_99. Part of ISIC 70_74 and 75_99 is not covered.

Table ME.2 VALEUR AJOUTÉE - VALUE ADDED

Millions de NM$ (Prix courants)

1989	1990	1991	1992	1993	1994	1995	1996			CITI révision 3	
..	..	..	..	..	..	..	..	..	**Agriculture, chasse et sylviculture**	A	01-02	
..	..	..	..	..	..	..	..	..	**Pêche**	B	05	
..	..	..	..	..	..	..	..	..	**Activités extractives**	C	10-14	
..	..	..	..	..	..	..	..	..	Extraction de charbon, de lignite et de tourbe		10	
..	..	..	..	..	..	..	..	..	Extraction de pétrole brut et de gaz naturel		11	
2 084	..	..	..	..	1 795	..	..	..	Extraction de minerais métalliques		13	
1 223	..	..	..	..	1 527	..	..	..	Autres activités extractives		14	
68 660	..	..	..	..	185 873	..	..	..	**Activités de fabrication**	D	15-37	
11 147	..	..	..	..	41 319	..	..	..	**Produits alimentaires et boissons**		15	
3 032	..	..	..	..	13 414	..	..	..	Boissons			155
1 611	..	..	..	..	4 886	..	..	..	**Produits à base de tabac**		16	160
3 579	..	..	..	..	8 808	..	..	..	**Textiles**		17	
2 365	..	..	..	..	3 362	..	..	..	Filature, tissage et achèvement des textiles			171
613	..	..	..	..	3 562	..	..	..	Autres articles textiles			172
602	..	..	..	..	1 884	..	..	..	Etoffes et articles de bonneterie			173
1 090	..	..	..	..	4 200	..	..	..	**Habillement; préparation, teinture des fourrures**		18	
931	..	..	..	..	3 765	..	..	..	Articles d'habillement autres qu'en fourrure			181
159	..	..	..	..	435	..	..	..	Préparation, teinture des fourrures; art. en fourrure			182
812	..	..	..	..	2 494	..	..	..	**Travail des cuirs; articles en cuir; chaussures**		19	
154	..	..	..	..	340	..	..	..	Apprêt et tannage des cuirs et articles en cuirs			191
659	..	..	..	..	2 154	..	..	..	Chaussures			192
2 195	..	..	..	..	5 903	..	..	..	**Bois et articles en bois et liège (sauf meubles)**		20	
326	..	..	..	..	393	..	..	..	Sciage et rabotage du bois			201
1 870	..	..	..	..	5 510	..	..	..	Articles en bois, liège, vannerie, sparterie			202
1 998	..	..	..	..	3 878	..	..	..	**Papier et carton; articles en papier et en carton**		21	
2 794	..	..	..	..	10 317	..	..	..	**Edition, imprimerie et reproduction**		22	
2 596	..	..	..	..	10 015	..	..	..	Edition			221
197	..	..	..	..	301	..	..	..	Imprimerie et activités annexes			222
..	..	..	..	..	..	..	..	..	Reproduction de supports enregistrés			223
4 987	..	..	..	..	9 032	..	..	..	**Cokéfaction; prod. pétroliers; comb. nucléaires**		23	
8 116	..	..	..	..	23 573	..	..	..	**Produits chimiques**		24	
6 128	..	..	..	..	16 526	..	..	..	Produits chimiques de base			241
1 596	..	..	..	..	5 886	..	..	..	Autres produits chimiques			242
393	..	..	..	..	1 161	..	..	..	Fibres synthétiques ou artificielles			243
1 068	..	..	..	..	2 050	..	..	..	**Articles en caoutchouc et en matières plastiques**		25	
1 068	..	..	..	..	2 050	..	..	..	Articles en caoutchouc			251
..	..	..	..	..	..	..	..	..	Articles en matières plastiques			252
3 903	..	..	..	..	12 161	..	..	..	**Autres produits minéraux non métalliques**		26	
1 165	..	..	..	..	2 821	..	..	..	Verre et articles en verre			261
2 739	..	..	..	..	9 340	..	..	..	Produits minéraux non métalliques, nca			269
4 471	..	..	..	..	6 596	..	..	..	**Produits métallurgiques de base**		27	
3 106	..	..	..	..	3 736	..	..	..	Sidérurgie et première transformation de l'acier			271
1 007	..	..	..	..	2 375	..	..	..	Métallurgie; métaux précieux et non ferreux			272
358	..	..	..	..	485	..	..	..	Fonderie			273
2 620	..	..	..	..	8 224	..	..	..	**Ouvrages en métaux, sauf machines et matériel**		28	
637	..	..	..	..	2 425	..	..	..	Constr. et menuiserie métal.; réservoirs; générateurs			281
1 983	..	..	..	..	5 799	..	..	..	Autres ouvrages en métaux			289
3 127	..	..	..	..	7 745	..	..	..	**Machines et matériel, nca**		29	
2 118	..	..	..	..	4 983	..	..	..	Machines d'usage général			291
1 010	..	..	..	..	2 762	..	..	..	Machines d'usage spécifique			292
..	..	..	..	..	..	..	..	..	Appareils domestiques, nca			293
682	..	..	..	..	920	..	..	..	**Mach. de bureau, comptables, matériel inform.**		30	
3 631	..	..	..	..	8 885	..	..	..	**Machines et appareils électriques, nca**		31	
1 655	..	..	..	..	3 034	..	..	..	Moteurs, génératrices et transformateurs électriques			311
..	..	..	..	..	..	..	..	..	Matériel électrique de distribution et de commande			312
..	..	..	..	..	..	..	..	..	Fils et câbles électriques isolés			313
161	..	..	..	..	852	..	..	..	Accumulateurs, piles électriques			314
192	..	..	..	..	586	..	..	..	Lampes électriques et appareils d'éclairage			315
1 622	..	..	..	..	4 414	..	..	..	Autres matériels électriques, nca			319
853	..	..	..	..	2 898	..	..	..	**Equip. et appar. de radio, TV, communication**		32	
456	..	..	..	..	1 885	..	..	..	Tubes et valves électroniques; autres composants			321
..	..	..	..	..	..	..	..	..	Emetteurs radio et TV; app. téléphonie, télégraphie			322
397	..	..	..	..	1 014	..	..	..	Récepteurs radio et TV et articles associés			323
268	..	..	..	..	981	..	..	..	**Instruments médicaux, de précision, d'optique**		33	
229	..	..	..	..	791	..	..	..	Appareils médicaux et de précision			331
31	..	..	..	..	155	..	..	..	Instruments d'optique ; matériel photographique			332
9	..	..	..	..	36	..	..	..	Horlogerie			333
9 188	..	..	..	..	19 990	..	..	..	**Véhicules automobiles et nemorques**		34	
333	..	..	..	..	488	..	..	..	**Autres matériels de transport**		35	
63	..	..	..	..	99	..	..	..	Construction et réparation de navires			351
116	..	..	..	..	108	..	..	..	Construction de matériel ferroviaire roulant			352
20	..	..	..	..	40	..	..	..	Construction aéronautique et spatiale			353
134	..	..	..	..	241	..	..	..	Autres équipements de transport			359
186	..	..	..	..	524	..	..	..	**Meubles; activités de fabrication, nca**		36	
..	..	..	..	..	..	..	..	..	Meubles			361
186	..	..	..	..	524	..	..	..	Activités de fabrication, nca			369
..	..	..	..	..	..	..	..	..	**Récupération**		37	
..	..	..	..	..	..	..	..	..	**Production et distrib. d'électricité, de gaz, d'eau**	E	40-41	
..	..	..	..	..	..	..	..	..	**Electricité, gaz, vapeur et eau chaude**		40	
..	..	..	..	..	..	..	..	..	Production, collecte et distribution d'électricité			401
..	..	..	..	..	..	..	..	..	**Captage, épuration et distribution d'eau**		41	410
..	..	..	..	..	..	..	..	..	**Construction**	F	45	
..	..	..	..	..	..	..	..	..	**Commerce de gros et de détail; réparation**	G	50-52	
3 501	..	..	..	..	14 374	..	..	..	**Hôtels et restaurants**	H	55	
..	..	..	..	..	..	..	..	..	**Transports, entreposage et communications**	I	60-64	
..	..	..	..	..	..	..	..	..	**Intermédiation financière**	J	65-67	
4 016	..	..	..	..	31 532	..	..	..	**Immobilier, locations, services aux entreprises**	K	70-74	
3 042	..	..	..	..	16 185	..	..	..	**Admin. publique; éducation; santé; autres**	L-Q	75-99	
								..	Grand total	A-Q	01-99	

Note: ISIC 1531 includes 1532 and 1549; 1541 includes 1544; 1721 includes 1723 and 1729; 1820 includes 1912; 2029 includes 2520; 2211 includes 2212, 2219, 2221 and 3691.
ISIC 2213 includes 2230, 2422 and 2429; 2411 includes 2423; 2899 includes 3699; 2912 includes 2913 and 2919; 2914 includes 2930; 2922 includes 2923; 2929 includes part of 70_74.
ISIC 3110 includes 3120, 3130; 3190 includes 3220; 3430 includes 3610; 3511 includes 3512; 3591 includes 3592; 55 includes part of 75_99. Part of ISIC 70_74 and 75_99 is not covered.

Statistiques des Structures Industrielles
OCDE, © 1998

Table ME.3 ESTABLISHMENTS - ETABLISSEMENTS

Units

ISIC revision 3			1989	1990	1991	1992	1993	1994	1995	1996
A	01-02	**Agriculture, hunting and forestry**	..	..	..	..	..	..	..	..
B	05	**Fishing**	..	..	..	..	..	..	..	..
C	10-14	**Mining and quarrying**	..	..	..	..	..	..	..	..
	10	Mining of coal and lignite; extraction of peat	..	..	..	..	..	..	..	..
	11	Crude petroleum & natural gas; related service activ.	..	..	..	..	..	..	..	..
	13	Mining of metal ores	537	..	..	..	..	188	..	..
	14	Other mining and quarrying	1 494	..	..	..	..	2 635	..	..
D	15-37	**Total manufacturing**	144 411	..	..	..	..	274 861	..	..
	15	**Food products and beverages**	49 916	..	..	..	..	91 264	..	..
	155	Beverages	1 717	..	..	..	..	3 861	..	..
	16	**Tobacco products**	22	..	..	..	..	26	..	..
	17	**Textiles**	3 777	..	..	..	..	14 372	..	..
	171	Spinning, weaving and finishing of textiles	1 224	..	..	..	..	3 750	..	..
	172	Other textiles	1 547	..	..	..	..	8 785	..	..
	173	Knitted and crocheted fabrics and articles	1 006	..	..	..	..	1 837	..	..
	18	**Wearing apparel dressing & dyeing of fur**	9 745	..	..	..	..	23 830	..	..
	181	Wearing apparel, except fur apparel	8 877	..	..	..	..	22 036	..	..
	182	Dressing and dyeing of fur; articles of fur	868	..	..	..	..	1 794	..	..
	19	**Tanning, dressing leather; leather artic.; footwear**	3 173	..	..	..	..	6 048	..	..
	191	Tanning, dressing leather; manuf. of leather articles	704	..	..	..	..	873	..	..
	192	Footwear	2 469	..	..	..	..	5 175	..	..
	20	**Wood and cork products, ex. furniture**	8 272	..	..	..	..	15 741	..	..
	201	Sawmilling and planing of wood	1 233	..	..	..	..	901	..	..
	202	Products of wood, cork, straw & plaiting material	7 039	..	..	..	..	14 840	..	..
	21	**Paper and paper products**	736	..	..	..	..	1 491	..	..
	22	**Publishing, printing & reprod. of recorded media**	8 344	..	..	..	..	16 046	..	..
	221	Publishing	7 184	..	..	..	..	14 398	..	..
	222	Printing and related service activities	1 160	..	..	..	..	1 648	..	..
	223	Reproduction of recorded media	..	..	..	..	..	..	..	..
	23	**Coke, refined petroleum products & nuclear fuel**	118	..	..	..	..	127	..	..
	24	**Chemicals and chemical products**	1 451	..	..	..	..	1 809	..	..
	241	Basic chemicals	935	..	..	..	..	1 037	..	..
	242	Other chemical products	497	..	..	..	..	750	..	..
	243	Man-made fibres	19	..	..	..	..	22	..	..
	25	**Rubber and plastic products**	533	..	..	..	..	792	..	..
	251	Rubber products	533	..	..	..	..	792	..	..
	252	Plastic products	..	..	..	..	..	..	..	..
	26	**Other non-metallic mineral products**	14 389	..	..	..	..	24 445	..	..
	261	Glass and glass products	476	..	..	..	..	785	..	..
	269	Non-metallic mineral products, nec	13 913	..	..	..	..	23 660	..	..
	27	**Basic metals**	1 663	..	..	..	..	1 365	..	..
	271	Basic iron and steel	575	..	..	..	..	191	..	..
	272	Basic precious and non-ferrous metals	280	..	..	..	..	125	..	..
	273	Casting of metals	808	..	..	..	..	1 049	..	..
	28	**Fabricated metal products, ex. machin. & equip.**	18 993	..	..	..	..	35 993	..	..
	281	Structural metal prod., tanks, reservoirs, generators	15 528	..	..	..	..	29 347	..	..
	289	Other fabricated metal products & service activities	3 465	..	..	..	..	6 646	..	..
	29	**Machinery and equipment, nec**	9 957	..	..	..	..	16 108	..	..
	291	General purpose machinery	3 161	..	..	..	..	5 616	..	..
	292	Special purpose machinery	6 796	..	..	..	..	10 492	..	..
	293	Domestic appliances, nec	..	..	..	..	..	..	..	..
	30	**Office, accounting and computing machinery**	100	..	..	..	..	93	..	..
	31	**Electrical machinery and apparatus, nec**	1 125	..	..	..	..	1 485	..	..
	311	Electric motors, generators and transformers	496	..	..	..	..	523	..	..
	312	Electricity distribution and control apparatus	..	..	..	..	..	..	..	..
	313	Insulated wire and cable	..	..	..	..	..	..	..	..
	314	Accumulators, primary cells and primary batteries	66	..	..	..	..	38	..	..
	315	Electric lamps and lighting equipment	302	..	..	..	..	581	..	..
	319	Other electrical equipment, nec	261	..	..	..	..	343	..	..
	32	**Radio, TV, communication equip. & apparatus**	214	..	..	..	..	354	..	..
	321	Electronic valves, tubes & other electronic compon.	156	..	..	..	..	297	..	..
	322	TV, radio transmitters & appar. for line teleph., telegr.	..	..	..	..	..	..	..	..
	323	TV, radio receivers and associated goods	58	..	..	..	..	57	..	..
	33	**Medical, precision, optical instr.; watches, clocks**	715	..	..	..	..	1 325	..	..
	331	Medical equip.; precision instruments and appliances	610	..	..	..	..	1 147	..	..
	332	Optical instruments and photographic equipment	89	..	..	..	..	168	..	..
	333	Watches and clocks	16	..	..	..	..	10	..	..
	34	**Motor vehicles, trailers, and semi-trailers**	10 660	..	..	..	..	20 949	..	..
	35	**Other transport equipment**	178	..	..	..	..	171	..	..
	351	Building and repairing of ships and boats	64	..	..	..	..	40	..	..
	352	Railway, tramway locomotives and rolling stock	15	..	..	..	..	18	..	..
	353	Aircraft and spacecraft	7	..	..	..	..	8	..	..
	359	Transport equipment, nec	92	..	..	..	..	105	..	..
	36	**Furniture; manufacturing, nec**	330	..	..	..	..	1 027	..	..
	361	Furniture	..	..	..	..	..	..	..	..
	369	Manufacturing, nec	330	..	..	..	..	1 027	..	..
	37	**Recycling**	..	..	..	..	..	..	..	..
E	40-41	**Electricity, gas and water supply**	..	..	..	..	..	..	..	..
	40	**Electricity, gas, steam and hot water supply**	..	..	..	..	..	..	..	..
	401	Production, collection and distribution of electricity	..	..	..	..	..	..	..	..
	41 410	**Collection, purification, distribution of water**	..	..	..	..	..	..	..	..
F	45	**Construction**	..	..	..	..	..	..	..	..
G	50-52	**Wholesale and retail trade; repairs etc**	..	..	..	..	..	..	..	..
H	55	**Hotels and restaurants**	124 692	..	..	..	..	202 805	..	..
I	60-64	**Transport, storage and communications**	..	..	..	..	..	..	..	..
J	65-67	**Financial intermediation**	..	..	..	..	..	..	..	..
K	70-74	**Real estate, renting and business activities**	38 264	..	..	..	..	81 940	..	..
L-Q	75-99	**Public admin.; education; health; other services**	110 393	..	..	..	..	189 154	..	..
A-Q	01-99	**Grand total**	..	..	..	..	..	..	..	..

Note: ISIC 1531 includes 1532 and 1549; 1541 includes 1544; 1721 includes 1723 and 1729; 1820 includes 1912; 2029 includes 2520; 2211 includes 2212, 2219, 2221 and 3691. ISIC 2213 includes 2230, 2422 and 2429; 2411 includes 2423; 2899 includes 3699; 2912 includes 2913 and 2919; 2914 includes 2930; 2922 includes 2923; 2929 includes part of 70_74. ISIC 3110 includes 3120, 3130; 3190 includes 3220; 3430 includes 3610; 3511 includes 3512; 3591 includes 3592; 55 includes part of 75_99. Part of ISIC 70_74 and 75_99 is not covered.

OECD Industrial Structure Statistics
OCDE OECD, © 1998

Table ME.4 EMPLOI, SALARIÉS - EMPLOYMENT, EMPLOYEES

Milliers

1989	1990	1991	1992	1993	1994	1995	1996			CITI révision 3	
..	..	..	..	..	..	..	..	..	**Agriculture, chasse et sylviculture**	**A**	**01-02**
..	..	..	..	..	..	..	..	..	**Pêche**	**B**	**05**
..	..	..	..	..	..	..	..	..	**Activités extractives**	**C**	**10-14**
..	..	..	..	..	..	..	..	..	Extraction de charbon, de lignite et de tourbe		**10**
..	..	..	..	..	..	..	..	..	Extraction de pétrole brut et de gaz naturel		**11**
47.9	..	..	..	..	26.2	..	..	..	Extraction de minerais métalliques		**13**
45.6	..	..	..	..	28.3	..	..	..	Autres activités extractives		**14**
2 470.9	..	..	..	..	2 909.4	..	..	..	**Activités de fabrication**	**D**	**15-37**
456.3	..	..	..	..	556.4	..	..	..	**Produits alimentaires et boissons**	**15**	
111.0	..	..	..	..	140.9	..	..	..	Boissons		155
5.1	..	..	..	..	4.7	..	..	..	**Produits à base de tabac**	**16**	160
201.4	..	..	..	..	225.2	..	..	..	**Textiles**	**17**	
110.5	..	..	..	..	88.5	..	..	..	Filature, tissage et achèvement des textiles		171
44.0	..	..	..	..	79.6	..	..	..	Autres articles textiles		172
46.9	..	..	..	..	57.1	..	..	..	Etoffes et articles de bonneterie		173
122.1	..	..	..	..	174.8	..	..	..	**Habillement; préparation, teinture des fourrures**	**18**	
111.3	..	..	..	..	159.1	..	..	..	Articles d'habillement autres qu'en fourrure		181
10.8	..	..	..	..	15.7	..	..	..	Préparation, teinture des fourrures; art. en fourrure		182
81.4	..	..	..	..	92.8	..	..	..	**Travail des cuirs; articles en cuir; chaussures**	**19**	
9.6	..	..	..	..	10.1	..	..	..	Apprêt et tannage des cuirs et articles en cuirs		191
71.8	..	..	..	..	82.7	..	..	..	Chaussures		192
133.6	..	..	..	..	158.7	..	..	..	**Bois et articles en bois et liège (sauf meubles)**	**20**	
32.2	..	..	..	..	21.1	..	..	..	Sciage et rabotage du bois		201
101.5	..	..	..	..	137.6	..	..	..	Articles en bois, liège, vannerie, sparterie		202
53.3	..	..	..	..	61.9	..	..	..	**Papier et carton; articles en papier et en carton**	**21**	
115.1	..	..	..	..	162.1	..	..	..	**Edition, imprimerie et reproduction**	**22**	
103.5	..	..	..	..	154.8	..	..	..	Edition		221
11.6	..	..	..	..	7.3	..	..	..	Imprimerie et activités annexes		222
..	..	..	..	..	..	..	..	..	Reproduction de supports enregistrés		223
48.8	..	..	..	..	27.1	..	..	..	**Cokéfaction; prod. pétroliers; comb. nucléaires**	**23**	
158.7	..	..	..	..	159.6	..	..	..	**Produits chimiques**	**24**	
115.5	..	..	..	..	102.4	..	..	..	Produits chimiques de base		241
35.9	..	..	..	..	42.7	..	..	..	Autres produits chimiques		242
7.3	..	..	..	..	14.5	..	..	..	Fibres synthétiques ou artificielles		243
30.2	..	..	..	..	32.6	..	..	..	**Articles en caoutchouc et en matières plastiques**	**25**	
30.2	..	..	..	..	32.6	..	..	..	Articles en caoutchouc		251
..	..	..	..	..	..	..	..	..	Articles en matières plastiques		252
128.9	..	..	..	..	145.8	..	..	..	**Autres produits minéraux non métalliques**	**26**	
34.5	..	..	..	..	34.2	..	..	..	Verre et articles en verre		261
94.4	..	..	..	..	111.6	..	..	..	Produits minéraux non métalliques, nca		269
116.0	..	..	..	..	74.0	..	..	..	**Produits métallurgiques de base**	**27**	
80.4	..	..	..	..	33.3	..	..	..	Sidérurgie et première transformation de l'acier		271
18.5	..	..	..	..	25.2	..	..	..	Métallurgie; métaux précieux et non ferreux		272
17.0	..	..	..	..	15.4	..	..	..	Fonderie		273
128.7	..	..	..	..	181.5	..	..	..	**Ouvrages en métaux, sauf machines et matériel**	**28**	
38.2	..	..	..	..	62.9	..	..	..	Constr. et menuiserie métal.; réservoirs; générateurs		281
90.6	..	..	..	..	118.6	..	..	..	Autres ouvrages en métaux		289
165.4	..	..	..	..	181.5	..	..	..	**Machines et matériel, nca**	**29**	
108.1	..	..	..	..	115.3	..	..	..	Machines d'usage général		291
57.3	..	..	..	..	66.2	..	..	..	Machines d'usage spécifique		292
..	..	..	..	..	..	..	..	..	Appareils domestiques, nca		293
18.8	..	..	..	..	18.9	..	..	..	**Mach. de bureau, comptables, matériel inform.**	**30**	
182.2	..	..	..	..	229.7	..	..	..	**Machines et appareils électriques, nca**	**31**	
73.0	..	..	..	..	74.6	..	..	..	Moteurs, génératrices et transformateurs électriques		311
..	..	..	..	..	..	..	..	..	Matériel électrique de distribution et de commande		312
..	..	..	..	..	..	..	..	..	Fils et câbles électriques isolés		313
6.9	..	..	..	..	8.3	..	..	..	Accumulateurs, piles électriques		314
12.3	..	..	..	..	17.5	..	..	..	Lampes électriques et appareils d'éclairage		315
90.1	..	..	..	..	129.3	..	..	..	Autres matériels électriques, nca		319
65.8	..	..	..	..	98.8	..	..	..	**Equip. et appar. de radio, TV, communication**	**32**	
36.5	..	..	..	..	67.8	..	..	..	Tubes et valves électroniques; autres composants		321
..	..	..	..	..	..	..	..	..	Emetteurs radio et TV; app. téléphonie, télégraphie		322
29.3	..	..	..	..	31.0	..	..	..	Récepteurs radio et TV et articles associés		323
19.7	..	..	..	..	31.5	..	..	..	**Instruments médicaux, de précision, d'optique**	**33**	
15.2	..	..	..	..	25.7	..	..	..	Appareils médicaux et de précision		331
3.4	..	..	..	..	5.0	..	..	..	Instruments d'optique ; matériel photographique		332
1.1	..	..	..	..	0.7	..	..	..	Horlogerie		333
204.4	..	..	..	..	257.0	..	..	..	**Véhicules automobiles et nemorques**	**34**	
19.4	..	..	..	..	14.1	..	..	..	**Autres matériels de transport**	**35**	
6.3	..	..	..	..	4.0	..	..	..	Construction et réparation de navires		351
5.8	..	..	..	..	1.7	..	..	..	Construction de matériel ferroviaire roulant		352
1.7	..	..	..	..	1.3	..	..	..	Construction aéronautique et spatiale		353
5.6	..	..	..	..	7.0	..	..	..	Autres équipements de transport		359
15.5	..	..	..	..	20.7	..	..	..	**Meubles; activités de fabrication, nca**	**36**	
..	..	..	..	..	..	..	..	..	Meubles		361
15.5	..	..	..	..	20.7	..	..	..	Activités de fabrication, nca		369
..	..	..	..	..	..	..	..	..	**Récupération**	**37**	
..	..	..	..	..	..	..	..	..	**Production et distrib. d'électricité, de gaz, d'eau**	**E**	**40-41**
..	..	..	..	..	..	..	..	..	**Electricité, gaz, vapeur et eau chaude**	**40**	
..	..	..	..	..	..	..	..	..	Production, collecte et distribution d'électricité		401
..	..	..	..	..	..	..	..	..	**Captage, épuration et distribution d'eau**	**41**	410
..	..	..	..	..	..	..	..	..	**Construction**	**F**	**45**
..	..	..	..	..	..	..	..	..	**Commerce de gros et de détail; réparation**	**G**	**50-52**
335.6	..	..	..	..	497.6	..	..	..	**Hôtels et restaurants**	**H**	**55**
..	..	..	..	..	..	..	..	..	**Transports, entreposage et communications**	**I**	**60-64**
..	..	..	..	..	..	..	..	..	**Intermédiation financière**	**J**	**65-67**
237.2	..	..	..	..	504.6	..	..	..	**Immobilier, locations, services aux entreprises**	**K**	**70-74**
296.4	..	..	..	..	460.3	..	..	..	**Admin. publique; éducation; santé; autres**	**L-Q**	**75-99**
								..	**Grand total**	**A-Q**	**01-99**

Note: ISIC 1531 includes 1532 and 1549; 1541 includes 1544; 1721 includes 1723 and 1729; 1820 includes 1912; 2029 includes 2520; 2211 includes 2212, 2219, 2221 and 3691.
ISIC 2213 includes 2230, 2422 and 2429; 2411 includes 2423; 2899 includes 3699; 2912 includes 2913 and 2919; 2914 includes 2930; 2922 includes 2923; 2929 includes part of 70_74.
ISIC 3110 includes 3120, 3130; 3190 includes 3220; 3430 includes 3610; 3511 includes 3512; 3591 includes 3592; 55 includes part of 75_99. Part of ISIC 70_74 and 75_99 is not covered.

Table ME.5 WAGES AND SALARIES, EMPLOYEES - SALAIRES ET TRAITEMENTS, SALARIÉS

Millions of NM$ (Current Prices)

ISIC revision 3				1989	1990	1991	1992	1993	1994	1995	1996
A	01-02		Agriculture, hunting and forestry	..	..	..	..	..	..	..	..
B	05		Fishing	..	..	..	..	..	..	..	..
C	10-14		Mining and quarrying	..	..	..	..	..	..	..	..
	10		Mining of coal and lignite; extraction of peat	..	..	..	..	..	..	..	..
	11		Crude petroleum & natural gas; related service activ.	..	..	..	..	..	..	..	..
	13		Mining of metal ores	315	..	..	..	..	542	..	..
	14		Other mining and quarrying	179	..	..	..	..	381	..	..
D	15-37		Total manufacturing	15 319	..	..	..	..	49 988	..	..
	15		Food products and beverages	2 401	..	..	..	..	8 613	..	..
		155	Beverages	625	..	..	..	..	2 616	..	..
	16	160	Tobacco products	42	..	..	..	..	179	..	..
	17		Textiles	1 117	..	..	..	..	3 138	..	..
		171	Spinning, weaving and finishing of textiles	682	..	..	..	..	1 409	..	..
		172	Other textiles	230	..	..	..	..	1 058	..	..
		173	Knitted and crocheted fabrics and articles	205	..	..	..	..	670	..	..
	18		Wearing apparel dressing & dyeing of fur	419	..	..	..	..	1 632	..	..
		181	Wearing apparel, except fur apparel	378	..	..	..	..	1 450	..	..
		182	Dressing and dyeing of fur; articles of fur	42	..	..	..	..	182	..	..
	19		Tanning, dressing leather; leather artic.; footwear	303	..	..	..	..	1 179	..	..
		191	Tanning, dressing leather; manuf. of leather articles	36	..	..	..	..	138	..	..
		192	Footwear	267	..	..	..	..	1 042	..	..
	20		Wood and cork products, ex. furniture	569	..	..	..	..	2 101	..	..
		201	Sawmilling and planing of wood	100	..	..	..	..	158	..	..
		202	Products of wood, cork, straw & plaiting material	470	..	..	..	..	1 944	..	..
	21		Paper and paper products	383	..	..	..	..	1 249	..	..
	22		Publishing, printing & reprod. of recorded media	703	..	..	..	..	3 342	..	..
		221	Publishing	643	..	..	..	..	3 236	..	..
		222	Printing and related service activities	60	..	..	..	..	106	..	..
		223	Reproduction of recorded media	..	..	..	..	..	..	..	..
	23		Coke, refined petroleum products & nuclear fuel	630	..	..	..	..	941	..	..
	24		Chemicals and chemical products	1 695	..	..	..	..	5 128	..	..
		241	Basic chemicals	1 271	..	..	..	..	3 452	..	..
		242	Other chemical products	359	..	..	..	..	1 299	..	..
		243	Man-made fibres	65	..	..	..	..	377	..	..
	25		Rubber and plastic products	265	..	..	..	..	762	..	..
		251	Rubber products	265	..	..	..	..	762	..	..
		252	Plastic products	..	..	..	..	..	..	..	..
	26		Other non-metallic mineral products	839	..	..	..	..	2 691	..	..
		261	Glass and glass products	281	..	..	..	..	792	..	..
		269	Non-metallic mineral products, nec	559	..	..	..	..	1 898	..	..
	27		Basic metals	904	..	..	..	..	1 701	..	..
		271	Basic iron and steel	683	..	..	..	..	1 004	..	..
		272	Basic precious and non-ferrous metals	132	..	..	..	..	449	..	..
		273	Casting of metals	88	..	..	..	..	248	..	..
	28		Fabricated metal products, ex. machin. & equip.	675	..	..	..	..	2 789	..	..
		281	Structural metal prod., tanks, reservoirs, generators	162	..	..	..	..	849	..	..
		289	Other fabricated metal products & service activities	513	..	..	..	..	1 939	..	..
	29		Machinery and equipment, nec	1 009	..	..	..	..	3 333	..	..
		291	General purpose machinery	651	..	..	..	..	2 036	..	..
		292	Special purpose machinery	358	..	..	..	..	1 297	..	..
		293	Domestic appliances, nec	..	..	..	..	..	..	..	..
	30		Office, accounting and computing machinery	138	..	..	..	..	395	..	..
	31		Electrical machinery and apparatus, nec	1 141	..	..	..	..	3 381	..	..
		311	Electric motors, generators and transformers	477	..	..	..	..	1 268	..	..
		312	Electricity distribution and control apparatus	..	..	..	..	..	..	..	..
		313	Insulated wire and cable	..	..	..	..	..	..	..	..
		314	Accumulators, primary cells and primary batteries	46	..	..	..	..	187	..	..
		315	Electric lamps and lighting equipment	68	..	..	..	..	251	..	..
		319	Other electrical equipment, nec	550	..	..	..	..	1 676	..	..
	32		Radio, TV, communication equip. & apparatus	358	..	..	..	..	1 400	..	..
		321	Electronic valves, tubes & other electronic compon.	210	..	..	..	..	928	..	..
		322	TV, radio transmitters & appar. for line teleph., telegr.	..	..	..	..	..	..	..	..
		323	TV, radio receivers and associated goods	147	..	..	..	..	473	..	..
	33		Medical, precision, optical instr.; watches, clocks	115	..	..	..	..	439	..	..
		331	Medical equip.; precision instruments and appliances	91	..	..	..	..	349	..	..
		332	Optical instruments and photographic equipment	19	..	..	..	..	78	..	..
		333	Watches and clocks	5	..	..	..	..	12	..	..
	34		Motor vehicles, trailers, and semi-trailers	1 420	..	..	..	..	5 108	..	..
	35		Other transport equipment	126	..	..	..	..	237	..	..
		351	Building and repairing of ships and boats	36	..	..	..	..	67	..	..
		352	Railway, tramway locomotives and rolling stock	49	..	..	..	..	43	..	..
		353	Aircraft and spacecraft	14	..	..	..	..	24	..	..
		359	Transport equipment, nec	27	..	..	..	..	103	..	..
	36		Furniture; manufacturing, nec	68	..	..	..	..	248	..	..
		361	Furniture	..	..	..	..	..	..	..	..
		369	Manufacturing, nec	68	..	..	..	..	248	..	..
	37		Recycling	..	..	..	..	..	..	..	..
E	40-41		Electricity, gas and water supply	..	..	..	..	..	..	..	..
	40		Electricity, gas, steam and hot water supply	..	..	..	..	..	..	..	..
		401	Production, collection and distribution of electricity	..	..	..	..	..	..	..	..
	41	410	Collection, purification, distribution of water	..	..	..	..	..	..	..	..
F	45		Construction	..	..	..	..	..	..	..	..
G	50-52		Wholesale and retail trade; repairs etc	..	..	..	..	..	..	..	..
H	55		Hotels and restaurants	1 151	..	..	..	..	4 477	..	..
I	60-64		Transport, storage and communications	..	..	..	..	..	..	..	..
J	65-67		Financial intermediation	..	..	..	..	..	..	..	..
K	70-74		Real estate, renting and business activities	1 376	..	..	..	..	10 932	..	..
L-Q	75-99		Public admin.; education; health; other services	1 195	..	..	..	..	6 789	..	..
A-Q	01-99		Grand total	..	..	..	..	..	..	..	..

Note: ISIC 1531 includes 1532 and 1549; 1541 includes 1544; 1721 includes 1723 and 1729; 1820 includes 1912; 2029 includes 2520; 2211 includes 2212, 2219, 2221 and 3691.
ISIC 2213 includes 2230, 2422 and 2429; 2411 includes 2423; 2899 includes 3699; 2912 includes 2913 and 2919; 2914 includes 2930; 2922 includes 2923; 2929 includes part of 70_74.
ISIC 3110 includes 3120, 3130; 3190 includes 3220; 3430 includes 3610; 3511 includes 3512; 3591 includes 3592; 55 includes part of 75_99. Part of ISIC 70_74 and 75_99 is not covered.

Table NL.1 **PRODUCTION - PRODUCTION**

Millions de Gld   (Prix courants)

1989	1990	1991	1992	1993	1994	1995	1996	Libellé		CITI révision 3	
..	..	..	..	..	..	..	..	**Agriculture, chasse et sylviculture**	A	01-02	
..	..	..	..	..	..	..	..	**Pêche**	B	05	
..	..	..	..	..	..	..	..	**Activités extractives**	C	10-14	
..	..	..	..	..	..	..	..	Extraction de charbon, de lignite et de tourbe		10	
..	..	..	..	..	..	..	..	Extraction de pétrole brut et de gaz naturel		11	
..	..	..	..	..	..	..	..	Extraction de minerais métalliques		13	
..	..	..	..	316	556	546	..	Autres activités extractives		14	
..	..	..	277 484	266 641	277 991	297 059	..	**Activités de fabrication**	D	15-37	
..	..	..	71 694	70 236	71 229	71 834	..	**Produits alimentaires et boissons**		15	
..	..	..	6 366	6 391	6 909	7 047	..	Boissons			155
..	..	..	6 229	6 621	6 932	7 289	..	**Produits à base de tabac**		16	160
..	..	..	4 801	4 726	4 645	4 603	..	**Textiles**		17	
..	..	..	1 928	1 721	1 732	1 604	..	Filature, tissage et achèvement des textiles			171
..	..	..	..	..	..	..	..	Autres articles textiles			172
..	..	..	..	..	..	..	..	Etoffes et articles de bonneterie			173
..	..	..	1 288	1 260	1 289	1 158	..	**Habillement; préparation, teinture des fourrures**		18	
..	..	..	1 288	1 260	1 289	1 158	..	Articles d'habillement autres qu'en fourrure			181
..	..	..	0	0	0	0	..	Préparation, teinture des fourrures; art. en fourrure			182
..	..	..	710	652	585	560	..	**Travail des cuirs; articles en cuir; chaussures**		19	
..	..	..	371	352	326	288	..	Apprêt et tannage des cuirs et articles en cuirs			191
..	..	..	338	300	259	272	..	Chaussures			192
..	..	..	2 369	2 371	2 452	2 736	..	**Bois et articles en bois et liège (sauf meubles)**		20	
..	..	..	..	..	..	..	..	Sciage et rabotage du bois			201
..	..	..	..	..	..	..	..	Articles en bois, liège, vannerie, sparterie			202
..	..	..	8 472	7 521	8 067	9 368	..	**Papier et carton; articles en papier et en carton**		21	
..	..	..	17 316	16 375	16 935	17 373	..	**Edition, imprimerie et reproduction**		22	
..	..	..	7 648	7 812	8 101	8 675	..	Edition			221
..	..	..	8 503	7 283	7 407	7 794	..	Imprimerie et activités annexes			222
..	..	..	1 165	1 280	1 427	904	..	Reproduction de supports enregistrés			223
..	..	..	17 291	19 029	18 164	17 549	..	**Cokéfaction; prod. pétroliers; comb. nucléaires**		23	
..	..	..	41 217	40 584	45 826	51 824	..	**Produits chimiques**		24	
..	..	..	25 119	23 979	28 321	32 545	..	Produits chimiques de base			241
..	..	..	..	..	..	..	..	Autres produits chimiques			242
..	..	..	..	..	..	..	..	Fibres synthétiques ou artificielles			243
..	..	..	8 206	7 687	8 156	8 633	..	**Articles en caoutchouc et en matières plastiques**		25	
..	..	..	1 097	1 043	1 039	919	..	Articles en caoutchouc			251
..	..	..	7 109	6 644	7 116	7 714	..	Articles en matières plastiques			252
..	..	..	7 801	7 559	8 268	8 455	..	**Autres produits minéraux non métalliques**		26	
..	..	..	1 451	1 466	1 559	1 631	..	Verre et articles en verre			261
..	..	..	6 350	6 093	6 710	6 825	..	Produits minéraux non métalliques, nca			269
..	..	..	8 390	7 874	9 045	10 477	..	**Produits métallurgiques de base**		27	
..	..	..	..	..	..	..	..	Sidérurgie et première transformation de l'acier			271
..	..	..	..	..	..	..	..	Métallurgie; métaux précieux et non ferreux			272
..	..	..	806	737	905	979	..	Fonderie			273
..	..	..	16 766	15 197	16 001	17 300	..	**Ouvrages en métaux, sauf machines et matériel**		28	
..	..	..	9 585	8 618	8 839	9 398	..	Constr. et menuiserie métal.; réservoirs; générateurs			281
..	..	..	7 181	6 579	7 162	7 902	..	Autres ouvrages en métaux			289
..	..	..	16 585	15 708	16 671	18 532	..	**Machines et matériel, nca**		29	
..	..	..	9 738	9 126	9 497	10 086	..	Machines d'usage général			291
..	..	..	6 336	6 093	6 728	8 007	..	Machines d'usage spécifique			292
..	..	..	511	489	446	438	..	Appareils domestiques, nca			293
..	..	..	2 809	2 382	2 353	3 333	..	**Mach. de bureau, comptables, matériel inform.**		30	
..	..	..	..	..	..	..	..	**Machines et appareils électriques, nca**		31	
..	..	..	1 050	1 109	740	641	..	Moteurs, génératrices et transformateurs électriques			311
..	..	..	1 209	1 138	1 620	1 863	..	Matériel électrique de distribution et de commande			312
..	..	..	922	799	848	1 113	..	Fils et câbles électriques isolés			313
..	..	..	..	..	..	..	..	Accumulateurs, piles électriques			314
..	..	..	..	..	..	..	..	Lampes électriques et appareils d'éclairage			315
..	..	..	..	..	..	..	..	Autres matériels électriques, nca			319
..	..	..	..	..	..	..	..	**Equip. et appar. de radio, TV, communication**		32	
..	..	..	..	..	..	..	..	Tubes et valves électroniques; autres composants			321
..	..	..	..	..	..	..	..	Emetteurs radio et TV; app. téléphonie, télégraphie			322
..	..	..	..	..	..	..	..	Récepteurs radio et TV et articles associés			323
..	..	..	..	..	..	..	..	**Instruments médicaux, de précision, d'optique**		33	
..	..	..	..	..	..	..	..	Appareils médicaux et de précision			331
..	..	..	..	..	..	..	..	Instruments d'optique ; matériel photographique			332
..	..	..	..	..	..	..	..	Horlogerie			333
..	..	..	..	..	..	..	..	**Véhicules automobiles et nemorques**		34	
..	..	..	..	..	..	..	..	**Autres matériels de transport**		35	
..	..	..	4 139	3 589	3 808	3 973	..	Construction et réparation de navires			351
..	..	..	..	..	..	..	..	Construction de matériel ferroviaire roulant			352
..	..	..	..	..	..	..	..	Construction aéronautique et spatiale			353
..	..	..	701	659	699	709	..	Autres équipements de transport			359
..	..	..	4 437	4 556	4 391	4 810	..	**Meubles; activités de fabrication, nca**		36	
..	..	..	3 599	3 663	3 605	3 835	..	Meubles			361
..	..	..	838	893	786	975	..	Activités de fabrication, nca			369
..	..	..	0	0	63	130	..	**Récupération**		37	
..	..	..	..	..	..	..	..	**Production et distrib. d'électricité, de gaz, d'eau**	E	40-41	
..	..	..	..	..	..	..	..	**Electricité, gaz, vapeur et eau chaude**		40	
..	..	..	..	..	..	..	..	Production, collecte et distribution d'électricité			401
..	..	..	..	..	..	..	..	**Captage, épuration et distribution d'eau**		41	410
..	..	..	..	79 886	82 707	87 772	..	**Construction**	F	45	
..	..	..	..	..	..	..	..	**Commerce de gros et de détail; réparation**	G	50-52	
..	..	..	..	..	..	..	..	**Hôtels et restaurants**	H	55	
..	..	..	..	..	..	..	..	**Transports, entreposage et communications**	I	60-64	
..	..	..	..	..	..	..	..	**Intermédiation financière**	J	65-67	
..	..	..	..	..	..	..	..	**Immobilier, locations, services aux entreprises**	K	70-74	
..	..	..	..	..	..	..	..	**Admin. publique; éducation; santé; autres**	L-Q	75-99	
..	..	..	..	..	..	..	..	Grand total	A-Q	01-99	

Statistiques des Structures Industrielles
OCDE, © 1998

NETHERLANDS

Table NL.2 VALUE ADDED - VALEUR AJOUTÉE

Millions of Gld (Current Prices)

ISIC revision 3			1989	1990	1991	1992	1993	1994	1995	1996
A	01-02	Agriculture, hunting and forestry	..	..	..	..	..	..	..	..
B	05	Fishing	..	..	..	..	..	..	..	..
C	10-14	Mining and quarrying	..	..	..	..	..	..	..	..
	10	Mining of coal and lignite; extraction of peat	..	..	..	..	..	..	..	..
	11	Crude petroleum & natural gas; related service activ.	..	..	..	..	..	..	..	..
	13	Mining of metal ores	..	..	..	..	..	..	..	..
	14	Other mining and quarrying	..	..	..	..	133	226	226	..
D	15-37	Total manufacturing	..	..	..	83 251	82 350	88 443	91 486	..
	15	Food products and beverages	..	..	..	15 224	15 353	15 769	15 446	..
	155	Beverages	..	..	..	3 161	3 137	3 440	3 299	..
16	160	Tobacco products	..	..	..	3 784	3 860	4 131	4 422	..
17		Textiles	..	..	..	1 663	1 641	1 598	1 527	..
	171	Spinning, weaving and finishing of textiles	..	..	..	801	731	718	630	..
	172	Other textiles	..	..	..	..	..	..	..	..
	173	Knitted and crocheted fabrics and articles	..	..	..	..	..	..	..	..
18		Wearing apparel dressing & dyeing of fur	..	..	..	394	388	372	316	..
	181	Wearing apparel, except fur apparel	..	..	..	394	388	372	316	..
	182	Dressing and dyeing of fur; articles of fur	..	..	..	0	0	0	0	..
19		Tanning, dressing leather; leather artic.; footwear	..	..	..	252	221	186	179	..
	191	Tanning, dressing leather; manuf. of leather articles	..	..	..	107	90	78	69	..
	192	Footwear	..	..	..	146	131	109	110	..
20		Wood and cork products, ex. furniture	..	..	..	819	845	835	912	..
	201	Sawmilling and planing of wood	..	..	..	..	..	..	..	..
	202	Products of wood, cork, straw & plaiting material	..	..	..	..	..	..	..	..
21		Paper and paper products	..	..	..	2 974	2 825	2 866	3 050	..
22		Publishing, printing & reprod. of recorded media	..	..	..	6 983	7 233	7 513	7 489	..
	221	Publishing	..	..	..	2 868	3 492	3 662	3 874	..
	222	Printing and related service activities	..	..	..	3 797	3 257	3 306	3 285	..
	223	Reproduction of recorded media	..	..	..	318	483	546	330	..
23		Coke, refined petroleum products & nuclear fuel	..	..	..	1 622	2 137	2 130	1 958	..
24		Chemicals and chemical products	..	..	..	11 470	11 429	14 984	17 075	..
	241	Basic chemicals	..	..	..	6 455	5 716	8 794	10 290	..
	242	Other chemical products	..	..	..	..	..	..	..	..
	243	Man-made fibres	..	..	..	..	..	..	..	..
25		Rubber and plastic products	..	..	..	3 005	2 862	3 021	2 930	..
	251	Rubber products	..	..	..	498	450	442	390	..
	252	Plastic products	..	..	..	2 507	2 412	2 578	2 540	..
26		Other non-metallic mineral products	..	..	..	3 290	3 316	3 661	3 757	..
	261	Glass and glass products	..	..	..	668	685	729	779	..
	269	Non-metallic mineral products, nec	..	..	..	2 622	2 631	2 932	2 978	..
27		Basic metals	..	..	..	3 053	3 001	3 565	4 047	..
	271	Basic iron and steel	..	..	..	..	..	..	..	..
	272	Basic precious and non-ferrous metals	..	..	..	..	..	..	..	..
	273	Casting of metals	..	..	..	384	340	402	412	..
28		Fabricated metal products, ex. machin. & equip.	..	..	..	6 098	5 645	5 846	6 085	..
	281	Structural metal prod., tanks, reservoirs, generators	..	..	..	3 135	2 847	2 878	2 945	..
	289	Other fabricated metal products & service activities	..	..	..	2 964	2 797	2 969	3 140	..
29		Machinery and equipment, nec	..	..	..	6 432	6 081	6 377	6 742	..
	291	General purpose machinery	..	..	..	3 825	3 493	3 532	3 591	..
	292	Special purpose machinery	..	..	..	2 435	2 422	2 696	3 008	..
	293	Domestic appliances, nec	..	..	..	172	166	150	143	..
30		Office, accounting and computing machinery	..	..	..	937	714	749	856	..
31		Electrical machinery and apparatus, nec	..	..	..	..	..	..	..	..
	311	Electric motors, generators and transformers	..	..	..	399	401	277	188	..
	312	Electricity distribution and control apparatus	..	..	..	563	479	646	721	..
	313	Insulated wire and cable	..	..	..	410	381	385	425	..
	314	Accumulators, primary cells and primary batteries	..	..	..	..	..	..	..	..
	315	Electric lamps and lighting equipment	..	..	..	..	..	..	..	..
	319	Other electrical equipment, nec	..	..	..	..	..	..	..	..
32		Radio, TV, communication equip. & apparatus	..	..	..	..	..	..	..	..
	321	Electronic valves, tubes & other electronic compon.	..	..	..	..	..	..	..	..
	322	TV, radio transmitters & appar. for line teleph., telegr.	..	..	..	..	..	..	..	..
	323	TV, radio receivers and associated goods	..	..	..	..	..	..	..	..
33		Medical, precision, optical instr.; watches, clocks	..	..	..	..	..	..	..	..
	331	Medical equip.; precision instruments and appliances	..	..	..	..	..	..	..	..
	332	Optical instruments and photographic equipment	..	..	..	..	..	..	..	..
	333	Watches and clocks	..	..	..	..	..	..	..	..
34		Motor vehicles, trailers, and semi-trailers	..	..	..	..	..	..	..	..
35		Other transport equipment	..	..	..	..	..	..	..	..
	351	Building and repairing of ships and boats	..	..	..	1 162	1 108	1 099	1 056	..
	352	Railway, tramway locomotives and rolling stock	..	..	..	..	..	..	..	..
	353	Aircraft and spacecraft	..	..	..	..	..	..	..	..
	359	Transport equipment, nec	..	..	..	209	195	206	204	..
36		Furniture; manufacturing, nec	..	..	..	1 698	1 779	1 739	1 818	..
	361	Furniture	..	..	..	1 349	1 387	1 381	1 415	..
	369	Manufacturing, nec	..	..	..	349	392	358	403	..
37		Recycling	..	..	..	0	0	21	44	..
E	40-41	Electricity, gas and water supply	..	..	..	..	..	..	..	..
	40	Electricity, gas, steam and hot water supply	..	..	..	..	..	..	..	..
	401	Production, collection and distribution of electricity	..	..	..	..	..	..	..	..
41	410	Collection, purification, distribution of water	..	..	..	..	..	..	..	..
F	45	Construction	..	..	..	..	27 427	27 481	28 894	..
G	50-52	Wholesale and retail trade; repairs etc	..	..	..	..	..	..	..	..
H	55	Hotels and restaurants	..	..	..	..	..	..	..	..
I	60-64	Transport, storage and communications	..	..	..	..	..	..	..	..
J	65-67	Financial intermediation	..	..	..	..	..	..	..	..
K	70-74	Real estate, renting and business activities	..	..	..	..	..	..	..	..
L-Q	75-99	Public admin.; education; health; other services	..	..	..	..	..	..	..	..
A-Q	01-99	Grand total	..	..	..	..	..	..	..	..

Table NL.3 INVESTISSEMENT - INVESTMENT

Millions de Gld   (Prix courants)

1989	1990	1991	1992	1993	1994	1995	1996			CITI révision 3	
..	..	..	..	..	..	..	..	Agriculture, chasse et sylviculture	A	01-02	
..	..	..	..	..	..	..	..	Pêche	B	05	
..	..	..	..	3 885	2 028	1 759	..	Activités extractives	C	10-14	
..	..	..	..	..	..	..	..	Extraction de charbon, de lignite et de tourbe		10	
..	..	..	..	..	..	..	..	Extraction de pétrole brut et de gaz naturel		11	
..	..	..	..	..	..	..	..	Extraction de minerais métalliques		13	
..	..	..	..	..	..	..	..	Autres activités extractives		14	
..	..	..	..	13 029	12 371	13 867	..	Activités de fabrication	D	15-37	
..	..	..	..	2 913	2 809	2 411	..	Produits alimentaires et boissons		15	
..	..	..	..	..	360	435	..	Boissons			155
..	..	..	..	249	157	142	..	Produits à base de tabac		16	160
..	..	..	..	212	186	185	..	Textiles		17	
..	..	..	..	..	81	54	..	Filature, tissage et achèvement des textiles			171
..	..	..	..	..	86	118	..	Autres articles textiles			172
..	..	..	..	..	19	12	..	Etoffes et articles de bonneterie			173
..	..	..	..	26	27	29	..	Habillement; préparation, teinture des fourrures		18	
..	..	..	..	..	..	..	..	Articles d'habillement autres qu'en fourrure			181
..	..	..	..	..	..	..	..	Préparation, teinture des fourrures; art. en fourrure			182
..	..	..	..	17	23	19	..	Travail des cuirs; articles en cuir; chaussures		19	
..	..	..	..	..	14	9	..	Apprêt et tannage des cuirs et articles en cuirs			191
..	..	..	..	..	8	10	..	Chaussures			192
..	..	..	..	109	99	137	..	Bois et articles en bois et liège (sauf meubles)		20	
..	..	..	..	..	6	13	..	Sciage et rabotage du bois			201
..	..	..	..	..	93	124	..	Articles en bois, liège, vannerie, sparterie			202
..	..	..	..	504	474	568	..	Papier et carton; articles en papier et en carton		21	
..	..	..	..	995	1 223	1 198	..	Edition, imprimerie et reproduction		22	
..	..	..	..	..	363	303	..	Edition			221
..	..	..	..	..	825	848	..	Imprimerie et activités annexes			222
..	..	..	..	..	35	46	..	Reproduction de supports enregistrés			223
..	..	..	..	765	707	447	..	Cokéfaction; prod. pétroliers; comb. nucléaires		23	
..	..	..	..	2 469	2 460	2 525	..	Produits chimiques		24	
..	..	..	..	..	1 631	1 642	..	Produits chimiques de base			241
..	..	..	..	..	830	883	..	Autres produits chimiques			242
..	..	..	..	..	..	..	..	Fibres synthétiques ou artificielles			243
..	..	..	..	737	562	556	..	Articles en caoutchouc et en matières plastiques		25	
..	..	..	..	..	66	78	..	Articles en caoutchouc			251
..	..	..	..	..	496	478	..	Articles en matières plastiques			252
..	..	..	..	550	661	770	..	Autres produits minéraux non métalliques		26	
..	..	..	..	..	142	140	..	Verre et articles en verre			261
..	..	..	..	..	519	629	..	Produits minéraux non métalliques, nca			269
..	..	..	..	284	349	360	..	Produits métallurgiques de base		27	
..	..	..	..	..	218	183	..	Sidérurgie et première transformation de l'acier			271
..	..	..	..	..	69	107	..	Métallurgie; métaux précieux et non ferreux			272
..	..	..	..	..	62	71	..	Fonderie			273
..	..	..	..	714	628	827	..	Ouvrages en métaux, sauf machines et matériel		28	
..	..	..	..	..	264	279	..	Constr. et menuiserie métal.; réservoirs; générateurs			281
..	..	..	..	..	364	548	..	Autres ouvrages en métaux			289
..	..	..	..	577	579	693	..	Machines et matériel, nca		29	
..	..	..	..	..	334	366	..	Machines d'usage général			291
..	..	..	..	..	245	328	..	Machines d'usage spécifique			292
..	..	..	..	..	..	..	..	Appareils domestiques, nca			293
..	..	..	..	160	91	103	..	Mach. de bureau, comptables, matériel inform.		30	
..	..	..	..	218	167	232	..	Machines et appareils électriques, nca		31	
..	..	..	..	..	19	14	..	Moteurs, génératrices et transformateurs électriques			311
..	..	..	..	..	53	84	..	Matériel électrique de distribution et de commande			312
..	..	..	..	..	25	62	..	Fils et câbles électriques isolés			313
..	..	..	..	..	17	13	..	Accumulateurs, piles électriques			314
..	..	..	..	..	..	..	..	Lampes électriques et appareils d'éclairage			315
..	..	..	..	..	53	59	..	Autres matériels électriques, nca			319
..	..	..	..	652	508	696	..	Equip. et appar. de radio, TV, communication		32	
..	..	..	..	..	..	..	..	Tubes et valves électroniques; autres composants			321
..	..	..	..	..	..	..	..	Emetteurs radio et TV; app. téléphonie, télégraphie			322
..	..	..	..	..	..	..	..	Récepteurs radio et TV et articles associés			323
..	..	..	..	262	146	166	..	Instruments médicaux, de précision, d'optique		33	
..	..	..	..	..	127	130	..	Appareils médicaux et de précision			331
..	..	..	..	..	19	37	..	Instruments d'optique ; matériel photographique			332
..	..	..	..	..	..	..	..	Horlogerie			333
..	..	..	..	337	323	1 592	..	Véhicules automobiles et nemorques		34	
..	..	..	..	..	..	..	..	Autres matériels de transport		35	
..	..	..	..	..	101	95	..	Construction et réparation de navires			351
..	..	..	..	..	2	2	..	Construction de matériel ferroviaire roulant			352
..	..	..	..	..	..	..	..	Construction aéronautique et spatiale			353
..	..	..	..	..	..	..	..	Autres équipements de transport			359
..	..	..	..	280	192	212	..	Meubles; activités de fabrication, nca		36	
..	..	..	..	..	146	162	..	Meubles			361
..	..	..	..	..	47	49	..	Activités de fabrication, nca			369
..	..	..	..	..	..	..	..	Récupération		37	
..	..	..	..	4 815	6 289	5 052	..	Production et distrib. d'électricité, de gaz, d'eau	E	40-41	
..	..	..	..	4 113	5 291	4 172	..	Electricité, gaz, vapeur et eau chaude		40	
..	..	..	..	..	..	..	..	Production, collecte et distribution d'électricité			401
..	..	..	..	702	998	880	..	Captage, épuration et distribution d'eau		41	410
..	..	..	..	1 813	1 722	1 778	..	Construction	F	45	
..	..	..	..	..	..	..	..	Commerce de gros et de détail; réparation	G	50-52	
..	..	..	..	..	..	..	..	Hôtels et restaurants	H	55	
..	..	..	..	..	..	..	..	Transports, entreposage et communications	I	60-64	
..	..	..	..	..	..	..	..	Intermédiation financière	J	65-67	
..	..	..	..	..	..	..	..	Immobilier, locations, services aux entreprises	K	70-74	
..	..	..	..	..	..	..	..	Admin. publique; éducation; santé; autres	L-Q	75-99	
..	..	..	..	..	..	..	..	Grand total	A-Q	01-99	

Note: When available: ISIC 1531 includes 1532; 1722 includes 1723 and 1729; 2102 includes 2109; 2410 includes 2430; 2691 includes 2692 and 2693; 2694 includes 2699; 2812 includes 2813; 2911 includes 2912 and 2913; 2914 includes 2915 and 2919; 2923 includes 2924, 2925, 2926 and 2929; 2927 includes 2930; 3140 includes 3150; 3320 includes 3313 and 3330; 3410 includes 3530; 3520 includes 3599; 3591 includes 3592; 3692 includes 3699; 3693 includes 3694.

Statistiques des Structures Industrielles
OCDE, © 1998

Table NL.4 INVESTMENT IN MACHINERY AND EQUIPMENT - DÉPENSES EN MACHINES ET ÉQUIPEMENT

Millions of Gld (Current Prices)

ISIC revision 3			1989	1990	1991	1992	1993	1994	1995	1996
A	01-02	**Agriculture, hunting and forestry**	..	..	..	..	..	..	..	..
B	05	**Fishing**	..	..	..	..	..	..	..	..
C	10-14	**Mining and quarrying**	..	..	..	..	2 434	1 203	1 005	..
	10	Mining of coal and lignite; extraction of peat	..	..	..	..	..	..	..	..
	11	Crude petroleum & natural gas; related service activ.	..	..	..	..	..	..	..	..
	13	Mining of metal ores	..	..	..	..	..	..	..	..
	14	Other mining and quarrying	..	..	..	..	..	..	..	..
D	15-37	**Total manufacturing**	..	..	..	..	9 957	9 759	10 962	..
	15	**Food products and beverages**	..	..	..	..	2 074	2 096	1 863	..
	155	Beverages	..	..	..	..	..	277	337	..
	16 160	**Tobacco products**	..	..	..	..	125	147	131	..
	17	**Textiles**	..	..	..	..	176	156	142	..
	171	Spinning, weaving and finishing of textiles	..	..	..	..	..	71	39	..
	172	Other textiles	..	..	..	..	..	68	92	..
	173	Knitted and crocheted fabrics and articles	..	..	..	..	..	17	11	..
	18	**Wearing apparel dressing & dyeing of fur**	..	..	..	..	17	16	18	..
	181	Wearing apparel, except fur apparel	..	..	..	..	..	..	..	..
	182	Dressing and dyeing of fur; articles of fur	..	..	..	..	..	..	..	..
	19	**Tanning, dressing leather; leather artic.; footwear**	..	..	..	..	13	14	16	..
	191	Tanning, dressing leather; manuf. of leather articles	..	..	..	..	..	9	7	..
	192	Footwear	..	..	..	..	..	5	9	..
	20	**Wood and cork products, ex. furniture**	..	..	..	..	68	68	91	..
	201	Sawmilling and planing of wood	..	..	..	..	..	5	8	..
	202	Products of wood, cork, straw & plaiting material	..	..	..	..	..	63	83	..
	21	**Paper and paper products**	..	..	..	..	446	392	460	..
	22	**Publishing, printing & reprod. of recorded media**	..	..	..	..	763	928	966	..
	221	Publishing	..	..	..	..	..	247	193	..
	222	Printing and related service activities	..	..	..	..	..	653	731	..
	223	Reproduction of recorded media	..	..	..	..	..	28	42	..
	23	**Coke, refined petroleum products & nuclear fuel**	..	..	..	..	666	651	400	..
	24	**Chemicals and chemical products**	..	..	..	..	2 053	2 071	2 059	..
	241	Basic chemicals	..	..	..	..	..	1 488	1 452	..
	242	Other chemical products	..	..	..	..	..	583	607	..
	243	Man-made fibres	..	..	..	..	..	..	..	..
	25	**Rubber and plastic products**	..	..	..	..	598	483	452	..
	251	Rubber products	..	..	..	..	..	55	55	..
	252	Plastic products	..	..	..	..	..	428	397	..
	26	**Other non-metallic mineral products**	..	..	..	..	435	498	562	..
	261	Glass and glass products	..	..	..	..	..	132	119	..
	269	Non-metallic mineral products, nec	..	..	..	..	..	366	443	..
	27	**Basic metals**	..	..	..	..	235	300	316	..
	271	Basic iron and steel	..	..	..	..	..	194	169	..
	272	Basic precious and non-ferrous metals	..	..	..	..	..	61	94	..
	273	Casting of metals	..	..	..	..	..	45	53	..
	28	**Fabricated metal products, ex. machin. & equip.**	..	..	..	..	481	455	573	..
	281	Structural metal prod., tanks, reservoirs, generators	..	..	..	..	..	163	171	..
	289	Other fabricated metal products & service activities	..	..	..	..	..	292	402	..
	29	**Machinery and equipment, nec**	..	..	..	..	361	390	456	..
	291	General purpose machinery	..	..	..	..	..	232	234	..
	292	Special purpose machinery	..	..	..	..	..	158	222	..
	293	Domestic appliances, nec	..	..	..	..	..	..	..	..
	30	**Office, accounting and computing machinery**	..	..	..	..	124	73	80	..
	31	**Electrical machinery and apparatus, nec**	..	..	..	..	152	122	174	..
	311	Electric motors, generators and transformers	..	..	..	..	..	12	9	..
	312	Electricity distribution and control apparatus	..	..	..	..	..	46	67	..
	313	Insulated wire and cable	..	..	..	..	..	21	54	..
	314	Accumulators, primary cells and primary batteries	..	..	..	..	..	8	8	..
	315	Electric lamps and lighting equipment	..	..	..	..	..	..	..	..
	319	Other electrical equipment, nec	..	..	..	..	..	35	37	..
	32	**Radio, TV, communication equip. & apparatus**	..	..	..	..	597	453	615	..
	321	Electronic valves, tubes & other electronic compon.	..	..	..	..	..	..	..	..
	322	TV, radio transmitters & appar. for line teleph., telegr.	..	..	..	..	..	..	..	..
	323	TV, radio receivers and associated goods	..	..	..	..	..	..	..	..
	33	**Medical, precision, optical instr.; watches, clocks**	..	..	..	..	145	108	118	..
	331	Medical equip.; precision instruments and appliances	..	..	..	..	..	93	92	..
	332	Optical instruments and photographic equipment	..	..	..	..	..	15	26	..
	333	Watches and clocks	..	..	..	..	..	..	..	..
	34	**Motor vehicles, trailers, and semi-trailers**	..	..	..	..	217	209	1 323	..
	35	**Other transport equipment**	..	..	..	..	..	..	..	..
	351	Building and repairing of ships and boats	..	..	..	..	..	61	53	..
	352	Railway, tramway locomotives and rolling stock	..	..	..	..	..	2	2	..
	353	Aircraft and spacecraft	..	..	..	..	..	..	..	..
	359	Transport equipment, nec	..	..	..	..	..	..	..	..
	36	**Furniture; manufacturing, nec**	..	..	..	..	211	129	148	..
	361	Furniture	..	..	..	..	..	96	113	..
	369	Manufacturing, nec	..	..	..	..	..	34	36	..
	37	**Recycling**	..	..	..	..	..	..	..	..
E	40-41	**Electricity, gas and water supply**	..	..	..	..	2 406	3 465	1 993	..
	40	**Electricity, gas, steam and hot water supply**	..	..	..	..	2 282	3 285	1 829	..
	401	Production, collection and distribution of electricity	..	..	..	..	..	..	..	..
	41 410	**Collection, purification, distribution of water**	..	..	..	..	124	179	164	..
F	45	**Construction**	..	..	..	..	1 106	1 027	953	..
G	50-52	**Wholesale and retail trade; repairs etc**	..	..	..	..	..	..	..	..
H	55	**Hotels and restaurants**	..	..	..	..	..	..	..	..
I	60-64	**Transport, storage and communications**	..	..	..	..	..	..	..	..
J	65-67	**Financial intermediation**	..	..	..	..	..	..	..	..
K	70-74	**Real estate, renting and business activities**	..	..	..	..	..	..	..	..
L-Q	75-99	**Public admin.; education; health; other services**	..	..	..	..	..	..	..	..
A-Q	01-99	**Grand total**	..	..	..	..	..	..	..	..

Note: When available: ISIC 1531 includes 1532; 1722 includes 1723 and 1729; 2102 includes 2109; 2410 includes 2430; 2691 includes 2692 and 2693; 2694 includes 2699; 2812 includes 2813; 2911 includes 2912 and 2913; 2914 includes 2915 and 2919; 2923 includes 2924, 2925, 2926 and 2929; 2927 includes 2930; 3140 includes 3150; 3320 includes 3313 and 3330; 3410 includes 3530; 3520 includes 3599; 3591 includes 3592; 3692 includes 3699; 3693 includes 3694.

Table NL.5 **ETABLISSEMENTS - ESTABLISHMENTS**

Unités

1989	1990	1991	1992	1993	1994	1995	1996		Description		CITI révision 3
..	..	..	..	..	..	..	..	..	**Agriculture, chasse et sylviculture**	A	01-02
..	..	..	..	..	..	..	..	..	**Pêche**	B	05
..	..	..	..	..	..	..	..	..	**Activités extractives**	C	10-14
..	..	..	..	..	..	..	..	..	Extraction de charbon, de lignite et de tourbe		10
..	..	..	..	..	..	..	..	..	Extraction de pétrole brut et de gaz naturel		11
..	..	..	..	..	..	..	..	..	Extraction de minerais métalliques		13
..	..	..	..	23	29	29	..	..	Autres activités extractives		14
..	..	..	6 601	6 681	6 716	6 404	..	..	**Activités de fabrication**	D	15-37
..	..	..	884	901	922	887	..	..	**Produits alimentaires et boissons**		15
..	..	..	34	34	34	35	..	..	Boissons		155
..	..	..	15	13	12	12	..	..	**Produits à base de tabac**	16	160
..	..	..	221	224	222	224	..	..	**Textiles**	17	
..	..	..	78	77	70	64	..	..	Filature, tissage et achèvement des textiles		171
..	..	..	..	..	..	..	..	..	Autres articles textiles		172
..	..	..	..	..	..	..	..	..	Etoffes et articles de bonneterie		173
..	..	..	124	108	126	92	..	..	**Habillement; préparation, teinture des fourrures**	18	
..	..	..	124	108	126	92	..	..	Articles d'habillement autres qu'en fourrure		181
..	..	..	0	0	0	0	..	..	Préparation, teinture des fourrures; art. en fourrure		182
..	..	..	74	72	63	53	..	..	**Travail des cuirs; articles en cuir; chaussures**	19	
..	..	..	34	31	27	24	..	..	Apprêt et tannage des cuirs et articles en cuirs		191
..	..	..	40	41	36	29	..	..	Chaussures		192
..	..	..	193	199	183	192	..	..	**Bois et articles en bois et liège (sauf meubles)**	20	
..	..	..	..	..	..	..	..	..	Sciage et rabotage du bois		201
..	..	..	..	..	..	..	..	..	Articles en bois, liège, vannerie, sparterie		202
..	..	..	165	156	156	166	..	..	**Papier et carton; articles en papier et en carton**	21	
..	..	..	761	753	754	693	..	..	**Edition, imprimerie et reproduction**	22	
..	..	..	170	173	162	157	..	..	Edition		221
..	..	..	578	565	578	523	..	..	Imprimerie et activités annexes		222
..	..	..	13	15	14	13	..	..	Reproduction de supports enregistrés		223
..	..	..	18	19	18	18	..	..	**Cokéfaction; prod. pétroliers; comb. nucléaires**	23	
..	..	..	282	306	309	304	..	..	**Produits chimiques**	24	
..	..	..	101	121	124	118	..	..	Produits chimiques de base		241
..	..	..	..	..	..	..	..	..	Autres produits chimiques		242
..	..	..	..	..	..	..	..	..	Fibres synthétiques ou artificielles		243
..	..	..	327	336	344	344	..	..	**Articles en caoutchouc et en matières plastiques**	25	
..	..	..	30	35	32	25	..	..	Articles en caoutchouc		251
..	..	..	297	301	312	319	..	..	Articles en matières plastiques		252
..	..	..	307	303	281	271	..	..	**Autres produits minéraux non métalliques**	26	
..	..	..	25	29	34	32	..	..	Verre et articles en verre		261
..	..	..	282	274	247	239	..	..	Produits minéraux non métalliques, nca		269
..	..	..	84	88	97	87	..	..	**Produits métallurgiques de base**	27	
..	..	..	..	..	..	..	..	..	Sidérurgie et première transformation de l'acier		271
..	..	..	..	..	..	..	..	..	Métallurgie; métaux précieux et non ferreux		272
..	..	..	45	47	47	45	..	..	Fonderie		273
..	..	..	1 066	1 089	1 110	1 023	..	..	**Ouvrages en métaux, sauf machines et matériel**	28	
..	..	..	581	593	585	525	..	..	Constr. et menuiserie métal.; réservoirs; générateurs		281
..	..	..	485	496	525	498	..	..	Autres ouvrages en métaux		289
..	..	..	944	953	986	918	..	..	**Machines et matériel, nca**	29	
..	..	..	519	519	528	488	..	..	Machines d'usage général		291
..	..	..	406	413	438	410	..	..	Machines d'usage spécifique		292
..	..	..	19	21	20	20	..	..	Appareils domestiques, nca		293
..	..	..	34	37	29	26	..	..	**Mach. de bureau, comptables, matériel inform.**	30	
..	..	..	..	..	..	..	..	..	**Machines et appareils électriques, nca**	31	
..	..	..	50	52	44	41	..	..	Moteurs, génératrices et transformateurs électriques		311
..	..	..	27	28	34	34	..	..	Matériel électrique de distribution et de commande		312
..	..	..	10	11	13	17	..	..	Fils et câbles électriques isolés		313
..	..	..	..	..	..	..	..	..	Accumulateurs, piles électriques		314
..	..	..	..	..	..	..	..	..	Lampes électriques et appareils d'éclairage		315
..	..	..	..	..	..	..	..	..	Autres matériels électriques, nca		319
..	..	..	..	..	..	..	..	..	**Equip. et appar. de radio, TV, communication**	32	
..	..	..	..	..	..	..	..	..	Tubes et valves électroniques; autres composants		321
..	..	..	..	..	..	..	..	..	Emetteurs radio et TV; app. téléphonie, télégraphie		322
..	..	..	..	..	..	..	..	..	Récepteurs radio et TV et articles associés		323
..	..	..	..	..	..	..	..	..	**Instruments médicaux, de précision, d'optique**	33	
..	..	..	..	..	..	..	..	..	Appareils médicaux et de précision		331
..	..	..	..	..	..	..	..	..	Instruments d'optique ; matériel photographique		332
..	..	..	..	..	..	..	..	..	Horlogerie		333
..	..	..	..	..	..	..	..	..	**Véhicules automobiles et nemorques**	34	
..	..	..	..	..	..	..	..	..	**Autres matériels de transport**	35	
..	..	..	143	142	137	137	..	..	Construction et réparation de navires		351
..	..	..	..	..	..	..	..	..	Construction de matériel ferroviaire roulant		352
..	..	..	..	..	..	..	..	..	Construction aéronautique et spatiale		353
..	..	..	29	28	30	29	..	..	Autres équipements de transport		359
..	..	..	384	409	393	383	..	..	**Meubles; activités de fabrication, nca**	36	
..	..	..	321	343	333	319	..	..	Meubles		361
..	..	..	63	66	60	64	..	..	Activités de fabrication, nca		369
..	..	..	0	0	6	11	..	..	**Récupération**	37	
..	..	..	..	..	..	..	..	..	**Production et distrib. d'électricité, de gaz, d'eau**	E	40-41
..	..	..	..	..	..	..	..	..	**Electricité, gaz, vapeur et eau chaude**	40	
..	..	..	..	..	..	..	..	..	Production, collecte et distribution d'électricité		401
..	..	..	..	..	..	..	..	..	**Captage, épuration et distribution d'eau**	41	410
..	..	..	..	25 816	27 489	30 004	..	..	**Construction**	F	45
..	..	..	..	..	..	..	..	..	**Commerce de gros et de détail; réparation**	G	50-52
..	..	..	..	..	..	..	..	..	**Hôtels et restaurants**	H	55
..	..	..	..	..	..	..	..	..	**Transports, entreposage et communications**	I	60-64
..	..	..	..	..	..	..	..	..	**Intermédiation financière**	J	65-67
..	..	..	..	..	..	..	..	..	**Immobilier, locations, services aux entreprises**	K	70-74
..	..	..	..	..	..	..	..	..	**Admin. publique; éducation; santé; autres**	L-Q	75-99
..	..	..	..	..	..	..	..	..	**Grand total**	A-Q	01-99

Statistiques des Structures Industrielles
OCDE, © 1998

NETHERLANDS

Table NL.6 EMPLOYMENT - EMPLOI

Thousands

ISIC revision 3			1989	1990	1991	1992	1993	1994	1995	1996
A	01-02	**Agriculture, hunting and forestry**	..	..	..	..	..	..	..	..
B	05	**Fishing**	..	..	..	..	..	..	..	..
C	10-14	**Mining and quarrying**	..	..	..	..	..	..	..	..
	10	Mining of coal and lignite; extraction of peat	..	..	..	..	..	..	..	..
	11	Crude petroleum & natural gas; related service activ.	..	..	..	..	..	..	..	..
	13	Mining of metal ores	..	..	..	..	..	..	..	..
	14	Other mining and quarrying	..	..	..	..	0.8	1.0	1.0	..
D	15-37	**Total manufacturing**	..	..	..	765.8	724.4	693.9	680.6	..
	15	**Food products and beverages**	..	..	..	121.1	118.9	114.2	109.0	..
	155	Beverages	..	..	..	11.4	11.2	11.2	11.0	..
16	160	**Tobacco products**	..	..	..	5.9	5.7	5.5	5.5	..
17		**Textiles**	..	..	..	19.6	18.7	17.4	16.5	..
	171	Spinning, weaving and finishing of textiles	..	..	..	8.8	8.1	7.2	6.3	..
	172	Other textiles	..	..	..	..	..	..	..	..
	173	Knitted and crocheted fabrics and articles	..	..	..	..	..	..	..	..
18		**Wearing apparel dressing & dyeing of fur**	..	..	..	6.9	6.2	5.9	5.1	..
	181	Wearing apparel, except fur apparel	..	..	..	6.9	6.2	5.9	5.1	..
	182	Dressing and dyeing of fur; articles of fur	..	..	..	0.0	0.0	0.0	0.0	..
19		**Tanning, dressing leather; leather artic.; footwear**	..	..	..	3.9	3.5	2.8	2.5	..
	191	Tanning, dressing leather; manuf. of leather articles	..	..	..	1.5	1.4	1.1	0.9	..
	192	Footwear	..	..	..	2.4	2.1	1.7	1.5	..
20		**Wood and cork products, ex. furniture**	..	..	..	11.3	11.1	10.7	11.4	..
	201	Sawmilling and planing of wood	..	..	..	..	..	..	..	..
	202	Products of wood, cork, straw & plaiting material	..	..	..	..	..	..	..	..
21		**Paper and paper products**	..	..	..	25.3	24.0	22.5	22.8	..
22		**Publishing, printing & reprod. of recorded media**	..	..	..	64.4	63.8	61.1	59.1	..
	221	Publishing	..	..	..	23.2	27.9	26.6	26.9	..
	222	Printing and related service activities	..	..	..	39.2	33.6	32.1	30.4	..
	223	Reproduction of recorded media	..	..	..	2.1	2.3	2.4	1.7	..
23		**Coke, refined petroleum products & nuclear fuel**	..	..	..	7.3	7.7	7.2	7.0	..
24		**Chemicals and chemical products**	..	..	..	86.9	79.3	76.4	72.5	..
	241	Basic chemicals	..	..	..	44.5	37.1	35.2	33.2	..
	242	Other chemical products	..	..	..	..	..	..	..	..
	243	Man-made fibres	..	..	..	..	..	..	..	..
25		**Rubber and plastic products**	..	..	..	30.6	29.3	28.4	27.1	..
	251	Rubber products	..	..	..	4.9	4.7	4.3	3.6	..
	252	Plastic products	..	..	..	25.7	24.6	24.1	23.5	..
26		**Other non-metallic mineral products**	..	..	..	29.1	27.9	27.3	27.3	..
	261	Glass and glass products	..	..	..	5.7	6.0	5.9	5.7	..
	269	Non-metallic mineral products, nec	..	..	..	23.4	21.9	21.4	21.7	..
27		**Basic metals**	..	..	..	29.6	26.6	26.0	26.0	..
	271	Basic iron and steel	..	..	..	..	..	..	..	..
	272	Basic precious and non-ferrous metals	..	..	..	..	..	..	..	..
	273	Casting of metals	..	..	..	4.8	4.5	4.4	4.5	..
28		**Fabricated metal products, ex. machin. & equip.**	..	..	..	71.5	67.5	65.7	65.7	..
	281	Structural metal prod., tanks, reservoirs, generators	..	..	..	37.3	35.7	34.0	33.9	..
	289	Other fabricated metal products & service activities	..	..	..	34.2	31.8	31.7	31.7	..
29		**Machinery and equipment, nec**	..	..	..	72.8	69.1	67.8	68.1	..
	291	General purpose machinery	..	..	..	41.5	39.3	38.2	37.9	..
	292	Special purpose machinery	..	..	..	29.3	27.8	28.0	28.5	..
	293	Domestic appliances, nec	..	..	..	2.0	2.0	1.6	1.7	..
30		**Office, accounting and computing machinery**	..	..	..	8.9	7.1	6.1	7.2	..
31		**Electrical machinery and apparatus, nec**	..	..	..	..	..	..	..	..
	311	Electric motors, generators and transformers	..	..	..	4.3	4.2	2.7	2.2	..
	312	Electricity distribution and control apparatus	..	..	..	5.6	5.1	6.8	6.7	..
	313	Insulated wire and cable	..	..	..	2.8	2.7	2.6	3.1	..
	314	Accumulators, primary cells and primary batteries	..	..	..	..	..	..	..	..
	315	Electric lamps and lighting equipment	..	..	..	..	..	..	..	..
	319	Other electrical equipment, nec	..	..	..	..	..	..	..	..
32		**Radio, TV, communication equip. & apparatus**	..	..	..	..	..	..	..	..
	321	Electronic valves, tubes & other electronic compon.	..	..	..	..	..	..	..	..
	322	TV, radio transmitters & appar. for line teleph., telegr.	..	..	..	..	..	..	..	..
	323	TV, radio receivers and associated goods	..	..	..	..	..	..	..	..
33		**Medical, precision, optical instr.; watches, clocks**	..	..	..	..	..	..	..	..
	331	Medical equip.; precision instruments and appliances	..	..	..	..	..	..	..	..
	332	Optical instruments and photographic equipment	..	..	..	..	..	..	..	..
	333	Watches and clocks	..	..	..	..	..	..	..	..
34		**Motor vehicles, trailers, and semi-trailers**	..	..	..	..	..	..	..	..
35		**Other transport equipment**	..	..	..	..	..	..	..	..
	351	Building and repairing of ships and boats	..	..	..	15.2	14.0	13.4	12.7	..
	352	Railway, tramway locomotives and rolling stock	..	..	..	..	..	..	..	..
	353	Aircraft and spacecraft	..	..	..	..	..	..	..	..
	359	Transport equipment, nec	..	..	..	2.5	2.3	2.4	2.3	..
36		**Furniture; manufacturing, nec**	..	..	..	21.8	21.6	20.3	20.9	..
	361	Furniture	..	..	..	18.1	17.9	17.0	17.1	..
	369	Manufacturing, nec	..	..	..	3.7	3.8	3.3	3.8	..
37		**Recycling**	..	..	..	0.0	0.0	0.1	0.3	..
E	40-41	**Electricity, gas and water supply**	..	..	..	..	..	..	..	..
	40	**Electricity, gas, steam and hot water supply**	..	..	..	..	..	..	..	..
	401	Production, collection and distribution of electricity	..	..	..	..	..	..	..	..
41	410	**Collection, purification, distribution of water**	..	..	..	..	..	..	..	..
F	45	**Construction**	..	..	..	..	378.6	378.9	393.6	..
G	50-52	**Wholesale and retail trade; repairs etc**	..	..	..	..	..	..	..	..
H	55	**Hotels and restaurants**	..	..	..	..	..	..	..	..
I	60-64	**Transport, storage and communications**	..	..	..	..	..	..	..	..
J	65-67	**Financial intermediation**	..	..	..	..	..	..	..	..
K	70-74	**Real estate, renting and business activities**	..	..	..	..	..	..	..	..
L-Q	75-99	**Public admin.; education; health; other services**	..	..	..	..	..	..	..	..
A-Q	01-99	**Grand total**	..	..	..	..	..	..	..	..

Table NL.7 **SALAIRES ET CHARGES SOCIALES , SALARIÉS - COMPENSATION OF LABOUR, EMPLOYEES**

Millions de Gld   (Prix courants)

1989	1990	1991	1992	1993	1994	1995	1996		Description		CITI révision 3	
..	..	..	..	..	..	..	..	..	**Agriculture, chasse et sylviculture**	A	01-02	
..	..	..	..	..	..	..	..	..	**Pêche**	B	05	
..	..	..	..	..	..	..	..	..	**Activités extractives**	C	10-14	
..	..	..	..	..	..	..	..	..	Extraction de charbon, de lignite et de tourbe		10	
..	..	..	..	..	..	..	..	..	Extraction de pétrole brut et de gaz naturel		11	
..	..	..	..	..	..	..	..	..	Extraction de minerais métalliques		13	
..	..	..	..	67	88	88		..	Autres activités extractives		14	
..	..	..	53 548	53 212	51 847	52 274		..	**Activités de fabrication**	D	15-37	
..	..	..	8 152	8 566	8 502	8 270		..	**Produits alimentaires et boissons**		15	
..	..	..	956	1 010	1 072	1 039		..	Boissons			155
..	..	..	487	526	513	519		..	**Produits à base de tabac**		16	160
..	..	..	1 173	1 166	1 089	1 038		..	**Textiles**		17	
..	..	..	566	543	492	431		..	Filature, tissage et achèvement des textiles			171
..	..	..	..	..	..	..		..	Autres articles textiles			172
..	..	..	..	..	..	..		..	Etoffes et articles de bonneterie			173
..	..	..	312	301	297	266		..	**Habillement; préparation, teinture des fourrures**		18	
..	..	..	312	301	297	266		..	Articles d'habillement autres qu'en fourrure			181
..	..	..	0	0	0	0		..	Préparation, teinture des fourrures; art. en fourrure			182
..	..	..	200	181	151	142		..	**Travail des cuirs; articles en cuir; chaussures**		19	
..	..	..	80	72	62	55		..	Apprêt et tannage des cuirs et articles en cuirs			191
..	..	..	120	109	89	87		..	Chaussures			192
..	..	..	646	657	644	698		..	**Bois et articles en bois et liège (sauf meubles)**		20	
..	..	..	..	..	..	..		..	Sciage et rabotage du bois			201
..	..	..	..	..	..	..		..	Articles en bois, liège, vannerie, sparterie			202
..	..	..	1 799	1 775	1 746	1 771		..	**Papier et carton; articles en papier et en carton**		21	
..	..	..	4 712	4 649	4 640	4 628		..	**Edition, imprimerie et reproduction**		22	
..	..	..	1 777	2 107	2 142	2 245		..	Edition			221
..	..	..	2 765	2 376	2 321	2 270		..	Imprimerie et activités annexes			222
..	..	..	169	167	177	114		..	Reproduction de supports enregistrés			223
..	..	..	834	1 032	881	870		..	**Cokéfaction; prod. pétroliers; comb. nucléaires**		23	
..	..	..	7 432	7 529	7 068	6 999		..	**Produits chimiques**		24	
..	..	..	4 141	4 054	3 547	3 591		..	Produits chimiques de base			241
..	..	..	..	..	..	..		..	Autres produits chimiques			242
..	..	..	..	..	..	..		..	Fibres synthétiques ou artificielles			243
..	..	..	1 941	1 941	1 941	1 903		..	**Articles en caoutchouc et en matières plastiques**		25	
..	..	..	322	336	317	273		..	Articles en caoutchouc			251
..	..	..	1 619	1 605	1 624	1 630		..	Articles en matières plastiques			252
..	..	..	1 966	1 942	1 984	2 038		..	**Autres produits minéraux non métalliques**		26	
..	..	..	409	443	456	472		..	Verre et articles en verre			261
..	..	..	1 557	1 499	1 528	1 567		..	Produits minéraux non métalliques, nca			269
..	..	..	2 350	2 254	2 128	2 219		..	**Produits métallurgiques de base**		27	
..	..	..	..	..	..	..		..	Sidérurgie et première transformation de l'acier			271
..	..	..	..	..	..	..		..	Métallurgie; métaux précieux et non ferreux			272
..	..	..	292	276	290	296		..	Fonderie			273
..	..	..	4 416	4 314	4 293	4 397		..	**Ouvrages en métaux, sauf machines et matériel**		28	
..	..	..	2 305	2 276	2 247	2 283		..	Constr. et menuiserie métal.; réservoirs; générateurs			281
..	..	..	2 111	2 039	2 045	2 113		..	Autres ouvrages en métaux			289
..	..	..	4 862	4 733	4 770	4 915		..	**Machines et matériel, nca**		29	
..	..	..	2 765	2 717	2 706	2 738		..	Machines d'usage général			291
..	..	..	1 983	1 905	1 964	2 079		..	Machines d'usage spécifique			292
..	..	..	115	111	99	98		..	Appareils domestiques, nca			293
..	..	..	607	535	491	563		..	**Mach. de bureau, comptables, matériel inform.**		30	
..	..	..	..	..	..	..		..	**Machines et appareils électriques, nca**		31	
..	..	..	275	293	181	151		..	Moteurs, génératrices et transformateurs électriques			311
..	..	..	393	359	490	491		..	Matériel électrique de distribution et de commande			312
..	..	..	211	208	207	238		..	Fils et câbles électriques isolés			313
..	..	..	..	..	..	..		..	Accumulateurs, piles électriques			314
..	..	..	..	..	..	..		..	Lampes électriques et appareils d'éclairage			315
..	..	..	..	..	..	..		..	Autres matériels électriques, nca			319
..	..	..	..	..	..	..		..	**Equip. et appar. de radio, TV, communication**		32	
..	..	..	..	..	..	..		..	Tubes et valves électroniques; autres composants			321
..	..	..	..	..	..	..		..	Emetteurs radio et TV; app. téléphonie, télégraphie			322
..	..	..	..	..	..	..		..	Récepteurs radio et TV et articles associés			323
..	..	..	..	..	..	..		..	**Instruments médicaux, de précision, d'optique**		33	
..	..	..	..	..	..	..		..	Appareils médicaux et de précision			331
..	..	..	..	..	..	..		..	Instruments d'optique ; matériel photographique			332
..	..	..	..	..	..	..		..	Horlogerie			333
..	..	..	..	..	..	..		..	**Véhicules automobiles et nemorques**		34	
..	..	..	..	..	..	..		..	**Autres matériels de transport**		35	
..	..	..	1 026	974	959	929		..	Construction et réparation de navires			351
..	..	..	..	..	..	..		..	Construction de matériel ferroviaire roulant			352
..	..	..	..	..	..	..		..	Construction aéronautique et spatiale			353
..	..	..	136	135	140	142		..	Autres équipements de transport			359
..	..	..	1 253	1 283	1 223	1 281		..	**Meubles; activités de fabrication, nca**		36	
..	..	..	1 029	1 038	1 008	1 040		..	Meubles			361
..	..	..	225	245	214	241		..	Activités de fabrication, nca			369
..	..	..	0	0	0	23		..	**Récupération**		37	
..	..	..	..	..	..	..		..	**Production et distrib. d'électricité, de gaz, d'eau**	E	40-41	
..	..	..	..	..	..	..		..	**Electricité, gaz, vapeur et eau chaude**		40	
..	..	..	..	..	..	..		..	Production, collecte et distribution d'électricité			401
..	..	..	..	..	..	..		..	**Captage, épuration et distribution d'eau**		41	410
..	..	..	..	22 855	22 942	23 679		..	**Construction**	F	45	
..	..	..	..	..	..	..		..	**Commerce de gros et de détail; réparation**	G	50-52	
..	..	..	..	..	..	..		..	**Hôtels et restaurants**	H	55	
..	..	..	..	..	..	..		..	**Transports, entreposage et communications**	I	60-64	
..	..	..	..	..	..	..		..	**Intermédiation financière**	J	65-67	
..	..	..	..	..	..	..		..	**Immobilier, locations, services aux entreprises**	K	70-74	
..	..	..	..	..	..	..		..	**Admin. publique; éducation; santé; autres**	L-Q	75-99	
..	..	..	..	..	..	..		..	**Grand total**	A-Q	01-99	

Statistiques des Structures Industrielles
OCDE, © 1998

NETHERLANDS

Table NL.8 WAGES AND SALARIES, EMPLOYEES - SALAIRES ET TRAITEMENTS, SALARIÉS

Millions of Gld (Current Prices)

ISIC revision 3			1989	1990	1991	1992	1993	1994	1995	1996
A	01-02	**Agriculture, hunting and forestry**	..	..	..	..	..	..	..	..
B	05	**Fishing**	..	..	..	..	..	..	..	..
C	10-14	**Mining and quarrying**	..	..	..	..	..	..	..	..
	10	Mining of coal and lignite; extraction of peat	..	..	..	..	..	..	..	..
	11	Crude petroleum & natural gas; related service activ.	..	..	..	..	..	..	..	..
	13	Mining of metal ores	..	..	..	..	..	..	..	..
	14	Other mining and quarrying	..	..	..	..	54	73	72	..
D	15-37	**Total manufacturing**	..	..	..	44 844	43 809	43 804	44 376	
	15	**Food products and beverages**	..	..	..	6 703	7 004	6 969	6 829	
	155	Beverages	..	..	..	807	819	843	847	
	16 160	**Tobacco products**	..	..	..	390	432	407	431	
	17	**Textiles**	..	..	..	945	960	909	876	
	171	Spinning, weaving and finishing of textiles	..	..	..	449	447	409	362	
	172	Other textiles	..	..	..	..	..	..	..	
	173	Knitted and crocheted fabrics and articles	..	..	..	..	..	..	..	
	18	**Wearing apparel dressing & dyeing of fur**	..	..	..	264	253	252	225	
	181	Wearing apparel, except fur apparel	..	..	..	264	253	252	225	
	182	Dressing and dyeing of fur; articles of fur	..	..	..	0	0	0	0	
	19	**Tanning, dressing leather; leather artic.; footwear**	..	..	..	164	148	127	122	
	191	Tanning, dressing leather; manuf. of leather articles	..	..	..	64	59	53	47	
	192	Footwear	..	..	..	99	89	75	75	
	20	**Wood and cork products, ex. furniture**	..	..	..	535	541	544	597	
	201	Sawmilling and planing of wood	..	..	..	..	..	..	..	
	202	Products of wood, cork, straw & plaiting material	..	..	..	..	..	..	..	
	21	**Paper and paper products**	..	..	..	1 516	1 482	1 483	1 522	
	22	**Publishing, printing & reprod. of recorded media**	..	..	..	3 910	3 887	3 931	3 943	
	221	Publishing	..	..	..	1 502	1 795	1 830	1 924	
	222	Printing and related service activities	..	..	..	2 269	1 950	1 950	1 920	
	223	Reproduction of recorded media	..	..	..	140	142	151	99	
	23	**Coke, refined petroleum products & nuclear fuel**	..	..	..	..	737	722	707	
	24	**Chemicals and chemical products**	..	..	..	6 180	5 980	5 875	5 823	
	241	Basic chemicals	..	..	..	3 406	3 113	2 588	2 993	
	242	Other chemical products	..	..	..	..	..	..	..	
	243	Man-made fibres	..	..	..	..	..	..	..	
	25	**Rubber and plastic products**	..	..	..	1 647	1 646	1 677	1 641	
	251	Rubber products	..	..	..	274	283	273	235	
	252	Plastic products	..	..	..	1 373	1 363	1 404	1 406	
	26	**Other non-metallic mineral products**	..	..	..	1 620	1 609	1 672	1 742	
	261	Glass and glass products	..	..	..	341	373	384	412	
	269	Non-metallic mineral products, nec	..	..	..	1 279	1 236	1 288	1 330	
	27	**Basic metals**	..	..	..	1 904	1 767	1 799	1 826	
	271	Basic iron and steel	..	..	..	..	..	..	..	
	272	Basic precious and non-ferrous metals	..	..	..	..	..	..	..	
	273	Casting of metals	..	..	..	245	231	251	259	
	28	**Fabricated metal products, ex. machin. & equip.**	..	..	..	3 715	3 606	3 702	3 819	
	281	Structural metal prod., tanks, reservoirs, generators	..	..	..	1 944	1 912	1 945	1 988	
	289	Other fabricated metal products & service activities	..	..	..	1 770	1 694	1 757	1 831	
	29	**Machinery and equipment, nec**	..	..	..	4 116	3 984	4 097	4 236	
	291	General purpose machinery	..	..	..	2 334	2 290	2 324	2 354	
	292	Special purpose machinery	..	..	..	1 685	1 602	1 688	1 797	
	293	Domestic appliances, nec	..	..	..	97	93	85	85	
	30	**Office, accounting and computing machinery**	..	..	..	517	439	431	507	
	31	**Electrical machinery and apparatus, nec**	..	..	..	..	..	..	..	
	311	Electric motors, generators and transformers	..	..	..	236	244	158	132	
	312	Electricity distribution and control apparatus	..	..	..	340	307	416	416	
	313	Insulated wire and cable	..	..	..	185	180	181	202	
	314	Accumulators, primary cells and primary batteries	..	..	..	..	..	..	..	
	315	Electric lamps and lighting equipment	..	..	..	..	..	..	..	
	319	Other electrical equipment, nec	..	..	..	..	..	..	..	
	32	**Radio, TV, communication equip. & apparatus**	..	..	..	..	..	..	..	
	321	Electronic valves, tubes & other electronic compon.	..	..	..	..	..	..	..	
	322	TV, radio transmitters & appar. for line teleph., telegr.	..	..	..	..	..	..	..	
	323	TV, radio receivers and associated goods	..	..	..	..	..	..	..	
	33	**Medical, precision, optical instr.; watches, clocks**	..	..	..	..	..	..	..	
	331	Medical equip.; precision instruments and appliances	..	..	..	..	..	..	..	
	332	Optical instruments and photographic equipment	..	..	..	..	..	..	..	
	333	Watches and clocks	..	..	..	..	..	..	..	
	34	**Motor vehicles, trailers, and semi-trailers**	..	..	..	..	..	..	..	
	35	**Other transport equipment**	..	..	..	..	..	..	..	
	351	Building and repairing of ships and boats	..	..	..	866	813	819	796	
	352	Railway, tramway locomotives and rolling stock	..	..	..	..	..	..	..	
	353	Aircraft and spacecraft	..	..	..	..	..	..	..	
	359	Transport equipment, nec	..	..	..	116	114	121	123	
	36	**Furniture; manufacturing, nec**	..	..	..	1 040	1 058	1 041	1 103	
	361	Furniture	..	..	..	855	860	862	899	
	369	Manufacturing, nec	..	..	..	185	197	179	204	
	37	**Recycling**	..	..	..	0	0	4	21	
E	40-41	**Electricity, gas and water supply**	..	..	..	..	..	..	..	
	40	**Electricity, gas, steam and hot water supply**	..	..	..	..	..	..	..	
	401	Production, collection and distribution of electricity	..	..	..	..	..	..	..	
	41 410	**Collection, purification, distribution of water**	..	..	..	..	..	..	..	
F	45	**Construction**	..	..	..	..	16 500	16 980	17 502	..
G	50-52	**Wholesale and retail trade; repairs etc**	..	..	..	..	..	..	..	
H	55	**Hotels and restaurants**	..	..	..	..	..	..	..	
I	60-64	**Transport, storage and communications**	..	..	..	..	..	..	..	
J	65-67	**Financial intermediation**	..	..	..	..	..	..	..	
K	70-74	**Real estate, renting and business activities**	..	..	..	..	..	..	..	
L-Q	75-99	**Public admin.; education; health; other services**	..	..	..	..	..	..	..	
A-Q	01-99	**Grand total**	..	..	..	..	..	..	..	..

OECD
OCDE   Industrial Structure Statistics
OECD, © 1998

Table NL.9 CHARGES SOCIALES DES EMPLOYEURS - EMPLOYERS' SOCIAL COSTS

Millions de Gld   (Prix courants)

1989	1990	1991	1992	1993	1994	1995	1996		Description		CITI révision 3	
..	..	..	..	..	..	..	..	..	**Agriculture, chasse et sylviculture**	A	01-02	
..	..	..	..	..	..	..	..	..	**Pêche**	B	05	
..	..	..	..	..	..	..	..	..	**Activités extractives**	C	10-14	
..	..	..	..	..	..	..	..	..	Extraction de charbon, de lignite et de tourbe		10	
..	..	..	..	..	..	..	..	..	Extraction de pétrole brut et de gaz naturel		11	
..	..	..	..	..	..	..	..	..	Extraction de minerais métalliques		13	
..	..	..	..	13	15	16	..	..	Autres activités extractives		14	
..	..	..	8 704	9 404	8 041	7 901	..	..	**Activités de fabrication**	D	15-37	
..	..	..	1 449	1 562	1 533	1 441	..	..	**Produits alimentaires et boissons**		15	
..	..	..	149	190	229	191	..	..	Boissons			155
..	..	..	98	94	105	88	..	..	**Produits à base de tabac**		16	160
..	..	..	228	206	180	163	..	..	**Textiles**		17	
..	..	..	117	96	83	69	..	..	Filature, tissage et achèvement des textiles			171
..	..	..	..	..	..	..	..	..	Autres articles textiles			172
..	..	..	..	..	..	..	..	..	Etoffes et articles de bonneterie			173
..	..	..	48	48	44	39	..	..	**Habillement; préparation, teinture des fourrures**		18	
..	..	..	48	48	44	39	..	..	Articles d'habillement autres qu'en fourrure			181
..	..	..	0	0	0	0	..	..	Préparation, teinture des fourrures; art. en fourrure			182
..	..	..	36	33	24	20	..	..	**Travail des cuirs; articles en cuir; chaussures**		19	
..	..	..	15	13	10	8	..	..	Apprêt et tannage des cuirs et articles en cuirs			191
..	..	..	21	20	14	12	..	..	Chaussures			192
..	..	..	111	116	100	100	..	..	**Bois et articles en bois et liège (sauf meubles)**		20	
..	..	..	..	..	..	..	..	..	Sciage et rabotage du bois			201
..	..	..	..	..	..	..	..	..	Articles en bois, liège, vannerie, sparterie			202
..	..	..	283	294	264	249	..	..	**Papier et carton; articles en papier et en carton**		21	
..	..	..	802	762	709	686	..	..	**Edition, imprimerie et reproduction**		22	
..	..	..	275	312	313	321	..	..	Edition			221
..	..	..	496	426	371	350	..	..	Imprimerie et activités annexes			222
..	..	..	29	25	26	15	..	..	Reproduction de supports enregistrés			223
..	..	..	..	295	159	163	..	..	**Cokéfaction; prod. pétroliers; comb. nucléaires**		23	
..	..	..	1 252	1 549	1 192	1 176	..	..	**Produits chimiques**		24	
..	..	..	735	941	558	599	..	..	Produits chimiques de base			241
..	..	..	..	..	..	..	..	..	Autres produits chimiques			242
..	..	..	..	..	..	..	..	..	Fibres synthétiques ou artificielles			243
..	..	..	294	295	264	262	..	..	**Articles en caoutchouc et en matières plastiques**		25	
..	..	..	48	54	44	38	..	..	Articles en caoutchouc			251
..	..	..	246	242	220	224	..	..	Articles en matières plastiques			252
..	..	..	346	333	312	296	..	..	**Autres produits minéraux non métalliques**		26	
..	..	..	68	70	72	60	..	..	Verre et articles en verre			261
..	..	..	278	263	240	236	..	..	Produits minéraux non métalliques, nca			269
..	..	..	446	487	330	393	..	..	**Produits métallurgiques de base**		27	
..	..	..	..	..	..	..	..	..	Sidérurgie et première transformation de l'acier			271
..	..	..	..	..	..	..	..	..	Métallurgie; métaux précieux et non ferreux			272
..	..	..	47	45	39	37	..	..	Fonderie			273
..	..	..	701	708	592	579	..	..	**Ouvrages en métaux, sauf machines et matériel**		28	
..	..	..	361	365	303	296	..	..	Constr. et menuiserie métal.; réservoirs; générateurs			281
..	..	..	341	345	289	283	..	..	Autres ouvrages en métaux			289
..	..	..	746	749	672	681	..	..	**Machines et matériel, nca**		29	
..	..	..	431	427	382	385	..	..	Machines d'usage général			291
..	..	..	298	303	276	282	..	..	Machines d'usage spécifique			292
..	..	..	18	18	14	14	..	..	Appareils domestiques, nca			293
..	..	..	90	96	59	56	..	..	**Mach. de bureau, comptables, matériel inform.**		30	
..	..	..	..	..	..	..	..	..	**Machines et appareils électriques, nca**		31	
..	..	..	39	49	23	19	..	..	Moteurs, génératrices et transformateurs électriques			311
..	..	..	53	52	74	75	..	..	Matériel électrique de distribution et de commande			312
..	..	..	26	29	26	37	..	..	Fils et câbles électriques isolés			313
..	..	..	..	..	..	..	..	..	Accumulateurs, piles électriques			314
..	..	..	..	..	..	..	..	..	Lampes électriques et appareils d'éclairage			315
..	..	..	..	..	..	..	..	..	Autres matériels électriques, nca			319
..	..	..	..	..	..	..	..	..	**Equip. et appar. de radio, TV, communication**		32	
..	..	..	..	..	..	..	..	..	Tubes et valves électroniques; autres composants			321
..	..	..	..	..	..	..	..	..	Emetteurs radio et TV; app. téléphonie, télégraphie			322
..	..	..	..	..	..	..	..	..	Récepteurs radio et TV et articles associés			323
..	..	..	..	..	..	..	..	..	**Instruments médicaux, de précision, d'optique**		33	
..	..	..	..	..	..	..	..	..	Appareils médicaux et de précision			331
..	..	..	..	..	..	..	..	..	Instruments d'optique ; matériel photographique			332
..	..	..	..	..	..	..	..	..	Horlogerie			333
..	..	..	..	..	..	..	..	..	**Véhicules automobiles et nemorques**		34	
..	..	..	..	..	..	..	..	..	**Autres matériels de transport**		35	
..	..	..	160	161	141	133	..	..	Construction et réparation de navires			351
..	..	..	..	..	..	..	..	..	Construction de matériel ferroviaire roulant			352
..	..	..	..	..	..	..	..	..	Construction aéronautique et spatiale			353
..	..	..	20	21	19	19	..	..	Autres équipements de transport			359
..	..	..	213	225	181	178	..	..	**Meubles; activités de fabrication, nca**		36	
..	..	..	174	177	146	141	..	..	Meubles			361
..	..	..	40	48	35	37	..	..	Activités de fabrication, nca			369
..	..	..	0	0	1	2	..	..	**Récupération**		37	
..	..	..	..	..	..	..	..	..	**Production et distrib. d'électricité, de gaz, d'eau**	E	40-41	
..	..	..	..	..	..	..	..	..	**Electricité, gaz, vapeur et eau chaude**		40	
..	..	..	..	..	..	..	..	..	Production, collecte et distribution d'électricité			401
..	..	..	..	..	..	..	..	..	**Captage, épuration et distribution d'eau**		41	410
..	..	..	..	6 313	6 052	6 178	..	..	**Construction**	F	45	
..	..	..	..	..	..	..	..	..	**Commerce de gros et de détail; réparation**	G	50-52	
..	..	..	..	..	..	..	..	..	**Hôtels et restaurants**	H	55	
..	..	..	..	..	..	..	..	..	**Transports, entreposage et communications**	I	60-64	
..	..	..	..	..	..	..	..	..	**Intermédiation financière**	J	65-67	
..	..	..	..	..	..	..	..	..	**Immobilier, locations, services aux entreprises**	K	70-74	
..	..	..	..	..	..	..	..	..	**Admin. publique; éducation; santé; autres**	L-Q	75-99	
..	..	..	..	..	..	..	..	..	**Grand total**	A-Q	01-99	

Statistiques des Structures Industrielles
OCDE, © 1998

Table NL.10 EXPORTS - EXPORTATIONS

Millions of Gld (Current Prices)

ISIC revision 3			1989	1990	1991	1992	1993	1994	1995	1996
A	01-02	**Agriculture, hunting and forestry**	..	..	..	..	..	..	..	..
B	05	**Fishing**	..	..	..	..	..	..	..	..
C	10-14	**Mining and quarrying**	..	..	..	..	..	..	..	..
	10	Mining of coal and lignite; extraction of peat	..	..	..	..	..	..	..	..
	11	Crude petroleum & natural gas; related service activ.	..	..	..	..	..	..	..	..
	13	Mining of metal ores	..	..	..	..	..	..	..	..
	14	Other mining and quarrying	..	..	..	..	90	206	110	..
D	15-37	**Total manufacturing**	..	..	..	124 062	125 179	132 681	145 950	..
	15	**Food products and beverages**	..	..	..	26 706	28 216	28 233	29 278	..
	155	Beverages	..	..	..	1 836	2 037	2 363	2 461	..
	16	160	**Tobacco products**	..	..	..	3 256	3 267	3 711	4 053	..
	17	**Textiles**	..	..	..	2 407	2 341	2 821	3 017	..
	171	Spinning, weaving and finishing of textiles	..	..	..	1 194	960	1 167	1 200	..
	172	Other textiles	..	..	..	..	..	..	..	..
	173	Knitted and crocheted fabrics and articles	..	..	..	..	..	..	..	..
	18	**Wearing apparel dressing & dyeing of fur**	..	..	..	456	508	484	445	..
	181	Wearing apparel, except fur apparel	..	..	..	456	508	484	445	..
	182	Dressing and dyeing of fur; articles of fur	..	..	..	0	0	0	0	..
	19	**Tanning, dressing leather; leather artic.; footwear**	..	..	..	239	238	255	248	..
	191	Tanning, dressing leather; manuf. of leather articles	..	..	..	161	162	182	162	..
	192	Footwear	..	..	..	78	76	73	86	..
	20	**Wood and cork products, ex. furniture**	..	..	..	358	413	374	468	..
	201	Sawmilling and planing of wood	..	..	..	..	..	..	..	..
	202	Products of wood, cork, straw & plaiting material	..	..	..	..	..	..	..	..
	21	**Paper and paper products**	..	..	..	3 766	3 613	4 431	5 016	..
	22	**Publishing, printing & reprod. of recorded media**	..	..	..	2 329	2 580	2 410	2 378	..
	221	Publishing	..	..	..	980	1 172	1 024	..	..
	222	Printing and related service activities	..	..	..	802	772	791	841	..
	223	Reproduction of recorded media	..	..	..	546	637	596	..	..
	23	**Coke, refined petroleum products & nuclear fuel**	..	..	..	7 054	9 106	8 299	8 389	..
	24	**Chemicals and chemical products**	..	..	..	29 055	29 147	33 700	37 816	..
	241	Basic chemicals	..	..	..	19 098	19 528	22 061	24 852	..
	242	Other chemical products	..	..	..	..	..	..	..	..
	243	Man-made fibres	..	..	..	..	..	..	..	..
	25	**Rubber and plastic products**	..	..	..	3 270	3 337	3 688	4 105	..
	251	Rubber products	..	..	..	618	535	616	602	..
	252	Plastic products	..	..	..	2 651	2 803	3 072	3 504	..
	26	**Other non-metallic mineral products**	..	..	..	1 798	1 714	1 935	2 028	..
	261	Glass and glass products	..	..	..	732	675	746	819	..
	269	Non-metallic mineral products, nec	..	..	..	1 066	1 039	1 189	1 209	..
	27	**Basic metals**	..	..	..	6 107	5 824	6 924	7 872	..
	271	Basic iron and steel	..	..	..	..	..	..	..	..
	272	Basic precious and non-ferrous metals	..	..	..	..	..	..	..	..
	273	Casting of metals	..	..	..	437	408	552	587	..
	28	**Fabricated metal products, ex. machin. & equip.**	..	..	..	4 947	4 431	4 869	5 334	..
	281	Structural metal prod., tanks, reservoirs, generators	..	..	..	2 221	1 992	2 113	2 264	..
	289	Other fabricated metal products & service activities	..	..	..	2 727	2 439	2 756	3 070	..
	29	**Machinery and equipment, nec**	..	..	..	7 959	7 835	8 190	9 816	..
	291	General purpose machinery	..	..	..	4 245	4 467	4 180	4 606	..
	292	Special purpose machinery	..	..	..	3 501	3 186	3 873	5 073	..
	293	Domestic appliances, nec	..	..	..	213	183	136	138	..
	30	**Office, accounting and computing machinery**	..	..	..	1 911	1 571	1 781	2 310	..
	31	**Electrical machinery and apparatus, nec**	..	..	..	..	..	..	..	..
	311	Electric motors, generators and transformers	..	..	..	385	420	264	210	..
	312	Electricity distribution and control apparatus	..	..	..	539	444	582	754	..
	313	Insulated wire and cable	..	..	..	194	183	226	287	..
	314	Accumulators, primary cells and primary batteries	..	..	..	..	..	..	..	..
	315	Electric lamps and lighting equipment	..	..	..	..	..	..	..	..
	319	Other electrical equipment, nec	..	..	..	..	..	..	..	..
	32	**Radio, TV, communication equip. & apparatus**	..	..	..	..	..	..	..	..
	321	Electronic valves, tubes & other electronic compon.	..	..	..	..	..	..	..	..
	322	TV, radio transmitters & appar. for line teleph., telegr.	..	..	..	..	..	..	..	..
	323	TV, radio receivers and associated goods	..	..	..	..	..	..	..	..
	33	**Medical, precision, optical instr.; watches, clocks**	..	..	..	..	..	..	..	..
	331	Medical equip.; precision instruments and appliances	..	..	..	..	..	..	..	..
	332	Optical instruments and photographic equipment	..	..	..	..	..	..	..	..
	333	Watches and clocks	..	..	..	..	..	..	..	..
	34	**Motor vehicles, trailers, and semi-trailers**	..	..	..	..	..	..	..	..
	35	**Other transport equipment**	..	..	..	..	..	..	..	..
	351	Building and repairing of ships and boats	..	..	..	2 028	1 692	1 927	2 004	..
	352	Railway, tramway locomotives and rolling stock	..	..	..	..	..	..	..	..
	353	Aircraft and spacecraft	..	..	..	..	..	..	..	..
	359	Transport equipment, nec	..	..	..	190	210	241	245	..
	36	**Furniture; manufacturing, nec**	..	..	..	1 173	1 182	1 119	1 290	..
	361	Furniture	..	..	..	730	720	717	811	..
	369	Manufacturing, nec	..	..	..	444	463	402	479	..
	37	**Recycling**	..	..	..	0	0	0	0	..
E	40-41	**Electricity, gas and water supply**	..	..	..	..	..	..	..	..
	40	**Electricity, gas, steam and hot water supply**	..	..	..	..	..	..	..	..
	401	Production, collection and distribution of electricity	..	..	..	..	..	..	..	..
	41	410	**Collection, purification, distribution of water**	..	..	..	..	..	..	..	..
F	45	**Construction**	..	..	..	..	..	..	..	..
G	50-52	**Wholesale and retail trade; repairs etc**	..	..	..	..	..	..	..	..
H	55	**Hotels and restaurants**	..	..	..	..	..	..	..	..
I	60-64	**Transport, storage and communications**	..	..	..	..	..	..	..	..
J	65-67	**Financial intermediation**	..	..	..	..	..	..	..	..
K	70-74	**Real estate, renting and business activities**	..	..	..	..	..	..	..	..
L-Q	75-99	**Public admin.; education; health; other services**	..	..	..	..	..	..	..	..
A-Q	01-99	**Grand total**	..	..	..	..	..	..	..	..

Table NZ.1 **ENTREPRISES – ENTERPRISES**

Unités 1988-89	1989-90	1990-91	1991-92	1992-93	1993-94	1994-95	1995-96			CITI révision 3	
86 247	84 249	83 749	84 740	86 166	74 070	74 554	71 966	**Agriculture, chasse et sylviculture**	A	01-02	
1 927	1 820	1 794	1 815	1 795	1 631	1 651	1 654	**Pêche**	B	05	
484	464	455	449	422	407	406	411	**Activités extractives**	C	10-14	
50	46	41	39	37	36	34	27	Extraction de charbon, de lignite et de tourbe		10	
64	62	67	78	77	75	68	66	Extraction de pétrole brut et de gaz naturel		11	
148	133	124	119	102	100	88	98	Extraction de minerais métalliques		13	
222	223	223	213	206	196	216	220	Autres activités extractives		14	
17 392	17 078	17 344	17 779	17 958	17 977	19 470	19 637	**Activités de fabrication**	D	15-37	
1 231	1 206	1 229	1 268	1 274	1 346	1 420	1 378	**Produits alimentaires et boissons**		15	
115	114	128	129	144	168	189	204	Boissons			155
5	4	4	4	3	3	2	2	**Produits à base de tabac**		16	160
726	700	683	702	717	722	774	768	**Textiles**		17	
138	128	116	116	130	125	139	134	Filature, tissage et achèvement des textiles			171
442	438	431	449	459	477	515	532	Autres articles textiles			172
146	134	136	137	128	120	120	102	Etoffes et articles de bonneterie			173
1 066	1 044	1 071	1 111	1 127	1 097	1 149	1 127	**Habillement; préparation, teinture des fourrures**		18	
..	..	..	..	..	..	..	..	Articles d'habillement autres qu'en fourrure			181
..	..	..	..	..	..	..	..	Préparation, teinture des fourrures; art. en fourrure			182
294	284	278	261	260	258	256	244	**Travail des cuirs; articles en cuir; chaussures**		19	
205	194	191	186	188	187	186	178	Apprêt et tannage des cuirs et articles en cuirs			191
89	90	87	75	72	71	70	66	Chaussures			192
1 456	1 441	1 504	1 520	1 579	1 656	1 795	1 837	**Bois et articles en bois et liège (sauf meubles)**		20	
355	358	372	389	402	498	528	541	Sciage et rabotage du bois			201
1 101	1 083	1 132	1 131	1 177	1 158	1 267	1 296	Articles en bois, liège, vannerie, sparterie			202
150	119	118	118	114	121	110	93	**Papier et carton; articles en papier et en carton**		21	
1 636	1 654	1 724	1 810	1 875	1 874	2 076	2 031	**Edition, imprimerie et reproduction**		22	
501	517	535	576	603	571	657	646	Edition			221
1 132	1 135	1 187	1 231	1 270	1 298	1 411	1 380	Imprimerie et activités annexes			222
3	2	2	3	2	5	8	5	Reproduction de supports enregistrés			223
31	27	28	26	26	25	30	27	**Cokéfaction; prod. pétroliers; comb. nucléaires**		23	
395	390	373	389	398	417	476	472	**Produits chimiques**		24	
..	..	..	..	..	..	..	..	Produits chimiques de base			241
261	251	240	249	255	250	288	286	Autres produits chimiques			242
..	..	..	..	..	..	..	..	Fibres synthétiques ou artificielles			243
520	513	517	554	511	513	540	544	**Articles en caoutchouc et en matières plastiques**		25	
81	86	84	95	92	89	91	77	Articles en caoutchouc			251
439	427	433	459	419	424	449	467	Articles en matières plastiques			252
678	650	634	619	654	608	666	647	**Autres produits minéraux non métalliques**		26	
134	132	128	129	147	125	139	118	Verre et articles en verre			261
544	518	506	490	507	415	455	459	Produits minéraux non métalliques, nca			269
171	160	157	162	166	203	211	215	**Produits métallurgiques de base**		27	
11	12	14	10	12	21	32	36	Sidérurgie et première transformation de l'acier			271
11	13	13	13	17	17	14	13	Métallurgie; métaux précieux et non ferreux			272
149	135	130	139	137	165	165	166	Fonderie			273
2 293	2 197	2 184	2 222	2 235	2 176	2 330	2 401	**Ouvrages en métaux, sauf machines et matériel**		28	
..	..	..	..	..	..	..	..	Constr. et menuiserie métal.; réservoirs; générateurs			281
..	..	..	..	..	..	..	..	Autres ouvrages en métaux			289
2 403	2 395	2 429	2 472	2 421	2 457	2 713	2 899	**Machines et matériel, nca**		29	
..	..	..	..	..	..	..	..	Machines d'usage général			291
..	..	..	..	..	..	..	..	Machines d'usage spécifique			292
49	48	45	46	43	46	53	55	Appareils domestiques, nca			293
47	48	57	67	56	59	57	55	**Mach. de bureau, comptables, matériel inform.**		30	
339	336	361	366	349	330	326	319	**Machines et appareils électriques, nca**		31	
..	..	..	..	..	..	..	..	Moteurs, génératrices et transformateurs électriques			311
..	..	..	..	..	..	..	..	Matériel électrique de distribution et de commande			312
11	13	12	10	7	8	10	9	Fils et câbles électriques isolés			313
4	4	4	5	6	6	5	5	Accumulateurs, piles électriques			314
55	55	51	52	56	49	51	53	Lampes électriques et appareils d'éclairage			315
269	264	294	299	280	267	260	252	Autres matériels électriques, nca			319
181	185	178	179	172	184	215	220	**Equip. et appar. de radio, TV, communication**		32	
126	130	121	117	120	129	161	166	Tubes et valves électroniques; autres composants			321
55	55	57	62	52	55	54	54	Emetteurs radio et TV; app. téléphonie, télégraphie			322
..	..	..	..	..	..	..	..	Récepteurs radio et TV et articles associés			323
235	245	241	237	228	224	244	259	**Instruments médicaux, de précision, d'optique**		33	
..	..	..	..	..	..	..	..	Appareils médicaux et de précision			331
23	24	26	24	25	20	23	25	Instruments d'optique ; matériel photographique			332
..	..	..	..	..	..	..	..	Horlogerie			333
567	533	529	542	569	559	584	564	**Véhicules automobiles et nemorques**		34	
435	424	409	403	411	591	662	700	**Autres matériels de transport**		35	
562	552	543	532	515	476	524	566	Construction et réparation de navires			351
1	1	..	..	..	..	..	..	Construction de matériel ferroviaire roulant			352
67	67	71	75	82	88	107	106	Construction aéronautique et spatiale			353
31	31	29	25	23	27	31	28	Autres équipements de transport			359
2 193	2 195	2 312	2 428	2 501	2 479	2 755	2 759	**Meubles; activités de fabrication, nca**		36	
1 381	1 370	1 428	1 471	1 496	1 539	1 718	1 720	Meubles			361
812	825	884	957	1 005	940	1 037	1 039	Activités de fabrication, nca			369
..	..	..	..	..	..	..	..	**Récupération**		37	
147	129	135	152	160	156	151	158	**Production et distrib. d'électricité, de gaz, d'eau**	E	40-41	
76	65	68	73	78	83	85	83	**Electricité, gaz, vapeur et eau chaude**		40	
63	54	57	59	61	70	72	72	Production, collecte et distribution d'électricité			401
71	64	67	79	82	73	66	75	**Captage, épuration et distribution d'eau**		41	410
24 901	24 533	25 702	26 127	25 533	24 271	28 330	30 642	**Construction**	F	45	
41 317	42 543	43 447	45 346	45 414	44 363	48 513	47 485	**Commerce de gros et de détail; réparation**	G	50-52	
6 187	6 485	6 764	7 014	7 204	7 051	7 732	7 872	**Hôtels et restaurants**	H	55	
9 980	9 763	10 457	11 384	11 330	10 618	12 026	12 636	**Transports, entreposage et communications**	I	60-64	
6 322	6 097	6 006	7 509	7 137	8 893	8 565	8 196	**Intermédiation financière**	J	65-67	
17 915	18 771	21 331	23 900	24 907	28 865	35 417	39 283	**Immobilier, locations, services aux entreprises**	K	70-74	
16 063	19 020	19 978	21 971	22 777	22 834	24 832	25 862	**Admin. publique; éducation; santé; autres**	L-Q	75-99	
212 904	215 190	221 134	231 755	234 165	224 451	243 461	247 469	**Grand total**	A-Q	01-99	

Note: Data refers to the fiscal year ending 31 March. Unless given separately, ISIC 1544 includes 1549; 2023 includes 2029; 2413 includes 2430; 2696 includes 2699; 2899 includes 2813;
319 includes 311 and 312; 321 includes 323; 3692 includes 3699; 3693 includes 3694; 102 includes 103. ISIC 35 excludes 352. Some ANZIC industries can not be converted directly to ISIC.
ISIC 29 includes ANZIC 2867 and 2869; ISIC 33 includes ANZIC 2839. Sub-totals may not always sum correctly due to the conversion between ANZIC and ISIC.

Statistiques des Structures Industrielles
OCDE, © 1998

Table NZ.2 EMPLOYMENT - EMPLOI

Thousands

	ISIC		Industry (ISIC revision 3)	1988-89	1989-90	1990-91	1991-92	1992-93	1993-94	1994-95	1995-96
A	01-02		Agriculture, hunting and forestry	151.7	176.0	158.4	152.5	152.9	148.0	158.3	166.7
B	05		Fishing	4.0	4.1	4.2	4.2	4.2	4.4	4.3	4.5
C	10-14		Mining and quarrying	4.4	4.0	4.2	4.1	3.8	4.0	4.2	4.2
	10		Mining of coal and lignite; extraction of peat	1.1	1.0	1.0	0.9	0.8	0.8	0.9	0.8
	11		Crude petroleum & natural gas; related service activ.	0.7	0.6	0.8	0.8	0.7	0.8	0.8	0.7
	13		Mining of metal ores	0.7	0.6	0.6	0.7	0.8	0.6	0.8	0.7
	14		Other mining and quarrying	1.9	1.7	1.7	1.7	1.5	1.8	1.7	1.7
D	15-37		Total manufacturing	267.2	256.8	235.2	225.6	231.0	244.6	252.4	257.7
	15		Food products and beverages	65.5	61.2	59.6	58.2	59.4	61.6	61.3	63.2
		155	Beverages	2.4	3.1	3.1	2.8	2.7	3.1	3.2	3.3
	16	160	Tobacco products	0.9	0.8	0.7	0.6	0.5	0.5	0.5	0.5
	17		Textiles	11.6	12.3	11.2	10.2	10.3	10.9	11.5	10.9
		171	Spinning, weaving and finishing of textiles	3.5	3.0	2.5	2.4	4.4	4.6	4.9	4.6
		172	Other textiles	4.7	6.0	5.8	5.2	3.7	4.2	4.5	4.5
		173	Knitted and crocheted fabrics and articles	3.4	3.4	3.0	2.6	2.2	2.1	2.1	1.8
	18		Wearing apparel dressing & dyeing of fur	15.6	14.8	13.6	12.6	12.8	13.2	13.0	11.8
		181	Wearing apparel, except fur apparel	..	..	..	..	..	..	..	..
		182	Dressing and dyeing of fur; articles of fur	..	..	..	..	..	..	..	..
	19		Tanning, dressing leather; leather artic.; footwear	4.5	4.9	4.3	3.9	4.0	4.6	4.6	4.3
		191	Tanning, dressing leather; manuf. of leather articles	2.5	2.5	2.3	2.4	2.5	2.7	2.8	2.6
		192	Footwear	2.1	2.4	2.0	1.5	1.5	1.9	1.8	1.6
	20		Wood and cork products, ex. furniture	14.0	14.8	14.0	14.0	15.1	17.1	15.8	19.5
		201	Sawmilling and planing of wood	6.8	6.9	6.7	7.0	7.7	8.8	7.1	10.6
		202	Products of wood, cork, straw & plaiting material	7.2	7.9	7.3	7.0	7.4	8.3	8.7	8.9
	21		Paper and paper products	10.3	8.6	9.6	9.0	8.7	8.7	9.4	9.1
	22		Publishing, printing & reprod. of recorded media	21.5	20.4	20.3	19.7	20.2	20.8	22.3	22.2
		221	Publishing	9.8	9.6	9.4	9.2	9.7	9.8	10.7	10.3
		222	Printing and related service activities	11.8	10.8	10.8	10.5	10.4	11.0	11.6	11.9
		223	Reproduction of recorded media	0.0	0.0	0.0	0.0	0.0	0.0	0.0	0.0
	23		Coke, refined petroleum products & nuclear fuel	1.6	0.9	1.0	1.0	0.9	0.8	0.8	0.8
	24		Chemicals and chemical products	13.6	10.9	10.4	11.1	11.1	11.3	11.2	11.2
		241	Basic chemicals	5.8	3.8	3.7	4.4	4.3	4.6	4.7	4.3
		242	Other chemical products	7.8	7.1	6.6	6.8	6.9	6.7	6.5	6.9
		243	Man-made fibres	..	..	..	..	..	..	..	..
	25		Rubber and plastic products	9.9	10.7	9.1	8.9	9.9	9.5	9.5	9.6
		251	Rubber products	2.4	3.0	2.0	1.9	3.0	2.0	1.9	1.9
		252	Plastic products	7.6	7.7	7.1	7.1	6.9	7.5	7.6	7.7
	26		Other non-metallic mineral products	7.9	6.8	6.3	6.1	6.5	6.6	7.0	7.7
		261	Glass and glass products	1.5	1.5	1.2	1.1	1.3	1.3	1.2	1.2
		269	Non-metallic mineral products, nec	6.4	5.2	5.1	5.0	5.2	4.4	4.8	5.5
	27		Basic metals	6.4	7.1	6.8	6.1	6.5	7.1	7.4	7.2
		271	Basic iron and steel	2.6	3.1	2.7	2.3	2.3	2.4	2.5	2.4
		272	Basic precious and non-ferrous metals	1.5	1.6	1.5	1.3	1.3	1.3	1.2	1.2
		273	Casting of metals	2.2	2.4	2.6	2.5	2.9	3.5	3.7	3.6
	28		Fabricated metal products, ex. machin. & equip.	21.2	19.6	17.6	16.8	16.9	18.5	20.4	21.6
		281	Structural metal prod., tanks, reservoirs, generators	..	..	..	..	..	..	..	..
		289	Other fabricated metal products & service activities	..	..	..	..	..	..	..	..
	29		Machinery and equipment, nec	18.5	18.9	17.9	17.1	17.8	21.2	22.5	22.9
		291	General purpose machinery	..	..	..	..	..	..	..	..
		292	Special purpose machinery	..	..	..	..	..	..	..	..
		293	Domestic appliances, nec	3.8	4.3	4.1	3.9	4.2	4.9	5.3	5.2
	30		Office, accounting and computing machinery	0.2	0.3	0.4	0.4	0.3	0.5	0.5	0.5
	31		Electrical machinery and apparatus, nec	4.9	4.8	5.0	4.5	4.5	4.7	5.0	4.9
		311	Electric motors, generators and transformers	..	..	..	..	..	..	..	..
		312	Electricity distribution and control apparatus	..	..	..	..	..	..	..	..
		313	Insulated wire and cable	0.8	0.7	0.7	0.6	0.5	0.6	0.6	0.6
		314	Accumulators, primary cells and primary batteries	0.5	0.5	0.5	0.4	0.4	0.3	0.1	0.1
		315	Electric lamps and lighting equipment	0.7	0.7	0.7	0.6	0.5	0.5	0.5	0.5
		319	Other electrical equipment, nec	2.9	3.0	3.1	2.9	3.1	3.3	3.8	3.7
	32		Radio, TV, communication equip. & apparatus	2.8	2.9	2.5	2.0	1.7	2.3	2.6	2.7
		321	Electronic valves, tubes & other electronic compon.	2.0	1.7	1.3	1.0	0.8	1.1	1.3	1.2
		322	TV, radio transmitters & appar. for line teleph., telegr.	0.8	1.2	1.2	0.9	1.0	1.1	1.4	1.5
		323	TV, radio receivers and associated goods	..	..	..	..	..	..	..	..
	33		Medical, precision, optical instr.; watches, clocks	1.3	1.6	1.5	1.6	1.5	1.1	1.3	1.4
		331	Medical equip.; precision instruments and appliances	..	..	..	..	..	..	..	..
		332	Optical instruments and photographic equipment	0.3	0.4	0.3	0.3	0.2	0.2	0.2	0.2
		333	Watches and clocks	..	..	..	..	..	..	..	..
	34		Motor vehicles, trailers, and semi-trailers	9.3	8.6	6.9	5.6	5.7	5.6	6.0	5.9
	35		Other transport equipment	3.7	3.6	3.1	3.2	3.1	3.5	4.5	4.6
		351	Building and repairing of ships and boats	2.8	2.6	2.3	2.3	2.3	2.6	3.5	3.6
		352	Railway, tramway locomotives and rolling stock	..	..	..	..	..	..	..	..
		353	Aircraft and spacecraft	0.7	0.8	0.6	0.7	0.7	0.8	0.8	0.8
		359	Transport equipment, nec	0.2	0.3	0.2	0.2	0.1	0.2	0.2	0.2
	36		Furniture; manufacturing, nec	12.1	13.7	12.8	12.4	12.5	13.9	14.5	14.5
		361	Furniture	8.4	9.2	8.8	8.4	8.5	9.4	9.9	10.1
		369	Manufacturing, nec	3.7	4.5	4.0	4.0	4.0	4.5	4.6	4.4
	37		Recycling	..	..	..	..	..	..	..	..
E	40-41		Electricity, gas and water supply	17.1	13.2	13.1	12.7	11.5	11.4	10.2	10.0
	40		Electricity, gas, steam and hot water supply	15.5	12.9	13.0	12.1	10.7	10.7	9.6	9.4
		401	Production, collection and distribution of electricity	14.6	12.1	12.1	11.1	9.7	9.7	8.7	8.2
	41	410	Collection, purification, distribution of water	1.6	0.3	0.2	0.7	0.7	0.7	0.6	0.6
F	45		Construction	82.2	79.4	75.8	70.4	69.2	74.1	85.1	92.9
G	50-52		Wholesale and retail trade; repairs etc	229.6	237.1	233.3	229.3	229.7	244.9	261.9	263.8
H	55		Hotels and restaurants	46.8	46.6	45.5	47.0	47.8	51.9	55.4	57.5
I	60-64		Transport, storage and communications	87.7	84.8	90.3	83.2	80.8	82.9	85.7	89.6
J	65-67		Financial intermediation	53.2	52.0	51.7	49.6	44.9	46.9	48.2	48.4
K	70-74		Real estate, renting and business activities	97.2	100.0	101.2	102.7	100.7	115.5	126.2	136.2
L-Q	75-99		Public admin.; education; health; other services	275.4	280.9	287.7	285.4	291.6	303.9	307.5	312.8
A-Q	01-99		Grand total	1 123.3	1 138.0	1 125.9	1 099.1	1 089.0	1 140.0	1 194.9	1 233.8

Note: Data refers to the fiscal year ending 31 March. Unless given separately, ISIC 1544 includes 1549; 2023 includes 2029; 2413 includes 2430; 2696 includes 2699; 2899 includes 2813; 319 includes 311 and 312; 321 includes 323; 3692 includes 3699; 3693 includes 3694; 102 includes 103. ISIC 35 excludes 352. Some ANZIC industries can not be converted directly to ISIC. ISIC 29 includes ANZIC 2867 and 2869; ISIC 33 includes ANZIC 2839. Sub-totals may not always sum correctly due to the conversion between ANZIC and ISIC.

Industrial Structure Statistics
OECD, © 1998

Table NZ.3 EMPLOI, SALARIÉS - EMPLOYMENT, EMPLOYEES

Milliers

1988-89	1989-90	1990-91	1991-92	1992-93	1993-94	1994-95	1995-96			CITI révision 3	
56.6	57.2	59.3	57.5	60.5	61.1	62.0	70.1	Agriculture, chasse et sylviculture	A	01-02	
1.9	2.0	2.1	2.1	2.1	2.4	2.3	2.4	Pêche	B	05	
4.0	3.6	3.8	3.7	3.5	3.7	3.8	3.8	Activités extractives	C	10-14	
1.1	1.0	1.0	0.9	0.8	0.7	0.8	0.8	Extraction de charbon, de lignite et de tourbe		10	
0.7	0.6	0.7	0.8	0.6	0.8	0.8	0.7	Extraction de pétrole brut et de gaz naturel		11	
0.5	0.5	0.5	0.6	0.7	0.5	0.7	0.9	Extraction de minerais métalliques		13	
1.7	1.6	1.6	1.5	1.3	1.7	1.5	1.5	Autres activités extractives		14	
244.9	235.2	213.6	202.9	208.0	220.7	226.9	232.0	Activités de fabrication	D	15-37	
63.6	59.8	58.3	56.6	57.9	59.9	59.5	61.5	Produits alimentaires et boissons		15	
2.3	3.0	3.0	2.6	2.5	2.9	3.0	3.1	Boissons			155
0.9	0.8	0.7	0.6	0.5	0.5	0.5	0.5	Produits à base de tabac		16	160
10.8	11.5	10.4	9.4	9.5	10.0	10.5	9.9	Textiles		17	
3.4	2.9	2.3	2.3	4.3	4.5	4.8	4.5	Filature, tissage et achèvement des textiles			171
4.2	5.4	5.2	4.7	3.1	3.6	3.8	3.8	Autres articles textiles			172
3.2	3.2	2.8	2.4	2.0	2.0	2.0	1.6	Etoffes et articles de bonneterie			173
14.2	13.4	12.2	11.2	11.3	11.8	11.5	10.3	Habillement; préparation, teinture des fourrures		18	
..	..	..	..	..	..	..	..	Articles d'habillement autres qu'en fourrure			181
..	..	..	..	..	..	..	..	Préparation, teinture des fourrures; art. en fourrure			182
4.2	4.5	3.9	3.6	3.7	4.2	4.2	4.0	Travail des cuirs; articles en cuir; chaussures		19	
2.2	2.2	2.1	2.2	2.3	2.4	2.6	2.4	Apprêt et tannage des cuirs et articles en cuirs			191
1.9	2.3	1.9	1.4	1.4	1.8	1.7	1.5	Chaussures			192
12.1	12.9	12.1	12.0	13.0	14.8	13.5	17.0	Bois et articles en bois et liège (sauf meubles)		20	
6.4	6.5	6.3	6.5	7.2	8.2	6.5	9.9	Sciage et rabotage du bois			201
5.7	6.4	5.9	5.4	5.9	6.6	7.0	7.1	Articles en bois, liège, vannerie, sparterie			202
10.1	8.5	9.5	8.9	8.6	8.6	9.3	9.0	Papier et carton; articles en papier et en carton		21	
19.4	18.2	18.0	17.4	17.7	18.2	19.5	19.4	Edition, imprimerie et reproduction		22	
9.3	9.1	8.9	8.6	9.1	9.1	10.0	9.6	Edition			221
10.2	9.1	9.2	8.8	8.6	9.1	9.5	9.9	Imprimerie et activités annexes			222
0.0	0.0	..	0.0	0.0	0.0	0.0	0.0	Reproduction de supports enregistrés			223
1.6	0.9	1.0	0.9	0.9	0.8	0.8	0.8	Cokéfaction; prod. pétroliers; comb. nucléaires		23	
13.2	10.5	10.0	10.7	10.7	10.8	10.7	10.7	Produits chimiques		24	
5.7	3.7	3.6	4.2	4.1	4.4	4.5	4.1	Produits chimiques de base			241
7.6	6.9	6.4	6.5	6.6	6.4	6.2	6.6	Autres produits chimiques			242
..	..	..	..	..	..	..	..	Fibres synthétiques ou artificielles			243
9.3	10.1	8.4	8.3	9.2	8.9	8.8	8.9	Articles en caoutchouc et en matières plastiques		25	
2.3	2.9	1.9	1.8	2.9	1.9	1.8	1.8	Articles en caoutchouc			251
7.0	7.2	6.5	6.5	6.4	7.0	7.0	7.1	Articles en matières plastiques			252
7.0	5.9	5.6	5.3	5.6	5.8	6.1	6.8	Autres produits minéraux non métalliques		26	
1.3	1.3	1.1	1.0	1.1	1.1	1.0	1.0	Verre et articles en verre			261
5.7	4.6	4.5	4.4	4.5	3.8	4.2	4.9	Produits minéraux non métalliques, nca			269
6.2	6.9	6.6	5.9	6.3	6.8	7.2	7.0	Produits métallurgiques de base		27	
2.6	3.1	2.7	2.3	2.3	2.3	2.5	2.3	Sidérurgie et première transformation de l'acier			271
1.5	1.6	1.5	1.3	1.3	1.2	1.2	1.2	Métallurgie; métaux précieux et non ferreux			272
2.1	2.2	2.4	2.3	2.7	3.3	3.5	3.4	Fonderie			273
18.3	16.8	14.8	13.9	14.0	15.5	17.3	18.5	Ouvrages en métaux, sauf machines et matériel		28	
..	..	..	..	..	..	..	..	Constr. et menuiserie métal.; réservoirs; générateurs			281
..	..	..	..	..	..	..	..	Autres ouvrages en métaux			289
15.4	15.7	14.8	13.9	14.7	17.9	18.9	19.0	Machines et matériel, nca		29	
..	..	..	..	..	..	..	..	Machines d'usage général			291
..	..	..	..	..	..	..	..	Machines d'usage spécifique			292
3.8	4.2	4.1	3.9	4.1	4.9	5.2	5.2	Appareils domestiques, nca			293
0.2	0.3	0.4	0.3	0.2	0.4	0.4	0.4	Mach. de bureau, comptables, matériel inform.		30	
4.5	4.4	4.6	4.0	4.1	4.2	4.6	4.5	Machines et appareils électriques, nca		31	
..	..	..	..	..	..	..	..	Moteurs, génératrices et transformateurs électriques			311
..	..	..	..	..	..	..	..	Matériel électrique de distribution et de commande			312
0.8	0.7	0.7	0.6	0.5	0.6	0.6	0.6	Fils et câbles électriques isolés			313
0.5	0.5	0.5	0.4	0.4	0.3	0.1	0.1	Accumulateurs, piles électriques			314
0.6	0.6	0.6	0.5	0.5	0.4	0.5	0.4	Lampes électriques et appareils d'éclairage			315
2.6	2.6	2.8	2.5	2.7	2.9	3.5	3.3	Autres matériels électriques, nca			319
2.6	2.7	2.3	1.7	1.5	2.0	2.4	2.4	Equip. et appar. de radio, TV, communication		32	
1.8	1.6	1.2	0.9	0.6	1.0	1.1	1.0	Tubes et valves électroniques; autres composants			321
0.8	1.2	1.1	0.9	0.9	1.1	1.3	1.4	Emetteurs radio et TV; app. téléphonie, télégraphie			322
..	..	..	..	..	..	..	..	Récepteurs radio et TV et articles associés			323
1.0	1.3	1.2	1.3	1.2	0.8	1.0	1.0	Instruments médicaux, de précision, d'optique		33	
..	..	..	..	..	..	..	..	Appareils médicaux et de précision			331
0.3	0.4	0.3	0.3	0.2	0.2	0.2	0.1	Instruments d'optique ; matériel photographique			332
..	..	..	..	..	..	..	..	Horlogerie			333
8.6	7.9	6.2	4.9	5.0	4.8	5.2	5.1	Véhicules automobiles et nemorques		34	
2.2	2.0	1.7	1.8	1.7	2.8	3.7	3.7	Autres matériels de transport		35	
2.1	1.9	1.6	1.7	1.7	2.0	2.8	2.9	Construction et réparation de navires			351
..	..	..	..	..	..	..	..	Construction de matériel ferroviaire roulant			352
0.6	0.7	0.5	0.6	0.6	0.7	0.7	0.7	Construction aéronautique et spatiale			353
0.2	0.3	0.2	0.2	0.1	0.1	0.1	0.1	Autres équipements de transport			359
9.2	10.8	9.8	9.2	9.2	10.5	10.8	10.9	Meubles; activités de fabrication, nca		36	
6.6	7.4	6.9	6.4	6.5	7.3	7.6	7.9	Meubles			361
2.7	3.5	2.9	2.7	2.7	3.2	3.2	3.0	Activités de fabrication, nca			369
..	..	..	..	..	..	..	..	Récupération		37	
17.0	13.1	13.1	12.6	11.3	11.3	10.2	9.9	Production et distrib. d'électricité, de gaz, d'eau	E	40-41	
15.5	12.9	12.9	12.1	10.7	10.7	9.6	9.4	Electricité, gaz, vapeur et eau chaude		40	
14.6	12.1	12.1	11.1	9.7	9.7	8.7	8.2	Production, collecte et distribution d'électricité			401
1.6	0.2	0.1	0.6	0.6	0.6	0.6	0.5	Captage, épuration et distribution d'eau		41	410
52.8	49.6	44.8	39.0	38.1	43.4	49.4	54.5	Construction	F	45	
176.8	180.5	176.7	169.3	168.9	183.6	195.9	199.1	Commerce de gros et de détail; réparation	G	50-52	
38.4	37.5	36.4	37.0	37.4	41.4	43.9	45.9	Hôtels et restaurants	H	55	
76.3	73.4	78.2	70.1	67.6	69.8	71.1	74.3	Transports, entreposage et communications	I	60-64	
50.8	49.7	49.4	47.2	42.4	43.0	44.3	44.6	Intermédiation financière	J	65-67	
71.7	75.7	74.8	73.4	70.2	81.3	85.3	90.9	Immobilier, locations, services aux entreprises	K	70-74	
259.1	263.6	269.5	265.1	270.3	281.9	284.3	288.4	Admin. publique; éducation; santé; autres	L-Q	75-99	
878.3	865.0	867.7	833.9	823.4	874.1	899.7	930.4	Grand total	A-Q	01-99	

Note: Data refers to the fiscal year ending 31 March. Unless given separately, ISIC 1544 includes 1549; 2023 includes 2029; 2413 includes 2430; 2696 includes 2699; 2899 includes 2813; 319 includes 311 and 312; 321 includes 323; 3692 includes 3699; 3693 includes 3694; 102 includes 103. ISIC 35 excludes 352. Some ANZIC industries can not be converted directly to ISIC. ISIC 29 includes ANZIC 2867 and 2869; ISIC 33 includes ANZIC 2839. Sub-totals may not always sum correctly due to the conversion between ANZIC and ISIC.

Statistiques des Structures Industrielles
OCDE, © 1998

Table NZ.4 EMPLOYMENT, FEMALES - EMPLOI, FEMMES

Thousands

	ISIC rev.3		Description	1988-89	1989-90	1990-91	1991-92	1992-93	1993-94	1994-95	1995-96
A	01-02		Agriculture, hunting and forestry	18.4	18.3	19.2	18.1	18.7	18.8	19.4	21.3
B	05		Fishing	0.2	0.2	0.3	0.2	0.3	0.3	0.2	0.3
C	10-14		Mining and quarrying	0.5	0.4	0.5	0.5	0.4	0.4	0.4	0.4
	10		Mining of coal and lignite; extraction of peat	0.1	0.1	0.1	0.1	0.1	0.1	0.1	0.1
	11		Crude petroleum & natural gas; related service activ.	0.2	0.1	0.2	0.2	0.1	0.1	0.1	0.1
	13		Mining of metal ores	0.1	0.1	0.1	0.1	0.1	0.1	0.1	0.1
	14		Other mining and quarrying	0.2	0.1	0.1	0.1	0.1	0.2	0.1	0.1
D	15-37		Total manufacturing	66.6	66.6	62.1	58.4	59.3	63.9	66.4	65.7
	15		Food products and beverages	15.2	15.3	15.4	14.8	15.0	17.3	17.9	18.1
		155	Beverages	0.6	0.9	0.8	0.8	0.8	0.8	0.9	1.0
	16	160	Tobacco products	0.4	0.4	0.3	0.2	0.2	0.2	0.2	0.2
	17		Textiles	5.0	5.3	4.6	4.1	4.2	4.6	4.8	4.5
		171	Spinning, weaving and finishing of textiles	1.1	1.0	0.8	0.7	1.3	1.3	1.5	1.3
		172	Other textiles	1.8	2.3	2.2	2.1	1.7	2.0	2.1	2.1
		173	Knitted and crocheted fabrics and articles	2.1	2.1	1.6	1.4	1.2	1.3	1.2	1.1
	18		Wearing apparel dressing & dyeing of fur	11.2	10.8	10.0	9.2	9.1	9.6	9.3	8.4
		181	Wearing apparel, except fur apparel	..	..	..	..	..	..	..	..
		182	Dressing and dyeing of fur; articles of fur	..	..	..	..	..	..	..	..
	19		Tanning, dressing leather; leather artic.; footwear	1.9	2.0	1.8	1.5	1.6	1.8	1.8	1.6
		191	Tanning, dressing leather; manuf. of leather articles	0.7	0.8	0.7	0.7	0.7	0.8	0.8	0.7
		192	Footwear	1.1	1.2	1.1	0.8	0.8	1.1	1.0	0.9
	20		Wood and cork products, ex. furniture	1.4	1.6	1.5	1.4	1.4	1.7	1.5	2.0
		201	Sawmilling and planing of wood	0.5	0.6	0.6	0.6	0.7	0.9	0.7	1.2
		202	Products of wood, cork, straw & plaiting material	0.9	1.0	0.9	0.8	0.7	0.8	0.8	0.8
	21		Paper and paper products	1.7	1.6	1.6	1.5	1.6	1.6	1.8	1.8
	22		Publishing, printing & reprod. of recorded media	8.0	7.9	7.7	7.5	7.6	7.7	8.5	8.4
		221	Publishing	4.2	4.4	4.3	4.3	4.6	4.6	5.1	5.0
		222	Printing and related service activities	3.8	3.5	3.4	3.1	3.0	3.2	3.4	3.4
		223	Reproduction of recorded media	..	..	..	..	0.0	0.0	0.0	0.0
	23		Coke, refined petroleum products & nuclear fuel	0.1	0.1	0.1	0.1	0.1	0.1	0.1	0.1
	24		Chemicals and chemical products	4.1	3.5	3.2	3.4	3.4	3.4	3.5	3.4
		241	Basic chemicals	1.2	0.8	0.7	0.9	0.9	0.9	0.9	0.8
		242	Other chemical products	2.9	2.7	2.5	2.5	2.6	2.5	2.6	2.6
		243	Man-made fibres	..	..	..	..	..	..	..	..
	25		Rubber and plastic products	2.5	2.3	2.1	2.1	2.1	2.1	2.1	2.2
		251	Rubber products	0.6	0.5	0.4	0.3	0.4	0.4	0.3	0.4
		252	Plastic products	2.0	1.8	1.7	1.7	1.7	1.8	1.8	1.9
	26		Other non-metallic mineral products	1.2	0.8	0.8	0.8	0.8	0.9	1.0	1.1
		261	Glass and glass products	0.2	0.2	0.2	0.2	0.2	0.2	0.2	0.2
		269	Non-metallic mineral products, nec	1.0	0.6	0.6	0.6	0.6	0.6	0.7	0.7
	27		Basic metals	0.4	0.8	0.8	0.7	0.8	0.8	0.8	0.7
		271	Basic iron and steel	0.1	0.4	0.3	0.3	0.3	0.3	0.3	0.2
		272	Basic precious and non-ferrous metals	0.1	0.1	0.1	0.1	0.1	0.1	0.1	0.1
		273	Casting of metals	0.2	0.3	0.4	0.3	0.4	0.4	0.5	0.5
	28		Fabricated metal products, ex. machin. & equip.	2.9	2.8	2.5	2.4	2.3	2.4	2.7	2.9
		281	Structural metal prod., tanks, reservoirs, generators	..	..	..	..	..	..	..	..
		289	Other fabricated metal products & service activities	..	..	..	..	..	..	..	..
	29		Machinery and equipment, nec	2.2	2.9	2.6	2.5	2.7	3.3	3.5	3.4
		291	General purpose machinery	..	..	..	..	..	..	..	..
		292	Special purpose machinery	..	..	..	..	..	..	..	..
		293	Domestic appliances, nec	0.9	1.5	1.3	1.3	1.4	1.7	1.8	1.8
	30		Office, accounting and computing machinery	0.0	0.1	0.1	0.1	0.0	0.1	0.1	0.1
	31		Electrical machinery and apparatus, nec	1.3	1.6	1.5	1.4	1.3	1.4	1.6	1.4
		311	Electric motors, generators and transformers	..	..	..	..	..	..	..	..
		312	Electricity distribution and control apparatus	..	..	..	..	..	..	..	..
		313	Insulated wire and cable	0.2	0.1	0.1	0.1	0.1	0.1	0.1	0.1
		314	Accumulators, primary cells and primary batteries	0.1	0.1	0.1	0.1	0.1	0.0	0.0	0.0
		315	Electric lamps and lighting equipment	0.2	0.2	0.2	0.2	0.2	0.2	0.2	0.2
		319	Other electrical equipment, nec	0.8	1.2	1.1	1.0	1.0	1.1	1.3	1.1
	32		Radio, TV, communication equip. & apparatus	1.2	1.0	0.9	0.6	0.6	0.7	0.9	0.9
		321	Electronic valves, tubes & other electronic compon.	0.9	0.5	0.4	0.3	0.2	0.3	0.3	0.3
		322	TV, radio transmitters & appar. for line teleph., telegr.	0.3	0.5	0.5	0.4	0.4	0.5	0.6	0.6
		323	TV, radio receivers and associated goods	..	..	..	..	..	..	..	..
	33		Medical, precision, optical instr.; watches, clocks	0.5	0.6	0.5	0.6	0.6	0.3	0.4	0.4
		331	Medical equip.; precision instruments and appliances	..	..	..	..	..	..	..	..
		332	Optical instruments and photographic equipment	0.1	0.2	0.1	0.1	0.1	0.1	0.1	0.1
		333	Watches and clocks	..	..	..	..	..	..	..	..
	34		Motor vehicles, trailers, and semi-trailers	1.8	1.6	1.2	1.0	1.0	0.9	1.0	1.0
	35		Other transport equipment	0.3	0.3	0.2	0.2	0.2	0.3	0.4	0.4
		351	Building and repairing of ships and boats	0.2	0.2	0.1	0.1	0.2	0.2	0.2	0.2
		352	Railway, tramway locomotives and rolling stock	..	..	..	..	..	..	..	..
		353	Aircraft and spacecraft	0.1	0.1	0.1	0.1	0.1	0.1	0.1	0.1
		359	Transport equipment, nec	0.0	0.0	0.0	0.0	0.1	0.1	0.1	0.0
	36		Furniture; manufacturing, nec	2.5	3.0	2.7	2.5	2.4	2.7	2.7	2.5
		361	Furniture	1.4	1.7	1.5	1.4	1.4	1.5	1.5	1.5
		369	Manufacturing, nec	1.0	1.3	1.2	1.1	1.0	1.1	1.1	1.0
	37		Recycling	..	..	..	..	..	..	..	..
E	40-41		Electricity, gas and water supply	2.8	2.2	2.3	2.2	2.1	2.2	2.1	2.1
	40		Electricity, gas, steam and hot water supply	2.6	2.2	2.2	2.2	2.0	2.1	2.0	2.0
		401	Production, collection and distribution of electricity	2.4	2.0	2.0	1.9	1.8	1.9	1.8	1.7
	41	410	Collection, purification, distribution of water	0.2	0.0	0.0	0.1	0.1	0.1	0.1	0.1
F	45		Construction	5.2	4.7	4.3	3.9	3.8	3.8	4.2	4.7
G	50-52		Wholesale and retail trade; repairs etc	73.7	78.2	75.8	72.9	73.4	79.4	84.4	85.7
H	55		Hotels and restaurants	21.9	22.4	21.6	21.9	22.5	25.0	26.7	28.0
I	60-64		Transport, storage and communications	24.0	23.8	24.0	22.5	20.7	21.4	22.1	23.8
J	65-67		Financial intermediation	29.6	29.9	30.0	28.6	25.8	25.6	26.1	26.6
K	70-74		Real estate, renting and business activities	37.7	40.1	40.0	38.2	37.2	42.3	44.5	47.3
L-Q	75-99		Public admin.; education; health; other services	150.3	151.9	158.5	158.4	162.0	170.3	172.1	179.8
A-Q	01-99		Grand total	375.6	381.4	386.2	377.0	375.7	398.9	411.3	429.2

Note: Data refers to the fiscal year ending 31 March. Unless given separately, ISIC 1544 includes 1549; 2023 includes 2029; 2413 includes 2430; 2696 includes 2699; 2899 includes 2813; 319 includes 311 and 312; 321 includes 323; 3692 includes 3699; 3693 includes 3694; 102 includes 103. ISIC 35 excludes 352. Some ANZIC industries can not be converted directly to ISIC. ISIC 29 includes ANZIC 2867 and 2869; ISIC 33 includes ANZIC 2839. Sub-totals may not always sum correctly due to the conversion between ANZIC and ISIC.

Table NY.1 **PRODUCTION - PRODUCTION**

Millions de NKr *(Prix courants)*

1989	1990	1991	1992	1993	1994	1995	1996			CITI révision 3
..	..	..	..	..	..	..	..	**Agriculture, chasse et sylviculture**	A	01-02
..	..	..	..	..	..	..	..	**Pêche**	B	05
..	..	..	..	..	..	143 080	..	**Activités extractives**	C	10-14
..	..	258	226	163	175	165	..	Extraction de charbon, de lignite et de tourbe		10
..	..	..	..	..	..	138 461	..	Extraction de pétrole brut et de gaz naturel		11
..	..	1 243	1 152	1 029	1 152	1 118	..	Extraction de minerais métalliques		13
..	..	2 357	1 973	1 974	2 188	3 336	..	Autres activités extractives		14
..	..	296 888	286 087	291 964	318 506	367 958	..	**Activités de fabrication**	D	15-37
..	..	79 083	79 743	80 514	84 733	..	..	**Produits alimentaires et boissons**		15
..	..	10 932	11 224	11 187	12 305	..	..	Boissons		155
..	..	..	..	..	..	..	..	**Produits à base de tabac**		16 160
..	..	3 302	3 247	3 205	3 401	3 520	..	**Textiles**		17
..	..	1 037	1 039	989	1 050	1 023	..	Filature, tissage et achèvement des textiles		171
..	..	1 732	1 598	1 586	1 694	2 039	..	Autres articles textiles		172
..	..	534	611	630	657	459	..	Etoffes et articles de bonneterie		173
..	..	942	964	1 033	1 170	1 431	..	**Habillement; préparation, teinture des fourrures**		18
..	..	884	906	983	1 122	1 377	..	Articles d'habillement autres qu'en fourrure		181
..	..	58	58	51	48	54	..	Préparation, teinture des fourrures; art. en fourrure		182
..	..	506	505	516	555	527	..	**Travail des cuirs; articles en cuir; chaussures**		19
..	..	318	336	340	378	283	..	Apprêt et tannage des cuirs et articles en cuirs		191
..	..	188	169	176	177	244	..	Chaussures		192
..	..	11 452	9 405	9 406	11 848	14 737	..	**Bois et articles en bois et liège (sauf meubles)**		20
..	..	5 747	4 800	4 541	6 005	6 823	..	Sciage et rabotage du bois		201
..	..	5 704	4 605	4 865	5 843	7 913	..	Articles en bois, liège, vannerie, sparterie		202
..	..	17 332	15 364	15 028	16 849	22 230	..	**Papier et carton; articles en papier et en carton**		21
..	..	20 469	18 857	19 295	20 601	25 927	..	**Edition, imprimerie et reproduction**		22
..	..	13 534	13 329	13 725	14 716	16 664	..	Edition		221
..	..	6 850	5 443	5 486	5 720	8 902	..	Imprimerie et activités annexes		222
..	..	85	85	85	165	361	..	Reproduction de supports enregistrés		223
..	..	15 430	14 766	16 518	15 698	13 425	..	**Cokéfaction; prod. pétroliers; comb. nucléaires**		23
..	..	22 990	22 775	24 320	26 966	29 532	..	**Produits chimiques**		24
..	..	16 326	15 331	16 340	18 924	20 785	..	Produits chimiques de base		241
..	..	6 663	7 443	7 979	8 042	8 747	..	Autres produits chimiques		242
..	..	0	0	0	0	0	..	Fibres synthétiques ou artificielles		243
..	..	5 231	4 333	4 433	5 146	6 507	..	**Articles en caoutchouc et en matières plastiques**		25
..	..	799	428	409	534	676	..	Articles en caoutchouc		251
..	..	4 432	3 905	4 023	4 611	5 831	..	Articles en matières plastiques		252
..	..	7 462	6 616	6 672	7 575	9 906	..	**Autres produits minéraux non métalliques**		26
..	..	..	..	1 189	1 372	1 505	..	Verre et articles en verre		261
..	..	..	..	5 483	6 203	8 401	..	Produits minéraux non métalliques, nca		269
..	..	27 774	25 217	25 408	31 713	37 113	..	**Produits métallurgiques de base**		27
..	..	6 864	6 722	..	7 655	8 891	..	Sidérurgie et première transformation de l'acier		271
..	..	20 711	18 350	18 429	22 894	26 816	..	Métallurgie; métaux précieux et non ferreux		272
..	..	199	145	..	1 164	1 406	..	Fonderie		273
..	..	10 919	9 560	9 474	9 992	13 793	..	**Ouvrages en métaux, sauf machines et matériel**		28
..	..	..	..	..	4 866	6 895	..	Constr. et menuiserie métal.; réservoirs; générateurs		281
..	..	..	..	..	5 126	6 898	..	Autres ouvrages en métaux		289
..	..	17 527	16 599	16 463	18 571	23 812	..	**Machines et matériel, nca**		29
..	..	10 745	10 444	9 954	11 343	14 543	..	Machines d'usage général		291
..	..	5 900	5 298	5 623	6 253	8 305	..	Machines d'usage spécifique		292
..	..	882	856	886	975	963	..	Appareils domestiques, nca		293
..	..	1 088	1 005	928	1 398	1 292	..	**Mach. de bureau, comptables, matériel inform.**		30
..	..	9 190	8 811	8 709	9 350	10 673	..	**Machines et appareils électriques, nca**		31
..	..	2 710	2 545	2 986	3 021	3 058	..	Moteurs, génératrices et transformateurs électriques		311
..	..	1 845	1 770	1 924	2 218	2 685	..	Matériel électrique de distribution et de commande		312
..	..	2 396	2 451	1 939	2 195	2 595	..	Fils et câbles électriques isolés		313
..	..	102	..	..	..	171	..	Accumulateurs, piles électriques		314
..	..	1 033	968	914	909	1 140	..	Lampes électriques et appareils d'éclairage		315
..	..	1 104	..	..	..	1 024	..	Autres matériels électriques, nca		319
..	..	3 489	3 701	3 766	4 554	5 672	..	**Equip. et appar. de radio, TV, communication**		32
..	..	401	526	570	610	804	..	Tubes et valves électroniques; autres composants		321
..	..	2 562	2 764	2 583	3 407	4 487	..	Emetteurs radio et TV; app. téléphonie, télégraphie		322
..	..	526	411	612	537	380	..	Récepteurs radio et TV et articles associés		323
..	..	3 367	3 530	3 842	4 221	5 859	..	**Instruments médicaux, de précision, d'optique**		33
..	..	3 179	..	..	4 047	5 631	..	Appareils médicaux et de précision		331
..	..	187	..	..	174	229	..	Instruments d'optique ; matériel photographique		332
..	..	0	..	..	0	0	..	Horlogerie		333
..	..	2 317	2 481	2 566	3 089	4 404	..	**Véhicules automobiles et nemorques**		34
..	..	30 090	32 016	33 327	33 603	36 097	..	**Autres matériels de transport**		35
..	..	26 170	28 093	29 445	28 747	31 315	..	Construction et réparation de navires		351
..	..	1 272	1 352	1 449	1 335	1 156	..	Construction de matériel ferroviaire roulant		352
..	..	2 292	2 180	2 041	3 052	3 147	..	Construction aéronautique et spatiale		353
..	..	357	391	393	469	482	..	Autres équipements de transport		359
..	..	6 795	6 460	6 407	7 252	8 835	..	**Meubles; activités de fabrication, nca**		36
..	..	5 059	4 663	4 667	5 521	6 611	..	Meubles		361
..	..	1 735	1 798	1 740	1 731	2 224	..	Activités de fabrication, nca		369
..	..	136	132	132	220	461	..	**Récupération**		37
..	..	..	..	..	..	..	..	**Production et distrib. d'électricité, de gaz, d'eau**	E	40-41
..	..	..	..	..	..	..	..	**Electricité, gaz, vapeur et eau chaude**		40
..	..	..	..	..	..	34 771	..	Production, collecte et distribution d'électricité		401
..	..	..	..	..	..	..	..	**Captage, épuration et distribution d'eau**		41 410
..	..	..	..	..	..	..	..	**Construction**	F	45
..	..	..	..	..	..	..	..	**Commerce de gros et de détail; réparation**	G	50-52
..	..	..	..	..	..	..	..	**Hôtels et restaurants**	H	55
..	..	..	..	..	..	..	..	**Transports, entreposage et communications**	I	60-64
..	..	..	..	..	..	..	..	**Intermédiation financière**	J	65-67
..	..	..	..	..	..	..	..	**Immobilier, locations, services aux entreprises**	K	70-74
..	..	..	..	..	..	..	..	**Admin. publique; éducation; santé; autres**	L-Q	75-99
..	..	..	..	..	..	..	..	**Grand total**	A-Q	01-99

Note: Unless given separetely, ISIC 155 includes 16.

Statistiques des Structures Industrielles
OCDE, © 1998

Table NY.2 VALUE ADDED - VALEUR AJOUTÉE

Millions of NKr (Current Prices)

ISIC revision 3			1989	1990	1991	1992	1993	1994	1995	1996
A	01-02	**Agriculture, hunting and forestry**	..	..	..	..	..	..	..	..
B	05	**Fishing**	..	..	..	..	..	..	..	..
C	10-14	**Mining and quarrying**	..	..	..	..	..	..	109 909	..
	10	Mining of coal and lignite; extraction of peat	..	..	55	76	32	23	32	..
	11	Crude petroleum & natural gas; related service activ.	..	..	..	..	..	..	108 065	..
	13	Mining of metal ores	..	..	377	411	271	437	348	..
	14	Other mining and quarrying	..	..	1 055	891	910	1 033	1 464	..
D	15-37	**Total manufacturing**	..	..	85 187	84 969	88 899	95 167	114 575	..
	15	**Food products and beverages**	..	..	17 022	19 183	19 965	20 568	..	..
	155	Beverages	..	..	8 022	8 450	8 407	8 880		..
	16 160	**Tobacco products**	..	..	..	1 801			..	..
	17	**Textiles**	..	..	1 285	1 294	1 252	1 242	1 298	..
	171	Spinning, weaving and finishing of textiles	..	..	410	409	391	404	390	..
	172	Other textiles	..	..	650	609	582	557	714	..
	173	Knitted and crocheted fabrics and articles	..	..	224	276	279	280	194	..
	18	**Wearing apparel dressing & dyeing of fur**	..	..	369	378	408	424	514	..
	181	Wearing apparel, except fur apparel	..	..	347	355	389	403	490	..
	182	Dressing and dyeing of fur; articles of fur	..	..	22	23	20	20	24	..
	19	**Tanning, dressing leather; leather artic.; footwear**	..	..	185	167	173	184	179	..
	191	Tanning, dressing leather; manuf. of leather articles	..	..	104	92	96	103	83	..
	192	Footwear	..	..	81	75	76	81	96	..
	20	**Wood and cork products, ex. furniture**	..	..	3 371	2 810	2 916	3 682	4 173	..
	201	Sawmilling and planing of wood	..	..	1 549	1 286	1 366	1 750	1 573	..
	202	Products of wood, cork, straw & plaiting material	..	..	1 821	1 524	1 549	1 932	2 601	..
	21	**Paper and paper products**	..	..	4 260	3 634	3 906	4 527	7 236	..
	22	**Publishing, printing & reprod. of recorded media**	..	..	8 961	8 466	8 911	9 438	11 616	..
	221	Publishing	..	..	5 977	6 038	6 435	6 860	7 700	..
	222	Printing and related service activities	..	..	2 935	2 380	2 428	2 484	3 712	..
	223	Reproduction of recorded media	..	..	48	48	48	94	205	..
	23	**Coke, refined petroleum products & nuclear fuel**	..	..	1 569	940	1 806	1 561	870	..
	24	**Chemicals and chemical products**	..	..	6 998	7 079	7 834	8 717	10 743	..
	241	Basic chemicals	..	..	4 623	4 316	4 772	5 824	7 251	..
	242	Other chemical products	..	..	2 375	2 828	3 062	2 893	3 492	..
	243	Man-made fibres	..	..	0	0	0	0	0	..
	25	**Rubber and plastic products**	..	..	1 860	1 680	1 701	1 876	2 294	..
	251	Rubber products	..	..	334	176	180	209	287	..
	252	Plastic products	..	..	1 526	1 505	1 521	1 667	2 007	..
	26	**Other non-metallic mineral products**	..	..	2 983	2 407	2 755	3 018	3 840	..
	261	Glass and glass products	..	..	..	..	501	567	646	..
	269	Non-metallic mineral products, nec	..	..	..	..	2 254	2 451	3 194	..
	27	**Basic metals**	..	..	5 942	5 560	6 017	7 548	9 867	..
	271	Basic iron and steel	..	..	1 534	1 528	..	1 884	2 408	..
	272	Basic precious and non-ferrous metals	..	..	4 322	3 978	4 182	5 122	6 827	..
	273	Casting of metals	..	..	86	54	..	542	632	..
	28	**Fabricated metal products, ex. machin. & equip.**	..	..	4 322	3 805	3 896	4 044	5 564	..
	281	Structural metal prod., tanks, reservoirs, generators	..	..	..	..	..	1 803	2 541	..
	289	Other fabricated metal products & service activities	..	..	..	..	..	2 240	3 024	..
	29	**Machinery and equipment, nec**	..	..	6 421	5 989	5 912	6 324	8 084	..
	291	General purpose machinery	..	..	3 781	3 534	3 341	3 615	4 703	..
	292	Special purpose machinery	..	..	2 286	2 132	2 223	2 321	3 031	..
	293	Domestic appliances, nec	..	..	354	322	348	388	351	..
	30	**Office, accounting and computing machinery**	..	..	337	334	283	390	352	..
	31	**Electrical machinery and apparatus, nec**	..	..	3 294	3 141	3 272	3 326	3 828	..
	311	Electric motors, generators and transformers	..	..	920	859	1 018	905	1 195	..
	312	Electricity distribution and control apparatus	..	..	758	710	736	849	972	..
	313	Insulated wire and cable	..	..	858	802	848	854	899	..
	314	Accumulators, primary cells and primary batteries	..	..	23	..	..	..	63	..
	315	Electric lamps and lighting equipment	..	..	392	365	359	363	425	..
	319	Other electrical equipment, nec	..	..	343	..	..	..	274	..
	32	**Radio, TV, communication equip. & apparatus**	..	..	1 520	1 338	1 477	1 660	1 976	..
	321	Electronic valves, tubes & other electronic compon.	..	..	164	214	203	230	312	..
	322	TV, radio transmitters & appar. for line teleph., telegr.	..	..	1 181	956	1 030	1 216	1 537	..
	323	TV, radio receivers and associated goods	..	..	175	169	244	215	127	..
	33	**Medical, precision, optical instr.; watches, clocks**	..	..	1 328	1 351	1 410	1 596	2 187	..
	331	Medical equip.; precision instruments and appliances	..	..	1 260	..	..	1 526	2 133	..
	332	Optical instruments and photographic equipment	..	..	68	..	..	69	55	..
	333	Watches and clocks	..	..	0	..	..	0	0	..
	34	**Motor vehicles, trailers, and semi-trailers**	..	..	800	851	955	1 082	1 464	..
	35	**Other transport equipment**	..	..	9 834	10 297	11 569	11 126	12 109	..
	351	Building and repairing of ships and boats	..	..	8 237	8 735	9 951	9 418	10 601	..
	352	Railway, tramway locomotives and rolling stock	..	..	486	520	566	507	429	..
	353	Aircraft and spacecraft	..	..	984	896	928	1 040	911	..
	359	Transport equipment, nec	..	..	127	144	124	161	169	..
	36	**Furniture; manufacturing, nec**	..	..	2 496	2 436	2 453	2 751	3 277	..
	361	Furniture	..	..	1 753	1 634	1 649	1 974	2 333	..
	369	Manufacturing, nec	..	..	742	802	804	778	944	..
	37	**Recycling**	..	..	31	29	29	84	163	..
E	40-41	**Electricity, gas and water supply**	..	..	..	..	..	..	..	..
	40	**Electricity, gas, steam and hot water supply**	..	..	..	..	..	..	..	..
	401	Production, collection and distribution of electricity	..	..	..	..	..	..	21 560	..
	41 410	**Collection, purification, distribution of water**	..	..	..	..	..	..	..	..
F	45	**Construction**	..	..	..	..	..	..	..	..
G	50-52	**Wholesale and retail trade; repairs etc**	..	..	..	..	..	..	..	..
H	55	**Hotels and restaurants**	..	..	..	..	..	..	..	..
I	60-64	**Transport, storage and communications**	..	..	..	..	..	..	..	..
J	65-67	**Financial intermediation**	..	..	..	..	..	..	..	..
K	70-74	**Real estate, renting and business activities**	..	..	..	..	..	..	..	..
L-Q	75-99	**Public admin.; education; health; other services**	..	..	..	..	..	..	..	..
A-Q	01-99	**Grand total**	..	..	..	..	..	..	..	..

Note: Unless given separetely, ISIC 155 includes 16.

Table NY.3 INVESTISSEMENT - INVESTMENT

Millions de NKr *(Prix courants)*

1989	1990	1991	1992	1993	1994	1995	1996			CITI révision 3
..	..	..	..	..	..	..	..	**Agriculture, chasse et sylviculture**	A	01-02
..	..	..	..	..	..	..	..	**Pêche**	B	05
..	..	..	..	..	..	1 468	..	**Activités extractives**	C	10-14
..	..	30	20	36	11	19	..	Extraction de charbon, de lignite et de tourbe		10
..	..	..	..	..	..	1 085	..	Extraction de pétrole brut et de gaz naturel		11
..	..	77	72	56	84	111	..	Extraction de minerais métalliques		13
..	..	190	168	136	146	253	..	Autres activités extractives		14
..	..	11 899	11 501	9 358	10 255	13 295	..	**Activités de fabrication**	D	15-37
..	..	2 520	2 314	2 511	2 554	..	..	**Produits alimentaires et boissons**		15
..	..	491	483	691	443	..	..	Boissons		155
..	..	..	37	..	..	..	..	**Produits à base de tabac**		16 160
..	..	117	78	160	143	171	..	**Textiles**		17
..	..	16	14	36	57	54	..	Filature, tissage et achèvement des textiles		171
..	..	86	40	103	60	94	..	Autres articles textiles		172
..	..	15	25	22	27	22	..	Etoffes et articles de bonneterie		173
..	..	11	9	13	26	34	..	**Habillement; préparation, teinture des fourrures**		18
..	..	10	9	11	25	32	..	Articles d'habillement autres qu'en fourrure		181
..	..	1	0	1	1	2	..	Préparation, teinture des fourrures; art. en fourrure		182
..	..	10	15	6	15	18	..	**Travail des cuirs; articles en cuir; chaussures**		19
..	..	5	13	3	7	16	..	Apprêt et tannage des cuirs et articles en cuirs		191
..	..	5	2	2	8	2	..	Chaussures		192
..	..	472	418	294	557	753	..	**Bois et articles en bois et liège (sauf meubles)**		20
..	..	327	287	157	332	400	..	Sciage et rabotage du bois		201
..	..	145	131	137	225	354	..	Articles en bois, liège, vannerie, sparterie		202
..	..	1 240	2 973	938	623	1 479	..	**Papier et carton; articles en papier et en carton**		21
..	..	623	644	619	895	1 243	..	**Edition, imprimerie et reproduction**		22
..	..	336	384	298	543	495	..	Edition		221
..	..	286	259	319	349	727	..	Imprimerie et activités annexes		222
..	..	1	1	1	3	21	..	Reproduction de supports enregistrés		223
..	..	263	206	345	261	176	..	**Cokéfaction; prod. pétroliers; comb. nucléaires**		23
..	..	1 907	1 164	1 025	1 171	1 126	..	**Produits chimiques**		24
..	..	1 430	830	656	756	875	..	Produits chimiques de base		241
..	..	476	334	369	416	251	..	Autres produits chimiques		242
..	..	0	0	0	0	0	..	Fibres synthétiques ou artificielles		243
..	..	270	155	204	270	360	..	**Articles en caoutchouc et en matières plastiques**		25
..	..	- 53	10	12	14	24	..	Articles en caoutchouc		251
..	..	323	145	192	256	336	..	Articles en matières plastiques		252
..	..	706	35	287	471	813	..	**Autres produits minéraux non métalliques**		26
..	..	..	..	27	35	78	..	Verre et articles en verre		261
..	..	..	..	260	437	735	..	Produits minéraux non métalliques, nca		269
..	..	1 208	898	519	897	1 134	..	**Produits métallurgiques de base**		27
..	..	308	152	..	303	420	..	Sidérurgie et première transformation de l'acier		271
..	..	887	732	398	554	647	..	Métallurgie; métaux précieux et non ferreux		272
..	..	13	14	..	39	67	..	Fonderie		273
..	..	338	436	246	232	443	..	**Ouvrages en métaux, sauf machines et matériel**		28
..	..	..	..	..	52	177	..	Constr. et menuiserie métal.; réservoirs; générateurs		281
..	..	..	..	..	180	266	..	Autres ouvrages en métaux		289
..	..	556	483	422	392	662	..	**Machines et matériel, nca**		29
..	..	323	291	263	204	316	..	Machines d'usage général		291
..	..	191	163	132	156	308	..	Machines d'usage spécifique		292
..	..	42	29	27	32	37	..	Appareils domestiques, nca		293
..	..	46	7	11	27	56	..	**Mach. de bureau, comptables, matériel inform.**		30
..	..	405	295	228	200	272	..	**Machines et appareils électriques, nca**		31
..	..	110	44	43	32	40	..	Moteurs, génératrices et transformateurs électriques		311
..	..	57	63	55	56	100	..	Matériel électrique de distribution et de commande		312
..	..	166	121	112	93	106	..	Fils et câbles électriques isolés		313
..	..	0	..	..	..	2	..	Accumulateurs, piles électriques		314
..	..	67	45	23	12	16	..	Lampes électriques et appareils d'éclairage		315
..	..	5	..	..	..	9	..	Autres matériels électriques, nca		319
..	..	164	110	134	170	178	..	**Equip. et appar. de radio, TV, communication**		32
..	..	15	10	16	26	35	..	Tubes et valves électroniques; autres composants		321
..	..	140	91	106	135	137	..	Emetteurs radio et TV; app. téléphonie, télégraphie		322
..	..	9	9	12	8	6	..	Récepteurs radio et TV et articles associés		323
..	..	79	118	117	174	273	..	**Instruments médicaux, de précision, d'optique**		33
..	..	77	..	..	172	263	..	Appareils médicaux et de précision		331
..	..	3	..	..	2	10	..	Instruments d'optique ; matériel photographique		332
..	..	0	..	..	0	0	..	Horlogerie		333
..	..	121	85	155	134	201	..	**Véhicules automobiles et nemorques**		34
..	..	584	839	912	787	846	..	**Autres matériels de transport**		35
..	..	519	744	729	664	698	..	Construction et réparation de navires		351
..	..	13	42	128	57	21	..	Construction de matériel ferroviaire roulant		352
..	..	40	46	37	54	118	..	Construction aéronautique et spatiale		353
..	..	11	7	18	10	9	..	Autres équipements de transport		359
..	..	259	180	211	246	342	..	**Meubles; activités de fabrication, nca**		36
..	..	148	94	129	189	266	..	Meubles		361
..	..	111	86	83	56	75	..	Activités de fabrication, nca		369
..	..	1	1	1	12	18	..	**Récupération**		37
..	..	..	..	..	..	..	..	**Production et distrib. d'électricité, de gaz, d'eau**	E	40-41
..	..	..	..	..	..	..	..	**Electricité, gaz, vapeur et eau chaude**		40
..	..	..	..	..	..	4 114	..	Production, collecte et distribution d'électricité		401
..	..	..	..	..	..	..	..	**Captage, épuration et distribution d'eau**		41 410
..	..	..	..	..	..	..	..	**Construction**	F	45
..	..	..	..	..	..	..	..	**Commerce de gros et de détail; réparation**	G	50-52
..	..	..	..	..	..	..	..	**Hôtels et restaurants**	H	55
..	..	..	..	..	..	..	..	**Transports, entreposage et communications**	I	60-64
..	..	..	..	..	..	..	..	**Intermédiation financière**	J	65-67
..	..	..	..	..	..	..	..	**Immobilier, locations, services aux entreprises**	K	70-74
..	..	..	..	..	..	..	..	**Admin. publique; éducation; santé; autres**	L-Q	75-99
..	..	..	..	..	..	..	..	**Grand total**	A-Q	01-99

Note: Unless given separetely, ISIC 155 includes 16.

Statistiques des Structures Industrielles
OCDE, © 1998

Table NY.4 INVESTMENT IN MACHINERY AND EQUIPMENT - DÉPENSES EN MACHINES ET ÉQUIPEMENT

Millions of NKr (Current Prices)

ISIC revision 3			1989	1990	1991	1992	1993	1994	1995	1996
A	01-02	**Agriculture, hunting and forestry**	..	..	..	..	..	..	..	..
B	05	**Fishing**	..	..	..	..	..	..	..	..
C	10-14	**Mining and quarrying**	..	..	..	..	..	..	..	..
	10	Mining of coal and lignite; extraction of peat	..	..	20	14	7	6	..	..
	11	Crude petroleum & natural gas; related service activ.	..	..	..	..	..	..	..	..
	13	Mining of metal ores	..	..	43	21	11	35	..	..
	14	Other mining and quarrying	..	..	139	108	105	118	..	..
D	15-37	**Total manufacturing**	..	..	8 309	6 658	6 093	7 283	..	..
	15	**Food products and beverages**	..	..	1 760	1 605	1 535	1 743	..	..
	155	Beverages	..	..	373	358	425	332	..	..
16	160	**Tobacco products**	..	..	..	19	..	..	..	..
17		**Textiles**	..	..	109	66	153	115	..	..
	171	Spinning, weaving and finishing of textiles	..	..	16	17	36	43	..	..
	172	Other textiles	..	..	82	26	98	47	..	..
	173	Knitted and crocheted fabrics and articles	..	..	11	23	20	24	..	..
18		**Wearing apparel dressing & dyeing of fur**	..	..	9	9	10	22	..	..
	181	Wearing apparel, except fur apparel	..	..	8	9	9	22	..	..
	182	Dressing and dyeing of fur; articles of fur	..	..	1	0	1	0	..	..
19		**Tanning, dressing leather; leather artic.; footwear**	..	..	8	11	4	11	..	..
	191	Tanning, dressing leather; manuf. of leather articles	..	..	4	9	1	4	..	..
	192	Footwear	..	..	4	2	2	7	..	..
20		**Wood and cork products, ex. furniture**	..	..	321	307	180	407	..	..
	201	Sawmilling and planing of wood	..	..	212	179	92	239	..	..
	202	Products of wood, cork, straw & plaiting material	..	..	109	128	88	169	..	..
21		**Paper and paper products**	..	..	576	582	513	503	..	..
22		**Publishing, printing & reprod. of recorded media**	..	..	559	499	634	767	..	..
	221	Publishing	..	..	294	258	369	432	..	..
	222	Printing and related service activities	..	..	263	241	264	330	..	..
	223	Reproduction of recorded media	..	..	1	1	1	4	..	..
23		**Coke, refined petroleum products & nuclear fuel**	..	..	198	32	61	87	..	..
24		**Chemicals and chemical products**	..	..	1 170	787	650	792	..	..
	241	Basic chemicals	..	..	821	522	355	502	..	..
	242	Other chemical products	..	..	348	266	295	290	..	..
	243	Man-made fibres	..	..	0	0	0	0	..	..
25		**Rubber and plastic products**	..	..	268	123	170	206	..	..
	251	Rubber products	..	..	4	8	13	9	..	..
	252	Plastic products	..	..	264	115	157	197	..	..
26		**Other non-metallic mineral products**	..	..	503	257	162	227	..	..
	261	Glass and glass products	..	..	..	..	22	30	..	..
	269	Non-metallic mineral products, nec	..	..	..	..	140	197	..	..
27		**Basic metals**	..	..	920	590	324	562	..	..
	271	Basic iron and steel	..	..	212	51	..	91	..	..
	272	Basic precious and non-ferrous metals	..	..	699	527	290	439	..	..
	273	Casting of metals	..	..	9	12	..	32	..	..
28		**Fabricated metal products, ex. machin. & equip.**	..	..	246	290	140	224	..	..
	281	Structural metal prod., tanks, reservoirs, generators	..	..	..	..	..	81	..	..
	289	Other fabricated metal products & service activities	..	..	..	..	..	143	..	..
29		**Machinery and equipment, nec**	..	..	448	424	310	337	..	..
	291	General purpose machinery	..	..	249	261	180	166	..	..
	292	Special purpose machinery	..	..	164	141	106	147	..	..
	293	Domestic appliances, nec	..	..	35	22	25	24	..	..
30		**Office, accounting and computing machinery**	..	..	46	6	11	24	..	..
31		**Electrical machinery and apparatus, nec**	..	..	295	179	181	222	..	..
	311	Electric motors, generators and transformers	..	..	92	38	34	68	..	..
	312	Electricity distribution and control apparatus	..	..	51	55	37	52	..	..
	313	Insulated wire and cable	..	..	103	45	83	82	..	..
	314	Accumulators, primary cells and primary batteries	..	..	0	..	..	..	..	..
	315	Electric lamps and lighting equipment	..	..	49	27	21	11	..	..
	319	Other electrical equipment, nec	..	..	0	..	..	..	..	..
32		**Radio, TV, communication equip. & apparatus**	..	..	158	108	128	164	..	..
	321	Electronic valves, tubes & other electronic compon.	..	..	13	9	14	20	..	..
	322	TV, radio transmitters & appar. for line teleph., telegr.	..	..	137	91	103	137	..	..
	323	TV, radio receivers and associated goods	..	..	9	8	11	8	..	..
33		**Medical, precision, optical instr.; watches, clocks**	..	..	69	111	94	158	..	..
	331	Medical equip.; precision instruments and appliances	..	..	67	..	..	156	..	..
	332	Optical instruments and photographic equipment	..	..	3	..	..	2	..	..
	333	Watches and clocks	..	..	0	..	..	0	..	..
34		**Motor vehicles, trailers, and semi-trailers**	..	..	129	82	141	112	..	..
35		**Other transport equipment**	..	..	309	411	506	382	..	..
	351	Building and repairing of ships and boats	..	..	257	359	376	282	..	..
	352	Railway, tramway locomotives and rolling stock	..	..	11	10	84	49	..	..
	353	Aircraft and spacecraft	..	..	31	35	29	44	..	..
	359	Transport equipment, nec	..	..	10	6	18	6	..	..
36		**Furniture; manufacturing, nec**	..	..	208	158	185	209	..	..
	361	Furniture	..	..	112	82	109	163	..	..
	369	Manufacturing, nec	..	..	96	76	76	46	..	..
37		**Recycling**	..	..	1	1	1	10	..	..
E	40-41	**Electricity, gas and water supply**	..	..	..	..	..	..	..	..
	40	**Electricity, gas, steam and hot water supply**	..	..	..	..	..	..	..	..
	401	Production, collection and distribution of electricity	..	..	..	..	..	..	..	..
41	410	**Collection, purification, distribution of water**	..	..	..	..	..	..	..	..
F	45	**Construction**	..	..	..	..	..	..	..	..
G	50-52	**Wholesale and retail trade; repairs etc**	..	..	..	..	..	..	..	..
H	55	**Hotels and restaurants**	..	..	..	..	..	..	..	..
I	60-64	**Transport, storage and communications**	..	..	..	..	..	..	..	..
J	65-67	**Financial intermediation**	..	..	..	..	..	..	..	..
K	70-74	**Real estate, renting and business activities**	..	..	..	..	..	..	..	..
L-Q	75-99	**Public admin.; education; health; other services**	..	..	..	..	..	..	..	..
A-Q	01-99	**Grand total**	..	..	..	..	..	..	..	..

Note: Unless given separetely, ISIC 155 includes 16.

Table NY.5 ETABLISSEMENTS - ESTABLISHMENTS

Unités

1989	1990	1991	1992	1993	1994	1995	1996			CITI révision 3	
..	..	..	..	..	..	..	..	**Agriculture, chasse et sylviculture**	A	01-02	
..	..	..	..	..	..	..	..	**Pêche**	B	05	
..	..	..	..	..	..	495	..	**Activités extractives**	C	10-14	
..	..	7	4	3	3	12	..	Extraction de charbon, de lignite et de tourbe		10	
..	..	..	..	..	..	142	..	Extraction de pétrole brut et de gaz naturel		11	
..	..	10	8	8	7	8	..	Extraction de minerais métalliques		13	
..	..	143	62	73	73	333	..	Autres activités extractives		14	
..	..	6 075	3 900	3 916	4 037	10 668	..	**Activités de fabrication**	D	15-37	
..	..	1 345	904	895	920	1 766	..	**Produits alimentaires et boissons**		15	
..	..	49	42	36	34	54	..	Boissons			155
..	..	..	6	..	..	2	..	**Produits à base de tabac**		16	160
..	..	182	120	115	117	307	..	**Textiles**		17	
..	..	31	26	24	22	53	..	Filature, tissage et achèvement des textiles			171
..	..	121	70	68	73	214	..	Autres articles textiles			172
..	..	30	24	23	22	40	..	Etoffes et articles de bonneterie			173
..	..	82	61	58	56	154	..	**Habillement; préparation, teinture des fourrures**		18	
..	..	74	56	53	51	136	..	Articles d'habillement autres qu'en fourrure			181
..	..	8	5	5	5	18	..	Préparation, teinture des fourrures; art. en fourrure			182
..	..	30	19	18	18	45	..	**Travail des cuirs; articles en cuir; chaussures**		19	
..	..	16	10	9	9	22	..	Apprêt et tannage des cuirs et articles en cuirs			191
..	..	14	9	9	9	23	..	Chaussures			192
..	..	571	303	286	297	959	..	**Bois et articles en bois et liège (sauf meubles)**		20	
..	..	212	125	122	125	297	..	Sciage et rabotage du bois			201
..	..	359	178	164	172	662	..	Articles en bois, liège, vannerie, sparterie			202
..	..	102	84	82	80	115	..	**Papier et carton; articles en papier et en carton**		21	
..	..	805	453	452	491	1 785	..	**Edition, imprimerie et reproduction**		22	
..	..	289	204	207	224	577	..	Edition			221
..	..	511	244	240	257	1 135	..	Imprimerie et activités annexes			222
..	..	5	5	5	10	73	..	Reproduction de supports enregistrés			223
..	..	22	11	59	65	78	..	**Cokéfaction; prod. pétroliers; comb. nucléaires**		23	
..	..	127	100	99	102	162	..	**Produits chimiques**		24	
..	..	54	47	50	52	65	..	Produits chimiques de base			241
..	..	73	53	49	50	97	..	Autres produits chimiques			242
..	..	0	0	0	0	0	..	Fibres synthétiques ou artificielles			243
..	..	197	116	126	144	337	..	**Articles en caoutchouc et en matières plastiques**		25	
..	..	31	15	16	24	63	..	Articles en caoutchouc			251
..	..	166	101	110	120	274	..	Articles en matières plastiques			252
..	..	274	143	177	173	500	..	**Autres produits minéraux non métalliques**		26	
..	..	35	29	30	27	57	..	Verre et articles en verre			261
..	..	239	114	147	146	443	..	Produits minéraux non métalliques, nca			269
..	..	81	65	67	83	116	..	**Produits métallurgiques de base**		27	
..	..	39	33	37	35	54	..	Sidérurgie et première transformation de l'acier			271
..	..	29	28	28	26	26	..	Métallurgie; métaux précieux et non ferreux			272
..	..	13	4	2	22	36	..	Fonderie			273
..	..	654	410	389	367	1 150	..	**Ouvrages en métaux, sauf machines et matériel**		28	
..	..	284	206	193	180	387	..	Constr. et menuiserie métal.; réservoirs; générateurs			281
..	..	370	204	196	187	763	..	Autres ouvrages en métaux			289
..	..	471	300	294	317	1 123	..	**Machines et matériel, nca**		29	
..	..	280	196	187	199	606	..	Machines d'usage général			291
..	..	171	91	94	104	489	..	Machines d'usage spécifique			292
..	..	20	13	13	14	28	..	Appareils domestiques, nca			293
..	..	12	6	6	6	21	..	**Mach. de bureau, comptables, matériel inform.**		30	
..	..	182	127	119	117	304	..	**Machines et appareils électriques, nca**		31	
..	..	36	31	31	29	65	..	Moteurs, génératrices et transformateurs électriques			311
..	..	51	31	33	38	74	..	Matériel électrique de distribution et de commande			312
..	..	16	12	14	14	15	..	Fils et câbles électriques isolés			313
..	..	3	2	2	2	5	..	Accumulateurs, piles électriques			314
..	..	20	16	15	13	38	..	Lampes électriques et appareils d'éclairage			315
..	..	56	35	24	21	107	..	Autres matériels électriques, nca			319
..	..	52	42	44	44	66	..	**Equip. et appar. de radio, TV, communication**		32	
..	..	14	13	15	16	29	..	Tubes et valves électroniques; autres composants			321
..	..	19	15	14	15	17	..	Emetteurs radio et TV; app. téléphonie, télégraphie			322
..	..	19	14	15	13	20	..	Récepteurs radio et TV et articles associés			323
..	..	76	55	55	55	285	..	**Instruments médicaux, de précision, d'optique**		33	
..	..	72	52	52	52	278	..	Appareils médicaux et de précision			331
..	..	4	3	3	3	7	..	Instruments d'optique ; matériel photographique			332
..	..	0	0	0	0	0	..	Horlogerie			333
..	..	85	57	52	54	91	..	**Véhicules automobiles et nemorques**		34	
..	..	354	283	300	292	582	..	**Autres matériels de transport**		35	
..	..	319	255	268	263	539	..	Construction et réparation de navires			351
..	..	9	9	9	8	9	..	Construction de matériel ferroviaire roulant			352
..	..	19	13	14	12	20	..	Construction aéronautique et spatiale			353
..	..	7	6	9	9	14	..	Autres équipements de transport			359
..	..	367	232	220	229	678	..	**Meubles; activités de fabrication, nca**		36	
..	..	270	165	169	178	461	..	Meubles			361
..	..	97	67	51	51	217	..	Activités de fabrication, nca			369
..	..	4	3	3	10	42	..	**Récupération**		37	
..	..	..	..	..	..	..	..	**Production et distrib. d'électricité, de gaz, d'eau**	E	40-41	
..	..	..	..	..	..	..	..	**Electricité, gaz, vapeur et eau chaude**		40	
..	..	..	..	..	..	326	..	Production, collecte et distribution d'électricité			401
..	..	..	..	..	..	..	..	Captage, épuration et distribution d'eau		41	410
..	..	..	..	..	..	..	..	**Construction**	F	45	
..	..	..	..	..	..	..	..	**Commerce de gros et de détail; réparation**	G	50-52	
..	..	..	..	..	..	..	..	**Hôtels et restaurants**	H	55	
..	..	..	..	..	..	..	..	**Transports, entreposage et communications**	I	60-64	
..	..	..	..	..	..	..	..	**Intermédiation financière**	J	65-67	
..	..	..	..	..	..	..	..	**Immobilier, locations, services aux entreprises**	K	70-74	
..	..	..	..	..	..	..	..	**Admin. publique; éducation; santé; autres**	L-Q	75-99	
..	..	..	..	..	..	..	..	**Grand total**	A-Q	01-99	

Note: Unless given separetely, ISIC 155 includes 16. From 1992 the annual enquiry covers, in general, all establishments with 10 or more persons. Previous annual enquiries covered, in general, all establishments with 5 or more persons engaged. From 1995 all establishments are covered by the annual enquiry. More detailed information available in the "Sources and definitions" Section of this publication.

Table NY.6 EMPLOYMENT - EMPLOI

Thousands

ISIC revision 3			1989	1990	1991	1992	1993	1994	1995	1996
A	01-02	**Agriculture, hunting and forestry**	..	..	..	..	..	..	859.0	..
B	05	**Fishing**	..	..	..	..	..	..	181.0	..
C	10-14	**Mining and quarrying**	..	..	..	..	..	..	25.2	..
	10	Mining of coal and lignite; extraction of peat	..	..	0.5	0.5	0.3	0.3	0.2	..
	11	Crude petroleum & natural gas; related service activ.	..	..	..	..	..	..	20.9	..
	13	Mining of metal ores	..	..	1.9	1.7	1.4	1.3	1.2	..
	14	Other mining and quarrying	..	..	2.4	1.7	1.8	1.8	2.9	..
D	15-37	**Total manufacturing**	..	..	256.4	234.9	234.8	240.5	277.1	..
	15	**Food products and beverages**	..	..	47.5	43.7	44.6	46.1	50.9	..
	155	Beverages	..	..	5.3	5.0	4.9	5.3	5.4	..
16	160	**Tobacco products**	..	..	..	..	..	..	0.5	..
17		**Textiles**	..	..	5.0	4.8	4.6	4.7	4.8	..
	171	Spinning, weaving and finishing of textiles	..	..	1.6	1.5	1.5	1.4	1.4	..
	172	Other textiles	..	..	2.4	2.2	2.0	2.0	2.5	..
	173	Knitted and crocheted fabrics and articles	..	..	1.1	1.2	1.1	1.3	0.8	..
18		**Wearing apparel dressing & dyeing of fur**	..	..	1.9	1.7	1.6	1.6	2.5	..
	181	Wearing apparel, except fur apparel	..	..	1.8	1.6	1.5	1.5	2.3	..
	182	Dressing and dyeing of fur; articles of fur	..	..	0.1	0.1	0.1	0.1	0.1	..
19		**Tanning, dressing leather; leather artic.; footwear**	..	..	0.8	0.8	0.7	0.8	0.8	..
	191	Tanning, dressing leather; manuf. of leather articles	..	..	0.4	0.4	0.4	0.4	0.3	..
	192	Footwear	..	..	0.4	0.4	0.4	0.4	0.4	..
20		**Wood and cork products, ex. furniture**	..	..	13.8	10.6	10.3	11.0	14.5	..
	201	Sawmilling and planing of wood	..	..	5.7	4.7	4.4	4.6	5.3	..
	202	Products of wood, cork, straw & plaiting material	..	..	8.1	6.0	5.9	6.5	9.2	..
21		**Paper and paper products**	..	..	11.0	10.4	10.2	10.2	10.7	..
22		**Publishing, printing & reprod. of recorded media**	..	..	31.6	29.1	29.2	30.3	36.0	..
	221	Publishing	..	..	23.0	22.4	22.6	23.3	25.6	..
	222	Printing and related service activities	..	..	8.4	6.6	6.5	6.7	10.0	..
	223	Reproduction of recorded media	..	..	0.1	0.1	0.1	0.2	0.4	..
23		**Coke, refined petroleum products & nuclear fuel**	..	..	1.4	1.3	1.6	1.6	1.6	..
24		**Chemicals and chemical products**	..	..	13.6	13.3	13.2	13.3	13.9	..
	241	Basic chemicals	..	..	8.4	8.2	8.2	8.3	8.4	..
	242	Other chemical products	..	..	5.2	5.1	5.0	4.9	5.4	..
	243	Man-made fibres	..	..	0.0	0.0	0.0	0.0	0.0	..
25		**Rubber and plastic products**	..	..	6.1	4.9	5.0	5.5	6.3	..
	251	Rubber products	..	..	1.2	0.6	0.6	0.7	0.9	..
	252	Plastic products	..	..	4.9	4.3	4.4	4.8	5.5	..
26		**Other non-metallic mineral products**	..	..	8.0	6.8	6.5	6.7	8.3	..
	261	Glass and glass products	..	..	1.7	1.6	1.5	1.6	1.8	..
	269	Non-metallic mineral products, nec	..	..	6.3	5.2	5.0	5.1	6.6	..
27		**Basic metals**	..	..	15.0	13.9	13.3	14.6	15.1	..
	271	Basic iron and steel	..	..	4.8	4.5	4.4	4.2	4.3	..
	272	Basic precious and non-ferrous metals	..	..	9.9	9.2	8.8	8.6	8.8	..
	273	Casting of metals	..	..	0.3	0.2	0.0	1.8	2.0	..
28		**Fabricated metal products, ex. machin. & equip.**	..	..	15.5	13.1	12.7	12.5	16.9	..
	281	Structural metal prod., tanks, reservoirs, generators	..	..	7.4	6.5	6.2	6.2	7.9	..
	289	Other fabricated metal products & service activities	..	..	8.1	6.5	6.5	6.3	9.0	..
29		**Machinery and equipment, nec**	..	..	19.9	18.3	18.1	18.4	22.0	..
	291	General purpose machinery	..	..	11.2	10.7	10.3	10.5	12.2	..
	292	Special purpose machinery	..	..	7.5	6.5	6.7	6.8	8.5	..
	293	Domestic appliances, nec	..	..	1.2	1.1	1.1	1.1	1.2	..
30		**Office, accounting and computing machinery**	..	..	1.0	0.9	0.8	0.8	0.9	..
31		**Electrical machinery and apparatus, nec**	..	..	9.9	8.6	8.3	8.0	9.3	..
	311	Electric motors, generators and transformers	..	..	2.8	2.5	2.7	2.2	2.9	..
	312	Electricity distribution and control apparatus	..	..	2.5	2.1	2.2	2.3	2.6	..
	313	Insulated wire and cable	..	..	1.6	1.3	1.4	1.4	1.4	..
	314	Accumulators, primary cells and primary batteries	..	..	0.1	0.1	0.1	0.1	0.2	..
	315	Electric lamps and lighting equipment	..	..	1.4	1.3	1.2	1.2	1.3	..
	319	Other electrical equipment, nec	..	..	1.4	1.2	0.8	0.8	0.9	..
32		**Radio, TV, communication equip. & apparatus**	..	..	4.3	3.6	3.9	4.1	4.2	..
	321	Electronic valves, tubes & other electronic compon.	..	..	0.6	0.7	0.7	0.8	0.9	..
	322	TV, radio transmitters & appar. for line teleph., telegr.	..	..	3.1	2.4	2.5	2.7	2.8	..
	323	TV, radio receivers and associated goods	..	..	0.6	0.5	0.7	0.6	0.4	..
33		**Medical, precision, optical instr.; watches, clocks**	..	..	3.2	3.3	3.4	3.6	5.2	..
	331	Medical equip.; precision instruments and appliances	..	..	3.1	3.2	3.3	3.5	5.0	..
	332	Optical instruments and photographic equipment	..	..	0.1	0.1	0.1	0.1	0.1	..
	333	Watches and clocks	..	..	0.0	0.0	0.0	0.0	0.0	..
34		**Motor vehicles, trailers, and semi-trailers**	..	..	3.2	3.2	3.2	3.2	4.6	..
35		**Other transport equipment**	..	..	33.0	33.5	34.6	34.1	35.8	..
	351	Building and repairing of ships and boats	..	..	27.3	28.3	29.4	29.0	30.9	..
	352	Railway, tramway locomotives and rolling stock	..	..	2.2	2.0	2.0	2.0	1.9	..
	353	Aircraft and spacecraft	..	..	3.0	2.7	2.6	2.4	2.5	..
	359	Transport equipment, nec	..	..	0.5	0.5	0.6	0.6	0.6	..
36		**Furniture; manufacturing, nec**	..	..	10.5	9.3	9.0	9.4	12.1	..
	361	Furniture	..	..	7.5	6.4	6.4	6.8	8.6	..
	369	Manufacturing, nec	..	..	3.0	2.9	2.6	2.6	3.5	..
37		**Recycling**	..	..	0.1	0.1	0.1	0.2	0.3	..
E	40-41	**Electricity, gas and water supply**	..	..	..	..	..	..	..	..
	40	**Electricity, gas, steam and hot water supply**	..	..	..	..	..	..	..	..
	401	Production, collection and distribution of electricity	..	..	..	..	..	..	19.5	..
	41	410	**Collection, purification, distribution of water**	..	..	..	..	..	..	..
F	45	**Construction**	..	..	..	..	..	..	..	..
G	50-52	**Wholesale and retail trade; repairs etc**	..	..	..	..	..	..	..	..
H	55	**Hotels and restaurants**	..	..	..	..	..	..	..	..
I	60-64	**Transport, storage and communications**	..	..	..	..	..	..	..	..
J	65-67	**Financial intermediation**	..	..	..	..	..	..	..	..
K	70-74	**Real estate, renting and business activities**	..	..	..	..	..	..	..	..
L-Q	75-99	**Public admin.; education; health; other services**	..	..	..	..	..	..	..	..
A-Q	01-99	**Grand total**	..	..	..	..	..	..	..	..

Note: Unless given separetely, ISIC 155 includes 16.

Table NY.7 EMPLOI, SALARIÉS - EMPLOYMENT, EMPLOYEES

Milliers

1989	1990	1991	1992	1993	1994	1995	1996		Code	CITI révision 3
..	..	..	..	..	..	..	..	**Agriculture, chasse et sylviculture**	A	01-02
..	..	..	..	..	..	..	..	**Pêche**	B	05
..	..	..	..	..	..	..	..	**Activités extractives**	C	10-14
..	..	0.5	0.5	0.3	0.3	..	..	Extraction de charbon, de lignite et de tourbe		10
..	..	..	..	..	..	..	..	Extraction de pétrole brut et de gaz naturel		11
..	..	1.9	1.7	1.4	1.3	..	..	Extraction de minerais métalliques		13
..	..	2.3	1.7	1.8	1.8	..	..	Autres activités extractives		14
..	..	255.8	234.7	234.7	240.4	..	..	**Activités de fabrication**	D	15-37
..	..	47.3	43.6	44.5	46.1	..	..	**Produits alimentaires et boissons**		15
..	..	5.3	5.0	4.9	5.3	..	..	Boissons		155
..	..	..	..	..	..	..	..	**Produits à base de tabac**		16 160
..	..	5.0	4.8	4.6	4.7	..	..	**Textiles**		17
..	..	1.6	1.5	1.5	1.4	..	..	Filature, tissage et achèvement des textiles		171
..	..	2.4	2.2	2.0	2.0	..	..	Autres articles textiles		172
..	..	1.1	1.2	1.1	1.3	..	..	Etoffes et articles de bonneterie		173
..	..	1.9	1.7	1.6	1.6	..	..	**Habillement; préparation, teinture des fourrures**		18
..	..	1.8	1.6	1.5	1.5	..	..	Articles d'habillement autres qu'en fourrure		181
..	..	0.1	0.1	0.1	0.1	..	..	Préparation, teinture des fourrures; art. en fourrure		182
..	..	0.8	0.8	0.7	0.8	..	..	**Travail des cuirs; articles en cuir; chaussures**		19
..	..	0.4	0.4	0.4	0.4	..	..	Apprêt et tannage des cuirs et articles en cuirs		191
..	..	0.4	0.4	0.4	0.4	..	..	Chaussures		192
..	..	13.7	10.6	10.3	11.0	..	..	**Bois et articles en bois et liège (sauf meubles)**		20
..	..	5.6	4.7	4.4	4.6	..	..	Sciage et rabotage du bois		201
..	..	8.0	6.0	5.9	6.5	..	..	Articles en bois, liège, vannerie, sparterie		202
..	..	11.0	10.4	10.2	10.2	..	..	**Papier et carton; articles en papier et en carton**		21
..	..	31.5	29.1	29.2	30.3	..	..	**Edition, imprimerie et reproduction**		22
..	..	23.0	22.4	22.6	23.3	..	..	Edition		221
..	..	8.4	6.5	6.5	6.7	..	..	Imprimerie et activités annexes		222
..	..	0.1	0.1	0.1	0.2	..	..	Reproduction de supports enregistrés		223
..	..	1.4	1.3	1.6	1.6	..	..	**Cokéfaction; prod. pétroliers; comb. nucléaires**		23
..	..	13.6	13.3	13.2	13.3	..	..	**Produits chimiques**		24
..	..	8.4	8.2	8.2	8.3	..	..	Produits chimiques de base		241
..	..	5.2	5.1	5.0	4.9	..	..	Autres produits chimiques		242
..	..	0.0	0.0	0.0	0.0	..	..	Fibres synthétiques ou artificielles		243
..	..	6.1	4.9	5.0	5.5	..	..	**Articles en caoutchouc et en matières plastiques**		25
..	..	1.2	0.6	0.6	0.7	..	..	Articles en caoutchouc		251
..	..	4.8	4.3	4.4	4.8	..	..	Articles en matières plastiques		252
..	..	8.0	6.8	6.5	6.7	..	..	**Autres produits minéraux non métalliques**		26
..	..	1.7	1.6	1.5	1.6	..	..	Verre et articles en verre		261
..	..	6.3	5.2	5.0	5.1	..	..	Produits minéraux non métalliques, nca		269
..	..	15.0	13.9	13.3	14.6	..	..	**Produits métallurgiques de base**		27
..	..	4.8	4.5	4.4	4.2	..	..	Sidérurgie et première transformation de l'acier		271
..	..	9.9	9.2	8.8	8.6	..	..	Métallurgie; métaux précieux et non ferreux		272
..	..	0.3	0.2	0.0	1.8	..	..	Fonderie		273
..	..	15.5	13.1	12.7	12.5	..	..	**Ouvrages en métaux, sauf machines et matériel**		28
..	..	7.4	6.5	6.2	6.2	..	..	Constr. et menuiserie métal.; réservoirs; générateurs		281
..	..	8.0	6.5	6.5	6.3	..	..	Autres ouvrages en métaux		289
..	..	19.9	18.3	18.1	18.4	..	..	**Machines et matériel, nca**		29
..	..	11.2	10.7	10.3	10.5	..	..	Machines d'usage général		291
..	..	7.4	6.5	6.7	6.8	..	..	Machines d'usage spécifique		292
..	..	1.2	1.1	1.1	1.1	..	..	Appareils domestiques, nca		293
..	..	1.0	0.9	0.8	0.8	..	..	**Mach. de bureau, comptables, matériel inform.**		30
..	..	9.9	8.6	8.3	8.0	..	..	**Machines et appareils électriques, nca**		31
..	..	2.8	2.5	2.7	2.2	..	..	Moteurs, génératrices et transformateurs électriques		311
..	..	2.5	2.1	2.2	2.3	..	..	Matériel électrique de distribution et de commande		312
..	..	1.6	1.3	1.4	1.4	..	..	Fils et câbles électriques isolés		313
..	..	0.1	0.1	0.1	0.1	..	..	Accumulateurs, piles électriques		314
..	..	1.4	1.3	1.2	1.2	..	..	Lampes électriques et appareils d'éclairage		315
..	..	1.4	1.2	0.8	0.8	..	..	Autres matériels électriques, nca		319
..	..	4.3	3.6	3.9	4.1	..	..	**Equip. et appar. de radio, TV, communication**		32
..	..	0.6	0.7	0.7	0.8	..	..	Tubes et valves électroniques; autres composants		321
..	..	3.1	2.4	2.5	2.7	..	..	Emetteurs radio et TV; app. téléphonie, télégraphie		322
..	..	0.6	0.5	0.7	0.6	..	..	Récepteurs radio et TV et articles associés		323
..	..	3.2	3.3	3.4	3.6	..	..	**Instruments médicaux, de précision, d'optique**		33
..	..	3.1	3.2	3.3	3.5	..	..	Appareils médicaux et de précision		331
..	..	0.1	0.1	0.1	0.1	..	..	Instruments d'optique ; matériel photographique		332
..	..	0.0	0.0	0.0	0.0	..	..	Horlogerie		333
..	..	3.2	3.2	3.2	3.2	..	..	**Véhicules automobiles et nemorques**		34
..	..	32.9	33.5	34.6	34.1	..	..	**Autres matériels de transport**		35
..	..	27.3	28.3	29.4	29.0	..	..	Construction et réparation de navires		351
..	..	2.2	2.0	2.0	2.0	..	..	Construction de matériel ferroviaire roulant		352
..	..	3.0	2.7	2.6	2.4	..	..	Construction aéronautique et spatiale		353
..	..	0.5	0.5	0.6	0.6	..	..	Autres équipements de transport		359
..	..	10.4	9.2	9.0	9.4	..	..	**Meubles; activités de fabrication, nca**		36
..	..	7.5	6.4	6.4	6.8	..	..	Meubles		361
..	..	3.0	2.9	2.5	2.6	..	..	Activités de fabrication, nca		369
..	..	0.1	0.1	0.1	0.2	..	..	**Récupération**		37
..	..	..	..	..	..	..	..	**Production et distrib. d'électricité, de gaz, d'eau**	E	40-41
..	..	..	..	..	..	..	..	**Electricité, gaz, vapeur et eau chaude**		40
..	..	..	..	..	..	..	..	Production, collecte et distribution d'électricité		401
..	..	..	..	..	..	..	..	**Captage, épuration et distribution d'eau**		41 410
..	..	..	..	..	..	..	..	**Construction**	F	45
..	..	..	..	..	..	..	..	**Commerce de gros et de détail; réparation**	G	50-52
..	..	..	..	..	..	..	..	**Hôtels et restaurants**	H	55
..	..	..	..	..	..	..	..	**Transports, entreposage et communications**	I	60-64
..	..	..	..	..	..	..	..	**Intermédiation financière**	J	65-67
..	..	..	..	..	..	..	..	**Immobilier, locations, services aux entreprises**	K	70-74
..	..	..	..	..	..	..	..	**Admin. publique; éducation; santé; autres**	L-Q	75-99
..	..	..	..	..	..	..	..	**Grand total**	A-Q	01-99

Note: Unless given separetely, ISIC 155 includes 16.

Statistiques des Structures Industrielles
OCDE, © 1998

Table NY.8 COMPENSATION OF LABOUR – SALAIRES ET CHARGES SOCIALES

Millions of NKr (Current Prices)

ISIC revision 3			1989	1990	1991	1992	1993	1994	1995	1996
A	01-02	**Agriculture, hunting and forestry**	..	..	..	..	..	..	3 280	..
B	05	**Fishing**			..		..	..	2 440	
C	10-14	**Mining and quarrying**	..	..	..	..	..	..	12 926	..
	10	Mining of coal and lignite; extraction of peat	..	..	123	141	113	122	144	
	11	Crude petroleum & natural gas; related service activ.	..	..	..	..	..	..	11 674	
	13	Mining of metal ores	..	..	431	388	373	411	319	
	14	Other mining and quarrying			554	440	471	481	789	
D	15-37	**Total manufacturing**	..	..	60 933	58 206	59 502	63 184	74 172	
	15	**Food products and beverages**			9 887	9 617	10 006	10 813		
	155	Beverages			1 394	1 385	1 416	1 618		
	16	**Tobacco products**	..	..	..		..		..	
	17	**Textiles**			923	906	884	948	963	
	171	Spinning, weaving and finishing of textiles	..	..	296	297	291	288	298	
	172	Other textiles			445	410	393	434	516	
	173	Knitted and crocheted fabrics and articles			182	200	199	226	149	
	18	**Wearing apparel dressing & dyeing of fur**	..	..	300	273	261	268	431	
	181	Wearing apparel, except fur apparel			282	258	243	250	405	
	182	Dressing and dyeing of fur; articles of fur			18	16	18	18	25	
	19	**Tanning, dressing leather; leather artic.; footwear**			137	130	133	141	144	
	191	Tanning, dressing leather; manuf. of leather articles			72	68	70	74	64	
	192	Footwear			65	62	63	66	80	
	20	**Wood and cork products, ex. furniture**			2 730	2 206	2 158	2 435	3 227	
	201	Sawmilling and planing of wood			1 151	992	951	1 014	1 206	
	202	Products of wood, cork, straw & plaiting material			1 579	1 214	1 206	1 420	2 021	
	21	**Paper and paper products**			2 659	2 585	2 569	2 708	3 033	
	22	**Publishing, printing & reprod. of recorded media**			7 103	6 465	6 637	7 004	8 778	
	221	Publishing			4 768	4 549	4 724	4 975	5 729	
	222	Printing and related service activities			2 292	1 873	1 871	1 968	2 925	
	223	Reproduction of recorded media			42	42	42	61	125	
	23	**Coke, refined petroleum products & nuclear fuel**			541	496	584	624	645	
	24	**Chemicals and chemical products**			4 063	4 123	4 182	4 347	4 850	
	241	Basic chemicals			2 620	2 661	2 658	2 796	2 994	
	242	Other chemical products			1 442	1 462	1 524	1 551	1 856	
	243	Man-made fibres			0	0	0	0	0	
	25	**Rubber and plastic products**			1 327	1 113	1 173	1 325	1 611	
	251	Rubber products			271	134	146	179	214	
	252	Plastic products			1 056	979	1 027	1 146	1 396	
	26	**Other non-metallic mineral products**			1 928	1 747	1 667	1 771	2 273	
	261	Glass and glass products			..	..	364	392	451	
	269	Non-metallic mineral products, nec			..	..	1 304	1 379	1 822	
	27	**Basic metals**			4 289	4 069	4 011	4 538	4 806	
	271	Basic iron and steel			1 292	1 242	..	1 233	1 317	
	272	Basic precious and non-ferrous metals			2 934	2 790	2 750	2 852	2 966	
	273	Casting of metals			62	37	..	453	524	
	28	**Fabricated metal products, ex. machin. & equip.**			3 477	3 063	3 017	3 113	4 331	
	281	Structural metal prod., tanks, reservoirs, generators			..	..	..	1 549	2 080	
	289	Other fabricated metal products & service activities			..	..	..	1 563	2 253	
	29	**Machinery and equipment, nec**			5 040	4 925	4 954	5 277	6 393	
	291	General purpose machinery			2 965	2 979	2 891	3 083	3 684	
	292	Special purpose machinery			1 813	1 697	1 816	1 916	2 408	
	293	Domestic appliances, nec			262	250	248	278	302	
	30	**Office, accounting and computing machinery**			298	264	260	289	272	
	31	**Electrical machinery and apparatus, nec**			2 541	2 414	2 401	2 413	2 853	
	311	Electric motors, generators and transformers			733	712	792	689	906	
	312	Electricity distribution and control apparatus			628	579	608	673	784	
	313	Insulated wire and cable			521	499	473	515	561	
	314	Accumulators, primary cells and primary batteries			38	..	..	..	48	
	315	Electric lamps and lighting equipment			305	296	283	284	319	
	319	Other electrical equipment, nec			316	..	..	..	234	
	32	**Radio, TV, communication equip. & apparatus**			1 283	1 045	1 119	1 269	1 395	
	321	Electronic valves, tubes & other electronic compon.			129	159	156	182	245	
	322	TV, radio transmitters & appar. for line teleph., telegr.			1 010	760	799	922	1 042	
	323	TV, radio receivers and associated goods			144	126	165	165	108	
	33	**Medical, precision, optical instr.; watches, clocks**			1 016	1 075	1 139	1 239	1 720	
	331	Medical equip.; precision instruments and appliances			990	..	..	1 209	1 686	
	332	Optical instruments and photographic equipment			26	..	..	30	35	
	333	Watches and clocks			0	..	..	0	0	
	34	**Motor vehicles, trailers, and semi-trailers**			709	718	761	807	1 194	
	35	**Other transport equipment**			8 618	9 050	9 674	9 735	10 526	
	351	Building and repairing of ships and boats			7 070	7 617	8 211	8 169	9 104	
	352	Railway, tramway locomotives and rolling stock			492	493	506	524	506	
	353	Aircraft and spacecraft			957	829	832	903	792	
	359	Transport equipment, nec			99	110	124	139	124	
	36	**Furniture; manufacturing, nec**			2 050	1 907	1 892	2 076	2 531	
	361	Furniture			1 409	1 276	1 290	1 455	1 740	
	369	Manufacturing, nec			641	631	603	621	791	
	37	**Recycling**			18	17	17	45	94	
E	40-41	**Electricity, gas and water supply**	..	..	..	..	..	..	5 726	..
	40	**Electricity, gas, steam and hot water supply**	..	..	..	..	..	..	..	..
	401	Production, collection and distribution of electricity	..	..	..	..	..	..	5 570	..
	41	410	**Collection, purification, distribution of water**	..	..	..	..	..	..	..
F	45	**Construction**	..	..	..	..	..	..	..	..
G	50-52	**Wholesale and retail trade; repairs etc**	..	..	..	..	..	..	..	..
H	55	**Hotels and restaurants**	..	..	..	..	..	..	..	..
I	60-64	**Transport, storage and communications**	..	..	..	..	..	..	..	..
J	65-67	**Financial intermediation**	..	..	..	..	..	..	..	..
K	70-74	**Real estate, renting and business activities**	..	..	..	..	..	..	..	..
L-Q	75-99	**Public admin.; education; health; other services**	..	..	..	..	..	..	..	..
A-Q	01-99	**Grand total**	..	..	..	..	..	..	..	..

Note: Unless given separetely, ISIC 155 includes 16.

Table NY.9 SALAIRES ET TRAITEMENTS, TOTAL - TOTAL WAGES AND SALARIES

Millions de NKr (Prix courants)

CITI révision 3

1989	1990	1991	1992	1993	1994	1995	1996		Code	CITI
..	..	..	..	..	..	..	..	**Agriculture, chasse et sylviculture**	A	01-02
..	..	..	..	..	..	..	..	**Pêche**	B	05
..	..	..	..	..	..	..	..	**Activités extractives**	C	10-14
..	..	121	138	113	121	..	..	Extraction de charbon, de lignite et de tourbe		10
..	..	..	..	..	..	..	..	Extraction de pétrole brut et de gaz naturel		11
..	..	402	362	352	391	..	..	Extraction de minerais métalliques		13
..	..	485	388	422	432	..	..	Autres activités extractives		14
..	..	52 917	50 574	52 688	55 982	..	..	**Activités de fabrication**	D	15-37
..	..	8 646	8 429	8 942	9 672	..	..	**Produits alimentaires et boissons**		15
..	..	1 203	1 196	1 248	1 430	..	..	Boissons		155
..	..	..	..	..	..	..	..	**Produits à base de tabac**		16 160
..	..	802	787	782	841	..	..	**Textiles**		17
..	..	258	259	259	256	..	..	Filature, tissage et achèvement des textiles		171
..	..	386	355	347	385	..	..	Autres articles textiles		172
..	..	158	173	175	200	..	..	Etoffes et articles de bonneterie		173
..	..	260	238	232	238	..	..	**Habillement; préparation, teinture des fourrures**		18
..	..	245	225	217	222	..	..	Articles d'habillement autres qu'en fourrure		181
..	..	15	13	15	16	..	..	Préparation, teinture des fourrures; art. en fourrure		182
..	..	118	112	117	124	..	..	**Travail des cuirs; articles en cuir; chaussures**		19
..	..	62	59	62	66	..	..	Apprêt et tannage des cuirs et articles en cuirs		191
..	..	56	53	59	59	..	..	Chaussures		192
..	..	2 374	1 920	1 916	2 165	..	..	**Bois et articles en bois et liège (sauf meubles)**		20
..	..	1 001	864	845	903	..	..	Sciage et rabotage du bois		201
..	..	1 373	1 055	1 070	1 263	..	..	Articles en bois, liège, vannerie, sparterie		202
..	..	2 291	2 226	2 253	2 378	..	..	**Papier et carton; articles en papier et en carton**		21
..	..	6 133	5 593	5 859	6 180	..	..	**Edition, imprimerie et reproduction**		22
..	..	4 126	3 943	4 179	4 394	..	..	Edition		221
..	..	1 971	1 613	1 643	1 732	..	..	Imprimerie et activités annexes		222
..	..	37	37	37	54	..	..	Reproduction de supports enregistrés		223
..	..	474	434	520	557	..	..	**Cokéfaction; prod. pétroliers; comb. nucléaires**		23
..	..	3 540	3 584	3 696	3 840	..	..	**Produits chimiques**		24
..	..	2 292	2 322	2 359	2 481	..	..	Produits chimiques de base		241
..	..	1 248	1 261	1 338	1 359	..	..	Autres produits chimiques		242
..	..	0	0	0	0	..	..	Fibres synthétiques ou artificielles		243
..	..	1 150	966	1 038	1 175	..	..	**Articles en caoutchouc et en matières plastiques**		25
..	..	235	116	129	159	..	..	Articles en caoutchouc		251
..	..	916	849	909	1 016	..	..	Articles en matières plastiques		252
..	..	1 658	1 494	1 467	1 563	..	..	**Autres produits minéraux non métalliques**		26
..	..	..	..	320	346	..	..	Verre et articles en verre		261
..	..	..	..	1 148	1 217	..	..	Produits minéraux non métalliques, nca		269
..	..	3 788	3 593	3 604	4 065	..	..	**Produits métallurgiques de base**		27
..	..	1 151	1 105	..	1 113	..	..	Sidérurgie et première transformation de l'acier		271
..	..	2 583	2 457	2 461	2 553	..	..	Métallurgie; métaux précieux et non ferreux		272
..	..	53	32	..	400	..	..	Fonderie		273
..	..	3 012	2 659	2 666	2 752	..	..	**Ouvrages en métaux, sauf machines et matériel**		28
..	..	..	..	..	1 376	..	..	Constr. et menuiserie métal.; réservoirs; générateurs		281
..	..	..	..	..	1 376	..	..	Autres ouvrages en métaux		289
..	..	4 359	4 263	4 376	4 651	..	..	**Machines et matériel, nca**		29
..	..	2 564	2 585	2 556	2 726	..	..	Machines d'usage général		291
..	..	1 569	1 463	1 602	1 683	..	..	Machines d'usage spécifique		292
..	..	226	215	218	243	..	..	Appareils domestiques, nca		293
..	..	256	226	226	250	..	..	**Mach. de bureau, comptables, matériel inform.**		30
..	..	2 204	2 094	2 117	2 126	..	..	**Machines et appareils électriques, nca**		31
..	..	635	613	695	601	..	..	Moteurs, génératrices et transformateurs électriques		311
..	..	542	500	533	591	..	..	Matériel électrique de distribution et de commande		312
..	..	456	439	420	459	..	..	Fils et câbles électriques isolés		313
..	..	33	..	..	..	..	..	Accumulateurs, piles électriques		314
..	..	263	255	249	250	..	..	Lampes électriques et appareils d'éclairage		315
..	..	275	..	..	..	..	..	Autres matériels électriques, nca		319
..	..	1 113	902	990	1 117	..	..	**Equip. et appar. de radio, TV, communication**		32
..	..	111	137	137	160	..	..	Tubes et valves électroniques; autres composants		321
..	..	878	656	709	812	..	..	Emetteurs radio et TV; app. téléphonie, télégraphie		322
..	..	124	109	144	145	..	..	Récepteurs radio et TV et articles associés		323
..	..	876	928	1 000	1 089	..	..	**Instruments médicaux, de précision, d'optique**		33
..	..	854	..	..	1 063	..	..	Appareils médicaux et de précision		331
..	..	22	..	..	26	..	..	Instruments d'optique ; matériel photographique		332
..	..	0	..	..	0	..	..	Horlogerie		333
..	..	613	621	674	714	..	..	**Véhicules automobiles et nemorques**		34
..	..	7 459	7 835	8 525	8 605	..	..	**Autres matériels de transport**		35
..	..	6 129	6 612	7 257	7 238	..	..	Construction et réparation de navires		351
..	..	422	409	426	445	..	..	Construction de matériel ferroviaire roulant		352
..	..	823	719	733	800	..	..	Construction aéronautique et spatiale		353
..	..	85	94	109	122	..	..	Autres équipements de transport		359
..	..	1 776	1 655	1 673	1 838	..	..	**Meubles; activités de fabrication, nca**		36
..	..	1 223	1 108	1 142	1 291	..	..	Meubles		361
..	..	553	548	531	547	..	..	Activités de fabrication, nca		369
..	..	15	15	15	40	..	..	**Récupération**		37
..	..	..	..	..	..	..	..	**Production et distrib. d'électricité, de gaz, d'eau**	E	40-41
..	..	..	..	..	..	..	..	**Electricité, gaz, vapeur et eau chaude**		40
..	..	..	..	..	..	..	..	Production, collecte et distribution d'électricité		401
..	..	..	..	..	..	..	..	**Captage, épuration et distribution d'eau**		41 410
..	..	..	..	..	..	..	..	**Construction**	F	45
..	..	..	..	..	..	..	..	**Commerce de gros et de détail; réparation**	G	50-52
..	..	..	..	..	..	..	..	**Hôtels et restaurants**	H	55
..	..	..	..	..	..	..	..	**Transports, entreposage et communications**	I	60-64
..	..	..	..	..	..	..	..	**Intermédiation financière**	J	65-67
..	..	..	..	..	..	..	..	**Immobilier, locations, services aux entreprises**	K	70-74
..	..	..	..	..	..	..	..	**Admin. publique; éducation; santé; autres**	L-Q	75-99
..	..	..	..	..	..	..	..	**Grand total**	A-Q	01-99

Note : Unless given separetely, ISIC 155 includes 16.

Statistiques des Structures Industrielles
OCDE, © 1998

NORWAY

Table NY.10 EMPLOYERS' SOCIAL COSTS – CHARGES SOCIALES DES EMPLOYEURS

Millions of NKr (Current Prices)

ISIC revision 3			1989	1990	1991	1992	1993	1994	1995	1996
A	01-02	**Agriculture, hunting and forestry**	..	..	..	..	..	..	..	..
B	05	**Fishing**	..	..	..	..	..	..	..	..
C	10-14	**Mining and quarrying**	..	..	..	..	..	..	..	..
	10	Mining of coal and lignite; extraction of peat	..	..	3	3	1	1	..	..
	11	Crude petroleum & natural gas; related service activ.	..	..	..	..	..	..	..	..
	13	Mining of metal ores	..	..	29	26	21	20	..	..
	14	Other mining and quarrying	..	..	69	53	49	49	..	..
D	15-37	**Total manufacturing**	..	..	8 016	7 632	6 814	7 202	..	..
	15	**Food products and beverages**	..	..	1 241	1 188	1 064	1 141	..	..
	155	Beverages	..	..	191	189	168	188	..	..
	16 160	**Tobacco products**	..	..	..	..	..	..	..	..
	17	**Textiles**	..	..	121	119	102	107	..	..
	171	Spinning, weaving and finishing of textiles	..	..	38	38	32	32	..	..
	172	Other textiles	..	..	59	55	46	49	..	..
	173	Knitted and crocheted fabrics and articles	..	..	24	27	24	26	..	..
	18	**Wearing apparel dressing & dyeing of fur**	..	..	39	35	29	30	..	..
	181	Wearing apparel, except fur apparel	..	..	37	33	27	27	..	..
	182	Dressing and dyeing of fur; articles of fur	..	..	2	2	2	2	..	..
	19	**Tanning, dressing leather; leather artic.; footwear**	..	..	18	18	16	16	..	..
	191	Tanning, dressing leather; manuf. of leather articles	..	..	10	9	8	9	..	..
	192	Footwear	..	..	9	8	8	8	..	..
	20	**Wood and cork products, ex. furniture**	..	..	356	286	242	270	..	..
	201	Sawmilling and planing of wood	..	..	150	128	106	112	..	..
	202	Products of wood, cork, straw & plaiting material	..	..	206	158	136	158	..	..
	21	**Paper and paper products**	..	..	368	359	316	329	..	..
	22	**Publishing, printing & reprod. of recorded media**	..	..	969	872	778	824	..	..
	221	Publishing	..	..	643	606	545	581	..	..
	222	Printing and related service activities	..	..	321	260	227	236	..	..
	223	Reproduction of recorded media	..	..	5	5	5	7	..	..
	23	**Coke, refined petroleum products & nuclear fuel**	..	..	68	62	64	67	..	..
	24	**Chemicals and chemical products**	..	..	523	539	486	507	..	..
	241	Basic chemicals	..	..	328	338	300	315	..	..
	242	Other chemical products	..	..	195	201	186	192	..	..
	243	Man-made fibres	..	..	0	0	0	0	..	..
	25	**Rubber and plastic products**	..	..	177	147	135	150	..	..
	251	Rubber products	..	..	36	17	17	20	..	..
	252	Plastic products	..	..	140	130	118	130	..	..
	26	**Other non-metallic mineral products**	..	..	270	253	200	208	..	..
	261	Glass and glass products	..	..	..	..	44	46	..	..
	269	Non-metallic mineral products, nec	..	..	..	..	156	161	..	..
	27	**Basic metals**	..	..	501	476	408	473	..	..
	271	Basic iron and steel	..	..	141	137	..	120	..	..
	272	Basic precious and non-ferrous metals	..	..	351	334	289	299	..	..
	273	Casting of metals	..	..	9	5	..	54	..	..
	28	**Fabricated metal products, ex. machin. & equip.**	..	..	465	405	351	361	..	..
	281	Structural metal prod., tanks, reservoirs, generators	..	..	..	..	..	173	..	..
	289	Other fabricated metal products & service activities	..	..	..	..	..	188	..	..
	29	**Machinery and equipment, nec**	..	..	681	662	579	625	..	..
	291	General purpose machinery	..	..	400	394	335	357	..	..
	292	Special purpose machinery	..	..	244	233	214	233	..	..
	293	Domestic appliances, nec	..	..	37	35	30	35	..	..
	30	**Office, accounting and computing machinery**	..	..	42	38	34	38	..	..
	31	**Electrical machinery and apparatus, nec**	..	..	337	320	284	287	..	..
	311	Electric motors, generators and transformers	..	..	97	98	97	87	..	..
	312	Electricity distribution and control apparatus	..	..	86	79	75	82	..	..
	313	Insulated wire and cable	..	..	65	59	52	56	..	..
	314	Accumulators, primary cells and primary batteries	..	..	5	..	..	..	..	..
	315	Electric lamps and lighting equipment	..	..	42	41	34	34	..	..
	319	Other electrical equipment, nec	..	..	41	..	..	..	..	..
	32	**Radio, TV, communication equip. & apparatus**	..	..	170	143	129	153	..	..
	321	Electronic valves, tubes & other electronic compon.	..	..	18	22	19	22	..	..
	322	TV, radio transmitters & appar. for line teleph., telegr.	..	..	132	104	90	110	..	..
	323	TV, radio receivers and associated goods	..	..	19	17	21	20	..	..
	33	**Medical, precision, optical instr.; watches, clocks**	..	..	140	147	139	150	..	..
	331	Medical equip.; precision instruments and appliances	..	..	136	..	..	146	..	..
	332	Optical instruments and photographic equipment	..	..	4	..	..	4	..	..
	333	Watches and clocks	..	..	0	..	..	0	..	..
	34	**Motor vehicles, trailers, and semi-trailers**	..	..	96	96	87	92	..	..
	35	**Other transport equipment**	..	..	1 159	1 215	1 149	1 130	..	..
	351	Building and repairing of ships and boats	..	..	941	1 005	954	931	..	..
	352	Railway, tramway locomotives and rolling stock	..	..	69	84	81	79	..	..
	353	Aircraft and spacecraft	..	..	135	110	99	103	..	..
	359	Transport equipment, nec	..	..	14	16	15	17	..	..
	36	**Furniture; manufacturing, nec**	..	..	274	251	219	238	..	..
	361	Furniture	..	..	186	168	147	164	..	..
	369	Manufacturing, nec	..	..	88	83	72	74	..	..
	37	**Recycling**	..	..	2	2	2	5	..	..
E	40-41	**Electricity, gas and water supply**	..	..	..	..	..	..	..	..
	40	**Electricity, gas, steam and hot water supply**	..	..	..	..	..	..	..	..
	401	Production, collection and distribution of electricity	..	..	..	..	..	..	..	..
	41 410	**Collection, purification, distribution of water**	..	..	..	..	..	..	..	..
F	45	**Construction**	..	..	..	..	..	..	..	..
G	50-52	**Wholesale and retail trade; repairs etc**	..	..	..	..	..	..	..	..
H	55	**Hotels and restaurants**	..	..	..	..	..	..	..	..
I	60-64	**Transport, storage and communications**	..	..	..	..	..	..	..	..
J	65-67	**Financial intermediation**	..	..	..	..	..	..	..	..
K	70-74	**Real estate, renting and business activities**	..	..	..	..	..	..	..	..
L-Q	75-99	**Public admin.; education; health; other services**	..	..	..	..	..	..	..	..
A-Q	01-99	**Grand total**	..	..	..	..	..	..	..	..

Note: Unless given separetely, ISIC 155 includes 16.

Table NY.11 HEURES OUVRÉES - HOURS WORKED

Milliers

1989	1990	1991	1992	1993	1994	1995	1996			CITI révision 3	
..	..	..	..	..	..	..	..	Agriculture, chasse et sylviculture	A	01-02	
..	..	..	..	..	..	..	..	Pêche	B	05	
..	..	..	..	..	..	..	..	Activités extractives	C	10-14	
..	..	835	739	551	550	..	..	Extraction de charbon, de lignite et de tourbe		10	
..	..	..	..	..	..	..	..	Extraction de pétrole brut et de gaz naturel		11	
..	..	3 005	2 689	2 350	2 125	..	..	Extraction de minerais métalliques		13	
..	..	3 908	2 785	2 992	3 004	..	..	Autres activités extractives		14	
..	..	401 723	371 114	371 973	383 836	..	..	Activités de fabrication	D	15-37	
..	..	74 994	70 240	71 469	73 367	..	..	Produits alimentaires et boissons		15	
..	..	9 250	8 919	8 837	9 570	..	..	Boissons			155
..	..	..	..	..	..	..	..	Produits à base de tabac		16	160
..	..	7 627	7 086	6 797	7 042	..	..	Textiles		17	
..	..	2 344	2 156	2 118	2 049	..	..	Filature, tissage et achèvement des textiles			171
..	..	3 707	3 256	3 036	3 213	..	..	Autres articles textiles			172
..	..	1 576	1 674	1 643	1 780	..	..	Etoffes et articles de bonneterie			173
..	..	2 816	2 420	2 305	2 260	..	..	Habillement; préparation, teinture des fourrures		18	
..	..	2 660	2 285	2 162	2 120	..	..	Articles d'habillement autres qu'en fourrure			181
..	..	156	136	143	140	..	..	Préparation, teinture des fourrures; art. en fourrure			182
..	..	1 172	1 079	1 099	1 141	..	..	Travail des cuirs; articles en cuir; chaussures		19	
..	..	600	566	575	599	..	..	Apprêt et tannage des cuirs et articles en cuirs			191
..	..	572	513	524	541	..	..	Chaussures			192
..	..	22 243	17 340	16 903	18 386	..	..	Bois et articles en bois et liège (sauf meubles)		20	
..	..	9 252	7 742	7 401	7 583	..	..	Sciage et rabotage du bois			201
..	..	12 990	9 598	9 502	10 803	..	..	Articles en bois, liège, vannerie, sparterie			202
..	..	18 046	16 829	16 721	16 983	..	..	Papier et carton; articles en papier et en carton		21	
..	..	40 914	35 798	36 525	37 352	..	..	Edition, imprimerie et reproduction		22	
..	..	26 876	24 702	25 674	25 991	..	..	Edition			221
..	..	13 793	10 851	10 606	11 002	..	..	Imprimerie et activités annexes			222
..	..	245	245	245	359	..	..	Reproduction de supports enregistrés			223
..	..	2 337	2 106	2 555	2 697	..	..	Cokéfaction; prod. pétroliers; comb. nucléaires		23	
..	..	22 596	22 565	22 601	22 924	..	..	Produits chimiques		24	
..	..	14 129	14 265	14 296	14 537	..	..	Produits chimiques de base			241
..	..	8 468	8 300	8 306	8 387	..	..	Autres produits chimiques			242
..	..	0	0	0	0	..	..	Fibres synthétiques ou artificielles			243
..	..	9 934	8 013	8 286	9 045	..	..	Articles en caoutchouc et en matières plastiques		25	
..	..	1 955	909	977	1 145	..	..	Articles en caoutchouc			251
..	..	7 978	7 104	7 309	7 900	..	..	Articles en matières plastiques			252
..	..	13 036	10 979	10 615	10 982	..	..	Autres produits minéraux non métalliques		26	
..	..	2 691	2 408	2 348	2 483	..	..	Verre et articles en verre			261
..	..	10 345	8 571	8 267	8 499	..	..	Produits minéraux non métalliques, nca			269
..	..	25 068	23 438	22 741	24 947	..	..	Produits métallurgiques de base		27	
..	..	8 029	7 695	7 650	7 254	..	..	Sidérurgie et première transformation de l'acier			271
..	..	16 592	15 508	15 054	14 939	..	..	Métallurgie; métaux précieux et non ferreux			272
..	..	447	235	37	2 754	..	..	Fonderie			273
..	..	24 823	21 243	20 594	20 387	..	..	Ouvrages en métaux, sauf machines et matériel		28	
..	..	12 080	10 756	10 179	10 163	..	..	Constr. et menuiserie métal.; réservoirs; générateurs			281
..	..	12 743	10 487	10 415	10 224	..	..	Autres ouvrages en métaux			289
..	..	32 487	30 437	30 387	31 274	..	..	Machines et matériel, nca		29	
..	..	18 665	18 081	17 380	18 164	..	..	Machines d'usage général			291
..	..	11 883	10 542	11 239	11 280	..	..	Machines d'usage spécifique			292
..	..	1 940	1 814	1 768	1 829	..	..	Appareils domestiques, nca			293
..	..	1 641	1 501	1 317	1 328	..	..	Mach. de bureau, comptables, matériel inform.		30	
..	..	16 171	14 079	13 795	13 010	..	..	Machines et appareils électriques, nca		31	
..	..	4 720	4 110	4 418	3 622	..	..	Moteurs, génératrices et transformateurs électriques			311
..	..	4 139	3 423	3 589	3 683	..	..	Matériel électrique de distribution et de commande			312
..	..	2 612	2 245	2 401	2 283	..	..	Fils et câbles électriques isolés			313
..	..	231	229	212	223	..	..	Accumulateurs, piles électriques			314
..	..	2 206	2 095	1 854	1 869	..	..	Lampes électriques et appareils d'éclairage			315
..	..	2 263	1 978	1 322	1 330	..	..	Autres matériels électriques, nca			319
..	..	7 055	6 107	6 488	6 936	..	..	Equip. et appar. de radio, TV, communication		32	
..	..	1 047	1 125	1 145	1 278	..	..	Tubes et valves électroniques; autres composants			321
..	..	5 021	4 190	4 259	4 662	..	..	Emetteurs radio et TV; app. téléphonie, télégraphie			322
..	..	987	792	1 084	996	..	..	Récepteurs radio et TV et articles associés			323
..	..	5 577	5 656	5 755	6 288	..	..	Instruments médicaux, de précision, d'optique		33	
..	..	5 406	5 502	5 596	6 115	..	..	Appareils médicaux et de précision			331
..	..	171	154	159	173	..	..	Instruments d'optique ; matériel photographique			332
..	..	0	0	0	0	..	..	Horlogerie			333
..	..	5 135	5 036	5 133	5 338	..	..	Véhicules automobiles et nemorques		34	
..	..	51 866	54 552	55 568	56 600	..	..	Autres matériels de transport		35	
..	..	42 735	46 198	47 077	48 259	..	..	Construction et réparation de navires			351
..	..	3 427	3 140	3 111	3 229	..	..	Construction de matériel ferroviaire roulant			352
..	..	5 005	4 451	4 506	4 176	..	..	Construction aéronautique et spatiale			353
..	..	698	764	874	936	..	..	Autres équipements de transport			359
..	..	16 055	14 486	14 193	15 257	..	..	Meubles; activités de fabrication, nca		36	
..	..	11 600	9 945	10 122	11 053	..	..	Meubles			361
..	..	4 454	4 541	4 071	4 204	..	..	Activités de fabrication, nca			369
..	..	131	124	124	294	..	..	Récupération		37	
..	..	..	..	..	..	..	..	Production et distrib. d'électricité, de gaz, d'eau	E	40-41	
..	..	..	..	..	..	..	..	Electricité, gaz, vapeur et eau chaude		40	
..	..	..	..	..	..	..	..	Production, collecte et distribution d'électricité			401
..	..	..	..	..	..	..	..	Captage, épuration et distribution d'eau		41	410
..	..	..	..	..	..	..	..	Construction	F	45	
..	..	..	..	..	..	..	..	Commerce de gros et de détail; réparation	G	50-52	
..	..	..	..	..	..	..	..	Hôtels et restaurants	H	55	
..	..	..	..	..	..	..	..	Transports, entreposage et communications	I	60-64	
..	..	..	..	..	..	..	..	Intermédiation financière	J	65-67	
..	..	..	..	..	..	..	..	Immobilier, locations, services aux entreprises	K	70-74	
..	..	..	..	..	..	..	..	Admin. publique; éducation; santé; autres	L-Q	75-99	
..	..	..	..	..	..	..	..	Grand total	A-Q	01-99	

Note: Unless given separetely, ISIC 155 includes 16.

Statistiques des Structures Industrielles
OCDE, © 1998

POLAND

Table PO.1 PRODUCTION - PRODUCTION

Millions of PLN (Current Prices)

ISIC revision 3			1989	1990	1991	1992	1993	1994	1995	1996
A	01-02	Agriculture, hunting and forestry	..	..	..	..	..	..	..	..
B	05	Fishing	..	..	..	..	..	..	..	..
C	10-14	Mining and quarrying	..	..	..	9 624	10 909	16 016	19 536	22 286
	10	Mining of coal and lignite; extraction of peat	..	..	..	5 804	8 372	12 145	14 329	16 832
	11	Crude petroleum & natural gas; related service activ.	..	..	..	..	..	..	..	..
	13	Mining of metal ores	..	..	..	..	..	..	..	..
	14	Other mining and quarrying	..	..	..	..	..	..	..	..
D	15-37	Total manufacturing	..	..	..	78 975	104 441	149 028	200 348	238 379
	15	Food products and beverages	..	..	..	20 592	26 293	36 539	46 658	59 861
	155	Beverages	..	..	..	..	..	..	..	..
	16 160	Tobacco products	..	..	..	1 601	2 200	3 042	1 816	2 228
	17	Textiles	..	..	..	2 857	3 486	5 203	6 399	6 890
	171	Spinning, weaving and finishing of textiles	..	..	..	..	..	..	..	..
	172	Other textiles	..	..	..	..	..	..	..	..
	173	Knitted and crocheted fabrics and articles	..	..	..	..	..	..	..	..
	18	Wearing apparel dressing & dyeing of fur	..	..	..	3 022	4 026	5 250	6 330	6 714
	181	Wearing apparel, except fur apparel	..	..	..	..	..	..	..	..
	182	Dressing and dyeing of fur; articles of fur	..	..	..	..	..	..	..	..
	19	Tanning, dressing leather; leather artic.; footwear	..	..	..	1 295	1 501	2 071	2 679	3 239
	191	Tanning, dressing leather; manuf. of leather articles	..	..	..	..	..	..	..	..
	192	Footwear	..	..	..	..	..	..	..	..
	20	Wood and cork products, ex. furniture	..	..	..	2 208	2 916	4 654	6 813	7 846
	201	Sawmilling and planing of wood	..	..	..	..	..	..	..	..
	202	Products of wood, cork, straw & plaiting material	..	..	..	..	..	..	..	..
	21	Paper and paper products	..	..	..	1 296	1 644	2 723	5 403	5 354
	22	Publishing, printing & reprod. of recorded media	..	..	..	2 001	2 928	4 350	6 473	7 879
	221	Publishing	..	..	..	..	..	..	..	..
	222	Printing and related service activities	..	..	..	..	..	..	..	..
	223	Reproduction of recorded media	..	..	..	..	..	..	..	..
	23	Coke, refined petroleum products & nuclear fuel	..	..	..	6 423	8 987	10 914	10 137	11 295
	24	Chemicals and chemical products	..	..	..	5 653	7 290	11 071	16 692	18 415
	241	Basic chemicals	..	..	..	..	..	..	..	..
	242	Other chemical products	..	..	..	..	..	..	..	..
	243	Man-made fibres	..	..	..	..	..	..	..	..
	25	Rubber and plastic products	..	..	..	2 396	3 417	5 231	7 770	8 908
	251	Rubber products	..	..	..	..	..	..	..	..
	252	Plastic products	..	..	..	..	..	..	..	..
	26	Other non-metallic mineral products	..	..	..	3 518	4 622	6 918	9 090	11 189
	261	Glass and glass products	..	..	..	..	..	..	..	..
	269	Non-metallic mineral products, nec	..	..	..	..	..	..	..	..
	27	Basic metals	..	..	..	5 864	7 511	11 277	16 057	17 106
	271	Basic iron and steel	..	..	..	..	..	..	..	..
	272	Basic precious and non-ferrous metals	..	..	..	..	..	..	..	..
	273	Casting of metals	..	..	..	..	..	..	..	..
	28	Fabricated metal products, ex. machin. & equip.	..	..	..	3 637	4 615	6 581	9 367	10 441
	281	Structural metal prod., tanks, reservoirs, generators	..	..	..	..	..	..	..	..
	289	Other fabricated metal products & service activities	..	..	..	..	..	..	..	..
	29	Machinery and equipment, nec	..	..	..	5 028	6 575	9 343	13 689	16 345
	291	General purpose machinery	..	..	..	..	..	..	..	..
	292	Special purpose machinery	..	..	..	..	..	..	..	..
	293	Domestic appliances, nec	..	..	..	..	..	..	..	..
	30	Office, accounting and computing machinery	..	..	..	117	179	172	479	716
	31	Electrical machinery and apparatus, nec	..	..	..	2 200	2 993	4 056	6 179	7 574
	311	Electric motors, generators and transformers	..	..	..	..	..	..	..	..
	312	Electricity distribution and control apparatus	..	..	..	..	..	..	..	..
	313	Insulated wire and cable	..	..	..	..	..	..	..	..
	314	Accumulators, primary cells and primary batteries	..	..	..	..	..	..	..	..
	315	Electric lamps and lighting equipment	..	..	..	..	..	..	..	..
	319	Other electrical equipment, nec	..	..	..	..	..	..	..	..
	32	Radio, TV, communication equip. & apparatus	..	..	..	1 053	1 546	2 356	3 347	4 082
	321	Electronic valves, tubes & other electronic compon.	..	..	..	..	..	..	..	..
	322	TV, radio transmitters & appar. for line teleph., telegr.	..	..	..	..	..	..	..	..
	323	TV, radio receivers and associated goods	..	..	..	..	..	..	..	..
	33	Medical, precision, optical instr.; watches, clocks	..	..	..	738	1 042	1 452	2 197	2 665
	331	Medical equip.; precision instruments and appliances	..	..	..	..	..	..	..	..
	332	Optical instruments and photographic equipment	..	..	..	..	..	..	..	..
	333	Watches and clocks	..	..	..	..	..	..	..	..
	34	Motor vehicles, trailers, and semi-trailers	..	..	..	2 639	4 153	5 819	8 704	13 694
	35	Other transport equipment	..	..	..	2 115	2 985	4 534	5 679	6 299
	351	Building and repairing of ships and boats	..	..	..	..	..	..	..	..
	352	Railway, tramway locomotives and rolling stock	..	..	..	..	..	..	..	..
	353	Aircraft and spacecraft	..	..	..	..	..	..	..	..
	359	Transport equipment, nec	..	..	..	..	..	..	..	..
	36	Furniture; manufacturing, nec	..	..	..	2 456	3 204	4 991	7 609	8 858
	361	Furniture	..	..	..	..	..	..	..	..
	369	Manufacturing, nec	..	..	..	..	..	..	..	..
	37	Recycling	..	..	..	269	329	483	780	782
E	40-41	Electricity, gas and water supply	..	..	..	11 162	14 953	19 361	24 549	27 987
	40	Electricity, gas, steam and hot water supply	..	..	..	10 037	13 492	17 412	22 441	25 542
	401	Production, collection and distribution of electricity	..	..	..	..	..	..	..	..
	41 410	Collection, purification, distribution of water	..	..	..	1 125	1 461	1 950	2 108	2 444
F	45	Construction	..	..	..	..	..	..	..	..
G	50-52	Wholesale and retail trade; repairs etc	..	..	..	..	..	..	..	..
H	55	Hotels and restaurants	..	..	..	..	..	..	..	..
I	60-64	Transport, storage and communications	..	..	..	..	..	..	..	..
J	65-67	Financial intermediation	..	..	..	..	..	..	..	..
K	70-74	Real estate, renting and business activities	..	..	..	..	..	..	..	..
L-Q	75-99	Public admin.; education; health; other services	..	..	..	..	..	..	..	..
A-Q	01-99	Grand total	..	..	..	..	..	..	..	..

Table PO.2 VALEUR AJOUTÉE - VALUE ADDED

Millions de PLN (Prix courants)

1989	1990	1991	1992	1993	1994	1995	1996			CITI révision 3	
..	..	..	7 658	10 287	13 100	18 428		**Agriculture, chasse et sylviculture**	**A**	**01-02**	
..	..	..	157	95	129	131		**Pêche**	**B**	**05**	
..	..	..	3 871	5 721	8 892	11 101	12 759	**Activités extractives**	**C**	**10-14**	
..	..	..	2 861	4 731	6 954	8 467	10 181	Extraction de charbon, de lignite et de tourbe		10	
..	..	..	..	..	..	..	..	Extraction de pétrole brut et de gaz naturel		11	
..	..	..	..	..	..	..	..	Extraction de minerais métalliques		13	
..	..	..	..	..	..	..	..	Autres activités extractives		14	
..	..	..	30 925	39 294	51 179	62 575	72 880	**Activités de fabrication**	**D**	**15-37**	
..	..	..	7 924	9 660	10 562	10 950	11 733	**Produits alimentaires et boissons**		**15**	
..	..	..	..	..	..	..	..	Boissons			155
..	..	..	1 149	1 459	1 936	453	596	**Produits à base de tabac**		**16**	160
..	..	..	1 194	1 334	1 901	2 285	2 685	**Textiles**		**17**	
..	..	..	..	..	..	..	..	Filature, tissage et achèvement des textiles			171
..	..	..	..	..	..	..	..	Autres articles textiles			172
..	..	..	..	..	..	..	..	Etoffes et articles de bonneterie			173
..	..	..	1 465	1 981	2 335	3 222	3 338	**Habillement; préparation, teinture des fourrures**		**18**	
..	..	..	..	..	..	..	..	Articles d'habillement autres qu'en fourrure			181
..	..	..	..	..	..	..	..	Préparation, teinture des fourrures; art. en fourrure			182
..	..	..	533	594	852	1 002	1 239	**Travail des cuirs; articles en cuir; chaussures**		**19**	
..	..	..	..	..	..	..	..	Apprêt et tannage des cuirs et articles en cuirs			191
..	..	..	..	..	..	..	..	Chaussures			192
..	..	..	812	1 075	1 830	2 078	2 714	**Bois et articles en bois et liège (sauf meubles)**		**20**	
..	..	..	..	..	..	..	..	Sciage et rabotage du bois			201
..	..	..	..	..	..	..	..	Articles en bois, liège, vannerie, sparterie			202
..	..	..	387	493	798	1 761	1 468	**Papier et carton; articles en papier et en carton**		**21**	
..	..	..	765	1 092	1 857	2 747	3 512	**Edition, imprimerie et reproduction**		**22**	
..	..	..	..	..	..	..	..	Edition			221
..	..	..	..	..	..	..	..	Imprimerie et activités annexes			222
..	..	..	..	..	..	..	..	Reproduction de supports enregistrés			223
..	..	..	2 665	3 411	3 971	1 737	1 370	**Cokéfaction; prod. pétroliers; comb. nucléaires**		**23**	
..	..	..	1 838	2 325	3 371	5 395	6 115	**Produits chimiques**		**24**	
..	..	..	..	..	..	..	..	Produits chimiques de base			241
..	..	..	..	..	..	..	..	Autres produits chimiques			242
..	..	..	..	..	..	..	..	Fibres synthétiques ou artificielles			243
..	..	..	926	1 365	1 933	2 953	3 306	**Articles en caoutchouc et en matières plastiques**		**25**	
..	..	..	..	..	..	..	..	Articles en caoutchouc			251
..	..	..	..	..	..	..	..	Articles en matières plastiques			252
..	..	..	1 412	1 807	2 731	3 550	4 566	**Autres produits minéraux non métalliques**		**26**	
..	..	..	..	..	..	..	..	Verre et articles en verre			261
..	..	..	..	..	..	..	..	Produits minéraux non métalliques, nca			269
..	..	..	1 517	1 743	2 572	4 092	4 037	**Produits métallurgiques de base**		**27**	
..	..	..	..	..	..	..	..	Sidérurgie et première transformation de l'acier			271
..	..	..	..	..	..	..	..	Métallurgie; métaux précieux et non ferreux			272
..	..	..	..	..	..	..	..	Fonderie			273
..	..	..	1 668	2 049	2 602	3 733	4 927	**Ouvrages en métaux, sauf machines et matériel**		**28**	
..	..	..	..	..	..	..	..	Constr. et menuiserie métal.; réservoirs; générateurs			281
..	..	..	..	..	..	..	..	Autres ouvrages en métaux			289
..	..	..	2 309	2 817	3 721	5 367	6 674	**Machines et matériel, nca**		**29**	
..	..	..	..	..	..	..	..	Machines d'usage général			291
..	..	..	..	..	..	..	..	Machines d'usage spécifique			292
..	..	..	..	..	..	..	..	Appareils domestiques, nca			293
..	..	..	63	65	115	188	247	**Mach. de bureau, comptables, matériel inform.**		**30**	
..	..	..	846	1 156	1 401	2 167	2 921	**Machines et appareils électriques, nca**		**31**	
..	..	..	..	..	..	..	..	Moteurs, génératrices et transformateurs électriques			311
..	..	..	..	..	..	..	..	Matériel électrique de distribution et de commande			312
..	..	..	..	..	..	..	..	Fils et câbles électriques isolés			313
..	..	..	..	..	..	..	..	Accumulateurs, piles électriques			314
..	..	..	..	..	..	..	..	Lampes électriques et appareils d'éclairage			315
..	..	..	..	..	..	..	..	Autres matériels électriques, nca			319
..	..	..	329	561	758	1 125	1 327	**Equip. et appar. de radio, TV, communication**		**32**	
..	..	..	..	..	..	..	..	Tubes et valves électroniques; autres composants			321
..	..	..	..	..	..	..	..	Emetteurs radio et TV; app. téléphonie, télégraphie			322
..	..	..	..	..	..	..	..	Récepteurs radio et TV et articles associés			323
..	..	..	396	580	630	964	1 386	**Instruments médicaux, de précision, d'optique**		**33**	
..	..	..	..	..	..	..	..	Appareils médicaux et de précision			331
..	..	..	..	..	..	..	..	Instruments d'optique ; matériel photographique			332
..	..	..	..	..	..	..	..	Horlogerie			333
..	..	..	832	1 370	1 450	2 023	3 105	**Véhicules automobiles et nemorques**		**34**	
..	..	..	751	881	1 798	1 869	2 228	**Autres matériels de transport**		**35**	
..	..	..	..	..	..	..	..	Construction et réparation de navires			351
..	..	..	..	..	..	..	..	Construction de matériel ferroviaire roulant			352
..	..	..	..	..	..	..	..	Construction aéronautique et spatiale			353
..	..	..	..	..	..	..	..	Autres équipements de transport			359
..	..	..	1 052	1 368	1 908	2 668	3 200	**Meubles; activités de fabrication, nca**		**36**	
..	..	..	..	..	..	..	..	Meubles			361
..	..	..	..	..	..	..	..	Activités de fabrication, nca			369
..	..	..	92	109	148	244	187	**Récupération**		**37**	
..	..	..	4 331	6 193	7 636	10 539	12 736	**Production et distrib. d'électricité, de gaz, d'eau**	**E**	**40-41**	
..	..	..	3 715	5 366	6 582	9 334	11 295	**Electricité, gaz, vapeur et eau chaude**		**40**	
..	..	..	..	..	..	..	..	Production, collecte et distribution d'électricité			401
..	..	..	616	827	1 054	1 205	1 441	**Captage, épuration et distribution d'eau**		**41**	410
..	..	..	8 932	10 150	11 999	14 990	..	**Construction**	**F**	**45**	
..	..	..	15 112	23 330	28 546	39 200	..	**Commerce de gros et de détail; réparation**	**G**	**50-52**	
..	..	..	832	10 150	11 999	1 519	..	**Hôtels et restaurants**	**H**	**55**	
..	..	..	7 101	9 496	12 531	16 153	..	**Transports, entreposage et communications**	**I**	**60-64**	
..	..	..	598	902	2 125	2 625	..	**Intermédiation financière**	**J**	**65-67**	
..	..	..	7 416	9 072	12 593	18 920	..	**Immobilier, locations, services aux entreprises**	**K**	**70-74**	
..	..	..	23 667	28 261	36 989	52 707	..	**Admin. publique; éducation; santé; autres**	**L-Q**	**75-99**	
..	..	..	110 599	152 951	197 716	248 887	..	**Grand total**	**A-Q**	**01-99**	

Statistiques des Structures Industrielles
OCDE, © 1998

Table PO.3 INVESTMENT - INVESTISSEMENT

Millions of PLN (Current Prices)

ISIC revision 3			1989	1990	1991	1992	1993	1994	1995	1996
A	01-02	**Agriculture, hunting and forestry**	..	..	..	640	780	1 030	1 559	2 391
B	05	**Fishing**	..	..	..	10	23	13	5	15
C	10-14	**Mining and quarrying**	..	..	..	888	1 032	1 444	1 674	1 840
	10	Mining of coal and lignite; extraction of peat	..	..	..	725	807	1 190	..	..
	11	Crude petroleum & natural gas; related service activ.	..	..	..	..	..	..	..	..
	13	Mining of metal ores	..	..	..	..	..	..	..	..
	14	Other mining and quarrying	..	..	..	..	..	..	..	..
D	15-37	**Total manufacturing**	..	..	..	4 580	4 965	8 396	11 733	17 215
	15	**Food products and beverages**	..	..	..	1 236	1 176	1 708	2 695	3 731
	155	Beverages	..	..	..	..	..	..	..	..
	16 160	**Tobacco products**	..	..	..	43	110	84	122	322
	17	**Textiles**	..	..	..	109	151	280	327	385
	171	Spinning, weaving and finishing of textiles	..	..	..	..	..	..	..	..
	172	Other textiles	..	..	..	..	..	..	..	..
	173	Knitted and crocheted fabrics and articles	..	..	..	..	..	..	..	..
	18	**Wearing apparel dressing & dyeing of fur**	..	..	..	115	124	191	233	258
	181	Wearing apparel, except fur apparel	..	..	..	..	..	..	..	..
	182	Dressing and dyeing of fur; articles of fur	..	..	..	..	..	..	..	..
	19	**Tanning, dressing leather; leather artic.; footwear**	..	..	..	42	36	51	80	98
	191	Tanning, dressing leather; manuf. of leather articles	..	..	..	..	..	..	..	..
	192	Footwear	..	..	..	..	..	..	..	..
	20	**Wood and cork products, ex. furniture**	..	..	..	100	157	321	510	562
	201	Sawmilling and planing of wood	..	..	..	..	..	..	..	..
	202	Products of wood, cork, straw & plaiting material	..	..	..	..	..	..	..	..
	21	**Paper and paper products**	..	..	..	94	239	453	489	687
	22	**Publishing, printing & reprod. of recorded media**	..	..	..	98	162	321	255	421
	221	Publishing	..	..	..	..	..	..	..	..
	222	Printing and related service activities	..	..	..	..	..	..	..	..
	223	Reproduction of recorded media	..	..	..	..	..	..	..	..
	23	**Coke, refined petroleum products & nuclear fuel**	..	..	..	183	306	561	709	1 254
	24	**Chemicals and chemical products**	..	..	..	388	451	911	1 181	1 554
	241	Basic chemicals	..	..	..	..	..	..	..	..
	242	Other chemical products	..	..	..	..	..	..	..	..
	243	Man-made fibres	..	..	..	..	..	..	..	..
	25	**Rubber and plastic products**	..	..	..	128	221	293	543	855
	251	Rubber products	..	..	..	..	..	..	..	..
	252	Plastic products	..	..	..	..	..	..	..	..
	26	**Other non-metallic mineral products**	..	..	..	212	308	609	845	1 279
	261	Glass and glass products	..	..	..	..	..	..	..	..
	269	Non-metallic mineral products, nec	..	..	..	..	..	..	..	..
	27	**Basic metals**	..	..	..	480	428	705	1 101	1 913
	271	Basic iron and steel	..	..	..	..	..	..	..	..
	272	Basic precious and non-ferrous metals	..	..	..	..	..	..	..	..
	273	Casting of metals	..	..	..	..	..	..	..	..
	28	**Fabricated metal products, ex. machin. & equip.**	..	..	..	126	171	357	326	580
	281	Structural metal prod., tanks, reservoirs, generators	..	..	..	..	..	..	..	..
	289	Other fabricated metal products & service activities	..	..	..	..	..	..	..	..
	29	**Machinery and equipment, nec**	..	..	..	200	217	378	584	773
	291	General purpose machinery	..	..	..	..	..	..	..	..
	292	Special purpose machinery	..	..	..	..	..	..	..	..
	293	Domestic appliances, nec	..	..	..	..	..	..	..	..
	30	**Office, accounting and computing machinery**	..	..	..	4	16	14	16	17
	31	**Electrical machinery and apparatus, nec**	..	..	..	179	190	261	381	557
	311	Electric motors, generators and transformers	..	..	..	..	..	..	..	..
	312	Electricity distribution and control apparatus	..	..	..	..	..	..	..	..
	313	Insulated wire and cable	..	..	..	..	..	..	..	..
	314	Accumulators, primary cells and primary batteries	..	..	..	..	..	..	..	..
	315	Electric lamps and lighting equipment	..	..	..	..	..	..	..	..
	319	Other electrical equipment, nec	..	..	..	..	..	..	..	..
	32	**Radio, TV, communication equip. & apparatus**	..	..	..	118	118	155	151	327
	321	Electronic valves, tubes & other electronic compon.	..	..	..	..	..	..	..	..
	322	TV, radio transmitters & appar. for line teleph., telegr.	..	..	..	..	..	..	..	..
	323	TV, radio receivers and associated goods	..	..	..	..	..	..	..	..
	33	**Medical, precision, optical instr.; watches, clocks**	..	..	..	33	34	60	91	133
	331	Medical equip.; precision instruments and appliances	..	..	..	..	..	..	..	..
	332	Optical instruments and photographic equipment	..	..	..	..	..	..	..	..
	333	Watches and clocks	..	..	..	..	..	..	..	..
	34	**Motor vehicles, trailers, and semi-trailers**	..	..	..	543	147	188	494	808
	35	**Other transport equipment**	..	..	..	55	88	207	197	247
	351	Building and repairing of ships and boats	..	..	..	..	..	..	..	..
	352	Railway, tramway locomotives and rolling stock	..	..	..	..	..	..	..	..
	353	Aircraft and spacecraft	..	..	..	..	..	..	..	..
	359	Transport equipment, nec	..	..	..	..	..	..	..	..
	36	**Furniture; manufacturing, nec**	..	..	..	85	103	250	378	423
	361	Furniture	..	..	..	..	..	..	..	..
	369	Manufacturing, nec	..	..	..	..	..	..	..	..
	37	**Recycling**	..	..	..	11	12	39	27	31
E	40-41	**Electricity, gas and water supply**	..	..	..	2 507	3 571	4 869	6 768	8 770
	40	**Electricity, gas, steam and hot water supply**	..	..	..	1 603	2 481	3 396	..	..
	401	Production, collection and distribution of electricity	..	..	..	..	..	..	..	..
	41 410	**Collection, purification, distribution of water**	..	..	..	904	1 090	1 473	..	..
F	45	**Construction**	..	..	..	956	1 025	1 556	2 157	3 845
G	50-52	**Wholesale and retail trade; repairs etc**	..	..	..	1 163	1 692	2 115	3 836	4 910
H	55	**Hotels and restaurants**	..	..	..	154	256	355	533	433
I	60-64	**Transport, storage and communications**	..	..	..	1 747	2 512	3 268	5 077	7 849
J	65-67	**Financial intermediation**	..	..	..	722	976	1 609	2 301	3 067
K	70-74	**Real estate, renting and business activities**	..	..	..	4 862	4 660	5 044	6 065	7 243
L-Q	75-99	**Public admin.; education; health; other services**	..	..	..	1 932	3 226	4 167	5 437	8 043
A-Q	01-99	**Grand total**	..	..	..	20 160	24 716	33 865	47 145	65 622

Table PO.4 **EMPLOI - EMPLOYMENT**

Milliers

1989	1990	1991	1992	1993	1994	1995	1996			CITI révision 3	
..	..	..	4 009.0	3 922.8	4 039.5	4 032.3	4 358.7	**Agriculture, chasse et sylviculture**	A	01-02	
..	..	..	17.9	15.5	14.9	13.6	12.8	**Pêche**	B	05	
..	..	..	454.2	398.8	376.8	357.1	339.1	**Activités extractives**	C	10-14	
..	..	..	..	..	..	..	..	Extraction de charbon, de lignite et de tourbe		10	
..	..	..	..	..	..	..	..	Extraction de pétrole brut et de gaz naturel		11	
..	..	..	..	..	..	..	..	Extraction de minerais métalliques		13	
..	..	..	..	..	..	..	..	Autres activités extractives		14	
..	..	..	3 069.8	2 985.5	3 071.4	3 102.5	3 158.8	**Activités de fabrication**	D	15-37	
..	..	..	491.5	499.2	517.5	529.7	552.4	**Produits alimentaires et boissons**		15	
..	..	..	..	..	..	..	..	Boissons			155
..	..	..	11.5	12.9	13.2	12.9	13.3	**Produits à base de tabac**		16	160
..	..	..	196.7	185.8	184.8	168.1	161.6	**Textiles**		17	
..	..	..	..	..	..	..	..	Filature, tissage et achèvement des textiles			171
..	..	..	..	..	..	..	..	Autres articles textiles			172
..	..	..	..	..	..	..	..	Etoffes et articles de bonneterie			173
..	..	..	279.5	278.2	297.6	319.9	316.3	**Habillement; préparation, teinture des fourrures**		18	
..	..	..	..	..	..	..	..	Articles d'habillement autres qu'en fourrure			181
..	..	..	..	..	..	..	..	Préparation, teinture des fourrures; art. en fourrure			182
..	..	..	99.5	93.5	91.6	90.2	90.9	**Travail des cuirs; articles en cuir; chaussures**		19	
..	..	..	..	..	..	..	..	Apprêt et tannage des cuirs et articles en cuirs			191
..	..	..	..	..	..	..	..	Chaussures			192
..	..	..	136.5	129.2	130.1	133.5	149.8	**Bois et articles en bois et liège (sauf meubles)**		20	
..	..	..	..	..	..	..	..	Sciage et rabotage du bois			201
..	..	..	..	..	..	..	..	Articles en bois, liège, vannerie, sparterie			202
..	..	..	38.5	37.7	44.9	41.5	42.7	**Papier et carton; articles en papier et en carton**		21	
..	..	..	76.2	72.3	80.4	82.5	90.0	**Edition, imprimerie et reproduction**		22	
..	..	..	..	..	..	..	..	Edition			221
..	..	..	..	..	..	..	..	Imprimerie et activités annexes			222
..	..	..	..	..	..	..	..	Reproduction de supports enregistrés			223
..	..	..	23.3	27.5	27.7	27.6	27.2	**Cokéfaction; prod. pétroliers; comb. nucléaires**		23	
..	..	..	141.5	135.3	147.3	141.1	141.0	**Produits chimiques**		24	
..	..	..	..	..	..	..	..	Produits chimiques de base			241
..	..	..	..	..	..	..	..	Autres produits chimiques			242
..	..	..	..	..	..	..	..	Fibres synthétiques ou artificielles			243
..	..	..	88.7	90.5	100.9	105.5	112.5	**Articles en caoutchouc et en matières plastiques**		25	
..	..	..	..	..	..	..	..	Articles en caoutchouc			251
..	..	..	..	..	..	..	..	Articles en matières plastiques			252
..	..	..	187.2	182.7	182.5	182.0	186.6	**Autres produits minéraux non métalliques**		26	
..	..	..	..	..	..	..	..	Verre et articles en verre			261
..	..	..	..	..	..	..	..	Produits minéraux non métalliques, nca			269
..	..	..	165.6	179.8	166.7	164.1	157.9	**Produits métallurgiques de base**		27	
..	..	..	..	..	..	..	..	Sidérurgie et première transformation de l'acier			271
..	..	..	..	..	..	..	..	Métallurgie; métaux précieux et non ferreux			272
..	..	..	..	..	..	..	..	Fonderie			273
..	..	..	185.5	172.0	177.9	192.1	208.0	**Ouvrages en métaux, sauf machines et matériel**		28	
..	..	..	..	..	..	..	..	Constr. et menuiserie métal.; réservoirs; générateurs			281
..	..	..	..	..	..	..	..	Autres ouvrages en métaux			289
..	..	..	330.7	306.4	303.9	299.7	291.2	**Machines et matériel, nca**		29	
..	..	..	..	..	..	..	..	Machines d'usage général			291
..	..	..	..	..	..	..	..	Machines d'usage spécifique			292
..	..	..	..	..	..	..	..	Appareils domestiques, nca			293
..	..	..	6.1	4.6	4.6	4.7	5.4	**Mach. de bureau, comptables, matériel inform.**		30	
..	..	..	93.3	93.4	99.6	99.7	99.4	**Machines et appareils électriques, nca**		31	
..	..	..	..	..	..	..	..	Moteurs, génératrices et transformateurs électriques			311
..	..	..	..	..	..	..	..	Matériel électrique de distribution et de commande			312
..	..	..	..	..	..	..	..	Fils et câbles électriques isolés			313
..	..	..	..	..	..	..	..	Accumulateurs, piles électriques			314
..	..	..	..	..	..	..	..	Lampes électriques et appareils d'éclairage			315
..	..	..	..	..	..	..	..	Autres matériels électriques, nca			319
..	..	..	63.5	56.1	53.5	51.1	46.6	**Equip. et appar. de radio, TV, communication**		32	
..	..	..	..	..	..	..	..	Tubes et valves électroniques; autres composants			321
..	..	..	..	..	..	..	..	Emetteurs radio et TV; app. téléphonie, télégraphie			322
..	..	..	..	..	..	..	..	Récepteurs radio et TV et articles associés			323
..	..	..	51.8	47.8	49.0	49.4	49.8	**Instruments médicaux, de précision, d'optique**		33	
..	..	..	..	..	..	..	..	Appareils médicaux et de précision			331
..	..	..	..	..	..	..	..	Instruments d'optique ; matériel photographique			332
..	..	..	..	..	..	..	..	Horlogerie			333
..	..	..	111.6	97.8	105.2	102.6	107.1	**Véhicules automobiles et nemorques**		34	
..	..	..	118.5	114.9	117.0	112.5	107.0	**Autres matériels de transport**		35	
..	..	..	..	..	..	..	..	Construction et réparation de navires			351
..	..	..	..	..	..	..	..	Construction de matériel ferroviaire roulant			352
..	..	..	..	..	..	..	..	Construction aéronautique et spatiale			353
..	..	..	..	..	..	..	..	Autres équipements de transport			359
..	..	..	166.4	162.0	167.5	185.0	194.3	**Meubles; activités de fabrication, nca**		36	
..	..	..	..	..	..	..	..	Meubles			361
..	..	..	..	..	..	..	..	Activités de fabrication, nca			369
..	..	..	6.2	6.2	8.0	7.1	7.8	**Récupération**		37	
..	..	..	254.3	257.1	268.8	269.2	259.4	**Production et distrib. d'électricité, de gaz, d'eau**	E	40-41	
..	..	..	..	..	..	..	..	**Electricité, gaz, vapeur et eau chaude**		40	
..	..	..	..	..	..	..	..	Production, collecte et distribution d'électricité			401
..	..	..	..	..	..	..	..	**Captage, épuration et distribution d'eau**		41	410
..	..	..	1 014.1	880.7	853.0	827.4	868.7	**Construction**	F	45	
..	..	..	1 871.3	1 982.2	1 892.2	1 903.1	1 900.3	**Commerce de gros et de détail; réparation**	G	50-52	
..	..	..	164.4	170.1	175.8	185.9	188.0	**Hôtels et restaurants**	H	55	
..	..	..	912.9	823.3	844.2	838.1	832.3	**Transports, entreposage et communications**	I	60-64	
..	..	..	188.3	221.6	252.1	268.2	285.8	**Intermédiation financière**	J	65-67	
..	..	..	542.8	570.6	529.6	554.3	594.4	**Immobilier, locations, services aux entreprises**	K	70-74	
..	..	..	2 511.0	2 533.0	2 605.7	2 616.2	2 689.1	**Admin. publique; éducation; santé; autres**	L-Q	75-99	
..	..	..	15 010.9	14 761.2	14 924.0	14 967.9	15 487.4	**Grand total**	A-Q	01-99	

Statistiques des Structures Industrielles
OCDE, © 1998

POLAND

Table PO.5 EMPLOYMENT, EMPLOYEES - EMPLOI, SALARIÉS

Thousands

ISIC revision 3				1989	1990	1991	1992	1993	1994	1995	1996
A	01-02		Agriculture, hunting and forestry	..	..	..	385.1	305.0	257.0	222.8	282.1
B	05		Fishing	..	..	..	18.5	14.8	12.9	11.4	9.8
C	10-14		Mining and quarrying	..	..	..	457.8	420.5	392.3	374.4	356.4
	10		Mining of coal and lignite; extraction of peat	..	..	..	369.5	351.2	326.5	307.8	293.1
	11		Crude petroleum & natural gas; related service activ.	..	..	..	..	..	..	..	..
	13		Mining of metal ores	..	..	..	..	..	..	..	..
	14		Other mining and quarrying	..	..	..	..	..	..	..	..
D	15-37		Total manufacturing	..	..	..	2 766.5	2 700.2	2 693.1	2 809.2	2 802.6
	15		Food products and beverages	..	..	..	461.1	466.5	454.4	484.2	486.0
		155	Beverages	..	..	..	..	..	..	..	..
	16	160	Tobacco products	..	..	..	11.0	12.1	12.4	12.4	12.4
	17		Textiles	..	..	..	183.7	172.2	171.1	164.6	153.3
		171	Spinning, weaving and finishing of textiles	..	..	..	..	..	..	..	..
		172	Other textiles	..	..	..	..	..	..	..	..
		173	Knitted and crocheted fabrics and articles	..	..	..	..	..	..	..	..
	18		Wearing apparel dressing & dyeing of fur	..	..	..	214.0	229.0	237.5	273.9	259.7
		181	Wearing apparel, except fur apparel	..	..	..	..	..	..	..	..
		182	Dressing and dyeing of fur; articles of fur	..	..	..	..	..	..	..	..
	19		Tanning, dressing leather; leather artic.; footwear	..	..	..	88.6	80.4	77.1	76.1	76.3
		191	Tanning, dressing leather; manuf. of leather articles	..	..	..	..	..	..	..	..
		192	Footwear	..	..	..	..	..	..	..	..
	20		Wood and cork products, ex. furniture	..	..	..	96.0	94.7	95.7	108.6	116.0
		201	Sawmilling and planing of wood	..	..	..	..	..	..	..	..
		202	Products of wood, cork, straw & plaiting material	..	..	..	..	..	..	..	..
	21		Paper and paper products	..	..	..	37.2	35.7	39.8	37.9	39.4
	22		Publishing, printing & reprod. of recorded media	..	..	..	59.2	58.2	59.1	66.3	68.8
		221	Publishing	..	..	..	..	..	..	..	..
		222	Printing and related service activities	..	..	..	..	..	..	..	..
		223	Reproduction of recorded media	..	..	..	..	..	..	..	..
	23		Coke, refined petroleum products & nuclear fuel	..	..	..	23.2	23.4	23.6	23.4	23.3
	24		Chemicals and chemical products	..	..	..	139.7	136.1	140.7	141.4	140.0
		241	Basic chemicals	..	..	..	..	..	..	..	..
		242	Other chemical products	..	..	..	..	..	..	..	..
		243	Man-made fibres	..	..	..	..	..	..	..	..
	25		Rubber and plastic products	..	..	..	71.4	77.0	85.4	89.1	95.4
		251	Rubber products	..	..	..	..	..	..	..	..
		252	Plastic products	..	..	..	..	..	..	..	..
	26		Other non-metallic mineral products	..	..	..	172.2	167.8	160.2	166.0	165.7
		261	Glass and glass products	..	..	..	..	..	..	..	..
		269	Non-metallic mineral products, nec	..	..	..	..	..	..	..	..
	27		Basic metals	..	..	..	166.4	165.1	154.0	150.1	153.6
		271	Basic iron and steel	..	..	..	..	..	..	..	..
		272	Basic precious and non-ferrous metals	..	..	..	..	..	..	..	..
		273	Casting of metals	..	..	..	..	..	..	..	..
	28		Fabricated metal products, ex. machin. & equip.	..	..	..	151.1	141.4	146.4	161.4	174.0
		281	Structural metal prod., tanks, reservoirs, generators	..	..	..	..	..	..	..	..
		289	Other fabricated metal products & service activities	..	..	..	..	..	..	..	..
	29		Machinery and equipment, nec	..	..	..	328.2	311.5	298.3	299.5	286.9
		291	General purpose machinery	..	..	..	..	..	..	..	..
		292	Special purpose machinery	..	..	..	..	..	..	..	..
		293	Domestic appliances, nec	..	..	..	..	..	..	..	..
	30		Office, accounting and computing machinery	..	..	..	6.5	4.8	3.9	4.2	4.1
	31		Electrical machinery and apparatus, nec	..	..	..	87.1	84.5	87.9	90.3	91.0
		311	Electric motors, generators and transformers	..	..	..	..	..	..	..	..
		312	Electricity distribution and control apparatus	..	..	..	..	..	..	..	..
		313	Insulated wire and cable	..	..	..	..	..	..	..	..
		314	Accumulators, primary cells and primary batteries	..	..	..	..	..	..	..	..
		315	Electric lamps and lighting equipment	..	..	..	..	..	..	..	..
		319	Other electrical equipment, nec	..	..	..	..	..	..	..	..
	32		Radio, TV, communication equip. & apparatus	..	..	..	61.3	52.9	48.6	45.2	42.2
		321	Electronic valves, tubes & other electronic compon.	..	..	..	..	..	..	..	..
		322	TV, radio transmitters & appar. for line teleph., telegr.	..	..	..	..	..	..	..	..
		323	TV, radio receivers and associated goods	..	..	..	..	..	..	..	..
	33		Medical, precision, optical instr.; watches, clocks	..	..	..	44.2	39.6	41.0	42.4	42.6
		331	Medical equip.; precision instruments and appliances	..	..	..	..	..	..	..	..
		332	Optical instruments and photographic equipment	..	..	..	..	..	..	..	..
		333	Watches and clocks	..	..	..	..	..	..	..	..
	34		Motor vehicles, trailers, and semi-trailers	..	..	..	110.7	97.3	101.5	99.1	100.5
	35		Other transport equipment	..	..	..	122.9	117.3	116.0	113.5	108.2
		351	Building and repairing of ships and boats	..	..	..	..	..	..	..	..
		352	Railway, tramway locomotives and rolling stock	..	..	..	..	..	..	..	..
		353	Aircraft and spacecraft	..	..	..	..	..	..	..	..
		359	Transport equipment, nec	..	..	..	..	..	..	..	..
	36		Furniture; manufacturing, nec	..	..	..	124.8	127.3	131.9	153.3	156.6
		361	Furniture	..	..	..	..	..	..	..	..
		369	Manufacturing, nec	..	..	..	..	..	..	..	..
	37		Recycling	..	..	..	6.0	5.4	6.6	6.3	6.3
E	40-41		Electricity, gas and water supply	..	..	..	243.3	271.1	276.0	277.5	277.0
	40		Electricity, gas, steam and hot water supply	..	..	..	..	..	..	..	..
		401	Production, collection and distribution of electricity	..	..	..	..	..	..	..	..
	41	410	Collection, purification, distribution of water	..	..	..	..	..	..	..	..
F	45		Construction	..	..	..	823.0	721.9	678.8	689.2	684.2
G	50-52		Wholesale and retail trade; repairs etc	..	..	..	1 042.1	999.4	996.1	1 078.6	1 119.7
H	55		Hotels and restaurants	..	..	..	101.6	105.3	122.5	128.2	133.8
I	60-64		Transport, storage and communications	..	..	..	794.7	746.5	728.1	723.4	721.9
J	65-67		Financial intermediation	..	..	..	185.5	209.8	225.2	237.4	248.6
K	70-74		Real estate, renting and business activities	..	..	..	426.7	381.1	366.4	414.4	425.3
L-Q	75-99		Public admin.; education; health; other services	..	..	..	2 330.3	2 287.8	2 357.3	2 393.5	2 418.4
A-Q	01-99		Grand total	..	..	..	9 575.1	9 163.4	9 105.7	9 360.0	9 479.8

Table PO.6 SALAIRES ET TRAITEMENTS, SALARIÉS - WAGES AND SALARIES, EMPLOYEES

Millions de PLN (Prix courants)

1989	1990	1991	1992	1993	1994	1995	1996			CITI révision 3
..	..	..	1102	1179	1332	1667	1879	**Agriculture, chasse et sylviculture**	A	01-02
..	..	..	57	59	70	80	89	**Pêche**	B	05
..	..	..	2613	3444	4918	6006	7171	**Activités extractives**	C	10-14
..	..	..	2214	2999	4265	5094	6085	Extraction de charbon, de lignite et de tourbe		10
..	..	..	40	4	5	8	10	Extraction de pétrole brut et de gaz naturel		11
..	..	..	207	257	399	559	653	Extraction de minerais métalliques		13
..	..	..	153	185	249	345	423	Autres activités extractives		14
..	..	..	8625	11709	15970	22097	27970	**Activités de fabrication**	D	15-37
..	..	..	1505	1967	2516	3535	4535	**Produits alimentaires et boissons**		15
..	..	..	..	..	..	..	..	Boissons		155
..	..	..	44	72	107	147	230	**Produits à base de tabac**		16	160
..	..	..	492	635	861	1073	1235	**Textiles**		17
..	..	..	..	..	..	..	..	Filature, tissage et achèvement des textiles		171
..	..	..	..	..	..	..	..	Autres articles textiles		172
..	..	..	..	..	..	..	..	Etoffes et articles de bonneterie		173
..	..	..	507	768	1024	1461	1676	**Habillement; préparation, teinture des fourrures**		18
..	..	..	..	..	..	..	..	Articles d'habillement autres qu'en fourrure		181
..	..	..	..	..	..	..	..	Préparation, teinture des fourrures; art. en fourrure		182
..	..	..	212	265	332	436	551	**Travail des cuirs; articles en cuir; chaussures**		19
..	..	..	..	..	..	..	..	Apprêt et tannage des cuirs et articles en cuirs		191
..	..	..	..	..	..	..	..	Chaussures		192
..	..	..	243	349	492	714	914	**Bois et articles en bois et liège (sauf meubles)**		20
..	..	..	..	..	..	..	..	Sciage et rabotage du bois		201
..	..	..	..	..	..	..	..	Articles en bois, liège, vannerie, sparterie		202
..	..	..	127	172	258	372	485	**Papier et carton; articles en papier et en carton**		21
..	..	..	230	312	433	648	856	**Edition, imprimerie et reproduction**		22
..	..	..	..	..	..	..	..	Edition		221
..	..	..	..	..	..	..	..	Imprimerie et activités annexes		222
..	..	..	..	..	..	..	..	Reproduction de supports enregistrés		223
..	..	..	130	203	289	390	462	**Cokéfaction; prod. pétroliers; comb. nucléaires**		23
..	..	..	503	706	1064	1512	1943	**Produits chimiques**		24
..	..	..	..	..	..	..	..	Produits chimiques de base		241
..	..	..	..	..	..	..	..	Autres produits chimiques		242
..	..	..	..	..	..	..	..	Fibres synthétiques ou artificielles		243
..	..	..	228	357	539	766	996	**Articles en caoutchouc et en matières plastiques**		25
..	..	..	..	..	..	..	..	Articles en caoutchouc		251
..	..	..	..	..	..	..	..	Articles en matières plastiques		252
..	..	..	510	689	932	1302	1642	**Autres produits minéraux non métalliques**		26
..	..	..	..	..	..	..	..	Verre et articles en verre		261
..	..	..	..	..	..	..	..	Produits minéraux non métalliques, nca		269
..	..	..	640	860	1173	1594	2092	**Produits métallurgiques de base**		27
..	..	..	..	..	..	..	..	Sidérurgie et première transformation de l'acier		271
..	..	..	..	..	..	..	..	Métallurgie; métaux précieux et non ferreux		272
..	..	..	..	..	..	..	..	Fonderie		273
..	..	..	452	594	829	1208	1655	**Ouvrages en métaux, sauf machines et matériel**		28
..	..	..	..	..	..	..	..	Constr. et menuiserie métal.; réservoirs; générateurs		281
..	..	..	..	..	..	..	..	Autres ouvrages en métaux		289
..	..	..	1039	1368	1795	2425	2994	**Machines et matériel, nca**		29
..	..	..	..	..	..	..	..	Machines d'usage général		291
..	..	..	..	..	..	..	..	Machines d'usage spécifique		292
..	..	..	..	..	..	..	..	Appareils domestiques, nca		293
..	..	..	22	27	28	38	49	**Mach. de bureau, comptables, matériel inform.**		30
..	..	..	283	406	580	789	1023	**Machines et appareils électriques, nca**		31
..	..	..	..	..	..	..	..	Moteurs, génératrices et transformateurs électriques		311
..	..	..	..	..	..	..	..	Matériel électrique de distribution et de commande		312
..	..	..	..	..	..	..	..	Fils et câbles électriques isolés		313
..	..	..	..	..	..	..	..	Accumulateurs, piles électriques		314
..	..	..	..	..	..	..	..	Lampes électriques et appareils d'éclairage		315
..	..	..	..	..	..	..	..	Autres matériels électriques, nca		319
..	..	..	185	244	310	399	480	**Equip. et appar. de radio, TV, communication**		32
..	..	..	..	..	..	..	..	Tubes et valves électroniques; autres composants		321
..	..	..	..	..	..	..	..	Emetteurs radio et TV; app. téléphonie, télégraphie		322
..	..	..	..	..	..	..	..	Récepteurs radio et TV et articles associés		323
..	..	..	140	186	268	373	473	**Instruments médicaux, de précision, d'optique**		33
..	..	..	..	..	..	..	..	Appareils médicaux et de précision		331
..	..	..	..	..	..	..	..	Instruments d'optique ; matériel photographique		332
..	..	..	..	..	..	..	..	Horlogerie		333
..	..	..	359	459	656	855	1159	**Véhicules automobiles et nemorques**		34
..	..	..	422	567	781	1009	1207	**Autres matériels de transport**		35
..	..	..	..	..	..	..	..	Construction et réparation de navires		351
..	..	..	..	..	..	..	..	Construction de matériel ferroviaire roulant		352
..	..	..	..	..	..	..	..	Construction aéronautique et spatiale		353
..	..	..	..	..	..	..	..	Autres équipements de transport		359
..	..	..	328	473	647	987	1230	**Meubles; activités de fabrication, nca**		36
..	..	..	..	..	..	..	..	Meubles		361
..	..	..	..	..	..	..	..	Activités de fabrication, nca		369
..	..	..	25	31	59	66	81	**Récupération**		37
..	..	..	1101	1800	2609	3363	4177	**Production et distrib. d'électricité, de gaz, d'eau**	E	40-41
..	..	..	896	1514	2213	2851	3522	**Electricité, gaz, vapeur et eau chaude**		40
..	..	..	..	..	..	..	..	Production, collecte et distribution d'électricité		401
..	..	..	205	286	396	512	655	**Captage, épuration et distribution d'eau**		41	410
..	..	..	2625	3075	3670	4763	6000	**Construction**	F	45
..	..	..	2510	3872	5224	7452	9664	**Commerce de gros et de détail; réparation**	G	50-52
..	..	..	225	330	537	756	974	**Hôtels et restaurants**	H	55
..	..	..	2776	3701	4875	6308	7941	**Transports, entreposage et communications**	I	60-64
..	..	..	966	1470	2072	2850	3904	**Intermédiation financière**	J	65-67
..	..	..	1535	1942	2480	3437	4840	**Immobilier, locations, services aux entreprises**	K	70-74
..	..	..	7547	10027	13423	18279	23549	**Admin. publique; éducation; santé; autres**	L-Q	75-99
..	..	..	31680	42608	57180	77058	98158	**Grand total**	A-Q	01-99

Statistiques des Structures Industrielles
OCDE, © 1998

Table SP.1 PRODUCTION - PRODUCTION

Billions of Ptas (Current Prices)

ISIC revision 3			1989	1990	1991	1992	1993	1994	1995	1996
A	01-02	Agriculture, hunting and forestry	..	..	..	..	..	..	..	..
B	05	Fishing	..	..	..	..	..	..	..	..
C	10-14	Mining and quarrying	..	..	..	..	574	576	652	..
	10	Mining of coal and lignite; extraction of peat	..	..	..	..	288	285	290	..
	11	Crude petroleum & natural gas; related service activ.	..	..	..	..	55	49	47	..
	13	Mining of metal ores	..	..	..	..	24	22	37	..
	14	Other mining and quarrying	..	..	..	..	208	220	279	..
D	15-37	Total manufacturing	..	..	..	..	30 568	34 872	39 708	..
	15	Food products and beverages	..	..	..	..	7 010	7 685	8 294	..
	155	Beverages	..	..	..	..	1 287	1 380	1 468	..
	16 160	Tobacco products	..	..	..	..	261	292	283	..
	17	Textiles	..	..	..	..	910	1 044	1 161	..
	171	Spinning, weaving and finishing of textiles	..	..	..	..	514	589	650	..
	172	Other textiles	..	..	..	..	222	288	329	..
	173	Knitted and crocheted fabrics and articles	..	..	..	..	174	167	182	..
	18	Wearing apparel dressing & dyeing of fur	..	..	..	..	812	873	863	..
	181	Wearing apparel, except fur apparel	..	..	..	..	774	824	824	..
	182	Dressing and dyeing of fur; articles of fur	..	..	..	..	38	49	40	..
	19	Tanning, dressing leather; leather artic.; footwear	..	..	..	..	604	728	816	..
	191	Tanning, dressing leather; manuf. of leather articles	..	..	..	..	208	254	226	..
	192	Footwear	..	..	..	..	396	475	589	..
	20	Wood and cork products, ex. furniture	..	..	..	..	672	740	889	..
	201	Sawmilling and planing of wood	..	..	..	..	91	97	121	..
	202	Products of wood, cork, straw & plaiting material	..	..	..	..	581	643	768	..
	21	Paper and paper products	..	..	..	..	808	965	1 266	..
	22	Publishing, printing & reprod. of recorded media	..	..	..	..	1 353	1 498	1 660	..
	221	Publishing	..	..	..	..	698	805	843	..
	222	Printing and related service activities	..	..	..	..	640	683	804	..
	223	Reproduction of recorded media	..	..	..	..	16	10	13	..
	23	Coke, refined petroleum products & nuclear fuel	..	..	..	..	1 125	1 157	1 255	..
	24	Chemicals and chemical products	..	..	..	..	2 959	3 470	3 883	..
	241	Basic chemicals	..	..	..	..	971	1 323	1 496	..
	242	Other chemical products	..	..	..	..	1 903	2 031	2 249	..
	243	Man-made fibres	..	..	..	..	85	116	138	..
	25	Rubber and plastic products	..	..	..	..	1 038	1 262	1 534	..
	251	Rubber products	..	..	..	..	302	359	433	..
	252	Plastic products	..	..	..	..	736	904	1 101	..
	26	Other non-metallic mineral products	..	..	..	..	1 828	2 004	2 221	..
	261	Glass and glass products	..	..	..	..	244	293	342	..
	269	Non-metallic mineral products, nec	..	..	..	..	1 583	1 711	1 879	..
	27	Basic metals	..	..	..	..	1 485	1 764	2 312	..
	271	Basic iron and steel	..	..	..	..	912	1 085	1 481	..
	272	Basic precious and non-ferrous metals	..	..	..	..	362	445	548	..
	273	Casting of metals	..	..	..	..	212	234	283	..
	28	Fabricated metal products, ex. machin. & equip.	..	..	..	..	1 849	2 099	2 583	..
	281	Structural metal prod., tanks, reservoirs, generators	..	..	..	..	655	770	947	..
	289	Other fabricated metal products & service activities	..	..	..	..	1 194	1 329	1 636	..
	29	Machinery and equipment, nec	..	..	..	..	1 410	1 717	1 963	..
	291	General purpose machinery	..	..	..	..	605	705	858	..
	292	Special purpose machinery	..	..	..	..	539	687	765	..
	293	Domestic appliances, nec	..	..	..	..	265	325	340	..
	30	Office, accounting and computing machinery	..	..	..	..	251	306	358	..
	31	Electrical machinery and apparatus, nec	..	..	..	..	891	1 014	1 195	..
	311	Electric motors, generators and transformers	..	..	..	..	139	154	182	..
	312	Electricity distribution and control apparatus	..	..	..	..	145	160	203	..
	313	Insulated wire and cable	..	..	..	..	113	149	179	..
	314	Accumulators, primary cells and primary batteries	..	..	..	..	54	57	56	..
	315	Electric lamps and lighting equipment	..	..	..	..	109	113	126	..
	319	Other electrical equipment, nec	..	..	..	..	332	382	449	..
	32	Radio, TV, communication equip. & apparatus	..	..	..	..	499	552	630	..
	321	Electronic valves, tubes & other electronic compon.	..	..	..	..	111	150	170	..
	322	TV, radio transmitters & appar. for line teleph., telegr.	..	..	..	..	256	250	278	..
	323	TV, radio receivers and associated goods	..	..	..	..	132	151	181	..
	33	Medical, precision, optical instr.; watches, clocks	..	..	..	..	245	257	283	..
	331	Medical equip.; precision instruments and appliances	..	..	..	..	206	215	243	..
	332	Optical instruments and photographic equipment	..	..	..	..	33	39	35	..
	333	Watches and clocks	..	..	..	..	6	3	6	..
	34	Motor vehicles, trailers, and semi-trailers	..	..	..	..	2 914	3 750	4 397	..
	35	Other transport equipment	..	..	..	..	592	572	640	..
	351	Building and repairing of ships and boats	..	..	..	..	267	251	289	..
	352	Railway, tramway locomotives and rolling stock	..	..	..	..	126	108	133	..
	353	Aircraft and spacecraft	..	..	..	..	143	146	139	..
	359	Transport equipment, nec	..	..	..	..	56	66	79	..
	36	Furniture; manufacturing, nec	..	..	..	..	1 024	1 077	1 174	..
	361	Furniture	..	..	..	..	739	777	850	..
	369	Manufacturing, nec	..	..	..	..	285	301	325	..
	37	Recycling	..	..	..	..	30	46	47	..
E	40-41	Electricity, gas and water supply	..	..	..	..	2 730	2 774	3 010	..
	40	Electricity, gas, steam and hot water supply	..	..	..	..	2 521	2 536	2 747	..
	401	Production, collection and distribution of electricity	..	..	..	..	2 310	2 296	2 469	..
	41 410	Collection, purification, distribution of water	..	..	..	..	209	238	263	..
F	45	Construction	..	..	..	..	..	..	..	..
G	50-52	Wholesale and retail trade; repairs etc	..	..	..	..	..	..	..	..
H	55	Hotels and restaurants	..	..	..	..	..	..	..	..
I	60-64	Transport, storage and communications	..	..	..	..	..	..	..	..
J	65-67	Financial intermediation	..	..	..	..	..	..	..	..
K	70-74	Real estate, renting and business activities	..	..	..	..	..	..	..	..
L-Q	75-99	Public admin.; education; health; other services	..	..	..	..	..	..	..	..
A-Q	01-99	Grand total	..	..	..	..	..	..	..	..

Table SP.2 VALEUR AJOUTÉE - VALUE ADDED

Milliards de Ptas (Prix courants)

1989	1990	1991	1992	1993	1994	1995	1996			CITI révision 3
..	..	..	..	..	..	..	..	**Agriculture, chasse et sylviculture**	A	01-02
..	..	..	..	..	..	..	..	**Pêche**	B	05
..	..	..	..	309	310	332	..	**Activités extractives**	C	10-14
..	..	..	..	197	192	191	..	Extraction de charbon, de lignite et de tourbe		10
..	..	..	..	19	18	14	..	Extraction de pétrole brut et de gaz naturel		11
..	..	..	..	8	8	12	..	Extraction de minerais métalliques		13
..	..	..	..	86	92	114	..	Autres activités extractives		14
..	..	..	..	9 777	10 731	11 760	..	**Activités de fabrication**	D	15-37
..	..	..	..	1 751	1 834	1 859	..	**Produits alimentaires et boissons**		15
..	..	..	..	455	443	466	..	Boissons		155
..	..	..	..	76	99	87	..	**Produits à base de tabac**	16	160
..	..	..	..	313	350	367	..	**Textiles**		17
..	..	..	..	178	191	204	..	Filature, tissage et achèvement des textiles		171
..	..	..	..	77	98	103	..	Autres articles textiles		172
..	..	..	..	58	60	60	..	Etoffes et articles de bonneterie		173
..	..	..	..	294	285	289	..	**Habillement; préparation, teinture des fourrures**		18
..	..	..	..	282	272	279	..	Articles d'habillement autres qu'en fourrure		181
..	..	..	..	12	13	10	..	Préparation, teinture des fourrures; art. en fourrure		182
..	..	..	..	158	173	179	..	**Travail des cuirs; articles en cuir; chaussures**		19
..	..	..	..	59	60	58	..	Apprêt et tannage des cuirs et articles en cuirs		191
..	..	..	..	99	113	121	..	Chaussures		192
..	..	..	..	229	239	275	..	**Bois et articles en bois et liège (sauf meubles)**		20
..	..	..	..	28	28	35	..	Sciage et rabotage du bois		201
..	..	..	..	201	211	241	..	Articles en bois, liège, vannerie, sparterie		202
..	..	..	..	246	293	375	..	**Papier et carton; articles en papier et en carton**		21
..	..	..	..	570	604	629	..	**Edition, imprimerie et reproduction**		22
..	..	..	..	263	304	292	..	Edition		221
..	..	..	..	301	297	333	..	Imprimerie et activités annexes		222
..	..	..	..	5	4	4	..	Reproduction de supports enregistrés		223
..	..	..	..	187	150	183	..	**Cokéfaction; prod. pétroliers; comb. nucléaires**		23
..	..	..	..	957	1 097	1 210	..	**Produits chimiques**		24
..	..	..	..	251	356	426	..	Produits chimiques de base		241
..	..	..	..	677	695	739	..	Autres produits chimiques		242
..	..	..	..	29	46	44	..	Fibres synthétiques ou artificielles		243
..	..	..	..	413	480	532	..	**Articles en caoutchouc et en matières plastiques**		25
..	..	..	..	139	162	182	..	Articles en caoutchouc		251
..	..	..	..	274	317	350	..	Articles en matières plastiques		252
..	..	..	..	708	818	902	..	**Autres produits minéraux non métalliques**		26
..	..	..	..	114	135	151	..	Verre et articles en verre		261
..	..	..	..	594	683	751	..	Produits minéraux non métalliques, nca		269
..	..	..	..	383	460	657	..	**Produits métallurgiques de base**		27
..	..	..	..	224	280	421	..	Sidérurgie et première transformation de l'acier		271
..	..	..	..	72	92	131	..	Métallurgie; métaux précieux et non ferreux		272
..	..	..	..	88	88	105	..	Fonderie		273
..	..	..	..	741	822	954	..	**Ouvrages en métaux, sauf machines et matériel**		28
..	..	..	..	253	286	309	..	Constr. et menuiserie métal.; réservoirs; générateurs		281
..	..	..	..	488	536	645	..	Autres ouvrages en métaux		289
..	..	..	..	595	674	725	..	**Machines et matériel, nca**		29
..	..	..	..	269	300	341	..	Machines d'usage général		291
..	..	..	..	229	264	287	..	Machines d'usage spécifique		292
..	..	..	..	97	109	97	..	Appareils domestiques, nca		293
..	..	..	..	104	115	114	..	**Mach. de bureau, comptables, matériel inform.**		30
..	..	..	..	350	385	426	..	**Machines et appareils électriques, nca**		31
..	..	..	..	51	57	60	..	Moteurs, génératrices et transformateurs électriques		311
..	..	..	..	60	69	78	..	Matériel électrique de distribution et de commande		312
..	..	..	..	35	44	53	..	Fils et câbles électriques isolés		313
..	..	..	..	22	20	20	..	Accumulateurs, piles électriques		314
..	..	..	..	39	38	43	..	Lampes électriques et appareils d'éclairage		315
..	..	..	..	142	157	173	..	Autres matériels électriques, nca		319
..	..	..	..	200	219	202	..	**Equip. et appar. de radio, TV, communication**		32
..	..	..	..	52	68	65	..	Tubes et valves électroniques; autres composants		321
..	..	..	..	118	114	102	..	Emetteurs radio et TV; app. téléphonie, télégraphie		322
..	..	..	..	30	36	34	..	Récepteurs radio et TV et articles associés		323
..	..	..	..	110	112	118	..	**Instruments médicaux, de précision, d'optique**		33
..	..	..	..	92	92	101	..	Appareils médicaux et de précision		331
..	..	..	..	16	19	15	..	Instruments d'optique ; matériel photographique		332
..	..	..	..	2	1	2	..	Horlogerie		333
..	..	..	..	744	887	1 005	..	**Véhicules automobiles et remorques**		34
..	..	..	..	244	234	245	..	**Autres matériels de transport**		35
..	..	..	..	101	103	107	..	Construction et réparation de navires		351
..	..	..	..	46	35	45	..	Construction de matériel ferroviaire roulant		352
..	..	..	..	80	78	73	..	Construction aéronautique et spatiale		353
..	..	..	..	17	18	20	..	Autres équipements de transport		359
..	..	..	..	398	390	418	..	**Meubles; activités de fabrication, nca**		36
..	..	..	..	288	284	304	..	Meubles		361
..	..	..	..	110	106	114	..	Activités de fabrication, nca		369
..	..	..	..	9	10	10	..	**Récupération**		37
..	..	..	..	1 671	1 659	1 725	..	**Production et distrib. d'électricité, de gaz, d'eau**	E	40-41
..	..	..	..	1 563	1 536	1 598	..	**Electricité, gaz, vapeur et eau chaude**		40
..	..	..	..	1 476	1 435	1 477	..	Production, collecte et distribution d'électricité		401
..	..	..	..	108	123	126	..	**Captage, épuration et distribution d'eau**	41	410
..	..	..	..	..	..	..	..	**Construction**	F	45
..	..	..	..	..	..	..	..	**Commerce de gros et de détail; réparation**	G	50-52
..	..	..	..	..	..	..	..	**Hôtels et restaurants**	H	55
..	..	..	..	..	..	..	..	**Transports, entreposage et communications**	I	60-64
..	..	..	..	..	..	..	..	**Intermédiation financière**	J	65-67
..	..	..	..	..	..	..	..	**Immobilier, locations, services aux entreprises**	K	70-74
..	..	..	..	..	..	..	..	**Admin. publique; éducation; santé; autres**	L-Q	75-99
..	..	..	..	..	..	..	..	**Grand total**	A-Q	01-99

Statistiques des Structures Industrielles
OCDE, © 1998

SPAIN

Table SP.3 INVESTMENT - INVESTISSEMENT

Billions of Ptas (Current Prices)

ISIC revision 3			1989	1990	1991	1992	1993	1994	1995	1996
A	01-02	**Agriculture, hunting and forestry**	..	..	..	..	..	..	..	..
B	05	**Fishing**	..	..	..	..	..	..	..	..
C	10-14	**Mining and quarrying**	..	..	..	..	57	62	72	..
	10	Mining of coal and lignite; extraction of peat	..	..	..	..	36	38	33	..
	11	Crude petroleum & natural gas; related service activ.	..	..	..	..	1	5	1	..
	13	Mining of metal ores	..	..	..	..	2	0	2	..
	14	Other mining and quarrying	..	..	..	..	17	19	35	..
D	15-37	**Total manufacturing**	..	..	..	..	1 322	1 250	1 502	..
	15	**Food products and beverages**	..	..	..	..	249	212	255	..
	155	Beverages	..	..	..	..	50	38	54	..
	16 160	**Tobacco products**	..	..	..	..	10	7	7	..
	17	**Textiles**	..	..	..	..	33	55	49	..
	171	Spinning, weaving and finishing of textiles	..	..	..	..	17	28	27	..
	172	Other textiles	..	..	..	..	10	20	15	..
	173	Knitted and crocheted fabrics and articles	..	..	..	..	6	7	7	..
	18	**Wearing apparel dressing & dyeing of fur**	..	..	..	..	11	20	16	..
	181	Wearing apparel, except fur apparel	..	..	..	..	10	20	16	..
	182	Dressing and dyeing of fur; articles of fur	..	..	..	..	1	1	0	..
	19	**Tanning, dressing leather; leather artic.; footwear**	..	..	..	..	9	11	12	..
	191	Tanning, dressing leather; manuf. of leather articles	..	..	..	..	2	4	4	..
	192	Footwear	..	..	..	..	7	7	8	..
	20	**Wood and cork products, ex. furniture**	..	..	..	..	20	24	33	..
	201	Sawmilling and planing of wood	..	..	..	..	2	2	4	..
	202	Products of wood, cork, straw & plaiting material	..	..	..	..	18	21	29	..
	21	**Paper and paper products**	..	..	..	..	47	50	62	..
	22	**Publishing, printing & reprod. of recorded media**	..	..	..	..	57	44	74	..
	221	Publishing	..	..	..	..	19	19	22	..
	222	Printing and related service activities	..	..	..	..	38	24	50	..
	223	Reproduction of recorded media	..	..	..	..	0	1	1	..
	23	**Coke, refined petroleum products & nuclear fuel**	..	..	..	..	42	34	32	..
	24	**Chemicals and chemical products**	..	..	..	..	131	131	163	..
	241	Basic chemicals	..	..	..	..	51	51	79	..
	242	Other chemical products	..	..	..	..	78	78	78	..
	243	Man-made fibres	..	..	..	..	2	2	6	..
	25	**Rubber and plastic products**	..	..	..	..	57	65	78	..
	251	Rubber products	..	..	..	..	16	15	21	..
	252	Plastic products	..	..	..	..	41	51	57	..
	26	**Other non-metallic mineral products**	..	..	..	..	94	86	128	..
	261	Glass and glass products	..	..	..	..	14	10	26	..
	269	Non-metallic mineral products, nec	..	..	..	..	79	76	102	..
	27	**Basic metals**	..	..	..	..	62	52	83	..
	271	Basic iron and steel	..	..	..	..	41	25	43	..
	272	Basic precious and non-ferrous metals	..	..	..	..	13	15	10	..
	273	Casting of metals	..	..	..	..	9	12	30	..
	28	**Fabricated metal products, ex. machin. & equip.**	..	..	..	..	92	84	96	..
	281	Structural metal prod., tanks, reservoirs, generators	..	..	..	..	24	18	18	..
	289	Other fabricated metal products & service activities	..	..	..	..	68	65	78	..
	29	**Machinery and equipment, nec**	..	..	..	..	44	56	57	..
	291	General purpose machinery	..	..	..	..	21	19	28	..
	292	Special purpose machinery	..	..	..	..	13	24	20	..
	293	Domestic appliances, nec	..	..	..	..	10	13	9	..
	30	**Office, accounting and computing machinery**	..	..	..	..	31	14	11	..
	31	**Electrical machinery and apparatus, nec**	..	..	..	..	30	30	43	..
	311	Electric motors, generators and transformers	..	..	..	..	2	2	4	..
	312	Electricity distribution and control apparatus	..	..	..	..	7	4	8	..
	313	Insulated wire and cable	..	..	..	..	3	4	5	..
	314	Accumulators, primary cells and primary batteries	..	..	..	..	2	3	2	..
	315	Electric lamps and lighting equipment	..	..	..	..	4	5	6	..
	319	Other electrical equipment, nec	..	..	..	..	10	12	18	..
	32	**Radio, TV, communication equip. & apparatus**	..	..	..	..	18	17	21	..
	321	Electronic valves, tubes & other electronic compon.	..	..	..	..	7	7	10	..
	322	TV, radio transmitters & appar. for line teleph., telegr.	..	..	..	..	5	5	7	..
	323	TV, radio receivers and associated goods	..	..	..	..	7	5	4	..
	33	**Medical, precision, optical instr.; watches, clocks**	..	..	..	..	4	4	8	..
	331	Medical equip.; precision instruments and appliances	..	..	..	..	6	3	7	..
	332	Optical instruments and photographic equipment	..	..	..	..	- 2	0	1	..
	333	Watches and clocks	..	..	..	..	0	0	0	..
	34	**Motor vehicles, trailers, and semi-trailers**	..	..	..	..	226	204	211	..
	35	**Other transport equipment**	..	..	..	..	18	17	17	..
	351	Building and repairing of ships and boats	..	..	..	..	7	7	7	..
	352	Railway, tramway locomotives and rolling stock	..	..	..	..	6	3	- 1	..
	353	Aircraft and spacecraft	..	..	..	..	4	5	6	..
	359	Transport equipment, nec	..	..	..	..	2	2	5	..
	36	**Furniture; manufacturing, nec**	..	..	..	..	34	33	43	..
	361	Furniture	..	..	..	..	24	24	35	..
	369	Manufacturing, nec	..	..	..	..	10	8	8	..
	37	**Recycling**	..	..	..	..	1	1	2	..
E	40-41	**Electricity, gas and water supply**	..	..	..	..	395	456	447	..
	40	**Electricity, gas, steam and hot water supply**	..	..	..	..	362	425	407	..
	401	Production, collection and distribution of electricity	..	..	..	..	320	381	326	..
	41 410	**Collection, purification, distribution of water**	..	..	..	..	34	31	41	..
F	45	**Construction**	..	..	..	..	..	..	..	..
G	50-52	**Wholesale and retail trade; repairs etc**	..	..	..	..	..	..	..	..
H	55	**Hotels and restaurants**	..	..	..	..	..	..	..	..
I	60-64	**Transport, storage and communications**	..	..	..	..	..	..	..	..
J	65-67	**Financial intermediation**	..	..	..	..	..	..	..	..
K	70-74	**Real estate, renting and business activities**	..	..	..	..	..	..	..	..
L-Q	75-99	**Public admin.; education; health; other services**	..	..	..	..	..	..	..	..
A-Q	01-99	**Grand total**	..	..	..	..	..	..	..	..

Table SP.4 ETABLISSEMENTS - ESTABLISHMENTS

Unités

1989	1990	1991	1992	1993	1994	1995	1996			CITI révision 3
..	..	..	..	..	..	..		Agriculture, chasse et sylviculture	A	01-02
				..	..	..		Pêche	B	05
..	..	..	..	1 873	1 655	1 809	..	**Activités extractives**	C	**10-14**
..	..	..	..	170	152	148		Extraction de charbon, de lignite et de tourbe		10
..	..	..	..	14	14	13		Extraction de pétrole brut et de gaz naturel		11
..	..	..	..	45	41	37		Extraction de minerais métalliques		13
..	..	..	..	1 644	1 448	1 611		Autres activités extractives		14
..	..	..	..	144 133	150 413	149 135	..	**Activités de fabrication**	D	**15-37**
..	..	..	..	25 006	27 320	27 507	..	**Produits alimentaires et boissons**		**15**
..	..	..	..	2 703	2 838	2 565		Boissons		155
..	..	..	..	36	35	34		**Produits à base de tabac**		**16** 160
..	..	..	..	6 151	6 360	5 625		**Textiles**		**17**
..	..	..	..	2 465	2 496	2 160		Filature, tissage et achèvement des textiles		171
..	..	..	..	2 527	2 606	2 359		Autres articles textiles		172
..	..	..	..	1 158	1 259	1 106		Etoffes et articles de bonneterie		173
..	..	..	..	10 167	10 612	10 638		**Habillement; préparation, teinture des fourrures**		**18**
..	..	..	..	9 626	10 057	10 205		Articles d'habillement autres qu'en fourrure		181
..	..	..	..	541	555	433		Préparation, teinture des fourrures; art. en fourrure		182
..	..	..	..	4 952	5 088	5 300		**Travail des cuirs; articles en cuir; chaussures**		**19**
..	..	..	..	1 494	1 551	1 573		Apprêt et tannage des cuirs et articles en cuirs		191
..	..	..	..	3 458	3 537	3 727		Chaussures		192
..	..	..	..	11 825	12 062	12 316		**Bois et articles en bois et liège (sauf meubles)**		**20**
..	..	..	..	1 410	1 432	1 610		Sciage et rabotage du bois		201
..	..	..	..	10 415	10 630	10 707		Articles en bois, liège, vannerie, sparterie		202
..	..	..	..	1 607	1 931	1 475		**Papier et carton; articles en papier et en carton**		**21**
..	..	..	..	11 569	11 615	12 044		**Edition, imprimerie et reproduction**		**22**
..	..	..	..	2 421	2 228	2 606		Edition		221
..	..	..	..	9 109	9 351	9 403		Imprimerie et activités annexes		222
..	..	..	..	39	35	36		Reproduction de supports enregistrés		223
..	..	..	..	27	25	20		**Cokéfaction; prod. pétroliers; comb. nucléaires**		**23**
..	..	..	..	3 621	3 651	3 294		**Produits chimiques**		**24**
..	..	..	..	946	947	768		Produits chimiques de base		241
..	..	..	..	2 639	2 671	2 489		Autres produits chimiques		242
..	..	..	..	37	33	36		Fibres synthétiques ou artificielles		243
..	..	..	..	3 972	4 426	4 279		**Articles en caoutchouc et en matières plastiques**		**25**
..	..	..	..	748	804	716		Articles en caoutchouc		251
..	..	..	..	3 224	3 622	3 563		Articles en matières plastiques		252
..	..	..	..	9 702	10 155	10 012		**Autres produits minéraux non métalliques**		**26**
..	..	..	..	1 026	1 103	1 163		Verre et articles en verre		261
..	..	..	..	8 676	9 051	8 849		Produits minéraux non métalliques, nca		269
..	..	..	..	1 446	1 558	1 591		**Produits métallurgiques de base**		**27**
..	..	..	..	552	453	444		Sidérurgie et première transformation de l'acier		271
..	..	..	..	243	308	258		Métallurgie; métaux précieux et non ferreux		272
..	..	..	..	650	797	889		Fonderie		273
..	..	..	..	21 963	23 377	23 380		**Ouvrages en métaux, sauf machines et matériel**		**28**
..	..	..	..	11 590	12 158	12 287		Constr. et menuiserie métal.; réservoirs; générateurs		281
..	..	..	..	10 373	11 219	11 092		Autres ouvrages en métaux		289
..	..	..	..	8 239	8 672	8 651		**Machines et matériel, nca**		**29**
..	..	..	..	3 367	3 045	3 125		Machines d'usage général		291
..	..	..	..	4 589	5 324	5 197		Machines d'usage spécifique		292
..	..	..	..	283	303	329		Appareils domestiques, nca		293
..	..	..	..	116	122	136		**Mach. de bureau, comptables, matériel inform.**		**30**
..	..	..	..	3 252	3 086	3 153		**Machines et appareils électriques, nca**		**31**
..	..	..	..	421	436	469		Moteurs, génératrices et transformateurs électriques		311
..	..	..	..	391	429	359		Matériel électrique de distribution et de commande		312
..	..	..	..	155	139	157		Fils et câbles électriques isolés		313
..	..	..	..	17	16	14		Accumulateurs, piles électriques		314
..	..	..	..	898	819	753		Lampes électriques et appareils d'éclairage		315
..	..	..	..	1 371	1 247	1 401		Autres matériels électriques, nca		319
..	..	..	..	741	831	662		**Equip. et appar. de radio, TV, communication**		**32**
..	..	..	..	444	492	426		Tubes et valves électroniques; autres composants		321
..	..	..	..	143	149	121		Emetteurs radio et TV; app. téléphonie, télégraphie		322
..	..	..	..	154	191	116		Récepteurs radio et TV et articles associés		323
..	..	..	..	1 922	1 754	1 766		**Instruments médicaux, de précision, d'optique**		**33**
..	..	..	..	1 736	1 628	1 527		Appareils médicaux et de précision		331
..	..	..	..	97	76	126		Instruments d'optique ; matériel photographique		332
..	..	..	..	88	50	113		Horlogerie		333
..	..	..	..	1 446	1 666	1 628		**Véhicules automobiles et nemorques**		**34**
..	..	..	..	1 120	1 214	1 075		**Autres matériels de transport**		**35**
..	..	..	..	882	963	879		Construction et réparation de navires		351
..	..	..	..	48	50	50		Construction de matériel ferroviaire roulant		352
..	..	..	..	53	59	53		Construction aéronautique et spatiale		353
..	..	..	..	136	142	92		Autres équipements de transport		359
..	..	..	..	15 064	14 633	14 415		**Meubles; activités de fabrication, nca**		**36**
..	..	..	..	11 843	11 365	11 133		Meubles		361
..	..	..	..	3 221	3 268	3 282		Activités de fabrication, nca		369
..	..	..	..	189	221	136		**Récupération**		**37**
..	..	..	..	1 166	1 158	1 264	..	**Production et distrib. d'électricité, de gaz, d'eau**	E	**40-41**
..	..	..	..	706	694	758	..	**Electricité, gaz, vapeur et eau chaude**		**40**
..	..	..	..	492	469	544	..	Production, collecte et distribution d'électricité		401
..	..	..	..	460	464	506	..	**Captage, épuration et distribution d'eau**		**41** 410
..	..	..	..	..	..	..	..	**Construction**	F	**45**
..	..	..	..	..	..	..	..	**Commerce de gros et de détail; réparation**	G	**50-52**
..	..	..	..	..	..	..	..	**Hôtels et restaurants**	H	**55**
..	..	..	..	..	..	..	..	**Transports, entreposage et communications**	I	**60-64**
..	..	..	..	..	..	..	..	**Intermédiation financière**	J	**65-67**
..	..	..	..	..	..	..	..	**Immobilier, locations, services aux entreprises**	K	**70-74**
..	..	..	..	..	..	..	..	**Admin. publique; éducation; santé; autres**	L-Q	**75-99**
..	..	..	..	..	..	..	..	**Grand total**	A-Q	**01-99**

Statistiques des Structures Industrielles
OCDE, © 1998
OECD / OCDE

SPAIN

Table SP.5 EMPLOYMENT - EMPLOI

Thousands

ISIC revision 3			1989	1990	1991	1992	1993	1994	1995	1996
A	01-02	Agriculture, hunting and forestry	..	..	..	..	..	..	..	..
B	05	Fishing	..	..	..	..	..	..	..	..
C	10-14	Mining and quarrying	..	..	..	..	55.7	50.1	49.5	..
	10	Mining of coal and lignite; extraction of peat	..	..	..	..	32.7	30.3	27.9	..
	11	Crude petroleum & natural gas; related service activ.	..	..	..	..	1.0	0.8	0.8	..
	13	Mining of metal ores	..	..	..	..	3.2	2.1	2.3	..
	14	Other mining and quarrying	..	..	..	..	18.8	16.8	18.5	..
D	15-37	Total manufacturing	..	..	..	..	2 222.1	2 197.6	2 205.1	..
	15	Food products and beverages	..	..	..	..	369.5	368.8	363.6	..
		155 Beverages	..	..	..	..	54.1	51.9	48.0	..
	16	160 Tobacco products	..	..	..	..	10.6	9.7	9.3	..
	17	Textiles	..	..	..	..	96.6	100.4	96.3	..
		171 Spinning, weaving and finishing of textiles	..	..	..	..	51.1	51.8	50.0	..
		172 Other textiles	..	..	..	..	26.2	28.6	28.6	..
		173 Knitted and crocheted fabrics and articles	..	..	..	..	19.3	20.0	17.7	..
	18	Wearing apparel dressing & dyeing of fur	..	..	..	..	132.2	123.5	119.2	..
		181 Wearing apparel, except fur apparel	..	..	..	..	128.1	119.5	115.8	..
		182 Dressing and dyeing of fur; articles of fur	..	..	..	..	4.1	4.0	3.4	..
	19	Tanning, dressing leather; leather artic.; footwear	..	..	..	..	57.9	61.2	61.5	..
		191 Tanning, dressing leather; manuf. of leather articles	..	..	..	..	17.9	17.7	17.3	..
		192 Footwear	..	..	..	..	40.1	43.5	44.2	..
	20	Wood and cork products, ex. furniture	..	..	..	..	88.3	86.1	89.9	..
		201 Sawmilling and planing of wood	..	..	..	..	10.8	10.9	12.1	..
		202 Products of wood, cork, straw & plaiting material	..	..	..	..	77.5	75.3	77.8	..
	21	Paper and paper products	..	..	..	..	48.1	47.6	46.5	..
	22	Publishing, printing & reprod. of recorded media	..	..	..	..	117.0	114.3	115.9	..
		221 Publishing	..	..	..	..	38.0	38.0	38.0	..
		222 Printing and related service activities	..	..	..	..	78.1	75.5	77.1	..
		223 Reproduction of recorded media	..	..	..	..	0.9	0.7	0.8	..
	23	Coke, refined petroleum products & nuclear fuel	..	..	..	..	8.3	7.7	7.5	..
	24	Chemicals and chemical products	..	..	..	..	138.6	135.0	130.0	..
		241 Basic chemicals	..	..	..	..	35.9	35.3	32.3	..
		242 Other chemical products	..	..	..	..	96.8	93.7	91.7	..
		243 Man-made fibres	..	..	..	..	5.8	6.0	6.0	..
	25	Rubber and plastic products	..	..	..	..	88.3	93.9	95.6	..
		251 Rubber products	..	..	..	..	26.6	28.7	29.0	..
		252 Plastic products	..	..	..	..	61.7	65.2	66.6	..
	26	Other non-metallic mineral products	..	..	..	..	155.8	153.5	156.4	..
		261 Glass and glass products	..	..	..	..	24.0	23.1	23.4	..
		269 Non-metallic mineral products, nec	..	..	..	..	131.9	130.4	133.1	..
	27	Basic metals	..	..	..	..	80.2	72.5	72.6	..
		271 Basic iron and steel	..	..	..	..	45.3	38.6	38.0	..
		272 Basic precious and non-ferrous metals	..	..	..	..	14.4	14.5	13.4	..
		273 Casting of metals	..	..	..	..	20.4	19.5	21.1	..
	28	Fabricated metal products, ex. machin. & equip.	..	..	..	..	215.1	221.4	232.8	..
		281 Structural metal prod., tanks, reservoirs, generators	..	..	..	..	89.1	93.4	96.9	..
		289 Other fabricated metal products & service activities	..	..	..	..	126.0	128.0	135.9	..
	29	Machinery and equipment, nec	..	..	..	..	138.7	141.1	142.6	..
		291 General purpose machinery	..	..	..	..	60.6	59.5	61.8	..
		292 Special purpose machinery	..	..	..	..	58.5	62.1	61.8	..
		293 Domestic appliances, nec	..	..	..	..	19.7	19.5	18.9	..
	30	Office, accounting and computing machinery	..	..	..	..	7.9	8.3	9.7	..
	31	Electrical machinery and apparatus, nec	..	..	..	..	76.7	75.8	74.5	..
		311 Electric motors, generators and transformers	..	..	..	..	12.1	11.0	11.5	..
		312 Electricity distribution and control apparatus	..	..	..	..	13.2	12.8	13.3	..
		313 Insulated wire and cable	..	..	..	..	8.1	7.9	7.5	..
		314 Accumulators, primary cells and primary batteries	..	..	..	..	3.4	3.2	2.5	..
		315 Electric lamps and lighting equipment	..	..	..	..	10.3	10.0	9.5	..
		319 Other electrical equipment, nec	..	..	..	..	29.6	31.0	30.2	..
	32	Radio, TV, communication equip. & apparatus	..	..	..	..	30.3	29.7	28.9	..
		321 Electronic valves, tubes & other electronic compon.	..	..	..	..	9.9	10.6	11.0	..
		322 TV, radio transmitters & appar. for line teleph., telegr.	..	..	..	..	14.7	13.2	12.0	..
		323 TV, radio receivers and associated goods	..	..	..	..	5.8	5.8	6.0	..
	33	Medical, precision, optical instr.; watches, clocks	..	..	..	..	24.3	21.9	22.6	..
		331 Medical equip.; precision instruments and appliances	..	..	..	..	20.4	18.4	19.1	..
		332 Optical instruments and photographic equipment	..	..	..	..	3.3	3.1	2.9	..
		333 Watches and clocks	..	..	..	..	0.6	0.3	0.6	..
	34	Motor vehicles, trailers, and semi-trailers	..	..	..	..	141.5	136.1	138.3	..
	35	Other transport equipment	..	..	..	..	52.0	50.4	51.7	..
		351 Building and repairing of ships and boats	..	..	..	..	29.4	28.2	29.6	..
		352 Railway, tramway locomotives and rolling stock	..	..	..	..	7.8	7.7	7.7	..
		353 Aircraft and spacecraft	..	..	..	..	10.9	10.7	10.6	..
		359 Transport equipment, nec	..	..	..	..	3.8	3.8	3.8	..
	36	Furniture; manufacturing, nec	..	..	..	..	142.2	136.6	137.9	..
		361 Furniture	..	..	..	..	110.3	106.0	107.1	..
		369 Manufacturing, nec	..	..	..	..	31.9	30.6	30.8	..
	37	Recycling	..	..	..	..	2.1	2.0	1.7	..
E	40-41	Electricity, gas and water supply	..	..	..	..	72.0	69.6	68.1	..
	40	Electricity, gas, steam and hot water supply	..	..	..	..	56.3	53.6	51.2	..
		401 Production, collection and distribution of electricity	..	..	..	..	51.2	48.4	46.2	..
	41	410 Collection, purification, distribution of water	..	..	..	..	15.7	16.1	16.8	..
F	45	Construction	..	..	..	..	..	..	..	..
G	50-52	Wholesale and retail trade; repairs etc	..	..	..	..	..	..	..	..
H	55	Hotels and restaurants	..	..	..	..	..	..	..	..
I	60-64	Transport, storage and communications	..	..	..	..	..	..	..	..
J	65-67	Financial intermediation	..	..	..	..	..	..	..	..
K	70-74	Real estate, renting and business activities	..	..	..	..	..	..	..	..
L-Q	75-99	Public admin.; education; health; other services	..	..	..	..	..	..	..	..
A-Q	01-99	Grand total	..	..	..	..	..	..	..	..

Table SP.6 EMPLOI, SALARIÉS - EMPLOYMENT, EMPLOYEES

Milliers

1989	1990	1991	1992	1993	1994	1995	1996			CITI révision 3	
..	..	..	..	..	..	..	..	**Agriculture, chasse et sylviculture**	A	01-02	
..	..	..	..	..	..	..	..	**Pêche**	B	05	
..	..	..	..	54.9	49.2	48.6	..	**Activités extractives**	C	10-14	
..	..	..	..	32.7	30.3	27.9	..	Extraction de charbon, de lignite et de tourbe		10	
..	..	..	..	0.9	0.8	0.8	..	Extraction de pétrole brut et de gaz naturel		11	
..	..	..	..	3.2	2.1	2.3	..	Extraction de minerais métalliques		13	
..	..	..	..	18.1	16.0	17.6	..	Autres activités extractives		14	
..	..	..	..	2 110.9	2 073.2	2 073.5	..	**Activités de fabrication**	D	15-37	
..	..	..	..	345.5	343.6	335.3	..	**Produits alimentaires et boissons**		15	
..	..	..	..	52.1	50.0	46.3	..	Boissons			155
..	..	..	..	10.6	9.7	9.3	..	**Produits à base de tabac**		16	160
..	..	..	..	92.4	95.3	92.0	..	**Textiles**		17	
..	..	..	..	49.8	50.2	48.5	..	Filature, tissage et achèvement des textiles			171
..	..	..	..	24.5	26.4	26.8	..	Autres articles textiles			172
..	..	..	..	18.1	18.8	16.7	..	Etoffes et articles de bonneterie			173
..	..	..	..	122.3	113.7	108.3	..	**Habillement; préparation, teinture des fourrures**		18	
..	..	..	..	118.8	110.2	105.3	..	Articles d'habillement autres qu'en fourrure			181
..	..	..	..	3.5	3.5	3.0	..	Préparation, teinture des fourrures; art. en fourrure			182
..	..	..	..	55.4	57.4	57.5	..	**Travail des cuirs; articles en cuir; chaussures**		19	
..	..	..	..	16.9	16.3	15.9	..	Apprêt et tannage des cuirs et articles en cuirs			191
..	..	..	..	38.4	41.1	41.6	..	Chaussures			192
..	..	..	..	78.0	74.2	77.2	..	**Bois et articles en bois et liège (sauf meubles)**		20	
..	..	..	..	9.7	9.6	10.4	..	Sciage et rabotage du bois			201
..	..	..	..	68.3	64.6	66.8	..	Articles en bois, liège, vannerie, sparterie			202
..	..	..	..	47.3	46.6	45.5	..	**Papier et carton; articles en papier et en carton**		21	
..	..	..	..	108.8	106.4	106.6	..	**Edition, imprimerie et reproduction**		22	
..	..	..	..	36.2	37.3	36.0	..	Edition			221
..	..	..	..	71.7	68.4	69.8	..	Imprimerie et activités annexes			222
..	..	..	..	0.9	0.7	0.8	..	Reproduction de supports enregistrés			223
..	..	..	..	8.3	7.7	7.5	..	**Cokéfaction; prod. pétroliers; comb. nucléaires**		23	
..	..	..	..	136.8	132.1	128.3	..	**Produits chimiques**		24	
..	..	..	..	35.5	34.8	32.2	..	Produits chimiques de base			241
..	..	..	..	95.5	91.4	90.2	..	Autres produits chimiques			242
..	..	..	..	5.8	6.0	5.9	..	Fibres synthétiques ou artificielles			243
..	..	..	..	85.8	91.8	92.7	..	**Articles en caoutchouc et en matières plastiques**		25	
..	..	..	..	26.1	28.3	28.5	..	Articles en caoutchouc			251
..	..	..	..	59.7	63.5	64.1	..	Articles en matières plastiques			252
..	..	..	..	148.9	146.0	148.5	..	**Autres produits minéraux non métalliques**		26	
..	..	..	..	23.3	22.2	22.5	..	Verre et articles en verre			261
..	..	..	..	125.7	123.8	126.0	..	Produits minéraux non métalliques, nca			269
..	..	..	..	79.6	71.7	71.3	..	**Produits métallurgiques de base**		27	
..	..	..	..	45.1	38.3	37.8	..	Sidérurgie et première transformation de l'acier			271
..	..	..	..	14.4	14.4	13.3	..	Métallurgie; métaux précieux et non ferreux			272
..	..	..	..	20.1	18.9	20.2	..	Fonderie			273
..	..	..	..	197.9	200.7	212.3	..	**Ouvrages en métaux, sauf machines et matériel**		28	
..	..	..	..	78.8	81.9	85.8	..	Constr. et menuiserie métal.; réservoirs; générateurs			281
..	..	..	..	119.0	118.8	126.5	..	Autres ouvrages en métaux			289
..	..	..	..	133.6	134.3	136.1	..	**Machines et matériel, nca**		29	
..	..	..	..	58.6	57.3	59.9	..	Machines d'usage général			291
..	..	..	..	55.4	57.7	57.6	..	Machines d'usage spécifique			292
..	..	..	..	19.5	19.3	18.7	..	Appareils domestiques, nca			293
..	..	..	..	7.9	8.3	9.6	..	**Mach. de bureau, comptables, matériel inform.**		30	
..	..	..	..	74.7	73.6	72.4	..	**Machines et appareils électriques, nca**		31	
..	..	..	..	11.8	10.8	11.1	..	Moteurs, génératrices et transformateurs électriques			311
..	..	..	..	12.9	12.5	13.2	..	Matériel électrique de distribution et de commande			312
..	..	..	..	8.1	7.9	7.5	..	Fils et câbles électriques isolés			313
..	..	..	..	3.4	3.2	2.5	..	Accumulateurs, piles électriques			314
..	..	..	..	9.9	9.2	9.0	..	Lampes électriques et appareils d'éclairage			315
..	..	..	..	28.6	30.1	29.2	..	Autres matériels électriques, nca			319
..	..	..	..	29.9	29.2	28.4	..	**Equip. et appar. de radio, TV, communication**		32	
..	..	..	..	9.5	10.3	10.5	..	Tubes et valves électroniques; autres composants			321
..	..	..	..	14.6	13.1	11.9	..	Emetteurs radio et TV; app. téléphonie, télégraphie			322
..	..	..	..	5.7	5.7	5.9	..	Récepteurs radio et TV et articles associés			323
..	..	..	..	22.8	20.4	21.1	..	**Instruments médicaux, de précision, d'optique**		33	
..	..	..	..	19.0	17.0	17.7	..	Appareils médicaux et de précision			331
..	..	..	..	3.3	3.1	2.9	..	Instruments d'optique ; matériel photographique			332
..	..	..	..	0.5	0.3	0.5	..	Horlogerie			333
..	..	..	..	140.9	135.1	137.3	..	**Véhicules automobiles et nemorques**		34	
..	..	..	..	51.2	49.6	51.1	..	**Autres matériels de transport**		35	
..	..	..	..	28.8	27.5	29.1	..	Construction et réparation de navires			351
..	..	..	..	7.8	7.6	7.6	..	Construction de matériel ferroviaire roulant			352
..	..	..	..	10.9	10.7	10.6	..	Construction aéronautique et spatiale			353
..	..	..	..	3.7	3.7	3.7	..	Autres équipements de transport			359
..	..	..	..	130.2	123.9	123.6	..	**Meubles; activités de fabrication, nca**		36	
..	..	..	..	100.6	95.8	95.3	..	Meubles			361
..	..	..	..	29.6	28.1	28.2	..	Activités de fabrication, nca			369
..	..	..	..	1.9	1.9	1.6	..	**Récupération**		37	
..	..	..	..	71.7	69.3	67.8	..	**Production et distrib. d'électricité, de gaz, d'eau**	E	40-41	
..	..	..	..	56.0	53.3	51.0	..	**Electricité, gaz, vapeur et eau chaude**		40	
..	..	..	..	51.0	48.2	46.1	..	Production, collecte et distribution d'électricité			401
..	..	..	..	15.6	16.0	16.8	..	**Captage, épuration et distribution d'eau**		41	410
..	..	..	..	..	..	..	..	**Construction**	F	45	
..	..	..	..	..	..	..	..	**Commerce de gros et de détail; réparation**	G	50-52	
..	..	..	..	..	..	..	..	**Hôtels et restaurants**	H	55	
..	..	..	..	..	..	..	..	**Transports, entreposage et communications**	I	60-64	
..	..	..	..	..	..	..	..	**Intermédiation financière**	J	65-67	
..	..	..	..	..	..	..	..	**Immobilier, locations, services aux entreprises**	K	70-74	
..	..	..	..	..	..	..	..	**Admin. publique; éducation; santé; autres**	L-Q	75-99	
..	..	..	..	..	..	..	..	**Grand total**	A-Q	01-99	

Statistiques des Structures Industrielles
OCDE, © 1998

Table SP.7 COMPENSATION OF LABOUR – SALAIRES ET CHARGES SOCIALES

Billions of Ptas (Current Prices)

ISIC revision 3			1989	1990	1991	1992	1993	1994	1995	1996
A	01-02	**Agriculture, hunting and forestry**	..	..	..	..	..	..	..	..
B	05	**Fishing**	..	..	..	..	..	..	..	..
C	10-14	**Mining and quarrying**	..	..	..	..	225	212	216	..
	10	Mining of coal and lignite; extraction of peat	..	..	..	..	150	148	139	..
	11	Crude petroleum & natural gas; related service activ.	..	..	..	..	5	5	5	..
	13	Mining of metal ores	..	..	..	..	15	8	12	..
	14	Other mining and quarrying	..	..	..	..	54	51	59	..
D	15-37	**Total manufacturing**	..	..	..	..	7 119	7 188	7 404	..
	15	**Food products and beverages**	..	..	..	..	1 039	1 064	1 064	..
		155 Beverages	..	..	..	..	230	229	221	..
	16	160 **Tobacco products**	..	..	..	..	56	53	50	..
	17	**Textiles**	..	..	..	..	234	245	247	..
		171 Spinning, weaving and finishing of textiles	..	..	..	..	136	136	139	..
		172 Other textiles	..	..	..	..	57	65	68	..
		173 Knitted and crocheted fabrics and articles	..	..	..	..	42	44	41	..
	18	**Wearing apparel dressing & dyeing of fur**	..	..	..	..	228	229	224	..
		181 Wearing apparel, except fur apparel	..	..	..	..	219	219	216	..
		182 Dressing and dyeing of fur; articles of fur	..	..	..	..	8	9	8	..
	19	**Tanning, dressing leather; leather artic.; footwear**	..	..	..	..	110	116	125	..
		191 Tanning, dressing leather; manuf. of leather articles	..	..	..	..	42	42	41	..
		192 Footwear	..	..	..	..	69	73	83	..
	20	**Wood and cork products, ex. furniture**	..	..	..	..	169	167	185	..
		201 Sawmilling and planing of wood	..	..	..	..	20	19	22	..
		202 Products of wood, cork, straw & plaiting material	..	..	..	..	149	148	163	..
	21	**Paper and paper products**	..	..	..	..	175	175	181	..
	22	**Publishing, printing & reprod. of recorded media**	..	..	..	..	386	396	402	..
		221 Publishing	..	..	..	..	172	183	177	..
		222 Printing and related service activities	..	..	..	..	211	210	222	..
		223 Reproduction of recorded media	..	..	..	..	3	2	2	..
	23	**Coke, refined petroleum products & nuclear fuel**	..	..	..	..	60	59	60	..
	24	**Chemicals and chemical products**	..	..	..	..	700	704	705	..
		241 Basic chemicals	..	..	..	..	205	204	188	..
		242 Other chemical products	..	..	..	..	468	470	487	..
		243 Man-made fibres	..	..	..	..	27	29	30	..
	25	**Rubber and plastic products**	..	..	..	..	331	338	353	..
		251 Rubber products	..	..	..	..	135	124	131	..
		252 Plastic products	..	..	..	..	195	213	221	..
	26	**Other non-metallic mineral products**	..	..	..	..	482	479	509	..
		261 Glass and glass products	..	..	..	..	84	81	85	..
		269 Non-metallic mineral products, nec	..	..	..	..	398	398	424	..
	27	**Basic metals**	..	..	..	..	342	327	331	..
		271 Basic iron and steel	..	..	..	..	195	184	186	..
		272 Basic precious and non-ferrous metals	..	..	..	..	72	70	67	..
		273 Casting of metals	..	..	..	..	74	74	77	..
	28	**Fabricated metal products, ex. machin. & equip.**	..	..	..	..	583	615	677	..
		281 Structural metal prod., tanks, reservoirs, generators	..	..	..	..	202	228	238	..
		289 Other fabricated metal products & service activities	..	..	..	..	381	388	438	..
	29	**Machinery and equipment, nec**	..	..	..	..	487	517	536	..
		291 General purpose machinery	..	..	..	..	216	226	241	..
		292 Special purpose machinery	..	..	..	..	195	214	221	..
		293 Domestic appliances, nec	..	..	..	..	75	77	74	..
	30	**Office, accounting and computing machinery**	..	..	..	..	81	79	81	..
	31	**Electrical machinery and apparatus, nec**	..	..	..	..	292	288	292	..
		311 Electric motors, generators and transformers	..	..	..	..	50	48	47	..
		312 Electricity distribution and control apparatus	..	..	..	..	49	49	52	..
		313 Insulated wire and cable	..	..	..	..	29	31	30	..
		314 Accumulators, primary cells and primary batteries	..	..	..	..	17	16	14	..
		315 Electric lamps and lighting equipment	..	..	..	..	31	30	29	..
		319 Other electrical equipment, nec	..	..	..	..	116	115	120	..
	32	**Radio, TV, communication equip. & apparatus**	..	..	..	..	145	141	144	..
		321 Electronic valves, tubes & other electronic compon.	..	..	..	..	36	40	43	..
		322 TV, radio transmitters & appar. for line teleph., telegr.	..	..	..	..	85	79	78	..
		323 TV, radio receivers and associated goods	..	..	..	..	24	22	23	..
	33	**Medical, precision, optical instr.; watches, clocks**	..	..	..	..	88	76	83	..
		331 Medical equip.; precision instruments and appliances	..	..	..	..	73	63	70	..
		332 Optical instruments and photographic equipment	..	..	..	..	14	13	11	..
		333 Watches and clocks	..	..	..	..	2	1	2	..
	34	**Motor vehicles, trailers, and semi-trailers**	..	..	..	..	599	592	610	..
	35	**Other transport equipment**	..	..	..	..	219	216	227	..
		351 Building and repairing of ships and boats	..	..	..	..	114	114	121	..
		352 Railway, tramway locomotives and rolling stock	..	..	..	..	37	36	38	..
		353 Aircraft and spacecraft	..	..	..	..	54	52	54	..
		359 Transport equipment, nec	..	..	..	..	14	15	14	..
	36	**Furniture; manufacturing, nec**	..	..	..	..	309	305	315	..
		361 Furniture	..	..	..	..	234	230	237	..
		369 Manufacturing, nec	..	..	..	..	75	75	78	..
	37	**Recycling**	..	..	..	..	6	6	6	..
E	40-41	**Electricity, gas and water supply**	..	..	..	..	430	433	434	..
	40	**Electricity, gas, steam and hot water supply**	..	..	..	..	364	360	354	..
		401 Production, collection and distribution of electricity	..	..	..	..	336	332	327	..
	41	410 **Collection, purification, distribution of water**	..	..	..	..	66	72	79	..
F	45	**Construction**	..	..	..	..	..	..	..	..
G	50-52	**Wholesale and retail trade; repairs etc**	..	..	..	..	..	..	..	..
H	55	**Hotels and restaurants**	..	..	..	..	..	..	..	..
I	60-64	**Transport, storage and communications**	..	..	..	..	..	..	..	..
J	65-67	**Financial intermediation**	..	..	..	..	..	..	..	..
K	70-74	**Real estate, renting and business activities**	..	..	..	..	..	..	..	..
L-Q	75-99	**Public admin.; education; health; other services**	..	..	..	..	..	..	..	..
A-Q	01-99	**Grand total**	..	..	..	..	..	..	..	..

Table SP.8 SALAIRES ET TRAITEMENTS, SALARIÉS - WAGES AND SALARIES, EMPLOYEES

Milliards de Ptas (Prix courants)

1989	1990	1991	1992	1993	1994	1995	1996			CITI révision 3	
..	..	..	..	..	..	..	..	**Agriculture, chasse et sylviculture**	A	01-02	
..	..	..	..	..	..	..	..	**Pêche**	B	05	
..	..	..	..	157	148	150	..	**Activités extractives**	C	10-14	
..	..	..	..	104	101	95	..	Extraction de charbon, de lignite et de tourbe		10	
..	..	..	..	4	4	4	..	Extraction de pétrole brut et de gaz naturel		11	
..	..	..	..	10	6	8	..	Extraction de minerais métalliques		13	
..	..	..	..	39	38	44	..	Autres activités extractives		14	
..	..	..	..	5 123	5 271	5 510	..	**Activités de fabrication**	D	15-37	
..	..	..	..	764	788	791	..	**Produits alimentaires et boissons**		15	
..	..	..	..	168	166	162	..	Boissons			155
..	..	..	..	37	36	35	..	**Produits à base de tabac**		16	160
..	..	..	..	173	184	186	..	**Textiles**		17	
..	..	..	..	100	102	104	..	Filature, tissage et achèvement des textiles			171
..	..	..	..	42	49	52	..	Autres articles textiles			172
..	..	..	..	31	34	31	..	Etoffes et articles de bonneterie			173
..	..	..	..	171	172	172	..	**Habillement; préparation, teinture des fourrures**		18	
..	..	..	..	165	165	166	..	Articles d'habillement autres qu'en fourrure			181
..	..	..	..	6	7	6	..	Préparation, teinture des fourrures; art. en fourrure			182
..	..	..	..	83	88	95	..	**Travail des cuirs; articles en cuir; chaussures**		19	
..	..	..	..	31	32	32	..	Apprêt et tannage des cuirs et articles en cuirs			191
..	..	..	..	52	55	64	..	Chaussures			192
..	..	..	..	124	124	141	..	**Bois et articles en bois et liège (sauf meubles)**		20	
..	..	..	..	15	14	17	..	Sciage et rabotage du bois			201
..	..	..	..	110	110	124	..	Articles en bois, liège, vannerie, sparterie			202
..	..	..	..	129	131	137	..	**Papier et carton; articles en papier et en carton**		21	
..	..	..	..	294	303	310	..	**Edition, imprimerie et reproduction**		22	
..	..	..	..	132	141	137	..	Edition			221
..	..	..	..	160	161	171	..	Imprimerie et activités annexes			222
..	..	..	..	2	2	2	..	Reproduction de supports enregistrés			223
..	..	..	..	42	41	42	..	**Cokéfaction; prod. pétroliers; comb. nucléaires**		23	
..	..	..	..	490	506	512	..	**Produits chimiques**		24	
..	..	..	..	136	142	134	..	Produits chimiques de base			241
..	..	..	..	337	344	358	..	Autres produits chimiques			242
..	..	..	..	18	20	21	..	Fibres synthétiques ou artificielles			243
..	..	..	..	225	247	259	..	**Articles en caoutchouc et en matières plastiques**		25	
..	..	..	..	82	88	94	..	Articles en caoutchouc			251
..	..	..	..	144	159	165	..	Articles en matières plastiques			252
..	..	..	..	349	354	381	..	**Autres produits minéraux non métalliques**		26	
..	..	..	..	58	57	61	..	Verre et articles en verre			261
..	..	..	..	292	297	319	..	Produits minéraux non métalliques, nca			269
..	..	..	..	245	235	243	..	**Produits métallurgiques de base**		27	
..	..	..	..	142	134	135	..	Sidérurgie et première transformation de l'acier			271
..	..	..	..	49	49	50	..	Métallurgie; métaux précieux et non ferreux			272
..	..	..	..	54	52	58	..	Fonderie			273
..	..	..	..	430	458	513	..	**Ouvrages en métaux, sauf machines et matériel**		28	
..	..	..	..	151	167	181	..	Constr. et menuiserie métal.; réservoirs; générateurs			281
..	..	..	..	279	290	332	..	Autres ouvrages en métaux			289
..	..	..	..	356	382	404	..	**Machines et matériel, nca**		29	
..	..	..	..	159	167	183	..	Machines d'usage général			291
..	..	..	..	144	159	167	..	Machines d'usage spécifique			292
..	..	..	..	52	55	55	..	Appareils domestiques, nca			293
..	..	..	..	44	47	50	..	**Mach. de bureau, comptables, matériel inform.**		30	
..	..	..	..	207	209	216	..	**Machines et appareils électriques, nca**		31	
..	..	..	..	35	36	37	..	Moteurs, génératrices et transformateurs électriques			311
..	..	..	..	35	36	39	..	Matériel électrique de distribution et de commande			312
..	..	..	..	21	22	23	..	Fils et câbles électriques isolés			313
..	..	..	..	11	12	10	..	Accumulateurs, piles électriques			314
..	..	..	..	22	21	21	..	Lampes électriques et appareils d'éclairage			315
..	..	..	..	83	83	86	..	Autres matériels électriques, nca			319
..	..	..	..	102	102	102	..	**Equip. et appar. de radio, TV, communication**		32	
..	..	..	..	27	30	32	..	Tubes et valves électroniques; autres composants			321
..	..	..	..	60	56	53	..	Emetteurs radio et TV; app. téléphonie, télégraphie			322
..	..	..	..	16	16	17	..	Récepteurs radio et TV et articles associés			323
..	..	..	..	61	57	63	..	**Instruments médicaux, de précision, d'optique**		33	
..	..	..	..	51	47	54	..	Appareils médicaux et de précision			331
..	..	..	..	9	10	8	..	Instruments d'optique ; matériel photographique			332
..	..	..	..	1	1	1	..	Horlogerie			333
..	..	..	..	407	419	447	..	**Véhicules automobiles et nemorques**		34	
..	..	..	..	154	154	166	..	**Autres matériels de transport**		35	
..	..	..	..	78	79	87	..	Construction et réparation de navires			351
..	..	..	..	25	26	27	..	Construction de matériel ferroviaire roulant			352
..	..	..	..	41	39	41	..	Construction aéronautique et spatiale			353
..	..	..	..	10	10	11	..	Autres équipements de transport			359
..	..	..	..	230	229	239	..	**Meubles; activités de fabrication, nca**		36	
..	..	..	..	173	172	179	..	Meubles			361
..	..	..	..	56	56	60	..	Activités de fabrication, nca			369
..	..	..	..	4	4	4	..	**Récupération**		37	
..	..	..	..	298	299	304	..	**Production et distrib. d'électricité, de gaz, d'eau**	E	40-41	
..	..	..	..	252	248	248	..	**Electricité, gaz, vapeur et eau chaude**		40	
..	..	..	..	232	229	228	..	Production, collecte et distribution d'électricité			401
..	..	..	..	46	51	56	..	**Captage, épuration et distribution d'eau**		41	410
..	..	..	..	..	..	..	..	**Construction**	F	45	
..	..	..	..	..	..	..	..	**Commerce de gros et de détail; réparation**	G	50-52	
..	..	..	..	..	..	..	..	**Hôtels et restaurants**	H	55	
..	..	..	..	..	..	..	..	**Transports, entreposage et communications**	I	60-64	
..	..	..	..	..	..	..	..	**Intermédiation financière**	J	65-67	
..	..	..	..	..	..	..	..	**Immobilier, locations, services aux entreprises**	K	70-74	
..	..	..	..	..	..	..	..	**Admin. publique; éducation; santé; autres**	L-Q	75-99	
..	..	..	..	..	..	..	..	**Grand total**	A-Q	01-99	

Statistiques des Structures Industrielles
OCDE, © 1998

SPAIN

Table SP.9 EMPLOYERS' SOCIAL COSTS – CHARGES SOCIALES DES EMPLOYEURS

Billions of Ptas (Current Prices)

ISIC revision 3			1989	1990	1991	1992	1993	1994	1995	1996
A	01-02	Agriculture, hunting and forestry	..	..	..	..	..	..	..	..
B	05	Fishing	..	..	..	..	..	..	..	..
C	10-14	Mining and quarrying	..	..	..	..	65	62	63	..
	10	Mining of coal and lignite; extraction of peat	..	..	..	..	46	46	44	..
	11	Crude petroleum & natural gas; related service activ.	..	..	..	..	1	1	1	..
	13	Mining of metal ores	..	..	..	..	5	2	3	..
	14	Other mining and quarrying	..	..	..	..	13	13	14	..
D	15-37	Total manufacturing	..	..	..	..	1 763	1 756	1 750	..
	15	Food products and beverages	..	..	..	..	247	255	251	..
	155	Beverages	..	..	..	..	54	54	51	..
	16	160	Tobacco products	..	..	..	..	16	16	14	..
	17	Textiles	..	..	..	..	56	58	58	..
	171	Spinning, weaving and finishing of textiles	..	..	..	..	33	33	33	..
	172	Other textiles	..	..	..	..	13	15	15	..
	173	Knitted and crocheted fabrics and articles	..	..	..	..	10	10	9	..
	18	Wearing apparel dressing & dyeing of fur	..	..	..	..	53	53	50	..
	181	Wearing apparel, except fur apparel	..	..	..	..	51	51	48	..
	182	Dressing and dyeing of fur; articles of fur	..	..	..	..	2	2	2	..
	19	Tanning, dressing leather; leather artic.; footwear	..	..	..	..	27	27	29	..
	191	Tanning, dressing leather; manuf. of leather articles	..	..	..	..	10	10	10	..
	192	Footwear	..	..	..	..	16	17	19	..
	20	Wood and cork products, ex. furniture	..	..	..	..	42	42	44	..
	201	Sawmilling and planing of wood	..	..	..	..	5	5	6	..
	202	Products of wood, cork, straw & plaiting material	..	..	..	..	37	37	38	..
	21	Paper and paper products	..	..	..	..	41	42	42	..
	22	Publishing, printing & reprod. of recorded media	..	..	..	..	84	86	84	..
	221	Publishing	..	..	..	..	36	39	36	..
	222	Printing and related service activities	..	..	..	..	48	47	48	..
	223	Reproduction of recorded media	..	..	..	..	1	0	0	..
	23	Coke, refined petroleum products & nuclear fuel	..	..	..	..	17	18	18	..
	24	Chemicals and chemical products	..	..	..	..	167	168	167	..
	241	Basic chemicals	..	..	..	..	53	54	50	..
	242	Other chemical products	..	..	..	..	107	107	109	..
	243	Man-made fibres	..	..	..	..	6	7	7	..
	25	Rubber and plastic products	..	..	..	..	98	85	86	..
	251	Rubber products	..	..	..	..	51	35	37	..
	252	Plastic products	..	..	..	..	46	50	49	..
	26	Other non-metallic mineral products	..	..	..	..	117	117	121	..
	261	Glass and glass products	..	..	..	..	20	21	22	..
	269	Non-metallic mineral products, nec	..	..	..	..	97	96	99	..
	27	Basic metals	..	..	..	..	93	90	85	..
	271	Basic iron and steel	..	..	..	..	53	50	50	..
	272	Basic precious and non-ferrous metals	..	..	..	..	21	20	16	..
	273	Casting of metals	..	..	..	..	19	20	19	..
	28	Fabricated metal products, ex. machin. & equip.	..	..	..	..	142	151	158	..
	281	Structural metal prod., tanks, reservoirs, generators	..	..	..	..	49	59	56	..
	289	Other fabricated metal products & service activities	..	..	..	..	92	93	102	..
	29	Machinery and equipment, nec	..	..	..	..	117	124	126	..
	291	General purpose machinery	..	..	..	..	51	53	56	..
	292	Special purpose machinery	..	..	..	..	48	51	51	..
	293	Domestic appliances, nec	..	..	..	..	19	19	18	..
	30	Office, accounting and computing machinery	..	..	..	..	31	14	14	..
	31	Electrical machinery and apparatus, nec	..	..	..	..	73	69	68	..
	311	Electric motors, generators and transformers	..	..	..	..	12	11	10	..
	312	Electricity distribution and control apparatus	..	..	..	..	11	11	12	..
	313	Insulated wire and cable	..	..	..	..	7	7	7	..
	314	Accumulators, primary cells and primary batteries	..	..	..	..	4	4	3	..
	315	Electric lamps and lighting equipment	..	..	..	..	8	7	7	..
	319	Other electrical equipment, nec	..	..	..	..	31	28	29	..
	32	Radio, TV, communication equip. & apparatus	..	..	..	..	31	32	33	..
	321	Electronic valves, tubes & other electronic compon.	..	..	..	..	8	9	10	..
	322	TV, radio transmitters & appar. for line teleph., telegr.	..	..	..	..	18	18	18	..
	323	TV, radio receivers and associated goods	..	..	..	..	5	5	5	..
	33	Medical, precision, optical instr.; watches, clocks	..	..	..	..	20	18	19	..
	331	Medical equip.; precision instruments and appliances	..	..	..	..	17	15	16	..
	332	Optical instruments and photographic equipment	..	..	..	..	3	3	3	..
	333	Watches and clocks	..	..	..	..	0	0	0	..
	34	Motor vehicles, trailers, and semi-trailers	..	..	..	..	157	157	154	..
	35	Other transport equipment	..	..	..	..	58	58	58	..
	351	Building and repairing of ships and boats	..	..	..	..	33	33	32	..
	352	Railway, tramway locomotives and rolling stock	..	..	..	..	9	9	10	..
	353	Aircraft and spacecraft	..	..	..	..	13	13	13	..
	359	Transport equipment, nec	..	..	..	..	3	4	3	..
	36	Furniture; manufacturing, nec	..	..	..	..	75	73	72	..
	361	Furniture	..	..	..	..	58	56	55	..
	369	Manufacturing, nec	..	..	..	..	17	18	17	..
	37	Recycling	..	..	..	..	1	1	1	..
E	40-41	Electricity, gas and water supply	..	..	..	..	131	131	127	..
	40	Electricity, gas, steam and hot water supply	..	..	..	..	111	110	104	..
	401	Production, collection and distribution of electricity	..	..	..	..	103	102	97	..
	41	410	Collection, purification, distribution of water	..	..	..	..	20	21	23	..
F	45	Construction	..	..	..	..	..	..	..	..
G	50-52	Wholesale and retail trade; repairs etc	..	..	..	..	..	..	..	..
H	55	Hotels and restaurants	..	..	..	..	..	..	..	..
I	60-64	Transport, storage and communications	..	..	..	..	..	..	..	..
J	65-67	Financial intermediation	..	..	..	..	..	..	..	..
K	70-74	Real estate, renting and business activities	..	..	..	..	..	..	..	..
L-Q	75-99	Public admin.; education; health; other services	..	..	..	..	..	..	..	..
A-Q	01-99	Grand total	..	..	..	..	..	..	..	..

Table SP.10 HEURES OUVRÉES - HOURS WORKED

Milliers

1989	1990	1991	1992	1993	1994	1995	1996			CITI révision 3	
..	..	..	..	..	..	..	..	**Agriculture, chasse et sylviculture**	A	01-02	
								Pêche	B	05	
..	..	..	..	86 223	75 896	74 731	..	**Activités extractives**	C	10-14	
..	..	..	..	46 857	42 516	38 114		Extraction de charbon, de lignite et de tourbe		10	
..	..	..	..	1 640	1 415	1 341		Extraction de pétrole brut et de gaz naturel		11	
..	..	..	..	5 170	3 580	3 923		Extraction de minerais métalliques		13	
..	..	..	..	32 556	28 385	31 353	..	Autres activités extractives		14	
..	..	..	..	3 696 926	3 633 857	3 637 130		**Activités de fabrication**	D	15-37	
..	..	..	..	616 410	609 799	591 672	..	**Produits alimentaires et boissons**		15	
..	..	..	..	92 583	88 538	81 784		Boissons			155
..	..	..	..	16 286	13 726	14 423		**Produits à base de tabac**		16	160
..	..	..	..	163 359	169 251	163 166		**Textiles**		17	
..	..	..	..	87 432	88 867	85 995		Filature, tissage et achèvement des textiles			171
..	..	..	..	43 284	46 848	48 076		Autres articles textiles			172
..	..	..	..	32 643	33 537	29 095		Etoffes et articles de bonneterie			173
..	..	..	..	216 311	198 246	188 078		**Habillement; préparation, teinture des fourrures**		18	
..	..	..	..	210 018	192 205	182 934		Articles d'habillement autres qu'en fourrure			181
..	..	..	..	6 293	6 041	5 144		Préparation, teinture des fourrures; art. en fourrure			182
..	..	..	..	98 780	101 135	102 639	..	**Travail des cuirs; articles en cuir; chaussures**		19	
..	..	..	..	29 927	28 796	27 839		Apprêt et tannage des cuirs et articles en cuirs			191
..	..	..	..	68 854	72 340	74 800		Chaussures			192
..	..	..	..	139 890	131 869	137 922		**Bois et articles en bois et liège (sauf meubles)**		20	
..	..	..	..	17 378	17 344	18 387		Sciage et rabotage du bois			201
..	..	..	..	122 512	114 525	119 534		Articles en bois, liège, vannerie, sparterie			202
..	..	..	..	84 231	83 031	81 012		**Papier et carton; articles en papier et en carton**		21	
..	..	..	..	192 645	188 573	187 816		**Edition, imprimerie et reproduction**		22	
..	..	..	..	62 602	64 847	60 943		Edition			221
..	..	..	..	128 531	122 488	125 536		Imprimerie et activités annexes			222
..	..	..	..	1 511	1 237	1 337		Reproduction de supports enregistrés			223
..	..	..	..	13 837	12 988	12 443		**Cokéfaction; prod. pétroliers; comb. nucléaires**		23	
..	..	..	..	240 407	232 374	226 404		**Produits chimiques**		24	
..	..	..	..	63 971	61 804	56 790		Produits chimiques de base			241
..	..	..	..	166 420	160 536	160 198		Autres produits chimiques			242
..	..	..	..	10 016	10 034	9 416		Fibres synthétiques ou artificielles			243
..	..	..	..	151 137	159 861	161 052		**Articles en caoutchouc et en matières plastiques**		25	
..	..	..	..	45 457	47 008	47 974		Articles en caoutchouc			251
..	..	..	..	105 680	112 853	113 078		Articles en matières plastiques			252
..	..	..	..	264 459	259 984	265 543		**Autres produits minéraux non métalliques**		26	
..	..	..	..	40 181	38 962	40 063		Verre et articles en verre			261
..	..	..	..	224 278	221 022	225 480		Produits minéraux non métalliques, nca			269
..	..	..	..	133 450	120 436	120 427		**Produits métallurgiques de base**		27	
..	..	..	..	74 941	62 793	61 764		Sidérurgie et première transformation de l'acier			271
..	..	..	..	25 177	24 951	22 986		Métallurgie; métaux précieux et non ferreux			272
..	..	..	..	33 332	32 692	35 677		Fonderie			273
..	..	..	..	348 898	355 003	375 228		**Ouvrages en métaux, sauf machines et matériel**		28	
..	..	..	..	141 446	145 726	152 202		Constr. et menuiserie métal.; réservoirs; générateurs			281
..	..	..	..	207 452	209 276	223 026	..	Autres ouvrages en métaux			289
..	..	..	..	232 628	234 677	240 509		**Machines et matériel, nca**		29	
..	..	..	..	103 294	101 282	106 613		Machines d'usage général			291
..	..	..	..	96 448	100 451	101 613		Machines d'usage spécifique			292
..	..	..	..	32 887	32 944	32 283		Appareils domestiques, nca			293
..	..	..	..	13 762	14 444	16 946		**Mach. de bureau, comptables, matériel inform.**		30	
..	..	..	..	130 725	129 521	127 317		**Machines et appareils électriques, nca**		31	
..	..	..	..	20 162	18 726	19 125		Moteurs, génératrices et transformateurs électriques			311
..	..	..	..	22 075	21 570	22 988		Matériel électrique de distribution et de commande			312
..	..	..	..	14 269	13 819	13 164		Fils et câbles électriques isolés			313
..	..	..	..	5 866	5 569	4 333		Accumulateurs, piles électriques			314
..	..	..	..	17 463	16 448	15 722		Lampes électriques et appareils d'éclairage			315
..	..	..	..	50 891	53 388	51 985		Autres matériels électriques, nca			319
..	..	..	..	52 340	50 909	48 979		**Equip. et appar. de radio, TV, communication**		32	
..	..	..	..	16 706	18 360	18 430		Tubes et valves électroniques; autres composants			321
..	..	..	..	25 549	22 309	20 157		Emetteurs radio et TV; app. téléphonie, télégraphie			322
..	..	..	..	10 086	10 240	10 393		Récepteurs radio et TV et articles associés			323
..	..	..	..	40 027	35 634	36 995		**Instruments médicaux, de précision, d'optique**		33	
..	..	..	..	33 393	29 617	31 066		Appareils médicaux et de précision			331
..	..	..	..	5 790	5 455	5 113		Instruments d'optique ; matériel photographique			332
..	..	..	..	844	563	816		Horlogerie			333
..	..	..	..	226 055	228 790	234 615	..	**Véhicules automobiles et nemorques**		34	
..	..	..	..	85 973	80 540	81 833	..	**Autres matériels de transport**		35	
..	..	..	..	47 581	45 639	45 917		Construction et réparation de navires			351
..	..	..	..	13 085	10 521	11 745		Construction de matériel ferroviaire roulant			352
..	..	..	..	18 987	18 465	17 819		Construction aéronautique et spatiale			353
..	..	..	..	6 321	5 916	6 352		Autres équipements de transport			359
..	..	..	..	231 905	219 702	219 243	..	**Meubles; activités de fabrication, nca**		36	
..	..	..	..	178 999	170 070	169 423		Meubles			361
..	..	..	..	52 906	49 632	49 820		Activités de fabrication, nca			369
..	..	..	..	3 410	3 364	2 866		**Récupération**		37	
..	..	..	..	121 086	115 939	114 792	..	**Production et distrib. d'électricité, de gaz, d'eau**	E	40-41	
..	..	..	..	94 202	88 725	85 808	..	**Electricité, gaz, vapeur et eau chaude**		40	
..	..	..	..	85 407	79 912	77 446		Production, collecte et distribution d'électricité			401
..	..	..	..	26 884	27 214	28 984		**Captage, épuration et distribution d'eau**		41	410
..	..	..	..	..	..	..	..	**Construction**	F	45	
..	..	..	..	..	..	..	..	**Commerce de gros et de détail; réparation**	G	50-52	
..	..	..	..	..	..	..	..	**Hôtels et restaurants**	H	55	
..	..	..	..	..	..	..	..	**Transports, entreposage et communications**	I	60-64	
..	..	..	..	..	..	..	..	**Intermédiation financière**	J	65-67	
..	..	..	..	..	..	..	..	**Immobilier, locations, services aux entreprises**	K	70-74	
..	..	..	..	..	..	..	..	**Admin. publique; éducation; santé; autres**	L-Q	75-99	
..	..	..	..	..	..	..	..	**Grand total**	A-Q	01-99	

Statistiques des Structures Industrielles
OCDE, © 1998

SWEDEN

Table SN.1 PRODUCTION - PRODUCTION

Millions of SKr (Current Prices)

ISIC revision 3			1989	1990	1991	1992	1993	1994	1995	1996
A	01-02	**Agriculture, hunting and forestry**	..	..	..	..	..	..	..	..
B	05	**Fishing**	..	..	..	..	..	..	..	..
C	10-14	**Mining and quarrying**	..	9 887	8 973	8 651	8 524	9 022	10 329	..
	10	Mining of coal and lignite; extraction of peat	..	408	457	493	493	594	617	..
	11	Crude petroleum & natural gas; related service activ.	..	..	..	..	..	..	..	..
	13	Mining of metal ores	..	6 565	5 828	5 827	5 625	6 080	6 996	..
	14	Other mining and quarrying	..	2 913	2 687	2 331	2 406	2 348	2 716	..
D	15-37	**Total manufacturing**	..	716 132	672 030	632 671	668 857	791 543	939 359	..
	15	**Food products and beverages**	..	91 129	88 989	87 868	91 065	98 816	100 634	..
	155	Beverages	..	8 538	9 149	9 388	9 216	11 004	11 212	..
	16 160	**Tobacco products**	..	1 976	2 169	2 433	2 306	2 479	2 497	..
	17	**Textiles**	..	7 864	6 938	6 369	6 406	7 005	7 632	..
	171	Spinning, weaving and finishing of textiles	..	2 170	2 250	1 993	2 027	1 967	2 118	..
	172	Other textiles	..	4 401	3 900	3 542	3 558	4 155	4 509	..
	173	Knitted and crocheted fabrics and articles	..	1 293	787	835	820	883	1 005	..
	18	**Wearing apparel dressing & dyeing of fur**	..	2 178	1 706	1 660	1 288	1 610	1 647	..
	181	Wearing apparel, except fur apparel	..	2 143	1 692	1 660	..	..	..	..
	182	Dressing and dyeing of fur; articles of fur	..	35	14	..	..	..	..	..
	19	**Tanning, dressing leather; leather artic.; footwear**	..	1 043	892	836	907	992	1 080	..
	191	Tanning, dressing leather; manuf. of leather articles	..	689	525	488	565	725	788	..
	192	Footwear	..	354	367	348	341	267	292	..
	20	**Wood and cork products, ex. furniture**	..	44 836	39 788	32 420	32 589	39 456	43 706	..
	201	Sawmilling and planing of wood	..	21 808	19 507	18 774	21 260	26 958	29 627	..
	202	Products of wood, cork, straw & plaiting material	..	23 028	20 281	13 646	11 329	12 498	14 079	..
	21	**Paper and paper products**	..	71 869	67 274	63 721	67 149	79 226	99 045	..
	22	**Publishing, printing & reprod. of recorded media**	..	39 935	39 610	37 939	39 599	43 387	47 364	..
	221	Publishing	..	17 183	17 455	17 060	18 807	25 691	28 133	..
	222	Printing and related service activities	..	22 752	22 155	20 879	20 792	17 697	19 231	..
	223	Reproduction of recorded media	..	..	..	..	..	..	..	..
	23	**Coke, refined petroleum products & nuclear fuel**	..	28 591	24 254	21 210	26 010	22 757	21 826	..
	24	**Chemicals and chemical products**	..	42 971	45 286	44 701	51 394	59 283	67 673	..
	241	Basic chemicals	..	21 246	21 007	19 385	21 316	23 714	28 188	..
	242	Other chemical products	..	..	..	..	..	35 569	39 485	..
	243	Man-made fibres	..	..	..	..	..	..	..	..
	25	**Rubber and plastic products**	..	16 108	15 672	14 923	15 277	18 803	21 664	..
	251	Rubber products	..	4 061	3 560	3 867	3 883	5 260	6 171	..
	252	Plastic products	..	12 047	12 112	11 056	11 395	13 543	15 493	..
	26	**Other non-metallic mineral products**	..	18 378	16 825	14 973	13 632	14 819	16 408	..
	261	Glass and glass products	..	4 386	3 891	3 616	3 407	3 831	4 138	..
	269	Non-metallic mineral products, nec	..	13 992	12 935	11 358	10 225	10 987	12 270	..
	27	**Basic metals**	..	53 892	47 102	43 416	51 325	65 279	80 736	..
	271	Basic iron and steel	..	39 890	35 354	33 532	39 868	51 570	64 118	..
	272	Basic precious and non-ferrous metals	..	14 002	11 695	9 853	11 288	13 516	16 339	..
	273	Casting of metals	..	..	54	31	169	193	279	..
	28	**Fabricated metal products, ex. machin. & equip.**	..	42 952	37 568	32 452	32 388	39 850	49 512	..
	281	Structural metal prod., tanks, reservoirs, generators	..	16 130	13 995	11 056	10 783	12 690	14 464	..
	289	Other fabricated metal products & service activities	..	26 822	23 572	21 396	21 605	27 160	35 048	..
	29	**Machinery and equipment, nec**	..	80 673	73 476	67 510	68 116	85 169	101 775	..
	291	General purpose machinery	..	39 979	36 180	34 192	33 652	41 869	50 764	..
	292	Special purpose machinery	..	34 296	31 062	27 613	28 364	36 265	43 629	..
	293	Domestic appliances, nec	..	6 398	6 235	5 705	6 100	7 034	7 382	..
	30	**Office, accounting and computing machinery**	..	8 110	7 512	6 134	4 649	4 002	3 595	..
	31	**Electrical machinery and apparatus, nec**	..	19 538	18 637	16 918	17 575	19 493	23 056	..
	311	Electric motors, generators and transformers	..	2 868	2 319	2 290	2 617	2 940	4 317	..
	312	Electricity distribution and control apparatus	..	5 476	5 114	4 737	4 503	5 079	6 046	..
	313	Insulated wire and cable	..	3 877	4 187	3 509	3 660	5 591	5 945	..
	314	Accumulators, primary cells and primary batteries	..	960	831	861	1 061	1 157	1 457	..
	315	Electric lamps and lighting equipment	..	2 616	2 361	2 221	2 186	2 166	2 312	..
	319	Other electrical equipment, nec	..	3 741	3 824	3 300	3 548	2 559	2 979	..
	32	**Radio, TV, communication equip. & apparatus**	..	23 221	23 915	25 008	31 784	45 380	65 708	..
	321	Electronic valves, tubes & other electronic compon.	..	2 251	2 089	1 871	2 473	3 001	3 431	..
	322	TV, radio transmitters & appar. for line teleph., telegr.	..	15 650	17 580	22 024	28 222	40 480	59 657	..
	323	TV, radio receivers and associated goods	..	5 320	4 246	1 113	1 090	1 899	2 620	..
	33	**Medical, precision, optical instr.; watches, clocks**	..	13 585	13 756	13 267	16 471	20 560	24 894	..
	331	Medical equip.; precision instruments and appliances	..	12 766	12 950	12 692	..	19 617	23 796	..
	332	Optical instruments and photographic equipment	..	818	806	575	836	943	1 098	..
	333	Watches and clocks	..	..	..	..	..	..	..	..
	34	**Motor vehicles, trailers, and semi-trailers**	..	74 464	66 881	66 020	67 574	89 497	118 264	..
	35	**Other transport equipment**	..	17 604	18 389	17 972	17 125	17 074	20 869	..
	351	Building and repairing of ships and boats	..	3 291	3 051	2 872	2 522	2 836	3 442	..
	352	Railway, tramway locomotives and rolling stock	..	4 155	4 431	4 221	4 280	4 484	4 717	..
	353	Aircraft and spacecraft	..	9 235	10 032	9 847	9 230	8 420	11 250	..
	359	Transport equipment, nec	..	923	875	1 032	1 093	1 334	1 459	..
	36	**Furniture; manufacturing, nec**	..	15 005	15 190	14 589	13 808	15 985	18 997	..
	361	Furniture	..	12 632	12 669	11 860	11 191	13 412	16 140	..
	369	Manufacturing, nec	..	2 373	2 521	2 729	2 617	2 572	2 857	..
	37	**Recycling**	..	211	203	329	420	622	775	..
E	40-41	**Electricity, gas and water supply**	..	..	..	..	..	..	..	..
	40	**Electricity, gas, steam and hot water supply**	..	..	..	..	..	..	..	..
	401	Production, collection and distribution of electricity	..	..	..	..	..	..	..	..
	41 410	**Collection, purification, distribution of water**	..	..	..	..	..	..	..	..
F	45	**Construction**	..	..	..	..	..	..	..	..
G	50-52	**Wholesale and retail trade; repairs etc**	..	..	..	..	..	..	..	..
H	55	**Hotels and restaurants**	..	..	..	..	..	..	..	..
I	60-64	**Transport, storage and communications**	..	..	..	..	..	..	..	..
J	65-67	**Financial intermediation**	..	..	..	..	..	..	..	..
K	70-74	**Real estate, renting and business activities**	..	..	..	..	..	..	..	..
L-Q	75-99	**Public admin.; education; health; other services**	..	..	..	..	..	..	..	..
A-Q	01-99	**Grand total**	..	726 018	681 003	641 322	677 381	800 565	949 689	..

Note: All period: ISIC 1549 includes 1544; 2222 includes 2230; 2695 includes part of 2691; 3320 includes 3330; 3592 includes 3591. In 1990, ISIC 272 includes 273. In 1991, ISIC 1810 includes 1820. In 1993, ISIC 2732 includes 2731. In 1995, ISIC 1549 includes 1542; 2411 includes 2412. In 1991, 1992, 1993 and 1995, ISIC 14 includes 11. From 1993 to 1995, ISIC 2429 includes 2430. In 1994 and 1995, ISIC 1030 includes 1010.

Table SN.2 VALEUR AJOUTÉE - VALUE ADDED

Millions de SKr (Prix courants)

1989	1990	1991	1992	1993	1994	1995	1996	Désignation		CITI révision 3
..	..				..	..	..	**Agriculture, chasse et sylviculture**	A	01-02
							..	**Pêche**	B	05
..	3 756	3 433	3 124	3 587	4 342	4 894	..	**Activités extractives**	C	10-14
..	169	193	261	224	279	253	..	Extraction de charbon, de lignite et de tourbe		10
..							..	Extraction de pétrole brut et de gaz naturel		11
..	2 414	2 100	1 928	2 432	3 128	3 586	..	Extraction de minerais métalliques		13
..	1 173	1 140	935	931	934	1 055	..	Autres activités extractives		14
..	235 066	225 241	213 175	229 430	268 560	307 953	..	**Activités de fabrication**	D	15-37
..	19 603	21 836	22 912	22 268	22 702	22 919	..	**Produits alimentaires et boissons**	15	
..	2 675	3 068	3 114	2 827	3 276	3 166	..	Boissons		155
..	1 073	1 209	1 392	1 290	1 443	1 416	..	**Produits à base de tabac**	16	160
..	3 000	2 728	2 582	2 574	2 840	2 977	..	**Textiles**	17	
..	838	897	790	779	750	805	..	Filature, tissage et achèvement des textiles		171
..	1 698	1 523	1 451	1 512	1 743	1 768	..	Autres articles textiles		172
..	464	309	340	283	347	404	..	Etoffes et articles de bonneterie		173
..	921	762	666	548	578	616	..	**Habillement; préparation, teinture des fourrures**	18	
..	908	755	666	..	..	..	..	Articles d'habillement autres qu'en fourrure		181
..	13	7	..	..	..	..	..	Préparation, teinture des fourrures; art. en fourrure		182
..	378	355	331	345	349	372	..	**Travail des cuirs; articles en cuir; chaussures**	19	
..	231	207	193	215	247	269	..	Apprêt et tannage des cuirs et articles en cuirs		191
..	148	148	138	130	102	103	..	Chaussures		192
..	13 424	10 927	8 627	9 570	12 359	12 384	..	**Bois et articles en bois et liège (sauf meubles)**	20	
..	6 222	4 647	3 969	5 442	7 974	7 553	..	Sciage et rabotage du bois		201
..	7 203	6 280	4 658	4 128	4 386	4 831	..	Articles en bois, liège, vannerie, sparterie		202
..	22 146	19 530	17 776	21 034	26 238	38 414	..	**Papier et carton; articles en papier et en carton**	21	
..	14 932	14 870	14 857	14 918	16 264	17 469	..	**Edition, imprimerie et reproduction**	22	
..	5 109	5 204	5 458	5 653	9 149	10 097	..	Edition		221
..	9 822	9 666	9 399	9 264	7 116	7 372	..	Imprimerie et activités annexes		222
..							..	Reproduction de supports enregistrés		223
..	8 789	5 844	2 489	3 633	3 110	2 907	..	**Cokéfaction; prod. pétroliers; comb. nucléaires**	23	
..	16 979	18 678	20 063	23 539	25 932	27 719	..	**Produits chimiques**	24	
..	7 305	6 585	6 280	7 209	8 410	10 564	..	Produits chimiques de base		241
..	..	..	..	..	17 522	17 155	..	Autres produits chimiques		242
..							..	Fibres synthétiques ou artificielles		243
..	6 356	6 425	6 169	6 085	7 577	8 096	..	**Articles en caoutchouc et en matières plastiques**	25	
..	1 572	1 565	1 578	1 543	2 166	2 321	..	Articles en caoutchouc		251
..	4 784	4 860	4 591	4 543	5 412	5 775	..	Articles en matières plastiques		252
..	8 276	7 719	6 733	6 139	6 226	6 982	..	**Autres produits minéraux non métalliques**	26	
..	1 813	1 646	1 468	1 500	1 572	1 769	..	Verre et articles en verre		261
..	6 464	6 073	5 265	4 639	4 654	5 213	..	Produits minéraux non métalliques, nca		269
..	12 892	11 157	10 571	13 019	17 427	21 708	..	**Produits métallurgiques de base**	27	
..	10 562	8 721	8 319	10 536	14 525	18 432	..	Sidérurgie et première transformation de l'acier		271
..	2 330	2 408	2 231	2 396	2 814	3 147	..	Métallurgie; métaux précieux et non ferreux		272
..	..	27	21	87	88	130	..	Fonderie		273
..	18 235	16 192	14 039	13 597	16 738	20 647	..	**Ouvrages en métaux, sauf machines et matériel**	28	
..	6 012	5 364	4 161	3 827	4 538	5 218	..	Constr. et menuiserie métal.; réservoirs; générateurs		281
..	12 222	10 828	9 879	9 770	12 201	15 429	..	Autres ouvrages en métaux		289
..	32 315	28 905	30 697	27 781	35 242	39 594	..	**Machines et matériel, nca**	29	
..	16 320	13 990	16 552	14 034	18 091	20 407	..	Machines d'usage général		291
..	13 882	12 754	12 045	11 747	14 622	16 752	..	Machines d'usage spécifique		292
..	2 113	2 161	2 100	2 000	2 529	2 435	..	Appareils domestiques, nca		293
..	2 580	3 056	2 326	1 887	1 797	1 590	..	**Mach. de bureau, comptables, matériel inform.**	30	
..	8 207	7 357	7 419	7 623	7 619	8 863	..	**Machines et appareils électriques, nca**	31	
..	1 284	1 177	1 157	1 213	1 310	1 702	..	Moteurs, génératrices et transformateurs électriques		311
..	2 489	2 041	2 234	2 320	2 126	2 525	..	Matériel électrique de distribution et de commande		312
..	1 495	1 443	1 311	1 325	1 748	1 765	..	Fils et câbles électriques isolés		313
..	455	329	404	465	459	636	..	Accumulateurs, piles électriques		314
..	985	889	829	804	859	924	..	Lampes électriques et appareils d'éclairage		315
..	1 498	1 477	1 484	1 496	1 117	1 310	..	Autres matériels électriques, nca		319
..	7 585	8 248	8 929	11 142	13 001	16 742	..	**Equip. et appar. de radio, TV, communication**	32	
..	1 272	1 252	974	1 307	1 278	2 001	..	Tubes et valves électroniques; autres composants		321
..	4 805	5 983	7 582	9 477	11 201	14 152	..	Emetteurs radio et TV; app. téléphonie, télégraphie		322
..	1 508	1 014	373	359	523	590	..	Récepteurs radio et TV et articles associés		323
..	6 851	7 039	6 727	8 105	9 680	10 753	..	**Instruments médicaux, de précision, d'optique**	33	
..	6 395	6 559	6 363	..	9 161	10 159	..	Appareils médicaux et de précision		331
..	455	479	364	450	519	594	..	Instruments d'optique ; matériel photographique		332
..	..	..	..		..		..	Horlogerie		333
..	18 156	19 018	14 797	22 082	28 768	31 444	..	**Véhicules automobiles et nemorques**	34	
..	6 462	7 741	7 510	7 052	6 784	7 251	..	**Autres matériels de transport**	35	
..	1 009	1 181	1 081	1 113	1 130	1 054	..	Construction et réparation de navires		351
..	1 688	1 906	1 732	1 710	1 897	1 764	..	Construction de matériel ferroviaire roulant		352
..	3 366	4 265	4 269	3 809	3 249	3 916	..	Construction aéronautique et spatiale		353
..	399	389	428	420	507	517	..	Autres équipements de transport		359
..	5 832	5 555	5 413	5 031	5 641	6 782	..	**Meubles; activités de fabrication, nca**	36	
..	4 659	4 367	4 223	3 895	4 602	5 442	..	Meubles		361
..	1 173	1 188	1 190	1 137	1 039	1 341	..	Activités de fabrication, nca		369
..	74	90	152	168	243	306	..	**Récupération**	37	
..	..	..	..	..	..	..	..	**Production et distrib. d'électricité, gaz, d'eau**	E	40-41
..	..	..	..	..	..	..	..	**Electricité, gaz, vapeur et eau chaude**	40	
..	..	..	..	..	..	..	..	Production, collecte et distribution d'électricité		401
..	..	..	..	..	..	..	..	**Captage, épuration et distribution d'eau**	41	410
..	..	..	..	..	..	..	..	**Construction**	F	45
..	..	..	..	..	..	..	..	**Commerce de gros et de détail; réparation**	G	50-52
..	..	..	..	..	..	..	..	**Hôtels et restaurants**	H	55
..	..	..	..	..	..	..	..	**Transports, entreposage et communications**	I	60-64
..	..	..	..	..	..	..	..	**Intermédiation financière**	J	65-67
..	..	..	..	..	..	..	..	**Immobilier, locations, services aux entreprises**	K	70-74
..	..	..	..	..	..	..	..	**Admin. publique; éducation; santé; autres**	L-Q	75-99
..	238 822	228 674	216 300	233 017	272 902	312 847	..	**Grand total**	A-Q	01-99

Note: All period: ISIC 1549 includes 1544; 2222 includes 2230; 2695 includes part of 2691; 3320 includes 3330; 3592 includes 3591. In 1990, ISIC 272 includes 273. In 1991, ISIC 1810 includes 1820. In 1993, ISIC 2732 includes 2731. In 1995, ISIC 1549 includes 1542; 2411 includes 2412. In 1991, 1992, 1993 and 1995, ISIC 14 includes 11. From 1993 to 1995, ISIC 1030 includes 1010.

Statistiques des Structures Industrielles
OCDE, © 1998

Table SN.3 ESTABLISHMENTS - ETABLISSEMENTS

Units

ISIC revision 3			1989	1990	1991	1992	1993	1994	1995	1996
A	01-02	**Agriculture, hunting and forestry**	..	..	..	..	..	..	..	..
B	05	**Fishing**	..	..	..	..	..	..	..	..
C	10-14	**Mining and quarrying**	..	198	188	175	166	158	160	..
	10	Mining of coal and lignite; extraction of peat	..	13	14	16	14	21	22	..
	11	Crude petroleum & natural gas; related service activ.	..	..	..	..	..	..	..	..
	13	Mining of metal ores	..	37	33	29	24	23	23	..
	14	Other mining and quarrying	..	148	141	130	128	114	115	..
D	15-37	**Total manufacturing**	..	9 509	9 284	8 754	8 153	8 210	8 510	..
	15	**Food products and beverages**	..	894	869	856	841	829	845	..
	155	Beverages	..	35	34	35	33	33	33	..
	16	160 **Tobacco products**	..	9	9	8	8	8	8	..
	17	**Textiles**	..	270	241	224	202	188	187	..
	171	Spinning, weaving and finishing of textiles	..	53	50	44	43	39	38	..
	172	Other textiles	..	166	147	138	121	114	112	..
	173	Knitted and crocheted fabrics and articles	..	51	44	42	38	35	37	..
	18	**Wearing apparel dressing & dyeing of fur**	..	165	127	100	71	62	60	..
	181	Wearing apparel, except fur apparel	..	156	124	100	..	..	..	..
	182	Dressing and dyeing of fur; articles of fur	..	9	3	..	..	..	..	..
	19	**Tanning, dressing leather; leather artic.; footwear**	..	50	44	38	39	32	34	..
	191	Tanning, dressing leather; manuf. of leather articles	..	27	22	19	19	18	20	..
	192	Footwear	..	23	22	19	20	14	14	..
	20	**Wood and cork products, ex. furniture**	..	806	797	773	673	688	709	..
	201	Sawmilling and planing of wood	..	383	386	381	357	370	373	..
	202	Products of wood, cork, straw & plaiting material	..	423	411	392	316	318	336	..
	21	**Paper and paper products**	..	274	267	266	252	248	256	..
	22	**Publishing, printing & reprod. of recorded media**	..	930	934	931	892	920	913	..
	221	Publishing	..	238	250	287	282	317	331	..
	222	Printing and related service activities	..	692	684	644	610	603	582	..
	223	Reproduction of recorded media	..	..	..	..	..	..	..	..
	23	**Coke, refined petroleum products & nuclear fuel**	..	27	23	20	21	19	17	..
	24	**Chemicals and chemical products**	..	316	320	313	308	322	315	..
	241	Basic chemicals	..	153	146	142	136	140	140	..
	242	Other chemical products	..	..	..	..	..	182	175	..
	243	Man-made fibres	..	..	..	..	..			..
	25	**Rubber and plastic products**	..	381	386	372	346	378	376	..
	251	Rubber products	..	70	72	65	64	76	77	..
	252	Plastic products	..	311	314	307	282	302	299	..
	26	**Other non-metallic mineral products**	..	429	419	410	390	376	356	..
	261	Glass and glass products	..	58	58	57	49	45	44	..
	269	Non-metallic mineral products, nec	..	371	361	353	341	331	312	..
	27	**Basic metals**	..	204	204	194	166	173	170	..
	271	Basic iron and steel	..	155	154	144	114	126	117	..
	272	Basic precious and non-ferrous metals	..	49	45	44	42	39	44	..
	273	Casting of metals	..	..	5	6	10	8	9	..
	28	**Fabricated metal products, ex. machin. & equip.**	..	1 571	1 510	1 316	1 228	1 252	1 415	..
	281	Structural metal prod., tanks, reservoirs, generators	..	567	538	460	420	402	423	..
	289	Other fabricated metal products & service activities	..	1 004	972	856	808	850	992	..
	29	**Machinery and equipment, nec**	..	1 415	1 388	1 277	1 152	1 168	1 201	..
	291	General purpose machinery	..	687	686	661	612	633	652	..
	292	Special purpose machinery	..	662	639	562	488	486	502	..
	293	Domestic appliances, nec	..	66	63	54	52	49	47	..
	30	**Office, accounting and computing machinery**	..	68	61	59	54	51	48	..
	31	**Electrical machinery and apparatus, nec**	..	363	364	371	315	319	332	..
	311	Electric motors, generators and transformers	..	52	44	43	38	35	45	..
	312	Electricity distribution and control apparatus	..	109	108	102	88	85	88	..
	313	Insulated wire and cable	..	30	36	35	34	33	36	..
	314	Accumulators, primary cells and primary batteries	..	8	9	8	10	11	12	..
	315	Electric lamps and lighting equipment	..	78	69	71	60	64	66	..
	319	Other electrical equipment, nec	..	86	98	112	85	91	85	..
	32	**Radio, TV, communication equip. & apparatus**	..	151	177	144	144	143	160	..
	321	Electronic valves, tubes & other electronic compon.	..	56	55	50	49	41	49	..
	322	TV, radio transmitters & appar. for line teleph., telegr.	..	66	94	70	67	70	77	..
	323	TV, radio receivers and associated goods	..	29	28	24	28	32	34	..
	33	**Medical, precision, optical instr.; watches, clocks**	..	195	195	185	232	237	266	..
	331	Medical equip.; precision instruments and appliances	..	167	167	159	..	212	237	..
	332	Optical instruments and photographic equipment	..	28	28	26	21	25	29	..
	333	Watches and clocks	..	..	..	..	..	..	..	..
	34	**Motor vehicles, trailers, and semi-trailers**	..	308	293	267	256	247	258	..
	35	**Other transport equipment**	..	174	166	164	143	140	154	..
	351	Building and repairing of ships and boats	..	71	63	55	48	44	55	..
	352	Railway, tramway locomotives and rolling stock	..	51	52	48	44	42	44	..
	353	Aircraft and spacecraft	..	26	25	30	25	25	24	..
	359	Transport equipment, nec	..	26	26	31	26	29	31	..
	36	**Furniture; manufacturing, nec**	..	499	481	456	409	397	412	..
	361	Furniture	..	399	385	367	333	331	345	..
	369	Manufacturing, nec	..	100	96	89	76	66	67	..
	37	**Recycling**	..	10	9	10	11	13	18	..
E	40-41	**Electricity, gas and water supply**	..	..	..	..	..	..	..	..
	40	**Electricity, gas, steam and hot water supply**	..	..	..	..	..	..	..	..
	401	Production, collection and distribution of electricity	..	..	..	..	..	..	..	..
	41	410 **Collection, purification, distribution of water**	..	..	..	..	..	..	..	..
F	45	**Construction**	..	..	..	..	..	..	..	..
G	50-52	**Wholesale and retail trade; repairs etc**	..	..	..	..	..	..	..	..
H	55	**Hotels and restaurants**	..	..	..	..	..	..	..	..
I	60-64	**Transport, storage and communications**	..	..	..	..	..	..	..	..
J	65-67	**Financial intermediation**	..	..	..	..	..	..	..	..
K	70-74	**Real estate, renting and business activities**	..	..	..	..	..	..	..	..
L-Q	75-99	**Public admin.; education; health; other services**	..	..	..	..	..	..	..	..
A-Q	01-99	**Grand total**	..	9 707	9 472	8 929	8 319	8 368	8 670	..

Note: All period: ISIC 1549 includes 1544; 2222 includes 2230; 2695 includes part of 2691; 3320 includes 3330; 3592 includes 3591. In 1990, ISIC 272 includes 273. In 1991, ISIC 1810 includes 1820. In 1993, ISIC 2732 includes 2731. In 1995, ISIC 1549 includes 1542; 2411 includes 2412. In 1991, 1992, 1993 and 1995, ISIC 14 includes 11. From 1993 to 1995, ISIC 2429 includes 2430. In 1994 and 1995, ISIC 1030 includes 1010.

OECD OCDE Industrial Structure Statistics
OECD, © 1998

Table SN.4 EMPLOI - EMPLOYMENT

Milliers

1989	1990	1991	1992	1993	1994	1995	1996		CITI révision 3	
..	..	..	..	..	..	..	..	**Agriculture, chasse et sylviculture**	A	01-02
..	..	..	..	..	..	..	..	**Pêche**	B	05
..	9.4	9.1	8.1	7.2	7.5	7.5	..	**Activités extractives**	C	10-14
..	0.5	0.4	0.4	0.4	0.5	0.5	..	Extraction de charbon, de lignite et de tourbe		10
..	..	..	..	..	..	..	..	Extraction de pétrole brut et de gaz naturel		11
..	6.4	6.2	5.5	4.8	5.2	5.1	..	Extraction de minerais métalliques		13
..	2.6	2.5	2.2	2.0	1.7	1.8	..	Autres activités extractives		14
..	773.0	713.0	639.7	585.5	598.7	633.8	..	**Activités de fabrication**	D	15-37
..	70.4	67.9	63.1	61.0	59.5	59.4	..	**Produits alimentaires et boissons**		15
..	5.2	4.9	4.7	4.4	4.2	4.5	..	Boissons		155
..	1.2	1.1	1.0	0.9	0.8	0.8	..	**Produits à base de tabac**	16	160
..	14.1	11.5	9.9	8.7	8.5	8.5	..	**Textiles**	17	
..	3.8	3.5	3.0	2.7	2.4	2.5	..	Filature, tissage et achèvement des textiles		171
..	7.5	6.3	5.4	4.8	5.0	4.9	..	Autres articles textiles		172
..	2.7	1.6	1.5	1.2	1.1	1.2	..	Etoffes et articles de bonneterie		173
..	6.1	4.2	3.3	2.2	2.1	2.1	..	**Habillement; préparation, teinture des fourrures**	18	
..	6.0	4.2	3.3	..	..	..	..	Articles d'habillement autres qu'en fourrure		181
..	0.1	0.0	..	..	..	..	..	Préparation, teinture des fourrures; art. en fourrure		182
..	2.0	1.5	1.3	1.2	1.1	1.2	..	**Travail des cuirs; articles en cuir; chaussures**	19	
..	1.2	0.8	0.7	0.7	0.7	0.8	..	Apprêt et tannage des cuirs et articles en cuirs		191
..	0.8	0.6	0.6	0.5	0.4	0.4	..	Chaussures		192
..	40.5	37.6	32.1	27.6	28.6	29.7	..	**Bois et articles en bois et liège (sauf meubles)**	20	
..	16.0	15.2	14.5	13.7	14.6	15.1	..	Sciage et rabotage du bois		201
..	24.4	22.4	17.6	13.9	14.0	14.6	..	Articles en bois, liège, vannerie, sparterie		202
..	54.4	50.5	46.2	43.5	43.0	44.1	..	**Papier et carton; articles en papier et en carton**	21	
..	55.1	52.4	45.3	43.4	45.6	45.8	..	**Edition, imprimerie et reproduction**	22	
..	16.9	16.0	13.1	13.6	25.2	26.7	..	Edition		221
..	38.3	36.4	32.2	29.9	20.4	19.1	..	Imprimerie et activités annexes		222
..	..	..	..	..	..	..	..	Reproduction de supports enregistrés		223
..	2.9	2.4	2.3	2.4	2.8	2.8	..	**Cokéfaction; prod. pétroliers; comb. nucléaires**	23	
..	34.7	33.9	31.7	29.7	32.1	33.9	..	**Produits chimiques**	24	
..	14.7	14.1	12.7	11.9	11.2	11.9	..	Produits chimiques de base		241
..	..	..	..	..	20.9	22.0	..	Autres produits chimiques		242
..	..	..	..	..	..	..	..	Fibres synthétiques ou artificielles		243
..	24.0	22.5	20.5	18.5	20.2	21.0	..	**Articles en caoutchouc et en matières plastiques**	25	
..	6.9	6.4	5.8	5.1	5.8	6.1	..	Articles en caoutchouc		251
..	17.1	16.1	14.7	13.4	14.4	14.8	..	Articles en matières plastiques		252
..	24.2	22.7	19.4	16.3	15.6	16.5	..	**Autres produits minéraux non métalliques**	26	
..	6.4	5.9	5.1	4.3	4.2	4.5	..	Verre et articles en verre		261
..	17.8	16.8	14.3	12.0	11.4	12.0	..	Produits minéraux non métalliques, nca		269
..	42.1	39.0	36.1	33.1	32.0	33.1	..	**Produits métallurgiques de base**	27	
..	33.7	31.3	29.1	26.6	25.8	26.7	..	Sidérurgie et première transformation de l'acier		271
..	8.5	7.5	6.9	6.2	5.9	6.1	..	Métallurgie; métaux précieux et non ferreux		272
..	..	0.1	0.1	0.3	0.3	0.3	..	Fonderie		273
..	64.4	55.1	46.9	42.6	45.6	51.7	..	**Ouvrages en métaux, sauf machines et matériel**	28	
..	20.9	17.9	14.4	12.8	13.2	14.3	..	Constr. et menuiserie métal.; réservoirs; générateurs		281
..	43.5	37.2	32.5	29.8	32.4	37.4	..	Autres ouvrages en métaux		289
..	114.3	103.6	92.9	81.2	84.4	89.9	..	**Machines et matériel, nca**	29	
..	57.1	50.2	48.6	40.4	43.9	46.5	..	Machines d'usage général		291
..	47.2	43.9	36.5	33.6	33.1	36.1	..	Machines d'usage spécifique		292
..	10.0	9.6	7.7	7.2	7.3	7.3	..	Appareils domestiques, nca		293
..	7.3	6.3	5.7	4.9	4.3	3.6	..	**Mach. de bureau, comptables, matériel inform.**	30	
..	28.8	25.5	23.6	20.2	19.2	21.8	..	**Machines et appareils électriques, nca**	31	
..	4.7	3.8	3.3	3.1	3.3	4.8	..	Moteurs, génératrices et transformateurs électriques		311
..	9.2	8.0	7.2	6.1	5.8	6.2	..	Matériel électrique de distribution et de commande		312
..	4.4	4.4	3.7	3.3	3.3	3.7	..	Fils et câbles électriques isolés		313
..	1.5	1.5	1.4	1.3	1.3	1.4	..	Accumulateurs, piles électriques		314
..	4.2	3.7	3.7	2.9	2.8	2.8	..	Lampes électriques et appareils d'éclairage		315
..	4.8	4.1	4.3	3.6	2.7	2.8	..	Autres matériels électriques, nca		319
..	30.7	31.9	28.9	29.0	30.6	36.1	..	**Equip. et appar. de radio, TV, communication**	32	
..	4.9	4.7	3.8	4.0	3.8	4.9	..	Tubes et valves électroniques; autres composants		321
..	19.2	21.1	23.2	23.9	25.1	29.3	..	Emetteurs radio et TV; app. téléphonie, télégraphie		322
..	6.6	6.1	1.9	1.1	1.6	2.0	..	Récepteurs radio et TV et articles associés		323
..	21.0	20.8	17.9	19.7	20.9	22.6	..	**Instruments médicaux, de précision, d'optique**	33	
..	19.3	19.1	16.6	..	19.6	21.2	..	Appareils médicaux et de précision		331
..	1.7	1.7	1.2	1.2	1.4	1.4	..	Instruments d'optique ; matériel photographique		332
..	..	..	..	..	..	..	..	Horlogerie		333
..	82.3	73.8	67.9	59.7	61.8	67.2	..	**Véhicules automobiles et nemorques**	34	
..	28.9	27.2	23.7	21.9	21.0	21.5	..	**Autres matériels de transport**	35	
..	4.4	4.8	4.4	3.5	3.3	3.6	..	Construction et réparation de navires		351
..	8.0	6.4	5.3	5.0	4.8	4.9	..	Construction de matériel ferroviaire roulant		352
..	15.0	14.5	12.6	12.2	11.7	11.6	..	Construction aéronautique et spatiale		353
..	1.5	1.5	1.5	1.2	1.3	1.3	..	Autres équipements de transport		359
..	23.4	21.6	19.6	17.5	18.5	19.9	..	**Meubles; activités de fabrication, nca**	36	
..	19.0	17.5	15.7	13.9	15.3	16.5	..	Meubles		361
..	4.4	4.1	3.9	3.6	3.2	3.4	..	Activités de fabrication, nca		369
..	0.2	0.2	0.3	0.2	0.4	0.4	..	**Récupération**	37	
..	..	..	..	..	..	..	..	**Production et distrib. d'électricité, de gaz, d'eau**	E	40-41
..	..	..	..	..	..	..	..	**Electricité, gaz, vapeur et eau chaude**		40
..	..	..	..	..	..	..	..	Production, collecte et distribution d'électricité		401
..	..	..	..	..	..	..	..	**Captage, épuration et distribution d'eau**	41	410
..	..	..	..	..	..	..	..	**Construction**	F	45
..	..	..	..	..	..	..	..	**Commerce de gros et de détail; réparation**	G	50-52
..	..	..	..	..	..	..	..	**Hôtels et restaurants**	H	55
..	..	..	..	..	..	..	..	**Transports, entreposage et communications**	I	60-64
..	..	..	..	..	..	..	..	**Intermédiation financière**	J	65-67
..	..	..	..	..	..	..	..	**Immobilier, locations, services aux entreprises**	K	70-74
..	..	..	..	..	..	..	..	**Admin. publique; éducation; santé; autres**	L-Q	75-99
..	782.3	722.1	647.9	592.7	606.2	641.3	..	**Grand total**	A-Q	01-99

Note: All period: ISIC 1549 includes 1544; 2222 includes 2230; 2695 includes part of 2691; 3320 includes 3330; 3592 includes 3591. In 1990, ISIC 272 includes 273. In 1991, ISIC 1810 includes 1820. In 1993, ISIC 2732 includes 2731. In 1995, ISIC 1549 includes 1542; 2411 includes 2412. In 1991, 1992, 1993 and 1995, ISIC 14 includes 11. From 1993 to 1995, ISIC 2429 includes 2430. In 1994 and 1995, ISIC 1030 includes 1010.

Statistiques des Structures Industrielles
OCDE, © 1998

Table SN.5 EMPLOYMENT, EMPLOYEES - EMPLOI, SALARIÉS

Thousands

ISIC revision 3			1989	1990	1991	1992	1993	1994	1995	1996
A	01-02	Agriculture, hunting and forestry	..	..	..	..	..	..	..	..
B	05	Fishing	..	..	..	..	..	..	..	..
C	10-14	Mining and quarrying	..	9.4	9.1	8.1	7.2	7.1	7.1	..
	10	Mining of coal and lignite; extraction of peat	..	0.5	0.4	0.4	0.4	0.5	0.5	..
	11	Crude petroleum & natural gas; related service activ.	..	..	..	..	..	..	..	..
	13	Mining of metal ores	..	6.4	6.2	5.5	4.8	4.8	4.8	..
	14	Other mining and quarrying	..	2.6	2.5	2.1	2.0	1.7	1.8	..
D	15-37	Total manufacturing	..	761.0	703.0	632.1	579.2	593.4	628.2	..
	15	Food products and beverages	..	68.7	66.4	61.9	59.8	58.3	58.3	..
	155	Beverages	..	5.1	4.9	4.7	4.3	4.1	4.5	..
	16	160 Tobacco products	..	1.1	1.1	1.0	0.9	0.8	0.8	..
	17	Textiles	..	14.0	11.4	9.9	8.7	8.5	8.5	..
	171	Spinning, weaving and finishing of textiles	..	3.8	3.5	3.0	2.7	2.4	2.4	..
	172	Other textiles	..	7.5	6.3	5.4	4.8	5.0	4.9	..
	173	Knitted and crocheted fabrics and articles	..	2.7	1.6	1.5	1.2	1.1	1.2	..
	18	Wearing apparel dressing & dyeing of fur	..	6.1	4.2	3.3	2.2	2.1	2.1	..
	181	Wearing apparel, except fur apparel	..	6.0	4.2	3.3	..	..	..	..
	182	Dressing and dyeing of fur; articles of fur	..	0.1	0.0	..	..	..	..	..
	19	Tanning, dressing leather; leather artic.; footwear	..	2.0	1.5	1.3	1.2	1.1	1.2	..
	191	Tanning, dressing leather; manuf. of leather articles	..	1.2	0.8	0.7	0.7	0.7	0.8	..
	192	Footwear	..	0.8	0.6	0.6	0.5	0.4	0.4	..
	20	Wood and cork products, ex. furniture	..	40.1	37.2	31.8	27.4	28.4	29.6	..
	201	Sawmilling and planing of wood	..	15.7	14.9	14.3	13.6	14.5	15.1	..
	202	Products of wood, cork, straw & plaiting material	..	24.4	22.3	17.6	13.9	13.9	14.5	..
	21	Paper and paper products	..	53.8	49.8	45.7	42.9	42.6	43.8	..
	22	Publishing, printing & reprod. of recorded media	..	54.6	51.6	44.9	43.0	45.3	45.4	..
	221	Publishing	..	16.7	15.8	13.0	13.4	25.0	26.4	..
	222	Printing and related service activities	..	37.9	35.8	31.9	29.5	20.3	19.0	..
	223	Reproduction of recorded media	..	..	..	..	..	..	..	..
	23	Coke, refined petroleum products & nuclear fuel	..	2.9	2.4	2.3	2.4	2.8	2.8	..
	24	Chemicals and chemical products	..	33.7	33.0	30.9	29.0	31.4	33.1	..
	241	Basic chemicals	..	13.9	13.6	12.4	11.6	10.8	11.5	..
	242	Other chemical products	..	..	..	..	..	20.6	21.5	..
	243	Man-made fibres	..	..	..	..	..	..	..	..
	25	Rubber and plastic products	..	23.2	21.8	19.9	18.0	19.6	20.7	..
	251	Rubber products	..	6.9	6.4	5.8	5.0	5.7	6.1	..
	252	Plastic products	..	16.3	15.5	14.2	12.9	13.9	14.7	..
	26	Other non-metallic mineral products	..	23.9	22.4	19.2	16.2	15.6	16.3	..
	261	Glass and glass products	..	6.4	5.9	5.1	4.3	4.2	4.5	..
	269	Non-metallic mineral products, nec	..	17.6	16.5	14.1	11.9	11.4	11.8	..
	27	Basic metals	..	41.2	37.7	35.2	32.8	31.8	33.0	..
	271	Basic iron and steel	..	33.2	30.5	28.5	26.5	25.6	26.5	..
	272	Basic precious and non-ferrous metals	..	8.1	7.2	6.6	6.0	5.9	6.1	..
	273	Casting of metals	..	..	0.1	0.1	0.3	0.3	0.3	..
	28	Fabricated metal products, ex. machin. & equip.	..	63.9	54.9	46.9	42.5	45.5	51.5	..
	281	Structural metal prod., tanks, reservoirs, generators	..	20.6	17.8	14.4	12.8	13.2	14.1	..
	289	Other fabricated metal products & service activities	..	43.3	37.1	32.5	29.8	32.4	37.3	..
	29	Machinery and equipment, nec	..	113.1	102.8	92.2	80.6	83.9	89.5	..
	291	General purpose machinery	..	56.5	49.7	48.2	40.0	43.7	46.3	..
	292	Special purpose machinery	..	46.8	43.6	36.3	33.4	32.9	36.0	..
	293	Domestic appliances, nec	..	9.8	9.5	7.7	7.2	7.3	7.3	..
	30	Office, accounting and computing machinery	..	6.9	6.0	5.3	4.9	4.3	3.6	..
	31	Electrical machinery and apparatus, nec	..	28.0	24.8	23.0	19.6	18.6	21.0	..
	311	Electric motors, generators and transformers	..	4.7	3.8	3.3	3.1	3.3	4.8	..
	312	Electricity distribution and control apparatus	..	8.6	7.4	6.6	5.6	5.2	5.6	..
	313	Insulated wire and cable	..	4.4	4.4	3.7	3.2	3.3	3.7	..
	314	Accumulators, primary cells and primary batteries	..	1.5	1.5	1.4	1.3	1.3	1.4	..
	315	Electric lamps and lighting equipment	..	4.2	3.7	3.7	2.9	2.8	2.8	..
	319	Other electrical equipment, nec	..	4.5	4.1	4.3	3.5	2.7	2.8	..
	32	Radio, TV, communication equip. & apparatus	..	30.6	31.8	28.8	29.0	30.6	36.1	..
	321	Electronic valves, tubes & other electronic compon.	..	4.9	4.6	3.8	4.0	3.8	4.9	..
	322	TV, radio transmitters & appar. for line teleph., telegr.	..	19.1	21.0	23.1	23.9	25.1	29.3	..
	323	TV, radio receivers and associated goods	..	6.6	6.1	1.9	1.1	1.6	1.9	..
	33	Medical, precision, optical instr.; watches, clocks	..	20.9	20.7	17.8	19.6	20.9	22.5	..
	331	Medical equip.; precision instruments and appliances	..	19.2	19.1	16.6	..	19.5	21.1	..
	332	Optical instruments and photographic equipment	..	1.7	1.6	1.2	1.2	1.3	1.4	..
	333	Watches and clocks	..	..	..	..	..	..	..	..
	34	Motor vehicles, trailers, and semi-trailers	..	80.2	72.9	67.4	59.3	61.4	66.8	..
	35	Other transport equipment	..	28.8	27.0	23.5	21.8	20.9	21.4	..
	351	Building and repairing of ships and boats	..	4.4	4.8	4.3	3.5	3.3	3.6	..
	352	Railway, tramway locomotives and rolling stock	..	7.9	6.3	5.2	4.9	4.7	4.8	..
	353	Aircraft and spacecraft	..	15.0	14.5	12.6	12.1	11.6	11.6	..
	359	Transport equipment, nec	..	1.5	1.5	1.5	1.2	1.2	1.3	..
	36	Furniture; manufacturing, nec	..	23.2	21.4	19.5	17.4	18.4	19.8	..
	361	Furniture	..	18.9	17.4	15.7	13.9	15.3	16.5	..
	369	Manufacturing, nec	..	4.3	4.0	3.8	3.5	3.2	3.4	..
	37	Recycling	..	0.2	0.2	0.3	0.2	0.4	0.4	..
E	40-41	Electricity, gas and water supply	..	..	..	..	..	..	..	..
	40	Electricity, gas, steam and hot water supply	..	..	..	..	..	..	..	..
	401	Production, collection and distribution of electricity	..	..	..	..	..	..	..	..
	41	410 Collection, purification, distribution of water	..	..	..	..	..	..	..	..
F	45	Construction	..	..	..	..	..	..	..	..
G	50-52	Wholesale and retail trade; repairs etc	..	..	..	..	..	..	..	..
H	55	Hotels and restaurants	..	..	..	..	..	..	..	..
I	60-64	Transport, storage and communications	..	..	..	..	..	..	..	..
J	65-67	Financial intermediation	..	..	..	..	..	..	..	..
K	70-74	Real estate, renting and business activities	..	..	..	..	..	..	..	..
L-Q	75-99	Public admin.; education; health; other services	..	..	..	..	..	..	..	..
A-Q	01-99	Grand total	..	770.3	712.1	640.2	586.4	600.5	635.3	..

Note: All period: ISIC 1549 includes 1544; 2222 includes 2230; 2695 includes part of 2691; 3320 includes 3330; 3592 includes 3591. In 1990, ISIC 272 includes 273. In 1991, ISIC 1810 includes 1820. In 1993, ISIC 2732 includes 2731. In 1995, ISIC 1549 includes 1542; 2411 includes 2412. In 1991, 1992, 1993 and 1995, ISIC 14 includes 11. From 1993 to 1995, ISIC 2429 includes 2430. In 1994 and 1995, ISIC 1030 includes 1010.

OECD
OCDE Industrial Structure Statistics
OCDE OECD, © 1998

Table SN.6 SALAIRES ET TRAITEMENTS, TOTAL - TOTAL WAGES AND SALARIES

Millions de SKr (Prix courants)

1989	1990	1991	1992	1993	1994	1995	1996		Description		CITI révision 3	
..	..	..	..	..	..	..	..	..	**Agriculture, chasse et sylviculture**	A	01-02	
..	..	..	..	..	..	..	..	..	**Pêche**	B	05	
..	1 574	1 690	1 559	1 456	1 656	1 759		..	**Activités extractives**	C	10-14	
..	68	70	77	77	102	94		..	Extraction de charbon, de lignite et de tourbe		10	
..	..	..	..	..	..	..		..	Extraction de pétrole brut et de gaz naturel		11	
..	1 093	1 168	1 091	1 019	1 219	1 287		..	Extraction de minerais métalliques		13	
..	413	451	391	361	336	378		..	Autres activités extractives		14	
..	116 726	116 621	113 992	109 447	117 198	131 711		..	**Activités de fabrication**	D	15-37	
..	9 630	9 859	10 172	10 173	10 473	11 056		..	**Produits alimentaires et boissons**		15	
..	838	844	899	869	844	916		..	Boissons			155
..	168	183	181	197	175	186		..	**Produits à base de tabac**		16	160
..	1 733	1 530	1 448	1 357	1 375	1 469		..	**Textiles**		17	
..	481	497	466	432	382	420		..	Filature, tissage et achèvement des textiles			171
..	959	852	795	764	827	861		..	Autres articles textiles			172
..	294	181	187	162	166	189		..	Etoffes et articles de bonneterie			173
..	627	483	425	303	298	322		..	**Habillement; préparation, teinture des fourrures**		18	
..	618	478	425	..	..	..		..	Articles d'habillement autres qu'en fourrure			181
..	8	4	..	..	..	..		..	Préparation, teinture des fourrures; art. en fourrure			182
..	220	188	178	168	168	193		..	**Travail des cuirs; articles en cuir; chaussures**		19	
..	132	109	100	99	111	131		..	Apprêt et tannage des cuirs et articles en cuirs			191
..	88	79	78	69	57	62		..	Chaussures			192
..	5 764	5 719	5 122	4 654	5 021	5 541		..	**Bois et articles en bois et liège (sauf meubles)**		20	
..	2 302	2 318	2 340	2 349	2 626	2 861		..	Sciage et rabotage du bois			201
..	3 462	3 402	2 782	2 305	2 395	2 680		..	Articles en bois, liège, vannerie, sparterie			202
..	8 862	8 909	8 824	8 607	8 981	9 652		..	**Papier et carton; articles en papier et en carton**		21	
..	8 759	8 804	8 385	8 428	8 809	9 475		..	**Edition, imprimerie et reproduction**		22	
..	2 944	2 963	2 847	2 983	4 849	5 467		..	Edition			221
..	5 815	5 842	5 538	5 444	3 960	4 007		..	Imprimerie et activités annexes			222
..	..	..	..	..	..	..		..	Reproduction de supports enregistrés			223
..	535	515	515	568	687	746		..	**Cokéfaction; prod. pétroliers; comb. nucléaires**		23	
..	6 065	6 387	6 424	6 385	7 318	8 026		..	**Produits chimiques**		24	
..	2 617	2 675	2 574	2 551	2 551	2 816		..	Produits chimiques de base			241
..	..	..	..	..	4 767	5 210		..	Autres produits chimiques			242
..	..	..	..	..	..	..		..	Fibres synthétiques ou artificielles			243
..	3 365	3 445	3 365	3 181	3 670	4 033		..	**Articles en caoutchouc et en matières plastiques**		25	
..	986	965	918	864	1 038	1 164		..	Articles en caoutchouc			251
..	2 378	2 480	2 448	2 316	2 632	2 869		..	Articles en matières plastiques			252
..	3 575	3 603	3 384	2 970	2 989	3 265		..	**Autres produits minéraux non métalliques**		26	
..	872	940	870	771	807	884		..	Verre et articles en verre			261
..	2 703	2 663	2 514	2 199	2 182	2 381		..	Produits minéraux non métalliques, nca			269
..	6 541	6 505	6 454	6 252	6 596	7 221		..	**Produits métallurgiques de base**		27	
..	5 298	5 278	5 292	5 096	5 377	5 875		..	Sidérurgie et première transformation de l'acier			271
..	1 243	1 212	1 148	1 103	1 174	1 282		..	Métallurgie; métaux précieux et non ferreux			272
..	..	15	14	52	45	64		..	Fonderie			273
..	9 275	8 592	7 762	7 274	8 258	9 977		..	**Ouvrages en métaux, sauf machines et matériel**		28	
..	3 091	2 903	2 439	2 228	2 430	2 759		..	Constr. et menuiserie métal.; réservoirs; générateurs			281
..	6 184	5 690	5 323	5 047	5 828	7 218		..	Autres ouvrages en métaux			289
..	17 630	17 239	17 330	15 482	16 841	19 253		..	**Machines et matériel, nca**		29	
..	9 161	8 456	9 350	7 858	8 836	10 060		..	Machines d'usage général			291
..	7 233	7 495	6 809	6 486	6 758	7 880		..	Machines d'usage spécifique			292
..	1 236	1 288	1 171	1 138	1 247	1 313		..	Appareils domestiques, nca			293
..	1 367	1 213	1 239	1 058	978	822		..	**Mach. de bureau, comptables, matériel inform.**		30	
..	4 330	4 277	4 222	3 973	3 814	4 623		..	**Machines et appareils électriques, nca**		31	
..	679	644	572	590	669	992		..	Moteurs, génératrices et transformateurs électriques			311
..	1 434	1 431	1 415	1 291	1 223	1 467		..	Matériel électrique de distribution et de commande			312
..	689	714	652	648	675	767		..	Fils et câbles électriques isolés			313
..	236	249	250	239	234	296		..	Accumulateurs, piles électriques			314
..	533	523	527	465	472	516		..	Lampes électriques et appareils d'éclairage			315
..	759	717	806	740	540	585		..	Autres matériels électriques, nca			319
..	4 812	5 517	5 296	5 652	6 367	7 799		..	**Equip. et appar. de radio, TV, communication**		32	
..	710	720	708	729	717	996		..	Tubes et valves électroniques; autres composants			321
..	3 096	3 834	4 337	4 719	5 345	6 383		..	Emetteurs radio et TV; app. téléphonie, télégraphie			322
..	1 006	964	252	205	305	420		..	Récepteurs radio et TV et articles associés			323
..	3 612	3 793	3 616	4 084	4 678	5 227		..	**Instruments médicaux, de précision, d'optique**		33	
..	3 349	3 521	3 418	..	4 399	4 920		..	Appareils médicaux et de précision			331
..	263	272	197	230	279	307		..	Instruments d'optique ; matériel photographique			332
..	..	..	..	..	..	..		..	Horlogerie			333
..	12 166	12 098	12 122	11 430	12 204	14 501		..	**Véhicules automobiles et nemorques**		34	
..	4 618	4 726	4 519	4 388	4 382	4 691		..	**Autres matériels de transport**		35	
..	677	814	818	663	649	751		..	Construction et réparation de navires			351
..	1 279	1 079	928	913	942	1 036		..	Construction de matériel ferroviaire roulant			352
..	2 462	2 620	2 529	2 590	2 554	2 641		..	Construction aéronautique et spatiale			353
..	200	214	244	222	237	263		..	Autres équipements de transport			359
..	3 038	2 997	2 948	2 810	3 033	3 536		..	**Meubles; activités de fabrication, nca**		36	
..	2 437	2 404	2 348	2 206	2 488	2 913		..	Meubles			361
..	601	593	599	605	546	623		..	Activités de fabrication, nca			369
..	35	35	62	52	84	95		..	**Récupération**		37	
..	..	..	..	..	..	..		..	**Production et distrib. d'électricité, de gaz, d'eau**	E	40-41	
..	..	..	..	..	..	..		..	**Electricité, gaz, vapeur et eau chaude**		40	
..	..	..	..	..	..	..		..	Production, collecte et distribution d'électricité			401
..	..	..	..	..	..	..		..	Captage, épuration et distribution d'eau		41	410
..	..	..	..	..	..	..		..	**Construction**	F	45	
..	..	..	..	..	..	..		..	**Commerce de gros et de détail; réparation**	G	50-52	
..	..	..	..	..	..	..		..	**Hôtels et restaurants**	H	55	
..	..	..	..	..	..	..		..	**Transports, entreposage et communications**	I	60-64	
..	..	..	..	..	..	..		..	**Intermédiation financière**	J	65-67	
..	..	..	..	..	..	..		..	**Immobilier, locations, services aux entreprises**	K	70-74	
..	..	..	..	..	..	..		..	**Admin. publique; éducation; santé; autres**	L-Q	75-99	
..	118 300	118 311	115 551	110 903	118 854	133 470		..	**Grand total**	A-Q	01-99	

Note: All period: ISIC 1549 includes 1544; 2222 includes 2230; 2695 includes part of 2691; 3320 includes 3330; 3592 includes 3591. In 1990, ISIC 272 includes 273. In 1991, ISIC 1810 includes 1820. In 1993, ISIC 2732 includes 2731. In 1995, ISIC 1549 includes 1542; 2411 includes 2412. In 1991, 1992, 1993 and 1995, ISIC 14 includes 11. From 1993 to 1995, ISIC 2429 includes 2430. In 1994 and 1995, ISIC 1030 includes 1010.

Statistiques des Structures Industrielles
OCDE, © 1998

OECD
OCDE

SWEDEN

Table SN.7 WAGES AND SALARIES, EMPLOYEES - SALAIRES ET TRAITEMENTS, SALARIÉS

Millions of SKr (Current Prices)

ISIC revision 3			1989	1990	1991	1992	1993	1994	1995	1996
A	01-02	Agriculture, hunting and forestry	..	..	..	..	..	..	..	..
B	05	Fishing	..	..	..	..	..	..	..	..
C	10-14	Mining and quarrying	..	1 571	1 683	1 552	1 451	1 495	1 617	..
	10	Mining of coal and lignite; extraction of peat	..	68	70	77	76	102	93	..
	11	Crude petroleum & natural gas; related service activ.	..	..	..	..	..	..	..	..
	13	Mining of metal ores	..	1 093	1 168	1 090	1 016	1 059	1 148	..
	14	Other mining and quarrying	..	410	444	385	359	335	376	..
D	15-37	Total manufacturing	..	114 384	114 490	112 207	107 851	115 665	130 100	..
	15	Food products and beverages	..	9 434	9 675	9 933	9 974	10 276	10 849	..
	155	Beverages	..	833	843	898	868	842	914	..
	16 160	Tobacco products	..	156	168	181	197	175	181	..
	17	Textiles	..	1 719	1 521	1 438	1 349	1 367	1 462	..
	171	Spinning, weaving and finishing of textiles	..	480	497	465	430	381	419	..
	172	Other textiles	..	948	846	790	761	824	859	..
	173	Knitted and crocheted fabrics and articles	..	291	179	183	158	161	184	..
	18	Wearing apparel dressing & dyeing of fur	..	621	479	420	301	296	320	..
	181	Wearing apparel, except fur apparel	..	613	474	420	..	..	..	..
	182	Dressing and dyeing of fur; articles of fur	..	8	4	..	..	..	..	..
	19	Tanning, dressing leather; leather artic.; footwear	..	219	187	176	166	167	192	..
	191	Tanning, dressing leather; manuf. of leather articles	..	131	108	99	97	110	130	..
	192	Footwear	..	87	79	78	69	57	62	..
	20	Wood and cork products, ex. furniture	..	5 705	5 669	5 079	4 618	4 992	5 522	..
	201	Sawmilling and planing of wood	..	2 256	2 277	2 306	2 322	2 605	2 849	..
	202	Products of wood, cork, straw & plaiting material	..	3 450	3 393	2 773	2 296	2 387	2 673	..
	21	Paper and paper products	..	8 726	8 773	8 696	8 430	8 828	9 515	..
	22	Publishing, printing & reprod. of recorded media	..	8 682	8 738	8 331	8 361	8 745	9 379	..
	221	Publishing	..	2 880	2 928	2 805	2 956	4 819	5 397	..
	222	Printing and related service activities	..	5 803	5 810	5 526	5 404	3 925	3 981	..
	223	Reproduction of recorded media	..	..	..	..	..	..	..	..
	23	Coke, refined petroleum products & nuclear fuel	..	527	515	515	568	687	746	..
	24	Chemicals and chemical products	..	5 843	6 165	6 201	6 185	7 100	7 783	..
	241	Basic chemicals	..	2 453	2 543	2 465	2 453	2 424	2 705	..
	242	Other chemical products	..	..	..	..	..	4 676	5 079	..
	243	Man-made fibres	..	..	..	..	..	..	..	..
	25	Rubber and plastic products	..	3 232	3 320	3 245	3 066	3 540	3 958	..
	251	Rubber products	..	974	961	898	843	1 015	1 137	..
	252	Plastic products	..	2 257	2 359	2 347	2 223	2 525	2 821	..
	26	Other non-metallic mineral products	..	3 525	3 562	3 357	2 942	2 972	3 240	..
	261	Glass and glass products	..	871	939	869	769	807	884	..
	269	Non-metallic mineral products, nec	..	2 654	2 623	2 487	2 173	2 165	2 356	..
	27	Basic metals	..	6 377	6 246	6 348	6 181	6 551	7 182	..
	271	Basic iron and steel	..	5 198	5 080	5 225	5 053	5 332	5 836	..
	272	Basic precious and non-ferrous metals	..	1 179	1 150	1 110	1 076	1 174	1 282	..
	273	Casting of metals	..	..	15	14	52	45	63	..
	28	Fabricated metal products, ex. machin. & equip.	..	9 201	8 559	7 749	7 261	8 240	9 935	..
	281	Structural metal prod., tanks, reservoirs, generators	..	3 055	2 888	2 436	2 226	2 426	2 725	..
	289	Other fabricated metal products & service activities	..	6 147	5 671	5 313	5 036	5 814	7 210	..
	29	Machinery and equipment, nec	..	17 323	16 962	17 113	15 269	16 644	19 054	..
	291	General purpose machinery	..	8 990	8 278	9 209	7 717	8 724	9 930	..
	292	Special purpose machinery	..	7 123	7 412	6 737	6 416	6 677	7 815	..
	293	Domestic appliances, nec	..	1 210	1 273	1 167	1 135	1 243	1 309	..
	30	Office, accounting and computing machinery	..	1 278	1 118	1 122	1 055	977	821	..
	31	Electrical machinery and apparatus, nec	..	4 080	4 071	4 023	3 753	3 588	4 356	..
	311	Electric motors, generators and transformers	..	679	643	572	590	669	991	..
	312	Electricity distribution and control apparatus	..	1 222	1 234	1 224	1 080	1 005	1 213	..
	313	Insulated wire and cable	..	689	714	652	647	675	767	..
	314	Accumulators, primary cells and primary batteries	..	236	249	250	239	234	291	..
	315	Electric lamps and lighting equipment	..	532	520	525	463	472	515	..
	319	Other electrical equipment, nec	..	723	711	800	734	533	579	..
	32	Radio, TV, communication equip. & apparatus	..	4 786	5 478	5 269	5 643	6 362	7 784	..
	321	Electronic valves, tubes & other electronic compon.	..	709	708	707	728	716	995	..
	322	TV, radio transmitters & appar. for line teleph., telegr.	..	3 071	3 807	4 311	4 710	5 341	6 379	..
	323	TV, radio receivers and associated goods	..	1 005	963	251	205	305	410	..
	33	Medical, precision, optical instr.; watches, clocks	..	3 596	3 773	3 598	4 057	4 655	5 201	..
	331	Medical equip.; precision instruments and appliances	..	3 344	3 513	3 412	..	4 387	4 907	..
	332	Optical instruments and photographic equipment	..	252	260	186	218	268	294	..
	333	Watches and clocks	..	..	..	..	..	..	..	..
	34	Motor vehicles, trailers, and semi-trailers	..	11 722	11 824	11 971	11 260	12 027	14 323	..
	35	Other transport equipment	..	4 590	4 677	4 450	4 372	4 369	4 678	..
	351	Building and repairing of ships and boats	..	663	798	794	663	649	749	..
	352	Railway, tramway locomotives and rolling stock	..	1 269	1 068	915	900	932	1 026	..
	353	Aircraft and spacecraft	..	2 462	2 598	2 519	2 588	2 552	2 641	..
	359	Transport equipment, nec	..	196	212	223	221	236	262	..
	36	Furniture; manufacturing, nec	..	3 006	2 973	2 931	2 792	3 024	3 524	..
	361	Furniture	..	2 431	2 398	2 346	2 203	2 485	2 909	..
	369	Manufacturing, nec	..	575	575	585	588	539	615	..
	37	Recycling	..	35	35	62	52	84	95	..
E	40-41	Electricity, gas and water supply	..	..	..	..	..	..	..	..
	40	Electricity, gas, steam and hot water supply	..	..	..	..	..	..	..	..
	401	Production, collection and distribution of electricity	..	..	..	..	..	..	..	..
	41 410	Collection, purification, distribution of water	..	..	..	..	..	..	..	..
F	45	Construction	..	..	..	..	..	..	..	..
G	50-52	Wholesale and retail trade; repairs etc	..	..	..	..	..	..	..	..
H	55	Hotels and restaurants	..	..	..	..	..	..	..	..
I	60-64	Transport, storage and communications	..	..	..	..	..	..	..	..
J	65-67	Financial intermediation	..	..	..	..	..	..	..	..
K	70-74	Real estate, renting and business activities	..	..	..	..	..	..	..	..
L-Q	75-99	Public admin.; education; health; other services	..	..	..	..	..	..	..	..
A-Q	01-99	Grand total	..	115 955	116 173	113 759	109 302	117 160	131 716	..

Note: All period: ISIC 1549 includes 1544; 2222 includes 2230; 2695 includes part of 2691; 3320 includes 3330; 3592 includes 3591. In 1990, ISIC 272 includes 273. In 1991, ISIC 1810 includes 1820. In 1993, ISIC 2732 includes 2731. In 1995, ISIC 1549 includes 1542; 2411 includes 2412. In 1991, 1992, 1993 and 1995, ISIC 14 includes 11. From 1993 to 1995, ISIC 2429 includes 2430. In 1994 and 1995, ISIC 1030 includes 1010.

Table SN.8 CHARGES SOCIALES DES EMPLOYEURS - EMPLOYERS' SOCIAL COSTS

Millions de SKr (Prix courants)

1989	1990	1991	1992	1993	1994	1995	1996			CITI révision 3	
..	..	..	..	..	..	..	..	**Agriculture, chasse et sylviculture**	A	01-02	
..	..	..	..	..	..	..	..	**Pêche**	B	05	
..	689	797	696	586	620	682	..	**Activités extractives**	C	10-14	
..	30	30	29	26	35	37	..	Extraction de charbon, de lignite et de tourbe		10	
..	..	..	..	..	..	..	..	Extraction de pétrole brut et de gaz naturel		11	
..	460	554	488	410	444	486	..	Extraction de minerais métalliques		13	
..	198	213	179	149	141	159	..	Autres activités extractives		14	
..	54 203	54 351	50 740	45 079	47 714	55 531	..	**Activités de fabrication**	D	15-37	
..	4 405	4 507	4 389	4 158	4 226	4 590	..	**Produits alimentaires et boissons**		15	
..	378	373	391	384	343	380	..	Boissons			155
..	77	83	78	75	66	70	..	**Produits à base de tabac**		16	160
..	792	714	625	550	557	606	..	**Textiles**		17	
..	212	238	200	166	145	165	..	Filature, tissage et achèvement des textiles			171
..	438	396	347	322	348	366	..	Autres articles textiles			172
..	143	81	78	61	64	74	..	Etoffes et articles de bonneterie			173
..	277	217	181	119	122	133	..	**Habillement; préparation, teinture des fourrures**		18	
..	273	215	181	..	..	..	..	Articles d'habillement autres qu'en fourrure			181
..	4	2	..	..	..	..	..	Préparation, teinture des fourrures; art. en fourrure			182
..	98	84	74	65	64	76	..	**Travail des cuirs; articles en cuir; chaussures**		19	
..	58	48	42	38	43	52	..	Apprêt et tannage des cuirs et articles en cuirs			191
..	39	36	32	27	22	24	..	Chaussures			192
..	2 565	2 538	2 184	1 824	1 944	2 241	..	**Bois et articles en bois et liège (sauf meubles)**		20	
..	1 039	1 034	1 002	924	1 025	1 177	..	Sciage et rabotage du bois			201
..	1 527	1 504	1 182	899	919	1 064	..	Articles en bois, liège, vannerie, sparterie			202
..	4 064	4 172	3 917	3 606	3 703	4 116	..	**Papier et carton; articles en papier et en carton**		21	
..	3 950	3 976	3 599	3 255	3 392	3 827	..	**Edition, imprimerie et reproduction**		22	
..	1 372	1 359	1 271	1 170	1 871	2 223	..	Edition			221
..	2 578	2 617	2 328	2 084	1 521	1 604	..	Imprimerie et activités annexes			222
..	..	..	..	..	..	..	..	Reproduction de supports enregistrés			223
..	243	244	232	216	279	317	..	**Cokéfaction; prod. pétroliers; comb. nucléaires**		23	
..	2 880	3 108	2 927	2 674	3 144	3 596	..	**Produits chimiques**		24	
..	1 197	1 242	1 113	1 034	1 001	1 176	..	Produits chimiques de base			241
..	..	..	..	..	2 144	2 420	..	Autres produits chimiques			242
..	..	..	..	..	..	..	..	Fibres synthétiques ou artificielles			243
..	1 563	1 579	1 481	1 308	1 498	1 701	..	**Articles en caoutchouc et en matières plastiques**		25	
..	485	452	449	396	466	520	..	Articles en caoutchouc			251
..	1 078	1 127	1 032	912	1 032	1 181	..	Articles en matières plastiques			252
..	1 737	1 720	1 523	1 248	1 198	1 367	..	**Autres produits minéraux non métalliques**		26	
..	407	427	369	296	292	344	..	Verre et articles en verre			261
..	1 331	1 292	1 155	952	906	1 023	..	Produits minéraux non métalliques, nca			269
..	3 008	2 996	2 832	2 503	2 676	3 043	..	**Produits métallurgiques de base**		27	
..	2 432	2 443	2 320	2 054	2 199	2 500	..	Sidérurgie et première transformation de l'acier			271
..	576	547	506	429	459	516	..	Métallurgie; métaux précieux et non ferreux			272
..	..	7	6	20	18	27	..	Fonderie			273
..	4 318	4 020	3 475	2 975	3 280	4 119	..	**Ouvrages en métaux, sauf machines et matériel**		28	
..	1 377	1 275	1 032	872	951	1 124	..	Constr. et menuiserie métal.; réservoirs; générateurs			281
..	2 941	2 745	2 443	2 103	2 329	2 995	..	Autres ouvrages en métaux			289
..	8 224	8 157	7 733	6 473	6 959	8 165	..	**Machines et matériel, nca**		29	
..	4 324	4 054	4 119	3 223	3 624	4 255	..	Machines d'usage général			291
..	3 306	3 479	3 063	2 772	2 862	3 368	..	Machines d'usage spécifique			292
..	594	623	551	478	473	542	..	Appareils domestiques, nca			293
..	664	573	536	420	397	337	..	**Mach. de bureau, comptables, matériel inform.**		30	
..	2 051	1 923	1 823	1 602	1 495	1 880	..	**Machines et appareils électriques, nca**		31	
..	314	296	240	227	257	399	..	Moteurs, génératrices et transformateurs électriques			311
..	687	646	636	550	490	585	..	Matériel électrique de distribution et de commande			312
..	322	315	282	248	254	314	..	Fils et câbles électriques isolés			313
..	103	108	103	97	85	132	..	Accumulateurs, piles électriques			314
..	258	227	220	192	196	215	..	Lampes électriques et appareils d'éclairage			315
..	366	330	342	288	212	235	..	Autres matériels électriques, nca			319
..	2 030	2 421	2 283	2 309	2 601	3 318	..	**Equip. et appar. de radio, TV, communication**		32	
..	355	350	309	300	299	422	..	Tubes et valves électroniques; autres composants			321
..	1 207	1 612	1 867	1 930	2 189	2 729	..	Emetteurs radio et TV; app. téléphonie, télégraphie			322
..	469	460	107	78	113	166	..	Récepteurs radio et TV et articles associés			323
..	1 764	1 830	1 650	1 757	1 942	2 204	..	**Instruments médicaux, de précision, d'optique**		33	
..	1 635	1 698	1 566	..	1 824	2 074	..	Appareils médicaux et de précision			331
..	129	132	83	101	117	130	..	Instruments d'optique ; matériel photographique			332
..	..	..	..	..	..	..	..	Horlogerie			333
..	5 950	5 876	5 848	4 917	5 020	6 366	..	**Véhicules automobiles et nemorques**		34	
..	2 163	2 240	2 073	1 912	1 938	1 990	..	**Autres matériels de transport**		35	
..	309	376	327	261	250	301	..	Construction et réparation de navires			351
..	598	491	408	383	388	411	..	Construction de matériel ferroviaire roulant			352
..	1 168	1 279	1 238	1 176	1 207	1 178	..	Construction aéronautique et spatiale			353
..	88	94	100	93	93	101	..	Autres équipements de transport			359
..	1 365	1 357	1 249	1 094	1 181	1 427	..	**Meubles; activités de fabrication, nca**		36	
..	1 079	1 085	995	852	957	1 165	..	Meubles			361
..	286	272	254	242	224	262	..	Activités de fabrication, nca			369
..	15	16	27	21	33	40	..	**Récupération**		37	
..	..	..	..	..	..	..	..	**Production et distrib. d'électricité, de gaz, d'eau**	E	40-41	
..	..	..	..	..	..	..	..	**Electricité, gaz, vapeur et eau chaude**		40	
..	..	..	..	..	..	..	..	Production, collecte et distribution d'électricité			401
..	..	..	..	..	..	..	..	**Captage, épuration et distribution d'eau**		41	410
..	..	..	..	..	..	..	..	**Construction**	F	45	
..	..	..	..	..	..	..	..	**Commerce de gros et de détail; réparation**	G	50-52	
..	..	..	..	..	..	..	..	**Hôtels et restaurants**	H	55	
..	..	..	..	..	..	..	..	**Transports, entreposage et communications**	I	60-64	
..	..	..	..	..	..	..	..	**Intermédiation financière**	J	65-67	
..	..	..	..	..	..	..	..	**Immobilier, locations, services aux entreprises**	K	70-74	
..	..	..	..	..	..	..	..	**Admin. publique; éducation; santé; autres**	L-Q	75-99	
..	54 892	55 148	51 437	45 665	48 333	56 213	..	**Grand total**	A-Q	01-99	

Note: All period: ISIC 1549 includes 1544; 2222 includes 2230; 2695 includes part of 2691; 3320 includes 3330; 3592 includes 3591. In 1990, ISIC 272 includes 273. In 1991, ISIC 1810 includes 1820. In 1993, ISIC 2732 includes 2731. In 1995, ISIC 1549 includes 1542; 2411 includes 2412. In 1991, 1992, 1993 and 1995, ISIC 14 includes 11. From 1993 to 1995, ISIC 2429 includes 2430. In 1994 and 1995, ISIC 1030 includes 1010.

Statistiques des Structures Industrielles
OCDE, © 1998

Table UK.1 PRODUCTION - PRODUCTION

Millions of £ (Current Prices)

ISIC revision 3			1989	1990	1991	1992	1993	1994	1995	1996
A	01-02	Agriculture, hunting and forestry	..	..	..	..	..	..	..	..
B	05	Fishing	..	..	..	..	..	..	..	..
C	10-14	Mining and quarrying	..	..	..	..	..	..	..	..
	10	Mining of coal and lignite; extraction of peat	..	..	..	..	..	..	..	..
	11	Crude petroleum & natural gas; related service activ.	..	..	..	..	..	..	..	..
	13	Mining of metal ores	..	..	..	..	..	..	..	..
	14	Other mining and quarrying	..	..	..	..	..	..	..	..
D	15-37	Total manufacturing	..	..	..	..	350 293	380 304	404 200	..
	15	Food products and beverages	..	..	..	..	57 723	59 678	62 222	..
	155	Beverages	..	..	..	..	10 596	11 019	12 145	..
	16 160	Tobacco products	..	..	..	..	7 601	7 543	8 260	..
	17	Textiles	..	..	..	..	9 216	9 757	10 346	..
	171	Spinning, weaving and finishing of textiles	..	..	..	..	3 684	4 104	3 655	..
	172	Other textiles	..	..	..	..	3 548	3 669	4 035	..
	173	Knitted and crocheted fabrics and articles	..	..	..	..	1 984	1 984	2 656	..
	18	Wearing apparel dressing & dyeing of fur	..	..	..	..	5 312	5 784	6 290	..
	181	Wearing apparel, except fur apparel	..	..	..	..	5 267	5 760	6 258	..
	182	Dressing and dyeing of fur; articles of fur	..	..	..	..	45	24	32	..
	19	Tanning, dressing leather; leather artic.; footwear	..	..	..	..	2 503	2 683	2 174	..
	191	Tanning, dressing leather; manuf. of leather articles	..	..	..	..	947	944	806	..
	192	Footwear	..	..	..	..	1 556	1 740	1 368	..
	20	Wood and cork products, ex. furniture	..	..	..	..	4 423	5 292	5 018	..
	201	Sawmilling and planing of wood	..	..	..	..	1 220	1 660	1 317	..
	202	Products of wood, cork, straw & plaiting material	..	..	..	..	3 203	3 633	3 701	..
	21	Paper and paper products	..	..	..	..	10 333	11 619	13 117	..
	22	Publishing, printing & reprod. of recorded media	..	..	..	..	21 112	23 123	22 931	..
	221	Publishing	..	..	..	..	11 002	11 806	12 469	..
	222	Printing and related service activities	..	..	..	..	9 515	10 724	9 719	..
	223	Reproduction of recorded media	..	..	..	..	595	593	743	..
	23	Coke, refined petroleum products & nuclear fuel	..	..	..	..	22 093	21 832	21 547	..
	24	Chemicals and chemical products	..	..	..	..	37 467	39 864	43 691	..
	241	Basic chemicals	..	..	..	..	14 259	15 080	17 580	..
	242	Other chemical products	..	..	..	..	22 109	23 821	24 966	..
	243	Man-made fibres	..	..	..	..	1 099	963	1 144	..
	25	Rubber and plastic products	..	..	..	..	14 668	16 301	17 245	..
	251	Rubber products	..	..	..	..	3 151	3 368	3 778	..
	252	Plastic products	..	..	..	..	11 517	12 933	13 467	..
	26	Other non-metallic mineral products	..	..	..	..	17 330	20 122	11 428	..
	261	Glass and glass products	..	..	..	..	2 197	2 465	2 856	..
	269	Non-metallic mineral products, nec	..	..	..	..	15 133	17 657	8 571	..
	27	Basic metals	..	..	..	..	..	..	18 871	..
	271	Basic iron and steel	..	..	..	..	..	..	10 498	..
	272	Basic precious and non-ferrous metals	..	..	..	..	4 916	5 077	6 319	..
	273	Casting of metals	..	..	..	..	1 671	1 996	2 055	..
	28	Fabricated metal products, ex. machin. & equip.	..	..	..	..	18 155	20 468	21 186	..
	281	Structural metal prod., tanks, reservoirs, generators	..	..	..	..	5 636	6 059	5 209	..
	289	Other fabricated metal products & service activities	..	..	..	..	12 518	14 408	15 976	..
	29	Machinery and equipment, nec	..	..	..	..	25 763	28 229	32 135	..
	291	General purpose machinery	..	..	..	..	13 461	14 969	16 738	..
	292	Special purpose machinery	..	..	..	..	10 034	10 785	12 985	..
	293	Domestic appliances, nec	..	..	..	..	2 267	2 475	2 412	..
	30	Office, accounting and computing machinery	..	..	..	..	11 150	10 714	12 678	..
	31	Electrical machinery and apparatus, nec	..	..	..	..	11 184	11 981	12 013	..
	311	Electric motors, generators and transformers	..	..	..	..	1 951	1 907	2 070	..
	312	Electricity distribution and control apparatus	..	..	..	..	2 706	3 022	3 372	..
	313	Insulated wire and cable	..	..	..	..	1 670	1 891	2 000	..
	314	Accumulators, primary cells and primary batteries	..	..	..	..	567	636	538	..
	315	Electric lamps and lighting equipment	..	..	..	..	1 313	1 394	1 153	..
	319	Other electrical equipment, nec	..	..	..	..	2 975	3 132	2 881	..
	32	Radio, TV, communication equip. & apparatus	..	..	..	..	9 622	12 389	14 917	..
	321	Electronic valves, tubes & other electronic compon.	..	..	..	..	3 284	4 186	5 328	..
	322	TV, radio transmitters & appar. for line teleph., telegr.	..	..	..	..	3 374	4 701	5 508	..
	323	TV, radio receivers and associated goods	..	..	..	..	2 965	3 502	4 081	..
	33	Medical, precision, optical instr.; watches, clocks	..	..	..	..	8 337	8 579	9 276	..
	331	Medical equip.; precision instruments and appliances	..	..	..	..	7 425	7 514	8 171	..
	332	Optical instruments and photographic equipment	..	..	..	..	813	914	981	..
	333	Watches and clocks	..	..	..	..	99	151	123	..
	34	Motor vehicles, trailers, and semi-trailers	..	..	..	..	26 715	30 989	33 575	..
	35	Other transport equipment	..	..	..	..	13 538	14 257	13 246	..
	351	Building and repairing of ships and boats	..	..	..	..	2 940	2 804	2 427	..
	352	Railway, tramway locomotives and rolling stock	..	..	..	..	1 117	1 184	925	..
	353	Aircraft and spacecraft	..	..	..	..	9 130	9 952	9 459	..
	359	Transport equipment, nec	..	..	..	..	352	317	434	..
	36	Furniture; manufacturing, nec	..	..	..	..	9 461	11 189	10 784	..
	361	Furniture	..	..	..	..	6 245	7 003	6 576	..
	369	Manufacturing, nec	..	..	..	..	3 216	4 186	4 208	..
	37	Recycling	..	..	..	..	..	838	1 252	..
E	40-41	Electricity, gas and water supply	..	..	..	..	..	..	..	..
	40	Electricity, gas, steam and hot water supply	..	..	..	..	..	..	..	..
	401	Production, collection and distribution of electricity	..	..	..	..	..	30 468	28 828	..
	41 410	Collection, purification, distribution of water	..	..	..	..	..	3 429	3 469	..
F	45	Construction	..	..	..	..	77 062	68 802	..	..
G	50-52	Wholesale and retail trade; repairs etc	..	..	..	..	..	..	..	..
H	55	Hotels and restaurants	..	..	..	..	..	..	..	..
I	60-64	Transport, storage and communications	..	..	..	..	..	..	..	..
J	65-67	Financial intermediation	..	..	..	..	..	..	..	..
K	70-74	Real estate, renting and business activities	..	..	..	..	..	..	..	..
L-Q	75-99	Public admin.; education; health; other services	..	..	..	..	..	..	..	..
A-Q	01-99	Grand total	..	..	..	..	..	..	..	..

Note: ISIC 1722 includes 1723 and 1729; 2699 includes 2710.

Table UK.2 **VALEUR AJOUTÉE - VALUE ADDED**

Millions de £ (Prix courants)

1989	1990	1991	1992	1993	1994	1995	1996			CITI révision 3
..	..	..	..	..	..	..	..	**Agriculture, chasse et sylviculture**	A	01-02
..	..	..	..	..	..	..	..	**Pêche**	B	05
..	..	..	..	..	..	..	..	**Activités extractives**	C	10-14
..	..	..	..	..	..	..	..	Extraction de charbon, de lignite et de tourbe		10
..	..	..	..	..	..	..	..	Extraction de pétrole brut et de gaz naturel		11
..	..	..	..	..	..	..	..	Extraction de minerais métalliques		13
..	..	..	..	..	..	..	..	Autres activités extractives		14
..	..	..	..	146 346	159 591	129 186	..	**Activités de fabrication**	D	15-37
..	..	..	..	20 456	21 384	15 711	..	**Produits alimentaires et boissons**		15
..	..	..	..	3 877	3 804	3 161	..	Boissons		155
..	..	..	..	1 620	1 660	1 428	..	**Produits à base de tabac**	16	160
..	..	..	..	4 330	4 487	3 846	..	**Textiles**		17
..	..	..	..	1 627	1 771	1 289	..	Filature, tissage et achèvement des textiles		171
..	..	..	..	1 706	1 719	1 444	..	Autres articles textiles		172
..	..	..	..	997	997	1 114	..	Etoffes et articles de bonneterie		173
..	..	..	..	2 605	2 978	2 392	..	**Habillement; préparation, teinture des fourrures**		18
..	..	..	..	2 586	2 964	2 377	..	Articles d'habillement autres qu'en fourrure		181
..	..	..	..	19	14	15	..	Préparation, teinture des fourrures; art. en fourrure		182
..	..	..	..	1 173	1 200	754	..	**Travail des cuirs; articles en cuir; chaussures**		19
..	..	..	..	411	371	244	..	Apprêt et tannage des cuirs et articles en cuirs		191
..	..	..	..	762	829	510	..	Chaussures		192
..	..	..	..	1 861	2 129	1 562	..	**Bois et articles en bois et liège (sauf meubles)**		20
..	..	..	..	393	504	272	..	Sciage et rabotage du bois		201
..	..	..	..	1 468	1 625	1 289	..	Articles en bois, liège, vannerie, sparterie		202
..	..	..	..	4 710	5 216	4 373	..	**Papier et carton; articles en papier et en carton**		21
..	..	..	..	13 149	14 474	10 520	..	**Edition, imprimerie et reproduction**		22
..	..	..	..	7 240	8 044	5 603	..	Edition		221
..	..	..	..	5 534	6 067	4 553	..	Imprimerie et activités annexes		222
..	..	..	..	375	363	364	..	Reproduction de supports enregistrés		223
..	..	..	..	3 108	3 125	2 845	..	**Cokéfaction; prod. pétroliers; comb. nucléaires**		23
..	..	..	..	16 994	18 110	15 121	..	**Produits chimiques**		24
..	..	..	..	5 052	5 642	5 412	..	Produits chimiques de base		241
..	..	..	..	11 499	12 112	9 279	..	Autres produits chimiques		242
..	..	..	..	443	356	431	..	Fibres synthétiques ou artificielles		243
..	..	..	..	7 271	7 995	6 245	..	**Articles en caoutchouc et en matières plastiques**		25
..	..	..	..	1 643	1 744	1 473	..	Articles en caoutchouc		251
..	..	..	..	5 628	6 250	4 771	..	Articles en matières plastiques		252
..	..	..	..	7 938	9 384	4 760	..	**Autres produits minéraux non métalliques**		26
..	..	..	..	1 165	1 313	1 096	..	Verre et articles en verre		261
..	..	..	..	6 772	8 071	3 663	..	Produits minéraux non métalliques, nca		269
..	..	..	..	..	..	5 508	..	**Produits métallurgiques de base**		27
..	..	..	..	..	..	3 173	..	Sidérurgie et première transformation de l'acier		271
..	..	..	..	1 371	1 499	1 469	..	Métallurgie; métaux précieux et non ferreux		272
..	..	..	..	922	1 027	867	..	Fonderie		273
..	..	..	..	9 660	10 456	8 999	..	**Ouvrages en métaux, sauf machines et matériel**		28
..	..	..	..	2 654	2 722	1 943	..	Constr. et menuiserie métal.; réservoirs; générateurs		281
..	..	..	..	7 006	7 735	7 055	..	Autres ouvrages en métaux		289
..	..	..	..	11 813	12 917	11 392	..	**Machines et matériel, nca**		29
..	..	..	..	6 390	7 098	6 205	..	Machines d'usage général		291
..	..	..	..	4 396	4 703	4 438	..	Machines d'usage spécifique		292
..	..	..	..	1 027	1 116	749	..	Appareils domestiques, nca		293
..	..	..	..	3 100	3 271	2 873	..	**Mach. de bureau, comptables, matériel inform.**		30
..	..	..	..	5 135	5 774	4 596	..	**Machines et appareils électriques, nca**		31
..	..	..	..	823	910	794	..	Moteurs, génératrices et transformateurs électriques		311
..	..	..	..	1 348	1 519	1 322	..	Matériel électrique de distribution et de commande		312
..	..	..	..	776	898	702	..	Fils et câbles électriques isolés		313
..	..	..	..	272	312	205	..	Accumulateurs, piles électriques		314
..	..	..	..	620	639	387	..	Lampes électriques et appareils d'éclairage		315
..	..	..	..	1 295	1 497	1 187	..	Autres matériels électriques, nca		319
..	..	..	..	4 120	5 221	4 948	..	**Equip. et appar. de radio, TV, communication**		32
..	..	..	..	1 597	2 018	2 127	..	Tubes et valves électroniques; autres composants		321
..	..	..	..	1 589	2 118	1 815	..	Emetteurs radio et TV; app. téléphonie, télégraphie		322
..	..	..	..	935	1 086	1 007	..	Récepteurs radio et TV et articles associés		323
..	..	..	..	4 429	4 702	3 822	..	**Instruments médicaux, de précision, d'optique**		33
..	..	..	..	3 924	4 132	3 302	..	Appareils médicaux et de précision		331
..	..	..	..	456	499	470	..	Instruments d'optique ; matériel photographique		332
..	..	..	..	50	71	50	..	Horlogerie		333
..	..	..	..	9 094	9 375	8 311	..	**Véhicules automobiles et nemorques**		34
..	..	..	..	6 846	7 414	5 044	..	**Autres matériels de transport**		35
..	..	..	..	1 595	1 652	1 110	..	Construction et réparation de navires		351
..	..	..	..	383	435	236	..	Construction de matériel ferroviaire roulant		352
..	..	..	..	4 716	5 180	3 531	..	Construction aéronautique et spatiale		353
..	..	..	..	151	147	167	..	Autres équipements de transport		359
..	..	..	..	4 642	5 611	3 888	..	**Meubles; activités de fabrication, nca**		36
..	..	..	..	3 030	3 372	2 370	..	Meubles		361
..	..	..	..	1 611	2 239	1 518	..	Activités de fabrication, nca		369
..	..	..	..	..	230	248	..	**Récupération**		37
..	..	..	..	..	..	..	..	**Production et distrib. d'électricité, de gaz, d'eau**	E	40-41
..	..	..	..	..	..	..	..	**Electricité, gaz, vapeur et eau chaude**		40
..	..	..	..	..	..	9 670	..	Production, collecte et distribution d'électricité		401
..	..	..	..	2 716	2 818	2 392	..	**Captage, épuration et distribution d'eau**	41	410
..	..	..	..	25 218	25 381	22 949	..	**Construction**	F	45
..	..	..	..	..	..	..	..	**Commerce de gros et de détail; réparation**	G	50-52
..	..	..	..	..	..	..	..	**Hôtels et restaurants**	H	55
..	..	..	..	..	..	..	..	**Transports, entreposage et communications**	I	60-64
..	..	..	..	..	..	..	..	**Intermédiation financière**	J	65-67
..	..	..	..	..	..	..	..	**Immobilier, locations, services aux entreprises**	K	70-74
..	..	..	..	..	..	..	..	**Admin. publique; éducation; santé; autres**	L-Q	75-99
..	..	..	..	..	..	..	..	**Grand total**	A-Q	01-99

Note: ISIC 1722 includes 1723 and 1729; 2699 includes 2710.

Statistiques des Structures Industrielles
OCDE, © 1998

Table UK.3 INVESTMENT - INVESTISSEMENT

Millions of £ (Current Prices)

ISIC revision 3			1989	1990	1991	1992	1993	1994	1995	1996
A	01-02	Agriculture, hunting and forestry	..	..	..	..	..	..	..	..
B	05	Fishing	..	..	..	..	..	..	..	..
C	10-14	Mining and quarrying	..	..	..	..	..	..	..	..
	10	Mining of coal and lignite; extraction of peat	..	..	..	..	..	..	..	..
	11	Crude petroleum & natural gas; related service activ.	..	..	..	..	..	..	..	..
	13	Mining of metal ores	..	..	..	..	..	..	..	..
	14	Other mining and quarrying	..	..	..	..	..	193	..	..
D	15-37	Total manufacturing	..	..	..	..	12 811	13 691	16 768	..
	15	Food products and beverages	..	..	..	..	2 199	2 135	2 284	..
	155	Beverages	..	..	..	..	515	507	570	..
	16 160	Tobacco products	..	..	..	..	86	85	88	..
	17	Textiles	..	..	..	..	314	357	343	..
	171	Spinning, weaving and finishing of textiles	..	..	..	..	116	174	139	..
	172	Other textiles	..	..	..	..	111	102	116	..
	173	Knitted and crocheted fabrics and articles	..	..	..	..	87	81	88	..
	18	Wearing apparel dressing & dyeing of fur	..	..	..	..	78	105	114	..
	181	Wearing apparel, except fur apparel	..	..	..	..	77	104	113	..
	182	Dressing and dyeing of fur; articles of fur	..	..	..	..	1	1	..	..
	19	Tanning, dressing leather; leather artic.; footwear	..	..	..	..	52	64	57	..
	191	Tanning, dressing leather; manuf. of leather articles	..	..	..	..	20	20	12	..
	192	Footwear	..	..	..	..	32	44	46	..
	20	Wood and cork products, ex. furniture	..	..	..	..	128	125	141	..
	201	Sawmilling and planing of wood	..	..	..	..	32	33	39	..
	202	Products of wood, cork, straw & plaiting material	..	..	..	..	96	92	102	..
	21	Paper and paper products	..	..	..	..	569	669	775	..
	22	Publishing, printing & reprod. of recorded media	..	..	..	..	1 038	1 049	1 161	..
	221	Publishing	..	..	..	..	391	358	452	..
	222	Printing and related service activities	..	..	..	..	622	664	645	..
	223	Reproduction of recorded media	..	..	..	..	25	28	64	..
	23	Coke, refined petroleum products & nuclear fuel	..	..	..	..	721	580	739	..
	24	Chemicals and chemical products	..	..	..	..	1 860	1 857	2 274	..
	241	Basic chemicals	..	..	..	..	725	662	821	..
	242	Other chemical products	..	..	..	..	1 071	1 139	1 362	..
	243	Man-made fibres	..	..	..	..	64	56	91	..
	25	Rubber and plastic products	..	..	..	..	753	749	906	..
	251	Rubber products	..	..	..	..	129	112	129	..
	252	Plastic products	..	..	..	..	624	637	777	..
	26	Other non-metallic mineral products	..	..	..	..	588	619	577	..
	261	Glass and glass products	..	..	..	..	140	133	173	..
	269	Non-metallic mineral products, nec	..	..	..	..	447	486	404	..
	27	Basic metals	..	..	..	..	..	..	503	..
	271	Basic iron and steel	..	..	..	..	..	..	273	..
	272	Basic precious and non-ferrous metals	..	..	..	..	112	91	116	..
	273	Casting of metals	..	..	..	..	66	83	113	..
	28	Fabricated metal products, ex. machin. & equip.	..	..	..	..	577	714	761	..
	281	Structural metal prod., tanks, reservoirs, generators	..	..	..	..	113	107	134	..
	289	Other fabricated metal products & service activities	..	..	..	..	464	607	627	..
	29	Machinery and equipment, nec	..	..	..	..	702	846	1 026	..
	291	General purpose machinery	..	..	..	..	355	438	542	..
	292	Special purpose machinery	..	..	..	..	256	311	386	..
	293	Domestic appliances, nec	..	..	..	..	92	96	98	..
	30	Office, accounting and computing machinery	..	..	..	..	235	313	363	..
	31	Electrical machinery and apparatus, nec	..	..	..	..	394	340	383	..
	311	Electric motors, generators and transformers	..	..	..	..	80	57	46	..
	312	Electricity distribution and control apparatus	..	..	..	..	110	75	100	..
	313	Insulated wire and cable	..	..	..	..	65	57	53	..
	314	Accumulators, primary cells and primary batteries	..	..	..	..	22	24	28	..
	315	Electric lamps and lighting equipment	..	..	..	..	38	35	35	..
	319	Other electrical equipment, nec	..	..	..	..	79	92	120	..
	32	Radio, TV, communication equip. & apparatus	..	..	..	..	541	738	1 270	..
	321	Electronic valves, tubes & other electronic compon.	..	..	..	..	281	394	848	..
	322	TV, radio transmitters & appar. for line teleph., telegr.	..	..	..	..	145	194	258	..
	323	TV, radio receivers and associated goods	..	..	..	..	116	150	164	..
	33	Medical, precision, optical instr.; watches, clocks	..	..	..	..	271	353	323	..
	331	Medical equip.; precision instruments and appliances	..	..	..	..	238	318	252	..
	332	Optical instruments and photographic equipment	..	..	..	..	..	31	63	..
	333	Watches and clocks	..	..	..	..	..	4	8	..
	34	Motor vehicles, trailers, and semi-trailers	..	..	..	..	982	1 258	1 937	..
	35	Other transport equipment	..	..	..	..	313	244	365	..
	351	Building and repairing of ships and boats	..	..	..	..	37	26	32	..
	352	Railway, tramway locomotives and rolling stock	..	..	..	..	14	- 21	63	..
	353	Aircraft and spacecraft	..	..	..	..	246	230	249	..
	359	Transport equipment, nec	..	..	..	..	15	8	20	..
	36	Furniture; manufacturing, nec	..	..	..	..	236	295	318	..
	361	Furniture	..	..	..	..	135	166	152	..
	369	Manufacturing, nec	..	..	..	..	101	129	165	..
	37	Recycling	..	..	..	..	..	23	61	..
E	40-41	Electricity, gas and water supply	..	..	..	..	..	..	..	..
	40	Electricity, gas, steam and hot water supply	..	..	..	..	..	..	..	..
	401	Production, collection and distribution of electricity	..	..	..	..	..	2 833	2 542	..
	41 410	Collection, purification, distribution of water	..	..	..	..	1 513	1 316	1 215	..
F	45	Construction	..	..	..	..	1 093	1 207	1 282	..
G	50-52	Wholesale and retail trade; repairs etc	..	..	..	..	..	..	..	..
H	55	Hotels and restaurants	..	..	..	..	..	..	..	..
I	60-64	Transport, storage and communications	..	..	..	..	..	..	..	..
J	65-67	Financial intermediation	..	..	..	..	..	..	..	..
K	70-74	Real estate, renting and business activities	..	..	..	..	..	..	..	..
L-Q	75-99	Public admin.; education; health; other services	..	..	..	..	..	..	..	..
A-Q	01-99	Grand total	..	..	..	..	..	..	..	..

Note: ISIC 1722 includes 1723 and 1729; 2699 includes 2710.

Table UK.4 **DÉPENSES EN MACHINES ET ÉQUIPEMENT - INVESTMENT IN MACHINERY AND EQUIPMENT**

Millions de £ *(Prix courants)*

1989	1990	1991	1992	1993	1994	1995	1996			CITI révision 3	
..	..	..	..	..	..	..	..	**Agriculture, chasse et sylviculture**	A	01-02	
..	..	..	..	..	..	..	..	**Pêche**	B	05	
..	..	..	..	..	..	..	..	**Activités extractives**	C	10-14	
..	..	..	..	..	..	..	..	Extraction de charbon, de lignite et de tourbe		10	
..	..	..	..	..	..	..	..	Extraction de pétrole brut et de gaz naturel		11	
..	..	..	..	..	..	..	..	Extraction de minerais métalliques		13	
..	..	..	..	..	150	..	..	Autres activités extractives		14	
..	..	..	..	10 426	11 241	13 409	..	**Activités de fabrication**	D	15-37	
..	..	..	..	1 615	1 606	1 776	..	**Produits alimentaires et boissons**		15	
..	..	..	..	373	349	430	..	Boissons			155
..	..	..	..	53	44	74	..	**Produits à base de tabac**		16	160
..	..	..	..	266	313	306	..	**Textiles**		17	
..	..	..	..	99	146	128	..	Filature, tissage et achèvement des textiles			171
..	..	..	..	95	96	97	..	Autres articles textiles			172
..	..	..	..	72	71	82	..	Etoffes et articles de bonneterie			173
..	..	..	..	72	96	100	..	**Habillement; préparation, teinture des fourrures**		18	
..	..	..	..	71	95	99	..	Articles d'habillement autres qu'en fourrure			181
..	..	..	..	1	1		..	Préparation, teinture des fourrures; art. en fourrure			182
..	..	..	..	46	54	51	..	**Travail des cuirs; articles en cuir; chaussures**		19	
..	..	..	..	18	18	12	..	Apprêt et tannage des cuirs et articles en cuirs			191
..	..	..	..	27	36	39	..	Chaussures			192
..	..	..	..	82	74	80	..	**Bois et articles en bois et liège (sauf meubles)**		20	
..	..	..	..	10	11	12	..	Sciage et rabotage du bois			201
..	..	..	..	72	63	69	..	Articles en bois, liège, vannerie, sparterie			202
..	..	..	..	473	582	716	..	**Papier et carton; articles en papier et en carton**		21	
..	..	..	..	798	856	848	..	**Edition, imprimerie et reproduction**		22	
..	..	..	..	257	272	297	..	Edition			221
..	..	..	..	518	557	499	..	Imprimerie et activités annexes			222
..	..	..	..	23	27	52	..	Reproduction de supports enregistrés			223
..	..	..	..	620	518	475	..	**Cokéfaction; prod. pétroliers; comb. nucléaires**		23	
..	..	..	..	1 458	1 473	1 868	..	**Produits chimiques**		24	
..	..	..	..	628	607	758	..	Produits chimiques de base			241
..	..	..	..	770	818	1 019	..	Autres produits chimiques			242
..	..	..	..	60	48	91	..	Fibres synthétiques ou artificielles			243
..	..	..	..	637	622	716	..	**Articles en caoutchouc et en matières plastiques**		25	
..	..	..	..	111	102	120	..	Articles en caoutchouc			251
..	..	..	..	526	520	595	..	Articles en matières plastiques			252
..	..	..	..	534	547	473	..	**Autres produits minéraux non métalliques**		26	
..	..	..	..	134	127	160	..	Verre et articles en verre			261
..	..	..	..	399	421	313	..	Produits minéraux non métalliques, nca			269
..	..	..	..	..	..	483	..	**Produits métallurgiques de base**		27	
..	..	..	..	..	..	268	..	Sidérurgie et première transformation de l'acier			271
..	..	..	..	104	84	115	..	Métallurgie; métaux précieux et non ferreux			272
..	..	..	..	53	66	100	..	Fonderie			273
..	..	..	..	450	518	565	..	**Ouvrages en métaux, sauf machines et matériel**		28	
..	..	..	..	77	72	88	..	Constr. et menuiserie métal.; réservoirs; générateurs			281
..	..	..	..	373	446	476	..	Autres ouvrages en métaux			289
..	..	..	..	538	644	832	..	**Machines et matériel, nca**		29	
..	..	..	..	253	308	464	..	Machines d'usage général			291
..	..	..	..	207	255	287	..	Machines d'usage spécifique			292
..	..	..	..	78	81	80	..	Appareils domestiques, nca			293
..	..	..	..	212	272	308	..	**Mach. de bureau, comptables, matériel inform.**		30	
..	..	..	..	307	296	342	..	**Machines et appareils électriques, nca**		31	
..	..	..	..	44	44	38	..	Moteurs, génératrices et transformateurs électriques			311
..	..	..	..	85	70	98	..	Matériel électrique de distribution et de commande			312
..	..	..	..	61	52	56	..	Fils et câbles électriques isolés			313
..	..	..	..	21	21	28	..	Accumulateurs, piles électriques			314
..	..	..	..	30	32	32	..	Lampes électriques et appareils d'éclairage			315
..	..	..	..	65	77	90	..	Autres matériels électriques, nca			319
..	..	..	..	470	653	872	..	**Equip. et appar. de radio, TV, communication**		32	
..	..	..	..	241	347	522	..	Tubes et valves électroniques; autres composants			321
..	..	..	..	131	177	235	..	Emetteurs radio et TV; app. téléphonie, télégraphie			322
..	..	..	..	99	129	115	..	Récepteurs radio et TV et articles associés			323
..	..	..	..	208	274	237	..	**Instruments médicaux, de précision, d'optique**		33	
..	..	..	..	183	240	187	..	Appareils médicaux et de précision			331
..	..	..	..	25	30	48	..	Instruments d'optique ; matériel photographique			332
..	..	..	..		3	3	..	Horlogerie			333
..	..	..	..	995	1 199	1 740	..	**Véhicules automobiles et nemorques**		34	
..	..	..	..	244	196	253	..	**Autres matériels de transport**		35	
..	..	..	..	20	13	33	..	Construction et réparation de navires			351
..	..	..	..	2	- 28	15	..	Construction de matériel ferroviaire roulant			352
..	..	..	..	207	202	189	..	Construction aéronautique et spatiale			353
..	..	..	..	14	8	15	..	Autres équipements de transport			359
..	..	..	..	191	231	245	..	**Meubles; activités de fabrication, nca**		36	
..	..	..	..	108	130	134	..	Meubles			361
..	..	..	..	84	102	111	..	Activités de fabrication, nca			369
..	..	..	..	..	23	49	..	**Récupération**		37	
..	..	..	..	..	..	..	..	**Production et distrib. d'électricité, de gaz, d'eau**	E	40-41	
..	..	..	..	..	2 580	2 298	..	**Electricité, gaz, vapeur et chaude**		40	
..	..	..	..	..	..	..	..	Production, collecte et distribution d'électricité			401
..	..	..	..	461	389	390	..	**Captage, épuration et distribution d'eau**		41	410
..	..	..	..	667	636	627	..	**Construction**	F	45	
..	..	..	..	..	..	..	..	**Commerce de gros et de détail; réparation**	G	50-52	
..	..	..	..	..	..	..	..	**Hôtels et restaurants**	H	55	
..	..	..	..	..	..	..	..	**Transports, entreposage et communications**	I	60-64	
..	..	..	..	..	..	..	..	**Intermédiation financière**	J	65-67	
..	..	..	..	..	..	..	..	**Immobilier, locations, services aux entreprises**	K	70-74	
..	..	..	..	..	..	..	..	**Admin. publique; éducation; santé; autres**	L-Q	75-99	
..	..	..	..	..	..	..	..	**Grand total**	A-Q	01-99	

Note: ISIC 1722 includes 1723 and 1729; 2699 includes 2710.

Statistiques des Structures Industrielles
OCDE, © 1998

OECD
OCDE

Table UK.5 ESTABLISHMENTS - ETABLISSEMENTS

Units

ISIC revision 3			1989	1990	1991	1992	1993	1994	1995	1996
A	01-02	**Agriculture, hunting and forestry**	..	..	..	..	..	..	..	..
B	05	**Fishing**	..	..	..	..	..	..	..	..
C	10-14	**Mining and quarrying**	..	..	..	..	..	..	..	..
	10	Mining of coal and lignite; extraction of peat	..	..	..	..	..	..	..	..
	11	Crude petroleum & natural gas; related service activ.	..	..	..	..	..	..	..	..
	13	Mining of metal ores	..	..	..	..	..	..	..	..
	14	Other mining and quarrying	..	..	..	..	..	..	..	..
D	15-37	**Total manufacturing**	..	..	..	..	161 625	156 941	170 283	..
	15	**Food products and beverages**	..	..	..	..	9 395	9 797	8 728	..
	155	Beverages	..	..	..	..	655	683	682	..
	16 160	**Tobacco products**	..	..	..	..	41	23	19	..
	17	**Textiles**	..	..	..	..	7 256	6 010	6 306	..
	171	Spinning, weaving and finishing of textiles	..	..	..	..	2 593	2 685	1 555	..
	172	Other textiles	..	..	..	..	3 581	2 244	3 684	..
	173	Knitted and crocheted fabrics and articles	..	..	..	..	1 082	1 081	1 067	..
	18	**Wearing apparel dressing & dyeing of fur**	..	..	..	..	7 499	7 917	8 399	..
	181	Wearing apparel, except fur apparel	..	..	..	..	7 444	7 855	8 338	..
	182	Dressing and dyeing of fur; articles of fur	..	..	..	..	55	62	61	..
	19	**Tanning, dressing leather; leather artic.; footwear**	..	..	..	..	2 156	1 683	1 539	..
	191	Tanning, dressing leather; manuf. of leather articles	..	..	..	..	1 536	1 101	1 014	..
	192	Footwear	..	..	..	..	620	582	525	..
	20	**Wood and cork products, ex. furniture**	..	..	..	..	7 767	7 178	8 269	..
	201	Sawmilling and planing of wood	..	..	..	..	1 976	1 924	1 471	..
	202	Products of wood, cork, straw & plaiting material	..	..	..	..	5 791	5 254	6 798	..
	21	**Paper and paper products**	..	..	..	..	3 094	3 269	3 190	..
	22	**Publishing, printing & reprod. of recorded media**	..	..	..	..	23 731	25 418	26 535	..
	221	Publishing	..	..	..	..	7 925	6 677	7 441	..
	222	Printing and related service activities	..	..	..	..	15 752	18 673	18 876	..
	223	Reproduction of recorded media	..	..	..	..	54	68	218	..
	23	**Coke, refined petroleum products & nuclear fuel**	..	..	..	..	199	221	441	..
	24	**Chemicals and chemical products**	..	..	..	..	3 809	3 856	4 561	..
	241	Basic chemicals	..	..	..	..	1 620	1 567	1 529	..
	242	Other chemical products	..	..	..	..	2 145	2 232	2 968	..
	243	Man-made fibres	..	..	..	..	44	57	64	..
	25	**Rubber and plastic products**	..	..	..	..	5 103	5 682	6 912	..
	251	Rubber products	..	..	..	..	577	649	873	..
	252	Plastic products	..	..	..	..	4 526	5 033	6 039	..
	26	**Other non-metallic mineral products**	..	..	..	..	4 946	4 495	5 252	..
	261	Glass and glass products	..	..	..	..	899	1 083	1 712	..
	269	Non-metallic mineral products, nec	..	..	..	..	4 047	3 412	3 540	..
	27	**Basic metals**	..	..	..	..	..	..	2 788	..
	271	Basic iron and steel	..	..	..	..	..	..	890	..
	272	Basic precious and non-ferrous metals	..	..	..	..	1 415	1 072	1 071	..
	273	Casting of metals	..	..	..	..	654	675	827	..
	28	**Fabricated metal products, ex. machin. & equip.**	..	..	..	..	26 170	27 729	28 855	..
	281	Structural metal prod., tanks, reservoirs, generators	..	..	..	..	3 687	3 645	4 493	..
	289	Other fabricated metal products & service activities	..	..	..	..	22 483	24 084	24 362	..
	29	**Machinery and equipment, nec**	..	..	..	..	11 636	12 816	15 570	..
	291	General purpose machinery	..	..	..	..	5 340	5 924	6 997	..
	292	Special purpose machinery	..	..	..	..	5 753	6 246	7 807	..
	293	Domestic appliances, nec	..	..	..	..	543	646	766	..
	30	**Office, accounting and computing machinery**	..	..	..	..	1 626	1 678	2 146	..
	31	**Electrical machinery and apparatus, nec**	..	..	..	..	5 529	6 103	5 690	..
	311	Electric motors, generators and transformers	..	..	..	..	1 688	1 489	1 233	..
	312	Electricity distribution and control apparatus	..	..	..	..	516	660	884	..
	313	Insulated wire and cable	..	..	..	..	382	359	377	..
	314	Accumulators, primary cells and primary batteries	..	..	..	..	49	61	93	..
	315	Electric lamps and lighting equipment	..	..	..	..	320	325	450	..
	319	Other electrical equipment, nec	..	..	..	..	2 574	3 209	2 653	..
	32	**Radio, TV, communication equip. & apparatus**	..	..	..	..	3 071	3 425	3 233	..
	321	Electronic valves, tubes & other electronic compon.	..	..	..	..	570	609	1 104	..
	322	TV, radio transmitters & appar. for line teleph., telegr.	..	..	..	..	1 147	1 248	1 051	..
	323	TV, radio receivers and associated goods	..	..	..	..	1 354	1 568	1 078	..
	33	**Medical, precision, optical instr.; watches, clocks**	..	..	..	..	3 676	4 281	6 526	..
	331	Medical equip.; precision instruments and appliances	..	..	..	..	3 289	3 826	5 758	..
	332	Optical instruments and photographic equipment	..	..	..	..	268	321	608	..
	333	Watches and clocks	..	..	..	..	119	134	160	..
	34	**Motor vehicles, trailers, and semi-trailers**	..	..	..	..	1 489	1 756	3 758	..
	35	**Other transport equipment**	..	..	..	..	2 215	2 600	3 108	..
	351	Building and repairing of ships and boats	..	..	..	..	1 479	1 754	1 600	..
	352	Railway, tramway locomotives and rolling stock	..	..	..	..	79	89	113	..
	353	Aircraft and spacecraft	..	..	..	..	502	572	1 146	..
	359	Transport equipment, nec	..	..	..	..	155	185	249	..
	36	**Furniture; manufacturing, nec**	..	..	..	..	15 072	19 137	17 894	..
	361	Furniture	..	..	..	..	6 403	7 624	7 187	..
	369	Manufacturing, nec	..	..	..	..	8 669	11 513	10 707	..
	37	**Recycling**	..	..	..	..	..	120	564	..
E	40-41	**Electricity, gas and water supply**	..	..	..	..	..	..	..	..
	40	**Electricity, gas, steam and hot water supply**	..	..	..	..	..	..	..	..
	401	Production, collection and distribution of electricity	..	..	..	..	..	111	145	..
	41 410	**Collection, purification, distribution of water**	..	..	..	..	57	55	76	..
F	45	**Construction**	..	..	..	..	199 363	195 374	187 260	..
G	50-52	**Wholesale and retail trade; repairs etc**	..	..	..	..	..	..	..	..
H	55	**Hotels and restaurants**	..	..	..	..	..	..	..	..
I	60-64	**Transport, storage and communications**	..	..	..	..	..	..	..	..
J	65-67	**Financial intermediation**	..	..	..	..	..	..	..	..
K	70-74	**Real estate, renting and business activities**	..	..	..	..	..	..	..	..
L-Q	75-99	**Public admin.; education; health; other services**	..	..	..	..	..	..	..	..
A-Q	01-99	**Grand total**	..	..	..	..	..	..	..	..

Note: ISIC 1722 includes 1723 and 1729; 2699 includes 2710.

Table UK.6 EMPLOI - EMPLOYMENT

Milliers

1989	1990	1991	1992	1993	1994	1995	1996		Code	CITI révision 3	
..	..	..	..	..	..	..	..	**Agriculture, chasse et sylviculture**	A	01-02	
..	..	..	..	..	..	..	..	**Pêche**	B	05	
..	..	..	..	..	..	..	..	**Activités extractives**	C	10-14	
..	..	..	..	..	..	..	..	Extraction de charbon, de lignite et de tourbe		10	
..	..	..	..	..	..	..	..	Extraction de pétrole brut et de gaz naturel		11	
..	..	..	..	..	..	..	..	Extraction de minerais métalliques		13	
..	..	..	..	..	..	..	..	Autres activités extractives		14	
..	..	..	..	4 218.2	4 249.9	4 205.4	..	**Activités de fabrication**	D	15-37	
..	..	..	..	551.3	542.7	512.4	..	**Produits alimentaires et boissons**		15	
..	..	..	..	57.4	56.2	55.2	..	Boissons			155
..	..	..	..	9.4	8.9	8.1	..	**Produits à base de tabac**		16	160
..	..	..	..	200.9	191.6	192.5	..	**Textiles**		17	
..	..	..	..	72.0	71.1	60.9	..	Filature, tissage et achèvement des textiles			171
..	..	..	..	74.6	69.6	68.2	..	Autres articles textiles			172
..	..	..	..	54.3	50.9	63.3	..	Etoffes et articles de bonneterie			173
..	..	..	..	183.6	169.7	181.6	..	**Habillement; préparation, teinture des fourrures**		18	
..	..	..	..	183.0	169.1	181.0	..	Articles d'habillement autres qu'en fourrure			181
..	..	..	..	0.6	0.6	0.6	..	Préparation, teinture des fourrures; art. en fourrure			182
..	..	..	..	57.1	57.7	52.2	..	**Travail des cuirs; articles en cuir; chaussures**		19	
..	..	..	..	17.1	16.3	14.3	..	Apprêt et tannage des cuirs et articles en cuirs			191
..	..	..	..	40.0	41.3	37.9	..	Chaussures			192
..	..	..	..	74.9	79.1	74.5	..	**Bois et articles en bois et liège (sauf meubles)**		20	
..	..	..	..	15.0	16.4	15.8	..	Sciage et rabotage du bois			201
..	..	..	..	59.9	62.7	58.8	..	Articles en bois, liège, vannerie, sparterie			202
..	..	..	..	125.5	125.8	122.9	..	**Papier et carton; articles en papier et en carton**		21	
..	..	..	..	317.7	330.9	315.1	..	**Edition, imprimerie et reproduction**		22	
..	..	..	..	140.6	144.9	141.8	..	Edition			221
..	..	..	..	172.9	182.3	167.8	..	Imprimerie et activités annexes			222
..	..	..	..	4.2	3.7	5.6	..	Reproduction de supports enregistrés			223
..	..	..	..	29.7	27.8	26.7	..	**Cokéfaction; prod. pétroliers; comb. nucléaires**		23	
..	..	..	..	270.4	265.1	276.5	..	**Produits chimiques**		24	
..	..	..	..	83.7	79.2	81.2	..	Produits chimiques de base			241
..	..	..	..	178.7	178.5	188.4	..	Autres produits chimiques			242
..	..	..	..	8.0	7.4	7.0	..	Fibres synthétiques ou artificielles			243
..	..	..	..	232.0	233.2	235.8	..	**Articles en caoutchouc et en matières plastiques**		25	
..	..	..	..	51.2	49.5	49.9	..	Articles en caoutchouc			251
..	..	..	..	180.8	183.7	185.8	..	Articles en matières plastiques			252
..	..	..	..	220.3	226.4	159.0	..	**Autres produits minéraux non métalliques**		26	
..	..	..	..	37.1	39.6	42.8	..	Verre et articles en verre			261
..	..	..	..	183.2	186.8	116.3	..	Produits minéraux non métalliques, nca			269
..	..	..	..	..	..	133.9	..	**Produits métallurgiques de base**		27	
..	..	..	..	..	..	63.8	..	Sidérurgie et première transformation de l'acier			271
..	..	..	..	37.3	33.1	32.6	..	Métallurgie; métaux précieux et non ferreux			272
..	..	..	..	36.7	36.5	37.4	..	Fonderie			273
..	..	..	..	368.1	382.1	392.9	..	**Ouvrages en métaux, sauf machines et matériel**		28	
..	..	..	..	93.3	90.3	81.5	..	Constr. et menuiserie métal.; réservoirs; générateurs			281
..	..	..	..	274.7	291.8	311.4	..	Autres ouvrages en métaux			289
..	..	..	..	386.7	392.9	400.8	..	**Machines et matériel, nca**		29	
..	..	..	..	209.8	215.9	216.4	..	Machines d'usage général			291
..	..	..	..	138.1	137.6	149.3	..	Machines d'usage spécifique			292
..	..	..	..	38.8	39.5	35.1	..	Appareils domestiques, nca			293
..	..	..	..	69.8	67.9	63.4	..	**Mach. de bureau, comptables, matériel inform.**		30	
..	..	..	..	185.0	194.7	183.6	..	**Machines et appareils électriques, nca**		31	
..	..	..	..	35.1	35.8	34.5	..	Moteurs, génératrices et transformateurs électriques			311
..	..	..	..	48.9	51.6	50.8	..	Matériel électrique de distribution et de commande			312
..	..	..	..	21.5	23.7	24.8	..	Fils et câbles électriques isolés			313
..	..	..	..	7.3	7.9	7.0	..	Accumulateurs, piles électriques			314
..	..	..	..	23.0	23.1	19.0	..	Lampes électriques et appareils d'éclairage			315
..	..	..	..	49.3	52.5	47.6	..	Autres matériels électriques, nca			319
..	..	..	..	117.3	132.4	137.0	..	**Equip. et appar. de radio, TV, communication**		32	
..	..	..	..	45.6	51.1	58.0	..	Tubes et valves électroniques; autres composants			321
..	..	..	..	38.7	46.3	42.8	..	Emetteurs radio et TV; app. téléphonie, télégraphie			322
..	..	..	..	33.0	35.0	36.2	..	Récepteurs radio et TV et articles associés			323
..	..	..	..	142.5	133.3	134.6	..	**Instruments médicaux, de précision, d'optique**		33	
..	..	..	..	125.8	117.0	118.5	..	Appareils médicaux et de précision			331
..	..	..	..	14.8	13.8	13.9	..	Instruments d'optique ; matériel photographique			332
..	..	..	..	1.9	2.4	2.2	..	Horlogerie			333
..	..	..	..	220.5	227.2	239.8	..	**Véhicules automobiles et nemorques**		34	
..	..	..	..	196.6	177.2	166.4	..	**Autres matériels de transport**		35	
..	..	..	..	48.1	41.5	38.7	..	Construction et réparation de navires			351
..	..	..	..	16.8	15.1	12.2	..	Construction de matériel ferroviaire roulant			352
..	..	..	..	125.6	114.4	108.9	..	Construction aéronautique et spatiale			353
..	..	..	..	6.0	6.2	6.6	..	Autres équipements de transport			359
..	..	..	..	185.0	210.0	188.6	..	**Meubles; activités de fabrication, nca**		36	
..	..	..	..	120.3	129.1	115.8	..	Meubles			361
..	..	..	..	64.7	80.9	72.8	..	Activités de fabrication, nca			369
..	..	..	..	..	3.5	7.1	..	**Récupération**		37	
..	..	..	..	..	..	..	..	**Production et distrib. d'électricité, de gaz, d'eau**	E	40-41	
..	..	..	..	..	..	..	..	**Electricité, gaz, vapeur et eau chaude**		40	
..	..	..	..	..	98.0	83.0	..	Production, collecte et distribution d'électricité			401
..	..	..	..	35.2	35.2	32.2	..	**Captage, épuration et distribution d'eau**		41	410
..	..	..	..	1 073.7	873.4	967.7	..	**Construction**	F	45	
..	..	..	..	..	..	..	..	**Commerce de gros et de détail; réparation**	G	50-52	
..	..	..	..	..	..	..	..	**Hôtels et restaurants**	H	55	
..	..	..	..	..	..	..	..	**Transports, entreposage et communications**	I	60-64	
..	..	..	..	..	..	..	..	**Intermédiation financière**	J	65-67	
..	..	..	..	..	..	..	..	**Immobilier, locations, services aux entreprises**	K	70-74	
..	..	..	..	..	..	..	..	**Admin. publique; éducation; santé; autres**	L-Q	75-99	
..	..	..	..	..	..	..	..	**Grand total**	A-Q	01-99	

Note: ISIC 1722 includes 1723 and 1729; 2699 includes 2710.

Statistiques des Structures Industrielles
OCDE, © 1998

OECD
OCDE

UNITED KINGDOM

Table UK.7 EMPLOYMENT, EMPLOYEES - EMPLOI, SALARIÉS

Thousands

ISIC revision 3			1989	1990	1991	1992	1993	1994	1995	1996
A	01-02	**Agriculture, hunting and forestry**	..	..	..	..	..	..	..	..
B	05	**Fishing**	..	..	..	..	..	..	..	..
C	10-14	**Mining and quarrying**	..	..	..	..	..	..	..	..
	10	Mining of coal and lignite; extraction of peat	..	..	..	..	..	..	..	..
	11	Crude petroleum & natural gas; related service activ.	..	..	..	..	..	..	..	..
	13	Mining of metal ores	..	..	..	..	..	..	..	..
	14	Other mining and quarrying	..	..	..	..	..	..	..	..
D	15-37	**Total manufacturing**	..	..	..	..	4 184.0	4 233.1	4 188.0	..
	15	**Food products and beverages**	..	..	..	..	546.0	540.1	510.2	..
	155	Beverages	..	..	..	..	57.4	56.2	55.2	..
	16 160	**Tobacco products**	..	..	..	..	9.4	8.9	8.1	..
	17	**Textiles**	..	..	..	..	198.7	190.7	191.7	..
	171	Spinning, weaving and finishing of textiles	..	..	..	..	71.2	70.6	60.7	..
	172	Other textiles	..	..	..	..	73.4	69.3	67.9	..
	173	Knitted and crocheted fabrics and articles	..	..	..	..	54.1	50.8	63.1	..
	18	**Wearing apparel dressing & dyeing of fur**	..	..	..	..	182.0	168.7	180.7	..
	181	Wearing apparel, except fur apparel	..	..	..	..	181.4	168.0	180.1	..
	182	Dressing and dyeing of fur; articles of fur	..	..	..	..	0.6	0.6	0.6	..
	19	**Tanning, dressing leather; leather artic.; footwear**	..	..	..	..	57.0	57.6	51.9	..
	191	Tanning, dressing leather; manuf. of leather articles	..	..	..	..	17.1	16.3	14.1	..
	192	Footwear	..	..	..	..	39.9	41.3	37.8	..
	20	**Wood and cork products, ex. furniture**	..	..	..	..	69.9	78.6	73.8	..
	201	Sawmilling and planing of wood	..	..	..	..	14.8	16.3	15.6	..
	202	Products of wood, cork, straw & plaiting material	..	..	..	..	55.1	62.3	58.3	..
	21	**Paper and paper products**	..	..	..	..	125.4	125.5	122.4	..
	22	**Publishing, printing & reprod. of recorded media**	..	..	..	..	309.8	329.7	313.4	..
	221	Publishing	..	..	..	..	137.3	144.9	141.5	..
	222	Printing and related service activities	..	..	..	..	168.3	181.1	166.4	..
	223	Reproduction of recorded media	..	..	..	..	4.2	3.7	5.6	..
	23	**Coke, refined petroleum products & nuclear fuel**	..	..	..	..	29.7	27.8	26.7	..
	24	**Chemicals and chemical products**	..	..	..	..	270.2	264.7	276.1	..
	241	Basic chemicals	..	..	..	..	83.6	79.1	81.0	..
	242	Other chemical products	..	..	..	..	178.7	178.2	188.1	..
	243	Man-made fibres	..	..	..	..	8.0	7.4	7.0	..
	25	**Rubber and plastic products**	..	..	..	..	230.3	232.5	234.7	..
	251	Rubber products	..	..	..	..	51.1	49.5	49.8	..
	252	Plastic products	..	..	..	..	179.2	183.1	184.9	..
	26	**Other non-metallic mineral products**	..	..	..	..	220.1	225.8	158.3	..
	261	Glass and glass products	..	..	..	..	37.1	39.5	42.5	..
	269	Non-metallic mineral products, nec	..	..	..	..	183.0	186.3	115.9	..
	27	**Basic metals**	..	..	..	..	..	..	133.5	..
	271	Basic iron and steel	..	..	..	..	..	..	63.7	..
	272	Basic precious and non-ferrous metals	..	..	..	..	37.3	33.1	32.5	..
	273	Casting of metals	..	..	..	..	36.6	36.4	37.3	..
	28	**Fabricated metal products, ex. machin. & equip.**	..	..	..	..	362.1	379.6	390.3	..
	281	Structural metal prod., tanks, reservoirs, generators	..	..	..	..	93.1	89.7	81.0	..
	289	Other fabricated metal products & service activities	..	..	..	..	268.9	290.0	309.2	..
	29	**Machinery and equipment, nec**	..	..	..	..	386.0	391.5	399.3	..
	291	General purpose machinery	..	..	..	..	209.4	214.8	215.7	..
	292	Special purpose machinery	..	..	..	..	137.9	137.2	148.4	..
	293	Domestic appliances, nec	..	..	..	..	38.8	39.5	35.1	..
	30	**Office, accounting and computing machinery**	..	..	..	..	69.8	67.9	63.3	..
	31	**Electrical machinery and apparatus, nec**	..	..	..	..	184.9	194.5	183.2	..
	311	Electric motors, generators and transformers	..	..	..	..	35.0	35.7	34.4	..
	312	Electricity distribution and control apparatus	..	..	..	..	48.9	51.6	50.8	..
	313	Insulated wire and cable	..	..	..	..	21.5	23.7	24.7	..
	314	Accumulators, primary cells and primary batteries	..	..	..	..	7.3	7.9	6.9	..
	315	Electric lamps and lighting equipment	..	..	..	..	22.9	23.1	18.9	..
	319	Other electrical equipment, nec	..	..	..	..	49.3	52.4	47.4	..
	32	**Radio, TV, communication equip. & apparatus**	..	..	..	..	117.2	132.2	136.7	..
	321	Electronic valves, tubes & other electronic compon.	..	..	..	..	45.5	51.1	57.8	..
	322	TV, radio transmitters & appar. for line teleph., telegr.	..	..	..	..	38.7	46.3	42.8	..
	323	TV, radio receivers and associated goods	..	..	..	..	33.0	34.8	36.1	..
	33	**Medical, precision, optical instr.; watches, clocks**	..	..	..	..	142.2	132.7	133.4	..
	331	Medical equip.; precision instruments and appliances	..	..	..	..	125.6	116.5	117.4	..
	332	Optical instruments and photographic equipment	..	..	..	..	14.7	13.8	13.8	..
	333	Watches and clocks	..	..	..	..	1.9	2.4	2.2	..
	34	**Motor vehicles, trailers, and semi-trailers**	..	..	..	..	220.1	227.0	239.5	..
	35	**Other transport equipment**	..	..	..	..	196.3	177.2	166.2	..
	351	Building and repairing of ships and boats	..	..	..	..	48.0	41.5	38.6	..
	352	Railway, tramway locomotives and rolling stock	..	..	..	..	16.8	15.1	12.2	..
	353	Aircraft and spacecraft	..	..	..	..	125.5	114.4	108.9	..
	359	Transport equipment, nec	..	..	..	..	6.0	6.2	6.6	..
	36	**Furniture; manufacturing, nec**	..	..	..	..	183.0	206.9	187.3	..
	361	Furniture	..	..	..	..	119.4	127.9	115.0	..
	369	Manufacturing, nec	..	..	..	..	63.6	79.0	72.3	..
	37	**Recycling**	..	..	..	..	..	3.5	7.0	..
E	40-41	**Electricity, gas and water supply**	..	..	..	..	..	..	..	..
	40	**Electricity, gas, steam and hot water supply**	..	..	..	..	..	..	..	..
	401	Production, collection and distribution of electricity	..	..	..	..	..	..	83.0	..
	41 410	**Collection, purification, distribution of water**	..	..	..	..	35.2	35.2	32.2	..
F	45	**Construction**	..	..	..	..	929.4	836.7	947.1	..
G	50-52	**Wholesale and retail trade; repairs etc**	..	..	..	..	..	..	..	..
H	55	**Hotels and restaurants**	..	..	..	..	..	..	..	..
I	60-64	**Transport, storage and communications**	..	..	..	..	..	..	..	..
J	65-67	**Financial intermediation**	..	..	..	..	..	..	..	..
K	70-74	**Real estate, renting and business activities**	..	..	..	..	..	..	..	..
L-Q	75-99	**Public admin.; education; health; other services**	..	..	..	..	..	..	..	..
A-Q	01-99	**Grand total**	..	..	..	..	..	..	..	..

Note: ISIC 1722 includes 1723 and 1729; 2699 includes 2710.

OECD OCDE Industrial Structure Statistics
OECD, © 1998

Table UK.8 **SALAIRES ET CHARGES SOCIALES , SALARIÉS - COMPENSATION OF LABOUR, EMPLOYEES**

Millions de £ *(Prix courants)*

1989	1990	1991	1992	1993	1994	1995	1996		CITI révision 3	
..	..	..	..	..	..	..	..	**Agriculture, chasse et sylviculture**	**A**	**01-02**
..	..	..	..	..	..	..	..	**Pêche**	**B**	**05**
..	..	..	..	..	..	..	..	**Activités extractives**	**C**	**10-14**
..	..	..	..	..	..	..	..	Extraction de charbon, de lignite et de tourbe		**10**
..	..	..	..	..	..	..	..	Extraction de pétrole brut et de gaz naturel		**11**
..	..	..	..	..	..	..	..	Extraction de minerais métalliques		**13**
..	..	..	..	..	..	..	..	Autres activités extractives		**14**
..	..	..	..	69 536	73 111	73 068	..	**Activités de fabrication**	**D**	**15-37**
..	..	..	..	7 766	8 058	7 847	..	**Produits alimentaires et boissons**	**15**	
..	..	..	..	1 087	1 200	1 226	..	Boissons		155
..	..	..	..	265	278	266	..	**Produits à base de tabac**	**16**	**160**
..	..	..	..	2 389	2 432	2 482	..	**Textiles**	**17**	
..	..	..	..	916	958	846	..	Filature, tissage et achèvement des textiles		171
..	..	..	..	907	902	893	..	Autres articles textiles		172
..	..	..	..	566	572	743	..	Etoffes et articles de bonneterie		173
..	..	..	..	1 541	1 641	1 673	..	**Habillement; préparation, teinture des fourrures**	**18**	
..	..	..	..	1 532	1 631	1 665	..	Articles d'habillement autres qu'en fourrure		181
..	..	..	..	9	9	8	..	Préparation, teinture des fourrures; art. en fourrure		182
..	..	..	..	677	655	592	..	**Travail des cuirs; articles en cuir; chaussures**	**19**	
..	..	..	..	253	197	181	..	Apprêt et tannage des cuirs et articles en cuirs		191
..	..	..	..	424	458	411	..	Chaussures		192
..	..	..	..	959	1 130	1 024	..	**Bois et articles en bois et liège (sauf meubles)**	**20**	
..	..	..	..	199	244	184	..	Sciage et rabotage du bois		201
..	..	..	..	760	886	840	..	Articles en bois, liège, vannerie, sparterie		202
..	..	..	..	2 222	2 316	2 318	..	**Papier et carton; articles en papier et en carton**	**21**	
..	..	..	..	5 750	6 523	6 064	..	**Edition, imprimerie et reproduction**	**22**	
..	..	..	..	2 642	2 941	2 898	..	Edition		221
..	..	..	..	3 023	3 508	3 045	..	Imprimerie et activités annexes		222
..	..	..	..	85	74	121	..	Reproduction de supports enregistrés		223
..	..	..	..	791	797	784	..	**Cokéfaction; prod. pétroliers; comb. nucléaires**	**23**	
..	..	..	..	6 019	6 098	6 523	..	**Produits chimiques**	**24**	
..	..	..	..	2 052	2 005	1 973	..	Produits chimiques de base		241
..	..	..	..	3 791	3 875	4 359	..	Autres produits chimiques		242
..	..	..	..	176	217	191	..	Fibres synthétiques ou artificielles		243
..	..	..	..	3 609	3 807	3 904	..	**Articles en caoutchouc et en matières plastiques**	**25**	
..	..	..	..	896	919	940	..	Articles en caoutchouc		251
..	..	..	..	2 713	2 888	2 964	..	Articles en matières plastiques		252
..	..	..	..	3 763	3 978	2 638	..	**Autres produits minéraux non métalliques**	**26**	
..	..	..	..	623	650	671	..	Verre et articles en verre		261
..	..	..	..	3 140	3 327	1 968	..	Produits minéraux non métalliques, nca		269
..	..	..	..	..	..	2 741	..	**Produits métallurgiques de base**	**27**	
..	..	..	..	..	..	1 453	..	Sidérurgie et première transformation de l'acier		271
..	..	..	..	672	623	638	..	Métallurgie; métaux précieux et non ferreux		272
..	..	..	..	572	614	651	..	Fonderie		273
..	..	..	..	5 890	6 169	6 110	..	**Ouvrages en métaux, sauf machines et matériel**	**28**	
..	..	..	..	1 643	1 629	1 398	..	Constr. et menuiserie métal.; réservoirs; générateurs		281
..	..	..	..	4 247	4 540	4 712	..	Autres ouvrages en métaux		289
..	..	..	..	6 864	7 248	7 537	..	**Machines et matériel, nca**	**29**	
..	..	..	..	3 776	3 986	4 134	..	Machines d'usage général		291
..	..	..	..	2 547	2 677	2 860	..	Machines d'usage spécifique		292
..	..	..	..	540	584	543	..	Appareils domestiques, nca		293
..	..	..	..	1 735	1 539	1 313	..	**Mach. de bureau, comptables, matériel inform.**	**30**	
..	..	..	..	2 942	3 118	3 024	..	**Machines et appareils électriques, nca**	**31**	
..	..	..	..	542	590	561	..	Moteurs, génératrices et transformateurs électriques		311
..	..	..	..	783	854	887	..	Matériel électrique de distribution et de commande		312
..	..	..	..	366	390	391	..	Fils et câbles électriques isolés		313
..	..	..	..	129	134	128	..	Accumulateurs, piles électriques		314
..	..	..	..	340	342	285	..	Lampes électriques et appareils d'éclairage		315
..	..	..	..	783	810	772	..	Autres matériels électriques, nca		319
..	..	..	..	1 960	2 409	2 535	..	**Equip. et appar. de radio, TV, communication**	**32**	
..	..	..	..	712	843	1 010	..	Tubes et valves électroniques; autres composants		321
..	..	..	..	764	990	966	..	Emetteurs radio et TV; app. téléphonie, télégraphie		322
..	..	..	..	484	577	559	..	Récepteurs radio et TV et articles associés		323
..	..	..	..	2 477	2 390	2 432	..	**Instruments médicaux, de précision, d'optique**	**33**	
..	..	..	..	2 222	2 124	2 153	..	Appareils médicaux et de précision		331
..	..	..	..	226	227	241	..	Instruments d'optique ; matériel photographique		332
..	..	..	..	28	38	38	..	Horlogerie		333
..	..	..	..	4 261	4 659	5 026	..	**Véhicules automobiles et nemorques**	**34**	
..	..	..	..	3 929	3 600	3 485	..	**Autres matériels de transport**	**35**	
..	..	..	..	945	776	737	..	Construction et réparation de navires		351
..	..	..	..	303	289	242	..	Construction de matériel ferroviaire roulant		352
..	..	..	..	2 603	2 451	2 410	..	Construction aéronautique et spatiale		353
..	..	..	..	78	83	96	..	Autres équipements de transport		359
..	..	..	..	2 483	2 977	2 642	..	**Meubles; activités de fabrication, nca**	**36**	
..	..	..	..	1 699	1 871	1 687	..	Meubles		361
..	..	..	..	784	1 106	955	..	Activités de fabrication, nca		369
..	..	..	..	..	55	108	..	**Récupération**	**37**	
..	..	..	..	..	..	..	..	**Production et distrib. d'électricité, de gaz, d'eau**	**E**	**40-41**
..	..	..	..	..	..	..	..	**Electricité, gaz, vapeur et eau chaude**	**40**	
..	..	..	..	..	2 704	2 407	..	Production, collecte et distribution d'électricité		401
..	..	..	..	637	665	622	..	**Captage, épuration et distribution d'eau**	**41**	**410**
..	..	..	..	13 541	13 983	14 670	..	**Construction**	**F**	**45**
..	..	..	..	..	..	..	..	**Commerce de gros et de détail; réparation**	**G**	**50-52**
..	..	..	..	..	..	..	..	**Hôtels et restaurants**	**H**	**55**
..	..	..	..	..	..	..	..	**Transports, entreposage et communications**	**I**	**60-64**
..	..	..	..	..	..	..	..	**Intermédiation financière**	**J**	**65-67**
..	..	..	..	..	..	..	..	**Immobilier, locations, services aux entreprises**	**K**	**70-74**
..	..	..	..	..	..	..	..	**Admin. publique; éducation; santé; autres**	**L-Q**	**75-99**
..	..	..	..	..	..	..	..	**Grand total**	**A-Q**	**01-99**

Note: ISIC 1722 includes 1723 and 1729; 2699 includes 2710. Compensation of labour for outworkers are included in the above figures.

Statistiques des Structures Industrielles
OCDE, © 1998

Table UK.9 WAGES AND SALARIES, EMPLOYEES - SALAIRES ET TRAITEMENTS, SALARIÉS

Millions of £ (Current Prices)

ISIC revision 3				1989	1990	1991	1992	1993	1994	1995	1996
A	01-02		**Agriculture, hunting and forestry**	..	..	..	..	..	..	..	..
B	05		**Fishing**	..	..	..	..	..	..	..	..
C	10-14		**Mining and quarrying**	..	..	..	..	..	..	..	..
	10		Mining of coal and lignite; extraction of peat	..	..	..	..	..	..	..	..
	11		Crude petroleum & natural gas; related service activ.	..	..	..	..	..	..	..	..
	13		Mining of metal ores	..	..	..	..	..	..	..	..
	14		Other mining and quarrying	..	..	..	..	..	..	..	..
D	15-37		**Total manufacturing**	..	..	..	..	61 384	64 313	64 173	..
	15		**Food products and beverages**	..	..	..	..	6 902	7 144	6 938	..
		155	Beverages	..	..	..	..	948	1 045	1 077	..
	16	160	**Tobacco products**	..	..	..	..	232	244	235	..
	17		**Textiles**	..	..	..	..	2 120	2 147	2 207	..
		171	Spinning, weaving and finishing of textiles	..	..	..	..	810	842	752	..
		172	Other textiles	..	..	..	..	805	797	787	..
		173	Knitted and crocheted fabrics and articles	..	..	..	..	505	508	669	..
	18		**Wearing apparel dressing & dyeing of fur**	..	..	..	..	1 395	1 410	1 456	..
		181	Wearing apparel, except fur apparel	..	..	..	..	1 387	1 402	1 449	..
		182	Dressing and dyeing of fur; articles of fur	..	..	..	..	8	8	7	..
	19		**Tanning, dressing leather; leather artic.; footwear**	..	..	..	..	608	580	540	..
		191	Tanning, dressing leather; manuf. of leather articles	..	..	..	..	233	174	161	..
		192	Footwear	..	..	..	..	376	405	378	..
	20		**Wood and cork products, ex. furniture**	..	..	..	..	854	992	932	..
		201	Sawmilling and planing of wood	..	..	..	..	172	216	167	..
		202	Products of wood, cork, straw & plaiting material	..	..	..	..	681	776	765	..
	21		**Paper and paper products**	..	..	..	..	1 960	2 029	2 036	..
	22		**Publishing, printing & reprod. of recorded media**	..	..	..	..	5 070	5 768	5 315	..
		221	Publishing	..	..	..	..	2 326	2 592	2 552	..
		222	Printing and related service activities	..	..	..	..	2 667	3 109	2 652	..
		223	Reproduction of recorded media	..	..	..	..	77	67	111	..
	23		**Coke, refined petroleum products & nuclear fuel**	..	..	..	..	669	672	658	..
	24		**Chemicals and chemical products**	..	..	..	..	5 179	5 239	5 625	..
		241	Basic chemicals	..	..	..	..	1 739	1 702	1 665	..
		242	Other chemical products	..	..	..	..	3 284	3 353	3 802	..
		243	Man-made fibres	..	..	..	..	157	184	158	..
	25		**Rubber and plastic products**	..	..	..	..	3 196	3 366	3 443	..
		251	Rubber products	..	..	..	..	788	806	814	..
		252	Plastic products	..	..	..	..	2 408	2 560	2 629	..
	26		**Other non-metallic mineral products**	..	..	..	..	3 321	3 507	2 319	..
		261	Glass and glass products	..	..	..	..	542	568	582	..
		269	Non-metallic mineral products, nec	..	..	..	..	2 780	2 939	1 737	..
	27		**Basic metals**	..	..	..	..	..	..	2 402	..
		271	Basic iron and steel	..	..	..	..	..	..	1 268	..
		272	Basic precious and non-ferrous metals	..	..	..	..	587	542	559	..
		273	Casting of metals	..	..	..	..	505	540	575	..
	28		**Fabricated metal products, ex. machin. & equip.**	..	..	..	..	5 259	5 505	5 453	..
		281	Structural metal prod., tanks, reservoirs, generators	..	..	..	..	1 474	1 465	1 257	..
		289	Other fabricated metal products & service activities	..	..	..	..	3 785	4 040	4 196	..
	29		**Machinery and equipment, nec**	..	..	..	..	6 072	6 415	6 629	..
		291	General purpose machinery	..	..	..	..	3 341	3 527	3 642	..
		292	Special purpose machinery	..	..	..	..	2 250	2 368	2 508	..
		293	Domestic appliances, nec	..	..	..	..	480	520	479	..
	30		**Office, accounting and computing machinery**	..	..	..	..	1 508	1 332	1 155	..
	31		**Electrical machinery and apparatus, nec**	..	..	..	..	2 618	2 750	2 669	..
		311	Electric motors, generators and transformers	..	..	..	..	481	515	490	..
		312	Electricity distribution and control apparatus	..	..	..	..	697	757	788	..
		313	Insulated wire and cable	..	..	..	..	325	347	350	..
		314	Accumulators, primary cells and primary batteries	..	..	..	..	111	116	112	..
		315	Electric lamps and lighting equipment	..	..	..	..	305	305	251	..
		319	Other electrical equipment, nec	..	..	..	..	699	710	677	..
	32		**Radio, TV, communication equip. & apparatus**	..	..	..	..	1 754	2 159	2 249	..
		321	Electronic valves, tubes & other electronic compon.	..	..	..	..	637	750	891	..
		322	TV, radio transmitters & appar. for line teleph., telegr.	..	..	..	..	682	888	854	..
		323	TV, radio receivers and associated goods	..	..	..	..	436	522	504	..
	33		**Medical, precision, optical instr.; watches, clocks**	..	..	..	..	2 189	2 113	2 123	..
		331	Medical equip.; precision instruments and appliances	..	..	..	..	1 963	1 877	1 873	..
		332	Optical instruments and photographic equipment	..	..	..	..	202	203	215	..
		333	Watches and clocks	..	..	..	..	24	33	35	..
	34		**Motor vehicles, trailers, and semi-trailers**	..	..	..	..	3 696	4 032	4 316	..
	35		**Other transport equipment**	..	..	..	..	3 484	3 156	3 056	..
		351	Building and repairing of ships and boats	..	..	..	..	838	678	641	..
		352	Railway, tramway locomotives and rolling stock	..	..	..	..	270	260	215	..
		353	Aircraft and spacecraft	..	..	..	..	2 307	2 144	2 115	..
		359	Transport equipment, nec	..	..	..	..	69	74	85	..
	36		**Furniture; manufacturing, nec**	..	..	..	..	2 204	2 627	2 328	..
		361	Furniture	..	..	..	..	1 515	1 665	1 494	..
		369	Manufacturing, nec	..	..	..	..	689	962	833	..
	37		**Recycling**	..	..	..	..	..	46	90	..
E	40-41		**Electricity, gas and water supply**	..	..	..	..	..	..	..	..
	40		**Electricity, gas, steam and hot water supply**	..	..	..	..	..	..	..	..
		401	Production, collection and distribution of electricity	..	..	..	..	..	2 212	1 980	..
	41	410	**Collection, purification, distribution of water**	..	..	..	..	538	560	523	..
F	45		**Construction**	..	..	..	..	12 054	12 441	..	..
G	50-52		**Wholesale and retail trade; repairs etc**	..	..	..	..	..	..	..	..
H	55		**Hotels and restaurants**	..	..	..	..	..	..	..	..
I	60-64		**Transport, storage and communications**	..	..	..	..	..	..	..	..
J	65-67		**Financial intermediation**	..	..	..	..	..	..	..	..
K	70-74		**Real estate, renting and business activities**	..	..	..	..	..	..	..	..
L-Q	75-99		**Public admin.; education; health; other services**	..	..	..	..	..	..	..	..
A-Q	01-99		**Grand total**	..	..	..	..	..	..	..	..

Note: ISIC 1722 includes 1723 and 1729; 2699 includes 2710.

Table UK.10 **CHARGES SOCIALES DES EMPLOYEURS - EMPLOYERS' SOCIAL COSTS**

Millions de £ (Prix courants)

1989	1990	1991	1992	1993	1994	1995	1996			CITI révision 3	
..	..	..	..	..	..	..	..	**Agriculture, chasse et sylviculture**	A	01-02	
..	..	..	..	..	..	..	..	**Pêche**	B	05	
..	..	..	..	..	..	..	..	**Activités extractives**	C	10-14	
..	..	..	..	..	..	..	..	Extraction de charbon, de lignite et de tourbe		10	
..	..	..	..	..	..	..	..	Extraction de pétrole brut et de gaz naturel		11	
..	..	..	..	..	..	..	..	Extraction de minerais métalliques		13	
..	..	..	..	..	..	..	..	Autres activités extractives		14	
..	..	..	..	8 152	8 631	8 741	..	**Activités de fabrication**	D	15-37	
..	..	..	..	864	914	908	..	**Produits alimentaires et boissons**		15	
..	..	..	..	139	155	150	..	Boissons			155
..	..	..	..	33	34	32	..	**Produits à base de tabac**		16	160
..	..	..	..	269	275	264	..	**Textiles**		17	
..	..	..	..	106	116	93	..	Filature, tissage et achèvement des textiles			171
..	..	..	..	102	98	100	..	Autres articles textiles			172
..	..	..	..	61	61	71	..	Etoffes et articles de bonneterie			173
..	..	..	..	147	153	145	..	**Habillement; préparation, teinture des fourrures**		18	
..	..	..	..	145	152	144	..	Articles d'habillement autres qu'en fourrure			181
..	..	..	..	1	1	1	..	Préparation, teinture des fourrures; art. en fourrure			182
..	..	..	..	69	71	49	..	**Travail des cuirs; articles en cuir; chaussures**		19	
..	..	..	..	21	21	19	..	Apprêt et tannage des cuirs et articles en cuirs			191
..	..	..	..	48	49	30	..	Chaussures			192
..	..	..	..	105	137	91	..	**Bois et articles en bois et liège (sauf meubles)**		20	
..	..	..	..	26	28	16	..	Sciage et rabotage du bois			201
..	..	..	..	79	109	74	..	Articles en bois, liège, vannerie, sparterie			202
..	..	..	..	263	281	279	..	**Papier et carton; articles en papier et en carton**		21	
..	..	..	..	681	754	747	..	**Edition, imprimerie et reproduction**		22	
..	..	..	..	316	348	346	..	Edition			221
..	..	..	..	357	399	390	..	Imprimerie et activités annexes			222
..	..	..	..	8	7	11	..	Reproduction de supports enregistrés			223
..	..	..	..	122	124	126	..	**Cokéfaction; prod. pétroliers; comb. nucléaires**		23	
..	..	..	..	839	858	897	..	**Produits chimiques**		24	
..	..	..	..	312	303	308	..	Produits chimiques de base			241
..	..	..	..	508	523	556	..	Autres produits chimiques			242
..	..	..	..	19	33	32	..	Fibres synthétiques ou artificielles			243
..	..	..	..	413	435	449	..	**Articles en caoutchouc et en matières plastiques**		25	
..	..	..	..	107	112	123	..	Articles en caoutchouc			251
..	..	..	..	306	323	326	..	Articles en matières plastiques			252
..	..	..	..	442	469	318	..	**Autres produits minéraux non métalliques**		26	
..	..	..	..	81	82	88	..	Verre et articles en verre			261
..	..	..	..	360	387	230	..	Produits minéraux non métalliques, nca			269
..	..	..	..	..	..	339	..	**Produits métallurgiques de base**		27	
..	..	..	..	..	..	185	..	Sidérurgie et première transformation de l'acier			271
..	..	..	..	85	80	79	..	Métallurgie; métaux précieux et non ferreux			272
..	..	..	..	67	74	76	..	Fonderie			273
..	..	..	..	631	660	653	..	**Ouvrages en métaux, sauf machines et matériel**		28	
..	..	..	..	169	164	139	..	Constr. et menuiserie métal.; réservoirs; générateurs			281
..	..	..	..	462	496	514	..	Autres ouvrages en métaux			289
..	..	..	..	792	829	904	..	**Machines et matériel, nca**		29	
..	..	..	..	435	457	491	..	Machines d'usage général			291
..	..	..	..	297	308	349	..	Machines d'usage spécifique			292
..	..	..	..	60	64	64	..	Appareils domestiques, nca			293
..	..	..	..	227	199	154	..	**Mach. de bureau, comptables, matériel inform.**		30	
..	..	..	..	323	352	346	..	**Machines et appareils électriques, nca**		31	
..	..	..	..	61	73	69	..	Moteurs, génératrices et transformateurs électriques			311
..	..	..	..	86	95	95	..	Matériel électrique de distribution et de commande			312
..	..	..	..	41	41	40	..	Fils et câbles électriques isolés			313
..	..	..	..	18	18	16	..	Accumulateurs, piles électriques			314
..	..	..	..	34	35	32	..	Lampes électriques et appareils d'éclairage			315
..	..	..	..	84	92	94	..	Autres matériels électriques, nca			319
..	..	..	..	205	248	284	..	**Equip. et appar. de radio, TV, communication**		32	
..	..	..	..	76	91	118	..	Tubes et valves électroniques; autres composants			321
..	..	..	..	81	101	112	..	Emetteurs radio et TV; app. téléphonie, télégraphie			322
..	..	..	..	48	55	54	..	Récepteurs radio et TV et articles associés			323
..	..	..	..	287	273	304	..	**Instruments médicaux, de précision, d'optique**		33	
..	..	..	..	259	244	274	..	Appareils médicaux et de précision			331
..	..	..	..	24	25	26	..	Instruments d'optique ; matériel photographique			332
..	..	..	..	4	5	4	..	Horlogerie			333
..	..	..	..	565	627	708	..	**Véhicules automobiles et nemorques**		34	
..	..	..	..	445	443	429	..	**Autres matériels de transport**		35	
..	..	..	..	107	99	95	..	Construction et réparation de navires			351
..	..	..	..	33	29	27	..	Construction de matériel ferroviaire roulant			352
..	..	..	..	296	307	295	..	Construction aéronautique et spatiale			353
..	..	..	..	9	9	11	..	Autres équipements de transport			359
..	..	..	..	280	333	295	..	**Meubles; activités de fabrication, nca**		36	
..	..	..	..	185	203	189	..	Meubles			361
..	..	..	..	95	129	106	..	Activités de fabrication, nca			369
..	..	..	..	..	9	18	..	**Récupération**		37	
..	..	..	..	..	..	..	..	**Production et distrib. d'électricité, de gaz, d'eau**	E	40-41	
..	..	..	..	..	..	..	..	**Electricité, gaz, vapeur et eau chaude**		40	
..	..	..	..	..	492	427	..	Production, collecte et distribution d'électricité			401
..	..	..	..	99	104	98	..	**Captage, épuration et distribution d'eau**		41	410
..	..	..	..	1 487	1 542	..	..	**Construction**	F	45	
..	..	..	..	..	..	..	..	**Commerce de gros et de détail; réparation**	G	50-52	
..	..	..	..	..	..	..	..	**Hôtels et restaurants**	H	55	
..	..	..	..	..	..	..	..	**Transports, entreposage et communications**	I	60-64	
..	..	..	..	..	..	..	..	**Intermédiation financière**	J	65-67	
..	..	..	..	..	..	..	..	**Immobilier, locations, services aux entreprises**	K	70-74	
..	..	..	..	..	..	..	..	**Admin. publique; éducation; santé; autres**	L-Q	75-99	
..	..	..	..	..	..	..	..	**Grand total**	A-Q	01-99	

Note: ISIC 1722 includes 1723 and 1729; 2699 includes 2710. Compensation of labour for outworkers are excluded from the above figures.

Statistiques des Structures Industrielles
OCDE, © 1998

Table UK.11 **EXPORTS - EXPORTATIONS**

Millions of £ (Current Prices)

ISIC revision 3			1989	1990	1991	1992	1993	1994	1995	1996
A	01-02	**Agriculture, hunting and forestry**	..	1 284	1 319	1 402	1 187	1 227	1 467	1 482
B	05	**Fishing**	..	271	316	317	244	286	293	307
C	10-14	**Mining and quarrying**	..	7 559	6 648	6 414	8 122	9 170	9 853	11 246
	10	Mining of coal and lignite; extraction of peat	..	98	80	52	60	56	57	73
	11	Crude petroleum & natural gas; related service activ.	..	5 262	4 430	4 427	5 035	6 059	6 640	7 639
	13	Mining of metal ores	..	19	7	11	15	15	30	19
	14	Other mining and quarrying	..	2 177	2 130	1 924	3 012	3 039	3 126	3 514
D	15-37	**Total manufacturing**	..	90 327	93 197	96 871	105 205	120 406	139 502	150 231
	15	**Food products and beverages**	..	5 455	5 820	6 546	7 277	8 251	9 106	8 873
		155	Beverages	..	2 230	2 376	2 584	2 760	3 010	3 162	3 322
	16	160	**Tobacco products**	..	642	765	948	636	855	1 127	1 201
	17	**Textiles**	..	2 535	2 441	2 603	2 702	3 175	3 448	3 592
		171	Spinning, weaving and finishing of textiles	..	1 241	1 140	1 216	1 272	1 501	1 603	1 626
		172	Other textiles	..	844	824	872	906	1 020	1 144	1 235
		173	Knitted and crocheted fabrics and articles	..	450	478	515	524	655	701	731
	18	**Wearing apparel dressing & dyeing of fur**	..	1 401	1 569	1 713	1 832	2 204	2 534	2 705
		181	Wearing apparel, except fur apparel	..	1 343	1 529	1 672	1 789	2 154	2 472	2 623
		182	Dressing and dyeing of fur; articles of fur	..	57	40	42	42	50	62	81
	19	**Tanning, dressing leather; leather artic.; footwear**	..	609	611	649	746	879	953	1 078
		191	Tanning, dressing leather; manuf. of leather articles	..	335	297	307	354	407	437	478
		192	Footwear	..	274	315	341	392	471	516	600
	20	**Wood and cork products, ex. furniture**	..	151	158	165	156	215	242	283
		201	Sawmilling and planing of wood	..	18	18	20	16	30	30	31
		202	Products of wood, cork, straw & plaiting material	..	132	140	145	140	185	212	253
	21	**Paper and paper products**	..	1 577	1 646	1 769	1 822	2 071	2 430	2 393
	22	**Publishing, printing & reprod. of recorded media**	..	1 500	1 541	1 591	1 883	2 176	2 436	2 481
		221	Publishing	..	1 181	1 209	1 279	1 531	1 750	2 030	2 024
		222	Printing and related service activities	..	318	332	312	352	426	406	457
		223	Reproduction of recorded media	..	0	0	0	0	0	0	0
	23	**Coke, refined petroleum products & nuclear fuel**	..	2 749	2 972	2 921	3 401	3 066	2 974	3 565
	24	**Chemicals and chemical products**	..	13 931	14 468	15 595	17 725	19 454	21 925	23 079
		241	Basic chemicals	..	5 991	6 062	6 350	7 201	7 749	8 566	8 672
		242	Other chemical products	..	7 293	7 746	8 585	9 905	11 043	12 593	13 605
		243	Man-made fibres	..	647	660	660	619	662	766	802
	25	**Rubber and plastic products**	..	2 451	2 548	2 767	2 883	3 318	3 889	4 119
		251	Rubber products	..	911	926	1 013	1 092	1 221	1 389	1 491
		252	Plastic products	..	1 540	1 622	1 754	1 792	2 097	2 500	2 628
	26	**Other non-metallic mineral products**	..	1 335	1 392	1 388	1 466	1 682	1 986	2 131
		261	Glass and glass products	..	406	458	446	460	522	599	601
		269	Non-metallic mineral products, nec	..	930	933	942	1 006	1 160	1 386	1 530
	27	**Basic metals**	..	5 914	5 560	5 269	5 653	6 525	8 091	7 580
		271	Basic iron and steel	..	3 304	3 225	3 183	3 449	3 926	4 736	4 408
		272	Basic precious and non-ferrous metals	..	2 610	2 334	2 086	2 204	2 600	3 355	3 123
		273	Casting of metals	..	0	0	0	0	0	0	49
	28	**Fabricated metal products, ex. machin. & equip.**	..	2 199	2 260	2 301	2 328	2 745	3 206	3 466
		281	Structural metal prod., tanks, reservoirs, generators	..	535	529	518	597	671	766	818
		289	Other fabricated metal products & service activities	..	1 664	1 730	1 783	1 731	2 075	2 440	2 648
	29	**Machinery and equipment, nec**	..	11 934	11 224	11 559	12 382	13 621	16 250	17 707
		291	General purpose machinery	..	5 451	5 450	5 596	6 149	6 703	7 962	8 692
		292	Special purpose machinery	..	5 992	5 269	5 416	5 633	6 217	7 470	8 126
		293	Domestic appliances, nec	..	491	505	548	600	701	818	889
	30	**Office, accounting and computing machinery**	..	6 343	6 588	6 636	8 063	9 588	11 799	12 126
	31	**Electrical machinery and apparatus, nec**	..	3 471	3 447	3 638	4 077	4 884	5 657	6 379
		311	Electric motors, generators and transformers	..	751	771	874	974	1 072	1 284	1 457
		312	Electricity distribution and control apparatus	..	779	842	874	972	1 119	1 284	1 453
		313	Insulated wire and cable	..	419	339	356	388	483	608	557
		314	Accumulators, primary cells and primary batteries	..	184	200	170	183	228	263	339
		315	Electric lamps and lighting equipment	..	223	215	228	277	333	383	430
		319	Other electrical equipment, nec	..	1 116	1 081	1 135	1 282	1 650	1 834	2 143
	32	**Radio, TV, communication equip. & apparatus**	..	4 553	4 876	5 218	7 099	9 322	12 228	13 187
		321	Electronic valves, tubes & other electronic compon.	..	2 033	2 083	2 523	3 740	4 729	5 954	5 788
		322	TV, radio transmitters & appar. for line teleph., telegr.	..	815	898	929	1 244	2 122	3 340	4 035
		323	TV, radio receivers and associated goods	..	1 705	1 896	1 765	2 115	2 470	2 933	3 364
	33	**Medical, precision, optical instr.; watches, clocks**	..	3 753	3 860	4 056	4 372	4 857	5 470	6 060
		331	Medical equip.; precision instruments and appliances	..	3 295	3 334	3 418	3 749	4 084	4 653	5 142
		332	Optical instruments and photographic equipment	..	359	440	509	463	553	575	654
		333	Watches and clocks	..	99	87	128	160	220	242	264
	34	**Motor vehicles, trailers, and semi-trailers**	..	8 376	9 677	10 065	9 443	11 089	13 380	16 104
	35	**Other transport equipment**	..	7 385	7 711	7 206	6 835	7 252	6 946	8 391
		351	Building and repairing of ships and boats	..	337	316	292	242	506	443	575
		352	Railway, tramway locomotives and rolling stock	..	88	104	89	133	494	104	77
		353	Aircraft and spacecraft	..	6 394	6 654	6 244	5 995	5 782	5 925	7 161
		359	Transport equipment, nec	..	567	637	581	465	469	475	578
	36	**Furniture; manufacturing, nec**	..	2 066	2 064	2 268	2 423	3 177	3 427	3 732
		361	Furniture	..	506	538	592	551	665	794	906
		369	Manufacturing, nec	..	1 560	1 527	1 676	1 871	2 512	2 634	2 826
	37	**Recycling**	..	0	0	0	0	0	0	0
E	40-41	**Electricity, gas and water supply**	..	25	0	0	0	0	2	2
	40	**Electricity, gas, steam and hot water supply**	..	25	0	0	0	0	2	2
		401	Production, collection and distribution of electricity	..	25	0	0	0	0	2	2
	41	410	**Collection, purification, distribution of water**	..	0	0	0	0	0	0	0
F	45	**Construction**	..	..	..	..	..	..	..	..
G	50-52	**Wholesale and retail trade; repairs etc**	..	..	..	..	..	..	..	..
H	55	**Hotels and restaurants**	..	..	..	..	..	..	..	..
I	60-64	**Transport, storage and communications**	..	..	..	..	..	..	..	..
J	65-67	**Financial intermediation**	..	..	..	..	..	..	..	..
K	70-74	**Real estate, renting and business activities**	..	..	..	..	..	..	..	..
L-Q	75-99	**Public admin.; education; health; other services**	..	..	..	..	..	..	..	..
A-Q	01-99	**Grand total**	..	103 694	104 819	108 507	117 313	133 878	153 875	166 327

Note: ISIC 1722 includes 1723 and 1729; 2699 includes 2710. The Grand total includes a figure for activities not adequately defined.

Table UK.12 IMPORTATIONS - IMPORTS

Millions de £ (Prix courants)

1989	1990	1991	1992	1993	1994	1995	1996			CITI révision 3	
..	4 295	4 150	4 315	4 306	4 780	5 267	5 734	**Agriculture, chasse et sylviculture**	A	01-02	
..	163	132	129	120	131	129	162	**Pêche**	B	05	
..	8 136	7 761	7 430	8 348	7 244	7 417	8 680	**Activités extractives**	C	10-14	
..	639	737	738	644	586	587	657	Extraction de charbon, de lignite et de tourbe		10	
..	4 553	4 342	4 138	4 403	3 475	3 345	4 152	Extraction de pétrole brut et de gaz naturel		11	
..	652	566	552	509	485	595	626	Extraction de minerais métalliques		13	
..	2 128	2 014	1 922	2 705	2 625	2 847	3 172	Autres activités extractives		14	
..	109 525	103 400	110 417	117 920	132 941	152 250	164 232	**Activités de fabrication**	D	15-37	
..	9 432	9 474	10 484	10 611	11 375	12 631	13 315	**Produits alimentaires et boissons**		15	
..	1 614	1 539	1 639	1 703	1 914	2 071	2 322	Boissons			155
..	139	161	161	166	186	222	241	**Produits à base de tabac**		16	160
..	4 177	4 082	4 351	4 354	4 914	5 286	5 654	**Textiles**		17	
..	2 322	2 151	2 224	2 198	2 574	2 739	2 780	Filature, tissage et achèvement des textiles			171
..	1 224	1 190	1 278	1 248	1 412	1 563	1 720	Autres articles textiles			172
..	630	741	849	908	928	985	1 154	Etoffes et articles de bonneterie			173
..	3 355	3 453	3 685	3 781	3 998	4 386	5 140	**Habillement; préparation, teinture des fourrures**		18	
..	3 329	3 434	3 662	3 764	3 974	4 359	5 092	Articles d'habillement autres qu'en fourrure			181
..	26	19	23	18	24	27	47	Préparation, teinture des fourrures; art. en fourrure			182
..	1 704	1 631	1 638	1 745	2 048	2 184	2 522	**Travail des cuirs; articles en cuir; chaussures**		19	
..	534	461	486	539	612	662	759	Apprêt et tannage des cuirs et articles en cuirs			191
..	1 169	1 170	1 152	1 206	1 435	1 522	1 763	Chaussures			192
..	2 361	1 867	1 871	1 959	2 390	2 211	2 259	**Bois et articles en bois et liège (sauf meubles)**		20	
..	1 365	1 006	987	1 046	1 328	1 115	1 136	Sciage et rabotage du bois			201
..	996	861	884	913	1 062	1 096	1 123	Articles en bois, liège, vannerie, sparterie			202
..	4 780	4 465	4 414	4 199	4 844	6 281	5 643	**Papier et carton; articles en papier et en carton**		21	
..	1 099	1 127	1 204	1 149	1 291	1 453	1 404	**Edition, imprimerie et reproduction**		22	
..	774	802	875	901	955	1 103	1 051	Edition			221
..	325	325	329	248	336	350	353	Imprimerie et activités annexes			222
..	0	0	0	0	0	0	0	Reproduction de supports enregistrés			223
..	2 696	2 432	1 982	2 000	1 996	1 753	2 149	**Cokéfaction; prod. pétroliers; comb. nucléaires**		23	
..	11 284	11 311	12 130	13 354	14 973	18 374	18 812	**Produits chimiques**		24	
..	6 176	5 956	6 073	6 531	7 351	9 536	9 238	Produits chimiques de base			241
..	4 542	4 809	5 461	6 228	6 951	8 071	8 805	Autres produits chimiques			242
..	566	546	596	595	671	767	770	Fibres synthétiques ou artificielles			243
..	3 126	3 077	3 380	3 368	3 961	4 545	4 649	**Articles en caoutchouc et en matières plastiques**		25	
..	923	914	1 050	1 110	1 316	1 528	1 638	Articles en caoutchouc			251
..	2 203	2 163	2 330	2 258	2 645	3 016	3 011	Articles en matières plastiques			252
..	1 617	1 470	1 496	1 419	1 655	1 779	1 868	**Autres produits minéraux non métalliques**		26	
..	676	652	676	669	746	826	834	Verre et articles en verre			261
..	941	818	820	750	909	954	1 034	Produits minéraux non métalliques, nca			269
..	6 441	5 823	5 701	5 951	6 587	8 485	8 464	**Produits métallurgiques de base**		27	
..	2 716	2 649	2 538	2 486	2 978	3 753	3 664	Sidérurgie et première transformation de l'acier			271
..	3 725	3 173	3 162	3 465	3 609	4 732	4 777	Métallurgie; métaux précieux et non ferreux			272
..	0	0	0	0	0	0	23	Fonderie			273
..	2 648	2 608	2 647	2 581	2 964	3 414	3 597	**Ouvrages en métaux, sauf machines et matériel**		28	
..	535	548	470	423	445	539	575	Constr. et menuiserie métal.; réservoirs; générateurs			281
..	2 113	2 060	2 178	2 158	2 519	2 875	3 022	Autres ouvrages en métaux			289
..	11 044	10 219	10 858	10 786	12 194	14 212	14 744	**Machines et matériel, nca**		29	
..	4 847	4 644	5 137	5 312	6 030	6 843	7 350	Machines d'usage général			291
..	5 187	4 520	4 646	4 406	4 984	6 083	6 123	Machines d'usage spécifique			292
..	1 009	1 055	1 075	1 069	1 180	1 287	1 270	Appareils domestiques, nca			293
..	7 716	7 592	8 360	10 023	10 707	12 401	12 801	**Mach. de bureau, comptables, matériel inform.**		30	
..	3 574	3 593	4 064	4 493	5 460	6 497	6 845	**Machines et appareils électriques, nca**		31	
..	703	701	840	844	979	1 201	1 440	Moteurs, génératrices et transformateurs électriques			311
..	1 002	974	1 096	1 174	1 294	1 517	1 603	Matériel électrique de distribution et de commande			312
..	379	381	406	486	561	729	723	Fils et câbles électriques isolés			313
..	224	221	248	352	418	492	439	Accumulateurs, piles électriques			314
..	347	327	383	424	500	563	581	Lampes électriques et appareils d'éclairage			315
..	919	988	1 091	1 213	1 708	1 994	2 059	Autres matériels électriques, nca			319
..	6 064	6 002	6 507	7 839	9 264	12 000	15 046	**Equip. et appar. de radio, TV, communication**		32	
..	2 684	2 783	3 070	3 903	4 376	5 801	7 688	Tubes et valves électroniques; autres composants			321
..	1 077	1 039	1 213	1 499	2 090	3 046	3 978	Emetteurs radio et TV; app. téléphonie, télégraphie			322
..	2 304	2 181	2 224	2 437	2 798	3 153	3 380	Récepteurs radio et TV et articles associés			323
..	3 694	3 745	3 925	4 298	4 584	5 175	5 885	**Instruments médicaux, de précision, d'optique**		33	
..	2 682	2 770	2 878	3 094	3 256	3 711	4 247	Appareils médicaux et de précision			331
..	652	656	689	757	856	963	1 082	Instruments d'optique ; matériel photographique			332
..	360	319	358	446	472	501	557	Horlogerie			333
..	13 196	10 763	12 786	14 692	16 940	19 167	21 683	**Véhicules automobiles et nemorques**		34	
..	5 839	5 157	4 939	4 917	5 989	5 041	6 143	**Autres matériels de transport**		35	
..	147	306	237	64	61	313	145	Construction et réparation de navires			351
..	72	91	148	243	730	223	63	Construction de matériel ferroviaire roulant			352
..	5 008	4 196	4 022	4 091	4 657	3 891	5 188	Construction aéronautique et spatiale			353
..	611	565	532	520	542	614	747	Autres équipements de transport			359
..	3 540	3 350	3 834	4 234	4 621	4 753	5 369	**Meubles; activités de fabrication, nca**		36	
..	1 098	988	1 035	942	1 081	1 177	1 355	Meubles			361
..	2 442	2 361	2 799	3 292	3 540	3 576	4 015	Activités de fabrication, nca			369
..	0	0	0	0	0	0	0	**Récupération**		37	
..	266	371	371	427	388	416	393	**Production et distrib. d'électricité, de gaz, d'eau**	E	40-41	
..	266	371	371	427	388	416	393	**Electricité, gaz, vapeur et eau chaude**		40	
..	266	371	371	427	388	416	393	Production, collecte et distribution d'électricité			401
..	0	0	0	0	0	0	0	**Captage, épuration et distribution d'eau**		41	410
..	..	..	..	..	..	..	..	**Construction**	F	45	
..	..	..	..	..	..	..	..	**Commerce de gros et de détail; réparation**	G	50-52	
..	..	..	..	..	..	..	..	**Hôtels et restaurants**	H	55	
..	..	..	..	..	..	..	..	**Transports, entreposage et communications**	I	60-64	
..	..	..	..	..	..	..	..	**Intermédiation financière**	J	65-67	
..	..	..	..	..	..	..	..	**Immobilier, locations, services aux entreprises**	K	70-74	
..	..	..	..	..	..	..	..	**Admin. publique; éducation; santé; autres**	L-Q	75-99	
..	126 087	118 872	125 867	133 723	148 192	168 125	181 970	**Grand total**	A-Q	01-99	

Note: ISIC 1722 includes 1723 and 1729; 2699 includes 2710. The Grand total includes a figure for activities not adequately defined.

Statistiques des Structures Industrielles
OCDE, © 1998

Section II

Disaggregated national accounts by industry
Comptes nationaux désagrégés par industrie

List of countries
Liste des pays

Table FN.14 PRODUCTION - PRODUCTION

Millions of Mk (Current Prices)

ISIC revision 3			1989	1990	1991	1992	1993	1994	1995	1996
A	01-02	**Agriculture, hunting and forestry**	..	42 589	36 886	34 435	34 980	38 026	32 703	31 285
B	05	**Fishing**	..	..	..	..	..	..	..	..
C	10-14	**Mining and quarrying**	3 550	3 454	3 287	3 334	3 225	3 523	3 816	3 852
	10	Mining of coal and lignite; extraction of peat	..	781	854	1 077	1 045	1 306	1 373	1 407
	11	Crude petroleum & natural gas; related service activ.	..	..	..	..	..	..	..	..
	13	Mining of metal ores	1 155	765	681	625	582	584	561	580
	14	Other mining and quarrying	1 788	1 908	1 752	1 632	1 598	1 633	1 882	1 865
D	15-37	**Total manufacturing**	293 085	297 738	265 223	269 231	292 201	326 149	382 076	394 354
	15	**Food products and beverages**	48 104	50 212	49 901	49 005	49 691	48 948	46 430	48 930
	155	Beverages	..	..	..	..	..	..	..	..
	16 160	**Tobacco products**	943	1 117	1 090	1 029	986	974	897	651
	17	**Textiles**	4 310	4 211	3 434	3 516	3 675	3 996	4 208	4 390
	171	Spinning, weaving and finishing of textiles	..	..	..	..	..	..	..	..
	172	Other textiles	..	..	..	..	..	..	..	..
	173	Knitted and crocheted fabrics and articles	..	..	..	..	..	..	..	..
	18	**Wearing apparel dressing & dyeing of fur**	4 327	3 654	2 944	2 326	2 282	2 673	2 540	2 526
	181	Wearing apparel, except fur apparel	..	..	..	..	..	..	..	..
	182	Dressing and dyeing of fur; articles of fur	..	..	..	..	..	..	..	..
	19	**Tanning, dressing leather; leather artic.; footwear**	1 629	1 550	1 258	1 188	1 141	1 251	1 297	1 302
	191	Tanning, dressing leather; manuf. of leather articles	..	..	..	..	..	..	..	..
	192	Footwear	..	..	..	..	..	..	..	..
	20	**Wood and cork products, ex. furniture**	18 684	19 280	14 869	14 754	16 606	20 624	21 201	20 540
	201	Sawmilling and planing of wood	..	..	..	..	..	..	..	..
	202	Products of wood, cork, straw & plaiting material	..	..	..	..	..	..	..	..
	21	**Paper and paper products**	47 862	44 666	40 870	43 375	48 558	55 552	73 354	67 218
	22	**Publishing, printing & reprod. of recorded media**	18 846	19 701	18 625	16 981	16 403	17 461	19 634	20 598
	221	Publishing	..	..	..	..	..	..	..	..
	222	Printing and related service activities	..	..	..	..	..	..	..	..
	223	Reproduction of recorded media	..	..	..	..	..	..	..	..
	23	**Coke, refined petroleum products & nuclear fuel**	8 855	12 023	11 492	11 389	12 616	12 767	11 226	13 768
	24	**Chemicals and chemical products**	17 319	17 114	16 065	16 680	17 981	20 133	22 127	22 031
	241	Basic chemicals	..	..	..	..	..	..	..	..
	242	Other chemical products	..	..	..	..	..	..	..	..
	243	Man-made fibres	..	..	..	..	..	..	..	..
	25	**Rubber and plastic products**	7 149	7 307	6 356	6 362	7 114	8 001	9 127	9 907
	251	Rubber products	..	..	..	..	..	..	..	..
	252	Plastic products	..	..	..	..	..	..	..	..
	26	**Other non-metallic mineral products**	10 381	10 770	8 932	7 443	6 948	7 499	7 963	8 660
	261	Glass and glass products	..	..	..	..	..	..	..	..
	269	Non-metallic mineral products, nec	..	..	..	..	..	..	..	..
	27	**Basic metals**	21 887	19 377	17 791	20 928	23 769	25 857	30 574	29 869
	271	Basic iron and steel	..	..	..	..	..	..	..	..
	272	Basic precious and non-ferrous metals	..	..	..	..	..	..	..	..
	273	Casting of metals	..	..	..	..	..	..	..	..
	28	**Fabricated metal products, ex. machin. & equip.**	14 360	14 589	12 307	11 629	13 023	14 089	17 519	18 487
	281	Structural metal prod., tanks, reservoirs, generators	..	..	..	..	..	..	..	..
	289	Other fabricated metal products & service activities	..	..	..	..	..	..	..	..
	29	**Machinery and equipment, nec**	28 585	30 561	24 720	24 392	27 456	31 936	40 709	47 605
	291	General purpose machinery	..	..	..	..	..	..	..	..
	292	Special purpose machinery	..	..	..	..	..	..	..	..
	293	Domestic appliances, nec	..	..	..	..	..	..	..	..
	30	**Office, accounting and computing machinery**	2 069	2 495	1 840	3 439	4 440	4 765	5 589	4 621
	31	**Electrical machinery and apparatus, nec**	7 900	8 077	7 039	7 565	8 369	10 066	12 276	13 649
	311	Electric motors, generators and transformers	..	..	..	..	..	..	..	..
	312	Electricity distribution and control apparatus	..	..	..	..	..	..	..	..
	313	Insulated wire and cable	..	..	..	..	..	..	..	..
	314	Accumulators, primary cells and primary batteries	..	..	..	..	..	..	..	..
	315	Electric lamps and lighting equipment	..	..	..	..	..	..	..	..
	319	Other electrical equipment, nec	..	..	..	..	..	..	..	..
	32	**Radio, TV, communication equip. & apparatus**	6 664	7 275	5 412	6 998	11 568	17 304	28 066	32 121
	321	Electronic valves, tubes & other electronic compon.	..	..	..	..	..	..	..	..
	322	TV, radio transmitters & appar. for line teleph., telegr.	..	..	..	..	..	..	..	..
	323	TV, radio receivers and associated goods	..	..	..	..	..	..	..	..
	33	**Medical, precision, optical instr.; watches, clocks**	2 771	2 878	2 895	3 066	3 625	3 990	5 076	5 860
	331	Medical equip.; precision instruments and appliances	..	..	..	..	..	..	..	..
	332	Optical instruments and photographic equipment	..	..	..	..	..	..	..	..
	333	Watches and clocks	..	..	..	..	..	..	..	..
	34	**Motor vehicles, trailers, and semi-trailers**	5 913	5 532	4 121	3 847	3 072	3 395	3 869	4 088
	35	**Other transport equipment**	7 414	8 141	6 990	7 532	7 359	8 772	11 256	10 069
	351	Building and repairing of ships and boats	..	..	..	..	..	..	..	..
	352	Railway, tramway locomotives and rolling stock	..	..	..	..	..	..	..	..
	353	Aircraft and spacecraft	..	..	..	..	..	..	..	..
	359	Transport equipment, nec	..	..	..	..	..	..	..	..
	36	**Furniture; manufacturing, nec**	7 113	7 208	6 272	5 787	5 519	6 096	6 706	7 042
	361	Furniture	..	..	..	..	..	..	..	..
	369	Manufacturing, nec	..	..	..	..	..	..	..	..
	37	**Recycling**	..	..	..	0	0	0	432	422
E	40-41	**Electricity, gas and water supply**	29 125	32 719	33 918	35 111	37 472	38 921	41 941	47 398
	40	**Electricity, gas, steam and hot water supply**	27 791	31 253	32 339	33 429	35 704	37 096	39 996	45 444
	401	Production, collection and distribution of electricity	..	..	..	..	..	..	..	..
	41 410	**Collection, purification, distribution of water**	1 334	1 466	1 579	1 682	1 768	1 825	1 945	1 954
F	45	**Construction**	..	102 189	88 306	69 004	56 951	57 077	62 457	65 114
G	50-52	**Wholesale and retail trade; repairs etc**	..	..	76 335	71 845	70 206	74 259	76 548	79 908
H	55	**Hotels and restaurants**	..	..	21 141	20 190	19 154	19 938	20 760	21 724
I	60-64	**Transport, storage and communications**	..	..	61 731	62 003	64 020	67 426	71 411	76 214
J	65-67	**Financial intermediation**	..	..	27 564	22 080	27 250	28 202	27 676	27 397
K	70-74	**Real estate, renting and business activities**	..	..	114 211	114 321	120 873	128 009	137 527	145 831
L-Q	75-99	**Public admin.; education; health; other services**	..	..	160 944	162 350	178 197	180 450	190 244	200 379
A-Q	01-99	**Grand total**	..	..	889 546	863 904	904 529	961 980	1 047 159	1 093 456

Table FN.15 VALEUR AJOUTÉE - VALUE ADDED

Millions de Mk (Prix courants)

1989	1990	1991	1992	1993	1994	1995	1996			CITI révision 3	
..	29 043	24 073	21 468	22 081	25 264	21 920	20 513	**Agriculture, chasse et sylviculture**	A	01-02	
..	..	..	..	..	..	..	..	**Pêche**	B	05	
2 037	1 733	1 729	1 800	1 687	1 936	1 958	1 952	**Activités extractives**	C	10-14	
..	..	377	610	577	810	859	871	Extraction de charbon, de lignite et de tourbe		10	
..	..	..	..	..	..	..	..	Extraction de pétrole brut et de gaz naturel		11	
799	436	391	353	297	279	183	170	Extraction de minerais métalliques		13	
921	986	961	837	813	847	916	911	Autres activités extractives		14	
105 225	105 383	89 667	92 426	101 816	112 737	128 831	129 211	**Activités de fabrication**	D	15-37	
11 291	11 753	12 510	12 604	13 095	12 371	12 103	12 244	**Produits alimentaires et boissons**		15	
..	..	..	..	..	..	..	..	Boissons			155
491	638	633	551	490	512	450	406	**Produits à base de tabac**		16	160
1 951	1 754	1 381	1 501	1 541	1 787	1 884	1 972	**Textiles**		17	
..	..	..	..	..	..	..	..	Filature, tissage et achèvement des textiles			171
..	..	..	..	..	..	..	..	Autres articles textiles			172
..	..	..	..	..	..	..	..	Etoffes et articles de bonneterie			173
2 017	1 680	1 475	1 195	1 154	1 226	1 142	1 072	**Habillement; préparation, teinture des fourrures**		18	
..	..	..	..	..	..	..	..	Articles d'habillement autres qu'en fourrure			181
..	..	..	..	..	..	..	..	Préparation, teinture des fourrures; art. en fourrure			182
710	647	538	538	507	551	569	544	**Travail des cuirs; articles en cuir; chaussures**		19	
..	..	..	..	..	..	..	..	Apprêt et tannage des cuirs et articles en cuirs			191
..	..	..	..	..	..	..	..	Chaussures			192
6 173	6 561	4 467	5 045	6 111	7 587	6 838	5 983	**Bois et articles en bois et liège (sauf meubles)**		20	
..	..	..	..	..	..	..	..	Sciage et rabotage du bois			201
..	..	..	..	..	..	..	..	Articles en bois, liège, vannerie, sparterie			202
15 542	13 459	10 282	12 359	15 475	18 275	24 073	20 704	**Papier et carton; articles en papier et en carton**		21	
8 371	8 558	8 100	7 418	7 192	7 653	8 251	8 528	**Edition, imprimerie et reproduction**		22	
..	..	..	..	..	..	..	..	Edition			221
..	..	..	..	..	..	..	..	Imprimerie et activités annexes			222
..	..	..	..	..	..	..	..	Reproduction de supports enregistrés			223
1 462	1 831	2 404	1 067	1 331	1 979	1 197	1 237	**Cokéfaction; prod. pétroliers; comb. nucléaires**		23	
6 909	6 759	5 905	6 713	7 169	7 956	8 242	7 910	**Produits chimiques**		24	
..	..	..	..	..	..	..	..	Produits chimiques de base			241
..	..	..	..	..	..	..	..	Autres produits chimiques			242
..	..	..	..	..	..	..	..	Fibres synthétiques ou artificielles			243
2 974	3 256	2 715	2 892	3 170	3 434	3 760	4 197	**Articles en caoutchouc et en matières plastiques**		25	
..	..	..	..	..	..	..	..	Articles en caoutchouc			251
..	..	..	..	..	..	..	..	Articles en matières plastiques			252
5 097	5 117	4 108	3 308	3 165	3 464	3 617	3 875	**Autres produits minéraux non métalliques**		26	
..	..	..	..	..	..	..	..	Verre et articles en verre			261
..	..	..	..	..	..	..	..	Produits minéraux non métalliques, nca			269
5 864	4 622	4 265	5 361	6 519	7 006	8 365	7 097	**Produits métallurgiques de base**		27	
..	..	..	..	..	..	..	..	Sidérurgie et première transformation de l'acier			271
..	..	..	..	..	..	..	..	Métallurgie; métaux précieux et non ferreux			272
..	..	..	..	..	..	..	..	Fonderie			273
6 295	6 404	5 445	5 083	5 391	5 718	6 576	7 070	**Ouvrages en métaux, sauf machines et matériel**		28	
..	..	..	..	..	..	..	..	Constr. et menuiserie métal.; réservoirs; générateurs			281
..	..	..	..	..	..	..	..	Autres ouvrages en métaux			289
12 551	13 648	11 046	10 554	11 790	13 081	16 100	18 587	**Machines et matériel, nca**		29	
..	..	..	..	..	..	..	..	Machines d'usage général			291
..	..	..	..	..	..	..	..	Machines d'usage spécifique			292
..	..	..	..	..	..	..	..	Appareils domestiques, nca			293
582	1 263	407	839	768	589	894	882	**Mach. de bureau, comptables, matériel inform.**		30	
3 750	3 708	3 228	3 672	3 885	4 409	5 192	5 741	**Machines et appareils électriques, nca**		31	
..	..	..	..	..	..	..	..	Moteurs, génératrices et transformateurs électriques			311
..	..	..	..	..	..	..	..	Matériel électrique de distribution et de commande			312
..	..	..	..	..	..	..	..	Fils et câbles électriques isolés			313
..	..	..	..	..	..	..	..	Accumulateurs, piles électriques			314
..	..	..	..	..	..	..	..	Lampes électriques et appareils d'éclairage			315
..	..	..	..	..	..	..	..	Autres matériels électriques, nca			319
3 091	3 534	2 083	2 972	4 489	5 828	8 667	9 875	**Equip. et appar. de radio, TV, communication**		32	
..	..	..	..	..	..	..	..	Tubes et valves électroniques; autres composants			321
..	..	..	..	..	..	..	..	Emetteurs radio et TV; app. téléphonie, télégraphie			322
..	..	..	..	..	..	..	..	Récepteurs radio et TV et articles associés			323
1 453	1 454	1 448	1 576	1 837	1 865	2 248	2 638	**Instruments médicaux, de précision, d'optique**		33	
..	..	..	..	..	..	..	..	Appareils médicaux et de précision			331
..	..	..	..	..	..	..	..	Instruments d'optique ; matériel photographique			332
..	..	..	..	..	..	..	..	Horlogerie			333
2 059	1 875	1 466	1 491	1 008	1 482	1 432	1 533	**Véhicules automobiles et nemorques**		34	
3 004	3 269	2 827	3 035	3 246	3 301	4 240	4 099	**Autres matériels de transport**		35	
..	..	..	..	..	..	..	..	Construction et réparation de navires			351
..	..	..	..	..	..	..	..	Construction de matériel ferroviaire roulant			352
..	..	..	..	..	..	..	..	Construction aéronautique et spatiale			353
..	..	..	..	..	..	..	..	Autres équipements de transport			359
3 588	3 593	2 934	2 652	2 483	2 663	2 914	2 953	**Meubles; activités de fabrication, nca**		36	
..	..	..	..	..	..	..	..	Meubles			361
..	..	..	..	..	..	..	..	Activités de fabrication, nca			369
..	..	..	0	0	0	77	64	**Récupération**		37	
9 245	9 504	11 059	11 003	11 334	12 281	12 984	13 641	**Production et distrib. d'électricité, de gaz, d'eau**	E	40-41	
8 249	8 390	9 886	9 748	10 019	10 893	11 487	12 140	**Electricité, gaz, vapeur et eau chaude**		40	
..	..	..	..	..	..	..	..	Production, collecte et distribution d'électricité			401
996	1 114	1 173	1 255	1 315	1 388	1 497	1 501	**Captage, épuration et distribution d'eau**		41	410
..	43 467	36 962	26 041	20 998	23 303	28 329	29 427	**Construction**	F	45	
..	..	43 549	40 616	40 139	43 178	44 871	46 951	**Commerce de gros et de détail; réparation**	G	50-52	
..	..	8 595	7 793	7 262	7 649	8 098	8 523	**Hôtels et restaurants**	H	55	
..	..	36 705	37 076	37 850	39 710	42 223	44 906	**Transports, entreposage et communications**	I	60-64	
..	..	17 984	12 983	17 388	16 665	17 566	17 988	**Intermédiation financière**	J	65-67	
..	..	65 273	67 008	71 055	74 503	79 221	84 674	**Immobilier, locations, services aux entreprises**	K	70-74	
..	..	107 509	108 011	103 837	104 342	110 108	115 072	**Admin. publique; éducation; santé; autres**	L-Q	75-99	
..	..	427 776	415 712	421 242	447 172	481 967	499 511	**Grand total**	A-Q	01-99	

Note: The Grand total includes imputed bank service charges.

Statistiques des Structures Industrielles
OCDE, © 1998

FINLAND

Table FN.16 INVESTMENT - INVESTISSEMENT

Millions of Mk (Current Prices)

ISIC revision 3			1989	1990	1991	1992	1993	1994	1995	1996
A	01-02	**Agriculture, hunting and forestry**	..	7 106	5 549	3 977	3 602	3 712	3 881	4 459
B	05	**Fishing**	..	..						
C	10-14	**Mining and quarrying**	375	278	173	136	122	176	410	385
	10	Mining of coal and lignite; extraction of peat	..	..	40	43	44	63	151	123
	11	Crude petroleum & natural gas; related service activ.	..	..	..	..	..	..	..	..
	13	Mining of metal ores	73	31	26	13	34	13	14	57
	14	Other mining and quarrying	267	216	107	80	44	100	245	205
D	15-37	**Total manufacturing**	21 822	21 770	15 888	14 102	12 759	14 091	18 821	21 551
	15	**Food products and beverages**	2 000	2 268	1 922	2 615	1 477	1 492	1 815	1 834
	155	Beverages	..	..	..	..	..	..	..	..
	16 160	**Tobacco products**	120	43	45	74	35	26	- 68	112
	17	**Textiles**	240	289	128	101	194	142	241	102
	171	Spinning, weaving and finishing of textiles	..	..	..	..	..	..	..	..
	172	Other textiles	..	..	..	..	..	..	..	..
	173	Knitted and crocheted fabrics and articles	..	..	..	..	..	..	..	..
	18	**Wearing apparel dressing & dyeing of fur**	111	62	27	31	17	13	59	73
	181	Wearing apparel, except fur apparel	..	..	..	..	..	..	..	..
	182	Dressing and dyeing of fur; articles of fur	..	..	..	..	..	..	..	..
	19	**Tanning, dressing leather; leather artic.; footwear**	61	48	25	21	18	34	38	40
	191	Tanning, dressing leather; manuf. of leather articles	..	..	..	..	..	..	..	..
	192	Footwear	..	..	..	..	..	..	..	..
	20	**Wood and cork products, ex. furniture**	1 376	1 334	1 026	788	826	1 065	1 111	808
	201	Sawmilling and planing of wood	..	..	..	..	..	..	..	..
	202	Products of wood, cork, straw & plaiting material	..	..	..	..	..	..	..	..
	21	**Paper and paper products**	7 142	6 841	5 272	4 091	3 978	3 449	3 977	8 415
	22	**Publishing, printing & reprod. of recorded media**	1 168	1 382	1 042	940	593	806	785	728
	221	Publishing	..	..	..	..	..	..	..	..
	222	Printing and related service activities	..	..	..	..	..	..	..	..
	223	Reproduction of recorded media	..	..	..	..	..	..	..	..
	23	**Coke, refined petroleum products & nuclear fuel**	474	283	616	712	559	137	232	253
	24	**Chemicals and chemical products**	1 835	1 965	1 002	1 060	1 214	1 149	2 236	1 240
	241	Basic chemicals	..	..	..	..	..	..	..	..
	242	Other chemical products	..	..	..	..	..	..	..	..
	243	Man-made fibres	..	..	..	..	..	..	..	..
	25	**Rubber and plastic products**	482	543	346	232	323	512	577	518
	251	Rubber products	..	..	..	..	..	..	..	..
	252	Plastic products	..	..	..	..	..	..	..	..
	26	**Other non-metallic mineral products**	866	1 154	463	314	333	372	451	429
	261	Glass and glass products	..	..	..	..	..	..	..	..
	269	Non-metallic mineral products, nec	..	..	..	..	..	..	..	..
	27	**Basic metals**	1 368	967	962	675	666	935	2 109	2 202
	271	Basic iron and steel	..	..	..	..	..	..	..	..
	272	Basic precious and non-ferrous metals	..	..	..	..	..	..	..	..
	273	Casting of metals	..	..	..	..	..	..	..	..
	28	**Fabricated metal products, ex. machin. & equip.**	1 053	1 090	672	359	333	338	672	610
	281	Structural metal prod., tanks, reservoirs, generators	..	..	..	..	..	..	..	..
	289	Other fabricated metal products & service activities	..	..	..	..	..	..	..	..
	29	**Machinery and equipment, nec**	1 538	1 543	984	669	406	848	1 416	1 368
	291	General purpose machinery	..	..	..	..	..	..	..	..
	292	Special purpose machinery	..	..	..	..	..	..	..	..
	293	Domestic appliances, nec	..	..	..	..	..	..	..	..
	30	**Office, accounting and computing machinery**	61	51	37	55	79	77	106	4
	31	**Electrical machinery and apparatus, nec**	290	405	235	315	325	458	451	474
	311	Electric motors, generators and transformers	..	..	..	..	..	..	..	..
	312	Electricity distribution and control apparatus	..	..	..	..	..	..	..	..
	313	Insulated wire and cable	..	..	..	..	..	..	..	..
	314	Accumulators, primary cells and primary batteries	..	..	..	..	..	..	..	..
	315	Electric lamps and lighting equipment	..	..	..	..	..	..	..	..
	319	Other electrical equipment, nec	..	..	..	..	..	..	..	..
	32	**Radio, TV, communication equip. & apparatus**	444	380	247	368	525	1 206	1 696	1 431
	321	Electronic valves, tubes & other electronic compon.	..	..	..	..	..	..	..	..
	322	TV, radio transmitters & appar. for line teleph., telegr.	..	..	..	..	..	..	..	..
	323	TV, radio receivers and associated goods	..	..	..	..	..	..	..	..
	33	**Medical, precision, optical instr.; watches, clocks**	151	169	92	90	135	148	142	158
	331	Medical equip.; precision instruments and appliances	..	..	..	..	..	..	..	..
	332	Optical instruments and photographic equipment	..	..	..	..	..	..	..	..
	333	Watches and clocks	..	..	..	..	..	..	..	..
	34	**Motor vehicles, trailers, and semi-trailers**	276	244	260	93	63	52	173	178
	35	**Other transport equipment**	248	337	231	206	546	646	342	332
	351	Building and repairing of ships and boats	..	..	..	..	..	..	..	..
	352	Railway, tramway locomotives and rolling stock	..	..	..	..	..	..	..	..
	353	Aircraft and spacecraft	..	..	..	..	..	..	..	..
	359	Transport equipment, nec	..	..	..	..	..	..	..	..
	36	**Furniture; manufacturing, nec**	518	372	254	293	114	186	232	200
	361	Furniture	..	..	..	..	..	..	..	..
	369	Manufacturing, nec	..	..	..	..	..	..	..	..
	37	**Recycling**	..	..	..	0	0	0	28	42
E	40-41	**Electricity, gas and water supply**	5 777	5 434	5 957	4 901	4 077	4 872	4 886	4 769
	40	**Electricity, gas, steam and hot water supply**	5 188	4 812	5 151	4 305	3 507	4 279	4 312	4 163
	401	Production, collection and distribution of electricity	..	..	..	..	..	..	..	..
	41 410	**Collection, purification, distribution of water**	589	622	806	596	570	593	574	606
F	45	**Construction**	..	2 856	1 865	374	131	611	927	1 160
G	50-52	**Wholesale and retail trade; repairs etc**	..	..	8 164	6 604	5 015	5 010	5 264	5 791
H	55	**Hotels and restaurants**	..	..	1 318	651	365	238	246	307
I	60-64	**Transport, storage and communications**	..	..	7 079	8 372	7 754	7 004	9 306	10 174
J	65-67	**Financial intermediation**	..	..	1 456	1 393	- 1 165	1 086	- 1 093	- 523
K	70-74	**Real estate, renting and business activities**	..	..	47 177	34 060	27 825	26 754	31 240	32 294
L-Q	75-99	**Public admin.; education; health; other services**	..	..	15 435	13 383	10 709	10 632	11 201	12 054
A-Q	01-99	**Grand total**	..	..	110 061	87 953	71 194	74 186	85 089	92 421

Table FN.17 DÉPENSES EN MACHINES ET ÉQUIPEMENT - INVESTMENT IN MACHINERY AND EQUIPMENT

Millions de Mk (Prix courants)

1989	1990	1991	1992	1993	1994	1995	1996			CITI révision 3	
..	3 525	2 510	1 502	1 457	1 793	2 060	2 358	**Agriculture, chasse et sylviculture**	A	01-02	
..	..	..	..	..	..	..	..	**Pêche**	B	05	
265	169	121	88	66	115	253	297	**Activités extractives**	C	10-14	
..	..	37	40	39	53	134	105	Extraction de charbon, de lignite et de tourbe		10	
..	..	..	..	..	..	..	..	Extraction de pétrole brut et de gaz naturel		11	
61	22	25	5	23	9	7	50	Extraction de minerais métalliques		13	
177	120	59	43	4	53	112	142	Autres activités extractives		14	
16 583	16 138	11 960	10 815	10 417	11 650	14 626	17 308	**Activités de fabrication**	D	15-37	
1 257	1 350	1 332	1 607	1 068	1 144	1 404	1 327	**Produits alimentaires et boissons**		15	
..	..	..	..	..	..	..	..	Boissons			155
60	33	41	71	34	25	- 68	75	**Produits à base de tabac**		16	160
201	186	107	75	183	112	191	117	**Textiles**		17	
..	..	..	..	..	..	..	..	Filature, tissage et achèvement des textiles			171
..	..	..	..	..	..	..	..	Autres articles textiles			172
..	..	..	..	..	..	..	..	Etoffes et articles de bonneterie			173
81	44	25	23	14	22	42	47	**Habillement; préparation, teinture des fourrures**		18	
..	..	..	..	..	..	..	..	Articles d'habillement autres qu'en fourrure			181
..	..	..	..	..	..	..	..	Préparation, teinture des fourrures; art. en fourrure			182
50	32	18	18	14	29	32	35	**Travail des cuirs; articles en cuir; chaussures**		19	
..	..	..	..	..	..	..	..	Apprêt et tannage des cuirs et articles en cuirs			191
..	..	..	..	..	..	..	..	Chaussures			192
1 002	995	750	632	585	801	856	632	**Bois et articles en bois et liège (sauf meubles)**		20	
..	..	..	..	..	..	..	..	Sciage et rabotage du bois			201
..	..	..	..	..	..	..	..	Articles en bois, liège, vannerie, sparterie			202
5 870	5 442	3 784	3 225	3 177	2 968	2 911	7 117	**Papier et carton; articles en papier et en carton**		21	
959	981	842	775	544	757	705	659	**Edition, imprimerie et reproduction**		22	
..	..	..	..	..	..	..	..	Edition			221
..	..	..	..	..	..	..	..	Imprimerie et activités annexes			222
..	..	..	..	..	..	..	..	Reproduction de supports enregistrés			223
373	198	336	568	468	102	188	181	**Cokéfaction; prod. pétroliers; comb. nucléaires**		23	
1 305	1 510	741	828	969	934	1 710	963	**Produits chimiques**		24	
..	..	..	..	..	..	..	..	Produits chimiques de base			241
..	..	..	..	..	..	..	..	Autres produits chimiques			242
..	..	..	..	..	..	..	..	Fibres synthétiques ou artificielles			243
372	440	315	217	276	415	484	427	**Articles en caoutchouc et en matières plastiques**		25	
..	..	..	..	..	..	..	..	Articles en caoutchouc			251
..	..	..	..	..	..	..	..	Articles en matières plastiques			252
586	808	372	264	264	318	361	353	**Autres produits minéraux non métalliques**		26	
..	..	..	..	..	..	..	..	Verre et articles en verre			261
..	..	..	..	..	..	..	..	Produits minéraux non métalliques, nca			269
1 251	808	829	560	628	809	1 705	1 604	**Produits métallurgiques de base**		27	
..	..	..	..	..	..	..	..	Sidérurgie et première transformation de l'acier			271
..	..	..	..	..	..	..	..	Métallurgie; métaux précieux et non ferreux			272
..	..	..	..	..	..	..	..	Fonderie			273
677	737	557	327	295	307	513	453	**Ouvrages en métaux, sauf machines et matériel**		28	
..	..	..	..	..	..	..	..	Constr. et menuiserie métal.; réservoirs; générateurs			281
..	..	..	..	..	..	..	..	Autres ouvrages en métaux			289
1 143	1 129	745	548	495	744	1 000	1 208	**Machines et matériel, nca**		29	
..	..	..	..	..	..	..	..	Machines d'usage général			291
..	..	..	..	..	..	..	..	Machines d'usage spécifique			292
..	..	..	..	..	..	..	..	Appareils domestiques, nca			293
59	46	33	51	79	77	88	13	**Mach. de bureau, comptables, matériel inform.**		30	
225	348	249	258	234	409	371	429	**Machines et appareils électriques, nca**		31	
..	..	..	..	..	..	..	..	Moteurs, génératrices et transformateurs électriques			311
..	..	..	..	..	..	..	..	Matériel électrique de distribution et de commande			312
..	..	..	..	..	..	..	..	Fils et câbles électriques isolés			313
..	..	..	..	..	..	..	..	Accumulateurs, piles électriques			314
..	..	..	..	..	..	..	..	Lampes électriques et appareils d'éclairage			315
..	..	..	..	..	..	..	..	Autres matériels électriques, nca			319
405	286	218	318	515	1 005	1 435	903	**Equip. et appar. de radio, TV, communication**		32	
..	..	..	..	..	..	..	..	Tubes et valves électroniques; autres composants			321
..	..	..	..	..	..	..	..	Emetteurs radio et TV; app. téléphonie, télégraphie			322
..	..	..	..	..	..	..	..	Récepteurs radio et TV et articles associés			323
109	96	77	65	83	109	120	141	**Instruments médicaux, de précision, d'optique**		33	
..	..	..	..	..	..	..	..	Appareils médicaux et de précision			331
..	..	..	..	..	..	..	..	Instruments d'optique ; matériel photographique			332
..	..	..	..	..	..	..	..	Horlogerie			333
160	147	208	70	50	55	110	177	**Véhicules automobiles et nemorques**		34	
153	283	166	152	338	352	275	247	**Autres matériels de transport**		35	
..	..	..	..	..	..	..	..	Construction et réparation de navires			351
..	..	..	..	..	..	..	..	Construction de matériel ferroviaire roulant			352
..	..	..	..	..	..	..	..	Construction aéronautique et spatiale			353
..	..	..	..	..	..	..	..	Autres équipements de transport			359
285	239	215	163	104	156	173	161	**Meubles; activités de fabrication, nca**		36	
..	..	..	..	..	..	..	..	Meubles			361
..	..	..	..	..	..	..	..	Activités de fabrication, nca			369
..	..	..	0	0	0	20	39	**Récupération**		37	
2 593	2 269	2 562	2 385	1 735	2 588	2 036	1 887	**Production et distrib. d'électricité, de gaz, d'eau**	E	40-41	
2 535	2 218	2 446	2 333	1 665	2 502	1 964	1 809	**Electricité, gaz, vapeur et eau chaude**		40	
..	..	..	..	..	..	..	..	Production, collecte et distribution d'électricité			401
58	51	116	52	70	86	72	78	**Captage, épuration et distribution d'eau**		41	410
..	2 023	1 379	384	277	587	764	1 008	**Construction**	F	45	
..	..	5 067	4 497	3 696	3 826	4 112	4 530	**Commerce de gros et de détail; réparation**	G	50-52	
..	..	674	317	172	182	196	215	**Hôtels et restaurants**	H	55	
..	..	4 753	6 080	5 406	4 654	6 234	6 501	**Transports, entreposage et communications**	I	60-64	
..	..	1 060	628	476	390	114	375	**Intermédiation financière**	J	65-67	
..	..	2 144	1 905	1 513	1 448	2 605	3 108	**Immobilier, locations, services aux entreprises**	K	70-74	
..	..	4 351	3 937	3 169	3 192	3 791	4 065	**Admin. publique; éducation; santé; autres**	L-Q	75-99	
..	..	36 581	32 538	28 384	30 425	36 791	41 652	**Grand total**	A-Q	01-99	

Statistiques des Structures Industrielles
OCDE, © 1998

FINLAND

Table FN.18 EMPLOYMENT - EMPLOI

Thousands

ISIC revision 3			1989	1990	1991	1992	1993	1994	1995	1996
A	01-02	Agriculture, hunting and forestry	..	206.9	197.5	187.1	174.4	169.0	158.0	147.3
B	05	Fishing	..	..	..	..	..	..	..	..
C	10-14	Mining and quarrying	5.5	5.4	5.1	5.1	4.2	4.2	4.2	4.2
	10	Mining of coal and lignite; extraction of peat	..	..	1.2	1.4	1.1	1.4	1.3	1.3
	11	Crude petroleum & natural gas; related service activ.	..	..	..	..	..	..	..	..
	13	Mining of metal ores	1.4	1.0	1.0	1.0	0.8	0.7	0.6	0.6
	14	Other mining and quarrying	2.8	3.0	2.9	2.7	2.3	2.1	2.3	2.3
D	15-37	Total manufacturing	482.2	474.6	440.3	398.3	372.4	374.3	390.9	394.6
	15	Food products and beverages	56.5	56.2	53.8	49.7	45.4	43.1	43.0	42.1
	155	Beverages	..	..	..	..	..	..	..	..
	16 160	Tobacco products	1.2	1.1	1.1	1.0	0.9	0.9	0.9	0.8
	17	Textiles	13.9	13.9	11.4	10.3	8.8	8.2	8.3	8.4
	171	Spinning, weaving and finishing of textiles	..	..	..	..	..	..	..	..
	172	Other textiles	..	..	..	..	..	..	..	..
	173	Knitted and crocheted fabrics and articles	..	..	..	..	..	..	..	..
	18	Wearing apparel dressing & dyeing of fur	20.4	16.2	13.2	9.5	8.4	7.7	7.4	6.9
	181	Wearing apparel, except fur apparel	..	..	..	..	..	..	..	..
	182	Dressing and dyeing of fur; articles of fur	..	..	..	..	..	..	..	..
	19	Tanning, dressing leather; leather artic.; footwear	6.2	5.7	4.7	4.0	3.5	3.5	3.5	3.3
	191	Tanning, dressing leather; manuf. of leather articles	..	..	..	..	..	..	..	..
	192	Footwear	..	..	..	..	..	..	..	..
	20	Wood and cork products, ex. furniture	36.4	35.7	31.9	28.2	26.0	27.3	27.2	26.2
	201	Sawmilling and planing of wood	..	..	..	..	..	..	..	..
	202	Products of wood, cork, straw & plaiting material	..	..	..	..	..	..	..	..
	21	Paper and paper products	45.7	44.5	41.8	39.8	38.7	38.6	38.1	38.2
	22	Publishing, printing & reprod. of recorded media	42.6	42.7	40.7	37.3	34.3	32.5	31.3	29.4
	221	Publishing	..	..	..	..	..	..	..	..
	222	Printing and related service activities	..	..	..	..	..	..	..	..
	223	Reproduction of recorded media	..	..	..	..	..	..	..	..
	23	Coke, refined petroleum products & nuclear fuel	4.0	3.8	4.0	3.9	3.7	3.6	3.6	3.7
	24	Chemicals and chemical products	20.0	20.0	19.8	18.8	18.1	17.9	18.5	18.2
	241	Basic chemicals	..	..	..	..	..	..	..	..
	242	Other chemical products	..	..	..	..	..	..	..	..
	243	Man-made fibres	..	..	..	..	..	..	..	..
	25	Rubber and plastic products	14.7	14.9	14.0	13.0	12.2	12.9	13.5	13.9
	251	Rubber products	..	..	..	..	..	..	..	..
	252	Plastic products	..	..	..	..	..	..	..	..
	26	Other non-metallic mineral products	21.2	21.7	19.5	16.3	13.3	12.8	12.6	12.4
	261	Glass and glass products	..	..	..	..	..	..	..	..
	269	Non-metallic mineral products, nec	..	..	..	..	..	..	..	..
	27	Basic metals	16.5	16.9	16.2	15.6	15.2	15.4	15.6	16.1
	271	Basic iron and steel	..	..	..	..	..	..	..	..
	272	Basic precious and non-ferrous metals	..	..	..	..	..	..	..	..
	273	Casting of metals	..	..	..	..	..	..	..	..
	28	Fabricated metal products, ex. machin. & equip.	32.4	33.3	30.5	26.2	24.6	24.8	27.1	27.5
	281	Structural metal prod., tanks, reservoirs, generators	..	..	..	..	..	..	..	..
	289	Other fabricated metal products & service activities	..	..	..	..	..	..	..	..
	29	Machinery and equipment, nec	58.4	59.8	56.2	49.6	46.9	48.3	53.1	56.6
	291	General purpose machinery	..	..	..	..	..	..	..	..
	292	Special purpose machinery	..	..	..	..	..	..	..	..
	293	Domestic appliances, nec	..	..	..	..	..	..	..	..
	30	Office, accounting and computing machinery	3.0	2.7	2.3	2.8	2.9	3.2	3.4	3.6
	31	Electrical machinery and apparatus, nec	17.2	17.3	15.3	13.9	12.9	14.2	16.9	17.6
	311	Electric motors, generators and transformers	..	..	..	..	..	..	..	..
	312	Electricity distribution and control apparatus	..	..	..	..	..	..	..	..
	313	Insulated wire and cable	..	..	..	..	..	..	..	..
	314	Accumulators, primary cells and primary batteries	..	..	..	..	..	..	..	..
	315	Electric lamps and lighting equipment	..	..	..	..	..	..	..	..
	319	Other electrical equipment, nec	..	..	..	..	..	..	..	..
	32	Radio, TV, communication equip. & apparatus	13.2	13.0	12.0	11.7	12.6	15.6	20.8	24.0
	321	Electronic valves, tubes & other electronic compon.	..	..	..	..	..	..	..	..
	322	TV, radio transmitters & appar. for line teleph., telegr.	..	..	..	..	..	..	..	..
	323	TV, radio receivers and associated goods	..	..	..	..	..	..	..	..
	33	Medical, precision, optical instr.; watches, clocks	7.1	7.2	7.0	6.5	6.4	6.8	7.9	8.2
	331	Medical equip.; precision instruments and appliances	..	..	..	..	..	..	..	..
	332	Optical instruments and photographic equipment	..	..	..	..	..	..	..	..
	333	Watches and clocks	..	..	..	..	..	..	..	..
	34	Motor vehicles, trailers, and semi-trailers	10.2	9.2	8.1	7.0	6.8	6.7	6.2	6.3
	35	Other transport equipment	20.3	18.0	17.4	16.7	15.9	16.0	17.0	16.2
	351	Building and repairing of ships and boats	..	..	..	..	..	..	..	..
	352	Railway, tramway locomotives and rolling stock	..	..	..	..	..	..	..	..
	353	Aircraft and spacecraft	..	..	..	..	..	..	..	..
	359	Transport equipment, nec	..	..	..	..	..	..	..	..
	36	Furniture; manufacturing, nec	21.1	20.8	19.4	16.5	14.9	14.3	14.7	14.7
	361	Furniture	..	..	..	..	..	..	..	..
	369	Manufacturing, nec	..	..	..	..	..	..	..	..
	37	Recycling	..	..	..	0.0	0.0	0.0	0.3	0.3
E	40-41	Electricity, gas and water supply	28.0	27.5	26.9	26.0	23.4	22.0	21.4	21.3
	40	Electricity, gas, steam and hot water supply	25.3	24.7	24.2	23.4	20.9	19.6	19.0	18.9
	401	Production, collection and distribution of electricity	..	..	..	..	..	..	..	..
	41 410	Collection, purification, distribution of water	2.7	2.8	2.7	2.6	2.5	2.4	2.4	2.4
F	45	Construction	..	207.5	181.8	152.1	128.0	117.0	122.4	125.5
G	50-52	Wholesale and retail trade; repairs etc	..	..	301.5	271.7	252.0	247.6	250.7	257.5
H	55	Hotels and restaurants	..	..	62.1	56.3	52.1	51.3	53.1	55.6
I	60-64	Transport, storage and communications	..	..	166.5	158.6	151.8	149.9	152.5	153.5
J	65-67	Financial intermediation	..	..	61.1	56.4	52.0	50.7	47.1	43.6
K	70-74	Real estate, renting and business activities	..	..	154.8	147.0	143.6	146.7	153.2	161.1
L-Q	75-99	Public admin.; education; health; other services	..	..	631.3	614.5	584.2	583.2	595.5	602.7
A-Q	01-99	Grand total	..	..	2 228.9	2 073.1	1 938.1	1 915.9	1 949.0	1 966.7

Table FN.19 EMPLOI, SALARIÉS - EMPLOYMENT, EMPLOYEES

Milliers

1989	1990	1991	1992	1993	1994	1995	1996			CITI révision 3	
..	..	..	46.3	43.9	42.6	43.0	38.2	**Agriculture, chasse et sylviculture**	A	01-02	
							..	**Pêche**	B	05	
..	..	..	4.4	3.8	3.7	3.7	3.7	**Activités extractives**	C	10-14	
..	..	..	0.9	0.9	1.1	1.0	1.0	Extraction de charbon, de lignite et de tourbe		10	
							..	Extraction de pétrole brut et de gaz naturel		11	
..	..	..	1.0	0.8	0.7	0.6	0.6	Extraction de minerais métalliques		13	
..	..	..	2.5	2.1	1.9	2.1	2.1	Autres activités extractives		14	
..	..	..	384.7	361.1	364.2	381.3	384.8	**Activités de fabrication**	D	15-37	
..	..	..	48.5	44.4	42.2	42.1	41.3	**Produits alimentaires et boissons**		15	
							..	Boissons			155
..	..	..	1.0	0.9	0.9	0.9	0.8	**Produits à base de tabac**		16	160
..	..	..	9.4	8.2	7.8	7.9	8.0	**Textiles**		17	
							..	Filature, tissage et achèvement des textiles			171
							..	Autres articles textiles			172
							..	Etoffes et articles de bonneterie			173
..	..	..	8.6	7.7	7.1	6.9	6.3	**Habillement; préparation, teinture des fourrures**		18	
							..	Articles d'habillement autres qu'en fourrure			181
							..	Préparation, teinture des fourrures; art. en fourrure			182
..	..	..	3.6	3.2	3.3	3.3	3.1	**Travail des cuirs; articles en cuir; chaussures**		19	
							..	Apprêt et tannage des cuirs et articles en cuirs			191
							..	Chaussures			192
..	..	..	26.1	24.7	26.1	26.1	25.1	**Bois et articles en bois et liège (sauf meubles)**		20	
							..	Sciage et rabotage du bois			201
							..	Articles en bois, liège, vannerie, sparterie			202
..	..	..	39.8	38.6	38.5	38.0	38.0	**Papier et carton; articles en papier et en carton**		21	
..	..	..	36.5	33.3	31.5	30.4	28.4	**Edition, imprimerie et reproduction**		22	
							..	Edition			221
							..	Imprimerie et activités annexes			222
							..	Reproduction de supports enregistrés			223
..	..	..	3.9	3.7	3.6	3.6	3.7	**Cokéfaction; prod. pétroliers; comb. nucléaires**		23	
..	..	..	18.8	18.1	17.8	18.4	18.1	**Produits chimiques**		24	
							..	Produits chimiques de base			241
							..	Autres produits chimiques			242
							..	Fibres synthétiques ou artificielles			243
..	..	..	12.7	12.0	12.7	13.3	13.7	**Articles en caoutchouc et en matières plastiques**		25	
							..	Articles en caoutchouc			251
							..	Articles en matières plastiques			252
..	..	..	15.8	12.9	12.5	12.3	12.1	**Autres produits minéraux non métalliques**		26	
							..	Verre et articles en verre			261
							..	Produits minéraux non métalliques, nca			269
..	..	..	15.6	15.2	15.4	15.6	16.1	**Produits métallurgiques de base**		27	
							..	Sidérurgie et première transformation de l'acier			271
							..	Métallurgie; métaux précieux et non ferreux			272
							..	Fonderie			273
..	..	..	23.9	22.7	23.2	25.6	26.2	**Ouvrages en métaux, sauf machines et matériel**		28	
							..	Constr. et menuiserie métal.; réservoirs; générateurs			281
							..	Autres ouvrages en métaux			289
..	..	..	48.0	45.4	46.8	51.7	55.2	**Machines et matériel, nca**		29	
							..	Machines d'usage général			291
							..	Machines d'usage spécifique			292
							..	Appareils domestiques, nca			293
..	..	..	2.8	2.9	3.2	3.4	3.6	**Mach. de bureau, comptables, matériel inform.**		30	
..	..	..	13.8	12.7	14.0	16.7	17.6	**Machines et appareils électriques, nca**		31	
							..	Moteurs, génératrices et transformateurs électriques			311
							..	Matériel électrique de distribution et de commande			312
							..	Fils et câbles électriques isolés			313
							..	Accumulateurs, piles électriques			314
							..	Lampes électriques et appareils d'éclairage			315
							..	Autres matériels électriques, nca			319
..	..	..	11.6	12.5	15.5	20.7	23.7	**Equip. et appar. de radio, TV, communication**		32	
							..	Tubes et valves électroniques; autres composants			321
							..	Emetteurs radio et TV; app. téléphonie, télégraphie			322
							..	Récepteurs radio et TV et articles associés			323
..	..	..	6.1	6.1	6.4	7.5	7.9	**Instruments médicaux, de précision, d'optique**		33	
							..	Appareils médicaux et de précision			331
							..	Instruments d'optique ; matériel photographique			332
							..	Horlogerie			333
..	..	..	6.9	6.6	6.6	6.1	6.2	**Véhicules automobiles et nemorques**		34	
..	..	..	16.4	15.6	15.8	16.8	16.0	**Autres matériels de transport**		35	
							..	Construction et réparation de navires			351
							..	Construction de matériel ferroviaire roulant			352
							..	Construction aéronautique et spatiale			353
							..	Autres équipements de transport			359
..	..	..	14.9	13.7	13.3	13.7	13.4	**Meubles; activités de fabrication, nca**		36	
							..	Meubles			361
							..	Activités de fabrication, nca			369
..	..	..	0.0	0.0	0.0	0.3	0.3	**Récupération**		37	
..	..	..	26.0	23.4	22.0	21.4	21.3	**Production et distrib. d'électricité, de gaz, d'eau**	E	40-41	
..	..	..	23.4	20.9	19.6	19.0	18.9	**Electricité, gaz, vapeur et eau chaude**		40	
							..	Production, collecte et distribution d'électricité			401
..	..	..	2.6	2.5	2.4	2.4	2.4	**Captage, épuration et distribution d'eau**		41	410
..	..	..	131.4	109.3	98.4	102.4	105.8	**Construction**	F	45	
..	..	..	233.8	215.1	208.0	212.2	219.2	**Commerce de gros et de détail; réparation**	G	50-52	
..	..	..	51.6	46.8	46.4	47.9	50.3	**Hôtels et restaurants**	H	55	
..	..	..	138.0	131.2	129.2	131.5	132.0	**Transports, entreposage et communications**	I	60-64	
..	..	..	56.4	52.0	50.7	47.1	43.6	**Intermédiation financière**	J	65-67	
..	..	..	139.6	134.2	136.2	142.1	150.3	**Immobilier, locations, services aux entreprises**	K	70-74	
..	..	..	590.0	561.6	560.3	571.9	578.4	**Admin. publique; éducation; santé; autres**	L-Q	75-99	
..	..	..	1 802.2	1 682.4	1 661.7	1 704.5	1 727.6	**Grand total**	A-Q	01-99	

Statistiques des Structures Industrielles
OCDE, © 1998

FINLAND

Table FN.20 TOTAL WAGES AND SALARIES - SALAIRES ET TRAITEMENTS, TOTAL

Millions of Mk (Current Prices)

	ISIC revision 3			1989	1990	1991	1992	1993	1994	1995	1996
A	01-02		Agriculture, hunting and forestry	..	4 108	4 203	3 790	3 517	3 504	3 643	3 408
B	05		Fishing	..	..						
C	10-14		Mining and quarrying	512	520	533	510	471	459	510	519
	10		Mining of coal and lignite; extraction of peat	..	..	91	99	106	115	129	132
	11		Crude petroleum & natural gas; related service activ.	..	..	..					
	13		Mining of metal ores	164	134	139	135	118	114	105	105
	14		Other mining and quarrying	263	300	303	276	247	230	276	282
D	15-37		Total manufacturing	47 900	50 931	48 505	45 553	44 041	46 727	52 970	55 292
	15		Food products and beverages	5 332	5 719	5 687	5 547	5 193	5 107	5 327	5 398
		155	Beverages	..	..	..	..	..	..	..	..
	16	160	Tobacco products	144	149	146	137	128	126	135	120
	17		Textiles	1 029	1 070	892	840	797	798	857	893
		171	Spinning, weaving and finishing of textiles	..	..	..	..	..	..	..	..
		172	Other textiles	..	..	..	..	..	..	..	..
		173	Knitted and crocheted fabrics and articles	..	..	..	..	..	..	..	..
	18		Wearing apparel dressing & dyeing of fur	1 353	1 086	940	687	619	616	637	602
		181	Wearing apparel, except fur apparel	..	..	..	..	..	..	..	..
		182	Dressing and dyeing of fur; articles of fur	..	..	..	..	..	..	..	..
	19		Tanning, dressing leather; leather artic.; footwear	410	397	346	292	273	284	299	291
		191	Tanning, dressing leather; manuf. of leather articles	..	..	..	..	..	..	..	..
		192	Footwear	..	..	..	..	..	..	..	..
	20		Wood and cork products, ex. furniture	3 066	3 163	2 753	2 498	2 522	2 864	3 092	3 054
		201	Sawmilling and planing of wood	..	..	..	..	..	..	..	..
		202	Products of wood, cork, straw & plaiting material	..	..	..	..	..	..	..	..
	21		Paper and paper products	5 633	5 976	5 916	5 782	5 792	6 068	6 545	6 776
	22		Publishing, printing & reprod. of recorded media	4 703	5 064	4 975	4 531	4 230	4 111	4 258	4 237
		221	Publishing	..	..	..	..	..	..	..	..
		222	Printing and related service activities	..	..	..	..	..	..	..	..
		223	Reproduction of recorded media	..	..	..	..	..	..	..	..
	23		Coke, refined petroleum products & nuclear fuel	529	549	610	621	611	590	626	663
	24		Chemicals and chemical products	2 241	2 448	2 539	2 472	2 458	2 535	2 795	2 826
		241	Basic chemicals	..	..	..	..	..	..	..	..
		242	Other chemical products	..	..	..	..	..	..	..	..
		243	Man-made fibres	..	..	..	..	..	..	..	..
	25		Rubber and plastic products	1 380	1 537	1 489	1 396	1 399	1 525	1 707	1 816
		251	Rubber products	..	..	..	..	..	..	..	..
		252	Plastic products	..	..	..	..	..	..	..	..
	26		Other non-metallic mineral products	2 060	2 320	2 088	1 716	1 473	1 496	1 579	1 589
		261	Glass and glass products	..	..	..	..	..	..	..	..
		269	Non-metallic mineral products, nec	..	..	..	..	..	..	..	..
	27		Basic metals	1 850	2 083	2 021	2 075	2 074	2 178	2 432	2 588
		271	Basic iron and steel	..	..	..	..	..	..	..	..
		272	Basic precious and non-ferrous metals	..	..	..	..	..	..	..	..
		273	Casting of metals	..	..	..	..	..	..	..	..
	28		Fabricated metal products, ex. machin. & equip.	3 100	3 314	3 012	2 620	2 549	2 752	3 357	3 552
		281	Structural metal prod., tanks, reservoirs, generators	..	..	..	..	..	..	..	..
		289	Other fabricated metal products & service activities	..	..	..	..	..	..	..	..
	29		Machinery and equipment, nec	6 215	6 773	6 372	5 893	5 769	6 305	7 685	8 553
		291	General purpose machinery	..	..	..	..	..	..	..	..
		292	Special purpose machinery	..	..	..	..	..	..	..	..
		293	Domestic appliances, nec	..	..	..	..	..	..	..	..
	30		Office, accounting and computing machinery	355	357	296	362	352	400	479	494
	31		Electrical machinery and apparatus, nec	1 695	1 858	1 715	1 645	1 580	1 822	2 204	2 378
		311	Electric motors, generators and transformers	..	..	..	..	..	..	..	..
		312	Electricity distribution and control apparatus	..	..	..	..	..	..	..	..
		313	Insulated wire and cable	..	..	..	..	..	..	..	..
		314	Accumulators, primary cells and primary batteries	..	..	..	..	..	..	..	..
		315	Electric lamps and lighting equipment	..	..	..	..	..	..	..	..
		319	Other electrical equipment, nec	..	..	..	..	..	..	..	..
	32		Radio, TV, communication equip. & apparatus	1 352	1 383	1 349	1 409	1 598	2 098	3 001	3 550
		321	Electronic valves, tubes & other electronic compon.	..	..	..	..	..	..	..	..
		322	TV, radio transmitters & appar. for line teleph., telegr.	..	..	..	..	..	..	..	..
		323	TV, radio receivers and associated goods	..	..	..	..	..	..	..	..
	33		Medical, precision, optical instr.; watches, clocks	767	845	813	802	812	887	1 086	1 182
		331	Medical equip.; precision instruments and appliances	..	..	..	..	..	..	..	..
		332	Optical instruments and photographic equipment	..	..	..	..	..	..	..	..
		333	Watches and clocks	..	..	..	..	..	..	..	..
	34		Motor vehicles, trailers, and semi-trailers	990	946	858	769	634	707	811	849
	35		Other transport equipment	2 032	2 168	2 064	2 046	1 885	2 082	2 488	2 293
		351	Building and repairing of ships and boats	..	..	..	..	..	..	..	..
		352	Railway, tramway locomotives and rolling stock	..	..	..	..	..	..	..	..
		353	Aircraft and spacecraft	..	..	..	..	..	..	..	..
		359	Transport equipment, nec	..	..	..	..	..	..	..	..
	36		Furniture; manufacturing, nec	1 664	1 726	1 624	1 413	1 293	1 376	1 535	1 553
		361	Furniture	..	..	..	..	..	..	..	..
		369	Manufacturing, nec	..	..	..	..	..	..	..	..
	37		Recycling	..	..	..	0	0	0	35	35
E	40-41		Electricity, gas and water supply	3 230	3 436	3 595	3 551	3 186	3 136	3 187	3 320
	40		Electricity, gas, steam and hot water supply	2 969	3 151	3 289	3 258	2 902	2 857	2 901	3 018
		401	Production, collection and distribution of electricity	..	..	..	..	..	..	..	..
	41	410	Collection, purification, distribution of water	261	285	306	293	284	279	286	302
F	45		Construction	..	24 008	21 747	18 107	14 723	13 541	14 803	15 667
G	50-52		Wholesale and retail trade; repairs etc	..	..	26 599	24 375	22 508	22 607	24 207	25 463
H	55		Hotels and restaurants	..	..	5 424	4 984	4 548	4 562	4 858	5 195
I	60-64		Transport, storage and communications	..	..	16 636	16 179	15 654	15 717	16 800	17 612
J	65-67		Financial intermediation	..	..	8 582	8 142	7 593	7 606	7 423	7 623
K	70-74		Real estate, renting and business activities	..	..	18 132	17 200	16 070	16 745	18 047	20 063
L-Q	75-99		Public admin.; education; health; other services	..	..	74 043	73 585	69 556	69 466	72 950	76 752
A-Q	01-99		Grand total	..	..	229 603	216 635	202 684	204 267	219 398	231 904

Note: The Grand total includes a figure for statistical discrepancy.

Table FN.21 CHARGES SOCIALES DES EMPLOYEURS - EMPLOYERS' SOCIAL COSTS

Millions de Mk (Prix courants)

1989	1990	1991	1992	1993	1994	1995	1996			CITI révision 3
..	..	..	911	930	948	976	859	Agriculture, chasse et sylviculture	A	01-02
			..	..	..	..	..	Pêche	B	05
..	..	..	132	140	141	156	151	Activités extractives	C	10-14
..	..	..	25	28	31	37	35	Extraction de charbon, de lignite et de tourbe		10
..	..	..	..	..	..	..	..	Extraction de pétrole brut et de gaz naturel		11
..	..	..	37	42	41	35	30	Extraction de minerais métalliques		13
..	..	..	70	70	69	84	86	Autres activités extractives		14
..	..	..	11 589	12 379	13 771	15 698	15 554	Activités de fabrication	D	15-37
..	..	..	1 446	1 488	1 527	1 610	1 562	Produits alimentaires et boissons		15
			..	..	..	..	..	Boissons		155
..	..	..	37	37	43	43	34	Produits à base de tabac		16 160
..	..	..	214	223	227	246	236	Textiles		17
			..	..	..	..	..	Filature, tissage et achèvement des textiles		171
			..	..	..	..	..	Autres articles textiles		172
			..	..	..	..	..	Etoffes et articles de bonneterie		173
..	..	..	161	163	164	166	151	Habillement; préparation, teinture des fourrures		18
			..	..	..	..	..	Articles d'habillement autres qu'en fourrure		181
			..	..	..	..	..	Préparation, teinture des fourrures; art. en fourrure		182
..	..	..	73	74	79	84	79	Travail des cuirs; articles en cuir; chaussures		19
			..	..	..	..	..	Apprêt et tannage des cuirs et articles en cuirs		191
			..	..	..	..	..	Chaussures		192
..	..	..	658	741	870	936	867	Bois et articles en bois et liège (sauf meubles)		20
			..	..	..	..	..	Sciage et rabotage du bois		201
			..	..	..	..	..	Articles en bois, liège, vannerie, sparterie		202
..	..	..	1 594	1 645	1 851	2 007	1 955	Papier et carton; articles en papier et en carton		21
..	..	..	1 089	1 124	1 142	1 219	1 130	Edition, imprimerie et reproduction		22
			..	..	..	..	..	Edition		221
			..	..	..	..	..	Imprimerie et activités annexes		222
			..	..	..	..	..	Reproduction de supports enregistrés		223
..	..	..	174	187	187	187	183	Cokéfaction; prod. pétroliers; comb. nucléaires		23
..	..	..	605	732	755	839	791	Produits chimiques		24
			..	..	..	..	..	Produits chimiques de base		241
			..	..	..	..	..	Autres produits chimiques		242
			..	..	..	..	..	Fibres synthétiques ou artificielles		243
..	..	..	338	391	445	490	510	Articles en caoutchouc et en matières plastiques		25
			..	..	..	..	..	Articles en caoutchouc		251
			..	..	..	..	..	Articles en matières plastiques		252
..	..	..	454	424	445	466	462	Autres produits minéraux non métalliques		26
			..	..	..	..	..	Verre et articles en verre		261
			..	..	..	..	..	Produits minéraux non métalliques, nca		269
..	..	..	545	595	677	730	733	Produits métallurgiques de base		27
			..	..	..	..	..	Sidérurgie et première transformation de l'acier		271
			..	..	..	..	..	Métallurgie; métaux précieux et non ferreux		272
			..	..	..	..	..	Fonderie		273
..	..	..	655	706	792	966	997	Ouvrages en métaux, sauf machines et matériel		28
			..	..	..	..	..	Constr. et menuiserie métal.; réservoirs; générateurs		281
			..	..	..	..	..	Autres ouvrages en métaux		289
..	..	..	1 494	1 620	1 881	2 347	2 477	Machines et matériel, nca		29
			..	..	..	..	..	Machines d'usage général		291
			..	..	..	..	..	Machines d'usage spécifique		292
			..	..	..	..	..	Appareils domestiques, nca		293
..	..	..	82	95	110	135	129	Mach. de bureau, comptables, matériel inform.		30
..	..	..	392	427	527	636	674	Machines et appareils électriques, nca		31
			..	..	..	..	..	Moteurs, génératrices et transformateurs électriques		311
			..	..	..	..	..	Matériel électrique de distribution et de commande		312
			..	..	..	..	..	Fils et câbles électriques isolés		313
			..	..	..	..	..	Accumulateurs, piles électriques		314
			..	..	..	..	..	Lampes électriques et appareils d'éclairage		315
			..	..	..	..	..	Autres matériels électriques, nca		319
..	..	..	327	423	580	853	949	Equip. et appar. de radio, TV, communication		32
			..	..	..	..	..	Tubes et valves électroniques; autres composants		321
			..	..	..	..	..	Emetteurs radio et TV; app. téléphonie, télégraphie		322
			..	..	..	..	..	Récepteurs radio et TV et articles associés		323
..	..	..	186	216	242	321	317	Instruments médicaux, de précision, d'optique		33
			..	..	..	..	..	Appareils médicaux et de précision		331
			..	..	..	..	..	Instruments d'optique ; matériel photographique		332
			..	..	..	..	..	Horlogerie		333
..	..	..	183	173	203	234	240	Véhicules automobiles et nemorques		34
..	..	..	529	540	628	740	643	Autres matériels de transport		35
			..	..	..	..	..	Construction et réparation de navires		351
			..	..	..	..	..	Construction de matériel ferroviaire roulant		352
			..	..	..	..	..	Construction aéronautique et spatiale		353
			..	..	..	..	..	Autres équipements de transport		359
..	..	..	353	355	396	433	425	Meubles; activités de fabrication, nca		36
			..	..	..	..	..	Meubles		361
			..	..	..	..	..	Activités de fabrication, nca		369
..	..	..	0	0	0	10	10	Récupération		37
..	..	..	1 021	958	1 033	1 045	1 019	Production et distrib. d'électricité, de gaz, d'eau	E	40-41
..	..	..	937	874	943	949	922	Electricité, gaz, vapeur et eau chaude		40
			..	..	..	..	..	Production, collecte et distribution d'électricité		401
..	..	..	84	84	90	96	97	Captage, épuration et distribution d'eau		41 410
..	..	..	5 015	4 294	4 286	4 502	4 354	Construction	F	45
..	..	..	6 374	6 358	6 407	6 405	6 433	Commerce de gros et de détail; réparation	G	50-52
..	..	..	1 171	1 201	1 190	1 228	1 267	Hôtels et restaurants	H	55
..	..	..	4 287	4 066	4 547	4 584	4 388	Transports, entreposage et communications	I	60-64
..	..	..	2 525	2 490	2 141	2 201	2 001	Intermédiation financière	J	65-67
..	..	..	4 148	4 192	4 388	4 607	4 896	Immobilier, locations, services aux entreprises	K	70-74
..	..	..	21 809	21 350	21 340	22 679	23 062	Admin. publique; éducation; santé; autres	L-Q	75-99
..	..	..	56 981	55 391	59 508	62 042	63 572	Grand total	A-Q	01-99

Statistiques des Structures Industrielles
OCDE, © 1998

FINLAND

Table FN.22 HOURS WORKED - HEURES OUVRÉES

Thousands

ISIC revision 3			1989	1990	1991	1992	1993	1994	1995	1996
A	01-02	Agriculture, hunting and forestry	..	479 900	446 400	436 600	416 200	404 000	376 700	357 100
B	05	Fishing	..	..	..	..	..	..	..	..
C	10-14	Mining and quarrying	9 800	9 500	8 800	8 900	7 700	7 300	7 500	7 400
	10	Mining of coal and lignite; extraction of peat	..	..	2 400	2 900	2 300	2 500	2 500	2 400
	11	Crude petroleum & natural gas; related service activ.								
	13	Mining of metal ores	2 200	1 700	1 600	1 500	1 300	1 200	1 000	1 000
	14	Other mining and quarrying	4 900	5 000	4 800	4 500	4 100	3 600	4 000	4 000
D	15-37	Total manufacturing	817 400	788 100	703 900	635 700	598 000	613 600	644 500	652 400
	15	Food products and beverages	97 200	94 500	88 600	82 600	75 500	72 500	71 000	70 100
	155	Beverages								
	16 160	Tobacco products	1 900	1 700	1 700	1 600	1 400	1 400	1 400	1 200
	17	Textiles	22 600	22 700	17 800	16 100	14 100	13 400	13 500	13 700
	171	Spinning, weaving and finishing of textiles	..	..	..	..	..	..	..	..
	172	Other textiles	..	..	..	..	..	..	..	..
	173	Knitted and crocheted fabrics and articles	..	..	..	..	..	..	..	..
	18	Wearing apparel dressing & dyeing of fur	33 600	26 100	20 500	15 200	13 100	12 200	11 700	10 900
	181	Wearing apparel, except fur apparel								
	182	Dressing and dyeing of fur; articles of fur								
	19	Tanning, dressing leather; leather artic.; footwear	10 200	9 400	7 500	6 500	5 700	5 600	5 600	5 300
	191	Tanning, dressing leather; manuf. of leather articles								
	192	Footwear								
	20	Wood and cork products, ex. furniture	62 400	60 400	49 300	44 000	42 000	45 600	45 500	43 700
	201	Sawmilling and planing of wood								
	202	Products of wood, cork, straw & plaiting material	..	..	..	..	..	..	..	..
	21	Paper and paper products	76 800	72 400	66 600	62 900	61 900	62 500	62 600	62 900
	22	Publishing, printing & reprod. of recorded media	68 000	66 400	62 200	55 900	52 000	50 200	48 200	46 200
	221	Publishing	..	..	..	..	..	..	..	..
	222	Printing and related service activities	..	..	..	..	..	..	..	..
	223	Reproduction of recorded media								
	23	Coke, refined petroleum products & nuclear fuel	6 700	6 300	6 500	6 500	6 100	5 900	6 000	6 200
	24	Chemicals and chemical products	33 800	32 700	32 300	30 400	30 000	29 400	30 600	30 100
	241	Basic chemicals	..	..	..	..	..	..	..	..
	242	Other chemical products	..	..	..	..	..	..	..	..
	243	Man-made fibres	..	..	..	..	..	..	..	..
	25	Rubber and plastic products	24 900	25 400	22 800	20 900	20 400	21 800	22 300	23 000
	251	Rubber products								
	252	Plastic products								
	26	Other non-metallic mineral products	36 600	36 200	30 900	25 300	21 100	20 800	20 700	20 500
	261	Glass and glass products								
	269	Non-metallic mineral products, nec	..	..	..	..	..	..	..	..
	27	Basic metals	27 900	28 100	26 000	25 400	25 000	25 700	26 000	26 600
	271	Basic iron and steel	..	..	..	..	..	..	..	..
	272	Basic precious and non-ferrous metals	..	..	..	..	..	..	..	..
	273	Casting of metals	..	..	..	..	..	..	..	..
	28	Fabricated metal products, ex. machin. & equip.	57 100	57 300	49 900	42 800	40 600	41 400	45 700	46 300
	281	Structural metal prod., tanks, reservoirs, generators	..	..	..	..	..	..	..	..
	289	Other fabricated metal products & service activities	..	..	..	..	..	..	..	..
	29	Machinery and equipment, nec	101 300	101 300	90 300	79 000	75 900	80 700	90 100	96 300
	291	General purpose machinery	..	..	..	..	..	..	..	..
	292	Special purpose machinery	..	..	..	..	..	..	..	..
	293	Domestic appliances, nec	..	..	..	..	..	..	..	..
	30	Office, accounting and computing machinery	5 100	4 700	3 900	4 600	4 700	5 300	5 600	5 700
	31	Electrical machinery and apparatus, nec	29 500	28 500	24 500	22 500	21 200	23 900	28 500	30 000
	311	Electric motors, generators and transformers	..	..	..	..	..	..	..	..
	312	Electricity distribution and control apparatus	..	..	..	..	..	..	..	..
	313	Insulated wire and cable	..	..	..	..	..	..	..	..
	314	Accumulators, primary cells and primary batteries	..	..	..	..	..	..	..	..
	315	Electric lamps and lighting equipment	..	..	..	..	..	..	..	..
	319	Other electrical equipment, nec	..	..	..	..	..	..	..	..
	32	Radio, TV, communication equip. & apparatus	22 900	21 500	19 600	19 100	21 100	26 200	34 700	39 900
	321	Electronic valves, tubes & other electronic compon.	..	..	..	..	..	..	..	..
	322	TV, radio transmitters & appar. for line teleph., telegr.	..	..	..	..	..	..	..	..
	323	TV, radio receivers and associated goods	..	..	..	..	..	..	..	..
	33	Medical, precision, optical instr.; watches, clocks	12 500	12 400	11 900	10 700	10 800	11 400	13 200	13 700
	331	Medical equip.; precision instruments and appliances	..	..	..	..	..	..	..	..
	332	Optical instruments and photographic equipment	..	..	..	..	..	..	..	..
	333	Watches and clocks	..	..	..	..	..	..	..	..
	34	Motor vehicles, trailers, and semi-trailers	17 700	15 000	12 400	10 700	8 700	9 900	9 900	10 300
	35	Other transport equipment	32 300	30 200	27 300	26 200	22 900	24 400	26 900	24 500
	351	Building and repairing of ships and boats	..	..	..	..	..	..	..	..
	352	Railway, tramway locomotives and rolling stock	..	..	..	..	..	..	..	..
	353	Aircraft and spacecraft	..	..	..	..	..	..	..	..
	359	Transport equipment, nec	..	..	..	..	..	..	..	..
	36	Furniture; manufacturing, nec	36 400	34 900	31 400	26 800	23 800	23 400	24 400	24 900
	361	Furniture	..	..	..	..	..	..	..	..
	369	Manufacturing, nec	..	..	..	..	..	..	..	..
	37	Recycling	..	..	..	0	0	0	400	400
E	40-41	Electricity, gas and water supply	46 800	45 300	43 900	41 600	37 400	35 300	34 300	34 100
	40	Electricity, gas, steam and hot water supply	42 500	40 900	39 600	37 600	33 500	31 600	30 400	30 200
	401	Production, collection and distribution of electricity	..	..	..	..	..	..	..	..
	41 410	Collection, purification, distribution of water	4 300	4 400	4 300	4 000	3 900	3 700	3 900	3 900
F	45	Construction	..	438 900	370 900	307 500	273 900	254 800	269 000	270 800
G	50-52	Wholesale and retail trade; repairs etc	..	..	526 100	476 000	444 300	448 400	450 700	467 800
H	55	Hotels and restaurants	..	..	110 400	101 800	94 500	95 200	96 600	101 300
I	60-64	Transport, storage and communications	..	..	297 200	283 700	270 700	268 900	273 900	276 600
J	65-67	Financial intermediation	..	..	103 100	99 800	90 700	77 800	75 900	72 300
K	70-74	Real estate, renting and business activities	..	..	262 900	250 300	246 300	261 100	273 700	289 800
L-Q	75-99	Public admin.; education; health; other services	..	..	995 100	968 700	919 400	920 300	951 800	960 500
A-Q	01-99	Grand total	..	..	3 868 700	3 610 600	3 399 100	3 386 700	3 454 600	3 490 100

Table HU.7 **PRODUCTION - PRODUCTION**

Millions de Ft (Prix courants) — CITI révision 3

1989	1990	1991	1992	1993	1994	1995	1996			
..	..	544 681	539 435	567 464	686 312	..	..	**Agriculture, chasse et sylviculture**	**A**	01-02
..	..	1 762	1 705	2 042	2 183	..	..	**Pêche**	**B**	05
..	..	145 438	66 565	48 285	49 154	..	..	**Activités extractives**	**C**	10-14
..	..	47 486	45 389	22 518	19 313	..	..	Extraction de charbon, de lignite et de tourbe		10
..	..	83 699	9 620	12 322	14 017	..	..	Extraction de pétrole brut et de gaz naturel		11
..	..	..	..	..	..	..	..	Extraction de minerais métalliques		13
..	..	6 028	5 933	7 279	10 456	..	..	Autres activités extractives		14
..	..	1 861 385	1 912 527	2 110 030	2 561 976	..	..	**Activités de fabrication**	**D**	15-37
..	..	509 778	510 198	560 543	682 515	..	..	**Produits alimentaires et boissons**		15
..	..	..	..	..	..	..	..	Boissons		155
..	..	10 998	14 460	18 403	23 755	..	..	**Produits à base de tabac**		16 160
..	..	65 346	57 736	66 749	71 955	..	..	**Textiles**		17
..	..	..	..	..	..	..	..	Filature, tissage et achèvement des textiles		171
..	..	..	..	..	..	..	..	Autres articles textiles		172
..	..	..	..	..	..	..	..	Etoffes et articles de bonneterie		173
..	..	36 111	46 059	51 456	61 625	..	..	**Habillement; préparation, teinture des fourrures**		18
..	..	..	..	..	..	..	..	Articles d'habillement autres qu'en fourrure		181
..	..	..	..	..	..	..	..	Préparation, teinture des fourrures; art. en fourrure		182
..	..	28 555	32 978	33 433	31 157	..	..	**Travail des cuirs; articles en cuir; chaussures**		19
..	..	..	..	..	..	..	..	Apprêt et tannage des cuirs et articles en cuirs		191
..	..	..	..	..	..	..	..	Chaussures		192
..	..	33 832	49 086	49 338	60 114	..	..	**Bois et articles en bois et liège (sauf meubles)**		20
..	..	..	..	..	..	..	..	Sciage et rabotage du bois		201
..	..	..	..	..	..	..	..	Articles en bois, liège, vannerie, sparterie		202
..	..	35 268	40 566	38 757	50 931	..	..	**Papier et carton; articles en papier et en carton**		21
..	..	66 918	75 074	85 946	104 242	..	..	**Edition, imprimerie et reproduction**		22
..	..	..	..	..	..	..	..	Edition		221
..	..	..	..	..	..	..	..	Imprimerie et activités annexes		222
..	..	..	..	..	..	..	..	Reproduction de supports enregistrés		223
..	..	160 938	174 905	193 586	198 787	..	..	**Cokéfaction; prod. pétroliers; comb. nucléaires**		23
..	..	194 790	186 575	207 057	256 860	..	..	**Produits chimiques**		24
..	..	..	..	..	..	..	..	Produits chimiques de base		241
..	..	..	..	..	..	..	..	Autres produits chimiques		242
..	..	..	..	..	..	..	..	Fibres synthétiques ou artificielles		243
..	..	52 630	56 130	62 618	89 166	..	..	**Articles en caoutchouc et en matières plastiques**		25
..	..	..	..	..	..	..	..	Articles en caoutchouc		251
..	..	..	..	..	..	..	..	Articles en matières plastiques		252
..	..	67 225	70 874	77 796	99 852	..	..	**Autres produits minéraux non métalliques**		26
..	..	..	..	..	..	..	..	Verre et articles en verre		261
..	..	..	..	..	..	..	..	Produits minéraux non métalliques, nca		269
..	..	140 722	103 186	90 819	111 198	..	..	**Produits métallurgiques de base**		27
..	..	..	..	..	..	..	..	Sidérurgie et première transformation de l'acier		271
..	..	..	..	..	..	..	..	Métallurgie; métaux précieux et non ferreux		272
..	..	..	..	..	..	..	..	Fonderie		273
..	..	90 269	103 004	119 022	161 852	..	..	**Ouvrages en métaux, sauf machines et matériel**		28
..	..	..	..	..	..	..	..	Constr. et menuiserie métal.; réservoirs; générateurs		281
..	..	..	..	..	..	..	..	Autres ouvrages en métaux		289
..	..	125 876	132 345	133 340	152 821	..	..	**Machines et matériel, nca**		29
..	..	..	..	..	..	..	..	Machines d'usage général		291
..	..	..	..	..	..	..	..	Machines d'usage spécifique		292
..	..	..	..	..	..	..	..	Appareils domestiques, nca		293
..	..	8 884	6 707	12 738	10 029	..	..	**Mach. de bureau, comptables, matériel inform.**		30
..	..	60 749	58 714	72 065	92 984	..	..	**Machines et appareils électriques, nca**		31
..	..	..	..	..	..	..	..	Moteurs, génératrices et transformateurs électriques		311
..	..	..	..	..	..	..	..	Matériel électrique de distribution et de commande		312
..	..	..	..	..	..	..	..	Fils et câbles électriques isolés		313
..	..	..	..	..	..	..	..	Accumulateurs, piles électriques		314
..	..	..	..	..	..	..	..	Lampes électriques et appareils d'éclairage		315
..	..	..	..	..	..	..	..	Autres matériels électriques, nca		319
..	..	35 355	32 523	41 048	53 584	..	..	**Equip. et appar. de radio, TV, communication**		32
..	..	..	..	..	..	..	..	Tubes et valves électroniques; autres composants		321
..	..	..	..	..	..	..	..	Emetteurs radio et TV; app. téléphonie, télégraphie		322
..	..	..	..	..	..	..	..	Récepteurs radio et TV et articles associés		323
..	..	32 184	41 042	44 109	57 318	..	..	**Instruments médicaux, de précision, d'optique**		33
..	..	..	..	..	..	..	..	Appareils médicaux et de précision		331
..	..	..	..	..	..	..	..	Instruments d'optique ; matériel photographique		332
..	..	..	..	..	..	..	..	Horlogerie		333
..	..	60 183	60 492	90 159	121 574	..	..	**Véhicules automobiles et nemorques**		34
..	..	6 219	9 269	10 126	13 902	..	..	**Autres matériels de transport**		35
..	..	..	..	..	..	..	..	Construction et réparation de navires		351
..	..	..	..	..	..	..	..	Construction de matériel ferroviaire roulant		352
..	..	..	..	..	..	..	..	Construction aéronautique et spatiale		353
..	..	..	..	..	..	..	..	Autres équipements de transport		359
..	..	37 952	49 917	50 218	54 661	..	..	**Meubles; activités de fabrication, nca**		36
..	..	..	..	..	..	..	..	Meubles		361
..	..	..	..	..	..	..	..	Activités de fabrication, nca		369
..	..	603	687	704	1 094	..	..	**Récupération**		37
..	..	311 119	294 846	326 571	334 558	..	..	**Production et distrib. d'électricité, de gaz, d'eau**	**E**	40-41
..	..	272 862	256 774	283 860	289 596	..	..	**Electricité, gaz, vapeur et eau chaude**		40
..	..	..	..	..	..	..	..	Production, collecte et distribution d'électricité		401
..	..	38 257	38 072	42 711	44 962	..	..	**Captage, épuration et distribution d'eau**		41 410
..	..	275 590	334 857	364 662	472 411	..	..	**Construction**	**F**	45
..	..	586 758	689 694	742 582	895 810	..	..	**Commerce de gros et de détail; réparation**	**G**	50-52
..	..	85 971	106 424	116 990	135 052	..	..	**Hôtels et restaurants**	**H**	55
..	..	348 212	439 484	492 117	599 261	..	..	**Transports, entreposage et communications**	**I**	60-64
..	..	152 155	163 984	209 264	326 080	..	..	**Intermédiation financière**	**J**	65-67
..	..	381 524	494 868	620 790	794 149	..	..	**Immobilier, locations, services aux entreprises**	**K**	70-74
..	..	629 556	841 809	1 136 298	1 318 302	..	..	**Admin. publique; éducation; santé; autres**	**L-Q**	75-99
..	..	5 324 151	5 886 198	6 737 095	8 175 248	..	..	**Grand total**	**A-Q**	01-99

Statistiques des Structures Industrielles
OCDE, © 1998

Table HU.8 VALUE ADDED - VALEUR AJOUTÉE

Millions of Ft (Current Prices)

ISIC revision 3			1989	1990	1991	1992	1993	1994	1995	1996
A	01-02	Agriculture, hunting and forestry	..	..	194 548	189 285	205 537	261 457	..	..
B	05	Fishing	..	..	590	594	558	814	..	..
C	10-14	Mining and quarrying	..	..	81 813	32 210	20 094	20 048	..	..
	10	Mining of coal and lignite; extraction of peat	..	..	22 437	23 558	7 864	5 645	..	..
	11	Crude petroleum & natural gas; related service activ.	..	..	54 272	3 721	5 945	7 460	..	..
	13	Mining of metal ores	..	..	..	..	..	..	..	..
	14	Other mining and quarrying	..	..	2 505	2 106	2 753	4 257	..	..
D	15-37	Total manufacturing	..	..	494 217	583 044	688 401	848 241	..	..
	15	Food products and beverages	..	..	113 298	120 763	138 515	160 812	..	..
	155	Beverages	..	..	..	..	..	..	..	..
	16 160	Tobacco products	..	..	2 734	3 290	3 798	6 282	..	..
	17	Textiles	..	..	16 741	18 689	22 943	25 733	..	..
	171	Spinning, weaving and finishing of textiles	..	..	..	..	..	..	..	..
	172	Other textiles	..	..	..	..	..	..	..	..
	173	Knitted and crocheted fabrics and articles	..	..	..	..	..	..	..	..
	18	Wearing apparel dressing & dyeing of fur	..	..	18 057	25 611	29 743	37 305	..	..
	181	Wearing apparel, except fur apparel	..	..	..	..	..	..	..	..
	182	Dressing and dyeing of fur; articles of fur	..	..	..	..	..	..	..	..
	19	Tanning, dressing leather; leather artic.; footwear	..	..	9 327	12 818	13 656	16 545	..	..
	191	Tanning, dressing leather; manuf. of leather articles	..	..	..	..	..	..	..	..
	192	Footwear	..	..	..	..	..	..	..	..
	20	Wood and cork products, ex. furniture	..	..	11 198	15 998	17 937	24 091	..	..
	201	Sawmilling and planing of wood	..	..	..	..	..	..	..	..
	202	Products of wood, cork, straw & plaiting material	..	..	..	..	..	..	..	..
	21	Paper and paper products	..	..	9 015	9 421	11 046	15 127	..	..
	22	Publishing, printing & reprod. of recorded media	..	..	18 297	22 689	29 968	38 640	..	..
	221	Publishing	..	..	..	..	..	..	..	..
	222	Printing and related service activities	..	..	..	..	..	..	..	..
	223	Reproduction of recorded media	..	..	..	..	..	..	..	..
	23	Coke, refined petroleum products & nuclear fuel	..	..	38 701	79 484	91 555	83 140	..	..
	24	Chemicals and chemical products	..	..	51 993	49 159	62 554	88 739	..	..
	241	Basic chemicals	..	..	..	..	..	..	..	..
	242	Other chemical products	..	..	..	..	..	..	..	..
	243	Man-made fibres	..	..	..	..	..	..	..	..
	25	Rubber and plastic products	..	..	16 016	16 452	20 991	28 044	..	..
	251	Rubber products	..	..	..	..	..	..	..	..
	252	Plastic products	..	..	..	..	..	..	..	..
	26	Other non-metallic mineral products	..	..	21 119	24 604	29 868	41 771	..	..
	261	Glass and glass products	..	..	..	..	..	..	..	..
	269	Non-metallic mineral products, nec	..	..	..	..	..	..	..	..
	27	Basic metals	..	..	19 784	15 949	16 134	20 827	..	..
	271	Basic iron and steel	..	..	..	..	..	..	..	..
	272	Basic precious and non-ferrous metals	..	..	..	..	..	..	..	..
	273	Casting of metals	..	..	..	..	..	..	..	..
	28	Fabricated metal products, ex. machin. & equip.	..	..	30 252	31 454	39 052	53 250	..	..
	281	Structural metal prod., tanks, reservoirs, generators	..	..	..	..	..	..	..	..
	289	Other fabricated metal products & service activities	..	..	..	..	..	..	..	..
	29	Machinery and equipment, nec	..	..	45 452	52 239	51 095	55 808	..	..
	291	General purpose machinery	..	..	..	..	..	..	..	..
	292	Special purpose machinery	..	..	..	..	..	..	..	..
	293	Domestic appliances, nec	..	..	..	..	..	..	..	..
	30	Office, accounting and computing machinery	..	..	2 122	1 681	2 819	2 117	..	..
	31	Electrical machinery and apparatus, nec	..	..	19 820	16 016	21 172	36 817	..	..
	311	Electric motors, generators and transformers	..	..	..	..	..	..	..	..
	312	Electricity distribution and control apparatus	..	..	..	..	..	..	..	..
	313	Insulated wire and cable	..	..	..	..	..	..	..	..
	314	Accumulators, primary cells and primary batteries	..	..	..	..	..	..	..	..
	315	Electric lamps and lighting equipment	..	..	..	..	..	..	..	..
	319	Other electrical equipment, nec	..	..	..	..	..	..	..	..
	32	Radio, TV, communication equip. & apparatus	..	..	6 943	8 401	13 683	18 959	..	..
	321	Electronic valves, tubes & other electronic compon.	..	..	..	..	..	..	..	..
	322	TV, radio transmitters & appar. for line teleph., telegr.	..	..	..	..	..	..	..	..
	323	TV, radio receivers and associated goods	..	..	..	..	..	..	..	..
	33	Medical, precision, optical instr.; watches, clocks	..	..	13 892	19 756	22 469	30 588	..	..
	331	Medical equip.; precision instruments and appliances	..	..	..	..	..	..	..	..
	332	Optical instruments and photographic equipment	..	..	..	..	..	..	..	..
	333	Watches and clocks	..	..	..	..	..	..	..	..
	34	Motor vehicles, trailers, and semi-trailers	..	..	14 212	15 073	24 877	32 437	..	..
	35	Other transport equipment	..	..	1 633	3 143	3 689	7 158	..	..
	351	Building and repairing of ships and boats	..	..	..	..	..	..	..	..
	352	Railway, tramway locomotives and rolling stock	..	..	..	..	..	..	..	..
	353	Aircraft and spacecraft	..	..	..	..	..	..	..	..
	359	Transport equipment, nec	..	..	..	..	..	..	..	..
	36	Furniture; manufacturing, nec	..	..	13 421	20 168	20 740	23 809	..	..
	361	Furniture	..	..	..	..	..	..	..	..
	369	Manufacturing, nec	..	..	..	..	..	..	..	..
	37	Recycling	..	..	190	186	97	242	..	..
E	40-41	Electricity, gas and water supply	..	..	90 486	102 003	115 923	125 265	..	..
	40	Electricity, gas, steam and hot water supply	..	..	69 730	81 071	93 018	99 931	..	..
	401	Production, collection and distribution of electricity	..	..	..	..	..	..	..	..
	41 410	Collection, purification, distribution of water	..	..	20 756	20 932	22 905	25 334	..	..
F	45	Construction	..	..	123 500	153 892	167 392	201 455	..	..
G	50-52	Wholesale and retail trade; repairs etc	..	..	307 185	284 026	353 792	420 586	..	..
H	55	Hotels and restaurants	..	..	48 458	57 589	63 743	73 207	..	..
I	60-64	Transport, storage and communications	..	..	209 907	245 244	276 967	333 774	..	..
J	65-67	Financial intermediation	..	..	101 815	109 144	145 595	245 125	..	..
K	70-74	Real estate, renting and business activities	..	..	234 815	317 265	412 178	525 158	..	..
L-Q	75-99	Public admin.; education; health; other services	..	..	411 657	549 973	692 147	864 304	..	..
A-Q	01-99	Grand total	..	..	2 298 991	2 624 269	3 142 327	3 919 434	..	..

Table NY.12 PRODUCTION - PRODUCTION

Millions de NKr (Prix courants)

1989	1990	1991	1992	1993	1994	1995	1996			CITI révision 3	
..	..	..	..	..	..	..	..	**Agriculture, chasse et sylviculture**	**A**	**01-02**	
..	..	..	..	..	..	..	..	**Pêche**	**B**	**05**	
92 948	113 160	119 827	122 921	132 272	135 748	139 864	..	**Activités extractives**	**C**	**10-14**	
..	..	..	..	..	..	..	..	Extraction de charbon, de lignite et de tourbe		**10**	
88 504	108 757	115 522	118 584	128 303	131 380	135 320	..	Extraction de pétrole brut et de gaz naturel		**11**	
1 405	1 394	1 186	1 116	982	1 058	1 015	..	Extraction de minerais métalliques		**13**	
2 813	2 788	2 879	3 016	2 853	3 171	3 402	..	Autres activités extractives		**14**	
289 455	300 877	302 828	303 982	311 566	338 762	366 194	..	**Activités de fabrication**	**D**	**15-37**	
67 270	69 370	74 293	78 146	78 848	82 482	85 277	..	**Produits alimentaires et boissons**		**15**	
3 538	3 629	4 217	4 114	4 111	5 022	5 030	..	Boissons			155
728	943	928	1 018	893	843	788	..	**Produits à base de tabac**		**16**	160
3 246	3 353	3 499	3 748	3 734	3 940	3 582	..	**Textiles**		**17**	
..	..	..	..	..	..	..	..	Filature, tissage et achèvement des textiles			171
..	..	..	..	..	..	..	..	Autres articles textiles			172
..	..	..	..	..	..	..	..	Etoffes et articles de bonneterie			173
936	1 020	1 034	1 111	1 189	1 332	1 475	..	**Habillement; préparation, teinture des fourrures**		**18**	
..	..	..	..	..	..	..	..	Articles d'habillement autres qu'en fourrure			181
..	..	..	..	..	..	..	..	Préparation, teinture des fourrures; art. en fourrure			182
455	529	542	583	589	636	538	..	**Travail des cuirs; articles en cuir; chaussures**		**19**	
..	..	..	..	..	..	..	..	Apprêt et tannage des cuirs et articles en cuirs			191
..	..	..	..	..	..	..	..	Chaussures			192
14 643	14 468	13 376	11 853	11 577	14 357	15 106	..	**Bois et articles en bois et liège (sauf meubles)**		**20**	
6 242	6 817	6 065	5 636	5 307	6 975	7 011	..	Sciage et rabotage du bois			201
8 401	7 651	7 311	6 217	6 270	7 382	8 095	..	Articles en bois, liège, vannerie, sparterie			202
18 352	18 268	17 449	15 548	15 796	17 754	23 344	..	**Papier et carton; articles en papier et en carton**		**21**	
21 409	22 382	22 927	23 045	24 291	25 902	27 202	..	**Edition, imprimerie et reproduction**		**22**	
13 931	14 499	14 955	15 038	15 880	17 040	17 644	..	Edition			221
..	..	..	..	..	..	..	..	Imprimerie et activités annexes			222
..	..	..	..	265	378	383	..	Reproduction de supports enregistrés			223
12 352	18 073	15 945	15 361	16 788	15 827	13 398	..	**Cokéfaction; prod. pétroliers; comb. nucléaires**		**23**	
22 688	23 407	23 198	23 270	24 973	27 597	29 807	..	**Produits chimiques**		**24**	
16 454	16 866	16 435	15 514	16 583	19 231	20 938	..	Produits chimiques de base			241
6 234	6 541	6 763	7 756	8 390	8 366	8 876	..	Autres produits chimiques			242
..	..	..	..	..	..	..	..	Fibres synthétiques ou artificielles			243
5 529	5 667	5 579	5 273	5 330	5 909	6 648	..	**Articles en caoutchouc et en matières plastiques**		**25**	
..	..	..	..	..	..	..	..	Articles en caoutchouc			251
..	..	..	..	..	..	..	..	Articles en matières plastiques			252
8 794	8 949	8 303	8 428	8 084	9 213	9 972	..	**Autres produits minéraux non métalliques**		**26**	
1 222	1 239	1 430	1 370	1 266	1 519	1 519	..	Verre et articles en verre			261
7 572	7 710	6 873	7 058	6 818	7 694	8 453	..	Produits minéraux non métalliques, nca			269
34 507	29 281	27 403	25 069	26 103	31 632	36 842	..	**Produits métallurgiques de base**		**27**	
7 764	7 266	6 843	6 706	6 921	7 707	8 908	..	Sidérurgie et première transformation de l'acier			271
26 572	21 838	20 353	18 136	18 213	22 697	26 538	..	Métallurgie; métaux précieux et non ferreux			272
171	177	207	227	969	1 228	1 396	..	Fonderie			273
11 373	11 993	11 924	11 628	11 141	12 267	14 151	..	**Ouvrages en métaux, sauf machines et matériel**		**28**	
..	..	..	..	..	..	..	..	Constr. et menuiserie métal.; réservoirs; générateurs			281
..	..	..	..	..	..	..	..	Autres ouvrages en métaux			289
16 858	18 066	18 686	20 125	18 825	21 388	24 322	..	**Machines et matériel, nca**		**29**	
9 740	10 956	11 630	11 866	11 192	12 859	14 766	..	Machines d'usage général			291
6 135	6 160	6 155	7 347	6 686	7 470	8 582	..	Machines d'usage spécifique			292
983	950	901	912	947	1 059	974	..	Appareils domestiques, nca			293
2 698	2 369	1 115	1 059	964	1 452	1 299	..	**Mach. de bureau, comptables, matériel inform.**		**30**	
9 159	9 526	9 451	9 445	9 419	10 099	10 714	..	**Machines et appareils électriques, nca**		**31**	
4 330	4 805	4 677	4 549	5 184	5 538	5 783	..	Moteurs, génératrices et transformateurs électriques			311
..	..	..	..	..	..	..	..	Matériel électrique de distribution et de commande			312
2 482	2 235	2 406	2 500	1 961	2 198	2 608	..	Fils et câbles électriques isolés			313
2 347	2 486	2 368	2 396	2 274	2 363	2 323	..	Accumulateurs, piles électriques			314
..	..	..	..	..	..	..	..	Lampes électriques et appareils d'éclairage			315
3 309	3 417	3 517	3 781	3 846	4 635	5 696	..	Autres matériels électriques, nca			319
2 928	2 916	3 008	3 356	3 211	4 077	5 312	..	**Equip. et appar. de radio, TV, communication**		**32**	
..	..	..	..	..	..	..	..	Tubes et valves électroniques; autres composants			321
381	501	509	425	635	558	384	..	Emetteurs radio et TV; app. téléphonie, télégraphie			322
2 561	3 008	3 448	3 725	4 441	4 846	5 901	..	Récepteurs radio et TV et articles associés			323
2 398	2 860	3 250	3 558	4 281	4 652	5 671	..	**Instruments médicaux, de précision, d'optique**		**33**	
163	148	198	167	160	194	230	..	Appareils médicaux et de précision			331
..	..	..	..	..	..	..	..	Instruments d'optique ; matériel photographique			332
3 180	2 789	2 388	2 683	2 516	3 157	4 371	..	Horlogerie			333
22 544	26 746	30 379	31 372	34 167	34 529	36 157	..	**Véhicules automobiles et nemorques**		**34**	
19 457	22 532	26 462	27 406	30 226	29 611	31 365	..	**Autres matériels de transport**		**35**	
1 023	1 421	1 256	1 337	1 440	1 331	1 155	..	Construction et réparation de navires			351
1 751	2 415	2 299	2 221	2 074	3 095	3 152	..	Construction de matériel ferroviaire roulant			352
313	378	362	408	427	492	485	..	Construction aéronautique et spatiale			353
6 871	7 250	7 440	7 705	7 620	8 473	9 117	..	Autres équipements de transport			359
5 212	5 450	5 487	5 472	5 478	6 319	6 810	..	**Meubles; activités de fabrication, nca**		**36**	
1 659	1 800	1 953	2 233	2 142	2 154	2 307	..	Meubles			361
3	3	4	6	432	492	487	..	Activités de fabrication, nca			369
28 700	30 096	31 825	31 028	30 421	29 102	31 830	..	**Récupération**		**37**	
27 019	28 300	29 917	29 093	28 375	26 930	29 613	..	**Production et distrib. d'électricité, de gaz, d'eau**	**E**	**40-41**	
26 852	28 103	29 650	28 807	28 081	26 660	29 301	..	**Electricité, gaz, vapeur et eau chaude**		**40**	
1 681	1 796	1 908	1 935	2 046	2 172	2 217	..	Production, collecte et distribution d'électricité			401
97 728	89 933	87 469	87 344	87 210	95 747	105 831	..	**Captage, épuration et distribution d'eau**		**41**	410
..	..	..	..	..	..	..	..	**Construction**	**F**	**45**	
..	..	..	..	..	..	..	..	**Commerce de gros et de détail; réparation**	**G**	**50-52**	
..	..	..	..	..	..	..	..	**Hôtels et restaurants**	**H**	**55**	
..	..	..	..	..	..	..	..	**Transports, entreposage et communications**	**I**	**60-64**	
..	..	..	..	..	..	..	..	**Intermédiation financière**	**J**	**65-67**	
..	..	..	..	..	..	..	..	**Immobilier, locations, services aux entreprises**	**K**	**70-74**	
..	..	..	..	..	..	..	..	**Admin. publique; éducation; santé; autres**	**L-Q**	**75-99**	
..	..	..	..	..	..	..	..	**Grand total**	**A-Q**	**01-99**	

Note: ISIC 1531 includes 1532; 2029 includes 2023; 2109 includes 2102; 2412 includes 2421; 2413 includes 243; 2692 includes 2691 and 2693; 2696 includes 2695 and 2699; 3120 includes 3110; 3150 includes 3140 and 3190; 3210 includes 3220; 3320 includes 3330; 3694 includes 3691, 3692, 3693 and 3699; and 453 includes 454.

Table NY.13 VALUE ADDED - VALEUR AJOUTÉE

Millions of NKr (Current Prices)

ISIC revision 3			1989	1990	1991	1992	1993	1994	1995	1996
A	01-02	**Agriculture, hunting and forestry**	..	..	..	..	..	..	..	..
B	05	**Fishing**	..	..	..	..	..	..	..	..
C	10-14	**Mining and quarrying**	72 799	90 826	94 595	95 113	99 736	103 740	111 503	..
	10	Mining of coal and lignite; extraction of peat	..	..	..	..	..	..	..	..
	11	Crude petroleum & natural gas; related service activ.	70 976	89 038	92 888	93 275	98 231	101 900	10 965	..
	13	Mining of metal ores	572	519	379	426	275	434	341	..
	14	Other mining and quarrying	1 194	1 222	1 275	1 340	1 193	1 377	1 481	..
D	15-37	**Total manufacturing**	85 750	84 196	85 839	88 327	94 667	100 297	111 072	..
	15	**Food products and beverages**	12 522	12 359	14 055	16 500	17 033	16 910	17 925	..
	155	Beverages	..	..	..	..	..	..	..	..
	16 160	**Tobacco products**	280	412	469	446	433	445	293	..
	17	**Textiles**	1 152	1 252	1 353	1 511	1 508	1 486	1 327	..
	171	Spinning, weaving and finishing of textiles	..	..	..	..	..	..	..	..
	172	Other textiles	..	..	..	..	..	..	..	..
	173	Knitted and crocheted fabrics and articles	..	..	..	..	..	..	..	..
	18	**Wearing apparel dressing & dyeing of fur**	389	384	406	451	488	501	527	..
	181	Wearing apparel, except fur apparel	..	..	..	..	..	..	..	..
	182	Dressing and dyeing of fur; articles of fur	..	..	..	..	..	..	..	..
	19	**Tanning, dressing leather; leather artic.; footwear**	166	181	198	201	207	207	181	..
	191	Tanning, dressing leather; manuf. of leather articles	..	..	..	..	..	..	..	..
	192	Footwear	..	..	..	..	..	..	..	..
	20	**Wood and cork products, ex. furniture**	4 411	4 356	3 857	3 694	3 673	4 367	4 242	..
	201	Sawmilling and planing of wood	1 861	2 003	1 633	1 604	1 597	1 913	1 587	..
	202	Products of wood, cork, straw & plaiting material	2 550	2 353	2 224	2 090	2 076	2 454	2 655	..
	21	**Paper and paper products**	4 928	4 803	4 239	3 639	3 969	4 617	7 223	..
	22	**Publishing, printing & reprod. of recorded media**	9 026	9 358	9 711	10 037	10 802	11 455	11 898	..
	221	Publishing	5 713	5 926	6 253	6 520	7 012	7 477	7 853	..
	222	Printing and related service activities	3 313	3 432	3 458	3 517	3 658	3 771	3 827	..
	223	Reproduction of recorded media	..	..	..	..	132	207	218	..
	23	**Coke, refined petroleum products & nuclear fuel**	884	1 364	1 600	1 021	1 847	1 594	839	..
	24	**Chemicals and chemical products**	7 428	7 382	6 748	7 014	8 028	8 883	10 759	..
	241	Basic chemicals	5 039	4 939	4 411	4 181	4 851	5 917	7 267	..
	242	Other chemical products	2 389	2 443	2 337	2 833	3 177	2 966	3 492	..
	243	Man-made fibres	..	..	..	..	..	..	..	..
	25	**Rubber and plastic products**	1 954	2 043	1 985	2 055	1 997	2 133	2 318	..
	251	Rubber products	..	..	..	..	..	..	..	..
	252	Plastic products	..	..	..	..	..	..	..	..
	26	**Other non-metallic mineral products**	3 240	3 296	3 207	2 945	3 243	3 577	3 893	..
	261	Glass and glass products	500	525	571	524	534	628	653	..
	269	Non-metallic mineral products, nec	2 740	2 771	2 636	2 421	2 709	2 949	3 240	..
	27	**Basic metals**	10 664	6 778	5 955	5 632	6 473	7 614	9 858	..
	271	Basic iron and steel	2 517	1 611	1 550	1 552	1 819	1 910	2 405	..
	272	Basic precious and non-ferrous metals	8 077	5 087	4 323	3 995	4 198	5 128	6 819	..
	273	Casting of metals	70	80	82	85	456	576	634	..
	28	**Fabricated metal products, ex. machin. & equip.**	4 517	4 733	4 817	4 766	4 732	5 196	5 726	..
	281	Structural metal prod., tanks, reservoirs, generators	..	..	..	..	..	..	..	..
	289	Other fabricated metal products & service activities	..	..	..	..	..	..	..	..
	29	**Machinery and equipment, nec**	6 291	6 679	7 024	7 105	6 819	7 475	8 288	..
	291	General purpose machinery	3 583	3 984	4 249	4 252	3 794	4 234	4 843	..
	292	Special purpose machinery	2 376	2 323	2 421	2 512	2 655	2 835	3 092	..
	293	Domestic appliances, nec	332	372	354	341	370	406	353	..
	30	**Office, accounting and computing machinery**	782	781	353	359	298	407	359	..
	31	**Electrical machinery and apparatus, nec**	3 259	3 161	3 417	3 497	3 676	3 689	3 896	..
	311	Electric motors, generators and transformers	1 571	1 706	1 726	1 671	1 916	1 856	2 206	..
	312	Electricity distribution and control apparatus	..	..	..	..	..	..	..	..
	313	Insulated wire and cable	844	541	857	819	865	857	905	..
	314	Accumulators, primary cells and primary batteries	844	914	834	1 007	895	976	785	..
	315	Electric lamps and lighting equipment	..	..	..	..	..	..	..	..
	319	Other electrical equipment, nec	..	..	..	..	..	..	..	..
	32	**Radio, TV, communication equip. & apparatus**	1 398	1 257	1 507	1 402	1 542	1 713	2 012	..
	321	Electronic valves, tubes & other electronic compon.	1 252	1 112	1 347	1 226	1 290	1 495	1 887	..
	322	TV, radio transmitters & appar. for line teleph., telegr.	..	..	..	..	..	..	..	..
	323	TV, radio receivers and associated goods	146	145	160	176	252	218	125	..
	33	**Medical, precision, optical instr.; watches, clocks**	1 056	1 157	1 341	1 485	1 710	1 910	2 179	..
	331	Medical equip.; precision instruments and appliances	1 019	1 104	1 276	1 420	1 655	1 833	2 125	..
	332	Optical instruments and photographic equipment	37	53	65	65	55	77	54	..
	333	Watches and clocks	..	..	..	..	..	..	..	..
	34	**Motor vehicles, trailers, and semi-trailers**	996	952	839	934	958	1 101	1 459	..
	35	**Other transport equipment**	7 800	8 815	9 965	10 641	12 163	11 515	12 315	..
	351	Building and repairing of ships and boats	6 184	6 970	8 377	9 044	10 499	9 795	10 804	..
	352	Railway, tramway locomotives and rolling stock	614	507	479	519	569	507	431	..
	353	Aircraft and spacecraft	899	1 209	982	925	961	1 046	914	..
	359	Transport equipment, nec	103	129	127	153	134	167	166	..
	36	**Furniture; manufacturing, nec**	2 604	2 690	2 789	2 986	2 975	3 315	3 372	..
	361	Furniture	1 851	1 927	1 925	1 991	1 955	2 331	2 392	..
	369	Manufacturing, nec	753	763	864	995	1 020	984	980	..
	37	**Recycling**	3	3	4	6	93	187	183	..
E	40-41	**Electricity, gas and water supply**	21 081	22 522	23 989	23 362	22 993	21 758	24 390	..
	40	**Electricity, gas, steam and hot water supply**	20 015	21 381	22 741	22 079	21 642	20 277	22 905	..
	401	Production, collection and distribution of electricity	19 937	21 280	22 618	21 961	21 592	20 204	22 757	..
	41 410	**Collection, purification, distribution of water**	1 066	1 141	1 248	1 283	1 351	1 481	1 485	..
F	45	**Construction**	34 710	31 145	29 308	29 714	27 519	30 037	33 537	..
G	50-52	**Wholesale and retail trade; repairs etc**	..	..	..	..	..	..	..	..
H	55	**Hotels and restaurants**	..	..	..	..	..	..	..	..
I	60-64	**Transport, storage and communications**	..	..	..	..	..	..	..	..
J	65-67	**Financial intermediation**	..	..	..	..	..	..	..	..
K	70-74	**Real estate, renting and business activities**	..	..	..	..	..	..	..	..
L-Q	75-99	**Public admin.; education; health; other services**	..	..	..	..	..	..	..	..
A-Q	01-99	**Grand total**	..	..	..	..	..	..	..	..

Note: ISIC 1531 includes 1532; 2029 includes 2023; 2109 includes 2102; 2412 includes 2421; 2413 includes 243; 2692 includes 2691 and 2693; 2696 includes 2695 and 2699; 3120 includes 3110; 3150 includes 3140 and 3190; 3210 includes 3220; 3320 includes 3330; 3694 includes 3691, 3692, 3693 and 3699; and 453 includes 454.

Table NY.14 **INVESTISSEMENT - INVESTMENT**

Millions de NKr   (Prix courants)

1989	1990	1991	1992	1993	1994	1995	1996			
..	..	..	..	..	..	..	..	..	**Agriculture, chasse et sylviculture** A	01-02
..	..	..	..	..	..	..	..	..	**Pêche** B	05
31 317	33 189	38 842	44 930	51 340	45 297	42 232	..	..	**Activités extractives** C	10-14
..	..	..	..	..	..	..	..	..	Extraction de charbon, de lignite et de tourbe	10
30 898	32 839	38 544	44 649	51 111	45 035	41 853	..	..	Extraction de pétrole brut et de gaz naturel	11
190	99	76	68	56	82	111	..	..	Extraction de minerais métalliques	13
198	235	195	194	135	170	249	..	..	Autres activités extractives	14
11 957	13 098	12 148	12 068	9 650	10 981	15 316	..	..	**Activités de fabrication** D	15-37
2 663	2 372	2 490	2 580	2 524	2 672	2 699	..	..	**Produits alimentaires et boissons**	15
361	275	421	444	683	423	360	..	..	Boissons		155
13	13	11	18	9	23	14	..	..	**Produits à base de tabac**	16	160
127	12	125	86	172	155	172	..	..	**Textiles**	17
..	..	..	..	..	..	..	..	..	Filature, tissage et achèvement des textiles		171
..	..	..	..	..	..	..	..	..	Autres articles textiles		172
..	..	..	..	..	..	..	..	..	Etoffes et articles de bonneterie		173
25	13	14	8	19	26	35	..	..	**Habillement; préparation, teinture des fourrures**	18
..	..	..	..	..	..	..	..	..	Articles d'habillement autres qu'en fourrure		181
..	..	..	..	..	..	..	..	..	Préparation, teinture des fourrures; art. en fourrure		182
12	8	10	17	5	18	15	..	..	**Travail des cuirs; articles en cuir; chaussures**	19
..	..	..	..	..	..	..	..	..	Apprêt et tannage des cuirs et articles en cuirs		191
..	..	..	..	..	..	..	..	..	Chaussures		192
657	763	484	459	290	767	756	..	..	**Bois et articles en bois et liège (sauf meubles)**	20
429	448	328	307	171	502	399	..	..	Sciage et rabotage du bois		201
228	315	156	152	119	265	357	..	..	Articles en bois, liège, vannerie, sparterie		202
630	1 139	1 244	2 976	942	625	1 482	..	..	**Papier et carton; articles en papier et en carton**	21
543	719	689	644	792	996	1 267	..	..	**Edition, imprimerie et reproduction**	22
303	387	350	406	411	578	511	..	..	Edition		221
240	332	339	238	365	408	734	..	..	Imprimerie et activités annexes		222
..	..	..	..	16	10	22	..	..	Reproduction de supports enregistrés		223
1 239	1 385	267	219	360	262	477	..	..	**Cokéfaction; prod. pétroliers; comb. nucléaires**	23
1 366	1 486	1 903	1 127	1 051	1 182	2 805	..	..	**Produits chimiques**	24
1 110	1 048	1 427	781	650	761	2 538	..	..	Produits chimiques de base		241
256	438	476	346	401	421	267	..	..	Autres produits chimiques		242
..	..	..	..	..	..	..	..	..	Fibres synthétiques ou artificielles		243
247	278	277	194	225	257	357	..	..	**Articles en caoutchouc et en matières plastiques**	25
..	..	..	..	..	..	..	..	..	Articles en caoutchouc		251
..	..	..	..	..	..	..	..	..	Articles en matières plastiques		252
773	895	758	68	307	528	807	..	..	**Autres produits minéraux non métalliques**	26
133	53	37	58	28	37	80	..	..	Verre et articles en verre		261
640	842	721	10	279	491	727	..	..	Produits minéraux non métalliques, nca		269
1 303	1 386	1 202	908	558	905	1 125	..	..	**Produits métallurgiques de base**	27
365	518	305	153	121	307	422	..	..	Sidérurgie et première transformation de l'acier		271
927	858	884	735	399	554	636	..	..	Métallurgie; métaux précieux et non ferreux		272
11	10	13	20	38	44	67	..	..	Fonderie		273
380	383	370	459	223	268	442	..	..	**Ouvrages en métaux, sauf machines et matériel**	28
..	..	..	..	..	..	..	..	..	Constr. et menuiserie métal.; réservoirs; générateurs		281
..	..	..	..	..	..	..	..	..	Autres ouvrages en métaux		289
522	590	591	544	440	463	678	..	..	**Machines et matériel, nca**	29
261	328	345	315	275	250	323	..	..	Machines d'usage général		291
219	220	203	198	138	180	314	..	..	Machines d'usage spécifique		292
42	42	43	31	27	33	41	..	..	Appareils domestiques, nca		293
- 212	..	45	6	11	28	58	..	..	**Mach. de bureau, comptables, matériel inform.**	30
439	430	413	321	242	224	276	..	..	**Machines et appareils électriques, nca**	31
153	177	169	114	103	99	141	..	..	Moteurs, génératrices et transformateurs électriques		311
..	..	..	..	..	..	..	..	..	Matériel électrique de distribution et de commande		312
179	165	167	116	112	92	106	..	..	Fils et câbles électriques isolés		313
107	88	77	91	27	33	29	..	..	Accumulateurs, piles électriques		314
..	..	..	..	..	..	..	..	..	Lampes électriques et appareils d'éclairage		315
..	..	..	..	..	..	..	..	..	Autres matériels électriques, nca		319
180	87	167	113	137	178	179	..	..	**Equip. et appar. de radio, TV, communication**	32
158	77	157	104	125	169	173	..	..	Tubes et valves électroniques; autres composants		321
..	..	..	..	..	..	..	..	..	Emetteurs radio et TV; app. téléphonie, télégraphie		322
22	10	10	9	12	9	6	..	..	Récepteurs radio et TV et articles associés		323
72	97	82	139	119	183	277	..	..	**Instruments médicaux, de précision, d'optique**	33
69	95	80	134	117	181	267	..	..	Appareils médicaux et de précision		331
3	2	2	5	2	2	10	..	..	Instruments d'optique ; matériel photographique		332
..	..	..	..	..	..	..	..	..	Horlogerie		333
99	97	125	89	86	135	200	..	..	**Véhicules automobiles et nemorques**	34
664	640	608	902	919	808	834	..	..	**Autres matériels de transport**	35
397	522	545	796	736	684	687	..	..	Construction et réparation de navires		351
17	22	13	42	129	57	21	..	..	Construction de matériel ferroviaire roulant		352
228	90	41	55	35	55	119	..	..	Construction aéronautique et spatiale		353
22	6	9	9	19	12	7	..	..	Autres équipements de transport		359
215	303	273	191	214	251	343	..	..	**Meubles; activités de fabrication, nca**	36
120	191	157	102	131	192	265	..	..	Meubles		361
95	112	116	89	83	59	78	..	..	Activités de fabrication, nca		369
..	2	..	..	5	27	18	..	..	**Récupération**	37
7 944	6 602	6 657	5 939	6 058	5 623	6 121	..	..	**Production et distrib. d'électricité, de gaz, d'eau** E	40-41
7 236	5 942	5 694	5 158	5 262	4 704	5 106	..	..	**Electricité, gaz, vapeur et eau chaude**	40
6 962	5 742	5 608	5 026	5 207	4 647	5 027	..	..	Production, collecte et distribution d'électricité		401
708	660	963	781	796	919	1 015	..	..	Captage, épuration et distribution d'eau	41	410
967	1 009	577	876	666	706	937	..	..	**Construction** F	45
..	..	..	..	..	..	..	..	..	**Commerce de gros et de détail; réparation** G	50-52
..	..	..	..	..	..	..	..	..	**Hôtels et restaurants** H	55
..	..	..	..	..	..	..	..	..	**Transports, entreposage et communications** I	60-64
..	..	..	..	..	..	..	..	..	**Intermédiation financière** J	65-67
..	..	..	..	..	..	..	..	..	**Immobilier, locations, services aux entreprises** K	70-74
..	..	..	..	..	..	..	..	..	**Admin. publique; éducation; santé; autres** L-Q	75-99
..	..	..	..	..	..	..	..	..	**Grand total** A-Q	01-99

Column heading (right): CITI révision 3

Note: ISIC 1531 includes 1532; 2029 includes 2023; 2109 includes 2102; 2412 includes 2421; 2413 includes 243; 2692 includes 2691 and 2693; 2696 includes 2695 and 2699; 3120 includes 3110; 3150 includes 3140 and 3190; 3210 includes 3220; 3320 includes 3330; 3694 includes 3691, 3692, 3693 and 3699; and 453 includes 454.

Statistiques des Structures Industrielles
OCDE, © 1998

Table NY.15 **INVESTMENT IN MACHINERY AND EQUIPMENT - DÉPENSES EN MACHINES ET ÉQUIPEMENT**

Millions of NKr (Current Prices)

ISIC revision 3			1989	1990	1991	1992	1993	1994	1995	1996
A	01-02	**Agriculture, hunting and forestry**	..	..	1 918	1 749	1 997	..	..	..
B	05	**Fishing**	..	..	147	151	203	..	..	..
C	10-14	**Mining and quarrying**	..	..	1 192	1 761	2 471	..	..	..
	10	Mining of coal and lignite; extraction of peat	..	..	20	14	9	..	..	..
	11	Crude petroleum & natural gas; related service activ.	..	..	1 017	1 623	2 347	..	..	..
	13	Mining of metal ores	..	..	34	19	12	..	..	..
	14	Other mining and quarrying	..	..	121	105	103	..	..	..
D	15-37	**Total manufacturing**	..	..	8 151	6 678	6 056	..	..	..
	15	**Food products and beverages**	..	..	1 594	1 601	1 465	..	..	..
	155	Beverages	..	..	295	299	421	..	..	..
	16 160	**Tobacco products**	..	..	6	11	7	..	..	..
	17	**Textiles**	..	..	109	67	160	..	..	..
	171	Spinning, weaving and finishing of textiles	..	..	..	..	..	..	..	..
	172	Other textiles	..	..	..	..	..	..	..	..
	173	Knitted and crocheted fabrics and articles	..	..	..	..	..	..	..	..
	18	**Wearing apparel dressing & dyeing of fur**	..	..	9	8	12	..	..	..
	181	Wearing apparel, except fur apparel	..	..	..	..	..	..	..	..
	182	Dressing and dyeing of fur; articles of fur	..	..	..	..	..	..	..	..
	19	**Tanning, dressing leather; leather artic.; footwear**	..	..	7	11	3	..	..	..
	191	Tanning, dressing leather; manuf. of leather articles	..	..	..	..	..	..	..	..
	192	Footwear	..	..	..	..	..	..	..	..
	20	**Wood and cork products, ex. furniture**	..	..	323	329	199	..	..	..
	201	Sawmilling and planing of wood	..	..	211	192	102	..	..	..
	202	Products of wood, cork, straw & plaiting material	..	..	112	137	97	..	..	..
	21	**Paper and paper products**	..	..	572	576	509	..	..	..
	22	**Publishing, printing & reprod. of recorded media**	..	..	570	439	674	..	..	..
	221	Publishing	..	..	284	241	367	..	..	..
	222	Printing and related service activities	..	..	286	198	291	..	..	..
	223	Reproduction of recorded media	..	..	..	..	16	..	..	..
	23	**Coke, refined petroleum products & nuclear fuel**	..	..	197	41	67	..	..	..
	24	**Chemicals and chemical products**	..	..	1 130	769	618	..	..	..
	241	Basic chemicals	..	..	810	516	353	..	..	..
	242	Other chemical products	..	..	320	253	265	..	..	..
	243	Man-made fibres	..	..	..	..	..	..	..	..
	25	**Rubber and plastic products**	..	..	270	150	188	..	..	..
	251	Rubber products	..	..	..	..	..	..	..	..
	252	Plastic products	..	..	..	..	..	..	..	..
	26	**Other non-metallic mineral products**	..	..	530	277	152	..	..	..
	261	Glass and glass products	..	..	28	34	23	..	..	..
	269	Non-metallic mineral products, nec	..	..	502	243	129	..	..	..
	27	**Basic metals**	..	..	937	590	349	..	..	..
	271	Basic iron and steel	..	..	231	50	32	..	..	..
	272	Basic precious and non-ferrous metals	..	..	697	526	289	..	..	..
	273	Casting of metals	..	..	9	14	28	..	..	..
	28	**Fabricated metal products, ex. machin. & equip.**	..	..	254	306	135	..	..	..
	281	Structural metal prod., tanks, reservoirs, generators	..	..	87	65	60	..	..	..
	289	Other fabricated metal products & service activities	..	..	167	241	75	..	..	..
	29	**Machinery and equipment, nec**	..	..	451	460	304	..	..	..
	291	General purpose machinery	..	..	250	270	175	..	..	..
	292	Special purpose machinery	..	..	167	168	105	..	..	..
	293	Domestic appliances, nec	..	..	34	22	24	..	..	..
	30	**Office, accounting and computing machinery**	..	..	46	7	11	..	..	..
	31	**Electrical machinery and apparatus, nec**	..	..	288	191	185	..	..	..
	311	Electric motors, generators and transformers	..	..	..	..	..	..	..	..
	312	Electricity distribution and control apparatus	..	..	139	95	74	..	..	..
	313	Insulated wire and cable	..	..	101	45	84	..	..	..
	314	Accumulators, primary cells and primary batteries	..	..	..	..	..	..	..	..
	315	Electric lamps and lighting equipment	..	..	48	51	27	..	..	..
	319	Other electrical equipment, nec	..	..	..	..	..	..	..	..
	32	**Radio, TV, communication equip. & apparatus**	..	..	157	106	128	..	..	..
	321	Electronic valves, tubes & other electronic compon.	..	..	..	..	..	..	..	..
	322	TV, radio transmitters & appar. for line teleph., telegr.	..	..	148	99	117	..	..	..
	323	TV, radio receivers and associated goods	..	..	9	7	11	..	..	..
	33	**Medical, precision, optical instr.; watches, clocks**	..	..	67	108	93	..	..	..
	331	Medical equip.; precision instruments and appliances	..	..	65	103	91	..	..	..
	332	Optical instruments and photographic equipment	..	..	2	5	2	..	..	..
	333	Watches and clocks	..	..	..	..	..	..	..	..
	34	**Motor vehicles, trailers, and semi-trailers**	..	..	131	84	105	..	..	..
	35	**Other transport equipment**	..	..	299	390	513	..	..	..
	351	Building and repairing of ships and boats	..	..	250	340	383	..	..	..
	352	Railway, tramway locomotives and rolling stock	..	..	10	9	83	..	..	..
	353	Aircraft and spacecraft	..	..	29	36	29	..	..	..
	359	Transport equipment, nec	..	..	10	5	18	..	..	..
	36	**Furniture; manufacturing, nec**	..	..	204	157	178	..	..	..
	361	Furniture	..	..	111	83	105	..	..	..
	369	Manufacturing, nec	..	..	93	74	73	..	..	..
	37	**Recycling**	..	..	..	..	1	..	..	..
E	40-41	**Electricity, gas and water supply**	..	..	2 552	2 456	3 013	..	..	..
	40	**Electricity, gas, steam and hot water supply**	..	..	2 529	2 435	2 991	..	..	..
	401	Production, collection and distribution of electricity	..	..	2 500	2 391	2 973	..	..	..
	41 410	**Collection, purification, distribution of water**	..	..	23	21	22	..	..	..
F	45	**Construction**	..	..	419	423	301	..	..	..
G	50-52	**Wholesale and retail trade; repairs etc**	..	..	6 616	6 731	6 985	..	..	..
H	55	**Hotels and restaurants**	..	..	366	381	536	..	..	..
I	60-64	**Transport, storage and communications**	..	..	3 763	4 209	4 547	..	..	..
J	65-67	**Financial intermediation**	..	..	748	854	924	..	..	..
K	70-74	**Real estate, renting and business activities**	..	..	2 014	1 721	2 177	..	..	..
L-Q	75-99	**Public admin.; education; health; other services**	..	..	8 170	8 879	9 257	..	..	..
A-Q	01-99	**Grand total**	..	..	36 056	35 993	38 467	..	..	..

Note: ISIC 1531 includes 1532; 2029 includes 2023; 2109 includes 2102; 2412 includes 2421; 2413 includes 243; 2692 includes 2691 and 2693; 2696 includes 2695 and 2699; 3120 includes 3110; 3150 includes 3140 and 3190; 3210 includes 3220; 3320 includes 3330; 3694 includes 3691, 3692, 3693 and 3699; and 453 includes 454.

Table NY.16 **EMPLOI - EMPLOYMENT**

Milliers

1989	1990	1991	1992	1993	1994	1995	1996			CITI révision 3	
..	..	..	..	..	..	..	..	**Agriculture, chasse et sylviculture**	**A**	**01-02**	
..	..	..	..	..	..	..	..	**Pêche**	**B**	**05**	
24.4	24.6	25.3	25.1	26.1	26.0	25.7	..	**Activités extractives**	**C**	**10-14**	
..	..	..	..	..	..	..	..	Extraction de charbon, de lignite et de tourbe		**10**	
18.4	19.0	20.0	20.3	21.4	21.4	21.2	..	Extraction de pétrole brut et de gaz naturel		**11**	
2.1	2.0	1.8	1.6	1.5	1.4	1.2	..	Extraction de minerais métalliques		**13**	
3.4	3.1	3.0	2.7	2.8	2.8	3.0	..	Autres activités extractives		**14**	
303.6	294.4	284.7	279.4	284.4	292.5	299.6	..	**Activités de fabrication**	**D**	**15-37**	
52.3	50.8	49.6	49.6	51.3	52.8	53.3	..	**Produits alimentaires et boissons**		**15**	
5.0	5.0	5.0	5.0	5.0	5.7	5.6	..	Boissons			155
0.8	0.7	0.7	0.7	0.6	0.6	0.6	..	**Produits à base de tabac**		**16**	160
7.2	6.8	6.3	6.5	6.5	6.6	5.9	..	**Textiles**		**17**	
..	..	..	..	..	..	..	..	Filature, tissage et achèvement des textiles			171
..	..	..	..	..	..	..	..	Autres articles textiles			172
..	..	..	..	..	..	..	..	Etoffes et articles de bonneterie			173
2.7	2.5	2.3	2.3	2.2	2.2	2.8	..	**Habillement; préparation, teinture des fourrures**		**18**	
..	..	..	..	..	..	..	..	Articles d'habillement autres qu'en fourrure			181
..	..	..	..	..	..	..	..	Préparation, teinture des fourrures; art. en fourrure			182
1.0	1.0	0.9	0.9	1.0	1.0	0.9	..	**Travail des cuirs; articles en cuir; chaussures**		**19**	
..	..	..	..	..	..	..	..	Apprêt et tannage des cuirs et articles en cuirs			191
..	..	..	..	..	..	..	..	Chaussures			192
22.0	19.6	17.7	15.5	15.6	16.4	16.6	..	**Bois et articles en bois et liège (sauf meubles)**		**20**	
7.9	7.5	6.8	6.6	6.3	6.3	6.2	..	Sciage et rabotage du bois			201
14.1	12.0	10.8	8.9	9.3	10.1	10.4	..	Articles en bois, liège, vannerie, sparterie			202
11.9	11.6	11.4	10.9	10.8	10.9	11.3	..	**Papier et carton; articles en papier et en carton**		**21**	
37.6	37.1	36.5	36.1	37.4	39.1	39.4	..	**Edition, imprimerie et reproduction**		**22**	
23.8	23.6	23.4	23.0	23.8	24.9	25.3	..	Edition			221
13.7	13.4	13.0	13.1	13.1	13.7	13.5	..	Imprimerie et activités annexes			222
0.1	0.1	0.1	0.1	0.5	0.5	0.6	..	Reproduction de supports enregistrés			223
1.9	1.8	1.9	1.8	2.0	2.0	1.9	..	**Cokéfaction; prod. pétroliers; comb. nucléaires**		**23**	
16.4	15.8	15.0	15.1	15.2	15.1	15.7	..	**Produits chimiques**		**24**	
10.3	9.9	9.1	9.0	9.1	9.0	9.4	..	Produits chimiques de base			241
6.1	5.8	6.0	6.1	6.2	6.1	6.4	..	Autres produits chimiques			242
..	..	..	..	..	..	..	..	Fibres synthétiques ou artificielles			243
6.8	6.4	6.1	5.5	5.8	5.8	6.0	..	**Articles en caoutchouc et en matières plastiques**		**25**	
..	..	..	..	..	..	..	..	Articles en caoutchouc			251
..	..	..	..	..	..	..	..	Articles en matières plastiques			252
10.8	10.3	9.0	8.6	8.2	8.5	8.5	..	**Autres produits minéraux non métalliques**		**26**	
1.7	1.6	1.7	1.6	1.5	1.6	1.6	..	Verre et articles en verre			261
9.1	8.6	7.3	6.9	6.6	6.9	6.9	..	Produits minéraux non métalliques, nca			269
17.8	17.2	16.8	15.4	16.1	16.4	16.6	..	**Produits métallurgiques de base**		**27**	
5.5	5.3	5.1	4.8	4.6	4.6	4.6	..	Sidérurgie et première transformation de l'acier			271
11.9	11.6	11.4	10.4	10.0	10.1	10.1	..	Métallurgie; métaux précieux et non ferreux			272
0.3	0.3	0.3	0.3	1.5	1.7	1.9	..	Fonderie			273
18.3	17.9	16.4	16.1	14.9	15.9	17.0	..	**Ouvrages en métaux, sauf machines et matériel**		**28**	
..	..	..	..	..	..	..	..	Constr. et menuiserie métal.; réservoirs; générateurs			281
..	..	..	..	..	..	..	..	Autres ouvrages en métaux			289
24.4	23.4	22.7	23.3	22.9	24.1	24.5	..	**Machines et matériel, nca**		**29**	
13.7	13.8	13.4	13.8	13.3	14.1	14.1	..	Machines d'usage général			291
9.5	8.4	8.1	8.4	8.6	8.8	9.3	..	Machines d'usage spécifique			292
1.4	1.2	1.1	1.1	1.1	1.1	1.1	..	Appareils domestiques, nca			293
3.4	3.0	1.3	1.1	1.1	1.1	1.0	..	**Mach. de bureau, comptables, matériel inform.**		**30**	
11.3	11.1	10.6	10.5	10.1	9.8	10.3	..	**Machines et appareils électriques, nca**		**31**	
5.8	6.0	5.7	5.5	5.8	5.4	6.1	..	Moteurs, génératrices et transformateurs électriques			311
..	..	..	..	..	..	..	..	Matériel électrique de distribution et de commande			312
2.2	2.0	2.0	2.0	1.8	1.9	2.0	..	Fils et câbles électriques isolés			313
3.3	3.1	2.9	3.0	2.5	2.6	2.3	..	Accumulateurs, piles électriques			314
..	..	..	..	..	..	..	..	Lampes électriques et appareils d'éclairage			315
..	..	..	..	..	..	..	..	Autres matériels électriques, nca			319
5.5	4.8	5.1	4.3	4.6	4.8	5.1	..	**Equip. et appar. de radio, TV, communication**		**32**	
4.9	4.2	4.5	3.8	3.9	4.2	4.7	..	Tubes et valves électroniques; autres composants			321
..	..	..	..	..	..	..	..	Emetteurs radio et TV; app. téléphonie, télégraphie			322
0.6	0.6	0.6	0.5	0.7	0.6	0.4	..	Récepteurs radio et TV et articles associés			323
4.0	4.0	4.2	4.7	5.5	5.6	6.2	..	**Instruments médicaux, de précision, d'optique**		**33**	
3.9	3.9	4.1	4.5	5.3	5.5	6.1	..	Appareils médicaux et de précision			331
0.2	0.2	0.1	0.1	0.1	0.1	0.1	..	Instruments d'optique ; matériel photographique			332
..	..	..	..	..	..	..	..	Horlogerie			333
3.8	3.4	3.0	3.2	2.9	3.2	4.4	..	**Véhicules automobiles et nemorques**		**34**	
32.0	33.9	36.0	34.8	38.7	38.1	38.6	..	**Autres matériels de transport**		**35**	
25.4	27.0	29.7	30.7	33.2	32.3	33.5	..	Construction et réparation de navires			351
2.7	2.1	1.9	1.8	1.8	1.9	1.8	..	Construction de matériel ferroviaire roulant			352
3.4	4.3	4.0	3.3	3.3	3.4	2.8	..	Construction aéronautique et spatiale			353
0.4	0.5	0.4	0.4	0.5	0.5	0.5	..	Autres équipements de transport			359
11.9	11.6	11.3	11.1	10.9	11.9	12.8	..	**Meubles; activités de fabrication, nca**		**36**	
8.5	8.2	7.8	7.5	7.5	8.3	8.7	..	Meubles			361
3.4	3.4	3.6	3.6	3.4	3.7	4.1	..	Activités de fabrication, nca			369
				0.4	0.5	0.5	..	**Récupération**		**37**	
20.9	20.8	20.6	20.7	20.6	20.7	20.7	..	**Production et distrib. d'électricité, de gaz, d'eau**	**E**	**40-41**	
20.2	20.0	19.7	19.9	19.7	19.7	19.9	..	**Electricité, gaz, vapeur et eau chaude**		**40**	
20.2	20.1	19.8	19.8	19.7	19.8	19.9	..	Production, collecte et distribution d'électricité			401
0.8	0.8	0.8	0.8	0.9	0.9	0.9	..	**Captage, épuration et distribution d'eau**		**41**	410
144.2	134.7	120.3	114.4	104.3	106.3	110.5	..	**Construction**	**F**	**45**	
..	..	..	..	..	..	..	..	**Commerce de gros et de détail; réparation**	**G**	**50-52**	
..	..	..	..	..	..	..	..	**Hôtels et restaurants**	**H**	**55**	
..	..	..	..	..	..	..	..	**Transports, entreposage et communications**	**I**	**60-64**	
..	..	..	..	..	..	..	..	**Intermédiation financière**	**J**	**65-67**	
..	..	..	..	..	..	..	..	**Immobilier, locations, services aux entreprises**	**K**	**70-74**	
..	..	..	..	..	..	..	..	**Admin. publique; éducation; santé; autres**	**L-Q**	**75-99**	
..	..	..	..	..	..	..	..	**Grand total**	**A-Q**	**01-99**	

Note: ISIC 1531 includes 1532; 2029 includes 2023; 2109 includes 2102; 2412 includes 2421; 2413 includes 243; 2692 includes 2691 and 2693; 2696 includes 2695 and 2699; 3120 includes 3110; 3150 includes 3140 and 3190; 3210 includes 3220; 3320 includes 3330; 3694 includes 3691, 3692, 3693 and 3699; and 453 includes 454.

Statistiques des Structures Industrielles
OCDE, © 1998

Table NY.17 EMPLOYMENT, EMPLOYEES - EMPLOI, SALARIÉS

Thousands

ISIC revision 3			1989	1990	1991	1992	1993	1994	1995	1996
A	01-02	**Agriculture, hunting and forestry**	..	..	17.2	16.3	16.6	..	..	..
B	05	**Fishing**	..	..	7.4	7.3	6.9	..	..	..
C	10-14	**Mining and quarrying**	..	..	24.6	24.4	25.5	..	..	..
	10	Mining of coal and lignite; extraction of peat	..	..	0.5	0.5	0.4	..	..	..
	11	Crude petroleum & natural gas; related service activ.	..	..	19.6	19.8	20.9	..	..	..
	13	Mining of metal ores	..	..	1.8	1.6	1.5	..	..	..
	14	Other mining and quarrying	..	..	2.7	2.5	2.7	..	..	..
D	15-37	**Total manufacturing**	..	..	259.5	253.7	257.7	..	..	..
	15	**Food products and beverages**	..	..	45.5	45.6	47.0	..	..	..
		155 Beverages	..	..	4.7	4.7	4.8	..	..	..
	16	160 **Tobacco products**	..	..	0.7	0.7	0.6	..	..	..
	17	**Textiles**	..	..	5.2	5.3	5.2	..	..	..
		171 Spinning, weaving and finishing of textiles	..	..	..	..	..	..	..	..
		172 Other textiles	..	..	..	..	..	..	..	..
		173 Knitted and crocheted fabrics and articles	..	..	..	..	..	..	..	..
	18	**Wearing apparel dressing & dyeing of fur**	..	..	1.7	1.6	1.5	..	..	..
		181 Wearing apparel, except fur apparel	..	..	..	..	..	..	..	..
		182 Dressing and dyeing of fur; articles of fur	..	..	..	..	..	..	..	..
	19	**Tanning, dressing leather; leather artic.; footwear**	..	..	0.8	0.8	0.8	..	..	..
		191 Tanning, dressing leather; manuf. of leather articles	..	..	..	..	..	..	..	..
		192 Footwear	..	..	..	..	..	..	..	..
	20	**Wood and cork products, ex. furniture**	..	..	15.4	13.3	13.3	..	..	..
		201 Sawmilling and planing of wood	..	..	6.0	5.6	5.4	..	..	..
		202 Products of wood, cork, straw & plaiting material	..	..	9.4	7.7	7.9	..	..	..
	21	**Paper and paper products**	..	..	11.0	10.5	10.4	..	..	..
	22	**Publishing, printing & reprod. of recorded media**	..	..	28.4	28.3	29.2	..	..	..
		221 Publishing	..	..	18.5	18.2	18.8	..	..	..
		222 Printing and related service activities	..	..	9.9	10.1	10.0	..	..	..
		223 Reproduction of recorded media	..	..	0.0	0.0	0.4	..	..	..
	23	**Coke, refined petroleum products & nuclear fuel**	..	..	1.9	1.8	1.9	..	..	..
	24	**Chemicals and chemical products**	..	..	14.6	14.6	14.7	..	..	..
		241 Basic chemicals	..	..	8.8	8.8	8.8	..	..	..
		242 Other chemical products	..	..	5.8	5.8	5.9	..	..	..
		243 Man-made fibres	..	..	..	..	..	..	..	..
	25	**Rubber and plastic products**	..	..	5.7	5.1	5.4	..	..	..
		251 Rubber products	..	..	..	..	..	..	..	..
		252 Plastic products	..	..	..	..	..	..	..	..
	26	**Other non-metallic mineral products**	..	..	8.2	7.9	7.5	..	..	..
		261 Glass and glass products	..	..	1.6	1.5	1.4	..	..	..
		269 Non-metallic mineral products, nec	..	..	6.6	6.4	6.1	..	..	..
	27	**Basic metals**	..	..	15.8	14.8	15.4	..	..	..
		271 Basic iron and steel	..	..	4.8	4.6	4.4	..	..	..
		272 Basic precious and non-ferrous metals	..	..	10.8	9.9	9.6	..	..	..
		273 Casting of metals	..	..	0.2	0.3	1.4	..	..	..
	28	**Fabricated metal products, ex. machin. & equip.**	..	..	15.3	14.6	13.4	..	..	..
		281 Structural metal prod., tanks, reservoirs, generators	..	..	7.2	6.9	6.5	..	..	..
		289 Other fabricated metal products & service activities	..	..	8.1	7.7	6.9	..	..	..
	29	**Machinery and equipment, nec**	..	..	21.1	21.4	21.0	..	..	..
		291 General purpose machinery	..	..	12.6	12.8	12.3	..	..	..
		292 Special purpose machinery	..	..	7.4	7.6	7.7	..	..	..
		293 Domestic appliances, nec	..	..	1.1	1.0	1.0	..	..	..
	30	**Office, accounting and computing machinery**	..	..	1.2	1.1	1.1	..	..	..
	31	**Electrical machinery and apparatus, nec**	..	..	10.2	10.0	9.6	..	..	..
		311 Electric motors, generators and transformers	..	..	..	..	..	..	..	..
		312 Electricity distribution and control apparatus	..	..	5.5	5.3	5.6	..	..	..
		313 Insulated wire and cable	..	..	2.0	1.9	1.7	..	..	..
		314 Accumulators, primary cells and primary batteries	..	..	..	..	..	..	..	..
		315 Electric lamps and lighting equipment	..	..	2.7	2.8	2.3	..	..	..
		319 Other electrical equipment, nec	..	..	..	..	..	..	..	..
	32	**Radio, TV, communication equip. & apparatus**	..	..	4.9	4.1	4.4	..	..	..
		321 Electronic valves, tubes & other electronic compon.	..	..	..	..	..	..	..	..
		322 TV, radio transmitters & appar. for line teleph., telegr.	..	..	4.3	3.6	3.8	..	..	..
		323 TV, radio receivers and associated goods	..	..	0.6	0.5	0.6	..	..	..
	33	**Medical, precision, optical instr.; watches, clocks**	..	..	4.0	4.3	5.1	..	..	..
		331 Medical equip.; precision instruments and appliances	..	..	3.9	4.2	5.0	..	..	..
		332 Optical instruments and photographic equipment	..	..	0.1	0.1	0.1	..	..	..
		333 Watches and clocks	..	..	..	..	..	..	..	..
	34	**Motor vehicles, trailers, and semi-trailers**	..	..	2.9	3.0	2.7	..	..	..
	35	**Other transport equipment**	..	..	34.2	34.3	36.7	..	..	..
		351 Building and repairing of ships and boats	..	..	28.0	28.9	31.3	..	..	..
		352 Railway, tramway locomotives and rolling stock	..	..	1.9	1.8	1.7	..	..	..
		353 Aircraft and spacecraft	..	..	3.9	3.2	3.2	..	..	..
		359 Transport equipment, nec	..	..	0.4	0.4	0.5	..	..	..
	36	**Furniture; manufacturing, nec**	..	..	10.8	10.6	10.4	..	..	..
		361 Furniture	..	..	7.4	7.1	7.2	..	..	..
		369 Manufacturing, nec	..	..	3.4	3.5	3.2	..	..	..
	37	**Recycling**	..	..	0.0	0.0	0.4	..	..	..
E	40-41	**Electricity, gas and water supply**	..	..	19.8	20.0	19.8	..	..	..
	40	**Electricity, gas, steam and hot water supply**	..	..	19.0	19.2	18.9	..	..	..
		401 Production, collection and distribution of electricity	..	..	18.8	19.0	18.7	..	..	..
	41	410 **Collection, purification, distribution of water**	..	..	0.8	0.8	0.9	..	..	..
F	45	**Construction**	..	..	95.1	90.0	81.2	..	..	..
G	50-52	**Wholesale and retail trade; repairs etc**	..	..	225.9	221.7	217.1	..	..	..
H	55	**Hotels and restaurants**	..	..	40.5	40.7	40.2	..	..	..
I	60-64	**Transport, storage and communications**	..	..	164.1	161.0	158.1	..	..	..
J	65-67	**Financial intermediation**	..	..	53.8	51.6	50.0	..	..	..
K	70-74	**Real estate, renting and business activities**	..	..	92.2	93.3	97.6	..	..	..
L-Q	75-99	**Public admin.; education; health; other services**	..	..	577.9	592.9	608.1	..	..	..
A-Q	01-99	**Grand total**	..	..	1 577.9	1 572.9	1 578.9	..	..	..

Note: ISIC 1531 includes 1532; 2029 includes 2023; 2109 includes 2102; 2412 includes 2421; 2413 includes 243; 2692 includes 2691 and 2693; 2696 includes 2695 and 2699; 3120 includes 3110; 3150 includes 3140 and 3190; 3210 includes 3220; 3320 includes 3330; 3694 includes 3691, 3692, 3693 and 3699; and 453 includes 454.

Table NY.18 SALAIRES ET CHARGES SOCIALES , SALARIÉS - COMPENSATION OF LABOUR, EMPLOYEES

Millions de NKr (Prix courants)

1989	1990	1991	1992	1993	1994	1995	1996			CITI révision 3
..	..	..	..	..	..	..	..	**Agriculture, chasse et sylviculture**	**A**	**01-02**
..	..	..	..	..	..	..	..	**Pêche**	**B**	**05**
9 054	9 604	10 640	11 269	12 070	12 680	12 892	..	**Activités extractives**	**C**	**10-14**
..	..	..	..	..	..	..	..	Extraction de charbon, de lignite et de tourbe		10
7 869	8 403	9 426	10 075	10 863	11 409	11 656	..	Extraction de pétrole brut et de gaz naturel		11
429	425	435	400	386	418	322	..	Extraction de minerais métalliques		13
632	660	652	646	702	725	800	..	Autres activités extractives		14
59 922	61 684	63 859	64 749	67 118	71 111	75 780	..	**Activités de fabrication**	**D**	**15-37**
9 245	9 525	10 009	10 349	10 879	11 623	12 189	..	**Produits alimentaires et boissons**		**15**
1 145	1 159	1 226	1 264	1 296	1 513	1 516	..	Boissons		155
167	169	186	184	180	169	153	..	**Produits à base de tabac**		**16** 160
951	984	973	1 029	1 026	1 105	985	..	**Textiles**		**17**
..	..	..	..	..	..	..	..	Filature, tissage et achèvement des textiles		171
..	..	..	..	..	..	..	..	Autres articles textiles		172
..	..	..	..	..	..	..	..	Etoffes et articles de bonneterie		173
304	309	318	309	298	313	437	..	**Habillement; préparation, teinture des fourrures**		**18**
..	..	..	..	..	..	..	..	Articles d'habillement autres qu'en fourrure		181
..	..	..	..	..	..	..	..	Préparation, teinture des fourrures; art. en fourrure		182
138	145	144	148	155	162	146	..	**Travail des cuirs; articles en cuir; chaussures**		**19**
..	..	..	..	..	..	..	..	Apprêt et tannage des cuirs et articles en cuirs		191
..	..	..	..	..	..	..	..	Chaussures		192
3 386	3 226	3 112	2 721	2 747	3 072	3 284	..	**Bois et articles en bois et liège (sauf meubles)**		**20**
1 195	1 232	1 208	1 165	1 125	1 179	1 222	..	Sciage et rabotage du bois		201
2 191	1 994	1 904	1 556	1 622	1 893	2 062	..	Articles en bois, liège, vannerie, sparterie		202
2 534	2 613	2 690	2 652	2 654	2 795	3 073	..	**Papier et carton; articles en papier et en carton**		**21**
7 135	7 380	7 613	7 749	8 099	8 641	8 983	..	**Edition, imprimerie et reproduction**		**22**
4 627	4 830	5 013	5 041	5 294	5 627	5 895	..	Edition		221
2 508	2 550	2 600	2 708	2 711	2 910	2 964	..	Imprimerie et activités annexes		222
..	..	..	94	104	124	..	..	Reproduction de supports enregistrés		223
506	514	588	573	638	671	653	..	**Cokéfaction; prod. pétroliers; comb. nucléaires**		**23**
3 870	4 023	4 148	4 312	4 399	4 540	4 979	..	**Produits chimiques**		**24**
2 557	2 685	2 660	2 723	2 755	2 888	3 073	..	Produits chimiques de base		241
1 313	1 338	1 488	1 589	1 644	1 652	1 906	..	Autres produits chimiques		242
..	..	..	..	..	..	..	..	Fibres synthétiques ou artificielles		243
1 358	1 376	1 411	1 339	1 432	1 510	1 650	..	**Articles en caoutchouc et en matières plastiques**		**25**
..	..	..	..	..	..	..	..	Articles en caoutchouc		251
..	..	..	..	..	..	..	..	Articles en matières plastiques		252
2 127	2 176	2 081	2 086	2 004	2 160	2 322	..	**Autres produits minéraux non métalliques**		**26**
344	349	405	396	382	431	457	..	Verre et articles en verre		261
1 783	1 827	1 676	1 690	1 622	1 729	1 865	..	Produits minéraux non métalliques, nca		269
4 060	4 151	4 337	4 164	4 448	4 636	4 862	..	**Produits métallurgiques de base**		**27**
1 253	1 286	1 311	1 264	1 251	1 269	1 335	..	Sidérurgie et première transformation de l'acier		271
2 742	2 804	2 961	2 831	2 800	2 890	2 997	..	Métallurgie; métaux précieux et non ferreux		272
65	61	65	69	397	477	530	..	Fonderie		273
3 729	3 876	3 818	3 828	3 610	4 015	4 443	..	**Ouvrages en métaux, sauf machines et matériel**		**28**
..	..	..	..	..	..	..	..	Constr. et menuiserie métal.; réservoirs; générateurs		281
..	..	..	..	..	..	..	..	Autres ouvrages en métaux		289
5 054	5 188	5 389	5 718	5 729	6 232	6 589	..	**Machines et matériel, nca**		**29**
2 852	3 072	3 214	3 407	3 348	3 673	3 826	..	Machines d'usage général		291
1 913	1 825	1 907	2 040	2 113	2 261	2 456	..	Machines d'usage spécifique		292
289	291	268	271	268	298	307	..	Appareils domestiques, nca		293
738	678	310	289	287	315	277	..	**Mach. de bureau, comptables, matériel inform.**		**30**
2 484	2 603	2 661	2 666	2 665	2 684	2 948	..	**Machines et appareils électriques, nca**		**31**
1 312	1 409	1 424	1 402	1 537	1 483	1 747	..	Moteurs, génératrices et transformateurs électriques		311
..	..	..	..	..	..	..	..	Matériel électrique de distribution et de commande		312
482	489	529	526	490	530	573	..	Fils et câbles électriques isolés		313
690	705	708	738	638	671	628	..	Accumulateurs, piles électriques		314
..	..	..	..	..	..	..	..	Lampes électriques et appareils d'éclairage		315
..	..	..	..	..	..	..	..	Autres matériels électriques, nca		319
1 220	1 116	1 307	1 103	1 184	1 332	1 438	..	**Equip. et appar. de radio, TV, communication**		**32**
1 098	984	1 160	968	1 008	1 157	1 330	..	Tubes et valves électroniques; autres composants		321
..	..	..	..	..	..	..	..	Emetteurs radio et TV; app. téléphonie, télégraphie		322
122	132	147	135	176	175	108	..	Récepteurs radio et TV et articles associés		323
860	925	1 036	1 173	1 416	1 514	1 721	..	**Instruments médicaux, de précision, d'optique**		**33**
825	890	1 007	1 145	1 382	1 475	1 686	..	Appareils médicaux et de précision		331
35	35	29	28	34	39	35	..	Instruments d'optique ; matériel photographique		332
..	..	..	..	..	..	..	..	Horlogerie		333
814	783	733	802	738	855	1 210	..	**Véhicules automobiles et nemorques**		**34**
7 163	7 779	8 788	9 336	10 197	10 221	10 760	..	**Autres matériels de transport**		**35**
5 673	6 153	7 209	7 849	8 683	8 603	9 313	..	Construction et réparation de navires		351
636	523	509	516	526	543	520	..	Construction de matériel ferroviaire roulant		352
757	999	970	856	857	930	801	..	Construction aéronautique et spatiale		353
97	104	100	115	131	145	126	..	Autres équipements de transport		359
2 078	2 144	2 206	2 217	2 254	2 437	2 583	..	**Meubles; activités de fabrication, nca**		**36**
1 475	1 503	1 507	1 475	1 537	1 695	1 772	..	Meubles		361
603	641	699	742	717	742	811	..	Activités de fabrication, nca		369
1	1	1	2	79	109	95	..	**Récupération**		**37**
4 844	4 958	5 154	5 331	5 513	5 721	5 923	..	**Production et distrib. d'électricité, de gaz, d'eau**	**E**	**40-41**
4 678	4 780	4 963	5 137	5 297	5 497	5 702	..	**Electricité, gaz, vapeur et eau chaude**		**40**
4 629	4 726	4 906	5 073	5 234	5 432	5 631	..	Production, collecte et distribution d'électricité		401
166	178	191	194	216	224	221	..	**Captage, épuration et distribution d'eau**		**41** 410
25 951	24 915	23 254	22 910	20 980	22 248	23 942	..	**Construction**	**F**	**45**
..	..	..	..	..	..	..	..	**Commerce de gros et de détail; réparation**	**G**	**50-52**
..	..	..	..	..	..	..	..	**Hôtels et restaurants**	**H**	**55**
..	..	..	..	..	..	..	..	**Transports, entreposage et communications**	**I**	**60-64**
..	..	..	..	..	..	..	..	**Intermédiation financière**	**J**	**65-67**
..	..	..	..	..	..	..	..	**Immobilier, locations, services aux entreprises**	**K**	**70-74**
..	..	..	..	..	..	..	..	**Admin. publique; éducation; santé; autres**	**L-Q**	**75-99**
..	..	..	..	..	..	..	..	**Grand total**	**A-Q**	**01-99**

Note : ISIC 1531 includes 1532; 2029 includes 2023; 2109 includes 2102; 2412 includes 2421; 2413 includes 243; 2692 includes 2691 and 2693; 2696 includes 2695 and 2699; 3120 includes 3110; 3150 includes 3140 and 3190; 3210 includes 3220; 3320 includes 3330; 3694 includes 3691, 3692, 3693 and 3699; and 453 includes 454.

Statistiques des Structures Industrielles
OCDE, © 1998

Table NY.19 TOTAL WAGES AND SALARIES - SALAIRES ET TRAITEMENTS, TOTAL

Millions of NKr (Current Prices)

ISIC revision 3			1989	1990	1991	1992	1993	1994	1995	1996
A	01-02	**Agriculture, hunting and forestry**	..	..	2 547	2 485	2 598	..	..	..
B	05	**Fishing**	..	..	1 740	1 778	1 746	..	..	..
C	10-14	**Mining and quarrying**	..	..	8 150	8 477	9 382	..	..	..
	10	Mining of coal and lignite; extraction of peat	..	..	111	108	84	..	..	..
	11	Crude petroleum & natural gas; related service activ.	..	..	7 135	7 509	8 379	..	..	..
	13	Mining of metal ores	..	..	362	332	330	..	..	..
	14	Other mining and quarrying	..	..	542	528	589	..	..	..
D	15-37	**Total manufacturing**	..	..	51 600	52 380	54 997	..	..	..
	15	**Food products and beverages**	..	..	8 173	8 493	9 079	..	..	..
		155 Beverages	..	..	977	1 015	1 047	..	..	..
	16	160 **Tobacco products**	..	..	138	144	133	..	..	..
	17	**Textiles**	..	..	803	853	874	..	..	..
		171 Spinning, weaving and finishing of textiles	..	..	..	..	..	..	..	..
		172 Other textiles	..	..	..	..	..	..	..	..
		173 Knitted and crocheted fabrics and articles	..	..	..	..	..	..	..	..
	18	**Wearing apparel dressing & dyeing of fur**	..	..	269	262	258	..	..	..
		181 Wearing apparel, except fur apparel	..	..	..	..	..	..	..	..
		182 Dressing and dyeing of fur; articles of fur	..	..	..	..	..	..	..	..
	19	**Tanning, dressing leather; leather artic.; footwear**	..	..	119	123	132	..	..	..
		191 Tanning, dressing leather; manuf. of leather articles	..	..	..	..	..	..	..	..
		192 Footwear	..	..	..	..	..	..	..	..
	20	**Wood and cork products, ex. furniture**	..	..	2 575	2 242	2 292	..	..	..
		201 Sawmilling and planing of wood	..	..	994	958	931	..	..	..
		202 Products of wood, cork, straw & plaiting material	..	..	1 581	1 284	1 361	..	..	..
	21	**Paper and paper products**	..	..	2 166	2 123	2 186	..	..	..
	22	**Publishing, printing & reprod. of recorded media**	..	..	6 075	6 209	6 495	..	..	..
		221 Publishing	..	..	3 956	4 000	4 189	..	..	..
		222 Printing and related service activities	..	..	2 119	2 209	2 223	..	..	..
		223 Reproduction of recorded media	..	..			83	..	..	..
	23	**Coke, refined petroleum products & nuclear fuel**	..	..	478	461	517	..	..	..
	24	**Chemicals and chemical products**	..	..	3 232	3 365	3 454	..	..	..
		241 Basic chemicals	..	..	2 069	2 120	2 169	..	..	..
		242 Other chemical products	..	..	1 163	1 245	1 285	..	..	..
		243 Man-made fibres	..	..	..	..	..	..	..	..
	25	**Rubber and plastic products**	..	..	1 150	1 096	1 180	..	..	..
		251 Rubber products	..	..	..	..	..	..	..	..
		252 Plastic products	..	..	..	..	..	..	..	..
	26	**Other non-metallic mineral products**	..	..	1 667	1 668	1 625	..	..	..
		261 Glass and glass products	..	..	322	312	311	..	..	..
		269 Non-metallic mineral products, nec	..	..	1 345	1 356	1 314	..	..	..
	27	**Basic metals**	..	..	3 455	3 294	3 586	..	..	..
		271 Basic iron and steel	..	..	1 039	1 016	1 030	..	..	..
		272 Basic precious and non-ferrous metals	..	..	2 363	2 222	2 224	..	..	..
		273 Casting of metals	..	..	53	56	332	..	..	..
	28	**Fabricated metal products, ex. machin. & equip.**	..	..	3 145	3 153	3 013	..	..	..
		281 Structural metal prod., tanks, reservoirs, generators	..	..	1 495	1 492	1 465	..	..	..
		289 Other fabricated metal products & service activities	..	..	1 650	1 661	1 548	..	..	..
	29	**Machinery and equipment, nec**	..	..	4 362	4 623	4 696	..	..	..
		291 General purpose machinery	..	..	2 617	2 773	2 756	..	..	..
		292 Special purpose machinery	..	..	1 529	1 629	1 716	..	..	..
		293 Domestic appliances, nec	..	..	216	221	224	..	..	..
	30	**Office, accounting and computing machinery**	..	..	242	225	231	..	..	..
	31	**Electrical machinery and apparatus, nec**	..	..	2 113	2 163	2 150	..	..	..
		311 Electric motors, generators and transformers	..	..	..	..	..	..	..	..
		312 Electricity distribution and control apparatus	..	..	1 138	1 147	1 249	..	..	..
		313 Insulated wire and cable	..	..	409	416	384	..	..	..
		314 Accumulators, primary cells and primary batteries	..	..	..	..	..	..	..	..
		315 Electric lamps and lighting equipment	..	..	566	600	517	..	..	..
		319 Other electrical equipment, nec	..	..	..	..	..	..	..	..
	32	**Radio, TV, communication equip. & apparatus**	..	..	1 015	893	987	..	..	..
		321 Electronic valves, tubes & other electronic compon.	..	..	..	..	..	..	..	..
		322 TV, radio transmitters & appar. for line teleph., telegr.	..	..	898	784	844	..	..	..
		323 TV, radio receivers and associated goods	..	..	117	109	143	..	..	..
	33	**Medical, precision, optical instr.; watches, clocks**	..	..	824	939	1 148	..	..	..
		331 Medical equip.; precision instruments and appliances	..	..	803	919	1 123	..	..	..
		332 Optical instruments and photographic equipment	..	..	21	20	25	..	..	..
		333 Watches and clocks	..	..	..	..	..	..	..	..
	34	**Motor vehicles, trailers, and semi-trailers**	..	..	597	652	608	..	..	..
	35	**Other transport equipment**	..	..	7 192	7 583	8 426	..	..	..
		351 Building and repairing of ships and boats	..	..	5 928	6 414	7 222	..	..	..
		352 Railway, tramway locomotives and rolling stock	..	..	387	383	388	..	..	..
		353 Aircraft and spacecraft	..	..	797	695	708	..	..	..
		359 Transport equipment, nec	..	..	80	91	108	..	..	..
	36	**Furniture; manufacturing, nec**	..	..	1 809	1 814	1 859	..	..	..
		361 Furniture	..	..	1 247	1 221	1 287	..	..	..
		369 Manufacturing, nec	..	..	562	593	572	..	..	..
	37	**Recycling**	..	..	1	2	68	..	..	..
E	40-41	**Electricity, gas and water supply**	..	..	4 178	4 333	4 431	..	..	..
	40	**Electricity, gas, steam and hot water supply**	..	..	4 023	4 175	4 252	..	..	..
		401 Production, collection and distribution of electricity	..	..	3 974	4 120	4 199	..	..	..
	41	410 **Collection, purification, distribution of water**	..	..	155	158	179	..	..	..
F	45	**Construction**	..	..	18 923	18 603	17 184	..	..	..
G	50-52	**Wholesale and retail trade; repairs etc**	..	..	41 815	42 485	42 860	..	..	..
H	55	**Hotels and restaurants**	..	..	7 369	7 678	7 774	..	..	..
I	60-64	**Transport, storage and communications**	..	..	30 193	30 646	31 406	..	..	..
J	65-67	**Financial intermediation**	..	..	11 711	11 727	11 951	..	..	..
K	70-74	**Real estate, renting and business activities**	..	..	20 326	21 403	23 352	..	..	..
L-Q	75-99	**Public admin.; education; health; other services**	..	..	103 564	109 997	116 254	..	..	..
A-Q	01-99	**Grand total**	..	..	302 117	311 992	323 934	..	..	..

Note: ISIC 1531 includes 1532; 2029 includes 2023; 2109 includes 2102; 2412 includes 2421; 2413 includes 243; 2692 includes 2691 and 2693; 2696 includes 2695 and 2699; 3120 includes 3110; 3150 includes 3140 and 3190; 3210 includes 3220; 3320 includes 3330; 3694 includes 3691, 3692, 3693 and 3699; and 453 includes 454.

Table NY.20 **CHARGES SOCIALES DES EMPLOYEURS - EMPLOYERS' SOCIAL COSTS**

Millions de NKr (Prix courants)

1989	1990	1991	1992	1993	1994	1995	1996			CITI révision 3	
..	..	411	466	421	..	..	..	**Agriculture, chasse et sylviculture**	A	01-02	
..	..	236	269	227	..	..	..	**Pêche**	B	05	
..	..	2 113	2 332	2 302	..	..	..	**Activités extractives**	C	10-14	
..	..	16	40	35	..	..	..	Extraction de charbon, de lignite et de tourbe		10	
..	..	1 930	2 129	2 115	..	..	..	Extraction de pétrole brut et de gaz naturel		11	
..	..	68	60	50	..	..	..	Extraction de minerais métalliques		13	
..	..	99	103	102	..	..	..	Autres activités extractives		14	
..	..	10 965	10 980	10 625	..	..	..	**Activités de fabrication**	D	15-37	
..	..	1 622	1 625	1 562	..	..	..	**Produits alimentaires et boissons**		15	
..	..	224	221	208	..	..	..	Boissons			155
..	..	45	37	42	..	..	..	**Produits à base de tabac**		16	160
..	..	147	151	130	..	..	..	**Textiles**		17	
..	..	..	..	..	..	..	..	Filature, tissage et achèvement des textiles			171
..	..	..	..	..	..	..	..	Autres articles textiles			172
..	..	..	..	..	..	..	..	Etoffes et articles de bonneterie			173
..	..	45	42	35	..	..	..	**Habillement; préparation, teinture des fourrures**		18	
..	..	..	..	..	..	..	..	Articles d'habillement autres qu'en fourrure			181
..	..	..	..	..	..	..	..	Préparation, teinture des fourrures; art. en fourrure			182
..	..	22	22	20	..	..	..	**Travail des cuirs; articles en cuir; chaussures**		19	
..	..	..	..	..	..	..	..	Apprêt et tannage des cuirs et articles en cuirs			191
..	..	..	..	..	..	..	..	Chaussures			192
..	..	476	420	383	..	..	..	**Bois et articles en bois et liège (sauf meubles)**		20	
..	..	193	186	167	..	..	..	Sciage et rabotage du bois			201
..	..	283	234	216	..	..	..	Articles en bois, liège, vannerie, sparterie			202
..	..	470	472	434	..	..	..	**Papier et carton; articles en papier et en carton**		21	
..	..	1 386	1 376	1 384	..	..	..	**Edition, imprimerie et reproduction**		22	
..	..	959	933	963	..	..	..	Edition			221
..	..	427	443	410	..	..	..	Imprimerie et activités annexes			222
..	..	..	..	11	..	..	..	Reproduction de supports enregistrés			223
..	..	98	100	114	..	..	..	**Cokéfaction; prod. pétroliers; comb. nucléaires**		23	
..	..	836	859	839	..	..	..	**Produits chimiques**		24	
..	..	539	546	518	..	..	..	Produits chimiques de base			241
..	..	297	313	321	..	..	..	Autres produits chimiques			242
..	..	..	..	..	..	..	..	Fibres synthétiques ou artificielles			243
..	..	232	214	216	..	..	..	**Articles en caoutchouc et en matières plastiques**		25	
..	..	..	..	..	..	..	..	Articles en caoutchouc			251
..	..	..	..	..	..	..	..	Articles en matières plastiques			252
..	..	372	374	323	..	..	..	**Autres produits minéraux non métalliques**		26	
..	..	76	75	62	..	..	..	Verre et articles en verre			261
..	..	296	299	261	..	..	..	Produits minéraux non métalliques, nca			269
..	..	795	782	814	..	..	..	**Produits métallurgiques de base**		27	
..	..	238	214	204	..	..	..	Sidérurgie et première transformation de l'acier			271
..	..	546	556	545	..	..	..	Métallurgie; métaux précieux et non ferreux			272
..	..	11	12	65	..	..	..	Fonderie			273
..	..	595	592	514	..	..	..	**Ouvrages en métaux, sauf machines et matériel**		28	
..	..	273	272	240	..	..	..	Constr. et menuiserie métal.; réservoirs; générateurs			281
..	..	322	320	274	..	..	..	Autres ouvrages en métaux			289
..	..	919	974	902	..	..	..	**Machines et matériel, nca**		29	
..	..	536	566	514	..	..	..	Machines d'usage général			291
..	..	337	364	350	..	..	..	Machines d'usage spécifique			292
..	..	46	44	38	..	..	..	Appareils domestiques, nca			293
..	..	53	49	41	..	..	..	**Mach. de bureau, comptables, matériel inform.**		30	
..	..	499	453	461	..	..	..	**Machines et appareils électriques, nca**		31	
..	..	..	..	..	..	..	..	Moteurs, génératrices et transformateurs électriques			311
..	..	263	231	260	..	..	..	Matériel électrique de distribution et de commande			312
..	..	108	98	94	..	..	..	Fils et câbles électriques isolés			313
..	..	..	..	..	..	..	..	Accumulateurs, piles électriques			314
..	..	128	124	107	..	..	..	Lampes électriques et appareils d'éclairage			315
..	..	..	..	..	..	..	..	Autres matériels électriques, nca			319
..	..	270	188	175	..	..	..	**Equip. et appar. de radio, TV, communication**		32	
..	..	..	..	..	..	..	..	Tubes et valves électroniques; autres composants			321
..	..	243	165	145	..	..	..	Emetteurs radio et TV; app. téléphonie, télégraphie			322
..	..	27	23	30	..	..	..	Récepteurs radio et TV et articles associés			323
..	..	194	211	239	..	..	..	**Instruments médicaux, de précision, d'optique**		33	
..	..	189	206	233	..	..	..	Appareils médicaux et de précision			331
..	..	5	5	6	..	..	..	Instruments d'optique ; matériel photographique			332
..	..	..	..	..	..	..	..	Horlogerie			333
..	..	121	133	113	..	..	..	**Véhicules automobiles et nemorques**		34	
..	..	1 416	1 551	1 539	..	..	..	**Autres matériels de transport**		35	
..	..	1 133	1 265	1 261	..	..	..	Construction et réparation de navires			351
..	..	112	123	128	..	..	..	Construction de matériel ferroviaire roulant			352
..	..	153	141	129	..	..	..	Construction aéronautique et spatiale			353
..	..	18	22	21	..	..	..	Autres équipements de transport			359
..	..	352	355	334	..	..	..	**Meubles; activités de fabrication, nca**		36	
..	..	230	221	208	..	..	..	Meubles			361
..	..	122	134	126	..	..	..	Activités de fabrication, nca			369
..	..	..	..	11	..	..	..	**Récupération**		37	
..	..	873	890	975	..	..	..	**Production et distrib. d'électricité, de gaz, d'eau**	E	40-41	
..	..	841	858	942	..	..	..	**Electricité, gaz, vapeur et eau chaude**		40	
..	..	834	850	933	..	..	..	Production, collecte et distribution d'électricité			401
..	..	32	32	33	..	..	..	**Captage, épuration et distribution d'eau**		41	410
..	..	3 710	3 705	3 138	..	..	..	**Construction**	F	45	
..	..	8 311	8 681	7 580	..	..	..	**Commerce de gros et de détail; réparation**	G	50-52	
..	..	1 271	1 429	1 261	..	..	..	**Hôtels et restaurants**	H	55	
..	..	5 574	6 330	5 555	..	..	..	**Transports, entreposage et communications**	I	60-64	
..	..	3 149	3 112	3 127	..	..	..	**Intermédiation financière**	J	65-67	
..	..	4 349	4 698	4 710	..	..	..	**Immobilier, locations, services aux entreprises**	K	70-74	
..	..	22 219	23 843	22 421	..	..	..	**Admin. publique; éducation; santé; autres**	L-Q	75-99	
..	..	63 181	66 733	62 341	..	..	..	**Grand total**	A-Q	01-99	

Note: ISIC 1531 includes 1532; 2029 includes 2023; 2109 includes 2102; 2412 includes 2421; 2413 includes 243; 2692 includes 2691 and 2693; 2696 includes 2695 and 2699; 3120 includes 3110; 3150 includes 3140 and 3190; 3210 includes 3220; 3320 includes 3330; 3694 includes 3691, 3692, 3693 and 3699; and 453 includes 454.

Statistiques des Structures Industrielles
OCDE, © 1998

SWEDEN

Table SN.9 PRODUCTION - PRODUCTION

Millions of SKr (Current Prices)

ISIC revision 3			1989	1990	1991	1992	1993	1994	1995	1996
A	01-02	Agriculture, hunting and forestry	..	..	50 994	49 291	48 382	50 548	56 904	..
B	05	Fishing	..	..	1 149	972	960	1 081	1 108	..
C	10-14	Mining and quarrying	..	..	10 266	10 106	9 676	10 368	11 997	..
	10	Mining of coal and lignite; extraction of peat	..	..	..	..	..	..	..	..
	11	Crude petroleum & natural gas; related service activ.	..	..	..	..	..	..	..	..
	13	Mining of metal ores	..	..	..	..	..	..	..	..
	14	Other mining and quarrying	..	..	..	..	..	..	..	..
D	15-37	Total manufacturing	..	..	757 939	711 995	753 513	882 017	1 041 585	..
	15	Food products and beverages	..	..	97 965	96 220	101 245	108 127	113 444	..
	155	Beverages	..	..	..	..	..	..	..	..
	16 160	Tobacco products	..	..	2 331	2 461	2 334	2 509	2 143	..
	17	Textiles	..	..	11 990	11 402	11 072	12 061	14 114	..
	171	Spinning, weaving and finishing of textiles	..	..	..	..	..	..	..	..
	172	Other textiles	..	..	..	..	..	..	..	..
	173	Knitted and crocheted fabrics and articles	..	..	..	..	..	..	..	..
	18	Wearing apparel dressing & dyeing of fur	..	..	..	..	..	..	..	..
	181	Wearing apparel, except fur apparel	..	..	..	..	..	..	..	..
	182	Dressing and dyeing of fur; articles of fur	..	..	..	..	..	..	..	..
	19	Tanning, dressing leather; leather artic.; footwear	..	..	..	..	..	..	..	..
	191	Tanning, dressing leather; manuf. of leather articles	..	..	..	..	..	..	..	..
	192	Footwear	..	..	..	..	..	..	..	..
	20	Wood and cork products, ex. furniture	..	..	45 552	36 916	36 494	44 621	52 090	..
	201	Sawmilling and planing of wood	..	..	21 713	20 788	21 746	28 158	31 820	..
	202	Products of wood, cork, straw & plaiting material	..	..	23 839	16 128	14 748	16 463	20 270	..
	21	Paper and paper products	..	..	69 504	65 796	69 440	80 791	106 784	..
	22	Publishing, printing & reprod. of recorded media	..	..	49 680	48 006	49 028	53 595	56 525	..
	221	Publishing	..	..	..	..	..	..	..	..
	222	Printing and related service activities	..	..	..	..	..	..	..	..
	223	Reproduction of recorded media	..	..	..	..	..	..	..	..
	23	Coke, refined petroleum products & nuclear fuel	..	..	24 606	21 521	26 552	24 771	25 822	..
	24	Chemicals and chemical products	..	..	48 900	48 187	55 124	63 053	71 586	..
	241	Basic chemicals	..	..	..	..	..	..	..	..
	242	Other chemical products	..	..	..	..	..	..	..	..
	243	Man-made fibres	..	..	..	..	..	..	..	..
	25	Rubber and plastic products	..	..	19 147	18 212	18 933	22 720	24 524	..
	251	Rubber products	..	..	..	..	..	..	..	..
	252	Plastic products	..	..	..	..	..	..	..	..
	26	Other non-metallic mineral products	..	..	19 825	17 603	16 219	17 309	19 140	..
	261	Glass and glass products	..	..	..	..	..	..	..	..
	269	Non-metallic mineral products, nec	..	..	..	..	..	..	..	..
	27	Basic metals	..	..	50 340	45 585	52 421	66 222	76 685	..
	271	Basic iron and steel	..	..	..	..	..	..	..	..
	272	Basic precious and non-ferrous metals	..	..	..	..	..	..	..	..
	273	Casting of metals	..	..	..	..	..	..	..	..
	28	Fabricated metal products, ex. machin. & equip.	..	..	46 610	40 221	42 301	51 127	63 879	..
	281	Structural metal prod., tanks, reservoirs, generators	..	..	..	..	..	..	..	..
	289	Other fabricated metal products & service activities	..	..	..	..	..	..	..	..
	29	Machinery and equipment, nec	..	..	84 785	78 240	78 767	97 209	118 224	..
	291	General purpose machinery	..	..	..	..	..	..	..	..
	292	Special purpose machinery	..	..	..	..	..	..	..	..
	293	Domestic appliances, nec	..	..	..	..	..	..	..	..
	30	Office, accounting and computing machinery	..	..	9 107	7 389	5 689	5 115	5 780	..
	31	Electrical machinery and apparatus, nec	..	..	48 513	47 560	55 445	68 779	93 451	..
	311	Electric motors, generators and transformers	..	..	..	..	..	..	..	..
	312	Electricity distribution and control apparatus	..	..	..	..	..	..	..	..
	313	Insulated wire and cable	..	..	..	..	..	..	..	..
	314	Accumulators, primary cells and primary batteries	..	..	..	..	..	..	..	..
	315	Electric lamps and lighting equipment	..	..	..	..	..	..	..	..
	319	Other electrical equipment, nec	..	..	..	..	..	..	..	..
	32	Radio, TV, communication equip. & apparatus	..	..	..	..	..	..	..	..
	321	Electronic valves, tubes & other electronic compon.	..	..	..	..	..	..	..	..
	322	TV, radio transmitters & appar. for line teleph., telegr.	..	..	..	..	..	..	..	..
	323	TV, radio receivers and associated goods	..	..	..	..	..	..	..	..
	33	Medical, precision, optical instr.; watches, clocks	..	..	16 506	16 187	19 139	23 694	24 308	..
	331	Medical equip.; precision instruments and appliances	..	..	..	..	..	..	..	..
	332	Optical instruments and photographic equipment	..	..	..	..	..	..	..	..
	333	Watches and clocks	..	..	..	..	..	..	..	..
	34	Motor vehicles, trailers, and semi-trailers	..	..	90 552	88 824	92 544	116 488	147 841	..
	35	Other transport equipment	..	..	..	..	..	..	..	..
	351	Building and repairing of ships and boats	..	..	..	..	..	..	..	..
	352	Railway, tramway locomotives and rolling stock	..	..	..	..	..	..	..	..
	353	Aircraft and spacecraft	..	..	..	..	..	..	..	..
	359	Transport equipment, nec	..	..	..	..	..	..	..	..
	36	Furniture; manufacturing, nec	..	..	22 026	21 665	20 766	23 826	25 245	..
	361	Furniture	..	..	..	..	..	..	..	..
	369	Manufacturing, nec	..	..	..	..	..	..	..	..
	37	Recycling	..	..	..	..	..	..	..	..
E	40-41	Electricity, gas and water supply	..	..	61 893	64 196	65 827	68 433	71 281	..
	40	Electricity, gas, steam and hot water supply	..	..	52 972	54 496	55 387	58 015	60 636	..
	401	Production, collection and distribution of electricity	..	..	..	..	..	..	..	..
	41 410	Collection, purification, distribution of water	..	..	8 921	9 700	10 440	10 418	10 645	..
F	45	Construction	..	..	187 054	171 577	157 173	153 038	155 400	..
G	50-52	Wholesale and retail trade; repairs etc	..	..	204 176	199 561	198 604	216 174	237 126	..
H	55	Hotels and restaurants	..	..	37 076	36 462	36 666	38 358	41 072	..
I	60-64	Transport, storage and communications	..	..	181 389	183 379	180 849	189 164	201 643	..
J	65-67	Financial intermediation	..	..	89 104	71 268	95 526	86 585	112 541	..
K	70-74	Real estate, renting and business activities	..	..	369 269	384 785	398 072	431 170	451 995	..
L-Q	75-99	Public admin.; education; health; other services	..	..	40 889	44 911	46 983	52 638	56 999	..
A-Q	01-99	Grand total	..	..	1 991 198	1 928 503	1 992 231	2 179 574	2 439 651	..

Note: ISIC 75-99 corresponds to ISIC 80-93.

Table SN.10 VALEUR AJOUTÉE - VALUE ADDED

Millions de SKr (Prix courants)

1989	1990	1991	1992	1993	1994	1995	1996			CITI révision 3	
34 301	34 204	30 467	28 906	26 910	28 337	34 417	..	**Agriculture, chasse et sylviculture**	A	01-02	
653	777	744	630	588	572	618	..	**Pêche**	B	05	
4 260	4 482	3 831	3 787	3 672	3 999	4 667	..	**Activités extractives**	C	10-14	
..	..	..	..	..	..	..	..	Extraction de charbon, de lignite et de tourbe		10	
..	..	..	..	..	..	..	..	Extraction de pétrole brut et de gaz naturel		11	
..	..	..	..	..	..	..	..	Extraction de minerais métalliques		13	
..	..	..	..	..	..	..	..	Autres activités extractives		14	
257 767	265 901	257 207	245 638	258 554	295 954	349 406	..	**Activités de fabrication**	D	15-37	
23 812	25 901	27 070	27 841	28 188	28 419	31 435	..	**Produits alimentaires et boissons**		15	
..	..	..	..	..	..	..	..	Boissons			155
1 115	1 294	1 548	1 749	1 667	1 828	1 500	..	**Produits à base de tabac**		16	160
5 263	5 406	5 144	4 966	4 757	5 021	5 615	..	**Textiles**		17	
..	..	..	..	..	..	..	..	Filature, tissage et achèvement des textiles			171
..	..	..	..	..	..	..	..	Autres articles textiles			172
..	..	..	..	..	..	..	..	Etoffes et articles de bonneterie			173
..	..	..	..	..	..	..	..	**Habillement; préparation, teinture des fourrures**		18	
..	..	..	..	..	..	..	..	Articles d'habillement autres qu'en fourrure			181
..	..	..	..	..	..	..	..	Préparation, teinture des fourrures; art. en fourrure			182
..	..	..	..	..	..	..	..	**Travail des cuirs; articles en cuir; chaussures**		19	
..	..	..	..	..	..	..	..	Apprêt et tannage des cuirs et articles en cuirs			191
..	..	..	..	..	..	..	..	Chaussures			192
14 217	15 715	13 373	9 825	10 140	13 382	14 942	..	**Bois et articles en bois et liège (sauf meubles)**		20	
5 665	6 171	4 578	3 658	4 472	7 309	7 472	..	Sciage et rabotage du bois			201
8 552	9 544	8 795	6 167	5 668	6 073	7 470	..	Articles en bois, liège, vannerie, sparterie			202
24 378	22 440	20 112	18 885	22 439	27 135	40 209	..	**Papier et carton; articles en papier et en carton**		21	
18 078	18 958	20 663	22 377	23 398	24 874	25 183	..	**Edition, imprimerie et reproduction**		22	
..	..	..	..	..	..	..	..	Edition			221
..	..	..	..	..	..	..	..	Imprimerie et activités annexes			222
..	..	..	..	..	..	..	..	Reproduction de supports enregistrés			223
5 269	6 453	6 823	4 121	6 031	5 314	5 641	..	**Cokéfaction; prod. pétroliers; comb. nucléaires**		23	
16 585	16 389	18 252	18 480	21 531	24 139	27 974	..	**Produits chimiques**		24	
..	..	..	..	..	..	..	..	Produits chimiques de base			241
..	..	..	..	..	..	..	..	Autres produits chimiques			242
..	..	..	..	..	..	..	..	Fibres synthétiques ou artificielles			243
7 946	7 916	7 925	7 880	8 167	9 477	10 134	..	**Articles en caoutchouc et en matières plastiques**		25	
..	..	..	..	..	..	..	..	Articles en caoutchouc			251
..	..	..	..	..	..	..	..	Articles en matières plastiques			252
8 231	8 751	8 411	7 669	7 177	7 646	8 320	..	**Autres produits minéraux non métalliques**		26	
..	..	..	..	..	..	..	..	Verre et articles en verre			261
..	..	..	..	..	..	..	..	Produits minéraux non métalliques, nca			269
15 015	14 517	12 514	11 476	13 418	17 317	21 802	..	**Produits métallurgiques de base**		27	
..	..	..	..	..	..	..	..	Sidérurgie et première transformation de l'acier			271
..	..	..	..	..	..	..	..	Métallurgie; métaux précieux et non ferreux			272
..	..	..	..	..	..	..	..	Fonderie			273
20 145	21 954	19 953	17 781	18 489	22 005	27 492	..	**Ouvrages en métaux, sauf machines et matériel**		28	
..	..	..	..	..	..	..	..	Constr. et menuiserie métal.; réservoirs; générateurs			281
..	..	..	..	..	..	..	..	Autres ouvrages en métaux			289
32 587	34 362	32 337	30 539	30 004	37 458	45 546	..	**Machines et matériel, nca**		29	
..	..	..	..	..	..	..	..	Machines d'usage général			291
..	..	..	..	..	..	..	..	Machines d'usage spécifique			292
..	..	..	..	..	..	..	..	Appareils domestiques, nca			293
3 585	3 772	3 568	2 947	2 174	2 000	2 218	..	**Mach. de bureau, comptables, matériel inform.**		30	
17 714	17 023	15 780	14 597	14 237	15 717	19 891	..	**Machines et appareils électriques, nca**		31	
..	..	..	..	..	..	..	..	Moteurs, génératrices et transformateurs électriques			311
..	..	..	..	..	..	..	..	Matériel électrique de distribution et de commande			312
..	..	..	..	..	..	..	..	Fils et câbles électriques isolés			313
..	..	..	..	..	..	..	..	Accumulateurs, piles électriques			314
..	..	..	..	..	..	..	..	Lampes électriques et appareils d'éclairage			315
..	..	..	..	..	..	..	..	Autres matériels électriques, nca			319
..	..	..	..	..	..	..	..	**Equip. et appar. de radio, TV, communication**		32	
..	..	..	..	..	..	..	..	Tubes et valves électroniques; autres composants			321
..	..	..	..	..	..	..	..	Emetteurs radio et TV; app. téléphonie, télégraphie			322
..	..	..	..	..	..	..	..	Récepteurs radio et TV et articles associés			323
6 068	7 336	7 709	7 428	8 428	10 299	9 960	..	**Instruments médicaux, de précision, d'optique**		33	
..	..	..	..	..	..	..	..	Appareils médicaux et de précision			331
..	..	..	..	..	..	..	..	Instruments d'optique ; matériel photographique			332
..	..	..	..	..	..	..	..	Horlogerie			333
30 036	29 099	27 768	28 576	30 291	34 939	42 477	..	**Véhicules automobiles et nemorques**		34	
..	..	..	..	..	..	..	..	**Autres matériels de transport**		35	
..	..	..	..	..	..	..	..	Construction et réparation de navires			351
..	..	..	..	..	..	..	..	Construction de matériel ferroviaire roulant			352
..	..	..	..	..	..	..	..	Construction aéronautique et spatiale			353
..	..	..	..	..	..	..	..	Autres équipements de transport			359
7 723	8 615	8 257	8 501	8 018	8 984	9 067	..	**Meubles; activités de fabrication, nca**		36	
..	..	..	..	..	..	..	..	Meubles			361
..	..	..	..	..	..	..	..	Activités de fabrication, nca			369
..	..	..	..	..	..	..	..	**Récupération**		37	
31 981	36 226	40 483	42 613	42 781	44 664	45 804	..	**Production et distrib. d'électricité, de gaz, d'eau**	E	40-41	
27 546	31 600	35 196	36 644	36 554	38 499	39 576	..	**Electricité, gaz, vapeur et eau chaude**		40	
..	..	..	..	..	..	..	..	Production, collecte et distribution d'électricité			401
4 435	4 626	5 287	5 969	6 227	6 165	6 228	..	**Captage, épuration et distribution d'eau**		41	410
83 644	94 090	98 536	91 790	79 490	74 686	74 016	..	**Construction**	F	45	
125 049	131 207	133 989	131 439	132 162	144 536	158 635	..	**Commerce de gros et de détail; réparation**	G	50-52	
19 330	19 139	20 250	20 438	20 001	20 506	21 800	..	**Hôtels et restaurants**	H	55	
71 379	81 120	87 538	89 319	84 616	89 621	97 387	..	**Transports, entreposage et communications**	I	60-64	
57 176	66 769	60 960	44 110	66 674	55 273	81 786	..	**Intermédiation financière**	J	65-67	
172 360	193 038	229 323	256 316	265 142	286 272	299 813	..	**Immobilier, locations, services aux entreprises**	K	70-74	
23 750	25 692	27 502	31 134	32 549	36 726	39 871	..	**Admin. publique; éducation; santé; autres**	L-Q	75-99	
881 650	952 645	990 830	986 120	1 013 139	1 081 146	1 208 220	..	**Grand total**	A-Q	01-99	

Note: ISIC 75-99 corresponds to ISIC 80-93.

Statistiques des Structures Industrielles
OCDE, © 1998

SWEDEN

Table SN.11 EMPLOYMENT - EMPLOI

Thousands

ISIC revision 3				1989	1990	1991	1992	1993	1994	1995	1996
A	01-02		**Agriculture, hunting and forestry**	166.0	163.6	155.8	150.7	149.8	150.5	145.3	..
B	05		**Fishing**	3.7	4.1	4.5	4.0	4.3	3.8	3.9	..
C	10-14		**Mining and quarrying**	10.9	10.8	10.5	10.1	9.0	9.4	9.8	..
	10		Mining of coal and lignite; extraction of peat	..	..	..	..	..	..	..	..
	11		Crude petroleum & natural gas; related service activ.	..	..	..	..	..	..	..	..
	13		Mining of metal ores	..	..	..	..	..	..	..	..
	14		Other mining and quarrying	..	..	..	..	..	..	..	..
D	15-37		**Total manufacturing**	957.6	925.9	868.1	789.9	731.3	744.4	770.3	..
	15		**Food products and beverages**	82.9	81.4	77.9	71.7	70.7	69.4	69.7	..
		155	Beverages	..	..	..	..	..	..	..	..
	16	160	**Tobacco products**	1.2	1.1	1.1	0.9	0.9	0.8	0.8	..
	17		**Textiles**	28.7	27.4	22.7	19.9	18.2	17.7	17.6	..
		171	Spinning, weaving and finishing of textiles	..	..	..	..	..	..	..	..
		172	Other textiles	..	..	..	..	..	..	..	..
		173	Knitted and crocheted fabrics and articles	..	..	..	..	..	..	..	..
	18		**Wearing apparel dressing & dyeing of fur**	..	..	..	..	..	..	..	..
		181	Wearing apparel, except fur apparel	..	..	..	..	..	..	..	..
		182	Dressing and dyeing of fur; articles of fur	..	..	..	..	..	..	..	..
	19		**Tanning, dressing leather; leather artic.; footwear**	..	..	..	..	..	..	..	..
		191	Tanning, dressing leather; manuf. of leather articles	..	..	..	..	..	..	..	..
		192	Footwear	..	..	..	..	..	..	..	..
	20		**Wood and cork products, ex. furniture**	47.8	47.3	44.4	39.8	36.2	37.1	39.2	..
		201	Sawmilling and planing of wood	19.8	19.3	18.4	17.6	16.8	17.5	17.9	..
		202	Products of wood, cork, straw & plaiting material	28.0	28.0	26.0	22.2	19.4	19.6	21.3	..
	21		**Paper and paper products**	60.6	58.1	54.4	49.1	45.5	45.0	45.1	..
	22		**Publishing, printing & reprod. of recorded media**	74.3	72.4	70.2	65.4	62.1	64.2	62.4	..
		221	Publishing	..	..	..	..	..	..	..	..
		222	Printing and related service activities	..	..	..	..	..	..	..	..
		223	Reproduction of recorded media	..	..	..	..	..	..	..	..
	23		**Coke, refined petroleum products & nuclear fuel**	3.2	3.3	3.1	2.8	2.9	2.8	2.4	..
	24		**Chemicals and chemical products**	39.4	36.3	35.5	33.0	31.7	32.8	34.7	..
		241	Basic chemicals	..	..	..	..	..	..	..	..
		242	Other chemical products	..	..	..	..	..	..	..	..
		243	Man-made fibres	..	..	..	..	..	..	..	..
	25		**Rubber and plastic products**	28.9	27.2	25.1	23.6	21.1	22.5	22.4	..
		251	Rubber products	..	..	..	..	..	..	..	..
		252	Plastic products	..	..	..	..	..	..	..	..
	26		**Other non-metallic mineral products**	30.1	29.6	28.5	24.8	21.0	19.7	19.7	..
		261	Glass and glass products	..	..	..	..	..	..	..	..
		269	Non-metallic mineral products, nec	..	..	..	..	..	..	..	..
	27		**Basic metals**	47.9	45.6	41.3	37.6	34.5	34.9	36.6	..
		271	Basic iron and steel	..	..	..	..	..	..	..	..
		272	Basic precious and non-ferrous metals	..	..	..	..	..	..	..	..
		273	Casting of metals	..	..	..	..	..	..	..	..
	28		**Fabricated metal products, ex. machin. & equip.**	85.1	82.6	75.2	66.9	61.2	64.9	69.2	..
		281	Structural metal prod., tanks, reservoirs, generators	..	..	..	..	..	..	..	..
		289	Other fabricated metal products & service activities	..	..	..	..	..	..	..	..
	29		**Machinery and equipment, nec**	130.9	129.4	120.2	109.6	99.5	102.7	103.3	..
		291	General purpose machinery	..	..	..	..	..	..	..	..
		292	Special purpose machinery	..	..	..	..	..	..	..	..
		293	Domestic appliances, nec	..	..	..	..	..	..	..	..
	30		**Office, accounting and computing machinery**	12.4	12.4	11.6	10.6	9.7	7.5	8.1	..
	31		**Electrical machinery and apparatus, nec**	73.8	65.5	63.2	55.8	51.8	53.1	62.9	..
		311	Electric motors, generators and transformers	..	..	..	..	..	..	..	..
		312	Electricity distribution and control apparatus	..	..	..	..	..	..	..	..
		313	Insulated wire and cable	..	..	..	..	..	..	..	..
		314	Accumulators, primary cells and primary batteries	..	..	..	..	..	..	..	..
		315	Electric lamps and lighting equipment	..	..	..	..	..	..	..	..
		319	Other electrical equipment, nec	..	..	..	..	..	..	..	..
	32		**Radio, TV, communication equip. & apparatus**	..	..	..	..	..	..	..	..
		321	Electronic valves, tubes & other electronic compon.	..	..	..	..	..	..	..	..
		322	TV, radio transmitters & appar. for line teleph., telegr.	..	..	..	..	..	..	..	..
		323	TV, radio receivers and associated goods	..	..	..	..	..	..	..	..
	33		**Medical, precision, optical instr.; watches, clocks**	20.8	23.0	22.6	20.9	20.5	22.1	21.6	..
		331	Medical equip.; precision instruments and appliances	..	..	..	..	..	..	..	..
		332	Optical instruments and photographic equipment	..	..	..	..	..	..	..	..
		333	Watches and clocks	..	..	..	..	..	..	..	..
	34		**Motor vehicles, trailers, and semi-trailers**	122.1	115.7	106.7	95.7	85.9	87.2	94.4	..
	35		**Other transport equipment**	..	..	..	..	..	..	..	..
		351	Building and repairing of ships and boats	..	..	..	..	..	..	..	..
		352	Railway, tramway locomotives and rolling stock	..	..	..	..	..	..	..	..
		353	Aircraft and spacecraft	..	..	..	..	..	..	..	..
		359	Transport equipment, nec	..	..	..	..	..	..	..	..
	36		**Furniture; manufacturing, nec**	67.5	67.6	64.4	61.8	57.9	60.0	60.2	..
		361	Furniture	..	..	..	..	..	..	..	..
		369	Manufacturing, nec	..	..	..	..	..	..	..	..
	37		**Recycling**	..	..	..	..	..	..	..	..
E	40-41		**Electricity, gas and water supply**	33.5	33.0	32.4	31.5	30.1	29.4	29.4	..
	40		**Electricity, gas, steam and hot water supply**	..	..	..	..	..	..	..	..
		401	Production, collection and distribution of electricity	..	..	..	..	..	..	..	..
	41	410	**Collection, purification, distribution of water**	..	..	..	..	..	..	..	..
F	45		**Construction**	297.3	299.2	297.2	267.8	229.6	213.9	214.5	..
G	50-52		**Wholesale and retail trade; repairs etc**	575.5	570.5	562.2	539.0	511.3	510.4	515.6	..
H	55		**Hotels and restaurants**	99.8	101.1	92.6	85.2	85.8	86.0	88.3	..
I	60-64		**Transport, storage and communications**	294.1	298.9	300.6	288.4	273.9	270.9	272.1	..
J	65-67		**Financial intermediation**	92.1	95.3	95.0	89.5	84.0	89.9	91.9	..
K	70-74		**Real estate, renting and business activities**	305.5	323.5	329.8	325.3	301.8	308.4	322.8	..
L-Q	75-99		**Public admin.; education; health; other services**	188.4	193.4	196.0	200.8	205.0	218.7	232.6	..
A-Q	01-99		**Grand total**	3 024.4	3 019.3	2 944.7	2 782.2	2 615.9	2 635.7	2 696.5	..

Note: ISIC 75-99 corresponds to ISIC 80-93.

Table SN.12 EMPLOI, SALARIÉS - EMPLOYMENT, EMPLOYEES

Milliers

1989	1990	1991	1992	1993	1994	1995	1996			CITI révision 3	
61.0	62.1	59.8	55.0	51.1	50.3	48.8	..	**Agriculture, chasse et sylviculture**	A	01-02	
0.7	0.8	0.9	0.7	0.8	0.7	0.7	..	Pêche	B	05	
10.6	10.4	10.1	9.4	8.5	8.8	9.1	..	**Activités extractives**	C	10-14	
..	..	..	..	..	..	..	..	Extraction de charbon, de lignite et de tourbe		10	
..	..	..	..	..	..	..	..	Extraction de pétrole brut et de gaz naturel		11	
..	..	..	..	..	..	..	..	Extraction de minerais métalliques		13	
..	..	..	..	..	..	..	..	Autres activités extractives		14	
935.4	903.2	843.5	763.6	705.5	719.3	743.7	..	**Activités de fabrication**	D	15-37	
80.2	78.5	75.3	69.8	68.6	66.9	67.2	..	**Produits alimentaires et boissons**		15	
								Boissons			155
1.2	1.1	1.1	0.9	0.9	0.8	0.8	..	**Produits à base de tabac**		16	160
26.1	24.7	20.0	17.6	15.6	15.1	14.9	..	**Textiles**		17	
..	..	..	..	..	..	..	..	Filature, tissage et achèvement des textiles			171
..	..	..	..	..	..	..	..	Autres articles textiles			172
..	..	..	..	..	..	..	..	Etoffes et articles de bonneterie			173
..	..	..	..	..	..	..	..	**Habillement; préparation, teinture des fourrures**		18	
..	..	..	..	..	..	..	..	Articles d'habillement autres qu'en fourrure			181
..	..	..	..	..	..	..	..	Préparation, teinture des fourrures; art. en fourrure			182
..	..	..	..	..	..	..	..	**Travail des cuirs; articles en cuir; chaussures**		19	
..	..	..	..	..	..	..	..	Apprêt et tannage des cuirs et articles en cuirs			191
..	..	..	..	..	..	..	..	Chaussures			192
45.2	44.4	41.3	36.2	32.8	33.9	35.9	..	**Bois et articles en bois et liège (sauf meubles)**		20	
18.8	18.2	17.2	16.3	15.5	16.3	16.7	..	Sciage et rabotage du bois			201
26.4	26.2	24.1	19.9	17.3	17.6	19.2	..	Articles en bois, liège, vannerie, sparterie			202
60.3	57.9	54.2	48.9	45.5	45.0	45.1	..	**Papier et carton; articles en papier et en carton**		21	
71.9	69.9	67.3	61.8	58.6	60.9	58.7	..	**Edition, imprimerie et reproduction**		22	
..	..	..	..	..	..	..	..	Edition			221
..	..	..	..	..	..	..	..	Imprimerie et activités annexes			222
..	..	..	..	..	..	..	..	Reproduction de supports enregistrés			223
3.2	3.3	3.1	2.8	2.9	2.8	2.4	..	**Cokéfaction; prod. pétroliers; comb. nucléaires**		23	
39.2	36.0	35.2	32.7	31.4	32.6	34.5	..	**Produits chimiques**		24	
..	..	..	..	..	..	..	..	Produits chimiques de base			241
..	..	..	..	..	..	..	..	Autres produits chimiques			242
..	..	..	..	..	..	..	..	Fibres synthétiques ou artificielles			243
28.7	27.0	24.9	23.4	20.9	22.4	22.3	..	**Articles en caoutchouc et en matières plastiques**		25	
..	..	..	..	..	..	..	..	Articles en caoutchouc			251
..	..	..	..	..	..	..	..	Articles en matières plastiques			252
29.0	28.5	26.8	22.7	19.4	18.2	18.2	..	**Autres produits minéraux non métalliques**		26	
..	..	..	..	..	..	..	..	Verre et articles en verre			261
..	..	..	..	..	..	..	..	Produits minéraux non métalliques, nca			269
47.6	45.2	40.9	37.1	34.2	34.4	36.1	..	**Produits métallurgiques de base**		27	
..	..	..	..	..	..	..	..	Sidérurgie et première transformation de l'acier			271
..	..	..	..	..	..	..	..	Métallurgie; métaux précieux et non ferreux			272
..	..	..	..	..	..	..	..	Fonderie			273
81.0	78.5	70.5	61.9	56.2	59.9	63.7	..	**Ouvrages en métaux, sauf machines et matériel**		28	
..	..	..	..	..	..	..	..	Constr. et menuiserie métal.; réservoirs; générateurs			281
..	..	..	..	..	..	..	..	Autres ouvrages en métaux			289
129.4	127.8	118.3	107.6	97.5	100.9	101.2	..	**Machines et matériel, nca**		29	
..	..	..	..	..	..	..	..	Machines d'usage général			291
..	..	..	..	..	..	..	..	Machines d'usage spécifique			292
..	..	..	..	..	..	..	..	Appareils domestiques, nca			293
12.3	12.3	11.5	10.5	9.6	7.4	8.0	..	**Mach. de bureau, comptables, matériel inform.**		30	
73.0	64.8	62.4	54.9	50.9	52.3	61.9	..	**Machines et appareils électriques, nca**		31	
..	..	..	..	..	..	..	..	Moteurs, génératrices et transformateurs électriques			311
..	..	..	..	..	..	..	..	Matériel électrique de distribution et de commande			312
..	..	..	..	..	..	..	..	Fils et câbles électriques isolés			313
..	..	..	..	..	..	..	..	Accumulateurs, piles électriques			314
..	..	..	..	..	..	..	..	Lampes électriques et appareils d'éclairage			315
..	..	..	..	..	..	..	..	Autres matériels électriques, nca			319
..	..	..	..	..	..	..	..	**Equip. et appar. de radio, TV, communication**		32	
..	..	..	..	..	..	..	..	Tubes et valves électroniques; autres composants			321
..	..	..	..	..	..	..	..	Emetteurs radio et TV; app. téléphonie, télégraphie			322
..	..	..	..	..	..	..	..	Récepteurs radio et TV et articles associés			323
20.7	23.0	22.6	20.9	20.5	22.1	21.6	..	**Instruments médicaux, de précision, d'optique**		33	
..	..	..	..	..	..	..	..	Appareils médicaux et de précision			331
..	..	..	..	..	..	..	..	Instruments d'optique ; matériel photographique			332
..	..	..	..	..	..	..	..	Horlogerie			333
121.5	115.2	106.0	95.0	85.2	86.6	93.7	..	**Véhicules automobiles et nemorques**		34	
..	..	..	..	..	..	..	..	**Autres matériels de transport**		35	
..	..	..	..	..	..	..	..	Construction et réparation de navires			351
..	..	..	..	..	..	..	..	Construction de matériel ferroviaire roulant			352
..	..	..	..	..	..	..	..	Construction aéronautique et spatiale			353
..	..	..	..	..	..	..	..	Autres équipements de transport			359
64.9	65.1	62.1	58.9	54.8	57.1	57.5	..	**Meubles; activités de fabrication, nca**		36	
..	..	..	..	..	..	..	..	Meubles			361
..	..	..	..	..	..	..	..	Activités de fabrication, nca			369
..	..	..	..	..	..	..	..	**Récupération**		37	
33.5	33.0	32.4	31.5	30.1	29.4	29.4	..	**Production et distrib. d'électricité, de gaz, d'eau**	E	40-41	
..	..	..	..	..	..	..	..	**Electricité, gaz, vapeur et eau chaude**		40	
..	..	..	..	..	..	..	..	Production, collecte et distribution d'électricité			401
..	..	..	..	..	..	..	..	**Captage, épuration et distribution d'eau**		41	410
253.4	255.3	254.4	222.6	186.4	173.1	173.8	..	**Construction**	F	45	
510.1	508.5	500.3	477.6	446.9	443.4	447.0	..	**Commerce de gros et de détail; réparation**	G	50-52	
89.0	89.5	81.5	74.7	72.4	73.5	75.3	..	**Hôtels et restaurants**	H	55	
269.8	275.3	276.6	263.4	249.1	246.3	246.9	..	**Transports, entreposage et communications**	I	60-64	
92.1	95.3	95.0	89.5	84.0	89.9	91.9	..	**Intermédiation financière**	J	65-67	
274.0	290.7	293.7	287.9	265.1	267.0	276.4	..	**Immobilier, locations, services aux entreprises**	K	70-74	
154.5	159.1	162.3	167.9	166.6	179.2	192.1	..	**Admin. publique; éducation; santé; autres**	L-Q	75-99	
2 684.1	2 683.2	2 610.5	2 443.8	2 266.5	2 280.9	2 335.1	..	**Grand total**	A-Q	01-99	

Note: ISIC 75-99 corresponds to ISIC 80-93

Statistiques des Structures Industrielles
OCDE, © 1998

SWEDEN

Table SN.13 COMPENSATION OF LABOUR – SALAIRES ET CHARGES SOCIALES

Millions of SKr (Current Prices)

ISIC revision 3			1989	1990	1991	1992	1993	1994	1995	1996
A	01-02	Agriculture, hunting and forestry	8 842	9 402	9 406	8 980	8 418	8 574	8 957	..
B	05	Fishing	109	124	131	115	123	144	136	..
C	10-14	Mining and quarrying	2 707	2 753	2 961	2 853	2 636	2 739	2 915	..
	10	Mining of coal and lignite; extraction of peat	..	..	..	..	..	..	..	..
	11	Crude petroleum & natural gas; related service activ.	..	..	..	..	..	..	..	..
	13	Mining of metal ores	..	..	..	..	..	..	..	..
	14	Other mining and quarrying	..	..	..	..	..	..	..	..
D	15-37	Total manufacturing	179 645	192 330	195 889	187 985	178 055	192 810	209 595	..
	15	Food products and beverages	14 059	14 991	15 815	15 744	15 551	16 063	16 494	..
	155	Beverages	..	..	..	..	..	..	..	..
	16 160	Tobacco products	249	258	248	233	228	239	247	..
	17	Textiles	4 024	4 040	3 721	3 407	3 070	3 167	3 182	..
	171	Spinning, weaving and finishing of textiles	..	..	..	..	..	..	..	..
	172	Other textiles	..	..	..	..	..	..	..	..
	173	Knitted and crocheted fabrics and articles	..	..	..	..	..	..	..	..
	18	Wearing apparel dressing & dyeing of fur	..	..	..	..	..	..	..	..
	181	Wearing apparel, except fur apparel	..	..	..	..	..	..	..	..
	182	Dressing and dyeing of fur; articles of fur	..	..	..	..	..	..	..	..
	19	Tanning, dressing leather; leather artic.; footwear	..	..	..	..	..	..	..	..
	191	Tanning, dressing leather; manuf. of leather articles	..	..	..	..	..	..	..	..
	192	Footwear	..	..	..	..	..	..	..	..
	20	Wood and cork products, ex. furniture	8 130	8 938	9 024	7 720	7 316	8 080	8 964	..
	201	Sawmilling and planing of wood	3 284	3 574	3 652	3 499	3 580	4 048	4 405	..
	202	Products of wood, cork, straw & plaiting material	4 846	5 364	5 372	4 221	3 736	4 032	4 559	..
	21	Paper and paper products	12 827	13 488	13 946	13 542	12 330	13 236	13 690	..
	22	Publishing, printing & reprod. of recorded media	14 718	15 867	16 101	15 476	14 768	15 727	16 538	..
	221	Publishing	..	..	..	..	..	..	..	..
	222	Printing and related service activities	..	..	..	..	..	..	..	..
	223	Reproduction of recorded media	..	..	..	..	..	..	..	..
	23	Coke, refined petroleum products & nuclear fuel	813	882	861	829	884	959	1 013	..
	24	Chemicals and chemical products	8 525	8 739	9 449	9 090	9 377	10 603	11 578	..
	241	Basic chemicals	..	..	..	..	..	..	..	..
	242	Other chemical products	..	..	..	..	..	..	..	..
	243	Man-made fibres	..	..	..	..	..	..	..	..
	25	Rubber and plastic products	5 588	5 857	5 785	5 870	5 492	6 312	6 407	..
	251	Rubber products	..	..	..	..	..	..	..	..
	252	Plastic products	..	..	..	..	..	..	..	..
	26	Other non-metallic mineral products	5 509	6 065	6 010	5 589	4 951	4 897	5 242	..
	261	Glass and glass products	..	..	..	..	..	..	..	..
	269	Non-metallic mineral products, nec	..	..	..	..	..	..	..	..
	27	Basic metals	9 376	9 885	9 665	9 233	8 973	9 604	10 683	..
	271	Basic iron and steel	..	..	..	..	..	..	..	..
	272	Basic precious and non-ferrous metals	..	..	..	..	..	..	..	..
	273	Casting of metals	..	..	..	..	..	..	..	..
	28	Fabricated metal products, ex. machin. & equip.	16 247	17 211	16 523	15 634	14 268	15 775	17 345	..
	281	Structural metal prod., tanks, reservoirs, generators	..	..	..	..	..	..	..	..
	289	Other fabricated metal products & service activities	..	..	..	..	..	..	..	..
	29	Machinery and equipment, nec	26 761	28 944	29 383	27 605	25 378	27 922	29 403	..
	291	General purpose machinery	..	..	..	..	..	..	..	..
	292	Special purpose machinery	..	..	..	..	..	..	..	..
	293	Domestic appliances, nec	..	..	..	..	..	..	..	..
	30	Office, accounting and computing machinery	2 698	2 929	3 062	2 904	2 624	2 306	2 216	..
	31	Electrical machinery and apparatus, nec	13 614	14 511	15 213	14 317	14 132	15 541	18 957	..
	311	Electric motors, generators and transformers	..	..	..	..	..	..	..	..
	312	Electricity distribution and control apparatus	..	..	..	..	..	..	..	..
	313	Insulated wire and cable	..	..	..	..	..	..	..	..
	314	Accumulators, primary cells and primary batteries	..	..	..	..	..	..	..	..
	315	Electric lamps and lighting equipment	..	..	..	..	..	..	..	..
	319	Other electrical equipment, nec	..	..	..	..	..	..	..	..
	32	Radio, TV, communication equip. & apparatus	..	..	..	..	..	..	..	..
	321	Electronic valves, tubes & other electronic compon.	..	..	..	..	..	..	..	..
	322	TV, radio transmitters & appar. for line teleph., telegr.	..	..	..	..	..	..	..	..
	323	TV, radio receivers and associated goods	..	..	..	..	..	..	..	..
	33	Medical, precision, optical instr.; watches, clocks	4 372	5 177	5 327	5 705	6 043	6 820	6 886	..
	331	Medical equip.; precision instruments and appliances	..	..	..	..	..	..	..	..
	332	Optical instruments and photographic equipment	..	..	..	..	..	..	..	..
	333	Watches and clocks	..	..	..	..	..	..	..	..
	34	Motor vehicles, trailers, and semi-trailers	23 500	24 963	25 690	25 044	23 010	25 236	29 968	..
	35	Other transport equipment	..	..	..	..	..	..	..	..
	351	Building and repairing of ships and boats	..	..	..	..	..	..	..	..
	352	Railway, tramway locomotives and rolling stock	..	..	..	..	..	..	..	..
	353	Aircraft and spacecraft	..	..	..	..	..	..	..	..
	359	Transport equipment, nec	..	..	..	..	..	..	..	..
	36	Furniture; manufacturing, nec	8 635	9 585	10 066	10 043	9 660	10 323	10 782	..
	361	Furniture	..	..	..	..	..	..	..	..
	369	Manufacturing, nec	..	..	..	..	..	..	..	..
	37	Recycling								
E	40-41	Electricity, gas and water supply	6 872	7 951	8 054	8 340	8 195	8 496	8 666	..
	40	Electricity, gas, steam and hot water supply	5 941	7 001	7 051	7 238	7 345	7 521	7 658	..
	401	Production, collection and distribution of electricity	..	..	..	..	..	..	..	..
	41 410	Collection, purification, distribution of water	931	950	1 003	1 102	850	975	1 008	..
F	45	Construction	65 029	74 624	78 637	70 693	61 920	58 960	59 753	..
G	50-52	Wholesale and retail trade; repairs etc	95 712	104 863	108 210	105 132	101 504	104 791	109 304	..
H	55	Hotels and restaurants	13 151	14 132	13 354	13 441	12 829	13 480	14 003	..
I	60-64	Transport, storage and communications	50 395	56 352	60 050	59 059	59 464	60 915	62 980	..
J	65-67	Financial intermediation	22 360	24 761	26 022	26 049	26 876	29 278	30 977	..
K	70-74	Real estate, renting and business activities	58 389	68 323	76 277	75 705	75 760	82 394	88 798	..
L-Q	75-99	Public admin.; education; health; other services	14 394	16 268	17 528	19 257	20 233	23 116	25 357	..
A-Q	01-99	Grand total	517 605	571 883	596 519	577 609	556 013	585 697	621 441	..

Note: ISIC 75-99 corresponds to ISIC 80-93

SUÈDE

Table SN.14 HEURES OUVRÉES - HOURS WORKED

Milliers

1989	1990	1991	1992	1993	1994	1995	1996		Catégorie		CITI révision 3
79 200	79 000	73 930	69 370	65 040	65 240	65 590	..		**Agriculture, chasse et sylviculture**	A	01-02
1 800	1 790	1 810	1 550	1 570	1 690	1 690	..		**Pêche**	B	05
17 990	17 090	16 220	15 170	14 300	14 480	15 190	..		**Activités extractives**	C	10-14
..	..	..	..	..	..	..	..		Extraction de charbon, de lignite et de tourbe		10
..	..	..	..	..	..	..	..		Extraction de pétrole brut et de gaz naturel		11
..	..	..	..	..	..	..	..		Extraction de minerais métalliques		13
..	..	..	..	..	..	..	..		Autres activités extractives		14
1 388 650	1 356 580	1 265 550	1 154 720	1 095 770	1 150 710	1 197 760	..		**Activités de fabrication**	D	15-37
116 470	113 980	108 370	103 830	104 150	105 830	108 480	..		**Produits alimentaires et boissons**		15
..	..	..	..	..	..	..	..		Boissons		155
1 850	1 670	1 650	1 540	1 510	1 500	1 470	..		**Produits à base de tabac**	16	160
37 400	34 810	28 400	24 660	22 450	23 130	22 520	..		**Textiles**		17
..	..	..	..	..	..	..	..		Filature, tissage et achèvement des textiles		171
..	..	..	..	..	..	..	..		Autres articles textiles		172
..	..	..	..	..	..	..	..		Etoffes et articles de bonneterie		173
..	..	..	..	..	..	..	..		**Habillement; préparation, teinture des fourrures**		18
..	..	..	..	..	..	..	..		Articles d'habillement autres qu'en fourrure		181
..	..	..	..	..	..	..	..		Préparation, teinture des fourrures; art. en fourrure		182
..	..	..	..	..	..	..	..		**Travail des cuirs; articles en cuir; chaussures**		19
..	..	..	..	..	..	..	..		Apprêt et tannage des cuirs et articles en cuirs		191
..	..	..	..	..	..	..	..		Chaussures		192
70 150	69 450	65 050	57 130	52 900	55 980	59 650	..		**Bois et articles en bois et liège (sauf meubles)**		20
29 860	29 320	27 780	26 360	25 330	27 640	28 410	..		Sciage et rabotage du bois		201
40 290	40 130	37 270	30 770	27 570	28 340	31 240	..		Articles en bois, liège, vannerie, sparterie		202
91 280	87 580	82 560	75 540	71 450	72 440	72 640	..		**Papier et carton; articles en papier et en carton**		21
107 040	105 770	102 400	90 800	89 350	91 250	90 500	..		**Edition, imprimerie et reproduction**		22
..	..	..	..	..	..	..	..		Edition		221
..	..	..	..	..	..	..	..		Imprimerie et activités annexes		222
..	..	..	..	..	..	..	..		Reproduction de supports enregistrés		223
5 440	5 580	5 210	4 750	5 030	5 250	4 630	..		**Cokéfaction; prod. pétroliers; comb. nucléaires**		23
58 210	53 640	52 530	50 150	48 890	52 900	55 050	..		**Produits chimiques**		24
..	..	..	..	..	..	..	..		Produits chimiques de base		241
..	..	..	..	..	..	..	..		Autres produits chimiques		242
..	..	..	..	..	..	..	..		Fibres synthétiques ou artificielles		243
42 010	39 610	36 610	34 420	31 960	35 190	34 450	..		**Articles en caoutchouc et en matières plastiques**		25
..	..	..	..	..	..	..	..		Articles en caoutchouc		251
..	..	..	..	..	..	..	..		Articles en matières plastiques		252
43 230	42 940	41 140	34 890	30 260	28 870	28 530	..		**Autres produits minéraux non métalliques**		26
..	..	..	..	..	..	..	..		Verre et articles en verre		261
..	..	..	..	..	..	..	..		Produits minéraux non métalliques, nca		269
71 050	66 850	59 460	55 250	52 070	53 780	57 570	..		**Produits métallurgiques de base**		27
..	..	..	..	..	..	..	..		Sidérurgie et première transformation de l'acier		271
..	..	..	..	..	..	..	..		Métallurgie; métaux précieux et non ferreux		272
..	..	..	..	..	..	..	..		Fonderie		273
120 780	118 260	107 420	94 060	87 670	96 920	101 910	..		**Ouvrages en métaux, sauf machines et matériel**		28
..	..	..	..	..	..	..	..		Constr. et menuiserie métal.; réservoirs; générateurs		281
..	..	..	..	..	..	..	..		Autres ouvrages en métaux		289
201 600	201 630	188 080	172 190	160 650	172 660	175 200	..		**Machines et matériel, nca**		29
..	..	..	..	..	..	..	..		Machines d'usage général		291
..	..	..	..	..	..	..	..		Machines d'usage spécifique		292
..	..	..	..	..	..	..	..		Appareils domestiques, nca		293
19 410	19 570	18 290	16 780	15 680	13 300	12 610	..		**Mach. de bureau, comptables, matériel inform.**		30
107 700	101 090	92 720	82 410	79 600	83 890	100 490	..		**Machines et appareils électriques, nca**		31
..	..	..	..	..	..	..	..		Moteurs, génératrices et transformateurs électriques		311
..	..	..	..	..	..	..	..		Matériel électrique de distribution et de commande		312
..	..	..	..	..	..	..	..		Fils et câbles électriques isolés		313
..	..	..	..	..	..	..	..		Accumulateurs, piles électriques		314
..	..	..	..	..	..	..	..		Lampes électriques et appareils d'éclairage		315
..	..	..	..	..	..	..	..		Autres matériels électriques, nca		319
..	..	..	..	..	..	..	..		**Equip. et appar. de radio, TV, communication**		32
..	..	..	..	..	..	..	..		Tubes et valves électroniques; autres composants		321
..	..	..	..	..	..	..	..		Emetteurs radio et TV; app. téléphonie, télégraphie		322
..	..	..	..	..	..	..	..		Récepteurs radio et TV et articles associés		323
31 640	36 210	34 630	31 990	32 830	36 070	35 540	..		**Instruments médicaux, de précision, d'optique**		33
..	..	..	..	..	..	..	..		Appareils médicaux et de précision		331
..	..	..	..	..	..	..	..		Instruments d'optique ; matériel photographique		332
..	..	..	..	..	..	..	..		Horlogerie		333
179 240	174 720	161 890	151 980	140 160	147 600	162 150	..		**Véhicules automobiles et nemorques**		34
..	..	..	..	..	..	..	..		**Autres matériels de transport**		35
..	..	..	..	..	..	..	..		Construction et réparation de navires		351
..	..	..	..	..	..	..	..		Construction de matériel ferroviaire roulant		352
..	..	..	..	..	..	..	..		Construction aéronautique et spatiale		353
..	..	..	..	..	..	..	..		Autres équipements de transport		359
84 150	83 220	79 140	72 350	69 160	74 150	74 370	..		**Meubles; activités de fabrication, nca**		36
..	..	..	..	..	..	..	..		Meubles		361
..	..	..	..	..	..	..	..		Activités de fabrication, nca		369
									Récupération		37
59 880	63 040	61 250	61 990	60 290	59 690	59 330	..		**Production et distrib. d'électricité, de gaz, d'eau**	E	40-41
..	..	..	..	..	..	..	..		**Electricité, gaz, vapeur et eau chaude**		40
..	..	..	..	..	..	..	..		Production, collecte et distribution d'électricité		401
..	..	..	..	..	..	..	..		**Captage, épuration et distribution d'eau**	41	410
448 820	447 180	441 530	393 370	334 820	321 000	323 190	..		**Construction**	F	45
767 740	768 160	751 630	727 600	686 950	697 110	707 160	..		**Commerce de gros et de détail; réparation**	G	50-52
131 280	132 690	117 130	111 240	105 790	107 790	110 040	..		**Hôtels et restaurants**	H	55
455 890	487 970	478 750	461 770	437 880	435 110	436 730	..		**Transports, entreposage et communications**	I	60-64
135 850	133 400	136 240	130 430	124 520	135 450	141 870	..		**Intermédiation financière**	J	65-67
404 650	425 880	425 410	422 310	399 800	411 680	421 670	..		**Immobilier, locations, services aux entreprises**	K	70-74
252 110	259 050	265 820	278 760	285 030	309 380	331 440	..		**Admin. publique; éducation; santé; autres**	L-Q	75-99
4 143 860	4 171 830	4 035 270	3 828 280	3 611 760	3 709 330	3 811 660	..		**Grand total**	A-Q	01-99

Note: ISIC 75-99 corresponds to ISIC 80-93.

Statistiques des Structures Industrielles
OCDE, © 1998

OECD
OCDE

Detailed ISIC Rev. 3 industry listing, 4-digit level

Extract from ISIC Revision 3

Tabulation Division Group Class	Detailed Description

A	**01-02**			**AGRICULTURE, HUNTING AND FORESTRY**
B	**05**			**FISHING**
C	**10-14**			**MINING AND QUARRYING**
	10			**Mining of Coal and Lignite; Extraction of Peat**
		101		Mining and agglomeration of hard coal
		102		Mining and agglomeration of lignite
		103		Extraction and agglomeration of peat
	11			**Extraction of Crude Petroleum and Natural Gas; Service Activities Incidental to Oil and Gas Extraction Excluding Surveying**
		111		Extraction of crude petroleum and natural gas
		112		Service activities incidental to oil and gas extraction excluding surveying
	12	**120**		**Mining of Uranium and Thorium Ores**
	13			**Mining of Metal Ores**
		131		Mining of iron ores
		132		Mining of non-ferrous metal ores, except uranium and thorium ores
	14			Other Mining and Quarrying
		141		Quarrying of stone, sand and clay
		142		Other mining and quarrying, n.e.c.
D	**15-37**			**TOTAL MANUFACTURING**
	15			**Manufacture of Food Products and Beverages**
		151		Production, processing and preservation of meat, fish, fruit, vegetables, oils and fats
			1511	Production, processing and preserving of meat and meat products
			1512	Processing and preserving of fish and fish products
			1513	Processing and preserving of fruit and vegetables
			1514	Manufacture of vegetable and animal oils and fats
		152		Manufacture of dairy products
		153		Manufacture of grain mill products, starches and starch products, and prepared animal feeds
			1531	Manufacture of grain mill products
			1532	Manufacture of starches and starch products
			1533	Manufacture of prepared animal feeds
		154		Manufacture of other food products, n.e.c.
			1541	Manufacture of bakery products
			1542	Manufacture of sugar
			1543	Manufacture of cocoa, chocolate and sugar confectionery
			1544	Manufacture of macaroni, noodles, couscous and similar farinaceous products
			1549	Manufacture of other food products, n.e.c.
		155		Manufacture of beverages
			1551	Distilling, rectifying and blending of spirits; ethyl alcohol production from fermented materials

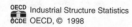

			1552	Manufacture of wines
			1553	Manufacture of malt liquors and malt
			1554	Manufacture of soft drinks; production of mineral waters

16   **160**   **Manufacture of Tobacco Products**

17   **Manufacture of Textiles**

      171   Spinning weaving and finishing of textiles
               1711   Preparation and spinning of textile fibres; weaving of textiles
               1712   Finishing of textiles
      172   Manufacture of other textiles
               1721   Manufacture of made-up textile articles, except apparel
               1722   Manufacture of carpets and rugs
               1723   Manufacture of cordage, rope, twine and netting
               1729   Manufacture of other textiles, n.e.c.
      173   Manufacture of knitted and crocheted fabrics and articles

18   **Manufacture of Wearing Apparel, Dressing and Dyeing of Fur**

      181   Manufacture of wearing apparel, except fur apparel
      182   Dressing and dyeing of fur; manufacture of articles of fur

19   **Tanning and Dressing of Leather; Manufacture of Luggage, Handbags, Saddlery, Harness and Footwear**

      191   Tanning and dressing of leather; manufacture of luggage, handbags, saddlery, harness and footwear
               1911   Tanning and dressing of leather
               1912   Luggage, handbags and the like, saddlery and harness
      192   Manufacture of footwear

20   **Manufacture of Wood and of Products of Wood and Cork, except Furniture; Manufacture of Articles of Straw and Plaiting Materials**

      201   Sawmilling and planing of wood
      202   Manufacture of products of wood, cork, straw and plaiting materials
               2021   Manufacture of veneer sheets; manufacture of plywood, laminboard, particle board and other panels and boards
               2022   Manufacture of builders' carpentry and joinery
               2023   Manufacture of wooden containers
               2029   Manufacture of other products of wood; articles of cork, straw and plaiting materials

21   **Manufacture of Paper and Paper Products**

      210   Manufacture of paper and paper products
               2101   Manufacture of pulp, paper and paperboard
               2102   Manufacture of corrugated paper and paperboard and containers of paper and paperboard
               2109   Manufacture of other articles of pulp and paperboard

22   **Publishing, Printing and Reproduction of Recorded Media**

      221   Publishing
               2211   Publishing of books, brochures, musical books and other publications
               2212   Publishing of newspapers, journals and periodicals
               2213   Publishing of recorded media
               2219   Other publishing
      222   Printing and service activities related to printing
               2221   Printing
               2222   Service activities related to printing
      223   Reproduction of recorded media

23   **Manufacture of Coke, Refined Petroleum Products and Nuclear Fuel**

      231   Manufacture of coke oven products

Statistiques des Structures Industrielles
OCDE, © 1998

	232		Manufacture of refined petroleum products
	233		Processing of nuclear fuel

24   **Manufacture of Chemicals and Chemical Products**

241   Manufacture of basic chemicals
     2411   Manufacture of basic chemicals, except fertilizers and nitrogen compounds
     2412   Manufacture of fertilizers and nitrogen compounds
     2413   Manufacture of plastics in primary forms and synthetic rubber
242   Manufacture of other chemical products
     2421   Manufacture of pesticides and other agro-chemical products
     2422   Manufacture of paints, varnishes and similar coatings, printing ink and mastics
     2423   Manufacture of pharmaceuticals, medicinal chemicals and botanical products
     2424   Manufacture of soap and detergents, cleaning and polishing preparations, perfumes and toilet preparations
     2429   Manufacture of other chemical products, n.e.c.
243   Manufacture of man-made fibres

25   **Manufacture of Rubber and Plastics Products**

251   Manufacture of rubber products
     2511   Manufacture of rubber tyres and tubes; retreading and rebuilding of rubber tyres
     2519   Manufacture of other rubber products
252   Manufacture of plastic products

26   **Manufacture of Other Non-Metallic Mineral Products**

261   Manufacture of glass and glass products
269   Manufacture of non-metallic mineral products, n.e.c.
     2691   Manufacture of non-structural non-refractory ceramic ware ("Pottery, china and earthenware")
     2692   Manufacture of refractory ceramic products
     2693   Manufacture of structural non-refractory clay and ceramic products
     2694   Manufacture of cement, lime and plaster
     2695   Manufacture of articles of concrete, cement and plaster
     2696   Cutting, shaping and finishing of stone
     2699   Manufacture of other non-metallic mineral products, n.e.c.

27   **Manufacture of Basic Metals**

271   Manufacture of basic iron and steel
272   Manufacture of basic precious and non-ferrous metals
273   Casting of metals
     2731   Casting of iron and steel
     2732   Casting non-ferrous metals

28   **Manufacture of Fabricated Metal Products, except Machinery and Equipment**

281   Manufacture of structural metal products, tanks, reservoirs and steam generators
     2811   Manufacture of structural metal products
     2812   Manufacture of tanks, reservoirs and containers of metal
     2813   Manufacture of steam generators, except central heating hot water boilers
289   Manufacture of other fabricated metal products; metal working service activities
     2891   Forging, pressing, stamping and roll-forming of metal; powder metallurgy
     2892   Treatment and coating of metals; general mechanical engineering on a fee or contract basis
     2893   Manufacture of cutlery, hand tools and general hardware
     2899   Manufacture of other fabricated metal products, n.e.c.

29   **Manufacture of Machinery and Equipment, not elsewhere classified**

291   Manufacture of general purpose machinery
     2911   Manufacture of engines and turbines, except aircraft, vehicle and cycle engines
     2912   Manufacture of pumps, compressors, taps and valves

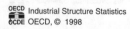

			2913	Manufacture of bearings, gears, gearing and driving elements
			2914	Manufacture of ovens, furnaces and furnace burners
			2915	Manufacture of lifting and handling equipment
			2919	Manufacture of other general purpose machinery
		292		Manufacture of special purpose machinery
			2921	Manufacture of agricultural and forestry machinery
			2922	Manufacture of machine-tools
			2923	Manufacture of machinery for metallurgy
			2924	Manufacture of machinery for mining, quarrying and construction
			2925	Machinery for food, beverage and tobacco processing
			2926	Manufacture of machinery for textile, apparel and leather production
			2927	Manufacture of machinery for weapons and ammunition
			2929	Manufacture of other special purpose machinery
		293		Manufacture of domestic appliances, n.e.c.

30   300   Manufacture of Office, Accounting and Computing Machinery

31   Manufacture of Electrical Machinery and Apparatus, not elsewhere classified

311	Manufacture of electric motors, generators and transformers
312	Manufacture of electricity distribution and control apparatus
313	Manufacture of insulated wire and cable
314	Manufacture of accumulators, primary cells and primary batteries
315	Manufacture of electric lamps and lighting equipment
319	Manufacture of other electrical equipment, n.e.c.

32   Manufacture of Radio, Television and Communication Equipment and Apparatus

321	Manufacture of Electronic valves and tubes and other electronic components
322	Manufacture of television and radio transmitters and apparatus for line telephony and line telegraphy
323	Manufacture of television and radio receivers, sound or video recording or reproducing apparatus, and associated goods

33   Manufacture of Medical, Precision and Optical Instruments, Watches and Clocks

331		Manufacture of medical appliances and instruments and appliances for measuring, checking, testing, navigating and other purposes, except optical instruments
	3311	Manufacture of medical and surgical equipment and orthopaedic appliances
	3312	Manufacture of instruments and appliances for measuring, checking, testing, navigating and other purposes, except industrial process control equipment
	3313	Manufacture of industrial process control equipment
332		Manufacture of optical instruments and photographic equipment
333		Manufacture of watches and clocks

34   Manufacture of Motor Vehicles, Trailers and Semi-trailers

341	Manufacture of motor vehicles
342	Manufacture of bodies (coachwork) for motor vehicles; manufacture of trailers and semi-trailers
343	Manufacture of parts and accessories for motor vehicles and their engines

35   Manufacture of Other Transport Equipment

351		Building and repairing of ships and boats
	3511	Building and repairing of ships
	3512	Building and repairing of pleasure and sporting boats
352		Manufacture of railway and tramway locomotives and rolling stock
353		Manufacture of aircraft and spacecraft
359		Manufacture of transport equipment, n.e.c.
	3591	Manufacture of motorcycles
	3592	Manufacture of bicycles and invalid carriages
	3599	Manufacture of other transport equipment, n.e.c.

	36			**Manufacture of Furniture; Manufacturing, not elsewhere classified**
		361		Manufacture of furniture
		369		Manufacturing, n.e.c.
			3691	Manufacture of jewellery and related articles
			3692	Manufacture of musical instruments
			3693	Manufacture of sports goods
			3694	Manufacture of games and toys
			3699	Other manufacturing, n.e.c.
	37			**Recycling**
		371		Recycling of metal waste and scrap
		372		Recycling of non-metal waste and scrap
E	**40-41**			**ELECTRICITY, GAS AND WATER SUPPLY**
	40			**Electricity, Gas, Steam and Hot Water Supply**
		401		Production, collection and distribution of electricity
		402		Manufacture of gas; distribution of gaseous fuels through mains
		403		Steam and hot water supply
	41	410		**Collection, Purification and Distribution of Water**
F	**45**			**CONSTRUCTION**
G	**50-52**			**WHOLESALE AND RETAIL TRADE; REPAIR OF MOTOR VEHICLES, MOTORCYCLES AND PERSONAL AND HOUSEHOLD GOODS**
H	**55**			**HOTELS AND RESTAURANTS**
I	**60**			**TRANSPORT, STORAGE AND COMMUNICATIONS**
J	**65-67**			**FINANCIAL INTERMEDIATION**
K	**70-74**			**REAL ESTATE, RENTING AND BUSINESS ACTIVITIES**
L-Q	**75-99**			**PUBLIC ADMINISTRATION AND DEFENCE; COMPULSORY SOCIAL SECURITY; EDUCATION; HEALTH; SOCIAL SERVICES; PRIVATE SERVICES; EXTRA-TERRITORIAL ORGANISATIONS AND BODIES**
A-Q	**01-99**			**GRAND TOTAL**

Liste industrielle détaillée de la CITI Rév. 3, au niveau 4-chiffres

Extrait de la CITI Révision 3

Catégorie	Division	Groupe	Classe	Description détaillée
A	01-02			**AGRICULTURE, CHASSE ET SYLVICULTURE**
B	05			**PECHE**
C	10-14			**ACTIVITES EXTRACTIVES**
	10			**Extraction de charbon et de lignite ; Extraction de tourbe**
		101		Extraction et agglomération de houille
		102		Extraction et agglomération de lignite
		103		Extraction et agglomération de tourbe
	11			**Extraction de pétrole brut et de gaz naturel ; Activités annexes à l'extraction de pétrole et de gaz, sauf prospection**
		111		Extraction de pétrole brut et de gaz naturel
		112		Activités annexes à l'extraction de pétrole et de gaz, sauf prospection
	12	120		**Extraction de minerais d'uranium et de thorium**
	13			**Extraction de minerais métalliques**
		131		Extraction de minerai de fer
		132		Extraction de minerais de métaux non ferreux autres que l'uranium et le thorium
	14			**Autres activités extractives**
		141		Extraction de pierres, de sables et d'argiles
		142		Activités extractives, n.c.a.
D	15-37			**ACTIVITES DE FABRICATION**
	15			**Fabrication de produits alimentaires et de boissons**
		151		Production, transformation et conservation de viande, de poisson, de fruits, de légumes ; fabrication d'huiles et graisses
			1511	Production, transformation et conservation de viande et de produits à base de viande
			1512	Transformation et conservation de poisson et de produits à base de poisson
			1513	Transformation et conservation de fruits et légumes
			1514	Fabrication d'huiles et graisses végétales et animales
		152		Fabrication de produits laitiers
		153		Travail des grains, fabrication de produits amylacés et d'aliments pour animaux
			1531	Travail des grains
			1532	Fabrication de produits amylacés
			1533	Fabrication d'aliments pour animaux
		154		Fabrication d'autres produits alimentaires
			1541	Boulangerie, pâtisserie, biscuiterie
			1542	Fabrication de sucre
			1543	Fabrication de cacao, chocolat et confiserie
			1544	Fabrication de pâtes alimentaires, de couscous et de produits farineux similaires
			1549	Fabrication de produits alimentaires n.c.a.
		155		Fabrication de boissons
			1551	Distillation, rectification et mélange de spiritueux ; fabrication d'alcool éthylique à partir de produits de fermentation
			1552	Fabrication de vin et de cidre
			1553	Fabrication de boissons alcoolisées à base de malt ; production de malt

Statistiques des Structures Industrielles
OCDE, © 1998

		1554	Fabrication de boissons non alcoolisées ; production d'eaux minérales
16	**160**		**Fabrication de produits à base de tabac**
17			**Fabrication de textiles**
	171		Filature, tissage et achèvement des textiles
		1711	Préparation et filature des fibres textiles ; tissage des textiles
		1712	Achèvement des textiles
	172		Fabrication d'autres articles textiles
		1721	Fabrication d'articles confectionnés en textile, sauf habillement
		1722	Fabrication de tapis et carpettes
		1723	Fabrication de cordes, câbles, ficelles et filets
		1729	Fabrication d'articles textiles n.c.a.
	173		Fabrication d'étoffes et d'articles de bonneterie
18			**Fabrication d'articles d'habillement ; Préparation et teinture des fourrures**
	181		Fabrication d'articles d'habillement autres qu'en fourrure
	182		Préparation et teinture des fourrures ; confection d'articles en fourrure
19			**Apprêt et tannage des cuirs ; Fabrication d'articles de voyage et de maroquinerie, d'articles de sellerie et de bourrellerie ; Fabrication de chaussures**
	191		Apprêt et tannage des cuirs ; Fabrication d'articles de voyage et de maroquinerie, d'articles de sellerie et de bourrellerie
		1911	Apprêt et tannage des cuirs
		1912	Fabrication d'articles de voyage et de maroquinerie, d'articles de sellerie et de bourrellerie
	192		Fabrication de chaussures
20			**Production de bois et d'articles en bois et liège (sauf fabrication de meubles) ; Fabrication d'articles de vannerie et de sparterie**
	201		Sciage et rabotage du bois
	202		Fabrication d'articles en bois, liège, vannerie et sparterie
		2021	Fabrication de feuilles de placage, de contre-plaqués et de panneaux
		2022	Fabrication d'ouvrages de charpenterie et de menuiserie de bâtiment
		2023	Fabrication d'emballages en bois
		2029	Fabrication d'autres ouvrages en bois ; fabrication d'ouvrages en liège, vannerie et sparterie
21			**Fabrication de papier, de carton, et d'articles en papier et en carton**
	210		Fabrication de papier, de carton, et d'articles en papier et en carton
		2101	Fabrication de pâte à papier, de papier et de carton
		2102	Fabrication de papier et carton ondulés et d'emballages en papier et carton
		2109	Fabrication d'autres articles en papier et carton
22			**Edition, imprimerie et reproduction de supports enregistrés**
	221		Edition
		2211	Edition de livres, brochures, œuvres musicales et autres publications
		2212	Edition de journaux et périodiques
		2213	Edition de supports enregistrés
		2219	Autres activités d'édition
	222		Imprimerie et activités annexes
		2221	Imprimerie
		2222	Activités annexes à l'imprimerie
	223		Reproduction de supports enregistrés
23			**Cokéfaction, Fabrication de produits pétroliers raffinés et de combustibles nucléaires**
	231		Cokéfaction

	232		Fabrication de produits pétroliers raffinés
	233		Traitement de combustibles nucléaires
24			**Fabrication de produits chimiques**
	241		Fabrication de produits chimiques de base
		2411	Fabrication de produits chimiques de base autres que les engrais et les produits azotés
		2412	Fabrication d'engrais et de produits azotés
		2413	Fabrication de matières plastiques et de caoutchouc synthétique sous formes primaires
	242		Fabrication d'autres produits chimiques
		2421	Fabrication de pesticides et d'autres produits agro-chimiques
		2422	Fabrication de peintures, vernis et produits similaires, d'encres d'imprimerie et de mastics
		2423	Fabrication de produits pharmaceutiques, de produits chimiques à usage médicinal et de produits d'herboristerie
		2424	Fabrication de savons et détergents, de produits d'entretien, de parfums et de produits pour la toilette
		2429	Fabrication d'autres produits chimiques n.c.a.
	243		Fabrication de fibres synthétiques ou artificielles
25			**Fabrication d'articles en caoutchouc et en matières plastiques**
	251		Fabrication d'articles en caoutchouc
		2511	Fabrication de pneumatiques et de chambres à air ; rechapage et resculptage de pneumatiques
		2519	Fabrication d'autres articles en caoutchouc
	252		Fabrication d'articles en matières plastiques
26			**Fabrication d'autres produits minéraux non métalliques**
	261		Fabrication de verre et d'articles en verre
	269		Fabrication de produits minéraux non métalliques n.c.a.
		2691	Fabrication de produits céramiques non réfractaires autres que pour la construction ("Grès, porcelaines et faïences")
		2692	Fabrication de produits réfractaires en céramique
		2693	Fabrication de matériaux de construction non réfractaires en céramique
		2694	Fabrication de ciment, chaux et plâtre
		2695	Fabrication d'ouvrages en béton, en ciment et en plâtre
		2696	Taille, façonnage et finissage de la pierre
		2699	Fabrication d'autres produits minéraux non métalliques n.c.a.
27			**Fabrication de produits métallurgiques de base**
	271		Sidérurgie et première transformation de l'acier
	272		Métallurgie et première transformation des métaux précieux et des métaux non ferreux
	273		Fonderie
		2731	Fonderie de métaux ferreux
		2732	Fonderie de métaux non ferreux
28			**Fabrication d'ouvrages en métaux (sauf machines et matériel)**
	281		Construction et menuiserie métalliques ; fabrication de citernes, réservoirs et générateurs de vapeur
		2811	Construction et menuiserie métalliques
		2812	Fabrication de réservoirs, citernes et conteneurs métalliques
		2813	Fabrication de générateurs de vapeur (sauf chaudières de chauffage central à eau chaude)
	289		Fabrication d'autres ouvrages en métaux ; activités de services du travail des métaux
		2891	Forge, emboutissage, estampage et profilage du métal ; métallurgie des poudres

	2892	Traitement et revêtement des métaux, activités de mécanique générale en sous-traitance
	2893	Fabrication de coutellerie, d'outils à main et de quincaillerie générale
	2899	Fabrication d'ouvrages en métaux n.c.a.

29   **Fabrication de machines et de matériels non classés ailleurs**

291   Fabrication de machines d'usage général

2911   Fabrication de moteurs et de turbines (sauf moteurs pour avions, automobiles et motocycles)

2912   Fabrication de pompes, de compresseurs et d'articles de robinetterie

2913   Fabrication de paliers, d'engrenages et d'organes mécaniques de transmission

2914   Fabrication de fours et de brûleurs

2915   Fabrication de matériel de levage et de manutention

2919   Fabrication d'autres machines d'usage général

292   Fabrication de machines d'usage spécifique

2921   Fabrication de machines agricoles et forestières

2922   Fabrication de machines-outils

2923   Fabrication de machines pour la métallurgie

2924   Fabrication de machines pour les mines, les carrières et la construction

2925   Fabrication de machines pour le traitement des produits alimentaires, des boissons et du tabac

2926   Fabrication de machines pour les industries du textile, de l'habillement et des cuirs

2927   Fabrication d'armes et de munitions

2929   Fabrication d'autres machines d'usage spécifique

293   Fabrication d'appareils domestiques n.c.a.

30   **300**   **Fabrication de machines de bureau, de machines comptables et de matériel de traitement de l'information**

31   **Fabrication de machines et de matériels électriques non classés ailleurs**

311   Fabrication de moteurs, génératrices et transformateurs électriques

312   Fabrication de matériel électrique de distribution et de commande

313   Fabrication de fils et câbles électriques isolés

314   Fabrication d'accumulateurs et de piles électriques

315   Fabrication de lampes électriques et d'appareils d'éclairage

319   Fabrication d'autres matériels électriques n.c.a.

32   **Fabrication d'équipements et appareils de radio, télévision et communication**

321   Fabrication de tubes et valves électroniques et d'autres composants électroniques

322   Fabrication d'émetteurs de radio et télévision, et d'appareils de téléphonie et de télégraphie

323   Fabrication de récepteurs de télévision et de radio, d'appareils d'enregistrement et de reproduction du son ou de l'image, et articles associés

33   **Fabrication d'instruments médicaux, de précision et d'optique et d'horlogerie**

331   Fabrication d'appareils médicaux et d'instruments et appareils pour la mesure, la vérification, le contrôle, la navigation et d'autres usages sauf les instruments d'optique

3311   Fabrication d'instruments et d'appareils médico-chirurgicaux et d'appareils d'orthopédie

3312   Fabrication d'instruments et appareils pour la mesure, la vérification, le contrôle, la navigation et d'autres usages, sauf les équipements de contrôle de processus industriels

3313   Fabrication d'équipements de contrôle de processus industriels

332   Fabrication d'instruments d'optique et de matériel photographique

333   Fabrication d'horlogerie

34   **Construction de véhicules automobiles, de remorques et de semi-remorques**

341   Construction de véhicules automobiles

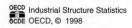

		342		Fabrication de carrosseries pour véhicules automobiles, fabrication de remorques et de semi-remorques
		343		Fabrication de pièces et accessoires pour véhicules automobiles et leurs moteurs
	35			**Fabrication d'autres matériels de transport**
		351		Construction et réparation de navires
			3511	Construction et réparation de navires de commerce
			3512	Construction et réparation de bateaux de plaisance et de sport
		352		Construction de matériel ferroviaire roulant
		353		Construction aéronautique et spatiale
		359		Fabrication d'autres équipements de transport
			3591	Fabrication de motocycles
			3592	Fabrication de bicyclettes et de véhicules pour invalides
			3599	Fabrication d'autres matériels de transport n.c.a.
	36			**Fabrication de meubles ; Activités de fabrication non classées ailleurs**
		361		Fabrication de meubles
		369		Activités de fabrication n.c.a.
			3691	Fabrication de bijouterie et d'articles similaires
			3692	Fabrication d'instruments de musique
			3693	Fabrication d'articles de sport
			3694	Fabrication de deux et jouets
			3699	Autres activités de fabrication n.c.a.
	37			**Récupération**
		371		Récupération de déchets et débris métalliques
		372		Récupération de déchets et débris non métalliques
E	**40-41**			**PRODUCTION ET DISTRIBUTION D'ELECTRICITE, DE GAZ ET D'EAU**
	40			**Production et distribution d'électricité de gaz, de vapeur et d'eau chaude**
		401		Production, collecte et distribution d'électricité
		402		Fabrication de gaz ; distribution par conduite de combustibles gazeux
		403		Production et distribution de vapeur et d'eau chaude
	41	410		**Captage, épuration et distribution d'eau**
F	**45**			**CONSTRUCTION**
G	**50-52**			**COMMERCE DE GROS ET DE DETAIL ; REPARATION DE VEHICULES AUTOMOBILES, DE MOTOCYCLES ET DE BIENS PERSONNELS ET DOMESTIQUES**
H	**55**			**HOTELS ET RESTAURANTS**
I	**60**			**TRANSPORTS, ENTREPOSAGE ET COMMUNICATIONS**
J	**65-67**			**INTERMEDIATION FINANCIERE**
K	**70-74**			**IMMOBILIER, LOCATIONS ET ACTIVITES DE SERVICE AUX ENTREPRISES**
L-Q	**75-99**			**ADMINISTRATION PUBLIQUE ET DEFENSE ; SECURITE SOCIALE OBLIGATOIRE ; EDUCATION ; SANTE ; SERVICES SOCIAUX ; SERVICES DOMESTIQUES ; ORGANISATIONS ET ORGANISMES EXTRATERRITORIAUX**
A-Q	**01-99**			**GRAND TOTAL**

METHODOLOGICAL INFORMATION

INFORMATIONS METHODOLOGIQUES

Section I

Sources and Definitions
Sources et définitions

Table of contents - Table des matières

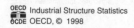

AUSTRALIA

I. INDUSTRIAL STATISTICS

Source

The information is provided by the Australian Bureau of Statistics (ABS). The data for mining and manufacturing industries are derived from the Manufacturing Survey, which is establishment-based. From 1990-91, all establishments have been surveyed. Data for other industries result from the Economic Activity Survey, which is based on enterprises ("management units"). The period covered is the fiscal year starting on 1 July.

Industrial Classification

Up to 1994, the classification used was the Australian Standard Industrial Classification (ASIC) in line with the ISIC Revision 2.

From 1995, the Australia and New Zealand Standard Industrial Classification (ANZSIC) is used. There is a correspondence between ANZSIC and ISIC Revision 3.

Concepts and Definitions of Variables

Production is turnover measured as sales and transfers out of goods whether or not produced by the establishment, income from services (such as manufacture or assembly on a fee or commission basis, repair and servicing, installation fees, delivery charges, sales or agency commissions, advertising income), rent, leasing and hiring income, government subsidies and bounties on production and capitalised wages and capitalised material costs of own account capital work.

Value added is calculated as turnover plus increase (or less decrease) in stocks minus selected expenses. Included in selected expenses are purchases and transfers of materials, fuels, containers and packaging materials and goods for resale, motor vehicle running expenses, rent, leasing and hiring expenses, repair and maintenance expenses, freight and cartage expenses, commission and subcontract expenses, advertising expenses, audit and other accounting fees, cleaning expenses, payments for data processing services, legal expenses, printing expenses, postal and courier service expenses, payments for secretarial, word processing and copying services, payments for staff training services, telecommunications expenses, travel, accommodation and entertainment expenses, other management and administrative expenses, land taxes and land rates, payroll based taxes and other operating expenses. Excluded from selected expenses are wages and salaries, superannuation expenses, workers' compensation and other insurance expenses, interest expenses, bank charges, royalties expenses, depreciation, bad debts, direct taxes, sales tax, excise, dividends and provisions.

From 1990-91, *employment* refers to the number of persons employed (including working proprietors and working partners of unincorporated businesses) at 30 June of each year. It includes all employees whether full time, part time, permanent, temporary or casual. It includes employees on paid leave at 30 June of each year. It excludes contractors, consultants, other self-employed persons providing services, unpaid helpers and volunteers.

Wages and salaries, employees are defined as gross wages and salaries paid/payable to employees for the year ended 30 June. They include wages, salaries, bonuses, commissions, overtime payments, penalty rates, leave payments and provisions for employee entitlements. They also include salaries and fees of directors and executives. They exclude payments to contractors, consultants and other self employed persons and the drawings of proprietors and partners of unincorporated businesses). They also exclude payroll-related taxes and reimbursements to employees for expenses incurred.

Numbers of *establishments* are at 30 June of the year indicated. An establishment is the smallest accounting unit of a business which controls its productive activities and is wholly contained within a single Australian State or Territory. The majority of establishments cover operations at a single location but a substantial minority incorporate more than one location.

Publications

i) *Census of manufacturing establishments*: summary of operations (Preliminary) by Industry subdivision, Australia (Catalogue No. 8201.0);

ii) *Manufacturing establishments,* summary of operations by Industry class, Australia (Catalogue No. 8202.0);

iii) *Manufacturing establishments,* details of operations by Industry class, Australia (Catalogue No. 8203.0) -- this is the main bulletin;

iv) *Business Operations and Industry Performance* (Catalogue No. 8140.0).

AUSTRIA

I. INDUSTRIAL STATISTICS

Source

Data are supplied by the Austrian Central Statistical Office.

Data for 1990-1994 are the results of the former annual Industrial Statistical Survey. This survey covered all establishments affiliated to the Industrial Section of the Federal Economic Chamber. t also covered establishments which affiliated to the "Gewerbe" Section but only with 20 or more employees. The statistical unit was the establishment ("Betrieb").

Data for 1995 are the results of the Non-agricultural Census. This census covers all enterprises in the non-agricultural sector (ISIC Revision 3 categories C to K and M to O). The statistical unit is the enterprise. Data for 1995 are not strictly comparable which the years before.

Industrial Classification

Up to 1994, the classification of economic activities used in Austria, "Betriebssystematik 1968", was in line with the ISIC Revision 2 classification. For hours worked, certain industries were not covered by the monthly survey: ISIC 324; ISIC 369; ISIC 385; ISIC 39.

From 1995, the classification used is the Austrian version of NACE Revision 1, so called "ÖNACE 1995". Up to the 4-digit level there is a complete correspondence between ÖNACE 1995 and NACE Revision 1, the 4-digit level being further subdivided into sub-classes. The ÖNACE 1995 is in line with the ISIC Revision 3.

Concepts and Definitions of Variables

1990-1994 data

The *establishment* corresponds to the local kind-of-activity unit (LKAU).

Production is gross output valued in producers' prices, including all indirect taxes but excluding value-added tax and all subsidies. It includes all products, net change of work in progress, work done on own account, services rendered, goods shipped in the same condition as received, electricity sold, fixed assets produced for own use, net changes in stock levels of finished goods, waste products, and goods made by homeworkers and handicraft workers.

Value added is based on the concept of "census" value added. It is calculated as the value of gross output less the cost of materials, fuels and other supplies, contract and commission work done by others, repair and maintenance work done by others, goods shipped in the same condition as received and electricity purchased with the input estimates made on a consumed basis. The cost of and receipts for non-industrial services are included. The valuation is in producers' prices, including all indirect taxes but excluding all subsidies and value added tax.

Employment data are given both for total number of persons engaged, and for employees, in terms of the number engaged or employed on 31 December of each year. Total employment includes working proprietors, unpaid family workers, self-employed persons, salaried employees, wage-earners, homeworkers, full- and part-time employees, and clerical workers or supervisory personnel performing functions closely related to the production process. *Hours worked* relate to actual hours worked (*i.e.* all paid hours less paid holiday and leave) by operatives and apprentices, according to the wage list. Included are: overtime, waiting time, rest periods, sick leave and public holidays. Casual and part-time workers are excluded. Supervisors and apprentices are included only if they appear on the wage list.

Investment is investment expenditure, defined as the value of purchases of fixed assets, including own-account construction of assets. The value of sales of fixed assets is not deducted. "Fixed assets" are those with a productive life of at least one year, including assets made by a unit's labour force; additions, alterations, repairs to existing assets; new assets, whether not yet in use, unused, previously used outside the country, or used assets. The valuation is at full cost including delivered price, cost of installation, fees and taxes (except value added tax). For assets produced by the unit, the cost of labour, material and other supplies, and an allocation for overheads are included. The value of sales of used assets is the actual amount realised. *Investment in machinery and equipment* is given in terms of investment expenditure defined as for total investment *i.e.* the value of the purchase of fixed assets plus own-account construction of assets. Included are transport equipment; industrial machinery and equipment; office machinery, equipment and furniture, professional instruments and equipment; alterations, improvements and repairs thereto.

Compensation of labour, employees covers wages and salaries, plus employers' contributions to social security schemes and pension funds. It includes regular and overtime payments, bonuses, cost-of-living allowances, vacation and sick leave pay, taxes and social insurance contributions payable by employees and deducted by employers, payments in kind and allowances (travelling, clothing expenses). *Employers' social costs* cover legally required and voluntary contributions, such as social security contributions (health, old-age, accident, unemployment insurance), contributions to the equalisation fund for child allowance, contributions to the residential construction fund and lodging allowance, and non-obligatory payments (e.g. in case of accident, disease or distress; canteen services; mileage allowance).

1995 data

The *enterprise* is generally the smallest legal unit which may consist of one or more establishments.

Production corresponds to turnover, including revenues out of capitalisation of services rendered for own account, excluding purchase of goods and services for resale in the same condition as received

Statistiques des Structures Industrielles OECD
OECD, © 1998 OCDE

(without foreign freights). It includes net change in stocks of commercial articles, finished products and work in progress.

Value added at factor costs is equal to value added at basic prices, excluding taxes and duties (without taxes of products), including subsidies (without subsidies on products). The value added at basic prices is calculated as the production value less foreign freights, purchase of material for working and processing, expenditure for repairs and maintenance done by other enterprises, expenditure for working done by other enterprises, payments for agency workers, purchase of fuels, expenditure for rents, expenditure for operational leasing of goods, other operating costs, expenditure for low-valued assets, taxes of products, including net change in stocks of fuels, raw materials and consumables and subsidies on products.

Employment data are given both for total number of persons engaged and for employees (on a fixed day: 31 December 1995). *Employment* includes working proprietors, unpaid family workers, self-employed persons, salaried employees, operatives, apprentices, homeworkers and part-time employees. *Employment, employees* includes salaried employees, operatives, apprentices, homeworkers and part-time employees.

Investment (capital formation) is investment expenditure, defined as the value of purchases of fixed assets, including own-account construction of assets. The value of sales of fixed assets is not deducted. Investments in land, in construction and alteration of buildings, in machinery and equipment, in tangible goods, in concessions, patents, licences, trade marks and in software are included. The valuation is at full cost including delivered price, cost of installation, fees and taxes (except turnover tax). *Investment in machinery and equipment* is given in terms of investment expenditure defined as for total investment i.e. the value of the purchase of fixed assets plus own-account construction of assets. Included are transport equipment, industrial machinery and equipment, office machinery, equipment and furniture, professional instruments and equipment, alterations, improvement and repairs.

Compensation of labour covers wages and salaries, employers' contributions to social security schemes and pension funds. Wages and salaries include regular and overtime payments, bonuses, cost-of-living allowances, vacation and sick leave pay, taxes and social insurance contributions payable by employees and deducted by employers, payments in kind and allowances. *Total wages and salaries* include the gross remuneration of salaried employees, operatives, apprentices, homeworkers and part-time employees. *Wages and salaries, employees* include the gross remuneration of salaried employees (without apprentices). *Employers' social costs* cover legally required and voluntary contributions, such as social security contributions (health, old-age, accident, unemployment insurance), contributions to the equalisation fund for child allowance, contributions to the residential construction fund and lodging allowance, and non-obligatory payments (e.g. in case of accident, disease or distress; canteen services; mileage allowance).

Hours worked by employees relate to actual hours worked (i.e. all paid hours less paid holiday leave) by salaried employees, operatives and apprentices, according to the wage list. Included are: overtime, waiting time, rest periods, sick leave and public holidays. Homeworkers and part-time workers are excluded.

Publications

All data to the 3-digit ISIC level are presented in the following publications:

i) *Industriestatistik*, 2. Teil, published by the Austrian Central Statistical Office in the framework of the publication series contribution for Austrian Statistics.

ii) *Gewerbestatistik*, 2. Teil, published by the Austrian *Central* Statistical Office in the framework of the publication series contribution for Austrian Statistics.

BELGIUM

I. GENERAL

The Belgian Institut des Comptes Nationaux (ICN) provided information on foreign trade and national accounts.

II. FOREIGN TRADE STATISTICS

Source

Trade data refer to the Belgium-Luxembourg Economic Union (BLEU). They are derived from returns which may be:

a) Customs imports and exports documents;

b) Statistical forms handed in at the Belgian-Dutch border;

c) Monthly magnetic tapes relating to imports originating in the Netherlands, passed to the ICN by the Dutch Centraal Bureau voor de Statistiek (CBS). These tapes assemble data on exports destined to the BLEU, as given to the CBS by Dutch exporters who have been given authorisation to provide summary figures;

d) Periodic statements from firms authorised to make overall import-export declarations (generally monthly) direct to the ICN.

Industrial Classification

The foreign trade service at the Banque Nationale de Belgique (BNB) establishes each year a converter between the national code for goods (the BNL) and the NACE-CLIO classification (version D, 1975). Data classified according to the SITC may be regrouped to ISIC using a fixed correlation table.

Concepts and Definitions of Variables

Special trade is given, *exports* fob, and *imports* cif.

Included are: state trading; commercial transactions in military equipment and supplies; foreign aid transactions; improvement and repair trade; transactions in new and second-hand ships and aircraft; electric energy and gas; industrial gold; gold and silver monies; old monies as collectors' items; bank notes, securities and other monies, etc.; printed or engraved in the BLEU or imported there after printing or engraving (these are taken at their commercial value -- i.e. value of paper and metal -- not their nominal value); sea products landed direct from the high seas. Only sea products landed by foreign ships are included in import statistics: those brought ashore by Belgian ships are regarded as national produce.

Excluded from the statistics are those movements of goods which represent no commercial interest. Full details of such operations are given in Articles 22, 24, 27, 28, 29, 30, 31 and 32 of Regulation 1736/75, relating to foreign trade statistics of the EC and trade among its Member countries. The text of these articles is available on request. In addition, there exists a level below which commercial transactions are not recorded. This limit is presently set at 14 500 Belgian Francs and 1 000 kg.

III. NATIONAL ACCOUNTS STATISTICS

Source

Number of establishments and remuneration of labour statistics are supplied by the Office national de sécurité sociale (ONSS). Employment data are provided by the Ministère de l'Emploi et du Travail.

Industrial Classification

Till 1992, the ONSS classified establishments and remuneration data according to NACE70. Since 1993, the original classification used, before regrouping to the ISIC, is NACE Revision 1. For this reason, data up to and including 1992 are not strictly comparable with those for later years.

Concepts and Definitions of Variables

Information is drawn up following the principles of national accounting (ESA 1979 -- the European System of Integrated Economic Accounts -- which is the European version of the SNA 1968, the United Nations' System of National Accounts).

Constant Price Data

Constant price statistics are, in principle, evaluated using a double-deflation method.

CANADA

I. GENERAL

Statistics Canada provided data and accompanying notes based on industrial statistics and national accounts.

II. INDUSTRIAL STATISTICS

Source

The Census of Manufactures (production, value added, employment, wages and salaries) conducted annually by Statistics Canada, is an establishment-based survey covering all units for the fiscal year.

Industrial Classification

Data have been regrouped to ISIC from the Canadian Standard Industrial Classification (1980), which has been in use since 1983. Data for 1982 were restated to this 1980 version. There are no major problems in reconciling the two systems.

Concepts and Definitions of Variables

Production is gross output (for manufacturing) including the full value of sales of all products, work done on own account, manufacturing services rendered, goods shipped in the same condition as received, electricity sold, fixed assets produced for own use, waste products, goods made by homeworkers and made by handicraft workers if the establishment has a pay deduction number, and revenue from rental of own products, allowing for net changes of work in progress and in stocks of finished goods. Canadian output for wholesale and retail trade is total sales and other revenue. The valuation is in factor values, including all subsidies and excluding all indirect taxes. The same valuation is used for the measurement of the "census" concept of *value added*, which is calculated as gross output less the cost of materials, fuels and other supplies, goods shipped in the same condition as received and electricity purchased. The cost of non-industrial services is not deducted. Value added includes receipts for various non-industrial services, but does not include interest or rental other than on machinery produced and rented. Canadian value added for wholesale and retail trade is output less the total "cost of goods sold" (total materials).

Employment, employees is based on the average number of employees throughout the year, whether full- or part-time. It includes salaried employees, and wage earners. Figures for *hours worked* cover the total number of hours worked in a year by operatives and include apprentices, casual and part-time workers. They are derived from an establishment-based census of firms covering all known incorporated firms (plus some unincorporated businesses) having shipments of manufactured goods in excess of $25 000 per annum, with estimates included for those smaller establishments for which data are obtained from taxation records. Included are: overtime, waiting time or time on call and rest periods. Annual leave, public holidays, sick leave and other paid leave are excluded.

Wages and salaries, employees include regular and overtime cash payments, bonuses and cost-of-living allowances, vacation and sick leave pay, taxes and social insurance contributions, etc., payable by employees and deduced by employers and payment in kind and allowances forming part of income.

Locations are given for *establishments* figures for wholesale and retail trade.

Publications

Annual Census of Manufactures, which includes 24 industry groups, and general publications.
Published by Statistics Canada.

CZECH REPUBLIC

1. INDUSTRIAL STATISTICS

Source

Data source is periodical sample surveys conducted by the Czech Statistical Office. The statistical unit is the enterprise.

The number of employees is decisive for the determination of the size category and derived reporting duty (more than 6 in 1997, 20 and more since 1998). Simple random sampling is used, stratified by the size of an enterprise and branch of industry (NACE).

Statistiques des Structures Industrielles OECD
OECD, © 1998 OCDE

Industrial Classification

Branch Classification of Economic Activities (OKEC) was introduced in 1992 and updated in 1994. OKEC uses 5-digit codes; they are taken over from NACE Revision 1 down to the 4th digit, the 5th digit is used for national specifics. OKEC is identical to ISIC Revision 3 down to the 2nd digit.

Concepts and Definitions of Variables

Production (gross output) is the sum of market and non-market outputs produced by domestic producers over a given period. It is equal to the sum of revenues from sales of own products, goods, works and services provided to the other establishments within the enterprise and included also changes in stocks of own production and work in progress. Costs incurred on sold goods and VAT are excluded. The valuation is in producer's prices, excluding VAT.

Value added is obtained by subtracting the value of inputs (the cost of materials, fuels and other supplies) from gross output.

Employment is the number of persons employed, including working proprietors, self-employed persons and salaried employees. *Employment, employees* encompasses all categories of permanent, temporary and seasonal employees contracted for work in the enterprise. The definition of this indicator is in line with the resolution concerning statistics of economically active population, employment, unemployment and underemployment, adopted by the 13th International Conference of Labour Statistics (Geneva, 1982) with the following exceptions: it excludes persons on maternity leave and apprentices.

Hours worked cover hours worked by manual workers.

Publications

i) Aggregate publications - distributed by the CSO:

Statistical Yearbook of the Czech Republic - available every year in December

Indicators of Social and Economic Development of the Czech Republic - 90th day after reference quarter

CSO Bulletin - January, April, July, October

ii) Statistical Information - series Industry - distributed by the CSO:

Czech Republic's Industry - 55th day

Czech Republic's Industry - Monthly Figures revised - June

DENMARK

I. GENERAL

The information was provided by Danmarks Statistik.

II. INDUSTRIAL STATISTICS

Source

Data are collected using a questionnaire based partly on the establishment as a local unit (employment, investments, remuneration data) and partly on kind-of-activity units (production, value added). The reference period is the calendar year for employment, exports, imports, and remuneration, and the accounting year for production, value added and investment data. Surveys with coverage of units with more than 19 persons are conducted every year for production, value added and investment data, supplemented by surveys every five years covering units with 0 to 19 employed in the enterprise.

Till 1989, the annual survey for employment and remuneration covered all units with six or more persons in the enterprise. From 1990, the figures for number of establishments, employment and remuneration are derived from the register-based statistics of establishments and employment. All establishments with any employment in manufacturing are covered.

Industrial Classification

The Danish national classification conforms to the ISIC, with some differences:

a) For production, value added and investment: ISIC 3829 includes 3821 and ISIC 3843 includes 3842;

b) For employment, remuneration and number of establishments: ISIC 3841 includes 3842 (up to and including 1989).

Concepts and Definitions of Variables

Production is given as gross output, valued in factor values, excluding all indirect taxes and including all subsidies. It includes the value of all products, net change of work in progress, work done on own account, services rendered, goods shipped in the same condition as received, electricity sold, fixed assets produced for own use, net changes in stock levels of finished goods, waste products, goods made by homeworkers and handicraft workers and other elements of turnover. The valuation is the same for *value added*, which is calculated from the value of gross output less the cost of materials, fuels and other supplies, contract and commission work done by others, goods shipped in the same condition as received and electricity purchased. The input estimates are on a consumed basis.

Employment (up to and including 1989) is given as the total number of persons engaged, as calculated from the average number of persons engaged at the end of March, June, September and November. Working proprietors, salaried employees, full-time employees, and part-time employees working a minimum of 15 hours per week are covered. Apprentices are also included. From 1990, the employment figures include all employees and all self-employed at end November in the establishments mentioned above. Both full-time and part-time employed are included, including secondary activities.

Statistiques des Structures Industrielles
OECD, © 1998

Investment (gross fixed capital formation) is given as the value of purchases of fixed assets, including own-account construction of assets, less the value of sales of fixed assets. Fixed assets are those with a productive life of more than three years, including assets made by a unit's labour force for its own use, additions, alterations and improvements to existing assets, new assets (whether or not in use) and used assets. The valuation is at full cost incurred, including the delivered price and the installation cost. For assets produced by the unit, the cost of work put in progress is used, including labour costs, costs of material and other supplies. The actual amount realised is taken when deducting sales of used assets. *Investment in machinery and equipment* is again gross fixed capital formation, and uses the same definition. Transport equipment, industrial machinery and equipment, office machinery, equipment and furniture, professional instruments and equipment, and alterations and improvements to all these are included.

Before 1990, *wages and salaries, employees* include wages to homeworkers. Regular and overtime cash payments, bonuses, cost-of-living allowances, vacation and sick leave pay are included. From 1990, the figures for wages and salaries include all outlays of these kinds reported to the tax authorities in establishments operating in manufacturing industry during the year. This means that even outlays in establishments which are not in activity at end November (but were in activity in manufacturing industry during some part of the year) are included in the figures.

Up to 1989, the number of *establishments* is given as the population of local units as it was ascertained in the annual survey for employment and remuneration. The data includes industrial establishments with 6 or more persons employed. From 1990, all establishments with any employment, in activity at end November, are covered.

Publications

i) Statistical Reports: *Industrial Statistics* (annual up to and including 1989);
ii) *Statistical News*, Series Industry and Energy;
iii) Statistical Reports: *Industrial Accounts Statistics*;
iv) *Statistical News*, Series General Economic Statistics and Internal Trade.

All are published by Danmarks Statistik.

FINLAND

I. GENERAL

Information has been provided by Statistics Finland, Helsinki for both industrial statistics and national accounts data.

II. INDUSTRIAL STATISTICS

Source

The data is derived from two sources: 1) the results of the Office's annual industrial statistics inquiry and 2) information from Tax Authorities Registers. The statistical unit which is used is the establishment and the survey covers chiefly the calendar year but in some instances the fiscal year is also used. There is a major break between the year 1994 and 1995. Up to 1994 all units employing five or more persons are surveyed. No attempt is made to account for units falling outside this limit, though the inquiry covers approximately 99% of gross output and 97% of all manufacturing employment.

In 1995 the cut-off limit for the units to be surveyed by statistical inquiry changed. The questionnaire was sent to all establishments that belong to an enterprise employing at least 10 persons. Data for units with less than 10 employees were compiled from information supplied by the Tax Administration. Since the year 1996 the cut-off limit has been 20 persons. Enterprises having less than 20 persons are regarded as single-unit enterprises.

Because of the major break between the year 1994 and 1995, the variables are not comparable between these years. Especially this holds true for the number of establishments. Furthermore, it is worth noting that, although the methods have remained basically the same since the year 1995, the number of plants is quite sensitive variable in present approach.

Industrial Classification

The classification, derived from NACE Revision 1, is the Finnish Standard Industrial Classification 1995 (SIC-95). It aligns with the ISIC Revision 3.

Concepts and Definitions of Variables

The *production* value is defined as turnover, plus or minus the changes in stocks of finished products, work in progress and goods and services purchased for resale, minus the purchases of goods and services for resale, plus capitalised production, plus other operating income. Incomes classified as extra-ordinary or financial in company accounts are excluded from production value (such as income from sales of tangible assets). The valuation is in factor values, excluding all indirect taxes and including all subsidies.

Value added is the gross income from operating activities. It can be calculated from gross operating surplus by adding personnel costs and by deducting income from sales of tangible assets. It is valued in factor costs, excluding indirect taxes and including subsidies.

Employment covers the total number of persons engaged, including working proprietors, unpaid family workers, salaried employees, wage earners and all full- and part-time employees and also persons on short-term leaves. It is based on the average number of employees throughout the year. *Employment, employees* covers total number of salaried employees excluding working proprietors and unpaid workers. *Hours worked* is measured by the actual hours worked by operatives during the accounting period.

Investment (capital formation) is expenditure on the purchase of fixed assets plus own-account construction of assets. Fixed assets include investments in equipment goods, buildings, other construction and other fixed assets and exclude investments in land and water resources. They are investments with a productive life of at least one year, and include assets made by a unit's labour force for its own use; additions, alterations, improvements and repairs to existing assets; new assets (whether or not in use) and used assets. The valuation is at full cost incurred, including delivered price, cost of installation and fees and taxes. *Investment in machinery and equipment* follows the same definition. Expenditure on transport equipment, industrial machinery and equipment, office machinery equipment and furniture, professional instruments and equipment are included together with alterations and improvements to these items.

Compensation of labour, employees is defined as wages, salaries and social costs. *Wages and salaries, employees* cover all paid regular and overtime wages and salaries, cash payments, bonuses, cost-of-living allowances, paid education, vacation and sick leave along with taxes and social insurance contributions payable by employees and deducted by employers, and payments in kind. *Supplements/employers' social costs* are employers' legally required supplements to wages and salaries. They cover statutory social insurance contributions and voluntary social insurance contributions of a statutory nature.

Publications

i)   *Preliminary Data on Finnish Industries,*

ii)   *Statistics on the Structure of Industry and Construction*

Both are published by Statistics Finland, Helsinki.

III. FOREIGN TRADE STATISTICS

Source

Data are derived from Board of Customs statistics.

Concepts and Definitions of Variables

General trade is given, *exports* fob, *imports* cif. Both include state trading, commercial transactions in military equipment, foreign aid transactions, transactions in new ships and aircraft, electric energy and gas, and specifically exclude direct transit trade, temporary exports or imports, monetary transactions and minor transactions of less than 1 000 Mk.

IV. NATIONAL ACCOUNTS STATISTICS

Source

National accounts data, covering the calendar year. All units are included.

Industrial Classification

The classification, derived from NACE Revision 1, is the Finnish Standard Industrial Classification 1995 (SIC-95). It aligns with the ISIC Revision 3.

Concepts and Definitions of Variables

Production is given as gross output in basic values, including the value of all products (allowing for net changes of work in progress and in stock levels of finished goods), work done on own account, services rendered, electricity sold, fixed assets produced for own use, and waste products. Goods made by homeworkers and handicraft workers are also included. *Value added* is again in basic values. It is calculated as gross output less the cost of materials, fuels and other supplies; contract and commission, repair and maintenance work done by others; and electricity purchased, using input estimates calculated on a consumed basis.

Employment covers the total number of persons engaged, based on the average number of employees throughout the year. Included are working proprietors, active business partners, unpaid family workers, the self-employed, homeworkers, salaried employees and wage earners, whether full- or part-time.

Investment is gross fixed capital formation, and takes the value of purchases of fixed assets (including own-account construction of assets), less the value of sales. Assets covered are those with a productive life of at least one year, including assets made by a unit's labour force for its own use and all alterations, additions and improvements. Repairs are excluded. New assets, if not yet in use or previously used outside the country, are covered. The valuation is at full cost incurred, including delivered price, cost of installation, fees and taxes. Gross fixed capital formation is also given for *investment in machinery and equipment*. It includes industrial machinery and equipment, office machinery, equipment and furniture, professional instruments and equipment, plus alterations and improvements to these items.

Total wages and salaries include regular and overtime cash payments, bonuses and cost-of-living allowances, vacation and sick leave pay, and payments in kind are covered, also taxes and social contributions payable by employees but deducted by employers.

Constant Price Data

Constant price data are calculated using price deflation, though for the agriculture division a double deflation-extrapolation method is used.

FRANCE

I. GENERAL

The data are of two types according to origin. Industrial statistics and foreign trade statistics have been supplied by SESSI (Ministry of Economy, Finances and Industry). National accounts information has been supplied by the French Institut National de la Statistique et des Etudes Economiques (INSEE).

1. INDUSTRIAL STATISTICS AND FOREIGN TRADE

Industrial Classification

The French classification is the NAF-1993 (Nomenclature des Activités Françaises). NAF-1993 is fully compatible with NACE Revision 1 and with ISIC Revision 3.

Concepts and Definitions of Variables

Production corresponds to the total value of goods and services, sold, stocked or immobilised, that have been produced during the year. Sold products include the margin realised by the enterprises. Stocked production and immobilised production are estimated at production cost. The immobilised production corresponds to the costs of work done by the enterprise on own account. *Value added* is defined as gross value added at factor costs. It is calculated as production, plus sold goods, less intermediate consumption (which corresponds to purchased goods, materials, fuels and other supplies, plus net change in stocks of goods, materials, fuels and other supplies, plus other external purchases and costs), plus subsidies and less taxes and assimilated payments.

Employment is defined as the average number of persons engaged throughout the year. *Employment, employees*, which corresponds to the average number of employees, is adjusted for net change of external workers (interim employed persons and workers on hire).

Investment data is the sum of the value of acquisitions and production of fixed capital. It includes fixed assets in progress but excludes intangible and financial assets and equipment financed by leasing.

Data for remuneration covers *wages and salaries, employees* paid by the employer during the year to compensate for the work of its employees (excluding interim employed persons and workers on hire). It excludes *employer's contributions to social security*, which are given separately.

Exports are defined as exported goods and services declared by enterprises. They include intra-Europe deliveries. They differ from exports registered by customs in that they correspond to direct exports only (i.e. not through a third party). Furthermore, the sector to which exports are classified is defined by the enterprise's main activity (i.e. secondary activity is classified to the same sector as the main activity).

III. NATIONAL ACCOUNTS STATISTICS

Source

France's national accounts are drawn up by INSEE (Paris), with the assistance of a number of other administrative bodies. National accounts of goods and services are based on kind-of-activity units for production, value added and employment. They cover the calendar year and are derived from a sample of all units.

The data are set out in accordance with international classifications and the rules of the UN System of National Accounts. However, the valuation method is based on French classifications and the rules of the "Système élargi de comptabilité nationale" (SECN), the French version of the European System of Integrated National Accounts (ESA). Input-output tables, with values at market prices, form an integral part of French national accounts and are published annually at the same time as the accounts.

Industrial Classification

Data were originally classified according to the NAP 100. The national conversion table was used to produce the ISIC-classified figures.

Concepts and Definitions of Variables

Production is gross output by branch in basic values. *Value added*, also in basic values, is calculated as gross output, less the cost of: materials, fuels and other supplies; contract and commission, repair and maintenance work done by others; goods shipped in the same condition as received; electricity purchased. Information on inputs is gathered on the basis of amount consumed.

Employment gives the number of persons engaged or employees (*employment-employees*) as the average number of employees (or persons engaged) throughout the year. Total employment includes working proprietors, active business partners, unpaid family workers, the self-employed, salaried employees, wage earners, homeworkers, and clerical workers or supervisory personnel performing functions closely related to the production process. Both full- and part-time employees are covered.

Exports are given fob and *imports* cif.

Gross fixed capital formation (*investment*) is the value of acquisitions of fixed capital (plus own-account construction) less the value of sales of own account construction. Fixed assets covered are those with a productive life of more than one year and include assets made by a unit's labour force for its own use; additions, alterations, improvements and repairs; new assets not yet in use and used assets. The valuation for new assets is the full cost incurred, including delivered price and installation charges, but excluding fees and taxes. Assets produced by the unit are valued at the cost of work put in progress, while for sales of used assets, the actual amount realised is taken.

Publications

Evaluation methods:

i) *Système Élargi de Comptabilité Nationale*, Volumes 198-199, Collections de l'INSEE, série C, no. 44.45, May 1976;

ii) *Sources et Méthodes d'Élaboration des Comptes Nationaux*, "les biens et services", Volume 397, Collections de l'INSEE, série C, no. 99, November 1981;

Constant price calculation:

iii) *Comptes nationaux des biens et services à prix constants*, volume 252, Collections de l'INSEE, série C, no. 59, March 1978;

Regular publication of accounts in:

iv) *Rapport sur les Comptes de la Nation*, Collections de l'INSEE.

GERMANY

I. GENERAL

The information is supplied by the Federal Statistical Office (Statistisches Bundesamt) in Wiesbaden. The data are of two types according to origin: industrial statistics, foreign trade statistics. Data prior to 1990 refer to western Germany (Federal Republic of Germany before the unification of Germany, including West Berlin). Data from 1991 onwards refer to unified Germany, except for data for value added, investment, and investment in machinery and equipment, which continue to refer to the former western Germany.

II. INDUSTRIAL STATISTICS

Source

In general, the figures for mining and manufacturing are derived from the monthly inquiry carried out by the Office. The inquiry covers, on a complete enumeration basis, local units belonging to enterprises with 20 or more persons engaged including production handicrafts and the industrial units of non-industrial activities.

For ISIC Major Division 4 all enterprises with 20 or more persons engaged are covered.

Industrial Classification

The data have been converted from the national classification (Systematik für die Statistik im Produzierenden Gewerbe -- SYPRO) to ISIC, in so far as details permit. The differences between the two nomenclatures are set out in the following paragraph.

Prefabricated building manufacturing, classified as construction under the national scheme, is not generally included; publishing (ISIC 342) is not surveyed; manufacture of natural stone products (ISIC 369) is included in ISIC 290; manufacture of mattresses (ISIC 332) in ISIC 321; manufacture of umbrellas (ISIC 390) in ISIC 322; manufacture of fur wearing apparel (ISIC 322) in ISIC 323; bookbinding (ISIC 342) in ISIC 341; manufacture of mixed lubricating oils and greases (ISIC 353, 354) in ISIC 351 and 352 combined; manufacture of unprocessed plastic pipes and tubes (ISIC 351) in ISIC 356; surface refinement and hardening plants (ISIC 381) in ISIC 371; manufacture of drawn steel wire and forged steel chains (ISIC 371), washing machines (ISIC 382) and assembly and repair of ventilation, heating and sanitary systems (ISIC Major Division 5) in ISIC 381; manufacture of lighting glassware (ISIC 362), recording of master tapes and records (ISIC Major Division 9) and manufacture of electric and electronic measuring instruments and meters (ISIC 385) in ISIC 383. The estimates of value added are generally compiled in the same manner as those for the inquiries but quarrying is included in ISIC 369, prefabricated building manufacturing is excluded for all years, erection of structural steel is included in ISIC 381 and the difference in respect of assembly and repair of ventilation, heating and sanitary systems has been adjusted.

In 1983, production and employment data were regrouped to the ISIC using an improved correlation table. However, this partly affects comparability with earlier years. The ISIC positions most affected are 371, 381 and 383.

Concepts and Definitions of Variables

The figures for *production* relate to turnover from own production based on invoice values and include proceeds from goods sold as purchased, from the sale of waste, power and similar items. Proceeds from non-industrial activities (e.g. interest payments, rentals, and dividends) are excluded. The value of shipments also excludes value added or turnover taxes but includes excise duties, costs for freight packing, postage and other changes. Shipments effected between units of the same enterprise are not recorded. Estimates for *value added* are net production or census value added. They are calculated as gross output less the cost of materials, fuels and other supplies, contract and commission work done by others, repair and maintenance work done by others, goods shipped in the same condition as received and electricity purchased. The cost of non-industrial services is excluded while receipts therefrom are included. Input estimates are on a received basis and adjustments have been made for changes in stocks of materials, fuels and other supplies. Valuation is done at producer price including all direct taxes (excluding turnover tax) and excluding all subsidies.

Employment figures are annual averages of all persons engaged at month's end. Included are working proprietors, active business partners, unpaid family workers, provided they are working for at least one third of the usual working time. Part-time and temporary employees are covered as well as apprentices. Homeworkers are excluded. *Hours worked* cover hours worked, including overtime, by operatives, which are defined as persons engaged who are subject to obligatory insurance in the workers' old age insurance funds. This includes industrial apprentices but not homeworkers. The following categories are also included: supervisors, casual and part-time workers.

The figures for total *investment* are obtained from an annual survey covering enterprises with 20 or more persons engaged. Handicraft industries are included. They represent gross fixed capital formation defined as the value of purchases of new and used fixed assets including own-account construction of assets and work in progress. The valuation is at full cost incurred including fees and taxes. Advance payments of investment goods not yet supplied are excluded.

Total wages and salaries exclude employer's contributions to social security. All payments for interim employed persons are included, and contributions to company old-age pensions institutions are excluded.

Publications

Fachserie 4, Reihe 4.1.1., *Beschäftigung, Umsatz und Energieversorgung der Unternehmen und Betriebe im Bergbau und im Verarbeitenden Gewerbe*, Statistisches Bundesamt, Wiesbaden.

III. FOREIGN TRADE STATISTICS

The foreign trade figures cover both general and special trade value cif/fob. They include state-trading, military equipment and supplies, transactions in new ships and aircraft, but exclude direct transit trade, monetary items. Merchandise transactions with the German Democratic Republic and goods imported by members of the military forces stationed are not covered. They are collected according to the national nomenclature ("Warengruppen und -zweigen des Warenverzeichnisses für Aussenhandelsstatistik (1975)") equated with ISIC. This process has meant assuming equivalence where the bulk of the product group is common to the definitions in both systems, so some imprecision must be expected in a few cases.

GREECE

I. INDUSTRIAL STATISTICS

Source

The data result from the Annual Industrial Survey, the Annual Statistical Survey on Mines, Quarries and Salterns and the Annual Electricity Survey conducted by the National Statistical Service of Greece. For the industrial survey, manufacturing establishments with 10 or more persons engaged are covered on the basis of a complete enumeration of establishments with 20 or more persons engaged and a stratified random sample of establishments with 10 to 19 persons. Government establishments are not included in the industrial survey. Electricity and gas surveys cover the two enterprises engaged in production and distribution for public use. Steam and water supply are not covered. The base unit is the establishment except for electricity and gas, where the enterprise is used.

Industrial Classification

The estimates are based on national classification and have been adjusted to ISIC as far as possible.

Concepts and Definitions of Variables

Production comprises the value of finished goods produced, receipts from contract work on account of others, receipts from repair work, receipts from the sale of goods sold in the same condition as purchased and other receipts (sales of self-produced steam, electric energy, processing waste, etc.; subsidies and reimbursements for re-export of products). The value is at ex-factory selling price, not including taxes. *Value added* is calculated as the value of the output less the cost of materials and supplies, purchased fuels and electricity consumed, the purchase value of goods sold in the same condition as purchased, and payments for contract and repair work.

Employment data relate to national averages based on enumeration in every other month in the year. Unpaid family workers are included if they work three hours a day or more. *Employment, employees* covers salaried employees, defined as persons receiving a monthly salary on a contractual basis irrespective of the amount of the remuneration, and wage earners, defined as persons receiving a daily pay or paid on a piece-work basis either in cash or in kind. *Days worked* cover days worked by operatives, relating to wage earners as defined earlier.

Investment (gross fixed capital formation) represents current expenditure on new and used fixed assets less sales and write-offs due to obsolescence. Own-account construction of fixed assets is included. The data for mining exclude salterns and the value of sales (insignificant) is generally not deducted.

Compensation of labour, employees covers wages, salaries, payments for overtime work and regular leave, bonuses, allowances, dismissal compensation and the value of receipts in kind. *Employers' social costs* cover employers' contributions to social security schemes on behalf of employees and wage earners.

Publications

i) *Annual Industrial Survey;*

ii) *Annual Statistical Survey on Mines, Quarries and Salterns;*

iii) *Statistical Yearbook;*

iv) *Monthly Statistical Bulletin.*

All are published by the National Statistical Service of Greece, Athens.

HUNGARY

I. GENERAL

The information is supplied by the Hungarian Central Statistical Office, for both industrial statistics and national accounts data.

II. INDUSTRIAL STATISTICS

Source

From 1992 onwards, all enterprises where two of three criteria are met in two consecutive years -- over 100 employees, over 300 million HUF annual turnover, 150 million HUF of total assets -- are covered. Only investments above 10 million HUF are reported. The employment data result from the Annual Employment and Earnings Survey, which covers enterprises with 20 or more employees.

Industrial Classification

Data are classified according to the Hungarian classification (TEÁOR 92), which is only fully compatible with ISIC Revision 3 at the two-digit level.

Concepts and Definitions of Variables

Employment, employees refers to the average staff number of paid employees. Only full-time workers are covered.

Investment (gross fixed capital formation) is defined as the value of the new and used fixed assets which are ready to use. The valuation is at full cost incurred, including VAT.

Wages and salaries of employees include bonuses and vacation pay. Benefits in kind and sick leave pay are excluded.

III. NATIONAL ACCOUNTS

Concepts and Definitions of Variables

Production (gross output*)* and *value added* are given using the SNA 93 concepts. The valuation is at basic prices.

Publications

i)   *Munkaügyi statisztika;*
ii)   *Beruházásstatisztika;*
iii)   *National Accounts Hungary, 1991-94,* Budapest, 1996.

All are published by the Hungarian Central Statistical Office.

ICELAND

I. NATIONAL ACCOUNTS STATISTICS

Source

Data are provided by the National Economic Institute of Iceland which annually draws a sample of financial statements out of tax records. The sample size covers around 50% of the total wage bill in various industries. The probability of an establishment being drawn into a sample increases with size. The reference period is the calendar year. Establishments and kind-of-activity units are used as basic reference units. For production and value added the stratified samples drawn are "grossed up" to the total size according to the proportion between the total wage bill and the sample wage bill. Employment figures are based on administrative registers of total coverage.

In 1994 figures were revised upwards. The revision improved the estimates in the following areas: gross fixed capital formation in dwellings; redefinition of the NATO base at Keflavík Airport outside Icelandic economic territory; inclusion of accrued pension liabilities in compensation of employees of central government; inflation adjustments to changes in inventories.

Industrial Classification

The national classification was based on ISIC Revision 1 from 1958; the data provided are converted to ISIC Revision 2 from 1968. NACE Revision 1 has been introduced and will be implemented in all statistics from 1996 onwards.

Concepts and Definitions of Variables

From 1992 onwards, gross output (*production*) is valued in basic prices, including all subsidies on products but excluding VAT; before 1992 gross output is valued in producers' prices, excluding all subsidies and VAT. The value of all products is taken, allowing for net changes of work in progress. *Value added* uses the "national accounting" concept of value added. It is calculated as the value of gross output less the cost of materials, fuels and other supplies, of contract and commission work done by others, of repair and maintenance work done by others and of electricity purchased. It includes receipts for non-industrial services but excludes the cost of non-industrial services. Input estimates are made on a consumed basis. The valuation is the same as for production.

Employment is calculated as the number of work years, based on the number of insured weeks of work provided by a register-based tax-source. Included are working proprietors, active business partners, unpaid family workers, self-employed, salaried employees and wage earners. Full-time and part-time employees are covered, as well as clerical workers or supervisory personnel performing functions closely related to the production process.

Remuneration of labour is here defined as the "national accounting" concept of "compensation of employees". It covers employees only, excluding the self-employed, and includes wages, salaries and social contributions incurred by employers.

Publications

  i) *Atvinnuvegaskyrslur (Industrial Statistics),* published annually;
  ii) *Historical Statistics,* published every other year;
  iii) *Compiling Icelandic National Accounts,* documentation of methods applied, output and expenditure approaches, Reykjavík, January 1996.

All the above are published by the National Economic Institute.

Statistiques des Structures Industrielles OECD
OECD, © 1998 OCDE

IRELAND

I. INDUSTRIAL STATISTICS

Source

Information was supplied by the Irish Central Statistics Office. Data are taken from the Annual Census of Industrial Local Units. This census relates to all units engaged in industrial activity which have on average three or more persons engaged during the year.

The extent to which separate returns are obtained in practice, however, depends on the availability of separate records in the business for the different local units.

Concepts and Definitions of Variables

Gross output (*production*) represents the net selling value of all goods manufactured in the year, whether sold or not, including work done and capital assets manufactured for own use. Operating subsidies related to the production or sales of the output are included in the value of gross output; excise duty and VAT are excluded. Prior to 1991, the value of capital work done on own account was included in gross output only in the case of two industries, namely electricity and turf production. Net output (*value added*) is the difference between gross output and industrial input. Industrial input consists of the industrial materials, industrial services and fuel and power used in the production of the output. Valuation is exclusive of deductible VAT.

Employment is the total number of persons engaged and represents the sum of all employees plus proprietors and unpaid family workers. Outside piece workers are excluded. The numbers given for each year refer to a week in September. For *employment, employees* (total employees), employees are persons who are paid a fixed wage or salary. Persons at work or temporarily absent because of illness, holidays, strikes, etc. are included, as are part-time workers. Outside piece workers i.e. homeworkers are excluded.

Investment is gross fixed capital formation (GFCF). Capital Assets (land, buildings, plant and equipment) are defined as goods with an expected useful life of more than one year intended for use by the local unit itself. Acquisitions include purchases from other local units and production by the local unit itself of capital goods for its own use. Major alterations, improvements and repairs that extend the useful life of an asset or increase its productivity are included. The value of work put in place during the year is included whether or not completed. Acquisitions are valued at total cost including installation charges and fees or duties but excluding deductible VAT and financial costs. Sales are valued at the price actually received excluding VAT. GFCF is the difference between the acquisitions and sales of capital assets. *Investment in machinery and equipment* is also GFCF, but relating to plant, machinery, equipment and vehicles only.

Wages and salaries, employees are defined as the gross amount paid to all employees, excluding outside piece-workers, before deduction of income tax, employees' contributions to social security etc. Overtime pay, bonuses, commissions, holiday pay and sick pay are included. Payments to working proprietors and home workers are excluded.

The number of local units (*establishments)* counted includes all the separate local units of multi-location enterprises even if separate details are not provided by the respondent.

ITALY

I. GENERAL

Information was provided by the Istituto Nazionale di Statistica (National Institute of Statistics), Rome.

II. INDUSTRIAL STATISTICS

Source

The Institute annually conducts total surveys on gross product and capital investments in the industrial sector. Enterprises with 20 or more persons engaged are covered, totalling about 55 000 enterprises in all sectors of economic activity. Information on such enterprises is obtained from the register resulting from the 1991 general census, updated annually using various sources. The coverage of the survey is estimated at 73% of the total industrial contribution (ISIC Major Divisions 1 to 5) to national added value (national accounts estimates) and at 81% of the manufacturing contribution. The survey covers about 58% of employment in the total industrial sector and 65% in manufacturing (the latter figure also based on the 1991 results). No attempt is made to account for units outside the scope of the survey. The inquiry covers the calendar year and takes the enterprise, classified by kind of activity, as its basic reference unit. Multi-unit enterprises with more than 250 persons engaged are required to furnish data separately for each unit. At the moment, figures on hours worked are taken from the Industrial Enterprise Survey. Starting from 1993, hours worked data will be derived from a special survey on employment, wages and hours worked taken from a sample of 18 000 enterprises with 10 to 199 employees and all enterprises (around 3 700) with more than 200 employees.

Industrial Classification

The national NACE-related classification is not fully convertible to ISIC. However, national conversion tables are used to produce 3-digit ISIC data and an effort is made to produce reliable estimation at the 4-digit level.

Concepts and Definitions of Variables

Production, or gross output net of indirect taxes and subsidies, is valued in selling prices, excluding VAT. Electricity sold, fixed assets produced for own use and goods made by other enterprises are included, making allowance for changes in stocks of finished goods and of work in progress. *Value added*, net of indirect subsidies and taxes, uses the "census" concept of value added. The valuation excludes all indirect taxes and subsidies. It is calculated as gross output plus receipts for non-industrial services, less the cost of materials, fuels and other supplies; contract and commission work done and repair and maintenance by others; electricity purchases; and non-industrial services. Input estimates are made on a received basis, making adjustment for stock changes in materials, fuels and other supplies.

Employment gives the number of persons engaged, based on the average number of employees through the year plus the total number of other persons engaged at four fixed dates. These dates are 31 March, 30 June, 30 September and 31 December. Working proprietors, active business partners, unpaid family workers, the self-employed, salaried employees and wage earners are all included. *Employment, employees* gives the separate figures for the average number of employees. *Hours worked* cover hours worked by manual workers, including overtime, rest periods and time on call. Annual leave, public holidays, sick leave and other paid leave are included. The following categories are excluded: employers, supervisors and apprentices.

Gross fixed capital formation (*investment*), value of sales not deducted, is defined as the value of purchases of fixed assets, including own-account construction. Fixed assets covered are those with a productive life of at least one year. Assets made by a unit's labour force for its own use; additions, alterations, improvements and repairs to existing assets; new assets (not yet in use, or previously used outside the country) and used assets are all included. The valuation is at full cost incurred, including installation expenses. Gross fixed capital formation in machinery and equipment, value of sales not deducted, is given for *investment in machinery and equipment*. Using the same definition, it covers transport equipment, industrial machinery, equipment and furniture, professional instruments and equipment. Alterations, improvements and repairs are also included.

Compensation of labour, employees covers wages and salaries, and employers' social costs. It includes regular and overtime cash payments, bonuses and cost-of-living allowances, vacation and sick leave pay, payments in kind and allowances. *Employers' social costs* are employers' contributions to social security schemes and to pension funds.

Establishments are kind-of-activity units.

Publications

Fatturato, prodotto lordo e investimenti delle imprese industriali: supplements to *Bollettino Mensile di Statistica*, ISTAT, Rome.

JAPAN

I. GENERAL

The information was supplied by the Japanese Ministry of International Trade and Industry (MITI) and the Ministry of Health and Welfare.

II. INDUSTRIAL STATISTICS

Source

The figures, excluding those for water works and water supply, are derived from MITI's Annual Census of Manufactures. This survey covers all establishments classified under Manufacturing except those belonging to the government and public service corporations. Since 1981, however, surveys have been conducted on all establishments (including those with three employees or less) only in years where the last digit is 0, 3, 5 or 8. In all other years, the survey is limited to those establishments with four or more employees. Investment figures cover establishments with 30 or more persons engaged. No attempt is made to account for units not covered. Mining figures result from the Survey of Mining Trends in Japan. This survey covers all establishments engaged in metal mining, coal and lignite mining and crude petroleum and natural gas drilling.

Figures for water works and supply are derived from the Ministry of Health and Welfare's "Statistics of Water Supply". For the number of establishments and employment variables, figures cover all establishments. For other variables, only bulk water and large water supply system establishments are covered.

Industrial Classification

The data are classified according to the Japanese Standard Industrial Classification (JSIC Rev. 10).

Concepts and Definitions of Variables

Gross output (*production*) represents the value of shipments of finished goods, adjusted for changes in stocks of finished goods and work in progress. In the case of mining, the value of production and other receipts is taken. Receipts for contract and repair and maintenance work are included. The value of goods shipped in the same condition as received is excluded. *Value added* is gross output less the cost of materials and fuels consumed, electricity purchases, contract work and indirect taxes, depreciation, including cost of non-industrial services and excluding receipts. Input estimates are made on a received basis, not allowing for changes in stock levels.

Employment is the number of persons engaged at the end of the year, full- or part-time. Persons engaged comprise employees (including apprentices and temporary workers, meeting minimum time requirements), working proprietors, unpaid family workers and contract workers (mining only). Other temporary and daily workers are excluded, though their remuneration is included in wages and salaries.

Investment is gross fixed capital formation, defined as value of purchases of fixed assets, including own account construction, less value of sales. Fixed assets covered are those with a productive life of more than one year and include repairs to existing assets, new assets whether not yet in use, unused, or previously used abroad, and used assets. The valuation is at full cost incurred, including delivered price, cost of installation and fees and taxes. For own-produced assets, the cost of work put in progress covers labour costs, materials and supplies and includes an allocation for overheads. The amount realised is taken for sales of used assets.

Wages and salaries, employees relate to total cash payments, including basic wages, bonuses and other premiums and allowances paid to employees. Mining figures include payments to contract workers. Figures for manufacturing include employees' retirement and termination allowances; these payments are not included in data for operatives.

Publications

   i) *Honpo Kogyo no Susei* (Mining Yearbook of Japan*);*
   ii) *Census of Manufactures* (annual).

Both published by MITI.

KOREA

I. INDUSTRIAL STATISTICS

Source

Data were provided by the National Statistical Office of Korea and are drawn from the results of the quinquennial Industrial Census and the annual Mining and Manufacturing Survey. The Industrial Census is conducted years ending in 3 and 8 (since 1973) and covers all establishments; the Mining and Manufacturing Survey is conducted in all other years and covers all establishments with five or more employees. The period covered is the calendar year.

Statistiques des Structures Industrielles OECD
OECD, © 1998 OCDE

Industrial Classification

The Korean industrial classification is the SIC (revised in 1992). It aligns with ISIC Revision 3.

Concepts and Definitions of Variables

Production is gross output measured as the total value of all goods produced and services rendered to others by the establishment during the year. In practice the calculation is as follows: the value of shipments, plus the net addition to inventories over the year of finished goods, semi-finished goods, and work-in-progress. *Value added* is derived by subtracting the cost of production from the value of gross output, i.e., it includes depreciation charges and overhead costs. Production costs refer to direct charges actually paid or payable for materials and services consumed or put into production during the year referred to, including freight charges and other direct charges incurred by the establishments in acquiring these goods and services. Included in production costs are the costs of: raw materials (including parts, components, containers and auxiliary materials - including those supplied to other establishments on a contract basis but excluding those received from others); fuel, electric and water expenses; contract work done for others; repair and maintenance of own assets; wages and retirement allowances; welfare expenses; rent and depreciation expenses; taxes; bad debt expenses; other costs such as insurance, transportation, warehousing, entertainment, advertising.

Employment refers to the average number of employees, working proprietors and unpaid family workers by month during the period of operation. Working proprietors and unpaid family workers include proprietors, partners of unincorporated firms and family members who work more than one-third the normal operating hours without regular remuneration. *Employment, employees* is the number of employees at the end of the year on the payroll - in terms of wages and salaries of operatives, administrative and related workers. Employees are included regardless of whether they are permanent, temporary or casual daily workers, or whether they are non-working persons on sick leave, on vacation, victims of accidents or on strike (except for: long-term -three months and more - absentees; members of the armed forces carried on active payrolls; workers in contracted establishments).

Investment is capital expenditure during the year on the acquisition, installation, expansion and capitalised repair of tangible fixed assets, less disposals. Tangible fixed assets are those with a productive life of one year or more. They include: land and assets such as buildings and structures; machinery and equipment; cars, ships and delivery equipment. The valuation is at book value ignoring fluctuations based on the revaluation and depreciation of fixed assets. When assets are purchased from other establishments, total acquisition cost is estimated as the cost of installation: when assets are constructed by the establishment itself, the estimated book value when completed is taken. The annual disposal of fixed assets is the amount of tangible fixed assets actually eliminated or lost during the year owing to their sale, transfer, donation, fire, disaster, theft, etc. The valuation of such assets is figured on the basis of the actual selling price, or, if this cannot be determined, the equivalent current market price of similar items.

Wages and salaries, employees are gross earnings paid to all employees on the payroll of the establishment during the period. Included are all forms of compensation of employees' labour such as salaries, wages, bonuses and allowances, irrespective of whether they are paid in cash or in kind. However, the following are excluded: payments to the retired, to long-term absentees, and to members of the armed forces. Payments accrued prior to the reference year but not actually paid till the reference year are excluded, while payment obligations accrued during the reference year but not actually paid are included. Cash payments are in gross terms, i.e. include tax deductions, compulsory savings, union dues, etc. Compensation in kind is valued by applying plant prices, if acquired internally, or purchase prices, if acquired externally.

The *establishment* is defined as a physical unit engaged in industrial activities, such as a factory, workshop, office or mine.

Publications

i) *Report on the Industrial Census*;

ii) *Report on the Mining and Manufacturing Survey*.

Both are published by the National Statistical Office of the Republic of Korea.

LUXEMBOURG

I. GENERAL

Information was supplied by the Service central de la statistique et des études économiques (STATEC), Luxembourg.

II. INDUSTRIAL STATISTICS

Source

The estimates are derived from the Annual Survey of Industrial Production undertaken by STATEC. All enterprises are covered, though those with less than an average of 20 persons engaged during the year are sampled.

Industrial Classification

Data were originally classified according to NACE 70. They have been regrouped as far as possible to the ISIC. Some industries are combined for reasons of confidentiality. In the tables:

a) ISIC 311 includes ISIC 312;

b) ISIC 313 includes ISIC 314;

c) ISIC 33 includes ISIC 39;

d) ISIC 351 also covers ISIC 354, 355 and 356 as well as the production of Thomas slag from ISIC 371;

e) ISIC 383 includes ISIC 385.

Concepts and Definitions of Variables

The estimates for output (*production*) relate to the value of sales effected during the year, adjusted for changes in the value of stocks of finished goods and work in progress, and receipts for services rendered. The value of work done on own account and the value of goods provided to employees as payments in kind are included. For goods sold in the same condition as received, the gross margin is used. The valuation is in factor values. The estimates of *value added* relate to the value of output less the cost of materials and supplies, and services purchased for use in the production process; adjustments are made for changes in the value of stocks of materials. The valuation is in factor values.

Employment is total persons engaged and represents the sum of the average number of working proprietors, unpaid family workers, wage earners and other employees. Homeworkers, whose contribution is considered negligible, are not covered.

Investment is gross fixed capital formation (GFCF) and represents the acquisition of new and used fixed assets, less sales. Included are own-account work and fixed capital formation in new establishments not yet in operation. Transactions are recorded at the time of delivery for movable capital goods. For immovable capital goods (buildings, etc.) and large-scale projects the value of work put in place is recorded, whether or not completed.

Publications

Annuaire statistique published by STATEC.

MEXICO

I. INDUSTRIAL STATISTICS

Source

The results of the Annual Industrial Survey for the United States of Mexico were supplied by the National Institute of Statistics, Geography and Information Technology (INEGI) via the Department of Statistics.

Up to 1991, this survey covered 129 types of economic activity in the manufacturing sector comprising 3218 establishments, which represented 72% of the statistical range used to calculate total gross output, based on the 1985 industrial census.

From 1992, the annual survey covers 205 types of economic activity in the manufacturing sector comprising 6884 establishments with more than 6 employees, which cover 80% of the total value of manufacturing production in each class of activity.

Industrial Classification

The classification system used by this survey is in line with international recommendations laid down by the Statistical Office of the United Nations. Some items are consolidated in order to make it comparable with the ISIC. In the ISIC revision 2 tables: ISIC 323, 353, 3821 and 3845 are not available; ISIC 3823 includes part of ISIC 3824 (manufacture, assembly and repair of machinery and equipment including tractors for the construction, extraction -- i.e. mining -- and other industries); ISIC 3849 is allocated to ISIC 3823 and 3843.

As from 1993, the classification used in surveys and censuses is the 1994 Mexican Classification of Economic Activities and Products (CMAP) which is based on ISIC Revision 3.

Concepts and Definitions of Variables

Production is total gross output. It is calculated as the total value of goods and services produced by a company, whether they are intermediate goods and services used in the production process or intended for final consumption. It includes the value of products made by the establishment using its own raw materials, plus income from assembly services, maintenance and other industrial services, rentals and leases, technology transfer, other non-industrial services, sale of electric power produced by the establishment, changes in stocks of work in progress, and the value of fixed assets produced by the establishment for its own use. *Value added*, or the gross domestic product, is obtained by subtracting the value of inputs (goods and services for intermediate consumption) from total gross output.

Employment, employees covers all permanent and temporary blue-collar and white-collar workers who, in the course of the reference year, worked within or outside the establishment, and who were managed or supervised by the establishment. It includes workers on strike or on paid or unpaid sick leave, holiday or short-term leave of absence. It excludes workers on indefinite leave of absence, pensioners, auditors, advisers, consultants, commission agents, other persons who, although not belonging to the establishment, provided professional services which were paid for solely on a commission basis or in the form of honorariums or fees, persons carrying out repair and maintenance duties in the establishment on behalf of other entities, and all home workers who do not appear on the payroll.

It is measured as a yearly average, i.e. as the total of blue- and white-collar workers employed each month over the year divided by twelve; alternatively, the number of months they worked generates a monthly average spread over a whole year. Blue-collar workers (operatives) are people who perform jobs that are predominantly manual or are linked to the operation of machinery or equipment (production and assembly), skilled supervisory staff, and staff employed on tasks linked to the production process such as cleaning, repairs, maintenance, dispatch and storage, shipment, delivery of raw materials and transport and who perform these services within or outside the establishment but under the establishment's direct control. White-collar workers include staff employed in planning, management, technical and administrative supervision related to the production process and ancillary services, and staff who perform tasks related to auditing, administration, records, research, sales, advertising, security and general office work. The variable includes owners, active partners and members of their families who are employed and receive regular pay.

Investment, or gross fixed capital formation, includes the following:

a) purchase of new fixed assets. This covers the total value of new fixed assets acquired by the establishment or received from other establishments within the same enterprise during the reference year. Included are: imported assets not previously used in the country even if they have been used abroad before they were imported, and partial payment for construction work;

b) purchase of used fixed assets. This represents the value of used fixed assets acquired by the establishment, or received from other establishments within the same enterprise, during the year under consideration. Includes fixed assets previously used in the country, whether made in the country or abroad. Land purchase during the year is to be considered a new acquisition;

c) fixed assets produced for own use. This covers the total value of fixed assets produced for own use during the reference year together with the establishment's materials and workforce. Work not finished during the year is valued on a pro rata basis. Included are: the value of fixed assets produced for rental and leasing, and for improvements, repairs and renovations carried out by the establishment on its assets during the year. Whenever such work prolongs the service life of such assets or increases their productivity. The following are excluded: expenditure on running repairs and maintenance, and on major improvements, repairs and renovations carried out by third parties on the establishment's fixed assets;

d) major improvements, repairs and renovations carried out by third parties on fixed assets belonging to the establishment. This covers the establishment's total expenditure on improvements, repairs and renovations carried out by third parties provided that they prolong the fixed assets' service life by more than a year, change their nature or increase their productivity. Specific inclusions are: the value of materials and the establishment's running costs in carrying out this type of work, and services received from other establishments within the same enterprise. Excluded are expenditure on running repairs and maintenance.

e) sale of fixed assets. Includes the total sales of the establishment's new and used fixed assets during the reference year, whether bought from third parties or produced by the establishment for its own use.

For *a)* to *d)* above, the valuation is based on prices actually invoiced. If these services have been received from other establishments within the same enterprise, they are assessed at their market value. Otherwise, the valuation is assigned prices that take into account labour and materials, adding in a margin to cover general expenses and profits. VAT is not included. For *e)* the valuation corresponds to sums

Statistiques des Structures Industrielles OECD
OECD, © 1998 OCDE

actually received and takes into account all charges invoiced to the purchaser. Excluded is interest charged on sales made on credit. VAT is not included.

Fixed assets are comprised of the following:

a) plant and equipment -- see investment in machinery and equipment below;

b) buildings and infrastructure -- refers to buildings and infrastructure owned by the establishment and linked directly or indirectly to the production process. Included are manufacturing plant, warehouses, offices, stores, installations for the purposes of piping water and steam and the supply of electricity, etc., and other structural items such as walkways, parking areas and land whose value cannot be assessed separately from that of the buildings themselves;

c) land (including repairs) -- refers to land that has not been built on, and is the property of the establishment but is not covered above;

d) transport -- includes all modes of transport such as ships, planes, carts, trucks, tractors with trailers, and other vehicles belonging to the establishment;

e) other fixed assets -- includes all fixed assets that are the property of the establishment which are not dealt with in the paragraphs above and whose service life is estimated to be more than one year.

The variable includes furniture, including office equipment such as computers and calculators, and equipment such as forklift trucks used for moving goods within the plant. It excludes intangible fixed assets such as patents and brand names. The criteria for evaluation are as follows. All fixed assets are valued at acquisition cost, defined as the purchase price plus transportation costs when carried out by third parties, installation costs, taxes (excluding VAT), insurance for goods in transit, and generally all expenditure incurred in transporting the assets to the establishment. The criteria for evaluation exclude interest paid on loans made to the establishment to finance the purchase of assets. Assets received from other establishments within the same enterprise are assessed as if purchased from a third party as defined above, failing which they are assessed at book value.

Investment in machinery and equipment is gross fixed investment in plant and equipment. It includes machinery and mechanical, electrical and any other type of equipment owned by the establishment and used in the production process and ancillary activities.

Compensation of labour, employees covers all expenditure on salaries or wages which the company has paid to salaried staff during the reference year, as well as money in the form of social security benefits, employers' social security contributions and profit-sharing.

Wages and salaries, employees can be split into wages paid to blue-collar workers and wages paid to white-collar workers.

Wages paid to blue-collar workers represent the total of all cash payments before deductions during the reference period to cover regular and non-recurrent work performed by permanent and temporary workers. It includes remuneration paid to blue-collar workers in the form of wages, bonuses, incentive payments, holiday pay and bonuses, and pay during short-term leave of absence. It excludes pensions paid to retired workers, to workers who are dismissed or whose contracts are otherwise terminated, and to home workers who do not appear on the payroll.

White-collar pay includes all cash payments before deductions during the reference period covering all regular and non-recurrent work performed by permanent and temporary staff. It includes remuneration to staff in the form of salaries, bonuses, incentive payments, holiday pay and bonuses, pay during short-term leave of absence and sales commission. It excludes pensions paid to retired workers, and payments such as honorariums, fees, and commission paid to individuals who have provided professional services to the establishment without being members of staff.

Social security benefits include the amounts blue- and white-collar workers received in cash, in services or in kind, these last being costed. Included are: the total of the cost to, and contributions made by, the establishment for food (canteen); child care and medical care; premiums for life insurance, occupational risks; dismissal and contract termination compensation; bonuses; assistance for transport and sport, etc.; and all payments that were the responsibility of employees but were in fact covered by the establishment. The following are excluded: the cost of uniforms and work clothes supplied to blue- and white-collar workers and refundable costs such as travelling expenses, entertainment expenses incurred by employees on behalf of the company.

Employers' social security contributions represent total payments made by the establishment during the reference year in the form of employers' contributions to the IMSS (Instituto Mejicano del Seguro Social -- Mexican Institute of Social Security), the INFONAVIT (Instituto del Fondo Nacional para la Vivienda de los Trabajadores -- Institute of the National Fund for Workers' Housing) and other official institutions.

Hours worked represent the number of regular and non-recurrent hours actually worked by paid permanent and temporary blue- and white-collar workers during the reference period. Included are: normal waiting time, time spent on preparing for work and, in the case of manual workers, time not worked owing to technical failures and on cleaning machinery tools used during the working day. Excluded are: time not spent working because of strikes, stoppages, holidays, sickness, natural phenomena, and any other exceptional suspension of work.

The *establishment* is the unit on which information has been requested for the Annual Industrial Survey. Each statistical unit represents one manufacturing industrial unit.

Publications

   i) *Estadística Industrial Anual;*

   ii) *Estadística Industrial Mensual.*

Both published by the Dirección General de Estadística, Secretariá de Programacíon y Presupuesto, Mexico.

NETHERLANDS

I. INDUSTRIAL STATISTICS

Source

Data were supplied by the Netherlands Central Bureau of Statistics and are based on the Bureau's own statistical inquiry.

From 1988 onwards, they cover, for the calendar year, all kind-of-activity units employing 20 or more persons (based on paid man-years per year), except the investments variables, where kind-of-activity units employing 10 or more persons have been surveyed. Up to and including 1987, units employing 10 or more persons were surveyed for all variables: however, in 1987, companies with 10-20 employees were surveyed on a sample basis. No estimation has been made for units falling outside the scope of the inquiry. Employment statistics are, for the more recent year, supplemented with information from the quarterly employment questionnaire.

Industrial Classification

Data up to and including 1992 were originally classified according to the Standard Industrial Classification of all economic activities, as formulated by the Central Bureau of Statistics of the Netherlands (SBI 1974), which is fully convertible to the ISIC. Following the introduction of NACE Revision 1 in 1993, the 1974 business register was replaced by the 1993 standard business register and for this reason data availability changes.

Concepts and Definitions of Variables

The value of gross output is given for *production* and includes all products, net change of work in progress, work done on own account, services rendered (included non-industrial services), goods shipped in the same condition as received, electricity sold, fixed assets produced for own use, net changes in stock levels of finished goods, waste products, and goods made by homeworkers and handicraft workers. The valuation is in producers' prices, including all indirect taxes but excluding all subsidies and VAT. *Value added*, which uses the "national accounts" concept of value added, is calculated from the value of gross output less the value of consumption (including costs of and receipts for non-industrial services). The cost of materials, fuels and other supplies, contract and commission work done by others, repair and maintenance work done by others, goods shipped in the same condition as received and electricity purchased are all deducted. Input estimates are on a received basis, adjusted for stock changes. The valuation is the same as for production.

Employment gives the total number of employees on 30 September. The coverage includes salaried employees, wage earners, homeworkers, full-time employees and part-time employees (liable to the Health Insurance Act).

Gross fixed capital formation (*investment*) is defined until 1988 as the value of purchases of fixed assets including own-account construction of assets. From 1988 on, investment is defined as the value of the fixed assets which have become available and are ready to use. They include not only the earlier mentioned, but also the leased and hired goods. Fixed assets are those with a productive life of at least one year, plus assets made by a unit's labour force for its own use, additions, alterations and improvements to existing assets, new assets (if previously unused or used outside the country) and used assets. The valuation is at full cost incurred, including delivered price, and cost of installation, including indirect taxes but excluding fees and VAT. For assets produced by the unit, the cost of work put in progress, including cost of labour, material and other supplies is taken. *Investment in machinery and equipment* is gross fixed capital formation in transport equipment (work trucks of the type used in factories, warehouses, etc., for short distance transport or for handling of goods), industrial machinery and equipment, office machinery, equipment and furniture, professional instruments and equipment, and alterations and improvements to the above.

Compensation of labour, employees is defined as wages, salaries, and employers' contributions to social security schemes and to pension funds. *Wages and salaries, employees* include regular and overtime cash payments, bonuses and cost-of-living allowances, vacation pay, taxes and social insurance contributions, payable by employees and deducted by employers, payments in kind and allowances. Sick leave pay is not included. *Employers' social costs* cover both obligatory and voluntary contributions. Contributions to the Health Insurance Act, Unemployment Insurance Act, General Family Allowances Act, General Widows' and Orphans' Pensions Act, Wage Earners Disablement Insurance Act all constitute legally required expenditure. Contributions to pension funds, supplements to payments by the social insurance acts, employers' contributions to medical insurance premiums, and allowances to foreign workers for lodging, food, travelling, etc., are voluntary.

Publications

i) *Yearly Production Statistics*. Separate publications for each major group of the national classification of the manufacturing industries (production, value added, employment and remuneration);

ii) *Yearly Statistics on Fixed Capital Formation in Industry* (investment data).

NEW ZEALAND

I. GENERAL

Statistics New Zealand, Wellington, supplied the information which is taken from industrial statistics.

II. INDUSTRIAL STATISTICS

Source

Data in ISIC Revision 2

Data are taken from the Manufacturing Census for 1978, 1981 and 1983. From 1985 onwards, they are taken from either the Annual Enterprise Survey, or the 5-yearly Economy Wide Census, or (for the employment variables from 1991 onwards) the Annual Business Directory Update (ABDU). They cover the fiscal year starting 1 April of the year given, though if this is not available, returns giving the last accounting year ending within the fiscal year specified are regarded as acceptable.

The Integrated Economic Census of Manufacturing takes the accounting unit as its basic reference unit, except for employment where the reference unit is the establishment. One-man businesses are excluded from all results prior to the 1983/84 census.

No estimation is made for units not covered by the survey.

Data in ISIC Revision 3

Data are taken from the Annual Business Frame Update, except that for Farming 1987-96 (source: Farm Production Survey). Data covers the fiscal year ending 31 March.

These statistics are derived from the Statistics New Zealand Business Directory. The Business Directory is a database of New Zealand businesses and their structure. The Annual Business Directory Update Survey (ABDU) is conducted in mid-February each year to update the details contained on the Business Directory.

From 1994, the population includes only businesses that were economically significant.

Industrial Classification

Data in ISIC Revision 2

The New Zealand Standard Industrial Classification (NZSIC) was originally used. There are no major problems involved in its conversion to the ISIC Revision 2. It has, however, an additional 5th level (Sub-Group) classification.

Data in ISIC Revision 3

The Australian and New Zealand Standard Industrial Classification (ANZSIC) was introduced in 1994. There is not a one-to-one relationship between NZSIC and ANZSIC; however there is a possible concordance between them and between ANZSIC and ISIC Revision 3.

The ANZSIC-based series from 1987-1993 is likely to be of a lower quality than the series from 1994 onwards because ANZSIC codes were added to the data retrospectively.

ABDU data is currently available in two time series. Only the data within these two time series is directly comparable. The two time series are:

- 1987 to 1994 data which was based on compulsory GST (Goods and Services Tax) registration and where 1994 data does not include the improvements in coverage made in 1994.

- 1994 to 1996 data which was based on economically significant units and where the 1996 data does not include the improvements in coverage made in 1996.

Concepts and Definitions of Variables from the 1985 Census Onwards

Employment is the number of full-time equivalent persons engaged, i.e. the sum of full time employees and working proprietors plus half part-time employees and working proprietors, at the end of February of the following year. It includes salaried employees, working proprietors, active business proprietors/partners, self-employees and wage earners.

Employment, employees excludes working proprietors.

Employment, females is the same, but for females only.

Enterprises in the private sector generally correspond to legal entities such as companies, partnerships, trusts, estates, incorporated societies, producer boards, sole proprietorships, etc. Some enterprises are defined by reference to other characteristics, such as a set of common objectives or the existence of an organisational structure. In this category are included government departments, local authorities, churches, voluntary organisations, etc.

Publications

i)   *Annual Enterprise Survey* releases;

ii)   *Annual New Zealand Business Activity* periodicals;

iii) *Key Statistics* periodicals

iv)   *Economic Census* releases (various, cyclical);

NORWAY

I. GENERAL

Industrial statistics and national accounts data are provided by Statistisk Sentralbyra, Statistics Norway, Oslo.

II. INDUSTRIAL STATISTICS

Source

From 1992 the annual enquiry covers, in general, all establishments in mining, quarrying and manufacturing industries with 10 or more persons engaged. Previous annual enquiries covered, in general, all establishments with 5 or more persons engaged. Information on oil and gas extraction is not included. For small establishments (less than 10 persons), information is collected yearly from administrative registers.

The reference unit is the establishment. The reference period is the calendar year.

Industrial Classification

From 1993 the revised Norwegian Standard Industrial Classification (SIC 94) has been used and caused some changes in the coverage of the statistics compared with the previous years. The classification has a six-level hierarchical structure.

SIC 94 is identical with NACE Rev.1 down to the 4-digit level, the 5-digit level being a subdivision for national needs. It has a concordance with ISIC Revision 3.

Concepts and Definitions of Variables

Gross output, *production*, is valued in producers' prices, excluding all subsidies, and including all indirect taxes but VAT. Included is the value of all goods produced on own account, repair work for others, mounting or installation of own products and merchandise, contract work, other work, own-account investment work, own-account repair work, rental receipts and gross profit of goods sold in the same condition as purchased.

Value added is valued – if nothing else is stated – at market prices and equal gross value of production less cost of goods and services consumed. It excludes all subsidies and including all taxes but VAT. The cost of materials, fuels and other supplies, contract and commission work done by others, repair and maintenance work done by others and electricity purchased are deducted from gross output. Cost of non-industrial services and receipts for non-industrial services are included. Input estimates are made on a consumed basis.

An *establishment* is defined as a functional unit which at a single physical location is engaged mainly in activities within a specific activity group of the Norwegian Standard Industrial Classification.

Employment gives the number of persons engaged, calculated as the average number of persons working in the establishment throughout the year, whether full- or part-time. Working proprietors, business partners, unpaid family workers, salaried employees, self-employed and wage earners are included, but not homeworkers and persons on military leave. *Employment, employees* comprise salaried managers and directors as well as transport workers, messengers, newsmen, watchmen and cleaning personnel.

Hours worked cover hours worked by employees, including overtime. Foremen and supervisors are included, also apprentices, casual workers and part-time workers.

Investment (Gross fixed capital formation) is defined as the acquisition of fixed durable assets, new and used, with an expected productive life of more than one year, including own account investment work, less receipts from sales of fixed durable assets. Acquisition of machinery, transport equipment etc. is recorded at the time when the assets are received, whether or not put into operation during the year. Purchase of buildings, structures, land etc. is treated alike. As for construction work in progress, the value of work carried out during the year is recorded, whether or not the project is completed within the period. The cost of acquisition means actual expenses incurred during the year, including investment levy, irrespective of time of payment. The figures on gross fixed capital formation do not comprise all capital used in mining, quarrying and manufacturing.

Investment in machinery and equipment is also capital formation, and follows the definition for total investment. Included are: transport equipment, industrial machinery and equipment, office machinery, equipment and furniture, professional instruments and equipment, and alterations and improvements to these items.

Compensation of labour covers wages and salaries and supplements. *Wages and salaries* comprise all payments, whether in cash or in kind, made by the employer in connection with work done, to all persons included in the count of employees (also employed outworkers). It includes taxes, social insurance and pension contributions payable by the employee, but deducted by the employer. Bonuses, production awards, holiday allowances and wages paid during periods of sickness, military leave or other absences, and commission earned by salesmen and representatives, are also included. Compensation of employees does not include compensation of individual proprietors, partners or family workers without regular wages. *Employers' social costs* include the other benefits for the employees and social expenses levied by law. Other benefits for the employees comprise employers' contributions to private pension, family allowance, health and casualty insurance, life insurance and similar schemes.

Publications

   i)   *Industristatistikk* (annual) -- Mining, Quarrying and Manufacturing;
   ii) *Elektrisitetstatistikk* (annual) -- Electricity and Gas Supply;
   iii) *Bygge- og anleggsstatistikk* (annual) -- Construction.

Published by Statistics Norway.

III. NATIONAL ACCOUNTS STATISTICS

Source

The figures are taken from National Accounts data (see "Publications"), and are based on results of Statistic Norway's statistical inquiries. The production statistics are fairly good for agriculture, forestry, fishing, oil activities, mining and manufacturing, electricity, water supply, transport and communication and a few other service activities. For most of the service industries the main sources are turnover and employment figures by industry from the Register of Establishments and Enterprises. The import and export statistics are satisfactory.

A weak spot in the system of production statistics is however the trade industries. For wholesale and retail trade the yearly basic statistics are not very useful for national accounting purposes. Output of wholesale and retail trade (combined) is in the national accounts calculated from the purchasers' values, *i.e.* from commodity by industry and commodity by final use figures. Trade margin coefficients, obtained by dividing for each commodity flow the value at purchaser price by the value at producer price for the previous year, are used to calculate trade margins. Thus, for each commodity, the trade coefficient is calculated for each category of use. The trade margin coefficients may be adjusted during the process of balancing supply and use of commodities in the national accounts. The basic statistics of inventories are very poor, giving only stocks by type by industry.

Industrial Classification

Imports are linked to an industry through the commodity specification. However, it is not possible to perform this specification for all imports. The grand total therefore includes a figure for these items. Examples are: goods for oil and gas pipeline transport, operating expenditure, expenditure on fixed assets, direct purchases abroad by Norwegian sailors.

Concepts and Definitions of Variables

Production is gross output, including the value of all products, net change of work in progress, work done on own account, services rendered, fixed assets produced for own use, waste products, goods made by homeworkers and handicraft workers. The valuation is in producers' prices, excluding all subsidies and including all indirect taxes but VAT, which is added later in the national accounts. The "National Accounts" concept is used for *value added*, which is calculated as the value of gross output less the cost of materials, fuels and other supplies, contract and commission work, repair and maintenance work done by others; rental expenses; and electricity purchased. Input estimates are on a consumed basis. The cost of non-industrial services is included in the above. The valuation is at market prices excluding VAT (again as it is added later in the national accounts).

Employment gives the total number of persons engaged based on the average number throughout the year. Working proprietors, salesmen, unpaid family workers, self-employed persons, salaried employees and wage earners are all included, whether full- or part-time.

Imports statistics give general trade (cif). They include state trading, commercial transactions in military equipment and supplies, foreign aid transactions, transactions in new ships and aircraft, electrical energy and gas, sea products landed direct from the high seas, and private donations and gifts. Direct transit trade, temporary imports, monetary items and minor transactions (less than 1 000 NKr) are all excluded.

Investment is gross fixed capital formation defined as the value of purchases of fixed assets, including own-account construction of assets, less the value of sales of fixed assets. Fixed assets are those with a productive life of at least one year, including assets made by a unit's labour force for its own use, additions, alterations and improvements to existing assets, new assets (if not yet in use or if previously used outside the country) and used assets. The valuation is the full cost incurred including the delivered price, the cost of installation, fees and taxes (but not VAT). For assets produced by the unit, the cost of work put in progress, including the cost of labour, materials and other supplies, is used. The actual amount realised is taken for sales of used assets.

Compensation of labour, employees covers wages and salaries paid to employees, employers' contributions to social security schemes and pension funds, and net contributions to the general fund for low-income trade union workers. It includes regular and overtime cash payments; bonuses and cost-of-living allowances; vacation and sick leave pay; taxes and social insurance contributions, payable by employees and deducted by employers; and payments in kind. *Employers' social costs* cover the legally required contributions to the general social insurance scheme, and voluntary payments to private pension, family allowance, health and casualty insurance, life insurance and similar schemes.

Constant Price Data

Constant price estimates were established using 1980 as the base year. Each and every item was chained on all aggregate levels separately, thus keeping intact the annual growth rates of the aggregates as arrived at through the genuine base year calculations. For this reason, the constant price aggregates cannot be reached by adding the detail (i.e. are non-additive).

Statistiques des Structures Industrielles
OECD, © 1998

Publications

i) *National Accounts Statistics* (annual);

ii) *National Accounts of Norway -- System and Methods of Estimation*, E. Flöttum.

The above are published by Statistics Norway, and are available in English.

POLAND

I. INDUSTRIAL STATISTICS

Source

The Central Statistical Office collects statistical data concerning economic activity of industrial enterprises. The statistical unit is enterprise.

All industrial enterprises are divided according to the number of employees into three groups: small enterprises (less than 5 persons), medium sized enterprises (6-50) and large enterprises (more than 50 persons).

All enterprises having more than 50 employees (in categories C and D) or more than 20 employees (in category E) are surveyed. Enterprises with 6-50 employees (in categories C and D) or 6-20 employees (in category E) are surveyed monthly by means of 10% samples and yearly in total. Enterprises having less then 6 employees are surveyed once a year by means of 8% samples.

In 1996, large enterprises accounted for 79% of the Poland's industrial production, medium sized enterprises for 16% and small enterprises for about 5%. In each of these three groups there were about 83%, 16% and 1% of persons employed in industry respectively.

Industrial classification

The Polish classification EKD (Europejska Klasyfikacja Dzia³alnoœci) was introduced into the Polish statistics in 1993. There is a direct correspondence with NACE Revision 1 and ISIC Revision 3.

Concepts and Definitions of Variables

The value of sold *production* is defined as revenue from selling own products (goods and services) and value of manufactured goods which are not included in the sale, but are treated on an equal basis (for example value of goods and services used for representative and advertisement needs). There is no adjustment for works in progress and for changes in stock of finished products. Transactions within establishments of the same enterprise are not included. Data for 1992 and 1993 include turnover tax, VAT (introduced on 5 July 1993) and excise tax. For 1993, 1994 and 1995, data include VAT and excise tax. For 1995 and 1996 VAT and excise tax are not included and price supplements are accounted for.

The variable gross *value added* is calculated for all units of the national economy, irrespective how many persons they employ. Since 1994, gross value added is measured at basic prices (before it was done at producers' prices). This change was caused by the introduction of a new tax system (July 5 1993), including VAT on goods and services, as well as excise tax. Basic prices exclude VAT and excise tax, but include subsidies on products. Gross value added is calculated as the value of output less the value of intermediate consumption. Different computation methods are applied for market and non-market units.

Investment outlays include financial or tangible outlays in order to create new fixed assets or improve (rebuild, enlarge, reconstruct, adapt or modernise) existing property, and outlays for primary equipment. Outlays for fixed assets include:

- buildings and structures, e.g. construction and assembly works, design and estimation of costs,
- machinery, technical equipment and tools (including instruments, movables and fittings),
- transport equipment,
- other, e.g. land amelioration, expenditures on purchase of land and second-hand fixed assets, livestock (since 1995), long-term planning and interests on credits and investment loans for the period of investment (data given exclusively at current prices). Other outlays include investments on primary equipment and costs of realisation of investment. These outlays do not include value of fixed assets.

Employment data refers to the number of persons engaged (at the end of the year), both full- and part-timers. They include persons on contracts, owners and co-owners of economic units, and members of their families, home-workers, agents and subagents, members of agricultural co-operatives. *Employment, employees* covers full- and part-timers on contracts. The latter are recalculated as full-time workers.

Wages and salaries are gross numbers and include personal earnings (excluding those of apprentices, home-workers and trainees), profit shares, balance surplus in co-operatives, bonuses from bonus funds and other remuneration arrangements made to selected groups of employees (journalists, authors of films and radio and TV programmes).

PORTUGAL

I. INDUSTRIAL STATISTICS

Source

Data are supplied by the National Institute of Statistics and are taken from annual surveys in manufacturing and mining industries, electricity, gas, building and public works.

Until 1989, data were collected via the Annual Enquiry into Manufacturing Industry, an establishment-based survey covering 11 500 units. In 1990 this survey was replaced by the Annual Enterprise Inquiry, an enterprise-based survey covering 65 000 enterprises in the mining, manufacturing and electricity, gas and water sectors. Figures for production, value added, employment, investment and number of enterprises cover the entire industry population. Figures for employment-employees, investment in machinery and equipment, wages and salaries, supplements to wages and salaries and hours worked cover enterprises employing 100 persons or more.

Concepts and Definitions of Variables

Production is given in terms of gross value of production, defined as the total value of finished goods produced by the establishment/"enterprise" (intermediate goods sold as such are considered as finished products), plus the value of fixed assets produced for own use, industrial works done for other users, electricity sold, waste products sold to third persons, less the value of work in progress at the beginning of the year. *Value added* is calculated as the gross value of output, plus the value of work done by the establishment/"enterprise" in the capacity of sub-contractor, less the value of materials, lubricants and energy consumed, hiring of machinery, and contract work done by others, the value of industrial work, repair and maintenance work done by others and non-industrial services received, and the value of duties paid for utilisation of manufacturing processes.

Employment covers all the persons, paid or unpaid, pursuing their principal activity in the establishment during the last week of the year. This includes all the persons working during the last week of the year, plus the persons on short leave (vacation and sick, strike...), but does not include the persons on military service or on the retired list. The paid personnel includes the management, the administrative, technical or office personnel and the manual workers; the unpaid personnel includes the proprietors, individual or collective, who actually participate in the work of the establishment without getting a regular wage and the unpaid family members who work at least a third of the normal working time. *Hours worked* cover hours worked by operatives.

Sales of fixed assets are deducted from *investment* and *investment in machinery and equipment.*

Remuneration corresponds to the wages and salaries paid during the year plus supplements to salaries and wages, plus employer's contributions.

Enterprise means any production unit, whether it is subsidiary to an establishment classed in another sector of activity, is under direct private management or is a public sector body carrying out work under direct management.

Publications

i) *Industrial Statistics* (Volume I and Volume II);
ii) *Statistics on Buildings and Dwellings.*

SPAIN

I. INDUSTRIAL STATISTICS

Source

The Spanish National Institute of Statistics (Instituto Nacional de Estadística, Ministerio de Economía y Hacienda) supplied the information. Statistics result from the Business Industrial Survey (Encuesta Industrial de Empresas), covering all industrial establishments employing one or more paid persons. Units with more than 20 persons engaged are surveyed exhaustively; units with less than 20 persons engaged are surveyed by sample. The total annual sample includes approximately 40 000 establishments.

Industrial Classification

The industrial nomenclature used in the survey is the revised National Classification of Economic Activities – 1993 (CNAE 1993). It is equivalent to NACE Revision 1 at the 4-digit level and has a correspondence with ISIC Revision 3.

Concepts and Definitions of Variables

Production follows the Spanish definition of gross output, this being the aggregate total of a) the output of goods and services for sale, including payments received for services and work performed by others and the value of electricity sold; b) goods resold in the same condition as received; c) payments for services rendered (rental of machines, technical assistance, etc.); d) products and work in progress; e) capital formation for own account (fixed assets produced for own use and the value of major repairs and improvements to own capital assets using own resources). The value of this gross output is calculated at factor values since operating subsidies have been added to the initial amount and taxes on manufacturing activity have not been included. *Value added* is calculated as the difference between the value of gross output at producer prices and intermediate consumption at purchaser prices, *i.e.,* value added at factor cost. Intermediate consumption includes the cost of a) raw materials and consumables; b) energy consumed for power and heating, steam, electricity, gas, etc.; c) purchases of industrial and non-industrial services; d) goods purchased for resale in the same condition as received.

Gross fixed capital formation at current prices (*investment*) is calculated by subtracting the value of sales of own fixed assets from the value of purchases of new and used fixed assets, major repairs and improvements to fixed assets performed by others, construction of assets for own account and major repairs and improvements to fixed assets carried out using own materials and labour.

Employment is calculated as the number of persons engaged, including both paid and unpaid staff and office staff as well as operatives. *Hours worked* corresponds to the total number of hours effectively worked by the persons engaged during the reference year.

Wages and salaries, employees is gross salary and wages paid during the reference year and payments in kind to the paid staff, excluding employers' social costs. *Employers' social costs* are social contributions paid by the employer (social security, pensions, and other social costs).

Publications

Encuesta Industrial Annual, Instituto Nacional de Estadística.

SWEDEN

I. GENERAL

The information is supplied by Statistics Sweden (Statistiska Centralbyran), Stockholm. The data are of three types according to origin: industrial statistics, foreign trade statistics and national accounts.

Industrial Classification

Data were originally classified according to ISIC. The SNI -- the Swedish Standard Industrial Classification -- equates to the 1968 version of ISIC to the 4-digit level.

II. INDUSTRIAL STATISTICS

Source

The data are taken from the Bureau's industrial statistics and are derived from its annual manufacturing inquiry. Until 1988, all establishments employing five or more persons were covered and no estimate was made for units not covered by the survey. From 1989, the survey covers manufacturing establishments (with five or more persons) in manufacturing enterprises employing ten or more persons and manufacturing establishments (with ten or more employees) in non-manufacturing enterprises. Non-respondents are estimated.

Industrial Classification

Until 1988 in all tables ISIC 342 (Printing and Publishing) did not include publishing, since this activity was not surveyed in the annual inquiry. Sand and clay pits (part of ISIC 29) were also excluded. From 1989 these activities are included.

Statistiques des Structures Industrielles OECD
OECD, © 1998 OCDE

Concepts and Definitions of Variables

Production is gross output, excluding all indirect taxes and including subsidies. The value of all products, net change of work in progress, services rendered, waste products and goods made by homeworkers are included. Until 1988, figures for "census" *value added*, excluding all indirect taxes and including subsidies, were calculated as the value of gross output less the cost of materials, fuels and other supplies, contract and commission work done by others and electricity purchased, excluding the cost of, and receipts for, non-industrial services. Since 1989, it has been calculated as production less total costs except wages and salaries (including social costs). Input estimates are on a consumed basis. Detailed information on the methods used to calculate the constant price series is available on request.

Employment data are taken from the average number of wage earners throughout the year, combined with the number of salaried employees at a certain date. They include working proprietors, active business partners, self-employed persons, salaried employees, wage earners. All full- and part-time employees are included, as well as clerical workers or supervisory personnel performing functions closely related to the production process. *Hours worked* cover hours worked by operatives and relate to wage earners.

Wages and salaries include regular and overtime cash payments, bonuses and cost-of-living allowances, vacation and sick leave pay, taxes and social insurance contributions, etc., payable by employees and deducted by employers and payments in kind. Social security costs are not included.

Publications

Manufacturing: Parts I and II in the series of *Official Statistics of Sweden* (SOS) published by Statistics Sweden. Also partly obtainable from the statistical databases at Statistics Sweden.

III. FOREIGN TRADE STATISTICS

Concepts and Definitions of Variables

The foreign trade statistics (shown in the same tables as industrial statistics) give general trade for the calendar year: *exports* fob, *imports* cif. Included are state trading; commercial transactions in military equipment and supplies; foreign aid transactions; transactions in new and used ships and aircraft; electric energy and gas; private donations and gifts and (for imports only) sea products landed direct from the high seas. Specific exclusions are direct transit trade, temporary exports, monetary items, some kinds of minor transactions of less than 2 000 SEK, and returned goods (recorded separately). Data were originally classified according to a Swedish version of ISIC.

Constant Price Data

Constant price data are deflated by using unit value for some products and exports and imports price indices for other products.

Publications

i) *Utrikeshandel,* manadsstatistik (monthly);
ii) *Utrikeshandel,* kvartalsstatistik (quarterly);
iii) Two annual publications.

Issued by Statistics Sweden. Also obtainable from the statistical databases at Statistics Sweden.

IV. NATIONAL ACCOUNTS STATISTICS

Concepts and Definitions of Variables

Gross output (*production*) is given in basic values, inclusive of non-commodity indirect taxes, exclusive of non-commodity subsidies. Included are: the value of all products, work done on own account, services rendered, electricity sold, goods made by home and handicraft workers, and fixed assets produced for own use. Adjustments are made for net changes of work in progress and in stock levels of finished goods. *Value added*, in basic values, is calculated as the value of gross output less the cost of materials, fuels and other supplies; contract and commission, repair and maintenance work done by others; and electricity consumed (estimates of inputs based on the amount consumed).

Employment gives the number of employed. Figures are derived from the average number of wage earners throughout the year, combined with the number of salaried employees at a certain date. They include all full- or part-time working proprietors, active business partners, self-employed persons and homeworkers. *Employment, employees* excludes entrepreneurs. *Hours worked* is hours worked by employees.

Total gross fixed capital formation is given for *investment*, and is the value of purchases of fixed assets, plus own-account construction, less the value of sales. It covers fixed assets with a productive life of at least three years and includes assets made by a unit's labour force for its own use, new assets and used assets (if previously used outside the country). Additions, alterations, improvements and capital repairs to existing assets are also included. The valuation for new assets is at full cost incurred, including delivered price, the cost of installation, fees and taxes. Assets produced by the unit take the cost of work put in progress, including labour, material and other supplies: sales of assets take the actual amount realised. *Investment in machinery and equipment* also gives gross fixed capital formation, uses the same calculation method and includes transport equipment; industrial machinery and equipment; office machinery, equipment and furniture; professional instruments and equipment. Alterations, improvements and capital repairs are also covered.

Compensation of labour covers wages, salaries and employers' contributions to social security schemes and to pensions funds. Included are: regular and overtime cash payments, bonuses and cost-of-living allowances; vacation and sick leave pay; taxes and social insurance contributions, etc., payable by employees and deducted by employers; and payments in kind. Employers' contributions cover only legally required expenditure.

Publications

Statistiska Meddelanden; series N.

SWITZERLAND

I. GENERAL

The data were prepared by the St. Galler Zentrum für Zukunftsforschung for the Bundesamt für Statistik - BFS (Office fédéral de la statistique - OFS).

II. FOREIGN TRADE STATISTICS

Concepts and Definitions of Variables

General trade is given for *exports* and *imports*. In both cases, state trading, commercial transactions in military equipment and supplies, foreign aid transactions, improvement and repair trade, transactions in new ships and aircraft, electric energy and gas, and private donations and gifts are included. Specific exclusions are: direct transit trade, temporary exports, monetary items, industrial precious metals and minor transactions.

III. NATIONAL ACCOUNTS STATISTICS

Source

The original survey uses the enterprise as the reference unit; it is conducted on a sample basis, no estimate is made for units falling outside this limit. Data cover the calendar year.

Industrial Classification

Data have been regrouped from the "Allgemeine Systematik der Wirtschaftszweige" (General Classification of Economic Activity). In the tables:

a) ISIC 3 includes ISIC 2;
b) ISIC 321 excludes ISIC 3213;
c) ISIC 322 also covers ISIC 323, 324 and 3213;
d) ISIC 33 (wood products and furniture) includes ISIC 3902 and 3903 (other manufacturing except jewellery);
e) ISIC 351 includes ISIC 352, 353, 354;
f) ISIC 355 includes ISIC 356;
g) ISIC 36 includes ISIC 2;
h) ISIC 37 (basic metal industries) includes ISIC 381/3813 (fabricated/structural metal products);
i) ISIC 38 excludes ISIC 381, 3813, 3853;
j) ISIC 382 includes ISIC 384 and 3851;
k) ISIC 383 includes ISIC 3852;
l) ISIC 385 excludes ISIC 3851, 3852, 3853;
m) ISIC 3901 (jewellery) includes ISIC 3853 (watches and clocks).

Concepts and Definitions of Variables

Gross output in producers' prices is given for *production*, and includes the value of all products. *Value added*, also in producers' prices, uses the national accounting concept of value added.

Employment gives the number of persons engaged, based on the average number of employees throughout the year. It includes working proprietors, active business partners, unpaid family workers, salaried employees, wage earners, full- and part-time employees.

Publications

Sources and methods are further described in:

i) P. Meier, *Daten für Branchenmodelle der schweizerischen Wirtschaft*, 1983;

ii) P. Meier, *Daten für den tertiären Sektor in der Schweiz, Wertschöpfung, Beschäftigung und Preise von 1960 bis 1982 für 18 Branchen*, 1984;

iii) H.G. Graf, F. Kneschaurek, Y. Wang, Vorleistungen, *Wertschöpfung und Produktivität in Industrie- und Dienstleistungsbranchen der Schweiz*, 1989;

iv) H.G. Graf, Das St. Galler *Branchenmodell: Stand der Revisionsarbeiten*, in: *Mitteilungen des SGZZ*, Ziff.2.3, Nr. 27, 1990.

Publications *i)* and *ii)* relate to the National Research Programme No. 9 and may be obtained from the programme management.

TURKEY

I. INDUSTRIAL STATISTICS

Source

Data are derived from the annual manufacturing survey conducted by the State Institute of Statistics, Ankara, except for 1992 for which data are derived from the Census of Industry and Establishments. Prior to 1992, all manufacturing establishments in the public sector and establishments employing 25 or more persons in the private sector were covered. From 1992 onwards, establishments employing 10 or more persons in the private sector are covered.

Industrial Classification

The Turkish classification is an adapted version of the ISIC. It contains an extra code, 3854 (other professional goods). The figures for 385 are therefore not equal to the sum of the published components. ISIC 4 (electricity, gas and water) excludes electricity.

Concepts and Definitions of Variables

Production, or output, is the value of output calculated by subtracting the value of the beginning of the year stock (finished and semi-finished goods) from the total of receipts from sales and services rendered to others, receipts from sales of transfers of electricity plus the end-of-year stock (finished and semi-finished goods) and the production value of fixed assets produced by the establishments' staff for own use. *Value*

Statistiques des Structures Industrielles OECD
OECD, © 1998 OCDE

added is obtained by subtracting the value of inputs from output. The value of inputs is calculated by subtracting the value of the end-of-year stock (raw materials, supplementary materials, packaging materials and fuel) from the total value of goods and services purchased or transferred, electricity purchased and the beginning-of-year stock (raw materials, supplementary materials, packaging materials and fuel).

Employment, or the average number of persons engaged, is obtained by adding the number of owners and partners and unpaid family workers, active in November, in the establishment to the average number of employees. The average number of employees is the arithmetic average of the number of employees in February, May, August and November. The *hours worked* in one year are calculated by multiplying the average number of production workers by the hours worked in one shift and the number of days worked in a year.

Investment is gross additions to the fixed assets during the year. It is calculated by subtracting the sales value of fixed assets sold during the year from total expenditures made on new or used fixed assets purchased from the domestic market, fixed assets imported new or used, fixed assets produced by the establishments' own staff, parts of fixed assets installed during the year purchased on a bid basis, major repairs and expenditures made on fixed assets, studies and plans, drawings, machinery, equipment, motor vehicle and building, other construction, office equipment and furniture (used by the establishment and expected to have a productive life of more than one year and recorded in the capital accounts) and expenditures on land and land improvements.

Remuneration (wages and salaries), or annual payments to employees, includes all payments in the form of wages and salaries and per diems gross of income tax, social security and pension fund premiums. It excludes social security and pension contributions and the like payable by the employer. It also includes overtime payments, bonuses, indemnities and payments in kind.

An *establishment* is a work place where single ownership or controlling status is established and generally where one type of economic activity occurs and which has the register and accounting sources necessary to fill in the questionnaires.

UNITED KINGDOM

I. GENERAL

The information is provided by the UK Office for National Statistics (formerly the Central Statistical Office) and is of two types: industrial and foreign trade statistics.

II. INDUSTRIAL STATISTICS

Source

From 1973 to 1977, the Annual Census of Production surveyed all establishments employing 20 or more persons. In 1978, a sampling scheme was introduced, the pattern of which has varied, but that established in the 1980 census was repeated from 1981 to 1983, and from 1985 to 1987. In these years forms were despatched to all establishments employing 100 persons or more and, in general, to samples of 1 in 2 of those employing 50 to 99, as well as 1 in 4 of those employing 20 to 49. 1984 was a benchmark census and forms were despatched to all establishments with 20 or more employed except for those in the 20 to 49 employment size band located in England, where, in general, a sample of 1 in 2 was taken. Estimates are made for each establishment falling outside the scope of the survey by calculating "average per head" ratios for census returns. These ratios are multiplied by the employment thought to exist in each non-responding or unselected establishment to yield an estimated value for that establishment. Though establishments are requested to provide calendar year data, returns for business years ending between 5 April of the year to which the census applies, and 6 April of the following year, are accepted.

The 1984 benchmark census made use of a new register of businesses. Extra, mainly small, units were added and some were reclassified from one industry to another. This change affected the estimates for all industries, a few significantly, and is reflected particularly in the figures for number of establishments.

The statistical unit is the establishment, defined as the smallest unit which can provide the information normally required for an economic census.

Industrial Classification

Results of the annual censuses from 1973 to 1979 were all based on the Standard Industrial Classification Revised 1968. Since 1980, censuses have been based on the Standard Industrial Classification Revised 1980. In order to provide a link between earlier results and those for 1980 and beyond, the 1979 results were reworked on the basis of the new classification.

Concepts and Definitions of Variables

Production, or gross output, is calculated by adjusting the value of total sales, work done and services rendered, by the net changes during the year of work in progress and stocks of finished goods. Total sales represents deliveries on sale of goods produced by establishments in the United Kingdom coming within the scope of the census and includes sales of goods made for establishments from materials given out by them to other organisations or to outworkers, and the sales of waste products and residues. The value of sales is the "net selling value", i.e. the amount charged to customers whether values "ex-works" or "delivered" less VAT, trade discounts, agents' commissions, etc., and allowances on returned goods. Where products attract excise duty, the value is inclusive of duty if goods are sold "duty-paid" and exclusive of duty if goods are sold in bond or exported. Sales of fixed assets are excluded. *Value added*, or gross value added at factor cost, is calculated as the value of gross output less the cost of purchases of materials for use in production and packaging, fuels, goods for merchanting or factoring, the cost of industrial and non-industrial services received, rates and the cost of licensing of motor vehicles. The value of purchases is adjusted for changes during the year of stocks of materials, stores and fuel. The valuation is in factor values, *i.e.* excluding indirect taxes and including subsidies.

Employment represents the number of persons engaged; it gives the average number of administrative, technical and clerical employees and operatives on payroll and the number of working proprietors employed during the year of return. Self-employed persons, active business partners, unpaid family workers working at least half normal hours, salaried employees and wage earners, whether full-time or part-time are all included, but homeworkers and casual workers are excluded. In comparison, *Employment, employees* does not include working proprietors, *i.e.* persons regarded as self-employed for national insurance purposes, members of their families who worked in the business without receiving a definite wage or salary for at least half the normal working hours and directors who worked in the business but did not receive a definite wage, salary or commission.

Investment, or gross fixed capital formation, is the value of purchases of fixed assets less the value of sales of such assets. The valuation is at full cost incurred, including the cost of installation and certain fees and taxes (namely legal fees, stamp duty, agents' commissions, etc.), and is inclusive of any amounts received or expected to be received in grants and/or allowances from government sources, statutory bodies or local authorities. In general, the value is that charged to capital account, together with any other amounts which rank as capital items for taxation purposes during the year. Where expenditure is spread over more than one census year, payments are included in the years in which they were made. Capital expenditure during the year in respect of production units where production had not started before the end of the year, and the value of capital goods produced for establishments' own use by establishments' own staff are included. The value of any assets acquired in taking over an existing business is excluded. The figures include non-deductible VAT but exclude deductible VAT. No allowance is made for depreciation, amortisation or obsolescence. *Investments in machinery and equipment* are the capital expenditure on

Statistiques des Structures Industrielles OECD
OECD, © 1998 OCDE

new and second-hand plant and machinery, office equipment and other capital equipment. Net capital expenditure on plant and machinery is the value of acquisitions less the value of disposals.

Compensation of labour, employees represents amounts paid during the year to employees. They include wages and salaries and supplements. Employers' National Insurance contributions etc. are included, as is outworkers remuneration. *Wages and salaries, employees* represent amounts paid during the year to employees. All overtime payments, bonuses, commissions, holiday pay and redundancy payments less any amounts reimbursed for this purpose from government sources are included. No deduction is made for income tax or employees' National Insurance contributions etc. Payments to working proprietors, payments in kind, travelling expenses, lodgings allowances etc. and employers' National Insurance contributions are excluded. *Employers' social costs* include employers' National Insurance contributions, i.e. employers' National Insurance contributions under the Social Security Pensions Act 1975, commercial insurance premiums for policies providing pensions, superannuation or other retirement benefits, sickness benefit, personal accident benefits, disability benefits or death benefits for employees or their dependants, and also outworkers remuneration which corresponds to amounts paid to outworkers, i.e. people who do work in their own homes generally on a piece work basis, whose names appear on the payroll. Amounts paid to outworkers by subcontractors are included in the cost of industrial services received. Estimates are not made for remuneration of outworkers for businesses not completing returns.

Publications

i) *Census of Production Introductory Notes* (Business Monitor PA 1001, published by the Office for National Statistics;

ii) *Annual Abstract of Statistics*, published by the Office for National Statistics, London.

III. FOREIGN TRADE STATISTICS

Source

Data are collected by Customs and Excise officials and subsequently passed on to the Office for National Statistics.

Industrial Classification

Customs and Excise compile statistics using the Standard International Trade Classification (SITC). They are then aggregated to the UK Standard Industrial Classification by the Office for National Statistics, which afterwards performs the conversion to the ISIC.

It should be noted that some detail has been suppressed for certain headings in some years. It has been added to sub-totals and totals where possible, and in any case to the grand total. Other items, which could not be classified to individual industries, have been included in the grand total: postal packages not classified to kind, continental shelf transactions, and low value transactions.

Concepts and Definitions of Variables

In both cases general trade is used. *Exports*, fob, are classified according to country of ultimate destination, *imports*, cif, according to country of consignment. In both cases state trading, commercial transactions in military equipment and supplies, foreign aid transactions, improvement and repair trade, transactions in new ships and aircraft, electric energy and gas, and private donations and gifts are included. Sea products landed direct from the high seas are also covered, though natural produce of the sea brought ashore by British registered vessels is excluded from imports. Direct transit trade and transactions in second-hand ships and aircraft are specifically excluded; temporary exports, monetary items, industrial gold and minor transactions are not.

Overseas Trade Statistics (monthly).

Published by HMSO.

UNITED STATES

I. GENERAL

The Bureau of the Census, U.S. Department of Commerce, supplied the information taken from industrial and foreign trade statistics.

II. INDUSTRIAL STATISTICS

Source

The data are derived from the Census Bureau's quinquennial census of manufactures and annual survey of manufactures. The quinquennial census covers years ending in 2 and 7 and covers all establishments with at least one employee; the annual survey takes a sample of around 55 000 establishments, representing a coverage of about two-thirds of total manufacturing employment. Beginning with the 1982 data, respondents were asked to report their end-of-year inventories at cost of market. Prior to 1982, respondents were permitted to value inventories using any generally accepted accounting method (FIFO, LIFO, market, to name a few). In 1982, LIFO users were asked to first report inventory values prior to the LIFO adjustment and then to report the LIFO reserve and the LIFO value after adjustment for the reserve. Because of this change in reporting instructions, the data for 1983 and onwards for value added and gross output are not comparable to prior year data.

Industrial Classification

Originally, the US Standard Industrial Classification (SIC) was used. With minor reservations, the industry data can be regrouped to the International Standard Industrial Classification (ISIC). The following are excluded from the national concept of manufacturing:

a) small-scale processing activities carried out as a secondary activity in agriculture;

b) custom work to the individual order of household consumers;

c) some repair activities and repair shops of railroads;

d) production of coke for own use by public utility companies;

e) manufacturing by retail establishments selling most of their products on their premises to household consumers;

f) manufacturing by construction contractors at the site.

Concepts and Definitions of Variables

Production or gross output is measured as deliveries in terms of shipments, fob, adjusted for change in inventory for work-in-process and finished goods. The goods shipped include goods produced in the establishments, those shipped in the same condition as received (resales), and receipts for industrial work done on materials owned by others or industrial services rendered to others. In a few industries where value of production is collected, the inventory adjustment is limited to work-in-process. In shipbuilding, the value of work done is collected and no inventory adjustment is made. The value of goods shipped is at producer prices, fob plant, exclusive of freight and taxes. In industries where the product is typically delivered, the value of shipments is in delivered prices. *Value added* is based on the "census" value added concept and is calculated as gross output less the cost of materials, fuels and other supplies, goods shipped in the same condition as received, contract and commission work done by others, and electricity purchased. The input estimates are on a consumed basis, though the cost of purchases is acceptable if close to the cost of goods put into production (if not, the respondent using purchase records is asked to adjust them for change in inventory to put them on a "use" basis). The valuation is the same as for production.

Employment figures are given for all full- and part-time employees on the payrolls of operating establishments. An average of four quarterly observations (taken on 12 March, May, August and November) is taken for production workers (operatives) and combined with the figure for all other employees that is taken annually on 12 March. Work hours include all production *hours worked*, including overtime hours, waiting time or time on call in the workplace, and rest periods, but excluding paid vacations. Overtime is in actual hours worked, not straight-time equivalent hours. The following categories are included: apprentices, casual workers, part-time employees. Employers, supervisors, family or unpaid workers and the self-employed are excluded.

Gross fixed capital formation (*investment*) relates to expenditure on new plant and equipment only. Included in the data is the value of new plant and equipment purchased and constructed by the unit's own labour force for its own used. Used plant and equipment purchased are excluded. While data on purchases of used assets are collected in the United States, they are not publishable for many industries because of confidentiality problems. Thus, data on total fixed assets acquired are not available by industry. Fixed assets are defined as those with a productive life of more than one year (following accounting practice and tax laws). The valuation of new fixed capital formation is at full cost and includes the valuation of additions, alterations, improvements and repairs to existing assets (if capitalised). Purchased new assets are at delivered prices and include the cost of installation but exclude fees and taxes. The value of new assets produced by the units includes labour, materials and other supply cost plus an allocation for overheads. For assets under construction but not fully in place at the end of the year, gross fixed capital formation (new) includes only the part of the total expenditures made during the specified year. *Investment in machinery and equipment* includes transport equipment; industrial machinery and equipment; office machinery and equipment; furniture, professional instruments and equipment, and alterations, improvements, and repairs to the above (if capitalised). Data on sales of fixed assets are not collected.

Remuneration covers gross earnings paid during the year, including wages, salaries and employers' contributions to pension funds and social security schemes. Regular and overtime cash payments, bonuses and cost-of-living allowances are included, as are vacation and sick leave pay, taxes and social insurance contributions payable by employees and deducted by employers, payments in kind (if significant and customary part of employee compensation), and allowances. With regard to contributions to social security schemes (*supplements to wages and salaries*), the Census Bureau distinguishes between those required by federal and state, or local legislation, and those voluntarily adopted by the employer on his own initiative or as a result of collective bargaining. They include such payments as Federal Old Age and Survivors' Insurance, unemployment compensation, and workers' compensation. Also included are payments for health insurance, life insurance, pension plans and stock purchase plans. *Wages and salaries* are based upon the remuneration minus the supplemental labour costs.

Publications

Data are published in:

i) Census of Manufactures;

ii) Annual Survey of Manufactures.

Both published by the Bureau of the Census, United States Department of Commerce, Washington D.C.

III. FOREIGN TRADE STATISTICS

Source

The United States Foreign Trade Statistics are compiled by the Bureau of the Census.

Foreign Trade Classification

The export data are originally compiled in accordance with Schedule B, Statistical Classification of Domestic and Foreign Commodities Exported from the United States and rearranged and summarised into the SIC and then regrouped to the ISIC. The import data are originally compiled using the Tariff Schedules of the United States annotated and summarised into the SIC and then regrouped to the ISIC.

Special Tabulations

Data are available from:

i) United States Exports, SIC Division by SIC-Based 2-Digit, 3-Digit and 4-Digit Product Code;

ii) United States Imports for Consumption and General Imports, SIC Division by SIC-Based 2-Digit, 3-Digit and 4-Digit Product Code.

Both issued by the Bureau of the Census, United States Department of Commerce, Washington D.C.

ALLEMAGNE

I. GÉNÉRALITÉS

Les informations émanent de l'Office Fédéral de Statistique (Statistisches Bundesamt) de Wiesbaden. On distingue deux types de données en fonction de leur origine : statistiques industrielles et statistiques du commerce extérieur. Les données relatives aux années antérieures à 1990 se réfèrent à l'Allemagne occidentale (République Fédérale d'Allemagne avant unification de l'Allemagne, y compris Berlin Ouest). Les données à partir de 1991 se réfèrent à l'Allemagne après unification, sauf les données concernant la valeur ajoutée, l'investissement et les dépenses en machines et équipement, qui continuent à ne couvrir que l'ancienne Allemagne occidentale.

II. STATISTIQUES INDUSTRIELLES

Source

En règle générale, les chiffres concernant les secteurs extractifs et manufacturiers sont tirés de l'enquête mensuelle menée par l'Office de Statistique. Cette enquête s'adresse à toutes les unités locales des entreprises de 20 salariés ou plus, y compris les artisanats de production et les unités de ces entreprises qui sont engagées dans des activités non industrielles.

Pour la branche 4 de la CITI, toutes les entreprises de 20 salariés ou plus sont prises en compte.

Classification industrielle

Les données, qui sont à l'origine exprimées en fonction de la classification nationale (Systematik für die Statistik im Produzierenden Gewerbe -- SYPRO), sont dans toute la mesure du possible ventilées selon la CITI. Les différences entre les deux nomenclatures sont indiquées ci-après.

La fabrication de bâtiments préfabriqués, qui relève du secteur de la construction dans la nomenclature nationale, n'est en général pas prise en compte ; les secteurs de l'imprimerie et de l'édition (CITI 342) ne sont pas couverts par l'enquête ; la fabrication d'objets en pierre (CITI 369) est incluse dans CITI 290, la fabrication de matelas (CITI 332) dans CITI 321, la fabrication de parapluies (CITI 390) dans CITI 322, la fabrication de vêtements en fourrure (CITI 322) dans CITI 323, la reliure (CITI 342) dans CITI 341, la fabrication d'huiles et graisses lubrifiantes composées (CITI 353, 354) dans les rubriques CITI 351 et 352, la fabrication de tuyaux et tubes en plastique brut (CITI 351) dans CITI 356, le traitement de surface et la cémentation (CITI 381) dans CITI 371, la fabrication de fils en acier étiré et de chaînes en acier forgé (CITI 371), de machines à laver (CITI 382) et l'assemblage et la réparation des systèmes de ventilation, de chauffage et de tuyauterie (branche 5 de la CITI) dans CITI 381, la fabrication d'articles en verre pour éclairage (CITI 362) et l'enregistrement de bandes et de disques (branche 9 de la CITI) ainsi que la fabrication d'appareils de mesure et de mètres électriques et électroniques (CITI 385) dans CITI 383. Les estimations de la valeur ajoutée sont en général calculées de la même manière que pour les enquêtes, mais les industries extractives sont incluses dans CITI 369, la fabrication de bâtiments préfabriqués est exclue pour toutes les années, le montage des profilés en acier est inclus dans CITI 381 et un ajustement est effectué pour le montage et la réparation des systèmes de ventilation, de chauffage et de tuyauterie.

En 1983, les données sur la production et l'emploi ont été ventilées en fonction de la CITI au moyen d'une table de conversion améliorée. Ceci affecte partiellement la comparabilité avec les chiffres des années antérieures. Les positions CITI pour lesquelles cela a l'incidence la plus notable sont les rubriques 371, 381 et 383.

Concepts et définitions des variables

Les chiffres sur la *production* indiquent le chiffre d'affaires tiré de la production de l'unité tel qu'il ressort des factures, y compris les recettes au titre des marchandises réexpédiées en l'état, de la vente des déchets de fabrication, d'électricité et autres articles similaires. Les recettes au titre des activités non industrielles (paiements d'intérêt, loyers, dividendes, par exemple) ne sont pas prises en compte. La valeur des livraisons ne tient pas non plus compte des taxes sur la valeur ajoutée ou le chiffre d'affaires, mais elle inclut les droits d'accise, les coûts d'emballage, d'affranchissement et autres frais. Les livraisons entre unités de la même entreprise ne sont pas comptabilisées. La *valeur ajoutée* est estimée à partir de la production nette, c'est-à-dire conformément au concept de valeur ajoutée «recensée». Elle est égale à la production brute déduction faite du coût des matériaux, combustibles et autres fournitures, des travaux exécutés sous contrat ou à la commande par d'autres unités, des travaux de réparation et d'entretien exécutés par d'autres unités, des marchandises réexpédiées en l'état et de l'électricité achetée. Le coût des services non industriels est exclu mais les recettes perçues à ce titre sont incluses. Les données relatives aux consommations sont estimées sur la base des quantités reçues et un ajustement est effectué pour tenir compte de la variation des stocks de matériaux, combustibles et autres fournitures. L'évaluation est faite aux prix à la production, y compris tous les impôts directs (à l'exclusion de la taxe sur le chiffre d'affaires) mais à l'exclusion de toutes les subventions.

Les chiffres sur l'*emploi* indiquent le nombre annuel moyen de personnes occupées en fin de mois. Y sont inclus les propriétaires exploitants, les associés actifs, les travailleurs familiaux non rémunérés, à condition qu'ils travaillent pendant un nombre d'heures équivalent à un tiers au moins de l'horaire normal. Les salariés à temps partiel et temporaires sont pris en compte de même que les apprentis. Les travailleurs à domicile sont exclus. Les *heures ouvrées* couvrent les heures travaillées, y compris les heures supplémentaires, par les ouvriers, qui sont définis comme les personnes occupées soumises à l'assurance obligatoire auprès des caisses de retraite des ouvriers. Cette définition englobe les apprentis, mais non les travailleurs à domicile. Elle comprend également les agents de maîtrise de même que les travailleurs occasionnels et à temps partiel.

Les chiffres concernant l'*investissement* total sont tirés d'une enquête annuelle s'adressant aux entreprises de 20 salariés ou plus. Les activités artisanales y sont prises en compte. Ces chiffres représentent la formation brute de capital fixe, qui est définie comme la valeur des acquisitions d'actifs fixes neufs et usagés, y compris ceux fabriqués par le personnel de l'établissement pour l'usage de ce dernier et les travaux en cours. L'évaluation est faite au prix de revient total, y compris les droits et redevances. Les paiements anticipés versés pour des actifs non encore reçus sont exclus.

Les données concernant les *salaires et traitements, total* ne comprennent pas les cotisations patronales de sécurité sociale. Toutes les sommes versées aux intérimaires sont incluses ; les cotisations aux caisses de retraite des sociétés sont exclues.

Publications

Fachserie 4, Reihe 4.1.1., *Beschäftigung, Umsatz und Energieversorgung der Unternehmen und Betriebe im Bergbau und im Verarbeitenden Gewerbe*, Statistisches Bundesamt, Wiesbaden.

III. STATISTIQUES DU COMMERCE EXTÉRIEUR

Les statistiques du commerce extérieur couvrent le commerce général ainsi que le commerce spécial, et sont évaluées CAF/FAB. Elles portent sur le commerce d'Etat, les transactions commerciales d'équipements et de fournitures militaires, les transactions portant sur les navires et avions neufs, mais excluent les échanges directs en transit et les articles monétaires. Les opérations sur marchandise avec la République Démocratique d'Allemagne et les biens importés par les membres des forces armées stationnées en Allemagne ne sont pas pris en compte. Les données sont recueillies selon la nomenclature nationale («Warengruppen und -zweigen des Warenverzeichnisses für Aussenhandelsstatistik (1975)») puis converties vers la CITI. Pour ce faire, on suppose qu'il y a équivalence entre les deux nomenclatures lorsque les groupes de produits considérés répondent pour l'essentiel à la même définition, de sorte qu'il faut parfois s'attendre à quelques imprécisions.

AUSTRALIE

I. STATISTIQUES INDUSTRIELLES

Source

Les informations émanent du Bureau Australien de Statistiques (ABS). Les données relatives aux industries manufacturières et extractives sont tirées de l'enquête «Manufacturing Survey», dont l'unité de base est l'établissement. Depuis 1990-91, l'enquête touche tous les établissements. Les données relatives aux autres industries proviennent de l'«Economic Activity Survey», dont l'unité de base est l'entreprise («management unit»). La période couverte est l'exercice budgétaire qui débute le 1er juillet.

Classification industrielle

Jusqu'en 1994, la classification utilisée était l'«Australian Standard Industrial Classification» (ASIC), alignée sur la CITI révision 2.

Depuis 1995, la classification utilisée est l'«Australian and New Zealand Standard Industrial Classification» (ANZSIC), alignée sur la CITI révision 3.

Concepts et définitions des variables

La *production* représente le chiffre d'affaires mesuré par les ventes et les transferts de biens, qu'ils soient produits par l'établissement ou non, plus les revenus provenant de services (tels qu'honoraires ou commissions versés pour la fabrication ou l'assemblage, recettes au titre de services et de réparations, frais d'installation, de livraisons, commissions de ventes et d'agences, revenus tirés de la publicité), les revenus provenant d'activités de location à bail, de crédit-bail et de louage, les subventions du gouvernement et les primes à la production, les salaires capitalisés et les coûts en matériaux intégrés au capital relatifs aux travaux d'équipements effectués pour le compte de l'établissement.

La *valeur ajoutée* est donnée par le chiffre d'affaires majoré (ou diminué) de la variation des stocks, déduction faite des dépenses diverses. Ces dernières comprennent les achats et transferts de matériaux, les combustibles, les containers et le matériel d'emballage, les biens pour la revente, les dépenses courantes pour les véhicules automobiles, les dépenses de location à bail, de crédit-bail et de louage, de réparations et d'entretien, de fret et de charriage, les frais de commissions, de sous-traitance et de publicité, les honoraires d'audit et de comptabilité, les frais de nettoyage, les paiements au titre de services de traitement de données, les frais d'acte, les frais d'impression et d'affranchissement, les paiements au titre de services de secrétariat, de traitement de textes, de photocopies, les dépenses pour la formation du personnel, pour les télécommunications, les voyages, le logement et les frais de représentation, les autres dépenses administratives, les taxes et impôts fonciers, les taxes fondées sur les salaires et les autres dépenses d'exploitation. En sont exclus les salaires et traitements, les retraites, les indemnités et autres assurances versées aux travailleurs, les intérêts, les frais de banques, les redevances, les amortissements, les mauvaises créances, les impôts directs et indirects, les dividendes et provisions.

A partir de 1990-1991, l'*emploi* indique le nombre de personnes employées (y compris les propriétaires exploitants et les associés pour les entreprises non constituées en sociétés) au 30 juin de chaque année. Sont compris tous les employés qu'ils soient à plein temps ou à temps partiel, permanents, temporaires ou saisonniers. Les employés en congé payé le 30 juin sont compris. En sont exclus les entrepreneurs, les consultants et les autres travailleurs indépendants fournissant des services ainsi que les aides et volontaires non payés.

Les *salaires et traitements, salariés* couvrent les salaires et traitements versés à tous les employés salariés de l'établissement pour l'année se terminant le 30 juin. Ils comprennent les salaires, les traitements, les primes et commissions, les paiements pour heures supplémentaires, les amendes, les congés payés et autres provisions. Les paiements versés aux entrepreneurs, consultants et autres travailleurs indépendants, et aux propriétaires et associés d'entreprises individuelles sont exclus, ainsi que les taxes relatives aux paiements et les remboursements aux employés pour frais encourus.

Le nombre d'*établissements* est comptabilisé au 30 juin de l'année considérée. L'établissement représente la plus petite unité comptable d'une entreprise au sein d'un état ou d'un territoire australien, ayant le contrôle de ses activités de production. En général, toutes les opérations d'un établissement sont réalisées sur un même lieu physique mais il se peut aussi qu'elles soient effectuées en des lieux différents.

Publications

i) *Census of manufacturing establishments*, summary of operations (Preliminary) by Industry subdivision, Australia (Catalogue No. 8201.0) ;

ii) *Manufacturing establishments*, summary of operations by Industry class, Australia (Catalogue No. 8202.0) ;

iii) *Manufacturing establishments,* details of operations by Industry class, Australia (Catalogue No. 8203.0) -- ce bulletin constitue la source principale ;

iv) *Business Operations and Industry Performance* (Catalogue No. 8140.0).

AUTRICHE

I. STATISTIQUES INDUSTRIELLES

Source

Les données émanent du Bureau central de statistique de l'Autriche.

Les données relatives aux années 1990-1994 sont le résultat de l'ancienne enquête statistique annuelle dans l'industrie. Cette enquête couvrait tous les établissements affiliés à la section industrielle de la Chambre économique fédérale. Elle couvrait également les établissements affiliés à la section "Gewerbe" mais seulement pour les établissements de plus de 20 employés. L'unité statistique était l'établissement ("Betriebe").

Les données pour 1995 sont le résultat du recensement non agricole. Ce recensement couvre toutes les entreprises du secteur non agricole (CITI révision 3 catégories C à K et M à O). L'unité statistique est l'entreprise. Les données de 1995 ne sont pas strictement comparables à celles des années précédentes.

Classification industrielle

Jusqu'en 1994, la classification des activités économiques («Betriebssystematik 1968») utilisée en Autriche était alignée sur la CITI révision 2. Pour les heures ouvrées, certaines industries n'étaient pas couvertes par l'enquête mensuelle : CITI 324 ; CITI 369 ; CITI 385 ; CITI 39.

A partir de 1995, la classification utilisée est la version autrichienne de la NACE révision 1, appelée "ÖNACE 1995". Elle est parfaitement comparable à la NACE révision 1 jusqu'au niveau à quatre chiffres, le quatrième niveau étant subdivisé en sous-classes. L'"ÖNACE 1995" est compatible avec la CITI révision 3.

Concepts et définitions des variables

Données 1990-1994

L'*établissement* correspond à l'unité locale par type d'activité.

La *production* correspond à la production brute évaluée aux prix à la production, y compris tous les impôts indirects, mais à l'exclusion de la taxe sur la valeur ajoutée et de toutes les subventions. Elle inclut tous les produits, la variation nette des travaux en cours, les travaux effectués par l'unité pour compte propre, les services rendus, les marchandises réexpédiées en l'état, l'électricité vendue, les actifs fixes produits par l'unité pour compte propre, la variation nette du niveau des stocks de produits finis, les déchets de fabrication et les biens fabriqués par des travailleurs à domicile et par des artisans.

La *valeur ajoutée* est établie conformément au concept de valeur ajoutée «recensée». Elle est donnée par la valeur de la production brute, déduction faite du coût des matériaux, combustibles et autres fournitures, des travaux exécutés sous contrat ou à la commande par d'autres unités, des travaux de réparation et d'entretien exécutés par d'autres unités, des marchandises réexpédiées en l'état et de l'électricité achetée, les estimations étant établies sur la base des quantités consommées. Y sont inclus le coût des services non industriels et les recettes perçues à ce titre. L'évaluation est faite aux prix à la production, y compris tous les impôts indirects mais à l'exclusion de toutes les subventions et de la taxe sur la valeur ajoutée.

Les données sur l'*emploi* indiquent, au 31 décembre de chaque année, le nombre total de personnes occupées et de salariés. Sont inclus dans l'emploi total les propriétaires exploitants, les travailleurs familiaux non rémunérés, les travailleurs indépendants, les employés, les salariés, les travailleurs à domicile, les salariés à temps complet et à temps partiel et le personnel de bureau et d'encadrement dont les fonctions sont étroitement liées au processus de production. Les *heures ouvrées* couvrent les heures travaillées (c'est-à-dire les heures payées moins les jours de congés et les jours fériés) par les ouvriers et les apprentis suivant le registre du personnel. Sont inclus : les heures supplémentaires, les heures passées à attendre et les périodes de repos, les congés de maladie et les jours fériés. Sont exclus les travailleurs occasionnels et à temps partiel. Les agents de maîtrise et les apprentis ne sont pris en compte que s'ils apparaissent sur le registre du personnel.

L'*investissement* correspond aux dépenses d'équipement, qui sont définies comme étant la valeur des acquisitions d'actifs fixes, y compris ceux fabriqués par le personnel de l'établissement pour l'usage de ce dernier. La valeur des ventes d'actifs fixes n'est pas déduite. Par actifs fixes, il faut entendre les biens qui ont une durée de vie productive d'un an au moins, y compris ceux qui sont fabriqués par le personnel de l'unité, les adjonctions, transformations et réparations d'actifs existants, les actifs neufs, non encore mis en service, inutilisés ou utilisés précédemment en dehors du pays, et les actifs usagés. L'investissement est évalué au prix de revient total, y compris le prix rendu, les frais d'installation, les droits et redevances (à l'exception de la taxe sur la valeur ajoutée). Dans le cas d'actifs produits par l'unité, les coûts de main-d'œuvre et le coût des matériaux et autres fournitures sont pris en compte ainsi qu'une provision pour frais généraux. La valeur des ventes d'actifs usagés est donnée par le montant réellement réalisé. Les *dépenses en machines et équipement* correspondent à la formation brute de capital fixe qui comprend, comme pour l'investissement total, les acquisitions d'actifs fixes y compris ceux qui sont fabriqués par le personnel de l'établissement pour l'usage de ce dernier. Y sont inclus : le matériel de transport, les machines et l'outillage industriel, les machines, les équipements et le mobilier de bureau, les instruments et équipements professionnels, les modifications, améliorations et réparations apportées à ces matériels.

Les *salaires et charges sociales* couvrent à la fois les salaires et traitements, et les cotisations patronales aux régimes de Sécurité sociale et de retraite. Elles incluent le paiement des heures normales et supplémentaires, les gratifications et indemnités de cherté de vie, les congés payés et congés de maladie, les impôts et cotisations d'assurance sociale dus par les salariés et retenus par l'employeur, les prestations en nature et les indemnités (déplacement, vêtements). Les *charges sociales des employeurs* englobent les dépenses exigées par la loi et les contributions volontaires, telles que cotisations de sécurité sociale (santé, vieillesse, accident, assurance chômage), les cotisations au fonds de péréquation des allocations familiales, les cotisations à la caisse de construction résidentielle et les indemnités de logement, ainsi que les paiements non obligatoires (par exemple en cas d'accident, de maladie ou de détresse matérielle, les services de restauration, les indemnités kilométriques).

Données 1995

L'*entreprise* est généralement la plus petite unité légale. Elle peut comprendre un ou plusieurs établissements.

La *production* correspond au chiffre d'affaires, y compris les revenus tirés de la capitalisation des services rendus pour son propre compte, non compris l'achat de biens et services destinés à la revente en l'état (sans frets étrangers). Elle comprend la variation nette des stocks d'articles commerciaux, des produits finis et des travaux en cours.

La *valeur ajoutée au coût des facteurs* est égale à la valeur ajoutée aux prix de base, non compris les impôts et redevances (sans les impôts sur les produits), y compris les subventions d'exploitation (sans les subventions sur les produits). La valeur ajoutée aux prix de base est calculée comme la valeur de la production moins les frets étrangers, les achats de matériaux pour les travaux et fabrications, les dépenses pour les réparations et l'entretien et pour les travaux effectués par d'autres entreprises, les dépenses pour les travailleurs intérimaires, l'achat de combustibles, les loyers, crédit-bail et autres coûts d'exploitation, les dépenses pour actifs faibles, les impôts sur les produits, y compris la variation nette des stocks de combustibles, de matières premières et matériaux consommés, les subventions sur les produits.

Des données de l'emploi sont données à la fois pour le nombre total de personnes occupées et pour le nombre de salariés. Sont inclus dans l'*emploi* total les propriétaires exploitants, les travailleurs familiaux non rémunérés, les travailleurs indépendants, les salariés (employés et ouvriers), les apprentis, les travailleurs à domicile et les travailleurs à temps partiel. L'*emploi, salariés* comprend les salariés (employés et ouvriers), les apprentis, les travailleurs à domicile et les travailleurs à temps partiel.

L'*investissement* (formation de capital) correspond aux dépenses d'équipement, qui sont définies comme étant la valeur des acquisitions d'actifs fixes, y compris ceux fabriqués par le personnel de l'établissement pour l'usage de ce dernier. La valeur des ventes d'actifs fixes n'est pas déduite. L'investissement comprend les terrains, les constructions et les modifications apportées aux constructions, les machines et équipements, les biens corporels, les concessions, les brevets, les licences et les logiciels. L'investissement est évalué au prix de revient total, y compris le prix rendu, les frais d'installation, les droits et redevances (à l'exception de la taxe sur la valeur ajoutée). Les *dépenses en machines et équipement* correspondent aux dépenses d'investissement, telles qu'elles sont définies ci-dessus, c'est-à-dire à la valeur des acquisitions d'actifs fixes, y compris ceux fabriqués par le personnel de l'établissement pour l'usage de ce dernier. Elles comprennent le matériel de transport, les machines et l'outillage industriel, les machines, les équipements et le mobilier de bureau, les instruments et équipements professionnels, les modifications, améliorations et réparations apportées à ces matériels.

Les *salaires et charges sociales* couvrent à la fois les salaires et traitements, et les cotisations patronales aux régimes de Sécurité sociale et de retraite. Les salaires et traitements incluent le paiement des heures normales et supplémentaires, les gratifications et indemnités de cherté de vie, les congés payés et congés de maladie, les impôts et cotisations d'assurance sociale dus par les salariés et retenus par l'employeur, les prestations en nature et les indemnités. Les *salaires et* traitements, total comprennent la rémunération brute des employés salariés, des ouvriers, des apprentis, des travailleurs à domicile et des travailleurs à temps partiel. Les *salaires et traitements, salariés* comprennent la rémunération brute des salariés, à l'exclusion des apprentis. Les *charges sociales des employeurs* englobent les dépenses exigées par la loi et les contributions volontaires, telles que cotisations de sécurité sociale (santé, vieillesse, accident, assurance chômage), les cotisations au fonds de péréquation des allocations familiales, les cotisations à la caisse de construction résidentielle et les indemnités de logement, ainsi que les paiements non obligatoires (par exemple en cas d'accident, de maladie ou de détresse matérielle, les services de restauration, les indemnités kilométriques).

Les *heures ouvrées* par les employés correspondent aux heures réellement travaillées (c'est-à-dire toutes les heures payées à l'exception des congés payés) par les salariés, employés et ouvriers, et apprentis, qui sont sur le registre des salaires. Les travailleurs à domicile et les travailleurs à temps partiel sont exclus.

Publications

Toutes les données sont fournies, avec une ventilation allant jusqu'aux positions à trois chiffres de la CITI, dans les publications suivantes :

i) *Industriestatistik*, 2. Teil ; qui émane du Bureau central de statistique de l'Autriche et sert, avec d'autres publications, à l'établissement des statistiques autrichiennes ;

ii) *Gewerbestatistik*, 2. Teil ; qui émane du Bureau central de statistique de l'Autriche et sert, avec d'autres publications, à l'établissement des statistiques autrichiennes.

BELGIQUE

I. GÉNÉRALITÉS

L'Institut des Comptes Nationaux (ICN) de la Belgique a fourni les renseignements ci-après concernant les statistiques du commerce extérieur et les comptes nationaux.

II. STATISTIQUES DU COMMERCE EXTÉRIEUR

Source

Les données sur les échanges se rapportent à l'Union Economique belgo-luxembourgeoise (UEBL). Elles sont tirées des déclarations suivantes :

a) Documents de douane à l'importation et à l'exportation ;

b) Formulaires statistiques remis à la frontière belgo-néerlandaise ;

c) Bandes magnétiques mensuelles relatives aux importations en provenance des Pays-Bas, transmises à l'ICN par le Centraal Bureau voor de Statistiek (CBS). Ces bandes magnétiques rassemblent les données concernant les exportations vers l'UEBL, fournies au CBS par les exportateurs néerlandais autorisés à faire des déclarations globales ;

d) Relevés périodiques des firmes autorisées à établir des déclarations (habituellement mensuelles) globales concernant leurs importations et leurs exportations et à les adresser directement à l'ICN.

Classification industrielle

Le Service du Commerce extérieur de la Banque Nationale de Belgique (BNB) établit chaque année une table de conversion entre le code national des marchandises (BNL) et la classification NACE-CLIO (version D de 1975). Les données ventilées selon la CTCI peuvent être ventilées selon la CITI au moyen d'une table fixe de conversion.

Concepts et définitions des variables

Pour le commerce spécial, les *exportations* sont évaluées FAB et les *importations* CAF.

Sont inclus : le commerce d'Etat, les transactions commerciales d'équipements et de fournitures militaires, les transactions d'aide extérieure, les améliorations et réparations, les transactions portant sur des navires et avions neufs et d'occasion, l'électricité et le gaz, l'or industriel, les monnaies d'or et d'argent, les monnaies anciennes de collection, les billets de banque, titres et autres actifs monétaires, etc., imprimés ou gravés en UEBL (qui sont comptabilisés à leur valeur commerciale -- c'est-à-dire à la valeur du papier ou du métal -- et non à leur valeur nominale), les produits de la mer provenant directement de haute mer. Seuls les produits de la mer amenés par des navires étrangers sont inclus dans les statistiques sur les importations ; ceux qui sont amenés par des navires belges sont considérés comme produit national.

Sont exclus du champ d'observation de la statistique, les mouvements de marchandises correspondant à des opérations qui ne présentent aucun intérêt sur le plan commercial. Ces opérations sont détaillées dans les articles 22, 24, 27, 28, 29, 30, 31 et 32 du règlement 1736/75 relatif aux statistiques du commerce extérieur des CE et du commerce entre leurs États Membres. Le texte de ces articles peut être obtenu sur demande. En outre, il existe un seuil en dessous duquel les transactions commerciales ne sont pas enregistrées. Ce seuil est actuellement fixé à 14 500 francs belges et 1 000 kg.

III. COMPTES NATIONAUX

Source

Les données sur le nombre d'établissements et sur la rémunération sont fournies par l'Office national de sécurité sociale (ONSS). Les statistiques sur l'emploi proviennent du Ministère de l'Emploi et du Travail.

Classification industrielle

Jusqu'en 1992, l'ONSS avait classé les données concernant les établissements et la rémunération suivant la NACE 70. A partir de 1993, la classification originale, avant transformation en CITI, est la NACE révision 1. Par conséquent, les données jusqu'en 1992 ne sont pas strictement comparables avec celles des années suivantes.

Concepts et définitions des variables

Les chiffres sont établis selon les principes de la comptabilité nationale (SEC 1979 -- le Système Européen de Comptes économiques intégrés -- qui est la version européenne du SCN 1968, le Système des Comptes Nationaux des Nations Unies).

Données à prix constants

Les statistiques à prix constants sont en principe établies par la méthode de la double déflation.

CANADA

I. GÉNÉRALITÉS

Les données émanent de Statistique Canada, de même que les notes explicatives concernant les statistiques industrielles et les comptes nationaux.

II. STATISTIQUES INDUSTRIELLES

Source

Le Recensement des Manufactures (production, valeur ajoutée, emploi, salaires et traitements) mené chaque année par Statistique Canada est une enquête dont l'unité de base est l'établissement, qui porte sur la totalité des unités et qui couvre l'exercice budgétaire.

Classification industrielle

Les données, à l'origine ventilées selon la classification industrielle type du Canada (1980), utilisée depuis 1983, sont exprimées en fonction de la CITI. Les données de 1982 sont alignées sur la version de 1980. Le passage d'un système à l'autre ne pose pas de problème majeur.

Concepts et définitions des variables

La *production* correspond à la production brute (des industries manufacturières) et comprend la valeur totale brute des ventes de tous les produits, des travaux effectués par l'unité pour son propre compte, des services manufacturiers rendus, des marchandises réexpédiées en l'état, de l'électricité vendue, des actifs fixes produits par l'unité pour son propre compte, des déchets de fabrication, des biens fabriqués par des travailleurs à domicile et par des artisans si l'établissement possède un numéro de code permettant la retenue à la source de l'impôt sur le revenu, ainsi que des recettes tirées de la location des produits, compte tenu de la variation nette des travaux en cours et des stocks de produits finis. L'évaluation est faite au coût des facteurs, y compris toutes les subventions et à l'exclusion de tous les impôts indirects. La production canadienne pour le commerce de gros et de détail est le total des ventes et de tous les autres revenus. La *valeur ajoutée*, qui est estimée conformément au concept de valeur ajoutée recensée, est évaluée de la même manière et est égale à la production brute déduction faite du coût des matériaux, combustibles et autres fournitures, des marchandises réexpédiées en l'état, et de l'électricité achetée. Le coût des services non industriels n'est pas déduit. La valeur ajoutée inclut les recettes provenant de divers services non industriels mais non les intérêts ou les loyers perçus sur des biens autres que les équipements produits et loués. La valeur ajoutée canadienne pour le commerce de gros et de détail est la production totale moins le coût total des marchandises vendues (total des matériaux).

L'emploi, salariés indique le nombre moyen de salariés, à temps complet ou à temps partiel, employés tout au long de l'année. Il inclut les employés et les salariés. Les chiffres concernant les *heures ouvrées* comprennent la totalité des heures travaillées pendant une année par les ouvriers, y compris les apprentis, les travailleurs occasionnels et les travailleurs à temps partiel. Ils proviennent d'un recensement effectué auprès des établissements de toutes les sociétés commerciales (plus quelques entreprises non constituées en société) dont les livraisons de produits manufacturés excèdent 25 000$ par an ; les résultats de cette enquête sont complétés par des estimations, établies à partir des registres fiscaux, pour les établissements plus petits. Sont incluses : les heures supplémentaires, les heures passées à attendre ou en astreinte et les périodes de repos. Les congés annuels, les jours fériés, les congés de maladie et autres absences payées sont exclus.

Les *salaires et traitements, salariés* englobent le paiement en espèces des heures normales et supplémentaires, les gratifications et indemnités de cherté de vie, les congés payés et congés de maladie, les impôts et cotisations d'assurance sociale, etc., dus par les salariés et retenus par l'employeur et les prestations en nature et les indemnités qui font partie intégrante du revenu.

Pour le commerce de gros et de détail, les chiffres pour les *établissements* se réfèrent aux locations physiques.

Publications

Annual Census of Manufactures, qui fournit des informations pour 24 secteurs industriels, et des publications de caractère général.

Ces publications émanent de Statistique Canada.

CORÉE

I. STATISTIQUES INDUSTRIELLES

Source

Les informations, qui émanent de l'Office national statistique de Corée, sont tirées du recensement industriel quinquennal et de l'enquête annuelle sur les industries extractives et manufacturières. Le recensement industriel est effectué les années dont le chiffre se termine par un 3 ou un 8 (depuis 1973) et s'adresse à tous les établissements ; l'enquête sur les industries extractives et manufacturières est effectuée les autres années et porte sur tous les établissements d'au moins 5 employés. La période de référence est l'année civile.

Classification industrielle

La classification coréenne type des activités industrielles est la SIC (révisée en 1992). Elle est compatible avec la CITI révision 3.

Concepts et définitions des variables

La *production* est la production brute mesurée comme la valeur totale de tous les biens produits et de tous les services rendus par l'établissement au cours de l'année. En pratique, le calcul se fait de la façon suivante : la valeur des livraisons, plus l'addition nette des stocks de l'année de produits finis, semi-finis et des travaux en cours. La *valeur ajoutée* est obtenue en soustrayant les coûts de production de la valeur de la production brute, c'est-à-dire qu'elle inclut les coûts d'amortissement et les frais généraux. Les coûts de production correspondent aux charges directes effectivement payées ou payables pour le matériel et les services consommés ou engagés dans la production pendant l'année à laquelle ils se réfèrent, y compris le fret et les autres charges directes supportées par les établissements pour l'acquisition de ces biens et services. Les coûts de production comprennent également le coût des matières premières (y compris les pièces détachées, les composants, les conteneurs et les fournitures auxiliaires -- celles fournies aux autres établissements sur une base contractuelle mais à l'exclusion de celles reçues d'autres établissements) ; les dépenses de fuel, d'électricité et d'eau ; les travaux sous contrat effectués pour d'autres ; la réparation et l'entretien des actifs propres ; les salaires et les indemnités de départ à la retraite ; les dépenses d'aide sociale ; les frais de location et d'amortissement ; les taxes ; les frais de contentieux ; les autres coûts tels que les assurances, les frais de transport, d'entreposage, de représentation et de publicité.

L'*emploi* indique le nombre moyen de salariés, de propriétaires exploitants et de travailleurs familiaux non rémunérés au cours de la période considérée. Les propriétaires exploitants et les travailleurs familiaux non rémunérés incluent les propriétaires, les associés des entreprises non constituées en société et les membres de la famille travaillant au moins un tiers de l'horaire normal, sans recevoir une rémunération régulière. L'*emploi, salariés* est le nombre de salariés apparaissant à la fin de l'année sur le registre du personnel de l'établissement - en termes de salaires et traitements - des ouvriers, du personnel administratif et des travailleurs apparentés. Les salariés sont inclus qu'il s'agisse de travailleurs permanents, temporaires ou journaliers ou qu'il s'agisse de personnes inactives en congé de maladie, en vacances, victimes d'accidents ou en grève (à l'exception : des absences de longue durée - supérieures à trois mois - ; des membres des forces armées continuant à figurer sur le registre du personnel actif ; des travailleurs des établissements sous contrat).

L'*investissement* correspond aux dépenses d'équipement au cours de l'année d'acquisition, d'installation, d'expansion et de réparation capitalisée des actifs fixes matériels, déduction faite des cessions. Par actifs fixes matériels, il faut entendre les biens qui ont une durée de vie productive supérieure à un an qui incluent : les terrains et actifs tels que les bâtiments et infrastructures ; les machines et équipements ; les voitures, bateaux et le matériel de livraison. L'évaluation est faite d'après la valeur comptable en ne tenant pas compte des fluctuations basées sur la réévaluation et la dépréciation des actifs fixes. Lors de l'achat d'actifs à d'autres établissements, le coût total d'acquisition est estimé comme le coût d'installation : quand les actifs sont construits par l'établissement lui-même, on prend la valeur comptable estimée lors de l'achèvement. La cession annuelle des actifs fixes est le montant des actifs fixes matériels effectivement détruits ou perdus au cours de l'année en raison de leur vente, transfert, donation, incendie, sinistre, vol, etc. L'évaluation de tels actifs s'effectue sur la base du prix de vente effectif ou, s'il ne peut être déterminé, du prix de marché d'articles équivalents.

Les *salaires et traitements, salariés* correspondent aux gains bruts payés à tous les employés apparaissant sur le registre du personnel de l'établissement au cours de la période. Sont incluses toutes les formes de rémunération des employés telles que salaires, traitements, gratifications et indemnités, qu'elles soient payées en nature ou en espèces. Toutefois, sont exclues : les indemnités de départ à la retraite et pour les congés de maladie de longue durée, et les indemnités aux membres des forces armées. Les paiements accumulés avant l'année de référence mais qui n'ont pas été effectivement payés jusqu'à l'année de référence sont exclus, tandis que les paiements obligatoires accumulés pendant l'année de référence mais qui n'ont pas effectivement été payés sont inclus. Les paiements en espèces sont exprimés en termes bruts, c'est-à-dire qu'ils comprennent les déductions fiscales, l'épargne obligatoire, les taxes syndicales, etc. Les rémunérations en nature sont évaluées au prix des équipements si l'acquisition est interne ou au prix d'achat si elle est externe.

L'*établissement* est défini comme une unité physique menant des activités industrielles, telle que les usines, les ateliers, les bureaux ou les mines.

Publications

i) *Report on the Industrial Census* ;
ii) *Report on the Mining and Manufacturing Survey*.

Toutes deux sont publiées par l'Office national de statistique de la République de Corée.

DANEMARK

I. GÉNÉRALITÉS

Les informations ci-après ont été fournies par Danmarks Statistik.

II. STATISTIQUES INDUSTRIELLES

Source

Les données sont recueillies au moyen d'une enquête par questionnaire qui utilise comme unité de référence, pour partie les établissements (pour les données sur l'emploi, l'investissement et les rémunérations), et pour partie les unités par type d'activité (pour les données sur la production et la valeur ajoutée). La période de référence est l'année civile pour l'emploi, les exportations, les importations et les rémunérations, et l'exercice comptable pour la production, la valeur ajoutée et l'investissement. Des enquêtes sur la production, la valeur ajoutée et l'investissement sont menées tous les ans auprès des unités de vingt salariés ou plus ; elles sont complétées par des enquêtes quinquennales s'adressant aux unités employant de 0 à 19 salariés.

Jusqu'en 1989, l'enquête annuelle sur l'emploi et les rémunérations s'adressait à toutes les unités de six salariés ou plus. Depuis 1990, les données sur le nombre d'établissements, l'emploi et les rémunérations proviennent des statistiques des établissements et de l'emploi découlant des registres. Tous les établissements du secteur manufacturier sont couverts.

Classification industrielle

La classification nationale danoise est alignée sur la CITI, aux quelques différences suivantes près :
- a) Pour la production, la valeur ajoutée et l'investissement : CITI 3829 comprend 3821 et CITI 3843 comprend 3842 ;
- b) Pour l'emploi, la rémunération et le nombre d'établissements : CITI 3841 comprend 3842 (jusqu'en 1989 inclus).

Concepts et définitions des variables

La *production* correspond à la production brute, évaluée au coût des facteurs, à l'exclusion de tous les impôts indirects, mais y compris toutes les subventions. Elle comprend la valeur de tous les produits, la variation nette des travaux en cours, les travaux effectués par l'unité pour compte propre, les services rendus, les marchandises réexpédiées en l'état, l'électricité vendue, les actifs fixes produits par l'unité pour compte propre, la variation nette du niveau des stocks de produits finis, les déchets de fabrication, les biens fabriqués par des travailleurs à domicile et des artisans et certains autres éléments du chiffre d'affaires. La procédure d'évaluation est la même pour la *valeur ajoutée*, qui est donnée par la valeur de la production brute déduction faite du coût des matériaux, combustibles et autres fournitures, des travaux exécutés sous contrat et à la commande par d'autres unités, des marchandises réexpédiées en l'état et de l'électricité achetée. Les estimations sont effectuées sur la base des quantités consommées.

L'*emploi* (jusqu'en 1989 inclus) indique le nombre total de personnes occupées tel qu'il ressort du nombre moyen de salariés employés à la fin des mois de mars, juin, septembre et novembre. Y sont pris en compte les propriétaires exploitants, les salariés à temps complet et les salariés à temps partiel travaillant au minimum 15 heures par semaine. Les apprentis sont également pris en compte. A partir de 1990, les données sur l'emploi comprennent tous les salariés et tous les travailleurs indépendants employés fin novembre dans les établissements mentionnés ci-dessus. Sont inclus les salariés à temps plein et les salariés à temps partiel, y compris ceux affectés aux activités secondaires.

L'*investissement* (formation brute de capital fixe) est donné par la valeur des acquisitions d'actifs fixes, y compris ceux qui sont fabriqués par le personnel de l'unité pour l'usage de ce dernier et déduction faite de la valeur des ventes de biens correspondants. Par actifs fixes, il faut entendre ceux dont la durée de vie productive est supérieure à trois ans, y compris ceux produits par le personnel de l'unité pour l'usage de ce dernier, les adjonctions, transformations et améliorations apportées aux actifs existants, les actifs neufs (qu'ils soient ou non en service) et les actifs usagés. L'évaluation est faite au prix de revient total, y compris le prix rendu et les frais d'installation. Dans le cas d'actifs produits par l'unité, on se base sur le coût des travaux en cours, y compris les coûts de main-d'œuvre et le coût des matériaux et autres fournitures. Pour la déduction des ventes d'actifs usagés, on utilise le montant réellement réalisé. Les *dépenses en machines et équipement* correspondent, elles aussi, à la formation brute de capital fixe et sont obtenues au moyen de la même définition que l'investissement total. Y sont inclus le matériel de transport, les machines et matériels industriels, les machines, équipements et mobilier de bureau, les instruments et équipements professionnels, ainsi que les modifications et améliorations apportées à ces matériels.

Pour les années antérieures à 1990, les *salaires et traitements, salariés* incluent les salaires versés aux travailleurs à domicile. Sont compris le paiement en espèces des heures normales et supplémentaires, les gratifications et indemnités de cherté de vie, les congés payés et les congés de maladie. Depuis 1990, les données relatives aux salaires et traitements comprennent toutes les dépenses de ce type déclarées aux autorités fiscales encourues dans les établissements du secteur manufacturier au cours de l'année. Par conséquent, même les dépenses des établissements qui ne sont pas en activité fin novembre (mais qui ont été en activité dans le secteur manufacturier au cours de l'année) sont incluses dans les chiffres.

Jusqu'en 1989, le nombre d'*établissements* était donné par le nombre d'unités locales tel qu'il ressortait de l'enquête annuelle sur l'emploi et les rémunérations. Les données recensaient les établissements industriels de six employés et plus. Depuis 1990, sont couverts tous les établissements, quel que soit le nombre d'employés, en activité fin novembre.

Publications

  i)   Statistical Reports : *Industrial Statistics* (annuel jusqu'en 1989 inclus) ;
 ii)   *Statistical News*, Series Industry and Energy ;
iii)   Statistical Reports : *Industrial Accounts Statistics* ;
iv)   *Statistical News*, Series General Economic Statistics and Internal Trade.

Toutes sont publiées par Danmarks Statistik.

ESPAGNE

I. STATISTIQUES INDUSTRIELLES

Source

Les informations émanent de l'Institut National de la Statistique d'Espagne (Instituto Nacional de Estadística, Ministerio de Economía y Hacienda). Les statistiques proviennent de l'enquête statistique annuelle qui couvre tous les établissements employant au moins une personne. Il s'agit d'une enquête exhaustive pour les établissements de plus de 20 employés et d'une enquête par échantillon pour les établissements de moins de 20 employés. L'échantillon total annuel comprend environ 40 000 établissements.

Classification industrielle

a) La classification industrielle utilisée dans l'enquête est la Classification Nationale des Activités Economiques, 1993 (CNAE, 1993). Elle est équivalente à la NACE révision 1 jusqu'au 4ème chiffre et est compatible avec la CITI révision 3.

Concepts et définitions des variables

La *production* correspond à la production brute au sens de la définition espagnole, qui comprend la somme de : *a)* la production de biens et services destinés à la vente, y compris les sommes perçues au titre de services et travaux réalisés par des tiers et de l'électricité vendue ; *b)* les marchandises réexpédiées en l'état ; *c)* la rémunération des services rendus (location de machines, assistance technique, etc.) ; *d)* les produits et travaux en cours ; *e)* la formation de capital pour compte propre (production par l'entreprise de biens d'équipements destinés à son propre usage et grosses réparations et améliorations apportées par l'unité à ses biens d'équipement avec ses propres moyens). Cette production brute est évaluée au coût des facteurs, c'est-à-dire inclut les subventions d'exploitation et exclut les impôts sur l'activité productive. La *valeur ajoutée* est donnée par la différence entre la production brute aux prix à la production et la consommation intermédiaire aux prix d'acquisition, c'est-à-dire qu'elle est exprimée au coût des facteurs. La consommation intermédiaire comprend le coût : *a)* des matières premières et matériaux consommés ; *b)* de l'énergie consommée pour obtenir force motrice, chaleur, vapeur, électricité, gaz, etc. ; *c)* des services industriels et non industriels achetés ; *d)* des marchandises achetées pour être revendues en l'état.

La formation brute de capital fixe aux prix courants (*investissement*) est égale à la valeur des achats de biens d'équipement neufs et usagés, des grosses réparations et améliorations apportées aux biens d'équipement par des tiers, de la production de biens d'équipement pour compte propre et des grosses réparations et améliorations apportées à ces biens au moyen de ressources propres en matériel et en main-d'œuvre, déduction faite de la valeur des actifs cédés.

L'*emploi* représente le nombre de personnes occupées. Il inclut les travailleurs rémunérés et non rémunérés qu'il s'agisse de personnel de bureau ou d'ouvriers. Les heures ouvrées correspondent au nombre total d'heures effectivement travaillées par les personnes occupées au cours de l'année de référence.

Les *salaires et traitements, salariés* englobent les traitements et salaires bruts en espèces et les prestations en nature versés au personnel rémunéré, à l'exclusion des charges sociales des employeurs. Les *charges sociales des employeurs* représentent les contributions sociales payées par les employeurs (sécurité sociale, retraite, autres coûts sociaux).

Publications

Encuesta Industrial Annual, Instituto Nacional de Estadística.

ÉTATS-UNIS

I. GÉNÉRALITÉS

Les informations relatives aux statistiques industrielles et aux statistiques du commerce extérieur sont fournies par le Bureau of the Census, Department of Commerce des Etats-Unis.

II. STATISTIQUES INDUSTRIELLES

Source

Les données sont tirées du recensement quinquennal des manufactures et de l'enquête annuelle des manufactures menées par le Bureau of the Census. Le recensement quinquennal porte sur les années dont le chiffre se termine par un 2 ou un 7 et s'adresse à tous les établissements employant un salarié au moins ; l'enquête annuelle couvre un échantillon de quelque 55 000 établissements, représentant les deux tiers environ de l'emploi manufacturier total. Depuis 1982, les stocks de fin d'année sont évalués aux prix du marché. Avant 1982, la valeur des stocks pouvait être déterminée à l'aide de toute méthode de calcul généralement acceptée en comptabilité (PEPS, DEPS, prix du marché, pour n'en citer que quelques unes). En 1982, les utilisateurs de la méthode PEPS ont été priés d'indiquer la valeur des stocks avant ajustement, puis la valeur de la réserve et enfin la valeur PEPS après ajustement compte tenu de la réserve. Du fait de ce changement dans les procédures de notification, les données pour l'année 1983 et les années suivantes ne sont pas comparables avec celles portant sur les années précédentes pour les stocks, la valeur ajoutée et la production brute.

Classification industrielle

A l'origine, la nomenclature utilisée est la classification industrielle type (SIC) des Etats-Unis. A quelques petites exceptions près, les données peuvent être ventilées selon la Classification Internationale Type par Industrie (CITI). La définition nationale des industries manufacturières exclut les activités suivantes :

a) transformation à petite échelle constituant une activité secondaire des entreprises agricoles ;

b) travaux réalisés à la commande pour des consommateurs du secteur des ménages ;

c) certaines activités de réparation et ateliers de réparation des chemins de fer ;

d) production, par les sociétés de services publics, de coke pour leur propre usage ;

e) activités de fabrication des établissements de vente au détail qui vendent la majorité de leurs produits sur place aux consommateurs du secteur des ménages ;

f) activités de fabrication sur le site des entrepreneurs du secteur de la construction.

Concepts et définitions des variables

La *production* ou production brute correspond aux livraisons, mesurées par les expéditions, FAB, avec un ajustement pour tenir compte de la variation des travaux en cours et des stocks de produits finis. Sont pris en compte les biens produits par l'établissement et ceux qui sont réexpédiés en l'état (reventes) ainsi que les recettes tirées de travaux industriels effectués sur des matériaux appartenant à d'autres unités ou de services industriels rendus à d'autres unités. Dans le cas de quelques industries où les données relevées correspondent à la valeur de la production, l'ajustement des stocks porte uniquement sur les travaux en cours. Pour la construction navale, le chiffre relevé correspond à la valeur des travaux réalisés et aucun ajustement n'est opéré pour les stocks.

L'évaluation est faite aux prix à la production, FAB départ usine, à l'exclusion du fret et des taxes. Pour les industries dont le produit est en général livré, la valeur des expéditions est exprimée au prix rendu. La *valeur ajoutée* est établie selon le concept de valeur ajoutée «recensée» et est donnée par la production brute déduction faite du coût des matériaux, combustibles, et autres fournitures, des marchandises réexpédiées en l'état, des travaux exécutés sous contrat ou à la commande par d'autres unités et de l'électricité achetée. Les données relatives aux consommations sont estimées sur la base des quantités consommées, mais on considère comme acceptable une évaluation au coût d'achat si ce dernier se rapproche du coût des biens utilisés pour la production (dans le cas contraire, l'unité déclarante qui se base sur la comptabilité des achats est invitée à procéder à un ajustement pour tenir compte de la variation des stocks afin d'obtenir le prix à la date de «consommation»). L'évaluation est faite de la même manière que pour la production.

Les chiffres sur l'*emploi* recensent l'ensemble des salariés, à temps complet et à temps partiel, apparaissant sur le registre du personnel des établissements en activité. Ils correspondent à une moyenne de quatre observations trimestrielles (le 12 des mois de mars, mai, août et novembre) pour les ouvriers de production, moyenne qui est combinée avec le chiffre observé tous les ans le 12 mars pour tous les autres salariés. Les *heures ouvrées* comprennent toutes les heures de production travaillées, y compris les heures supplémentaires, les heures passées à attendre ou en astreinte sur le lieu de travail et les périodes de repos, mais à l'exclusion des congés payés. Les heures supplémentaires sont calculées en heures réellement travaillées et non pas en équivalence heures-ajustées. Sont compris : les apprentis, les travailleurs occasionnels et à temps partiel. Sont exclus : les employeurs, les agents de maîtrise, les travailleurs non rémunérés ou membres de la famille, et les travailleurs indépendants.

La formation brute de capital fixe (*investissement*) concerne uniquement les dépenses d'installations et d'équipements neufs. Elle englobe la valeur des installations et biens d'équipement neufs achetés et fabriqués par le personnel de l'unité pour l'usage de ce dernier. Les achats d'installations et de biens d'équipement usagés sont exclus. Bien que des données sur les achats d'actifs usagés soient recueillies aux Etats-Unis, elles ne peuvent être publiées pour beaucoup d'industries à cause de problèmes de confidentialité. Par conséquent, il n'existe pas de données par industrie sur le total des actifs fixes. Les actifs couverts sont ceux qui ont une durée de vie productive de plus d'un an (conformément aux procédures comptables et à la législation fiscale). L'évaluation de la formation de capital fixe neuve est faite au prix de revient total, y compris celui des adjonctions, modifications, améliorations et réparations apportées aux actifs existants (dans la mesure où elles sont portées au compte de capital). Les actifs neufs achetés sont comptabilisés à leur prix rendu, y compris les frais d'installation, mais à l'exclusion des honoraires et des taxes. La valeur des actifs neufs produits par les unités comprend les coûts de main-d'œuvre ainsi que celui des matériaux et autres fournitures et qu'une provision pour frais généraux. Pour les actifs en construction, mais pas encore terminés à la fin de l'année, la formation brute de capital fixe (neuve) comprend seulement la part des dépenses totales faite pendant l'année considérée. Les *dépenses en machines et équipement* englobent le matériel de transport, les machines, équipement et mobilier de bureau, les instruments et équipements professionnels, et les modifications et réparations apportées à ces matériels (si elles sont portées au compte de capital). Aucune donnée n'est recueillie sur les ventes d'actifs fixes.

La *rémunération* couvre les gains bruts au cours de l'année : elle comprend les salaires, les traitements et les cotisations patronales aux caisses de sécurité sociale et aux fonds de retraite. Sont inclus : le paiement en espèces des heures normales et supplémentaires, les gratifications et indemnités de cherté de vie, de même que les congés payés et congés de maladie, les impôts et cotisations d'assurance sociale dus par les salariés et retenus par l'employeur, les prestations en nature (si elles correspondent à un montant important et font habituellement partie de la rémunération des salariés) et les indemnités. Pour les cotisations aux caisses de Sécurité sociale (*compléments des salaires et traitements*), le Bureau of the Census établit une distinction entre celles qui sont obligatoires aux termes de la législation fédérale, de l'Etat ou locale, et celles qui sont volontaires, soit de la propre initiative de l'employeur, soit parce qu'elles constituent le résultat d'une négociation collective. Sont compris les paiements comme : assurance fédérale vieillesse réversible («Federal Age and Survivors' Pension»), assurance-chômage, autre assurance. Sont également compris les cotisations pour l'assurance-maladie, pour l'assurance-vie, les plans de retraite et plans d'acquisitions d'actions. Les *salaires et traitements* sont fondés sur la rémunération, à l'exclusion des coûts salariaux supplémentaires.

Publications

Les données sont publiées dans :
i) *Census of Manufactures* ;
ii) *Annual Survey of Manufactures*.

Toutes deux émanent du Bureau of the Census, US Department of Commerce, Washington D.C.

III. STATISTIQUES DU COMMERCE EXTÉRIEUR

Source

Les statistiques du commerce extérieur des Etats-Unis sont établies par le Bureau of the Census.

Classification du commerce extérieur

A l'origine, les données sur les exportations sont établies selon le Schedule B de la Statistical Classification of Domestic and Foreign Commodities Exported, des Etats-Unis ; elles sont ensuite réarrangées et ventilées selon la SIC, puis selon la CITI. Pour les importations, les données sont d'abord établies sur la base du Tariff Schedules (barème douanier) des Etats-Unis, puis annotées et regroupées selon la SIC et enfin ventilées selon la CITI.

Tableaux spéciaux

Les données sont disponibles dans :
i) *United States Exports*, SIC Division by SIC-based 2-digit, 3-digit and 4-digit Product Code ;
ii) *United States Imports for Consumption and General Imports*, SIC Division by SIC-based 2-digit, 3-digit and 4-digit Product Code.

Ces deux documents émanent du Bureau of the Census, Department of Commerce des Etats-Unis, Washington D.C.

FINLANDE

I. GÉNÉRALITÉS

Les informations relatives aux statistiques industrielles et aux comptes nationaux émanent de l'Office central de statistique de la Finlande à Helsinki.

II. STATISTIQUES INDUSTRIELLES

Source

Les données sont tirées de deux sources : l'enquête annuelle dans l'industrie menée par l'Office de statistique et les registres fiscaux. L'unité statistique de référence est l'établissement. Si l'enquête porte principalement sur l'année civile, l'exercice budgétaire est utilisé dans certains cas. Il y a une rupture importante entre l'année 1994 et l'année 1995. Jusqu'en 1994, l'enquête s'adresse à toutes les unités de cinq salariés ou plus. Aucune estimation n'est faite pour tenir compte des unités d'une taille inférieure, mais l'enquête couvre approximativement 99 pour cent de la production brute et 97 pour cent de l'emploi manufacturier total.

En 1995, le seuil est modifié : le questionnaire est envoyé à tous les établissements appartenant à une entreprise employant au moins 10 personnes. Pour les unités employant moins de 10 personnes, les informations ont été fournies par l'administration fiscale. Depuis 1996, le seuil a été porté à 20 personnes. Les entreprises ayant moins de 20 employés sont considérées comme des entreprises à établissement unique.

Du fait de cette importante rupture entre 1994 et 1995, les données relatives à ces deux années ne sont pas comparables entre elles, en particulier en ce qui concerne le nombre d'établissements. En outre, il faut signaler que, bien que les méthodes soient restées fondamentalement les mêmes depuis 1995, le nombre d'usines est une variable relativement sensible.

Classification industrielle

La classification nationale, dérivée de la NACE révision 1, est la Classification Industrielle Type Finlandaise de 1995 (SIC-95). Elle est alignée sur la CITI révision 3.

Concepts et définitions des variables

La *production* correspond au chiffre d'affaires augmenté de la variation nette des stocks de produits finis, des travaux en cours et des marchandises et services achetés pour la revente, diminué des achats de biens et services destinés à la revente. Elle comprend la production capitalisée et les autres revenus d'exploitation. Les revenus considérés comme extraordinaires ou financiers sur les comptes de l'entreprise sont exclus de la valeur de la production (comme les revenus tirés de la vente d'actifs corporels). La production est évaluée au coût des facteurs, à l'exclusion de tous les impôts indirects, mais y compris toutes les subventions.

La *valeur ajoutée* correspond au revenu brut provenant d'activités d'exploitation. Elle peut se calculer à partir de l'excédent brut d'exploitation, plus les coûts du personnel et déduction faite des revenus provenant de la vente d'actifs corporels. Elle est évaluée au coût des facteurs à l'exclusion de tous les impôts indirects, mais y compris toutes les subventions.

L'*emploi* comprend le nombre total de personnes occupées, et englobe les propriétaires exploitants, les travailleurs familiaux non rémunérés, et les employés et ouvriers, à temps complet ou à temps partiel, ainsi que toutes les personnes en congé de courte durée. Il est calculé sur la base du nombre moyen de salariés employés tout au long de l'année. L'*emploi, salariés* couvre le nombre total de salariés, non compris les propriétaires exploitants et les travailleurs familiaux non rémunérés. Les *heures ouvrées* correspondent aux heures réellement effectuées par les ouvriers au cours de la période sous revue.

L'*investissement* (formation de capital) correspond aux acquisitions d'actifs fixes, y compris ceux fabriqués par le personnel de l'établissement pour l'usage de ce dernier. Par actifs fixes, il faut entendre les biens d'équipement, les bâtiments et autres constructions, et les autres actifs fixes ; sont exclus les investissements en terrains et en ressources en eau. Ils correspondent aux investissements dont la durée de vie productive est d'un an au moins, y compris ceux fabriqués par le personnel de l'établissement pour l'usage de ce dernier, les adjonctions, transformations, améliorations et réparations d'actifs existants, les actifs neufs (qu'ils soient ou non mis en service) et les actifs usagés.

L'évaluation est faite au prix de revient total, y compris le prix rendu, les frais d'installation et les droits et redevances. Les *dépenses en machines et équipement* sont obtenues sur la base de la même définition. Y sont incluses les dépenses en matériel de transport, machines et matériels industriels, machines, équipement et mobilier de bureau, instruments et équipements professionnels ainsi que les modifications et améliorations apportées à ces matériels.

Les *salaires et charges sociales, salariés* sont définis comme correspondant aux salaires, traitements et charges sociales. Les *salaires et traitements, salariés* comprennent le paiement des heures normales et supplémentaires, les paiements en espèces, les gratifications et indemnités de cherté de vie, la formation, les congés payés et les congés de maladie ainsi que les impôts et cotisations d'assurance sociale dus par les employés et retenus par les employeurs et les prestations en nature. Les *suppléments/charges sociales des employeurs* correspondent aux sommes que les employeurs sont légalement tenus de payer en sus des traitements et salaires. Ils couvrent les cotisations d'assurance sociale obligatoires et les cotisations d'assurance sociale volontaires de nature statutaire.

Publications

i) *Preliminary Data on Finnish Industries* ;
ii) *Statistics on the Structure of Industry and Construction.*

Toutes deux sont publiées par l'Office central de statistique de la Finlande à Helsinki.

III. STATISTIQUES DU COMMERCE EXTÉRIEUR

Source

Les données sont tirées des statistiques du Board of Customs (service des douanes).

Concepts et définitions des variables

Les données portent sur le commerce général, les *exportations* étant exprimées FAB et les *importations* CAF. Sont inclus dans les deux cas : le commerce d'État, les transactions commerciales d'équipements militaires, les transactions d'aide à l'extérieur, les transactions portant sur les navires et avions neufs, l'électricité et le gaz. Par contre, sont expressément exclus : les échanges directs en transit, les exportations ou importations temporaires, les transactions monétaires et les opérations d'un montant inférieur à 1 000 Mk.

IV. COMPTES NATIONAUX

Source

Les données de comptabilité nationale portent sur l'année civile. Elles couvrent toutes les unités.

Classification industrielle

La classification nationale, dérivée de la NACE révision 1, est la Classification Industrielle Type Finlandaise de 1995 (SIC-95). Elle est alignée sur la CITI révision 3.

Concepts et définitions des variables

La *production* est égale à la production brute en valeur de base, y compris la valeur de tous les produits (compte tenu de la variation nette des travaux en cours et du niveau de stocks des produits finis), des travaux effectués par l'unité pour compte propre, des services rendus, de l'électricité vendue, des actifs fixes produits par l'unité pour compte propre et des déchets de fabrication. Les biens fabriqués par des travailleurs à domicile et par des artisans sont aussi pris en compte. La *valeur ajoutée* est, elle aussi, fournie en valeur de base. Elle est donnée par la production brute déduction faite du coût des matériaux, combustibles et autres fournitures, des travaux exécutés sous contrat ou à la commande par d'autres unités, des travaux de réparation et d'entretien exécutés par d'autres unités et de l'électricité achetée, les données relatives aux consommations étant estimées sur la base des quantités consommées.

L'*emploi* englobe le nombre total de personnes occupées et est calculé sur la base du nombre moyen de salariés employés tout au long de l'année. Sont inclus : les propriétaires exploitants, les associés actifs, les travailleurs familiaux non rémunérés, les travailleurs indépendants, les travailleurs à domicile, les employés et les salariés à temps complet et à temps partiel.

L'*investissement* correspond à la formation brute de capital fixe et comprend la valeur d'acquisition des actifs fixes (y compris les biens d'équipement fabriqués par le personnel de l'établissement pour l'usage de ce dernier) déduction faite de la valeur des ventes. Les actifs fixes couverts sont ceux qui ont une durée de vie productive d'un an au moins, y compris ceux fabriqués par le personnel de l'établissement pour l'usage de ce dernier et toutes les transformations, adjonctions et améliorations. Les réparations ne sont pas prises en compte. Les actifs neufs le sont, à condition qu'ils n'aient pas encore été mis en service ou aient été utilisés précédemment en dehors du pays. L'évaluation est faite au prix de revient total, y compris le prix rendu, les frais d'installation, les droits et redevances. Pour les *dépenses en machines et équipement*, le concept utilisé est aussi celui de formation brute de capital fixe. Elles incluent les dépenses en machines et matériels industriels, machines, équipement et mobilier de bureau, instruments et équipements professionnels, ainsi que les transformations et améliorations apportées à ces matériels.

Les *salaires et traitements, total* comprennent le paiement en espèces des heures normales et supplémentaires, les gratifications et indemnités de cherté de vie, les congés payés et congés de maladie et les prestations en nature, ainsi que les impôts et cotisations d'assurance sociale dus par les salariés et retenus par l'employeur.

Données à prix constants

Les données à prix constants sont obtenues par simple déflation, bien que pour l'agriculture on utilise une méthode de double déflation par extrapolation.

FRANCE

I. GÉNÉRALITÉS

Les informations émanent de l'Institut National de la Statistique et des Etudes Economiques (INSEE).

II. STATISTIQUES INDUSTRIELLES ET STATISTIQUES DU COMMERCE EXTERIEUR

Classification industrielle

La classification française est la Nomenclature des Activités Françaises (NAF-1993). Elle est parfaitement compatible avec la NACE révision 1 et avec la CITI révision 3.

Concepts et définitions des variables

La *production*, ou production propre, correspond à la valeur totale des biens et services produits dans l'exercice, qu'ils soient vendus, stockés ou immobilisés. Les produits vendus incorporent la marge réalisée par l'entreprise. La production stockée et la production immobilisée sont estimées au coût de production. La production immobilisée correspond au coût des travaux faits par l'entreprise pour elle-même. La *valeur ajoutée* est définie comme la valeur ajoutée brute au coût des facteurs. Elle se calcule comme suit : production propre, plus ventes de marchandises, moins la consommation intermédiaire au sens large (c'est-à-dire les achats de marchandises, de matières premières et autres approvisionnements, plus la variation de stocks de marchandises, de matières premières et autres approvisionnements, plus les autres achats et charges externes), plus les subventions d'exploitation, moins les impôts, taxes et versements assimilés.

L'*emploi* est défini comme la moyenne annuelle des effectifs occupés. L'*emploi, salariés* est égal à la moyenne annuelle des effectifs salariés, corrigé du solde des effectifs extérieurs (intérimaires ou pris en location) et prêtés en location à une autre entreprise.

Les données d'*investissement* correspondent à la somme des dépenses consacrées par les entreprises à l'acquisition ou à la création de moyens de production. Elles comprennent les immobilisations en cours, mais excluent les immobilisations incorporelles et financières et les équipements financés par crédit-bail.

Les *salaires et traitements, salariés* couvrent les rémunérations payées par l'employeur au cours de l'année en compensation du travail de ses propres employés (à l'exclusion du personnel loué et du personnel intérimaire). Ils ne comprennent pas les *charges sociales des employeurs*, qui sont données séparément.

Les *exportations* sont les ventes à l'exportation déclarées par les entreprises. Elles comprennent les livraisons intra-communautaires. Ces exportations diffèrent de celles qui sont recensées par les douanes car elles correspondent aux seules exportations directes (c'est-à-dire qui ne passent pas par une société tiers) réalisées par les entreprises. De plus, les exportations d'un secteur comprennent les exportations des entreprises du secteur réalisées pour l'ensemble de leurs activités confondues.

III. COMPTES NATIONAUX

Source

En France, l'élaboration des comptes de la nation est assurée par l'INSEE (Paris), avec le concours de certains autres organismes administratifs. Dans la comptabilité nationale française sur les biens et services, l'unité de référence est le type d'activité de l'unité pour la production, la valeur ajoutée et l'emploi. Les données portent sur l'année civile et sont obtenues auprès d'un échantillon d'unités.

Les évaluations sont présentées ici en conformité avec les nomenclatures internationales et avec les règles du système des comptes nationaux de l'ONU (SCN). Il convient toutefois de noter qu'elles sont élaborées selon les nomenclatures françaises et les règles du «Système élargi de comptabilité nationale» (SECN), version française du «Système européen de comptes économiques intégrés» (SEC). Les tableaux entrées-sorties, valorisés aux prix du marché, sont partie intégrante des comptes nationaux français et sont publiés, annuellement, en même temps.

Classification industrielle

A l'origine, les données sont ventilées selon la NAP 100. Une table de conversion nationale est utilisée pour établir des chiffres ventilés selon la CITI.

Concepts et définitions des variables

La *production* correspond à la production brute des branches exprimée en valeur de base. La *valeur ajoutée*, qui est aussi exprimée en valeur de base, est égale à la production brute déduction faite du coût des matériaux, combustibles et autres fournitures, des travaux exécutés sous contrat ou à la commande par d'autres unités, des travaux de réparation et d'entretien exécutés par d'autres unités, des marchandises réexpédiées en l'état, et de l'électricité achetée. Les données relatives aux consommations sont recueillies sur la base des quantités consommées.

L'*emploi* correspond au nombre de personnes occupées ou nombre de salariés (emploi salarié) tel qu'il ressort du nombre moyen de salariés (ou personnes occupées) employés tout au long de l'année. Y sont inclus les propriétaires exploitants, les associés actifs, les travailleurs familiaux non rémunérés, les travailleurs indépendants, les employés, les salariés, les travailleurs à domicile ainsi que le personnel de bureau et d'encadrement dont les fonctions sont étroitement liées au processus de production. Sont pris en compte aussi bien les salariés à temps complet que les salariés à temps partiel.

Les *exportations* sont évaluées FAB et les *importations* CAF.

La formation brute de capital fixe (*investissement*) est égale à la valeur des acquisitions d'actifs fixes (y compris les biens fabriqués par le personnel de l'établissement pour l'usage de ce dernier) déduction faite de la valeur des ventes. Les actifs fixes couverts sont ceux dont la durée de vie productive est supérieure à un an et ils englobent ceux fabriqués par le personnel de l'établissement pour l'usage de ce dernier, les adjonctions, transformations, améliorations et réparations, les actifs fixes neufs non encore mis en service et les actifs usagés. L'évaluation des actifs fixes neufs est faite au prix de revient total, y compris le prix rendu et les frais d'installation, mais à l'exclusion des droits et redevances. Pour l'évaluation des actifs fixes produits par l'unité, on prend en compte le coût des travaux en cours, mais pour celles des ventes d'actifs usagés, on se base sur le montant effectivement réalisé.

Publications

Méthodes d'évaluation :

i) *Système Elargi de Comptabilité Nationale*, volumes 198-199, Collections de l'INSEE, série C, n°44.45, mai 1976 ;

ii) *Sources et Méthodes d'Elaboration des Comptes Nationaux*, «les biens et services», volume 397, Collections de l'INSEE, série C, n°99, novembre 1981 ;

Evaluation à prix constants :

iii) *Comptes nationaux des biens et services à prix constants, volume 252, Collections de l'INSEE, série C, n°59, mars 1978 ;*

Publication régulière des comptes nationaux dans :

iv) *Rapport sur les Comptes de la Nation, Collections de l'INSEE.*

GRÈCE

I. STATISTIQUES INDUSTRIELLES

Source

Les données sont tirées de l'Enquête Annuelle dans l'Industrie, de l'Enquête Statistique Annuelle dans les Industries Extractives («Mines, Quarries and Salterns») et de l'Enquête Annuelle dans l'Electricité, effectuées par l'Office National de Statistique de la Grèce. L'enquête dans l'industrie porte sur les établissements manufacturiers de 10 salariés et plus ; elle s'adresse à tous les établissements de 20 salariés ou plus et à un échantillon aléatoire stratifié des établissements employant de 10 à 19 personnes. Les établissements publics ne sont pas inclus dans l'échantillon. Les enquêtes sur l'électricité et le gaz couvrent les deux entreprises engagées dans la production et la distribution pour l'usage public. La distribution de vapeur et d'eau n'est pas incluse. L'unité de référence est l'établissement sauf pour l'électricité et le gaz où c'est l'entreprise.

Classification industrielle

Les données sont établies en fonction de la classification nationale et ventilées selon la CITI, dans la mesure du possible.

Concepts et définitions des variables

La *production* comprend la valeur de la production de produits finis, les recettes au titre des travaux effectués sous contrat pour le compte d'autres unités, des travaux de réparation et de la vente de marchandises réexpédiées en l'état, et d'autres opérations (ventes de vapeur, d'énergie électrique, de déchets de fabrication, etc., produits par l'unité ; subventions et remboursements au titre de la réexportation de marchandises). L'évaluation est faite au prix de vente départ usine, hors taxes. La *valeur ajoutée* est donnée par la valeur de la production déduction faite du coût des matériaux et autres fournitures, des combustibles achetés et de l'électricité consommée, des marchandises réexpédiées en l'état et des travaux effectués sous contrat ainsi que des travaux de réparation.

L'*emploi* correspond à une moyenne nationale fondée sur un comptage bimensuel. Les travailleurs familiaux non rémunérés sont pris en compte s'ils travaillent au moins trois heures par jour. L'*emploi, salariés* couvre à la fois les employés, c'est-à-dire les personnes qui reçoivent un salaire mensuel sur une base contractuelle quel que soit le montant de la rémunération, et les ouvriers définis comme les personnes qui reçoivent un salaire journalier ou qui sont payées à la pièce soit en espèces soit en nature. Les *jours ouvrés* sont les jours de travail effectués par les ouvriers tels qu'ils sont définis ci-dessus.

L'*investissement* (formation brute de capital fixe) représente les dépenses courantes au titre d'actifs fixes, neufs ou usagés, déduction faite des ventes et des réductions de capital dues à l'obsolescence. La fabrication de biens d'équipement par le personnel de l'établissement pour l'usage de ce dernier est incluse. Les données relatives aux industries extractives ne comprennent pas l'extraction du sel et la valeur des ventes (insignifiante) n'est généralement pas déduite.

Les *salaires et charges sociales, salariés* couvrent les salaires et traitements, le paiement des heures supplémentaires et des congés réguliers, les gratifications, les indemnités, l'indemnité de licenciement et la valeur des recettes en nature. Les *charges sociales des employeurs* comprennent les contributions patronales aux caisses de sécurité sociale en faveur des employés et salariés.

Publications

   i) *Enquête Annuelle dans l'Industrie* ;
   ii) *Enquête Statistique Annuelle dans les Industries Extractives* («Mines, Quarries and Salterns») ;
   iii) *Annuaire Statistique* ;
   iv) *Bulletin Statistique Mensuel.*

Toutes sont publiées par l'Office National de Statistique de la Grèce, à Athènes.

HONGRIE

I. GÉNÉRALITÉS

Les informations émanent de l'Office Central Statistique de Hongrie, aussi bien pour les statistiques industrielles que pour les données des comptes nationaux.

II. STATISTIQUES INDUSTRIELLES

Source

A partir de 1992, toutes les entreprises qui répondent à deux des trois critères ci-dessous pendant deux années consécutives sont couvertes par l'enquête : plus de 100 salariés, plus de 300 millions de Forint de chiffres d'affaire annuel, 150 millions de Forint de capital total. Seuls les investissements de plus de 10 millions de Forint sont déclarés. Les données d'emploi résultent de l'enquête annuelle sur l'emploi et les salaires qui couvre les entreprises de 20 salariés et plus.

Classification industrielle

La classification hongroise est la TEÁOR 92 qui est compatible avec la CITI révision 3 jusqu'au 2ème chiffre.

Concepts et définitions des variables

L'*emploi, salariés* se rapporte à la moyenne des effectifs de salariés rémunérés. Il ne couvre que l'emploi à plein temps.

L'*investissement* (formation brute de capital fixe) est défini comme la valeur des actifs nouveaux et usagés prêts à l'emploi. Il est évalué au prix de revient total, y compris la TVA.

Les *salaires et traitements, salariés* comprennent les primes et congés payés. Les prestations en nature et les congés de maladie sont exclus.

III. COMPTES NATIONAUX

Concepts et définitions des variables

La *production* (production brute) et la valeur ajoutée sont établis selon les concepts de la comptabilité SNA 93. Elles sont évaluées aux prix de base.

Publications

i)   *Munkaügyi statisztika* ;

ii)   *Beruházásstatisztika* ;

iii)   *National Accounts Hungary, 1991-94,* Budapest, 1996.

Toutes sont publiées par l'Office Central Statistique de Hongrie.

IRLANDE

I. STATISTIQUES INDUSTRIELLES

Source

Les informations ont été fournies par le Bureau central de statistiques de l'Irlande. Les données sont tirées du «Census of Industrial Local Units» (recensement annuel des unités locales industrielles). Ce recensement porte sur toutes les unités menant une activité industrielle qui occupaient en moyenne trois personnes ou plus pendant l'année considérée. La possibilité d'obtenir des déclarations distinctes pour chaque unité dépend toutefois de la disponibilité de relevés séparés dans l'entreprise pour les différentes unités locales.

Concepts et définitions des variables

La production brute (*production*) représente la valeur marchande nette de tous les biens fabriqués au cours de l'année, qu'ils soient ou non vendus, y compris la valeur du travail exécuté et la valeur des travaux d'équipement effectués pour compte propre. Les subventions d'exploitation relatives à la production ou à la vente de la production sont incluses dans la valeur de la production brute ; le droit d'accise et la TVA en sont exclus. Jusqu'en 1990 inclus dans le cas de deux industries, à savoir la production d'électricité et de tourbe, la valeur des travaux d'équipement effectués pour compte propre était incluse dans la production brute. La production nette (*valeur ajoutée*) correspond à la différence entre la production brute et la consommation intermédiaire de l'industrie. La consommation intermédiaire de l'industrie comprend les matériaux industriels, les services industriels ainsi que le combustible et l'énergie utilisés dans la production. L'évaluation ne tient pas compte de la TVA récupérable.

L'*emploi* représente le nombre total de personnes occupées et correspond à la somme de l'ensemble des salariés et des propriétaires et travailleurs familiaux non rémunérés. Les ouvriers à la pièce qui travaillent à domicile ne sont pas pris en compte. *L'emploi, salariés* (nombre total de salariés) couvre les personnes qui reçoivent un salaire ou un traitement fixe. Les personnes au travail ou celles qui sont temporairement absentes pour des raisons de maladie, de congé, de grève, etc.

sont prises en compte, de même que les travailleurs à temps partiel. Les ouvriers à la pièce qui travaillent à domicile ne sont pas pris en compte.

L'investissement correspond à la formation brute de capital fixe (FBCF). Par actifs fixes (terrains, bâtiments, installations et équipements), on entend les biens dont la durée de vie utile prévue est supérieure à un an et qui sont destinés à être utilisés par l'unité locale elle-même. Les acquisitions comprennent les achats auprès d'autres unités et la production par l'unité elle-même de biens d'équipement pour son propre usage. Les modifications, améliorations et réparations importantes qui prolongent la durée de vie utile d'un actif ou en accroissent la productivité sont prises en compte. La valeur du travail entrepris au cours de l'année est incluse, que ce travail soit ou non achevé. L'évaluation des acquisitions est faite au prix de revient total, y compris les frais d'installation et les droits ou redevances, mais à l'exclusion de la TVA récupérable et des frais financiers. L'évaluation des ventes est faite au prix réellement perçu, déduction faite de la TVA. La FBCF représente la différence entre les acquisitions et les ventes d'actifs fixes. Les *dépenses en machines et équipement* correspondent, elles aussi, à la FBCF mais concernent uniquement les machines et équipements.

Les *salaires et traitements, salariés* représentent le montant brut payé aux employés, à l'exception des ouvriers à la pièce qui travaillent à domicile, avant déduction des impôts sur le revenu, les cotisations de sécurité sociale dues par les salariés, etc. Sont inclus les paiements pour les heures supplémentaires, les gratifications, les commissions, les congés payés et les congés de maladie. Sont exclus les paiements aux propriétaires exploitants et aux travailleurs à domicile.

Par *établissement*, on entend toutes les unités locales situées sur des sites de production distincts des entreprises implantées sur plusieurs sites, même si le répondant ne fournit pas de détails particuliers à leur sujet.

ISLANDE

I. COMPTES NATIONAUX

Source

Les données émanent du National Economic Institute de l'Islande, qui tire chaque année un échantillon d'états financiers à partir des registres de l'administration fiscale. L'échantillon couvre environ 50 pour cent de la masse salariale des diverses branches. La probabilité d'appartenir à l'échantillon augmente avec la taille de l'établissement. La période de référence est l'année civile. L'établissement et l'unité d'activité économique sont utilisés comme unités statistiques de base. La production et la valeur ajoutée de l'échantillon stratifié sont converties à l'échelle de l'ensemble du secteur industriel à l'aide de la part de l'échantillon dans la masse salariale totale. Les chiffres relatifs à l'emploi sont fondés sur des registres administratifs qui couvrent la totalité du secteur industriel.

En 1994 les chiffres ont été révisés en hausse. Cette révision a amélioré les estimations dans les domaines suivants : formation brute de capital fixe sous forme de logements ; reclassement de la base de l'OTAN à l'aéroport de Keflavik hors du territoire économique islandais ; inclusion des droits accumulés pour la retraite dans la rémunération des salariés de l'administration centrale ; ajustement des variations de stocks pour tenir compte de l'inflation.

Classification industrielle

La classification nationale s'appuyait depuis 1958 sur la CITI révision 1 ; les données fournies sont ventilées d'après la deuxième révision de cette classification à partir de 1968. La NACE révision 1 a été adoptée et sera appliquée dans toutes les statistiques à compter de 1996.

Concepts et définitions des variables

A partir de 1992, la production brute (*production*) est évaluée aux prix de base, y compris toutes les subventions sur les produits, mais à l'exclusion de la TVA ; avant 1992, elle est évaluée aux prix à la production, à l'exclusion de toutes les subventions et de la TVA. Elle comprend la valeur de tous les produits, compte tenu de la variation nette des travaux en cours. La *valeur ajoutée* correspond à la notion de valeur ajoutée de la comptabilité nationale. Elle est donnée par la valeur de la production brute, déduction faite du coût des matériaux, combustibles et autres fournitures, des travaux effectués sous contrat ou à la commande par d'autres unités, ainsi que des travaux de réparation et d'entretien exécutés par d'autres unités et de l'électricité achetée. Elle comprend les recettes au titre des services non industriels, mais elle en exclut les coûts. Les estimations relatives aux consommations sont établies sur la base des quantités consommées. L'évaluation est faite de la même manière que pour la production.

L'*emploi* est mesuré par le nombre d'années de travail, calculé d'après le nombre de semaines de travail assurées qui ressort des registres fiscaux. Sont compris les propriétaires exploitants, les associés actifs, les travailleurs familiaux non rémunérés, les travailleurs indépendants et les salariés. Les données englobent les salariés à temps complet et à temps partiel ainsi que le personnel de bureau et d'encadrement dont les fonctions sont étroitement liées au processus de production.

Par *rémunération* du travail on entend ici la «rémunération des salariés» au sens de la comptabilité nationale. Elle couvre uniquement les salariés, à l'exclusion des travailleurs indépendants, et comprend les salaires et les cotisations de sécurité sociale à la charge des employeurs.

Publications

i) *Atvinnuvegaskyrslur (Statistiques industrielles)*, publiées annuellement ;

ii) *Historical Statistics (Statistiques rétrospectives)*, publiées tous les deux ans ;

iii) *Compiling Icelandic National Accounts (L'établissement des comptes nationaux islandais)*, méthodes appliquées, optiques de la production et de la dépense, Reykjavik, janvier 1996.

Ce sont toutes des publications du National Economic Institute.

ITALIE

I. GÉNÉRALITÉS

Les informations émanent de l'Istituto Nazionale di Statistica (Institut National de Statistique), à Rome.

II. STATISTIQUES INDUSTRIELLES

Source

L'Institut de statistique mène chaque année des enquêtes globales sur le produit brut et les investissements en biens d'équipement dans le secteur industriel. Cette enquête s'adresse aux entreprises de 20 salariés ou plus, soit au total quelque 55 000 entreprises dans tous les secteurs d'activité économique. Les informations concernant ces entreprises sont tirées du registre qui a été établi à la suite du recensement général de 1991 et qui est mis à jour tous les ans à partir de sources diverses. D'après les estimations, l'enquête couvre 73 pour cent de la contribution de l'ensemble du secteur industriel (branches 1 à 5 de la CITI) à la valeur ajoutée nationale (estimations des comptes nationaux) et 81 pour cent de celle du secteur manufacturier. Elle couvre 58 pour cent environ de l'emploi dans l'ensemble du secteur industriel et 65 pour cent de l'emploi dans le secteur manufacturier (ce dernier chiffre est aussi basé sur les résultats de 1991). Aucune estimation n'est faite pour tenir compte des unités qui ne sont pas couvertes par l'enquête. L'enquête porte sur l'année civile et utilise comme unité de référence l'entreprise, avec une classification par type d'activité. Les entreprises de plus de 250 salariés qui se composent de plusieurs unités sont tenues de fournir une réponse distincte pour chacune de leurs unités. A l'heure actuelle, les chiffres sur les heures ouvrées sont tirés de l'enquête sur les entreprises industrielles. A partir de 1993, les données relatives aux heures ouvrées seront tirées d'une enquête spéciale sur l'emploi, les salaires et les heures ouvrées menée auprès d'un échantillon de 18 000 entreprises de dix à 199 salariés et auprès de toutes les entreprises (environ 3 700) de 200 salariés et plus.

Classification industrielle

Les rubriques de la classification nationale, qui est inspirée de la NACE révision 1, ne peuvent pas toutes être ramenées à des rubriques de la CITI révision 3. Néanmoins, il existe des tables de conversion nationales qui permettent l'établissement de données au niveau des rubriques à 3 chiffres de la CITI révision 3, et des efforts sont faits pour produire des estimations fiables au niveau des rubriques à 4 chiffres.

Concepts et définitions des variables

La *production*, ou production brute nette des impôts indirects et subventions, est évaluée aux prix de vente, hors TVA. L'électricité vendue, les actifs fixes produits par l'unité pour son propre usage et les biens fabriqués par d'autres entreprises sont inclus, compte tenu de la variation des stocks de produits finis et de la variation nette des travaux en cours. La *valeur ajoutée*, nette des subventions et impôts indirects, est établie selon le concept de valeur ajoutée «recensée». Elle est évaluée à l'exclusion de tous les impôts indirects et subventions. Elle correspond à la production brute majorée des recettes au titre des services non industriels, déduction faite du coût des matériaux, combustibles et autres fournitures, des travaux exécutés sous contrat ou à la commande par d'autres unités, des travaux de réparation et d'entretien réalisés par d'autres unités, de l'électricité achetée et des services non industriels. Les estimations relatives aux consommations sont effectuées sur la base des quantités reçues, avec un ajustement pour tenir compte de la variation des stocks de matériaux, combustibles et autres fournitures.

L'*emploi* indique le nombre de personnes occupées, tel qu'il ressort du nombre moyen de salariés employés tout au long de l'année et du nombre total d'autres personnes employées à quatre dates précises, à savoir le 31 mars, le 30 juin, le 30 septembre et le 31 décembre. Les propriétaires exploitants, associés actifs, travailleurs familiaux non rémunérés, travailleurs indépendants, employés et salariés sont tous pris en compte. L'*emploi, salariés* permet d'isoler le nombre moyen d'employés. Les *heures ouvrées* correspondent aux heures travaillées par les ouvriers, y compris les heures supplémentaires, les heures de repos et les heures passées à attendre. Sont compris les congés annuels, les jours fériés, les congés de maladie et autres congés payés. Sont exclus : les employeurs, les agents de maîtrise et les apprentis.

La formation brute de capital fixe (*investissement*), déduction non faite de la valeur des ventes, est égale à la valeur des acquisitions d'actifs fixes, y compris ceux fabriqués par le personnel de l'établissement pour l'usage de ce dernier. Les actifs fixes couverts sont ceux dont la durée de vie productive est au moins égale à un an. Sont pris en compte : les actifs fabriqués par le personnel de l'établissement pour l'usage de ce dernier, les adjonctions, transformations, améliorations et réparations d'actifs existants, les actifs fixes neufs (non encore en service ou précédemment utilisés en dehors du pays) et les actifs usagés. L'évaluation est faite au prix de revient total, y compris les frais d'installation. Les *dépenses en machines et équipement* correspondent à la formation brute de capital fixe en machines et équipement, valeur des ventes non déduite. Elles reposent sur la même définition que l'investissement total et englobent le matériel de transport, les machines, équipement et mobilier industriels, les instruments et équipements professionnels. Les modifications, améliorations et réparations sont également prises en compte.

Les *salaires et charges sociales, salariés* couvrent les traitements, les salaires et les charges sociales des employeurs. Ils comprennent le paiement en espèces des heures normales et supplémentaires, les gratifications et indemnités de cherté de vie, les congés payés et congés de maladie, les prestations en nature et les indemnités. Les *charges sociales des employeurs* couvrent le coût total des contributions patronales aux caisses de sécurité sociale et aux caisses de retraite.

Les *établissements* sont définis en fonction du type d'activité de l'unité.

Publications

Fatturato, prodotto lordo e investimenti delle imprese industriali : suppléments au *Bollettino Mensile di Statistica*, ISTAT, Rome.

JAPON

I. GÉNÉRALITÉS

Les informations émanent du Ministère japonais du Commerce International et de l'Industrie (MITI) et du Ministère de la Santé et des Affaires Sociales.

II. STATISTIQUES INDUSTRIELLES

Source

Les données, sauf celles concernant les installations de distribution d'eau, proviennent de l'«Annual Census of Manufactures» du MITI. Cette enquête couvre tous les établissements définis comme manufacturiers à l'exception de ceux appartenant à des entreprises publiques ou de service public. Depuis 1981, tous les établissements (y compris ceux employant trois personnes ou moins) ne sont cependant plus interrogés que les années dont le chiffre se termine par 0, 3, 5 ou 8. Les autres années, l'enquête se limite aux établissements employant quatre personnes ou plus. Les données sur l'investissement concernent les établissements de 30 salariés ou plus. Aucune estimation n'est opérée pour tenir compte des unités non couvertes. Les chiffres concernant les activités extractives et minières proviennent de la «Survey of Mining Trends in Japan». Cette enquête s'adresse à tous les établissements engagés dans des activités d'extraction de métal, charbon et lignite et de forage de pétrole et de gaz naturel.

Les chiffres pour le captage, l'épuration et la distribution de l'eau sont dérivés des «Statistiques de Distribution d'Eau», publiés par le Ministère de la Santé et des Affaires Sociales. Pour les variables concernant le nombre d'établissements et l'emploi, tous les établissements sont couverts. Pour d'autres variables, seuls les établissements de captage, d'épuration et de distribution de l'eau de taille importante sont couverts.

Classification industrielle

Les données sont ventilées selon la classification japonaise type des activités industrielles (JSIC révision 10).

Concepts et définitions des variables

La production brute (*production*) indique la valeur des livraisons de produits finis ajustée pour tenir compte de la variation des stocks de produits finis et des travaux en cours. Dans le cas des activités extractives, en plus de la valeur de production il est tenu compte d'autres recettes. Les recettes au titre des travaux réalisés sous contrat ainsi que des travaux de réparation et d'entretien sont incluses. Par contre, la valeur des produits réexpédiés en l'état est exclue. La *valeur ajoutée* est donnée par la production brute déduction faite du coût des matériaux et combustibles, de l'électricité achetée, des travaux exécutés sous contrat et des impôts indirects, ainsi que des amortissements, y compris le coût des services non industriels mais à l'exclusion des recettes à ce titre. Les données relatives aux consommations sont estimées sur la base des quantités reçues et aucun ajustement n'est opéré pour tenir compte de la variation du niveau des stocks.

L'*emploi* indique le nombre de personnes occupées à la fin de l'année, à temps complet ou partiel. Il comprend les salariés (y compris les apprentis et les travailleurs temporaires sous réserve de certains critères concernant la durée minimale du travail), les propriétaires exploitants, les travailleurs familiaux non rémunérés et les travailleurs sous contrat (activités minières et extractives seulement). Les autres travailleurs temporaires et journaliers sont exclus, bien que leur rémunération soit incluse dans la valeur des salaires et traitements.

L'*investissement* correspond à la formation brute de capital fixe, définie comme la valeur des acquisitions d'actifs fixes, y compris ceux fabriqués par le personnel de l'établissement pour l'usage de ce dernier, déduction faite de la valeur des ventes. Par actifs fixes, il faut entendre les biens qui ont une durée de vie productive supérieure à un an, les réparations d'actifs existants, les actifs neufs non encore en service, inutilisés ou utilisés précédemment en dehors du pays, et les actifs usagés. L'évaluation est faite au prix de revient total, y compris le prix rendu, les frais d'installation et les droits et redevances. Dans le cas d'actifs produits par l'unité, le coût des travaux en cours couvre les coûts de main-d'œuvre, le coût des matériaux et fournitures ainsi qu'une provision pour frais généraux. Pour l'évaluation des ventes d'actifs usagés, on se fonde sur le montant effectivement réalisé.

Les *salaires et traitements, salariés* correspondent au total des paiements en espèces versés aux personnes employées, y compris le salaire de base, les gratifications et autres primes et indemnités. Pour les industries minières et extractives, les chiffres comprennent les sommes versées aux travailleurs à la tâche. Pour les industries manufacturières, les chiffres couvrent les indemnités de départ à la retraite et de licenciement des employés, mais pas celles des ouvriers.

Publications

  i) *Honpo Kogyo no Susei* (Mining Yearbook of Japan) ;
  ii) *Census of Manufactures* (annuel).

  Toutes deux sont publiées par le MITI.

LUXEMBOURG

I. GÉNÉRALITÉS

Les informations émanent du Service central de la statistique et des études économiques (STATEC), Luxembourg.

II. STATISTIQUES INDUSTRIELLES

Source

Les estimations sont tirées de l'Enquête annuelle sur la production industrielle, menée par STATEC. Toutes les entreprises sont couvertes ; cependant celles qui, pendant l'année, ont employé, en moyenne, moins de 20 personnes sont estimées à partir d'un échantillon.

Classification industrielle

Les données qui à l'origine étaient établies selon la NACE 70, ont été regroupées dans la mesure du possible selon la CITI. Certaines industries sont regroupées pour des raisons de confidentialité. Dans les tableaux :

a) CITI 311 inclut CITI 312 ;

b) CITI 313 inclut CITI 314 ;

c) CITI 33 inclut CITI 39 ;

d) CITI 351 englobe CITI 354, 355 et 356 de même que la production de scories Thomas (du secteur CITI 371) ;

e) CITI 383 inclut CITI 385.

Concepts et définitions des variables

Les estimations pour la *production* correspondent à la valeur des ventes effectuées pendant l'année, ajustée pour tenir compte de la variation de la valeur des stocks de produits finis et des travaux en cours, et des recettes pour services rendus. Sont incluses la valeur des travaux effectués pour compte propre et la valeur des biens fournis aux employés comme prestations en nature. Pour les marchandises réexpédiées en l'état, on utilise la marge brute. L'évaluation se fait au coût des facteurs. Les estimations pour la *valeur ajoutée* représentent la valeur de la production moins les coûts des matériaux et autres fournitures, et services achetés pour servir dans le processus de production ; on effectue des ajustements pour tenir compte de la variation de la valeur des stocks de matériaux. L'évaluation se fait au coût des facteurs.

L'*emploi* comprend la totalité des personnes engagées et correspond à la somme des nombres moyens de propriétaires exploitants, de travailleurs familiaux non rémunérés, de salariés et d'autres employés. Les travailleurs à domicile, dont la contribution est considérée comme négligeable, sont exclus.

L'*investissement*, ou formation brute de capital fixe (FBCF), représente les acquisitions d'actifs fixes neufs et usagés, moins les ventes. Sont compris les travaux pour compte propre et la formation de capital fixe en nouveaux établissements non encore mis en opération. Les dépenses en biens meubles sont enregistrées au moment où ils sont livrés. Les dépenses en biens immeubles (par exemple, bâtiments, grosses réparations) et les nouvelles implantations correspondent à la valeur des travaux mis en œuvre pendant l'année de référence, que ces travaux soient achevés ou non à la fin de cette même année.

Publications

Annuaire statistique publié par STATEC.

MEXIQUE

I. STATISTIQUES INDUSTRIELLES

Source

Les résultats de l'enquête annuelle dans l'industrie des Etats-Unis du Mexique émanent de l'Institut national des statistiques, de la géographie et des technologies de l'information (INEGI), par l'intermédiaire du Département des statistiques.

Jusqu'en 1991, cette enquête portait sur 129 catégories d'activités économiques du secteur manufacturier, soit sur 3 218 établissements qui représentent eux-mêmes 72 pour cent du champ statistique servant au calcul du produit brut total, fondé sur le recensement industriel de 1985.

A partir de 1992, l'enquête annuelle porte sur 205 catégories d'activités économiques du secteur manufacturier, soit sur 6 684 établissements de plus de 6 salariés, qui couvrent 80 pour cent de la valeur totale de la production manufacturière dans chaque classe d'activité.

Classification industrielle

Le système de classification utilisé dans l'enquête est conforme aux recommandations internationales du Bureau de statistique des Nations Unies. Certains postes sont regroupés afin de garantir la comparabilité avec la CITI. Dans les tableaux CITI révision 2 : les secteurs CITI 323, 353, 3821 et 3845 ne sont pas disponibles ; le secteur CITI 3823 inclut une partie de CITI 3824 (fabrication, montage et réparation de machines et de matériel y compris les tracteurs destinés aux industries de la construction, aux industries extractives et à d'autres industries) ; le secteur CITI 3849 est allouée aux CITI 3823 et 3843.

A partir de 1993, la classification utilisée dans les enquêtes et les recensements est la Classification Mexicaine des Activités Economiques et des Produits (CMAP 1994) qui se fonde sur la CITI révision 3.

Concepts et définitions des variables

La *production* correspond à la production brute totale. Elle est donnée par la valeur totale des biens et services produits, qu'il s'agisse de produits et services intermédiaires entrant dans le processus de production ou de produits destinés à la consommation finale. Elle inclut la valeur des produits fabriqués par l'établissement au moyen de matières premières lui appartenant, ainsi que les revenus provenant des services d'assemblage, d'entretien et autres services industriels, des locations et locations-ventes, des transferts de technologie, d'autres services non industriels, de la vente d'électricité produite par l'établissement, de la variation des stocks de travaux en cours et de la valeur des actifs fixes produits par l'établissement pour son propre usage. La *valeur ajoutée*, ou produit intérieur brut, est donnée par le produit brut total, déduction faite de la valeur des entrants (biens et services destinés à la consommation intermédiaire).

L'*emploi, salariés* englobe tous les travailleurs manuels et non manuels, permanents et temporaires, qui, au cours de l'année de référence, ont travaillé dans l'établissement ou en dehors de celui-ci et qui étaient dirigés ou supervisés par celui-ci. Y sont inclus les travailleurs en grève ou en congés de maladie, payés ou non, en vacances ou absents pour une courte durée. En sont exclus les travailleurs absents pour une durée indéterminée, les retraités, les auditeurs, les conseillers, les consultants, les commissionnaires en marchandises et autres personnes qui, bien que n'appartenant pas au personnel de l'établissement, ont rendu à ce dernier des services qui leur ont été rémunérés uniquement à la commission ou sous forme d'honoraires, les personnes qui ont effectué des travaux de réparation et d'entretien dans l'établissement pour le compte d'autres unités et tous les travailleurs à domicile qui n'apparaissent pas sur le livre de paie.

Le chiffre de l'emploi est une moyenne annuelle, obtenue en divisant par douze la somme annuelle du nombre de travailleurs manuels et non manuels employés chaque mois ; une autre possibilité serait de se référer au nombre de mois de travail effectué par chaque travailleur pour obtenir la répartition moyenne sur l'ensemble de l'année. Par travailleurs manuels (ouvriers), il faut entendre les personnes dont l'emploi est avant tout manuel ou est lié au fonctionnement des machines et équipements (de production et d'assemblage), les agents de maîtrise qualifiés et le personnel affecté à des tâches liées au processus de production comme le nettoyage, la réparation, l'entretien, l'expédition et le stockage, l'affrètement, l'acheminement des matières premières et le transport, et qui exécutent ces tâches à l'intérieur ou à l'extérieur de l'établissement, mais sous le contrôle direct de ce dernier. Par travailleurs non manuels, il faut entendre le personnel affecté à des tâches de planification, de gestion et de supervision technique ou administrative, liées au processus de production et de services annexes ainsi que le personnel affecté à des tâches de vérification, d'administration, de comptabilité, de recherche, de vente, de publicité et de sécurité ou à tout travail de bureau en général. Le chiffre de l'emploi inclut les propriétaires, les partenaires actifs et les membres de leurs familles employés par l'établissement dès lors qu'ils reçoivent un salaire régulier.

L'*investissement*, ou formation brute de capital fixe, comprend les éléments suivants :

a) Achats d'actifs fixes neufs. Ceux-ci couvrent la valeur totale des actifs fixes neufs acquis par l'établissement ou reçus par lui d'autres établissements de la même entreprise au cours de l'année de référence. Y sont inclus les actifs importés qui n'ont jamais été utilisés dans le pays même s'ils ont été utilisés à l'étranger avant leur importation, et les paiements partiels versés au titre de travaux de construction ;

b) Achats d'actifs fixes usagés. Ceux-ci représentent la valeur des actifs fixes usagés acquis par l'établissement ou reçus par ce dernier d'autres établissements de la même entreprise au cours de l'année de référence. Y sont inclus les actifs fixes précédemment utilisés dans le pays, qu'ils aient ou non été fabriqués dans le pays. Les achats de terrains au cours de l'année sont considérés comme des achats d'actifs neufs ;

c) Actifs fixes produits par l'établissement pour son propre usage. Ceux-ci correspondent à la valeur totale des actifs fixes produits, pendant l'année de référence, par le personnel de l'établissement, pour l'usage de ce dernier, au moyen de matériaux lui appartenant. Les travaux en cours sont évalués sur une base proportionnelle. Sont inclus les actifs fixes destinés à la location ou à la location-vente ainsi que les améliorations, réparations et rénovations apportées par l'établissement à ses propres actifs pendant l'année de référence, dès lors que ces travaux prolongent la durée de vie de ces actifs ou en accroissent la productivité. Sont exclus les dépenses de réparation et d'entretien courant, ainsi que les gros travaux d'amélioration, de réparation et de rénovation exécutés par des tiers sur les actifs fixes de l'établissement ;

d) Gros travaux d'amélioration, de réparation et de rénovation exécutés par des tiers sur des actifs fixes appartenant à l'établissement. Ils correspondent au total des dépenses faites par l'établissement pendant l'année de référence au titre de travaux d'amélioration, de réparation et de rénovation exécutés par des tiers dès lors que ces travaux prolongent la durée de vie des actifs fixes de plus d'un an, en modifient la nature ou en accroissent la productivité. Sont spécifiquement pris en compte la valeur des matériaux et les frais de fonctionnement encourus par l'établissement pour ce type de travaux, ainsi que les services reçus d'autres établissements de la même entreprise. Sont exclues les dépenses de réparation et d'entretien courant ;

e) Ventes d'actifs fixes. Elles représentent la valeur totale des ventes d'actifs fixes, neufs et usagés, réalisées par l'établissement pendant l'année de référence, que ces actifs aient été acquis auprès de tiers ou fabriqués par l'établissement pour son propre usage.

Pour les éléments a) à d) ci-dessus, l'évaluation se fonde sur le prix effectivement facturé. Lorsque les services ont été reçus d'autres établissements de la même entreprise, ils sont évalués aux prix du marché ou, à défaut, à un prix fictif qui inclut le coût de la main-d'œuvre et des matières premières, auquel s'ajoute une marge pour tenir compte des frais généraux et des bénéfices. La TVA n'est pas incluse. Pour l'élément e), l'évaluation se fonde sur le montant effectivement reçu et prend en compte tous les frais facturés à l'acheteur, à l'exclusion des intérêts perçus sur les ventes à crédit. La TVA n'est pas incluse.

Les actifs fixes comprennent les éléments suivants :

a) Machines et équipement -- se reporter à la rubrique investissement en machines et équipement, ci-après ;

b) Bâtiments et infrastructures -- à savoir les bâtiments et infrastructures appartenant à l'établissement et liés directement ou indirectement au processus de production. Sont inclus les ateliers de fabrication, les entrepôts, les bureaux, les magasins, les installations d'acheminement de l'eau, de la vapeur et de l'électricité, ainsi que les autres structures telles qu'allées piétonnières et aires de stationnement et les terrains dont la valeur ne peut être dissociée de celle des bâtiments eux-mêmes ;

c) Terrains (réfections incluses) -- à savoir les terrains non bâtis qui appartiennent à l'établissement et n'entrent pas sous la rubrique précédente ;

d) Matériel de transport -- comprend tous les modes de transport tels que navires, avions, wagons, camions, tracteurs à remorque et autres véhicules appartenant à l'établissement ;

e) Autres actifs fixes -- à savoir tous les actifs fixes, qui appartiennent à l'établissement, qui n'entrent pas dans les rubriques précédentes et dont la durée de vie est estimée à plus d'un an.

Sont inclus le mobilier, y compris les équipements de bureaux tels que les ordinateurs et machines à calculer, et les engins du genre chariot élévateur utilisés pour déplacer des marchandises à l'intérieur de l'établissement. Sont exclus les actifs fixes immatériels tels que les brevets et marques de fabrique. L'évaluation repose sur les principes suivants : tous les actifs fixes sont évalués à leur coût d'acquisition, qui comprend le prix d'achat ainsi que les frais de transport lorsque ce dernier est effectué par des tiers, les frais d'installation, les taxes (à l'exclusion de la TVA), l'assurance des biens en transit et, d'une manière générale, tous les frais encourus pour le transport des actifs jusqu'à l'établissement. Sont exclus les intérêts payés au titre des prêts contractés par l'établissement pour financer ses achats d'actifs. Les actifs reçus d'autres établissements de la même entreprise sont évalués sur la base des mêmes principes que ceux achetés à des tiers comme il a été précisé ci-dessus ou, à défaut, à leur valeur comptable.

Les *dépenses en machines et équipement* correspondent à la formation brute de capital fixe en machines et équipement. Elles comprennent les machines et autres équipements mécaniques, électriques et autres appartenant à l'établissement et utilisés dans le processus de production ou pour des activités annexes.

Les *salaires et charges sociales, salariés* couvrent l'ensemble des dépenses au titre des traitements et salaires versés par l'établissement au personnel salarié au cours de l'année de référence ainsi que des prestations sociales, des contributions patronales de sécurité sociale et de l'intéressement.

Les *salaires et traitements, salariés* se décomposent en salaires des travailleurs manuels et salaires des travailleurs non manuels.

Les salaires des travailleurs manuels correspondent au montant brut des sommes versées en espèces avant déductions au cours de la période de référence en rémunération des tâches normales et non récurrentes effectuées par le personnel permanent et temporaire. Sont incluses les sommes versées aux travailleurs manuels sous forme de salaires, de primes, de bonifications, de congés et indemnités payés ainsi que les sommes versées pendant les absences de courte durée. Sont exclus les pensions servies aux retraités, les indemnités versées aux travailleurs licenciés ou dont le contrat vient à échéance, et les sommes versées aux travailleurs à domicile qui n'apparaissent pas sur le livre de paie.

Les salaires des travailleurs non manuels comprennent l'ensemble des sommes versées en espèces avant déductions au cours de la période de référence en rémunération des tâches normales et non récurrentes effectuées par le personnel permanent et temporaire. Sont incluses les sommes versées sous forme de salaires, de primes, de bonifications, de congés payés et indemnités ainsi que les sommes versées pendant les absences de courte durée et les commissions sur ventes. Sont exclues les pensions servies aux retraités ainsi que les honoraires, rétributions et commissions versés aux prestataires de services non-membres du personnel de l'établissement.

Les prestations sociales correspondent aux paiements que reçoivent les travailleurs manuels et non manuels, qu'ils soient en espèces, sous forme de services ou en nature ; dans les deux derniers cas, elles sont évaluées à leur coût. Sont inclus le montant total des frais supportés par l'établissement et des contributions versées par lui au titre de l'alimentation (cantine), de la garde d'enfants et des soins médicaux, des primes d'assurance-vie et d'assurance contre les risques professionnels, des indemnités de licenciement et de fin de contrat, des primes, des allocations de transport, de sport, etc., ainsi que tous les paiements normalement à la charge des salariés mais qui, en réalité, sont pris en charge par l'établissement. Sont exclus le coût des uniformes et vêtements de travail fournis aux travailleurs manuels et non manuels et les dépenses récupérables, comme les frais de déplacement et les frais de représentation, encourues par les employés au nom de l'entreprise.

Les contributions patronales de sécurité sociale correspondent à l'ensemble des sommes versées par l'établissement, pendant l'année de référence, au titre des cotisations patronales à l'IMSS (Instituto Mejicano del Seguro Social -- Caisse mexicaine de sécurité sociale), à l'INFONAVIT (Instituto del Fondo Nacional para la Vivienda de los Trabajadores -- Caisse nationale d'aide au logement des travailleurs) et à d'autres organismes officiels.

Les *heures ouvrées* indiquent le nombre d'heures, normales ou non récurrentes, réellement effectué par le personnel manuel et non manuel, permanent et temporaire, pendant la période de référence. Sont inclus les temps d'attente normaux, les temps de préparation et, dans le cas des travailleurs manuels, les heures non travaillées en raison de défaillances techniques et le temps passé à nettoyer les outils et machines utilisés pendant la journée de travail. Sont exclues les heures non travaillées pour cause de grève, d'arrêt de travail, de vacances, de maladie, de mauvais temps et autres motifs exceptionnels.

L'unité sur laquelle portent les informations demandées dans l'enquête annuelle dans l'industrie est l'*établissement*. Chaque entité industrielle correspond à une unité statistique.

Publications

i) *Estadística Industrial Anual* ;
ii) *Estadística Industrial Mensual.*

Toutes les deux émanent de la Dirección General de Estadística, Secretariá de Programacíon y Presupuesto, Mexique.

NORVÈGE

I. GÉNÉRALITÉS

Les statistiques industrielles et les données de comptabilité nationale émanent de Statistik Sentralbyra (Bureau Central de statistiques de Norvège), à Oslo.

II. STATISTIQUES INDUSTRIELLES

Source

A partir de 1992, l'enquête annuelle s'adresse, en règle générale, à tous les établissements des industries extractives et manufacturières de 10 salariés ou plus. Les enquêtes annuelles précédentes couvraient, en règle générale, tous les établissements de 5 salariés ou plus. Les informations sur l'extraction de pétrole et de gaz ne sont pas incluses. Pour les petits établissements (de moins de 10 personnes), les informations proviennent chaque année des registres administratifs.

L'unité de référence est l'établissement. La période de référence est l'année civile.

Classification industrielle

A partir de 1993, l'adoption de la classification industrielle type de Norvège, révisée (SIC 94) a entraîné quelques modifications dans la couverture des statistiques par rapport aux années précédentes. La classification a une structure hiérarchique à 6 niveaux.

La SIC 94 est identique à la NACE révision 1 jusqu'au 4ème niveau, le 5ème chiffre étant une subdivision pour les besoins nationaux. Elle est compatible avec la CITI révision 3.

Concepts et définitions des variables

La *production* correspond à la production brute évaluée aux prix à la production, à l'exclusion de toutes les subventions, mais y compris tous les impôts indirects, sauf la TVA. Elle inclut la valeur de tous les biens produits par l'établissement pour son propre compte, des travaux de réparation effectués pour d'autres unités, du montage ou de l'installation de ses propres biens et produits, des travaux exécutés sous contrat, des autres travaux, des travaux d'investissement et de réparation effectués par l'unité pour son propre compte, des revenus de locations, et des profits bruts tirés de la revente de biens en l'état.

La *valeur ajoutée* est évaluée – sans affirmation contraire – aux prix du marché et est égale à la valeur brute de la production diminuée du coût des biens et services consommés. Elle exclut toutes les subventions, mais comprend tous les impôts indirects, sauf la TVA. Les coûts des matériaux, combustibles et autres fournitures, des travaux exécutés sous contrat ou à la commande par d'autres unités, des travaux de réparation et d'entretien exécutés par d'autres unités et de l'électricité achetée sont déduits de la valeur de la production brute. Les coûts des services non industriels sont inclus de même que les recettes à ce titre. Les données relatives aux consommations intermédiaires sont estimées sur la base des quantités consommées.

Un *établissement* se définit comme une unité fonctionnelle qui mène, en un seul endroit, une activité principale appartenant à un groupe d'activités spécifique de la classification industrielle type de la Norvège.

L'*emploi* indique le nombre de personnes occupées et est calculé sur la base du nombre moyen de salariés travaillant dans l'établissement tout au long de l'année, à temps complet ou à temps partiel. Il comprend les propriétaires exploitants, les associés, les travailleurs familiaux non rémunérés, les employés et les salariés ainsi que les travailleurs indépendants mais non les travailleurs à domicile et les travailleurs en congé militaire. L'*emploi, salariés* comprend les gérants et directeurs salariés, les employés des entreprises de transport, les commissionnaires, les marchands de journaux, les gardiens, et le personnel d'entretien. Les *heures ouvrées* correspondent aux heures effectuées par les salariés et comprennent les heures supplémentaires. Sont compris les contremaîtres et agents de maîtrise, les apprentis, les travailleurs occasionnels et les travailleurs à temps partiel.

La formation brute de capital fixe (*investissement*) est définie comme la valeur des acquisitions d'actifs fixes, neufs ou usagés, dont la durée de vie productive est d'un an au moins, y compris ceux fabriqués par le personnel de l'établissement pour l'usage de ce dernier, déduction faite de la valeur des ventes d'actifs durables. L'acquisition de machines, d'équipement de transport, etc. est enregistrée à la date de réception des actifs, qu'ils soient ou non mis en œuvre dans l'année. L'achat de bâtiments, structures, terrains, etc. est traité de la même façon. Comme pour les travaux de construction en cours, la valeur des travaux effectués au cours de l'année est enregistrée même s'ils ne sont pas achevés dans l'année. Par coût d'acquisition on entend les dépenses réelles encourues pendant l'année, y compris les prélèvements sur l'investissement, quelle que soit la date de paiement. Les chiffres sur la formation de capital fixe ne comprennent pas tout le capital utilisé dans les industries extractives et manufacturières.

Les *dépenses en machines et équipement* correspondent, elles aussi, à la formation de capital et reposent sur la même définition que l'investissement total. Y sont inclus le matériel de transport, les machines et matériels industriels, les machines, équipement et mobilier de bureau, les instruments et équipements professionnels, ainsi que les modifications et améliorations apportées à ces matériels.

Les *salaires et charges sociales* englobent les salaires et traitements et les suppléments. Les salaires et traitements comprennent tous les paiements, en espèces ou en nature, effectués par l'employeur en compensation du travail effectué, à toutes personnes inscrites sur le registre des salariés (y compris les travailleurs à domicile). Ils comprennent les impôts, assurances sociales, et contributions au système des pensions dus par l'employé, mais retenus par l'employeur. Sont également inclus les gratifications, les primes de production, les congés payés, congés de maladie et congés militaires, les commissions des vendeurs et des représentants. Ils ne comprennent pas les salaires et charges relatives aux propriétaires indépendants, aux associés et aux travailleurs familiaux qui ne perçoivent pas de revenus réguliers. Les suppléments correspondent aux *charges sociales des employeurs*. Ils recouvrent les dépenses sociales légales et les autres prestations données aux employés, à savoir les contributions patronales aux régimes privés de pensions, les allocations familiales, les assurances maladie-accidents, les assurances sur la vie et les autres régimes similaires.

Publications

i) *Industristatistikk* (annuelle) -- Industries extractives et manufacturières ;

ii) *Elektrisitetstatistikk* (annuelle) -- Industries de l'électricité et du gaz ;

iii) *Bygge- og anleggsstatistikk* (annuelle) -- Construction.

Toutes sont publiées par le Bureau de statistique de la Norvège.

III. COMPTES NATIONAUX

Source

Les chiffres sont tirés des comptes nationaux publiés (*cf.* la rubrique «Publications») et sont établis à partir des résultats d'enquêtes menées par le Bureau de statistique. Les statistiques sur la production sont relativement fiables pour l'agriculture, la sylviculture, la pêche, les activités liées à l'exploitation du pétrole, les industries extractives et manufacturières, l'électricité, la distribution d'eau, les transports et communications et quelques autres activités de service. Pour la plupart des industries de services, la principale source d'information est fournie par les données sur le chiffre d'affaires et l'emploi par industrie tirées du registre des établissements et des entreprises. Les statistiques sur les importations et les exportations sont satisfaisantes.

Un des points faibles des statistiques sur la production concerne les industries du commerce. Pour le commerce de gros et de détail, les séries annuelles originales ne sont guère utiles pour l'établissement des comptes nationaux. Dans ces derniers, la production du commerce de gros et de détail (considérés ensemble) est calculée à partir de la valeur d'achat, c'est-à-dire des chiffres par produit ventilés par industrie et par utilisation finale. Des coefficients de marge donnés, pour chaque produit de bien, par le rapport entre le prix d'achat et le prix à la production de l'année précédente, sont utilisés pour déterminer les marges commerciales. Ainsi, pour chaque produit, un coefficient de marge est calculé pour chaque catégorie d'utilisation. Les coefficients de marge commerciale peuvent être révisés dans le cadre de la procédure d'équilibrage de l'offre et des emplois de produits réalisée lors de l'établissement des comptes nationaux. Les séries originales sur les stocks sont très médiocres et fournissent uniquement une ventilation par type et par branche d'activité.

Classification industrielle

Les importations sont affectées à telle ou telle industrie en fonction des caractéristiques du produit. Cependant, il n'est pas toujours possible de spécifier ces caractéristiques. Dans ce cas, les chiffres sont intégrés directement dans le total général. C'est ce qui se passe notamment pour les biens servant au transport par oléoduc et gazoduc, les dépenses d'exploitation, les dépenses en actifs fixes, les achats directs à l'étranger des marins norvégiens.

Concepts et définitions des variables

La *production* correspond à la production brute, y compris la valeur de tous les produits, de la variation nette des travaux en cours, des travaux effectués par l'établissement pour compte propre, des services rendus, des actifs fixes produits par l'établissement pour son propre usage, des déchets de fabrication, des biens fabriqués par des travailleurs à domicile et des artisans. L'évaluation est faite aux prix à la production, à l'exclusion de toutes les subventions mais y compris tous les impôts indirects, à l'exception de la TVA qui est rajoutée par la suite dans les comptes nationaux. La *valeur ajoutée* est calculée selon le concept de valeur ajoutée de la comptabilité nationale ; elle est donnée par la valeur de la production brute déduction faite du coût des matériaux, combustibles et autres fournitures, des travaux exécutés sous contrat ou à la commande, des travaux de réparation et d'entretien exécutés par d'autres unités, des dépenses de location et de l'électricité achetée. Les données relatives aux consommations sont estimées sur la base des quantités consommées. Le coût des services non industriels est inclus. L'évaluation est faite aux prix du marché, compte non tenu de la TVA (dans ce cas aussi elle est rajoutée plus tard dans les comptes nationaux).

L'*emploi* indique le nombre total de personnes occupées tel qu'il ressort du nombre moyen de salariés employés tout au long de l'année. Il inclut les propriétaires exploitants, les vendeurs, les travailleurs familiaux non rémunérés, les travailleurs indépendants, les employés et les salariés, à temps complet et à temps partiel.

Les statistiques sur les *importations* portent sur le commerce général (CAF). Elles englobent le commerce d'Etat, les transactions commerciales d'équipements et de fournitures militaires, les transactions d'aide extérieure, les transactions portant sur les navires et avions neufs, l'électricité et le gaz, les produits de la mer provenant directement de haute mer et les donations et dons privés. Sont exclus les échanges directs en transit, les importations temporaires, les articles monétaires et les petites transactions (d'un montant inférieur à 1 000 KrN).

L'*investissement* correspond à la formation brute de capital fixe et est défini comme étant égal à la valeur des acquisitions d'actifs fixes, y compris ceux fabriqués par le personnel de l'établissement pour l'usage de ce dernier, déduction faite des ventes. Les actifs fixes couverts sont ceux qui ont une durée de vie d'un an au moins, y compris ceux fabriqués par le personnel de l'établissement pour l'usage de ce dernier, les adjonctions, transformations et améliorations d'actifs fixes existants, les actifs fixes neufs (à condition qu'ils n'aient pas encore été mis en service ou aient été utilisés précédemment en dehors du pays) et les actifs fixes usagés. L'évaluation est faite au prix de revient total, y compris le prix rendu, les frais d'installation, les droits et redevances (mais non la TVA). Pour les actifs fixes produits par l'unité, on utilise le coût des travaux en cours, y compris les coûts de main-d'œuvre et le coût des matériaux et autres fournitures. Pour les ventes d'actifs fixes usagés, on se base sur le montant réellement réalisé.

Les *salaires et charges sociales, salariés* couvrent les salaires et traitements versés aux salariés, les cotisations patronales aux caisses de sécurité sociale et de retraite et les cotisations nettes au fonds général d'aide aux travailleurs à faible revenu. Elle inclut le paiement en espèces des heures normales et supplémentaires, les gratifications et indemnités de cherté de vie, les congés payés et congés de maladie, les impôts et les cotisations d'assurance sociale dus par les salariés et retenus par l'employeur, ainsi que les prestations en nature. Les *charges sociales des employeurs* englobent les cotisations exigées par la loi au régime général de l'assurance sociale et les contributions volontaires aux caisses privées de retraite, d'allocations familiales, d'assurance santé et accident, d'assurance-vie et autres.

Données à prix constants

Les estimations à prix constants utilisent 1980 comme année de référence. Un indice en chaîne est établi pour chaque produit à chaque niveau d'agrégation, de sorte que le taux de croissance annuel des divers agrégats soit identique à celui qui aurait été obtenu en utilisant l'année réelle de référence. Par conséquent, les agrégats à prix constants ne peuvent pas être obtenus par la somme de leurs composantes.

Publications

  i) *National Accounts Statistics* (annuelle) ;

  ii) *National Accounts of Norway -- System and Methods of Estimation,* E. Flöttum.

  Elles émanent du Bureau de statistique de la Norvège et sont disponibles en langue anglaise.

NOUVELLE-ZÉLANDE

I. GÉNÉRALITÉS

Les informations relatives aux statistiques industrielles émanent de Statistics New Zealand, Wellington.

II. STATISTIQUES INDUSTRIELLES

Source

Données en CITI révision 2

Les données proviennent du Manufacturing Census pour 1978, 1981 et 1983. A partir de 1985, elles sont tirées soit de l'«Annual Enterprise Survey» soit de l'«Economy Wide Census» réalisé tous les cinq ans, soit encore (pour les chiffres sur l'emploi à partir de 1991) de l'«Annual Business Directory Update». Elles portent sur l'exercice budgétaire qui débute le 1er avril, mais si les données ne sont pas disponibles pour cette période, on considère comme acceptables les réponses portant sur le dernier exercice comptable qui se termine dans le courant de l'exercice budgétaire considéré.

L'«Integrated Economic Census of Manufacturing» utilise comme unité de référence l'unité comptable, sauf pour l'emploi où l'unité de référence est l'établissement. Les entreprises d'une seule personne sont exclues de toutes les données antérieures au recensement de 1983/84.

Par ailleurs, aucune estimation n'est faite pour tenir compte des unités qui ne sont pas couvertes par l'enquête.

Données en CITI révision 3

Les données proviennent de l'«Annual Business Frame Update», sauf pour la branche agricole pour les années 1987-1996 (source : enquête sur la production agricole). Elles portent sur l'exercice budgétaire qui se termine le 31 mars.

Ces statistiques sont dérivées du répertoire «Statistics New Zealand Business Directory» qui est une banque de données sur les entreprises néo-zélandaises et sur leur structure. L'enquête annuelle «Annual Business Directory Update Survey» (ABDU) est menée chaque année, mi-février, pour mettre à jour les détails contenus dans le répertoire d'entreprises.

A partir de 1994, la population ne comprend que les entreprises économiquement significatives.

Classification industrielle

Données en CITI révision 2

La classification utilisée à l'origine est la «New Zealand Standard Industrial Classification» (NZSIC). La ventilation des données selon la CITI ne pose pas de problèmes majeurs. La classification néo-zélandaise comporte toutefois une position supplémentaire à cinq chiffres (sous-groupe).

Données en CITI révision 3

La classification «Australian and New Zealand Standard Industrial Classification» (ANZSIC) a été introduite en 1994. Il n'existe pas de relation directe entre la NZSIC et l'ANZSIC : toutefois, une concordance est possible entre elles d'une part, et entre l'ANZSIC et la CITI révision 3 d'autre part.

Il est probable que les séries fondées sur l'ANZSIC de 1987 à 1993 soient d'une qualité moindre que les séries à partir de 1994 parce qu'elles ont été reclassifiées selon l'ANZSIC rétrospectivement.

Les données ABDU sont actuellement disponibles dans deux types de séries temporelles. Seules les données appartement à chacun de ces sous-ensembles sont directement comparables entre elles :

- les données de 1987 à 1994 fondées sur un enregistrement obligatoire GST (Taxe sur les biens et services), les chiffres de 1994 n'incluant pas les améliorations apportées en 1994 à leur couverture ;
- les données de 1994 à 1996 qui sont fondées sur les unités économiquement significatives, les chiffres de 1996 n'incluant pas les améliorations apportées en 1996 à leur couverture.

Concepts et définitions des variables à partir du recensement de 1985

L'emploi est le nombre de personnes occupées en équivalent plein temps, c'est-à-dire le nombre total de salariés et de propriétaires exploitants occupés à plein temps, plus la moitié du nombre de salariés et de propriétaires exploitants occupés à temps partiel à la fin du mois de février de l'année suivante. Il comprend les employés, salariés et ouvriers, les propriétaires exploitants, les propriétaires et associés actifs et les travailleurs indépendants.

L'emploi, salariés exclut les propriétaires exploitants.

L'emploi, femmes repose sur la même définition que l'emploi, salariés mais pour les femmes seulement.

Les *entreprises* du secteur privé correspondent généralement à des entités légales telles que sociétés, sociétés en nom collectif, fiducies, patrimoines, entreprises non constituées en société, centrales de production, entreprises individuelles, etc. Certaines entreprises sont définies par référence à d'autres caractéristiques, telles qu'un ensemble d'objectifs communs ou l'existence d'une structure organisationnelle. Dans cette catégorie sont compris les services de l'administration publique, les collectivités locales, les églises, les organisations caritatives, etc.

Publications

i) Communiqué de l'*Annual Enterprise Survey* ;

ii) Périodiques *Annual New Zealand Business Activities* ;

iii) Périodiques *Key Statistics* ;

iv) Communiqué (variable, cyclique) du *Economic Census*.

PAYS-BAS

I. STATISTIQUES INDUSTRIELLES

Source

Les données émanent du Bureau Central de Statistique des Pays-Bas et sont tirées de l'enquête statistique menée par le Bureau.

Depuis 1988, elles couvrent, pour l'année civile, toutes les unités d'activité économique de 20 salariés ou plus (sur la base du nombre d'années-personnes rémunérées par an), à l'exception des données sur les investissements qui se rapportent à toutes les unités d'activité économique de 10 salariés ou plus. Jusqu'en 1987, les unités d'activité économique de 10 salariés ou plus ont été couvertes : cependant en 1987, les entreprises de 10 à 20 employés ont été interrogées dans le cadre d'une enquête par sondage. Aucune estimation n'est faite pour tenir compte des unités qui ne sont pas couvertes par l'enquête. Les données sur l'emploi sont, pour l'année la plus récente, complétées par les informations provenant du questionnaire trimestriel sur l'emploi.

Classification industrielle

Jusqu'en 1992, les données étaient ventilées à l'origine selon la classification industrielle type de toutes les activités économiques qui a été établie par le Bureau Central de Statistique des Pays-Bas (SBI 1974) et qui est totalement compatible avec la CITI. Suite à l'introduction de la NACE révision 1 en 1993, le registre standard de 1993 a remplacé le registre des entreprises de 1974 et pour cette raison la disponibilité des chiffres change.

Concepts et définitions des variables

La *production* correspond à la valeur de la production brute et inclut tous les produits, la variation nette des travaux en cours, les travaux effectués par l'unité pour compte propre, les services rendus (y compris les services non industriels), les marchandises réexpédiées en l'état, l'électricité vendue, les actifs fixes produits par l'unité pour son propre usage, la variation nette des stocks de produits finis, les déchets de fabrication et les biens fabriqués par des travailleurs à domicile et des artisans. L'évaluation est faite aux prix à la production, y compris tous les impôts indirects mais à l'exclusion de toutes les subventions et de la TVA. La *valeur ajoutée*, définie selon le concept de valeur ajoutée de la comptabilité nationale, est donnée par la valeur de la production brute déduction faite de la valeur des consommations (y compris les coûts et recettes au titre des services non industriels). Sont déduits le coût des matériaux, combustibles et autres fournitures, des travaux exécutés sous contrat ou à la commande par d'autres unités, des travaux de réparation et d'entretien exécutés par d'autres unités, des marchandises réexpédiées en l'état et de l'électricité achetée. Les données relatives aux consommations sont estimées sur la base des quantités reçues et un ajustement est effectué pour tenir compte des variations de stocks. L'évaluation est faite de la même manière que pour la production.

L'*emploi* indique le nombre total de salariés au 30 septembre. Les chiffres couvrent les employés, les salariés, les travailleurs à domicile, les salariés à temps complet et les salariés à temps partiel (assujettis à la législation sur l'assurance-maladie).

Avant 1988, la formation brute de capital fixe (*investissement*) est définie comme correspondant à la valeur des acquisitions d'actifs fixes, y compris ceux fabriqués par le personnel de l'établissement pour l'usage de ce dernier. A partir de 1988, l'investissement est défini comme la valeur des actifs fixes qui sont devenus disponibles et sont prêts à servir. Ils comprennent non seulement les actifs mentionnés ci-dessus, mais également les biens en location ou en leasing. Les actifs fixes couverts sont ceux qui ont une durée de vie productive d'un an au moins, plus ceux fabriqués par le personnel de l'établissement pour l'usage de ce dernier, les adjonctions, transformations et améliorations d'actifs existants, les actifs neufs (à condition qu'ils aient été inutilisés auparavant ou utilisés en dehors du pays) et les actifs usagés. L'évaluation est faite au prix de revient total, y compris le prix rendu et les frais d'installation et les impôts indirects, mais à l'exclusion des droits et redevances et de la TVA. Pour les actifs produits par l'unité, on utilise le coût des travaux en cours, y compris les coûts de main-d'œuvre, le coût des matériaux et autres fournitures. Les *dépenses en machines et équipement* correspondent à la formation brute de capital fixe en matériel de transport (du type de ceux qui sont utilisés dans les usines, entrepôts, etc., pour le transport sur courte distance ou la manutention des marchandises), machines et matériels industriels, machines, équipement et mobilier de bureau, instruments et équipements professionnels, et elles incluent les modifications et améliorations apportées à ces matériels.

Les *salaires et charges sociales, salariés* correspondent aux salaires, traitements et cotisations patronales aux caisses de sécurité sociale et de retraite. Les *salaires et traitements, salariés* incluent le paiement en espèces des heures normales et supplémentaires, les gratifications et indemnités de cherté de vie, les congés payés, les impôts et cotisations d'assurance sociale dus par les salariés et retenus par l'employeur, les prestations en nature et les indemnités. Les congés de maladie ne sont pas pris en compte. Les *charges sociales des employeurs* couvrent à la fois les dépenses exigées par la loi et les contributions volontaires. Les dépenses exigées par la loi comprennent les cotisations versées au titre de la législation sur l'assurance-maladie, sur l'assurance-chômage, sur les allocations familiales, sur la retraite des veuves et des orphelins et sur l'assurance-invalidité des salariés. Les contributions volontaires comprennent les cotisations aux fonds de retraite venant s'ajouter aux paiements au titre de la législation sur l'assurance sociale, les cotisations aux assurances médicales complémentaires et les indemnités de logement, de nourriture et de déplacement, etc., versées aux travailleurs étrangers.

Publications

i) *Yearly Production Statistics.* Une publication distincte paraît pour chaque catégorie de la classification nationale des industries manufacturières (Production, valeur ajoutée, emploi et rémunération) ;

ii) *Yearly Statistics on Fixed Capital Formation in Industry* (données sur l'investissement).

POLOGNE

I. STATISTIQUES INDUSTRIELLES

Source

Le Bureau Central de Statistique collecte les données statistiques relatives à l'activité économique des entreprises industrielles. L'unité statistique est l'entreprise.

Toutes les entreprises industrielles sont réparties en trois groupes selon le nombre de salariés : les petites entreprises (moins de 5 personnes), les entreprises de taille moyenne (de 6 à 50 personnes) et les grandes entreprises (plus de 50 personnes).

Toutes les entreprises de plus de 50 personnes (dans les catégories C et D) ou plus de 20 (dans la catégorie E) sont interrogées. Les entreprises employant entre 6 et 50 personnes (dans les catégories C et D) ou entre 6 et 20 (dans la catégorie E) sont interrogées tous les mois au moyen d'un échantillon représentant 10 pour cent des entreprises, et une fois par an dans leur totalité. Les entreprises de moins de 6 employés sont interrogées une fois par an au moyen d'un échantillon représentant 8 pour cent de leur population.

En 1996, les grandes entreprises ont été responsables de 79 pour cent de la production industrielle, les entreprises moyennes 16 pour cent et les petites entreprises environ 5 pour cent. Ces trois groupes employaient respectivement 83 pour cent, 16 pour cent et 1 pour cent des personnes salariées dans l'industrie.

Classification industrielle

La classification polonaise EKD (Europejska Klasyfikacja Dzia³alnoœci) a été introduite dans les statistiques de Pologne en 1993. Il existe une correspondance directe avec la NACE révision 1. Et avec la CITI révision 3.

Concepts et définitions des variables

La valeur de la *production* vendue est définie comme le revenu provenant de la vente des produits (biens et services) de l'entreprise et la valeur des biens fabriqués qui ne sont pas inclus dans les ventes mais sont traités sur une base égale (par exemple, la valeur des biens et services utilisés pour des raisons de représentation et de publicité). Aucun ajustement n'est effectué pour les travaux en cours et pour les variations des stocks de produits finis. Les transactions entre établissements d'une même entreprise ne sont pas incluses. Les données de 1992 et 1993 incluent la taxe sur le chiffre d'affaires, la TVA (introduite le 5 juillet 1993) et les droits d'assise. Pour 1993, 1994 et 1995 les données incluent la TVA et les droits d'assise. En 1995 et 1996, la TVA et les droits d'assise ne sont pas compris et les suppléments de prix sont comptés.

La variable *valeur ajoutée* brute est calculée pour toutes les unités de l'économie nationale, quel que soit le nombre de personnes qu'elles emploient. Depuis 1994, la valeur ajoutée brute est mesurée aux prix de base (antérieurement elle l'était aux prix départ-usine). Ce changement est dû à l'introduction d'un nouveau système de taxes (le 5 juillet 1993), incluant la TVA sur les biens et services ainsi que les droits d'assise. Les prix de base ne comprennent pas la TVA et les droits d'assise mais incluent les subventions sur les produits. La valeur ajoutée brute est calculée comme la valeur de la production diminuée de la valeur des consommations intermédiaires. Différentes méthodes de calcul sont utilisées pour les unités marchandes et non marchandes.

Les dépenses d'*investissement* comprennent les dépenses financières ou matérielles effectuées pour créer de nouveaux actifs ou pour améliorer (reconstruction, agrandissement, adaptation ou modernisation) les actifs existants, et les dépenses effectuées pour des équipements primaires. Les dépenses de capital fixe comprennent :

- Bâtiments et infrastructures, c'est-à-dire travaux de construction et d'assemblage, devis et estimation des coûts ;
- Machines, équipement technique et outils (y compris instruments, mobiliers et installations) ;
- Matériel de transport ;
- Autres, à savoir amélioration des terrains, dépenses d'achats de terrains et de capital fixe d'occasion, bétail (depuis 1995), planification à long terme, intérêts sur les crédits et les emprunts pour la période d'investissement (données exclusivement à prix courants). D'autres dépenses incluent les investissements sur l'équipement primaire et les coûts de réalisation de l'investissement mais n'incluent pas la valeur du capital fixe.

Les données d'*emploi* correspondent au nombre de personnes occupées (à la fin de l'année), que ce soit à temps plein ou à temps partiel. Elles comprennent les personnes sous contrat, les propriétaires et copropriétaires d'unités économiques et les membres de leurs familles, les travailleurs à domicile, les agents et sous-agents, et les membres des coopératives agricoles. L'*emploi, salariés* couvre les salariés à temps complet et à temps partiel sous contrat. Les données relatives à ces derniers sont recalculées en équivalence plein-temps.

Les *salaires et traitements* sont des données brutes et incluent les gains individuels (à l'exclusion de ceux des apprentis, des travailleurs à domicile et des stagiaires), les participations aux bénéfices, les excédents de soldes dans les coopératives, les gratifications des fonds de primes, et autres types de rémunérations données à des groupes d'employés particuliers (journalistes, auteurs de films et de programme TV ou radio).

PORTUGAL

I. STATISTIQUES INDUSTRIELLES

Source

Les données, qui émanent de l'Institut National de Statistique, sont tirées des enquêtes annuelles réalisées dans les industries manufacturières et extractives, l'électricité, le gaz, ainsi que dans le bâtiment et les travaux publics.

Jusqu'en 1989, les données étaient tirées de l'Enquête Annuelle sur l'Industrie Manufacturière, auprès de 11 500 établissements. En 1990 elle a été remplacée par l'Enquête Annuelle aux Entreprises, qui touche 65 000 entreprises dans l'industrie extractive, l'industrie manufacturière et le secteur électricité, gaz et eau. Les chiffres pour la production, la valeur ajoutée, l'emploi, les investissements et le nombre d'entreprises englobent la totalité du secteur industriel. Les chiffres pour l'emploi des salariés, les dépenses en machines et équipement ainsi que les compléments des salaires et traitements n'englobent que les entreprises ayant 100 salariés ou plus.

Concepts et définitions des variables

La *production* est la valeur brute de production, définie comme la valeur totale des produits finis fabriqués par l'établissement/«entreprise» (les produits intermédiaires vendus en l'état sont considérés comme des produits finis), à laquelle s'ajoute celle des actifs fixes produits par l'unité, pour son propre usage, des travaux industriels exécutés pour des tiers, de l'électricité vendue, et des déchets de fabrication vendus à des tiers, déduction faite de la valeur des produits en cours de fabrication au début de l'année. La *valeur ajoutée* est obtenue en ajoutant à la valeur brute de production les travaux de sous-traitance exécutés par l'établissement/«entreprise», déduction faite de la valeur des matériaux, combustibles et énergie consommés, de la location de machines, des travaux de sous-traitance exécutés par des tiers, des travaux industriels ou d'entretien et de réparation exécutés par des tiers, ainsi que des services non industriels reçus, et des droits acquittés pour l'utilisation de procédés de fabrication.

L'*emploi* couvre le personnel, rémunéré ou non rémunéré, qui, pendant la dernière semaine de l'année, exerce dans l'établissement sa profession principale. Sont prises en considération toutes les personnes en activité dans l'établissement pendant la dernière semaine de l'année, et celles qui sont absentes pour une courte durée (maladie, vacances, grève, etc.), mais non les personnes qui effectuent leur service militaire ou qui sont à la retraite. Le personnel rémunéré comprend les cadres, le personnel administratif, technique et de bureau et le personnel ouvrier ; le personnel non rémunéré englobe les propriétaires, en nom individuel ou collectif, qui participent réellement à l'activité de l'établissement sans recevoir de salaire régulier, et les membres de la famille qui travaillent au moins pendant un tiers de la durée normale sans recevoir de salaire en échange de leur travail. Les *heures ouvrées* couvrent les heures travaillées par les ouvriers.

Les ventes des actifs fixes sont déduites des chiffres pour l'*investissement* et les *dépenses en machines et équipement*.

La *rémunération* correspond au total des traitements et salaires versés pendant l'année, auquel s'ajoutent les compléments des salaires et traitements et les cotisations patronales aux régimes de Sécurité sociale et de retraite.

Par *entreprise*, on entend toute entité productrice, qu'elle soit auxiliaire d'un établissement classé dans un autre secteur d'activité, qu'elle soit dirigée par des particuliers en régime d'administration directe ou encore qu'elle corresponde à une entité du secteur public exécutant des travaux en régime d'administration directe.

Publications

i) *Industrial Statistics* (volume I et volume II) ;
ii) *Statistics on Building and Dwellings.*

REPUBLIQUE TCHEQUE

I. STATISTIQUES INDUSTRIELLES

Source

La source des données est une enquête périodique par échantillon menée par l'Office Statistique Tchèque. L'unité statistique est l'entreprise.

Le nombre de salariés joue un rôle décisif pour la détermination de la classe de taille et pour le devoir de réponse qui en découle (plus de 6 salariés en 1997 ; 20 et plus à partir de 1998). L'Office Statistique utilise une enquête par échantillon aléatoire, stratifiée par la taille de l'entreprise et par le secteur industriel (NACE).

Classification industrielle

La classification industrielle des activités économiques (OKEC) a été introduite en 1992 et mise à jour en 1994. L'OKEC est divisée en 5 niveaux, les quatre premiers comparables à ceux de la NACE révision 1, le cinquième ajouté pour les besoins du pays. L'OKEC est identique à la CITI révision 3 jusqu'au niveau 2.

Concepts et définitions des variables

La *production* (valeur brute de production) est la somme des biens et services marchands et non-marchands élaborés par des producteurs intérieurs sur une période donnée. Elle est égale à la somme des revenus tirés des ventes des produits de l'entreprise, des biens, travaux et services fournis à d'autres établissements de l'entreprise et inclut les variations de stocks de sa propre production et des travaux en cours. Les frais encourus sur les produits vendus et la TVA sont exclus. L'évaluation se fait aux prix départ-usine, non compris la TVA.

La *valeur ajoutée* est obtenue en soustrayant la valeur des consommations intermédiaires (coûts des matières premières, combustibles et autres fournitures) à la valeur de la production brute.

L'*emploi* est le nombre de personnes occupées. Il comprend les propriétaires exploitants, les entrepreneurs individuels et les salariés. L'*emploi, salariés* inclut toutes les catégories de salariés permanents, temporaires et saisonniers ayant un contrat de travail dans l'entreprise. La définition de cet indicateur est conforme à la résolution concernant les statistiques de population économiquement active, d'emploi, de chômage et de sous-emploi, adoptée par la 13ème Conférence Internationale sur les Statistiques de l'Emploi (Genève, 1982) avec les exceptions suivantes : les personnes en congé de maternité et les apprentis sont exclus.

Les *heures ouvrées* couvrent les heures travaillées par les ouvriers.

Publications

i) Publications agrégées – diffusées par le CSO
    Annuaire statistique de la République tchèque - disponible chaque année en décembre ;
    Indicateurs du Développement Economique et Social de la République tchèque – 90 jours après le trimestre de référence ;
    Bulletin du CSO – janvier, avril, mai et octobre ;
ii) Information Statistique – série Industrie – diffusée par le CSO
    Industrie de la République tchèque – 55ème jour
    Industrie de la République tchèque – chiffres mensuels révisés – juin.

ROYAUME-UNI

I. GÉNÉRALITÉS

Les informations émanent de l'«Office for National Statistics» (anciennement le «Central Statistical Office») du Royaume-Uni et concernent deux catégories de données : les statistiques industrielles et les statistiques du commerce extérieur.

II. STATISTIQUES INDUSTRIELLES

Source

De 1973 à 1977, l'Annual Census of Production (Recensement annuel de la production) s'adressait à tous les établissements de 20 salariés ou plus. En 1978, on a adopté un système d'échantillonnage dont la forme a varié, mais celui qui a été mis au point pour le recensement de 1980 a été réutilisé de 1981 à 1983, et de 1985 à 1987. Pour ces années-là, des questionnaires ont été envoyés à tous les établissements comptant 100 salariés ou plus et, d'une façon générale, à des échantillons composés d'un établissement sur deux parmi ceux comptant 50 à 99 salariés, et d'un établissement sur quatre parmi ceux comptant 20 à 49 salariés. Pour le recensement de 1984, qui devait servir au calage des données, des formulaires ont été envoyés à tous les établissements comptant 20 salariés ou plus, à l'exception de ceux employant entre 20 et 49 personnes situés en Angleterre, dont 1 sur 2 a été inclus dans l'échantillon. Des estimations sont effectuées pour chacun des établissements qui ne sont pas couverts par l'enquête, en ce sens que l'on calcule une «moyenne par tête» à partir des réponses au recensement. Les chiffres obtenus sont multipliés par le nombre de salariés supposés être employés dans chacun des établissements non sélectionnés ou qui n'ont pas répondu, ce qui permet d'obtenir une estimation pour ledit établissement. Il est demandé aux établissements de fournir des données portant sur l'année civile, mais on accepte les réponses concernant l'exercice comptable se terminant entre le 5 avril de l'année sur laquelle porte le recensement et le 6 avril de l'année suivante.

Le recensement de 1984 a exploité un nouveau registre des entreprises. Des unités supplémentaires (généralement de petite taille) ont été rajoutées, et d'autres ont été reclassées d'un secteur industriel vers un autre. Ce changement a affecté les estimations pour toutes les industries, quelques-unes d'une façon significative, particulièrement celles concernant le nombre d'établissements.

L'unité statistique est l'établissement, défini comme la plus petite unité qui puisse fournir l'information normalement requise dans le cadre d'un recensement.

Classification industrielle

Les résultats des recensements annuels effectués entre 1973 et 1979 étaient ventilés selon la Standard Industrial Classification, version révisée de 1968. Depuis le recensement de 1980, les chiffres sont ventilés selon la version de 1980 de cette classification. Afin de relier les données des premiers recensements à celles qui ont été obtenues en 1980 pour les années suivantes, les chiffres de 1979 ont été recalculés sur la base de la nouvelle classification.

Concepts et définitions des variables

La *production*, ou production brute, est donnée par la valeur des ventes totales, des travaux exécutés et des services rendus, corrigée de la variation nette, durant l'année considérée, des travaux en cours et des stocks de produits finis. Les ventes totales correspondent aux livraisons de biens produits par les établissements couverts par l'enquête implantés au Royaume-Uni, et comprennent les ventes de biens fabriqués à l'intention de ces établissements à partir de matériaux fournis par ces derniers à d'autres établissements ou à des travailleurs extérieurs, ainsi que les ventes de déchets et de résidus. La valeur des ventes correspond à la valeur nette, autrement dit la somme demandée aux clients -- prix départ-usine ou prix rendu -- déduction faite de la TVA, des remises, des commissions des représentants, etc., ainsi que de la valeur des retours. Lorsque les produits sont soumis à un droit d'accise, celui-ci est inclus si les biens sont vendus «après paiement des droits» et exclu si les biens sont vendus sous douane ou s'ils sont exportés. Les ventes d'actifs fixes ne sont pas prises en compte. La *valeur ajoutée* ou la valeur ajoutée brute au coût des facteurs, correspond à la valeur de la production brute déduction faite du coût des matériaux utilisés dans la production et le conditionnement, des combustibles, des biens nécessaires pour la vente ou l'affacturage, du coût des services industriels et non industriels reçus, des impôts locaux et des taxes de mise en circulation des véhicules. La valeur des achats est corrigée des variations, durant l'année considérée, des stocks de matériaux, de fournitures et de combustibles. L'évaluation est faite au coût des facteurs à l'exclusion des impôts indirects mais y compris les subventions.

L'*emploi* représente le nombre de personnes occupées ; il indique le nombre moyen d'agents administratifs, de techniciens, d'employés de bureau et d'ouvriers inscrits sur le registre du personnel de l'établissement en question durant l'année du recensement, ainsi que le nombre de propriétaires exploitants occupés durant cette même année. Sont inclus les travailleurs indépendants, les associés actifs, les travailleurs familiaux non rémunérés travaillant au moins la moitié de l'horaire normal, les salariés payés au mois ou à la semaine, employés à temps complet ou à temps partiel, mais sont exclus les travailleurs à domicile ainsi que les travailleurs occasionnels. Pour sa part, l'*emploi, salariés* ne comprend pas les propriétaires exploitants, c'est-à-dire les personnes considérées comme des travailleurs indépendants par l'assurance sociale, les membres de leurs familles travaillant dans l'entreprise au moins la moitié de l'horaire normal, sans véritablement recevoir ni salaire ni traitement ainsi que les directeurs travaillant dans l'entreprise qui n'ont pas précisément reçu de salaire, traitement ou commission.

L'*investissement*, ou formation brute de capital fixe, représente la valeur des acquisitions d'actifs fixes déduction faite des ventes. L'évaluation est faite au prix de revient total, y compris les frais d'installation et certains droits et redevances (frais d'acte, droit de timbre, commissions de représentants, etc.) et comprend tout montant reçu ou attendu de l'Etat, d'organismes officiels ou des collectivités locales, sous forme de subventions et/ou déductions pour investissement. En règle générale, la valeur retenue correspond au montant porté au compte de capital auquel s'ajoute toute autre somme qui, aux fins de l'imposition durant l'année en question, est considérée comme du capital. Lorsque les dépenses sont étalées sur plusieurs années, les paiements sont comptabilisés l'année où ils ont été effectués. Sont incluses les dépenses d'équipement encourues durant l'année du recensement par des unités de production où la production n'a pas commencé avant la fin de l'année considérée, ainsi que la valeur des biens d'équipement produits par le personnel de l'établissement pour l'usage de ce dernier. Est exclue la valeur de tout actif acquis à l'occasion du rachat d'une entreprise existante. Les chiffres comprennent le montant de la TVA non récupérable, mais ne comprennent pas celui de la TVA récupérable. Aucune provision n'est prévue pour amortissement ou obsolescence. Les *dépenses en machines et équipement* correspondent aux dépenses d'équipement consacrées à l'achat, à l'état neuf ou usagé, d'installations et de machines industrielles et de bureau ainsi que d'autres types d'équipement. Les dépenses nettes d'équipement et de machines sont données par la valeur des acquisitions déduction fait des mises au rebut.

Les *salaires et charges sociales, salariés* correspondent aux sommes versées durant l'année du recensement aux agents administratifs, aux techniciens, aux employés de bureau ainsi qu'aux ouvriers. Ils comprennent les salaires et traitements et les contributions patronales. Les contributions patronales au régime national d'assurance, etc. sont incluses de même que la rémunération des travailleurs extérieurs. Les *salaires et traitements, salariés* représentent les sommes versées pendant l'année aux salariés. Tous les paiements au titre d'heures supplémentaires, les gratifications, les commissions, les congés payés ainsi que les indemnités de licenciement après déduction des montants remboursés par l'Etat sont compris. Aucune déduction n'est effectuée au titre des impôts sur le revenu, des assurances, des retraites obligatoires, etc. Sont exclus les sommes prélevées par les propriétaires exploitants, les prestations en nature, les frais de déplacement, les indemnités de logement. Les *charges sociales des employeurs* comprennent les contributions des employeurs à l'assurance sociale, surcharge comprise, prévues aux termes de la Social Security Pensions Act de 1975 ainsi que les primes versées, pour le compte des salariés ou des personnes à leur charge, aux caisses privées d'assurance à divers titres : pensions, retraite ou autres, assurance-maladie, accident, invalidité, décès. Elles comprennent également les rémunérations des travailleurs extérieurs c'est-à-dire les sommes qui sont versées aux personnes qui travaillent à leur domicile généralement sur la base d'un travail à la pièce et dont les noms apparaissent sur le registre. Les sommes versées aux travailleurs extérieurs par les sous-traitants sont incluses dans le coût des services industriels reçus. Les rémunérations versées aux travailleurs à domicile ne sont pas estimées pour les entreprises qui n'ont pas retourné leur réponse.

Publications

i) *Census of Production Introductory Notes* (Business Monitor PA 1001), publié par le «Business Statistics Office», Office for National Statistics ;

ii) *Annual Abstract of Statistics,* publié par l'«Office for National Statistics», Londres.

III. STATISTIQUES DU COMMERCE EXTÉRIEUR

Source

Les données sont recueillies par les fonctionnaires des douanes et de la régie puis transmises à l'«Office for National Statistics».

Classification industrielle

Les statistiques des douanes et de la régie sont établies selon la classification type du commerce international (CTCI). Elles sont ensuite regroupées selon la «Standard Industrial Classification» du Royaume-Uni par l'«Office for National Statistics» qui les ventile alors selon la CITI.

On notera que les données relatives à certains postes détaillés ont été négligées pour certaines positions et pour certaines années. Les chiffres correspondants ont été intégrés dans les sous-totaux et les totaux, dans la mesure du possible, et en tout état de cause dans le total général. D'autres opérations, impossibles à affecter à une industrie particulière, ont été directement intégrées dans le total général : les paquets postaux de nature indéterminée, les transactions concernant le plateau continental et celles de faible valeur.

Concepts et définitions des variables

Les données portent sur le commerce général, aussi bien pour les exportations que pour les importations. Les *exportations*, exprimées FAB, sont ventilées en fonction du pays de destination finale et les *importations*, exprimées CAF, selon le pays d'expédition. Sont inclus dans les deux cas : le commerce d'Etat, les transactions commerciales d'équipement et de fournitures militaires, les transactions extérieures, le commerce d'entretien et de réparation, les transactions portant sur les navires et avions neufs, l'électricité et le gaz, ainsi que les donations et dons privés. Les produits de la mer provenant directement de haute mer sont aussi pris en compte, mais les produits naturels de la mer amenés par des navires immatriculés au Royaume-Uni sont exclus des importations. Sont spécifiquement exclus : les échanges directs en transit et les transactions portant sur des navires et avions d'occasion, mais non les exportations temporaires, les articles monétaires, l'or industriel et les petites transactions.

Publications

Overseas Trade Statistics (mensuel).
Publié par HMSO.

SUÈDE

I. GÉNÉRALITÉS

Les informations émanent du Bureau de statistique de la Suède (Statistiska Centralbyran), à Stockholm. Les données se répartissent en trois catégories, selon leur origine : statistiques industrielles, statistiques du commerce extérieur et comptes nationaux.

Classification industrielle

A l'origine, les données sont ventilées selon la CITI. La SNI -- classification industrielle type de la Suède -- est alignée sur la version 1968 de la CITI jusqu'aux positions à quatre chiffres.

II. STATISTIQUES INDUSTRIELLES

Source

Les données proviennent du fichier de statistiques industrielles du Bureau et sont tirées de son enquête annuelle dans les industries manufacturières. Jusqu'en 1988, tous les établissements de cinq salariés ou plus étaient pris en compte et aucune estimation n'était faite pour tenir compte des unités non couvertes par l'enquête. Depuis 1989, l'enquête s'adresse aux établissements manufacturiers (de 5 salariés ou plus) des entreprises manufacturières de dix salariés ou plus et aux établissements manufacturiers (de dix salariés ou plus) des entreprises non manufacturières. Des estimations sont effectuées pour tenir compte des réponses manquantes.

Classification industrielle

Jusqu'en 1988, l'édition n'était pas prise en compte dans CITI 342 (imprimerie et édition) dans tous les tableaux, cette activité n'étant pas couverte par l'enquête annuelle. Les carrières de sable et d'argile (comprises dans CITI 29) étaient également exclues. Depuis 1989, ces activités sont incluses.

Concepts et définitions des variables

La *production* correspond à la production brute, à l'exclusion des impôts indirects mais y compris toutes les subventions. Elle inclut la valeur de tous les produits, la variation nette des travaux en cours, les services rendus, les déchets de fabrication et les biens fabriqués par les travailleurs à domicile. Jusqu'en 1988, la *valeur ajoutée* correspondant au concept de valeur ajoutée recensée, à l'exclusion des impôts indirects mais y compris les subventions, était donnée par la valeur de la production brute déduction faite du coût des matériaux, combustibles et autres fournitures, des travaux exécutés sous contrat ou à la commande par d'autres unités et de l'électricité achetée, à l'exclusion des coûts et recettes au titre des services non industriels. Depuis 1989, elle est égale à la production déduction faite des coûts totaux, hors salaires et traitements (charges sociales incluses). Les données relatives aux consommations sont estimées sur la base des quantités consommées. Des informations détaillées concernant les méthodes utilisées pour établir les séries à prix constants peuvent être obtenues sur demande.

Les données sur l'*emploi* indiquent le nombre moyen d'ouvriers occupés tout au long de l'année auquel on ajoute le nombre d'employés occupés à certaines dates. Sont pris en compte les propriétaires exploitants, les associés actifs, les travailleurs indépendants, les employés et les salariés. Les salariés à temps complet et à temps partiel sont pris en compte, de même que le personnel de bureau et d'encadrement dont les fonctions sont étroitement liées au processus de production. Les *heures ouvrées* couvrent les heures travaillées par les salariés.

Les *salaires et traitements* comprennent le paiement en espèces des heures normales et supplémentaires, les gratifications et indemnités de cherté de vie, les congés payés et congés de maladie, les impôts et cotisations d'assurance sociale, etc., dus par les salariés et retenus par l'employeur ainsi que les prestations en nature. Les charges de sécurité sociale ne sont pas prises en compte.

Publications

Industries manufacturières : parties I et II de la série *Official Statistics of Sweden* (SOS) publiée par le Bureau de statistique. Une partie des séries est également disponible dans les banques de données du Bureau de statistique.

III. STATISTIQUES DU COMMERCE EXTÉRIEUR

Concepts et définitions des variables

Les statistiques du commerce extérieur (qui apparaissent dans les mêmes tableaux que les statistiques industrielles) portent sur le commerce général et concernent l'année civile : les *exportations* sont exprimées FAB et les *importations* CAF. Elles incluent le commerce d'Etat, les transactions commerciales d'équipement et de fournitures militaires, les transactions d'aide extérieure, les transactions portant sur les navires et avions neufs et usagés, l'électricité et le gaz, les donations et dons privés et (uniquement dans le cas des importations) les produits de la mer provenant directement de haute mer. Sont spécifiquement exclus les échanges directs en transit, les exportations temporaires, les articles monétaires, certaines petites transactions portant sur des montants inférieurs à 2 000 KrS et les retours (qui sont enregistrés à part). A l'origine, les données sont ventilées selon une version suédoise de la CITI.

Données à prix constants

Les données à prix constants sont obtenues, pour certains produits, au moyen de la valeur unitaire, et pour d'autres, de l'indice des prix des exportations et des importations.

Publications

i) *Utrikeshandel,* manadsstatistik (mensuel) ;

ii) *Utrikeshandel,* kvartalsstatistik (trimestriel) ;

iii) Deux publications annuelles.

Documents publiés par le Bureau de statistique de la Suède. Les chiffres sont également disponibles dans les banques de données du Bureau de statistique.

IV. COMPTES NATIONAUX

Concepts et définitions des variables

La production brute (*production*) est donnée en valeur de base, y compris les impôts indirects ne s'appliquant pas aux produits mais à l'exclusion des subventions ne s'appliquant pas aux produits. Elle inclut la valeur de tous les produits, des travaux effectués par l'unité pour son propre compte, les services rendus, de l'électricité vendue, les biens fabriqués par des travailleurs à domicile et des artisans et des actifs fixes produits par l'unité pour son propre usage. Un ajustement est opéré pour tenir compte de la variation nette des travaux en cours et des stocks de produits finis. La *valeur ajoutée*, exprimée en valeur de base, est donnée par la valeur de la production brute déduction faite du coût des matériaux, combustibles et autres fournitures, des travaux exécutés sous contrat ou à la commande par d'autres unités, des travaux de réparation et d'entretien exécutés par d'autres unités et de l'électricité consommée. Les données relatives aux consommations sont estimées sur la base des quantités consommées.

L'*emploi* indique le nombre de salariés. Les chiffres sont obtenus à partir du nombre moyen d'ouvriers employés tout au long de l'année et du nombre d'employés à certaines dates. Ils incluent les propriétaires exploitants, les associés actifs, les travailleurs indépendants et les travailleurs à domicile, à temps complet et à temps partiel. L'*emploi, salariés* exclut les chefs d'entreprise. Les *heures ouvrées* couvrent les heures travaillées par les salariés.

L'*investissement* correspond à la formation brute totale de capital fixe et est donné par la valeur des acquisitions d'actifs fixes, y compris ceux fabriqués par le personnel de l'établissement pour l'usage de ce dernier, déduction faite des ventes. Les actifs fixes couverts sont ceux qui ont une durée de vie productive de trois ans au moins et ils englobent ceux fabriqués par le personnel de l'établissement pour l'usage de ce dernier, les actifs fixes neufs et usagés (précédemment utilisés en dehors du pays). Les adjonctions, transformations, améliorations et réparations d'actifs existants sont aussi prises en compte. Pour les actifs fixes neufs, l'évaluation est faite au prix de revient total, y compris le prix rendu, les frais d'installation et les droits et redevances. Pour ceux produits par l'unité, on utilise le coût des travaux en cours, y compris les coûts de main-d'œuvre et le coût des matériaux et autres fournitures ; pour les ventes d'actifs fixes, on se base sur le montant effectivement réalisé. Les *dépenses en machines et équipement* correspondent, elles aussi, à la formation brute de capital fixe et sont calculées selon la même méthode que l'investissement total ; elles portent sur le matériel de transport, les machines et matériels industriels, les machines, équipement et mobilier de bureau, les instruments et équipements professionnels. Les modifications, améliorations et réparations apportées à ces matériels sont aussi prises en compte.

Les *salaires et charges sociales* correspondent à la rémunération des salariés, y compris les charges sociales. Elle englobe donc les salaires, les traitements et les cotisations patronales aux caisses de sécurité sociale et de retraite. Y sont inclus : le paiement en espèces des heures normales et supplémentaires, les gratifications et indemnités de cherté de vie, les congés payés et congés de maladie, les impôts et cotisations d'assurance sociale, etc., dus par les salariés et retenus par l'employeur, et les prestations en nature. Les cotisations patronales couvrent uniquement les dépenses exigées par la loi.

Publications

Statistiska Meddelanden ; série N.

SUISSE

I. GÉNÉRALITÉS

Les données sont établies par le St. Galler Zentrum für Zukunftsforschung à l'intention du Bundesamt für Statistik -- BFS (Office fédéral de la Statistique -- OFS).

II. STATISTIQUES DU COMMERCE EXTÉRIEUR

Concepts et définitions des variables

Les données portent sur le commerce général, aussi bien pour les *exportations* que pour les *importations*. Sont inclus dans les deux cas : le commerce d'Etat, les transactions commerciales d'équipement et de fournitures militaires, les transactions d'aide extérieure, le commerce d'entretien et de réparation, les transactions portant sur les navires et avions neufs, l'électricité et le gaz, ainsi que les donations et dons privés. Sont spécifiquement exclus les échanges directs en transit, les exportations temporaires, les articles monétaires, les métaux précieux industriels et les petites transactions.

III. COMPTES NATIONAUX

Source

A l'origine, l'enquête utilise l'entreprise comme unité de référence ; elle se fait par échantillonnage, mais aucune estimation n'est effectuée pour tenir compte des unités qui ne sont pas touchées par l'enquête. Les données portent sur l'année civile.

Classification industrielle

Les données sont ventilées selon l'«Allgemeine Systematik der Wirtschaftszweige» (Nomenclature générale de l'activité économique). Dans les tableaux :
  a) CITI 3 inclut CITI 2 ;
  b) CITI 321 exclut CITI 3213 ;
  c) CITI 322 englobe CITI 323, 324 et 3213 ;
  d) CITI 33 (fabrication d'ouvrages en bois et de meubles) inclut CITI 3902 et 3903 (autres industries manufacturières sauf bijouterie) ;
  e) CITI 351 inclut CITI 352, 353, 354 ;

f) CITI 355 inclut CITI 356 ;

g) CITI 36 inclut CITI 2 ;

h) CITI 37 (industrie métallurgique de base) inclut CITI 381/3813 (fabrication d'ouvrages en métaux, d'éléments de construction en métal) ;

i) CITI 38 exclut CITI 381, 3813, 3853 ;

j) CITI 382 inclut CITI 384 et 3851 ;

k) CITI 383 inclut CITI 3852 ;

l) CITI 385 exclut CITI 3851, 3852, 3853 ;

m) CITI 3901 (bijouterie) inclut CITI 3853 (fabrication de montres et horloges).

Concepts et définitions des variables

La *production* correspond à la production brute exprimée aux prix à la production et inclut la valeur de tous les produits. La *valeur ajoutée*, qui est, elle aussi, exprimée aux prix à la production, est calculée selon le concept de valeur ajoutée de la comptabilité nationale.

L'*emploi* indique le nombre de personnes occupées tel qu'il ressort du nombre moyen de salariés employés tout au long de l'année. Il inclut les propriétaires exploitants, les associés actifs, les travailleurs familiaux non rémunérés, les employés et les salariés, à temps complet et à temps partiel.

Publications

On trouvera une description plus détaillée des sources et méthodes dans les ouvrages suivants :

i) P. Meier, *Daten für Branchenmodelle der schweizerischen Wirtschaft, 1983* ;

ii) P. Meier, *Daten für den tertiären Sektor in der Schweiz, Wertschöpfung, Beschäftigung und Preise von 1960 bis 1982 für 18 Branchen*, 1984 ;

iii) H.G. Graf, F. Kneschaurek, Y. Wang, *Vorleistungen, Wertschöpfung und Produktivität in Industrie- und Dienstleistungsbranchen der Schweiz*, 1989 ;

iv) H.G. Graf, *Das St. Galler Branchenmodell : Stand der Revisionsarbeiten, in : Mitteilungen des SGZZ*, Ziff.2.3, Nr.27, 1990.

Les publications *i)* et *ii)* concernent le Programme National de Recherche N° 9 et peuvent être obtenues auprès de ses responsables.

TURQUIE

I. STATISTIQUES INDUSTRIELLES

Source

Les données proviennent de l'enquête annuelle dans les industries manufacturières réalisée par l'Institut public des statistiques d'Ankara, sauf en 1992 où les données sont tirées du Recensement de l'Industrie et des Etablissements. Jusqu'en 1992, tous les établissements manufacturiers du secteur public ainsi que ceux du secteur privé employant 25 personnes ou plus sont couverts par l'enquête. A partir de 1992, tous les établissements du secteur privé employant 10 personnes ou plus sont couverts

Classification industrielle

La classification turque est une adaptation de la CITI. Elle contient une rubrique supplémentaire, 3854 (autres matériels professionnels). En conséquence les chiffres pour CITI 385 ne sont pas égaux à la somme des composantes publiées. CITI 4 (électricité, gaz et eau) exclut l'électricité.

Concepts et définitions des variables

La *production* est donnée par la valeur totale des ventes de biens et services et des transferts d'électricité, à laquelle on ajoute la valeur des stocks (de produits finis et semi-finis) en fin d'année et celle des actifs fixes produits par l'unité pour son propre usage et dont on déduit la valeur des stocks en début d'année (de produits finis et semi-finis). La *valeur ajoutée* est donnée par la production déduction faite de la valeur des consommations intermédiaires. Cette dernière correspond à la valeur totale des produits et services achetés ou transférés, de l'électricité achetée et de la valeur des stocks en début d'année après déduction de la valeur des stocks en fin d'année (matières premières, fournitures, matériel d'emballage et combustibles).

L'*emploi*, ou le nombre moyen de personnes occupées, est donné par le nombre de propriétaires, de partenaires et de travailleurs familiaux non rémunérés, en activité au mois de novembre dans l'établissement, auquel on ajoute le nombre moyen de salariés. Ce dernier est égal à la moyenne arithmétique du nombre de salariés employés en février, mai, août et novembre. Les *heures ouvrées* dans une année correspondent au produit du nombre moyen d'ouvriers par le nombre d'heures ouvrées dans une équipe postée et le nombre de jours travaillés dans l'année.

L'*investissement* représente les acquisitions brutes d'actifs fixes au cours de l'année. Il est donné par le coût total des actifs fixes neufs ou usagés acquis sur le marché intérieur, des actifs fixes neufs ou usagés importés, des actifs fixes produits par le personnel de l'établissement, des actifs fixes installés pendant l'année et achetés aux enchères, des grosses réparations et des dépenses faites sur les actifs fixes, des études, plans et dessins, des machines, équipement, véhicules et construction, du matériel et mobilier de bureau (à condition qu'ils soient utilisés dans l'établissement, qu'ils aient une espérance de vie productive supérieure à un an et qu'ils soient portés au compte de capital) et aux dépenses d'acquisition et d'amélioration des terrains, déduction faite des ventes.

La *rémunération* (traitements et salaires), correspond aux sommes versées aux salariés au cours de l'année et comprend tous les paiements au titre de salaires, traitements et indemnités journalières, avant déduction de l'impôt sur le revenu, des cotisations d'assurance sociale et de retraite. Elle exclut les cotisations patronales aux caisses de sécurité sociale, de retraite et autres. Elle inclut le paiement des heures supplémentaires, les gratifications, les indemnités et les prestations en nature.

Un *établissement* est un lieu de travail où il existe un statut unique de propriété ou de contrôle, où, en général, un seul type d'activité économique est réalisé et qui dispose des sources comptables et du registre nécessaire pour remplir les questionnaires.

Statistiques des Structures Industrielles
OCDE, © 1998
OECD OCDE

Section II

Exchange rates and purchasing powers parities for GDP
Taux de change et parités de pouvoir d'achat du PIB

Statistiques des Structures Industrielles
OCDE, © 1998

Exchange Rates - national currency per US dollar -
Taux de change - monnaie nationale par dollar É-U -

	1987	1988	1989	1990	1991	1992	1993	1994	1995	1996	
Australia	1.4282	1.2799	1.2646	1.2811	1.2838	1.3617	1.4706	1.3678	1.3490	1.2779	Australie
Austria	12.643	12.348	13.231	11.370	11.676	10.989	11.632	11.422	10.082	10.587	Autriche
Belgium	37.334	36.768	39.404	33.418	34.148	32.150	34.597	33.457	29.480	30.962	Belgique
Canada	1.3260	1.2307	1.1840	1.1668	1.1457	1.2087	1.2901	1.3656	1.3724	1.3635	Canada
Czech Republic ...	..	..	..	21.145	27.920	28.370	29.153	28.785	26.541	27.145	République Tchèque
Denmark	6.8403	6.7315	7.3102	6.1886	6.3965	6.0361	6.4839	6.3606	5.6024	5.7987	Danemark
Finland	4.3956	4.1828	4.2912	3.8235	4.0440	4.4794	5.7123	5.2235	4.3667	4.5935	Finlande
France	6.0107	5.9569	6.3801	5.4453	5.6421	5.2938	5.6632	5.5520	4.9915	5.1155	France
Germany	1.7974	1.7562	1.8800	1.6157	1.6595	1.5617	1.6533	1.6228	1.4331	1.5048	Allemagne
Greece	135.43	141.86	162.42	158.51	182.27	190.62	229.25	242.60	231.66	240.71	Grèce
Hungary	46.971	50.413	59.066	63.206	74.735	78.988	91.933	105.16	125.68	152.65	Hongrie
Iceland	38.677	43.014	57.042	58.284	58.996	57.546	67.603	69.944	64.692	66.500	Islande
Ireland	0.6729	0.6565	0.7055	0.6046	0.6213	0.5877	0.6773	0.6686	0.6237	0.6250	Irlande
Italy	1 296.1	1 301.6	1 372.1	1 198.1	1 240.6	1 232.4	1 573.7	1 612.4	1 628.9	1 543.0	Italie
Japan	144.64	128.15	137.96	144.79	134.71	126.65	111.20	102.21	94.06	108.78	Japon
Korea	822.57	731.47	671.46	707.76	733.35	780.65	802.67	803.45	771.27	804.45	Corée
Luxembourg	37.334	36.768	39.404	33.418	34.148	32.150	34.597	33.457	29.480	30.962	Luxembourg
Mexico	1.3782	2.2731	2.4615	2.8126	3.0184	3.0949	3.1156	3.3751	6.4194	7.5995	Mexique
Netherlands	2.0257	1.9766	2.1207	1.8209	1.8697	1.7585	1.8573	1.8200	1.6057	1.6859	Pays-Bas
New Zealand	1.6946	1.5264	1.6722	1.6762	1.7335	1.8618	1.8505	1.6865	1.5239	1.4549	Nouvelle Zélande
Norway	6.7375	6.5170	6.9045	6.2597	6.4829	6.2145	7.0941	7.0576	6.3352	6.4498	Norvège
Poland	0.0265	0.0431	0.1439	0.9500	1.0576	1.3626	1.8115	2.2723	2.4250	2.6961	Pologne
Portugal	140.88	143.95	157.46	142.56	144.48	135.00	160.80	165.99	151.11	154.24	Portugal
Spain	123.48	116.49	118.38	101.93	103.91	102.38	127.26	133.96	124.69	126.66	Espagne
Sweden	6.3404	6.1272	6.4469	5.9188	6.0475	5.8238	7.7834	7.7160	7.1333	6.7059	Suède
Switzerland	1.4912	1.4633	1.6359	1.3892	1.4340	1.4062	1.4776	1.3677	1.1825	1.2360	Suisse
Turkey	857.22	1422.4	2121.7	2608.6	4171.8	6872.4	10 984.6	29 608.7	45 845.1	81 404.9	Turkuie
United Kingdom ...	0.6119	0.5622	0.6112	0.5632	0.5670	0.5698	0.6668	0.6534	0.6337	0.6410	Royaume-Uni
United States	1.0000	1.0000	1.0000	1.0000	1.0000	1.0000	1.0000	1.0000	1.0000	1.0000	États-Unis

Source: OECD. Statistics Directorate.

Source : OCDE. Direction des statistiques

Purchasing power parities for GDP - national currency per US dollar -
Parités de pouvoir d'achat du PIB - monnaie national par dollar É-U -

	1987	1988	1989	1990	1991	1992	1993	1994	1995	1996	
Australia	1.2829	1.3432	1.3839	1.3870	1.3666	1.3712	1.3530	1.3378	1.2911	1.2994	Australie
Austria	14.709	14.389	14.161	14.040	14.170	13.976	13.865	13.918	13.787	13.579	Autriche
Belgium	40.467	39.811	39.905	39.450	39.158	37.782	37.303	37.289	36.887	36.823	Belgique
Canada	1.3057	1.3139	1.3186	1.3030	1.2873	1.2817	1.2630	1.2508	1.1863	1.1853	Canada
Czech Republic . . .	..	..	..	5.2441	7.6474	8.3495	9.4604	10.390	10.845	11.690	République Tchèque
Denmark	9.4538	9.4134	9.4779	9.3930	9.1768	9.1447	8.7859	8.7093	8.4498	8.3278	Danemark
Finland	6.0080	6.1928	6.2943	6.3840	6.2987	6.3528	6.0862	6.1468	5.8845	5.8858	Finlande
France	6.8008	6.7526	6.6863	6.6140	6.5095	6.4172	6.5728	6.6231	6.4856	6.5718	France
Germany	2.2037	2.1532	2.1067	2.0880	2.0931	2.0655	2.1029	2.0694	2.0236	2.0274	Allemagne
Greece	99.835	111.14	121.81	140.80	161.17	170.06	184.34	196.21	203.88	213.90	Grèce
Hungary	..	..	..	26.099	32.649	37.078	43.218	51.170	60.743	72.551	Hongrie
Iceland	54.348	64.297	73.768	82.630	85.725	83.131	82.926	84.057	76.171	76.755	Islande
Ireland	0.7218	0.7177	0.7254	0.6902	0.6664	0.6379	0.6548	0.6384	0.6372	0.6725	Irlande
Italy	1 315.6	1 353.0	1 377.5	1 421.0	1 462.5	1 458.5	1 533.8	1 533.4	1 556.4	1 583.0	Italie
Japan	210.16	203.80	199.17	195.30	193.06	188.16	184.31	180.59	168.80	165.62	Japon
Korea	492.49	506.11	510.57	537.85	590.73	585.59	591.42	618.16	617.14	629.24	Corée
Luxembourg	41.643	40.390	40.030	39.680	39.477	38.879	39.620	40.005	39.025	39.707	Luxembourg
Mexico	0.5363	1.0304	1.2488	1.5335	1.8854	2.0162	2.1217	2.2762	2.9667	3.7894	Mexique
Netherlands	2.3370	2.2772	2.2079	2.1650	2.1835	2.1353	2.1344	2.1242	2.0354	2.0447	Pays-Bas
New Zealand	1.5504	1.6161	1.6348	1.6090	1.5640	1.5115	1.5117	1.5022	1.4715	1.4779	Nouvelle Zélande
Norway	9.5499	9.6537	9.7752	9.7310	9.5977	8.9806	8.9309	9.1192	9.1802	9.1140	Norvège
Poland	..	..	..	0.3014	0.4666	0.6040	0.7579	1.0007	1.1416	1.3647	Pologne
Portugal	83.22	89.10	95.94	103.70	109.93	115.55	116.96	118.11	119.54	122.39	Portugal
Spain	102.00	103.79	106.47	109.50	110.39	114.76	116.96	121.32	122.56	123.68	Espagne
Sweden	8.4334	8.6487	8.9496	9.3360	9.9438	9.7962	9.8332	9.8985	9.7664	9.6780	Suède
Switzerland	2.2489	2.2275	2.1993	2.1980	2.2308	2.1627	2.1316	2.0980	2.0188	2.0524	Suisse
Turkey	358.57	584.83	982.99	1 491.0	2 280.2	3 667.2	5 989.8	12 096.2	22 404.7	39 274.7	Turkuie
United Kingdom . . .	0.5634	0.5755	0.5905	0.6023	0.6349	0.6157	0.6373	0.6456	0.6565	0.6440	Royaume-Uni
United States	1.0000	1.0000	1.0000	1.0000	1.0000	1.0000	1.0000	1.0000	1.0000	1.0000	États-Unis

Source: OECD, Statistics Directorate.
Exchange rates and purchasing power parities are given for information. If used to convert the data presented in this publication for purposes of international comparison, care should be taken to understand the limitations of the validity of such comparisons. These are due to the different survey and estimation techniques used in each country to compile national industrially disaggregated datasets. All information made available to the Secretariat is given in Part C: 'Sources and Definitions'.

Source : OCDE, Direction des statistiques.
Leur utilisation pour convertir les données contenues dans cette publication afin de permettre des comparaisons internationales devrait être accompagnée d'une compréhension des limites de telles comparaisons. Ces limites sont dûes aux différentes techniques d'enquêtes et d'estimations utilisées dans chaque pays pour compter des ensembles de données nationales désagrégées par secteur. Toutes les informations fournies au Secrétariat sont décrites en Partie C: 'Sources et Définitions'.

OECD PUBLICATIONS, 2, rue André-Pascal, 75775 PARIS CEDEX 16
PRINTED IN FRANCE
(30 1999 03 3 P) ISBN 92-64-05854-0 – No. 50759 1999